CH
AN

sional Education, Law School

Visit our website for further information or details of open days

2003

nove

1 vacatio applica
norton r

4 universit law fair

6 universit law fair

7 universit law fair

12 universit law fair

13 universit law fair (

14 vacatio applica
clifford c (christm
herbert s
lovells (c

15 universit law fair

17 universit law fair

19 queen's law fair

20 city univ universit law fair
universit law fair

21 universit law fair

septem

24 **training contract application deadline:**
foot anstey sargent
freshfields bruckhaus deringer (law grads)

31 **training contract application deadline:**
allen & overy (law students)
bristows (for september interviews)
cadwalader, wickersham & taft
field fisher waterhouse
ford & warren
hewitsons
jones day gouldens
keoghs
laytons
leboeuf, lamb, greene & macrae
lovells
shadbolt & co
stevens & bolton
wedlake bell

30 **training con application deadline:**
cumberland ellis peirs
orchard
taylor walton

teacher stern selby

Published by Chambers and Partners Publishing
(a division of Orbach & Chambers Ltd)
Saville House, 23 Long Lane, London EC1A 9HL
Tel: (020) 7606 1300 Fax: (020) 7600 3191
email: info@ChambersandPartners.co.uk
www.ChambersandPartners.com

Our thanks to the many students, trainees, pupils, solicitors, barristers and graduate recruitment personnel who assisted us in our research. Also to Chambers and Partners recruitment team for their knowledge and assistance and to the researchers of Chambers UK 2003-2004 and Chambers Global 2003 from which all firm rankings are drawn.

ISBN: 0-85514-306-1

Publisher: Michael Chambers
Managing Editor: Fiona Boxall
Editor: Anna Williams
Writers: Joanne O'Connor, Anna Saunders, Hannah Langworth, Michael Lovatt, Mark Knowles, Katherine Hardcastle, Ian Malone
Database: Nigel Birch
A-Z Co-ordinators: Jill Tugwell, Hayley Whiting
Production: Paul Cummings, Jasper John, John Osborne, Laurie Griggs
Business Development Manager: Brad D. Sirott
Business Development Team: Neil Murphy, Richard Ramsay, Jane Walker
Proofreaders: Rita Perry, Sarah Reardon, Sarah Weise, Tom Stevens, Ian Cowmeadow

Printed by: Polestar Wheatons Limited

CONTENTS

first steps

choices

solicitors

specialist practice areas

international firms... international locations

the true picture

put down that firm brochure and get the true picture here. we interviewed hundreds of trainees and newly qualified solicitors at our top 120 firms and asked them to tell us about their training contracts in their own words... and they did!

solicitors a-z

barristers

First Steps

CONTACTS

The Law Society:	113 Chancery Lane, London WC2A 1PL Tel: 020 7242 1222 E-mail: info.services@lawsociety.org.uk www.lawsoc.org.uk
Legal Education and Training Department:	Tel: 0870 606 2555 E-mail: legaled@lawsociety.org.uk www.training.lawsociety.org.uk
Trainee Solicitors Group:	The Law Society 113 Chancery Lane, London WC2A 1PL Helpline: 08000 856 131 E-mail: info@tsg.org www.tsg.org.uk
The Bar Council:	3 Bedford Row, London WC1R 4DB Tel: 020 7242 0082 www.barcouncil.org
Education and Training Department:	2/3 Cursitor Street, London EC4A 1NE Tel: 020 7440 4000 www.legaleducation.org.uk
Gray's Inn, Education Department:	8 South Square. Gray's Inn, London WC1R 5ET Tel: 020 7458 7950 www.graysinn.org.uk
Inner Temple, Education & Training Department:	Treasury Office, Inner Temple, London EC4Y 7HL Tel: 020 7797 8250 www.innertemple.org.uk
Lincoln's Inn, Students' Department:	Treasury Office, Lincoln's Inn, London WC2A 3TL Tel: 020 7405 0138 www.lincolnsinn.org.uk
Middle Temple, Students' Department:	Treasury Office, Middle Temple, London EC4Y 9AT Tel: 0207 427 4800 www.middletemple.org.uk
Career Development Loans:	Freepost, Warrington WA4 6FB Tel: (freephone) 0800 585505 www.lifelonglearning.co.uk/cdl
Government Legal Service:	Recruitment Team GLS Secretariat, Queen Anne's Chambers, 28 Broadway, London SW1H 9JS Tel: 020 7210 3574/3304/3386 E-mail: recruit@gls.gsi.gov.uk www.gls.gov.uk
Crown Prosecution Service:	50 Ludgate Hill, London EC4M 7EX Tel: 020 7796 8053 www.cps.gov.uk

CONTACTS

The Law Centres Federation:	Duchess House, 18-19 Warren Street, London W1T 5LR Tel: 020 7387 8570 E-mail: info@lawcentres.org.uk www.lawcentres.org.uk
Institute of Chartered Secretaries and Administrators:	16 Park Crescent, London W1B 1AH Tel: 020 7580 4741 www.icsa.org.uk
The Institute of Legal Executives:	Kempston Manor, Kempston, Bedfordshire MK42 7AB Tel: 01234 841000 E-mail: info@ilex.org.uk www.ilex.org.uk
Chartered Institute of Patent Agents:	95 Chancery Lane, London WC2A IDT Tel: 020 7405 9450 E-mail: mail@cipa.org.uk www.cipa.org.uk
Institute of Trade Mark Attorneys:	Canterbury House, 2-6 Sydenham Road, Croydon, Surrey CR0 9XE Tel: 020 8686 2052 www.itma.org.uk
Free Representation Unit:	Fourth Floor, Peer House, 8-14 Verulam Street, London WC1X 8LZ Tel: 020 7831 0692 www.fru.org.uk
The Law Commission:	Conquest House, 37-38 John Street, Theobalds Road, London WC1N 2BQ Tel: 020 7453 1220 E-mail: secretary@lawcommission.gsi.gov.uk www.lawcom.gov.uk
Citizens Advice Bureaux:	Head Office, Myddleton House, 115-123 Pentonville Road, London N1 9LZ Tel: 020 7833 2181 Volunteer Hotline: 08451 264264 www.nacab.org.uk
Legal Services Commission:	Head office, 85 Gray's Inn Road, London WC1X 8TX Tel: 020 7759 0000 www.legalservices.gov.uk
CPE Central Applications Board:	P.O. Box No. 84, Guildford, Surrey GU3 1YX Tel: 01483 451080 www.lawcabs.ac.uk
LPC Central Applications Board:	P.O. Box No. 84, Guildford, Surrey GU3 1YX Tel: 01483 301282 www.lawcabs.ac.uk
Online Pupillage Application System:	Technical Assistance Helpline: 01491 828918 E-mail: olpas@gti.co.uk http://olpas.gti.co.uk

so you want to be a lawyer...

Whether you're studying law at university or thinking of converting your non-law degree into professional qualifications, we hope that this book will help you to focus on your future career and achieve your goal. Your first decision must be whether to become a barrister or a solicitor, and this decision should be based on two things: the nature of the work and your chances of success.

barrister

As soon as you announce your desire to become a barrister, the world and his wife will tell you to think carefully about your decision. In the wake of cautionary advice, many wannabe barristers become despondent and resign themselves to training as solicitors. The Bar embraces only the very best of candidates and, on numbers alone, it is far easier to become a solicitor. For many Bar school applicants the chances of a lasting career at the Bar are poor, but the converse is also true: good chambers are desperate for high-calibre candidates and are concerned that the City law firms will snap up the brightest young talent. The debate rages about how to reconcile the mismatch of student numbers to pupillages and tenancies. Reducing the number of Bar School places by weeding out inappropriate or less qualified applicants seems a sensible solution, yet it flies in the face of the Bar Council's stated aim to make the Bar more accessible. So, as things stand, you have the unenviable task of self-evaluating your chances of sucess in gaining pupillage.

To choose the Bar half-heartedly is unwise, but it's equally unwise to throw away a long-held dream. Match your passion with realism when you decide if the Bar is for you. If your academic record and interpersonal skills are excellent, read on...

If you're still with us, then your next step is to make sure your preconceptions of a career at the Bar are accurate. Don't just rely on your image of *Rumpole of the Bailey* or the roles portrayed in *This Life* and *North Square.* A barrister sets himself apart from a solicitor by the services he provides. His two main functions are advocacy and specialist opinion. If advocacy is what draws you to the law, the Bar is an obvious place for you, but it is no longer the only place. The gradual erosion of the Bar's monopoly on advocacy has been hastened by the Access to Justice Act 1999. The basic principle is that appropriately qualified solicitors must have equal rights of audience. If you want to read more on this topic turn to the **Litigation/Dispute Resolution** practice area section. Even as a barrister, the amount of advocacy you'll undertake will depend on the area of law in which you specialise. For details read the **Practice Areas at the Bar** section. If you choose an advocacy-heavy area of practice though, you'll need to develop a sophisticated, persuasive, clear and concise style. If you've always hated mooting, you should question your fitness for this career.

Advocacy is not the be-all and end-all. The smart young barrister will specialise and secure career success by offering genuine expertise in a particular field. There will always be a demand from solicitors for a second legal opinion on complex cases, and in some areas of work, advocacy plays only a small role in the service a barrister provides.

When researching the Bar sections of *Chambers UK*, our colleagues get plenty of feedback from solicitors and lay clients as to what makes a good barrister. Even the most admired of them don't all excel in every aspect of the job, but they do all have at least one aspect in which they are superb. Some are magnificent on their feet in court, and those who can modify their performance appropriately for judges, witnesses and (where relevant) jury are especially valued. Some barristers may not be the smoothest of advocates, but their knowledge of the law and the industry sector for which they work is unparalleled. Solicitors frequently describe such barristers as not just bright, but "*fearfully bright*." In today's legal profession solicitors are continually asking themselves "Why buy a dog if I can bark myself?" Well, if the dog can bark better...

As a barrister, your working environment will be completely different to that of your solicitor peers. You'll be self-employed for a start and that means you'll have to pay rent in chambers, VAT on your earnings and organise your own tax returns. You'll also be the master of your own destiny. Establishing your own client base – and keeping it – is essential, even though the majority of barristers work with others in sets, sharing premises called chambers and the services of professional managers called clerks. But you'll not be sharing your fees with fellow members of your set. Notions of partnership are absent. You'll rise or fall on your own merits.

For the first time this year, we have sent our *True Picture* team to the Bar. We've visited and researched 24 leading sets to try and work out what makes them tick. If you're a strong candidate, then reading the **Chambers Reports** section may help you decide which set should become your professional home...perhaps for the rest of your working life!

Seeking funding for Bar school will be an important task. Rich parents will prove enormously useful, but face it – you don't all have them. Before you start looking at your family in a completely different (and less than loving) light, read the **Funding** section and **Money, money, money....** The young Bar is feeling the pinch at the moment with dwindling fees, increased competition from solicitors and fewer cases reaching court. On the plus side, all pupillages must now be funded by chambers and this is making an enormous difference to pupils and some lucky BVC students. However, both factors are having an impact on the number of pupillages available and there are some indications that the number of pupillages offered in 2003 was lower than in previous years.

solicitor

Most budding lawyers qualify as solicitors rather than as barristers. Over 5,000 trainees start contracts each year, while the number of pupillages available is about one tenth of this figure. The career path of a solicitor is regarded as being smoother and more certain. Unless you plan to take a year out for travel or other experience, if you want to train in a commercial firm (as opposed to a high street practice) the decision-making process should start in the second year of a three-year law degree or the final year of a non-law degree. Commercial firms generally offer training contracts two years in advance; leave it too late and your preferred firms will no longer be recruiting for the year you want to start.

After your degree, law school awaits. Law graduates need spend only one year on the Legal Practice Course (LPC). Those with a non-law degree must also complete the CPE/PgDL before being eligible for the LPC. Larger commercial firms often offer scholarships to cover course fees and some maintenance for the LPC and, if necessary, the CPE/PgDL. A handful of big City firms require students to attend one of the three law schools that offer the 'City LPC', which is tailored for those embarking on a career in corporate and finance work. Many smaller firms – those in general or high street practice – tend not to offer law school sponsorship and recruit closer to the start date of the training contract. For students headed for this type of firm, the CPE and LPC years can be an uncertain and expensive time.

Selecting the right firm for you is a crucial decision because the client base, work and reputation of the firm you train at will determine the experience you gain and your future marketability as a lawyer. In addition to finding out about the size and location of a firm and the work it handles, you should research the firm's reputation and learn about its culture. At Chambers and Partners, we've made it our business to know who does what, how well they do it and what it might be like working at a particular firm. In the **Practice Areas** section of this book, you'll find the core results of the research carried out for *Chambers UK 2003-2004*. Our league tables will help you work out which firms command greatest respect from clients and other professionals in different areas of practice. An enormous amount of additional information is available in *Chambers UK*, including details of law firms' top clients and deals. Copies of the book should be available in your university careers office or law department library, or you can read the whole thing online at www.chambersandpartners.com. If you want to throw your research net even wider, you can find out about a firm's international work and reputation in *Chambers Global* and *Chambers US*.

In **The True Picture** we've profiled 120 of the leading firms in England and Wales. That part of the book should help you understand what kind of firm might suit you and the kind of work you can expect to receive when you get there. Law firms come in all shapes and sizes, so do your research, do a bit of navel-gazing and work out what's best for you.

magic circle: Slaughter and May, Clifford Chance, Freshfields, Allen & Overy and Linklaters. These are seen by many as the elite and are high paying, hard working and very corporate and finance-oriented. The prestige that attaches to a magic circle training is undeniable and, to that end, there are many students who'd consider going nowhere else. Whether this is because of the advice they are given by course directors, careers advisors, friends already at these firms or plain herd mentality, the fact is that these firms do have the pick of the brightest students and offer a superb training. Their size and big-money deals will definitely not appeal to all students and it's important that those who'd fare better in a different or smaller environment feel able to make an alternative choice.

london : The top ten City of London firms account for around 1,000 training contracts between them, representing around 20% of all training contracts registered with the Law Society. There's not a huge difference between the magic circle and firms such as Lovells, Herbert Smith and others of their ilk. In the largest commercial firms, work is almost entirely focused around business law, although a tiny number retain specialists in family law and private client practice. Hours are often long, but the money is very good. Expect high-profile work. Expect to be pushed and, at times, be prepared to give 110%. If you are working against a deadline on a deal then you will be expected to stay until it is finished. This can mean working through the night and coming in at weekends from time to time.

The pace is less frenetic in West End firms and there will also be less of an emphasis on financial and corporate transactions. Many smaller West End firms have specialisms in, say, media and entertainment or property work.

To get into a respected London firm you will need a consistently excellent academic record, from A-levels through to your first and second-year exam results or final degree. Unfortunately you'll need to go right to the back of a very long queue if you failed to gain at least a 2:1. Recruitment personnel in City firms are also keen to ensure that prospective trainees possess commercial awareness. In other words, understanding what businesses want, how they work and what lawyers can do to help them. You need to show that you have an interest in law, an interest in business and an interest in the firm you are going to. If you can't, there's something wrong with your decision.

regionals: The City of London may be the beating heart of big, blue-chip international business, but there's more to life than an EC postcode. Out in the regions, firms such as Dickinson Dees, Burges Salmon and Wragge & Co – to name but a few – offer top-notch clients and some international work. While some regional firms might as well be top London firms that just happen to be based in the regions, others focus on regional clients and work.

Regional firms can be every bit as difficult to get into as City firms. In some cases you are statistically more likely to get into a magic circle firm; a quick glance at the **Solicitors A-Z profiles** will show you why. If a City firm has refused you, don't assume you'll walk into a top regional firm...they are unimpressed by sloppy-seconds applications. If you are applying to join a firm in Bristol, for example, and have studied and lived in London all your life, be prepared to be asked why you want to move to the area. The last thing firms want is to spend a fortune on training only for newly qualified lawyers to swan off to jobs in the City. Recruitment personnel at the top regional practices are looking for exactly the same abilities and experience as the top City firms.

Salaries are lower outside London, in some cases significantly so, but the cost of living is much more reasonable than in the capital. You will also benefit from less frenetic hours than at the City-based practices. Regional firms have a reputation for being a bit friendlier, a bit calmer and a bit more human than those in the City. As you will see in **The True Picture**, however, it is all about finding a firm that suits you.

nationals: National firms have offices in a number of UK cities. Eversheds has ten offices in England and Wales; DLA has eight in England and Scotland. Hammonds and Pinsents each have four in London, Birmingham, Leeds and Manchester, while Addleshaw Goddard skips the Birmingham option. Some nationals avoid these major cities: Shoosmiths operates in smaller towns and cities from the South Coast up to Nottingham. Beachcroft Wansbroughs, Laytons, Bevan Ashford and others offer multiple offices. Each of these firms has a different approach to recruitment and whether or not trainees move around the country, so make sure you know the policy adopted by your chosen firm.

niche: Particularly in London, there are a variety of niche firms to choose from. Construction, entertainment, IP, insurance litigation, family...the list goes on. If you are absolutely certain that you want to specialise in a particular practice area (especially if you have already worked in the relevant industry) a niche firm is a sound choice. Be aware that many firms described as niche practices actually offer other types of work. Be aware also that some niche firms do try to woo students by stressing their other areas of practice.

general practice/high street: Practices range from substantial, long-established firms in large town centres to sole practitioners working above shops in the suburbs. These firms act for legally-aided clients, individuals funding themselves and local businesses. Staple work includes matrimonial, landlord and tenant, personal injury, employment, family, wills and probate and crime. It's increasingly likely that firms have an additional specialism in small-ticket commercial work for local businesses. Be prepared to earn considerably less than your peers in commercial practice. Commonly, you'll be paid at or around the minimum salary level recommended by the Law Society – £13,600pa for the provinces and £15,300pa for inner London. The hours can be unsociable if you find yourself working in crime, but in this kind of firm you will get to handle clients and real work from a very early stage. You'll grow up fast and you'll also see how the law actually affects individuals and the community in which you practice. Unlike commercial firms, most do not recruit two years in advance and most do not sponsor students through the LPC. Larger firms may take on four or five trainees a year, while the smallest will recruit on an ad hoc basis.

government legal service

About 30 training positions are available with the Government Legal Service every year. The majority are in London with the occasional one in Manchester. Positions are available for both trainee solicitors and pupil barristers and, according to Peter Beecroft, Recruitment Manager for the Service, the split was roughly even between the two types last year. "*We don't mind which branch of the profession they wish to pursue, it's their good mind, communication skills and commitment to become a good Government lawyer we're after.*" Various departments take trainees/pupils every year, namely: Customs & Excise; Inland Revenue; the DTI; the Department for Work & Pensions/Department of Health; the Treasury Solicitor's Department; the Home Office; Department for Environment, Food and Rural Affairs; the Department for Constitutional Affairs and the Office of the Deputy Prime Minister/Department for Transport. Some departments take one trainee, others up to half a dozen. Legal teams vary in size from a single lawyer in some of the smaller bodies to up to 300 in larger departments and agencies, in particular the Treasury Solicitor's Department and the Department for Constitutional Affairs.

Successful candidates are asked to nominate the area in which they would like to work. Trainee solicitor 'seats' are allocated after discussion with trainees. *"If they're in a large department, they might be able to get all the experience they need,"* says Peter, adding that they may be trained in more than one department if that is what's needed to give them the right experience. The training involves a variety of work concerned with both public and private law, including *"learning about litigation, working on government contracts and giving advice to ministers or administrators."* However, trainees are unlikely to get involved with drafting legislation, although *"maybe they would observe the process from the fringe."*

For pupil barristers, some departments follow the traditional 'two six' system, whereby six months are spent in barristers chambers and the other six within the GLS. Other departments have adopted the newer 'four four four' system, starting pupils in the department then sending them out to barristers chambers before bringing them back to the department. The first stage in securing training with the GLS is to contact its recruitment team, rather than the departments themselves. The GLS recruits two years before the pupillage/training contract begins and all vacancies are advertised in the national press and on the GLS website. Sponsorship for the LPC/BVC is available. A vacation scheme offers two or three-week work placements. Refer to www.gls.gov.uk.

local government

There are hundreds of local authority legal departments in the UK, some of which offer training contracts. There's no centralised list of vacancies and no single recruitment office, so you must contact each legal department separately and keep an eye open for advertisements in the legal and national press.

Training contracts usually conform to the four six-month seat system that's prevalent in private practice and you'll move between different teams to experience a number of areas of law. What's on offer? How about property, planning and environmental law; litigation and prosecution work; consumer protection, housing, education and childcare; employment, personal injury, administrative and commercial/contracts. The good news for aspiring advocates is that LA trainees have rights of audience before judges in chambers, something for which your peers in private practice must wait until after qualification. Your client will always be the local authority, although instructions will come from different officers within the authority. Without doubt the variety of work and experiences to be gained is wide, and for many there's real appeal in working for a public sector organisation that's closely involved with the local environment and community.

Most local government lawyers remain in the public sector, but the job is portable. Local authority legal departments exist everywhere in the UK, and lawyers can also transfer to the GLS or CPS or even go into private practice. Working conditions are good; family-friendly is not a dirty word; part-time working and job sharing are not uncommon. Some local authorities operate their legal departments along commercial principles and all must adhere to the principle of 'Best Value'.

Law School sponsorship is rare, but there are opportunities for both vacation work and/or paralegalling. For further information on a career in local government try www.lgcareers.com.

crown prosecution service

If you have a passion for criminal law and the idea of billable hours and contract drafting leaves you cold, the CPS may appeal. The service employs around 2,500 lawyers in England and Wales to handle cases involving some 1.4 million defendants each year.

prosecutors review and prosecute criminal cases following investigation by the police and advise the police on matters of criminal and evidence law. Prosecutors are stationed in one of two units. Criminal Justice Units were established within police stations to combat the problem of failed prosecutions. Lawyers here advise police on the appropriate charge for the crime. They spend one day in the office preparing cases and the next in the magistrates' court, dealing with administrative matters relating to each case. Lawyers in the Trial Unit deal with Crown Court cases, including murder, rape and robbery. Because Crown Court matters are more serious, prosecutors often act as instructing counsel, although they can become Higher Court Advocates and conduct prosecutions themselves. You won't be stranded in either unit as the CPS regularly rotates staff.

While it may lack the grit and glamour of *Law and Order*, the work of the CPS is exciting and varied. "*You never have the same day twice.*" You can expect to deal with 30 or 40 cases each day, and you must be on top of them all! Although they don't have the same degree of intense client contact as do defence lawyers, CPS prosecutors interact with everyone from magistrates, clerks, solicitors, probation officers and police, to civilian and expert witnesses, and even serving prisoners. They also liaise with victims' support and racial equality agencies. Where a prosecution is abandoned, the prosecutor must inform the victims of the reasons why. It's easy to see why one prosecutor told us: "*You must be flexible and prepared for anything!*" CPS lawyers must also be fairly "*bulletproof.*" The service sometimes gets bad press for failed prosecutions, so at times you'll not be the most popular person at the party, although you're guaranteed to have some pretty entertaining anecdotes!

Traditionally the CPS only recruited qualified lawyers, but last year it took on 22 trainees. Whether it will do the same again remains to be seen. Contact the CPS recruitment office to find out. A prosecutor's starting salary is around £22,500, rising to around £50,000, but you must be prepared to transfer to anywhere in the UK.

caseworkers assist prosecutors by researching cases and making recommendations on information required and charges to be brought; liaising with counsel, witnesses, police and court staff; and providing support to witnesses and victims. They also attend court to assist counsel on a regular basis. London caseworkers will usually be able to do a three-month stint at the Old Bailey. Impressive organisational skills and an ability to relate to people are essential. The starting salary is just shy of £17,000.

The way to the CPS can often be a circuitous one. Jim Federick, a trainee lawyer, graduated with a non-law degree in 1998 and got a job in finance at the CPS, later becoming a caseworker. The CPS allowed him a career break for two years, during which time he completed his CPE and the LPC. He is now stationed in a Criminal Justice Unit in Brighton. Melanie Walfall began her legal career in private practice, completing her training with a criminal defence firm before moving to the CPS. She is now working in a Criminal Justice Unit.

The CPS is a famously supportive employer, providing ongoing training and educational opportunities to its staff as well as decent benefits and flexitime. Individual area offices run work experience schemes so if you are interested contact your local service centre. Demand for placements is high, especially in London, so apply early.

All those we spoke to were proud to be a part of an institution that is dedicated to "*serving the public.*" As Jim told us, you can sleep soundly at night knowing that "*you are doing good work, and are making the world a safer place.*" To the Batmobile!

law centres

From its roots in North Kensington in 1970, the network of UK Law Centres has grown to around 54 today, each set up as either a registered charity or a not-for-profit company and run by its own local management committee. Advice is given to the public without charge as funding comes from local government grants (approx 60%) or the Legal Services Commission by way of 'Legal Help' certificated legal aid payments. The kinds of legal problems handled by a law centre may vary from one to another, but they can all be described as social welfare law specialists. Employment, discrimination, housing, immigration and public law (eg education and community care) form the main diet. Crime is not handled.

Law Centres see themselves as more than just providers of legal advice to the public; they tend to take on cases that have a wider social impact. A client who has a dispute with their window cleaner or a consumer problem is less likely to be taken on than someone who is affected by, say, a decision of a local authority on how rent arrears are dealt with. The number of cases brought by social landlords for rent arrears has increased to around 30,000 a year. Because law centres regard this as a trend that adversely affects a sufficiently large number of people, they believe their lawyers' time will be well spent on tackling individual problems while also trying to bring about policy change.

Law Centres employ qualified solicitors and barristers. Most work is carried out by these lawyers with only around 10% of the typical centre's hours being clocked up by volunteers assisting at evening drop-in sessions. The majority of law centre lawyers will have originally come from private practice, although some will have earned their stripes in a law centre. Traditionally, those lawyers who have qualified while working at a law centre have done so by combining part-time study with work. This is the route most commonly followed by experienced advice workers.

From 2003 the Legal Services Commission is funding some 20 or so training contracts in 14 law centres up and down the country. These will mirror the typical training contract in private practice with trainees spending periods of time with different lawyers to learn about their specialist areas of work. Before you go rushing down to the post box with your CV, take note: an equal opps policy means that candidates will only be considered if they respond to an advertisement. Look for these in *The Guardian* (Wednesdays), local newspapers, a two-monthly publication called *Legal Action* (your university law library should have it), and on the Law Centres Federation website www.lawcentres.org.uk.

Salaries for qualified lawyers are around £24-30,000 (or more in London). At the junior level this compares favourably with high street practice, but the gap widens the more senior you get. Law centres operate along different lines to private practices; less hierarchy, more of an equal say for staff at all levels – some even operate as collectives with all staff drawing the same salary. Terms and conditions at work emulate those in local government and, as such, pension and holiday provisions etc. are good, while flexible and part-time working is common.

Most law centres employ 10-15 lawyers and, if you're attracted to working with colleagues who share your ideals and social conscience, you may want to investigate a career in the sector. See the section called **Are you a strong candidate?** for info on volunteering while still studying.

in-house

A small number of large companies and banks offer training contracts and pupillages. For information on in-house legal teams registered to take trainees check the Law Society's website and for pupillages, refer to the Bar Council. Information in this area can be hard to come by, but you can refer to *Chambers UK* for the contact details of legal teams in the FTSE 100 companies.

court clerk

The Court Service is an executive agency of the Department for Constitutional Affairs and is responsible for the daily business of the court system. Launched in 1995, it fulfils the administrative functions of the court, such as providing ushers and dealing with court timetabling, and is also engaged in modernising the physical appearance of courts. Because it is an administrative agency, there are few opportunities for lawyers, however, the service recruits Judicial Assistants at various times throughout the year. JA appointments are temporary, and each lasts for a three-month term. JAs undertake legal tasks for the Lord Justices in the Civil Division of the Court of Appeal at the Royal Courts of Justice, including legal research, advice and providing assistance in drafting judgments.

Applicants must be qualified lawyers who have completed pupillage or traineeship. They also need to demonstrate intellectual ability, with a minimum 2:1 degree, the ability to work under pressure as part of a team and word processing skills. JA appointments pay around £80 per day. The Service advertises positions in *The Times* weekly law supplement and in the *Law Society's Gazette*.

There are longer term careers available too. We spoke to magistrates' clerks who relished their role as legal advisors to lay magistrates and managers of the court. Approximately 430 magistrates' courts operate in England and Wales, and between them they handle the majority of the country's criminal proceedings. In a busy port city like Hull, for instance, in addition to the usual TV licence and traffic offences, the clerks will see drug trafficking cases and other serious crimes. A rural court is likely to be quieter and crimes of violence will be less common, while clerks in busy metropolitan centres will experience the greatest variety of cases.

A court clerk needs to be able to think on their feet and deal confidently with people. The clerks we spoke to told us that the vast majority of defendants speak to them with respect and are quite easy to handle. Occasionally they exercise the power to order individuals into custody for contempt of court, but this is rare! Confidence is an essential trait; the magistrates need to know they can rely on you for sound advice on issues like self-defence, identification of suspects, and inferences from the silence of defendants after arrest. After just a few years, there are unlikely to be many occasions when you're faced with a situation you've not handled before.

A shift in recruitment policy has seen the traditional route (by which even those without degrees could train while studying for the Diploma in Magisterial Law) overtaken by the recruitment of LPC and BVC graduates as trainee court clerks.

As the trainee progresses through a structured training programme, the number and complexity of their court duties will increase until ultimately they are advising lay magistrates on points of law and procedure. Most courts operate nine or ten sessions a week and most clerks will be in court for the majority of these. The remaining time will be spent exercising powers delegated to them by the magistrates, like issuing summonses, for example.

Individual courts recruit trainee clerks and general staff as and when they need them. Vacancies are advertised in a weekly publication called *Justice of the Peace and Local Government Law* and also in local papers. Those with legal qualifications seeking training contracts should contact the Association of Magistrates' Courts (tel: 020 7723 1975 or www.ccmcc.co.uk).

paralegal work

Many students spend time working as paralegals in law firms. If you have time to fill before starting your training or while you are still trying to find a training contract, this is an excellent way to fill it. Paralegalling can also be a full-time career for some, although qualifying as a legal executive may be better in the long term. Sadly, at the time of writing, the market for paralegals is poor.

are you a strong candidate?

Make no mistake, your dream job is not going to fall from the sky and land on you. It will require effort, and those who think otherwise are either ridiculously intelligent or ridiculously stupid. Thankfully, these days it's rarely 'who you know' and mostly 'who you are' that will get you a job. There's a lot you can do to increase your appeal to recruiters, but some things you are or you aren't, you have or you don't.

i am what i am...

A non-law degree is absolutely no drawback whatsoever; indeed, students with language skills and science degrees score especially highly with recruiters in solicitors firms and we noted a preponderence of classics and humanities grads at the leading sets at the Bar. Overall, non-law grads perform **very** well.

Whether they admit it or not, firms and chambers tend to subscribe to the idea that there's a pecking order of universities. Graduates from Oxford, Cambridge and a number of other favoured redbricks and London colleges dominate the City firms and London sets. For details of our 2002 'Preferred Universities' survey of solicitors' firms check the Chambers Student website.

Regional firms and sets often feel more comfortable recruiting those with a local connection – perhaps family ties or an education in the area. They want to know that whoever they take on will be committed to a long-term career in the region.

Many older applicants assume they are at a disadvantage. Far from it! So long as you have something to show for your extra years, you may find it easier to impress recruiters. You already know how to work, your people/client-handling skills are probably better developed, and you may even offer specific industry experience. We've come across successful barristers and solicitors who've done everything from secretarial work, pub management and film production to police work. Certain past-life work experiences – healthcare, the armed forces, accountancy and engineering – make candidates particularly interesting.

It's official! Travel does broaden the mind. Recruiters know this too, so don't feel that you need to play down the time you've spent exploring the world.

drifting freshers

Year after year, new students are tempted into the drifting fresher trap, only to be washed up on the beach near Lamejobsville in later years. "It's just my first year, it doesn't actually count" and "I can always resit," they say. What they don't mutter over the vodka redbulls and purple nasties is that you may be applying for training contracts in your second year, and if the only marks you have to show firms are the amazing Thirds you netted in your first year, it's not going to look good. You'll need to pull good grades throughout your time at uni – you really don't want to end up touting around a 2:2 or a Third when you leave.

Nonetheless, your first year is a time to explore your newfound independence and practically unlimited opportunities. Almost every uni will have a wide range of societies, meeting groups or sports clubs. At the vast majority, if your leisure pursuit of choice is not on offer, they'll give you the cash to set it up, provided you can rustle up a handful of like-minded individuals. Commitment to your interests will give an extra dimension to both your university experience and, crucially, your CV.

don't swim with your eyes shut

Sometimes the flood of info from university bodies such as the students' union and careers service can be so heavy you feel like you are drowning in e-mails, flyers and posters telling you of this job vacancy, that Amnesty meeting, or the other CV workshop. Resist the temptation to let it all wash over you. Relevant work experience is vital to almost every successful job application, so keep your eyes open for suitable positions, and use them to test your own ideas of what you would like to do. Many universities run law-specific career seminars in association with firms of solicitors or sets of chambers. Michael Hunting, grad recruitment guru at Eversheds, places real value in the 30 university visits the firm makes each year. *"If candidates are prepared and know how to promote themselves, they come across much better – people sometimes ask if we are giving secrets away at these sessions, and we say 'Yes, why be secretive about it?'"* Earlier in 2003 we attended a large session for students hosted by Devereux Chambers. A number of barristers tackled various topics and made themselves available for questions both in the lecture room and over drinks afterwards. Attending such sessions will really help.

If you want to be a commercial lawyer, a bit of business savvy will also be required. You could read the *FT* now and again, or find an internet site that will give you headline bulletins in bite-sized chunks. Keep up to date in a way that suits you, just don't be oblivious to the events going on around you at national and international level.

step forward

Volunteering goes a long way to showing what sort of person you are. For almost every area of interest you can find a parallel voluntary position; joining an organisation or society that works in or promotes your chosen area of interest will keep you up to date and demonstrate your commitment. Barristers chambers and law firms really value such practical experience, and to some it is as important as your academic qualifications. Again, take advantage of the info available at uni – your student law society, students' union and careers service should have links with voluntary organisations. If not, check the internet for volunteering opportunities. For general volunteering try www.knowuk.co.uk, a directory of UK voluntary agencies. If you are interested in human rights and civil liberties, www.justice.org.uk and www.amnesty.org are good places to start. As well as having good links to similar organisations, they welcome volunteers and offer internships. For local law centres, visit www.lawcentres.org.uk, but be aware you are unlikely to be able to give legal advice – they may need help with translating and general office duties though.

We spoke to the Citizens Advice service, which has over 22,000 volunteers in over 2,000 bureaux. Those with real commitment and enough time can train with the CAB on its Open College Network-accredited Adviser Training Programme (lasting 40 weeks on a part-time basis). This is a widely recognised qualification that may subsequently enable the period of your law firm training contract to be reduced. Not all volunteers have the time or the inclination to train as advisers, and if admin, IT or reception work is enough for you, why not request one of these roles. Debt, benefits, housing, employment, consumer issues, family matters and immigration are the most commonly raised problems, some six million of which are handled each year. Statistical monitoring enables CABx to work out which issues it regards suitable for Government lobbying and campaigning. For more info see www.citizensadvice.org.uk/join-us. Aspiring barristers, especially should read the section on the Free Representation Unit (FRU) on page 601.

on an even keel

Barristers chambers and firms of solicitors are looking for those who have covered plenty of bases: good or excellent academic performance, a bit of sport and/or music/arts and plenty of interaction with others. Do make an effort to get involved in a range of things – you don't want to end up walking away, 2:1 safely in hand and thinking *"I wish I'd done more at university..."* But in your bid to be president of this or that society, don't forget that the degree itself is why you are there.

cpe/pgdl/gdl: law for non-lawyers

The Law Society determines the training requirements for qualification as a solicitor in England and Wales. There are two stages to the training process, academic and vocational. The vocational bit is the LPC and the academic bit can be satisfied in one of three ways: by completing a qualifying law degree, or the CPE, or the Institute of Legal Executives ILEX exams, which enable people already in legal employment to qualify while they are working. Similarly, the Bar Council requires those who want to be barristers, but do not have a qualifying law degree, to undergo the CPE course.

Don't be intimidated by the array of names for the CPE. The difference between the Postgraduate Diploma in Law, the Common Professional Examination and the Graduate Diploma in Law is simply one of nomenclature. From both the Law Society's and the Bar Council's points of view, all are equally valid. For simplicity, we will use the term CPE throughout this book.

admission requirements

The standard requirement for admission to the CPE is a degree from a university in the UK or the Republic of Ireland. However, some other non-standard qualifications are recognised, such as certain overseas degrees and degree equivalent or professional qualifications. Additionally, non-graduate mature persons who have gained considerable experience and shown exceptional ability in academic, professional, business or administrative fields may be considered.

the course

This will be no walk in the park. Full-time CPE courses last for a minimum of 36 weeks during which you'll be expected to undertake 45 hours of lectures, tutorials, private study and research per week. Consequently some students opt to study part-time over two years.

The course covers seven "foundations of legal knowledge":

- **Contract**
- **Tort**
- **Criminal law**
- **Equity and trusts**
- **EU law**
- **Property law**
- **Public law**

Assessment is usually by way of written exams – these will mostly be traditional three-hour papers – and many institutions also require you to submit coursework assignments and/or a dissertation. No two CPE courses are the same, so do your research. Contact institutions to request a prospectus, speak to former students and find out what course suits you best. Depending on where you go, the CPE can either be characterised by the need to memorise great swathes of photocopied material and parrot learn cases and legislation, or it can be a challenge that excites the brainiest of brainiacs. City Uni is seen to offer a rigorous and academic course and is favoured by aspiring barristers. One pupil at a leading London set noted: *"They work you harder at City, but you're allowed to use your brain. It's not simply learning by rote."*

Typically, the teaching is a combination of lectures and classes, for which you'll have to prepare material in readiness for a grilling by your tutors. Some institutions (City Uni among them) will also require you to write several academic essays per term. At law schools that favour a more practical approach, such as BPP or the College of Law, you'll have to prepare solutions to problem questions which you'll then tackle in tutorials.

At first, the material you're learning and the way you're expected to think may seem alien, but don't expect a gentle induction. This is a fast-track course, and if you don't get up to speed with the essentials in the first few weeks, there's a real danger of falling behind. If you're really bright, you may find it is easy to cruise through the course – those photocopied manuals get you out of a whole lot of reading; however, you **will** need to put the hours in if you're going to pass. And remember, if you're being sponsored, your firm won't be impressed if you just scrape through.

If you're well-organised and keep up to date with the work, it is possible to do very well without being in the library 24/7 – many people manage to squeeze in part-time jobs and plenty of fun. Essentially, it's a case of applying the skills you already have to industrial quantities of new material. If you do this in bite-sized chunks as you go along, the whole process is relatively palatable. If you worked hard at university and got a good degree, you're perfectly capable of succeeding on the CPE – some people even find themselves enjoying it!

applications

Those wishing to study the CPE full-time must apply through the Central Applications Board (See contact details on page 7). To ensure the best chance of securing a place at your college of choice, apply early in the calendar year and in the first round of applications. It is possible to apply for a place in the second round in the late spring but popular, oversubscribed schools are unlikely to still have places. If you are hoping to do your LPC at a very popular school it is really worthwhile trying to get a CPE place there. Most schools guarantee LPC places to those of their students who are successful at the CPE.

The course is now offered at 33 different universities and colleges in England and Wales. Look on our website at www.chambersandpartners.com for a full list and for details of course fees.

When to do it

When you join your class on the first day of your CPE, you'll probably discover that the student population is more varied than you imagined. Of course, there will be plenty of new and recent graduates, but there will also be people who have left other careers to train as lawyers and people who have already worked in law firms in a non-qualified capacity. If you're considering a career in law there is no need to embark on the CPE immediately – many students are richer for a period of time away from academia. There's a whole world of adventure and useful experiences out there beyond the classroom and you'll find that it is easier to take time out before starting your career.

the legal practice course

The LPC is the year-long course undertaken by prospective solicitors after either a qualifying law degree or the CPE. It is designed to equip students with the skills needed for practice rather than as a further period of scholarship. The first two-thirds of the year is spent on compulsory elements: knowledge areas including litigation, conveyancing and business law, and legal skills such as interviewing, advocacy, drafting and IT. After taking exams on these compulsory sections, the remaining months are devoted to three elective subjects. The range of options varies from one school to another – there's a full list of who offers what on our Chambers student website.

the city lpc

Those with training contracts from the eight City consortium firms (A&O, Clifford Chance, Freshfields, Herbert Smith, Linklaters, Lovells, Norton Rose and Slaughter and May) must study the 'City LPC' at BPP in London, Nottingham Law School or Oxford Institute of Legal Practice. The City LPC is a challenging course that is closely focused on the type of work City trainees will undertake. Consortium firm students are required to choose the private acquisitions, debt finance and equity finance electives.

Places are also available to students going to non-consortium firms, but the course is appropriate only for those headed for City practice. A non-City LPC is also offered by these three institutions, but competition is ferocious as a large quota of places at each are reserved for City LPC students and the schools' own successful CPE students. City electives are offered at other schools, so not studying at BPP, Oxford or Nottingham is no bar to gaining a City-compatible LPC. Consortium firms' students are put in a ballot to decide whether they'll go to BPP, Nottingham or Oxford. While asked about their preferences, they are not always guaranteed their first-choice school.

how do you choose a law school?

Applications are administered centrally by the LPC Central Applications Board (see page 7). Before filling in the LawCabs application form, get hold of as much information as possible — read LawCabs' literature, request prospectuses, chat to representatives visiting your university and current students. When choosing a school, there are plenty of considerations:

career issues: For non-consortium firm students who already have a training contract offer, a future employer may have a preferred list of schools and a view on what electives should be taken. At the very least, your future employer should be able to give you advice, and if it is paying your fees it's probably only polite to ask. If you don't yet have a training contract, think about the quality of careers advice on offer at different schools. Have they a good record for getting students placements and/or training contracts with the kind of firm you want to work for? In the summer of 2002 we surveyed law firms in England and Wales to identify their preferred LPC providers. The results can be found on our website, although for the most part (and particularly outside the City), firms usually indicated a preference for schools with a good assessment grade.

electives: Find out which schools offer the electives best suited to the type of practice you want to move into. Some may have restrictions on elective combinations or run electives only when there is sufficient demand.

assessment grades and pass rates: Pass rates are published on the Law Society's website each autumn, but be aware that direct comparisons are impossible as each institution examines and marks independently. The Law Society visits and inspects each institution and then publishes an 'Ofsted-style' report on its website along with an assessment grade. The grades are set out in the following table.

LAW SOCIETY ASSESSMENT GRADES – SEPT 2003	
Anglia Polytechnic University	Good
Bournemouth University	Good
BPP Law School	Very Good
Bristol Institute of Legal Practice at UWE	Excellent
Cardiff Law School	Excellent
College of Law at Birmingham	Very Good
College of Law at Chester	Very Good
College of Law at Guildford	Very Good
College of Law at London	Very Good
College of Law at York	Very Good
De Montfort University	Good
Inns of Court School of Law	Very Good
Leeds Metropolitan University	Satisfactory
Liverpool John Moores University (p/t)	Good
London Metropolitan University	Good
Manchester Metropolitan University	Good
Nottingham Law School	Excellent
Oxford Institute of Legal Practice	Very Good
Staffordshire University	Very Good
Thames Valley University	Good
University of Central England	Satisfactory
University of Central Lancashire	Very Good
University of Exeter	Good
University of Glamorgan	Good
University of Hertfordshire (p/t)	Good
University of Huddersfield	Good
University of Northumbria	Good
University of Sheffield	Very Good
University of Westminster	Very Good
University of Wolverhampton	Good

teaching methods: Most institutions timetable around 14 hours of classes per week. In some places you might be able to catch up on sleep in the back row of a lecture theatre; at others you'll be swanning around mock offices during sessions designed to replicate a morning in a firm. Exam and assessment methods also vary with some institutions offering significantly more coursework. As for exams, some are entirely open-book while others only allow statutes and practitioner texts into the exam room. A larger provider may not be right for you, if you like to be more than a number to your tutors. Then again, relative anonymity may appeal.

tactics: The most popular institutions require you to put them as first choice on the LawCabs form before they will even consider you. Check whether your university or CPE provider or your law firm has an agreement with an LPC provider.

money and fees: Fees vary – City LPC providers charge the most – and you should check whether they include the cost of textbooks, Law Society membership, etc. Even if you have sponsorship, living expenses still need to be taken into account and London, especially, can be a nasty shock if you haven't lived there before. For the latest info on fees, we've a table on our website.

location: For many students, tight finances restrict their choice of school. Living at home with the olds will save you a packet...if you can stand it! If you're lucky enough to be able to strike out on your own, it's worth considering what you like and don't like about your university or CPE provider, and whether you want to prolong your undergraduate experience or escape it. And remember, some LPC providers are dominated by graduates of local universities. While some providers are part of a university law faculty; elsewhere, elaborate floral arrangements and acres of plate glass may make you feel like you're studying for your LPC in the offices of a City law firm.

social mix: Some institutions have a very diverse intake, with students heading off to all types of practice; others are dominated by particular groups, eg future City slaves or regional devotees. It's worth thinking about whether you'd prefer to be somewhere with students on a similar career path or whether you want to mix it up with a wider cross-section of people. Size also matters: it can be harder to bond with your cohort where you're one of several hundred. Past students have reported a better social scene in smaller schools. Studenty cities such as Nottingham and Bristol are always a lot of fun; however, students in the Big Smoke warn us that often everyone turns into pumpkins when classes end.

lpc providers – the inside story

We have taken a closer look at ten LPC providers that take 100 or more students per year and also have "Excellent" or "Very good" Law Society ratings. These reports are based on the answers to questions posed to course directors, Law Society reports and interviews with current and former students.

bpp law school, london

number of places: 756 full-time, 144 part-time

The law school is just one part of this professional education business: accountants, lawyers, insolvency practitioners, financial types, marketing types and MBAs the world over have qualified with BPP. It comes as no surprise that it won the contract for the sole provider of the City LPC in London. It is even less shocking to find that around 80% of BPP students have either studied a CPE there, or will train with one of the eight firms for which the City LPC was developed. Jenny Barnes, the school's client liaison manager, explained: "*Up to two-thirds of our places are available to consortium firms.*" Competition for the remaining places is fierce – last year BPP attracted 2,684 applications for the full-time course.

As is increasingly the case elsewhere, the course focuses on black letter law and primary sources that will become a trainee's stock-in-trade. However, the compulsory subjects are weighted towards City practice, and this bent carries through into the electives offered – Family Law and the hard-to-find Advanced Criminal Litigation option are perhaps the only two that are not obviously 'City'. As Jenny told us: "*The most popular were Debt Finance, Equity Finance and Private Acquisitions, as many students were required by their firms to take these electives, or wanted to do so as they planned to pursue a career in a City practice.*" As a result, students choosing the 'non-City' pathway are apt to find that, like polyfilla, their timetables fit nicely into the gaps left by the City classes. In an effort to counter allegations of City bias, the non-commercial electives are designed with the help of specialists in those fields, ensuring the quality is on par with the rest.

Expect to work hard – there's around 15 hours of weekly class time and a respectable 18 students per tutor in seminars, so preparation and participation are unavoidable, even for determined slackers. But then you won't find slackers at BPP; the majority of students have at least a 2:1 and 15% of the 2002 entrants had Firsts. In short, if you don't want to put the effort in, don't apply. The social side suffers a bit from the lack of campus life, and the students we spoke to commented that many stuck to an established circle of friends. Again, showing BPP's awareness of the downsides and the desire to tackle them, it stumps up the cash for dinner and drinks for each tutor group at the beginning of the year. The cynical will argue this comes out of your fees, but chances are these will have come from a law firm and not your own pocket.

apply here if:

- your consortium firm expects you to
- you are heading for City practice
- you're a legal genius with City-bound chums

bristol institute of legal practice at uwe

number of places: 320 full-time, 80 part-time

UWE was the first institution to receive an 'Excellent' rating from the Law Society and has retained this grading ever since. Full of praise for its teaching and organisation, the Law Society on its last assessment visit only singled out UWE's IT provision for improvement, a complaint also echoed by some students. But not all. One said: *"I thought the facilities were excellent, computers were always available."* The moans of most former students were reserved, however, for the location, with one student going as far as to say: *"If I were a first-year undergraduate turning up there I'd be distressed."*

Students were generally positive about the quality of *"approachable"* teachers, although as at other institutions, the course was accepted as a necessary hurdle to qualification. *"It was nothing at all like being at university, they piled on the work and you had to turn up...in fact it was more like going to work than university!"* A wide range of electives is on offer and teaching is more weighted towards small group work than elsewhere; marathon three-hour workshops predominate, with the occasional overview lecture and support clinic. An LL.M in Advanced Legal Practice is offered as a top-up qualification. Competition for places is intense (it's wise to put UWE as first choice on your form) and the course mainly attracts students aiming for large and medium firms in Bristol and London.

UWE is located on the edge of the student mecca of Bristol, but the campus can be a tad tricky to get to; parking is a *"nightmare"* and public transport not always reliable. Despite this, living in one of the student enclaves, such as Cotham or Redland near the city centre, rather than the campus, comes highly recommended.

apply here if:

- you're after great teaching in small groups
- you want a wide range of electives
- you love Bristol to bits

cardiff law school

number of places: 160 full-time

Take the best bits of London, knock off the really tall bits, wash the really dirty bits and what's left will look a bit like Cardiff, fast becoming one of the best British cities in which to live and work. Throw in one of only three LPC providers to bear the 'Excellent' badge and you have the beginnings of a very attractive LPC year. Then sprinkle liberally with the facilities offered by a university ranked seventh in the UK for research (don't forget the student union, sports and accommodation services, library facilities, counselling, health and daycare). As a final dressing, the law school organises a wide range of social and sporting events, and unlike the majority of providers, offers a graduation ceremony at which mum and dad can do their best to embarrass you.

The small intake means close working relationships between staff and students. Ian Brookfield, the LPC course leader, pointed out: *"We can do things with 160 people that other places will struggle to do."* Moreover, the college has fostered such strong links with local firms, that the careers service can guarantee a work placement for all of the 60% of students starting the course without a training contract. A slim majority eventually go to firms in Wales and the rest into a full range of practices from Newcastle to Norwich. *"We are aiming to be a full-service provider...for all branches of the profession,"* Ian told us. Accordingly, *"if students choose appropriate electives,"* they will be fit for all types of public and private sector employers. We're told Cardiff has *"never not run an elective if students want to do it."*

Students heaped praise on the school. *"The course is very well run; a lot of thought has been put into it."* Cardiff had more than two first-choice applicants per place for 2003. Ian warned: *"To get here* [students] *must put Cardiff first on their application."* Most have at least a 2:1, but *"the degree is just one of the criteria we consider. It is possible that a 2:2 student with a training contract and good work experience might get an offer in favour of a 2:1 student who doesn't score well in other areas."*

apply here if:

- you want a top-flight, intimate institution
- you want a wide range of electives to choose from
- a thriving social/professional community appeals

college of law

The College of Law is the country's largest LPC provider, spread across five different locations. The institution suffered a blow when it failed to win a contract to provide the City LPC to trainees of the eight consortium firms, but quickly picked itself up and is now marketing its LPC on the basis of its breadth and accessibility. All the locations have an impressive 'Very good' rating from the Law Society and a broad range of electives is on offer. In line with most other LPC providers, the College of Law teaches in a mixture of small and large groups, timetabling in around 14 hours a week. Some say the course is not as challenging as it could be, but don't be lulled into a false sense of security; there's a lot of it and you need to keep on top of all your classes and coursework.

The same course is taught all over the country, but the same problems with the course are also found in all five locations. Acting on Law Society recommendations, the College of Law is currently introducing more small group sessions and increasing IT facilities and IT-based elements of the course. In some branches it has been running trials of a new Computer Assisted Learning programme (CAL). There have been suggestions from the Law Society that sessions could be more challenging, and some students do feel that too much spoon-feeding goes on, but in fairness this is a criticism we hear about most LPC providers. On the plus side, popular student pro bono schemes are up and running in all locations and participation can really enhance a student's experience of the year, both in terms of motivation and learning vital client-handling skills.

Around 30% of students start the course with training contracts; future City stars (minus those from the big eight consortium firms) tend to cluster in London and Guildford, with the other branches having strong regional appeal and links. Generally, a good time is had by all socially, although the five locations have very different characters.

store street, london

number of places: 1,248 full-time, 192 part-time

Just off Tottenham Court Road, this is the country's largest law school. Many students tend to view the LPC as a necessary evil and see Store Street as more of a factory than a temple of learning. This may be a fashionable view to hold (we note the same thing among Bar students at the biggest BVC provider, ICSL), but it's probably a poor attitude to go in with. Even without the City LPC, the London site is still full of future Square Mile trainees. If you'd rather study with students who are headed for all sections of the solicitors' profession, this is the London provider to choose. Remember, as always in London, everyone lives too far apart to co-ordinate fun and games easily. It's worth making the effort though and the West End is on your doorstep.

birmingham

number of places: 480 full-time, 60 part-time

The course here has only been running for two years and so students enjoy a brand new building in an excellent and central location in Birmingham's Jewellery Quarter. The first year of the course may have been dogged by teething troubles (a ceiling fell down and there were workmen banging around for a while), but we understand the set-up is just peachy now. The Birmingham branch has taken the initiative with the CAL trials, although at the time of writing we had no details on how they were received by students. The College offers good links with Midlands firms.

chester

number of places: 600 full-time, 60 part-time

Students love life in Chester and its cheap and cheerful accommodation, but the branch here is actually located just outside the town, so unless you want to use public transport, you may need a car...or a friend with a car. A range of students come here, from those destined for top commercial firms in London right down to the good old high street practice. Unfortunately, they're not all as glamorous as the ones featured on *Hollyoaks*, but you can't have it all!

guildford

number of places: 720 full-time, 100 part-time

Guildford used to be the LPC provider of choice for the pashmina and chinos brigade. These days there are fewer smart convertibles in the car park as students headed to consortium firms are directed elsewhere. This has had the beneficial effect of making the school less cliquey. As in all four locations, the careers service does a sterling job and students speak positively of the leafy manor in which the COL is housed. With so mant students, the social scene is good, although Guildford's clubs and bars can, at best, be described as tacky. London is just 40 minutes away if you need a fix of city living after too many evenings in country pubs.

york

number of places: 492 full-time, 60 part-time.

Students rave about their time in this small and friendly city. Most tend to have a northern connection, having grown up locally or studied at a northern university; others intend to train in the region. This really is the place to go if you are heading for one of Yorkshire's law firms, as you'll quickly make friends with your future colleagues and rivals. *Coronation Street*-style housing is readily available, and if you want to keep an eye on the horses, the college (which is contained within an old school) is practically trackside.

apply here if:

- you want a highly regarded LPC
- you want a broad choice of electives
- pro bono experience appeals

inns of court school of law, city university, london

number of places: 120 full-time

The Inns of Court School of Law has been providing legal education for a very long time, but until 2000 it only trained barristers. In 2002, it became a department within City University's Faculty of Law, but perhaps due to the newness of the arrangement, the accompanying perks (sports facilities, student union, counselling services and, perhaps best of all for those from out of town, accommodation services) are, as yet, underused by ICSL students.

A common allegation levelled at LPC providers is a tendency to spoon-feed students, leading to decreased motivation. Not here. Course leader Paul Aber has instigated some cultural changes. He tells us: "*Everyone will come to all sessions, they will come on time and be prepared.*" You've been warned! With large groups of around 80, small groups of 16 and skills groups of just eight, students are expected to "*take responsibility for their own work.*" Such small groups also assist effective feedback.

The quality of LPC teaching has always been praised and ICSL has a 'Very good' rating, but as it continues its post-millennial evolution facilities have also improved. The Morrison Hall, built in the late 80s yet still managing to resemble a grim Welsh chapel, has been split in two and dramatically made over. On top is a spacious refectory, below is a hi-tech lecture theatre boasting IT facilities that allow real-time, on-screen interaction between tutor and students. IT also features heavily in the library and every classroom If your PC skills are shaky, there are classes to get you up to speed.

The gardens and squares of Gray's Inn are ideal for cultivating your budding sense of lawyer-self, especially as the Royal Courts of Justice and Chancery Lane are close by. Most ICSL students will be studying for the Bar but, as an LPC student, you'll have your own subset and tutors will make the effort to get to know you.

The course is heavy on black letter law and commercially focused. As the school attracts students destined for a wide range of firms, the electives also cater to a range of specialist practices. The calibre of students is rather good – nothing less than a 2:1 will do unless you have a damn good CV. ICSL now receives ten applications per available place. Sounds like it's entitled to be a little fussy about grades…

apply here if:

- barrister mates are going there
- you want an intimate LPC within a large school
- only the epicentre of English law will do

nottingham law school

number of places: 650 full-time, 70 part-time

Nottingham Law School stands out from the crowd, and not just because it won the approval of the eight consortium law firms that sponsor the City LPC. A proud bearer of the Law Society's 'Excellent' seal of approval, Nottingham excels across the board. If we had a pound for every glowing recommendation we've heard from past students, we'd have given up wet London Mondays for a yacht in the Whitsundays. Unsurprisingly, the course is oversubscribed and, as a result, virtually all students have a 2:1 or a First.

Of these 650-plus bright young things, around 70% have a training contract offer before starting and a third end up at consortium firms. Bob White, the director of graduate development, said: *"It's not part of the selection process; the fact is, the people who get in are the type who have a training contract – if you are good, we want you."* Its desire for able students doesn't stop at City and commercial types. Nottingham reserves 100 places for people who don't want to follow a corporate pathway, preferring instead *"a package designed for…general commercial practice." "We aren't prepared to sell ourselves body and soul to one part of the market."*

Last year we noted that some 'non-City' students felt a little marginalised. Bob conceded: *"You could have a sense that this is a corporate place,"* but points out that *"good 'hard' legal skills are important whether you are going to a big firm or a single-partner practice."* Moreover, in class, you won't find yourself the odd family wannabe in a group of City slickers. *"We do a lot of social engineering to get the dynamics right – we try to make sure there is a cross section in classes."*

One past student conveyed the buzz that often surrounds the school: *"I'd heard it was the best – people raved about it – and I really enjoyed it. As well as really good teaching, I also had really good fun. Practically the whole course goes out some nights – 600 people in one place!"* So if you are bright, there's perhaps only one 'restriction' left. The school is in Nottingham, and as Bob neatly put it: *"It wouldn't suit someone who has never been north of Watford and doesn't want to."*

apply here if:

- you have an excellent academic record
- you are looking for a broad range of electives
- you are/are not heading to a consortium firm

oxford institute of legal practice

number of places: 353 full-time

Winning the prestigious tender to provide the City LPC has meant a rapid growth in student numbers, buildings and facilities at OILP. However, some students have questioned whether quality was sacrificed for quantity: in 2002 the shine rubbed off when a student petition emerged after lower than expected pass rates. We are not aware of any kind of uprising in 2003.

The range of electives on offer is standard for an institution mainly catering to the needs of students heading to City firms, as is the teaching structure – a mixture of lectures and small group sessions (around 17 students) totalling around 14 hours per week. On the plus side, communication between tutors and students seems to be good, with the Law Society rating the personal tutor programme and the staff-student liaison committee. However, as in other schools, some students complain of spoon-feeding. Internal organisation and assessment methods also came under fire, particularly the closed-book exams. As one student pointed out: *"We are not in a profession that needs to know everything without being able to look it up in a book."* Oxford is not the only school to examine in this way.

These future lawyers are a brainy lot. 96% of the class of 2003 had a 2:1 or better, reflecting the intense competition to get in; this year there were 1,627 applications for 353 places. There seems to be an element of cliqueyness at the Institute; those not in possession of an undergraduate degree from Oxford and non-City students may feel a bit excluded. However, there's no denying the appeal of this student paradise of a city, and student membership of OILP opens up the facilities of the two universities. The institute itself also has good facilities and offers the chance to be involved in pro bono schemes.

apply here if:

- you're a consortium firm student
- you can't bear to leave Oxford
- you've fab grades and are happy to work hard

university of sheffield

number of places: 180 full-time, 64 part-time

After a marketing drive that has dramatically increased the number of applicants, Sheffield has expanded its LPC course to cater for 180 students – almost 30% up on last year. It's been given the green light by the Law Society to increase this further to 216 for the 2005 start. The University has also retained its 'Very good' rating. As a school that actively resisted the City LPC, Sheffield provides a broad range of electives to a similarly broad range of students.

In order to understand Sheffield's rejection of the City course and the approach it prefers, we spoke to course director, Elizabeth Smart: *"Actively resist is perhaps the wrong word,"* she began. *"We aim to provide a course that will equip students to work in a breadth of areas; we prefer to give breadth and good grounding."* As a result, there are no places reserved for students who begin the course with a training contract, and the University offers ten electives including that rarest of beasts, Advanced Criminal Litigation. Talking of ACL, Elizabeth said: *"We run two groups each year, and it is certainly something students come here for."* Indeed, the elective is to be found at only two other schools.

Sheffield is keen to maintain its intimate feel, despite the planned expansion. With a maximum of 18 students in each class, attractive premises and a new *"street cafe"* common room complete with refreshments and internet access, it looks set to achieve this. That's not to say the school is a small and isolated place. As Elizabeth explained: *"We are a fully integrated part of the University of Sheffield Law Department, and students that come here really are part of the university."* Another plus, this time trumpeted by the Law Society, is its 'steering community', which has good links with law firms, both locally and nationally.

Of the students at Sheffield, 30% start with training contracts. The majority of students have 2:1s, with most of the rest holding 2:2s, although there are a handful of Firsts and Thirds. Demand outstrips supply, with 665 applications for the 180 places last year.

apply here if:

- you're after a quality LPC provider in the north
- you want a broad choice of electives
- you want an authentic university experience

staffordshire university

number of places: 150 full-time/part-time

Staffordshire is committed to integrating IT into its teaching methods, including the use of computers in class. Course facilities also include mock courtrooms and simulated solicitors' offices. The Staffordshire

LPC is rated as 'Very good' by the Law Society; staff offer weekly surgeries and work groups are of no more than 16 students. Should you want to prolong your time as a student even further, students successfully completing the LPC can take the LL.M in Legal Practice as a top-up qualification.

Staffordshire's practical approach also seems to extend to its attitudes on recruitment; LPC course director Rosemary Evans stresses that the university likes to keep an open mind on admissions. But be warned, as with other good LPC institutions, there are still many more applicants than places. Once you're in, however, the word is that the relatively small numbers of students on the course means you'll find it easier to get to know your peers. The law school is located on the university's Stoke site – forget all those dreary Arnold Bennett novels, this is the birthplace of Robbie Williams! The university boasts strong links to the local profession, most notably a mentoring scheme that matches every student to a local solicitor. However, if you're not strongly committed to the Midlands, you may find the careers assistance too regionally focused. The school seems to do a good job of providing a good value LPC for those who still need to get a training contract – only 25% of students start the course with one. Priority is given to those applicants who live locally and to Staffordshire Uni graduates.

apply here if:

- you have links to the Midlands or want them
- you want plenty of hands-on careers advice
- you're happy to get to grips with technology

university of westminster

number of places: 120 full-time, 64 part-time

The University of Westminster's law school is located in a pulsating area of London, right near Oxford Circus. It utilises its location by nurturing links with neighbouring law firms, and many of the teaching staff maintain contact with practice. These links are immediately evident (particularly so on the fledgling immigration course) with practitioners teaching all the electives. Local firms also sponsor individual electives, giving prizes to those who perform well or offering work experience.

As with the other smaller LPC providers, the school highlights the benefits of the close relationship between staff and students. With small group sessions of between 15-20 students, class sizes are about average, yet with less than 200 students in total the school offers an intimate environment. The students who choose Westminster tend to be a little older, with many (re)turning to study later in life. Almost a third have come through the CPE route, and although there's the usual group of City-bound students, this is smaller than at other London LPC providers. Only 15–20% of students begin with training contracts because the majority head for high street practice or smaller commercial partnerships where the practice of hiring trainees one or two years in advance is far less common. Miles MacLeod, LPC supervisor at the school, told us: *"No places are specifically reserved for students with training contracts, but Westminster obviously looks upon these applicants favourably."*

Yet another big difference is the number of students with the minimum entry requirement of a 2:2 – 44% of the student body have a lower second, which means they will probably be paying their own fees. This doesn't mean the school is second rate; indeed it takes a lot of effort and investment to secure a 'Very good' rating from the Law Society. Good news for those paying own fees: Westminster's course costs over £1,000 less than that of BPP and the College of Law.

apply here if:

- you want value for money in London
- you like the personal touch
- the bright lights of the city mesmerise you

the bar vocational course

The BVC is the practical training hoop through which aspiring barristers must jump. Following completion of the BVC, you will be called to the Bar and can start pupillage. Eight institutions receive the Bar Council's seal of approval, and this year it has changed its assessment requirements such that, wherever you go, there will be continual and fairly intensive assessment throughout the latter part of the course. While the Bar Council strives to ensure that all providers work to the same standard with comparable facilities, there are still variations between courses and institutions. You would be well advised to investigate each provider, find out what barristers and students think of each one, read prospectuses and consider which suits you best. Applications are made centrally through BVC Online.

The BVC is not an academic course, instead it teaches basic procedural knowledge, written skills and advocacy (the most popular aspect of the course). The compulsory components are civil litigation and remedies, criminal litigation and sentencing, evidence, and professional ethics. Drafting and conferencing skills are taught in workshops, while civil and criminal procedure and evidence are taught in lectures. These elements are assessed through multiple-choice tests. In addition to the compulsory components, you'll also study two option subjects. Check our student website for a table showing the options on offer at each BVC provider and course fees.

The required focus on practical skills (conferencing, advocacy, negotiation, opinion writing, drafting, case preparation and legal research) can be frustrating for even the brightest students. Some find the course a walkover, complaining: *"The BVC is a complete waste of time"* and *"the most abysmal intellectual experience of my life."* Many students told us they felt the BVC could be completed intensively in around five months (or less) as opposed to the current nine. But you must remember that the raison d'être of the BVC is the transformation of academic law students into practising (and practical) barristers. One school asks its students to write an opinion over their first weekend. *"They give us terrific academic essays,"* the course director explained, *"but they come to absolutely no conclusions! By the end of the year, they're offering clear advice with a client in mind."* Another told us: *"The pleasure of teaching this course is that you see the students transform."* Whether or not they realise it, apparently!

how to choose a school

Students are influenced by many factors in selecting a school. Some opt for smaller institutions where they will benefit from more individual attention, location is the main concern for others, and of course cost is also a big issue. There is no reason to assume that the best BVC providers are in London. Indeed, you may wish to bear in mind that regional providers are invariably cheaper and can offer strong links to their local Bar.

If you're worried about becoming distanced from the London Bar, you'll be pleased to hear that many regional providers have taken steps to prevent this. When choosing a school, it is also worth considering whether or not it is attached to another institution. One affiliated with a university is likely to benefit from large library collections, sporting facilities and extensive student support functions. Look into the elective subjects offered at your preferred school and make sure that they appeal to you.

bpp law school, london

number of places: 216 full-time, 48 part-time

BPP Plc is an international professional training company and the law school is just one aspect of its business. As Richard Holt, the BVC course leader told us: *"We are a service provider, and although we have obligations to the Bar Council, we are a business first and foremost. The students are our clients."* Students find the course refreshingly rigorous, with one describing the learning curve as *"almost vertical."* It draws near-universal acclaim from students who praise *"excellent teaching and facilities"* and acknowledge that the course offered *"a good grounding for practice."* Its small group seminars are renowned for being challenging, but *"not intimidating."* In an attempt to emulate practice, briefs used earlier in the course, say in a knowledge-based area, will resurface later for another component such as advocacy, *"so there is linkage and integration in the course."* There are nine elective subjects on offer, including some less-common choices like international trade and intellectual property.

BPP's modern, glass-fronted building is kitted out with six mock courtrooms, each fully equipped with video, PowerPoint and smart boards. Not smart enough to do your knowledge assessments for you, but such is life. The library has super long opening hours seven days a week. Only 10% of your classes will be taken in large herds; the rest of the time, you'll be in small groups of 12, and for advocacy training, smaller clusters of six. This small-group system seems to be working, and students told us that although they only ever saw the work of the other 11 students, *"it worked really well and we're still in touch with each other."* Happily, *"everyone was up to a good standard."* For advocacy workshops the school mixes up the groups to ensure that students see a range of advocacy styles. BPP also runs a two-year part-time BVC with weekend classes once a month.

bristol institute of legal practice at uwe

number of places: 120 full-time

The BVC at Bristol is taught by practitioners and aims to replicate practice as closely as possible. Validated to take 120 students, the school prefers to limit the intake to just 96 per year. It provides each tutorial group with its own dedicated room containing practitioners' books, a TV and computer facilities. This system of teams operating out of base rooms is intended to emulate real barristers chambers, and collaborative learning is a key part of the Bristol ethos. The course includes two placement weeks in a range of possible locations, including the Crown Prosecution Service, judge marshalling, chambers and even the ECJ. It is structured in such a way that two major case studies run throughout the course, one civil and one criminal.

A wide range of optional subjects includes clinical negligence, company, employment and family law, international trade, the Mercantile Court and construction, arbitration and adjudication. A popular option is the Free Legal Representation Service in which students assist with cases referred by the local Citizens Advice Bureau. Cases might include mortgage repossessions, small claims court matters or employment and welfare law.

Students take pupillages across the country, although mostly in the South West or London. The school prides itself on the level of pastoral support, brought about by plenty of staff-student interaction, including lunches with personal tutors. Student praise is reserved mainly for the advocacy element (*"immediate feedback was fantastic"*), views on some other areas were mixed. Bristol is, of course, one of the best cities in which to be a student. Alas, the location and ambience of the UWE campus does not inspire the same fond memories in former students.

cardiff law school

number of places: 60 full-time

With only 60 places, Cardiff is the smallest BVC provider and one of the most oversubscribed. Teaching is directed at groups of 12, although advocacy is taught in smaller groups of six. The course is structured such that several case scenarios *"weave in and out of the course in different streams."* This means that you might revisit the same fact scenario in opinion writing and drafting and later in conferencing or advocacy. As Andrew Jerram, course coordinator points out: *"It ensures that students can focus on developing their skills, rather than having to learn new fact patterns all the time."* Cardiff wants its students to be familiar with the texts they'll come across in practice, so provides them with the White Book (the civil procedure manual) and Blackstone's Criminal Practice in addition to the ICSL manuals.

Although most students who gain pupillage head to Welsh chambers, recent former students have gone to London, Manchester, Bournemouth and even as far as Malaysia, Gibraltar, Mauritius, Cyprus and Kenya. Around one third of Cardiff's BVC cohort is from overseas and as such there is a strong international flavour to the place, which makes for an interesting year.

To keep tutors on point with legal developments, each course has its own consultant who is a member of the local practising Bar. There are options available in company law, international trade, pupillage advocacy, family, criminal and employment law. From 2004, Cardiff also hopes to offer alternative dispute resolution. As part of the course, students spend five days with a barrister in chambers and five days with a circuit judge. Andrew told us: *"It's the best way for students to put into context what they're learning."* Anyone hesitant about moving to south Wales could do well to heed the words of one former student: *"Everything is cheaper in Cardiff, there is a better quality of life and nice sunny people."* Shame the weather isn't always so bright.

the college of law, store street, london

number of places: 120 full-time

The College of Law has been the UK's largest provider of postgraduate legal education since the Pleistocene era. Its Store Street branch started life as an LPC-only school churning out prospective solicitors. Now it also caters for BVC students, who share the premises and facilities with around 650 full-time LPC students. As the smallest BVC school in London, the COL offers Bar students an intimate atmosphere and *"familiar faces."* Students praised the *"personal teaching,"* and *"attentive staff."* The programme is intense and you can expect to be at college from nine to five most days.

On your first day you'll be allocated to a training group of six students, and you'll stay with them for the entirety of the course. Over 80% of your classes will be conducted in this training group; it's a system that promotes collaborative learning. Other classes are taken in larger groups, but don't expect to be sitting passively – preparation is essential. The mini advocacy exercises, taken in groups of six, come strongly recommended, although some students wished there were more of them. If there was a criticism, it was the at times overwhelming preponderance of *"handouts that say nothing."* There is a dazzling array of options including advanced civil and advanced criminal litigation, tribunals practice, judicial review practice, family law, commercial practice and a popular pro bono option. Participation in the COL pro bono scheme is a great way for students to hone their research and interviewing skills and students can also experience the cut and thrust of tribunal advocacy in the college's Tribunal Representation Service. Mooting and negotiation is also taken seriously, and recently its team came second in the international negotiation finals in Sydney. There is a strong collegiate atmosphere, the social scene is good, and the student body has a strong international flavour.

the inns of court school of law, city university, london

number of places: up to 600 (most full-time)

Biggest and oldest of the BVC providers, ICSL has undergone a few changes in the last 18 months. In 2002 the school became a department of the Faculty of Law at City University, thus opening up library, sports and student facilities to those on the BVC course. Its premises have been revamped and there is now a brand new refectory area overlooking the beautiful gardens of Gray's Inn, a state of the art lecture hall with interactive IT facilities and an expanded library with long opening hours.

The sheer size and impersonality of the place has been a commonly voiced concern, but to its credit ICSL has taken this criticism on board and the student body is now divided into four groups, each with its own course leader and designated staff. Some students had also criticised the variable teaching quality, with one remarking that *"staff are hit and miss between absolute brilliance and, worryingly, disinterest."* Further, some students expressed concern about apparently arbitrary marking schemes, and we were somewhat surprised to hear that the school charges £67 for an assessment to be remarked. But the civil procedure course was roundly praised, as was the *"invaluable"* advocacy training.

What ICSL has over many other providers is experience; illustrating this, its course materials have been syndicated to other institutions. And of course, one of the best things is its location in the beating heart of Barrister Central. Another is the fact that the school offers options not available at most other providers such as immigration and competition law. There is also a FRU option in which students can experience real employment and social security tribunals first hand, and a pro bono clinic run in conjunction with the LPC course. Oh, and one more thing…most of your friends will be there with you.

manchester metropolitan university

places: 100 full-time

In August 2004 the entire law school at Manchester Met will be moving to newly refurbished premises. Future BVC students will benefit from state of the art lecture rooms, complete with video equipment and all the trimmings. Facilities aside, the school boasts a good staff to student ratio, with one teacher for every nine students. From your first day you'll be assigned to a syndicate group of 12. These groups have their own base rooms,which are designed to replicate barristers chambers. Each base room is fitted with an authentic library and all small-group sessions are conducted in there.

Manchester Met has strong links to the Northern Circuit, whose members take the professional conduct classes, and local chambers mentor each syndicate group. In addition to the ordinary advocacy courses, there is a weekly two-hour masterclass. On Wednesdays, you can listen to guest speakers addressing issues ranging from how pupils should interact with barristers to alternative career choices.

There is a good range of options available, including child law, Chancery and European competition law. The course is run over a four-day week, so you'll have Fridays to recover from Thursday nights out. And although most BVC students who get pupillage go on to practice on the Northern and North Eastern Circuits, subsidies are available for students to travel to London to dine at their Inn.

At just £7,345 for the year, Manchester is a bargain of a BVC. Alan Gibb, the course director, told us that to win a place you'd need to list Manchester first or second on the BVC-online application. Regional connections will win you extra points, but you'll still need a *"very, very strong"* academic track record and *"clear evidence of some commitment to the Bar."* Mini-pupillages, mooting or public speaking all look good.

university of northumbria at newcastle

number of places: 80 full-time plus up to 40 LL.B students

In addition to its full-time BVC course, Northumbria offers a unique legal training, whereby LLB students can undertake the BVC (or the LPC) as part of their LLB degree course. The choice as to whether to take an LPC route or a BVC route is made before the start of the third year and students are then exempted from further professional training once they finish their four-year degree. We spoke to a number of students who had completed 'exempting degrees' from this university and all of them reported on the programme in glowing terms.

Operating from dedicated base rooms, established study groups have their own IT facilities and library. Part and parcel of the BVC experience, and offering a free legal service for members of the public, the university's Student Law Office is the largest and most comprehensive student-run facility in the UK. Students interview clients, analyse the case and research the law, manage their own time, draft documents and give advice, even presenting cases in tribunals and assisting in court hearings. Aside from giving students an extremely realistic taste of life in practice, the high-profile SLO has even won plaudits from senior QCs.

Not so long ago, the university shifted an entire courtroom from Morpeth, so now students can practice in the (albeit displaced) real thing. There are good links with the local Bar and regular visits from recorders, judges, police and forensic experts. Those successful at the BVC go on to practise in all parts of the country and overseas.

Advocacy experience will help you stand out from the crowd, as the course is oversubscribed; students from the region are also favoured. In the past, around 30% of students have gained pupillage by the time they finish the course, although the figure rises after completion.

nottingham law school

number of places: 120 full-time

Nottingham smells of law students. With two universities offering law degrees and a superior LPC attracting top-grade students, it's no wonder prospective BVC students want a piece of the action. As such, the school can afford to accept only high-calibre applicants. Nottingham is looking for students who put it first on the BVC-online application, and you'll need a First or a 2:1 plus demonstrated commitment to the profession and to public speaking *"in the broadest sense."* Mini pupillages, time in a law firm and mooting or debating are all considered favourably.

The course is taught using seven briefs – four criminal and three civil – which you'll work with throughout the year. The school tries to simulate practice as closely as possible and, rather than providing students with study manuals, it has chosen Archbold (a crime practitioners' book) and the White Book (the practitioners' book for civil procedure). This is a boon since they cost around £250 a pop. Students are *"thrown in at the deep end"* with these texts, and according to course leader James Wakefield: *"They get a better understanding of real court advocacy"* since *"judges expect you to refer to these books in court."* Validated to take 120 students, Nottingham aims for just 95 per year. James said: *"If you're willing to engage, teachers will train you and invest in you."* Knowledge-based courses are conducted in groups of 12, while advocacy classes are half that size. The advocacy course is held in the old Guildhall Court Rooms – its Victorian wood panelling is guaranteed to bring out the Rumpole in anyone. There are seven electives available: advanced criminal, advanced civil, immigration, landlord & tenant, family, commercial and employment.

Despite its location, the school has a healthy Inns of Court life and organises regular bus trips to London to enable students to dine. Chances are loads of your friends will be on the LPC course so the year could be a lot of fun.

funding

You've already got a student debt from uni that probably outstrips the mortgage on your parent's house, so how on earth are you going to get through law school? You're not the bank robbing type...

grants

Although there are no centrally administered mandatory awards available, there is a slim chance (just above blood-from-stone) that you will qualify for a Local Education Authority grant. You and your folks will have to complete a fistful of forms, as discretionary awards are means tested. Pay close attention to the criteria – whether you are a mature student, single parent or independent student can make a big difference. Your chances will improve if you apply early; such funds are normally extremely limited. The Department for Education and Skills website www.dfes.gov.uk/studentsupport has more info.

hardship funds, access funds and charities

Your LEA may be able to point you in the direction of local charities or trusts that could be good for an award. Another source of information is your course provider itself, so ask if it knows of any possible funds. Many law schools operate a hardship fund, which may come in handy if you are reduced to spending shirt buttons. Pop along, find out what is on offer and see if you qualify – it could turn out to be your lucky day.

bank loans

Already got a huge overdraft? No problem! You could still qualify for a special package from a high street bank. Perhaps believing the 'rich lawyer' stereotype, many will go out of their way to provide further funding to impoverished CPE/LPC/BVC students. The interest rates are low – usually around 1% above base – and the repayment terms can be very favourable. Have a look at what your own bank is offering, then spend some time researching others to get the best deal. Many banks will give enhanced packages to students at specific colleges, so ask your law school if they have any such arrangements in place. It's worth spending a little time scouting around for the deal that best suits your needs. Before you sign on the dotted line:

- make sure you really understand the nuts and bolts of the deal, especially what will you have to repay and when
- Remember that course fees are usually required well in advance, so get on the case early
- Don't borrow more than you really need or you could find yourself struggling to make the repayments when the time comes
- Consider drawing down funds on a monthly basis (your bank may insist on this anyway)

career development loans

Barclays Bank, the Co-operative Bank and the Royal Bank of Scotland provide these on behalf of the DfES. Full details are at www.lifelonglearning.co.uk/cdl. In essence, if you don't get a Government grant or employer sponsorship, you can borrow up to £8,000 towards 80% of your fees, and the Government will pay the interest for the year of the grant and one month after.

benefits, benefactors, begging...

You may find yourself in a privileged position whereby your family can keep your head above water, but remember they will be expecting results so work hard to keep them happy. Ditto for those holding training contracts or pupillages which come with law school funding. No matter how much (or how little) funding you have been given, at the very least your firm or chambers will want to see a good record on results and attendance. Bear in mind that you won't be able to claim benefits while at college. Whatever you decide, do take advantage of the benevolence of everyone from hairdressers to train companies – student discounts can help keep your piggy bank rattling for longer.

part-time work

Officially, full-time courses are exactly that – full-time. This applies even on those courses where you have a large chunk of the day away from the classroom. Most colleges accept that students may need to work a few hours a week or during holidays, but think long and hard about your ability to work while you study. Lack of time or energy to study could lead to failed exams, so if you need to earn a significant amount just to keep afloat, might a part-time course be more realistic?

solicitors

law firm sponsorship: you may be one of the lucky ones who has secured a training contract, in which case your firm may put up the cash for LPC fees, and perhaps CPE fees, if you need these too. On top of this, it may even give you a modest maintenance grant to help you through the year(s). Our **Salaries Table** on page 68 details the funding on offer from leading firms. However, very many students start their course without the guarantee of a training contract offer. For them it's a gamble as to whether they will get any funding, or even a training contract, and there's no easy way around the problem of having to commit to course fees before knowing if it will all be worth it in the end.

law society: The society has its own bursary scheme and application forms can be obtained from them from February to April. Be quick though; the closing date is 30 April in the year your course starts. Well worth investigating are various trust funds advertised on the Law Society's website.

barristers

Students studying the CPE and/or BVC and pupils can apply for a range of scholarships from the four Inns of Court. All Bar students must join an Inn, and many of them base their decision as to which one to join on the likelihood of their getting their hands on some of the £3 million plus that is paid out each year by the Inns. We've produced a quick summary of what's on offer on page 587 in our **Table of Scholarships from the Inns.** You should also contact the Inns for further details and then research their awards before applying – some are merit-based, while others consider financial hardship. Each of the Inns produces a detailed brochure that should help you work your way through the maze of scholarships and awards. You can only apply to one Inn, so apply only once you are fully armed with all the relevant info.

Since 1 January 2003 all pupillages are required to be backed by a minimum chambers award of £10,000. Some sets pay far in excess of this sum – the highest is presently £40,000 from Chancery set Maitland Chambers – and a growing number of them allow students to draw on these awards while studying the BVC. The majority of students however still have to depend on bank loans and/or parental support. The subject is discussed further in our **Barristers** section.

Universities and Law Schools A-Z

BPP Professional Education

68-70 Red Lion Street, London WC1R 4NY
Tel: (020) 7430 2304 Fax: (020) 7430 1389
Email: law@bpp.com
Website: www.bpp.com

college profile

BPP is the leading provider of professional legal education in the country with over 2,000 full, part time and distance-learning law students. The School has three Law Schools situated in Leeds, London (Holborn) and London (Waterloo). Because of BPP's reputation for quality and professionalism in providing legal education, it has been selected by eight of the top city and international law firms as one of only three law schools nationally to train their trainee solicitors. The teaching team on the Bar Vocational Course also maintains close links with Chambers. The Law Society has rated the Legal Practice Course at BPP as excellent (one of only four providers in the country to have this rating). All of BPP's courses are taught by professional, trained tutors and practitioners using a range of hi-tech facilities. The college has a specialist careers service designed to help all its students reach their full potential.

graduate diploma in law

The Graduate Diploma in Law conversion course at BPP is taught with a practical student centred approach. A comprehensive range of manuals and books are provided within the course fees. Students who successfully complete the School's Graduate Diploma in Law are guaranteed a place on the full or part time Legal Practice Course and can progress on to the full or part time Bar Vocational Course at BPP. The course is offered as a full time, part time (weekends or evenings) and distance learning course.

legal practice course

BPP's LPC benefits from close collaboration with a number of the top legal firms in the country and uses a range of realistic problem scenarios and transactions designed to prepare students for practice as a trainee solicitor. The LPC is avaiable on a full time and part time (evening or weekend) basis.

bar vocational course

The BVC at BPP concentrates on developing the essential barristerial skills of drafting, opinion writing, advocacy, negotiation and conference. These skills are practiced in tutorial groups as small as six and take place in one of the Law School's realistic courtrooms. The BVC is available on a full time and part time (monthly / weekend) basis.

contact

GDL full time: Steve Wallace
Tel: (020) 7430 7050
Email: stevewallace@bpp.com

GDL part time: Rachel Timperlake
Tel: (020) 7430 5655
Email: racheltimperlake@bpp.com

LPC full time: Cathy Burrows
Tel: (020) 7430 7004
Email: cathyburrows@bpp.com

LPC part time: Paul Kendall
Tel: (020) 7430 7040
Email: paulkendall@bpp.com

BVC: Veena Solanki
Tel: (020) 7430 7053
Email: veenasolanki@bpp.com

Cardiff Law School

Cardiff Law School, Cardiff University, PO Box 294, Cardiff CF10 3UX
Tel: (029) 2087 4964 Fax: (029) 2087 4984
Email: Brookfield@Cardiff.ac.uk
Website: www.cardiff.ac.uk/claws/cpls

university profile

Cardiff Law School is long established, well-resourced and enjoys an international reputation for its teaching and research. In the most recent assessment of research quality conducted by the Higher Education Funding Council, Cardiff achieved a grade 5 rating, placing it in the top law schools in the country. Cardiff offers opportunities for students to pursue postgraduate study by research leading to the degrees of M.Phil and Ph.D. In addition, taught Masters degrees in the areas of canon, commercial, European legal studies, marine affairs and medical law are offered in full and part-time mode.

legal practice course and bar vocational course

Within the Law School, the Centre for Professional Legal Studies is validated to offer both the Legal Practice Course and the Bar Vocational Course. Students are taught by experienced solicitors and barristers who have been specifically recruited for this purpose. Placements with solicitors' firms or sets of Chambers are available to students pursuing the vocational courses, while students studying the Bar Vocational Course additionally enjoy a one week placement with a Circuit or District Judge. Cardiff's Legal Practice Course has four times been rated 'Excellent' by the Law Society; one of only three providers of this course to hold the top ranking.

facilities

Recent developments within the Law School include extensive IT provision together with dedicated accommodation for the vocational courses which house a practitioner library, courtroom facilities, and fixed and movable audio visual equipment for recording inter-active practitioner skills activities. In addition, the main law library contains one of the largest collections of primary and secondary material within the UK. The Law School is housed in its own building at the heart of the campus, itself located in one of the finest civic centres in Britain and only a short walk from the main shopping area. The University has its own postgraduate centre, together with a full range of sporting and social facilities.

contact

LPC: Mr Ian C Brookfield
Tel: (029) 2087 4941

BVC: Mr Andrew Jerram
Tel: (029) 2087 4964

Other postgraduate law courses:
The Postgraduate Registry
Tel: (029) 2087 4351

University of Central England in Birmingham

School of Law, Franchise Street, Perry Barr, Birmingham B42 2SU
Tel: (0121) 331 6600/6614 Fax: (0121) 331 6622

college profile

UCE School of Law has been a major centre for legal education and training in the city for over 30 years. UCE is committed to providing a service that meets your needs – whether academic, professional or personal. It can be seen in the distinctly informal staff-student relationships, in the extensive support provision and learning facilities that you would expect to find in a large university such as UCE, including a legal practice resource centre, IT workrooms and mock courtroom, and of course in the quality and relevance of its courses.

postgraduate diploma in legal practice/lpc (full or part-time)

UCE's LPC maintains a generalist approach, reflecting the fact that the majority of students progress to general practice in small and medium size firms. However, UCE is also committed to making sure that this is not at the cost of those students who aim for commercial practice – UCE offers distinctive electives for this sector including mergers and acquisitions, commercial property and commercial law. UCE aims to develop the problem-solving skills, commercial awareness and self-sufficiency that a trainee solicitor needs. Small class sizes and accessible staff ensure that individual study needs are met and that you receive the support you need to maximize personal development.

graduate diploma in law/cpe (full or part-time)

The CPE course is designed for non-law graduates wishing to enter the profession as solicitors or barristers. The purpose of the CPE is to provide legal training, which although primarily academic in nature, also reflects the demands that legal practice will place on that academic knowledge. UCE's teaching emphasises participation and student-centred learning. A variety of teaching methods are employed in order to develop the legal skills which form the basis of a successful career in law. An 'open door' policy and a commitment to individual personal development ensures you receive the support needed to maximize your potential.

pgcert/pgdip/llm corporate and business law (subject to validation)

Explores relevant and topical legal issues relating to the corporate and business world.

pgcert/pgdip/ma immigration & refugee policy, law & practice

Examines the implications of current law and practice in the UK.

pgdip/llm international human rights

USA Pathway: Explores the conflict between the US Death Penalty and international standards. Students may undertake a semester's internship in the USA.

European Pathway: Studies the increasing importance of Human Rights in the UK and European law, including international environmental law and conflict, and refugees.

ma legal practice

An opportunity for practising solicitors and LPC graduates to 'top up' studies to Master's level.

contact

Apply to:
Full-time CPE and LPC courses
Central Applictions Board
Part-time CPE and LPC courses
Direct to university
Other courses
Direct to university

contact names

CPE and LPC
Keith Gompertz
Other postgraduate courses
Karen D'Arcy

Email: lss@uce.ac.uk
Website: www.uce.ac.uk

City University, London - Institute of Law

City University, Institute of Law, Northampton Square, London EC1V 0HB
Tel: Dept of Law: (020) 7040 8301 ICSL: (020) 7404 5787
Fax: Dept of Law: (020) 7040 8578 ICSL: (020) 7831 4188
Email: Dept of Law: cpe@city.ac.uk ICSL: ICSLcourses@city.ac.uk
Website: www.city.ac.uk/law

college profile

Law has been taught at City since 1977. In 2001 the Inns of Court School of Law (ICSL) joined the established Department of Law to form a new Institute of Law. This formalised a long-standing relationship, and made City the first university in London to offer courses for students and practitioners in both branches of the profession at all stages of legal education. In addition to postgraduate legal training for both solicitors and barristers ICSL offers a well-established CPD programme which includes the PSC for trainee solicitors and Higher Rights training. Its successful Pro Bono project gives vocational course students the opportunity to work with live clients at the School's Advice Clinic or to work with a voluntary partner.

courses

cpe/diploma in Law (full or part time) Designed to enable non-law graduates to complete the first stage of professional training, this CPE course is one of the largest and most respected CPE courses in the UK, with a long-standing reputation with the Bar and a strong and growing reputation amongst City law firms.

graduate entry llb (two years full time) A well-established broader conversion course providing an opportunity to develop special interests.

llm programme (full or part time) A modular programme in International Law, with opportunities to specialise in human rights or environmental law, and a unique LLM in Criminal Litigation (icsl).

bar vocational course (ICSL - full or part-time) A forward looking IT based course focusing on the needs of the modern bar, particularly advocacy.

legal practice course (ICSL - full or part-time) Rated Very Good by the Law Society.

contact

Full course brochures are available from the Department of Law or ICSL as appropriate

department of law

Tel: (020) 7040 8301
Fax (020) 7040 8578
Email: cpe@city.ac.uk

icsl

Tel: (020) 7404 5787
Fax: (020) 7831 4188
Email: ICSLcourses@city.ac.uk

The College of Law

Braboeuf Manor, Portsmouth Road, Guildford GU3 1HA
Freephone: (0800) 328 0153 Fax: (01483) 460460
Email: admissions@lawcol.co.uk
Website: www.college-of-law.co.uk

college profile

The College of Law, the largest legal training establishment in Europe, has centres in Birmingham, Chester, Guildford, London and York. The College has an excellent reputation with law firms and chambers, and its teaching staff are professionally qualified as solicitors or barristers. The College's Careers Service uses its specialist knowledge and extensive contacts to help students gain training contracts and pupillages. The College offers the following courses:

graduate diploma in law (full-time, part-time or distance learning)

The GDL is the law conversion course for graduates of disciplines other than law who wish to become solicitors or barristers. Students will receive in-depth tuition in seven foundation subjects from tutors with a proven track record in providing legal education. Successful students receive a Diploma in Law and are guaranteed a place on the College's Legal Practice Course.

legal practice course (full-time, part-time, or block learning)

The LPC is the vocational stage of training for prospective solicitors. The College's LPC has been developed in consultation with both City and provincial firms to address the real needs of today's legal profession, and ensure the course meets the demands of life in practice.

bar vocational course (full-time)

The BVC is the vocational stage of training for prospective barristers and is available at the College's London Centre. It has been developed in conjunction with practising barristers to prepare students for life in their early years at the Bar. Practitioners from highly respected sets of chambers also contribute to the delivery of the course.

For further information about courses at any of the College's centres, please contact Admissions.

contact

Freephone:
(0800) 328 0153
Email:
admissions@lawcol.co.uk

London Metropolitan University

Department of Law, Governance and International Relations,
London City campus, 84 Moorgate, London EC2M 6SQ
Tel: (020) 7320 1616 Fax: (020) 7320 1163
Email: enquiries.city@londonmet.ac.uk
Website: www.londonmet.ac.uk

course enquiries
(020) 7320 1616

university profile

London Metropolitan University was created on 1 August 2002 following the merger of London Guildhall University and the University of North London. The University offers a wide range of professional law courses available in full-time and part-time day and evening modes. The teaching style of these courses is considered to be one of the friendliest and most thorough available. The University prides itself on giving students personal and individual attention; it is committed to keeping class numbers low; and its IT facilities include a number of the software programmes that are found in practice. Students receive training that is relevant, professional and geared towards ensuring success. There is easy access to underground and mainline stations.

legal practice course (full-time or part-time day or evening)

Many of the teaching staff are either in practice or have recently left practice, so that the emphasis is on the provision of professional training. Welfare and commercial electives are offered, including subjects such as immigration and international trade.

Class sizes are limited and skills training is provided in smaller groups to ensure personal and individual attention. Computers are utilised within the classroom along with video to ensure that the latest training and practitioner tools are made available to students. A unique (to London) part-time day course is offered to provide flexibility in training modes. The part-time day and evening mode is also run in collaboration with South Bank University.

common professional examination/postgraduate diploma in Law (full-time or part-time day or evening)

Training is both by lectures and tutorials with an emphasis on the seven foundations of legal knowledge. The course prides itself on the personal and individual attention offered to all students. A variety of teaching and assessment methods are utilised including research assignments, case and statute analysis, and case studies. Fee assistance is provided to those students wishing to continue with the LPC at London Metropolitan University. The University also offers a flexible mode of study, which enables students from a wide range of backgrounds to undertake the course.

Manchester Metropolitan University

School of Law, All Saints West, Lower Ormond Street, Manchester M15 6HB
Tel: (0161) 247 3050 Fax: (0161) 247 6309
Email: law@mmu.ac.uk

contact

Contact the Admissions Tutor for the relevant course

college profile

The School of Law is one of the largest providers of legal education in the UK, and enjoys an excellent reputation for the quality and range of its courses. It is one of only six providers that offer the full range of law courses LLB, GDipL, LPC and BVC. The School's courses are well designed and taught, combining rigorous academic standards with practical application. In September 2003, the School moved into a brand new, state of the art building, in the heart of Manchester.

bar vocational course (full-time)

This course provides the vocational stage of training for intending practising barristers. Adopting a Syndicate Group approach, the BVC is activity based and interactive. Extensive IT and audio visual facilities combine with dedicated, well equipped premises to provide an enjoyable and stimulating experience. Excellent student support is provided including mentoring by practising barristers and an Additional Professional Programme which is designed to bridge the gap betweeen student and professional life.

legal practice course (full-time or part-time)

This course is for those wishing to qualify as a solicitor. Offering a full range of commercial and private client electives the Legal Practice Course, taught by professionally qualified staff, prepares you for every day practice. There is a dedicated Resource Centre and an excellent pastoral care programme for LPC students. Consistently recognised by the Law Society for its high quality.

postgraduate diploma in law/cpe (full-time or part-time)

An increasing number of graduates enter the legal profession this way, with employers attracted by the applicant's maturity and transferable skills. The course places emphasis on the acquisition of legal research and other relevant legal skills. On completion students normally join the School's LPC or BVC Course. This means that if the full-time mode is followed a non-law graduate can become professionally qualified in two years.

Middlesex University

UK/EU Admissions, Middlesex University, Bounds Green Road, London N11 2NQ
Tel: (020) 8411 5898
Email: admissions@mdx.ac.uk
Website: www.mdx.ac.uk

college profile

Middlesex University Business School is the largest business school in London and is located at the Hendon campus, within 30 minutes of Central London by underground rail. The law group has been offering both undergraduate and postgraduate programmes for over 25 years and hosts the Centre for Research in Industrial and Commercial Law, with current projects in Employment Law (Whistleblowing), Environmental Law and European Law.

undergraduate programmes

The University offers two qualifying law degrees which provide exemption from the first stage of professional legal education for those seeking a professional career in law. Those are: the LLB Honours Business Law and BA Honours Law. A combined honours, non-qualifying degree is also offered in Law.

postgraduate programmes - llm

LLM (with specialisation in International Business Law or International Economic Law.) A flexible programme for law graduates or practitioners who wish to specialise in a particular area. The University specialises in international business law or international economic law. Students can also study a generic LLM.

llm in employment law

Designed for practising lawyers, human resource practitioners, trade union officials and advice workers. Applications from students with a non-law background are welcomed. Students who have not practised law previously will undertake a pre-course block on legal principles and methods.

pg diploma in law/cpe (full-time and distance learning)

Designed for non-law graduates who wish to pursue a career in law. The programmes are recognised by the Law Society and the General Bar Council, while the CPE board approves the CPE programmes. The Pg Diploma is studied one year full-time, whilst the CPE is offered as a two year distance learning course. The programmes provide the academic stage to your legal education that leads to qualification as a barrister or solicitor. Students who successfully pass the programme have a guaranteed place on the full-time LPC at the College of Law.

Middlesex University
Business School London

contact

UK/EU Admissions,
Middlesex University
Bounds Green Road,
London N11 2NQ
Tel: (020) 8411 5898
Email: admissions@mdx.ac.uk
Website: www.mdx.ac.uk

Middlesex
University

Northumbria University

School of Law, Northumbria University, Sutherland Building,
Newcastle-upon-Tyne NE1 8ST
Tel: (0191) 227 4494
Fax: (0191) 227 4557
Website: http://law.northumbria.ac.uk

college profile

The School of Law at Northumbria University is known for its excellence in the provision of academic and professional legal education. Situated in central Newcastle, the School has over 60 full-time teaching staff and is one of the largest departments in the University. Full-time, part-time and distance learning modes of study are available. The School is validated to run the Bar Vocational Course, the Legal Practice Course and the Common Professional Examination/Diploma in Law Course. It also offers the Professional Skills Course and an extensive LLM programme, including courses in Mental Health Law, Medical Law, Commercial Law, European Law, International Trade Law and Commercial Property. The Law School has dedicated lecture and workshop accommodation together with its own Law Skills Centre which includes a large practitioner library, court room and offices with full CCTV facilities plus open access IT equipment.

lpc (full-time or part-time)

- the vocational training course for students who wish to qualify as solicitors
- a wide range of corporate and private client electives
- practical workshops

bvc (full-time)

- the vocational training course for students who wish to qualify as barristers
- practical skills training in dedicated accommodation
- strong practitioner participation

cpe (full-time or distance learning)

- the academic stage of training for non-law graduates who wish to qualify as solicitors or barristers
- structured study materials
- opportunity to obtain a law degree with an additional study programme
- opportunities for successful CPE students on the Legal Practice Course at Northumbria.

contact

School of Law Admissions Office
Tel: (0191) 227 4494
Fax: (0191) 227 4557
Email: la.information@northumbria.ac.uk

Nottingham Law School

Nottingham Law School, Belgrave Centre, Nottingham NG1 5LP
Tel: (0115) 848 6871 Fax: (0115) 848 6878
Email: linda.green2@ntu.ac.uk
Website: www.nls.ntu.ac.uk

bar vocational course

Nottingham Law School has designed its BVC to develop to a high standard a range of core practical skills, and to equip students to succeed in the fast-changing environment of practice at the Bar. Particular emphasis is placed on the skill of advocacy. Advocacy sessions are conducted in groups of six and the School uses the Guildhall courtrooms for most sessions. The BVC is taught entirely by qualified barristers, and utilises the same integrated and interactive teaching methods as all of the School's other professional courses. Essentially, students learn by doing and Nottingham Law School provides an environment in which students are encouraged to realise, through practice and feedback, their full potential.

legal practice course

The LPC is offered by full-time and part-time block study. This course has been designed to be challenging and stimulating for students and responsive to the needs of firms, varying from large commercial to smaller high street practices.

Nottingham Law School's LPC features: integration of the transactions and skills, so that each advances the other, whilst ensuring the transferability of skills between different subject areas. Carefully structured interactive group work which develops an ability to handle skills and legal transactions effectively, and in an integrated way. A rigorous assessment process that nevertheless avoids 'assessment overload', to maintain a teaching and learning emphasis to the course. A professionally qualified team, retaining substantial links with practice. An excellent rating from The Law Society's Assessment Panel in every year of its operation.

the graduate diploma in law (full-time)

The Nottingham Law School GDL is a one year conversion course designed for any non-law graduate who intends to become a solicitor or barrister in the UK. The intensive course effectively covers the seven core subjects of an undergraduate law degree in one go. It is the stepping stone to the LPC or the BVC at Nottingham Law School, and a legal career thereafter. It is a graduate Diploma (Dip Law) in its own right and operates on a similar basis to the LPC (see above), though inevitably it has a more academic basis.

contact

Nottingham Law School
Belgrave Centre
Nottingham NG1 5LP
Tel: (0115) 848 6871
Fax: (0115) 848 6878
Email:linda.green2@ntu.ac.uk
Website:www.nls.ntu.ac.uk

University of the West of England, Bristol

Faculty of Law, Frenchay Campus, Coldharbour Lane, Bristol BS16 1QY
Tel: (0117) 328 2604 Fax: (0117) 328 2268
Email: law@uwe.ac.uk
Website: www.uwe.ac.uk

college profile

The Bristol Institute of Legal Practice, which is part of the Faculty of Law at the University of the West of England, Bristol, is one of the largest providers of professional legal education in the United Kingdom. The Law Society has recognised the quality of its Legal Practice Courses by awarding them an 'Excellent' rating. It is also proud to be one of only seven providers outside London to be validated by the Bar Council to run the Bar Vocational Course. Moreover, the Higher Education Funding Council for England and Wales rated teaching across the Faculty as a whole as 'Excellent'.

courses

The Bristol Institute of Legal Practice offers the following courses:

legal practice course - lpc (full-time and part-time) The Institute's Legal Practice Courses have a national reputation for quality, which has been recognised by the Law Society with its award of an 'Excellent' rating. Moreover, it currently offers more elective subjects (13) than any other provider in the country. The Faculty has very good links with both local and national firms of solicitors.

bar vocational course - bvc (full-time) In 1996 the UWE Faculty of Law was successfully validated by the Bar Council to run the Bar Vocational Course. When validating the course the Chairman of the Bar Council remarked among other factors taken into account was 'the standard of the facilities to be made available for the Course and the strength of support from the local Bar'.

common professional examination (full-time and part-time) The Faculty has run CPE courses for over 20 years. Both the full-time and part-time versions of the course are recognised nationally as being high quality. They are also very popular and highly respected by the Legal Profession. The courses have very high pass rates and, on the successful completion of the Bristol CPE, students also receive a Postgraduate Diploma in Law.

contact

Faculty of Law
Tel: (0117) 328 2604
Fax: (0117) 328 2266
Email: bilpinfo@uwe.ac.uk

University of Wolverhampton

School of Legal Studies, Molineux Street, Wolverhampton WV1 1SB
Tel: (01902) 321000 Fax: (01902) 321570

college profile

Based in Wolverhampton and offers courses for students intending to follow a variety of careers within the legal profession. The law school has been offering these courses for over 20 years. Its LPC programme has had consistently good ratings. The lecturers are drawn from experienced solicitors, barristers, academics and individuals from business and industry. There are excellent IT facilities, a well-stocked library, bookshop and a sports centre. The School also offers an LLM in International Corporate and Financial Law, which draws together a number of legal issues with an international dimension such as the regulation of financial services and financial crime. It also deals with matters such as international banking law, international corporate finance and international corporate. The School also offers an MA in Practice Management a course developed in connection with the management section of the Law Society. It is taught on a flexible, part-time, block-delivery basis and is designed to provide an outlet to complex managerial and organisational issues facing practice managers.

legal practice course (full/part-time)

The vocational training course for those intending to practise as solicitors, the University's LPC offers a sound basis for a professional career. The core subjects of Business, Litigation and Conveyancing are taught, together with a range of commercial and private client options. Professional skills courses, practical workshops and seminars are all part of the training. Additional benefits include close links with local practitioners, mentoring, CV distribution and group social activities. The Legal Practice Course is housed in modern purpose-built dedicated accommodation which includes a court room, LPC Resources room and solicitors offices. The course is taught by experienced professionally-qualified staff with close links with the local profession. It has active personal tutor support, in-house and guest practitioners, a Practitioner Liaison Committee and a careers tutor.

common professional examination (full/part-time)

The academic stage of training for non-law graduates wishing to become solicitors or barristers. A full programme of lectures and tutorials is offered on this demanding course. Students are taught by experienced practitioners. Places on the LPC are guaranteed for successful students. New flexible studying choices are under discussion. Teaching methods on the CPE are varied and include lectures, group-led discussion and debate, workshops, oral presentations and independent research. The course includes an intensive induction programme involving use of library, methodology and an introduction to IT. The course as a whole is designed to provide the essential skills necessary for a successful career in law.

contact

Ms Loraine Houlton
Head of Corporate & Professional Division
Tel: (01902) 321999
Fax: (01902) 321567

Solicitors

SOLICITORS TIMETABLE

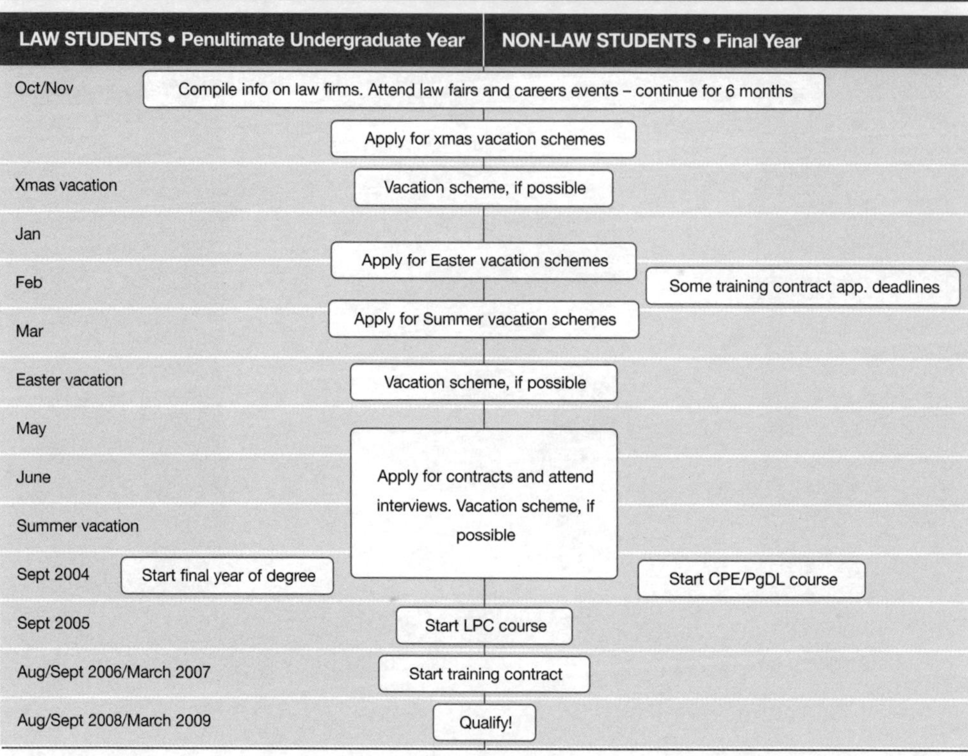

Notes

1 *It is important to check application closing dates for each firm as these will vary.*

2 *Some firms will only accept applications for vacation schemes from penultimate year students whether law or non-law. See A-Z pages for further information.*

3 *Some firms require very early applications from non-law graduates. See A-Z pages for further information.*

4 *The timetable refers primarily to those firms that recruit two years in advance. Smaller firms often recruit just one year in advance or for immediate vacancies.*

vacation schemes

A vacation scheme can be a vital first step to a training contract. Stephen Wilkinson, grad recruitment partner at Herbert Smith, describes the firm's vac scheme as: *"An integral part of the graduate recruitment process."* In some firms, you even complete the same form for both the summer vacation scheme and the training contract. Be aware that applications generally far outnumber the places available and selection interviews can be as tough as training contract interviews. But if you are successful, take comfort from the fact that your application was selected from a mountain of others and this means that the firm likes you on paper. Be attentive, show that you are keen to learn, and use the opportunity to your full advantage.

artificial flavouring?

Although schemes are generally well organised, the work you'll see – perhaps some simple research or reviewing files – will, at best, only give you a general flavour of the firm. Don't fool yourself that the firm is looking for case-winning legal thought; you aren't likely to be given anything too demanding. If your interest lies in a specialist area of practice then do ask to spend time in that department.

As anyone who has ever been on a vac scheme will tell you, there's a chance you will be more involved in the social scene than in the work, and it is here that many students come a cropper. Perhaps due to bug-under-a-microscope nervousness, combined with the enthusiasm of the trainees charged with responsibility for showing you a good time, rumours abound of drunken student antics. One hapless student at a magic circle firm drank a little too much one lunchtime, only to spend the afternoon on the telephone back at the office – the big white porcelain one. Not clever. But we have yet to hear of UK students behaving as badly as some did in Sydney in 2003. At an end-of-summer bash thrown by several of the city's top firms, booze-fuelled summer clerks trashed a hotel, causing thousands of dollars worth of damage. Much of the action was caught on CCTV. We tracked down one of these students, who told us that many of the offenders hadn't received the job offers they were expecting. Take heed and be sensible when partying with potential employers.

woo who?

Inevitably you get a somewhat distorted view of the training experience, but it's possible to look beyond the best behaviour and boosted party budget. Figure out what sort of cases and deals the lawyers are working on. And what sort of people the lawyers are. Can you spot how partners and assistants behave towards each other? Can you see yourself as one of them, turning up for work day-in, day-out, year after year… Leave the nerves at home and concentrate on being friendly, focused, prompt and enthusiastic.

It is a common misconception that the 'certificate' (which you won't get) saying: "I did a vac scheme at Bing, Bong & Bang" will help get you a job elsewhere. Usually it won't. Fact is, when shown to another firm, it isn't worth very much at all – at best it shows you've cast around for a firm you like. Do too many schemes and it could demonstrate a lack of initiative on your part. Recruiters would certainly be more impressed by someone with one or two schemes under their belt and then a trip rafting the Zambezi or guanaco herding in the high Andes. The pay may be decent but don't become a scheme junkie, and don't fret if you miss out on a scheme with a firm that you are really interested in. Many firms, including Clifford Chance and Slaughter and May, insist students should not be put off from applying to them for training contracts just because they didn't get vac scheme places.

VACATION SCHEMES

FIRM NAME	NUMBER OF PLACES	DURATION	REMUN-ERATION	2004 DEADLINE
Addleshaw Goddard	75	2 weeks	Not known	13 February 2004
Allen & Overy	90	3 weeks	£250 p.w.	31 January 2004
Arnold & Porter	Yes	Not known	Not known	6 February 2004
Ashurst Morris Crisp	Easter (graduates & final year non-law); Summer (penultimate year law)	Easter: 2 weeks Summer: 3 weeks	£250 p.w.	31 January 2004
Baker & McKenzie	London: 30 International: 3-5*	3 weeks *6-12 weeks in Lon/o'seas office	£250 p.w.	31 January 2004
Barlow Lyde & Gilbert	Yes, plus open days and drop in days	Not known	Not known	27 February 2004
Berwin Leighton Paisner	50	2 weeks	Not known	28 February 2004
Bevan Ashford	80	Not known	Not known	31 March 2004
Bird & Bird	18	3 weeks	£220 p.w.	30 January 2004
Bristows	Yes	Christmas/Easter: 1 week summer: 2 weeks	200 p.w.	Christmas: 29 November 2003; Easter/summer: 28 February 2004
Burges Salmon	40	2 weeks	£175 p.w.	30 January 2004
Capsticks	Yes	2 weeks	Not known	28th February 2004
Clifford Chance	Yes - Christmas, Easter and summer (some overseas)	2-4 weeks	£270 p.w.	Christmas: 14 Nov 2003 Easter/Summer: 31 Jan 2004
Clyde & Co	Yes	3 weeks	Not known	27 February 2004
CMS Cameron McKenna	55	2 weeks	£225 p.w.	Not known
Cobbetts	6 in April; 24 in summer	Not known	Not known	Not known
Coffin Mew & Clover	Open week in July	Not known	Not known	Not known
Covington & Burling	16	Not known	Not known	28 February 2004
Davenport Lyons	10	2 weeks	£175 p.w.	January 2004
Dechert	12, plus 20-30 open days at both Easter and summer	2 weeks	Min. £225 p.w.	Vac scheme: 27 February 2004
Denton Wilde Sapte	45 (plus 25 open days)	1 week	Not known	(OD: 5 December 2003) 27 February 2004

VACATION SCHEMES

FIRM NAME	NUMBER OF PLACES	DURATION	REMUN-ERATION	2004 DEADLINE
Dickinson Dees	36	1 week	£125 p.w.	29 February 2004
DLA	200	1 week	£210 p.w (Lon) £160 p.w (Ors)	28 February 2004
DMH	Yes	1 week	Unpaid	31 January 2004
DWF	Open days	n/a	n/a	Not known
Eversheds	150	2 weeks	Regional variations	31 January 2004
Farrer & Co	32: Easter and summer	2 weeks	£220 p.w.	31 January 2004
Field Fisher Waterhouse	Yes	Not known	Not known	1 January to 28 February 2004
Foot Anstey Sargent	Yes	Not known	Not known	31 March 2004
Freshfields Bruckhaus Deringer	100	2 weeks	£500 total	14 February 2004 (apply asap after 1 December 2003)
Gateley Wareing	12	2 weeks	Not known	13 February 2004
Halliwell Landau	40	2 weeks	£126 p.w.	31 March 2004
Hammonds	64	3 weeks	£230 p.w. (Lon) £180 p.w. (Ors)	29 February 2004
Herbert Smith	115 (Christmas: non-law; Easter/summer: law and non-law) some o/seas	Not known	Not known	Christmas: 14 November 2003 Easter/summer: 30 January 2004
Hewitsons	Yes	1 week	Not known	Not known
Hill Dickinson	Yes	1 week	Not known	30th April 2004
Holman Fenwick & Willan	16	2 weeks	£250 p.w.	1 January to 14 February 2004
Howes Percival	Yes	Not known	Not known	Not known
Hugh James	Yes	Not known	Not known	Not known
Ince & Co	18	2 weeks	£250 p.w.	13 February 2004
Irwin Mitchell	50	1 week	£75 p.w.	31 January 2004
Jones Day Gouldens	16 in Christmas: non-law 16 in Easter: non-law 40 in summer: law	2 weeks	£275 p.w.	Christmas: 31 Oct 2003 Easter/summer: 14 February 2004
Kendall Freeman	12	2 weeks	Not known	29 February 2004
KLegal	10	4 weeks	£250 p.w.	21 February 2004
Lawrence Graham	40 in Easter & summer	2 weeks	£220 p.w.	31 January 2004
Laytons	6	1 week	Not known	31 March 2004

VACATION SCHEMES

FIRM NAME	NUMBER OF PLACES	DURATION	REMUN-ERATION	2004 DEADLINE
Lester Aldridge	8	2 weeks	£75 p.w.	31 March 2004
Linklaters	30 in Christmas (non-law), 60 in summer (law), some o/seas	Not known	£250 p.w.	Not known
Lovells	90 Christmas, Easter and summer	Not known	Not known	Xmas: 14 Nov 2003 Easter/summer: 13 February 2004
Macfarlanes	40	2 weeks	£250 p.w.	27 February 2004; places offered from end of Jan
Manches	Aprox. 23	1 week	Under review	31 January 2004
Masons	Approx 18 in London, approx 5 in Manchester	2 weeks	Not known	20 February 2004
Mayer, Brown, Rowe & Maw LLP	25 Easter and summer	2 weeks	Not known	Not known
McCormicks	Yes	Not known	Not known	27 February 2004
Mills & Reeve	Yes	2 weeks	Not known	1 March 2004
Mishcon de Reya	12	2 weeks	£200 p.w.	14 March 2004
Morgan Cole	6 open days	n/a	n/a	31 March 2004
Nabarro Nathanson	60	3 weeks	Not known	28 February 2004
Nicholson Graham & Jones	open days	n/a	n/a	Not known
Norton Rose	15 in Christmas 45 in summer 5 or 6 six open days	Christmas: 2 weeks summer: 3 weeks	£250 p.w.	1 November 2003 31 January 2004
Olswang	Yes	2 weeks	£250 p.w.	1 March 2004
Orchard	Yes	Not known	Not known	Not known
Osborne Clarke	20-25 Easter and summer	1 week	£175-200 p.w.	31 January 2004
Pannone & Partners	50 Easter and summer	1 week	None	Easter: 30 January 2004 summer: 27 February 2004
Penningtons	London: 60 Easter open day places + some summer vac places	Not known	Expenses	Days: 15 February 2004; Vac scheme: 15 April 2004
Pinsents	90	2 weeks	Not known	20 February 2004
Prettys	One day placements	n/a	n/a	Not known
RadcliffesLeBrasseur	20	2 weeks	Travel exp	31 March 2004
Reed Smith	12	4 weeks (Lon) 2 weeks (Mids)	£800 (Lon) £300 (Mids)	31 January 2004
Reynolds Porter Chamberlain	12	2 weeks	£250 p.w.	27 February 2004

VACATION SCHEMES

FIRM NAME	NUMBER OF PLACES	DURATION	REMUN-ERATION	2004 DEADLINE
Richards Butler	30 in London plus overseas placements	2 weeks	£200 p.w.	13 February 2004
Shadbolt & Co	6	2 weeks	£170 p.w.	16 March 2004
Shoosmiths	30	2 weeks	£160 p.w.	28 February 2004
Simmons & Simmons	30-40	4 weeks	£250 p.w.	20 February 2004
SJ Berwin	60	2 weeks	£225 p.w.	31 January 2004
Slaughter and May	60 (penult. year of degree)	2 weeks	£250 p.w.	6 February 2004
Speechly Bircham	12	3 weeks	£250 p.w.	14 February 2004
Steeles	Yes	Not known	Not known	Not known
Stephenson Harwood	16	2 weeks	£250 p.w.	20 February 2004
Taylor Walton	8	Up to 4 weeks	Agreed w/trainee	30 April 2004
Taylor Wessing	24	2 weeks	£225 p.w.	20 February 2004
Teacher Stern Selby	Approx 10	Not known	Not known	Not known
TLT Solicitors	8	1 week	Not known	Not known
Travers Smith Braithwaite	45 summer + Christmas & Easter places	2 weeks	£250	31 January 2004
Trowers & Hamlins	25-30 plus open days	2 weeks	£225 p.w.	1 March 2004
Walker Morris	45	1 week	£150 p.w.	28 February 2004
Ward Hadaway	Yes	1 week	Not known	30 April 2004
Watson, Farley & Williams	30	2 weeks	£200 p.w.	27 February 2004
Wedlake Bell	6	3 weeks	£150 pw	29 February 2004
Weil, Gotshal & Manges	12	Not known	Not known	14 February 2004
White & Case	40-50	2 weeks	£250 p.w.	31 January 2004
Withers LLP	6 in Easter and 24 in summer	2 weeks	Not known	30 January 2004
Wragge & Co LLP	Easter and summer	Not known	Not known	31 January 2004

applications and selection

applications

You've done your research, you've read this book cover to cover, and you know where you want to work and why. The next step is to start sending in those applications. The vast majority of firms work to a strict timetable and most commercial firms fill their training vacancies two years in advance, so make sure you don't miss the boat. Unless they want to take time out, law students should apply towards or during the summer vacation before their final degree year and non-law students should apply before starting the CPE. Smaller firms accept applications just one year in advance or even closer to the start of the contract.

Blanket applications are spotted easily and will get you nowhere. Tailor each and every application, considering things such as the firm's areas of speciality, its size, location, international presence, culture and ethos. You should consider the ways in which your skills, qualifications and interests are relevant to the firm. **The True Picture** and **Solicitors A-Z** sections of this guide, together with the rankings in the **Practice Areas** will prove useful. For more on the work and reputations of firms, consult *Chambers UK*.

Obviously your application must grab the attention of the reader. But if you can't dazzle them with your genius, don't be tempted to blind them with cheap gimmicks. One applicant stapled a teabag to his application with an invitation to "relax and enjoy!" Others use bizarre fonts and lurid paper. Never include a photograph of yourself on your application – the assessors will have plenty of time to look at you during the interview. Your application should speak for itself. It should be clear, concise, and individually tailored to the particular firm.

Writing job applications can be a lonely and anxious experience. Don't be afraid to consult friends and family members who have been through the same thing or may simply be happy to proofread your application. You'd be amazed at the number of errors a fresh pair of eyes can uncover. Check our website for more detailed advice on application forms and CVs.

what are firms looking for?

At the very least good academics – commercial firms usually require a minimum 2:1, and many are now examining A-level grades too. But brains alone are not enough. Firms often get applications from *"people who look great on paper, but when they get into an interview situation they find it hard to relate to real life and to be more practical."* Most sought after are applicants with the potential to develop commercial acumen. As Kate Turner-Robson from Herbert Smith told us: *"We want people who can use their academic ability in practical situations in the workplace. We want people with good teamwork skills, with flexibility. Obviously they're going to be the brightest of the bright, but are also able to relate to people."*

Do not be deterred if you didn't complete a vacation scheme, if you have little practical experience of the law, or if law was not your first degree. Commercial firms are looking for business acumen, problem-solving ability, pragmatism and teamwork. Summer retail work, travel, organising a college function, mooting and sporting activities can all demonstrate these things to a greater or lesser degree. For all students, a clear understanding of what is involved in commercial practice and a genuine commitment to commercial law are essential. Claire Harris from Lovells told us: *"We're recruiting for the long run; we're recruiting people who will shape and develop the business and who understand what the firm is about."* As Slaughter and May's Charlotte Houghton put it: *"We are looking for people who will be able to relate to clients."* Pretty simple, really.

preparing for an interview or selection day

Read your application and have it fresh in your mind for the interview. Study the firm's recruitment literature and browse their website. You should also be up to date with goings on in the commercial world and in the area of law in which you hope to practice. Read the legal press such as *The Lawyer*, *Legal Week*, the *Law Society's Gazette*, as well as Tuesday's law section of *The Times*. In the weeks leading up to the interview, pay attention to the news and form some opinions, or at the very least be aware of the issues of the day.

When you are invited to an interview, find out who will be conducting it. With the names of the interviewing partners, you can do a little web research on them. Find out about their practice area, their career progression and interests. Consult *Chambers UK* – if they are listed you might even see what their peers and clients say about them!

Do rehearsal interviews with your friends/ careers service/parents, in order to hone your answers. Anticipate what interviewers will ask you! There are a series of very obvious questions that you should be ready to answer. They include old faithfuls like "Why do you want to work for us?" "What attracts you to the law?" and "Tell us about a time when you demonstrated teamwork." It can be a real challenge when you are asked about your strengths and weaknesses. Be honest, but not too forthcoming! It is imperative that you try to provide examples of how you counteract your weaknesses.

the interview

Despite the proliferation of psychometric testing and assessment days, many firms still rely on the simple application + interview . Slaughter and May, Herbert Smith and Allen & Overy all offer interviews with two partners, or a partner and an HR bod. At Herbert Smith, you'll be given a business case study and 45 minutes to read through it, take notes and prepare answers to the questions the partners will then ask you during the interview. Herbert Smith's partner in charge of recruitment, Stephen Wilkinson, stressed that the case study doesn't discriminate against non-law students.

Be sure to have a good night's sleep, and a proper breakfast on the day of the interview (yes mum!). Hunger-induced delirium might be okay in the modelling industry, but is not so cool in law.

Although quite a few firms have a business casual dress policy, err on the side of formality. Business attire – a suit, a clean, pressed shirt and neat hair are best.

Plan your journey beforehand and arrive in the vicinity of the firm with an hour to spare. Sit in a cafe, read the newspaper, read over your application and your interview notes. Calm down and relax! If you think an hour sounds excessive, you'd be amazed to hear of the numbers of candidates who turn up to interviews ten, 15, 20 minutes late, flustered and needing to use the toilet. **Do not be late.** Remember that partners and HR staff are extremely busy people, and to keep them waiting is simply self-sabotage.

Keep in mind that you are being assessed from the moment you enter the firm's offices. Be polite and courteous to everyone you meet, from secretarial staff to partners, cleaners to HR representatives. Potential candidates are crossed off lists after arrogant behaviour towards support staff.

During the interview, **think** before you answer questions. A brief pause before you speak is infinitely preferable to 5 minutes of incoherent rambling. Also, try to avoid starting each answer with "*Well...*" or "*Um...*" When you're speaking, be clear and measured, and make eye contact with each of the interviewers. Be positive, friendly and enthusiastic. Avoid cynicism. Watch your body language and be relaxed, but not too laid back.

And, of course, when they ask: "Do you have any questions for us?" make sure you have saved at least one or two good questions. It is perfectly acceptable to take notes into your interview, so write down a series of questions you want to ask beforehand. After all, it's easy to forget them in all the stress and hoopla surrounding interviews. This is your chance to find out what the partners are like, and what they like about the firm. Claire Harris of Lovells points out: *"It's a good opportunity to put partners on the spot as to what they find rewarding about their career."* But don't be too probing – asking a partner what they earn, as did one interviewee, will raise some giggles and a few eyebrows, but won't win you any favours.

Finally, play safe and don't accept food in an interview. This is a trap for young players. It's difficult enough to handle nerves in a job interview and to enunciate intelligent answers to tricky questions, without worrying about spraying crumbs over the desk or negotiating a rogue cup and saucer. Food complicates matters, just stick with mineral water.

an assessment day in the life of...

A typical assessment day consists of a written test, a group exercise, an interview and perhaps a presentation to some partners.

Lovells' assessment day starts at 10am, when you are introduced to the other candidates. The day kicks off with a presentation by a partner, followed by a question and answer session. This gives applicants the chance to *"grill the partner, get behind the publicity and find out the direction of the business."* Do try to ask something at this stage, but don't take the grilling process into aggressive Paxman-style questioning.

Candidates then take a test based on the Watson Glaser critical thinking analysis, developed by the British Psychological Society. Calm down: there are no electrodes, just tests to assess your ability to deduce information from given facts. The idea is that the 40-minute test replicates live conditions at work. While there's not a lot you can do to prepare yourself, any degree requiring research and analysis should be preparation enough.

Following this, the applicants have lunch with trainee solicitors. Although many firms, including Lovells, tell us they never ask for a report from the trainees, the lunch is still an important part of the day. You are also assessing the firm and deciding whether you like it or not! As Claire puts it: *"It's a two-way exercise – we're on show too!"* Make the most of lunch by asking questions about the responsibility trainees are given, what the work is like and which are the best departments to work in.

In the afternoon group exercise your group will be given a brief to read in ten minutes and then 25 minutes to discuss it. The partners who'll be interviewing you will oversee the process, trying to spot evidence of teamwork, analytical skills, commercial sense and business acumen.

Finally, there's an interview that lasts for about 45 minutes, and is conducted by two partners or a partner and a senior HR manager. The interview involves open, probing questions based on your application form. You'll be tested on your ability to relate to the business world, the quality of your thinking and the clarity of your communication. And, of course, how well you can think on your feet. You should demonstrate an understanding of what's involved in commercial law and an understanding of the firm you're applying to.

gaffes and bloopers

Remember your old cub scout motto: Be Prepared. Recruiters make allowances for youth, inexperience and nervousness, but they do not make allowances for lack of preparation. One HR representative told us: *"One of the major reasons people get turned down is that they have not prepared for the interview, or when they don't have questions for us. Why would we invest money in someone who hasn't given us any thought apart from 'It's well paid and all my mates are doing it'?"*

It's natural to highlight your qualities and to point out your successes, but be careful about over-egging the pudding. Recruiters can always tell when a story doesn't quite ring true and are rarely impressed by an arrogant applicant.

Bringing your parents is another no-no. One candidate brought her mother to her interview and was surprised when mum was asked to wait in reception and have a cup of tea. Bless!

APPLICATIONS AND SELECTION

FIRM NAME	METHOD OF APPLICATION	SELECTION PROCESS	DEGREE CLASS	NUMBER OF CONTRACTS	NUMBER OF APPLICATIONS
Addleshaw Goddard	See website	Interview, assessment centre	2:1	50	3,000
Allen & Overy	Application form & online	Interview	2:1	120	4,000
Arnold & Porter	Application form	Interview	2:1	3-5	Not known
asb law	See website	2 interviews & assessments	2:1	10	500
Ashurst Morris Crisp	Online	1 interview with assistant & another with 2 partners	2:1	50	2,500
B P Collins	Handwritten letter & CV	Screening interview & selection day	Not known	Not known	Not known
Baker & McKenzie	Letter & app form/online	Oral presentation, interview with 2 partners & meet a trainee	2:1	30	2,000
Barlow Lyde & Gilbert	Application form & covering letter	Interview day	Not known	16-18	2,000
Beachcroft Wansbroughs	Application form	Assessment centre & panel interview	2:1 preferred	26	Not known
Berwin Leighton Paisner	Online application form	Assessment day & partner interview	2:1	35	2,000
Bevan Ashford	Application form	Not known	2:1	25	Not known
Bircham Dyson Bell	CV & covering letter	2 interviews with ptnrs & HR	2:1	6	Not known
Bird & Bird	Online application form	Assessment morning	2:1	14	1,500
Blake Lapthorn Linnell	Application form	Assessment; second interview	2.1	5-7	500
Boyes Turner	Letter & CV/online	2 interviews & 1 week work placement	2:1	4	Not known
Brabners Chaffe Street	Application form	Interview & assessment day	2:1/post-grad	7	Not known
Brachers	Handwritten letter & CV	Interview day with partners	2:1	6	400
Bristows	Application form	2 interviews	2.1 preferred	Up to 10	3,500
Browne Jacobson	CV & covering letter/online	Assessment centre	2:1	8	1,500
Burges Salmon	Application form	Not known	2:1	20-25	1,500
Cadwalader, Wickersham & Taft	CV & covering letter	2 interviews	2:1	6-8	400
Capsticks	Application form	Summer placement then interview with Training Principal & partners	2:1 or above	4-5	Approx 200
Charles Russell	Letter & app form/online	Assessment day	2:1	8-10	Approx 2,000
Clarks	Application form or letter & CV	Open day/interview; second interview & written tests	Usually 2:1 or above	3-4	1,000

APPLICATIONS AND SELECTION

FIRM NAME	METHOD OF APPLICATION	SELECTION PROCESS	DEGREE CLASS	NUMBER OF CONTRACTS	NUMBER OF APPLICATIONS
Clifford Chance	Online application	Assessment day: interview + group exercise & verbal reasoning test	2:1	125	2,000
Clyde & Co	Application form & covering letter	Assessment session+interview with 2 partners	2:1	20	1,300+
CMS Cameron McKenna	Online application form	Initial interview followed by assessment centre	2:1	80	1,500
Cobbetts	Application form	Half-day assessments	2:1	15	1,000
Coffin Mew & Clover	CV & covering letter	Interview	2:1 (usually)	4-5	400+
Coudert Brothers	Letter & CV	2 interviews with partners	2:1	4	Not known
Covington & Burling	Application form & covering letter	2 interviews	2:1	4	Not known
Cripps Harries Hall	Online application form	1 interview with managing partner & head of HR	2.1	8	Up to 750
Cumberland Ellis Peirs	Letter & covering CV	2 interviews with partners	2:1	2	500
Davenport Lyons	CV & covering letter	Interviews	2:1	5	1,500
Dechert	Online application form	Communication exercises & interviews	2:1	18	Over 1,500
Denton Wilde Sapte	Application form	First interview; selection test; second interview	2:1	35	2,000
Devonshires	Online application form	Not known	2:1 and higher	6	400
Dickinson Dees	Online application	Interview + in-tray exercises & personality questionnaire	2:1	15	700
DLA	Application form	1st interview, 2nd interview & assessment afternoon	2:1	85+	2,000
DMH	Application form	1st interview & assessments; work experience & 2nd interview	2:1	6-7	400
DWF	Application form	Two-stage interview/selection process	2:1 preferred	6	Approx 1,000
Edwards Geldard	Application form	Interview & summer placement	2:1 desirable	8	400
Eversheds	Online	Selection day: group & individual exercises, presentations & interview	2:1	92	4,000
Farrer & Co	Application form & covering letter	Interviews with GR manager and partners	2:1	8	1,500
Field Fisher Waterhouse	Application form & covering letter	Interview	2:1	10-12	2,000
Finers Stephens Innocent	CV & covering letter	2 interviews with the training partners	2:1	4	1,200
Foot Anstey Sargent	Letter & CV or online form	Assessment day	2:1 preferred	8	Not known
Forbes	Handwritten letter & CV	Interview with partners	2:1	4	350

APPLICATIONS AND SELECTION

FIRM NAME	METHOD OF APPLICATION	SELECTION PROCESS	DEGREE CLASS	NUMBER OF CONTRACTS	NUMBER OF APPLICATIONS
Ford & Warren	Handwritten letter & CV	Interviews & exercise	2:1	6	700
Forsters	Application form	1st interview with HR manager & GR partner; 2nd with 2 partners	Not known	Not known	Not known
Freethcartwright LLP	Application form	Interview & selection day	Not known	Not known	Not known
Freshfields Bruckhaus Deringer	Application form	Interview with 2 partners & written test	2:1	100	c.2,500
Gateley Wareing	See website	Not known	2:1	Not known	Not known
Goodman Derrick	CV & covering letter	2 interviews	2:1 min	2-3	900
Halliwell Landau	Application form	Written paper, presentation & interview	2:1	10	1,000
Hammonds	Online application form	2 interviews	2:1	40	1,800
Harbottle & Lewis LLP	CV & letter	Interview	2:1	4	800
Henmans	Online application form	Interview with HR manager & partners	Not known	3	450
Herbert Smith	Application form	Case study & interview	2:1	up to 100	1,139
Hewitsons	Application form	Interview	2:1 min	8	1,400
Hill Dickinson	CV & letter by email	Assessment day	Not known	Not known	Not known
Holman Fenwick & Willan	Application form	2 interviews with partners & written exercise	2:1	8	1,000
Howes Percival	Letter, CV & application form	Assess. centre & 2nd interview with training principal & partner	2:1	7	300
Hugh James	Application form	Assessment day	2:2	7	350
Ince & Co	Letter & CV	Interview with HR; interview with 2 partners & written test	2:1	8	1,500
Irwin Mitchell	Application form & covering letter	Assessment centre and interview; second interview	Not known	15	1,000
Jones Day Gouldens	CV & letter online	2 interviews with partners	2:1	20	1,700
Kendall Freeman	Online application	Interview with 2 partners	2:1	6-7	Not known
Keoghs	CV & covering letter	Two-stage interview	2:1	4	800
KLegal	Online application	2 interviews & assessment centre	2:1	10-12	Not known
Lawrence Graham	Application form	Interview	2:1	18	1,000
Laytons	Application form	2 interviews	1 or 2:1	8	2,000
LeBoeuf, Lamb, Greene & MacRae	CV & covering letter	2 interviews	2:1	4	1,000

APPLICATIONS AND SELECTION

FIRM NAME	METHOD OF APPLICATION	SELECTION PROCESS	DEGREE CLASS	NUMBER OF CONTRACTS	NUMBER OF APPLICATIONS
Lee Bolton & Lee	Letter & CV	Panel interview	2:1	3	800
Lester Aldridge	Letter, CV & application form	Interview by a panel of partners	2:1	5	300
Lewis Silkin	Application form	Assessment day: interview with 2 partners & analytical exercise	2:1	6	1,000
Linklaters	Application form	2 interviews & commercial case study	2:1	125	2,500
Lovells	Online application form	Assessment day: critical thinking test, group exercise, interview	2:1	75	1,500
Lupton Fawcett	Application form & handwritten letter	Interviews & assessment days	2:1 preferred	2-3	300
Mace & Jones	Covering letter & CV	Interview with partners	2:1	varies	1,500
Macfarlanes	Online application	Assessment day	2:1	25	1,500
Manches	Application form	Interview with 2 partners. 2nd interview & assessments	2:1	10	1,000
Martineau Johnson	Online application form	Half-day assessment centre	2:1	10-12	650
Masons	Online application form	Assessment day & an interview	2:1	15-17	1,600
Mayer, Brown, Rowe & Maw LLP	Online application form	Selection workshop: interview, business analysis exercise & group exercise	2:1	25-30	720
McCormicks	Application form	Interview with 2 partners	2:1	4	300
McDermott, Will & Emery	CV & covering letter	Not known	Not known	Not known	Not known
Mills & Reeve	Application form	One day assessment centre	2:1	15-20	Approx 500
Mishcon de Reya	Application form	Not known	2:1	6	800+
Morgan Cole	Apply online	Assessment centre & interview	2.1 preferred	Not known	Not known
Nabarro Nathanson	Application form	Interview & assessment day	2:1	30	1,500
Nicholson Graham & Jones	Online	Interview & assessment	2:1	10	1,500
Norton Rose	Online application form	Interview & group exercise	2:1	70	3,500+
Olswang	Online	Business case scenario, interview, psychometric test + written exercises	2:1	Up to 20	2,500
Orchard	Application form	2 interviews	2:1	4-6	350
Osborne Clarke	Online application form	Assessment day: interviews, group exercises etc; 2nd interview + presentation	2:1 preferred	20-25	1,000-1,500

APPLICATIONS AND SELECTION

FIRM NAME	METHOD OF APPLICATION	SELECTION PROCESS	DEGREE CLASS	NUMBER OF CONTRACTS	NUMBER OF APPLICATIONS
Pannone & Partners	Application form & CV	1st interview; 2nd interview comprises tour of firm & lunch	2:1	10	700
Payne Hicks Beach	Letter & CV	Interview	2:1	3	1,000
Penningtons	Covering letter, CV & application form	Interview with a partner and director of studies	2:1	11	1,000
Pinsents	Online application form	Assessment centre including interview	2:1	35	2,000
Prettys	Application letter & CV	Not known	2:1 preferred	4-5	Not known
Pritchard Englefield	Application form	Interview	Generally 2:1	3	300-400
RadcliffesLeBrasseur	CV & covering letter	2 interviews with partners	2:1	4	1,000
Reed Smith	Application form & covering letter	Assessment day: 2 interviews, aptitude test & presentation	2:1	6	1,000
Reynolds Porter Chamberlain	Online	Assessment day	2.1	10	1,000
Richards Butler	Online application form	Selection exercise & interview	2:1	20	2,000
Salans	Handwritten letter & CV	Interviews & workshop	2:1	3 or 4	500+
Shadbolt & Co	Application form	Interview & written assessment	2:1	4	100
Shearman & Sterling	Application form	Interviews	2:1	6	Not known
Shoosmiths	Application form	Full-day selection centre	2:1	10	1,000
Sidley Austin Brown & Wood	Covering letter & application form	Interview(s)	2:1	6-8	500
Simmons & Simmons	Online	Assessment day: interview & written & document exercises	2:1	50-60	2,700
SJ Berwin	Online application form	2 interviews	2:1	35	2,500
Slaughter and May	Covering letter & CV or online	Interview	2:1	Approx 85	2,500+
Speechly Bircham	Application form	Interview	2:1	5	1,000
Steeles	Online or CV & covering letter	Interview/assessment day	2:1	6	300-400
Stephenson Harwood	Application form	Assessment centre	2:1	16-18	Not known
Stevens & Bolton	Letter & application form	2 interviews	2:1	3	600
Tarlo Lyons	Application form	2 interviews with partners & skills assessment	2:1	3	300

APPLICATIONS AND SELECTION

FIRM NAME	METHOD OF APPLICATION	SELECTION PROCESS	DEGREE CLASS	NUMBER OF CONTRACTS	NUMBER OF APPLICATIONS
Taylor Walton	CV & covering letter	First & second interviews	2:1 or above	Not known	Not known
Taylor Wessing	Application form	2 interviews, 1 with a partner	2:1	24	1,600
Teacher Stern Selby	Letter & application form	2 interviews	2:1 (not absolute)	3-6	1,000
Thomson Snell & Passmore	Handwritten letter & app form	1 interview with Training Partner and 1 other partner	2:1	4	Approx 500
TLT Solicitors	Application form	Assessment day	2:1 preferred	8	750
Travers Smith Braithwaite	CV and covering letter	Interviews (2 stage process)	2:1	25	2,500
Trowers & Hamlins	Letter, application form & CV	Interview(s), essay & practical test	2:1+	12-15	1,600
Walker Morris	Application form	Telephone & face-to-face interviews	2:1	15	Approx 800
Ward Hadaway	Application form & handwritten letter	Interview	2:1	8	400+
Watson, Farley & Williams	Online application	Assessment centre & interview	2:1 min	12	1,000
Wedlake Bell	CV & covering letter	Interviews	2:1	4 or 6	Not known
Weightman Vizards	Online	Not known	Not known	Not known	Not known
Weil, Gotshal & Manges	Online application form	Not known	2:1	12	Not known
White & Case	Online application	Interview	2:1	20-25	1,500
Wiggin & Co	CV	2 interviews	2:1	3	300
Withers LLP	Application form	2 interviews	2:1	12	1,200
Wollastons	CV & application form	Interviews (2 stage)	2:1	2	500
Wragge & Co	Online or application form	Telephone discussion & assessment day	2:1	25	1,300

offer and acceptance

After all your hard work in trying to secure a training contract, you'll need to know what to do when you actually land one. If you've already studied contract law you'll know the basic principles of offer and acceptance; if you've not yet been introduced to the timeless delights of Carlill v The Carbolic Smokeball Co, what better time to learn!

By accepting a training contract offer you enter into a legally binding contract with the law firm, so accept the right offer. Appreciating the minefield into which inexperienced students step, the Law Society has issued guidelines by which law firms should manage the recruitment process. The guidelines are detailed and we advise any student who is unsure about their position to read them – they are published on the society's website. However, to give you a feel for things, here are the main points.

If you're a law undergraduate, training contract interviews can only be scheduled for 1 September onwards in your final undergraduate year. If you've impressed the firm on a vacation scheme, it must wait until this date before offering you a contract.

An offer should be made in writing; however, many recruiters now make initial offers by phone. You need not accept a verbal offer, so be polite and ask them to send the offer in writing.

Unless the training contract is due to start within 12 months, the offer ought not to be made subject to a deadline for acceptance. Nevertheless, the guidelines do allow a deadline to be set, although it must be at least three weeks after the offer is made. But here's the saver – no deadline should expire before 1 November in a law undergrad's final year or a non-law grad's CPE year. If a firm is paying your law school fees, it should set out the terms and conditions of the arrangement in the training contract offer letter.

We get calls from students who want to hang on to an offer from one firm while they pursue applications with others. In the initial wave of relief, it's easy to forget that the balance of power has shifted in your favour. We've heard from too many trainees who simply took the first offer they got because the firm was prepared to fund their LPC and/or CPE. As long as you understand and respect the rules concerning offers, our advice is to sit on one (or two) while your remaining applications run their course. Of course, if your top choice firm offers you a job, and you're confident it's the one for you, then go for it.

Unfortunately, some non-law grads may find there is a very long gap between an offer made by a big City firm that deliberately interviews early on in the academic year and the interviews timetabled by the majority of commercial firms. If you want to hang on to an offer then do so, and don't be guilt-tripped into accepting it until you're ready. You may be phoned up – perhaps too regularly for your liking – so be clear and polite about why you are delaying your decision and when you think you will be able to give an answer. These firms are making offers early; you are merely keeping step with the normal schedule.

Your obligations? You need to respond to a firm that's made an offer as quickly as you can. Either accept it, refuse it or simply explain that you need time to consider it. You need to tell the firm how much more time you need. Do not go beyond the 1 November date mentioned above, save in exceptional circumstances. Ask the firm to confirm its agreement to wait until the chosen date.

You can't collect offers like Pokémon cards; you can hold only two at a time and must reject the rest. When you accept an offer, you must do so in writing. You should also then confirm to other firms that you are withdrawing your application. This is, after all, only fair to recruiters (who are really overworked at this time of year) and other applicants (who may not get an interview if you are still hogging the shortlist).

SALARIES AND BENEFITS

FIRM NAME	1ST YEAR SALARY	2ND YEAR SALARY	SPONSORSHIP/ AWARDS	OTHER BENEFITS	QUALIFICATION SALARY
Addleshaw Goddard	£20,000 (Manch/Leeds) £28,000 (London)	£22,000 (Manch/Leeds) £30,000 (London)	CPE & LPC: fees + maintenance grant of £4,500	Corporate gym m'ship, STL, subsd restaurant, pension	£33,000 (Manch/Leeds) £48,000 (London)
Allen & Overy	£28,500	£32,000	CPE & LPC: fees + £5,000 p.a. maintenance (£4,500 outside London, Oxford & Guildford)	Pte healthcare scheme, PMI, STL, subsd restaurant, gym m'ship, 6 weeks unpaid leave on qual	£50,000
Arnold & Porter	Minimum £30,000	Not known	CPE & LPC: sponsorship	PHI, STL, life ass	£59,000
asb law	£16,750	£18,750	Interest free loan	Life ass, PMI	£27,500
Ashurst Morris Crisp	£28,000-29,000	£31,000-32,000	CPE & LPC: fees + £5,000 p.a. maintenance (£4,500 outside London & Guildford), £500 LPC distinction award, language tuition bursaries	PHI, pension, life ass, STL, gym m'ship	£48,000
Baker & McKenzie	£28,000 + £3,000 'golden hello'	£32,000	CPE & LPC: fees + £5000 p.a. maintenance + laptop or £2,000 for LPC	PHI, life ins, PMI, group personal pension, subsd gym m'ship, STL, subsd staff restaurant	£50,000-£52,000
Barlow Lyde & Gilbert	£28,000	£30,000	CPE & LPC: fees + maintenance	Not known	£47,000
Beachcroft Wansbroughs	£27,000 (London) £19,500 (regions)	£29,500 (London) £22,000 (regions)	CPE & LPC fees + £3,500 bursary	Flexible scheme (buy & sell benefits, inc. holiday, pension, pte healthcare)	Not known
Berwin Leighton Paisner	£28,000	£32,000	CPE & LPC: fees + £4,500 p.a. maintenance	Flexible package inc. PHI, PMI, subsd conveyancing, subsd gym m'ship	£48,000
Bevan Ashford	Not known	Not known	LPC: yes CPE: sometimes	Not known	Not known
Bircham Dyson Bell	£26,000	£27,000	Not known	Pension, life ass, PHI	Not known
Bird & Bird	£26,000	£28,000	CPE & LPC: fees + £3,500 p.a. maintenance	BUPA, STL, subsd sports club m'ship, life cover, PHI, pension	£43,000
Blake Lapthorn Linnell	£16,500	£18,000	Not known	Not known	£29,000
Boyes Turner	£17,500	£18,500	LPC: £3,000 interest-free loan	Pension, life ass	Not known
BP Collins	£17,000	£18,000	50% LPC costs refund when TC starts	Not known	Not known
Brabners Chaffe Street	£17,000	Not known	Not known	Not known	Not known

Notes: PHI = Permanent Health Insurance; STL = Season Travel Ticket Loan; PMI = Private Medical Insurance

SALARIES AND BENEFITS

FIRM NAME	1ST YEAR SALARY	2ND YEAR SALARY	SPONSORSHIP/ AWARDS	OTHER BENEFITS	QUALIFICATION SALARY
Brachers	£16,500	£18,200	LPC/CPE: £6,000 discretionary award	Not known	£27,500-£30,000
Bristows	£26,000	£28,000	CPE & LPC: fees + £5,000 p.a. maintenance	Pension, life ass & health ins	£43,000
Browne Jacobson	£18,500	Not known	CPE & LPC: funding	Not known	Regional variations
Burges Salmon	£20,000	£21,000	CPE & LPC: fees + maintenance £4,500 for LPC only (£3,500 p.a. if studying both)	Bonus, pension, mobile phone, laptop, gym m'ship, social club, xmas gift	£34,000
Cadwalader, Wickersham & Taft	£30,000	£33,600	CPE & LPC: fees + £4,500 p.a maintenance	PHI, STL, BUPA (dental & health), life ass	£65,000
Capsticks	Not known	Not known	CPE & LPC: scholarship contributions	Bonus, pension, PHI, death in service, STL	£40,500
Charles Russell	£27,000	£29,500	London: CPE & LPC fees + £4,500 p.a. maintenance Chelt/Guildford: one off LPC grants	BUPA, PHI, life ass	£44,000
Clarks	£17,750	£19,000	LPC: fees + maintenance	Pension, free conveyancing	Not known
Clifford Chance	£28,500	£32,000	CPE & LPC: fees + £5,000 p.a. maintenance (Lon/Guild/Oxf), £4,500 p.a. (elsewhere), prizes for first class degree & LPC distinction	Interest-free loan, pte health ins, subsd restaurant, fitness centre, life ass, occupational health service, PHI	£48,000
Clyde & Co	£27,000	£30,000	CPE & LPC: fees + maintenance (provided where no LEA funding)	Subsd sports club, STL, staff restaurant, weekly free bar	£46,000
CMS Cameron McKenna	£28,000	£32,000	CPE & LPC: fees + £5,000 p.a. maintenance (Lon/Guild/Oxf), £4,500 (elsewhere)	Not known	£48,000
Cobbetts	Competitive	Competitive	CPE & LPC: grant available	Social club, LA Fitness pool & gym	Not known
Coffin Mew & Clover	Competitive	Competitive	CPE & LPC: discussed with candidates	Not known	£26,000+
Coudert Brothers	£28,000	£32,000	CPE & LPC: fees + £4,000 p.a. maintenance (discretionary)	Pension, health ins, subsd gym m'ship, STL, pte med & dental care	Not known
Covington & Burling	£28,000	£32,000	CPE & LPC: fees + £5,000 p.a. maintenance	Pension, PHI, pte health cover, life ass, STL	Not known
Cripps Harries Hall	£17,000	£19,000	LPC fees: 50% interest free loan, 50% bursary (discretionary)	Not known	£30,000
Cumberland Ellis Peirs	Not known	Not known	None	STL, luncheon vouchers	Not known

Notes: PHI = Permanent Health Insurance; STL = Season Travel Ticket Loan; PMI = Private Medical Insurance

SALARIES AND BENEFITS

FIRM NAME	1ST YEAR SALARY	2ND YEAR SALARY	SPONSORSHIP/ AWARDS	OTHER BENEFITS	QUALIFICATION SALARY
Davenport Lyons	Not known	Not known	Not normally	STL, client intro bonus, contrib to gym m'ship, discretionary bonus	Not known
Dechert	£28,000	£32,000	LPC: fees + £4,500 p.a. maintenance (where no LEA grant)	PHI, life ass, subsd gym m'ship, STL	c.£48,000
Denton Wilde Sapte	£27,000-28,000	£30,000-31,000	CPE & LPC: fees + £4,500 p.a. maintenance (£5,000 in London)	Flexible (includes pte health cover, sports m'ship, PHI, life ass, dental) meal allowance, STL	£48,000
Devonshires	Market rate	Market rate	LPC: funding considered	STL, healthcare scheme, subsd health-club m'ship	Negotiable
Dickinson Dees	£18,000	£19,500	CPE & LPC: fees + £4,000 interest free loan	Not known	£30,000
DLA	£28,000 (London) £20,000 (regions) £16,000 (Scotland)	£31,000 (London) £22,000 (regions) £18,000 (Scotland)	CPE & LPC: fees + maintenance	Contributory pension, health ins, life ass, sports & social facilities, car scheme	£48,000 (London) £33,000 (Birmingham) £32,500 (other English) £30,000 (Scotland)
DMH	£17,000	£19,500	Not known	Not known	£29,000
DWF	£16,750	Not known	LPC: fees	Life ass, pension	Not known
Edwards Geldard	£16,000	£17,000	LPC: fees; CPE: £3,000	Life ass at 3 x salary	£29,000
Eversheds	£28,000 (London)	£31,000 (London)	CPE & LPC: fees + maintenance	Regional variations	£46,000 (London)
Farrer & Co	£26,000	£28,000	CPE & LPC: fees + £4,500 p.a. mainte-nance	Health & life ins, subsd gym m'ship, STL	£40,000
Field Fisher Waterhouse	£26,000	£29,120	CPE & LPC: fees + maintenance	STL, PMI, life ass	£43,000
Finers Stephens Innocent	Highly competitive	Highly competitive	LPC & CPE: fees	Pension, PMI, life ins, long-term disability ins, STL	Highly competitive
Foot Anstey Sargent	£15,600	£17,680	LPC: £8,000	Contributory pension	£27,825
Forbes	At least Law Soc min	£16,000	Not known	Not known	Highly competitive
Forsters	£24,500	£26,500	None	STL, PHI, life ins, subsd gym m'ship	£41,000

Notes: PHI = Permanent Health Insurance; STL = Season Travel Ticket Loan; PMI = Private Medical Insurance

SALARIES AND BENEFITS

FIRM NAME	1ST YEAR SALARY	2ND YEAR SALARY	SPONSORSHIP/ AWARDS	OTHER BENEFITS	QUALIFICATION SALARY
Freethcartwright	£16,000	Not known	Not known	Not known	Not known
Freshfields Bruckhaus Deringer	£28,000	£32,000	CPE & LPC: fees + £5,000 p.a. maintenance (Lon/Oxf), £4,500 p.a. (elswhere)	Life ass, PHI, group personal pension, interest-free loan, STL, PMI, subsd staff restaurant, gym	£50,000
Gateley Wareing	£18,500	£20,500	LPC: fees + £4,000 maintenance CPE: fees	Bonus scheme (up to 10% of salary)	£32,000
Goodman Derrick	£24,500	£25,750	LPC: fees + maintenance	Med health ins, STL, pension	Not known
Halliwell Landau	£21,000	£22,000	CPE & LPC: fees + £2,000 maintenance	Pension, subsd gym m'ship	£32,000
Hammonds	£20,500	£23,000	CPE & LPC fees paid & maintenance grant of £4,500 p.a.	Subsd accom (rotational trainees), flexible benefits scheme	£46,500 (London) £33,000-34,000 (other)
Harbottle & Lewis LLP	£24,250	£25,250	LPC: fees + interest-free loan	Lunch, STL	£41,000
Henmans	£16,275	£17,850	Not known	Not known	£27,000
Herbert Smith	£28,500	£32,000	CPE & LPC: fees + £5,000 p.a. maintenance	Profit share, PHI, PMI, STL, life ass, gym, group personal accident ins, matched contrib. pension	£50,000
Hewitsons	£17,500	£18,500	None	Not known	£31,500
Hill Dickinson	£17,500	£19,000	LPC: fees (further funding under review)	Not known	Not known
Holman Fenwick & Willan	£28,000	£30,000	CPE & LPC: fees + £5,000 p.a. maintenance	PMI, PHI, accident ins, subsd gym m'ship, STL	Not known
Howes Percival	£18,750	£20,000	CPE & LPC: funding	Contributory pension, pte health ins	Not known
Hugh James	Competitive	Competitive	Not known	Contribution to stakeholder pension	Competitive
Ince & Co	£27,000	£30,000	LPC: fees + £4,750 grant (London), £4,000 (elsewhere), CPE: discretionary	STL, corporate health cover, PHI, contributory pension	£47,000
Irwin Mitchell	£17,500 (outside London)	£19,500 (outside London)	CPE & LPC: fees + £3,000 maintenance	Not known	Not known

Notes: PHI = Permanent Health Insurance; STL = Season Travel Ticket Loan; PMI = Private Medical Insurance

SALARIES AND BENEFITS

FIRM NAME	1ST YEAR SALARY	2ND YEAR SALARY	SPONSORSHIP/ AWARDS	OTHER BENEFITS	QUALIFICATION SALARY
Jones Day Gouldens	£33,000	£37,000	CPE & LPC: fees + £5,000 p.a. maintenance	Pte healthcare, STL, subsd sports club m'ship, group life cover	£55,000
Kendall Freeman	£26,000-27,000	£28,000-29,000	CPE & LPC: fees + maintenance	Not known	£48,000
Keoghs	Under review	Under review	Not known	Not known	£27,500
KLegal	£28,000	£32,000	CPE & LPC: fees + £4,500 p.a. maintenance	Flextra (flexible scheme inc. life ass, pension, lunch allowance)	Not known
Lawrence Graham	£28,000	£32,000	CPE & LPC: fees + £4,000 p.a. maintenance	STL, on-site gym	£46,000
Laytons	Market rate	Market rate	CPE & LPC: funding considered	Not known	Market rate
LeBoeuf, Lamb, Greene & MacRae	£33,000	£37,000	CPE & LPC: fees + £4,500 maintenance	PMI, STL, subsd restaurant	£65,000
Lee Bolton & Lee	£21,000	£22,000	LPC: contribution	STL, discretionary bonus	£39,000
Lester Aldridge	£16,500-17,000	£17,500-18,000	LPC: discretionary loan	Life ass, pension	£29,000
Lewis Silkin	£27,000	£29,000	LPC: fees	Life ass, critical illness cover, health ins, STL, pension, subsd gym m'ship	£43,000
Linklaters	£28,500	£32,000	CPE & LPC: fees + £4,500-£5,000 p.a. maintenance.	Health & w'wide travel ins, life ass, pension, STL, subsd gym m'ship	£50,000 + bonus
Lovells	£28,000	£32,000	CPE & LPC: fees + £5,000 p.a. maintenance (Lon/Guild/Oxf), £4,500 p.a.(elsewhere), £500 bonus & £1,000 salary advance on joining, £500 prize for first class degree	PPP med ins, life ass, PHI, STL, in-house gym, staff restaurant, in-house dentist, doctor & physio, local retail discounts	£50,000
Lupton Fawcett	Competitive	Competitive	LPC: interest-free loan, funding can be discussed	Health ins, STL	Competitive
Mace & Jones	£15,000	£15,500	Not known	Not known	Negotiable

Notes: PHI = Permanent Health Insurance; STL = Season Travel Ticket Loan; PMI = Private Medical Insurance

SALARIES AND BENEFITS

FIRM NAME	1ST YEAR SALARY	2ND YEAR SALARY	SPONSORSHIP/ AWARDS	OTHER BENEFITS	QUALIFICATION SALARY
Macfarlanes	£28,000	£32,000	CPE & LPC: fees + £5,000 p.a. maintenance (Lon/Guild/Oxf), £4,500 (elsewhere), prizes for LPC distinction or commendation	STL, pension, PHI*, PMI*; subsd conveyancing/ health club/gym m'ship/restaurant, subscriptions to City of London Law Soc/TSG *After 12 months	£50,000
Manches	£26,500 (London)	£30,000 (London)	CPE & LPC: fees + £4,000 p.a. maintenance	STL, BUPA after 6 months, PHI, life ins, pension after 3 months	£40,250 (London)
Martineau Johnson	£18,000	£19,500	CPE & LPC: fees + £3,500 p.a. maintenance	Not known	£33,000
Masons	Starts £25,000 (London) (varies between offices)	Rises to £27,000 (London) (varies between offices)	CPE & LPC: fees + maintenance	Life ass, pte health care (all offices) Subsd restaurant & STL (London)	£43,000 (London)
Mayer, Brown, Rowe & Maw LLP	£28,000	Not known	CPE & LPC: + £4,500 p.a. maintenance (£5,000 for Lon/Guild)	STL, subsd sports club m'ship, pte health scheme	£50,000
McCormicks	Highly competitive	Highly competitive	Not known	Not known	Highly competitive
McDermott, Will & Emery	£30,000	Not known	CPE & LPC: fees + maintenance	Pte med & dental ins, life ass, PHI, STL, subisidised gym m'ship, employee assistance programme	Not known
Mills & Reeve	£20,000	£21,000	LPC: fees + maintenance CPE: fees	Life ass, contrib pension, bonus, subsd gym, BUPA discount	£31,500-32,500
Mishcon de Reya	£25,000	£27,000	CPE & LPC: fees + bursary	Med cover, subsd gym m'ship, STL, PHI, life ass, pension	Not known
Morgan Cole	Competitive	Competitive	CPE & LPC: fees + maintenance	Not known	Not known
Nabarro Nathanson	£28,000 (Lond/Reading) £20,000 (Sheffield)	£32,000 (Lond/Reading) £22,000 (Sheffield)	CPE & LPC: fees + £5,000 p.a. maintenance (Lon/Guild), £4,500 (elsewhere)	PMI, pension, STL, subsd restaurant, subsd corporate gym m'ship	£46,000 (London) £31,000 (Sheffield)
Nicholson Graham & Jones	£28,000	£31,000	CPE & LPC: fees + £4,000 p.a. maintenance	Life ass, STL, subsd gym m'ship, BUPA	£44,000

Notes: PHI = Permanent Health Insurance; STL = Season Travel Ticket Loan; PMI = Private Medical Insurance

SALARIES AND BENEFITS

FIRM NAME	1ST YEAR SALARY	2ND YEAR SALARY	SPONSORSHIP/ AWARDS	OTHER BENEFITS	QUALIFICATION SALARY
Norton Rose	£28,500	£32,000	CPE & LPC: fees + £5,000 p.a. maintenance, £1,000 travel scholarship	£800 loan on arrival, life ass, pte health ins, STL, subsd gym m'ship, 4 weeks unpaid leave on qual	Not known
Olswang	£26,500	£30,000	CPE & LPC: fees + £4,500 p.a. fees + maintenance, (London) or £4,000 (o/s London)	After 6 months: pension, med cover, life cover, dental scheme, STL, subsd gym m'ship. After 12 months: PHI	£46,000
Osborne Clarke	£25,000 (London/TV) £19,000 (Bristol)	Not known	CPE & LPC: fees + £3,000 p.a. maintenance	Pension contributions, pte healthcare cover, STL, PHI, group life ass	£47,000 (London) £43,000 (TV) £34,000 (Bristol)
Pannone & Partners	£19,000	£21,000	LPC: fees	Not known	£32,000
Payne Hicks Beach	£25,000	£27,500	CPE & LPC: fees	STL, life ass, PHI, pension	Not known
Penningtons	£25,500 (London)	£27,500 (London)	LPC: fees + maintenance, award for commendation or distinction	Subsd sports & social club, life ass, pte med, STL	£38,000 (London)
Pinsents	£28,000	£32,000	CPE & LPC: fees + maintenance (CPE: £3,000, LPC: £5,000)	Not known	Approx £48,000
Prettys	Not known	Not known	Discretionary	Not known	Not known
Pritchard Englefield	£20,750	£21,250	LPC: fees	Some subsd training, luncheon vouchers	£34,000
RadcliffesLeBrasseur	£23,500 (London) £15,000 (Leeds)	£26,000 (London) £16,500 (Leeds)	LPC: fees	Health ins, STL, life ass, PHI, pension	£38,000 (London)
Reed Smith	£27,000	£31,000	CPE & LPC: fees + maintenance + interest-free loan	BUPA, STL, life ass, PHI, pension contributions	£48,000
Reynolds Porter Chamberlain	£27,000	£29,000	CPE & LPC: fees + £4,000 p.a. maintenance	Bonus, PMI, income protection, STL, subsd gym m'ship	£45,000
Richards Butler	£28,000	£31,000	CPE & LPC: fees + £5,000 p.a. maintenance	Bonus, life ins, BUPA, STL, subsd staff restaurant, conveyancing allowance	£48,000 + bonus
Salans	£26,500	£28,500	LPC: fees	Pte healthcare, pension, STL	Variable

Notes: PHI = Permanent Health Insurance; STL = Season Travel Ticket Loan; PMI = Private Medical Insurance

SALARIES AND BENEFITS

FIRM NAME	1ST YEAR SALARY	2ND YEAR SALARY	SPONSORSHIP/ AWARDS	OTHER BENEFITS	QUALIFICATION SALARY
Shadbolt & Co	£22,000	£26,000	LPC: 50% fee refund when TC starts	Pte healthcare, PHI, life ass, paid study leave, STL, bonus, prof m'ships + subs	£35,000
Shearman & Sterling	£30,000	£34,000	CPE & LPC: fees + £4,500 maintenance	Not known	£55,000
Shoosmiths	Competitive	Competitive	LPC: £12,500 split between fees & maintenance	Life ass, pension after 3 months, various staff discounts, Xmas bonus	Market rate
Sidley Austin Brown & Wood	£28,500	£32,000	CPE & LPC: fees + maintenance	Healthcare, disability cover, life ass, contrib to gym m'ship, STL	Not known
SJ Berwin	£28,000	£32,000	CPE & LPC: fees + £4,500 p.a. maintenance (£5,000 in London)	Corporate sports m'ship, free lunch, health ins	£48,000
Simmons & Simmons	£28,000	£32,000	CPE & LPC: fees + £5,000 p.a. maintenance (Lon/Guild/Oxf), £4,500 (elsewhere)	STL, fitness loan, trav ins, accident ins, death in service, med cover, staff restaurant	£48,000
Slaughter and May	£29,000	£32,500	CPE & LPC: fees + maintenance	BUPA, STL, pension, subsd health club m'ship, 24-hour accident cover	£50,000
Speechly Bircham	£26,000-27,000	£28,000-29,000	CPE & LPC: fees + maintenance	STL, PMI, life ass	£45,000
Steeles	Not known	Not known	Not known	Pension, accident ins, legal services, STL, gym m'ship loan	Not known
Stephenson Harwood	£26,000	£29,000	CPE & LPC: fees + maintenance	Subsd health club m'ship, pte health ins, BUPA, STL	£46,000
Stevens & Bolton	£20,000	£22,000	CPE & LPC: £5,000 towards fees + £4,000 p.a. maintenance	PMI, life ass, pension, STL, PHI	£38,000
Tarlo Lyons	£25,000 (on average)	£28,000 (on average)	LPC: fees	Bonus, pte health scheme, pension plan, subsd health club m'ship	£42,000
Taylor Wessing	£26,000	£29,000	CPE & LPC: fees + £4,500 p.a. maintenance	Pte med care, PHI, STL, subsd staff restaurant, pension	£48,000
Teacher Stern Selby	£24,000	Not known	LPC: occasional funding	Not known	£35,000
Thomson Snell & Passmore	£16,500	£18,000	LPC: grant & interest free loan	Not known	£27,500
TLT Solicitors	Not known	Not known	LPC: fees + maintenance	Pension, subsd health ins, subsd sports & health club m'ship, life ass	Market rate

Notes: PHI = Permanent Health Insurance; STL = Season Travel Ticket Loan; PMI = Private Medical Insurance

SALARIES AND BENEFITS

FIRM NAME	1ST YEAR SALARY	2ND YEAR SALARY	SPONSORSHIP/ AWARDS	OTHER BENEFITS	QUALIFICATION SALARY
Travers Smith Braithwaite	£28,000	£32,000	LPC & CPE: fees + 5,000 p.a. maintenance (£4,500 o/side Lon)	Pte health ins, permanent sickness cover, life ass, STL, refreshment credit, subsd sports club m'ship	£48,000
Trowers & Hamlins	£26,000	£27,500	CPE & LPC: fees + £4,250–£4,500 p.a. maintenance	STL, pte healthcare after 6 months, employee assistance programme, bonus, death in service	£43,500
Walker Morris	£20,000	£22,000	CPE: fees + £3,500 maintenance, LPC: fees + £4,500 maintenance	Not known	£32,000
Ward Hadaway	£17,000	£18,000	LPC: fees + £2,000 int-free loan	Death in service insurance, pension	Min £30,000
Watson, Farley & Williams	£28,500	£32,500	CPE & LPC: fees + £4,500 p.a. maintenance (£4,000 o/side London)	Life ass, PHI, BUPA, STL, pension, subsd gym m'ship	Min £50,000
Wedlake Bell	Not known	Not known	LPC & CPE: fees + £2,500 p.a. maintenance (if no LEA grant)	Pension, STL, subsd gym m'ship. On qual: life ass, med ins, PHI	Not known
Weightman Vizards	Not known	Not known	CPE & LPC: fees	Pension, health cover, life ass	Not known
Weil, Gotshal & Manges	£35,000	Not known	CPE & LPC: fees + main-tenance	Bonus, health screens, pension, PHI, pte health cover, life ass, subsd gym m'ship, STL	Not known
White & Case	£33,000-34,500	£36,000-37,500	CPE & LPC: fees + £5,500 p.a. maintenance, prize for LPC commendation or distinction	BUPA, gym m'ship con-trib, life ins, pension, PHI, STL, bonus	£60,000
Wiggin & Co	£21,900	£29,700	CPE & LPC: fees + £3,000 p.a. maintenance	Life ass, pte health cover, pension scheme, PHI	£41,600
Withers LLP	£27,000	£29,000	CPE & LPC: fees + £4,500 p.a. maintenance, prize for CPE/LPC distinction or commendation	STL, PMI, life ass, Xmas bonus, subsd cafe	£45,000
Wragge & Co LLP	£21,000	£24,000	CPE & LPC: fees + £4,500 p.a. maintenance, prizes for first class degree & LPC distinction	£1,000 int-free loan, pen-sion, life ass, PHI, travel schemes, PMI, sports & social club, indep fin advice, subsd gym m'ship, Xmas gift	£33,000

Notes: PHI = Permanent Health Insurance; STL = Season Travel Ticket Loan; PMI = Private Medical Insurance

after qualification

doom and gloom?

A year ago we reported that the market for newly qualifieds had tightened considerably. Unfortunately, by the autumn of 2003 it had tightened even further; in fact things haven't been as bad since the beginning of the 1990s. The glut of NQs is a consequence of increased trainee recruitment in the late 90s colliding with a sluggish economy that has now left many firms over-lawyered. Junior solicitor redundancies have exacerbated the problem for NQs – at the moment, certainly in commercial firms, there are simply too many inexperienced solicitors.

To find out more about what is happening we spoke to Paul Thomas of Chambers and Partners Recruitment. *"Fewer NQs have voluntarily put themselves out into the job market,"* Paul told us. *"If more of them did, there might be more jobs."* It is wholly understandable that NQs are playing it safe and taking what's on offer at the firm that has trained them, even if this means they are accepting second or third-choice jobs. Anxieties about not getting a job has meant that many NQs are mismatched in their new positions. They will either learn to live with this or they will become disillusioned with their work, maybe even leaving private practice or the profession entirely. Sadly, once started on the road to specialisation it is difficult for lawyers to change.

crunching the numbers

Paul says: *"Despite everything, firms have been trying hard to keep their NQs."* The lesson they learned in the late 90s – too few experienced assistants to handle work leading to competition and salary hikes – is not one they want to repeat. But that said, NQ salaries are so much higher than they ever were before (many would say NQs are grossly overpaid) and firms can't afford to keep everyone. In *The True Picture* we report on the retention rates of our subject firms in September 2003. A number of them retained a high proportion of their NQs while others fared much worse. If you wish to see the pattern of retention for individual firms, we will be publishing a table on our website towards the end of 2003.

hot or not?

We heard reports that there were only five corporate finance vacancies for external NQ applicants in the City this autumn. If true, this indicates just how tough the market has been. However, the picture is not as gloomy in all practice areas. At the worst end of the scale we see corporate (private equity not as bad as M&A), TMT and IP; finance (including project finance) is throwing up slightly more vacancies, as is litigation; performing best are commercial property, private client and residential conveyancing. Paul says: *"Actually, there are some red-hot conveyancing jobs at really good firms, yet few NQs will even consider a career in this area."* Positions in popular practice areas like employment and tax are rarer than hen's teeth as they are filled quickly by internal candidates.

The London market has been the worst hit, so if you are a good candidate looking to relocate to the regions from the capital, there is hope. As with trainee recruitment, most regional firms will look more favourably on candidates who present a convincing reason for moving to their area – painful memories of the brain drain to the City are still fresh.

Most of our readers will qualify in 2008, by which time we hope the market will have improved dramatically, but for the benefit of any trainees reading this, and for the sake of giving students some good advice early on, we asked Paul for some tips on how to manage your training:

- However you feel about a particular seat, give 100% at all times during your training contract. You can't afford to clock up mediocre appraisal reports.
- If you're at a firm with a dominant area of practice, then recognise that most NQ jobs will be in that

area. If you want to maximise your chances then construct a seat plan that fits the firm's focus. At A&O, for example, you might be better off doing three or four seats that all complement each other around the finance hub.

- If you are at a smaller firm, you might want to keep your options open by getting a spread of experience.
- Double or repeat seats can make all the difference.
- Consider the benefits/downsides of a seat overseas or seconded to a client. Consider when might be the best time to take such an opportunity and when it might be better to be visible in the office. These factors may be firm-specific.
- Keep a thorough record of everything that you do. If you need to go to an interview and can't explain what you did in your litigation seat 20 months ago, you begin to look like a poor candidate.
- Get involved in the life of the firm, schmooze partners (don't stalk them or behave too obsequiously though) and socialise with your team.
- If you find yourself out in the cold in a tight job market after training, then try to get work as quickly as you can. There's a temptation to go off travelling, but when March and September comes around the following year, recruiters will have fresh, eager NQs to pick from; you will have a great suntan and a new talent for playing the guitar, but you'll appear 'stale'. Only if the job market is blooming with health should you consider anything more than an extended holiday.
- If it gets to the stage when you have to compromise and accept a position that is not your ideal job, you might want to follow the 'two out of three' rule – practice area, type of firm, location. If the job ticks two of these three, take it.

going in-house

It's easy to see the allure of the in-house culture – more predictable working hours, more opportunities to become involved in business decisions, and incentivised pay structures, which have the potential to translate into bonuses or share options. But for some, the lack of infrastructure and hands-on supervision may act as a deterrent.

Commonly most in-house positions are broad commercial roles with an emphasis on negotiating commercial contracts and managing, in conjunction with outside lawyers, property, litigation and other day-to-day legal issues. If you're considering moving in-house, you'll benefit from a broad mix of commercial work during your training contract and would be well advised to qualify into a corporate or commercial department. Specialist opportunities for litigators and property lawyers are more limited, though positions do exist for an in-house 'expert', say in IP/IT or employment. In a really buoyant market there are also opportunities for corporate lawyers to manage the acquisition and disposal of group companies.

Positions within banks are usually highly paid, but specialised and transaction-focused. Most banks are looking for candidates with some prior legal experience in banking and/or capital markets, so successful applicants tend to come from the magic circle or other leading finance firms.

"In any one year, there aren't many in-house jobs for newly qualifieds," says Stuart Morton of Chambers and Partners' in-house recruitment team. *"Legal departments are relatively small and business people are relatively demanding, so there's not much time to train up junior lawyers."* Positions tend to come up as and when the need arises, not just in March/September when most training contracts end. *"The best advice is to position yourself well in a law firm and register with a reputable consultancy, like Chambers, who will let you know when a suitable job arises.But be prepared for it to take a while."*

Whether it's banking or industry, much of a candidate's success has to do with their attitude. *"Teams are small and employers are keen to find the right 'fit'. Personality often takes precedence over experience,"* advises Stuart. Employers want to be sure you can spot the commercial reality of business situations, which is not really a legal skill. Finally, when applying for a job in-house, there's no substitute for enthusiasm and good research into the company.

Specialist Practice Areas

banking & finance

banking: Work centres on commercial loan agreements – the documentation of lending money and arranging its signing and completion. The banking lawyer's work frequently overlaps with corporate finance work, particularly mergers and acquisitions. **capital markets:** The issuance of 'debt' or 'equity' securities and related areas such as securitisation, repackaging and structured finance, plus the whole range of 'derivatives' products. If that's left you confused already, don't worry. **'debt'** relates to publicly tradeable financial instruments, which are listed on a stock exchange, but traded off the exchange by bond traders. A company raises money by issuing bonds and a bank or group of banks will underwrite the issue. The bonds will pay interest until they are redeemable. **'equity'** is slightly sexier than debt. It's all about public offerings (including IPOs) of shares and company flotations. As shares are riskier and more volatile than bonds, the returns are higher.

Both debt and equity transactions involve a company presenting itself to investors by way of a prospectus and documents recording the issue of security for cash. A typical capital markets transaction might involve, say, a company raising several million pounds sterling via the issue of a bond sold into Europe or a public offering of equity. The proceeds might then be swapped into dollars and perhaps used for the acquisition of another company. Lawyers will assist with the structuring of the deal and ensure compliance with securities laws.

type of work

Top-level banking and capital markets work is concentrated in the world financial centres – London, Frankfurt, New York, Hong Kong and Paris. The most complex transactions are handled by City law firms, whose clients tend to be international banks. At the biggest firms, lawyers are usually specialised. In the regions finance work is of a simpler and more domestic type for clients that are usually UK banks and building societies and the companies they lend to.

The demands on lawyers are intensive because of the cyclical nature of transaction management. A normal 50-hour week can rise to 75 or 100 hours as a deal nears completion; however, banking lawyers speak of the buzz of completing a deal. It's a major motivational force. Andrew O'Keeffe, a banking solicitor at Simmons & Simmons, described most clients as *"very driven people, but pretty decent. They expect high standards."* A capital markets lawyer working in-house in a large international bank echoed his sentiments on the buzz: *"My work is exciting, fast and snappy. I have to make decisions quickly and give on the spot advice to a wide variety of people – anyone from the corporate treasurer of a multinational to the mayor of the City of Moscow. I also like interacting with the traders on the floor."*

You need to be a bright spark to do well in finance law. Andrew told us: *"You are faced with incredibly complex formulae in documents so the job is intellectually challenging."* Equally important is commercial awareness: *"We have to cater for the 'what if' scenario. Someone has a great idea and sells it to the banks. When we put the documentation together we are there to cater for the downside; anything that could possibly happen. You feel like a business advisor not a lawyer sometimes."* The bottom line: finance lawyers enable the work of most other commercial lawyers to reach fruition. *"Nothing moves without money. Money is the petrol in the engine that is the world economy. Banking lawyers are at the centre of things."*

It's widely accepted that banking and capital markets are not law-intensive areas of practice. They are not regulated heavily by case law and statutes. You won't be doing masses of research into black letter law, but you will be researching market sectors.

In this sense your career won't be stagnant.

"Things change and markets develop. Ten years ago there was no project finance." Thankfully, the language isn't archaic and the more senior you get, the more time you spend managing deals and the less time you spend drafting. International travel will be a part of your working life if you join a firm handling cross-border deals. Our in-house capital markets lawyer told us: *"I travel all over the world and find out about all manner of things. I've been to a Mexican tortilla factory and an Indonesian textile manufacturer to learn about the production of rayon."*

a day in the life of...

9.30am: After short commute from trendy docklands apartment to rather grand office in EC2, check e-mails from NY counterparts and London clients with workaholic tendencies.
11.00am: E-postbag dealt with, call client to clarify instructions on financing of purchase of property portfolio. Draft set of new clauses into primary loan agreement following client's instructions.
1.00pm: Haul (expanding) belly and sense of guilt into office gym. (January is such a hateful month.)
2.15pm: Venezuelan oil pipeline project team meeting. Have sufficiently senior role on team to avoid any dogsbody tasks. Partner in charge praises my performance so far on drafting the loan agreement.
3.30pm: Venezuelan pipeline clients and other lawyers arrive. Our team batting for lenders. Negotiations tough but fair. Held own in negotiating controls that bank will have over borrower's business.
7.00pm: Meeting concludes. Send off latest draft of this morning's property loan document by courier. Faff around on e-mail to friends.
7.45pm: Depart for home clutching *FT*.

skills needed

...practical intelligence... analytical skills... interest in business and international finance... ability to dedicate to the task... accuracy and care... capacity to do routine work in the early days... love the rush of adrenalin... stamina... good interpersonal skills...

You must have confidence in yourself and be quite tough as sometimes people can be unpleasant in the way they negotiate with you. The full-on nature of the work will affect your personal life at times, so do make sure that the world of international finance and business interests you. To prime yourself for a career as a finance lawyer, read the business pages in your daily newspaper (ideally a salmon pink one!). Work experience in the finance sector will help you gain a better idea of how you'll take to this world. And, lastly, don't worry if you're not a mathematical wizard!

career options

This is a big-money world and salaries in private practice and all related areas are high. Some deals keep you in the office from 9-7pm, some keep you there into the early hours of the morning and, through your choice of firm, you can gravitate towards the type of deal that suits you. Top City firms' lawyers specialise to a high degree. For some this has real appeal; for others it's a turn off and they talk of the finance "factory firms." In smaller practices, lawyers are broader-based and enjoy a variety of deals, albeit lower profile. Read more about the leading finance practices in *Chambers UK* and *Chambers Global*.

Some City solicitors view banking law as an ideal platform for a subsequent career in the financial markets, but if you already know you want to become a banker, then become a banker, not a lawyer. It's really that simple.

Even at trainee level, secondments to international banks are available from City firms and can give a taste of things to come. Moves in-house at banks are common, especially in capital markets, where some find the job gets them *"one step closer to the business; thinking of deals and knocking ideas around."* There's less drafting and a lot of ad hoc queries from different parts of the bank. *"Some lawyers sit on trading floors; others set policies and help in deciding on risk."* Remember though, while the business of a law firm is law, the business of a bank is banking and a lawyer 'in a bank', has a back office function. For some, the ego needs to be pandered by a law firm partnership, but others just appreciate the better hours in-house. Financial Services Regulation now employs ever-greater numbers of compliance lawyers. As credit risk departments and capital adequacy requirements become increasingly important so does the advisory role of the lawyers involved.

LEADING FIRMS FROM CHAMBERS UK 2003-2004

BANKING & FINANCE: LARGER DEALS ■ LONDON

Rank	Firm
1	**Allen & Overy**
	Clifford Chance LLP
2	**Linklaters**
3	**Freshfields Bruckhaus Deringer**
4	**Ashurst Morris Crisp**
	Norton Rose
5	**Lovells**
	Shearman & Sterling
	Simpson Thacher & Bartlett
	Slaughter and May
6	**Denton Wilde Sapte**
	Herbert Smith
	Latham & Watkins
	White & Case

BANKING & FINANCE ■ MIDLANDS

Rank	Firm
1	**Eversheds** Birmingham
	Pinsents Birmingham
2	**Wragge & Co LLP** Birmingham
3	**DLA** Birmingham
	Gateley Wareing Birmingham
4	**Martineau Johnson** Birmingham
5	**Browne Jacobson** Nottingham
	Hammonds Birmingham
6	**Lee Crowder** Birmingham
	Needham & James Birmingham

BANKING & FINANCE: MEDIUM DEALS ■ LONDON

Rank	Firm
1	**Baker & McKenzie**
	CMS Cameron McKenna
	DLA
2	**Berwin Leighton Paisner**
	Macfarlanes
	Simmons & Simmons
3	**Dickson Minto WS**
	Jones Day Gouldens
	Travers Smith Braithwaite
4	**Addleshaw Goddard**
	Eversheds
	SJ Berwin
	Taylor Wessing
	Watson, Farley & Williams

BANKING & FINANCE ■ WALES

Rank	Firm
1	**Eversheds** Cardiff
	Morgan Cole Cardiff
2	**Edwards Geldard** Cardiff

BANKING & FINANCE ■ EAST ANGLIA

Rank	Firm
1	**Eversheds** Cambridge, Norwich
	Mills & Reeve Cambridge, Norwich
2	**Taylor Vinters** Cambridge

BANKING & FINANCE ■ NORTH EAST

Rank	Firm
1	**Dickinson Dees** Newcastle upon Tyne
	Eversheds Newcastle upon Tyne
2	**Ward Hadaway** Newcastle upon Tyne
3	**Robert Muckle** Newcastle upon Tyne

BANKING & FINANCE: ■ THE SOUTH & SOUTH WEST

Rank	Firm
1	**Burges Salmon** Bristol
	Osborne Clarke Bristol
2	**Bond Pearce** Bristol Southampton
3	**Blake Lapthorn Linnell** Southampton
4	**CMS Cameron McKenna** Bristol
5	**Rickerbys** Cheltenham
6	**asb law** Brighton Crawley
	Clarke Willmott Bristol
	Foot Anstey Sargent Exeter, Plymouth

BANKING & FINANCE ■ NORTH WEST

Rank	Firm
1	**DLA** Liverpool, Manchester
2	**Addleshaw Goddard** Manchester
	Eversheds Manchester
	Halliwell Landau Manchester
3	**Hammonds** Manchester
4	**Cobbetts** Manchester
	Pinsents Manchester
5	**DWF** Liverpool, Manchester
6	**Brabners Chaffe Street** Liverpool
	Kuit Steinart Levy Manchester

BANKING & FINANCE ■ YORKSHIRE

Rank	Firm
1	**Addleshaw Goddard** Leeds
2	**DLA** Leeds
	Eversheds Leeds
3	**Hammonds** Leeds
	Pinsents Leeds
	Walker Morris Leeds

competition

This section is devoted to UK and European competition law. The basic aim of the regulatory authorities is to ensure that markets function effectively on the basis of fair and open competition. Competition law in the UK is intrinsically tied to EU Articles 81 and 82 and their UK analogues – Chapters I and II of the Competition Act 1998. These address anti-competitive agreements (such as price-fixing cartels) and the abuse of dominant market positions (eg by way of excessive or predatory pricing). It's easy to find examples of these types of behaviour. Recently there have been huge fines for the various household name producers of vitamins that clubbed together to keep prices high. The regulators make it their business to bust open these smoke-filled rooms deals. In addition to industry-wide enquiries (eg CDs, new cars, banking services, supermarkets), the behaviour of individual companies is scrutinised, particularly those who dominate their market and flex their commercial muscle so as to harm consumers.

Some competition lawyers specialise even further in areas such as anti-dumping (preventing companies exporting a product at a price lower than normally charged on its own home market) and State Aid (eg national governments propping up underperforming flag carrier airlines). Other lawyers specialise in particular industries such as electricity, gas, water, telecoms and media, each of which has an additional layer of sector-specific regulatory laws and a sector-specific regulator.

type of work

Non-contentious competition work commonly takes the form of merger control advice and clearance for both UK and European mergers, or structuring commercial agreements and other business practices so as to comply with competition laws. It is fast moving, high profile work. Contentious work traditionally referred to High Court litigation which had a competition element, while work defending regulatory investigations (eg cartel investigations, 'abuse of market dominance cases' or industry investigations such as the recent Competition Commission inquiry into supermarkets) fell somewhere in between. Competition lawyers traditionally specialised in either contentious or non-contentious work, however, these days they have to be expert in both in order to be fully effective.

Domestic competition law brings practitioners into close contact with regulatory bodies. In the UK these include the Office of Fair Trading (OFT), the Competition Commission, the Competition Appeals Tribunal and industry-specific regulators, such as Ofcom (media and telecoms) and GEMA (gas and electricity). At EU level the relevant regulator is the European Commission, with appeals being heard by the Court of First Instance and, ultimately, the European Court of Justice.

There are examples of important M&A deals that failed to get clearance. In 2000 the EU regulators refused to allow a $20 billion tie-up between EMI and Time Warner's music subsidiary on the grounds that it would have placed 80% of Europe's record industry in the hands of just four global giants. Yet there is also a growing trend towards appealing regulators' 'block' decisions. Airtours (now MyTravel) is a recent high-profile example of an EC Commission decision to block a merger being overturned on appeal to the European Courts.

Competition law requires the lawyer to gain a thorough understanding of how industries and their markets operate. Rod Carlton, a competition partner at Freshfields Bruckhaus Deringer, couldn't stress this enough. For him, it's what appeals most about the work: over the last ten years he's learnt a fair bit about retail, the music industry, pay TV, telecoms, public transport, cinema, newspapers and perfume. *"I've never been bored by the job; quite the contrary,"* he told us. *"You analyse companies and sectors in order to understand why they do what they do. There's a comparison with what management consultants, such as McKinsey, do. We look at everything from the minutiae to the grand plans."*

UK regulators have had greater teeth and claws since the Competition Act 1998 and Enterprise Act 2003. Rod told us: *"The OFT and sector regulators now have more people and greater powers to root out anti-competitive behaviour. There's a much more contentious feel to the work. And the potential exposure to heavy corporate fines and personal criminal sanctions – including imprisonment – really concentrates the client's mind."*

Most competition firms have a Brussels office and are keen to send junior lawyers on placements there. Although some UK firms do the majority of active work on-site domestically, a presence in Belgium is useful for keeping eyes and ears open and maintaining close contact with the politicians and power brokers. Anti-dumping and trade law is one area of competition that remains very heavily Brussels-driven. For information on the firms with the best national and international competition practices, we recommend *Chambers UK* and *Chambers Global*.

a day in the life...

Dean Murray is an assistant at Newcastle firm Dickinson Dees. He told us about the OFT's habit of conducting 'dawn raids'. *"We might get a 9.30am call from the person in charge of a company or site that is about to be raided. Our dawn raid team (which can be up to ten people; we take as many as there are investigators from the OFT), go to the premises and handle the raid."* The team will try to get an idea of what the OFT is looking for. *"During the raid itself it's man-for-man marking almost. We make sure they are not looking at things they shouldn't; we take copies of whatever they take and make sure they don't ask questions that are out of order. Normally a raid goes on for most of the day. They are usually looking for evidence that something suspicious is going on, such as the existence of anti-competitive agreements. The event itself is exciting but the real work is only just beginning."*

Back in the office, the team conducts its own investigation of the company's activities. The OFT will issue a 'Rule 14 Notice' detailing what the client is alleged to have done wrong. The lawyers will then make written and oral submissions about the statement and eventually the OFT's decision will be given. It can be appealed before the Competition Appeals Tribunal and then, in some cases, in the Court of Appeal. But not all OFT actions are fought all the way. Sometimes the lawyers find their clients are not whiter than white and will go for a leniency procedure, with the client holding its hands up to wrongdoing in the hope of getting a lower fine. Dawn raids are a rarity: not every day is as action-packed. Much of the lawyer's time will be spent researching company and market information and drafting and reviewing merger notification documents. It's not a tick-the-box exercise though, as Rod said: *"You start with a blank piece of paper each time; there are no standard forms to follow."*

skills needed

... clear, analytical mind... good judgement and confident in relying on gut instincts... articulate, both orally and on paper... good mediation and lobbying skills... thoroughness... attention to detail... numeracy... decisiveness... linguistic ability... enthusiasm...

Diplomacy, common sense and a desire to understand business are prerequisite traits. Junior lawyers work directly under the guidance of experienced partners and in the early years can't expect to fly far by themselves. Web research, 'market' research, talking to clients about their business, honing drafting skills and developing gut instinct are plenty to be getting on with. The work involves the exercise of advocacy skills, both written and oral. If you enjoy constructing an argument for an essay and then expressing it clearly, backing up your points with the necessary evidence, you're already on the right road. Academically gifted and skill-rich lawyers populate the area. Not only is there a lot of law to learn, the principles of economics and international trade have to become second nature.

The international nature of the work means overseas trips to learn about the practicalities of clients' businesses. Rod told us: *"I've been out to California to help plan a major merger... yet I've also been to Wimbledon to find out how holiday snaps are processed."*

career options

At the junior end, EU/competition can be difficult to break into, but don't be put off. The number of active firms and the size of competition departments are set to carry on growing with the increased enforcement activity of the European and UK regulators. The type of firm will determine the nature of the work available: while heavy-duty matters (especially merger work) are usually handled by the top London firms, there is still both UK and EU work being carried out in the regions. A young lawyer must invest for future career success and, in time, the benefits of patience become clear. Rod told us: *"Clients are extremely grateful; our work makes a real difference. Competition lawyers, like tax and financial services lawyers, are regarded as premium advisors."*

Few competition lawyers leave private practice, although some do go overseas. Usually only global giants like Coca-Cola, Microsoft, Vodafone and Diageo can support a specialist team in-house. Some lawyers might turn gamekeeper and join the OFT or one of the UK sector regulators like Oftel. Dean talked of the OFT having emulated the US Dept. of Justice's "revolving-door policy" whereby lawyers move to the regulator, gain experience and go back out into private practice. EU Commission jobs crop up.

LEADING FIRMS FROM CHAMBERS UK 2003-2004

COMPETITION ■ LONDON	
1	**Freshfields Bruckhaus Deringer**
	Herbert Smith
	Slaughter and May
2	**Linklaters**
3	**Ashurst Morris Crisp**
	Lovells
	SJ Berwin
4	**Allen & Overy**
	Baker & McKenzie
	Clifford Chance LLP
	Denton Wilde Sapte
	Norton Rose
	Simmons & Simmons
5	**Addleshaw Goddard**
	Bristows
	CMS Cameron McKenna
	Eversheds
	Macfarlanes
	Mayer, Brown, Rowe & Maw LLP
	Richards Butler

COMPETITION ■ THE SOUTH	
1	**Burges Salmon** Bristol
2	**Bond Pearce** Plymouth, Southampton

COMPETITION ■ THE NORTH	
1	**Eversheds** Leeds, Manchester
2	**Addleshaw Goddard** Leeds, Manchester
3	**Dickinson Dees** Newcastle upon Tyne

COMPETITION ■ MIDLANDS	
1	**Pinsents** Birmingham
2	**Wragge & Co LLP** Birmingham
3	**Eversheds** Birmingham
	Martineau Johnson Birmingham
4	**Edwards Geldard** Derby

COMPETITION ■ WALES	
1	**Eversheds** Cardiff
	Morgan Cole Cardiff

construction & projects

construction

Once upon a time, construction lawyers drafted contracts for developers and construction companies. Buildings would go up, but often the parties fell into dispute. They'd call the lawyers back in to commence litigation that sometimes took years. Other parties, eg architects or subcontractors, would get caught up in the dispute; everyone spent huge amounts of money and working relationships ended up in tatters.

type of work

The main aspects of construction law: developing the contractual arrangements prior to building work and dispute resolution (when it all goes horribly wrong) are still the staple, but there's a different approach taken these days. Tom Pemberton, an assistant at Shadbolt & Co, talked about the new philosophy in construction – partnering – where all concerns try to achieve a common goal rather than sue the hide off each other. It seems to have had an effect: parties are increasingly working with each other when things go wrong. For example, most contracts now contain a mandatory arbitration procedure to be adopted in case of dispute. Adjudication of disputes has become the industry norm and it follows a swift 28-day timetable. Tom explains that it's only in the last few years since partnering concepts have become established that the old practice of recouping construction costs through claims has begun to die. Now, *"lawyers drafting contracts are really put under pressure. Clients don't want you to pick up too many points or cause too many headaches, but you do have to advise the client of where the risks lie."*

It's an unpretentious area of the law, according to Sally Davies, a partner at Mayer, Brown, Rowe & Maw. For the record, she thinks it's an area that's just as open to women as it is to the lads. Sally's gone into the contentious side of things and she recommends that you pick your team according to your natural inclination. *"Normally people have a natural bias for contentious or non-contentious work,"* so if you want to concentrate on one rather than the other, be aware that some firms like their construction lawyers to handle both aspects of the work. *Chambers UK* contains details of the leading construction practices across the country.

skills needed

...attention to detail... excellent drafting... good judgement... down-to-earth attitude... comfortable with technical information... industry background a major boon... stamina... imagination... team worker... good interpersonal skills...

Some pretty seminal legal decisions have arisen out of construction disputes – they deal with complex relationships between parties, which define the boundaries of contract and tort. You need to have an affinity with case law and be prepared to keep up to date with the reports as well as industry trends and thinking. But can you combine legal know-how with practical advice and real imagination?

Sally says: *"You don't have to be frightened of dealing with a huge volume of documentation. You don't have to read it all, but you do have to sift out the wheat from the chaff and home in on the detail... You feel a bit like a forensic investigator when you're going through documents, working out what's relevant and what's not."*

Since the Technology and Construction Court introduced its Pre-action Protocol, many more disputes have been resolved through mediation and this, in turn, has changed the way lawyers must operate. *"It requires a whole different skill set,"* according to Sally. *"You become more of a negotiator and your role is much more hands-on."*

It's important that you get on with all sorts of people. Sally explains: *"You might be dealing with some real boffins – for example, geotechnical engineers and structural engineers who produce reports that you have to interpret. Some contractor and subcontractor clients are extremely down to earth; on the other hand, you have clients who are corporate types or in-house lawyers with whom you must speak on a more sophisticated level."* Some lawyers make a name for themselves based partly on their social skills. We're not belittling their legal talents; generally speaking, construction industry clients like to bond with their advisors. A lawyer who can put the client at ease and be 'one of the lads' (male or female) goes far.

projects

Major projects are located worldwide and projects lawyers hail from every major jurisdiction. Be it a power station or a motorway, specialist construction lawyers work hand in hand with finance and corporate lawyers to enable projects to come to fruition. A few City firms and the largest US practices dominate the biggest international projects, but there's work for projects lawyers all over the UK.

In the UK, the Private Finance Initiative (PFI), a part of the Public Private Partnerships (PPP), is an important source of work. PFI introduces private funding and management into areas that were previously the domain of government, eg the building and operation of hospitals. Over the last 15 years, the PFI/PPP sector has grown; once the preserve of City firms, lawyers all over the UK are now involved.

type of work

Projects vary from oil pipelines in far-flung places to PFI prisons in Liverpool. The exact nature of the legal work depends on the type, size and location of the project and the firm's clients. Some consistently act for the project company – usually a special purpose company established to build, own and operate, say, a power station. Often the project company is a joint venture between a number of sponsors who contribute equity to part-fund the project. Project sponsors could include the manufacturer of the gas turbines installed in the power station, the construction company that will erect the plant, and the power company that will buy the electricity. The company could also be partially owned by a government body or banks.

Other firms act for the project promoter – the organisation that commissions the project. It could be an NHS trust that wants a new hospital or a foreign government that wants a privately financed motorway. Then there are the firms that act purely on the finance side for banks, guarantors, export credit agencies, governments, and international funding agencies. Other categories of client include the contractors, operators and so on. Each party requires its own legal representation.

Malcolm Austwick, a partner in Beachcroft Wansbroughs, explained just how long projects could go on for. After the initial tender process, in which bids are built up over a couple of years, the successful bidder is selected to manage the project. It then has to secure the finance, obtain the necessary planning permission and agree construction, service and employment contracts. Lawyers advising on any of these contracts must understand the big picture. They have to see how changing one contractual term will have a knock-on effect throughout the entire transaction.

"Because they're so complicated," says Malcolm, *"the only thing to do is to put in deadlines for the different stages. It's a real challenge putting together something so complicated."* There were few precedents in the early years, but now PFI/PPP is widespread and more boilerplate contracts are employed by the lawyers. Every project is unique, though.

skills needed

...prepared to travel/live overseas (international work)... commercial awareness... patience... tact and diplomacy... strong client skills... good on contract and tort... good drafting... comfortable with long, complex documents... stamina...

If you enjoy the challenge of creating a scheme and figuring out all its possibilities and pitfalls, you're reading the right section of this book.

The ability to work with a team of people, be they your own colleagues and clients or other lawyers and professionals, funders or subcontractors, is crucial. As projects go on for years, you need to build relationships with all those involved.

career options

Nearly all international projects are governed (to varying degrees) by English or New York law, so experience in this field is internationally marketable. American law firms, in particular, are recruiting experienced English lawyers, which has forced up salaries to make international projects one of the highest paid specialisms. Those who want to become solicitor advocates will have the opportunity; some will even find a niche in international arbitration.

The construction industry has lawyers working in-house. The role may be as a general corporate counsel or more specifically as a litigator. Companies like AMEC, Balfour Beatty, Sir Robert McAlpine and Carillion all have their own legal teams. Some lawyers also join clients in a project management role.

LEADING FIRMS FROM CHAMBERS UK 2003-2004

Rank	PROJECTS ■ LONDON
1	**Allen & Overy**
	Clifford Chance LLP
	Linklaters
2	**Freshfields Bruckhaus Deringer**
	Norton Rose
	Shearman & Sterling
	White & Case
3	**Denton Wilde Sapte**
	Lovells
	Milbank, Tweed, Hadley & McCloy LLP
	Slaughter and May
4	**Ashurst Morris Crisp**
	Baker & McKenzie
	CMS Cameron McKenna
	Herbert Smith
	Simmons & Simmons
	Vinson & Elkins RLLP

Rank	PFI/PPP ■ LONDON
1	**Allen & Overy**
	Clifford Chance LLP
	Linklaters
2	**Ashurst Morris Crisp**
	Freshfields Bruckhaus Deringer
3	**CMS Cameron McKenna**
	Herbert Smith
	Lovells
	Norton Rose
4	**Berwin Leighton Paisner**
	Denton Wilde Sapte
	Masons
	Simmons & Simmons
5	**Addleshaw Goddard**
	DLA
	Mayer, Brown, Rowe & Maw LLP
	Pinsents
	Slaughter and May
	Trowers & Hamlins

Rank	PROJECTS/PFI ■ THE SOUTH & WALES
1	**Bevan Ashford BBL** Bristol
2	**Burges Salmon** Bristol
	Eversheds Cardiff
3	**Masons** Bristol
4	**Beachcroft Wansbroughs** Bristol
	Morgan Cole Cardiff

Rank	PROJECTS/PFI ■ MIDLANDS & EAST ANGLIA
1	**Pinsents** Birmingham
	Wragge & Co LLP Birmingham
2	**DLA** Birmingham
	Eversheds Nottingham
	Mills & Reeve Cambridge
3	**Martineau Johnson** Birmingham

Rank	PROJECTS/PFI ■ THE NORTH
1	**Addleshaw Goddard** Manchester
2	**Dickinson Dees** Newcastle upon Tyne
	DLA Leeds
	Eversheds Leeds
	Pinsents Leeds
3	**Masons** Leeds, Manchester
	Nabarro Nathanson Sheffield

CONSTRUCTION ■ LONDON

1 **Masons**

2 **CMS Cameron McKenna**
Mayer, Brown, Rowe & Maw LLP
Shadbolt & Co

3 **Berwin Leighton Paisner**
Fenwick Elliott
Linklaters

4 **Allen & Overy**
Clifford Chance LLP
Freshfields Bruckhaus Deringer
Herbert Smith
Lovells
Norton Rose
Taylor Wessing

5 **Ashurst Morris Crisp**
Denton Wilde Sapte
Hammonds
Kennedys
Macfarlanes
Nicholson Graham & Jones
Trowers & Hamlins

6 **Baker & McKenzie**
Beale and Company
Berrymans Lace Mawer
Campbell Hooper
Corbett & Co
Davies Arnold Cooper
Eversheds
Glovers
Lane & Partners
Nabarro Nathanson
SJ Berwin
Winward Fearon

CONSTRUCTION ■ THE SOUTH

1 **Shadbolt & Co** Reigate

2 **Blake Lapthorn Linnell** Fareham, Soton
Cripps Harries Hall Tunbridge Wells

3 **Lester Aldridge** Bournemouth
Thomas Eggar Reigate

CONSTRUCTION ■ THAMES VALLEY

1 **Blake Lapthorn Linnell** Oxford
Clarks Reading
Morgan Cole Oxford, Reading

2 **Shoosmiths** Reading

CONSTRUCTION ■ SOUTH WEST

1 **Bevan Ashford BBL** Bristol
Bevan Ashford EPL Exeter
Masons Bristol

2 **Burges Salmon** Bristol
Osborne Clarke Bristol

3 **Beachcroft Wansbroughs** Bristol

4 **Bond Pearce** Plymouth
Laytons Bristol

CONSTRUCTION ■ WALES

1 **Eversheds** Cardiff
Hugh James Cardiff
Morgan Cole Cardiff

CONSTRUCTION ■ MIDLANDS

1 **Wragge & Co LLP** Birmingham

2 **Gateley Wareing** Birmingham

3 **Hammonds** Birmingham

4 **Eversheds** Birmingham, Nottingham
Freethcartwright LLP Nottingham
Pinsents Birmingham

5 **Browne Jacobson** Nottingham
DLA Birmingham
Lee Crowder Birmingham
Martineau Johnson Birmingham
Shoosmiths Birmingham, Northampton

CONSTRUCTION ■ EAST ANGLIA

1 **Eversheds** Cambridge, Ipswich, Norwich
Mills & Reeve Cambridge

2 **Birketts** Ipswich
Greenwoods Peterborough
Hewitsons Cambridge

CONSTRUCTION ■ NORTH WEST

1 **Masons** Manchester

2 **Hammonds** Manchester
Mace & Jones Liverpool, Manchester

3 **Addleshaw Goddard** Manchester

4 **DLA** Liverpool

5 **Halliwell Landau** Manchester
Hill Dickinson Liverpool

6 **Elliotts** Manchester
Eversheds Manchester
Pannone & Partners Manchester

CONSTRUCTION ■ YORKSHIRE

1 **Addleshaw Goddard** Leeds
Hammonds Leeds

2 **DLA** Leeds, Sheffield
Masons Leeds

3 **Pinsents** Leeds
Walker Morris Leeds

4 **Eversheds** Leeds
Nabarro Nathanson Sheffield

CONSTRUCTION ■ NORTH EAST

1 **Dickinson Dees** Newcastle upon Tyne
Watson Burton Newcastle upon Tyne

2 **Eversheds** Newcastle upon Tyne

3 **Hay & Kilner** Newcastle upon Tyne
Ward Hadaway Newcastle upon Tyne

corporate law

Corporate transactions are the lifeblood of commercial firms and experienced corporate lawyers are among the highest paid in the profession, earning seven-figure rewards in some instances.

type of work

Large City firms act for companies listed on stock exchanges, while smaller City and regional firms tend to advise leading regional private companies and a handful of the FTSE 250.

Mergers and acquisitions (M&A) and corporate restructurings are the core business and are interlinked with finance (banking and capital markets work), hence the umbrella term 'corporate finance'. Companies fund their acquisitions by a variety of means. They may restructure, disposing of certain assets not considered essential to their core business. If they are privately held, they may raise finance by 'going public' – offering shares to the public and institutional investors on any of the public stock exchanges. If they are already public companies, they may make a rights issue (offer of new shares). They may also raise money via debt, eg loans from the market (bonds) or from banks or other financial institutions. A complex, high-value deal may need to be financed by a combination of these methods.

Since the mid-80s private equity or venture capital has been a focus. At the top end of the work is the 'buyout', which might be as straightforward as the present management of a company raising capital to take control (an MBO). As the management wouldn't normally have the cash for the deal, the majority comes from venture capital companies and/or banks. Sometimes the venture capital company will itself pinpoint the deal and take a controlling interest in the target company. At the other end of the scale are the 'development capital' deals where the management of a company might seek between, say, £250,000 and £20 million to start up or expand.

Irrespective of the type of deal, there are three key phases to the work: negotiating and drafting the agreements, arranging the financing, and carrying out 'due diligence'. Due diligence is a time-consuming but necessary task to ensure the accuracy of information passed from the target to the bidder or from the company raising capital to the funder. If a target claims to be the largest baked beans canner in the country, then due diligence will reveal whether or not this is true and whether or not there is outstanding litigation or any other factors that could harm profitability after a takeover or buyout. Whereas a trainee can expect to be involved in one or two deals at a time, newly qualifieds can expect to be working on several at once.

Private companies have few shareholders (owners), whereas stock exchange-listed companies can have millions. This makes the latter vulnerable to hostile takeover bids from rival companies seeking a controlling stake. To help public companies combat this threat, the City developed a detailed takeover code to govern both friendly and hostile M&A activity. Although voluntary, the code is universally followed. It sets a strict timetable for companies to make bids and respond to potential bidders and has guidelines for the treatment of shareholders. Lawyers need to know this code inside out.

a day in the life...

Michelle Thomas is a partner in Eversheds' Cardiff office. She used to work at a magic circle firm and is able to contrast the types of deals the different firms handle. *"If you work outside the City you must be able to handle all types of transactions. In a large City firm you might become very specialised, for example in IPOs or public takeovers. In a regional firm you might work on an IPO one day, be acting for the target of a public takeover the next and handle a private acquisition the next."* If you work in a City megafirm a high proportion of the work will have an international flavour. If you want international work in the regions, judge a firm by its overseas offices, associations and client base.

There are other key differences between firms, most notably hours and the increased chances of a junior lawyer getting close to the front-line action. The largest City firms handle the biggest transactions so, naturally, a trainee or junior assistant will not carry a huge amount of responsibility. As Michelle says: *"There will always be an element of tedium on any job. If you are a trainee working on a £2 billion deal, the reality is that you are not going to get much more responsibility than some research and managing a data room."* Essential yet administrative tasks on huge deals will hopefully be interspersed with greater responsibility on smaller transactions. Andrew Jolly, an assistant at Slaughter and May, feels that even as a very junior lawyer *"you're presented with a problem that you have to solve, either working within a team or working on your own. There's a good mix of independence and working with others."*

Team spirit is essential. Working three 20-hour days in a row may be rare, but it does happen. Much has been said about killer hours in corporate, about all-nighters and the loss of life and love in the quest for career progression. It's true that corporate departments tend to work the longest hours, but it's equally true that market conditions affect the time spent at work. Simon Beddow, a partner at Ashurst Morris Crisp, wonders if the hours are a little overstated. *"It's a fact of modern life that if you want to get on you have to put in the effort. The real strain comes when you are about 5-6 years PQE and you are really productive as lead fee earner behind a partner on two or three deals at any one time."* Certainly the current economic conditions mean that corporate lawyers are far less busy than they were three or four years ago. With M&A activity at barely half its earlier levels, it's easy to see why corporate teams are at best taking it easy, and at worst shedding staff.

skills needed

...not for the faint-hearted... stamina... a touch of the glory seeker...handling demanding, intelligent clients... comfortable with big price tags... good presentation... decisiveness... confidence... tact and clear communication... eye for detail... a good all-rounder...

Most corporate lawyers accept that there's a bit of brash ego-led behaviour around, but it's inevitable when you've got highly motivated lawyers acting for equally motivated clients under tight deadlines. There is an element of showmanship involved. Simon says: *"As the lawyer, you try and get everything organised in advance, but there are always points at issue between the parties until the last moment. It may come down to a crunch meeting when it's all about who blinks first. When that's happened, the lawyer can document it, but until you know where everything will land, you can't finalise the deal."*

Some specialist lawyers contend that corporate lawyers' jobs are all about doing deals and have very little to do with pure law. As a corporate lawyer you do have to be a jack of all trades. Merger control, IP/IT, employment, tax, etc. all need to be understood and the basics communicated to the client. OK, the corporate lawyer will call upon the skills of specialists, but they need to know when to do that.

Andrew highlighted certain essential skills: practical things and good old-fashioned common sense. *"You must have the ability to see through the rubbish and pick out important bits of information from a lot of documentation. Knowing which bits to focus on requires an analytical mind."* He certainly believes that *"drafting skills are underrated – it's so important that what you draft is clear and understandable."* Lastly, Andrew thinks that *"general people skills – getting on with others,"* are vital. You'll spend a lot of time in meetings, much of it thrashing out points of agreement, but also making small talk with your client.

Those who excel in corporate work seem to thrive in pressured situations. Simon told us: *"You have to keep driving yourself when sometimes all you want to do is stop."* Deadlines are almost always genuine – eg the end of an accounting year – and sometimes this means there aren't enough hours in a day. If you're going to have a problem with the working pattern, you should choose another area of law.

career options

The market has suffered in the last couple of years and remains flat in 2003. But activity will increase again, perhaps with a new twist or flavour of deal. Regional firms' deals are usually of lower value, but can still be cross-border. The reward for working in a large commercial department of a smaller firm (both in the regions and in London) is involvement in clients' affairs at an earlier stage. Larger regional firms, like their City counterparts, allow qualified lawyers to be seconded to major clients. A sound grounding in corporate finance makes an excellent springboard for working in industry. Many lawyers move in-house to major companies, tempted by decent hours and salaries.

Some lawyers join the banking world, either as in-house lawyers, corporate finance execs or analysts. Those who make the transition from lawyer to client enjoy the dynamic pace of life and are glad to shed the advisory role. Such moves generally occur early on, but high-profile moves of senior partners to investment banks do happen. Company secretarial positions suit lawyers with a taste for variety and responsibility. Our best advice to budding corporate lawyers is to make the *FT* your friend. You don't need to study it religiously, just make sure you know what the big stories are. To find out more about the strengths of the different corporate law practices, read *Chambers UK* and *Chambers Global.*

LEADING FIRMS FROM CHAMBERS UK 2003-2004

CORPORATE FINANCE ■ THE SOUTH

Band	Firm
1	**Blake Lapthorn Linnell** Southampton
2	**Bond Pearce** Southampton
	Shadbolt & Co Reigate
	Stevens & Bolton Guildford
3	**asb law** Crawley
	Clyde & Co Guildford
	Cripps Harries Hall Tunbridge Wells
	Paris Smith & Randall Southampton
	Rawlison Butler Crawley
	Thomas Eggar Chich, Horsham, Reigate, Worthing
4	**Coffin Mew & Clover** Southampton
	Davies Lavery Maidstone
	DMH Brighton, Crawley
	Lester Aldridge Bournemouth, Soton
	Mundays Cobham
	Shoosmiths Fareham
	Thomson Snell & Passmore Tunbridge Wells

CORPORATE FINANCE ■ SOUTH WEST

Band	Firm
1	**Burges Salmon** Bristol
	Osborne Clarke Bristol
2	**Bond Pearce** Bristol, Exeter, Plymouth
	TLT Solicitors Bristol
3	**Bevan Ashford BBL** Bristol
	Bevan Ashford EPL Exeter
4	**BPE Solicitors** Cheltenham
	Charles Russell Cheltenham
	Clark Holt Swindon
	Foot Anstey Sargent Exeter, Plymouth
5	**Clarke Willmott** Bristol, Taunton
	Laytons Bristol
	Lyons Davidson Bristol
	Michelmores Exeter
	Stephens & Scown Exeter, St Austell, Truro
	Veale Wasbrough Bristol

CORPORATE FINANCE ■ THAMES VALLEY

Band	Firm
1	**Osborne Clarke** Reading
2	**Clarks** Reading
	Kimbells LLP Milton Keynes
	Manches Oxford
	Nabarro Nathanson Reading
	Pitmans Reading
3	**Boyes Turner** Reading
	Hale and Dorr Oxford
	Howes Percival Milton Keynes
	Shoosmiths Reading

CORPORATE FINANCE ■ EAST ANGLIA

Band	Firm
1	**Eversheds** Cambridge, Norwich
	Mills & Reeve Cambridge, Norwich
2	**Hewitsons** Cambridge
	Taylor Vinters Cambridge
3	**Birketts** Ipswich
	Prettys Ipswich
	Taylor Wessing Cambridge
4	**Greene & Greene** Bury St Edmunds
	Greenwoods Peterborough
	Howes Percival Norwich
5	**Wilkin Chapman** Lincoln, Louth

CORPORATE FINANCE: LARGER DEALS ■ LONDON

Rank	Firm
1	Freshfields Bruckhaus
	Linklaters
	Slaughter and May
2	Allen & Overy
	Clifford Chance LLP
	Herbert Smith
3	Ashurst Morris Crisp
4	Lovells
	Macfarlanes
5	Norton Rose
6	CMS Cameron McKenna
	Simmons & Simmons

CORPORATE FINANCE ■ WEST MIDLANDS

Rank	Firm
1	**Eversheds** Birmingham
	Wragge & Co LLP Birmingham
2	**Pinsents** Birmingham
3	**DLA** Birmingham
	Gateley Wareing Birmingham
	Hammonds Birmingham
4	**Martineau Johnson** Birmingham
5	**Heatons** Birmingham
	Lee Crowder Birmingham

CORPORATE FINANCE ■ EAST MIDLANDS

Rank	Firm
1	**Browne Jacobson** Nottingham
	Eversheds Nottingham
2	**Edwards Geldard** Derby, Nottingham
	Freethcartwright LLP Nottingham
	Gateley Wareing Leicester, Nottingham
	Shoosmiths Northampton, Nottingham
3	**Howes Percival** Leicester, Northampton
4	**Harvey Ingram Owston** Leicester
	Hewitsons Northampton

CORPORATE FINANCE ■ NORTH EAST

Rank	Firm
1	**Dickinson Dees** Newcastle upon Tyne
2	**Ward Hadaway** Newcastle upon Tyne
3	**Eversheds** Newcastle upon Tyne
	Robert Muckle Newcastle upon Tyne
4	**Watson Burton** Newcastle upon Tyne

CORPORATE FINANCE: MEDIUM DEALS ■ LONDON

Rank	Firm
1	Jones Day Gouldens
	Mayer, Brown, Rowe & Maw LLP
	Travers Smith Braithwaite
2	Baker & McKenzie
	SJ Berwin
	Weil, Gotshal & Manges
3	Berwin Leighton Paisner
	Denton Wilde Sapte
4	Addleshaw Goddard
	Hammonds
	Olswang
	Pinsents
	Taylor Wessing
5	Dechert
	DLA
	Eversheds
	Nabarro Nathanson
	Osborne Clarke
	White & Case

CORPORATE FINANCE ■ WALES

Rank	Firm
1	**Morgan Cole** Cardiff
2	**Berry Smith** Cardiff
	Edwards Geldard Cardiff
	Eversheds Cardiff
	M and A Solicitors Cardiff
3	**Dolmans** Cardiff

CORPORATE FINANCE ■ NORTH WEST

Rank	Firm
1	**Addleshaw Goddard** Manchester
	DLA Liverpool, Manchester
	Eversheds Manchester
2	**Halliwell Landau** Manchester
3	**Hammonds** Manchester
4	**Brabners Chaffe Street** Liverpool, Manchester
	Cobbetts Manchester
	DWF Liverpool, Manchester
5	**Kuit Steinart Levy** Manchester
	Mace & Jones Liverpool, Manchester
	Pannone & Partners Manchester
	Pinsents Manchester
	Wacks Caller Manchester

CORPORATE FINANCE: SMALLER DEALS ■ LONDON

Rank	Firm
1	Bird & Bird
	Lawrence Graham
	Memery Crystal
	Richards Butler
	Stephenson Harwood
2	Field Fisher Waterhouse
	Harbottle & Lewis LLP
	Lewis Silkin
	Nicholson Graham & Jones
	Reed Smith
3	Charles Russell
	Faegre Benson Hobson Audley
	Fox Williams
4	Howard Kennedy
	Kendall Freeman
	Marriott Harrison
	Watson, Farley & Williams
5	Barlow Lyde & Gilbert
	Finers Stephens Innocent
	Middleton Potts
6	Beachcroft Wansbroughs
	Clyde & Co
	Reynolds Porter Chamberlain
	Steptoe & Johnson
	Wedlake Bell

CORPORATE FINANCE ■ YORKSHIRE

Rank	Firm
1	**Addleshaw Goddard** Leeds
	DLA Leeds, Sheffield
2	**Eversheds** Leeds
	Walker Morris Leeds
3	**Hammonds** Leeds
	Pinsents Leeds
4	**Lupton Fawcett** Leeds
5	**Andrew M Jackson** Hull
	Cobbetts Leeds
	Gordons Bradford, Leeds
	Irwin Mitchell Leeds, Sheffield
6	**Gosschalks** Hull
	Lee & Priestley Leeds
	Nelson & Co Leeds
	Rollits Hull, York

crime

Forget gripping courtroom dramas in which cases are neatly wrapped up in an hour (including commercial breaks). What you'll be handling is real life.

Criminal lawyers act for defendants in Magistrates' Courts, Crown Courts and Courts Martial. However serious the charge, the basic process is the same; the difference is in the detail. Lesser offences are dealt with in the Magistrates' Courts where defendants are usually represented by solicitors. More serious cases are tried in the Crown Courts, where most clients still prefer to use a barrister. In addition to criminal law and procedure, lawyers need to be familiar with mental health, immigration and extradition issues, particularly in criminal fraud.

type of work

general crime: Most criminal lawyers live on a diet of 'everyday crime', giving plenty of opportunities for advocacy. Expect to visit police stations, prisons and Magistrates' Courts on a daily basis. Vanessa Lloyd of London firm Lewis Nedas told us about the early days of her career: *"I was quite often sent to prisons for instructions. I also got to sift through evidence, listen to tapes of interviews and visit crime scenes. You're dealing with clients face-to-face from the beginning; you're not just paper shuffling from behind your desk."* Because the work is date-driven, cases have a quick turnover. Even murders are usually dealt with in under a year. Lawyers see the fruits of their labours relatively quickly, particularly those accredited to work as Duty Solicitors in the Magistrates' Courts.

In 2001 the Legal Aid Board was replaced by the Legal Services Commission, which introduced a franchise system limiting the number of firms that handle publicly funded criminal defence. Further changes are expected in 2004 that are likely to result in even fewer firms being able to work on publicly funded crime matters.

So-called 'top-end' criminal firms like Burton Copeland and Kingsley Napley get a fair amount of private criminal work, usually through recommendations from existing clients or commercial law firms without a crime capability. Even some high street firms get a small amount of this private work. However, now that the means test for criminal legal aid has been removed, defendants no longer have to prove that they are poor enough. As Vanessa says: *"Now even a millionaire will qualify for 'legal aid',"* and so private client work in this field is increasingly rare.

Over the last ten years there has been a succession of Crime Bills, each tinkering with aspects of the criminal justice system. Mode of trial issues, the abolition of the double jeopardy rule, changes to PACE, and modifications to sentencing guidelines – crime specialists need to keep their wits about them and must be prepared to keep up with changes as and when they happen.

The Human Rights Act has impacted too. Stephen Gentle, a partner at Kingsley Napley, thinks it's made *"a cultural difference – people are more clued-up and conscious of fairness in proceedings and evidence generally."* Specific articles dealing with the right to privacy, the right to a fair trial and freedom of expression seem the most obviously applicable, but the full effects of the HRA are still unclear. It's an interesting time to become a criminal lawyer.

criminal fraud: Only firms on the Legal Services Commission's Serious Fraud Panel may undertake this work. Stephen distinguishes it from general crime work: *"95% of all criminal trials are in the Magistrates' Court, but we only do cases in the Crown Courts, ie the other 5%. There are a large number of firms on the Serious Fraud Panel but there's only about four to five firms in London that do the really big fraud cases."* There's a whole other set of skills and knowledge you need to acquire. *"You actually need to learn about* *people's businesses in order to defend them properly. You don't need to know how an armed robber spends his day to be able to defend him."* As a result, *"it can be a much more intellectual exercise than blood and guts crime."*

a day in the life...

Criminal lawyers lead hectic lives. You might get into the office at 8.30am, having already spent some of the night at a police station. At 9.30am it's off to the Magistrates' Court for procedural and remand hearings or a plea in mitigation. After lunch on the hoof, you might be interviewing clients and conferring with counsel. There is still paperwork to deal with and you could be back in the police station tonight. Home at last, but you'll have to spend some of your free time preparing for the next day in court.

While trainees used to be thrown in at the deep end, the Law Society has now introduced an accreditation process. Until accredited, they are no longer able to attend police station interviews by themselves, nor are they able to make Magistrates' Court appearances. Vanessa explained the police station accreditation process: *"You start off by going to watch a solicitor do a number of interviews, then a solicitor will watch you do it on your own. There are written and oral tests at the end of this. All up, it takes about a year to become accredited, during which time you can build up a portfolio of police station work."*

skills needed...

...an eye for detail... sharp and resolute on your feet... excellent people skills... empathy... good organisational and IT skills... 100% commitment... willing to work without huge financial reward...

Dealing with criminal clients can be challenging: they may come from deprived backgrounds with drink, drug and/or psychiatric problems. Vanessa says: *"This doesn't necessarily make them difficult to deal with, it just means you must be aware of any problems they have. Most clients appreciate that you're there to help them."* Michael Mackey, a partner at Burton Copeland in Manchester, explains: *"The relationship between a criminal lawyer and their clients is more dependent on fundamental trust than, say, for commercial or conveyancing clients. We deal with their liberty."* As Stephen says: *"For most clients, their predicament will be the worst thing that's ever happened to them... A bad result could mean ten years away from their family, not watching their kids grow up."* There's a real camaraderie amongst criminal solicitors as they're always meeting peers in police stations and courts. Added to this, criminal lawyers are not up against each other; they're facing a 'common enemy', as it were, in the CPS.

Michael told us how important it is to be enthusiastic about your work, as clients will be relying heavily on you for *"something, which is very, very important to them."* You also have to be direct. If you mislead the client (especially if you are over-optimistic about their prospects) this leads to real problems for them... and you. Stephen agrees that you can't be frightened of giving unwelcome advice: *"If you tell a client they've got a good chance, but you've read the case and they don't, they're not going to thank you when they get five years."*

In handling casework, there's also a certain element of detective work. When you speak with your client and sift through the evidence, you'll be looking for things the police have missed. In addition to your clients and the police, depending on the case, you'll be dealing with a number of expert witnesses – medical, forensic, ballistics, blood... You have to be a bit savvy and very questioning. If you're known for your gullibility, are you looking at the right career?

career options

If you're seeking a good criminal practice look at our parent publication, *Chambers UK*, or alternatively ask a Citizens Advice Bureau or your local Law Society which firms specialise in crime. Training contracts at specialist criminal firms offering high-profile work are rare, but at general criminal firms there may be more openings. Under the new franchise system the idea is to take on as many cases as possible and so firms now need the personnel to bring in and handle the work. Some lawyers actively promote the idea of trying paralegal work for a while or outdoor clerking for solicitors or barristers. Additionally, work in the voluntary sector is a practical way of gaining a realistic view of people and real life. As Stephen says: "*You can't be starry-eyed when you start this job or you'll get your hands burnt very quickly.*" The downside is the salary. Vanessa revealed: "*Friends who qualified at the same time as me are now earning three times as much in the City, but if you want this job you're not looking to be a City solicitor!*" Michael adds: "*It's very demanding, very time consuming and not as well paid, but I couldn't contemplate doing anything else.*"

Refer to the **So you want to be a lawyer** section on page 13 for information on careers with the CPS.

LEADING FIRMS FROM CHAMBERS UK 2003-2004

CRIME ■ SOUTH WEST

Band	Firm
1	**Douglas & Partners** Bristol
2	**Bobbetts Mackan** Bristol
	Kelcey & Hall Bristol
	Sansbury Campbell Bristol
3	**Bay Advocates** Torquay
	Nunn Rickard Solicitor Advocates Exeter
	St James Solicitors Exeter
	Stones Exeter
4	**Russell Jones & Walker** Bristol
	Stephen Walker Plymouth
	Wolferstans Plymouth

CRIME ■ WALES

Band	Firm
1	**Martyn Prowel Solicitors** Cardiff
2	**Colin Jones** Barry
	Goldstones Swansea
	Graham Evans & Partners Swansea
	Huttons Cardiff
	Spiro Grech & Harding Roberts Solicitors
	Wilson Devonald Swansea
3	**Clarke & Hartland** Cardiff
	Douglas-Jones Mercer Swansea
	Gamlins Rhyl
	Howe & Spender Port Talbot
	Robertsons Cardiff
	Savery Pennington Cardiff

CRIME ■ MIDLANDS

Band	Firm
1	**Cartwright King** Nottingham
	Fletchers Nottingham
	The Johnson Partnership Nottingham
2	**Glaisyers** Birmingham
	Kieran Clarke Solicitors Chesterfield
	Nelsons Nottingham
	The Smith Partnership Derby
3	**Banner Jones Middleton** Chesterfield
	Elliot Mather Chesterfield
	Jonas Roy Bloom Birmingham
	Purcell Parker Birmingham
	Tyndallwoods Birmingham
	Varley Hadley Siddall Nottingham
	Woodford-Robinson Northampton
4	**Barrie Ward & Julian Griffiths** Nottingham
	Bate Edmond Snape Coventry

CRIME ■ EAST ANGLIA

Band	Firm
1	**Belmores** Norwich
	Overbury Steward Eaton & Woolsey Norwich
	TMK Solicitors Southend-on-Sea
2	**David Charnley & Co** Romford
	Fosters Norwich
	Hatch Brenner Norwich
	Lucas & Wyllys Great Yarmouth
	Norton Peskett Lowestoft
	TNT Solicitors (Thanki Novy Taube) Harlow
3	**Coles** Great Yarmouth
	Copleys Huntingdon
	Gepp & Sons Chelmsford, Colchester
	Hunt & Coombs Peterborough

CRIME ■ NORTH EAST

Band	Firm
1	**David Gray Solicitors** Newcastle upon Tyne
	Grahame Stowe, Bateson Leeds
	Henry Hyams Leeds
	Sugaré & Co Leeds
2	**Graysons Solicitors** Sheffield
	Howells Sheffield
	Irwin Mitchell Sheffield
	Levi & Co Leeds
	McCormicks Leeds
	The Max Gold Partnership Hull
	Williamsons Solicitors Hull

CRIME ■ LONDON

1. Bindman & Partners
   Birnberg Peirce & Partners
   Edward Fail Bradshaw & Waterson
   Kingsley Napley
   Taylor Nichol
2. Hallinan, Blackburn, Gittings & Nott
   Henry Milner & Co
   Hickman & Rose
   Hodge Jones & Allen
   Powell Spencer & Partners
   Saunders & Co
   Tuckers
   Victor Lissack & Roscoe
3. Burton Copeland (London)
   Edwards Duthie
   Reynolds Dawson
   Russell Jones & Walker
   Russell-Cooke
   Simons Muirhead & Burton
   TNT Solicitors (Thanki Novy Taube)
   TV Edwards
4. Andrew Keenan & Co
   Claude Hornby & Cox
   Corker Binning Solicitors
   Iliffes Booth Bennett (IBB) Uxbridge
   Joy Merriam & Co
   McCormacks
   Stokoe Partnership
   Venters Solicitors
5. Alistair Meldrum & Co Enfield
   Bark & Co
   Birds Solicitors
   Fisher Meredith
   Kaim Todner
   Moss & Co
   Whitelock & Storr

CRIME ■ NORTH WEST

1. Brian Koffman & Co Manchester
   Burton Copeland (North) Liverpool, Manchester
   JMW Solicitors Manchester
   Tuckers Manchester
2. Betesh Fox & Co Manchester
   Cobleys Salford
   Draycott Browne Manchester
   Kristina Harrison Solicitors Salford
   Maidments Manchester
   Olliers Manchester
   Pearson Fielding Partnership Liverpool
   RM Broudie & Co Liverpool
   Rowlands Manchester
   Russell & Russell Bolton
3. Cunninghams Manchester
   Farleys Blackburn
   Forbes Blackburn
   Jackson & Canter Liverpool

FRAUD: CRIMINAL ■ LONDON

1. Burton Copeland (London)
   Kingsley Napley
   Peters & Peters
2. Irwin Mitchell
3. Byrne & Partners
   Corker Binning Solicitors
   Russell Jones & Walker
4. Garstangs
   Simons Muirhead & Burton
5. Claude Hornby & Cox
   Victor Lissack & Roscoe

FRAUD: CRIMINAL ■ SOUTH & SOUTH WEST

1. Blake Lapthorn Linnell Fareham
   Hodkinsons Solicitors Locks Heath
2. Bobbetts Mackan Bristol

FRAUD: CRIMINAL ■ WALES

1. Martyn Prowel Solicitors Cardiff
   Roy Morgan & Co Cardiff

FRAUD: CRIMINAL ■ MIDLANDS

1. Cartwright King Nottingham
   Richard Nelson solicitors Nottingham
2. Glaisyers Birmingham
   Nelsons Nottingham

FRAUD: CRIMINAL ■ THE NORTH

1. Cooper Kenyon Burrows Manchester
2. Pannone & Partners Manchester
3. Betesh Fox & Co Manchester
   DLA Manchester
   Irwin Mitchell Sheffield
4. Burton Copeland (north) Manchester
   David Hanman Associates Manchester
5. Russell Jones & Walker Manchester

employment law

Are you fascinated by human nature, curious about the forces at play in employer/employee relations and eager to be involved in cases provoking legislative and social changes affecting everyone who has ever had a job? Then think about employment law.

Specialist employment teams are normally divided along partisan lines. Commercial firms (corporate client base and higher fees) work for employers and highly paid senior executives. These departments are often combined with or allied to pensions law teams. The 'right on' firms act mainly for trade union clients and other individuals. Some have allied practices in claimant personal injury. Almost every high street practice and Citizens Advice Bureau purports to give employment advice to individuals. In fact, the practice area is now so law-intensive that even full-time specialists have a hard time keeping up with the almost weekly changes from the European and domestic courts.

type of work

The work of an employment lawyer is a rich and varied mix of advisory, pre-emptive, contractual and litigious work. Contentious matters are heard in employment tribunals, County Courts or the High Court. Some employment cases, which start in an employment tribunal, become test cases appealed to the higher courts and a few may even reach the Court of Appeal, House of Lords or even the European Court of Justice. In tribunals, employees ('applicants') may claim for redundancy pay, unfair dismissal, breach of contract, and sex, race and disability discrimination against their employers ('respondents'). Claims for breach of contract may also be made in the High Court or County Courts depending on the value of the claim. In January 2001, Julie Bower, a former City analyst won almost £1.5 million in a breach of contract case after the size of her bonus payment in 1998 was found to be derisory when compared to those earned by male colleagues and other aspects of her working environment were deemed to have been discriminatory.

Although the awards in most cases (save discrimination) will be capped at £53,500, the high value of some awards makes it easy to see why individuals are increasingly willing to bring claims and why employers defend them. Many firms (especially those outside the City) prefer their employment lawyers to handle most of their own advocacy and consequently this is one area of the law where the Ally McBeal experience is not a million miles from the truth. It's not a bad area for those who may have once thought about becoming a barrister.

The Government intends to widen the field in terms of discrimination. By 2005 we are likely to see anti-age discrimination laws, and legislation to prevent discrimination on the grounds of religion may come in even sooner. Given their experiences following the creation of laws against sex, race and disability discrimination, employment lawyers predict a wave of new claims from applicants following the introduction of these new laws. The employment lawyers we spoke to also reported an increase in work following recent legal requirements for workforce consultation prior to corporate disposals and large-scale redundancies. All of this is great news for budding employment lawyers.

Although acting for employees doesn't always put a lawyer on the side of the angels, those acting for trade unions and their members are often ideologically motivated. A lawyer may find himself representing thousands of union members in their campaigns to change working practices or the law on, say, pension rights for part-time workers. Employment law is, by its nature, highly politicised, regulating, as it does, the relationship between workers and employers. Dr John McMullen, the national head of employment law at Pinsents, which acts mainly for employers, emphasises this. *"It's one of the few subjects that can combine topical issues of politics, industrial relations and people alongside the intellectual disciplines studied at university."*

Employment lawyers see themselves as somewhat different from corporate lawyers although they find themselves working closely with them on transactions, with employment advice increasingly becoming a vital ingredient in the deal. The hours are usually not as relentless as those experienced in the corporate departments though. Chris Goodwill, an employment partner at Clifford Chance, says: *"I'm glad you asked me and not my wife. The hours are absolutely fine and I've never missed a play or a film or a dinner or a Leeds match because of work. Can I uncross my fingers now?"* More seriously, he points out: *"The worst thing about an employment lawyer's hours is not so much the number of them, but the unpredictability of when they might have to be put in."*

a day in the life of...

8.45am: Arrive at employment tribunal to greet white-faced HR director and head of IT from important corporate client. Client is defending an unfair dismissal claim brought by ex-employee sacked for downloading v. dodgy porn at work. Applicant is using somewhat teenage argument that 'everyone else was doing it', but has not managed to rally any colleagues in support of this.

10am: Explain to clients that the hearing will be relatively informal and the morning will be spent reading out their witness statements to the tribunal panel (which is supposed to be neutral like Switzerland). Witnesses perform fabulously under my guidance and can't help thinking their performance is the result of own superb preparation of case.

1.30pm: After behaving like contortionists, tribunal panel stop bending over backwards to be helpful towards hapless (and unrepresented) ex-employee. He has no supporting witnesses and no way of proving his claim (of not being a sleazy, porn-obsessed time-waster). Suppress urge to do one-person Mexican wave as tribunal finds for my client.

2.30pm: Back in office. Scoff sandwich at desk (celebratory lunch with victorious client arranged for next week) and turn attention to phone messages. Return call to a client whose staff have got themselves into what is technically termed 'an intriguing pickle'.

Following an office quiz night in a local bar, two teams had gone onto a club where some pretty steamy and v. public antics had ensued between drunk female employee and two male members of staff. Worried onlookers have reported the events. Employer now concerned that the participants may complain of sexual harassment (though who was harassing who?). Consider whether events could be deemed to have taken place in the course of employment and, if so, whether they amount to sexual harassment. Client calls back to say the participants are shamefaced and can't remember much about it. Conclude it should be seen as high spirits out of work and suggest no disciplinary action be taken.

5pm: Call rather rambunctious partner in corporate department with advice on how TUPE regulations affect his client's acquisition of a rival's business. Persuade him that buyer can't just discontinue the seller's rather generous maternity scheme because "the place for women is at home with the babies." Put call on speakerphone so all nearby colleagues can appreciate just how impossible and mad (and loud) he is. Conclude that it is as much my dulcet tones as it is the soundness of advice that wins him over. Prepare memo summarising advice for the client.

7pm: Catch homeward bound train with good intention of perusing case updates...

skills needed

...being a people person... sensitivity and calmness... sense of humour... versatility... excellent communication and negotiation skills... a talent for advocacy...

practicality... an ability to quickly assimilate changes in strategy and advice... knowing when to be tough... detailed knowledge of relevant law...

John points out: *"The law is so fast-moving that continuous education and development is vital for the employment law practitioner. Added to this, with dimensions of European law, discrimination, human rights, strikes and industrial action and dismissal disputes, no day is boring."* Hilary O'Connor, a partner at SJ Berwin, agrees: *"A good memory is essential. However, in some cases the legal solution to a problem is not the cheapest or quickest solution for the client, so you need good business judgement and good instincts to know which one to choose. It is very people-oriented, so patience, tact, empathy and the ability to inspire confidence is essential."* But it's not all about being warm and cuddly. Chris thinks that you have to be versatile in your approach to the work. *"An employment lawyer needs to be one part academic, one part agony aunt and one part hit man!"*

career options

Those hoping for a career as an employment lawyer face stiff competition. Most commercial firms have at least a small, dedicated department and even the smallest high street firm will have clients seeking employment advice. Like most litigation, the volume of work increases in times of recession. As Hilary confirms: *"In times of recession we get instructions on redundancies and terminations. In times of economic strength there's more corporate-led advice needed."* Chris agrees, saying: *"The chameleonic nature of the employment lawyer's work seems to add a bit of job security."*

Employers such as the Post Office and BA have in-house employment lawyers, but more usually a move in-house would combine employment law with general commercial advice. Many partners in leading employment practices combine their practice with part-time tribunal chairs. Know-how lawyers are dedicated to keeping their colleagues up to date on changes in the law and draft client newsletters etc.

LEADING FIRMS FROM CHAMBERS UK 2003-2004

Band	EMPLOYMENT ■ NORTH EAST
1	**Dickinson Dees** Newcastle upon Tyne
	Eversheds Newcastle upon Tyne
	Short Richardson & Forth Newcastle upon Tyne
2	**Crutes Law Firm** Newcastle upon Tyne
	Jacksons Stockton on Tees
	Samuel Phillips & Co Newcastle upon Tyne
	Thompsons Newcastle upon Tyne
	Ward Hadaway Newcastle upon Tyne
	Watson Burton Newcastle upon Tyne

Band	EMPLOYMENT ■ NORTH WEST
1	**Addleshaw Goddard** Manchester
	Eversheds Manchester
2	**Cobbetts** Manchester
	DLA Liverpool, Manchester
	Hammonds Manchester
	Mace & Jones Liverpool, Manchester
3	**DWF** Liverpool, Manchester
	Whittles Manchester
4	**Halliwell Landau** Manchester
	Thompsons Liverpool, Manchester
5	**Berg & Co** Manchester
	Brabners Chaffe Street Liverpool, Manchester
	Keoghs Bolton
	Pannone & Partners Manchester
	Weightman Vizards Liverpool

Band	EMPLOYMENT ■ YORKSHIRE
1	**Pinsents** Leeds
2	**Addleshaw Goddard** Leeds
	Cobbetts Leeds
	DLA Leeds, Sheffield
	Eversheds Leeds
	Ford & Warren Leeds
	Hammonds Leeds
3	**Gordons** Bradford, Leeds
	Walker Morris Leeds
4	**Irwin Mitchell** Sheffield
	Lupton Fawcett Leeds
	Nelson & Co Leeds
	Rollits Hull

EMPLOYMENT: RESPONDENT ■ LONDON

1. Allen & Overy
   Simmons & Simmons
2. Baker & McKenzie
   Lewis Silkin
3. Fox Williams
   Herbert Smith
   Lovells
   Mayer, Brown, Rowe & Maw LLP
4. Beachcroft Wansbroughs
   Charles Russell
   Clifford Chance LLP
   Dechert
   Eversheds
   Hammonds
   Linklaters
   McDermott, Will & Emery
   Nabarro Nathanson
   Olswang
5. Addleshaw Goddard Boodle Hatfield
   CMS Cameron McKenna
   Denton Wilde Sapte
   Farrer & Co
   Freshfields Bruckhaus Deringer
   Macfarlanes
   Norton Rose
   Osborne Clarke
   Salans
   Slaughter and May
   Speechly Bircham
   Travers Smith Braithwaite
6. Archon
   Ashurst Morris Crisp
   Barlow Lyde & Gilbert
   Berwin Leighton Paisner
   Bird & Bird
   Doyle Clayton
   Lawrence Graham
   Masons
   SJ Berwin
   Stephenson Harwood
   Taylor Wessing
   Withers LLP

EMPLOYMENT: APPLICANT ■ LONDON

1. Pattinson & Brewer
   Russell Jones & Walker
2. Thompsons
3. Rowley Ashworth
4. Bindman & Partners
   Irwin Mitchell
   Lawfords

EMPLOYMENT ■ THE SOUTH

1. **Blake Lapthorn Linnell** Portsmouth
   DMH Brighton, Crawley
2. **Bond Pearce** Southampton
3. **Paris Smith & Randall** Southampton
   Rawlison Butler Crawley
4. **asb law** Crawley
   Clyde & Co Guildford
   Cripps Harries Hall Tunbridge Wells
5. **Brachers** Maidstone
   Lester Aldridge Bournemouth, Southampton
   Pattinson & Brewer Chatham
   Stevens & Bolton Guildford
   Thomson Snell & Passmore Tunbridge Wells

EMPLOYMENT ■ THAMES VALLEY

1. **Clarks** Reading
2. **Osborne Clarke** Reading
3. **Henmans** Oxford
   Morgan Cole Oxford, Reading
   Olswang Thames Valley Reading
   Pitmans Reading
   Underwoods Hemel Hempstead

EMPLOYMENT ■ WALES

1. **Eversheds** Cardiff
2. **Morgan Cole** Cardiff, Swansea
3. **Edwards Geldard** Cardiff
4. **Hugh James** Cardiff

EMPLOYMENT ■ SOUTH WEST

1. **Bevan Ashford BBL** Bristol
   Burges Salmon Bristol
   Osborne Clarke Bristol
2. **Bond Pearce** Plymouth
3. **Burroughs Day** Bristol
   TLT Bristol
   Veale Wasbrough Bristol
4. **Pattinson & Brewer** Bristol
   Thompsons Bristol
   Thring Townsend Bath, Swindon
5. **Clarke Willmott** Taunton
   Michelmores Exeter
   Stephens & Scown Exeter
   Wolferstans Plymouth

EMPLOYMENT ■ MIDLANDS

1. **Eversheds** Birmingham, Nottingham
   Wragge & Co LLP Birmingham
2. **Hammonds** Birmingham
3. **Pinsents** Birmingham
4. **Browne Jacobson** Nottingham
   DLA Birmingham
   Martineau Johnson Birmingham
5. **Bevan Ashford BBL** Birmingham
   Freethcartwright LLP Nottingham
   Higgs & Sons Brierley Hill, Dudley
   Shakespeares Birmingham

EMPLOYMENT ■ EAST ANGLIA

1. **Eversheds** Cambridge, Norwich
   Mills & Reeve Cambridge, Norwich
2. **Greenwoods** Peterborough
   Hewitsons Cambridge
   Taylor Vinters Cambridge
3. **Prettys** Ipswich
   Steeles Norwich
4. **Hegarty & Co** Peterborough

environmental law

While there are careers for tree-hugging, planet-saving heroes, these are unlikely to be in private practice. Most environmental lawyers work for corporate clients seeking damage limitation, pre-emptive advice and defence from prosecution. Additionally, there's a volume of corporate support work, ensuring environmental liability is fully understood and apportioned between corporate entities. As Caroline May, a partner at Hammonds, states: *"You don't have to be an environmentalist to be an environmental lawyer, but you do have to have a keen interest in environmental issues."*

type of work

Mike Nash, a partner at Simmons & Simmons, told us: *"Environmental law is a real Tardis. It looks small from the outside, but get inside and it's gigantic."* Administrative law, property, planning, contract and corporate law, EU law, international law and, increasingly, human rights. This sounds like an interdisciplinary free-for-all, so picture the work grouped into three broad areas:

- transactional, project and property support;
- compliance and regulatory advice; and
- litigation (encompassing criminal and civil disputes, judicial reviews and statutory appeals).

The environmental lawyer's caseload will usually be split between contentious and non-contentious matters. Contentious work may involve defending clients from criminal prosecution for breach of regulations. Indeed, there's been an upturn in prosecutions since the authorities began to flex their muscles a couple of years ago. You might find yourself in the Magistrates' Court running an argument on abuse of process or you might be arguing that the regulator has interpreted the law incorrectly. On the civil side there are tortious claims ('toxic torts') brought by those who suffer loss as a result of environmental impact.

On the non-contentious side environmental lawyers have a vital role on the sale and purchase of businesses or land, drafting contractual provisions for the allocation of risk. There's also standalone work, such as advice to clients on the extent of their obligations under new EU regulations. These may cover issues such as waste, pollution control, water abstraction and nature conservation.

Environmental law is still relatively new and there's a substantial amount of research and interpretation of legislation to be done. A trainee can come into their own given that they might, almost by accident, become the team's expert on a new piece of legislation or EU directive. Increasingly, the Human Rights Act has an impact, particularly in terms of the right to peaceful enjoyment of property. Mike says: *"The HRA was primarily brought in to protect individuals, but many people don't realise that it also gives human rights to companies and can be used to protect those rights as well."*

a day in the life...

What about a typical day? Caroline stresses: *"No two days are alike. Today I've dealt with a health and safety prosecution; I've been meeting a client and then dealing with a regulator; I've been meeting with clients to get ongoing authorisation for compliance issues; I've been in court for criminal and civil litigation; and I've been talking to government ministers about contaminated land."* Phew! A mix of public, private, civil, criminal and general compliance work then. She added: *"A lot of environmental issues are mucky issues: waste and sludge and sewers and spills."* Sounds a bit grim. *"It can be, particularly if you've got to go wander around a riverbed in your wellies."* Mike has similar comments: *" Lawyers in this area actually go out and visit sites. Corporate lawyers for example may do a deal involving 100 sites yet never go near any of them."* His days are equally as varied. He might be in the office drafting a letter of advice or a warranty for a corporate sale and then get a call from a client saying, "The Environment Agency's arrived. Should we talk to them or hand over the documents they are asking for?" This is part of the appeal. *"If you're someone who enjoys an organised routine and a thoroughly methodical day, it's not really for you."*

Junior lawyers can find it a challenging area to get to grips with. There's a substantial body of environmental law to get your head around, plus corporate, property and litigation procedures. As environmental teams are quite small, junior lawyers probably get more responsibility than in many other areas. Mike points out: *"You often get bite-sized chunks of work. If there's a specific regulatory issue to advise on, for example, a relatively junior person can take responsibility for it rather than just be part of a larger project."*

skills needed

...deal with intellectual problems commercially... be an all-rounder... understand corporate structures... interest in environmental issues... a grasp of science... research, interpretation and presentation skills...

Mike says: *"It's a mix of the rarefied and absurdly practical. There are aspects of the job that are intellectually demanding, but the client doesn't want you to answer just for fun or do a dissertation for a year; they want you to weigh up the risks, decide whether they're acceptable and go with it."*

You're often giving regulatory advice over a number of years – it's not like a transaction where you do a deal and everyone goes home. You might be advising at board level in relation to strategic issues, but you'll also meet and deal with people on site visits, some of whom might have scientific or engineering backgrounds. In addition to engineering and manufacturing clients generally, those in the waste, chemicals, ports, energy, rail, construction, food and water industries will feature. We wondered if there was any industry sector that wasn't involved. Mike identified one: *"The dot.com world – there's no one spilling anything or impacting on the environment there. They leave us cold."* Brrrr!

career options

It's a popular and, therefore, competitive area. Just over a decade ago solicitors got pretty excited about the emerging work, but commercial reality has tempered attitudes. According to Caroline: *"City law firms thought environment law would be the next big thing and pumped masses of people into it, many of whom jumped out with equal speed when it became clear that it was still very much secondary – or even third – to banking and corporate finance work."* The market for new lawyers is merely *"trundling along about level,"* but more students are studying the subject and thinking about it as a career. Mike told us: *"We always have more trainees wanting to specialise in it than we can take on."* Why is it so popular? Caroline thinks it may go back to the *"misguided notion that it's going to involve saving whales, seals and trees."*

The local authority route is an alternative to private practice. You'll handle regulatory work, planning issues, waste management and air pollution cases, and have a role in advising the authority on its own liability. In-house positions for environmental lawyers are few and far between in corporate Britain, however, organisations such as Greenpeace, Friends of the Earth and RSPB have in-house lawyers.

The Department for Environment, Food and Rural Affairs (DEFRA) employs over 80 lawyers, including trainees on GLS-funded schemes. Work covers litigation, drafting of subordinate legislation, straight advisory work and contract drafting. The Environment Agency for England and Wales has responsibility for protecting and enhancing the environment through regulation of those corporate activities that have the greatest potential to pollute. The legal workload is diverse and requires a number of different legal skills. The Agency is the prosecution body for environmental crime and a number of Agency lawyers are full-time prosecutors. In addition there's a large amount of other enforcement work. As well as this, lawyers are involved in advice work at either the policy or operational level, which spans guidance on new regulations to advising on a licence for a particular site. Agency policy lawyers work closely with government lawyers on implementing and drafting legislation. The scope of work covers water quality, waste management, Integrated Pollution Prevention and Control, contaminated land, water resources, flood defence, fisheries, navigation and conservation, as well as other areas such as Environmental Impact Assessment and information law. Oh...and another little matter – regulating the disposal of radioactive waste! Around 70 work from Bristol and eight regional offices. Contact the relevant regional solicitor for more info.

LEADING FIRMS FROM CHAMBERS UK 2003-2004

ENVIRONMENT ■ LONDON
1 Allen & Overy
Freshfields Bruckhaus Deringer
2 Ashurst Morris Crisp
Barlow Lyde & Gilbert
Clifford Chance LLP
CMS Cameron McKenna
Denton Wilde Sapte
Leigh, Day & Co
Linklaters
Mayer, Brown, Rowe & Maw LLP
Simmons & Simmons
Slaughter and May
3 Berwin Leighton Paisner
Hammonds
Jones Day Gouldens
Lovells
Nabarro Nathanson
SJ Berwin
4 Baker & McKenzie
Herbert Smith
Lawrence Graham
Nicholson Graham & Jones
Norton Rose
Trowers & Hamlins
5 Addleshaw Goddard
Stephenson Harwood

ENVIRONMENT ■ THE SOUTH
1 **Bond Pearce** Southampton
2 **Blake Lapthorn Linnell** Southampton
3 **Brachers** Maidstone
DMH Brighton
Horsey Lightly Fynn Newbury
Stevens & Bolton Guildford

ENVIRONMENT ■ SOUTH WEST
1 **Bond Pearce** Plymouth
Burges Salmon Bristol
2 **Clarke Willmott** Bristol, Taunton
Osborne Clarke Bristol
3 **Bevan Ashford BBL** Bristol
4 **Veale Wasbrough** Bristol

ENVIRONMENT ■ WALES
1 **Edwards Geldard** Cardiff
Morgan Cole Cardiff
2 **Eversheds** Cardiff
3 **Hugh James** Cardiff

ENVIRONMENT ■ EAST ANGLIA
1 **Mills & Reeve** Cambridge
Richard Buxton Cambridge
2 **Eversheds** Norwich
3 **Hewitsons** Cambridge

ENVIRONMENT ■ MIDLANDS
1 **Wragge & Co LLP** Birmingham
2 **Browne Jacobson** Nottingham
Eversheds Birmingham, Nottingham
Hammonds Birmingham
Pinsents Birmingham
3 **Kent Jones and Done** Stoke-on-Trent

ENVIRONMENT ■ NORTH WEST
1 **Eversheds** Manchester
2 **Hammonds** Manchester
Leigh, Day & Co Manchester
3 **Addleshaw Goddard** Manchester
4 **WDL Solicitors** Chester

ENVIRONMENT ■ NORTH EAST
1 **Eversheds** Leeds
Nabarro Nathanson Sheffield
2 **DLA** Sheffield
3 **Addleshaw Goddard** Leeds
Hammonds Leeds
4 **Dickinson Dees** Newcastle upon Tyne
Pinsents Leeds

family law

Family lawyers deal with the fallout from marital breakdown and a wide range of issues concerning children. The work ranges from the restructuring of a client's finances and companies at the high end of the private market, to issues of adoption, access and custody in the field of children's law, most of which falls in the public domain. Whether they were working in a high street firm alongside social services on a case involving child abuse, or from a 'boutique' firm trying to save a client's offshore investments, all the lawyers we spoke to echoed the sentiment that *"these are issues that really do matter; things that change the lives of individuals."* As a family lawyer you are in a position to help your client through one of life's most traumatic experiences and, with 40% of marriages ending in divorce these days, you're unlikely to be short of work.

type of work

Known for his ability to handle the more excitable client, Alex Carruthers, a partner in niche practice Hughes Fowler Carruthers, specialises in all aspects of matrimonial and family law at the top end of the market. Here you'll need to gain an understanding of tax, trusts, pensions and property issues and have *"an appreciation of money and how it works, combined with an insight into human nature."* While you may spend time crunching numbers, you must remember that there are feelings as well as finances at stake and never lose sight of the fact that *"you're going for the best overall deal, which involves money and emotions."*

Stephen Foster, head of family law at Lester Aldridge in Bournemouth, came to family law after practising commercial litigation in the City. With the area becoming increasingly technical, a sound knowledge of corporate law puts you at a distinct advantage. For Stephen, one of the main attractions of 'high-end' work is that it has become increasingly international and genuinely exciting. *"You're dealing with entrepreneurs who are positive people, full of drive and vigour. These are people for whom life poses no obstacles. It's a real buzz working with them."*

Work in the public arena is less glamorous and potentially more traumatic, since your cases are more likely to involve child abuse and domestic violence than trophy wives and offshore accounts. Michael Devlin, a partner at Stephensons in Salford, specialises in children's law and adoption issues. He specialised initially in criminal work and subsequently moved into family law. Typically a trainee will go into family law and then carve out a niche in an area like divorce or children's law within an established practice. As a family lawyer dealing with the general public, you will represent and work with local authorities, family members, children's guardians and, occasionally, children in their own right. This is a multidisciplinary area, so you'll have a lot of contact with social workers, psychologists, probation officers and medical professionals who are *"well qualified and committed to what they do."* Much of your time will be spent in court, with spare moments taken up with correspondence, client meetings or conferences. Michael warns that, while *"professional satisfaction is very high, the work is publicly funded so there are no fortunes to be made."* Setting yourself up as a high street family lawyer can be a commercially viable proposition however, just so long as you have a bit of nous and can build a strong following.

Family law may not be as intellectually rigorous as tax law or pensions, but actually you do need to have a level of understanding of these areas. According to Michael: *"You shouldn't regard it as next door to being a social worker." "Strong academics make you stand out,"* but it is equally important to have a life outside the law. You need to have some experience of people, relationships and the ways of the world. Stephen's practice took on a lawyer who used to run his own business and so is well positioned to understand the stresses and strains on their entrepreneurial clients.

There are increasing opportunities for advocacy as a family lawyer. Professional standards are generally considered to be high and *"there are not so many sharks and egos floating around. People tend to operate within the limits of openness, honesty and fairness."* The Human Rights Act has opened up new possibilities in the area of children's law and the Adoption and Children Act 2002 will also make big waves. Since the 1991 Children's Act, the area has been very *"vibrant,"* and there have been continual case law developments.

a day in the life of...

One of the attractions of family law is that no two clients and no two days are ever the same. A typical day for a lawyer in high-end private practice might involve meeting with a client in a five-star hotel to discuss the evolution of their companies and spending the afternoon in court up against a senior barrister, before heading back to the office for a three-hour phone call with an emotional client, which *"should really have lasted for 15 minutes."* A high street lawyer is likely to spend much of their time in court and in meetings with clients and the social services, with the beginning and end of the day taken up with correspondence. You won't be pulling all-nighters like your friends in City firms, but there's likely to be paperwork to take home in the evening.

As a junior lawyer in private practice you can expect to go to court with a partner, take notes and prepare bundles of case documentation. It's an easy area to become immersed in and it offers a good mixture of responsibility and interesting work.

Stephen warns, however, that there is a steep learning curve for the newly qualified lawyer. You will immediately become exposed to difficult and complex issues. *"It could come as a shock to a 23-year-old who is naïve in the ways of the world to see how adults of their parents' age are behaving towards one another."*

skills needed

...listening skills... life experience... professional distance... compassion... a real interest in human relations... wisdom... intelligence... numeracy... ability to remain non-confrontational... interest in advocacy... commercial acumen... non-judgemental...

According to Alex, those who are likely to succeed in this area will be gregarious and sensitive, and will combine a keen eye for detail with a real interest in people. *"We tend to be people with big personalities."* Stephen looks out for *"intellectual voltage"* in those he recruits.

One of the key qualities that you need as a family lawyer is sensitivity, but *"this should not be mistaken for being soft."* What the client needs is firm and realistic advice. You must be interested in people and understand what motivates them. You must also be able to understand the psychodynamics of relationships and relationship breakdowns. *"Clients will often be driven by subconscious issues and so it is up to you to understand what people really want and to deliver it as far as possible."* Professional detachment is a must. Michael explains: *"You need to draw the line right from the start or else they could start thinking of you as a friend. You need to make it clear that you're not there to dance to whatever tune they're playing."*

career options

There are in-house positions with local authorities and some big charities, but in terms of hands-on, client-focused work, there is no substitute for private practice. High street opportunities abound for well-qualified and skilled applicants, but positions in commercial firms are far less common than ten to 15 years ago as many of these firms shut down their family departments. High-end work is handled by a tight pool of firms, the best of which are identified and discussed in *Chambers UK*.

LEADING FIRMS FROM CHAMBERS UK 2003-2004

FAMILY/MATRIMONIAL ■ LONDON

1 Manches
Withers LLP

2 Alexiou Fisher Philipps
Charles Russell
Hughes Fowler Carruthers
Levison Meltzer Pigott
Miles Preston & Co
Payne Hicks Beach
Sears Tooth

3 Bindman & Partners
Collyer-Bristow
Dawson Cornwell
Farrer & Co
Goodman Ray
Gordon Dadds
Kingsley Napley
Mishcon de Reya
Reynolds Porter Chamberlain

4 Clintons
Family Law In Partnership
International Family Law Chambers

5 Anthony Gold
Barnett Sampson
CKFT
Dawsons
Fisher Meredith
Forsters
Hodge Jones & Allen
Margaret Bennett
Osbornes
Russell-Cooke
Stephenson Harwood

FAMILY/MATRIMONIAL ■ THE SOUTH

1 **Lester Aldridge** Bournemouth

2 **Blake Lapthorn Linnell** Portsmouth
Brachers Maidstone
Paris Smith & Randall Southampton
Thomson Snell & Passmore Tunbridge Wells

3 **Coffin Mew & Clover** Portsmouth
Cripps Harries Hall Tunbridge Wells
Ellis Jones Bournemouth
Max Barford & Co Tunbridge Wells
Williams Thompson Christchurch

FAMILY/MATRIMONIAL ■ THAMES VALLEY

1 **Blandy & Blandy** Reading
Manches Oxford

2 **Boodle Hatfield** Oxford
Darbys Oxford
Henmans Oxford
Morgan Cole Oxford

3 **Horsey Lightly Fynn** Newbury
Iliffes Booth Bennett (IBB) Uxbridge

FAMILY/MATRIMONIAL ■ SOUTH WEST

1 **Burges Salmon** Bristol
Foot Anstey Sargent Plymouth
Stephens & Scown Exeter
TLT Bristol
Tozers Exeter, Plymouth
Wolferstans Plymouth

2 **Clarke Willmott** Bristol
Gill Akaster Plymouth
Ian Downing Family Law Practice Plymouth

3 **Hartnells Family Law Practice** Exeter
Hooper & Wollen Torquay
Stone King Bath
Stones Exeter
Woollcombe Beer Watts Newton Abbot

4 **E David Brain & Co** St Austell
Ford Simey Exeter
Veale Wasbrough Bristol
Withy King Bath

FAMILY/MATRIMONIAL ■ WALES

1 **Hugh James** Cardiff
Larby Williams Cardiff
Nicol Denvir & Purnell Cardiff
Wendy Hopkins & Co Cardiff

2 **Martyn Prowel Solicitors** Cardiff
Robertsons Cardiff

3 **Harding Evans** Newport
Howells Cardiff
Leo Abse & Cohen Cardiff

FAMILY/MATRIMONIAL ■ MIDLANDS

1 **Blair Allison & Co** Birmingham
Challinors Lyon Clark West Bromwich
Rupert Bear Murray Davies Nottingham

2 **Nelsons** Nottingham
Tyndallwoods Birmingham

3 **Anthony Collins Solicitors** Birmingham
Hadens Walsall
Lanyon Bowdler Shrewsbury
Osborne & Co Birmingham
Turnbull Garrard Shrewsbury
Wace Morgan Shrewsbury
Young & Lee Birmingham

4 **Blythe Liggins** Leamington Spa
Freethcartwright LLP Nottingham

FAMILY/MATRIMONIAL ■ EAST ANGLIA

1 **Mills & Reeve** Cambridge, Norwich

2 **Buckles** Peterborough
Hunt & Coombs Peterborough
Silver Fitzgerald Cambridge

3 **Cozens-Hardy & Jewson** Norwich
Gotelee & Goldsmith Ipswich
Hansells Norwich
Hatch Brenner Norwich
Rudlings & Wakelam Thetford

FAMILY/MATRIMONIAL ■ NORTH WEST

1 **Pannone & Partners** Manchester

2 **Addleshaw Goddard** Manchester
Cobbetts Manchester
Cuff Roberts Liverpool

3 **Burnetts** Carlisle
Green & Co Manchester
JMW solicitors Manchester
Laytons Manchester
Mace & Jones Knutsford, Liverpool
Morecroft Urquhart Liverpool
Stephensons Leigh

FAMILY/MATRIMONIAL ■ YORKSHIRE

1 **Addleshaw Goddard** Leeds

2 **Gordons** Bradford
Grahame Stowe, Bateson Leeds
Irwin Mitchell Leeds, Sheffield
Jones Myers Gordon Leeds

3 **Andrew M Jackson** Hull
Lupton Fawcett Leeds
Zermansky & Partners Leeds

4 **Kirbys** Harrogate
Walker Morris Leeds

FAMILY/MATRIMONIAL ■ NORTH EAST

1 **Dickinson Dees** Newcastle upon Tyne, Stockton on Tees

2 **Hay & Kilner** Newcastle upon Tyne
Mincoffs Newcastle upon Tyne
Samuel Phillips & Co Newcastle upon Tyne
Sinton & Co Newcastle upon Tyne
Ward Hadaway Newcastle upon Tyne

intellectual property

Intellectual property law can be defined by its two halves: patent work (hard IP), ie the protection of inventions and processes; and non-patent work (soft IP), ie trademarks, design rights, copyright, passing off, anti-counterfeiting and confidential information. Both overlap with IT (information technology), telecommunications, broadcasting and internet work. The work often extends into Europe and beyond.

type of work

There are three main UK intellectual property rights providing owners with a complete monopoly. Patents protect new, industrially applicable inventions. They provide the proprietor with a monopoly to work the invention for a certain period. A registered trademark provides the owner with a limited monopoly to use that mark on certain goods or services. Finally, a registered design gives the owner an exclusive right to use the design. There are also more limited rights. For example, a work attracting copyright protection gives the owner of the copyright the right to prevent others copying the work.

IP clients include manufacturers and suppliers of hi-tech, engineering, pharmaceutical and agrochemical products, leading brand owners, universities, scientific institutions and media clients. IP work can be contentious or non-contentious. Disputes usually revolve around arguments of infringement or the existence of one or more intangible property rights in an invention, a literary/artistic work, a trademark or a product, or whether any IP rights exist at all. Patent litigation, in particular, can be very complex indeed, with cases running for years – usually there's a lot at stake. Kerry Griffin, an assistant at Bird & Bird, told us: *"The larger contentious cases tend to be patent matters as the parties are often multinational companies and the financial consequences can be enormous; often the trademark infringement or cybersquatting cases settle out of court."* Carl Steele, an assistant at Taylor Wessing, sees how much effort is put into patent disputes: *"It's all-consuming. For example, two big drug companies going head-to-head – they need as much time as you can give them and will spend a lot of money for the best lawyers."*

Carl doesn't generally handle patent cases, preferring to concentrate on other IP work, especially trademarks. He thinks: *"Trademark issues can be conceptually as difficult as patents. Patent cases are all about understanding the science and framing a really good expert's report. Trademark cases often succeed and fail on the reactions of the public to a rival's trademark (which can be unpredictable to say the least!) and you really need to know your law. Copyright issues can also be horrendously complicated."* If one of his publisher clients wanted to buy the rights to a series of books, for example, Carl would have to review the 'title' or chain of ownership of copyright to these literary works, rather like reviewing the title to a piece of land.

Passing off disputes often focus on the get-up and packaging of a product. The Jif lemon case, which turned on the shape of the bottle, is a leading authority in this area. More recently, there's been the ongoing saga of Arsenal v Reed, in which the club tried to prevent a street trader selling unofficial club merchandise.

The internet has also kept IP lawyers busy in the last few years. Cybersquatting (domain name disputes) have become commonplace, and there's little doubt that convergence in telecoms and IT will give rise to even more opportunities for the IP lawyer keen to work for clients in the technology sector.

a day in the life...

In some senses Carl's a jack of all trades. His work involves a multitude of things from advising on the results of basic trademark searches to trademark opposition work (stopping a rival registering a new mark), advising on a worldwide trademark filing strategy and drafting trademark-related agreements, for example sponsorship, endorsement and merchandising contracts. Then there's the excitement of the commencement or defence of trademark infringement procedings. These activities see him working either solo or with a small team of other IP specialists. On the other hand, there are times when he will be called upon to work as a part of a multidisciplinary team on a large corporate transaction. For some companies a portfolio of IP rights is one of the most valuable assets they own and even the humblest of companies will have issues to explore. Carl will have to advise on the IP warranties given or received by the parties to the transaction and perhaps check the title to the rights that are claimed.

Kerry can get caught up in mammoth pan-European pharmaceutical patent infringement cases (like the glaucoma drug litigation she's currently handling for a US pharmaceuticals client), or she can find herself handling a series of smaller non-contentious agreements – patent and trademark licences, Research & Development agreements, assignments of rights and material transfer agreements. Her workload is about 70/30 contentious/non-contentious. Sometimes the big disputes mean getting bogged down for months on end in the preparation of evidence and production of relevant documents (called disclosure), but there are also opportunities to carry out her own advocacy on small pre-trial points.

skills needed

patent law...a basic understanding of science (minimum A-levels; ideally a degree)... aptitude for technical matters and concepts... well-organised... precise drafting...

general IP...curiosity for all things creative, artistic and technological... handle quirky/eccentric/artistic types... interest in the internet... up with consumer trends...

Carl and Kerry illustrate a crucial point very well. He has no science background and has found a career in areas of IP other than patents. On the other hand, Kerry, as a science graduate, has chosen an area of work in which only scientists tend to thrive. *"A lot of scientists who come into law don't like research, those days in a lab plating out bacteria – just horrendous! But with patent law they can use their science background and effectively get a kick-start to their career. As an IP lawyer you're right at the front of scientific developments and you even get to talk to Nobel prize-winners – that's exciting."* She says that hopefully clients can talk to her in the same technical terms as if she were someone junior in their lab.

Drafting skills, precision and accuracy (or as some put it, being *"picky"*) are absolutely crucial, particularly in patent work. It's all about getting beneath the surface of information and being dogged in your assessment of it. Kerry told us she sometimes has to play devil's advocate: *"As a non-expert you must examine the evidence and make sure it makes sense."* Time becomes your enemy. *"The trick is to be precise enough and get everything done in time. Things go incredibly rapidly – imagine having 99 CD-ROMs to look through for relevant documents or a witness statement to produce in less than 24 hours."*

With general IP you'll need to have a good sense of commercial strategy and branding issues and be innovative in the way you think. Ideas and public perceptions, images and symbols will be your stock-in-trade. Maybe in another life you'd have worked in an advertising agency.

Few students know much about IP when they begin their training contracts, which is why many large firms send newly qualifieds on a course in Bristol run by the Intellectual Property Lawyers Association. The residential course counts as half an LL.M and is taught by partners from major IP firms.

career options

If you choose the right firm you'll probably be able to do at least one IP seat during training. Carl says: *"If you want to be a patent litigator you'd be well advised to join a specialist firm... but if you want to go for the publishing/music/ privacy/breach of confidence work then a West End firm may be a better option if you want to work with famous celebrities. Clients like that don't want to pay the fees of a big, City, corporate-oriented law firm. If you want a bit of everything, then go to a large commercial practice with a good IP/media department."* Although IP lawyers in London will tell you that the capital is where it's at, there are other hot spots. The Thames Valley has a concentration of IT companies and Cambridge's 'Silicon Fen' has grown on the back of the hi-tech and biotech companies that have spun out of the university. *Chambers UK* identifies the leading IP practices in the UK and gives details of their particular specialisms and clients.

IP knowledge is valued outside private practice. Manufacturing, pharmaceutical and research companies employ patent specialists and there are in-house legal teams at all the large pharmaceutical companies, for example, Procter & Gamble, Reckitt Benckiser and Unilever. Non-patent lawyers find their way into the media world: all major publishers and television companies have in-house IP lawyers. Many broadcasting companies now employ lawyers in positions such as head of business and legal affairs. Additionally, firms of trademark agents and patent attorneys are often keen to recruit those with a legal training.

LEADING FIRMS FROM CHAMBERS UK 2003-2004

INTELLECTUAL PROPERTY: PATENT LITIGATION ■ LONDON	
1	**Bird & Bird**
	Bristows
2	**Linklaters**
	Simmons & Simmons
	Taylor Wessing
3	**Herbert Smith**
	Lovells
	Wragge & Co LLP
4	**Baker & McKenzie**
	Clifford Chance LLP
	Olswang
5	**Roiter Zucker**

INTELLECTUAL PROPERTY ■ THE SOUTH	
1	**Laytons** Guildford
2	**Blake Lapthorn Linnell** Fareham
	DMH Brighton
3	**Bond Pearce** Southampton
	Lester Aldridge Bournemouth
	Shadbolt & Co Reigate

INTELLECTUAL PROPERTY ■ THAMES VALLEY	
1	**Willoughby & Partners** Oxford
2	**Nabarro Nathanson** Reading
	Olswang Thames Valley Reading
3	**Manches** Oxford
4	**Osborne Clarke** Reading
	Shoosmiths Milton Keynes
	The Law Offices of Marcus J O'Leary Wokingham

INTELLECTUAL PROPERTY ■ SOUTH WEST	
1	**Bevan Ashford bbL** Bristol
	Osborne Clarke Bristol
2	**Beachcroft Wansbroughs** Bristol
	Burges Salmon Bristol
3	**Humphreys & Co Solicitors** Bristol
4	**Laytons** Bristol

INTELLECTUAL PROPERTY ■ WALES	
1	**Edwards Geldard** Cardiff
2	**Eversheds** Cardiff
	Morgan Cole Cardiff

INTELLECTUAL PROPERTY: GENERAL ■ LONDON

1. Bird & Bird
   Taylor Wessing
2. Bristows
   Linklaters
   Simmons & Simmons
3. Baker & McKenzie
   Herbert Smith
   Lovells
   Willoughby & Partners
4. Ashurst Morris Crisp
   Clifford Chance LLP
   Denton Wilde Sapte
   Field Fisher Waterhouse
   Wragge & Co LLP
5. Allen & Overy
   Freshfields Bruckhaus Deringer
   Jones Day Gouldens
   Olswang
   Slaughter and May
6. Addleshaw Goddard
   Briffa
   Hammonds
   Howrey Simon Arnold & White
   Mayer, Brown, Rowe & Maw LLP
   Richards Butler
   Roiter Zucker
   SJ Berwin
   White & Case
   Withers LLP

INTELLECTUAL PROPERTY ■ MIDLANDS

1. **Wragge & Co LLP** Birmingham
2. **Pinsents** Birmingham
3. **Browne Jacobson** Nottingham
   Martineau Johnson Birmingham

INTELLECTUAL PROPERTY ■ EAST ANGLIA

1. **Eversheds** Cambridge
   Mills & Reeve Norwich
2. **Greenwoods** Peterborough
   Taylor Vinters Cambridge
   Taylor Wessing Cambridge

INTELLECTUAL PROPERTY ■ NORTH EAST

1. **Addleshaw Goddard** Leeds
2. **DLA** Leeds
   Eversheds Leeds
   Hammonds Leeds
   Irwin Mitchell Leeds
   Pinsents Leeds
   Walker Morris Leeds
3. **Dickinson Dees** Newcastle upon Tyne
   Lupton Fawcett Leeds

INTELLECTUAL PROPERTY ■ NORTH WEST

1. **Addleshaw Goddard** Manchester
   Halliwell Landau Manchester
2. **DLA** Liverpool, Manchester
   Eversheds Manchester
   Hill Dickinson Liverpool
3. **Berg & Co** Manchester
   Cobbetts Manchester
4. **Hammonds** Manchester
   Kuit Steinart Levy Manchester
   Taylors Blackburn
5. **Pannone & Partners** Manchester

litigation/dispute resolution

If you watched *Ally McBeal* you'd be forgiven for thinking that litigation is all about silver-tongued lawyers cross-examining thin-lipped corporate sharks in neat, hour-long disputes. Think again. Most disputes never reach trial, and as a rule clients aren't interested in having their 'day in court'. Every litigator knows that, almost without exception, the best approach is to reach a commercial settlement quickly and cheaply.

Unless they can be settled by correspondence, disputes are concluded in one of three ways. The first is through litigation itself – the issue and pursuit of court proceedings, which can be expensive and time-consuming. For this reason, contracts often provide for disputes between the parties to be referred to the second method, namely binding arbitrations, which are usually conducted by an expert in the subject matter where it is particularly specialised. Unlike court proceedings, arbitrations are confidential. They are particularly common in the shipping, insurance and construction industries. The third method is Alternative Dispute Resolution (ADR). Although it can take various forms, the most common form of ADR is mediation. This involves structured negotiations between the parties, which are overseen and directed by an independent mediator. Less common forms of ADR include neutral evaluation, expert determination and conciliation. The parties retain the right to litigate if they find it impossible to reach an agreement.

type of work

General commercial litigators handle a variety of business disputes, but most cases will be contractual, encompassing anything from a dispute over the sale of a multimillion pound business to an argument over the meaning of a term in a tenancy agreement. Such so-called generalists might also deal with negligence claims by companies against their professional advisors. Some litigators specialise in certain industry sectors, such as construction, shipping, insurance, property or media; however, the majority of skills will be common to all areas of commercial litigation as will the majority of procedures.

Quite simply, litigation is a process. Once a case has been commenced, it follows a predetermined course laid down by the rules of court: statement of case, disclosure of documents, witness statements, various procedural applications and, in a small number of cases, trial. In a major case this process can take several years. The mutual disclosure of relevant documents can be a particularly protracted and expensive affair despite the Civil Procedure Rules (CPR), which came into force in April 1999 following the Woolf reforms to the civil justice system. Managing this process is the litigator's primary role and this requires not only a mastery of the rules, but also a keen appreciation of tactics and detail.

Opportunities for litigators have increased in the last few years, which is to some extent due to the extension of High Court rights of audience to solicitors. Although solicitors were always entitled to draft statements of case – the formal documents setting out the claimant's claim and the defendant's response – and some even trained to act as advocates in High Court procedural hearings, they rarely did so. Instead such work was normally referred to barristers. However, there is now scope for change. While there hasn't been a flood of solicitor advocates into the High Court, many firms are aiming to keep more advocacy in-house. This phenomenon is particularly marked in the large City firms. Lovells and Herbert Smith, for example, both have advocacy policies whereby solicitor advocates are used in most cases other than major hearings or full trials, while firms like Clifford Chance, Linklaters and Norton

Rose are putting an increasing number of their own solicitors through advocacy training programmes.

Looking more closely at Lovells, its litigators have been encouraged to attain higher rights of audience. The firm went one step further in September 2002, when a three-day advocacy accreditation course was included in the firm's annual foundation training course for newly qualified litigators. Lovells' partner Patrick Sherrington believes that *"It's no more than the natural evolution of the legal market. As restrictive practices have disappeared, there has been a blurring of the edges as to what solicitors and barristers do."* Stephen Brown, a dispute resolution partner at Mayer, Brown, Rowe & Maw, says: *"We're very keen for our junior people to get higher rights and to do their own drafting. Both disciplines – advocacy and case preparation – are crucial to becoming good dispute resolvers."* Stephen thinks that advocacy training can really benefit solicitors: *"It has made us think more like barristers; to think about winnable cases and not just arguable cases."*

The choice to bring in a barrister will be made on a case-by-case basis and will always be a question of what is in the client's best interests. As Patrick says: *"Certainly I'd be happy to appear in many different situations, but would I appear in a highly complex matter where the case would turn on intricate and specialist evidential rules and impeccable cross-examination skills honed over years of higher court advocacy? Of course not – I'd engage an experienced barrister."* It goes without saying that students who are aspiring litigators and are looking to become solicitor advocates should check firms' policies before applying, ie will becoming a solicitor advocate at the firm be possible at all, purely optional, actively encouraged or mandatory? A word of warning though, if you want to advocate non-stop then go to the Bar. Also, specialist litigation practices handling smaller cases will provide greater scope for advocacy than large City firms.

The current economic doldrums have meant that litigators also have an advisory role as clients begin to contemplate their options under contracts that they might have entered into in more prosperous times.

a day in the life...

In a large City firm a qualified litigator may work on just a few big cases at a time. The caseload will probably be more varied in smaller litigation departments. Sarah Armstrong, an associate at Lovells, typically has three to four different cases on the go, all of which are at different stages of the litigation process. There's the factual investigation stage, whereby documents have been sent to her and she needs to work out the key facts. Then there's the stage of calling and meeting with counsel and clients, advising on developments and reviewing the case generally – tactical stuff. Next comes the advocacy element, where mediations, for example, can tie her up for one to two days at a time.

Sarah told us: *"We don't generally go to court all that much as we are dealing with fewer cases, but there are inevitably interlocutory hearings."* This raises an interesting question. When you're starting out as a litigator, is there much opportunity to do your own advocacy? Depending on the firm you're at, the potential is definitely there. The bigger and more valuable the cases your firm takes on, the more likely you are to be a 'cog in the machine' in terms of researching and helping with case preparation rather than doing any advocacy yourself. However, *"You've always got the chance to build up your advocacy experience on pro bono cases and other smaller cases, and you can seize advocacy opportunities in the interlocutory stages of any case."* Sarah also mentions the advocacy required in client meetings. Eh? *"You're explaining points to clients who don't necessarily want to hear the answer. This takes just as much skill – if not more – than when you're advocating in court or at a mediation."* Ah.

As a junior litigator or even a trainee in a firm that handles lower value cases, you'll frequently make undisputed court applications and ask for adjournments, which will enable you to practice your advocacy skills. You'll also be analysing an awful lot of documents, and, as a result, your research and legal analysis skills will develop quickly. The trickier task is then applying the law to all the facts.

skills needed

....drive... commercial awareness... be a tactician... natural toughness... enjoy formulating and articulating arguments... must like to win... assimilate information quickly... think laterally... good negotiator... thick-skinned but still sensitive to clients' needs...

As well as being able to conceive ideas and arguments, you also need to communicate them to your client, counsel or, for junior lawyers, to the partner supervising you. In this respect, as Sarah says: "*The partners you're working with in the early years are really your clients in a way – you're building up their trust so that they'll then let you loose on real clients.*" Sarah's experience is in sharp contrast to the young litigator in firms that handle smaller value cases (eg personal injury claims) in which the activities carried out by megafirm partners would be done by juniors, and full responsiblity for a case is theirs from day one.

Good judgement, instinct and common sense are invaluable. Stephen adds: "*By the time you're one to two years into it, people will be depending on you. I can only read so much of the material on each case and I have to depend on the assistants in my team to read and conclude what they do in terms of case preparation and strategy formulation.*" He also says: "*You can be the brightest person in the world, but if you can't handle criticism or pressure, or you muse indefinitely instead of making decisions, then you'll never make it as a litigator.*" His synopsis of litigation: "*It's about thinking it through, forming a view, making sure it's as watertight as possible and then being prepared to stand up for it.*"

Corporate clients see litigation as part of business risk; they take your advice and pay your fees and they can absorb whatever happens. For private individuals (such as minority shareholders) the impact of litigation on their lives shouldn't be underestimated – it can mean the difference between life going on and ruination. While this leads to important differences in handling the two types of client, both will be concerned with efficiency, good management and costs. It's important to develop good relationships with your clients so that they trust you to make decisions on their behalf. As Stephen says: "*Winning litigation for clients is not just an academic exercise – these are real people.*"

career options

Every commercial firm has a litigation department and some regard it as their primary practice area. The Law Society requires all trainees to undertake contentious work in their training contract and most know within the space of six months whether they click with litigation. We need say no more than that!

If you're looking to be a specialist litigator then experience in the relevant industry sector will help. However, when you're starting out it's probably best to focus on establishing a broad caseload. The consensus amongst our interviewees was that junior litigators should spend a few years – perhaps three to four – building up their general skills and then move into a specialist area. You'll be more marketable as a litigator if you've accumulated general skills from an early stage, as this will ensure you'll be less vulnerable to market trends, particularly in recessionary times. That said, a career in a top-rated niche department or firm is not to be sniffed at.

In-house opportunities are not that common, although banks, insurance, construction and shipping companies sometimes employ specialist litigators. As a rule, only the very largest in-house departments need general commercial litigators. Stephen expresses his preference for private practice well: "*In-house you'll always be a bolt-on to the business, whereas in private practice you are the business.*"

LEADING FIRMS FROM CHAMBERS UK 2003-2004

LITIGATION: GENERAL COMMERCIAL (MEDIUM TEAMS) ■ LONDON

Band	Firm
1	**Eversheds**
	Jones Day Gouldens
	Macfarlanes
	Mayer, Brown, Rowe & Maw LLP
	Stephenson Harwood
2	**Berwin Leighton Paisner**
	Dechert
	Masons
	Nabarro Nathanson
	Nicholson Graham & Jones
	Reynolds Porter Chamberlain
3	**Hammonds**
	Ince & Co
	Kendall Freeman
	Pinsents
	Shook, Hardy & Bacon
	Taylor Wessing
	Watson, Farley & Williams
4	**Addleshaw Goddard**
	Charles Russell
	Lawrence Graham
	Lewis Silkin
	Memery Crystal
	Mishcon de Reya
	Morgan, Lewis & Bockius
	Olswang
	Travers Smith Braithwaite
	White & Case

LITIGATION: GENERAL COMMERCIAL (LARGER TEAMS) ■ LONDON

Band	Firm
1	**Herbert Smith**
2	**Clifford Chance LLP**
	Freshfields Bruckhaus Deringer
3	**Allen & Overy**
	Linklaters
	Lovells
	Slaughter and May
4	**Ashurst Morris Crisp**
	Barlow Lyde & Gilbert
	Norton Rose
	Simmons & Simmons
5	**Baker & McKenzie**
	Clyde & Co
	CMS Cameron McKenna
	Denton Wilde Sapte
	Richards Butler
	SJ Berwin

LITIGATION: GENERAL COMMERCIAL ■ SOUTH WEST

Band	Firm
1	**Burges Salmon** Bristol
	Osborne Clarke Bristol
2	**Beachcroft Wansbroughs** Bristol
	Bevan Ashford EPL Exeter
	Bond Pearce Bristol, Exeter, Plymouth
	TLT Bristol
	Veale Wasbrough Bristol
3	**Bevan Ashford bbl** Bristol
	Clarke Willmott Bristol, Taunton
	Foot Anstey Sargent Exeter, Plymouth
4	**Bevans** Bristol
	BPE Solicitors Cheltenham
	Charles Russell Cheltenham
	Laytons Bristol
	Michelmores Exeter
	Rickerbys Cheltenham

LITIGATION: GENERAL COMMERCIAL ■ THE SOUTH

Band	Firm
1	**Blake Lapthorn Linnell** Fareham
2	**Bond Pearce** Southampton
	Clyde & Co Guildford
	Cripps Harries Hall Tunbridge Wells
	DMH Brighton
	Paris Smith & Randall Southampton
	Thomas Eggar Chichester, Reigate, Worthing
3	**asb law** Crawley, Maidstone
	Brachers Maidstone
	Charles Russell Guildford
	Lester Aldridge Bournemouth
	Stevens & Bolton Guildford
4	**Barlows** Guildford
	Shadbolt & Co Reigate
	Shoosmiths Fareham

LITIGATION: GENERAL COMMERCIAL ■ THAMES VALLEY

1 **Clarks** Reading
Morgan Cole Oxford, Reading
Nabarro Nathanson Reading

2 **Boyes Turner** Reading
Manches Oxford
Pitmans Reading
Shoosmiths Reading

3 **Matthew Arnold & Baldwin** Watford

4 **Henmans** Oxford

LITIGATION: GENERAL COMMERCIAL ■ MIDLANDS

1 **Wragge & Co LLP** Birmingham

2 **Eversheds** Birmingham, Nottingham
Pinsents Birmingham

3 **Hammonds** Birmingham

4 **Gateley Wareing** Birmingham
Lee Crowder Birmingham
Martineau Johnson Birmingham

5 **Browne Jacobson** Nottingham
DLA Birmingham
Freethcartwright LLP Nottingham

6 **Challinors Lyon Clark** West Bromwich
George Green Cradley Heath
Kent Jones and Done Stoke-on-Trent
Moran & Co Tamworth
Shakespeares Birmingham
Shoosmiths Northampton

LITIGATION: GENERAL COMMERCIAL ■ WALES

1 **Edwards Geldard** Cardiff
Eversheds Cardiff
Hugh James Cardiff
Morgan Cole Cardiff

2 **Palser Grossman** Cardiff Bay

LITIGATION: GENERAL COMMERCIAL ■ EAST ANGLIA

1 **Eversheds** Cambridge, Norwich
Mills & Reeve Cambridge, Norwich

2 **Hewitsons** Cambridge
Taylor Vinters Cambridge

3 **Birketts** Ipswich
Greenwoods Peterborough
Howes Percival Norwich
Prettys Ipswich
Steeles Norwich

LITIGATION: GENERAL COMMERCIAL ■ NORTH WEST

1 **Addleshaw Goddard** Manchester
Eversheds Manchester

2 **DLA** Liverpool, Manchester

3 **Brabners Chaffe Street** Liverpool, Preston
Cobbetts Manchester
Halliwell Landau Manchester
Hammonds Manchester
Wacks Caller Manchester

4 **Berg & Co** Manchester
DWF Liverpool, Manchester
Hill Dickinson Liverpool
Pannone & Partners Manchester

5 **Cuff Roberts** Liverpool
Kuit Steinart Levy Manchester
Mace & Jones Liverpool, Manchester
Rowe Cohen Manchester

6 **Davies Arnold Cooper** Manchester
Kershaw Abbott Manchester

LITIGATION: GENERAL COMMERCIAL ■ YORKSHIRE

1 **DLA** Leeds, Sheffield
Eversheds Leeds
Hammonds Leeds

2 **Addleshaw Goddard** Leeds
Pinsents Leeds

3 **Irwin Mitchell** Sheffield
Walker Morris Leeds

4 **Gordons** Bradford, Leeds
Keeble Hawson Leeds
Lupton Fawcett Leeds

5 **Andrew M Jackson** Hull
Brooke North Leeds
Cobbetts Leeds
Nabarro Nathanson Sheffield
Rollits Hull

LITIGATION: GENERAL COMMERCIAL ■ NORTH EAST

1 **Ward Hadaway** Newcastle upon Tyne

2 **Dickinson Dees** Newcastle upon Tyne
Eversheds Newcastle upon Tyne

3 **Hay & Kilner** Newcastle upon Tyne
Robert Muckle Newcastle upon Tyne

4 **Jacksons** Gateshead
Watson Burton Newcastle upon Tyne

media and entertainment

We have divided this section into three categories: advertising and marketing, defamation, and entertainment law.

advertising & marketing

Firms with advertising and marketing clients handle both 'pure' and general advertising law. 'Pure' advertising law focuses on the products or advertisements produced by clients, ensuring the content is legal and appropriate. General advertising law encompasses commercial contracts with suppliers, clients and the rest of the media, as well as corporate transactions, litigation and employment issues as they affect advertising clients.

type of work: Copy clearance lawyers advise clients on ad campaigns for all types of media – TV, radio, poster, internet, etc. Issues include comparative advertising (copy denigrating rivals), unauthorised references to living individuals and parodies of films or TV shows. A thorough understanding of defamation and intellectual property law is essential. Legislation such as the Lotteries and Amusements Act and the Consumer Protection Act feature, and copy clearance work is further governed by regulatory codes such as those of the Advertising Standards Authority (ASA) and Ofcom (which has just taken over from the Independent Television Commission). The lawyer must help the client to say exactly what it wants to say without falling foul of these regulations.

The lawyer may have to defend the client against allegations that their work has infringed the rights of third parties or advise whether an ad should be pulled. This *"can take some nerve,"* according to Brinsley Dresden, a partner at Lewis Silkin, and the action may well go *"right to the wire"* before the third party backs down (if they do at all). At times you may go on the offensive, helping clients to bring complaints about competitors' advertising to the ASA or Ofcom. This may arise when a competitor is 'knocking copy' (making disparaging references to your client's products) or when a competitor is making claims that your client wouldn't be allowed to make.

Brinsley's clients are *"creative and lively individuals – well-educated, intelligent and demanding, but always good fun to deal with."* They want fast and practical advice: *"You can't simply tell people 'no' because often they're committed to a course of action before they speak to you. Often you can only advise them on how to minimise the risks involved."* Rarely is anything black and white; it's about risk management in grey areas and it's up to the lawyer to identify the risks and, if not eliminate them, manage them as best they can.

This is not a dry, document-intensive area of law. By all accounts advertising lawyers simply don't have the time to do hours of research. It's fast in and fast out, which keeps it fresh. *"It's great fun and very satisfying to advise on a TV commercial and then, when you're at home watching TV, suddenly there's your commercial. It's certainly immediate in terms of seeing the results of your labour."*

There isn't a huge demand for these specialist advisors so competition is reasonably tough. While not essential, working in an ad agency prior to training could be a real help, as you'll already know about the culture and how advertising is produced.

defamation

Until they bring back duelling, defamation laws will continue to be used to protect a person's honour and good name. Individuals and organisations can be defamed by written word, which constitutes libel, or by spoken word, which constitutes slander. The majority of actions undertaken in the field are for libel.

type of work: Non-contentious work includes pre-publication or pre-broadcast advice to authors, editors and TV companies. Contentious lawyers act for either claimants (individuals or companies alleging that publishers/broadcasters have damaged their reputation) or defendants. According to Jason McCue, a partner at H2O: *"The first decision to make is whether you want to act for claimants or defendants."* The work is quite different. It's mainly investigative work for defendants as *"there are only so many basic defences to a libel action,"* whereas for claimants *"you've got more control over shaping the action."*

Defamation hinges on questions of personal honour and the right to freedom of expression. Unlike most areas of law, these matter more to clients than money, and consequently clients may insist on their day in court even when they have a near hopeless case. Principles can be expensive.

Clients range from high-profile politicians or pop stars to unknown businessmen. Client contact is likely to begin at junior level and many see it as critical to career progression to build up personal links with clients and in-house lawyers as quickly as possible. But there are important differences between various types of clients. Jason says: *"If you're dealing with a lawyer at a newspaper, rest assured they know what they're talking about; they've done it all before and know all the rules."* By contrast, a pop singer may know nothing about the process. Certain high-profile matters might make you think libel law is all about trials. However, most libel lawyers have only one or two full trials a year, if they're lucky. Like any other type of litigation, most cases settle before they get to the door of the court.

You definitely need to keep up with ever-shifting societal values, and socio-political awareness is crucial, Jason explained. *"People are much more brand-conscious and media-aware these days"* and 'reputation management' is the new buzz phrase.

Nothing is more embarrassing for a media lawyer than if a client rings up and says 'politician X has done something...' and you have to ask not only what party the politician belongs to but also who he or she actually is! You're expected to know these things and be au fait with the latest news and views: *"Otherwise, what right do you have to call yourself a media lawyer?"* In short, listen to the radio, watch the TV, read newspapers...and *Hello!* Previous experience in the media will help, whether it's working on TV documentaries, on newspapers or as a press secretary to an MP. These jobs expose you to research tasks and a conception of *"what's going on in the world."* As Jason says: *"The law is easy to learn. Learning about the media industry can take a lifetime, but you can get a head start by working in it."*

And what of the Human Rights Act? *"It's now gone through its childhood and is starting to bite. It will continue to mature so it's important to come to grips with it. Lawyers weren't sure how it was going to work at first and didn't know what the courts were going to do. But now we have precedents and people are getting more cocky in using it."* Two of the biggies are Article 8 (the right to privacy) and Article 10 (the right to freedom of expression). Regarding privacy, the law is still confused and the two cases of note in the last year – brought by Sara Cox and Catherine Zeta Jones/Michael Douglas – have not clarified matters. Cox settled out of court and the Douglases did not win their claim on privacy grounds.

entertainment

Do you want to be in the world of money or the world of ideas? If you want the former, then become a corporate or banking lawyer. If you want something less institutionalised, entertainment law may just be for you. We have divided this section into film & broadcasting, music, theatre and publishing.

type of work: Clients of all types need contract, employment and litigation advice, and an understanding of commercial law is key to almost everything. Intellectual property is the other main legal discipline you'll need to apply.

film & broadcasting

Look at films or TV programmes as being like any other commercial product. You have to develop the product, finance it, produce it and then sell it. All of these elements require legal advice of one kind or another. The work is a combination of commercial contract law (with an element of banking and secured lending) and the law of copyright. The film lawyer would normally see the process through from start to finish. For just one film production you may have seven different types of finance, four producers and 58 separate agreements to deal with! At the other end of the scale, you might be asked to give swift and concise clearance and classification advice to the British Board of Film Classification.

music

Clients come from all sectors of the music industry, including record labels, production companies, managers and the artists themselves. Some firms lean more towards acting for talent, others for the record labels. Contract work is central to everything. High-profile litigation sometimes arises when there is a dispute over contract terms or ownership of rights in compositions. When band members split with each other or with their management, lawyers are brought in to fight their client's corner in the process of sorting out who is entitled to what. Whether they're specialising in contentious or non-contentious work, music lawyers have to be fully versed in all aspects of copyright as well as contract law. Specialist music firms may also advise on the incorporation and development of new record labels and joint venture agreements between larger and smaller labels.

theatre

There are a few practitioners in London who thrive off the theatrical world. Some work within broader media firms, others in niche outfits that attract clients by virtue of their own reputation. Clients include theatre and opera companies, producers, theatrical agents and actors. Theatre lawyers will spend a lot of time in contract negotiations for their clients; relationships between the constituent parties to a new production all need to be established and regulated through these contracts. A lawyer will usually find himself involved from the inception of the idea for a production right through to the opening curtain and beyond and, increasingly, lawyers will become involved in arrangements for the funding of a new production.

publishing

Work in this sector includes contractual, licensing, copyright and libel advice for newspapers and publishing houses. Most of this is carried out in-house or by libel lawyers, so there are only a few London firms that can be said to specialise in publishing law. An interest in language and literature is an obvious requirement. More and more work is for internet-based publications.

skills needed

...people skills... flexibility... understanding of basic psychology... same outlook and language as clients... understanding how creative people work... *"you need to do a lot of hand-holding"*... patience... prepared to immerse yourself in the industry... a thorough knowledge of contract and copyright law... creativity in problem solving... commercial aptitude... methodical nature... inquisitiveness...

In the early stage of your career you must learn quickly how the industry works; clients value experience. Abigail Payne, a partner at Harbottle & Lewis, explained that clients are creative people looking for commercial solutions. *"This isn't an area where you can just pull out a precedent and fill in the blanks – you actually need a lot of commercial acumen and you need to be innovative."* She also makes the point that *"you're very rarely instructed as to what to do, unlike in the big City firms, where large corporate clients often structure the commercial deals themselves and then instruct lawyers to document them."* Social skills are important: *"There's an awful lot of client development work... Entertainment lawyers at niche firms are expect-*

ed to bring clients in... You need to be creative to do this. For example, I go to American film festivals every year and meet with US producers and financiers. I also go to the Cannes Film Festival." In addition, she gets invited to the premieres of the films she's worked on. Awful!

career options

It's not easy becoming an entertainment lawyer; there aren't many firms that do the work and competition for training contracts is as stiff as it gets. There are two basic routes in – train at a niche entertainment firm or train at a large City firm with a specialism in entertainment. Abigail thinks it's more difficult to move to a City firm after training at an entertainment firm, as City firms are generally looking for someone with a wider commercial background. However, at Harbottle & Lewis, "*We quite often take on people from bigger City firms at the six months to one year-qualified level.*" Remember though, it's an area in which many vacancies will come up by word of mouth. It really is a case of who you know.

Lawyers transfer between private practice and in-house jobs at media and entertainment organisations more readily than they did a few years ago. The money is generally perceived to be better in-house and the hours are considered more favourable – you don't need to go out looking for new clients, for example. In-house legal counsel can come from both specialist media firms and general commercial firms. A lack of stiffness and formality is characteristic of the entertainment industry generally, which often translates through to the working environment. Casual dress, less hierarchy and involvement in a fair degree of non-legal business management tasks can make for a refreshing contrast to the usual experience of a commercial lawyer.

Abigail worked in-house at the BBC for two years after she qualified, handling independent drama financing work. "*The people are more relaxed than in private practice, there's less pressure and you're never scared to ask things. You're given a lot more responsibility. I was the main lawyer involved in financing films with £3-4 million budgets, doing the work of a two-year qualified even though I had just completed a training contract!*" How did the vacancy come up? "*By word of mouth.*" Naturally.

LEADING FIRMS FROM CHAMBERS UK 2003-2004

DEFAMATION/ REPUTATION MANAGEMENT ■ THE REGIONS
1 **Foot Anstey Sargent** Exeter
Wiggin & Co Cheltenham
2 **Brabners Chaffe Street** Liverpool
Cobbetts Manchester
3 **Pannone & Partners** Manchester

MEDIA & ENTERTAINMENT ■ THE REGIONS
1 **Manches** Oxford
McCormicks Leeds
Morgan Cole Cardiff, Swansea
Wiggin & Co Cheltenham

ADVERTISING & MARKETING ■ LONDON

1. Lewis Silkin
   Macfarlanes
   Osborne Clarke
2. The Simkins Partnership
3. Addleshaw Goddard
   Hammonds
   Taylor Wessing
4. Harrison Curtis
   Olswang
5. Lawrence Graham
   Mayer, Brown, Rowe & Maw LLP
6. Baker & McKenzie
   CMS Cameron McKenna
   Field Fisher Waterhouse
   Lovells

DEFAMATION/ REPUTATION MANAGEMENT ■ LONDON

1. Addleshaw Goddard
   Davenport Lyons
   Farrer & Co
   Olswang
   Peter Carter-Ruck and Partners
   Schillings
2. David Price Solicitors & Advocates
   Reynolds Porter Chamberlain
3. Charles Russell
4. Bindman & Partners
   Clifford Chance LLP
   Goodman Derrick
   Lovells
   Mishcon de Reya
   Russell Jones & Walker
   Simons Muirhead & Burton
   Wiggin & Co
5. Finers Stephens Innocent
   Harbottle & Lewis LLP
   Lee & Thompson
   Lewis Silkin
   Richards Butler
   Taylor Wessing

MEDIA & ENTERTAINMENT: FILM FINANCE ■ LONDON

1. Richards Butler
   SJ Berwin
2. Davenport Lyons
   Denton Wilde Sapte
   Olswang
3. Addleshaw Goddard
   The Simkins Partnership

MEDIA & ENTERTAINMENT: FILM & TV PRODUCTION ■ LONDON

1. Olswang
2. Harbottle & Lewis LLP
   Lee & Thompson
3. Davenport Lyons
   Richards Butler
4. Denton Wilde Sapte
   SJ Berwin
   The Simkins Partnership
5. Addleshaw Goddard
   Harrison Curtis
   Simons Muirhead & Burton

MEDIA & ENTERTAINMENT: BROADCASTING ■ LONDON

1. Denton Wilde Sapte
   Olswang
2. Goodman Derrick
   Wiggin & Co
3. Clifford Chance LLP
   Richards Butler
4. Davenport Lyons
   Field Fisher Waterhouse
   Harbottle & Lewis LLP
   Herbert Smith
   SJ Berwin
5. Allen & Overy
   Lovells
   The Simkins Partnership
   Travers Smith Braithwaite

MEDIA & ENTERTAINMENT: PUBLISHING ■ LONDON

1. Denton Wilde Sapte
2. Taylor Wessing
3. Finers Stephens Innocent
   Harbottle & Lewis LLP
   The Simkins Partnership
4. Lovells
   Olswang

MEDIA & ENTERTAINMENT: MUSIC ■ LONDON

1. Russells
2. Clintons
   Lee & Thompson
3. Sheridans
   The Simkins Partnership
4. Addleshaw Goddard
   Bray & Krais
   Davenport Lyons
5. Hamlins
   Harbottle & Lewis LLP
   Mishcon de Reya
6. Eversheds
   Harrison Curtis
   Marriott Harrison
   Searles
   Spraggon Stennett Brabyn

MEDIA & ENTERTAINMENT: THEATRE ■ LONDON

1. Clintons
2. The Simkins Partnership
3. Bates, Wells & Braithwaite
   Harrison Curtis
   Tarlo Lyons
4. Campbell Hooper
   Harbottle & Lewis LLP

personal injury & clinical negligence

PI and clinical negligence firms come in two flavours: claimant and defendant. Firms acting for defendants of personal injury claims act for insurance companies in the main and firms who defend clinical negligence claims represent health authorities, hospital trusts, other public bodies and insurers. Usually a firm with a strong defendant client base will not risk a conflict of interest by taking on claimant cases (which could be against its own client or a potential new client).

type of work

personal injury: PI cases can be small, such as pavement 'slippers and trippers' and whiplash claims arising from road traffic accidents (RTAs). At the other end of the scale are huge multiparty industrial disease claims against large companies. Deafness, diseases resulting from exposure to asbestos, Vibration White Finger (VWF) in miners... sadly there are plenty of examples.

'Lower end' (ie low value and high volume) PI work may be carried out by paralegals and trainees, while qualified solicitors at specialist firms take on more serious cases, such as major road accidents or accidents at work. Legal Aid is no longer available for PI cases, so almost all of the work is undertaken on a conditional fee agreement (CFA). This is what's called 'no win, no fee' and those of you who watch far too much daytime TV will all know the ads! The dramatic demise of Claims Direct and TAG showed how the area is vulnerable to a number of pressures and, indeed, there has been a lot of litigation over the conduct and costs of no win, no fee cases. This type of work involves stringent risk assessment by firms and claims companies before they agree to take on a case, to ensure it has a good enough chance of winning. The Civil Procedure Rules (CPR) have streamlined litigation procedure so that as much preparation and investigation of the claim as is possible takes place before trial. The aim is to promote greater transparency between the parties to ensure settlement is reached in many more cases.

PI work nowadays entails a lot of paperwork. This involves getting to grips with detailed medical reports, drafting witness statements and keeping clients updated on their case. It's not all paper pushing though. The work takes solicitors out of the office to see clients, some of whom may not be able to get out of the house because of their injuries, or perhaps to a conference with a barrister. They may also need to go and investigate the site of an accident or incident.

Defendant personal injury firms work on panels appointed by insurance companies. As the majority of insurance claims fall into the 'lower end' category, this kind of work is the daily staple of defendant firms. However, higher value and law-making cases are of more interest. In 2002, one of the most important cases was *Fairchild v Glenhaven* in which the House of Lords decided that even though it was impossible to decide which of two employers had been responsible for the victim's asbestos-related illness, his widow should be entitled to sue either. Practitioners expect to see mediation and fixed costs schemes impacting more and more on their work in the coming years.

clinical negligence: Quite simply, claimant clients are the victims of medical treatment that went wrong. Action taken on their behalf could be against a hospital or health authority for negligent treatment by one or more of their medical practitioners, or perhaps a pharmaceutical company arising out of the use of unsafe drugs. Additionally, there are public enquiries, such as that into the Bristol heart babies, and cases which involve issues of patient confidentiality, mental health or consent to treatment, for instance where an abortion was performed very close to the legal time limit. The clients, while usually individual claimants, can be a part of a group action (eg MMR). Some firms have professional bodies as their clients. Welsh firm Hugh James, for instance, is on the panel of firms acting for the Royal College of Nursing in claims pertaining to back injuries and stress.

Claimant clinical negligence work necessitates first and foremost building up a rapport with the client. Not only have they suffered great personal tragedy, but they often mistrust professionals, having been let down by the one professional they feel they should most be able to trust – their doctor. As with PI, there's considerable paperwork required in preparation for trial and broadly the same client handling activities.

In 2002 there was a significant change in this area – the streamlining of the number of firms who defend claims against the NHS. The National Health Service Litigation Authority (NHSLA) has a panel of 16 firms to handle all its work. Capsticks is one of these firms and since April 2002 most of its clinical defence work has come from the NHSLA. According to Sarah Stanton, a partner at the firm, the NHSLA runs various schemes rather like an insurance company, but is a part of the NHS and reports to the Department of Health. Consequently the NHSLA won't usually know the particular health professionals involved in the case in question. It is up to the solicitors to get the professionals' views on the case. "*The doctors and nurses involved in the case are witnesses and the solicitor has to make sure they understand the difference between being negligent and not. They often don't realise how much detail is required during the case.*"

The spiralling costs of negligence claims against the NHS prompted the Government's Chief Medical Officer to propose a number of changes. These include the mediation of more claims, the creation of a National Patient Safety Agency to help record and root out the causes of claims, and the 'Resolve' scheme that was piloted in England to deal more cost effectively with cases worth less than £15,000. Practitioners are also looking towards the formalisation of structured settlements and the periodic payment of costs rather than large lump sum payments to claimants.

a day in the life...

Sarah will typically start her day with her postbag and a bit of general admin. She'll spend the greater part of the morning on 'heavy duty' paper work, such as drafting a witness statement or an advisory report to a client, although there are always a number of phone calls that interrupt the flow. The afternoon is filled with routine correspondence, chasing people for information, updating clients etc. and there may well be a meeting with the rest of her team to discuss one of their cases. Part of one day a week will be spent out of the office either at court or visiting witnesses – the doctors and nurses. Once or twice a month there will be an evening case conference with a barrister.

Life as a trainee is rewarding. Working under Sarah you would be "*fully involved... you can expect to be part of the team in a true sense and make a valuable contribution.*" The standard trainee job is research, which may be into medical matters, duty of care, procedure or quantum (the level of damages the claimant should get). There is no escaping preparing trial bundles for any trainee in contentious work, but more interesting work might involve drafting instructions to an expert witness. Advocacy is also greatly encouraged for trainees so, if on a claimant case, you could expect to make an application to court, for instance to approve the level of damages to be made to a child claimant.

skills needed

...confidence in your own decisions... communication skills... good bedside manner... clear and logical thinker... sympathy for client... eye for detail... firm negotiator... interest in medical issues... interest in people... tact with professionals (they don't like being criticised!)... calm... organised...

Lawyers in this area, like any other, must have an eye for detail. More importantly, says Sarah, because the work involves wading through swathes of medical documents, you learn to expect the unexpected. *"A document can seem insignificant, then it gets to trial and it's really significant."* A medical background is not necessary and although *"it helps in the early days, you do pick up the knowledge along the way."* That said, leading clinical negligence practices often have their fair share of former medical professionals. It's not an ideal practice area if you are squeamish as the facts of some cases can be harrowing. It can be an incredibly stressful area, but does not provide the massive financial compensations of City firms. Simply put, money is not what motivates solicitors in this area.

Trainees learn to stand on their own two feet quickly. According to Stephen Webber, an assistant solicitor at Hugh James, the biggest difference between this kind of work and commercial work is that rather than having the partner make all the decisions, a trainee handling a PI caseload makes their own decisions on a daily basis.

It can be difficult remaining detached from the client when a case takes three or four years and the relationship becomes more intense as you near trial. To overcome this difficulty, *"you have to focus on proving the case and getting the best result."* But a sense of great personal reward can come from the intensity of the relationship: *"The defendant is generally insured and can get the best advice. The claimant isn't and often doesn't understand the legal process. You can help them get justice using your professional training."* Stephen told us: *"The serious cases do motivate you. When you see a claimant who's been treated badly, they do deserve to be compensated. Getting them compensation means there's one less thing for them to worry about and it gives them closure."*

Ann Alexander, managing partner of Alexander Harris, loves her work most of all because she not only makes a difference to one person's life, but can also change the system. Since she took on and won a case involving patients who were awake but paralysed under anaesthetic, she says, *"there has been a complete rethink on training anaesthetists and preventing this happening again. They have developed a method of testing if people are awake. Things have changed in healthcare due to our work."*

career options

Sarah and Stephen trained in firms that carried out PI and clinical negligence work. Things were a bit different for Ann, who started off doing general high street contentious work, such as hearings in Magistrates' Courts and care proceedings. The reason she took on her first clinical negligence case is that she was recommended as a solicitor who would listen! The best start in this area is to gain a coveted training contract at one of the specialist firms. An alternative route in is applying for a paralegal position after your degree and LPC and to show the firm just what you can do. Alexander Harris and Hodge Jones & Allen recruit lots of their trainees from their paralegal departments, but still look for a 2:1, such is the competition for places.

After training there are few opportunities outside private practice. Some lawyers move in-house to the NHSLA or other defence organisations, such as the Medical Defence Union. Stephen has diversified his work by taking on PI-related cases with a human rights aspect. He saw his practice take on a new dimension recently when he won a Court of Appeal case pertaining to psychological damage suffered by a mother who witnessed the misdiagnosis and subsequent death of her baby in hospital.

PI and clinical negligence lawyers tend to stay with the job. As they gain experience, the cases they handle become more serious. Ultimately, this could mean class actions, breaking law, and managing matters in the glare of the media spotlight. You can see the appeal – even to a lawyer with hundreds of cases under their belt already. The trend for work to flow to larger, specialist practices rather than high street PI/clin neg dabblers is likely to continue.

LEADING FIRMS FROM CHAMBERS UK 2003-2004

PERSONAL INJURY: MAINLY CLAIMANT ■ LONDON

1 **Irwin Mitchell**
Leigh, Day & Co
Stewarts

2 **Field Fisher Waterhouse**

3 **Alexander Harris**
Russell Jones & Walker

4 **Evill and Coleman**
Pattinson & Brewer
Rowley Ashworth
Thompsons

5 **Anthony Gold**
Hodge Jones & Allen
O H Parsons & Partners

6 **Bolt Burdon**

PERSONAL INJURY: MAINLY DEFENDANT ■ LONDON

1 **Barlow Lyde & Gilbert**
Beachcroft Wansbroughs

2 **Berrymans Lace Mawer**
Kennedys
Vizards Wyeth

3 **Davies Arnold Cooper**
Davies Lavery
Greenwoods

4 **Plexus Law**
Watmores

PERSONAL INJURY: MAINLY CLAIMANT ■ THE SOUTH

1 **Lamport Bassitt** Southampton
Thomson Snell & Passmore TunbridgeWells

2 **George Ide, Phillips** Chichester
Moore & Blatch Southampton

3 **Shoosmiths** Basingstoke

PERSONAL INJURY: MAINLY DEFENDANT ■ THE SOUTH

1 **Beachcroft Wansbroughs** Winchester
Berrymans Lace Mawer Southampton
Clarke Willmott Southampton
Davies Lavery Maidstone

2 **Bond Pearce** Southampton
Palser Grossman Southampton

PERSONAL INJURY: MAINLY CLAIMANT ■ THAMES VALLEY

1 **Boyes Turner** Reading
Osborne Morris & Morgan Leighton Buzzard

2 **Thring Townsend** Swindon

3 **Harris Cartwright** Slough

4 **Fennemores** Milton Keynes
Field Seymour Parkes Reading

PERSONAL INJURY: MAINLY DEFENDANT ■ THAMES VALLEY

1 **Morgan Cole** Reading

2 **Henmans** Oxford

PERSONAL INJURY: MAINLY CLAIMANT ■ SOUTH WEST

1 **Bond Pearce** Plymouth

2 **Lyons Davidson** Bristol
Veale Wasbrough Bristol

3 **Rowley Ashworth** Exeter
Thompsons Bristol, Plymouth

PERSONAL INJURY: MAINLY DEFENDANT ■ SOUTH WEST

1 **Beachcroft Wansbroughs** Bristol

2 **Veitch Penny** Exeter

3 **Bond Pearce** Bristol
Cartwrights Insurance Partners Bristol

4 **Bevan Ashford BBL** Bristol

PERSONAL INJURY: MAINLY CLAIMANT ■ WALES

1 **Hugh James** Cardiff
Leo Abse & Cohen Cardiff

2 **John Collins & Partners** Swansea
Thompsons Cardiff

3 **Edwards Geldard** Cardiff
Loosemores Cardiff
Russell Jones & Walker Cardiff

PERSONAL INJURY: MAINLY DEFENDANT ■ WALES

1 **Hugh James** Cardiff
Morgan Cole Cardiff

2 **Palser Grossman** Cardiff Bay

3 **Dolmans** Cardiff

4 **Douglas-Jones Mercer** Swansea

PERSONAL INJURY: MAINLY CLAIMANT ■ MIDLANDS

1. **Irwin Mitchell** Birmingham
2. **Rowley Ashworth** Birmingham, Wolverhampton
   Thompsons Birmingham
3. **Alexander Harris** Solihull
   Barratt, Goff & Tomlinson Nottingham
   Freethcartwright LLP Nottingham
   Russell Jones & Walker Birmingham
4. **Flint, Bishop & Barnett** Derby
   Higgs & Sons Stourbridge

PERSONAL INJURY: MAINLY DEFENDANT ■ MIDLANDS

1. **Beachcroft Wansbroughs** Birmingham
   Buller Jeffries Birmingham
   Weightman Vizards Birmingham Leicester
2. **Browne Jacobson** Nottingham
3. **DLA** Birmingham
   Everatt & Company Evesham
   Keoghs Coventry
   Palser Grossman Birmingham

PERSONAL INJURY: MAINLY CLAIMANT ■ EAST ANGLIA

1. **Cunningham John** Thetford
2. **Morgan Jones & Pett** Great Yarmouth
   Taylor Vinters Cambridge
3. **Edwards Duthie** Ilford
   Leathes Prior Norwich

PERSONAL INJURY: MAINLY DEFENDANT ■ EAST ANGLIA

1. **Eversheds** Ipswich
   Mills & Reeve Norwich
2. **Prettys** Ipswich
3. **Edwards Duthie** Ilford
   Kennedys Brentwood

PERSONAL INJURY: MAINLY CLAIMANT ■ NORTH WEST

1. **Pannone & Partners** Manchester
2. **Leigh, Day & Co** Manchester
   Thompsons Liverpool, Manchester
3. **Donns Solicitors** Manchester
   Hugh Potter & Company Manchester
   John Pickering & Partners Manchester, Oldham
   Russell Jones & Walker Manchester
4. **Linder Myers** Manchester

MAINLY DEFENDANT ■ NORTH WEST

1. **James Chapman & Co** Manchester
2. **Berrymans Lace Mawer** Liverpool, Manchester
   Keoghs Bolton
   Weightman Vizards Liverpool, Manchester
3. **Beachcroft Wansbroughs** Manchester
   Halliwell Landau Manchester
   Hill Dickinson Liverpool, Manchester

PERSONAL INJURY: MAINLY CLAIMANT ■ YORKSHIRE

1. **Irwin Mitchell** Leeds, Sheffield
2. **Russell Jones & Walker** Leeds, Sheffield
3. **Morrish & Co** Leeds
   Pattinson & Brewer York
   Rowley Ashworth Leeds
4. **Bridge McFarland Solicitors** Grimsby

PERSONAL INJURY: MAINLY DEFENDANT ■ YORKSHIRE

1. **Beachcroft Wansbroughs** Leeds
   DLA Sheffield
2. **Nabarro Nathanson** Sheffield
3. **Eversheds** Leeds
   Irwin Mitchell Leeds, Sheffield
   Keeble Hawson Leeds, Sheffield
   Langleys York
   Praxis Partners Leeds

PERSONAL INJURY: MAINLY CLAIMANT ■ NORTH EAST

1. **Thompsons** Newcastle upon Tyne
2. **Browell Smith & Co** Newcastle upon Tyne
   Hay & Kilner Newcastle upon Tyne
   Marrons Newcastle upon Tyne
3. **Beecham Peacock** Newcastle upon Tyne
   Gorman Hamilton Solicitors Newcastle upon Tyne
   Russell Jones & Walker Newcastle upon Tyne

PERSONAL INJURY: MAINLY DEFENDANT ■ NORTH EAST

1. **Eversheds** Newcastle upon Tyne
   Jacksons Stockton on Tees
2. **Crutes Law Firm** Newcastle upon Tyne
   Hay & Kilner Newcastle upon Tyne
   Sinton & Co Newcastle upon Tyne

CLIN NEG: MAINLY CLAIMANT ■ LONDON

1 **Leigh, Day & Co**

2 **Irwin Mitchell**

3 **Alexander Harris**
Kingsley Napley
Parlett Kent

4 **Bindman & Partners**
Charles Russell
Evill and Coleman
Field Fisher Waterhouse
Russell Jones & Walker

CLIN NEG: MAINLY DEFENDANT ■ LONDON

1 **Capsticks**

2 **Hempsons**

3 **Bevan Ashford BBL**

4 **Kennedys**
RadcliffesLeBrasseur
Weightman Vizards

CLIN NEG: MAINLY CLAIMANT ■ THE SOUTH

1 **Blake Lapthorn Linnell** Portsmouth
Thomson Snell & Passmore Tunbridge Wells

2 **Penningtons** Godalming
Wynne Baxter Brighton

3 **Moore & Blatch** Southampton

CLIN NEG: MAINLY DEFENDANT ■ THE SOUTH

1 **Beachcroft Wansbroughs** Winchester

2 **Brachers** Maidstone

CLIN NEG: MAINLY CLAIMANT ■ SOUTH WEST

1 **Barcan Woodward** Bristol
Parlett Kent Exeter

2 **Clarke Willmott** Bristol
Preston Goldburn Falmouth
Withy King Bath
Wolferstans Plymouth

3 **John Hodge & Co** Weston-super-Mare

4 **Over Taylor Biggs** Exeter

CLIN NEG: MAINLY DEFENDANT ■ SOUTH WEST

1 **Bevan Ashford BBL** Bristol

2 **Beachcroft Wansbroughs** Bristol

CLIN NEG: MAINLY CLAIMANT ■ THAMES VALLEY

1 **Boyes Turner** Reading

2 **Osborne Morris & Morgan** Leighton Buzzard

3 **Harris Cartwright** Slough

CLIN NEG: MAINLY CLAIMANT ■ WALES

1 **Huttons** Cardiff

2 **Hugh James** Cardiff

3 **Harding Evans** Newport
John Collins & Partners Swansea

4 **Edwards Geldard** Cardiff

CLIN NEG: MAINLY DEFENDANT ■ WALES

1 **RadcliffesLeBrasseur** Cardiff

CLIN NEG: MAINLY CLAIMANT ■ MIDLANDS

1 **Anthony Collins Solicitors** Birmingham
Challinors Lyon Clark Birmingham
Freethcartwright LLP Nottingham
Irwin Mitchell Birmingham

2 **Alexander Harris** Solihull
Brindley Twist Tafft & James Coventry

CLIN NEG: MAINLY DEFENDANT ■ MIDLANDS

1 **Browne Jacobson** Birmingham

2 **Bevan Ashford BBL** Birmingham
Weightman Vizards Birmingham, Leicester

CLIN NEG: MAINLY CLAIMANT ■ EAST ANGLIA

1 **Cunningham John** Thetford

2 **Attwater & Liell** Harlow
Gadsby Wicks Chelmsford
Scrivenger Seabrook St Neots

3 **Morgan Jones & Pett** Great Yarmouth

CLIN NEG: MAINLY DEFENDANT ■ EAST ANGLIA

1 **Kennedys** Newmarket

CLIN NEG: MAINLY CLAIMANT ■ NORTH WEST

1 **Alexander Harris** Altrincham
Pannone & Partners Manchester

2 **JMW Solicitors** Manchester

3 **Edwards Abrams Doherty** Liverpool
Leigh, Day & Co Manchester
Linder Myers Manchester

4 **Donns Solicitors** Manchester
Maxwell Gillott Lancaster

CLIN NEG: MAINLY DEFENDANT ■ NORTH WEST

1 **Hempsons** Manchester
Hill Dickinson Liverpool

2 **George Davies Solicitors** Manchester

CLIN NEG: MAINLY CLAIMANT ■ YORKSHIRE

1 **Irwin Mitchell** Sheffield

2 **Lester Morrill** Leeds

3 **Heptonstalls** Goole

CLIN NEG: MAINLY DEFENDANT ■ YORKSHIRE

1 **Hempsons** Harrogate

CLIN NEG: MAINLY CLAIMANT ■ NORTH EAST

1 **Peter Maughan & Co** Gateshead
Samuel Phillips & Co Newcastle upon Tyne

2 **Ben Hoare Bell** Sunderland
Hay & Kilner Newcastle upon Tyne

CLIN NEG: MAINLY DEFENDANT ■ NORTH EAST

1 **Eversheds** Newcastle upon Tyne

2 **Ward Hadaway** Newcastle upon Tyne

private client

Private client lawyers act for individuals, families, trusts and charities, as opposed to corporate entities. The work that falls under the 'private client' banner will vary depending on the type of firm you join. In a high street firm, your clients may be any member of the public, regardless of wealth or background; in a central London firm, clients are most likely to be wealthy (aka high net worth individuals). A general private client lawyer will advise on the acquisition, disposal and management of the personal assets of individuals and families, some will even handle matrimonial matters. Some focus on specialist tax and trusts advice plus wills and probate, and a few will branch out related areas of work such as heritage property and charities law. In most cases, the work is primarily advisory, although litigation is on the increase.

type of work

trusts, probate and personal tax: Few people stumble into private client work by accident. You'll probably already know you're more interested in working for and helping individuals rather than faceless corporations, and you'll probably feel inclined towards trusts and related subjects at college.

Trusts are a popular way of holding assets and avoiding tax. They allow family members to access funds, while enabling the donor to retain a degree of control over the funds' ultimate destination. Many students find trusts law a bit turgid, and if you're one of them, private client may not be your cup of tea – there is an awful lot of law involved. Often trusts are most effectively held in an offshore jurisdiction, in which case this requires the lawyer to apprise his client of the system of law behind the trust to ensure he understands the foreign law implications. As well as handling offshore trusts in conjunction with overseas lawyers and trust companies, lawyers advise an increasing number of overseas clients seeking to invest in the UK. Offshore and private banks may also need advice about their clients' UK interests.

The private client solicitor is necessarily a party to very personal information – private details of family circumstances and finances – about his clients, and must be able to listen to without being judgemental. Impartiality is essential: the solicitor must simply offer sound, practical advice and respect the clients' privacy. Chris Belcher, a solicitor at Farrer & Co, points out: "*You have to be able to step back and maintain a professional, objective point of view.*"

Will drafting and probate – the management of a deceased's affairs – form a significant part of the work. From early on, as a young lawyer you can get very involved in this work, handling your own small files. Chris noted that the work is much more hands-on from day one, and while your friends in the corporate department might be paginating and bundling, you will be drafting wills and handling the practical aspects of a client's affairs, such as organising house clearances and shipping furniture – this is where all that black letter law gets balanced out with common sense, and the true variety of the work becomes apparent.

charities: This related area of practice would see you acting for clients from well-known national charities to lower-profile and local, private charitable trusts. Work consists of charity registrations and reorganisations, Charity Commission investigations, the development of trading subsidiaries and advising charitable clients on other issues, such as tax, trusts or property matters. Many firms, especially the smaller ones, frequently specialise in advising particular types of organisation, for example religious, educational or environmental charities. Plenty of charities law is quasi-corporate in nature, so if you are torn between private clients and commercial clients, charities law could be ideal for you.

heritage property: Heritage work involves handling a variety of issues relating to heritage chattels – individual items or collections that may be of cultural value or significance. The work involves organising export licences, arranging loans or sales of specific artworks or collections, and providing the tax planning related to the ownership of such property. Chris explained: *"Even though you may be looking at a boring trust law point, the subject matter is very interesting."* One day he found himself helping to carry valuable works of art into a meeting at the National Gallery, something no banking or corporate lawyer could ever aspire to in the normal course of business.

skills needed

...common sense... lateral thinking... communication and people skills... pragmatism... objectivity... organised mind... curiosity... eye for detail... desire to help people... good bedside manner...

Private client lawyers are often thought of as the archetypal old-fashioned 'man of affairs', but Chris pointed out that the image of the *"Jack of all trades, who is on the golf course on Friday afternoons"* is changing. While this type of law doesn't have the same stresses of the fast and furious deals and rapid deadlines of corporate work, it demands other, equally important skills. Even without strict deadlines, time-management and the ability to prioritise are vital. Likewise, with all that tax and accounts work, it helps to be numerate, though *"you don't have to be Einstein!"* Private client work can be technical and you have to be interested in the academic side, but practical skills and a personable nature are equally important.

Private client departments are not the best places to flex macho muscles, but if people and their personal affairs are what make you tick you'll be in your element. However, if it's a glamorous, jet-setting, champagne-fuelled career you are after, private client work probably isn't for you. While it is not all little old ladies, and some clients can be famous or important individuals, *"this is not really very sexy work."* But remember; no matter how exciting your clients are, the highly confidential nature of the work means you won't be able to namedrop with your mates in the pub.

Chris was very clear that *"there is no typical lawyer as there is no typical client."* They are not all Colonel Snooty and Lady Farquhar-Farquharson; more and more clients have made their money through property, business or even a lottery win, so a public school education and country retreat are not essential.

career options

Most private client lawyers spend their entire career in private practice, some specialising in international clients; others in UK clients. Training at an established private client firm, such as Withers, Farrer & Co or Boodle Hatfield, will give the very best possible start. City firms such as Allen & Overy and Macfarlanes have continued to offer these services, allowing trainees to combine private client work with a corporate training. But there are excellent private client practices all over the country, and although moves between the high street and the firms servicing wealthy individuals are not that common, either kind of training will set you up well for provincial practice.

In the 1990s, large commercial firms shed private client departments, but the area is now experiencing growth again and three new Trustee Acts in the last few years have seen the sector evolving. Additionally, general trends in the way families are organised and greater life expectancy are each having an impact. In-house opportunities are limited, although a few offshore trust companies and private banks do have their own legal advisors, and banks in, say, the Bahamas, Cayman Islands and Channel Islands employ lawyers in advisory or risk control positions. Those who want to spend time in an offshore, tropical haven will find job ads offering positions.

For charities specialists there is less scope in terms of specialist law firms, but they do exist. With the opportunity to make strong contacts with clients, there is always the possibility of moving into a more general role within the charities sector. For details of the leading private client and charities firms, refer to *Chambers UK*.

LEADING FIRMS FROM CHAMBERS UK 2003-2004

TRUSTS & PERSONAL TAX ■ LONDON

1 Macfarlanes
Withers LLP

2 Allen & Overy
Charles Russell
Currey & Co
Lawrence Graham

3 Baker & McKenzie
Boodle Hatfield
Farrer & Co
Forsters
Payne Hicks Beach
Speechly Bircham
Taylor Wessing

4 Berwin Leighton Paisner
Bircham Dyson Bell
Harcus Sinclair
Hunters
Linklaters
May, May & Merrimans
Nicholson Graham & Jones
Simmons & Simmons

5 Collyer-Bristow
Davenport Lyons
Dawsons
Herbert Smith
Howard Kennedy
Lee & Pembertons
RadcliffesLeBrasseur
Rooks Rider
Smyth Barkham
Stephenson Harwood
Trowers & Hamlins
Wedlake Bell

TRUSTS & PERSONAL TAX ■ WALES

1 Edwards Geldard Cardiff
Hugh James Cardiff

2 Margraves Llandrindod Wells

TRUSTS & PERSONAL TAX: CONTENTIOUS ■ LONDON

1 Allen & Overy
Baker & McKenzie
Berwin Leighton Paisner
Boodle Hatfield
Charles Russell
Clifford Chance LLP
Farrer & Co
Herbert Smith
Lawrence Graham
Laytons
Macfarlanes
Norton Rose
Withers LLP

TRUSTS & PERSONAL TAX ■ THAMES VALLEY

1 Boodle Hatfield Oxford

2 B P Collins Gerrards Cross
Blandy & Blandy Reading
Boyes Turner Reading
Henmans Oxford, Woodstock
Iliffes Booth Bennett (IBB) Chesham, Ingatestone
Matthew Arnold & Baldwin Watford

3 Penningtons Newbury
Pictons Hemel Hempstead, Central Milton Keynes
Stanley Tee Bishops Stortford

TRUSTS & PERSONAL TAX ■ NORTH WEST

1 Halliwell Landau Manchester

2 Addleshaw Goddard Manchester
Birch Cullimore Chester
Brabners Chaffe Street Liverpool
Cobbetts Manchester
Cuff Roberts Liverpool
Pannone & Partners Manchester

TRUSTS & PERSONAL TAX ■ THE SOUTH

1 Cripps Harries Hall Tunbridge Wells
Thomas Eggar Chichester, Horsham

2 Paris Smith & Randall Southampton
Penningtons Godalming
Stevens & Bolton Guildford
Thomson Snell & Passmore Tunbridge Wells

3 Adams & Remers Lewes
Blake Lapthorn Linnell Portsmouth
Brachers Maidstone
Charles Russell Guildford
DMH Brighton
Lester Aldridge Bournemouth
Moore & Blatch Lymington
Mundays Cobham
White & Bowker Winchester

4 Barlows Guildford
Buss Murton Tunbridge Wells
Godwins Winchester
Griffith Smith Brighton
Rawlison Butler Crawley
Whitehead Monckton Maidstone

TRUSTS & PERSONAL TAX ■ MIDLANDS

1 Martineau Johnson Birmingham

2 Browne Jacobson Nottingham
Hewitsons Northampton
Higgs & Sons Brierley Hill
Lodders Stratford-upon-Avon

3 Lee Crowder Birmingham
Pinsents Birmingham
Wragge & Co LLP Birmingham

4 Edwards Geldard Derby, Nottingham
Freethcartwright LLP Nottingham
Gateley Wareing Birmingham
Hallmarks Worcester
Shakespeares Birmingham

TRUSTS & PERSONAL TAX ■ SOUTH WEST

1 **Burges Salmon** Bristol
Wilsons Salisbury

2 **Charles Russell** Cheltenham
Osborne Clarke Bristol
Wiggin & Co Cheltenham

3 **Bond Pearce** Plymouth
Foot Anstey Sargent Exeter, Plymouth

4 **Clarke Willmott** Bristol, Taunton
Hooper & Wollen Torquay
Michelmores Exeter, Sidmouth

5 **Coodes** St Austell
Rickerbys Cheltenham
TLT Bristol
Veale Wasbrough Bristol

TRUSTS & PERSONAL TAX ■ EAST ANGLIA

1 **Mills & Reeve** Cambridge, Norwich

2 **Hewitsons** Cambridge
Willcox & Lewis Norwich
Taylor Vinters Cambridge

3 **Greene & Greene** Bury St Edmunds
Howes Percival Norwich

4 **Ashton Graham** Bury St Edmunds, Ipswich
Birketts Ipswich
Cozens-Hardy & Jewson Norwich
Hansells Norwich
Hood Vores & Allwood Dereham
Prettys Ipswich
Roythorne & Co Spalding
Wollastons Chelmsford

CHARITIES ■ THE SOUTH

1 **Blake Lapthorn Linnell** Portsmouth

2 **Griffith Smith** Brighton
Thomson Snell & Passmore Tunbridge Wells

3 **Barlows** Guildford
Cripps Harries Hall Tunbridge Wells
Lester Aldridge Bournemouth
Thomas Eggar Chichester

TRUSTS & PERSONAL TAX ■ NORTH EAST

1 **Dickinson Dees** Newcastle upon Tyne
Wrigleys Leeds, Sheffield

2 **Addleshaw Goddard** Leeds
Pinsents Leeds, Sheffield

3 **Andrew M Jackson** Hull
Grays York
Irwin Mitchell Sheffield

4 **Gordons** Leeds
Lupton Fawcett Leeds
Rollits Hull
Ward Hadaway Newcastle upon Tyne

CHARITIES ■ LONDON

1 **Bates, Wells & Braithwaite**
Farrer & Co

2 **Withers LLP**

3 **Nabarro Nathanson**
Russell-Cooke
Stone King

4 **Allen & Overy**
Berwin Leighton Paisner
Bircham Dyson Bell
Claricoat Phillips

5 **Campbell Hooper**
Charles Russell
RadcliffesLeBrasseur

6 **CMS Cameron McKenna**
Harbottle & Lewis LLP
Hempsons
Herbert Smith
Lawrence Graham
Macfarlanes
Speechly Bircham
Trowers & Hamlins
Winckworth Sherwood

CHARITIES ■ THAMES VALLEY

1 **Blake Lapthorn Linnell** Oxford
Henmans Oxford

2 **BrookStreet Des Roches** Witney
Manches Oxford
Winckworth Sherwood Oxford

CHARITIES ■ THE SOUTH WEST

1 **Stone King** Bath

2 **Osborne Clarke** Bristol

3 **Burges Salmon** Bristol
Rickerbys Cheltenham
Wilsons Salisbury

4 **Bond Pearce** Plymouth
Foot Anstey Sargent Exeter
Thring Townsend Bath
Tozers Exeter
Veale Wasbrough Bristol

CHARITIES ■ MIDLANDS

1 **Anthony Collins Solicitors** Birmingham
Martineau Johnson Birmingham

2 **Lee Crowder** Birmingham
Wragge & Co LLP Birmingham

3 **Pinsents** Birmingham

CHARITIES ■ EAST ANGLIA

1 **Mills & Reeve** Norwich
Taylor Vinters Cambridge

2 **Greenwoods** Peterborough
Hewitsons Cambridge

CHARITIES ■ NORTH WEST

1 **Brabners Chaffe Street** Liverpool
Halliwell Landau Manchester
Oswald Goodier & Co Preston

2 **Birch Cullimore** Chester
Pannone & Partners Manchester

CHARITIES ■ NORTH EAST

1 **Wrigleys** Leeds

2 **Dickinson Dees** Newcastle upon Tyne
Rollits York

3 **Addleshaw Goddard** Leeds

4 **Grays** York
Irwin Mitchell Sheffield
McCormicks Leeds

property/real estate

Let's face facts, most students find land law simply dull, dull, dull. Why on earth would anyone choose to become a property lawyer? There's one fairly simple reason: property work involves real projects – things you can actually touch and real people, who you deal with right from the get go. Forget Re: Vandervell's Trusts, think of developing a new cinema in Leicester Square or converting an old factory site into a residential complex. Property deals are big, fat and tangible and, if you like, you can go and walk around in them. As Sophie Hamilton, senior partner at leading property firm Forsters, says: *"I don't understand Eurobonds and Futures other than in an intellectual way. I can't get hold of them in my hand and I wouldn't get excited about a 90-page document dealing with them, but properties are real."*

There's another simple reason why some trainees have a Road to Damascus experience with property – you get buckets of client contact from an early stage, handle your own cases and make a real difference from the outset. It appeals to those with a sense of independence. Wragge & Co associate, Mark Chester, dispelled the dull as ditch water myth: *"Don't be frightened off by the crap you go through at university and law school. Messrs. Megarry and Wade are enough to send you into a coma, but practice is different."*

type of work

Work is divided between transactional matters and one-off management advice. Sophie gave us some examples of the sort of non-transactional advice clients may need: *"The owner of an investment property might ring and say 'Enron have just gone bust and we let them a large amount of office space 18 months ago. What do we do now?' Or the occupier of a small property might ring and say, 'Someone's just dumped a skip in my yard? How do I get rid of it?'"* When does a Eurobonds lawyer ever have to deal with a skip load of anything?

Most work is transactional and the best-informed property lawyers are those who keep themselves apprised of what's going on in the industry – the movers, the shakers and the deals. They are more likely to be reading *Property Week* and *The Estates Gazette* than Megarry and Wade. In the first couple of years, you'll learn how to do *"bog standard"* work – sales and purchases, leases and transfers of leases, consents for the alteration or subletting of buildings. Mark told us that it's important to learn the basics inside and out before stepping up into more specialised work. Even the deals at *"the pointy end"* strip back to the fundamentals of the basic deals you cut your teeth on.

Across the country, most property lawyers act for a wide variety of clients: homeowners, small business tenants, landlords, investors and banks. They see the property market from all angles and must be able to champion the cause of these different parties. A varied workload is part of the appeal for many, but it does mean that the lawyer must continually adapt his or her style of communication and advice to suit the client. Only in the very largest firms will the property solicitor be pigeonholed into acting for just one type of client – usually large investors or banks. For Sophie: *"The most interesting clients are the developers; entrepreneurs who are coming up with the deals and the new projects."* Mark agrees with her.

Property lawyers need to keep on top of changes in the law. To illustrate this, we need only to look at a brand new way of owning land that will follow after commonhold legislation comes into effect at the end of 2003. Neil Toner, a partner in Lewis Silkin's property department, told us: *"It's a fundamental change in land law The property industry has been talking about it for years, but now it's actually happening."* As well as understanding how this new 'third way' of owning land actually works, lawyers will have to respond very quickly to the market's reaction. "*In residential property we think it will be hugely popular,*" Neil said. "*Commercial property developers are less aware of its potential. That means property lawyers need to be more clued up on what commonhold offers, so that they can advise clients of the range of options available when structuring development schemes.*" Whatever the response from the market, practitioners will have to abandon some very long-held legal principles for some very new ones.

Arguably, the fundamental decision to be made is between being a litigator and a commercial lawyer. Having chosen the latter, becoming a property lawyer simply means that you chose a job where deals are centred on land and buildings instead of, say, company shares (or maybe those Eurobonds). Certainly, the property lawyer's job will touch upon various other disciplines: company law, finance, revenue law, trusts, liquor licensing, health and safety, telecommunications, environmental law, agricultural law, insolvency, project finance and planning. Pretty quickly you learn about the roles of surveyors and property agents, engineers and architects; you'll interact with the Inland Revenue, local authorities, the Land Registry, Companies House, banks and mortgage lenders, brokers, designers...and the list goes on. A property lawyer will get to know most of their contemporaries in the surveying firms locally. Surveyors are more gregarious than lawyers and Friday lunchtimes see hordes of them in city bars. Brave property lawyers are genuinely welcomed and valuable contacts are often made. You'll become an integral part of the professional world of property and you'll understand that clients regard you as a business adviser not the dull academic that you feared you'd become in land law lectures at uni.

day in the life of...

9am: Consider 'Things To Do' list, which has become constant companion. Calculate that, without interruptions, list can be eliminated in two days. Fat chance! Morning post has now doubled said list. Receive latest draft of complex supermarket development agreement from counterpart acting for landowner. Said counterpart has a sneaky habit of never remembering to draft clauses to reflect points agreed in negotiations. Must check document with hawk's eye and redraft where necessary. Answer half a dozen short and simple letters and turn to supermarket project.

11.30am: Mortgage funds arrive for purchase of totally gorgeous Chelsea penthouse for chairman of senior partner's most important client. Quick calculation confirms that we have total purchase money in firm's account; it's time to complete the deal and allow a cool £1.8 million to zing across electronically to seller's solicitors. Client is excited as an eight-year-old on a sugar high. (Bodes well for gift of flowers).

2.10pm: Double espresso in world-dominating coffee franchise has added to wonderful 'edgy' feeling, which always accompanies deal completion. Call from seller's solicitor to say all money received and sale is completed. Call delighted and gushing client. (Flowers now a dead cert.)

2.45pm: Start lengthy task of reading purchase contract and lease for restaurant client opening new, themed eatery in old watermill. Must become expert on all matters of a watery nature, read surveyor's report closely and look into the limitations imposed on listed buildings.

4pm: Eyes beginning to glaze over with volume of small print. Decide to have a fast and furious 90 minutes on itty-bitty elements of 'To Do' list. Interrupted by call from client whose financially troubled tenant has missed rent payment. Look at lease and advise anxious client. Agree to draft letter to send to errant tenant.

5.15pm: Sign outgoing letters. Big bouquet still not showed up. Turn attention to watermill documents.

7pm: Enough is enough. Tomorrow's another day...

skills needed

...good on paper... good negotiator... persuasive in argument... precision and care... respect and understanding of black letter law... the ability to multitask... well-organised mind and paperwork... lateral thought... numeracy... an interest in the property world... team player... work well alone... flexibility...

The amount of documentation to be considered and amended requires you to be well organised, calm and ready to embrace detail. Successful property lawyers combine the capacity for new ideas and clever strategy with a willingness to sit down and turn the ideas, word by word, into watertight agreements. Negotiation skills are key. In addition to being able to argue a point well, you've got to know when to push, when to dig your heels in and when to give in. In this respect, pernickety lawyers do not make the best practitioners! Skills will come (in time) from practice, common sense and a good knowledge of what the property market will allow you to get away with. It's also your job to uncover everything there is to know about a property so tenacity is important. Ideally, you'll be one part private detective, one part horse trader and one part draftsman.

Your dealings with clients, other lawyers and property professionals will be both on the phone and in meetings. You'll need to express yourself clearly and confidently. Generally, both sides have the same goal and so the real trick is to get the best deal for your client within the time scale that they set for you. The most successful and satisfied property lawyers actually get on very well with their opposite numbers. Sophie told us: *"It makes all the difference in a transaction...everyone comes to the party at the end of the deal."*

At times in the largest firms, a young lawyer might be a part of the team working on just one (albeit big) project. More typically, a property lawyer will have scores of different cases on the go at any one time, so you have to be pretty adept at juggling them all. You learn early on how to prioritise tasks. And you also learn that the list of 'Things To Do' never goes away!

career options

Just as the fortunes of the property market have been cyclical, the fortunes of property lawyers rise and fall accordingly. No longer just a support for more glamorous and bigger-billing departments, deals are more sophisticated in their structuring than ever before and property lawyers can hold their heads up high.

Some in-house lawyers perform much the same function as those in private practice. Clerical Medical has a large in-house legal department with specialist property lawyers handling the fund's property deals in tandem with solicitors in private practice. At Warner Bros, lawyers act more like clients, instructing firms to carry out the work for them.

Know-how jobs crop up regularly as do public sector roles, say at the Land Registry or in a local authority. Some property lawyers even turn into developers...after all, why waste all that experience?

LEADING FIRMS FROM CHAMBERS UK 2003-2004

REAL ESTATE: LARGER DEALS ■ LONDON

1 Linklaters

2 Clifford Chance LLP

3 Berwin Leighton Paisner
Freshfields Bruckhaus Deringer
Herbert Smith
Lovells

4 Ashurst Morris Crisp
Nabarro Nathanson
SJ Berwin

5 Allen & Overy
CMS Cameron McKenna

REAL ESTATE: MEDIUM DEALS ■ LONDON

1 Denton Wilde Sapte
Jones Day Gouldens
Macfarlanes

2 Dechert
Forsters
Lawrence Graham
Norton Rose

3 Mayer, Brown, Rowe & Maw LLP
Olswang
Slaughter and May

4 Eversheds
Simmons & Simmons

5 Field Fisher Waterhouse
Richards Butler

REAL ESTATE: SMALLER DEALS ■ LONDON

1 Boodle Hatfield
Maxwell Batley
Travers Smith Braithwaite

2 Nicholson Graham & Jones
Speechly Bircham

3 Finers Stephens Innocent
Manches
Trowers & Hamlins

4 Fladgate Fielder
Julian Holy
Mishcon de Reya
Stepien Lake Gilbert & Paling
Taylor Wessing

5 Addleshaw Goddard
Davies Arnold Cooper
Hamlins
Osborne Clarke
Park Nelson

REAL ESTATE ■ MIDLANDS

1 **Eversheds** Birmingham
Wragge & Co LLP Birmingham

2 **Pinsents** Birmingham

3 **DLA** Birmingham
Hammonds Birmingham

4 **Freethcartwright LLP** Nottingham
Lee Crowder Birmingham
Shoosmiths Birmingham, Northampton

5 **Browne Jacobson** Nottingham
Edwards Geldard Derby
Martineau Johnson Birmingham

6 **Harvey Ingram Owston** Leicester
Knight & Sons Newcastle-under-Lyme
Wright Hassall Leamington Spa

REAL ESTATE ■ THE SOUTH

1 **Blake Lapthorn Linnell** Fareham, Ports, Soton

2 **Bond Pearce** Southampton
Cripps Harries Hall Tunbridge Wells
Paris Smith & Randall Southampton

3 **Clyde & Co** Guildford
DMH Brighton, Crawley
Stevens & Bolton Guildford

4 **GCL Solicitors** Guildford
Lester Aldridge Bournemouth
Rawlison Butler Crawley
Shoosmiths Fareham
Thomas Eggar Chichester, Horsham, Reigate, Worthing
Thomson Snell & Passmore Tunbridge Wells

5 **Brachers** Maidstone
Coffin Mew & Clover Portsmouth, Southampton
Mundays Cobham
Penningtons Basingstoke, Godalming
Steele Raymond Bournemouth

6 **asb law** Crawley, Horsham, Maidstone
Davies Lavery Maidstone
Laytons Guildford
Moore & Blatch Southampton

REAL ESTATE ■ WALES

1 **Edwards Geldard** Cardiff
Eversheds Cardiff

2 **Berry Smith** Cardiff
Palser Grossman Cardiff Bay

3 **Hugh James** Cardiff
Morgan Cole Cardiff
Morgan LaRoche Swansea
Robertsons Cardiff

REAL ESTATE ■ THAMES VALLEY

1 **Pitmans** Reading

2 **BrookStreet Des Roches** Witney
Clarks Reading
Denton Wilde Sapte Milton Keynes
Iliffes Booth Bennett (IBB) Uxbridge

3 **Blake Lapthorn Linnell** Oxford
Boyes Turner Reading
Harold Benjamin Harrow
Manches Oxford
Matthew Arnold & Baldwin Watford
Morgan Cole Oxford
Nabarro Nathanson Reading

4 **Blandy & Blandy** Reading
BPC Business Lawyers Gerrards Cross
Fennemores Milton Keynes
Field Seymour Parkes Reading
Pictons Luton
Stanley Tee Bishop's Stortford

REAL ESTATE ■ EAST ANGLIA

1 **Hewitsons** Cambridge
Mills & Reeve Cambridge

2 **Eversheds** Cambridge, Norwich
Taylor Vinters Cambridge

3 **Birketts** Ipswich

4 **Ashton Graham** Bury St Edmunds
Few & Kester Cambridge
Greene & Greene Bury St Edmunds
Greenwoods Peterborough
Prettys Ipswich

REAL ESTATE ■ SOUTH WEST

1 **Burges Salmon** Bristol

2 **Beachcroft Wansbroughs** Bristol
Bevan Ashford BBL Bristol
Bevan Ashford EPL Exetor, Plymouth, Taunton
Osborne Clarke Bristol

3 **Bond Pearce** Bristol, Exeter, Plymouth
Clarke Willmott Bristol
Michelmores Exeter
TLT Bristol

4 **BPE Solicitors** Cheltenham
Charles Russell Cheltenham
Davies and Partners Gloucester
Rickerbys Cheltenham
Veale Wasbrough Bristol

5 **Clark Holt** Swindon
Davitt Jones Bould Taunton
Foot Anstey Sargent Plymouth
Stephens & Scown Exeter, Liskeard, St Austell, Truro
Thring Townsend Bath, Swindon

REAL ESTATE ■ NORTH WEST

1 **Addleshaw Goddard** Manchester
Bullivant Jones Liverpool
Cobbetts Manchester
DLA Liverpool
Eversheds Manchester

2 **Halliwell Landau** Manchester
Hammonds Manchester

3 **Beachcroft Wansbroughs** Manchester
DWF Liverpool
Field Cunningham & Co Manchester

4 **Brabners Chaffe Street** Liverpool
Cuff Roberts Liverpool
Hill Dickinson Chester
JMW solicitors Manchester
Mace & Jones Manchester
Masons Manchester
Pannone & Partners Manchester

REAL ESTATE ■ YORKSHIRE

1 **Addleshaw Goddard** Leeds
Walker Morris Leeds

2 **DLA** Leeds, Sheffield
Pinsents Leeds

3 **Cobbetts** Leeds
Eversheds Leeds

4 **Andrew M Jackson** Hull
Hammonds Leeds
Nabarro Nathanson Sheffield

5 **Gordons** Bradford, Leeds
Irwin Mitchell Sheffield
Keeble Hawson Sheffield

6 **Denison Till** York
Gosschalks Hull
Rollits Hull
Shulmans Leeds
Wake Smith Sheffield

REAL ESTATE ■ NORTH EAST

1 **Dickinson Dees** Newcastle upon Tyne

2 **Eversheds** Newcastle upon Tyne

3 **Robert Muckle** Newcastle upon Tyne
Ward Hadaway Newcastle upon Tyne
Watson Burton Newcastle upon Tyne

public interest

civil liberties and human rights

type of work

When most of us look at a case, even if it seems unfair, we are likely to resign ourselves to the fact that nothing can be done because the law is the law. Civil liberties lawyers such as Danny Simpson, head of the criminal and civil liberties department at Howells in Sheffield, believe that *"we ought to be able to use the existing law to challenge injustices."*

This kind of work stems from an attitude of mind. Civil liberties or human rights aspects will be found in many cases if you look for them. It is fast reaching the point when almost every case, civil or criminal, will contain at least one of these elements. In the civil context, cases may involve discrimination at work, for example, where people are unfairly passed over for promotion, miss out on maternity and holiday leave, or do not receive equal, fair pay for equal work. Family law is also a growing area involving civil liberties, increasingly in the areas of child access and residency. Child access cases mainly involve separated fathers and the term 'reasonable access' – even quite recently, courts have ruled one day per month to be reasonable, but this is due to be appealed. The right to family life enshrined in the Human Rights Act is frequently the basis of arguments in family proceedings. Human rights concerns have also been raised in cases concerning housing tenancies, where the issue might be a gay or lesbian partner's right to succeed to a tenancy previously held by a deceased partner.

Miscarriages of criminal justice involve bringing convictions before the Criminal Cases Review Board to take them to the Court of Appeal.

The administrative law dimension involves the judicial review of decisions by public bodies. With recent case law appearing to expand the definition of a public body, it seems likely that this field of work will continue to grow. One such challenge involved a patient in a private psychiatric hospital objecting to changes in the way her ward was being run. The judge declared that the hospital was in effect exercising the powers of a public authority and was therefore susceptible to judicial review.

a day in the life...

A typical day for Danny often involves going to court for criminal proceedings. On other days he may visit people in jail to discuss their grievances over how they are being treated. In the office there's plenty of client contact and a large caseload. Danny has a habit of taking on cases that no one else will take, even if that means doing it for free, as he believes *"it's no good just letting things lie if they are morally or politically offensive."* Even junior lawyers can expect to conduct their own advocacy, attend the Coroner's Court, see clients in prison and deal with miscarriage of justice cases.

skills needed

...passion... determination... demonstrated commitment... creativity... showing initiative... communicate well with joe public and with the court... love of advocacy...

career options

If you're looking for a training contract with one of the firms that specialise in human rights and civil liberties, be aware that this is an incredibly competitive area. However, firms with criminal and family departments that take on cases with civil liberties aspects, often find it difficult to recruit talented and committed trainees. The problem, of course, is that the work largely legally aided (or done for free if no funding is available). These firms cannot offer the salaries that attract trainees to commercial firms. A firm might create a job for you, if you can convince them that you are worth taking on. Demonstrate your passion and commitment by carrying out voluntary work and joining relevant organisations. Law centres and voluntary work are the alternatives to private practice, and it is not uncommon for dedicated lawyers to move between the two.

immigration law

type of work

Immigration covers two areas: business and personal. Business immigration tends to be practised in larger firms with corporate clients that want to bring over employees and their families to live and work in the UK. There are some individual clients, for instance under the Highly Skilled Migrants Programme, which according to the Government aims to tackle the current skills shortage in the UK.

Personal immigration work is summed up by Lanis Levy, a solicitor at Glazer Delmar in South London: *"A client is asking you to address one of the most fundamental issues in their life – the question of whether they will be permitted to live and work or study in the country they choose."* For many, this will be a truly heartfelt issue, determining whether they can be together with their spouse/partner and family.

Immigration work is certainly varied and involves more than the basic assistance given to those who want to become British through the process of naturalisation. Most people are familiar with asylum work, which aims to enable those who fear persecution at home to stay in Britain. But your work might also involve arranging for someone to visit relatives in the UK or for a student to come to study here. A more unusual case might see you representing a prisoner facing deportation after serving a sentence for a relatively minor conviction, even though they had lived in Britain for 20 years.

a day in the life...

There is absolutely no typical day for Lanis. In the office there are calls to be returned to clients, such as a woman with a child who has been abandoned in her flat by her partner. She has no idea how she will pay next month's rent as her immigration status does not entitle her to claim any benefits. Lanis admits: *"I like to take on cases where people have come to the end of the line."* Another client is having difficulties in getting support from social services. Next there is an appeal hearing to rearrange because the interpreter who showed up to the last hearing didn't speak the same dialect as the client. Attendance at an appeal will then necessitate a trip out of the office, with Lanis carrying out her own advocacy. Once every couple of weeks she will visit a client in prison. Lanis is clearly passionate about her job: *"It can be the most rewarding work imaginable!"* From early on, a trainee will take instructions from clients and attend interviews at the Home Office or the Immigration Service. They will prepare statements and representations to the Home Office or chase up pending claims. With support from more senior colleagues, they will take on their own cases.

skills needed

...sensitivity... compassion and commitment... able to deal with emotional and distressed clients... tenacity... willing to question decisions by authorities... language skills may be a real boon...

career options

Most of the interesting and challenging work is publicly funded, but proposals to reuce the funds available on asylum claims represent a threat to solicitors' immigration practices. Working in the voluntary sector can be more satisfying as funding constraints do not hamper the progress of a case. This is the only real alternative to private practice, and any kind of experience you can get with law centres, refugees' or human rights' organisations will be invaluable. You can also keep up to date in this fast-moving area by joining organisations like the Joint Council for the Welfare of Immigrants, or by becoming a student member of the Immigration Law

Practitioners Association. Not all immigration lawyers do their own advocacy, but it means an enormous amount to the client to have the same person take their case from start to finish. If advocacy is important to you, there's plenty of opportunity to develop this skill as an immigration lawyer.

education

type of work

This is a multi-disciplinary practice area, advising educational institutions on all aspects of the law. Its distinguishing features are an underlying public law dimension and a regulatory system that is particular to educational institutions. Further and higher education institutions may also be incorporated as companies and so require the same business advice as any other corporate client. "*This has to be tempered by a recognition of the fact that they are charities and publicly funded, with a set of ethics and a keen sense of academic freedom,*" stresses John Hall, head of the education law group at Eversheds.

The work may involve advice on generating different sources of income or on buying IT equipment. Just like any business, colleges and universities need advice on all the usual aspects of their day-to-day running, such as employment, property, planning, construction and PFI/PPP. Universities also have IP-rich spin-off businesses, which require advice. Occasionally advice will be needed following a complaint from a student and a different firm will represent the student.

a day in the life...

A typical day for John might involve advising on a strategic partnership between a university and industry, followed by phone calls to the DfES to discuss regulations or clear policy issues. At lunchtime there could be an education team meeting with employment lawyers to review internal procedures at a university following a claim of discrimination. In the afternoon he might meet his main contacts at a college with a funding deficit to chat generally about how the firm might be able to advise them. Perhaps the college ought to decrease the number of campuses from five to three, which would then involve decreasing the amount of accommodation and restructuring staff. Getting governing body approval, bringing in consultants and carrying out an options feasibility study would be prerequisites and it would be likely that the college would want to invest in new IT and refurbish some of its buildings. Many different areas of law are, therefore, involved in just one meeting.

skills needed

...commercial outlook... the self confidence to 'take a view'... teamwork... pragmatism combined with common sense and ethics... multi-disciplinary approach... keeping up with changes in the sector... ability to get under the client's skin...

career options

As education is high on the political agenda, this area is subject to an enormous amount of change. This is especially the case with structural and funding aspects of the post-16 education system. Education law would suit a person who is interested in giving "*commercial advice with an approach driven by public sector values.*" The only real alternative to training in private practice is to apply to a local authority for a training contract. This will provide a wide training in all areas of local government, after which the newly qualified could specialise in education issues.

Choose a niche firm if you wish to advise children, students and parents on education issues like exclusions from school, bullying or provisions for students with special needs. *Chambers UK* identifies leading education firms by their specialism. Once qualified, there are a few opportunities to work in the Department for Education and Skills and an increasing number of opportunities to work in-house at universities.

LEADING FIRMS FROM CHAMBERS UK 2003-2004

HUMAN RIGHTS: TRADITIONAL ■ LONDON

Band	Firm
1	Bhatt Murphy
	Bindman & Partners
2	Christian Khan
3	Birnberg Peirce & Partners
	Hickman & Rose
4	Leigh, Day & Co
	Scott-Moncrieff, Harbour & Sinclair
	Simons Muirhead & Burton
5	CCL
	Deighton Guedalla
	Taylor Nichol

HUMAN RIGHTS: COMMERCIAL ■ LONDON

Band	Firm
1	Clifford Chance LLP
	Herbert Smith
2	Freshfields Bruckhaus Deringer
	Lovells

HUMAN RIGHTS ■ MIDLANDS

Band	Firm
2	**Tyndallwoods** Birmingham

HUMAN RIGHTS ■ THE NORTH

Band	Firm
1	**Howells** Sheffield
2	**Harrison Bundey & Co** Leeds
	Irwin Mitchell Sheffield
3	**A S Law** Liverpool
4	**Robert Lizar** Manchester

IMMIGRATION: PERSONAL ■ LONDON

Band	Firm
1	Bindman & Partners
	Birnberg Peirce & Partners
	Wesley Gryk
2	Deighton Guedalla
	Luqmani Thompson
	Wilson & Co
3	Bartram & Co
	Bates, Wells & Braithwaite
	DJ Webb & Co
	Gill & Co
	Glazer Delmar
	Powell & Co

IMMIGRATION: BUSINESS ■ LONDON

Band	Firm
1	CMS Cameron McKenna
	Kingsley Napley
2	Bates, Wells & Braithwaite
	Magrath & Co
	Reed Smith
3	Baker & McKenzie
	Laura Devine Solicitors
	Sturtivant & Co
4	Harbottle & Lewis LLP
	Lovells
	Mishcon de Reya
	Penningtons
5	DJ Webb & Co
	Fox Williams
	Gulbenkian Harris Andonian
6	Gherson & Co
	Taylor Wessing

IMMIGRATION ■ THE SOUTH

Band	Firm
1	**Darbys** Oxford
	Turpin Miller & higgins Oxford

IMMIGRATION ■ MIDLANDS

Band	Firm
1	**The Rights Partnership** Birmingham
	Tyndallwoods Birmingham
2	**Elizabeth Davidge Solicitor** Birmingham

IMMIGRATION ■ EAST ANGLIA

Band	Firm
1	**Gross & Co** Bury St Edmunds
	Leathes Prior Norwich
	Wollastons Chelmsford

IMMIGRATION ■ THE NORTH

Band	Firm
1	**David Gray Solicitors** Newcastle upon Tyne
2	**Harrison Bundey & Co** Leeds
3	**A S Law** Liverpool
	Howells Sheffield
	James & Co Bradford
4	**Davis Blank Furniss** Manchester
	Henry Hyams Leeds
	Jackson & Canter Liverpool
	Samuel Phillips & Co Newcastle upon Tyne

EDUCATION: INSTITUTIONS ■ LONDON

1 **Eversheds**
2 **Beachcroft Wansbroughs**
3 **Farrer & Co**
Winckworth Sherwood
4 **Berrymans Lace Mawer**
Lawfords
Lee Bolton & Lee
Reynolds Porter Chamberlain

EDUCATION: INDIVIDUALS ■ LONDON

1 **Levenes**
Teacher Stern Selby
2 **Coningsbys** Croydon
Fisher Meredith
3 **Bennett Wilkins**
Gills Southall
John Ford Solicitors
4 **Ashok Patel & Co**

EDUCATION: INSTITUTIONS ■ WALES

1 **Eversheds** Cardiff
Morgan Cole Cardiff

EDUCATION: INDIVIDUALS ■ WALES

1 **Russell Jones & Walker** Cardiff

EDUCATION: INSTITUTIONS ■ THE SOUTH & SOUTH WEST

1 **Veale Wasbrough** Bristol
2 **Rickerbys** Cheltenham
Stone King Bath
3 **Beachcroft Wansbroughs** Bristol
Bond Pearce Plymouth
DMH Brighton
4 **Michelmores** Exeter
Osborne Clarke Bristol
Thomas Eggar Chichester
Tozers Exeter

EDUCATION: INDIVIDUALS ■ THE SOUTH & SOUTH WEST

1 **AE Smith & Son** Stroud
2 **Blake Lapthorn Linnell** Fareham

EDUCATION: INSTITUTIONS ■ THAMES VALLEY

1 **Blake Lapthorn Linnell** Oxford
Manches Oxford
Morgan Cole Oxford
Winckworth Sherwood Oxford

EDUCATION: INSTITUTIONS ■ THE NORTH

1 **Eversheds** Leeds, Manchester, Newcastle upon Tyne
2 **Pinsents** Leeds
3 **Robert Muckle** Newcastle upon Tyne

EDUCATION: INDIVIDUALS ■ THE NORTH

1 **Maxwell Gillott** Lancaster
2 **Irwin Mitchell** Sheffield

EDUCATION: INSTITUTIONS ■ MIDLANDS

1 **Martineau Johnson** Birmingham
2 **Eversheds** Birmingham, Nottingham
3 **Browne Jacobson** Nottingham
Pinsents Birmingham
Wragge & Co LLP Birmingham

EDUCATION: INSTITUTIONS ■ EAST ANGLIA

1 **Mills & Reeve** Cambridge
2 **Eversheds** Cambridge
3 **Birkett Long** Colchester
Wollastons Chelmsford

shipping

definition of terms

P&I Club: Protection and Indemnity Club – a marine insurance club run mutually by and for shipowners.

Charter party: a commercial instrument – essentially a contract for the hire of an entire ship for the purpose of import or export of goods.

Bill of Lading: a receipt for goods loaded given by the master of the ship, a contract of carriage between the owners of the ships and the owners of the goods and a negotiable certificate of title for the goods themselves.

Salvage: reward payable by owners of ships and goods saved at sea by 'salvors'.

Shipping. What images come to mind? Greek shipping magnates chomping cigars? 17th century West Country ne'er-do-wells scouring the high seas for treasure and thrills under the lawless (and give-away) banner of the Jolly Roger? The reality of shipping law is that it's an area filled with variety, complexity and, depending on the strand you go into, unpredictability. As Chris Hobbs, head of Norton Rose's Greek office, says: *"You never quite know what's going to happen during an average day, but whatever does happen is quite often exciting."* Shipping is truly international in terms of the travel potential and the people and places you deal with. Someone who likes a simple, unvarying routine and the safety of staying in their office is unlikely to be suited for a career as a shipping lawyer.

type of work

Unsurprisingly, shipping law concerns ships, and more specifically the carriage of goods or people by sea. It can be either contentious or non-contentious.

Contentious work is broken down into wet ('Admiralty') work and dry ('marine') work. Unsurprisingly again, the terms 'wet' and 'dry' are key indicators to the nature of the work. Wet work concerns disputes arising from accidents or misadventure at sea, ie collision, salvage, total loss and yes, even modern-day piracy. Wet lawyers are often former naval officers or ex-mariners (in the main *sans* dead albatrosses hanging from their necks). Dry work concerns disputes over contracts made on dry land, such as charter parties, bills of lading, cargo or sale of goods contracts.

Non-contentious work is primarily ship finance and ship building contracts, sale and purchase agreements, employment contracts for crew members, affreightment contracts, registration and re-flagging of ships. Further niche areas include yachting or fishing, which usually involve regulatory matters. As James Gosling, a partner at Holman Fenwick & Willan, states: *"You really get a good handle on the basics of contract law and drafting,"* and it goes without saying that this will be invaluable to your career as a lawyer – whether or not in shipping.

Few shipping lawyers handle both contentious and non-contentious work and those that do generally work in smaller firms or overseas offices. The type of firm you train with normally pre-determines your post-qualification specialism. There are a number of specialist shipping firms in London such as Ince & Co, Holman Fenwick & Willan and Clyde & Co, where contentious work will take up the majority of the training contract. Other more general corporate firms such as Norton Rose are known predominantly for their non-contentious shipping practices (ship finance in particular) and yet maintain contentious shipping teams as well as offering a wide training in other areas of law.

a day in the life of....

The global nature of the client base means you're acutely aware of the different time zones that you're working to on any given day, and you plan your time accordingly. A wet lawyer *"might come trudging in on Monday thinking the world's fallen in, and the next thing you know you're on a plane to Tahiti."* Not every day's as glamorous, of course, and *"you may be asked to go to some pretty unpleasant places and told to just get on with it."* James told us: *"For me at least, it sure beats conveying a house in North Finchley!"*

Many cases are high-profile, attracting media interest. Think about the Herald of Free Enterprise, the Braer oil spillage and the Sea Empress – all have involved lawyers in various capacities. James says of wet work: *"Getting involved in casualty cases is a real adrenalin rush. You often have to get to a ship as quickly as you can to preserve evidence and make sure you get the right story from the witnesses."* You then have to get the right 'forum' – the most beneficial jurisdiction for your client – as quickly as possible. Wet lawyers need to act fast. Any delay to a ship, howsoever caused, costs money. Your client expects you to analyse problems quickly and come up with sensible answers.

As for non-contentious work, don't be under any illusions; ship finance is nowhere near as exciting as casualty work, nor does it offer the same opportunities for travel. In the main, you'll be drafting, and considering finance agreements and other standard contracts relating to ships and their crew.

It's a controversial question: how do women fare in the rather macho world of shipping? Regrettably, shipping clients from some cultures have traditionally been rather male-oriented when it comes to business. It remains true that most of the top shipping lawyers are male, but things are changing. James told us: *"Virtually half the clients on the insurance side are women."* More women are making their presence known in ship finance and dry work, but it's a different story in wet work. Why? James explained: *"The plain and simple truth is you'd be asking for trouble if you sent a woman to investigate a collision between a Greek vessel and a Mexican vessel somewhere in West Africa. It's not the safest place for a man, never mind a woman."* In addition, *"a lot of masters of vessels find it difficult telling a man what they did wrong, let alone a woman."*

skills needed

dry/wet:...no place for shrinking violets... abreast of legal developments/industry trends... firm grip on contract, tort and court procedure... flexible over hours... available to travel... good communicator... sense of humour... common sense... team spirit and self motivation... **wet:** ...previous experience of life at sea helpful (but not essential)... guts/sense of adventure...

Dry lawyers need to develop a good knowledge of conflicts (as distinct from forum shopping) as well as contract and tort. As for wet lawyers, they need to be bold, as they will face adversity and the unexpected. You also need to be *"an engaging person with a broad outlook on life."* You'll be interacting with a vast range of people from different cultures and different ends of the social scale; many will have been schooled in the university of life. These clients – shipowners, operators, traders and charterers through to P&I clubs, other insurers and hull underwriters – are a real mixed bag. *"Claims handlers in P&I clubs are usually English and middle class, whereas salvors are often hulking great Dutchmen who've done salvages in some of the wildest places in the world."* Clients all tend to be larger than life – as James says: *"Whether they're hull underwriters or shipowners, they're risk-takers by their very nature, and they enjoy it."*

A keen analytical mind and a commercial outlook won't go astray. Chris says: *"A lot of people write us off as a bunch of partying, rather frivolous animals but if you look at the law of contract, and to an extent the law of tort, a lot of the cases that laid down fundamental principles are shipping cases."* Other than having been a mariner or naval officer, is there any experience that can help? *"Well, if you've seen a bit and done a bit and know a bit about the world, that can help."* At the end of the day, being a good lawyer in this field is just as much about common sense as *"knowing all the legal stuff."* Oh, *"a good liver"* also comes in handy!

"Ships are quite romantic things," James told us. *"Very few people get into shipping law and then leave it during a mid-life crisis to go and do M&A, for example."* We wondered just how romantic he was feeling

when he told us: *"I've been shot at and I've been on sinking ships..."*

career options

Jobs outside London are relatively few, as shipping work is limited to larger port towns. In the firms with overseas offices, assistants can work abroad for a few years or even permanently. This is generally considered a good career move, particularly with regard to partnership prospects back home. If, following qualification, you decide shipping is not for you, as a contentious shipping lawyer you'll have gained a solid grounding as a commercial litigator. If you've been doing non-contentious work, you should have little problem shifting into general finance or corporate work.

If private practice does not appeal, P&I clubs, shipowners, operators and marine insurers all have openings for specialist lawyers, but the financial rewards will be less than in private practice, as will the legal component of the position. Shipowners or operators would want you to have knowledge or experience of the industry before approaching them for an in-house position. The predominance of English law in international shipping makes it relatively easy for in-housers to walk the plank back into private practice. Alternatively, you could convey houses in North Finchley!

LEADING FIRMS FROM CHAMBERS UK 2003-2004

SHIPPING ■ LONDON

Band	Firm
1	**Holman Fenwick & Willan**
	Ince & Co
2	**Clyde & Co**
3	**Bentleys, Stokes & Lowless**
	Hill Taylor Dickinson
	Richards Butler
4	**Barlow Lyde & Gilbert**
	Holmes Hardingham
	More Fisher Brown
	Shaw and Croft
	Stephenson Harwood
	Thomas Cooper & Stibbard
	Waltons & Morse
5	**Clifford Chance LLP**
	Middleton Potts
	Norton Rose
	Watson, Farley & Williams
6	**Curtis Davis Garrard** Feltham
	Fishers
	Hill Dickinson
	Jackson Parton
	Lawrence Graham
	Waterson Hicks

SHIPPING: FINANCE ■ LONDON

Band	Firm
1	**Norton Rose**
2	**Allen & Overy**
	Stephenson Harwood
	Watson, Farley & Williams
3	**Clifford Chance LLP**
	Denton Wilde Sapte

SHIPPING ■ THE SOUTH & SOUTH WEST

Band	Firm
1	**Davies, Johnson & Co** Plymouth
	Foot Anstey Sargent Exeter, Plymouth
2	**Bond Pearce** Plymouth, Southampton
	Lester Aldridge Southampton

SHIPPING ■ EAST ANGLIA

Band	Firm
1	**Dale & Co** Felixstowe
	John Weston & Co Felixstowe
2	**Prettys** Ipswich

SHIPPING ■ THE NORTH

Band	Firm
1	**Andrew M Jackson** Hull
	Eversheds Newcastle upon Tyne
	Mills & Co Newcastle upon Tyne
	Rayfield Mills Newcastle upon Tyne
2	**DLA** Liverpool, Manchester
	Hill Dickinson Liverpool, Manchester

sports law

Strictly speaking, sports law is more an industry focus rather than a discipline in its own right and, consequently, sports lawyers practice a broad range of law. However, there is a distinct and ever developing body of law specifically concerning sports-related issues. This is best illustrated when national law and particular sports regulations collide, such as in the Bosman case, wherein football regulations governing player transfers were at odds with European employment regulations.

Sporting regulatory bodies are increasingly being taken to court (and hit for six) for imposing rules which conflict with the prevailing laws of the land. There was no doubt in the minds of the sports lawyers we spoke to that the continuing trends of increased professionalism and the globalisation of sporting concerns will lead to more sports-related law-making, whether through legislation or judicial decisions. Further specific industry regulation is inevitable.

type of work

Lawyers entering the area can expect to become familiar with trademark issues, data protection issues, sponsorship and broadcasting agreements and general contractual law as well as more specific sports-related issues like player transfers. The work is nearly always contractual, with a strong IP bias in terms of intangible rights.

Sports law can be broken down into three main components:

- The regulatory, disciplinary, criminal and personal injury advice given to individuals, teams and ruling bodies
- Media/sponsorship and advertising
- Corporate and commercial advice, eg the Stock Exchange listing of a football club

Most firms with a sports practice will have a leaning to one or other of these aspects of the work. It would be worth your while ascertaining who acts for who and what type of work each concentrates on. As usual, we recommend you use *Chambers UK* for your research.

Sportspeople being sportspeople, there is a need for advice on crime, personal injury and of course employment law. In addition, EU and competition issues are increasingly coming into play. The subject matter of sports law is as wide as a Gareth Southgate penalty miss. Fraser Reid of Addleshaw Goddard's sports group makes the point that *"to be lucrative, a sports practice must focus on commercial matters rather than sports governance – unless you're acting for the leading sporting bodies."* He adds: *"Commercialism has firmly taken over from administration, both in the marketplace in the roles of administrators and in law firms' sports practices."* Of course, the fortunes of the sector are cyclical and, sadly, the last year has seen a decline in the volume of commercial activity. The collapse of both ITV Digital and Leo Kirch's media empire certainly played a part in this. As a result, rights holders in UK sport hope that the forthcoming Communications Bill, with its proposed changes to the rules governing foreign ownership of media organisations, will provide a welcome shot in the arm for the sports broadcasting industry in the UK and help stimulate competition for rights fees once more.

Yet, other areas of work continue unabated. There's so much capital injected into and generated by sport that *"there's a real need for lawyers to become involved and provide advice on areas such as the protection and exploitation of sporting commercial rights."* Indeed, several of the year's leading cases involved the misuse of commercial rights and included the Eddie Irvine image rights case, in which the

Formula 1 driver successfully sued Talk Sport for passing off, after the radio station used a photo of him in an advertisement. Also, the Arsenal v Matthew Reed case, in which the football club attempted to prevent a street trader from selling merchandise containing the Arsenal name and certain other trademarks.

It's definitely a more established and structured practice area than it used to be. Jonathan Hall, RFU Secretary and Legal Officer, remembers the early 90s: *"A few people were beginning to practise sports law, but it was more the case that IP lawyers would advise in relation to sports-related trademark work or the corporate department would advise in relation to an acquisition of a sports company, for example."* This evolution has taken place over the course of the last ten years, and particularly since the emergence of PayTV. Why so? *"It's tagged along with the growth in new media and technology – there are now far more ways of getting access to sport in general, and football in particular."* You don't need to be a sports lawyer to realise that the stratospheric rise in money and publicity associated with the industry means more rights to be looked after, more regulation and more deals. In short, more legal work! Even the current crisis in football will provide plenty of legal work.

a day in the life...

Our interviewees would have us believe that there's simply no such thing as a typical day, but one thing is clear, sports lawyers don't, as a rule, regularly spend eight hours poring over one document. True, junior lawyers can expect to spend a lot of their time drafting basic sponsorship and broadcasting agreements and giving written advice on various IP issues such as trademark and copyright, but much of the time is spent meeting and speaking with clients, and forming good relationships with them. Fraser told us: *"My career is in the law – it's what I'm qualified to do – and I love sport, so combining the two is perfect. If I wasn't a lawyer, I would want to be a sportsman and if I wasn't a sportsman I would want to be a lawyer."*

skills needed

...basic legal skills... commercial nous... good interpersonal skills... background reading (and watching)... innovation... proactivity... it's what you know and who you know...

In this industry more than most, people really do know you by your name and personality counts for a lot. You don't necessarily need unbridled passion for sport (such as a propensity to paint your face with team colours and sing largely risible team anthems). You do need to show a genuine interest in the industry – to follow it, keep up with developments and talk enthusiastically and cogently about it. It's an embryonic market and extremely competitive to break into so you need to be technically excellent and innovative. People love to be associated with famous names. Lawyers are no different, and they're generally protective of their relationships with sporting clients and guarded against new entrants.

It's not an area where you can just sit back and watch from the sidelines; you must be ahead of the game and, just as importantly, you must be seen to be ahead of it. Rights holders, sports agents and broadcasters alike will have commercial nous and they won't expect their lawyer to be without it. A quick mental jog through the sporting year makes you realise how many events have thrown up legal issues. Looking solely at the Cricket World Cup, there was the Shane Warne doping scandal, the political and legal problems arising out of the England team's refusal to play in Zimbabwe, and the reluctance of the Indian players to sign up to restrictions on their personal sponsorship arrangements during a period before, during and after the event. There was even an incident whereby a spectator was removed on from a particular venue because he was a drinking a can of Coke rather than a can of Pepsi!

career options

In private practice, sports specialists have moved into this area both by accident and design. Sports lovers often try to steer their careers in this direction, while corporate, litigation, IP or personal injury lawyers who have acquired a sporting clientele may suddenly find themselves being referred to as sports lawyers. In the last couple of years, some lucky young assistants have been able to specialise on qualification and become a junior part of the few dedicated sports law teams that do exist.

There are various opportunities in the industry, in particular in the larger federated governing bodies (such as the FA, the MCC or the RFU). You could also work for a sports broadcaster negotiating rights, or as an agent for sports personalities or teams. One possible advantage of moving in-house is outlined by the RFU's Jonathan Hall. A lot of law firms may not have the variety or volume to give you a broad range of experience in the industry. Jonathan says: *"A lot of them focus on a very narrow area and you'll get very good experience in that area, but that's about it."* So it's all happening in-house then? *"I certainly think so. The chances are that you will find yourself dealing with sports law issues almost all of the time, although there are clearly non-sports law issues to address, as with any organisation."*

There's no doubt that sports law as a practice area is very much geared towards self-described 'sports nuts', namely people who like to combine their professional qualifications with something in which they have a strong personal interest. And how many other practice areas really offer that opportunity to combine your career with your passion? Probably about as many as the number of countries which field truly world-class rugby league teams. Anyone who doesn't know the answer to that question probably isn't cut out to be a sports lawyer!

LEADING FIRMS FROM CHAMBERS UK 2003-2004

SPORT: COMMERCIAL/MEDIA ■ LONDON	
1	Denton Wilde Sapte
2	Bird & Bird
	Hammonds
	Nicholson Graham & Jones
	Olswang
3	Addleshaw Goddard
	Freshfields Bruckhaus Deringer
	Harbottle & Lewis LLP
	SJ Berwin
	The Simkins Partnership
4	Clintons
	Collyer-Bristow
	Couchman Harrington Associates
	Farrer & Co
	Field Fisher Waterhouse
	Fladgate Fielder
	Herbert Smith

SPORT: REGULATORY ■ LONDON	
1	Denton Wilde Sapte
2	Farrer & Co
	Hammonds
	Max Bitel, Greene
3	Charles Russell
	Freshfields Bruckhaus Deringer
	Simmons & Simmons
	The Simkins Partnership

SPORT ■ THE SOUTH & SOUTH WEST	
1	**Clarke Willmott** Bristol, Southampton
2	**Osborne Clarke** Bristol
3	**Wiggin & Co** Cheltenham

SPORT ■ WALES	
1	**Hugh James** Cardiff

SPORT ■ MIDLANDS	
1	**Freethcartwright LLP** Nottingham

SPORT ■ THE NORTH	
1	**James Chapman & Co** Manchester
2	**McCormicks** Leeds
3	**Addleshaw Goddard** Manchester
4	**Cramers Solicitors** Leeds
	George Davies Solicitors Manchester
	Hill Dickinson Liverpool, Manchester
	Walker Morris Leeds

tax

"Nothing pleases finance directors more than saving some tax. If you give advice that saves your clients tax in the commercial world, then they're going to be very happy people." These words from Jonny Gillespie, an associate at Pinsents in Leeds, neatly summarise the immense and enduring value of corporate tax lawyers. Their primary role is to advise as to the most tax-efficient means of structuring and running business. Tax work is highly client-focused; a good deal of the work is for repeat clients who invariably want quick and commercial answers to complex questions. If you're looking to avoid dealing with people by sequestering yourself away in a tiny office with dusty statute books and dodgy lighting, don't become a tax lawyer.

type of work

The voluminous and ever evolving nature of tax law requires constant attention to black letter law, but it's not the case that you'll be forever poring over the minutiae while your colleagues in sexier areas get to close deals and pop champagne corks. There is a wide variety of tax work on offer – transactional, contentious and general advisory – not to mention an increasingly international aspect to the transactional work in particular, where the relevant laws of a number of jurisdictions need to be considered. Tax is a crucial component of every major deal undertaken by commercial firms. Whether the matter is corporate, finance or property-related, you can be sure that tax lawyers will be among the key advisors.

Greg Sinfield, head of indirect taxes at Lovells, told us: *"It takes a long time for young lawyers to build up the experience necessary to advise in a wide range of situations. People shouldn't think that they'll become an expert in less than four to five years."* There's a huge quantity of law relevant to the area and, when giving advice, practitioners need to take into account not only tax legislation and cases, but also other areas of law that may be relevant. While you don't need to have your eyes shifted to the side of your head, you do need to develop all-round vision.

Tax law evolves at a far greater rate than the majority of other practice areas so you'll need to be constantly on the lookout for change. As Alasdair Douglas, a partner at Travers Smith Braithwaite, says: *"Other types of lawyers get their knickers in a twist if there's new legislation once every ten years. But we're used to it. There's a huge amount of new law in tax every year. Last year there was a 400 page Finance Act, and this year it will probably be just as big."* Jonny adds: *"The thing about tax is that no matter how qualified or senior you are, you will never know everything because it's changing all the time – it doesn't stand still."*

a day in the life...

You'd be forgiven for thinking that most of a tax lawyer's work involves dealing with numbers and doing mathematical calculations. But you'd be wrong. Douglas French, a partner at Clifford Chance, says: *"Tax lawyers don't do a lot of the boring stuff; we don't do compliance work, we don't file returns, we don't do due diligence or computations."* So what does a typical day involve? Researching law, advising on deals, advising on how to structure business activities...and basic fire-fighting! That said, Alasdair stresses how much corporate support work there is. *"In most commercial firms, junior tax lawyers will work on acquisitions and disposals of businesses and companies till it's coming out of their ears!"* However, he adds that *"tax law has the greatest intellectual challenge as a junior lawyer simply because it's so difficult to get your head around as an area of law. Secondly, tax lawyers are dealing with law all the day, not working out the logistics of getting a deal done or shuffling bits of paper."*

As far as the work/life balance goes, Jonny thinks that *"it's much better than in a lot of other depart-*

ments. We do work hard but we usually manage to do it within normal working hours... If you like burning the midnight oil and having lots of 4am corporate completions, then tax may not be for you." Why are the hours so reasonable? It's mainly the nature of the work itself that allows it to be completed within normal working hours, which links in nicely with the fact that *"tax lawyers are so in demand that firms generally treat them well."* Another bonus of the job, according to Alasdair, is the fact that you deal with and get to know lawyers from right around the firm on a day-to-day basis. *"You get to work on the corporate deals, the property deals and the banking deals."*

skills needed

... good academics... analytical mind... thinking outside the box... willing to challenge and test... clear communication... commerciality... technical excellence... great interpretation of black letter law... no anorak required!

One of the most important things you must do as a tax lawyer is to get complex messages across to your clients in a concise and understandable manner. By and large, your clients will not be tax experts and they will not want a lengthy academic discussion as to tax theory. What they will want is to know the commercial effect of the relevant legislation on their business and they will want to know it quickly.

Tax lawyers have to be commercially minded and able to communicate really complex ideas to non-experts. But as Douglas states: *"While the vast majority of us aren't anoraks, tax law is likely to appeal to lawyers who like law – reading statutes and cases."* The studious or academic side does need to be there but remember, it's just a part of the picture. Douglas goes on to say: *"One of the most valuable qualities a tax lawyer can have is creativity and innovation; the ability to think outside the box, to think about a set of facts from all angles and save some tax."*

career options

It's interesting to note that some of the most respected tax barristers have only been at the Bar for a few years. It's not that they have defied the logic of everything we've said so far, it's because a number of them had already achieved a successful track record as a tax solicitor. Excellent news: this part of the Bar is known for its super-high earnings.

As for the alternatives to private practice, in a nutshell, your options are pretty clear. You can work in-house in the tax department of a large corporate or bank, or you can work for the government in Inland Revenue or Customs & Excise. Greg makes the point that *"if you go in-house at a corporate or bank, you only have the one client, which if you're lucky will give you an array of matters to deal with. If you work for the government, you get a fantastic range of matters because the government deal with all types of tax issues."* Although the working pressures are less under a public paymaster, unfortunately so are the financial rewards. As Jonny observes: *"The flow tends to be the other way people usually join a commercial law firm from Inland Revenue or Customs & Excise and get paid much more after getting valuable knowledge and practical experience of tax law in the civil service."*

Some solicitors move to accountancy firms in a tax consultancy role (as distinct from working for the legal arm of an accountancy firm). While *"it's very similar to working for law firms,"* according to some there are *"certain cultural differences,"* which can make for a rather bumpy adjustment to the new job.

Overall, the skills and knowledge gained through working in private practice are portable at all levels of qualification. There's certainly no shortage of positions in private practice for those who want them, provided they're *"made of the right stuff."* After just a few years of bedding down in the area, junior tax lawyers become a very marketable commodity. As Jonny states: *"Firms are always keen to have a decent tax lawyer, and this is reflected in the salaries."* There's just one draw back – the public image. As one of our tax lawyers said: *"When I meet a girl a party and I tell her what I do, it tends to kill conversation stone dead!"*

LEADING FIRMS FROM CHAMBERS UK 2003-2004

TAX: CORPORATE ■ LONDON

Band	Firm
1	**Freshfields Bruckhaus Deringer**
	Linklaters
	Slaughter and May
2	**Allen & Overy**
	Clifford Chance LLP
3	**Ashurst Morris Crisp**
	Herbert Smith
4	**Berwin Leighton Paisner**
	Lovells
	Macfarlanes
	Norton Rose
	Simmons & Simmons
	SJ Berwin
	Travers Smith Braithwaite
5	**CMS Cameron McKenna**
	Denton Wilde Sapte
	Nabarro Nathanson
	Olswang
	Shearman & Sterling
	Watson, Farley & Williams
6	**Addleshaw Goddard**
	Clyde & Co
	Field Fisher Waterhouse
	McDermott, Will & Emery
	Weil, Gotshal & Manges

TAX: CORPORATE ■ THE SOUTH & SOUTH WEST

Band	Firm
1	**Burges Salmon** Bristol
	Osborne Clarke Bristol
2	**Blake Lapthorn Linnell** Fareham
	TLT Bristol
	Wiggin & Co Cheltenham

TAX: CORPORATE ■ MIDLANDS & EAST ANGLIA

Band	Firm
1	**Pinsents** Birmingham
	Wragge & Co LLP Birmingham
2	**DLA** Birmingham
	Eversheds Birmingham, Nottingham
3	**Hammonds** Birmingham
	Mills & Reeve Cambridge

TAX: CORPORATE ■ THE NORTH

Band	Firm
1	**Addleshaw Goddard** Leeds, Manchester
	Pinsents Leeds
2	**Eversheds** Leeds, Manchester
	Hammonds Leeds, Manchester
3	**Dickinson Dees** Newcastle upon Tyne
	Walker Morris Leeds
4	**Irwin Mitchell** Leeds

tmt

TMT (Technology, Media & Telecoms) is an ever-changing practice area and just as the technology industry evolves with rapidity, so must the lawyers servicing it. Kim Nicholson is a TMT partner at Olswang. She says: *"You need to be a driven and questioning person – constantly asking 'what's next?'"*

Michael Chissick is the head of the technology group at Field Fisher Waterhouse. He told us: *"It's an area of law where you have to be a bit more nimble than others. You have to keep reinventing yourself."* He started out in computer law in the late 80s and by 1996 e-commerce had arrived. In the mid-90s multi-media came and went. When digital TV hit, he and his colleagues got up to speed on that. When the dot.com bubble burst they had to adjust to the fact that the lucrative start-up market was disappearing. Michael and his team now find that 'e-government' is their hot topic, given the Government's stated aim of delivering services on-line.

So what kind of clients do TMT lawyers work for?

- IT and telecoms suppliers and their customers;
- huge multinationals with offices across Europe and the US;
- small entrepreneurs or start-ups;
- local and central government and charities;
- web-based businesses, software developers, hardware suppliers and maintainers, disaster recovery suppliers;
- 23-year-olds winning and losing fortunes from their dad's garages!

The concept of 'convergence' keeps TMT lawyers on their toes these days. Telecommunications, TV and the internet are becoming so interrelated and interchangeable that lawyers in the sector must learn to master each of these media. As Michael told us: *"It's all going to come together; you'll be watching TV on your phone and sending e-mail from your TV. Will phone lines win or will BskyB take over? It will change the way we all work. I might have to get involved in more content issues as my telecoms clients might become involved in buying-in content. We will have understand all the new developments and develop all the necessary skills. We may have to become more of a one-stop shop."* Kim agrees: *"If someone's predominant field is IT contracts, they still have to understand regulatory telecoms stuff; they must know the likely hurdles. There's a necessity for lawyers to work really closely together."*

type of work

IT and internet-based work involves a lot of commercial contract drafting, for example, terms and conditions for a website, software development agreements, computer games licences or outsourcing (where outside IT specialists are brought in to set up and run a company's computer systems). Clients will seek advice on issues such as data protection compliance or cyber-squatting (domain name disputes). Lawyers are also drawn into a support role, working with their corporate colleagues on M&A transactions. Competition law rears its head, for example, where large IT suppliers are accused of abusing a dominant position in the market place.

Some matters may even lead on to litigation and, at this stage, non-contentious TMT lawyers will enlist the help of specialist TMT litigators. Richard Yates is a two-year qualified TMT lawyer in Nabarro Nathanson's Reading office. These contentious lawyers regularly handle disputes over contracts to provide IT services (hardware/software/maintenance/disaster recovery etc.). If a piece of software simply doesn't do what the customer thought it would, their primary goal is to get to the point where the software will work. In these circumstances, lawyers need to handle matters in a way that doesn't ruin the relationship between the parties. Richard says: *"Our clients look for alternatives to traditional litigation; for many it's all about getting the next deal moving."* Then there are disputes between competitors, perhaps over intellectual property in software or the name or design of a website. Even without a customer-supplier relationship to protect, mediation, expert determination and other less formal methods of dispute resolution are very popular with TMT clients. TMT lawyers are likely to spend less time in court than ordinary commercial litigators, and more time advising clients on strategies for negotiating settlements to disputes. Major IT suppliers are often keen to avoid the publicity of litigation at a time when poor sector performance is being reported in the press. But not all cases are resolved amicably. Big multi-million pound disputes do reach the High Court and TMT litigators may be called upon to rush to court on very short notice to apply for emergency injunctions (eg to prevent ongoing breach of copyright in a client's software).

Lawyers acting for telecoms clients are additionally called upon to give advice on the regulatory regimes, which govern the sector and are designed to protect the interests of consumers. There's been so much legislation from Brussels in last few years that Kim says: *"Even at 15 years qualified I still need to bone up on new law. I need to be constantly thinking of new risks and opportunities."* There's a heavy transactional side to telecoms law and any observer will have noted the consolidation in the industry in the last couple of years. The big issue of recent times has been the 3G mobile phone licenses issued by governments across Europe, and Broad Band and Wireless Local Loop are very 'now'. If these terms baffle and leave you cold, you're not destined for TMT!

a day in the life...

Michael told us that there are periods when he's involved in really big deals that occupy all his time and take him out of the office with a team of lawyers and clients. *"That's maybe three or four times a year. Usually my day is more varied though. After I've picked up my e-mails to find out what's happening in the US, there are normally a couple of small agreements around for me to advise on. It's a very rare day when I don't have a meeting, either with lawyers or a client."* 80% of the typical TMT lawyer's work is transactional in nature, be it a large M&A deal or a smaller commercial contract. Michael says: *"We are becoming more like corporate lawyers in large outsourcing deals; we co-ordinate other parts of the firm – employment, property, pensions, banking, tax, etc. IT lawyers today are what corporate lawyers were ten years ago."*

The reality is that as a TMT lawyer you exist to service the many needs of your client sector. New laws and cases appear and your job is to navigate a path through these as well as being a good all-round commercial advisor. Good news: TMT lawyers normally get the chance to go on secondment to clients. Young solicitors at Field Fisher Waterhouse enjoy spells at clients such as Colt Telecom, Northgate, Ordnance Survey, the BBC and Accenture.

skills needed

...general grounding in corporate and contract law... commercial... ability to be a deal-maker... understand 'hard' regulatory matters... sensitive to the needs of 'creatives'... keep up to speed with new technology... comfortable with technical jargon... industry knowledge... gut feel for the issues... be thrilled by change... innovative... knowledge of competition law and copyright matters... a sensible approach to risk...

Are you always the first of your friends to buy gadgets? Michael confesses to this; he's fascinated by technology. Having a background in the technology sector will help, but is by no means essential. If this all sounds rather boysie, rest assured that as many women go into the area as men. Kim confirms: *"The business people are quite logically minded,"* and certainly the techies are that way. *"For example, software programming is a structured mental process."* And as for the lawyers, like Michael, Kim says: *"I am quite a gadget person. Most people here do like gadgets!"*

Commercial draftsmanship is a core skill. Commonly, there are no precedents for what you're trying to achieve – there were none for 3G mobile phone licences – so you must not be put off by a blank piece of paper. You have to be innovative and come up with some 'outside the box' thinking. Richard says: *"Sometimes we need to advise our clients that there is no point in spending £5K on the perfect legal case, when a cheaper route is just as likely to achieve the right result."* Little in this area of law is traditional. Innovative technology clients call for innovative legal advisors.

Before you start your training you can help yourself enormously by keeping up with developments in technology. Michael has a monthly legal column in *Internet Magazine* and also recommends *Computing, Internet World* and *Computer Weekly*. Kim recommends *New Media Age* as it gives an overview of what the main companies are doing. If you're already up to speed with the movers and shakers in the sector and how the market has shifted, then when you start your training you can spend more time developing legal skills and less time grasping the basics of the sector.

What you definitely don't need to be is a nerdy no-mates. People skills are vital and you'll learn to deal with clients who are poles apart in terms of needs and temperament. Richard explained: *"Dispute management is part of everyday life for large multi-national clients and instructions come from in-house lawyers familiar with disputes. Emotions can run stronger in disputes involving smaller clients where the outcome may make or break the business, and may have a direct personal impact on the company director who is giving you instructions."*

career options

As it's still seen as a sexy area of law, it's quite competitive at the junior end. It's not been the best of markets since the technology slump, but the lawyers we spoke to were adamant that if you have a passion for the sector then you should pursue your dream job. Twinning your interests with your legal training is the route to job satisfaction. Teams within law firms tend to be quite stable, but some lawyers do move in-house and often find their role becomes wider ranging than in private practice. These jobs are almost certainly going to be on the non-contentious side.

LEADING FIRMS FROM CHAMBERS UK 2003-2004

INFORMATION TECHNOLOGY ■ LONDON

1 **Allen & Overy**
Baker & McKenzie
Bird & Bird
Clifford Chance LLP

2 **Lovells**
Masons

3 **Field Fisher Waterhouse**
Kemp Little LLP
Linklaters
Taylor Wessing

4 **Denton Wilde Sapte**
Freshfields Bruckhaus Deringer
Mayer, Brown, Rowe & Maw LLP
Nabarro Nathanson
Olswang
Osborne Clarke
Shaw Pittman LLP
Simmons & Simmons
Slaughter and May
Tarlo Lyons

5 **Berwin Leighton Paisner**
Bristows
DLA
Harbottle & Lewis LLP
Herbert Smith
Norton Rose

INFORMATION TECHNOLOGY ■ THE SOUTH

1 **Bond Pearce** Southampton
DMH Brighton

2 **Clyde & Co** Guildford

INFORMATION TECHNOLOGY ■ THAMES VALLEY

1 **Nabarro Nathanson** Reading
Law Offices of Marcus J O'Leary

2 **Olswang Thames Valley** Reading
Osborne Clarke Reading

3 **Boyes Turner** Reading
Clark Holt Swindon
Manches Oxford

4 **Willoughby & Partners** Oxford

INFORMATION TECHNOLOGY ■ SOUTH WEST

1 **Osborne Clarke** Bristol

2 **Beachcroft Wansbroughs** Bristol
Bevan Ashford BBL Bristol
Burges Salmon Bristol

3 **Foot Anstey Sargent** Plymouth

INFORMATION TECHNOLOGY ■ WALES

1 **Edwards Geldard** Cardiff
Eversheds Cardiff
Morgan Cole Cardiff

INFORMATION TECHNOLOGY ■ MIDLANDS & EAST ANGLIA

1 **Wragge & Co LLP** Birmingham

2 **Eversheds** Birmingham, Nottingham

3 **Hewitsons** Cambridge, Northampton
Pinsents Birmingham
V-Lex Ltd Worksop

INFORMATION TECHNOLOGY ■ THE NORTH

1 **Addleshaw Goddard** Leeds, Manchester

2 **Masons** Leeds, Manchester

3 **Eversheds** Leeds, Manchester
Pinsents Leeds

4 **Halliwell Landau** Manchester
Hammonds Leeds, Manchester
Irwin Mitchell Leeds, Sheffield

TELECOMMUNICATIONS ■ LONDON

1 **Allen & Overy**
Bird & Bird
Clifford Chance LLP

2 **Baker & McKenzie**
Linklaters
Olswang

3 **Field Fisher Waterhouse**
Freshfields Bruckhaus Deringer
Simmons & Simmons

4 **Ashurst Morris Crisp**
Denton Wilde Sapte
Mayer, Brown, Rowe & Maw LLP
Norton Rose
Taylor Wessing

5 **Charles Russell**
Herbert Smith
Kemp Little LLP
Osborne Clarke
Slaughter and May
Wilmer, Cutler & Pickering

TELECOMMUNICATIONS ■ THE REGIONS

1 **Eversheds** Leeds
Wragge & Co LLP Birmingham

international firms...international locations

Several UK law firms have had overseas offices for a number of years, but there's no doubt that in the last five the profession has become even more outward looking. In the race to plant their flags all over Europe and Asia, City firms have set up new offices, merged with foreign law firms and built alliances. Now that the majority of quality law firms in Europe have already tied themselves to UK or US firms, they have embarked on a phase of transatlantic mergers. In 2002 we saw the creation of Mayer, Brown, Rowe & Maw, and in 2003 all eyes were on Jones Day Gouldens and the near miss merger of Ashurst Morris Crisp with New York firm Fried, Frank, Shriver, Harris & Jacobson. US firms view London as the gateway to Europe and, consequently, have great interest in the London legal market. Save for one or two notable exceptions, the US law firms already in London have expanded their British operations.

Plenty of firms pride themselves on their international reach, boasting about how many offices they have in various jurisdictions, and many students now consider this aspect to be the determining factor when choosing where to train. If you share this view of what is important and you are determined to spend part of your training contract overseas then you certainly have plenty of choice. Pick the right firm and you can effectively guarantee time in an overseas office.

the top international players

We consulted our colleagues on *Chambers Global* to identify the leading 15 international law firms. The position of a firm in the following table reflects the number of times it is ranked in *Chambers Global 2003-2004* for its work. Each ranking (the total number is shown in brackets) is for a separate area of practice, be this projects in Kazakhstan, shipping in Hong Kong, IP in Spain and so on. For detailed information on any law firm's global practice, refer to *Chambers Global* on **www.chambersandpartners.com** or consult the copy in your university's careers library or law department.

TOP 15 GLOBAL FIRMS	
1	Clifford Chance (116)
2	Freshfields Bruckhaus Deringer (99)
3	Baker & McKenzie (96)
4	Allen & Overy (95)
5	Linklaters (73)
6	White & Case LLP (55)
7	Shearman & Sterling (42)
8	Lovells (41)
9	Skadden, Arps, Slate, Meagher & Flom (38)
10	Herbert Smith (36)
11	Norton Rose (33)
12	Cleary Gottlieb Steen & Hamilton (32)
13	Denton Wilde Sapte (31)
14	Ashurst Morris Crisp (30)
15	Weil, Gotshal & Manges (29)

From Chambers Global 2003-2004

pack your bags!

Although time abroad gives you experience of working in another jurisdiction, you'll not normally practise foreign law. An overseas seat is without doubt a very rewarding and challenging experience. It will almost always be taken in an office that is smaller than the firm's UK office and you should find that you are working on tasks offering greater responsibility. The trick to securing the most popular overseas seats is to wage an effective campaign of self-promotion and to get the prerequisite experience in the UK office before you go. The key to getting a particular seat may be as simple as having the right second language, but remember that language skills may also act as a handcuff. Quite simply, if the firm has a Moscow office and you are the only Russian-speaking trainee you won't be going to New York – the purpose of sending you abroad is so you can work for the best interests of the firm, not have a fab holiday!

It may be hard work. It may be an eye opener. It may even be lonely if you're in a less popular location; nevertheless, the overwhelming feeling is that time abroad is very worthwhile. To give you a taste of what's on offer in the most-visited cities, we've picked our top trainee getaways...

amsterdam

Legend has it that Amsterdam was founded by two fishermen and a seasick dog after the dog jumped ship to deposit the contents of its stomach. If you think Amsterdam is only good for stag weekends, clogs and plant exports – marijuana and tulips – then think again. This city is one of the world's most liveable and loveable. Cars and buses give way to scores of bicycles, and some 100 kms of romantic tree-lined canals weave between distinctive 17th century town houses and more museums per square inch than anywhere else in the world. Amsterdam offers the exuberance and cultural vibrancy of a big city, with the manageability of a small town. And although the city is known for its liberal, and often experimental attitudes to drugs and prostitution, it also has a reputation for tolerance and safety. Hop on your bike for a social and cultural awakening that might just blow your mind.

Work: Several firms offer trainee seats in Amsterdam. Both Clifford Chance and Allen & Overy send three trainees: one to corporate and two to finance. Clifford Chance's corporate operation is a Dutch department, although it operates a policy whereby if there is a non-Dutch speaker present, everyone must speak English. Being in a smaller office, you can expect much more responsibility so don't be surprised if you find yourself regularly meeting with clients or running a due diligence exercise by yourself. However, the Dutch are famously laid back, and have a *"fantastic approach to the work/life balance – you need a very good reason to work past 6pm."* Accordingly, partners are often more approachable than in the UK...and don't be shocked by their more relaxed attitudes. On the subject of smoking, whether it's tobacco or something more exotic, it lacks the stigma in Holland that it has in the UK. Smoking tobacco in offices and at your desk is not uncommon. If you're easily offended, this is probably not the place for you – the Dutch can also be blunt to the point of apparent rudeness. As one trainee put it: *"If you're doing something badly, they'll just say 'That's appalling!'"*

Rest and Play: Like the seasick dog, trainees might find the city's social scene at times a little dizzying. But fear not, should the bars, restaurants and clubs become overwhelming, a sobering visit to one of the many galleries and museums housing Van Gogh, Rembrandt and Vermeer will perk you up. Forget the tube, trainees are offered firm bicycles upon their arrival. Spacious apartments are centrally located in *"trendy"* canal districts, like Nieuwmarkt or Keizersgracht. Most cycle canalside to work in around five minutes. A CC trainee remarked: *"It has given me an extra two hours a day!"* An A&O trainee said: *"There's something really great about being able to open your window and look out onto a canal."* Flexible licensing hours allow trainees to go home after work, eat and then walk to the bars or brown cafes. Just remember to tip the bouncers on leaving – they never forget a face. Eating out is cheaper than in London and the city boasts a banquet of world cuisines. You'll have a ready-made set of friends to dine with – the city is home to some 15 UK trainees at any one time. In summer, the locals take to the pavement cafes and descend naked on Vondelpark. At weekends you can cycle to the pretty Monacon Dam, about 15 kms to the north, to eat pancakes and drink beer before wobbling your way back. There's no shortage of boat owners at the major UK firms, so you'll often find yourself baking on the deck of a barge. In winter, when the canals freeze over, it's all about ice skating and sipping on hot chocolate.

Best Things: Canal culture, Biking to work, Legalised marijuana.
Worst Things: Constant hangovers, Tipping bouncers, Dutch directness.

brussels

Home of commerce, bureaucracy and Tintin, Brussels is the heart of new Europe and plays host to the headquarters of many EU institutions. 159 embassies are based there, in addition to 120 IGOs and 1,400 NGOs. Political powerhouse it may be, but it is probably fair to say that you can cram most of Brussels' attractions into a weekend. So what about spending a whole six months out there? When speaking to Brussels trainees it was hard to tell whether they had been spending too much time with the city's 2,500 diplomats or whether there just wasn't that much to reveal about the place; they proved to be hard nuts to crack. Frequent references were made to chocolate, mussels and beer, but the city's more obscure delights, including the museums of fencing, lace, trams and comic strip art, had eluded most of them.

Work: Competition for Brussels seats is *"not exactly fierce,"* as most trainees opt for warmer, more romantic climes. If you have a particular interest in EU or competition law, or you want to be close to home, or the possibility of rejection makes you anxious, Brussels could be for you. Several trainees opted for the city because they spoke French and wanted to improve it, but language skills are not considered to be a particular advantage, especially since many firms will provide tuition. *"Competition law can be quite intense at times,"* but all-nighters and Saturdays in the office are *"very rare."* In addition to EU law, *"there is also a lot of quality trade work coming through the city."* A DLA trainee said her work was characterised by *"big deals, lots of research and lots of responsibility."* Much of her day was spent monitoring public affairs and reviewing EU publications and websites. Don't underestimate the volume of research-based tasks that will come your way. *"You won't get much client contact but there are a lot more conferences and seminars to attend."*

Rest and Play: Baker & McKenzie's one-bedroom apartment affords lovely views of the office, two streets away and DLA's beautiful Art Nouveau flat is in the city centre. Many trainees live in the Schumann area near to the Commission buildings and tend to flock together; tours and events are laid on by the many firms in the city. The climate may be English but there's *"a much better quality of life and much better food."* Brussels is only two and a half hours and £75 away from the UK, so persuading friends and family to visit won't prove difficult. Said one trainee: *"I haven't had a weekend on my own since I got here."* Brussels is a manageable city with a pleasant pace of life. Of course, Brussels' most famous symbol is the Mannekin Pis, a small statue of a boy relieving himself into a fountain, but if the excitement wears off after a couple of visits, you could always follow the lead of the trainees who hired a car and made a pilgrimage to Ostend, Belgian refuge of the late, great Marvin Gaye.

Best Things: Restaurants, European lifestyle, Internationalism.
Worst Things: Cobblestones in high heels, Poodles.

frankfurt

Frankfurt is the ideal habitat for the UK Finance Trainee. It is the European capital of Capital and is *"clean, cosmopolitan and friendly."* If you want an unforgettable time in a radically different environment then politely decline, but Frankfurt is a good place to live in the basic sense of the verb. *"It's the nicest place I've been for everyday living. You never get that busy feeling. There's always space."* The city is famous for its huge airport (incorporating a nightclub and adult cinema) and business conventions; most visitors see little else of the place. Even though most business is done in English, being able to speak German is of real advantage in terms of *"building up a rapport with clients and locals and making the most of your time there."* The consensus was that the ski season is the best time of year to be in Frankfurt, but in the summer you can enjoy lovely parks and open-air pools. Think Tooting Lido, but clean and green and pleasant.

Work: Linklaters offers the quintessential Frankfurt experience: a capital markets seat on the 32nd floor of a skyscraper. At most firms the work is paper-intensive and finance all the way. Much is done in English and pertains to English law, but *"you can't be afraid of German law."* A Lovells trainee described a corporate and banking seat very similar to the ones back in London. There's not a lot of client contact and, as in other European capitals, there is some mundane translation work. Sadly, a lot of the work involves *"taking an old precedent and then changing the figures for a new transaction,"* but it was refreshing to hear that *"there is no culture where you feel you have to stay late."*

Rest and Play: The *"classy"* Linklaters apartment has a balcony, is one minute from the office and located right above an English pub. *"Except for clothes, you won't need to bring anything. It's a bit like living in a hotel."* The Lovells flat is also within easy walking distance of the office which means that, compared to the London commute, *"you gain two hours every day."* All the UK trainees are clustered in the same part of town so you've a ready made social circle, if you so desire. The best thing about the bars and clubs is that you never have to stand up or queue. *"Frankfurt's waiters have excellent memories."* If it all seems just too nice and you need to exorcise rebellious urges, it's cheap to hire a Merc and go for a cruise down the Autobahn, where the only speed limitation is your nerve.

Best Things: Standard of living, Structure.
Worst Things: Lazy shopkeepers and erratic opening hours.

hong kong

Back with the Chinese after 99 years of British rule, Hong Kong has become the boisterous love child of Chairman Mao and Ronald McDonald. A city obsessed with money, shopping and branded goods, *"when it's all lit up at night you feel like an extra from Blade Runner."* Yet despite the pace, the political contradictions, the crowds and the smog, HK residents must be doing something right since they enjoy very high life expectancy. When the hum of money gets too much for you, you can take a free T'ai Chi class in the park or visit one of the region's Buddhist temples and remote islands. September to March is mild; otherwise it gets very hot and sweaty.

Work: A Stephenson Harwood trainee spoke of his desire to work in a *"hugely challenging"* and *"radically different"* culture. *"Much of the time you can't answer a question easily and you keep having to go back to the books...There is no comfort zone."* Mostly trainees will deal with general commercial work, but a Simmons & Simmons trainee told us that if you have the requisite language skills, you might find yourself assisting on more corporate transactions. Herbert Smith offers litigation seats and one trainee we spoke to had spent much of her time on IP law. You must be ready to master a whole new set of traditions and etiquette before you can deal effectively with clients and colleagues. Many of the firms are staffed with local lawyers as well as westerners, and trainees get the chance to mix with them and their families. *"You are treated as a guest and are encouraged to get out and enjoy yourself."*

Rest and Play: Many firms have apartments on The Levels, a residential hill where your relative altitude reflects your wealth. Most trainees live halfway up with the expats, where there's a pleasant village feel. *"Hong Kong is definitely the most hedonistic place to go overseas,"* one Norton Rose trainee said. You can certainly take the *"out until 6am"* route through your time on the island, visiting Wanchai, the old sailors' hangout just ten minutes from the CBD or Lan Kwai Fong, with its concentration of expat bars. If you find yourself lured into the murky underworld of the karaoke clubs *"you'd better learn your song properly. Locals take it very seriously and often practice in their lunch breaks."* The Chinese Opera is another quintessential HK entertainment although one trainee said: *"It's like nothing I've ever seen and something I never want to see again."* You can easily get to mainland China for a round of golf or to pick up counterfeit goods and many firms have a junk for harbour cruises. Sports fans should time their visit to coincide with Rugby Sevens.

Best Things: Lifestyle, Nightlife, Waterskiing and beach picnics.
Worst Things: Pollution, Humidity, Spending habits.

madrid

Having come through a bloody civil war and spent decades languishing under Franco, Spain has played a hard game of catch-up with its neighbours, but now, according to one trainee we spoke to, *"Spain is really starting to move on the international scene... it's an exciting time to be out here."* Madrid is everything a capital city should be: vibrant, affordable and fun. *"For young, single people it is ideal."* You would be wise to avoid a summer seat, however, since Madrid can become scorching hot and the savvy locals all flee to the coast.

Work: Being a trainee solicitor is not the best way to soak up the easy going 'mañana' ethos for which the locals are famous. Madrid is a regional commercial centre like Paris or Frankfurt, and you can expect to be handling the same kind of commercial and corporate work, with plenty of private M&A and corporate housekeeping, etc. Good Spanish is essential, since you will mostly be handling Spanish law. *"You end up working just as hard as in London, but people are less likely to come up to you and tell you that something's urgent."* SJ Berwin's offices are dress-down on Friday, but the working environment is *"smart and conservative." "In Madrid you generally see a lot more people wearing suits."* There is a fair bit of *"translation and checking, but when there's chargeable work on, it always takes priority."* A two- or three-hour siesta in the middle of the day can jar with Protestant sensibilities and, when there's a lot of work on, the long lunch break means you can be in the office until 10 or 11pm. *"People guard their weekends quite jealously,"* said a trainee from Linklaters.

Rest and Play: SJ Berwin's apartment is smart, central and only a 25-minute walk to the office. The Linklaters' apartment is allegedly *"the best by quite a long way,"* near Colon and right in the centre of things. Madrid is a real cultural oasis in the otherwise barren central plains of Spain. Bar culture figures highly and the city boasts three of the best art collections in Europe: the Prado, the Reina Sofia and the Thyssen. Queues for the latest movies stretch twice around the block, but tickets cost a quarter of what you'd pay in the West End. Madrid is an ideal base for trips to the surrounding countryside and *"you are positively encouraged to get away at weekends."* The locals are open and friendly and it is easy to immerse yourself in Spanish life. Whether you want to go to a bullfight, hang out in cafés or watch some proper football, Madrid has it all, including our man Golden Balls.

Best Things: Food, Social life, Weather, Beckham.
Worst Things: Long days, Having to go out so late, Dishonest cabbies.

the middle east

The business centres of the Middle East offer guaranteed fine weather, high-profile work and exotic glitz. Oil has turned Abu Dhabi from a small fishing village into one of the richest cities in the world in just 40 years, and skyscrapers and palm trees now predominate. *"The city is incredibly anglicised and the culture shock is minimal."* If Abu Dhabi isn't to your liking, *"stunningly beautiful"* Muscat offers a more authentic taste of life in the Gulf. March to September is the best time to go, although you'll be air conditioned all year round.

Work: In the Gulf *"they have a different way of doing business,"* but they still tend to do it in English. Commercial work predominates and there's an emphasis on projects and finance. A Trowers & Hamlins trainee told us that work is *"split between dealing with UAE Government departments and multinational consortiums that want to set up business in the UAE."* Another dealt with *"a vast range of things from enormous power stations to people worried about lost luggage."* There's plenty of client contact, including PR and marketing experiences you'd never get back in London. The working day runs from 8am–1pm and then 4pm–7pm, and the lunch break is best spent *"swimming, waterskiing or taking a nap."* The week runs from Saturday to Wednesday, with some trainees required to work Thursday mornings. Because there are only three days in common with foreign offices the pressure can build up fast. *"When someone phones up and asks for something to be done by the end of the week, it often means it has to be done there and then." "Work becomes much more a part of your daily life than it is back in London,"* but then there's not much to do in Muscat once you've been to the Souk and admired the views.

Rest and Play: *"Fabulous"* apartments with sea views are par for the course and come with all mod cons short of gold taps and fittings. Free memberships of swanky health clubs also come as standard, as do cars and free petrol. If it's culture you're after, think twice about Abu Dhabi, since *"there isn't much."* There's an *"excellent quality of life"* however, and with the Maldives, Oman and Petra all within striking distance, holidays become a major expense. The expat community and office colleagues make up a big part of a trainee's social life, with Abu Dhabi's 'Brit Club' playing an important part. The scene in Muscat is quieter and socialising takes place in the city's half dozen hotels. By the end of your six months *"the waiters will know exactly what you are going to drink and where you are going to sit."* The expat lifestyle is something you love or hate, and in either case you must *"put up with the slight superficiality of it."* The smaller pool of Brit-lawyers in Muscat means you're more likely to build a wider group of friends, including teachers, engineers and oil workers. *"The rolling turnover of trainees also means you acquire your predecessor's friends."* Better hope they made some...

Best Things: Lifestyle, Quality work, Desert and wadi exploration.
Worst Things: Heat, Isolation, Boredom.

moscow

If you have a taste for adventure and are concerned that a lifetime of due diligence won't give you any good stories to tell the grandchildren, you should consider the Wild East. *"Moscow doesn't attract applicants like Singapore does. Most people in Moscow have an interesting story and a real interest in it."* With its fascinating history, stunning architecture and a metro system with more chandeliers than your average palace, Moscow is rounded off with *"an appealing edge of madness." "There's no routine, something always happens..."* As in any frontier town, there is a fair amount of crime and punishment, and things change fast. *"People have preconceptions of Moscow which are not true. You can't sell jeans and you won't have to queue for food. It is very Western. You're not going to starve."* Winter is the best time to be there if you're not out to get a tan. Expect plenty of *"fresh, crisp snow"* and temperatures of down to 30°C.

Work: Many firms offer energy work in addition to a regular diet of banking and corporate. A Denton Wilde Sapte trainee worked on a Black Sea gas pipeline case that touched on complex ownership issues and maritime law. The workload for all the trainees we spoke to was described as *"steady." "You can expect to do things that are well beyond trainee level. It gives you a lot of confidence."* English is the language of the office, but pidgin Russian is helpful, if only to get around the city and make sense of the *"mind-boggling"* Cyrillic alphabet. Levels of autonomy in one Moscow office were so high that London proved a disappointment for one trainee who *"felt crushed by the full weight of the hierarchy"* on his return. Trainees of the world unite! You have nothing to lose but your contracts!

Rest and Play: Most firms provide trainees with good-sized apartments within the Zone 1 Garden Ring; others provide an allowance for suitable accommodation. Even in the plusher buildings, *"water and heating can go off quite sporadically."* You'll never be at a loss for things to do in Moscow. *"Things happen,"* reported one trainee, mysteriously. The usual tourist attractions – Lenin's Mausoleum and Red Square – are impressive although the view of St Basil's Cathedral is somewhat marred by the *"endless procession of women in white wedding dresses who want their photo taken in front of it."* Russian food is *"heavy,"* but you won't be limited to the *"greasy potato patties"* that one trainee recalled fondly from a trip in the early 90s. Travelwise you can get as far as St Petersburg on an overnight train and there's a circuit of picturesque towns around the city known as 'The Golden Ring'. Any final pearls of wisdom before you defect? *"There are many things that you should know before you go out there, but half the fun is discovering them for yourself."*

Best Things: Surreal social life, Anarchy.
Worst Things: Hassle from the police, Bribery, Traffic and pollution.

new york

When asked what they liked most about New York, trainees tend to give us the same answer as the Pope. *"Tutti buoni,"* he told reporters, *"everything is good."* *"Manhattan life is 24/7 and people do everything for you."* Convenience comes at a price, however. *"You'll need to get used to giving away dollar bills."* Despite overseas allowances and cheap taxis, trainees coming from London found it *"extremely expensive."* The city famously picked itself up and carried on after the tragic events of 9/11, and its mayor is now leading the bid for the 2012 Olympic Games, whose ancient motto 'Swifter, higher, stronger' (whatever that is in Greek) could easily be adopted by the city itself. The best time to be out there is in the fall, when the city is *"absolutely beautiful"* and you don't have to put up with intense heat or cold.

Work: New York law is reasonably similar to UK law and trainees are likely to come in contact with similar work. Finance figures highly and a lot of work from Latin America comes through the city. Clifford Chance offers its trainees a capital markets seat, dealing mainly with south american banks, plus one in project finance and one in corporate. The atmosphere in its New York office was more formal than in the UK, with a good old-fashioned partner hierarchy dictating where people sit and the size of the office. One trainee we spoke to had regularly been in the office after midnight during a busy period, but generally, 9am to 8pm are typical hours. *"Before I went out there I was worried that I would never see the light of day,"* admitted an Allen & Overy trainee. Any language barriers? One trainee told us: *"I find I have to speak more loudly and repeat myself."*

Rest and Play: Trainees get apartments with fantastic views on the Upper East and Upper West sides but, from the sound of things, don't spend much time at home. You'll need a head for heights and a taste for concierges and marble atria. Beyond the daily cost of living, the main expense is *"jetting off for the weekend."* One trainee talked of trips to New Orleans and Bermuda, and when you tire of the Sex and the City lifestyle, you can do the West Wing and Ally McBeal thing in Washington and Boston. There's skiing upstate in the winter and summer weekends in the Hamptons. *"Manic"* is how one trainee described the social life. *"There are a million bars and the best restaurants in the world."* Locals eat out all the time and the good places are booked up months in advance. Culturally, New York is in a league of its own and between them the Whitney, the Met, the Guggenheim and the Moma contain some of the most important art of the last century. Sustained by a potent mix of caffeine and Cosmopolitans, one trainee confided to us: *"When I get back to London I'm going to sleep for a week."*

Best Things: Convenience, Lifestyle, Diversity
Worst Things: Tipping, Hours

paris

Get a bottle of red wine, a pack of Gauloise and some Godard movies, and ask someone with a husky voice to whisper a list of Parisian monuments in your ear. If this does it for you, and you have at least GCSE French, then make a beeline for the capital of romance, style, art and haughty grandeur. Whether you're more at home in the cafés of the Left Bank or on the leather sofas at the National Bank, there is everything a young bourgeois or bohemian could wish for, from haute couture to basement jazz clubs. The best time to go is March to September. In May it's not too hot and there are no tourists around; it's the perfect time to invite friends across. *"I had so many people come out to visit that I got to know the sites of Paris far better than most tour guides,"* claimed one trainee.

Work: Clifford Chance has several seats for trainees, most of which deal with broad-based finance issues covering projects, asset finance, general banking and structured finance. There's also a fair bit of corporate and property work coming through the city. Eversheds offers a seat in public international law. One of its trainees found she was working for US and UK lawyers on arbitrations between countries and governments, which tended to be *"quite academic."* Trainees have to manage themselves far more in Paris than in London, and find they are given a lot more rope. *"Long term it's very beneficial, but there were times when you wish you could have an easier life."* The hours are varied but reasonable, so *"work won't be keeping you in every night."*

Rest and Play: Clifford Chance's apartments afford amazing views from the 30th floor of a building in the 15th arrondissement in the south west of the city and only ten minutes' walk from the office. Eversheds has an apartment in Le Marais, right in the centre of things. If you want it, there's a ready-made, e-mail-run social scene for the numerous UK trainees in the city, and *"some people spend every night in the Firkin."* Bars are open until 2am and the club scene is of similar quality to London's. Long gone are the days when French music meant Serge Gainsbourg or Johnny Hallyday; Paris has had a revival of late, giving the locals all the more reason to be snooty to foreigners. Travel is a great temptation since *"Paris is an ideal springboard to the rest of Europe."* Depending on the time of year, you can be on the slopes or the sands within a few hours thanks to the high speed TGV. Parisian restaurants are spectacular and dining out is likely to take care of your surplus euros. *"I tend to eat out four or five times a week,"* claimed one trainee, but with the rent taken care of and a living allowance, *"you're still onto a bit of a money spinner."*

Best Things: Food, Wine, Romance.
Worst Things: French TV, No bacon sarnies, The attitude towards the English.

piraeus/athens

Home to Alexander the Great, Socrates and moussaka, Greece is a delight for hellenophiles, historians, and hedonists alike. The enduring images of Athens in recent times – the Acropolis and Mount Olympus aside – are of a smog-choked city of traffic jams and eyeball-searing heat, but don't believe the horror stories. Athens is no more polluted than London, and while temperatures can reach 40°C in summer, this is compensated for by post-work swims at the beach. If Athens is the cradle of civilisation, Piraeus is its hospital waiting room. Other guidebooks would have you believe it's the sort of place you end up in when waiting for a ferry to take you somewhere better…in our case, you just have to be a trainee. Piraeus is a port city, and although this means lots of ships and less than inspiring architecture, there's also an abundance of sunshine, seafood and sailors. If that's not enough, Athens is only nine kms and a three quid taxi fare away, and the blinding white sands of the Greek islands are at your feet. Whether it's weekend island hopping, the sleep-when-you're-dead nightlife, or the spectacular ruins of the Acropolis, a trainee seat in Piraeus or Athens is sure to be no Greek tragedy.

Work: If your interest lies in shipping, then a seat in Piraeus will float your boat. Most trainees spent their time in ship finance, with the occasional piece of litigation. The law is largely English, and transactions are handled mainly in the mother tongue, although knowledge of Greek definitely helps. By contrast, work in Athens tends to be corporate finance, with Greek law playing a greater role. At Norton Rose, solicitors speak in Greek, so if it's all Greek to you, best stay in London. All our trainee sources spoke of *"extraordinary"* levels of responsibility relative to the UK. You can expect to be drafting your own loan agreements, attending closing and signing meetings solo, and plenty of contact with often colourful shipping clients. One Watson, Farley & Williams trainee was sent from Piraeus to Germany to Russia, representing a financier for the purchaser of a new vessel. Working hours are more or less the same as in the UK; so although offices open later, expect to work later too. Thanks be to Zeus that the bars stay open late for post-toil retsina and post-deal plate smashing.

Rest and Play: Norton Rose's Piraeus trainees live in an *"amazing"* fourth floor apartment overlooking the Marina Zea, a ten-minute walk from the office. The deal is much the same at Stephenson Harwood and Watson, Farley & Williams, both of which offer trainees two-bedroom flats just minutes from work. Of course, add an extra 15 minutes for each street you have to cross. Young Athenians at Norton Rose are set up in apartments half an hour from the office, but there are good public transport links. Most of the trainees we spoke to already had contacts in Greece, with one using his time outside office hours to make plans for his very own Big Fat Greek Wedding. But for those who don't, there is a trainee welcoming committee ready and willing to introduce you to everything from hip hop clubs to downing the retsina to the tune of Zorba's Dance in harbour-front bars. Where London trainees might find themselves drinking in All Bar One, the Greek contingent can kick up their heels at bouzouki nights and enjoy hair-raising spins around go-kart tracks before breakfasting in a taverna. All on a school night too! Verdicts on the food varied: some trainees wax lyrical about Greece's epicurean delights, while others decry the ubiquitous *"grease and cheese pie."* Either way, a seat in Greece is a baklava-sweet deal. Earning a London salary, living rent-free in a relatively inexpensive and vibrant city with easy access to the Greek islands every weekend leaves the Central Line and the occasional weekend in Stow-on-the-Wold flailing in its wake.

Best Things: Fresh seafood, Bouzouki nights, Watching ferries come into port from your office window.
Worst Things: Stifling summer heat, Traffic.

prague

Like sleeping beauty, Prague has awoken from her 40 years of hibernation under Soviet rule and reappeared as a magical fairyland of spires, towers, cobbled streets and endless churches. Only Prague could have described her emergence from communism as the Velvet Revolution, and indeed, the city brims with elegance and romance. Situated on the Vltava River, the entire city is a UNESCO world heritage site dominated by a castle. Weekends hold trips to the western spa towns, while the Sumava Mountains of south Bohemia offer superb hiking. Prague has reclaimed her cultural, artistic and musical life, and from the eclectic mixture of artistic and architectural styles from gothic to art deco, cubist to high renaissance, to the clink and chatter of Czechs enjoying a post-work drink, Prague will enchant even the most cynical trainee. As one put it, *"I've been here six months now and every time I leave the office and walk into the main square, I think 'Wow, this is fantastic!'"*

Work: Work will be a dab of corporate here, a dash of finance there, spots of litigation and privatisation, the occasional joint venture and a splash of IP. *"Whatever lands on our desks really."* It's the sort of broad-based, diverse experience you would expect of a high street practice, but with the sort of support (and let's face it, money) that a major commercial firm can offer. Interaction with the local authorities provided some trainees with a lesson in post-communist bureaucracy, and one spoke of the *"frustrations of dealing with the competition authorities."* Reflecting the diversity of the city itself, the work and culture in the office are very international in flavour. This is doubtless why the offices are English speaking, and you can *"survive easily with little or no Czech."* You'll be surrounded by the Czech Republic's brightest and best. *"Amazing people. Those who were first in their class at law school."* Not surprising then, trainees also noted a deferential attitude towards partners, who are often *"truly exceptional"* lawyers. Nevertheless, the office atmosphere is relaxed and quintessentially Czech: *"Everyone makes an effort to go out for a proper lunch every day."* White & Case maintains an intimate festive tradition of meeting at the Christmas market in the old town square to *"have a hot drink and cuddle up for half an hour"* before returning to the office.

Rest and Play: CMS Cameron MacKenna's flat is a ridiculous two-minute walk from work, and trainees don't even set their alarms until 9am. White & Case, Clifford Chance and Allen & Overy also offer *"impressive"* and centrally located apartments. Visiting mothers: don't be alarmed by the austere communist entrance to the trainees' digs, the interiors are modern and completely refurbished by the firms. *"While it's all dour soviet misery outside, it's Ikea-tastic on the inside!"* Prague boasts a large expat community, but *"it's nice to broaden your horizons. You can hear about life behind the Iron Curtain."* You can still eat and drink in Prague cheaply, and although fairly *"stodgy"* and *"not to everyone's tastes,"* the traditional Czech menu of meat, potatoes and dumplings will certainly keep you warm in the winter, if not super-model svelte. In any case, you can walk off those extra pounds, since the city is safe and best experienced on foot. Drinking is the most popular pastime: *"You tend to take over a whole cocktail bar, there's no closing time and staff don't go home until you've finished."* When you're not listening to the strains of Dvorak wafting out of the apartment downstairs, you can get into live jazz, opera, rock and dance music for a fraction of London prices. You certainly won't be short of visitors, since *"you suddenly grow all these friends who want to stay on weekends!"*

Best Things: Hot drinks and cuddles at the Christmas market, Reading Kundera in an old town square cafe.

Worst Things: Aloof customer service, Czech bureaucracy, Leaving.

milan/rome

Italy's business and fashion capital, Milan, is home to the Italian Stock Exchange and most of its major banks and corporates. Although *"not the most beautiful city in the world,"* it is wealthy, glamorous and fast paced. Nestled in the plains of the Po Valley, it's a short journey into the Alps or to the beautiful lakes region. The Eternal City, Rome, meanwhile, remains Italy's traditional regulatory centre. It lacks the relentless commercial pace of Milan, but none of its style, and is *"the most stunning city in the world,"* according to one besotted trainee. Milan's winters can be cool, with temperatures falling below zero. In the summer, both cities become hot and muggy, and Rome can be stifling. Sensibly, the locals flee to the coast, and you'd be well advised to do the same whenever you can.

Work: Competition for Italian seats is tough and language skills are essential. Work-wise, expect either corporate and equity capital markets or banking and finance. We spoke to trainees at Freshfields and Clifford Chance who had been busy drafting advices and prospectuses in addition to the usual pre-transaction review work. One trainee helped worked for Italian designers, jewellers and luxury goods houses, from Prada to Bulgari, and his mother is now one of the luckiest and best-dressed women around. Expect more finance and securitisation work in Rome, but as with most foreign offices, *"it was the equivalent of doing three seats in terms of variety."* Forget Starbucks, you'll be quaffing real coffee here, and you'll need it, since working hours are much the same as London, and sometimes longer. While this will be no Roman Holiday, you will enjoy long lunches, regular coffee breaks and a generally relaxed office environment. Trainees noted a more deferential attitude towards partners, who tend to be older and highly academically qualified. *"There's a real focus on the partners being everything, and to be fair, it's mostly true."* Despite this, trainees spoke of a *"warm"* atmosphere in the office. *"If you make an effort to speak Italian, you'll be rewarded."* As one put it, *"it's almost like a family."* Not to be confused, of course, with The Family.

Rest and Play: The sparsity of UK trainees in Rome means you need to *"try quite hard to make friends."* But Italians are famously welcoming, and as one trainee told us: *"I loved being alone in Rome, I wasn't going to Irish bars and talking English the entire time."* Linklaters hosts a football tournament where you can take on the locals, and one trainee reported that he'd made an eclectic group of English friends *"from translaters to novelists."* Linklaters presently provides a budget for accommodation, while Clifford Chance offers an apartment overlooking the Roman Forum. One source described his journey to work on a Vespa, whizzing past the Colosseum. Whether it's sipping an £8 espresso in Piazza Navona, getting lost in cobbled streets, or admiring the views from atop St Peter's Basilica, there'll be something about Rome that'll have you tossing a coin in the Trevi Fountain.

By contrast, you don't have to enjoy Milan alone. *"We really pool the friendship resources."* When you're not bankrupting yourself at Prada, you can enjoy one of Italy's *"most civilised traditions,"* the aperetivo. This involves evening drinks served with anything from sushi to salami. In what one trainee called a *"rather barbaric practice,"* some Italian lawyers will go out for aperetivo from 6-9pm and then return to the office afterwards! Miraculously, you can just turn up at football games in the afternoon and get tickets to see the city's famous clubs – AC Milan or Inter Milan. Freshfields' apartment is *"huge and runs for miles,"* although according to one trainee, Italian central heating can be *"a little too savage; I find myself climbing into the fridge at night!"*

Best Things: Real coffee, the food, the shopping, the football…everything. Just everything.
Worst Things: Queuing for the Sistine Chapel, Bankruptcy/Shopping addiction, Bum-pinching.

singapore

The Singapore of today, with its three million inhabitants is a far cry from the fishing village Stamford Raffles found in 1819. With its polyglot society, 90% home ownership and general all-round efficiency, Singapore is seen by many as a model city state. The opium dens and rickshaws of its colonial past have been swept aside to make way for a brave, new civic utopia where the streets are safe and clean, everything is air conditioned, and an automated taxi system means never waiting more than four minutes for a cab. Singapore is known as 'The Fine City' as much for its rigorously enforced penalties as for its splendour. You're liable to be fined for jaywalking, failing to flush the toilet or importing packs of chewing gum that are surplus to personal use. *"It's like living in a very nice bubble,"* admitted one trainee. Singapore is non-seasonal, but the humidity can be a shock and you'll feel like you're walking out into soup as you leave Changi Airport. Many people take a spare shirt to work and peel off the moist one upon arriving in the office.

Work: Singapore is much more developed than its ASEAN counterparts, yet its legal profession has experienced both a recession and SARS of late. Some international firms have abandoned their joint venture agreements with local law firms or left the jurisdiction entirely, but fear not: a number of firms remain heavily engaged in the market and will remain so. Their trainees are mostly involved in litigation, project finance and corporate work and shipping also figures highly in smaller niche firms, offering a variety of work that overlaps with other practice areas. A few firms also deal with aviation law. Don't be deceived by the *"efficient and relaxed atmosphere,"* as in times of plenty, you'll be rushed off your feet and working beyond the standard 9am-6pm. *"Everything in the city works,"* and that will include you.

Rest and Play: Norton Rose trainees share a *"vast"* apartment with its own pool, just behind Orchard Road, Singapore's version of Oxford Street. If you're addicted to designer labels, whoop for joy because *"shopping is the national pastime."* Many of the other firms' trainees live centrally in the expat enclave, which was variously considered *"great fun"* or *"quite claustrophobic."* Foodies will love the city's culinary offerings; home cooking is nonsensical as you can eat out after work very cheaply while exploring different districts, such as China Town and Little India. For those who can't resist (or are hosting Ma and Pa for a week or two), there's always the Raffles Hotel and their world famous gin slings. A well-established social scene amongst UK trainees and expats means all new arrivals find *"a ready made set of new friends."* One trainee told us how over the previous weekend a group of 25 trainees hired a private Indonesian island for three days. *"And next weekend we're all going off diving from this island off Malaysia."* She'd only arrived in Singapore three weeks earlier!

Best Things: Travel opportunities, Cultural difference, Food.
Worst Things: Claustrophobia, Sweating.

tokyo

Japan has emerged from the 90s as a schizoid hybrid of Advanced Capitalism and Zen Buddhism. At some point something's got to give, but for now the tensions that run through the capital like fault lines make it a vital, edgy and exciting place to be; *"Tokyo is off the planet."* Crowded, cramped, noisy and hectic, it is the *"archetypal concrete jungle, but with a real charm to it."* While you can get yourself the latest all-singing all-dancing mobile phone for barely more than a tenner, you may surprise yourself by spending six quid on a can of baked beans. Go in September and you'll miss the rainy season and get some skiing. March is a month of *"blue skies and cherry blossoms;"* a time when the Japanese go to extraordinary lengths to celebrate the passing of the seasons.

Work: Tokyo offers mainly banking work, but Denton Wilde Sapte trainees get to have a crack at whatever comes into the office, from energy to litigation work. You need to have *"a lot of stamina."* You are likely to be handling your own cases and *"you won't feel like a trainee."* You're unlikely to get much client contact unless you are a master of oriental languages and etiquette, but you will be involved in marketing. Expect to work long hours and some weekends if things hot up.

Rest and Play: DWS has a brand new western-style apartment while other firms provide more traditional Japanese-style accommodation complete with tatami matting. Ashursts has a central place in Hiroo, *"the Hampstead of Tokyo."* A trainee e-mail list *"gives you a good base to expand from,"* so you'll not feel isolated. Expect to go out with colleagues, but the Japanese are notoriously reserved. *"They have very distinct professional and personal personas and they are difficult to get to know."* It's easy enough to work and play in the same district, but make the effort to get out of Roppongi. *"There's lots of expat bars and English pubs, but it's not a nice area, it's quite sleazy."* For traditional entertainment, *"karaoke is a must."* The

Japanese do it in a booth with their friends; it's not about embarrassing yourself in front of strangers. At weekends, bullet trains can take you to Hiroshima, Miya Jima and Nikko for day trips and in winter you can be on the slopes in an hour and a half. Gentlemen, unless you're tiny, take plenty of clothes with you, as you're unlikely to find much that fits. Ladies, retail therapy will not be at all therapeutic as you'll probably need to buy size extra large unless you have the hips of a nine-year-old.

Best Things: Visual stimulation, Safety, Cheap electronics.
Worst Things: Language problems, Hard to get to know the Japanese.

warsaw

Let's be honest, Warsaw is hardly the city of choice for those about to play the trainee game of musical chairs. Often viewed as a bleak, post-communist purgatory, it suffers from a serious image problem. By the end of World War II, the entire city was rubble, its spectacular old town lay in ruins and its population was decimated. It is a testament to the determination and spirit of the city that it has completely rebuilt itself. The old town was painstakingly reconstructed and, in 1980, was awarded its place on the UNESCO World Heritage List. The left bank of the Vistula river monopolises the main attractions, the city centre, the Royal Way and the old town, while the right bank contains the increasingly hip Praga district. Socialist realist art and architecture stand alongside renaissance and gothic styles. Poland's post-communist transformation throws up many surprises, such as former Solidarnosc leader and president, Lech Walesa now presenting a weekly angling show on TV3.

Work: At the time of research, Poland was in a recession, and some trainees found themselves doing a fair bit of proofreading and checking the English in documents. In less lean times, you'll be doing a broad range of corporate and commercial work, from drafting contracts and advice work to document review. Expect to work on *"almost anything that comes into the firm;"* smaller offices and fewer staff will ensure a broad legal education of the kind that is rare in London. The hours are slightly better than back home, although there are *"fewer people to absorb the work when things get hectic."* The atmosphere in Warsaw offices is friendly, although, elements of communist bureaucratic culture remain. *"When you ask for something to be done, it's always on Poland time."*

Rest and Play: UK trainees form a tight-knit group and go out several nights a week, but English is prevalent among young Warsawites, who are a tolerant and open bunch, and making friends is easy. The city buzzes after dark, with cool and knowledgeable crowds descending on the many bars and clubs. There's everything from spit and sawdust drinking dens to ultra hip lounge bars with cocktails and DJs, and international acts are increasingly attracted to the city. In summer, you can relax in leafy parks – the famous Lazienki Park plays host to live Chopin concerts. For beautiful scenery, try the Hanseatic city of Gdansk, the Baltic coastline or the Mazurian Lakes and mountains. The medieval city of Krakow is another weekend favourite. The biggest drawback is the food. Local supermarkets are pretty basic, however, hypermarkets are springing up outside the centre. For eating out, there's everything from milk bars (workmen's cafes) to high-quality restaurants, but the general view on Polish food is that it's *"pretty bland,"* and the concept of vegetarianism doesn't really exist. *"You'll find bits of meat floating in your 'vegetable' soup."* Everyone we spoke to loved the experience of an *"exciting, raw and untouched"* place. In years to come, you'll be able to smugly say: *"Warsaw was better five years ago, before the tourists ruined it."*

Best Things: The Russian Market on Sunday morning, Vodka.
Worst Things: Pickled herrings for breakfast, Communist architecture, Lloyd Webber musicals in Polish.

OVERSEAS SEATS – WHO GOES THERE?

LOCATION	FIRM
Abu Dhabi	Richards Butler, Simmons & Simmons, Trowers & Hamlins
Amsterdam	Allen & Overy, Baker & McKenzie, Clifford Chance, CMS Cameron McKenna, Freshfields Bruckhaus Deringer, Herbert Smith, Linklaters, Norton Rose, Slaughter and May
Athens	Norton Rose, Richards Butler, Thomas Cooper & Stibbard
Australia	Baker & McKenzie
Bahrain	Norton Rose, Trowers & Hamlins
Bangkok	Allen & Overy, Linklaters, Watson, Farley & Williams, Freshfields Bruckhaus Deringer
Beijing	Freshfields Bruckhaus Deringer, Norton Rose
Berlin	Hammonds
Bratislava (Slovakia)	Allen & Overy
Brussels	Addleshaw Goddard, Allen & Overy, Ashurst Morris Crisp, Baker & McKenzie, Blake Lapthorn Linnell, Cleary, Gottlieb, Steen & Hamilton CMS Cameron McKenna, Clifford Chance, Cobbetts, Coudert Bros, Dechert, Dickinson Dees, DLA, Eversheds, Freshfields Bruckhaus Deringer, Hammonds, Herbert Smith, KLegal, Linklaters, Lovells, Mayer, Brown, Rowe & Maw, Nabarro Nathanson, Norton Rose, Olswang, Pinsents, Simmons & Simmons, SJ Berwin, Slaughter and May, Taylor Vinters, Taylor Wessing, White & Case, Wragge & Co.
Boston	Dechert
Bucharest	Linklaters
Budapest	Allen & Overy, CMS Cameron McKenna, Linklaters
California	Osborne Clarke, Weil Gotshal & Manges
Chicago	Baker & McKenzie
Cologne	Freshfields Bruckhaus Deringer, Osborne Clarke
Copenhagen	Slaughter and May
Dubai	Clifford Chance, Clyde & Co, Denton Wilde Sapte, Norton Rose, Trowers & Hamlins
Düsseldorf	Simmons & Simmons, Slaughter and May
Frankfurt	Allen & Overy, Ashurst Morris Crisp, Clifford Chance, Freshfields Bruckhaus Deringer, Linklaters, Lovells, Norton Rose, SJ Berwin, Slaughter and May, White & Case
Hamburg	Allen & Overy, CMS Cameron McKenna
Helsinki	Slaughter and May
Hong Kong	Allen & Overy, Baker & McKenzie, Barlow Lyde & Gilbert, Bird & Bird, Clifford Chance, Clyde & Co, CMS Cameron McKenna, Denton Wilde Sapte, Freshfields Bruckhaus Deringer, Herbert Smith, Holman, Fenwick & Willan, Linklaters, Lovells, Norton Rose, Richards Butler, Shearman & Sterling, Simmons & Simmons, Slaughter and May, Stephenson Harwood, White & Case
Lisbon	Simmons & Simmons
Luxembourg	Allen & Overy, Slaughter and May
Madrid	Allen & Overy, Ashurst Morris Crisp, Baker & McKenzie, Clifford Chance, Linklaters, Hammonds, Simmons & Simmons, SJ Berwin, Slaughter and May
Milan	Allen & Overy, Ashurst Morris Crisp, Clifford Chance, Freshfields Bruckhaus Deringer, Herbert Smith, Lovells, Norton Rose, Simmons & Simmons, Slaughter and May, White & Case
Monaco	Lawrence Graham
Moscow	Allen & Overy, Baker & McKenzie, Freshfields Bruckhaus Deringer, Herbert Smith, Linklaters, Norton Rose, White & Case
Munich	Clifford Chance, Norton Rose, SJ Berwin
New York	Allen & Overy, Clifford Chance, Dechert, Freshfields, Lovells, Simmons & Simmons, Slaughter and May, Weil Gotshal & Manges
Oman	Trowers & Hamlins
Oslo	Slaughter and May

OVERSEAS SEATS – WHO GOES THERE?

LOCATION	FIRM
Paris	Allen & Overy, Ashurst Morris Crisp, Bird & Bird, Clifford Chance, CMS Cameron McKenna, DWS, Eversheds, Freshfields Bruckhaus Deringer, Hammonds, Herbert Smith, Holman Fenwick & Willan, Linklaters, Lovells, Norton Rose, Richards Butler, Shadbolt & Co, Shearman & Sterling, Simmons & Simmons, Slaughter and May, SJ Berwin, TSB, Watson, Farley & Williams, White & Case, Weil, Gotshal & Manges
Philadelphia	Dechert
Piraeus	Holman Fenwick & Willan, Ince & Co, Norton Rose, Stephenson Harwood, Watson, Farley & Williams
Prague	Allen & Overy, Clifford Chance, CMS Cameron McKenna, Linklaters, Norton Rose, White & Case
Rome	Allen & Overy, Clifford Chance
Rotterdam	Simmons & Simmons
Sao Paolo	Clifford Chance, Linklaters, Richards Butler
Shanghai	Freshfields Bruckhaus Deringer, Herbert Smith, Stephenson Harwood

LOCATION	FIRM
Singapore	Allen & Overy, Clifford Chance, Freshfields Bruckhaus Deringer, Herbert Smith, Linklaters, Norton Rose, Shearman & Sterling, Slaughter and May , Stephenson Harwood, Watson, Farley & Williams, White & Case
Stockholm	Linklaters, Slaughter and May
Stuttgart	CMS Cameron McKenna, Herbert Smith
Tokyo	Allen & Overy, Clifford Chance, Denton Wilde Sapte, Freshfields Bruckhaus Deringer, Herbert Smith, Linklaters, Simmons & Simmons, Slaughter and May, White & Case
Turin	Hammonds
Utrecht	CMS Cameron McKenna
Warsaw	Allen & Overy, Clifford Chance, Linklaters
Washington	Baker & McKenzie, CMS Cameron McKenna, Dechert, Freshfields Bruckhaus Deringer

The True Picture

the true picture

In compiling *The True Picture*, we spoke to trainees and newly qualified solicitors at 120 of the leading law firms in England and Wales. Many of the larger firms have been covered in the previous six editions of the *Student Guide* and we've become very familiar with them; however, this year we have included some firms for the first time. Our website will have an archive section so that you can read past reviews of some of this year's 'no shows'.

how we do our research

Firms provide us with complete lists of their trainees and NQs. Having checked that the lists are complete, we then randomly select a sample of individuals who we interview over the phone. Our sources are guaranteed anonymity. We try to capture the general mood in a firm, looking for commonly held opinions rather than sensational stories. If we refer to trainee moans, it is because the issues in question have been raised by a number of individuals.

The True Picture is not forwarded to the law firms prior to publication; they see it for the first time when you do. We feel that this makes our work unique. Call us cynical, but we see little value in the well-crafted testimonials that appear in various other publications. If we're honest, we're also bored by the tired old lines in many recruitment brochures. You know the ones which promise that XYZ & Co is unique because it is a friendly firm where everybody is down to earth and approachable partners operate an open door policy. Few of our trainee sources seemed to believe us when we told them we heard these expressions several times every day. We have tried to burrow deeper than such clichés, but please forgive us if any have evaded the find-and-delete function! It's not that we don't think that law firms are like this, just that it doesn't make any one firm unique (don't believe anyone who tries to convince you otherwise).

our findings

Last year we found that trainees were sometimes edgy and more critical of their firms than during the past three or four years. This year, with the NQ job market even worse than it was last year, we sensed that many were either world weary or eternally grateful to have been kept on. We have tried to look beyond the current market conditions when writing the *True Picture*, as we recognise that things will have changed by the time our readers start their training. There are several facts that affect training contracts up and down the country.

- Levels of responsibility vary between departments. In property you might have your own small files. In corporate you will generally work in a very junior capacity as part of a team.
- The experience in litigation depends entirely on the type of cases your firm undertakes; you may take small cases all the way through to settlement, or you may be stuck for months on documentation in larger cases.
- In times of plenty, corporate means long hours, which commonly climax in dreaded all-nighters. In 2002 and 2003 there has been a shortage of corporate work, so hours have been more manageable. By the way, we often use the word **coco** to refer to company-commercial departments.
- **Grunt work** is almost inescapable, especially in larger firms. This delightful expression covers more administrative, yet essential, tasks like compiling court bundles and scheduling documents in litigation, and putting together completion bibles (copies of all relevant documents), or supervising visitors to data rooms in transactional departments. The photocopier can rear its head in any department.
- Most firms offer four six-month seats, some a six by four-month rotation and others still have their own pattern. Trainees switch departments,

either sharing a room and working for a partner or senior assistant, or working for a number of lawyers, perhaps in an open-plan environment.
- The Law Society has raised its minimum salary level, but salaries in commercial firms have stopped rising. Some NQ salaries have fallen.

Your choice of firm will be based partly on location, partly on size and partly on the practice areas available...then it's a matter of chemistry. Some firms are stuffier than others; some are more industrious; some are happier to directly involve trainees with clients; and some seem obsessed with brand identity rather than allowing staff to think and act independently. It's important that you find the firm that best fits you. During our interviews we noticed that different issues affect trainees at different types of firms:

consider the magic circle if:

- You are happy being one of hundreds of trainees and an even greater number of staff
- You desperately want to go overseas
- Self-determination isn't that important to you and you are happy to make big sacrifices in terms of your social life
- You want a top name on your CV
- You believe no expense should be spared on office support and facilities
- You believe patience is a virtue – your role will be small until post-qualification
- Money is important to you

consider mid-sized firms if:

- You'd hate to be one of hundreds of trainees – you're a name and not a number
- You want partners and staff to know who you are and you want to be able to get to know a majority of people at the firm
- The finance and corporate focus of the big City players doesn't get you excited
- An overseas seat is not the be-all and end-all
- You want to be well paid

consider national firms if:

- You want the confidence of a nationally known name on your CV
- You want to be among the best paid in the region where you work
- You believe that strength lies in numbers, even if they are spread across the country
- You want to be one of a reasonable number of trainees in your office
- You're happy moving between cities either during or after your training (investigate the policies of different national firms)
- It doesn't bother you that there are bigger deals and clients to be had at City firms

consider regional firms if:

- You think that rat-race London living would be a nightmare
- You're proud of where you come from and want to build a career there (older trainees with local roots and previous careers often do really well)
- You want to know the people you work with
- You want to be able to get to know and regularly see the powers that be in your firm – being run from another city just doesn't appeal
- You don't live just to work – you want your friends to still recognise you after work
- Your long-time squeeze is already settled and you value love over money

consider niche firms if:

- You really know what you want to qualify into.
- You have relevant industry experience.
- You have what it takes to see off the competition

and finally...

We hope *The True Picture* will help you decide what sort of firms you want to target. The most important thing is to understand what type of work a firm does and what type of place it is, because no matter how hard or how easy you'll find it to secure a training contract, you'll want to end up with the right one.

THE TRUE PICTURE 120 FIRMS

BY SIZE	FIRM NAME	CITY	TOTAL TRAINEES	PAGE NUMBER
1	Eversheds	London*	201	254
2	Clifford Chance LLP	London	235	223
3	Allen & Overy	London	247	179
4	Linklaters	London	250	315
5	DLA	London*	171	246
6	Freshfields Bruckhaus Deringer	London	181	270
7	Herbert Smith	London	180	285
8	CMS Cameron McKenna	London*	115	228
9	Addleshaw Goddard	Leeds*	99	177
10	Lovells	London	119	318
11	Hammonds	London*	87	280
12	Denton Wilde Sapte	London*	100	242
13	Pinsents	Birmingham*	64	356
14	Norton Rose	London	147	345
15	Slaughter and May	London	162	381
16	Beachcroft Wansbroughs	London*	54	194
17	Ashurst Morris Crisp	London	97	185
18	Wragge & Co LLP	Birmingham*	48	428
19	Nabarro Nathanson	London*	62	339
20	Simmons & Simmons	London	111	376
21	Berwin Leighton Paisner	London	61	196
22	SJ Berwin	London	78	378
23	Osborne Clarke	Bristol*	40	349
24	Mayer, Brown, Rowe & Maw LLP	London	50	329
25	Bevan Ashford	Bristol*	49	198
26	Masons	London*	43	326
27	Baker & McKenzie	London	67	187
28	Morgan Cole	Cardiff*	31	336
29	KLegal	London*	28	303
30	Barlow Lyde & Gilbert	London*	34	190
31	Taylor Wessing	London*	48	394
32	Halliwell Landau	Manchester*	27	278
33	Olswang	London*	46	347
34	Clyde & Co	London*	38	226
35	Bird & Bird	London	29	203
36	Field Fisher Waterhouse	London	24	260
37=	Mills & Reeve	Cambridge*	39	333
37=	Shoosmiths	Northampton*	23	371
39	Charles Russell	London*	26	221
40	Richards Butler	London	44	366

** Indicates branches elsewhere in England and Wales. Only head office location listed.*

THE TRUE PICTURE 120 FIRMS

BY SIZE	FIRM NAME	CITY	TOTAL TRAINEES	PAGE NUMBER
41	Blake Lapthorn Linnell	Portsmouth*	20	205
42	Lawrence Graham	London	35	306
43	Burges Salmon	Bristol	36	217
44	Irwin Mitchell	Sheffield*	30	297
45	Stephenson Harwood	London	30	388
46	Hill Dickinson	Liverpool*	19	287
47=	Dickinson Dees	Newcastle*	28	244
47=	Reynolds Porter Chamberlain	London*	20	363
49	Jones Day Gouldens	London	40	299
50	Cobbetts	Manchester*	26	231
51=	Macfarlanes	London	45	320
51=	Travers Smith Braithwaite	London	42	406
53	DWF	Liverpool*	14	250
54	Trowers & Hamlins	London*	28	408
55	Pannone & Partners	Manchester	19	352
56	Browne Jacobson	Nottingham*	20	215
57	Penningtons	London*	22	354
58	White & Case	London	38	423
59	Freethcartwright LLP	Nottingham*	14	268
60	Walker Morris	Leeds	31	413
61	Holman Fenwick & Willan	London	18	291
62=	Dechert	London	27	242
62=	Withers LLP	London	23	425
64	Edwards Geldard	Cardiff*	21	252
65	Weil, Gotshal & Manges	London	20	421
66	Manches	London*	20	322
67=	Speechly Bircham	London	10	384
67=	Farrer & Co	London	13	258
69	Ward Hadaway	Newcastle	15	415
70	Hugh James	Cardiff*	17	293
71=	Thomas Eggar	Chichester*	12	398
71=	Nicholson Graham & Jones	London	19	343
73	RadcliffesLeBrasseur	London*	13	360
74=	Ince & Co	London	24	295
74=	Martineau Johnson	Birmingham*	22	325
74=	Veale Wasbrough	Bristol	13	411
77	Mishcon de Reya	London	16	334
78=	Lewis Silkin	London	13	313
78=	Watson, Farley & Williams	London	20	417
80	Cripps Harries Hall	Tunbridge Wells*	14	238

** Indicates branches elsewhere in England and Wales. Only head office location listed.*

THE TRUE PICTURE 120 FIRMS

BY SIZE	FIRM NAME	CITY	TOTAL TRAINEES	PAGE NUMBER
81	Sidley Austin Brown & Wood	London	15	374
82	Bristows	London	17	213
83	TLT Solicitors	Bristol	15	402
84=	Brabners Chaffe Street	Liverpool*	17	209
84=	Laytons	London*	11	308
86	Lester Aldridge	Bournemouth*	11	311
87=	Foot Anstey Sargent	Plymouth*	12	262
87=	Gateley Wareing	Birmingham*	13	274
89	Bircham Dyson Bell	London*	10	201
90	Boodle Hatfield	London*	10	207
91	Wedlake Bell	London	10	419
92	Capsticks	London	12	219
93	Reed Smith	London*	12	361
94=	Harbottle & Lewis LLP	London	8	283
94=	Russell-Cooke	London	10	368
96	Thring Townsend	Swindon*	12	400
97	Taylor Vinters	Cambridge	10	390
98	Ford & Warren	Leeds	11	264
99=	Bates, Wells & Braithwaite	London*	8	192
99=	DMH	Brighton*	13	249
101	Andrew M Jackson	Hull	10	182
102=	Hodge Jones & Allen	London	8	289
102=	Shadbolt & Co	Reigate*	8	370
104	Taylor Walton	Luton*	10	392
105	Kendall Freeman	London	15	301
106	Coffin Mew & Clover	Fareham*	9	232
107=	Brachers	Maidstone*	10	211
107=	Collyer-Bristow	London	8	234
107=	Gosschalks	Hull	8	276
110	LeBoeuf, Lamb, Greene & MacRae LLP	London	8	310
111	Prettys	Ipswich	9	358
112	Teacher Stern Selby	London	9	396
113	Steeles	Norwich*	11	386
114	McCormicks	Leeds	8	331
115=	Coudert Brothers	London	8	236
115=	Fosters	Norwich*	13	266
117	Nelson & Co	Leeds	9	341
118	Anthony Gold	London	9	183
119	TMK Solicitors	Southend on Sea*	9	404
120	Galbraith Branley	London	10	273

Firms are listed in order of size as measured by partner and assistant figures provided to Chambers UK

Addleshaw Goddard

the facts

Location: Manchester, Leeds, London
UK ranking by size: 9
Total number of trainees: 99
Seats: 4x6 months
Alternative seats: Brussels, secondments
Extras: Pro-bono – Manchester Uni Legal Advice Centre, Springfield Legal Advice Centre

This firm is the result of a merger between northern giant Addleshaw Booth and City firm Theodore Goddard. It's early days of course, but both sides certainly brought plenty of good things to the party.

opposites attract

The consensus among trainees is that the merger took place because Addleshaws wanted *"a London office as big as Leeds and Manchester,"* while TG was keen to join forces to gain greater national presence. We feel that's a generous interpretation of TG's needs; in truth, it had bounced painfully from one set of merger talks to another and the cracks of frustration were beginning to show. Suffice to say TG *"couldn't expand as it was and there was a danger the firm was going to be left behind. The management needed to take a more modern approach and merge for the good of the firm."* Addleshaws has brought softly spoken TG *"a much needed marketing edge,"* and the northerners tell us their house style is now more refined. *"Documents and letters have become more City looking, plainer and sleeker."* Said one: *"I think the firm will be aiming to have a solid couple of years and then go international."* Let's wait and see.

We wondered how the signing of the treaty had been received by the humble foot soldiers. As far as the northerners are concerned, it's business as usual and our spies in London (where change is most obvious) reported that everything was going smoothly so far. However, as the old saying goes: *"It's difficult to merge two law firms without ruffling a few feathers."* While the merger is accepted to be the right step forward, in the TG camp we sensed nostalgia for the old days. According to one: *"There's a perception that some of the good things about the firm will change."* For example, there was some regret at the loss of a *"gentlemanly culture"* in favour of increased bureaucracy and aggressive target setting. Also on the endangered list is TG's tradition of guaranteeing a qualification job to all trainees. For your information, in September 2003, 28 of the 37 qualifiers stayed with the new firm.

up north

We've decided to comment on the northern and London offices separately rather than drawing premature conclusions. Most trainees spend their entire training contract in one office and this doesn't bother anyone because *"the kind of people Addleshaws recruits in Manchester or Leeds want to stay in the north."* Quite apart from friends and family, there are plenty of reasons making them content to stay. Across both cities, the firm is ranked by *Chambers UK* in the top two firms in 40 areas of practice from banking to healthcare and IT, and each office offers pretty much the same seat selection. Trainees must do a corporate or banking seat, a contentious seat and a property seat.

Corporate finance is *"one of the best departments to be in."* Trainees get bite-sized chunks of big deals, such as drafting ancillary documents or assisting with due diligence; however, our sources weren't stuck in document rooms the whole time and didn't suffer from small-cog syndrome. One satisfied customer told us: *"At the beginning of a deal, my supervisor would sit down with me and explain what my role would be."* There's plenty of client contact and trainees were often responsible for negotiating and amending small contract clauses. If you were the kind of person at uni who left all your work until the last minute and then pulled a few all-nighters to finish it, you'll love the *"binge-working"* culture of this department. *"The corporate department has a bit of a reputation for slacking off when it's quiet,"* but when a deal's nearing completion, you'll certainly be putting the late nights in.

In the *"massive"* commercial property department, there is a lot of tedious document scheduling, but trainees also enjoyed running up to 40 of their own files. And because the working day is generally a very regular 9am till 6pm, there's plenty of time to have fun. We loved the cute (if simplistic) analysis of one trainee: *"Law school gives you the impression that property lawyers are stuck in a room full of deeds, but in fact they're always going out on Friday nights."*

In litigation you might be able to do some advocacy yourself, perhaps applying for charging orders over properties. Again, client contact is there for the taking and you'll learn to *"keep clients calm while letting them know what's happening."* The most hotly contested seats are employment and IP. If you want one or other, *"it's a combination of making an early request and working hard in your early seats. Getting known as a good trainee helps."* We got the impression that at school, the Addleshaws' trainees would have been the ones sat in the front row sticking their hands up to answer every question. One trainee told us: *"We are all hard workers."*

misspent youth

There's time for fun as well. In Manchester we heard about departmental weekends in seaside cottages and five-a-side football. On a Friday night, trainees gather in the Pitcher and Piano conveniently located underneath the office. Manchester TSG events are popular and the firm even pays for your summer ball ticket. There's also a firm summer party, last year held in Barca in Castlefield which, we hear, is owned by Mick Hucknall. (Readers may insert their own joke here.)

For some reason, Leeds trainees were keener to talk about their Christmas party, a glamorous event held at a swanky hotel with *"fantastic raffle prizes."* Apparently, one trainee went home the proud recipient of a Playstation 2. The Leeds social committee organises trips to Blackpool, its own five-a-side football league, days at the races and *"lots of pool nights."* The office local is a bit more exotic – on a Friday everyone heads to a Greek bar called Homaru, which has *"a balcony bit with umbrellas"* and two-for-one drinks.

Both of the northern offices occupy city centre premises. The Mancunians told us about a *"space age"* atrium complete with glass lift and palm trees, and trainees in Leeds were full of praise for their café and a giant chessboard with knee-high pieces. *"We never want to move them in case someone's playing a game."* Go on, we'll send a fiver to the first trainee who e-mails us a jpeg evidencing play.

down south

And what of London? Addleshaws' office was small, but the firm had always planned to grow it. The tie-up with TG now means the London operation has an entirely new feel. TG was well known as a mid-size City player with a twist of media and entertainment work. Said one source: *"They're a bit off the wall and like to see themselves as a bit wacky. One of the older partners is into mad sports like tobogganing."* Those craaazy media lawyers, right? Wrong. The real characters are in the tax department where *"they all wear Jarvis Cocker-style black glasses and outrageous shirts. Some of them look like they should be on holiday in the Caribbean."* A seat in tax is no holiday though; the law is very technical and so, as a trainee, expect lots of research. Corporate seats are where you can *"get your hands dirty."* Trainees here get stuck into the nitty-gritty of big deals. But beware, when things get going you can expect long hours: *"The worst was getting four hours' sleep between Monday and Wednesday."* A secondment is available to Psion Films, which is headed by an ex-TG lawyer.

What about those juicy IP and media seats? We heard a lot of positive comment on IP, where trainees become the first point of contact on Acid, a legal helpline set up to combat copyright theft. Before you go and buy a new designer suit, *"it's mainly design work from trade organisations that make things like fireplaces and lampshades."* In IP you'll also get to visit trade fairs as an undercover *"legal rover"* and get involved in mediations. A lucky few experience media law, perhaps focusing on advertising and e-commerce or the music biz. Defamation is also hot and you even get to read *Heat* and *Hello!* as homework – the firm acts for international celebrities such as Michael Douglas, Catherine Zeta Jones and Steve Bing.

thank goddard it's friday

As we were interviewing, the firm was busy organising its London staff into coherent departments across the two offices. The smaller but *"much nicer"* Cannon Street office is being retained for the time being, in addition to TG's Aldersgate Street building, just a stone's throw from the hub of the *Student Guide* intelligence operation. We know for a fact that this building is the brownest place on planet earth, and several of our sources were no more charitable in their descriptions. No one was too sure about the *"horrendous art,"* which turns out to be *"photos of old men and aerial views of farmland."* Best of all we were told of *"the duff car park that doesn't work."* Huh? *"There's a concrete ramp that goes nowhere. We heard a story that they botched it up when it was built."* Sounds like a job for Handy Andy.

Fortnightly end-of-week firm drinks have been known to finish at four or five in the morning. It seems that *"however old you are, you never say no to a free drink!"* Whether it's in sports bar Extra Time, Ye Olde Red Cow or Smiths of Smithfield, there's a good deal of mingling between staff. But *"there's no great compunction to go out and get lashed"* and there are plenty of non-alcoholic social events. The firm is strong on sport, especially rugby and football.

and finally...

Everything points to a bright future for Addleshaw Goddard. It may not have much to shout about internationally at the moment, but there's no law that says you must have this at the top of your agenda.

Allen & Overy

the facts

Location: London
UK ranking by size: 3
Total number of trainees: 247
Seats: 3 or 6 months long
Alternative seats: Overseas seats, secondments
Extras: Pro bono – Battersea Legal Centre, Privy Council death row appeals, language training

Allen & Overy is a card-carrying member of the magic circle clique. For the lucky initiates, this means blue-chip clients, massive deals, outrageous salaries and even more outrageous hours. Although A&O is best known for its stellar finance practice, the firm has an excellent reputation in almost every single practice area. From employment to energy and from capital markets to charities, there is something for everyone City-minded. Just be aware that you may have to fight to get into the most popular niche departments.

banking on success

A&O is in the finance premier league, acting for most of the leading banks and financial institutions in the UK and worldwide. ABN AMRO, Bank of America, Barclays Capital, BNP Paribas, Citibank, Deutsche Bank, HSBC...just believe us, and our parent publication *Chambers UK*, when we say that for banks, A&O is *"first stop for heavy structural and securitisation work."* It maintained its vice-like grip on the jumbo financing market, securing seven of the top ten European loans in 2002. The asset finance team scooped the role of European counsel to Qantas. It is top dog for finance litigation, and its trust, asset tracing and fraud group is the pre-eminent practice in the UK. By now, you'll have begun to get a picture of day-to-day business.

Twelve months of the training contract must be spent in the banking, corporate and international capital markets groups, but for most trainees, this is far from onerous. *"The work is so wide-ranging,"* said one. *"In corporate, I was doing energy work, while in banking, half the work I did was corporate restructuring and insolvency. I got to see both sides of the coin – drafting facility agreements and then seeing what happens when things go wrong."* Banking is split into global loans, financial services regulatory, leveraged finance, restructuring and projects. Corporate encompasses M&A, equity capital markets, financial institutions, private equity, competition, communications, media and technology, energy & utilities and environment. In leveraged finance, trainees work with *"big names"* on high-profile transactions. The hours are variable, ranging from the blissful (*"if you're not doing much, you can be out at 5.30pm"*) to the plain insane (*"the next night you might work all night, all through the following day and not leave until 10pm, 36 hours later"*). Red Bull and coffee are the order of the day, preferably together. Equity capital markets offers deals with an international flavour, while debt capital markets is a popular group, renowned for making trainees *"feel a part of the team."* Appropriately, we heard of a project called Red Bull – a utility company restructuring and bond issue.

Litigation polarises trainees into those who can't get enough and those who certainly can. Most opt for a swift three-month seat, although people who want six months can ask to extend. While some trainees *"just sat through it hoping it would end,"* others enjoyed quality work, civil fraud in particular. As you might expect, most trainees find themselves working on huge matters, often doing the more mundane tasks. However, for those who push, there is also the chance to take more responsibility on smaller matters.

a spoonful of sugar

We won't harp on, but the finance practice is undoubtedly the most important. Yet A&O excels in other areas too. Despite rumours of fee earner departures, the employment group has made a dazzling charge up the charts, being promoted to the top tier in *Chambers UK*. No mean feat. Trainees who step into the employment, pensions and incentives group should see a broad range of work, which might include attending tribunal hearings, drafting trust deeds and responding to complaints from pensioners. And trainees love it *"because it's more personal, it's more tangible."* As is the experience in the private client team, which advises its wealthy corporate exec clientele.

A vast international empire almost guarantees a seat overseas. If this is on your agenda, expect to tender for a posting (usually a 4th seat) by stating why you want a particular office, what experience you've already had and what type of work you'd like to cover. You can pick from cities in Europe, Asia and the US, but if you want somewhere really popular, you'll have to pass muster. The selection process includes an examination of your previous assessments and discussions with past supervisors – a real incentive to show willing in all your earlier seats. Overseas seats can offer high levels of responsibility in a more intimate setting than at home. On the whole, however, our sources reported receiving a good dose of sweet client contact throughout their training, making the medicinal grunt work that much easier to swallow.

suffer the little children...

The highly accurate bullshit-o-meter installed in each *Student Guide* researcher's inner ear goes berserk every time we hear the words 'approachable partners' (ooh, there it goes) and 'open-door policy'. But we can't deny the sincerity of the trainees who praised these aspects of A&O. We heard about a utopian approach to staffing transactions: *"Trainees work together with paralegals, and support staff are given responsibility to look after files and understand transactions and come to meetings. We're all merging together into something where teamwork becomes the most important aspect."* Additionally: *"We're encouraged to pick up the phone or to walk into someone's office rather than send an e-mail."* And another source said: *"As a trainee, it's important to be able to ask questions and feel comfortable with partners. Guy Beringer* [senior partner] *knew my name and he still smiles at me in the corridor."* Like Jesus to a child...

harpers and queen...

The amorphous haze of A&O's legendary friendliness

has crystallised into something called Values into Action. It's easy to chuckle about *"management consultant speak,"* but trainees feel the values are true of the firm. It seems there's no escaping the insidious Values. In their first week they attend a seminar about them and *"the screensavers have them rolling around all day."* We won't recite all six (you'll have plenty of time to do that once you join), but our sources were particularly fond of the *"working together as one firm"* and *"excellence in everyone and everything"* bits.

At a time when most firms are happily selling their grannies to protect partner profits, this year the firm announced a 10.5% bonus to all staff, regardless of job description or geography. Furthermore, of those in the magic circle, the firm boasts the highest number of female partners. We should also mention that in 2002 the British Toilet Association deposited the 'Loo of the Year' award on the firm. We only hope that the dapper crappers will be faithfully reproduced at the firm's new digs when it moves in 2006. Something that perhaps will not be reproduced in the new Spitalfields office is the firm's current reception area decor. It's all *Country Life* and Chesterfields – hardly what you'd expect from the magic circle, and certainly not in keeping with its business-casual dress code.

keeping the troops happy

Can a firm hold onto a warm and fuzzy reputation while also relentlessly driving towards world domination? Maybe the man who knows the answer is Partha Bose, the business motivation expert and author of *Alexander The Great's Art of Strategy,* who has been hired by the firm. Of course, Alexander was a brutal Macedonian military leader who built a huge global empire. And yet he was into positive reinforcement for his men, arranging games and contests for them on their days off from fighting. Accompanying the invading armies were scientists, doctors, engineers, surveyors, architects, scientists and historians. In a similar vein, the troops at One New Change are provided with doctors, dentists, physiotherapists, a gym, a canteen and a bar. And of course, there are the requisite sports teams, reading groups and chess assemblages. Not quite, but you get our drift.

And in spite of being part of one of the largest trainee populations, our interviewees were adamant that they *"don't feel like just a number."* The firm has a trainee solicitors' liaison committee of eight that meets monthly with HR and partners to raise issues and make suggestions. It covers anything from the procedure for applying for overseas seats to the quality of sandwiches served up in seminars. We were shocked to hear that the latter is one area in which *"the values into action are sadly lacking."* One outcome has been the introduction of trainee feedback on their supervisors, surely the job of the *Student Guide.*

It all sounds too good to be true, doesn't it? We heard several times that *"it's not part of the culture to moan here."* And when we asked one trainee what the firm looks for in new recruits, he replied: *"The ability to get on with things and not whine when you have had a long journey or a lot of work." "They want people who will get the work done."* Another trainee put it this way: *"We're no-nonsense lawyers, people who do the job and go home."* A&O recently told associates they must clock up 2,200 recorded hours a year (as distinct from chargeable hours and including pro bono, reading on the train, etc) and there have been mutterings of discontent.

In 2003, amidst trainee purges across the City, A&O retained 102 of its 114 NQs. But a few years down the track, many troops go in-house or to smaller firms. Although *"you don't get the sense that everybody is passing through,"* no one we spoke to had partnership aspirations. One summed it up by saying: *"The beauty about working at a firm like this is you can do either. If you want to stay long term, that's encouraged. If you want to leave, you can go anywhere you like."* So true.

and finally...

Prestigious clients and deals means the Allen & Overy name on your CV is a golden ticket to anywhere. Be clear about the sort of work you want to do and understand that the demands of the job are high. Shall we group hug now?

Andrew M Jackson

the facts

Location: Hull
UK ranking by size: 162
Total number of trainees: 10
Seats: 4x6 months
Alternative seats: None

Apologies in advance for the poor effort to recreate the brilliant Hull accent, but if the words "Ello and welcurme to 'ull trains, the bufeah is orpern and selling a selectshurne of curkes and 'ot snacks" mean anything at all to you, you are probably already familiar with Andrew M Jackson. The firm has serviced the commercial needs of Humberside for well over a century, so if you are looking for an established practice that values home-grown talent, you're on the right track.

cold hands, warm heart

AMJ attracts clients from small owner-operated affairs to large nationals including MFI, Carpetrite, Cannons Health Clubs, Associated British Ports, P&O North Sea Ferries and Seven Seas. There's even a small amount of international work, much of it in the maritime and freight forwarding sectors. The firm's Hull-centricity flavours the smaller value work, and AMJ has a reciprocal respect for local business: *"It sees itself as part of and supporting local commerce, and makes a lot of having good relationships with businesses."* Proving that not all business is local, the maritime lawyers handled a major criminal case in the south west of England involving fishing and fish processing companies that had come under the eagle eye of DEFRA. Meanwhile, the commercial property group acts on warehousing and retail projects across the country.

From the firm's trainee info-starved website to the client-focused packs handed out at law fairs, you would be forgiven for thinking that AMJ is an overly business-like place. It's not. It is simply that the firm chooses to rely on its reputation to attract both clients and personnel, rather than puff and bluster. *"It prides itself on word of mouth rather than big glossy adverts,"* said a source. This austere, almost distant exterior belies a warm heart. The majority of trainees are home grown, as are many of the senior lawyers. We were told: *"It does like to grow from within."* And it wants people who know their way around this part of the world.

having a go

From shipping law (or, as one trainee corrected us, *"Admiralty"*) origins, AMJ has developed and expanded into a wide range of areas. Commercial property is now by far the biggest department, with the next largest – shipping, litigation and corporate – being more than able craft in their own right. A flotilla of smaller departments, such as family, employment, and wills and probate, follow in their wake. But beware: although we spoke to trainees who had been placed in private client departments for their first six months, *"the firm would like you to go into commercial seats and, ultimately, into the commercial side of the firm."*

Seat-wise, *"there's nothing compulsory at all, and there's enough work to fit everyone into what they want."* The current favourites are corporate and commercial litigation. Apparently, *"it's just the nature of these departments. Even if people can't see themselves qualifying into either, they at least want to have a go."*

contact sports

One trainee who had spent time in the corporate department said: *"You can get really involved, be it MBOs, shareholder agreements, new company formations...it's a lot of hands-on experience."* Being the right-hand man (or woman) of the lead lawyer on a deal is a treat to be savoured. Similar levels of involvement and responsibility are to be found throughout the firm, although the specific tasks differ. Generally, there is *"good contact with clients,"* and plenty of opportunities to *"get involved and make a contribution,"* be it doing PI or contentious probate (among a myriad of other things) in general litigation, *"appearing in tribunals on TUPE matters"* in employment, *"doing chambers applications in relation to insolvency and debt collection"* in commercial litigation, or *"standard divorce cases to more complex situations"* in family.

"They have done a lot to change the training regime over the last two years," said one source. Grumbles over feedback from supervisors are definitely fading: some departments, such as coco, are now *"very into feedback."* Jolly good. Additionally, AMJ now has mentors in the form of designated partners *"to get them interested in training matters and to be a point of contact for trainees."* Trainees meet with their mentor on a monthly basis: *"It takes a while to get to know what you can say to them, but after a while it is very helpful,"* said one trainee. Charged with *"looking after pastoral care,"* the new regime has yet to fully develop, but a trainee's lot looks even better than it did this time last year, if you can overlook the salary.

whatever next?

How AMJ will develop in the future is anyone's guess. To date, *"it has gone for organic growth rather than quick growth through amalgamation."* As one source told us: *"That might change...I can't see that they can stay in Hull forever, if it wants to grow more."* Occupying *"the top five floors of a small tower block,"* space in the *"modestly decorated"* office is increasingly at a premium. Desk arrangements vary from department to department; in corporate, trainees sit together in a bay, in others they share with a junior solicitor, and in yet others they share with a partner. A source warned: *"It's okay taking people on, but accommodation may become a problem in the next two years. I've heard that the firm might be doing something about it."* If the retention of four out of the five 2003 qualifiers is anything to go by, that sounds like a good idea.

24-minute party people

The social scene? *"We try to go out as a firm, all the trainees together, once a month, and we are involved with the TSG stuff, and we do know most of the trainees in the city."* As you would expect, there are favoured ale houses: *"Lloyds on a Friday night or the Jazz Bar. If its going to be anywhere it usually starts off at one of those,"* said one source. Football and cricket, a firm-wide summer barbie and occasional nights out seem perfectly adequate for most as they usually have an ample supply of friends outside work.

and finally...

If you are after really big-ticket work, Hull takes second place to Leeds and Sheffield in Yorkshire. That said, if Humberside is where you want to be, you're going to want to apply to Andrew M Jackson. From there, you'll have the chance to aim your guns at the opposition in Leeds, London, and sometimes beyond.

Anthony Gold

the facts

Location: London
UK ranking by size: 434
Total number of trainees: 9
Seats: Flexible (often 1x12 + 2x6)
Alternative seats: None

Anthony Gold was born in 1963, the year JFK was assassinated and Beatlemania swept the UK. Forty years on and the firm has a great name in family and PI. With a foot in the City, it is equally happy catering to commercial clients or the man in the street.

golden wonder

We doubt it goes so far as to see itself as a beacon of enlightened lawyering, but there's a passing resemblance between the lighthouse on the firm's website and the firm's seventh floor London Bridge office. *"The view just blew me away,"* said one trainee when citing his reasons for joining (though unfortunately you need to qualify before you get a desk enabling you to gaze out over Southwark and St Paul's Cathedrals). Anthony Gold also has offices in slightly less picturesque Streatham and, as a result of a recent merger, an outpost in Elephant & Castle. Compared to some, this legal blind date seems to have been successful: *"We were given lots of notice of it; people were introduced beforehand. I think it will work,"* pronounced one source.

Trainees can spend time in all three offices, although none of our sources had yet visited the Elephant, which handles housing, community care, judicial review and residential conveyancing. Although there will be familiar faces, moving between the offices is not always easy. One trainee was looking forward to the buzz of working in the centre of London after a spell in Streatham, but admitted that she felt like she was about to start a new job. Although the work may be broadly similar, the offices look and feel different. Streatham has a high-streety atmosphere (*"it's not plush"*) and handles legal aid work; London Bridge caters to commercial and privately paying clients. In Streatham you can expect to sit with your supervisor, whereas at London Bridge trainees are grouped together primary school-style. But you won't find them passing notes and flicking rulers; they are a mature and sensible lot – around half of the class of 2003 are on their second careers. And there's no pinching and hair pulling about who gets to go where: *"There's no reason for us to be competitive, there are enough seats for everyone. You don't always get a seat when you want it, but you will get it at some point."*

mending minds

The firm's biggest departments are family, spread across both offices, and PI in London Bridge. In family you can expect *"proper hands-on experience"* on a full spread of cases from children in care to housing work and domestic violence. In PI, clients include those who have suffered brain damage and/or mental illness following an accident. Any reader heading for a City giant may wish to note that the firm also acts for those suffering psychiatric damage caused by excess stress at work. Rather than acting on block instructions for unions or insurers, Anthony Gold operates on a claimant by claimant basis under conditional fee agreements.

Trainees do two seats chosen from family, PI and housing as this is where much of the firm's work lies. Happily, this is no problem as most come to the firm with a strong attraction to these particular areas. Usually trainees opt to do a 12-month seat in an department of their choice: with double the amount of time and experiences, *"you get really comfortable."* Trainees also usually do a seat in the commercial department, although the majority only choose six months of commercial work. According to our sources, *"commercial work is not really the main focus of the firm,"* yet there's more than enough to sample – commercial litigation, professional indemnity, commercial property and employment. Your chances of retention are good, particularly if you're interested in working for private clients. In September 2003, four of the six qualifiers stayed.

saving souls

Over the two years, trainees can expect lots of responsibility. According to one source: *"It's sometimes a bit scary, but you learn so much more."* You won't be chained to your desk, as there will be plenty of court visits (usually weekly in family seats) and we spoke to some who had been involved in asylum cases and judicial reviews. The hours are generally 9am to 5pm, with late nights infrequent but not unknown. Trainees report a better quality of life than law school comrades in the City, but before you get too excited, remember it's called selling your soul for a reason: *"The firm's no good if you want to make money,"* one interviewee sighed. Some trainees also felt that, at times, the job could be emotionally demanding: *"You worry about the dire situations some of our clients find themselves in – their lives are very close to yours."*

banged up

You shouldn't choose Anthony Gold expecting a laugh-a-minute training as *"most of the time it's heads down in the office;"* yet, clearly, this firm is stuffed full of lawyers who are truly dedicated to improving the lives of their clients and have a genuine pride in their work. Having said that, it's not all about righting wrongs and saving south London – Anthony Gold's

Christmas bash is *"always brilliant."* Last year the bubbly flowed freely in The Clink at London Bridge, a dungeon-like gaol turned party venue, offering upmarket prison food and guided tours of the cells. Generally, the London Bridge office is the more social of the two in which the trainees do time. *"There are more people there, so more goes on,"* although staff from the other offices do sometimes meet up. Some of the more daring inmates gave high-minded principles a new meaning earlier this year when they undertook a charity abseil from the top of Guy's Hospital.

and finally...

If you already have a strong bent for family or personal injury, you're going to love Anthony Gold. If you also want to gain experience in commercial law then it could be a perfect match.

Ashurst Morris Crisp

the facts

Location: London
UK ranking by size: 17
Total number of trainees: 97
Seats: 4x6 months
Alternative seats: Overseas seats, secondments
Extras: Pro bono – Islington and Toynbee Hall Legal Advice Centres, Disability Law service, Business in the Community, death row appeals, language training

Ashurst Morris Crisp has built itself a fine reputation for corporate work. It may not have the bulk of a magic circle firm, but it's expert at scooping up good deals from big-name clients. Following the failure of its third merger bid in as many years, the firm now says it is committed to life as a lone ranger.

breaking new ground...

Ashursts (by the time you read this, there's a good chance the firm will have dropped its full name) has been a tightly woven part of the rich tapestry of the City since 1822. Its founding partners were William Ashurst, a leading radical and proponent of the Reform Act; John Morris, a leading City figure; and the Victorian eccentric Sir Frank Crisp. Despite radical beginnings, the firm is now perceived to be one of the more traditional in the City. And it seems that this is just the way trainees like it. Said one: *"It's a traditional firm with well-established, long-term clients. The traditional aspect appealed to me."* Another told us: *"I wasn't keen to go to a firm that focused on new media...some allegedly cutting-edge outfit. I didn't want to wait to see if it would cut the edge – I wanted one already there."*

Wherever *"there"* is, the firm has been there for a very long time. Back in the day, Ashursts masterminded the rescue of a number of banks in the City crash of 1866, and was involved in the reorganisation of the Grand Trunk Railway Company of Canada and the completion of the Inner Circle Line on the London Underground. Has nothing changed in 150 years? It recently advised sponsors supporting the Metronet consortium in the London Underground PPP. And international infrastructure projects work continues to this day; Ashursts recently acted for Dragados and Bouygues on their bid to build the first high-speed rail link between France and Spain. Further afield, Ashursts' energy lawyers are advising Kuwait Petroleum Corporation on gas importation to Kuwait through a subsea pipeline.

...and trying new things

A corporate seat is mandatory for all trainees, and Ashursts also asks you do two seats from real estate, litigation and international finance. On the likelihood of getting what you want, one trainee pointed out: *"It depends on how proactive you are in communicating your choice."* Another agreed: *"If you just keep your head down, the firm will default to the template options. Of course, everybody accepts that you have to spend some time in data rooms. If you're happy to do that and don't volunteer for more, you'll get data rooms."* You have been warned.

At the heart of the corporate practice is a highly respected private equity group. For trainees, this means *"plenty of really high-responsibility work,"* including drafting bits of due diligence reports, working on verification and attending meetings. Private equity partners give *"lots of responsibility and are happy to give you the freedom to try new things."* In mainstream corporate finance, trainees become embroiled in hefty deals, so don't expect a raft of responsibility from the off. But *"if you're interested and you ask,"* supervisors will usually explain the details of the transaction to you and you'll be in the company of *"helpful junior associates."*

space junk

As you'd expect in a decent coco department, the hours can be gruelling. One trainee *"did about three nights on the trot. On the second night, you go home and sleep for four or five hours, then come back in."* Phew! *"It's amazing,"* said one, *"the adrenalin keeps you going"* and *"it can be quite amusing when people are stupidly tired."* Hmmm... Despite its image, international finance includes plenty of bits and pieces that are ideal for trainees to chew on. You'll be drafting or reviewing documents for smaller overdraft facilities, as well as getting involved *"in a support role"* on bigger deals. This department is expanding and boasts a *"hard-working and supportive"* atmosphere.

The firm's media practice has been absorbed into the technology, media and communications group. Trainees are exposed to the corporate side of media work, mainly drafting verification notes, and during busier periods they can also expect to have a go at software licences and agency agreements, research into advertising standards and regulatory issues including, recently, the Communications Bill. The group is largely occupied with satellite procurement, and trainees are included in the picture, attending meetings (possibly abroad), taking notes and helping to draft ancillary documentation. Said one: *"It was so global, it was unreal. We were in a meeting room with 20 people of different nationalities."*

Opinion was divided on litigation. Some lucky trainees were involved in smaller matters, revelling in *"real drafting work, good responsibility and client contact."* Others weren't. They got *"caught up in big deals* [sic] *doing nothing but due diligence* [sic again]." Frankly, it was easy to spot those who regarded a contentious seat as a necessary evil. Trainees' experiences and views of litigation are *"very split. If you'd spoken to someone three doors down, they would say it's horrific – nothing but boxing files."* For those after a bigger slice of the responsibility pie, the advice is to get yourself into employment or IP where you'll have a better chance of sinking your teeth into more discrete matters.

monkey business

IP is *"the fun group,"* where trainees can don fake moustaches (Okay, not really) and go undercover in the hunt for trademark infringements by *"dodgy T-shirt manufacturers."* And joy of joys, they see a good dose of court work, even appearing before High Court masters on small applications. In real estate (*"a great department"*), trainees run their own smaller files, as well as getting involved in *"the more corporate side of real estate deals."* They work for several fee earners at a time, and *"quite often a partner will just say 'Can you help me out on this?' and it will be just the two of you working together."* Snug as bugs in a rug.

Aside from client secondments (eg. IBM), postings are also available in overseas offices, namely Brussels, Frankfurt, Madrid, Milan and Paris. Although the firm has offices in Singapore and Tokyo, trainees have not been sent there for some time. The firm did reasonably well on NQ retention in September 2003: 44 of the 51 qualifiers stayed.

summer lovin'

It's virtually beyond dispute that Ashursts is a traditional firm, but whether this translates into an oppressive hierarchy is another matter entirely. *"You work closely with partners in all departments"* and, according to one source, partners are *"keen to avoid the hierarchy Ashursts is known for."* While there are *"the older partners who are still a bit 'like that', the more powerful partners are in favour of flat levels of communication and recognise there's little point in hierarchy."* For some, the firm's traditional image is *"no bad thing."* Said one trainee: *"I suppose it's fairly accurate: we have a traditional approach to client care, taking clients to lunch and so on."* To put it another way: if you go to a university law fair, *"some firms will be handing out jammy dodgers and stress balls. Ashursts doesn't do that."* We like a firm that doesn't resort to beads and mirrors to win new friends.

Aaah yes, friendship. Ashursts has a good friend in New York called Fried, Frank, Harris, Shriver & Jacobson. They started out by paying each other compliments; then there were gifts of client referrals and days and nights together on shared deals, followed by a public courtship (at first denied) and a promise to take things 'all the way'. Alas, it came to nothing and Ashursts merely reinforced its growing reputation as an altar bolter. Nonetheless, some rivals, clients (and clearly partners) believe the failure to merge is no bad thing. Just as it's okay to diss your best friend's ex, you hear people whispering that Fried Frank's culture was unlikely to fit with Ashursts' more genteel ethos. Having decided to go it alone, the firm is now working on building its own US practice in London.

going for gold

The firm is admired for its *"gentlemanly"* approach to transactions. Unfortunately, 'gentlemanly' is a rather gender-specific word that implies the firm is a bit of a boys' club. True, Ashursts has suffered from the allegation that it had almost no female partners, but having checked the list of their names, we noted that a clutch of women have now made partnership. One female trainee said quite firmly: *"I would be angry if this was an issue for us, but it's not."* Moving on... The firm is proud of its reputation for sporting prowess, boasting a stack of Olympian, national and international sportsmen. Regular trips to the gym are the pinnacle of achievement for most trainees.

home sweet gnome

It seems somewhat incongruous that one of the founders of this firm was an eccentric and prolific garden gnome collector. Frank Crisp's riverside home in Berkshire was eventually bought by ex-Beatle George Harrison, who restored its lavish and downright bizarre gardens and caverns to their former glory. Harrison even wrote a song about the Victorian lawyer who, he claimed, sent him gardening tips from the grave. You might feel like one of the walking dead after an all-nighter in corporate, but other than that we suspect the firm's offices are a pretty pleasant place to be. You'll bump into your peers in the staff restaurant, where fancy new caterers cook such delights as mori mori fish with mango salad. The Light is still the bar of choice for trainees, although in summer it competes with Exchange Square. If feeling particularly trendy, and not too self-conscious in their suits, it's Cantaloupe. And on Friday mornings, when they're struggling with sore heads, the restaurant serves up a heart-stopping full English for just £2.20.

and finally...

To use a woefully over-worn phrase, Ashursts punches above its weight. It has a long history of excellence, and now a renewed sense of pride in its unique culture and independence.

Baker & McKenzie

the facts

Location: London
UK ranking by size: 27
Total number of trainees: 67
Seats: 4x6 months
Alternative seats: Overseas seas, secondments
Extras: Pro bono – Waterloo Advice Centre, death row appeals

Once upon a time in America, some chap called Baker had a dream of an international law firm, without nationality. Dreams are normally gone by the morning, but this particular dream-weaver went on to help create Baker & McKenzie. From a single office in Chicago, Bakers now has a mind-bending 615 partners in 66 offices across 36 jurisdictions, most of which are staffed by local lawyers. London serves as a hub for Europe, co-ordinating many of the multi-jurisdictional transactions. Despite this global reach, the firm has managed to keep a mid-sized feel.

as if by magic

Last year we commented that the firm's recruitment website seemed rather childish, à la Mr Benn of 52 Festive Road. Well, the strange interchangeable jackets idea is still there, but the lurid colours that accompanied them are gone. We doubt it's because of our gentle teasing; it's more likely a reflection of Bakers' tendency to continually evolve – this firm is not the type to stand still. A source told us: *"The firm is looking to develop, particularly its corporate work, and also its relationships with both Baker Mac offices worldwide and important existing clients."* The firm is *"always looking for new ways to tap into new clients,"* and having added three new overseas offices in the past year, internationally, this Baker has fingers in more pies than Little Jack Horner.

In London, the firm offers a full range of services including anti-trust, banking, corporate, IP, IT, dispute resolution, employment, insurance, project finance, real estate, and tax services to an impressive client roster. Avis Europe, Cisco Systems, Compaq, DaimlerChrysler, Japan Tobacco, Shell and Sony all turn to Baker Mac when they need a friendly legal ear.

my mate

Trainees in London follow a standard four by six months training schedule. Following the national trend, employment, IP and IT are the favourite seats. One source reported: *"Employment is always very popular...we have a good employment department here. The work is excellent as we have great clients, and the people are great too."* Great. IP and IT received praise in equal measure, being component parts of a sort of crossover department. As one source explained: *"It's a big department, with people who are totally at the IP end and people totally at the IT end, and then there are people in the middle doing things like copyright and software."* IP, IT and telecoms law are fields in which Baker & McKenzie has excelled the world over. The clients of these departments offer prestige and glamour and so it's not surprising that most trainees want a piece of the action. The existence of these trainee hotspots means there's no certainty that you will get exactly what you crave. The advice is to *"think carefully about it"* and then to push hardest for what matters most. That's not to say the firm doesn't aim to please: *"HR are very good and always try to accommodate your first choice."*

We heard mixed reports about the compulsory corporate seat. One source noted: *"Lots of trainees are scared of corporate, and you have to do it in your second or third seat. Yeah, it can be intimidating, but as soon as you are part of it, you really enjoy it – the teams are great, and there is a great work ethic; everyone puts in 100% and the partners are really good."* Great. Another source put it in marmite terms: *"People either love corporate or hate it. They get a regular flow of people wanting to qualify into the department, so some must like it, but others see it as something that must be done here, and just got through."*

happy medium

Overall, trainees reported a good level of involvement in the work, and a fair deal of client contact. It seems curious to speak of one of the biggest law firms on the planet as offering a mid-sized firm experience, but that's exactly what trainees get. One who had spent time in dispute resolution told us: *"I was given a couple of relatively small claims to manage myself and was trusted with quite a lot really."* On lower value matters, say contractual disputes, *"files are passed from associates and you are asked to contact clients to get more information and to then get the claim in order."* Even when not in charge of a file, there are few occasions where you'll feel like you are interchangeable with any one of a dozen other trainees. *"You get disputes that are small enough for you to be the one trainee in the department who is working on them...you are continually used, going to meetings, doing some drafting, and then random bits of research."*

It's the same story in the employment department, which happens to have one of the most respected teams in the UK. A past tenant of the seat told us: *"I've always been treated with respect, told what my role is going to be and given responsibility. You are expected to be able to do work in the first place, but if you show yourself to be willing, keen and capable, you'll really reap rewards."* By now you'll have got the picture – this is a rewarding training environment.

book of the week

Which really only leaves us with the task of telling you about the parties and people that will be a part of your life as a trainee. Oh, and the brilliant overseas opportunities! In 2003 eight foreign offices received visits from trainees – Chicago, Washington, Amsterdam, Brussels, Madrid, Moscow, Hong Kong and Singapore. Even if you stay in the UK, you'll be constantly liaising with lawyers across the constellation of Baker Mac offices.

And in London, you'll get a very decent office to work in. Just like the old website, colour is the order of the day. *"There are great stained glass windows in the entrance and the sunlight puts little colours on the walls."* Great. And there's more colour in the central courtyard and in the artwork. *"It varies, but there's quite a lot. There's one that caused a bit of controversy: a man with his head in a horse. It's just one of those pictures you have a reaction to – it's as if the horse's neck is open and the man is rummaging around inside."* For a change, the Damien Hirst works in the staff restaurant don't even register on the shock-o-meter.

Socially, the firm gels well and the demarcation between partners and staff is not rigid. One trainee tried to communicate this by telling us that *"at monthly Friday night drinks you'll see people from managing partners right down through to support staff...if I should even use the words 'down through to'."* We hear that some of the trainees have just started a book group, *"well, it's more about girls getting together and having a drink!"* The quiz nights too seem to be another excuse to just get together for a drink – *"they are not too competitive, pretty light-hearted affairs."* Perhaps the best social gathering we heard about was the team who celebrated completing a deal 20 minutes earlier than their seven o'clock deadline...seven in the morning that is. After a glass of bubbly, they sped off to Smithfield Market for breakfast and a couple of pints in the pub and then headed home to bed. Separately, we assume.

playing to your strengths

One thing that bugs us quite a bit is the way trainees up and down the country claim that their firms recruit a really diverse range of trainees, when clearly, blatantly, many of them don't. Generally, firms recruit in their own image, thus perpetuating the culture already in place. Baker & McKenzie is no different, but its culture is already diverse. In its case, we can genuinely report that the trainee population is diverse in terms of age and background, nationality and temperament. There are ex-barristers, people with non-law first careers, working parents, young whippersnappers, extroverts and quiet types – all sorts in fact. One trainee felt that the firm was good at identifying people's strengths and then playing to them. Laudable, but there is a down side: *"You seem to be able to score brownie points by going along to graduate recruitment events, but there doesn't seem to be a democratic way of dishing out those events. There are favourites."*

In September 2003, the final tally saw 18 of the 25 second-year trainees staying on post-qualification.

and finally...

If there's ever a time when we don't hear really positive feedback about Baker & McKenzie's training scheme, we promise we'll eat our keyboards. No two ways about it, this is a great pick for anyone after an international training in a mid-sized firm.

Barlow Lyde & Gilbert

the facts

Location: London, Oxford
UK ranking by size: 30
Total number of trainees: 34
Seats: 4x6 months
Alternative seats: Occasional secondments
Extras: Pro bono – St Botolph's Project, lang. training

Barlow Lyde & Gilbert is a break from the norm. It's not only its location in Aldgate that puts daylight between this firm and the typical City outfit: unlike most big players, BLG is not corporate led, offering instead a litigation-heavy training.

web of intrigue

Something of a *"dark horse,"* BLG is best known for its litigation practice and its work for the insurance industry. An impressive roster of clients includes Churchill, AXA, Direct Line and Admiral, and growing non-contentious teams act for the likes of Barclays and Tesco and, from Oxford, a cluster of pharmaceutical and technology companies. However, success in the insurance sector casts a big shadow: *"It might not be that well known to the man in the street, but those in insurance will know Barlows' name."* True enough. Of course, the non-contentious lawyers also owe much to insurance clients as many of their deals come off the back of relationships originally forged by their litigating colleagues. In June 2003, for example, the corporate group acted for the executive management team of Churchill Insurance on the £1.1 billion acquisition of the company by Royal Bank of Scotland.

At a time when some firms are withdrawing from the TMT arena, BLG seems to be gaining ground there. Of its Oxford branch, we were told, *"it has made some lateral hires lately, and is getting some good deals and top-notch clients."* These are? Companies like Oxford University spin-out, Spinox, established to develop silk-spinning techniques for clinical and other purposes with 'seedcorn' funding from Germany.

Trainees spend time in four departments on a six-month seat plan. BLG has lots of mini-specialist practice areas within larger groups, so for example: *"You could come into the shipping department and not even know there is an aerospace department."* What this means is trainees have a wide choice of seats, with the added benefit that *"they will try to give you your first choice in all seats."* You won't avoid litigation (if that's your intention, turn the page now) – trainees typically do one non-contentious and three litigious seats, although more and more are doing a 50/50 split these days.

soft touch?

Litigation-led firms have an advantage over corporate and finance firms – lawyers can plan the working day/week such that extreme highs and lows are less common. One source said: *"I was told at the beginning I would work reasonable hours, and I actually do."* Another added: *"If you were here regularly after 8pm they would think you were slow."* When longer hours do hit, extra effort is recognised. As one trainee told us: *"I worked 8.30am to 7.30pm for a while, making bundles, but what made it more bearable was that my supervisor was grateful, gave me a lot of feedback, and took me out to say thank you."*

But BLG is no soft option. You won't walk into a job here unless you make the right impression, in the first instance on the grad recruitment head honcho Caroline Walsh. Her name popped up in every interview – something that would normally turn our Acme Brochure-Speak detector into a smoking mess – but there seems to be a genuine appreciation of her efforts. One source advised: *"You won't get in if you aren't friendly and outgoing,"* because *"there is no room for back-room lawyers, those who are socially inept and sit in the corner being all academic. They only take on people who are capable of meeting clients."* Basically, *"being interesting is about as important as academic ability."*

team talk

The professional liability and com lit department makes up around a third of the firm. Most trainees visit one or more of its subgroups *"simply because it is* so big." A popular department, it is "*oversubscribed on qualification, as it is most people's first or second choice.*" Separate teams handle negligence actions concerning accountants, financial services, lawyers, insurance brokers and IT consultants. You'll even find big law firm clients alongside professionals' insurers.

Comprising several smaller teams, including PI and clinical negligence, the general insurance department has risen in popularity too. One fan told us: "*There is a fair amount of advocacy and you get to work on case management conferences and infant settlements.*" A PI seat can be "*a fantastic experience if you want to be a litigator – you might be given a £2K trip-and-slip case that you can get on with as you wish.*" Interestingly, a fair amount of this work emanates from the aerospace department: "*We get big clients with big cases, but they don't want to go to other firms for the small stuff, so trainees run these files themselves with a partner supervising.*" BLG acted for two airlines, SAA and QANTAS, in the recent wave of claims for compensation for DVT.

Reinsurance is an altogether different beast, ideally suited to big-brained people who thrive on intellectual challenges. Is this why we hear that "*there are a few trainees who really want to do it, but it doesn't have the same mass appeal,*" and "*it is still seen as a bit nerdy as it is so specialist and so technical.*" We investigated BLG's world-beating reputation. From advising London market reinsurers on issues arising out of the collapse of Enron to a spate of film financing cases, its lawyers are at the forefront of international reinsurance industry disputes. Major air disasters, post-9/11 issues, Latin American pollution losses and political risk coverage, will all plunge the trainee into a vortex of unfamiliar concepts and terminology, such as '*facultative reinsurance*', '*commutation recovery*' and '*long-tail US programmes*'. Baffling.

...should you choose to accept it

Our sources reported a good supervision, but it is more hands-off than hands-on, requiring those who need advice to seek it. This can cause problems (think overworked partner) but we were told: "*you never feel unable to go back to someone for help.*" While trainees are given "*a good level of work and responsibility,*" inevitably, "*you get your fair share of photocopying, but we have a good paralegal team – you aren't being trained to paginate!*"

In 2002, following a visit from management consultants, BLG began a drive to promote cross-firm communication. Having "*decided not to have a mission statement,*" it did introduce several "*attainable goals,*" although our trainee sample could only remember three – "*supportive,*" "*communicative,*" and "*client-focused.*" By way of example, we were told that the firm has gone to great lengths to improve links with the tech-centric Oxford office: "*They've made a conscious effort to get everyone to go to work in Oxford for a day.*" Additionally, there are now cohort-based "*lateral communication groups across the firm*" to get people mingling. In September 2003, 13 of the 18 qualifiers stayed with the firm to carry on mingling.

bloody marble-ous

The large glass atrium in the office is the venue for "*lots of meet and greets.*" The "*pride and joy of Barlows,*" the atrium used to start on the seventh floor and go right up to the roof of the building that BLG shares with other businesses. Right up to the roof...until Richards Butler built over it. "*I think we persuaded them into doing up our library and seminar rooms at the same time,*" joked one trainee. Throughout, "*the decor is nice, not Olswang offices, but nice.*" "*I've seen other places where the client area is really swish, and then you see the offices and think 'Oh my god,' but it isn't like that here,*" said a source. The only part of the building that drew negative comments is the bit clients see first: "*The reception is an 80s throwback, a bit Dynasty and shoulder pads.*" Um...isn't that how we described it in 2001?

The trainee social scene gets full marks. "*The Slug & Lettuce opposite is a favourite – you'll always see a few friendly faces on a Friday. Sometimes we pretend we are going somewhere else but we never do.*" There's even a bit of intra-office dating: "*I know of at least four couples who are out, and a couple who are getting married,*" whispered the office gossip. BLG also gets good marks for its sporting endeavours, and there are teams for a number of pursuits, from women's football to hockey.

and finally...

For those looking to get stuck into some real litigation at an early stage, Barlow Lyde & Gilbert offers a plethora of opportunities, as well as several nice sidelines if you fancy a change. Recognition must be given to the expanding non-contentious departments, but litigation is still the fat kid on the see-saw.

Bates, Wells & Braithwaite

the facts

Location: London
UK ranking by size: 152
Total number of trainees: 8
Seats: 2x6 + 3x4 months
Alternative seats: Occasional secondments
Extras: Numerous pro bono activities

It was a happy day when, earlier this year, the *Student Guide* crossed paths with Bates, Wells & Braithwaite. So, with apologies to those of our past readers with a strong sense of social conscience, we now introduce the nation's top charity lawyers.

doing the right thing

The firm's roots stretch back over 100 years to rural Suffolk, but as everyone was a bit hazy on the subject we'll start the clock ticking from 1970 when the London office opened. BWB's real strengths lie in the services it provides to the charities sector, immigration clients and entertainment organisations, particularly theatre companies. For trainees of a certain persuasion, this makes the firm a highly attractive prospect. *"It's a firm for people who want to carve out a career that's a bit different from the norm; people who want to make an impact in an area that is specialist and socially valuable."* One source said it values *"do-gooding, in the best sense of the word."* Within the 2003 trainee cohort was someone who'd worked for Amnesty and the Organization for Security and Co-operation in Europe; someone who'd been a teacher and a psychiatric nurse; and someone who'd worked for an environmental group. Breathe easy if you're still wet behind the ears – the odd youngster does come straight from uni. What all successful applicants seem to have done is *"thought through the questions 'Why am I on this planet?' and 'What are the social or moral reasons why I should do this or that with my life?'."*

If you think BWB's work is limited in scope, you'd be wrong. Charities need advice beyond the specialist constitutional, registration and lottery funding issues that are peculiar to them – try property, employment, commercial transactions and general litigation. Factor in a busy immigration team and you'll see that two years is hardly long enough to experience all that's on offer. Trainees all do two six-month seats in their first year, chosen from charities/private client, litigation, commercial and immigration. Second-years do three four-month seats chosen from pure charity, litigation, employment and property. A couple of trainees have done short secondments with TV production companies TalkBack and Hat Trick.

"The system is designed such that whatever you do, you spend at least one seat in the charity and social enterprise department." Excuse us? Social enterprise? *"Yes, the department has rebranded itself. It's because the social enterprise movement has been growing rapidly in the last couple of years. It's basically people who want to do good while running a business that makes profits...it's a big growth area for the firm."*

gobbledegook and verse

Having been introduced to some new jargon, we wondered if new recruits had to learn a whole new language on arrival at BWB. One source put our minds at rest: *"There's a certain amount of jargon that clients use, and it helps to become familiar with it, but that happens in all firms. We try not to use all that jargon when we can."* And on getting to grips with law that you'll not have come across before: *"People here are good about giving you little five minute tutorials."* As anywhere, the effort made by supervisors depends on who you get. In the experience of one trainee: *"There are at least two partners who are really excellent and made time and answered my questions about first principles. There were others who were friendly and approachable, although they didn't especially dedicate effort. No one is a disaster or hostile and undermining."* Glad to hear it.

At partner level there are certainly some intriguing characters. One source freely admitted that some were *"eccentric and traditional...there's a slight feeling of it being an equity old boys club."* But then, almost in the same breath, they spoke about how it was easy for trainees to *"step outside the sense of hierarchy"* and for partners and trainees to *"shout and take the piss out of each other."* Many partners are described simply as *"inspirational"* because they manage to combine successful legal careers with a passion for something else beyond law. For one it is poetry. *"She runs Poetry in the City and gets various poets to bring along their favourite pieces to various places in the City, including this one."* Hence the collection of umbrellas in reception that bear the group's branding.

waterloo sunset

You might need one of those umbrellas when making a dash from the main office to the overflow office just around the corner. *"Until recently we were all in fairly scruffy premises in Cheapside, but we have recently split in two and now charities and immigration are in an open-plan office."* The immigration team is a big attraction for trainees. Every six months, one of them gets to work with the two partners, nationality expert and junior solicitor, dividing their time between business immigration (applications under the Highly Skilled Migrant Programme, etc), privately paying clients and asylum cases. If your main interest is in the Human Rights Act, you'll probably find this is where it will most often be brought into play. *"We certainly use the right to family and private life in immigration cases,"* a source explained. Trainees' tasks in immigration are varied and include making applications for leave to remain and entry clearance, corresponding with the Home Office, attending asylum appeals, liaising with medical and academic experts, and conducting research into the political situation in clients' countries. Sometimes you might attend interviews at an airport or Waterloo Station. There's just one thing (something you might already be aware of if you keep abreast of the subject): proposals for changes in the funding of legal advice to asylum seekers threaten many firms' ability to continue providing this kind of service. BWB is not immune, so watch this space.

frantic antics

If you want to attend seminars on how to deal with clients then go to another firm; here, you learn *"through osmosis."* As one trainee told us: *"You absorb and do."* You'll have structured appraisals at the end of seats and an annual review, but most of the time, *"you just know if you are OK"* by the reactions of your seniors. As impressive as they may be at work, we're really not sure you want to follow the example set by some partners at the Christmas party. In 2002, they performed an intriguing sketch. We didn't really want to probe too deeply once we realised it involved a senior bod donning rubber gloves to perform some sort of underwear inspection on another male partner (who was wearing a nightie). *"It all ended in a general scrummage."* No, no, no, no, no.

More generally, the social scene is relaxed. Local pubs are less than inspiring, but there are one or two *"unfavourites"* and a social committee organises the odd wine tasting *"and so forth"* and a summer day out. In September 2003, one of the three qualifying trainees stayed on, with another joining the civil service's European Fast Stream and the other moving up north.

and finally...

Bates, Wells & Braithwaite offers inspiration and social conscience in place of slickness and deal trophies. Don't mistake it for a haven for wishy-washy, cardigan-wearing liberals, even though the founder of the London office is a Liberal life peer.

Beachcroft Wansbroughs

the facts

Location: Birmingham, Bristol, Leeds, London, Manchester, Winchester

UK ranking by size: 16

Total number of trainees: 54

Seats: 4x6 months

Alternative seats: Secondments

National firm Beachcroft Wansbroughs' strengths lie in insurance litigation, services to the health sector and, increasingly, projects and PFI. Training is available in four of its six offices – Bristol, London, Leeds, and Manchester.

fe fi fo fum

In 1999, Wansbroughs Willey Hargrave, a leading insurance litigation firm in Leeds, Sheffield, Bristol and Winchester merged with London commercial firm Beachcroft Stanleys and another smaller insurance litigation player in Manchester called Vaudreys. By 2001 the Sheffield branch had closed and a new Birmingham office was open. Four years on and there's a greater sense of shared identity than before, certainly at trainee level, although admittedly our sources were all post-merger recruits.

After interviewing, we're left with an image of a sleeping giant. It's not that BW is snoozing its way into the 21st century, but it does seem to leave rather light footprints for such a large creature. Some trainees thought the firm needed to stomp a bit louder, to let everyone know what it is achieving. To illustrate, one said: *"If you look at our website you'll find it's under construction."* Indeed it was, although we saw some attractive grad recruitment pages. The good news is that we see signs of the giant waking up to the idea of more noise. And Beachcrofts has plenty of good news to share: bucking the trend and proving itself to be weatherproof, in 2003 it posted an 18% profit increase, retained 23 of its 26 qualifying trainees and continued to hire senior lawyers from other top firms.

a fair day's work

Almost all our sources spoke about Beachcrofts' assessment day. *"It had six parts...each one looked at you from a different angle,"* said one. Another agreed the day had been very fair and went further to talk about how the firm was a fair place generally. *"It is ethically minded and strives to be fair. For example, in professional indemnity cases the lawyers act for the insurer and the insured; they have to be ringmaster and play fair for both."* Everyone was happy with the hours they worked. *"Hours are considered to be one of the best things about Beachcrofts. We all reckon that we have traded a higher salary for a better working life."* You get the impression that people really enjoy working here; of his peers, one trainee said: *"They have an equanimity about things. Nobody goes out of their way to be needlessly aggressive."*

mickey mouse job

Bristol is the administrative centre, but we were told the managing and senior partners are London-based...but then a Leeds trainee claimed the managing partner was actually in his office. *"No, he's definitely here,"* a London trainee countered. Baffled by his omnipresence, we wondered if, like Mickey Mouse in Disneyland, there might be several of him, each working to a carefully planned schedule so as not to be seen in two places at once. *"He is on the road a lot,"* a reliable source informed us.

Definitely a London man, senior partner and former Tory cabinet minister, Lord Hunt of Wirral has good reason to be pleased. 2002 brought the inauguration of the International Criminal Court in The Hague, something for which he'd campaigned. Amazingly, one Lord Hunt isn't enough for this lot. Its second, Lord Hunt of Kings Heath, is a former Labour health minister (you may recall his resignation over the war in Iraq) and one-time chief exec of the NHS Confederation. We're reliably informed that both are permitted to be present in the same room at the same time and none of the other four Lord Hunts kicking around in Parliament have any connection with Beachcrofts.

london: treasured hunts

London has the most trainees and seat options. Stints in property, corporate finance and projects/PFI are all likely; the contentious element of your training can be satisfied in 'litigation solutions', professional indemnity, insurance/reinsurance, IT/IP, property litigation or employment. *"They're quite open minded and willing to let you try the things you want;"* apparently, there are more seats than trainees so people don't have to fill the same positions every six months. Spread between Fetter Lane and Eastcheap in the City's insurance district, the firm services insurance companies and NHS trusts, plus other public and private sector clients. The quality of trainee work is enhanced by the presence of paralegals. *"In litigation there are some mind-numbing and seemingly inane tasks – they are an essential part of the process and have got to be done by someone who knows what they are doing – but you're not overburdened by them."* Unless on secondment to Unilever, trainees share an office with their supervisor, although they work for several fee earners, gaining exposure to a variety of cases and working styles.

There have been jokes about the Lords Hunt – hunt balls etc, etc. *"We do have Country Life in reception and there are some public school types who might enjoy hunting and fishing,"* but they are a minority. Another impression is that the firm has hordes of *"dowdy"* people, trudging on with NHS and public law work. Also inaccurate: *"Property, for example, do a lot of work for the NHS and local authorities, and even there they are having to get more hard nosed."* There are monthly drinks in the in-house restaurant Café 100 and two popular pubs close by – The Mucky Duck and The Printers Devil (*"a proper old blokes' pub with a pool table and a jukebox"*). The whole office comes together for the annual black tie dinner dance.

bristol: zero tolerance

Bristol offers professional indemnity, PI and commercial litigation as well as non-contentious seats like corporate, employment and property. It's not uncommon to do three contentious seats, but there's sufficient variety in these. *"In [defendant] PI, I dealt with a case myself – not massively high value – and I assisted on other people's cases."* Cases include small RTAs and accidents as well as more serious injuries including those incurred in high-speed police chases. You'll speak to solicitors on the other side, attend case management conferences and even do small court applications. Apparently, one supervisor had pronounced: *"I want you to learn how to think about litigation, not just be given boxes of paperwork."* The training committee is *"stringent about the kind of things they're prepared to let trainees do. There is one bad trainee supervisor who is not being allowed to have one again until he proves himself."*

If clin neg is your thing then step on up. When the NHSLA chopped back its panel of approved defence firms, the Bristol office retained its position, but *"the NHSLA asked for its ball back from the London office."* Beachcrofts occupies a city centre location not too far from Cattle Green Park. After work, you can nip down to the trainees favourite on the waterfront, Bar Coda. You can also practice talking to grown ups as there's plenty of departmental socialising too.

leeds: yes…yes…yes

Leeds means loads of litigation, especially defendant clin neg and PI. It's begun to take more trainees now that some of the non-contentious departments are big enough to offer seats; however, corporate is not available. Instead, try professional indemnity, health advice, employment, property, construction, projects and defendant insurance, which is both complex fast track (*"cases under £15,000 that won't spiral out of control"*) and multi-track (*"more catastrophic injuries"*). Low-value claims are handled by big teams of 'analysts' in Birmingham and Manchester in a separate division called Mutual Law. Trainees reported enthusiastically on PI: *"I did a wide range of drafting tasks, instructed experts, spoke to witnesses...and trainees are allowed to do settlements and simple case management conferences, and you do genuine advocacy on your own."* A PI seat is great for chalking up the tasks on the Law Society's checklist: *"You go through the form at the end of the seat and it's 'yes, yes, yes' all the way down!"* The office is on the square featured in TV Bar-dram *North Square.* Walking through the small, Georgian-fronted reception, you soon realise that, just like J-Lo, it's really big behind. All Bar One remains popular after work.

manchester: party animals

Manchester also tends towards the contentious, although it has more seat choices. Trainees all do PI or professional indemnity, but property and employment also offer good experiences. NHS trusts and other public sector clients dominate alongside large insurers, but again, there is a distinct corporate client base and ad hoc secondments are an alternative to the office. Described as *"all very normal,"* the trainees are keen to help each other out with any tricky questions: *"You get a lot of e-mails between trainees."* If your peers don't know the answer, then it's time to ask your supervisor or another fee earner. On the standard of trainee work we had good reports: *"I'm happy with the support and supervision I get and I've run some of my own files. You're allowed to liaise with clients and go to site meetings and investigate things yourself."*

In the city centre, overlooking St. Anne's Church, the open-plan office is pretty swish and boasts a bar complete with table football and Sky TV. It sounds like the party office of the firm. As in Leeds, there's a monthly '100 Club' draw (£100 prize money) as well as different events. *"In September there's an annual trip to Blackpool, in October Halloween Olympics, November…um, can't remember what we did…in December we had the Christmas ball with a cabaret act by second-year trainees..."* We stopped our source there.

and finally...

All the vital signs are looking good for Beachcroft Wansbroughs. Trainees are delighted with the firm's bedside manner and recommend it to anyone keen on a litigation-heavy training. Those keen on working for heath sector clients and/or on projects/PFI will also want to apply.

Berwin Leighton Paisner

the facts

Location: London
UK ranking by size: 21
Total number of trainees: 61
Seats: 4x6 months
Alternative seats: Secondments

In 2001,Berwin Leighton and Paisner & Co merged to produce BLP. Commercial property remains the mainstay of the firm, with associated practices in property finance and property litigation, but the firm's corporate and finance practices are on the up. Its international ambitions were realised this year, when it tied itself to New York real estate boutique Kramer Levin Naftalis & Frankel. And it's expanding its European network, allying itself to the Milan-based real estate firm Studio Santa Maria.

wiring brains telephone

In an attempt to get our heads around the firm's practice, we picked the brains of the editor of *Chambers UK.* After 20 minutes of finance speak, our minds wandered to thoughts of St. Lucia and sex on the beach. The cocktail, that is. If the same thing happens to you, apply to a crime firm. But if you reckon real estate finance is even better than sex (on the beach or elsewhere) read on.

BLP's obsession with anagrams continues unabated. Just look at the website, if you doubt us. Her Nine Rainbow Piglets remains a firm seriously into its branding. But this isn't a case of style over substance. *Chambers UK* awards BLP prestigious rankings in real estate and related litigation and finance matters, PFI, smaller corporate work, environment, planning, local government advice and a host of other more specialist areas. Its stellar client list includes giant property industry names like British Land, Argent, Hammerson and Land Securities, but you'll probably be more familiar with clients like the MoD, Whitbread, JD Wetherspoon, Sheraton, Marriott and

Holiday Inn. The firm also manages the day-to-day property profile of its star client Tesco.

It's a little known fact, but we feel duty bound to tell you that BLP was recently awarded the honour of 'Switchboard of the Year', based on the excellent response time, clarity and handling skills of its receptionists. In our job, that's nothing to be sniffed at.

inhibit on peer wrangles

The training system is the standard four by six-months arrangement. While the firm maintains that the only compulsory is a contentious seat, the majority of trainees do a stint in the core real estate practice. No surprise, given its size and fine reputation. Not that you should mind. Trainees gave the real estate seat a standing ovation. It's a hard-working group, and *"you're at the coalface with your head down all day."* Although individual teams vary according to the character of the partner in charge, most are collegial and tight-knit with trainees welcomed along to group lunches and drinks. Those who tried real estate later on in their training appreciated being able to draw upon skills they'd learned in corporate, finance and litigation seats. Large-scale project and development work is mixed up with the autonomy of managing your own smaller files. Expect *"outstanding responsibility"* and a wide array of work, with supervisors who *"get you involved fully."* Just remember that BLP works *"for huge institutional clients on massive transactions. You shouldn't have the conception that you'll be selling houses."*

In these seats you need to keep your ears open and your mind alert, just to understand what the deals are all about. Outsourcing is a bit of a buzzword. Simply put, it's the transfer of management and service responsibilities from a large property owner to a company that will step into its shoes…for a price. In this field, BLP has acted for both clients that divest themselves of responsibilities – central and local government, universities and educational establishments, healthcare providers, etc. – and the clients that take up these responsibilities. More traditional real estate deals have involved the firm in well-known developments such as Birmingham's Brindleyplace, Paradise Street in Liverpool, every single NCP carpark in the UK (Royal Bank of Scotland bought the whole portfolio at auction for £821 million), 400 Little Chef restaurants and 200 Travelodges (sold by client Compass), and some very prestigious addresses in the City of London.

new pong in the libraries

Corporate finance is a department on the rise, and this year *Chambers UK* elevated it to band 3 for medium-sized deals. Corporate garnered mixed reactions from our interviewees. While most found themselves basking in *"proper work"* and even relishing the *"customary all-nighter"* (*"you should do it, just for the bravado!"*), one or two reported they had trouble negotiating the structure of the group. Those who snagged good work found themselves at client meetings, and assisting with drafting on major finance transactions.

Yet again, loud praise for corporate tax, where trainees immerse themselves into research on VAT structuring and loan relationships on billion-pound deals. You may also end up writing articles for publication (client news updates etc.) and helping out on the business development side. The best thing about tax is that it touches almost every area of legal practice, so you'll be working with most departments in the firm – a great way to get your face known. If the stresses of corporate tax get too much, a seat in the planning and environment group can offer a decidedly *"unCityish"* experience. Trainees loved the public policy context of this area of law and appreciated that their work was in pursuit of a *"tangible goal."*

brain on while pestering

Although the vibe in real estate litigation is somewhat older and more *"serious,"* it *"kicks you into gear early on."* This is a *"good nuts and bolts seat,"* offering you your own files and client contact, working for pension funds and large private property portfolios. Those who want to step away from London Bridge for a seat can choose to spend time on a client secondment.

These are currently available with Tesco (alas, our standard shelf-stacking joke is too worn out this year), construction client Arup, Toyota and Ford.

wherein plainest boring?

BLP is known for its strong connections in the Jewish community, but before anyone else contacts us to ask if that will make it easier for them to secure a training contract, let's be quite clear that BLP recruits in the same manner as any other commercial firm. In previous editions, we've described trainees as a fairly safe lot, *"hard-working and keen to please."* Perhaps keen to dispel this image, this year trainees described themselves as *"lively, well-rounded and bloody good at what they do."* Most puzzlingly, they also claimed to be *"unorthodox,"* but whether this was meant in comparison to other City trainees or people in general, we couldn't decide! *"You'd have a hard time walking over the people here. They're not happy to be told to be quiet."* So, this year at least, BLP is full of petulant Kelly Osbourne-types!

Whatever the case, the trainees we spoke to were interested, enthusiastic and certainly willing to speak their minds. Unfortunately, like many firms, BLP can have its political corners, but on the positive side trainees felt that they would emerge from their two years of trainee incubation as competent practitioners: *"We get good training, good resources, and we are treated pretty well."* Each department organises its own training programmes to ensure trainees are kept up to date on legal developments.

sip wine, linger on breath

Having been split between Adelaide House at London Bridge and another office in Fleet Street, this year the firm became one happy cohabiting family after it annexed the building next door to Adelaide House. The social life is *"there if you want it,"* apparently *"'if' being the operative word."* For those who do, there are themed firm-wide drinks nights. Recently one took on a hoedown flavour. Unsurprisingly, most of our sources were mysteriously on hoe-liday at the time. On a more regular basis, and avoiding any kind of costume drama, trainees just *"dive into a pub"* – usually FOB (below Adelaide House), The Fine Line or The Borough Bar. For lunch you can head to Alibi, the staff restaurant, or you can sit by the river. One of our sources conducted his interview gazing into the murky depths of the Thames from atop London Bridge. We checked back with him the next day...he hadn't jumped. On the subject of not jumping, 25 of the 31 NQs stayed with BLP in September 2003.

fly and nail...

If you want to work in international money markets and time zones, or you want to be in on the biggest of cross-border transactions, this isn't the place for you. But if you hanker after quality training in an environment where *"everyone knows your name,"* BLP is indeed a good choice. The firm's growing corporate finance practice and its international expansion prove that it's looking beyond its old stomping grounds – the property industry and the public sector.

Bevan Ashford

the facts

Location: Tiverton, Taunton, Plymouth, Exeter, Bristol, London, Birmingham
UK ranking by size: 25
Total number of trainees: 49
Seats: 4x6 months
Alternative Seats: Secondments
Extras: Pro bono – Tiverton legal drop-in centre

Bevan Ashford is an established regional firm with seven offices spread across its two profit centres, one in the West Country and the other comprising London, Bristol and Birmingham. Whilst the latter boasts an outstanding reputation for healthcare litigation and PFI work alongside a developing commercial practice, the West Country grouping covers the full gamut of commercial, matrimonial, criminal and PI.

a tale of two partnerships

In the eyes of a credulous world, and through the lens of its own website, press releases and recruitment materials, Bevan Ashford has long appeared a prosperous firm, united in its singular push for regional and national prominence. But although there are no dark forces at work, be under no illusions that Bevan Ashford is two distinct entities operating under a single banner. Each has its own character, objectives, core practice areas, territory and trainees. This peculiar state of affairs arose following the 1986 merger of Devon's Ashford Spark and Bristol's Bevan Hancock, which never progressed to full profit sharing or integration. The vibrations along the EPL (Exeter, Plymouth, Tiverton, Taunton, London) and BBL (Bristol, Birmingham, London) fault line have caused speculation about a prospective split. A deliberate decision to rent separate workspace in the capital has drawn attention to a strategic internal review being undertaken by the firm. Due in February, it had not yet filtered out to the watching public by the time we went to press, but with both partnerships equally profitable the firm can afford to take its time. From a prospective trainee's point of view, it is vital to be aware of "*the absolute divide*" between BBL and EPL, and to make an informed choice about which you select. Only very rarely can you work in the other one.

14 hours to save the earth

Swoosh! Log on to the firm's website and you're immediately exposed to a Flash shower of meteorites. As hard as we looked for Ming the Merciless, he never materialised, so we must assume the meteorites are intended to underline the firm's energy and progressive outlook. If so, it seems a fair reflection of the ambition and healthy growth across the BBL axis. As one trainee declared: "*We are working to achieve a more national profile*" (obviously when not busy building a giant laser to annihilate the moon).

The hub of the axis, the Bristol office, has nationally recognised expertise in clinical negligence and healthcare issues and boasts a long association with the NHS. Complex medical claims in the fields of obstetrics, neurosurgery and infection are defended by a team that has been retained by the NHS Litigation Authority and won instructions from other healthcare bodies. Although BBL would clearly suit anyone with a preference for clin neg or clinical policy work, particularly someone with experience in the health sector, these clients also send it commercial, projects, employment, IP/IT, and general litigation instructions. One trainee practically hyperventilated when they told us: "*There's been a lot of recruitment and one of our main clients is still the NHS but we're moving away from just claims and there's lots of public sector commercial work and we won an audit relations partnership with Bristol City Council and...*" Calm down, breathe deeply, we get the picture. The firm now has a roughly 50/50 public/private sector client base, with impressive private sector clients including Orange and Intel (which both offer secondments for trainees).

bright-eyed and bushy-tailed

Described as "*not clinically, horribly modern, but no chandeliers,*" the Bristol office is "*squirreling into surrounding buildings*" to accommodate new staff. Centrally located, the firm's local The Three Sugar Loaves on Christmas Steps is "*only two minutes away from work, and the best fish and chip shop in the world is only 30 seconds from the pub.*" Could you ask for more? With sports teams, outdoor pursuits and social events, all in a city within easy reach of the countryside, we doubt it. And nor did the trainee who told us: "*I chose Bristol because I'd worked in London for a few years and I thought the quality of life factor would kick in here. It has!*"

The London and Birmingham offices began as healthcare and clin neg outposts when the Bristol office extended its reach beyond its capabilities. While maintaining close contact, both have been given their head in gaining new work in new practice areas. From its 26th floor Birmingham office, BBL has recently wangled sole appointment as advisor to Birmingham and The Black Country Strategic Health Authority. Presently, there are four trainees in Brum who "*feel very much part of the firm"* and with new coco, employment and projects teams, the scope and scale of work means it's likely to increase the trainees intake. The BBL London office on Chancery Lane has also had a growth spurt, with new commercial and IP/IT teams, and a banking team in the offing. Reflecting on this expansion, one trainee opined: *"The new BBL CEO is very forward thinking; there are going to be lots of changes."*

Whilst Bristol is the epicentre, it is easy for a Bristol trainee to take at least one of their four seats in another office and vice versa. What's more, the firm isn't hung up on trainees having a local connection, although it is *"looking for a commitment to staying in the office where you apply."* The only downside we could find was in Bristol, where the loathed morning post room duty is back after two years of banishment.

go west young man

Turning to the EPL partnership, Exeter is the largest and most commercial of the four offices and has *"a key focus on company commercial work"* that includes advice to smaller local companies as well as *"multimillion pound regional mergers and acquisitions."* With an even spread of private clients, private sector concerns and public sector organisations, trainees can work in coco, commercial property, commercial litigation, criminal, matrimonial, insolvency, probate or IP in various contexts. Here, as across other EPL offices, there isn't the PFI or healthcare focus that characterises the BBL partnership, yet links to local authorities and NHS trusts are good. Client secondments such as an IP placement at Exeter University Innovation Group are common.

The commercial atmosphere informs the working culture in Exeter to a greater extent than in any other office, and not always to happy effect. Following on from certain experiences we reported in previous years, some individuals expressed concerns about *"disciplinary procedures and the way they're enforced."* Without knowing the specifics, perhaps we should simply say that a stricter atmosphere suits some people better than others. While you must be *"suited and booted"* at all times, and we did hear tell of one partner memo-ing instructions via his secretary to a trainee in the office next door, generally office life is less authoritarian than these examples might suggest. Socially there's *"always something on the boil."* That something can be anything from carousing on the Southernhay strip (actually the closest you'll get to a bar room brawl will be a tense moment on day three of the trainee bonding weekend at Longleat Center Parcs) to sailing, surfing or hiking. Additionally, there's a busy TSG, in which trainees are key figures. The firm plans to move from its central location to premises on the outskirts of the city, and the feeling is that this may propel the office even further into a commercial outlook.

bridge on the river parrett

The Plymouth, Tiverton and Taunton offices all share the quality of being smaller, quieter, and more family-oriented, notwithstanding that the quality of work is extremely high. This comment refers to Taunton, but from what we heard, stands true for all three: *"Everyone knows everyone, and they have all worked together for ages. People only leave to have kids then come back."* An *"easy-going"* atmosphere was largely met with approval from our sources, although one said: *"I liked it, but I know others who found it too cliquey."* However, given that trainees shuttle around between offices for each of their four seats, you'll get ample opportunity to suss out which location you like best.

The Tiverton office has an excellent reputation for advising West Country estates (that means landed gentry and farmers) on agricultural, rural and probate matters, in addition to handling commercial litigation and PI. Both Taunton and Plymouth also cover family and crime, and excel in property. The latter has strong links to Plymouth City Council, with a regular secondment to its childcare department available to trainees. Although there are usually only a couple of trainees per office at any one time, don't imagine that infers social isolation because the firm organises frequent events, including drinks, dinners, and trainee away days. At the Dorset Games in Exeter, trainees competed in netball, volleyball and other less formal pursuits against teams from councils, housing associations, community groups and local law firms.

EPL places importance on community involvement, a view that clearly extends to the recruitment of trainees. Most of the current crop have links with the South West, yet rather than implying insularity, their decisions to stay in the region were for all the right reasons. Piece together this fragment of our interview notes and you'll understand why – *"Lifestyle amazing home by 6.30 bbq on the beach jealous City friends."* The firm did well on retention in September 2003, BBL kept ten of its 14 qualifiers and EPL kept 14 of its 16.

and finally...

This firm is open-minded about recruitment and appreciates what candidates from non-standard backgrounds bring to the job. Remember that Bevan Ashford is two firms in one, and pick the right one.

Bircham Dyson Bell

the facts

Location: London, Cardiff, Edinburgh
UK ranking by size: 124
Total number of trainees: 10
Seats: 4x6 months
Alternative seats: None

With top-flight parliamentary work, a high-class private clientele and one eye fixed on the commercial ball, for the discerning applicant, Westminster-based Bircham Dyson Bell offers a very civilised training.

chuffin' trains

Steaming ahead on parliamentary matters, the firm is on the legal panel for Transport for London, covers Transport and Works Act Orders, Light Railway Orders and general rail and infrastructure issues. The firm is also a big engine on Scottish parliamentary matters. However, it's not all Puffing Billy and parliamentary bluster: in addition to highly respectable private client work, since acquiring much of niche City practice Bower Cotton in 2000, the firm has been navigating a more commercial landscape. A diverse client list sees individuals' commercial ventures rub shoulders with AIM-listed companies like Mobilefutures. The firm also handles everything from property to IP, family to employment. You might be aware that Birchams represented the interests of the family of Dr David Kelly in the Hutton Inquiry.

jiggling

In the standard four by six months' training, your first seat is allocated, and thereafter you have some say in where you go. *"The firm is receptive to what you want to do"* and *"if they can jiggle it for you, they will."* While no seat is compulsory, *"because private client is the biggest department, you are unlikely to get through without one seat there."* Good news for budding employment lawyers, a new seat is being created for them. And anyone not looking forward to litigation will be pleased to hear that a seat in the parliamentary group also takes care of the Law Society's stipulated contentious training requirement. By no means all the trainees are budding politicos: *"There are those who apply here because they are interested in it, and those who regard it as a nice, interesting thing tacked on the side."*

The offices in Cardiff and Edinburgh don't play a big part in the training. *"You couldn't do a whole seat in Cardiff, but you might get sent there for a couple of days."* Trainees aren't enticed into the firm with offers of client secondments or overseas seats; instead, it offers recruits the kind of hands-on, mature experience that the City's fun-lovin', jet-settin' crowd can only hope they may one day have. Trainees spoke of having *"the ideal balance between responsibility and supervision,"* adding: *"It is up to you to manage your own time here – nobody is babysitting you."* Across the board, *"trainees have genuine work to do so there are support staff to do the small stuff."* In property, expect up to 70 of your own files and to be *"very much number one in the firing line."* In cocom, too, you will have a few things of your own, but in private client you'll handle discrete matters on larger files. Trainees try out their fledgling advocacy skills, but in litigation there is also a danger that they must flex their bundling muscles, though even here *"the partner involved will be there helping you do it."*

maiden speeches

Of late, training has become more formalised – the private client department offers the most lunchtime sessions (up to four a week), while in litigation, every fortnight trainees must give a 20-minute presentation on a relevant topic. In keeping with Birchams' grown-up attitude to work, *"there is a certain amount of pressure to leave on time...people have been told to go home."* No, that is not a misquote. Apparently, *"the partners are hot on making sure you are out the door on time."* They are also pretty hot on feedback: as well as mid-seat and end-of-seat appraisals, *"you are encouraged to say if you aren't getting enough feedback."* Also, partners don't just tell the trainees when they've done well, *"they are good at conveying things like that to each other too."* Moreover, while there is no official trainee forum, *"we have a very open dialogue with the partners and the people at the top."* Even though *"we aren't all buddies, there are no walls between people"* and *"there is a strong sense of decency."* Hopefully all this adult conversation won't make you feel like you've moved to Dawson's Creek.

spot the rug

As we suspected all along, Birchams *"really is very civilised."* One trainee described how *"a few years ago you could have legitimately described it as a country firm that had been picked up and dumped in central London – it was very traditional, friendly and polite."* A move to new premises in Broadway at the end of 2001 has seen it depart from the old style and make headway as a more up-to-date firm. The Georgian façade conceals *"a very modern interior."* However, sources felt the firm *"still retains an element of the traditional image"* and has meeting rooms decked out to appeal to the tastes of its different clients. Private clients will be escorted to rooms with antiques, Persian rugs and ticking clocks; commercial clients get swish minimalism and *"sharp-edged furniture."* Reception *"mixes the two."*

Birchams often recruits maturer applicants. An environmental activist works alongside a former opera singer, who rubs shoulders with an ex-army officer. Between them staff dabble in music, sport, painting and cookery outside work. Sounds like a perfect dinner party guest list. We were told quite categorically: *"The 22-year-old automaton with a law degree, a legal family and no other focus probably won't get a job."* That said, some of the new recruits aren't exactly over the hill and there's a lot to be said for the idea that *"if you have something to offer, it doesn't matter how old you are."* In short, maturity counts for a lot, but wrinkles and hair loss are not a prerequisite. All three September 2003 qualifiers stayed with the firm.

cream quackers

In keeping with the sophistication of the firm, and its recruits, Birchams' trainees are more likely to be found wine tasting or taking a stroll in nearby St James' Park than propping up a bar every night. That said, Friday nights do see trainees heading for The Two Chairmen at Queen Anne's Gate, and there is the usual repertoire of quiz nights, karaoke, cricket and tennis. The summer and Christmas parties are both memorable affairs: last year's Christmas party at the Connaught Rooms had an Abba theme, but it did not extend to gold lurex fancy dress or bad-taste wigs. Birchams' style is more good conversation, fine wine, and fantastic food. Perhaps in pursuit of this, once a month a complete mix of staff from receptionists up to senior fee earners gather for a sit-down lunch courtesy of the firm's *"unbelievable"* in-house chef. The rest of the time, *"you can eat your lunch with the ducks in the park."*

and finally...

Bircham Dyson Bell's traditional façade belies the presence of a growing commercial focus. We suspect it would get the thumbs-up from the Dinner Party Inspectors too.

Bird & Bird

the facts

Location: London
UK ranking by size: 39
Total number of trainees: 29
Seats: 4x6 months
Alternative seats: Overseas seats, secondments
Extras: Language training

Bird & Bird is best known for its leading practices in IP, technology and communications, and e-commerce, yet it has also proved its worth in sport, media, corporate and employment. Start preening those feathers and plan your flight path.

flying around

The firm's literature indicates that three of your four seats will be spent in company, litigation and property. However, trainees seem to have found ways around this general rule. A tax seat, for example, might count as time in company, and a contentious IP seat could fulfil the litigation requirement. While you have no choice over your first seat, the firm listens to your views on your second and third, and many trainees return to their favourite department for their final seat and a smooth run into qualification.

Bird & Bird is best known for its TMT and IP practices, but numerous other areas of work are available for trainees looking for more traditional spheres in which to test their wings. Corporate and general commercial seats are available, and Commercial 1 offers plenty of drafting, mainly software licence agreements, hardware agreements and precedents for IT clients. The atmosphere in the corporate department proper is slightly *"stiffer"* than elsewhere and typically the hours longer. As to what the corporate finance lawyers actually do, deals have included: Adobe Systems' acquisition of the Canadian internet server, Accelio, after a bidding war; BT instructed them on the unwinding of their global joint venture with AT&T; and Imperial College London came to them on a partial divesting of its interest in 38 companies. It's easy to see the TMT theme in much of the department's work.

The perennial favourite seat – employment – won continued praise, since *"it's the sort of area where, if they trust you, you can get a lot of interesting work."* Alas, just before we went to press two employment partners and three assistants left the firm to set up as a niche practice. Tax (yes, TAX!) has emerged as the sleeper hit of the trainee year. The department offers one seat every six months and thus far the seat has been filled every time. It is renowned for being the most intellectually stimulating department; a place where you can expect to sink your beak into complex research.

bird brain

Rumours abound that you must have a PhD to even get an interview at Bird & Bird. This is clearly not the case, and indeed, as one trainee told us: *"The appeal of science graduates is vastly overstated."* While some trainees are self-confessed *"techies,"* most are humanities or *"plain old law"* graduates with no science experience whatsoever. However, if you do have a science degree or PhD, or perhaps even some relevant post-graduate work experience, it will certainly be welcomed enthusiastically by the IP department.

Chambers UK gives the firm top rankings in both patent litigation and general (softer) IP work. The IP lawyers' reputation stretches worldwide and they are involved with very many of the most important cases around. For the sweet-toothed: it represented Nestlé on appeals concerning Trade Marks Registry decisions over the phrase 'Have A Break' and the shapes of the Polo mint and the Viennetta ice cream.

keep your pecker up

Work in the firm's traditional stronghold of pharmaceuticals is often international in nature. Examples include actions regarding the anti-depressant Citalopram and others manufactured by Dutch clients. Proving just how protracted patent matters are, since 1999 the firm has acted for both Transkaryotic Therapies and Aventis in one of the longest ever UK patent trials concerning the use of genetic engineering to treat anaemia. But even the non-scientists among you will recognise the name Viagra. Bird & Bird is standing firm for Pfizer in its bid to keep old men feeling young. Patent work is tricky, and it's easy to see why science grads find life easier in this department.

Even in general commercial litigation, trainees find themselves doing some hardcore research work. We only heard of one incident of true grunt work: *"We had to haul 25 archive boxes from the basement. Everyone hoped that this particular matter would not rear its ugly head."* But of course, when it did, *"it was the trainees who lugged the dusty boxes."* It was fairly quiet across the City when we interviewed trainees, so our sources at Bird & Bird said nothing exceptional when they confirmed: *"We're not very busy at the moment and, to be blunt, we haven't been for a good few months."* Right now, these fledglings are being fed on a reasonable amount of *"slightly scrappy work and less of the meaty stuff."* They are each allocated a supervisor, either a partner or an associate, but *"you're not hamstrung by a single supervisor. You can wander around and get work off anyone and you're encouraged to go out and get it."*

spreading your wings

A shaken tech sector and a doom and gloom economy aside, the firm is flying reasonably high under the leadership of a bold and ambitious management and it has opened four new offices in as many years in The Hague, Düsseldorf, Munich and Milan. The benefits of working with an international firm are already apparent: two trainees did a seat in the firm's Hong Kong office recently, and another went out to Paris. Everyone we spoke to was optimistic about the chances of flying the coop and perching somewhere exotic at some stage. NQs go to European offices for seminars and meetings with counterparts, and a twinning system ensures that more senior staff can spend two weeks or more in another part of the European nestwork...sorry network, *"mostly doing precedent work and just getting to know the office."*

Closer to home, the firm is split across two offices. The Furnival Street office houses IP and real estate, while the remainder of the firm is in the newly refurbished Fetter Lane office, which is now v. chichi with lots of glass and *"sleeping bag-blue"* sofas. However, pity the trainee who had spent a seat in a room that featured *"no window, a wall, a book shelf and a rather resilient plant."* And how did the plant cope in these less than ideal conditions? *"Better than the human occupants,"* came the witty reply. Despite its supersexy client base, this is not a firm *"slavishly chasing trends like an advertising agency."* It's suits and ties most days, although IP is *"pretty trendy"* with a less formal dress code. Thursday is the new Friday at Walkers and The Castle. More serious boozers might find themselves at Shoeless Joe's or Walkabout. (Puh-lease)

nest building material

Motivations for joining the firm were varied and, we sensed, less focused than in previous years. It was Bird & Bird's enviable reputation for IP work that attracted some trainees; others were won over by its compact size. Yet, for the first time we heard a half-hearted: *"It just seemed like a good idea at the time."* But once installed into their training contracts, trainees spoke of the sense of pride they felt when a client or colleague *"would come to me as an expert on something."* OK, they lamented that things were not busier but, even during this quieter period, there remains a sense of dynamism in the firm. Above all things, the Bird & Bird trainee is confident and self-motivated in an *"unpretentious, understated"* way. Year after year we've heard about how partners here *"don't suffer fools gladly."* But while they might occasionally need to slip on a thicker skin, almost all our sources felt able to ask questions of their seniors. Apparently an egg-shaped head is not essential. *"Some trainees are geniuses, others are sharp operators,"* said one trainee, perhaps not fully understanding the connotations of the expression.

How ambitious are these youngsters? *"I'm not absolutely fixated on achieving partnership at this firm,"* but *"some are keen, and others are scarily keen!"* Wherever they sit on the eager beaver scale, all share a willingness to *"get stuck in."* Just as well, this is no nanny-style training. And just as our source was telling us how trainees muck in and *"roll their sleeves up,"* he observed a trainee hauling a large bin past his office. Aah, the sweet smell of shredded paper.

If there was one gripe, it was that management could be more transparent: *"There is a sense of bureaucracy operating above our heads."* The 2002 qualifiers who stayed with the firm were placed on a six-month probation period. It left a *"nasty taste in the mouth"* for many. The same thing happened in September 2003 for the seven out of 12 qualifiers that stayed.

and finally...

Bird & Bird's success was built on industry focus. It was never aiming to be all things to all people, but it's certainly all things to its TMT and IP clients. Its nest seems to have wobbled less, or perhaps less obviously, than some of its peers' in this tougher climate, indicating good design and construction.

Blake Lapthorn Linnell

the facts

Location: Fareham, Portsmouth, Southampton, London, Oxford
UK ranking by size: 47
Total number of trainees: 20
Seats: 4x6 months
Alternative seats: Brussels, secondments

Already one of the most recognised names in the southern counties, Blake Lapthorn decided that 2003 was a year for living dangerously. On 1 May, sticking two fingers up to a lousy economy, it joined forces with one of Oxford's best firms, Linnells. We trust the Magdalen College Choir singing to the crowds on the bridge that morning did a quick number in honour of the merger.

battle plans

As this is the first year we've spoken to recruits to the Oxford firm, we hope they will forgive our better knowledge of the Blake Lapthorn side of things. Over the last four years or so we've watched as BL shifted into a higher gear and looked more seriously at its training scheme and trainees. Fed up with the NQ brain drain to London, it cut the size of its trainee intake by half, concentrating on applicants with a good reason to stick around after qualification, and it made funding available for law school. Trainee salaries and self-worth have increased as a result.

The merger with Linnells is not the first for Blake Lapthorn. In November 2001 it pulled off a successful union with Portsmouth insolvency specialists Sherwin Oliver, which by all accounts has been rather successful. Before that it had already completed two small mergers with firms in London and Southampton. While all this augers well for the latest merger, everyone we spoke to acknowledged that stepping further from home to the Thames Valley represented a bigger challenge. With one likening the idea to *"the invasion of the daleks,"* some trainees hinted that it might be just the start of a phase that will bring more mergers; certainly, the management has indicated that the new firm is aiming to grow both on the south coast and in Oxford. While some critics have questioned the logic of a tie-up between firms in seemingly unconnected regions, we believe there are opportunities ripe for picking in the Oxford/Thames Valley area. In September 2003, seven of the nine qualifiers stayed on.

feast or famine

Trainees from Southampton Uni and others in the region fare well, as do those with even deeper roots there. Trainees sense the firm is likely to want recruits with a leaning towards commercial practice, although the four-seat training does offer experience on both sides of the client fence. *"The idea is to give us a good mix of training experiences."* And mixed it is. *"Trainers can vary enormously in the amount of responsibility they allow and the chargeable work they will give.*

Some people have been in seats where they have hated every minute of it, as they are given nothing but leftovers and rubbish to do. In other seats there are endless amounts of responsibility." And in some, the responsibilities are "*quite immense.*"

Full six-month client secondments are offered to some trainees. In the past these have been with ICI and Zurich Insurance; just a couple of the best names on a very healthy client roster that also includes major retail banks, RAC, South West Trains, Thames Television, Lockheed Martin, RSPCA, Kerry Foods, PwC, Grant Thornton, BAA, Whitbread and more. For those looking for a spell further from home there's a three-month posting to an associated Brussels firm, Renouf & Co. London, however, does not offer seats to trainees at this time.

driving to work

The three south coast offices are very different from each other. Kings Court in Southampton houses almost all the commercial departments and is very popular. Unlike Portsmouth and Segensworth (Fareham), it benefits from a city centre location and is felt to be the most sociable. "*Clearly, it's the best office,*" chuckled one trainee who only five minutes earlier had told us: "*In each of the three offices people will say their office is the best.*" Just 30 seconds away from cafés, shops and banks, "*there's millions of things to do at lunchtime and it has a younger feel.*" Most of the go-ahead, commercial partners are based here and there's a real feeling of "*this is where it's at.*"

New Court in Segensworth is the first of two identical purpose-built offices in side-of-motorway business parks. "*It's all litigation in Segensworth;*" much of it claimant personal injury, both fast-track and more serious head and spinal cases. There is also a niche in abuse claims against LEAs and schools. A top-ranked clinical negligence team handles claims against the NHS for bungled treatment and has been selected to participate in the new 'Resolve' scheme that's been set up to settle lower-value claims more quickly. Other breeds of litigation include debt recovery, professional indemnity and general commercial claims. Unlike Southampton there's not loads to do at lunchtime, unless you jump in your car and drive for five minutes. On the opposite side of the M27 is a TGI Friday, but none of our sources saw themselves as TGI types. The thing that bugged people most was the "*great big*" electricity pylon towering over the office. "*It fizzes when it rains,*" one source said anxiously.

Harbour Court in Portsmouth is a mirror image of the building in Segensworth (but without the pylon). It hosts the private client lawyers and a few remnants of commercial teams that have either escaped or forgotten to move to Southampton. It has also been the administrative hub, with the HR and accounts teams making it "*easy to keep up to date with what's going on in the firm.*" "*Harbour Court is a bit more relaxed than the others,*" one trainee thought, although, again, you have to get in your car to go anywhere at lunchtime. Tesco's coffee shop is the nearest place to grab lunch: "*Usually we'd meet up for a sandwich and a pot of tea.*"

driven to drama

Whichever office they are working from, trainees all go through the same three-monthly appraisals, which are "*taken very seriously.*" They also follow the same pattern of formal training sessions. The PSC is run in conjunction with Law South – a collection of some of the better firms in the region – and there are regular screenings of LNTV videos. "*There's also a stream of external courses which are advertised and you can go on.*" What with the external courses and the switching between offices for different seats and the lunchtime trips to Tesco, "*you do need a car as a trainee.*"

Despite being split between three offices, the south coast trainees get on well as a group. They all seemed quite pleased by the recent merger with Linnells, and although it was still early days, they'd received a visit from their new colleagues and were looking forward to going up to Oxford for a lunch. They anticipated that in the future they'd have a shot at an Oxford seat, although in terms of the daily commute this would be better suited to someone who'd chosen to join the colony of younger fee earners living in Winchester.

We love tales of office high jinks, especially pantomimes, and the BLL didn't disappoint on the latter. Blake Lapthorn partners take to the stage to entertain staff: last Christmas they performed a unique version of Snow White and the Seven Dwarves. As one trainee explained: *"There's a fair few people here into amateur dramatics…in more ways than one!"* Say no more.

oxford: battle of the sexes

Oxford firm Linnells has enjoyed a city centre existence for more than 90 years, but in Autumn 2003 it will move out to a new purpose-built office near the ring road on the Botley side. Apparently there's still a Mr Linnell working at the firm as a consultant, but, unless he has a portrait of Dorian Gray in his attic, we doubt very much if he is the original founder! Recruiting just three trainees each year, this partner-heavy firm has been initiating them into the ways of both commercial and private client practice. A four-seat training system allows them relative freedom in choosing the seats that most appeal. Everyone does a property and a litigation seat, and beyond that *"it's pretty much up to you, if there is a business need for a trainee in your desired department."* The choices on offer: private client, family, PI (largely claimant), company/commercial, non-contentious media and technology (the firm has some interesting publishing clients), employment, residential and/or commercial property and commercial litigation.

The advantage of working as one of a few trainees is *"more responsibility and individual attention."* We heard about regular trips to court and conferences with counsel in London, plenty of client meetings and ample opportunities to perfect drafting skills. *"I have prepared a list of documents on a few files,"* one trainee admitted, but as for an oversupply of boring chores: *"No, there's not much – we have two paralegals."* Expect to put in *"pretty normal hours"* – around 8.30am till 5.45pm is usual. Linnells sounds like the sort of place where it's easy to fit in: lawyers work open-plan, which is *"excellent, as it really puts the focus on teamwork and it makes it so much easier to integrate and chat to people."* For anyone labouring under the illusion that regional firms are behind their City peers on IT and office systems, take note: *"All that is great here. We have digital dictation and our IT system is really sophisticated, more so than Blake Lapthorn's actually."* There's a whole heap of after-hours activities, including a deadly serious boys versus girls rivalry. *"It's been going on for a while now. We've had different boys v girls events…things like netball, Qasar, an evening at the dogs to see who can win more money, bowling and that kind of thing."* Vernon Kaye would be proud.

and finally...

Blake Lapthorn Linnell now boasts 79 partners, 600 staff and five offices. We're told to expect more growth… although hopefully without the problems that some other cross-region firms have experienced.

Boodle Hatfield

the facts

Location: London, Oxford
UK ranking by size: 126
Total number of trainees: 10
Seats: 4x6 months
Alternative seats: Secondments

Boodle Hatfield is a West End thoroughbred specialising in property and private client work and counting the Duke of Westminster's Grosvenor Estate among its clients. It is top-ranked in London for smaller property deals, and for trusts and personal tax. As it has been doing it for more than 275 years, we'd be pretty surprised if it hadn't got the hang of it by now.

a tour of the estate

Boodle Hatfield's main offices are located in Mayfair, just a short stroll from Oxford Street. Listen up ladies: *"You can go shopping at lunchtime."* The firm is unlikely to move from this agreeable corner of London because of its connection to the Grosvenor Estate and easy access for *"various high net worth individuals"* and other organisations that constitute its principal client base. All property and corporate deals are now undertaken in London, as are the litigation and private client matters; its Oxford branch handles some employment, contentious family and financial planning work. The two offices seem quite chummy, but as a trainee your training will almost certainly be based entirely in London. We heard mutterings about recruiting a trainee to spend time in both offices, but no more than this.

Like a tightly packed suitcase, the firm has something for all occasions. In descending order of size, the divisions are property, tax and financial planning (private client), corporate, employment, and litigation (including family law). When we asked the trainees where Boodle Hatfield's real preoccupations lay, they told us: *"The firm has a strong private client and property focus. The other departments are seen as support departments, although employment is coming into its own."* You'll do seats in four out of the five departments, but you won't quite have a totally free choice. It can be a little awkward getting an employment seat as it's oversubscribed; litigation and property are compulsory. We've said this before, and we'll say it again – we think it's a terrible shame that a firm with so many pats on the back for its real estate work manages to recruit so many trainees who couldn't care less. Practically every trainee we spoke to told us they had no real interest in property matters; however, although six months was always enough, nearly everyone enjoyed it once they got going. We'll venture to suggest that, if you're a budding property lawyer, Boodle Hatfield will give you a real chance to shine.

huffing and puffing

Choosing to champion the other departments, our sources talked about the *"very nice"* corporate people and the *"lovely"* litigation department, describing them as younger, buzzier and a bit more sociable. One trainee liked being left alone to run his own files in litigation, whereas for another the real high points were the opportunities to *"get creative and write nasty letters."* Steady on, Woolf and all that! Despite it being a very small department, trainees still feel they see a good variety of work. Acting for corporate clients and individuals, trainees get stuck into all sorts – from professional negligence claims to the unlawful 'professional' activities of a client's tenant who was running a brothel just round the corner from the office. While in litigation, trainees can specialise in contentious family work…but they have to ask nicely.

Many of the current trainees were attracted to the firm for its private client work and generally just love hobnobbing with *"dotty old Duchesses"* and drawing up wills for the minor aristocracy. One trainee surpassed him/herself when they described a stint in private client as a time for *"developing knowledge of a niche area of fiscal law."* In the words of another: *"It's basically all about advising rich clients about how to avoid inheritance tax."* A new three-month secondment to auction house Christie's is currently on trial.

Aspiring trainees should be aware that at this firm there's less distinction between the private client and corporate departments than elsewhere. One trainee felt that the standard coco tag was misleading: *"The clients aren't plcs or listed companies, but entrepreneurs and small businesses. It's not M&A work at all – private client stuff comes over and you'll be working on projects for private individuals."* For example, you might find yourself sorting out some offshore issues for a wealthy lord or lady, or dealing with a billionaire who has set up his own company. This focus was rather attractive to the trainees who were more interested in private client work, and for those who wanted a taste of the big time, the popular six-month ICI secondment fits the bill. There, trainees were involved in bigger transactions, merger work and large-scale financings.

a nip to the air

Boodle Hatfield is steeped in tradition – stay with the firm and you might be there to celebrate its 300th birthday. Among its clients are some of the country's wealthiest landowners and individuals, so do you need to have an equally distinguished pedigree to fit in here? Not really. Although, *"someone who's scruffy wouldn't fit in!"* Trainees did agree that attendance at *"a reputable university"* is certainly preferred, as *"in a former life the firm was very academic and you can still see this to a certain extent in the property department – some of the senior partners like to do everything by the book."* But if you think traditionalism can't be combined with contemporary values, you'd be wrong. The number of female role models is commendable: around one in three partners are women.

The winds of change have blown across Grosvenor Square and up Brook Street lately and trainees tell us of management consultants marching in and coming out with *"the usual nonsense."* Nevertheless, *"there has been some impact on the internal mechanics of the firm."* One trainee said: *"It has been a shock to the system, but if the firm wanted to become more profitable, then it had no choice."* As for newly qualifieds, things seem no more difficult here than in the average firm: of the four trainees qualifying in September 2003, two were hired.

pitched just right

This is not a firm that permits itself to get hot under the collar. Boodle Hatfield believes in civilised working practices and, generally, you'll only find a handful of people in the office after 7pm. As one trainee explained: *"The firm expects you to have a social life."* Lest we labour under any misapprehensions, the young man added: "I *wouldn't want anyone to think it's a doddle – you do have to get stuck in when you're in the office."* But of course.

The social calendar revolves around an unorthodox, yet intriguing, combination of softball in Hyde Park and karaoke. Trainees freely admit that the former is probably *"more drinking than actually playing softball."* When it's raining or they simply can't agree who gets to go on first base, there are favoured *"traditional haunts"* such as The Old Monk on Maddox Street. The Christmas party is always a sophisticated affair, held in recent years at the Café Royale and the Hilton on Park Lane. Another much-loved fixture in the Boodle Hatfield diary is an annual games night where the firm's finest compete against a team from the Grosvenor Estate in a number of events including snooker and darts. Admittedly, the lawyers generally don't cover themselves in glory: *"They take it a lot more seriously than us and we pride ourselves on that. We always end up with the wooden spoon."* Always the best idea.

and finally...

If it's top-end private client or property work you're searching for, you've found the right place.

Brabners Chaffe Street

the facts

Location: Liverpool, Manchester, Preston
UK ranking by size: 109
Total number of trainees: 17
Seats: 4x6 months
Alternative seats: Secondments

Brabners Chaffe Street is a medium-sized North West firm servicing predominantly commercial clients. After a series of mergers and shake-ups, the all-new Brabners is now settling into itself.

wedded bliss

A year and a half after they tied the knot, we can report that Liverpool and Preston firm Brabners and Manchester-based Chaffe Street (that's Chaif, not Chaff) seem to be happily settled. Trainees from both sides of the firm report that communication (always the secret of a happy marriage) and co-operation is generally good: *"It does feel like the offices have been quite well integrated. It's not like one big office – there are always going to be local differences – but the merger has been successful because we have a very similar client base."* Departments often train and socialise together across the offices, and all staff from all three locations get together for an annual conference. In the future it looks likely that trainees will be able to move between offices during their training. When we spoke to them, ten trainees were working in Liverpool and four in Manchester, which reflects, so far as the training scheme is concerned, the relative importance of the two sites.

swap shop

The Liverpool side of the operation is clearly dominant; Preston has 15 fee earners and Manchester has just 20 or so fee earners to Liverpool's 90-odd. In terms of their size, the big guns are the property, corporate and litigation departments; in Liverpool employment and private client teams bring up the rear. You'll do four seats from these five departments, but don't count on getting exactly what you want all of the time. A new system will mean that your first two seats will be allocated to you when you start, after that you'll have some input in where you go. This should please trainees who up till now have sometimes had to engage in a spot of bartering with each other. Said one source: *"I managed to change [one seat] as I found someone willing to swap."*

The hot seat is employment, partly because *"it's very hands-on. You can manage files by yourself,"* and partly because the small department has a good vibe. *"The employment department is all open plan rather than individuals' offices and that helps to improve the atmosphere – people really feel part of a team."* There are regular departmental nights out and we also heard of a summer party at a partner's house. Litigation is also popular; a seat here might entail general contentious work including professional negligence or insolvency cases, or it could be focused on construction or media. The media litigation team is ranked by *Chambers UK* as one of the best defamation practices outside London, and boasts an impressive client roster of radio stations, newspaper clients (including the *Manchester Evening News* and the *Liverpool Daily Post & Echo),* sports personalities and soap stars.

Far from being out on a limb, there's cross-referral between the commercial departments and the private client team. As one of two trainees in private client, you might find yourself assisting a partner on tax planning advice for individuals who work for the firm's corporate clients or a partner who handles probate matters. Again, we heard of trainees agreeing to swap seats, so splitting your seat between the different types of work seems perfectly possible. We're guessing there are sports personalities and soap stars on offer here too! A sixth option is a secondment to one of the firm's most important local clients, Mersey Docks and Harbour Company. This secondment can replace any seat and trainees can choose to focus on either property or corporate work, or to do a mixture of both. Mersey Docks is typical of the type of client you'll get to work with at Brabners.

oi! chatterbox!

There are formal end-of-seat appraisals and *"more informally, partners are happy to chat through things for ten minutes."* In Manchester a trainee told us: *"Typical hours are 8.30am to 6pm, but the emphasis is on getting work done during the day and being efficient. We are all proud of being quite hard working."* It's much the same in Liverpool, although corporate offers the longest hours with some late nights.

If you think it's all work, work, work in this office, you'd be sorely mistaken; in one particularly fun-filled department, *"we waste an hour or so a week on practical jokes."* Oooh! You too? Alternatively, if you find yourself at a loose end, you might go and have a chat with managing partner Michael Brabner, who (if our spies are to be trusted) seems to pop up all over the place on a regular basis. Said one: *"I'll be walking down the corridor and Michael Brabner will be walking the other way and he'll always say hello."* From another: *"He often seems to appear when I'm chatting with someone at the photocopier – he always joins in."* End-of-month drinks in the Liverpool office are a prime spot, if you're after a guaranteed sighting of the main man. These monthly events (*"they used to be held in the boardroom until they redecorated it"*) certainly get the seal of approval from trainees: *"Staff turn up from Manchester and Preston and it tends to turn into a very big night out."*

And speaking of which, the office in the centre of Liverpool's business district is well placed for extra-curricular activities. The Brabners gang usually end up in The Living Room or Late Lounge, rubbing shoulders with the likes of John Barnes, Jamie Redknapp and the *Hollyoaks* blondes.

performance anxiety

The highlight of the Brabners year is an annual sketch show that is written and performed by trainees for the 'enjoyment' of all at the Christmas party. *"We dress up as partners and take the mick out of their nice cars,"* said one thesp. If you're happy to perform in front of a difficult client, but too coy to mimic your boss in front of a hundred or so of your colleagues, a training contract at Brabners may not be for you. Basically, *"if you're just going to sit at your desk all day and not speak then you'll find it very hard."* Most of the current batch were either born in the North West or went to one of the region's universities; one trainee went so far as to say that such a connection was a prerequisite for joining the firm. However, if you didn't already have a social network in Manchester or Liverpool, it sounds like you can soon find one: *"Liverpool has such a work hard, play hard culture that it's very difficult not to meet people if you're social."* The city's Trainee Solicitors Group was described as being particularly active and a great way to meet people, and the Brabners trainees have traditionally been heavily involved with it.

Fast growth, good value, reliable service – is Brabners the Ryanair of the legal world? You might want to mull over this idea as you're handed a free glass of wine by the firm's recruiters at a university law fair...of course, that's more than you'll get on a Ryanair flight. In September 2003, six out of the ten qualifiers stayed on with the firm.

and finally...

Rollocking good fun and a thorough training together in one package. Sounds like a good deal to us.

Brachers

the facts

Location: Maidstone, London
UK ranking by size: 205
Total number of trainees: 10
Seats: 4x6 months
Alternative seats: Occasionally Lille

A Kent-based firm with offices in Maidstone and London, Brachers has strong commercial, private client and family groups and expertise in clinical negligence work. Trainees looking for quality, broad-based training in this part of the South East should read on...

the garden of england

Brachers retains a coveted place on the NHS Litigation Authority panel, alongside 14 other firms, making it one of the few outfits with lawyers practising clinical negligence defence work. The firm is also powered by its regional connections, acting for a largely Kentish client base of small to medium-sized businesses, some nationals, and private clients, ranging from landowners to those who own substantial share portfolios. This densely populated part of the county is set to become even more crowded – the Government's recent 'Communities Plan' indicates four growth areas in the South East, one of which is to be Ashford, just down the M20 from Maidstone.

The litigation diet is a mix of private and commercial matters, while the employment group acts for both applicants and respondents. Curiously, the family team also acts in some criminal cases, advising the RSPCA on its animal cruelty litigation. Sadly, the corporate department suffered a blow in early 2003, when high-profile partner Stuart Butler-Gallie left the firm, taking with him a young and dynamic team. *"Things looked unsteady for a while,"* according to one source, *"but are now looking up."* New partners have joined Brachers, including one from Herbert Smith and the former in-house counsel for Eurotunnel. Result? An increasing emphasis on corporate/commercial litigation at the time we interviewed. If corporate deals light your fire, quiz the firm on its strategy and find out more about the work you can expect.

fifty fifty

Trainees were lured by the promise of City-style training and support, with high street levels of responsibility and, in a way, the firm is a hybrid of the two. There's no doubt that if it's responsibility you want, Brachers is the place to get it. It's *"pretty sink or swim,"* although you'll be within reach of a lifeline. *"You can always tell them if you think it's too much."*

Since the matters being handled are smaller than in the City, there are times when you'll find yourself running the show. We heard about one trainee who attended employment tribunals, and we don't just mean to take notes. Apparently, by his third seat he'd run an entire employment tribunal hearing for the applicant, in which he prepared and conducted the examination-in-chief and the cross-examination of witnesses. You could be in the City for years without getting that sort of experience. The passive or timid may not be suited to this high-pressure environment, but for the motivated and the brave it can be exhilarating. One trainee told us: *"I do what I want unless people tell me otherwise. My approach has been to take a step above the instructions and to do the work myself."*

bracher yourselves!

Brachers is a firm in transition. As well as undergoing personnel shifts, the corporate department has been restructured such that property, M&A and employment lawyers are now all within easy reach of each other, creating a broader and *"commercial facing department."* Additionally, refurbishment has given the firm a new look; the offices are now kitted out with funky new furniture (okay, maybe funky is an exaggeration) and arty photographs of sailboats and desert scenes. The library has been relocated from a basement meeting room (*"a pain in the backside, frankly"*) to its own room upstairs, complete with resident librarian. Yet the period features have been retained.

In all respects, Brachers is a melding of the old and the new, of the traditional and the modern. Trainees believe that the firm is *"becoming more progressive,"* although the mood varies according to which department you're in. Property, for example, is fairly informal, while probate is more traditional in style. We sense the atmosphere in each department mirrors its client base. Trainees' seat choices are usually accommodated and the firm does look to the subjects you studied to determine where your interests lie. Those with a demonstrated interest in a particular practice area will get preference over others.

It struck us that Brachers has a straightforward approach to most things. Training contract interviews were described as a delight compared to the ordeal at some other firms. On the topic of winning new business, one source said: *"Our philosophy is that if you deliver service at an affordable price, that's the best form of marketing. We don't try to be clever about it."* And on the best way to guide trainees: *"Monthly meetings took in everything I'd done in the month. I'd simply talk to the supervising partner to see where I was going and what I was going to do next month, etc."*

the one minute dash

This year our sources were more restrained in their comments about Maidstone, leaving us to wonder if we'd been too harsh before. Maidstone is on the up, we learned. A massive redevelopment in the town centre means new clubs, bars and restaurants aplenty, but it still doesn't evoke great affection in trainees. Indeed, some commute from London every day, which is fine if you're in one of the two London employment seats, but otherwise financially crippling and quite tiring. Travelling against the flow of commuters, at least you'll get a carriage to yourself. The solution for two trainees is to take up residence in the firm's cottage, only a minute from the Maidstone offices. As long as you leave the house before the opening bars of the *Kilroy* tune, you're laughing.

Brachers clearly places little emphasis on regional connections when recruiting trainees. There are a few

Kent natives in the current batch, but others are from London and as far afield as Wales. One of Brachers' key draw cards is its NHS Litigation Authority work, another is the 'deep end of the pool' training, and the third is the chance for trainees to sample from a wide variety of areas of law. Some sources also stressed that they didn't want to *"work like dogs"* in the City. One confessed: *"To be frank, I don't want to spend my early 30s burning out in a London firm."* Here the hours are a regular 9am–5.15pm, with the occasional late night when required. On qualification, the thorny issue of money rears its head. Property is expensive, but regional salaries low in comparison to London. Brachers pays a market rate for Kent, but this doesn't make things any easier for those contemplating life as an NQ. Two of the four September 2003 qualifiers stayed on.

coming together

Staff and partners from each of the three Maidstone office buildings (*"the sprawling empire along the London Road"*) gather on a Thursday to share a buffet lunch. It pays dividends in terms of aiding cohesion. On a wider note, the firm is a member of the Law South network, through which the PSC and other training is organised. As a trainee you'll study alongside your peers at firms like Blake Lapthorn Linnell and Wilsons. The trainees have a social fund with which to indulge themselves in whatever manner they see fit. In addition to meals and drinks, last year they attended an open-air concert at Leeds Castle. Good? *"It was a complete piss-up and the best night out I had last year,"* according to one trainee. There are regular go-karting and bowling nights and, once a year, all staff embark on a junket to France at the firm's expense.

and finally...

"Best of both worlds" is how trainees sum up Brachers. If you're seeking responsibility amongst lawyers who handle a broad range of quality matters for decent clients and, for the most part, work very manageable hours, Brachers is going to be of interest. But do remember: you've got to want to be in Kent.

Bristows

the facts

Location: London
UK ranking by size: 107
Total number of trainees: 17
Seats: 3 to 6 months long
Alternative seats: Secondments
Extras: German classes

Over the last 160 years, Bristows has built its business on clients with valuable interests in IP and technology. If you aspire to IP work – really top-flight, gutsy stuff – then you should target this market leader.

dexter's laboratory?

Bristows works with clients in industry sectors ranging from pharmaceuticals, electronics, IT and telecommunications to consumer products, television and entertainment. Texas Instruments, DuPont, Gillette, Tupperware, Rizla, Pitney Bowes, Kimberly-Clark, Novartis, Monsanto, 3M, Sara Lee...its many household name clients could easily take care of most of your needs, including the three 'S's of personal hygiene and even a little late night relaxation.

In stressing the high academic standards, we mustn't dissuade those without a PhD or science-boffin tendencies from applying. Bristows is in the enviable position of only needing to select a few recruits from masses of applicants. If you have a law or an arts degree, you'll not be disadvantaged, but an MSc or even grander letters after your name will be of real interest. Usually, around half of the new intake will have a science or technical background, but all of them will have a brilliant academic record and a very clear understanding of why they want to train at the firm. While some trainees come straight from university and law school, *"they want people with life experience. A higher proportion of trainees here have done things and are a little older."* As for the type best suited to Bristows, academically gifted individuals also need to be *"vibrant and chatty"* with a bit of *"zing."*

Some 60% of the firm's fee income comes from IP litigation, so *"if you want IP, you are guaranteed nine months of it."* Trainees spend three months in commercial IP working on, for example, licensing and research and development agreements. A longer six-month spell in contentious IP sucks them into a vortex of heavyweight patent cases, which requires determined effort when *"reading in,"* and some longer hours. The powers that be try to match the talents of the super-qualified scientist trainees with partners who handle cases closest to their area of experience. Non-scientists feel their way around the department more cautiously.

coping with depression

Many patent cases run for years. The case involving the antidepressant drug Citalopram (which has worldwide sales of nearly £1 billion) has been a swift one, yet it is still a good example of the IP lit department's work. A Danish company developed Citalopram in the 1970s and then, in 2002, Bristows' client, Novartis, hoped to manufacture and market a generic version of it. However, they feared that the Danes might injunct them from doing so. The Bristows' team determined that Novartis should verify and then show the Danish company that the proposed process of manufacturing generic Citalopram would not actually be covered by the subsisting patent. Expert reports were prepared, various experiments were conducted and two NQs went over to Secunderabad in India to inspect the manufacture of the generic drug. Faced with all this evidence, the Danes had to drop their application for an interim injunction and Novartis has been able to sell its version of the drug. The case involved a team of six Bristows lawyers – three assistants and three partners, one of whom is a solicitor advocate.

international inspectors

The case illustrates a number of important points about Bristows' core work. First, these big cases are handled by teams: *"Everyone fits in like cogs in a wheel, everyone has responsibilities."* Unfortunately for the littlest trainee cogs, this can mean getting *"stung"* with photocopying and bundle preparation. Second, the work is frequently international: *"You're not jetting off to a sunny beach every day,"* but lawyers are forever flying to Europe and the US. *"I've found it quite refreshing to be dealing with Americans one day and Germans the next,"* one trainee told us. The US link is particularly strong, so if you're a California dreamer and you display good rainmaking skills after qualification, you may be making a few trips stateside.

Our third point is that having scientific or techy tendencies can transform your training contract. Just as NQs went to India on Citalopram, on another case a couple of trainees flew to the US to observe experiments. *"Trainees with PhDs or technical skills are seen as really valuable in these situations."* Finally, the team running the case included a solicitor advocate. There are now five such advocates in the firm and the intention is that more litigators will qualify with full rights of audience.

round the houses

We asked trainees to consider how they felt about working on such cases, assuming that they'd focus on the feel-good aspects of assisting with the introduction of important new drugs. Indeed, some did, telling us: *"You sometimes think 'In a few years this could be saving people'."* But we also heard a more considered, and perhaps cynical, view of the patents game. *"You see the impact of the work in the real world when you read the FT. If a drugs patent is knocked out, you see one company's share price drop. It's basically two big companies fighting over market share. It's definitely all about commercial considerations and, coming from science, that's one of the first things you realise."*

But wait! It's not all IP. Bristows offers more general advice to clients, and this means a selection of trainee assignments. Expect a seat in property (*"two partners, lovely and small, and now with two ex-Lovells assistants"*), where you'll have your own small files and you'll assist other fee earners on theirs. Expect time in commercial litigation ("*a lot of employment, debt recovery and contract disputes*") and corporate ("*five partners, some of whom are pretty senior*"). You could opt for a secondment to a client, or if that doesn't appeal, you could try a seat in competition law. Whichever seat you're in, it sounds like you'll have the Bristows way of working drummed into you. And that is? "*Thoroughness*" and "*checking your work, again and again...and again.*" In September 2003, only three of the seven qualifying trainees were asked to stay and continue working in the Bristows way.

aah! bristows

The firm was once under the control of the Cooke family. There's still a Cooke in the partnership, but it has grown and modernised in the last decade. Trainees talk of a younger generation of partners now playing an important role in the firm's development, of new marketing staff, of press releases and seminars for clients, and of a new head of corporate with "*a new view on how to win business.*" As forward looking and brand spanking as this sounds, don't go imagining anything space age when it comes to the offices or the firm's style. Occupying five Georgian buildings in Lincoln's Inn, there's still a touch of old-school formality around the place, noticeable in a determination to keep the dress code strictly to business attire. And it's perhaps also noticeable in the cherished annual tradition of the black-tie ball for staff – somewhere sophisticated like Claridges or the Mandarin Oriental ("*very civilised this year with no casualties of war!*").

Trainees describe an easy-mannered firm: "*You don't feel scared of asking questions and it's not like you wait until the end of the day to leave a piece of work on your supervisor's desk and then run away quickly.*" In the absence of macho culture, politeness and familiarity thrive. Imagine late nights in the office only when absolutely necessary and imagine never having to meet a billing target. Imagine working from a room with a fireplace and a view of Lincoln's Inn Fields (although we heard of one poor soul whose view was of a cupboard and nothing more). Throw in a bit of banter between partners, e-mails amongst trainees endlessly debating which pub to visit on Friday night (will it be The George or The Seven Stars or Truckles?), no wonder our sources were satisfied.And that's before we factor in the benefits of a small trainee population that prefers to picnic lunch and learn to rollerblade together rather than vie for the attention of partners. Trainees get noticed:"*You are like gold dust – partners have to fight over trainees!*" This probably explains why one of our sources said: "*Usually you sit with a partner, but you are not stapled to their desk.*" Pain-free training? We reckon so.

and finally...

Most big City firms keep their IP departments ticking on a diet of corporate support. If that doesn't excite you and you'd prefer complex IP litigation, then either choose to train here or, once you become sufficiently frustrated with your lot, try and move here.

Browne Jacobson

the facts

Location: Nottingham, Birmingham, London
UK ranking by size: 64
Total number of trainees: 20
Seats: 4x6 months
Alternative Seats: None

While Browne Jacobson's name has been built on insurance matters, non-contentious commercial practice now makes up an equal proportion of the firm's workload. The recent expansion of the Birmingham office underlines a determination to establish itself beyond familiar East Midlands territory.

a match made in nottingham

Few outsiders associate Nottingham with anything more than the Robin Hood legend and quaint handicrafts, but the city has given us more than Kevin Costner in tights and enough lace to stretch to the moon and back. How about DH Lawrence or Lord Byron? Then, of course, there's Torvill and Dean... None of our trainee sources at Browne Jacobson skated around the issue of why they selected this firm to train them. Most hailed from somewhere in the Midlands and the rest tended to have been students in Nottingham and couldn't bear to leave after graduation. All came to the firm with open eyes and clear expectations: *"I applied to a few City firms, but didn't like them. Browne Jacobson was relaxed and so unstuffy compared to experiences I had at City firms."*

When we asked 'What one thing would you change about your firm?', no less than three people said: *"Get a vending machine."* It's hard not to suspect that a little covert brainwashing is going on when the most contentious issue concerns the location of the next snack. But our hard-hitting investigative tendencies were put to shame, and we quickly concluded that BJ trainees must simply be very happy. Without implying complacency or stagnation (the firm has just posted an 11% increase in turnover), there's something very comfortable about the place. One trainee asked us to assimilate a novel concept – *"relaxed ambition."* In the minds of some, *"in the local Nottingham market it stands out,"* and *"it is seen locally and regionally as being ambitious."* But? *"The London office will probably stay the same size it has done for years."* Good news for trainees who already like what they see.

the full spectrum

You've heard the phrase 'shades of grey'. Here it's more a case of finely gradated shades of insurance. The huge insurance and public risk department is *"the most popular amongst trainees."* It incorporates the green team, the red team, the orange team, and the indigo, purple and violet teams. The red team is the largest group and handles medical and educational negligence and defendant personal injury work for local authorities. Its remit spans cases including defence of NHS trusts and LEAs against child abuse cases and bullying charges, on which matters it also drafts policy wordings for insurers. Some trainees have had experience of groundbreaking 'failure to educate' cases concerning LEA responsibilities towards autistic children. It doesn't take a genius to work out that the green team handles insurance matters in respect of the environment, among them habitat and species protection. Clients include English Nature. Less logically, the orange team deals with employer's liability and public liability from *"industrial disease to slips and trips"* for a variety of companies and insurers including Municipal Mutual and St. Paul International. The purplish teams all handle clinical negligence claims against the NHSLA and other healthcare providers

The firm enjoys a hefty slice of the corporate transactions up for grabs in the East Midlands, acting both for banks and private companies with top-end deals hitting the £20-30 million mark. It recently received instructions from RBS/NatWest on the £22 million management buy out of the Leger Travel business from MyTravel, and also advised Notts County FC's shareholders on the sale of their interests.

Across the board, the common song was of initiative rewarded: *"I expressed interest and got more work because of it."* One trainee said: *"In commercial litigation, I even got my own case load and made strategic decisions on it."* Regular hours tend to be a pleasant 9am to 5.30pm or 6.30pm, and even in corporate, *"9pm at the latest if you have a deal on, but you'll normally get told to go home if you're there at 8pm!"* An added bonus is that with an *"excellent general office,"* there's very little grunt work.

revolution? what revolution?

A new initiative in seat allocation now means that every fresh intake of trainees will be consulted in advance as to their preferences for seats and office location. Thereafter, three months before each seat changeover trainees say where they want to visit next. *"The firm tries hard to fit everyone in,"* and whilst inevitably not everyone is satisfied, the feeling is that *"it balances out over the two years."* Trainees think the expansion of the Birmingham office from *"more a high street concern to a genuine corporate team"* will lead to an increase in trainee traffic to the city. As for London, there are two seats, offering the possibility of engaging with an associated office in Paris and the overseas end of BJ's corporate work.

Whether it's working across the desk from your supervisor or enjoying a pint in the local pub The Royal Children after work, it's clear that a fairly flat hierarchy is operating to a positive effect. Apparently, *"the firm is so open you could go anywhere and talk to anyone."* Listening to trainees, you sense like has sought out like, not least because the qualities trainees value in BJ are the very same terms they use to describe each other. They speak of being *"dedicated and loyal," "relaxed, grounded and down to earth," "not not ambitious, but valuing the social side of things too."* The most telling thing we heard? *"Really single-minded people might not fit in, especially if you take yourself too seriously."*

A few trainees sat on the social committee that came up with this year's It's A Knock Out-themed summer party (replete with impossible tasks, giant inflatables and the ubiquitous buckets of water), whilst others had substantial input on a proposal to redesign the website. All trainees attend quarterly meetings, chaired by trainees with partners in attendance, to discuss pertinent issues. Among its successes, the forum can claim a change in the assessment regime such that appraisals now take place more regularly. We're not sure if we should cry 'Vive La Résistance!' or 'Vive La République!' at this point.

In September 2003, all nine of the qualifying trainees accepted jobs at the firm – hardly surprising as the place hardly comes across as a hotbed of dissatisfaction and unrest. One of them told us: *"There really is no reason why this couldn't be a job for life – you could be a partner here."*

and finally...

If you want a good grounding in contentious work without cutting off your transactional options, then Browne Jacobson offers just this. With decent hours, recognisable faces every which way you turn and plenty of fun, it's a good Midlands pick.

Burges Salmon

the facts

Location: Bristol
UK ranking by size: 49
Total number of trainees: 36
Seats: 6x4 months
Alternative seats: Secondments
Extras: Pro bono – Bristol University Law Clinic, Bristol Neurological Unit, Drug Addiction & Recovery Agency, Bristol & Avon Enterprise Agency

This is the big fish in the Bristol shoal. Offering heavyweight clients, excellent work and a first-rate name without the headaches and house prices of London, Burges Salmon is a pretty good catch.

cash cows

Burges Salmon has netted an enviable portfolio of clients that includes EMI, Reuters, Orange, Honda and Coca-Cola. If this list isn't proof enough that *"it is so not true that we just work for farmers,"* then understand that 75% of its business emanates from outside the region. Burges Salmon is fishing in deeper waters, casting its net around big deals like Connaught Plc's £21.7 million acquisition of GasForce and BBA Group's sale of its Signature Aircraft Engineering and Aircraft Charter Business to PremiAir Aviation Group.

And, um, then there's the farming deals...the restructuring of the Milk Link co-operative and the £55 million acquisition of businesses from Express Dairies and Tanner Foods. The firm can't escape being known as the national leader on agricultural matters, and in truth this was a definite attraction for some sources. BS acts for The National Trust and The Crown Estate, and came into its own over the foot-and-mouth crisis. It's often at the forefront of cases in the European Courts as well as the House of Lords and Court of Appeal. If neither corporates nor cows do it for you, BS maintains a top-notch reputation for everything from family to private client and partnership law.

fish out of water?

So what type of firm mixes farmers and financiers? Despite aspirations to *"move away from the regional identity, and into the Top 20,"* BS remains committed to being *"Bristol-based with a long reach."* It is *"single site and wants to stay that way."* And it's less an office full of farmers' sons in suits and more City-boys in wellies: *"Many of the fee earners and partners are ex-City."* If the firm's range of expertise and clients wasn't enough to make it stand out from the crowd, its signature pink notepaper certainly does. *"It is the colour of salmon..."* Really? *"Like, organic salmon, not farmed salmon..."* Yes? *"You know, more poached than smoked."* If in doubt, check out the firm's website. The *FT*, Thomas Pink, pink gin – we rather think its keeping good company. One candid source admitted: *"It might be a sign of snobbery – they are deliberately trying to be different."*

The firm offers six seats of four months each. Coco, property, either commercial litigation or APLE (agric/property lit/environment), and either employment/pensions or tax & trusts are compulsory. After this, there's an option seat and a final qualification seat, which is pretty self-explanatory. Four months can feel short: *"In your early seats moving isn't easy, but as you go on it becomes easier to adapt."* And besides, *"four months in a bad seat is manageable. Plus, if you love one, you can always go back."* In addition to spending the final seat in their qualification department, several sources had also spent their option seat there too. The system is ideal for someone with very little idea about what they want to do, and can also be tailored to suit more decisive recruits. *"Everyone thinks it is brilliant."* IP and employment were the popular seats this year; none seem particularly unpopular. There are also client secondments (eg Orange), for which it's more a case of being invited than applying to go.

all talk

After the PSC there are internal lectures firm-wide. Trainees are encouraged to attend these lectures and are also obliged to give two 15-minute presentations to the other trainees in their first year. One presentation must be on a legal topic; the other on a general item of interest. Expect to be schooled on matters such as the World Cup, wine tasting and chocolate. Sounds like a good excuse to drink, eat and talk footie.

Generally, trainees benefit from high levels of responsibility and *"aren't given donkey work – we have support staff for that."* Most of our sources worked from 9am-6pm with the odd late-night horror story. It seems that *"the hours are growing with the quality of work."* In return for your efforts, the appraisal system incorporates mid and end-of-seat appraisals and in-between times *"you tend to get feedback on everything you have done. Even if your supervisor is swamped they will get back to you at a later date."* We also heard of trainees mucking in to help each other. In short, *"you are never left dangling."*

As you'd expect, *"the Bristol location is a common draw."* Though all our sources denied that it was a firm policy to only recruit from the area, they all admitted to some connection, be it family or university. In the past we have commented that a lot of trainees here are more mature, and embarking on a second career. This year, there's almost a 50:50 split between older fish and young smolts. *"If you have had a previous career, and can prove its worth, it is a huge advantage."* That said, anybody hankering after an easy ride outside the Big Smoke should be aware that the firm expects its trainees to be as ambitious as it is. Bright, jolly and receptive, well-balanced hard workers, these trainees are good, honest, salt-of-the-earth types, and in September 2003 the firm hung on to 19 of its 21 qualifiers.

top shelf

Foolishly, we asked about the social life without being entirely prepared for the answer. An endless list of sports include rugby, hockey, horse riding, surfing, netball, sailing and dragon boat racing (in pink wigs, naturally). For the less energetic: shopping trips, theatre visits, trips to France, paintballing and karaoke. A while back, using 'charidee' as a thinly veiled excuse to step out of their legal briefs, some partners and staff posed for a naked calendar. *"It was very tastefully done*

– there were lots of strategically placed files and FTs!" Women's Institute, eat your heart out. Many a Friday night is lost in the Pitcher & Piano, and the firm-wide interdepartmental quiz 'Universally Challenged' guarantees some form of ritual humiliation or another. And let's reflect briefly on senior partner, Richard Wynn Jones, who has not only appeared at work in cow-print trousers (and naked) in the name of charity, but was last sighted astride a bucking bronco. Explanations for his behaviour on a postcard please.

the litmus test

Trainees made us sick with envy as they described not only great views of Bristol's redeveloped waterfront, but a plethora of bars and a central location within walking distance of Clifton and other more affordable areas. In terms of location, *"there is not much missing."* Of its two buildings, *"one is modern and air conditioned, the other is past its sell-by date and hot."* Regulation magnolia walls and pink carpets pale in comparison to the firm's super loos. *"The toilets are really posh – you just have to wave at them to make them flush."*

And so we reach the question of whether or not the firm lives up to a reputation for being traditional and conservative. Is the 'Bourgeois Salmon' nickname a fair one? Pointing to the glutton's portion of fun that comes with the serious business of training, one source simply said: *"If it was stuffy and traditional you wouldn't have all that."* Some might argue that the crazy social life and permanent dress-down policy could all be an attempt to mask inherent traditionalism. Either way, none of our sources would want the firm any different, saying: *"If they wanted to change their image they would change the colour of the paper."*

and finally...

For indisputable quality of work and clients, a broad training and cracking good fun, we recommend you cast your net in Burges Salmon's direction. But, *"if you want to do the London thing, you need to get it out of your blood before coming here."* And do remember that your application will need to be seriously impressive.

Capsticks

the facts

Location: London
UK ranking by size: 129
Total number of trainees: 12
Seats: 6x4 months
Alternative seats: Secondments
Extras: Pro bono – Putney Law Centre

The name Capsticks is synonymous with healthcare. Half of the firm's profits come from its core practice in clinical law and most of the rest is derived from other services to its biggest client – the NHS – which is a huge landowner and the biggest employer in Europe.

cubism

Capsticks has recently rebranded. The most obvious change is the arrival of *"a large, red plastic cube"* in reception that we're told might represent *"the fire, determination and forward thinking of the firm."* Well, possibly. Trainees hadn't noticed any other differences because *"the rebranding represented a change that had already happened; it just brought the image up to date."* As one explained: *"The firm went through one transition to expand into property and employment work, and now we're moving into the overall healthcare market. We now do a lot of charity, regulation and private sector healthcare work."*

At least one of your six four-month seats will be spent in clinical law. A negligence seat might cover *"anything from a small, fractured wrist claim up to brain-damaged babies."* Early on, you tend not to run cases in your own name, instead working on *"little bits of the bigger ones."* Nevertheless, there is *"lots of contact with clients and experts"* and you'll be *"drafting instructions to counsel, doing progress reports for clients, sorting out the litigation forms or working on defences."* The seat comes with a good dose of responsibility and *"you do anything you might do when qualified, just under supervision."* Trainees see a spread of different types of cases, but those who qualify in this field become specialists: *"We try and offer clinical expertise attached to a lawyer."* Don't worry, no one will expect you to wield a scalpel, and bad handwriting isn't mandatory.

second opinions

It's far from the case that Capsticks only does NHS clinical negligence work. Even within the clinical department, there's now a whole lot more on offer. Half of the clinical law lawyers specialise in non-contentious work, advising NHS trusts and the private healthcare sector in areas such as data protection, consent to treatment and policy matters. You could find yourself grappling with headline-hitting issues such as organ retention and hospital closure. One of the clinical seats focuses on enquiry work, ensuring that tough decisions made by the NHS will not be left open to judicial review in the future. Get out that white coat – during these seats, it's common to be seconded to a hospital for one or two days a week. If so, you might find yourself assisting on claims management or taking witness statements for a big case.

Time in property or a commercial department is highly likely. In property, *"everything we do has a health-service angle."* Expect all the usual leases, licences and title research but normally for NHS properties. Supervision is *"close"* and you're unlikely to get your own files – as the seat will probably only be four months long, *"they're less willing to put the file in your name for such a short time."* Employment is hands-on (*"you get to do so much so early"*) and the work is *"very people-based and fast-moving."* On unfair dismissal, sex or race discrimination cases Capsticks always uses in-house advocates. You'll be *"helping prepare the case and trotting along to court."* The general dispute resolution department handles a lot of property litigation as the NHS owns so much land, but the work is *"really diverse"* – you might need to go to court for an injunction to prevent an abusive individual from hassling NHS staff.

bedside manner

Capsticks does a lot of pillow fluffing and temperature taking. One source said: *"You'll be protected by your supervisor, who will sit down with you and explain the work."* Another felt: *"It's good that they start you on easy tasks and increase the level of responsibility."* Assessments during and after each seat mean *"fairly continuous appraisal."* There is also plenty of external training. Aside from the PSC, trainees can sit in on the sessions that Capsticks runs for its Open University Diploma in Risk Management. *"It is quite useful as you get to look at something from the client's perspective."* There are also lunchtime talks given by doctors, barristers and experts from within the firm.

"We're all lovely!" enthused one trainee when we asked what kind of people train at Capsticks. So there you have it – the nasty and unsightly need not apply. Capsticks doesn't expect you to have a medical or even a scientific background; however, the clinical dimension is undoubtedly a draw for plenty of applicants. One trainee mused: *"I think lots of people are fascinated by clinical issues – hence the popularity of Casualty."* (Perhaps they've simply nothing better to do on a Saturday night.) Some of the lawyers at the firm have been doctors or nurses, but *"the firm isn't full of medical people on second careers; there are more of us who were interested in working for the health services or the public sector in general."* Always remember that Capsticks isn't only looking for clinical lawyers; it also needs to recruit those with commercial experience or inclinations. In September 2003, four out of the seven NQs stayed with the firm.

If you're tempted by Capsticks then you should apply for a place on its vacation scheme as it is *"the firm's main way of recruiting."* During this two-week placement, you'll sample different areas of work and get a fairly good idea of what life as a trainee will be like. *"It's not a two-week grilling session – you won't be tested on your knowledge of CPR."* If you do get offered a training contract, you'll be invited back to do another placement the following summer.

chicken tonight and every night

One trainee described the office in *"nice, leafy Putney"* as *"a big, white, seven-floored palace,"* whereas another felt the *"fairly nondescript 1970s tower block"* was, appropriately, *"a bit like a hospital."* With a snigger, they added: *"There's no beds in the corridor though, unlike in the City!"* Putney is *"good for food"* and *"right on the river"* and a lot of people walk to work. Capsticks is a sociable place, although many of the fee earners have young families so *"it's not a heavy-drinking firm."* When some do *"toddle over the road"* at the end of the day (a civilised 5.30pm), wine bar *"Piaf's is the place."* People also meet up for lunch: *"A small contingent go to Nando's every day for peri peri chicken; others try to limit themselves to three times a week."* Every year there's a five-a-side football tournament for six teams put together at randon. The boys are *"outnumbered and outplayed."* There are also trips to the theatre, ice-skating and a visit to the notorious Body Worlds exhibition by Gunther von Hagens was *"a big hit with the clinical negligence department."*

and finally...

Those with a taste for blood and guts should put Capsticks at the top of their list, but don't assume it's all clinical negligence. Anyone with an affiliation for public health matters or looking for a career in which law meets healthcare will be in their element.

Charles Russell

the facts

Location: London, Guildford, Cheltenham
UK ranking by size: 45
Total number of trainees: 26
Seats: 4x6 months
Alternative seats: Secondments
Extras: Pro bono – Bethnal Green Law Centre

Charles Russell is a medium-sized commercial firm. While its provincial branches are leading local names, the London practice is the main operation. It may not be the biggest or the highest paying firm in the capital, but boy does it have some interesting work.

two in one

With 30% of the firm's business coming from private individuals and 70% from commercial organisations, trainees can clamber over the client fence. Some applicants will be attracted by claimant clinical negligence, family law and estates and trusts work; others by telecoms, media, defamation and sports law; others still will simply have a hazy idea that they want to combine commercial practice with areas of greater human interest. All these aspirations are appropriate at Charles Russell. However, one second-year said: *"In my intake of ten people, a lot of us wanted at least one seat on the private client side, but I think Charles Russell is now looking for more commercial people. The year below me shows that the firm is on target with that."*

Smaller City firms attract a certain type of applicant: those who appreciate that the size of a firm impacts on the role that a new recruit can be given. If the experiences of our sources are anything to go by there's little scope for complaint at CR. *"Insurance & reinsurance is a small team and you work for one of the partners who is very willing to give you responsibility. The group does a range of cases from substantial reinsurance claims to smaller direct insurance claims. I was supervised well on my own smaller cases."* In corporate you might assist a team of three lawyers on a larger deal, and on smaller deals you'll handle component tasks, perhaps even taking a vital role in the completion meeting. Whatever the size of the matter, you'll be kept in the loop: *"When a deal came in I went to the first client meeting and then had contact with the client throughout."*

We were told that the firm had no paralegals and so the grunt work was falling to trainees. But even if you are spending time on, say, bundling duties in litigation, you'll also be charged with responsibility for more interesting tasks like preparing witness statements. One satisfied customer of the property department reported: *"I had a small amount of residential conveyancing – one sale and one purchase – to do on my own, the rest was commercial. I also did some corporate support and drafted leases and licences to assign, taking clients through them. I really enjoyed having my own files."*

up close and personal

In clinical negligence cases, *"clients might be very ill or dying and you need to show sympathy,"* yet you still have to act the consummate professional at all times. It's exactly the same story in family, a seat that *"some love and some hate." "The traditional view is that we are quite expensive. Admittedly none of our clients are on the bread-line, but they're not all hugely rich. We act for husbands and wives equally. It's more financial than children's law but we do have a legal aid franchise for child abduction work, which trainees and junior lawyers do because we're cheaper."*

If you enjoy family, you'll also enjoy private client. The client base mirrors that of the family department: *"old money with lots of trusts and tax issues"* as well as new-money clients, who are often referred from the commercial departments. Trainees need to be *"quite confident in dealing with people, as some of them are amazingly wealthy and used to getting what they want."*

let them eat cake

The firm has quite a few meeja-types and celebs on its client roster. Worth mentioning too are a whole stack of magazine publishers, including *Hello!* (CR acted on the wedding cake-scoffing spat with CZJ and Michael Douglas), *Elle, Red, B, Sugar* and *Men's Health*. Client research – it's the perfect excuse for thumbing through a glossy at work. Better still, CR recently won Pop-bitch as a client and the firm has gone from strength to strength in media and defamation work. No disrespect to the more conventional commercial departments, but the media team illustrates perfectly how the firm is transforming its image from crusty old family firm into a bigger, bolder commercial practice. We doubt that just a few years ago it would have put out a jazzy-looking recruitment brochure like its last offering, which portrays lawyers with paper bags on their heads, a young lady bound with rope and a lad with an alarm clock down his pants.

But perhaps we underestimate the firm just because it's been kicking around since the 1760s; after all, in the closing years of the 19th century, it did champion Oscar Wilde in his sexuality-based court cases. The firm is at a crossroads: look one way and you see a fuddy-duddy, wood-panelled law firm; look the other and it's a media outfit. In the reception area, oil paintings of past Russell family lawyers hang alongside a plasma screen TV. *"Some people have had misgivings about the plasma screen, thinking it's too modern and a risky idea,"* one source whispered, but as we all know, being all things to all people can be difficult. Charles Russell is making a reasonable job of it though, and the loyalty of clients like Scoot.com, Cable & Wireless, Channel 4, ITN and Sony prove this.

guildford: digging for gold

The Guildford office hosts six trainees, presenting them with a spread of work and departments. It attracts those wanting to practice in a respected firm, while eschewing the long hours and filth of city living. Best known to law students for its College of Law, Guildford was first settled by Saxons after the Roman legions departed. Archaeologists have also discovered the earliest known remains of CR's office – a high street practice named Bulldocks. These days the town is home to Michael Buerk, Chris and Billie, commuters, professionals and anyone else who can afford to live there; all in all it offers a healthy private client base. However, just as in London, commercial work rules the roost and, according to one trainee: *"The managing partner has a vision for this office to become a centre of excellence for insolvency and property litigation."*

Trainees choose four seats from property (residential or commercial), family, private client, company /commercial, litigation (with specialist units including insolvency, property, employment and personal injury) and IP. Our sources spoke well of the firm and the training; plenty of client contact, good IT and library facilities, ample space in a well-fitted and centrally located office, a warm environment, and decent hours (although in some seats, trainees spend 45 minutes opening the post every morning – a pain if you have a full diary). On the downside, *"sometimes we have a hard time convincing London that we are not country bumpkins."* Far from it – the office has plenty to shout about including mid-range corporates and public sector clients in coco, and a stack of big names in property and property lit including ntl, Village Cinemas, Warner Bros, Sun Life Assurance, and Marconi.

Mixed reviews on the social front, including a call for more enthusiasm for organised office-wide activities like the summer BBQ. Fair dues to those who are game (if yours is cricket, get your whites washed), especially the lawyers who stepped off the top of a six-storey building (roped up and in the name of charity, not out of desperation). Guildford is a funny place. According to one of our colleagues, a long-time resident, it's sleeping deeply during the day and kicking and screaming at night. There are plenty of restaurants, picturesque ruins and cobbled streets, the Yvonne Arnaud Theatre, and an ice disco at the Spectrum sports centre.

cheltenham: the prom queen

Alas, we're unable to devote more than a paragraph to eulogising Cheltenham (or 'Nam as some of the locals call it). Charles Russell's office on The Promenade is one of the largest in this Regency town; however, at the time of our research it was trainee-less. Usually it hires at least one, so if you hanker after a commercial/private client training in this gorgeous town, you should seriously consider it. Cheltenham boasts sophisticated architecture, several renowned literature and music festivals, top retail opportunities and a race course that's viewed as a Mecca for the Irish. All this and the Cotswolds too. Last year, trainees spoke favourably of their training, so we'll assume this bodes well for future hires.

Across the firm ten of the 13 qualifying trainees stayed on in September 2003.

and finally...

Charles Russell only wants ten trainees a year, so it can be choosy. Yet we sense that, people skills aside, there's no single 'type' it's looking for. Yes, it has some strong niche areas, but don't worry if you're not ready to be pigeonholed just yet.

Clifford Chance LLP

the facts

Location: London
UK ranking by size: 2
Total number of trainees: 235
Seats: 4x6 months
Alternative seats: Overseas seats, secondments
Extras: Pro bono – Hackney and Tooting Advice Centres, language training

The largest law firm in the world, the name Clifford Chance has become synonymous with international transactions, overseas offices and ambitious plans for world domination.

once upon a time...

There were two English law firms, Coward Chance and Clifford Turner. In 1987, their merger created... well, you know what. In 1992, it became the first major non-US firm to practice US law outside the United States, and in January 2000, it merged with New York's Rogers & Wells, creating the largest international law firm. Then German firm Punder, Volhard, Weber & Axter joined in the party, as did Tokyo's Tanaka & Akita. All the while, across the globe, new offices were set up from scratch. CC now has some 3,000 lawyers in 32 cities worldwide.

The client list reads like a roll-call of leading international financial institutions and corporate movers and shakers. Of late it has advised First Aqua Group on its £2.05 billion acquisition of Southern Water Group, and Philip Morris on the US$5.6 billion merger of Miller Brewing with South African Breweries. Sadly, reports of beer flowing freely in the office remain unsubstantiated. It advised General Electric on its US$2.3 billion acquisition of the Structured Finance business of ABB Ltd, and in Paris it acted for France Telecom on the sale of its transmission tower business, Télédiffusion de France to a private equity consortium for €1.9 billion. Everything at CC is giant-sized, especially deal price tags.

financially astute

Clifford Chance is a finance-heavy firm. We assumed that a finance seat would be compulsory, so we checked with grad recruitment. They told us it wasn't, but that in practice all trainees did one. (We also asked if a corporate seat was compulsory. They told us it wasn't, but that in practice all trainees did one.) If the mere mention of the f-word makes you wince, look away now. CC's stellar client list includes Morgan Stanley, Royal Bank of Scotland, Citigroup, Crédit Lyonnais, CSFB and Goldman Sachs.

General banking seats won near universal acclaim for offering *"good responsibility, lots of client contact and great people."* The subject matter is less technical than in many finance groups, and perfect for trainees to test their wheels. For the most part, *"the clients are happy to deal with trainees."* Capital markets also seemed quite popular with trainees assisting on bond issues for, among other things, major PFI projects. Asset finance involves aircraft financings, and to the joy of many trainees, a good deal of drafting. Once again this year, *"most of the horror stories come from securitisation,"* although whether it lives down to its reputation is hotly debated. The department is extremely busy, and at times, lawyers can be *"less sensitive to the delicate feelings of trainees."* We should stress that for every trainee who had moaned, we spoke to another who'd enjoyed the seat. Perhaps it was because *"I was working for the nicest people in the group,"* one suggested.

thirsty work

CC has been in on some of the biggest corporate restructurings, from Energis and Marconi to British Energy. In yet another booze-related deal, it acted for Nomura's principal finance group on the £2.013 billion disposal of the Unique and Voyager pub groups, comprising some 4,189 pubs. If your mouth is watering at these tasty transactions, just remember the size of the deal is inversely proportional to the amount of responsibility a trainee can expect. A corporate trusts seat offers an overview of capital markets and loan agreements, and although there is a large dose of admin and document review to be swallowed, it is sweetened with drafting work on ancillary agreements and letters. In investment funds trainees see a mix of regulatory and transactional work. Somehow private equity has come to be viewed as the warm and cuddly end of corporate: *"They were willing to take me through the work and let me make mistakes."* Real estate seats are less popular, but those who do them relish the chance to manage their own smaller files and it is almost guaranteed to *"immerse you from the start."*

The litigation groups were said to have a distinctive *"old-school"* and *"formal"* atmosphere. Trainees reported less interaction with partners and doses of tiresome bundling. A good way to chalk up contentious experience is in the international arbitration group. However, cases are long-running – there's a legendary matter on which the partner in charge worked as a trainee. Those with a social conscience can ask to be considered for a placement at Liberty or Law4All. These, and the more niche seats away from corporate and finance are quite difficult to secure. IP and competition seats are also especially popular, so if you want time in either, make your preference known at the outset. Usually spending only three months in litigation, most CC trainees are intent on transactional work and nothing more. A total opt-out (a short course) will soon be available.

the lonely planet

In the giant-sized game of musical chairs a tip sheet is essential. A full-sized guidebook to the firm, written by trainees for trainees means you can read ahead before travelling to your next department. Avoiding grunt work; info on which departments have the longest opening hours; and where the locals are friendliest – it's all there to fill you in on *"the bigger picture"* on deals. Said one trainee: *"A lot of the time I didn't understand what I was doing or how it fitted into the grand scheme. That would have made it worthwhile and made the work I did better."*

Overseas seats can offer the levels of responsibility that some trainees crave at home and, as a truly global firm, CC can offer all of its trainees six months away. However, you must accept that your posting won't necessarily be to the place you want most. Although there are seats available in glamorous locations like Hong Kong, Singapore and New York, *"the reality is that if you speak German, you'll go to Frankfurt. If you speak French, they'll send you to Paris."* In a cruel twist of fate, those lacking in foreign language skills often fare best when the flight tickets are handed out. With languages, it's a case of live by the CV, die by the CV – if you caught the attention of the firm's recruiters by flicking your foreign tongue, you must expect to use it whenever and wherever you are asked.

chopper squad

We asked if there was an archetypal CC lawyer. The denials came in floods. *"Absolutely not,"* said one trainee, *"how can there be in a firm of this size?"* A cursory glance at the website will confirm that CC has staff from all backgrounds and nationalities and with all manner of experiences. And with size and variety come people you like and admire and people you don't. While there are impeccably mannered lawyers with interpersonal skills and standards of behaviour beyond reproach, there's also an element of the *"inappropriate and embarrassing."* CC lands itself in the legal press virtually daily, and it's not always for its work-related successes. Undoubtedly, it is a tall poppy in the vast field of law firms, and there are many who would want to see it chopped down to size. While Clifford Chance *"may not be the most politically correct firm in the world,"* as one trainee told us, *"that's not always a bad thing."* Others were rather proud of its roguish charm, insisting: *"At least there are characters here. The partners aren't all cardboard cut-outs."* Few would disagree with the idea that *"there is no scope for progression in this firm on any grounds other than merit."*

farewell gotham city

In August 2003 the Clifford Chance Empire moved away from the City and into a new purpose-built edifice in Canary Wharf. Despite its distance from west London or south London or…anywhere apart from east London, trainees were enthusiastic about moving. *"It will be good to get out of Aldersgate,"* said one, *"things are looking a bit dated, and for the past couple of years, the firm's sort of stopped trying with the place."* Alas, this enthusiasm isn't repeated throughout the ranks and we've heard discontented mutterings from other lawyers. Gazing from the windows of the *Student Guide's* offices just won't be the same knowing that there'll be no Clifford Chance towering over us.

CC has an image of itself as a trailblazer. It takes pride in getting everywhere before anyone else. The first transatlantic merger, the first City player with a decent presence in California, the first UK City firm to move wholesale to Docklands: somehow these things matter to it. And size matters too…a lot. That said, our trainees were adamant that despite the size of the firm, they felt supported by the institution. And if, like them, you think of CC as a series of smaller practice groups and limit your sights to getting to know just some of them, it all becomes more manageable.

Why Clifford Chance? For some, choosing the firm was as inevitable as delays on the Northern Line or Tim Henman getting knocked out of Wimbledon. Some are simply attracted to the most recognisable brand in the City; some have their eyes on the international offices; others are drawn to the idea of a well-structured training scheme…and the salary. As a truly global firm, it can offer foreign seats to everyone who wants them. With its vast resources, it can provide excellent formal training in terms of seminars and lectures. However, you should be clear that in terms of day-to-day work, the experience can be as variable as it is in any large firm. Everything depends on the group you find yourself in, the individual supervisor to whom you are allocated, and timing. In the larger departments you will be *"one of an army of trainees,"* largely regarded as a *"business resource."* You fit in where you are needed. We wouldn't go as far as to say that production line values reign, but if you want to make a name for yourself or you are highly individualistic, this is not the most obvious choice.

your firm needs you

We've mentioned in previous editions that it's almost a mantra that the needs of the firm come first. The firm's website proudly proclaims that its people *"believe in one approach."* Trainees accept this mantra completely, saying resignedly: *"You go where the business needs you."* Whether it's a seat in Warsaw or staying late at the office to complete a piece of work, the business needs are paramount. Hours vary from department to department, and we won't lie to you – they can be gruelling. For many trainees, the biggest difficulty came from the not knowing: *"I've gone home at 6pm quite a few times, but you don't realise that you'll be leaving early until 5.45pm."* Said another: *"No matter how much you speak to people before you start, and no matter how much people warn you about the hours, you never quite believe it until you start."* But as one sensible trainee told us: *"If you're not prepared to work long hours, you shouldn't come to the City."* And you should certainly stay away from the magic circle.

There is no point in us trying to discuss a trainee group social life. The trainee body is simply *"too vast for us to descend en masse to Smiths of Smithfield."* As you progress through your contract, you'll make friends with a group of your peers, and your nights out will happen largely on an informal basis with these select chums. By the time you read this, the CC trainees will have found a few favourite bankers' bars in Canary Wharf. Stay posted for next year's in-depth analysis on Docklands nightlife. In September 2003, 56 of the 63 qualifying trainees took jobs with the firm.

and finally...

If size matters to you, Clifford Chance wins hands down. If you want a trailblazing empire of a firm with ambitious world vision, it's just that. And if you crave a name with gravitas, it's got that too. Just bear in mind that finance and corporate deals power the firm, and be prepared for the personal sacrifices – the job can feel consuming.

Clyde & Co

the facts

Location: London, Guildford, Cardiff
UK ranking by size: 38
Total number of trainees: 38
Seats: 4x6 months
Alternative seats: Overseas seats, secondments
Extras: Pro bono – RCJ CAB, Lambeth, Mary Ward, Surrey & Kingston Law Centres, Brent CAB, language training

With traditional strengths in shipping, insurance and reinsurance, Clyde & Co's international compass points to the shores of almost every place with a port. Don't be fooled into thinking these areas are the be-all and end-all though; Clydes has plenty more to offer.

there for...

Clyde & Co is a truly international law firm, having made its name as a facilitator of international commerce. The firm's 400+ lawyers are qualified in 17 jurisdictions and speak 25 languages. With offices in Belgrade, Caracas, Dubai, Hong Kong, Paris, Piraeus, Singapore and St Petersburg, you can't fail to see that this firm works across latitudes and longitudes, day in and day out. As well as greasing the wheels of trade through its insurance, corporate, commercial, tax and marine & transport departments, like the Yellow Pages, Clydes is also there for the nasty things in life via its litigation, arbitration and mediation services.

town and country

Back on limey soil, most of the lawyers have settled in London and Guildford and each site offers the same spread of work, including litigation, shipping and insurance/reinsurance as well as banking, corporate/commercial, energy and property. The firm is litigation-heavy in both locations – when we interviewed, 25 of the 43 trainees were in some sort of lit seat. However, the Guildford office is now home to the Business Law Group, *"targeting the M4 corridor"* (despite the fact it is nearer the M3) and picking up on the region's tech businesses. The group consists of non-contentious commercial property, IT, IP, employment and corporate teams and a general comlit team. Firm-wide, IT/telecoms clients include Oracle, Nokia, Hewlett-Packard, Ericsson, Dell, Cable & Wireless, Orange and Psion.

In London you'll find something approaching the stereotypical 'City' work environment. Of the 43 trainees, 24 were in London and 14 in Guildford, with the remainder on secondment or overseas. Although not compulsory, at trainee level there is *"definitely crossover between the two offices."* Trainees attend events and seminars at both sites, and we spoke to several sources who had completed seats in each. Commenting on the pros and cons of working in Guildford, our sources said:*"You can get London experience in Guildford;" "you get paid the same, it is a nice work environment, and you get to sit in sunny pub gardens at lunchtime."* One felt it was *"really laid-back, a better quality of life."* Not everyone relishes the prospect of time in Surrey: *"Certain personalities would find it worse than purgatory,"* but *"if you like that sort of thing, it is a nice touch."*

the beating heart

Despite the development of new practice groups, *"the heart of the firm"* remains in shipping and insurance. Even though there are no compulsory seats, trainees invariably spend six months in one or the other, if not both, of these departments. One source was at pains to point out that *"although you are likely to do one of them, you can get through the two years without them."* The pragmatists noted: *"You ought to do shipping; otherwise you won't understand the heart of the firm."* In a similar vein: *"If you are sensible, you will want to do the best work the firm has to offer, and you won't find that in the corporate seat."* Perhaps this icy logic explains why shipping litigation is one of the more popular seats, usually joined by the nation's favourite, employment.

While *"none are particularly horrific," "if you get a dull seat, human resources take a lot of care to make it up to you."* Indeed, HR seems to have its finger on the pulse: *"Sometimes they move you in a direction you didn't expect, but one that will suit you better. The initial reaction was 'Oh, I didn't ask for that', but three months later I was saying 'Thanks for ignoring what I said!'"* Those who know that shipping is what they want are indulged. *"You do get people who say 'I want to be a shipping lawyer' and want four shipping seats, and they usually get them."*

wanted: new roommate

Most trainees reported *"plenty of client contact, face-to-face, and supervision at a necessary level."* In some departments it is possible that *"they will let you off the reins fairly early if they feel comfortable with your work."* That said: *"If you are working on larger cases, it is a different ball game."* Expect your experiences to vary wildly from seat to seat – you might be doing research for a partner in international trade and energy, preparing arbitration packs in marine casualty, working on disclosure, prepping witness statements and trial bundles in insurance, or running your own cases under supervision in employment. Much of the work is complex; finance, for example, is *"very technical, with a steep learning curve, but once you get there you have extremely marketable skills. It's the big boys' playground."* Frequently, *"it's in at the deep end, so you must swim quickly,"* but *"you mostly get the feeling you are doing good work."* Across the firm we spoke to trainees who insisted they were *"yet to experience a paginator."*

Trainees used to each have their own rooms, but space is now at a premium and a number are sharing with another trainee or a qualified solicitor. Although you will be assigned a supervisor, they won't be breathing down your neck the whole time. After a little probing on the subject, we worked out that, depending on the supervisor and/or the proactivity of the trainee, the level of feedback received can be either a lot or a little. *"You just get on with it and at the end of your seat, you get feedback. You can ask for ongoing feedback, but they don't come forward with it,"* said one person. Another, who pointed out that you might work for more than one lawyer, said: *"The others you work for throughout the seat feed back to the supervisor, and you can just pull up to the partner and ask 'How far have I come, What do I need to improve on?' – that kind of thing."*

feelin' hot, hot, hot

Some trainees fly to Dubai for a stint in one of its two corporate/commercial seats; others choose to litigate in Singapore. *"The Dubai office prefers third or fourth-seat trainees,"* said one source, but *"trainees are less keen to go in the fourth seat"* as it is *"more astute to be in the UK when qualification decisions are made."* In such circumstances, the seats are opened up to first-years. Once you get out to the Far East, *"temperatures can hit 45° C in the summer, 25 in the winter."* Thanks to air-con and the bundle of other benefits such as a rent-free apartment, car and mobile phone *"it's certainly not a bum deal out there."* Um...preaching...converted.

you are what you eat

Clydes' wealth of clients in international trade and transportation has had an acute effect on its development, largely due to the people involved. As one source explained: *"A lot of the people we deal with are 'cut to the chase' people; they're not interested in bullshit, so that leads to a certain straightforwardness here."* It's *"not brutal at all"* nor is it *"a comfy pair of slippers"* – it is *"just positive."* We wondered if all of this, in turn, attracts a certain type of trainee. Coming from a wide range of backgrounds and nations, they are undoubtedly all quite individual, yet there is a common gene. Those we spoke to were uniformly bright and forthright: *"We are all pretty positive and bubbly,"* confessed one. Clydes is not awash with *"men in pinstriped double-breasted suits, smoking cigars;"* yet *"some could be described as eccentric,"* confessed one source, *"scarily bright but eccentric."* Clearly, *"individuality is respected."* When our researcher asked one trainee how she compared to the bulls and bears often found in the City, she replied that she was *"ferret-like."* Enough said.

In both offices, hours are *"pretty reasonable."* One trainee said: *"I have worked to 10.30pm or 11pm on a couple of nights, and I know in the past people have done all-nighters, but it can get quite exciting and you live on the adrenalin."* After work you'll find quite a lot going on. *"We spend too much time in the pub,"* giggled one lass, although *"there isn't a perception that you have to hang out with people from work."* On Friday evenings (already dressed-down since breakfast), a number of the trainees, associates and partners can be found in the nearby pub, The Tup. There are various sports teams, although we heard some grumbles over the number of activities offered for women. In September 2003, 15 of the 20 qualifying trainees stayed at the firm.

and finally...

If you have a taste for insurance, and don't mind a sea-salt flavour, Clyde & Co should feature high on your list. You've got to want a litigation-heavy training, but if you do, this one comes highly recommended.

CMS Cameron McKenna

the facts

Location: London, Bristol, Aberdeen
UK ranking by size: 8
Total number of trainees: 115
Seats: 4x6 months
Alternative seats: Overseas seats, secondments
Extras: Pro bono – Islington Law Centre, language training

A top-ten City firm, CMS Cameron McKenna is known among students for its 'nice' reputation, but with big-name clients and international business, we suggest the firm has a lot more going for it. Its training brochure asks 'Will the real CMS Cameron McKenna please stand up?' And that was exactly our question, so when quizzing trainees we tried to ban the phrase 'friendly and down to earth'. See how they fared...

are two heads better than one?

In 2003, Cameron McKenna again won a place in *The Sunday Times'* '100 Best Companies To Work For' survey. Our sources wholeheartedly endorsed the ranking, saying *"they are all so nice," "it's so casual and laid back"* and *"I know it's a cliché, but it really is very very friendly."* Ahem...F-word! Thankfully, some bright sparks had cottoned on to the fact that the firm can give them more than group hugs and a rosy glow. For almost every trainee content to simply talk about how *"happy,"* *"cheerful"* and *"comfortable"* they were, there was someone else ready to discuss the firm's *"focus and drive on cleaning up more of the corporate marketplace,"* international opportunities and *"great training that touches on diverse areas of the law."*

Last year trainees baffled us with a laissez-faire attitude that seemed at cross-purposes with the firm's stated aim of *"raising its game and going for the bigger work."* This year we've concluded that there are two paths you can go down, and the firm doesn't seem to mind which one you take. So whether you are looking for a gentle stroll through the City or a gateway to exciting opportunities, the firm offers both.

eastern promises

The firm has advanced internationally under its CMS banner, following a programme of alliance building to boost an existing network of offices. Years before others showed any interest, it was launching into Eastern Europe. It has continued to fulfil its Eastern European promise, although last year it closed its Beijing office, and significantly reduced its Hong Kong presence. Whereas last year trainees were vague about the CMS strategy, this year more of our sources were clued-up, although, inevitably, those who'd done overseas seats had more to say on the matter. In our humble, hack opinion some trainees have spotted the real opportunities that CMS can offer them, while for others CMS remains a choice of letterhead and no more.

The Eastern European focus goes hand in hand with a top-notch energy practice; undoubtedly, for this work, you'll struggle to find a better employer. The firm is also the leading name in product liability defence, health and safety law and business immigration, and our interviewees happily endorsed the variety of their experiences, saying *"smaller nichey seats are always popular."* Yet, while they clearly understand the firm's resolve to boost its corporate and finance presence, our sources were quick to note that *"if top-tier finance work is all that interests you, you should go elsewhere."* Yet, the firm has handled some pretty hefty transactions in the last couple of years, including the £1.9 billion acquisition of Meridien Hotels for Nomura and the £1.28 billion financing of Enterprise Inn's bids for three large pub estates. Cross-border work is best illustrated by transactions in the energy sector: the sale of the 13-country upstream oil and gas business of Veba for US$2 billion, the sale of Burmah Oil Nederlands Exploration to a Kuwaiti company, and the sale of the Forties oilfield to Apache.

there's no place like home

Trainees choose four six-month seats from corporate, banking, real estate, litigation and the group entitled energy, projects and construction. A few grumbles led to a consultation on seat allocation between trainees and management. The problem stemmed from *"a lack of transparency with the procedure."* Full marks: *"The firm didn't just sweep it under the carpet and everyone really appreciated the consultation."* The main problem has been that *"trainees aren't linear in their focus – people come here for the variety, not to be thrown into corporate and banking for the rest of their life – there is competition for the niche stuff."* One source went so far as to cite banking and corporate as least popular seats.

The only seats that are regarded as *"a really thorny issue"* are in Aberdeen (oil and gas) and Bristol (insurance, banking lit and corporate recovery). These are not compulsory, but *"you don't get away with refusing!"* *"People always leave for Aberdeen very bitter, and come back having really enjoyed it."* After a series of interviews with people who had never left the London office, we were bewildered as to why anyone would pass up six months overseas for the grit and grind of London. We were told: *"There are people who will do anything to go and those who would loathe even the star destinations,"* and *"many people are settled in their lives and relationships."* We'd obviously unearthed subscribers to the 'lovely comfortable Cameron McKenna' school of thought. More adventurous recruits found overseas seats to be the highlight of their training and that, rather than being stuck in hick town outposts, they were *"working in offices that have a big presence in their own right, and have work and clients they could never get in London."* The globetrotting contingent also handled greater responsibilities than they'd had back home.

wee timorous beasties

How would we pick out the Camerons lot in a room full of City trainees? *"We wouldn't be standing in the corner on our own,"* said one source. Another went further: *"We would be the first on the dance floor and the last off it...and we would be making arrangements to meet up later."* Social skills in abundance, but what else? *"You wouldn't be able to pick us out on age, gender or nationality."* True, but you might be able to pick them out on university – we noted a high proportion of graduates from Scottish unis, and it's clear that the firm is looking beyond Oxbridge. However, the real common denominator is a desire for a City experience, but *"without the workload or the pressure."*

While you are unlikely to find yourself signing away your social life, our sources warned that *"if you want to go home at 5.30pm every day, don't come here."* Everyone had done some late nights and a few had the dubious pleasure of weekend working. Thankfully, well-trained supervisors ensure that *"no one is really chucked in at the deep end, or spends six months chained to the photocopier."* While we heard of one poor soul who spent several nights on the trot paginating until 3am, we were also told of an *"all hands on deck"* culture, making such tasks less lonely. *"It would be rare to meet a client on your own,"* but trainees are not locked away – client contact via e-mail and phone is normal.

In addition to a formal appraisal system, fee earners are forthcoming with advice and pats on the back. Each department organises a programme of training sessions and there are trainee-specific courses on top of that. Client secondments (eg Wellcome Trust, Lloyds TSB) are popular after the event, if not actively pursued by trainees.

asylum seekers

Thursday is the new Friday – Smiths of Smithfield, Bed, The Living Room, The Butchers Hook & Cleaver...you name it, this lot have been there. A *"legendary"* annual trainee ball is supplemented by trips to the dogs, curry nights and karaoke evenings for *"voluntary humiliation."* Everyone spoke warmly of peers, and we weren't surprised to find that groups of trainees spend weekends away and holidays together.

One source described the office as *"square with a square hole in the middle."* Others spoke of a client floor that *"looks like a hotel. It's all thick carpets and expensive floral arrangements."* The fee earning areas are *"all white and a bit clinical"* and *"you can't open the windows, which is very disturbing."* One inventive source compared it to a mental hospital. To be fair, the inmates are actually *"relatively sane."*

k.o.

The firm is, according to our sources, *"not so hung up on being in the magic circle any more."* However, with a new managing partner and a hoard of management consultants drawing diagrams and writing plans on the top floor, it is *"rolling out a whole new strategy at the moment."* Trainees are not immune to the firm's ambitions to get its hands on bigger work, telling us that to attain this *"they are trying to make people a bit punchier."* The firm they described is a far cry from the aggressive, heavyweight fighters in the magic circle ring; it's a place where *"everyone stops and says hello, be it to the postboy or a partner,"* where dress-down is the order of the day and many people have chosen it for a calmer life. While some trainees were attracted to a firm that *"is up-and-coming with places to go,"* we sensed that many were quite content with the status quo. 29 of the 34 September 2003 qualifiers stayed.

and finally...

CMS Cameron McKenna can accommodate those who are excited by all the opportunities on offer, as well as those who are happy to settle with the security of a good, honest, home-grown training.

Cobbetts

the facts

Location: Manchester, Leeds
UK ranking by size: 56
Total number of trainees: 26
Seats: 4x6 months
Alternative seats: Brussels, secondments

Cobbetts is a success story. Originally a North West firm, it has an excellent reputation in property law and an appetite for growth. Importantly for the trainees of 2006, it has variety and new cities on its mind.

dare we?

There is a telephone that sits in a neglected corner of the *Student Guide* office. It's hung about with cobwebs and covered in a thick coat of dust. A yellowing A4 notepad lies next to it, and a dried-up bic ballpoint with a chewed end sits forlornly on the desktop. The phone hasn't been touched for nearly a year, not since the hardy researcher who last interviewed Cobbetts' trainees flung the receiver into the cradle with a final despairing lunge, cutting off in mid-flow the stream of praise that had driven him to the very edges of human tolerance. Shall we try the line? They couldn't still be there could they? Do we dare lift the handset and see? *"...it's getting bigger and more dynamic but it still has a regional feel and it's so friendly," "there's no personal conflict or in-fighting," "it's olde-worldly and nice but not stuck in the past," "we all respect one another," "it's really friendly," "it's really friendly..."* And so it was; a new year, a new group of trainees and yet the same joyous carol; clearly Cobbetts is doing something right.

all roads leeds to manchester

Residence in a stately building on one of Manchester's shopping streets sums up the balance between old and new, corporate ambition and a staff-friendly ethos. This kind of statement was typical: *"You're getting the best of all worlds; it's ambitious and dynamic, but still in contact with what made it what it is."* We asked for clarification: *"We've got a reputation for good client care, and want to maintain a regional base, but over time be seen as a national force."*

Having undergone several mergers in the last decade, the most recent with Leeds' outfit Read Hind Stewart, the *"progressive ambition"* trainees described is obviously no phantom. They told us they had *"the potential to grow with the firm"* and *"a sense of anticipation about going into work,"* and frankly it's easy to see why. Cobbetts has been in merger talks with established Birmingham practice Lee Crowder for some months, and if the green light is given in October 2003, the two firms aim to unite by the following May. We've been watching Lee Crowder too: it's obviously gearing up for something as partners have been joining and leaving.

How well does Cobbetts adjust to change? One trainee told us: *"When I started just after the* [Leeds] *merger, it was two separate firms, but there's been a real effort to integrate."* That effort has included exchange visits across the Pennines, social events galore, and a drive to unify IT/procedural/marketing systems that sports the rather dubious title 'One Virtual Office'. But there is nothing virtual about the recruitment drive and expansion in Leeds – its quota for new trainees is now five or six per year.

home of the whopper

A trainee's first year consists of a seat in litigation and a seat in property. Ah yes, the p- word... read no further until you have digested the idea that Cobbetts has built its foundations on a bed of good quality property work. An array of large clients takes in charities, housing associations, local authorities, and property investors. This is not forgetting select big names like Orange, Burger King or Peel Holdings. In practical terms, this all boils down to the most trainee responsibility of any seat in the firm: *"I have run files from beginning to end under supervision."* Of the atmosphere in the department, one source told us: *"It is less pressurised. With longer term deadlines it's much easier to manage your time."* Expect to work on anything from day-to-day sales and leasing for medium-sized businesses to large-scale development projects. However, also be aware that several trainees described this as *"the most desk-bound seat in the firm."*

Cobbetts' recent growth has begun to even the balance between property and commercial, and as one trainee suggested, *"the division is 50/50."* Admittedly, few students think of themselves as property lawyers, but if you do and you want to train in the north, an application to Cobbetts is essential. But what if you have other career designs? One of our sources told us: *"I made clear that I wasn't interested in property after the first seat, and they were responsive."* Commercial (including IP and IT), banking or litigation seats offer *"a chance to do advocacy or agency bits and pieces for banks and building societies, inside and outside Manchester"* and involvement in high-worth deals. On the downside, the trainees we spoke to suggested that *"there's less autonomy; you involve yourself with the partner who runs the files."* Or to put it more bluntly: *"You get your share of legwork!"* For those looking to leave the office for a while, there are regular secondments at Orange or the Royal Bank of Scotland, and one three-month seat each year with an associated firm in Brussels.

x marks the spot

While the word 'personable' recurred more times than we'd like to mention, trainees described a definite Cobbetts type, much along these lines: *"A bit of a perfectionist, good all round, academic, reasonable personality and likeable,"* and *"maybe a little bit of the x-factor in everyone."* From varied backgrounds and with many having previous work experience, the firm may seek out a certain genus of trainee, but this is not an attack-of-the-clones scenario. Indeed, trainees praised *"the work done by training execs in selecting trainees they think will fit the firm and its ethos, and the support they offer you subsequently."* In their first year, trainees have a feedback session with a training partner each month and seat appraisals every three months. *"They really go out of their way to accommodate your changing needs."*

like it? i bought a house

Many trainees meet for lunch *"most days,"* go out on school nights and join in with the firm-wide Friday night powwows in Chez Gerard. Then you've got to add in regular drinks parties hosted by each department in turn – for example, a *Stars In Their Eyes* themed night in commercial litigation – and for a paltry £2 a week you can subscribe to the Social Club, which arranges trips to Doncaster Races and the like. Last but definitely not least we must report on the Christmas party, which, in a gesture to the merger, was held equidistant between Leeds and Manchester last year in the McAlpine Stadium in Huddersfield. It involved more food, booze and dancing than could reasonably be handled and was topped off by a pantomime in which partners lampooned one another mercilessly. Small wonder *"lots of us have put down roots, even those who didn't plan to stay past training."* In September 2003, six of the nine qualifying trainees stayed with the firm.

and finally...

Anyone who derides northern values as antique or homely would find Cobbetts hard to quantify. Both loyal, and inspiring loyalty, it works hard for its trainees and expects them to reciprocate fully. An expanding firm, not to be ignored.

Coffin Mew & Clover

the facts

Location: Portsmouth, Southampton, Fareham, Gosport
UK ranking by size: 196
Total number of trainees: 9
Seats: 6x4 months
Alternative seats: None

One of the largest firms on the south coast with a broad sphere of practice, Coffin Mew & Clover is steadily evolving away from the smaller, more dispersed firm it was just a few years ago.

the first rule of coffin club

Over 100 years of practice had left our subject firm with numerous offices dotted along the south coast and a genial but out-of-shape identity aching for a lifestyle makeover. A burst of Trinny & Susannah meets Mr Motivator-style activity saw it shape up, trim down and acquire funky new premises as it consolidated into four main offices. Unlike post-New Year lifestyle changes that inevitably collapse in a hail of broken training regimes and recriminations, all viewed through a cloud of cigarette smoke, CMC has carried on working out this year. Departments have been rearranged into more flexible outfits and the firm has flexed its growing corporate muscles with confidence. All in all, it's less Fat Club and more Fight Club.

Firmly settled into a new open-plan building, the Southampton office *"has a lot more cohesion."* With more staff and trainee seats than other offices, and the lion's share of commercial work, it has witnessed the sharp end of the firm's evolution. Family and social housing law is a mainstay, although it is in the large new North Harbour office in Portsmouth that trainees had most experience of such work .

By contrast, trainees found the Fareham office *"not quite as sociable, perhaps because there's less to do,"* with *"a relaxed atmosphere, a lot more private client work"* and only *"a small commercial department."* Trainees had little more than passing acquaintance with the Gosport office, which was considered to be *"on the same scale as Fareham."* The four offices are all relatively close to each other, and although opinion was divided as to whether you need a car or not (some trainees said you couldn't live without one, others raved about *"excellent public transport"*), you'll not find it a strain switching between offices during your training.

an embarrassment of riches

The six four-month seat training is a *"rounded grounding."* It allows trainees to focus on their preferred areas once they have sampled business services, private client and, ideally, property. And, given the breadth of the firm's practice, you could be forgiven for wanting to try a little of everything. Commercially minded, Madam? How about coco, commercial litigation, employment, IP or finance/business regulation? In any of those seats you'll work closely with partners and gain exposure to decent deals for private limited companies. Although the trade-off on larger matters is that *"you do the legwork,"* trainees can still take on more responsibility, for example attending court hearings in litigation. And if you're not satisfied with the level of work you're getting, a quick word in your superior's shell-like should put things straight: *"I asked for more advocacy, and I got it,"* said one trainee.

Would Sir prefer something a little more private? May we recommend conveyancing, PI, mental health, clinical negligence, family or crime? Many of these areas involve client contact at an intimate level: *"In family, I attended interviews and was listening to emotional stories."* The crime seat, on the other hand, is the province of *"crazy hours"* and *"nights spent in police stations."* The nature of work in these areas means it's possible for trainees to run their own files, as the following example highlights. *"In PI, I was shown a filing cabinet with 24 cases in it and told 'They're yours!'"*

Last, but definitely not least, we couldn't omit reference to the speciality of the house – social housing. This department has a reputation for handling all aspects of housing associations' public and commercial business, including corporate structures, leasehold management, key worker developments and, at its contentious end, commercial litigation. Clients include Downland HA, Hampshire Voluntary HA, Portsmouth HA, Southampton City Council and Richmond Housing Partnership. It may not automatically present itself as the most fashionable area of practice, but suck it and see – it's good stuff. Perhaps you'll end up like this trainee who remembered social housing clients with a fond reverence normally reserved for senile relations: *"They're funny old creatures, but we know them well."*

Overall, the only trainee role that sits awkwardly is the morning duty of opening the post, *"an archaic tradition"* that many would like to see the back of.

the sixth sense

Sensing that one could easily become bewildered by the wealth of opportunities, trainees recommend you come to the firm with an open mind and be reassured that you won't be left alone to pick a path through the maze. *"I had a great deal of choice, they always listened to what I had to say and then structured my training to match it,"* chirped one. And if all rational and logical efforts fail to give you direction, you can always fall back on the strange powers of training partner and resident psychic Malcolm Padgett, who possesses *"a sixth sense about placing trainees."* Sceptical? So were we until we heard this: *"I thought I'd hate litigation, but Malcolm said 'I think you're a litigator', so I reluctantly tried it, and now I'm qualifying into litigation!"* We like his style...

the melting pot

Trainees hail from as far afield as Wales, Scotland, Hull and the Midlands, and have a miscellany of previous experience, be it a first career, travelling or a freshly printed degree certificate. A local connection may not be important, but you'll need to develop an attachment to the south coast because *"it isn't London life in or out of work, there isn't that intensity."* And there isn't the same salary either. But whether it's enjoying a Friday lunchtime tuna melt together at the Orange Rooms, attending one of the regular dinner parties, or dancing the night away at a CM&C party, trainees are unequivocal about the value of fun. *"If there's work to do you do it, the firm has a professional attitude, but I can plan a social life too. I can be windsurfing at Poole or climbing near the Solent by 6.30pm most days."* This is a firm where it's easy to make friends: *"Some of my best friends at the firm are the people who supervised me in my first seat,"* one source reflected. In 2003, all five qualifiers were offered positions and four stayed.

and finally...

Coffin Mew & Clover is working hard to expand its commercial base, while still maintaining links to the community. Perfect for those wanting a broad training on the south coast.

Collyer-Bristow

the facts

Location: London
UK ranking by size: 205
Total number of trainees: 8
Seats: 4x6 months
Alternative seats: None

Whether it's pop stars, office dating, sailors or boring old good training you're interested in, the distinctly artistic temperament of this London mid-sizer might just tickle your fancy.

rockin' all over the world

As well as the classics of corporate, property and litigation, there's also a well-regarded sports group that frequently works on sponsorship issues and numbers Sport England among its clients. Away from track and field, you'll also find C-B lawyers wooing new clients at the Cannes Music Festival. The firm actually has enough pop star clients to produce its own CD, including up-and-coming singer songwriter Damien Rice, drum and bass artist Blade, Deep Purple and…er…Status Quo. As if all this isn't interesting enough, its website boasts affiliations with lawyers in far flung places. Trainee reports back this up – we heard about cases coming from all over including Thailand, and an associate who speaks six languages.

There are no compulsories other than a contentious seat. Beyond litigation, your other three seats come from the remaining four departments: property, private client, matrimonial and coco. Litigation is the biggest department and it's perfectly possible to spend a year there. Its caseload is broad and trainees get involved in anything from overseas fraud and air carriage to RTAs and IP. The good news is that *"you get responsibility right from the word go and can get your hands dirty running small cases by yourself."* The bad news is that you may find yourself getting stuck into bundling and other grunt work but, as one trainee told us: *"I never felt like I was stuck at the photocopier."*

Coco is smaller, but growing and very popular with trainees. Clients range from international giants to small businesses, among them Destination Group, which was bought by lastminute.com for £12 million, Willmott Dixon and Middlesex University. You might just get the chance to go abroad while in this seat; we heard of trainees sent on visits to a client in Switzerland. But it was the matrimonial department that got all the rave reviews. Trainees mostly work on divorces, generally for people with serious money, including millionaire businessmen, Middle Eastern clients and Nigerian aristocracy. You also might even experience some child abduction work.

The firm prefers its trainees to do either a property or a private client seat *"because you have your own files and so you get used to billing."* Private client came across as the Rothko of the firm's practices; some hated it, everyone found it hard to get into, but those who persevered ended up loving it. Those we spoke to who'd done a seat there were given a huge amount of responsibility and work. Much of its business concerns the administration of estates, but there's a lot of variety within this. *"We had a real mix of clients – some people with very large estates and also some very ordinary people with complicated problems, for instance, disputes over which was the last will."* The property department has some excellent development and investment work and boasts clients such as Antler Property Investments, Crest Nicholson and Philip Morris.

As far as seat allocation goes, *"no one's been pouting."* In fact it's Mona Lisa smiles all round; trainees feel that the system is *"fair and transparent"* and tell us that the attitude of the firm is that *"nothing's final until everyone's happy."* We even hear that trainee foot stamping has led to the creation of a new coco seat. All three September 2003 NQs stayed with the firm…just like last year.

bedford row conspiracy

When we asked our sources about the firm's character, they painted a picture of a *"quirky, fun"* all rounder. This is a firm that collects avant-garde Christmas trees to display in its very own gallery and sponsors Olympic sailor Ben Ainslie. Sometimes when law firms try to be trendy it's as embarrassing as watching your dad dancing, but this one lives up to the hype. There's not much room for artistic licence in the dress code, so forget that paint smattered smock and beret because it's suits all the way here. There is a monthly dress-down Friday, but unfortunately you can't even wear your Status Quo T-shirt: *"There are so many rules that all meaning is taken out of it. Everyone's pretty conservative."* Even on not-so-dress-down Friday, if you're anywhere where you might be spotted by a client, don't even think about taking that jacket off.

Trainees told us that the firm is quite preoccupied with art; indeed, you'd be forgiven for thinking you'd walked into a gallery not solicitors' offices. The works of art are spread around the ground floor and the client meeting rooms and are changed every six to eight weeks. Generally, Collyer-Bristow's taste seems to be good, although we did hear of some questionable choices, including a *"pretty dreadful" "big picture of a pink poodle"* and *"some very rude pictures"* (although, as one male trainee added, *"none of my mates were offended."*) It's art, honest!

Upstairs in the lawyer bits of the Bedford Row premises, the *"pokey offices"* feel a bit garret-like, although, despite one trainee moaning about the lack of *"a whacking great salary,"* no one's starving. The firm has grown through lateral hires so space is a problem and this has meant that the litigators are camping out in an annexe round the corner in Raymond Buildings. The word is that the firm intends to get everyone under the same roof in the next year or so.

wish it could be christmas every day

We had high hopes for juicy office gossip after hearing that assistant Laura O'Connor is a bit of an expert on 'love contracts', that is, the clauses in employment contracts or staff handbooks that discourage or ban workplace relationships. But no, the best we got out of this lot was: *"There's a netball team and occasional bowling outings."* Although the partners put their credit cards behind a local bar once a month, the firm isn't *"a big everyone-down-the-pub place."* If you want to socialise with your workmates, you can, but there's no pressure to join in if you don't want to. The trainees seem like a contented bunch, happy to go out for meals together – sometimes to entertain future recruits; they even meet up at each other's homes for drinks. There are parties in the summer and at Christmas, but the real high spot on the social calendar is the switching on of the fairy lights on the Collyer-Bristow novelty tree; last year a specially commissioned ceramic creation. It's clearly an unmissable moment.

and finally...

It's wall-to-wall barristers in Bedford Row and the streets around Gray's Inn, and we suspect that some of the character and novelty of the Bar has rubbed off on this particular firm. Collyer-Bristow is definitely one for the independent-minded, not the City flock.

Coudert Brothers LLP

the facts

Location: London
UK ranking by size: 324
Total number of trainees: 8
Seats: 4x6 months
Alternative seats: Overseas seats
Extras: Language training

Born in the USA in 1853 of French parents, Coudert Brothers (or Frères depending on where you are in the world) has 31 offices in 19 countries. The London outpost may be small, but since 1960 it has been discreetly getting on with some high-class international work.

from russia with love

Apart from the property department which acts for housing associations and the owners of shopping malls, the work of this office has a cross-border flavour. Admittedly, trainees were reticent to talk about what exactly they were doing, but from what we could gather, much of the work is referred from other Coudert offices in Europe, Asia and the US. Our colleagues at *Chambers Global* tell us it is top ranked in the Russian corporate and energy markets. One trainee conceded that *"the focus has always been there, but it's getting stronger at the moment."* To illustrate the point, it has recently been involved in an arbitration worth hundreds of millions of dollars concerning the construction of an oil terminal in the Baltic region. It is also advising clients on commercial contracts in Kazakhstan and giving English legal opinions on agreements for the supply of energy in Russia.

the world is not enough

Coudert's work is pretty solid but it has to be said that other American law firms, many of whom have been in London for less time, have greater presence in the capital. When we asked why the firm hasn't made greater efforts to expand, the best explanation we heard was that *"worldwide, the firm's offices tend not to be huge and tend to be focused on individuals who build up relationships over time."* One trainee said it was the stated intention of the sinister sounding ExCom (Executive Committee) that the firm would grow in London, but *"other US firms have taken some big risks; we prefer cautious growth."* Make that very cautious growth. It's had 40 years after all, so don't bank on big changes all of a sudden. In 2003, two of the firm's four qualifying trainees added to the headcount.

The international focus of the work will be very apparent during the course of your training. While Coudert doesn't guarantee a seat abroad, *"most people get to go to Brussels."* The only language training currently on offer is Russian but the firm will consider setting up classes if there is enough demand.

licence to bill

Back in the London office, corporate and litigation seats are a must and you'll usually spend time in property. This latter seat offers a different experience from the rest, but trainees report on *"an excellent and well run department."* Partners let them loose on residential conveyancing for staff – a great warm-up to the commercial work of the department. Trainees like running their own files and also praised partners who *"are very good at training you rather than expecting you to do lots of billable hours."*

In all departments, you'll be used as a team resource, and this means variety. It's particularly apparent in the corporate seat, which could bring company secretarial work, competition, banking or projects. As far as tasks go, you'll be asked to draft minutes or small contracts as well as conducting research into anything from EC law to arbitrage, where an investment house will speculate on whether a merger will go ahead. This is the department where you might get sent on missions abroad if you're lucky; we heard of one past trainee fluent in Russian who got to jet off to Eastern Europe on a regular basis. Averaging 9.30am to 6.30pm, the hours are *"pretty cushy"* for a 'US firm'; however, in corporate you may end up doing *"quite long hours for a while, which then get back to normal – and the adrenalin makes it feel worth doing."*

Litigation is predominantly international with some domestic property litigation. Most of the matters the firm takes on are large (apparently, one trainee spent a year working on one case) so this means advocacy opportunities are effectively non-existent. It also means that grunt work (photocopying and bundling, etc) is likely, although not all-consuming.

on her majesty's secret service

So how do you get in to Coudert? Forget loud marketing; Coudert recruits a very select intake from those in the know. Trainees say the firm looks for two things: languages and *"that little bit extra;" "they want you to have done more than come out of a straight law degree and the LPC." "Most people have a couple of languages"* and trainees have all travelled or worked in other industries before being recruited. Once you're in, as with many small firms and top-secret organisations, it's a close and supportive environment – *"everyone knows each other, we all pop into each other's offices."* But don't forget the bigger picture. Coudert has agents in 30 offices across 18 countries and trainees feel *"it's good to be part of a larger network."* Meetings for all the European lawyers, including trainees, are held every year (this year Dublin): *"It should be good fun and it's useful to know the people on the other end of the phone."*

casino royale

The London office on Cannon Street is outwardly unremarkable and, to our disappointment, pretty unremarkable inside as well. Fairly traditional, *"it's not an open-plan funkily architect-designed building,"* but trainees do like the boardroom with its views over St Paul's and the *"fantastic toilets"* are a bit of a focal point. *"They have a marble floor and are very comfortable – I'd happily spend a quarter of an hour in there."* As we reported last year, the lifts are *"full of surprises;" "you press the button and the lift might turn up or it might not."*

In 2003, Coudert is celebrating its 150th birthday and had planned big parties in two of the firm's oldest offices, New York and Paris. We wondered if such a special occasion warranted bringing out a few bottles of the firm's very own wine, the impressive sounding Château Coudert Saint-Émilion Grand Cru. Alas, the trainees had never tasted it and didn't particularly want to: *"I've heard rumours it's undrinkable – I'm hoping for something much nicer."* Every year, the firm has a Christmas party in a smart hotel and a summer 'event.' This year staff were invited along to a US-themed treasure hunt, held on the 4th of July and set off by a Marilyn Monroe look-alike in Grosvenor Square. Throughout the year, there are drinks every month – shaken not stirred, of course – as well as informal gatherings in The Hatchet. Trainees might meet up for lunch, but pointed out that with so few of them, *"it's not like freshers' week all over again."*

and finally...

One for those whose focus is more global than City and who like the idea of being one of a select few.

Cripps Harries Hall

the facts

Location: Tunbridge Wells, London
UK ranking by size: 103
Total number of trainees: 14
Seats: usually 6 of varying length
Alternative seats: None

Not a National Trust property, but one of the leading firms in the southern Home Counties, Cripps Harries Hall is experiencing a period of ambitious expansion and the odd headline-hitting new venture.

a feast fit for a king

More than half Cripps' work is spread between the commercial, finance and investment departments, with the remainder split between dispute resolution and private client. It acts for a range of regional businesses, household names, plcs, government departments, start-ups and private clients. News-making clients include Benjamin Pell (aka Benji the Binman) and it is also representing law firm Lawrence Graham in a case against a disgraced former partner. What all this means is that a Kent location does not come at the expense of great quality work. Trainees said: *"The firm is ambitious about increasing its turnover, and this is the backdrop against which we have been working for the past two years." "They are getting big hitters from the capital and making a grab for London work."*

The firm's ever-growing property profile has been bolstered by the arrival of DJ Freeman's former senior property partner and several other lawyers. The department hit the headlines for its part in City firm Lovells' Mexican Wave scheme. Developed for the Prudential's property investment arm, the scheme sees Lovells farming out less complex work to smaller firms that operate at lower cost. While this might sound like the leftovers from someone else's feast, actually it's a pretty tasty banquet in itself. One source described it as *"clear evidence that the firm is trying to expand and establish relationships with firms and clients in London."* The arrival of the firm's first IP partner last year, plus a whole raft of new faces into private client, hasn't passed unnoticed.

country seats

Cripps has a small London office, but training means two years in the country residence, rather than the City pied-à-terre. The seat system makes for a hectic schedule, and at the beginning of the contract a six-seat plan is worked out for everyone. Seats vary from three to six months and everything is subject to change, depending on where the firm needs more bodies. The system is ideal for those who start without fixed ideas – *"It's nice to try a little bit of everything to find out what you do and don't like"* and it makes for a *"rounded legal education."*

There are *"no specific rules"* about compulsory seats, although *"there are some tacit ones."* Commercial property has traditionally been a busy department, and *"you will be there for six months unless you have a good reason not to."* Conversely, employment is a small department and incredibly popular, so you are unlikely to spend more than three months there. Otherwise, the firm accommodates requests to extend a short seat. Formal training is taken pretty seriously, with sessions about once a week. Video seminars are mixed in with lunchtime discussions led by fee earners and afternoon sessions by external speakers. *"There is a three-line whip for first-years;"* in the second year *"you are given more leeway to choose."* Supervisors (usually partners) check trainees' work at the end of each month and at the end of each seat there is a *"rigorous"* appraisal. Inevitably, when supervisors are pushed for time, feedback is less forthcoming, but nobody we spoke to felt they were short-changed, and we heard of some trainees sitting down with their supervisor at the end of each day to go through what they had done, *"be it good or bad."*

mum's the word

All our sources described impressive levels of responsibility and client contact. One talked of taking client meetings on her own, while advocacy is *"there if you want it,"* and in departments where it is appropriate (eg private client and conveyancing) you will be handed your own files. While everyone chips in, no one talked of lengthy bonding sessions with the photocopier. Even if you can't take a lead on your own, *"you will never just sit there doing boring admin jobs."*

Over the years, Cripps has developed a reputation for easy hours, and this year's interviewees suggested that little has changed. The 9am-5.15pm day can be done, apparently, though most of our sources stayed a little longer. *"No one will frown on you for leaving at 5.30pm."* Best of all, everyone gets a 75-minute lunch break, ideal for shopping, indigestion-free eating or a daily fix of soap. Over the last two years we have tried to get to the bottom of the trainees' telly habits. Once the story was that you could be home in time to watch Neighbours at 5.35pm; then the myth was quashed entirely. This year one honest soul told us (in strictest confidence of course) that so many people live so close to the office *"it is really easy to go round for a cup of tea at lunchtime and do the Neighbours thing."* However, the obsession has *"fizzled out a bit since Holly Vallance left."*

Tunbridge Wells and the outlying countryside is picturesque and a great place for taking your Mum out for tea. However, sophistication comes at a price and in the past trainees have been quite candid about the disparity between salary and cost of living, although the firm does offer discretionary bursaries and interest-free loans to ease the financial burden at law school. This year our sources were diplomatic and kept schtum on the subject of pay. All we'll say is that, where possible, some trainees do live at home, which means that Mum is the one treating them to tea.

keeping up appearances

The elegant Georgian spa town of Tunbridge Wells was granted its Royal prefix in 1909, but fear not, it's not all polo matches and dinner parties. On a Friday evening, many people end up at Sankeys wine bar, and at the end of the month there are firm-wide drinks. There are cricket, football and netball teams, a racquet club and a whole host of other sporting interests. Departmental dinners and bowling nights are also popular and the summer ball was a hot topic of conversation this year. Organised by the second-year trainees, this year's masquerade was held at a local country house and vineyard. If this sounds a little too sophisticated for your tastes, you might try Da Vinci's (or 'Davs'). We were cautioned against paying a visit ourselves, but one source confessed that *"Cripps people do saunter down there..."*

The firm occupies five period buildings on two sides of one street (we are assured it is a quiet road and nipping between departments is not too perilous). Last year we were told the office was two minutes' walk from the town centre, this year it's only *"sixty seconds"* so all that sport is clearly paying off. The offices are open plan and described as *"quite modern, quite pleasant"* and lacking *"anything quirky."* The IT system won rave reviews from our sources.

You'll be expected to dress formally, as *"Tunbridge clients are looking for that;"* however, we were also told that *"the firm is more down-to-earth than you'd think."* Everyone we spoke to was incredibly diplomatic and utterly polite, almost to the extent that we wondered if the masked summer ball had exerted a lasting influence. And on the subject of lasting influences, in the past the firm's website has emphasised Cripps' 150-year history, but no longer: *"It has a history, but is not trapped by it and can still move on,"* one source told us. Another added: *"The firm is moving away from its past, but is not cutting all its ties. It is proud of its age and doesn't want to upset its clients."* Fair enough. In September 2003, four of the seven qualifying trainees stayed to continue the firm's best traditions.

and finally...

If you hanker for the big city and bright lights, Tunbridge Wells probably isn't for you, but if Kent is your thing, you'll be pushed to find a better firm. We're not suggesting that Cripps Harries Hall is bling bling, but there is certainly more to it than twinsets and pearls.

Dechert

the facts

Location: London
UK ranking by size: 76
Total number of trainees: 27
Seats: 6x4 months
Alternative seats: Overseas seats, secondments
Extras: Pro bono – North Kensington Law Centre

The unequivocal GI Bride, the firm formerly known as Titmus Sainer Dechert is now settled in the marital home since hitching up with US hotshot Dechert Price & Rhoads in 2000. So is it marital bliss in the Dechert household now the honeymoon period is over?

the pre-nup

A mid-sized corporate practice with a strong reputation for medium-sized corporate litigation and real estate deals, Dechert also prizes its finance work, *"especially the hedge fund aspect and real estate finance."* In corporate, you can expect to see *"AIM floats and takeovers – the standard range of a corporate department,"* while in real estate the team acts for Land Securities and The Crown Estate in a practice that has branched out from its roots in retail property. Despite the loss of the criminal and civil fraud team earlier this year, successful niches are to be found in product liability, VAT, investment funds and property litigation. Spotting a theme? In this marriage, the pre-nup agreement focused firmly on the property and the bank balance.

Dechert doesn't seem in need of any marriage guidance just yet. This is a *"cosy"* coupling, a *"good blend"* of US and UK influences. Take a look at the firm's website and you could be forgiven for missing the British blood: it's all jazzy graphics and video shows. Our sources thought that *"all UK firms have something to learn from the US attitude to business – the US is a few years ahead in that respect."* While the union has brought 'can-do' energy to the Brits, *"UK clients want the UK style, they don't want people slapping them on the back and offering them a hamburger every five minutes."* So this has definitely been a meeting of minds rather than the brainwashing of a British product? Absolutely! *"If you compare us with Weil Gotshal and Cadwaladers, we are Bridget Jones."* All that said, come to Dechert, and expect to hear an American twang: quite apart from visitors from stateside, there's no getting away from the fact that *"the HQ is in Philly and the policy is written in the States."* An *"increasingly transatlantic thrust"* is visible in the deals, but you'll still be servicing the likes of *The Telegraph*, Dixons, Tesco and the designers of the London Eye. Dechert hasn't traded the bowler for a baseball cap just yet: this City outfit still has a *"chilled and personable culture."*

small world

On arrival at Dechert, you will be swept off to the States to visit the in-laws in Philadelphia, but don't start packing the kitchen sink – you'll be back in less than a week. The firm has opted for six four-month training seats: *"It increases your chances of seeing the seats you want and it is good to have a chance to go back later as a seasoned trainee."* There are no compulsories, though there is *"definitely a preference for you to get a taste for business and property."* This year, employment and corporate were the most popular, but the latter at least takes on five trainees, so there is room for everyone. Every trainee has to do something contentious, however, *"they are good at finding you a suitable seat, if litigation isn't your thing."* If it is your thing, you are advised to speak up, especially if you want to *"play Perry Mason for the odd afternoon."*

As a member firm of the Inn Group (which includes solicitors and barristers), Dechert trainees attend masses of lectures and seminars held by outside speakers. With plenty of internal lectures too, we heard of trainees clocking up more than double their required hours, simply because they couldn't get enough. Barmy. For those wishing to make the most of the firm's small European presence, there's a secondment to Brussels, offering research galore on competition law and close working with the US operation. For people who want to go the whole hog, there are opportunities to be seconded to Philadelphia, Boston, New York or Washington for a six to eight-week stint near the end of their training.

your firm needs you

When we asked trainees about the kind of work and responsibility they got, one replied: *"I was thrown in at the deep end with no water wings at all."* Another said: *"It is quite hair-raising and a bit nerve-racking;"* and *"with less staff there is more juicy stuff for trainees."* Far from being a place for wilting English roses, Dechert is *"in favour of giving you jobs that will stretch you."* Expect to run files, manage the administration of deals, attend client meetings, take witness statements, appear in front of masters and effect small closures. Alone.

The only problem with a smaller firm is that there aren't the vast troops of paralegals and support staff standing to attention, so *"there is grunt work, and at times you will ask yourself, 'I went to university for this?'"* We suspect, wherever you go, that thought will flash through your mind at some point or another; here the trade-off is *"a fantastic feeling when work goes out with your name on it."* In return for your efforts, there is a tip-top support system. Ex-College of Law head Bernard George has won the hearts and minds of his young troops with his efficient and compassionate battle drills. A team of *"faultless"* supervisors are as rigorously trained as their charges, and an effective appraisal system and mature attitude on all fronts enables training to be performed as *"a very subtle art."*

When all's quiet on the Western Front, *"there is no problem with upping sticks and going home."* However, we did hear of some long nights and the odd Sunday in the office. All our sources were early birds, and liked to be at their desks at around 8.30am, leaving at about 6.30pm. This seems to be as much a reflection on their enthusiasm as the firm's diktat. When things do get hairy, no one seems to mind. One source, when describing an all-nighter, said: *"The whole team stayed, we ordered pizzas – there was almost a wartime feel as everyone got down to it."* That's the ticket!

code breakers

Mixing English charm and manners with American vitality, we found the Dechert brigade chatty in the extreme. Gushing with enthusiasm, they are *"robust and slightly thick-skinned,"* yet *"a fairly relaxed bunch overall."* Apparently, *"if you are incredibly driven, want to speed up the ranks and thrive on pressure, it is probably too laid back for you."* In the face of a total dress-down policy, shirt and chinos are a pretty standard uniform for the men and the ladies dress tidily too – *"As long as you don't wear your AC/DC T-shirt you'll be fine."* Unfortunately Dechert trainees do not live up to the wartime sweethearts image we portrayed last year when we reported on a flurry of inter-departmental valentines. The truth of the matter is that on February 14th the firm's internal newsletter publishes a series of anonymous love messages.

In a bid to shed old English traditions the partners' dining room has been replaced with the *"terribly exciting, meritocratic"* Dechert Deli. You won't find powdered eggs and corned beef rissoles in this officer's mess, however. And while we're on the subject of mess, let us briefly consider the office. We knew Dechert trainees had retained their finely tuned British sarcasm when we were told that *"the offices are special."* Indeed from the outside they are – red brick, leaded windows, castellated walls, a courtyard complete with soothing fountain – on the inside they are also about as British as can be, with *"battered steel filing cabinets,"* no air con, and a reception area that looks like an airport lounge. All is not lost as plans are afoot to make a move to something more modern and with a good address. One source commented: *"The US offices all have fantastic addresses and Sergeants' Inn is the same. If they turned round tomorrow and said we are moving to the erotic gherkin that would be a great address, but we won't be moving to Clerkenwell."* Sadly, a number of the September 2003 qualifiers won't be around to find out: this year only nine of the 16 were able to stay.

It's not all about keeping up appearances; trainees do let their hair down too. Old favourite The Clachan recently rebranded itself as Sergeants, but hasn't lost its faithful following. In addition to spontaneous drinks, the firm runs a *"rugged"* social programme that includes trips to the dog track, summer soirées in the courtyard, cricket, a boat trip down the Thames, Christmas parties, and of course a party for the 4th of July. All ranks mix socially and it is not unusual to go out for a drink with your supervisor. *"It's not cheesy like 'everyone is my best mate', but it is informal."*

and finally...

For an energetic, hands-on commercial experience, Dechert offers just that. If you're in any doubt as to who wears the trousers in the Dechert marriage, remember, *"one can learn much from the Americans."* Except how to cope in a blackout, of course.

Denton Wilde Sapte

the facts

Location: London
UK ranking by size: 12
Total number of trainees: 100
Seats: 4x6 months
Alternative seats: Overseas seats, secondments
Extras: Pro bono – The Prince's Youth Trust

In last year's *Student Guide*, we reported on a City firm cruising along quite nicely; trainees were happy with their lot in life and the firm retained over 80% of its qualifiers. Since then, DWS has featured heavily in the legal press, and not always for the right reasons.

africa calling

Denton Wilde Sapte is the product of the 2000 merger of energy and media specialists Denton Hall and banking outfit Wilde Sapte. The more staid and conservative banking firm Wilde Sapte was hailed as the perfect foil for the cooler media and energy types at Denton Hall. The merger dust settled, revealing a glistening new firm with offices spanning Europe, Asia and the Middle East.

OK let's get all the unpleasantness out of the way in one hit (DWS certainly did). In 2003, only 28 of the 48 qualifying trainees were retained, 70 fee earners and support staff were made redundant, and the start dates for some of the new trainees were deferred. The firm disbanded its European referral network, Denton International, and hopes for a US connection faded with the collapse of merger talks with New York's Pillsbury Winthrop. There is good news. DWS remains a force in the Middle East and Eastern Europe, and is now blazing a trail in Africa, positioning itself as the major UK firm on the continent and developing alliances with local firms in Botswana, Ghana (chocaholics take note: the firm advises Ghana Cocoa), Tanzania and Uganda among others.

Its UK energy and natural resources practice remains pre-eminent, as does its aviation (regulatory) practice and those in broadcasting, sport and rail transport. The banking department is well respected, and here the firm acts for a range of financial institutions including Royal Bank of Scotland, Crédit Lyonnais, Barclays, Deutsche Bank and ABN Amro. On the electricity front, the firm is acting for London Electricity on its acquisition of Seeboard for £1.4 billion, and is advising the Government of the Sultanate of Oman on the restructuring and privatisation of the country's electricity and water industries. It also advises on oil and gas infrastructure projects in such far-flung locations as Iran, China and Kazakhstan.

don't call us

We would love to tell you that we spoke to a broad sample of DWS trainees. We can't. The problem lies in the fact that few people were open to the idea of talking to us. Boy did we find it a struggle. And then the clouds parted and, joy of joys, some trainees actually answered their phones. All of those we spoke to fell into the lucky half who had been offered NQ jobs. Perhaps it was gratitude, perhaps it was an inability to entertain the possibility that their firm has been suffering lately, perhaps it was love – whatever the case, DWS had certainly inspired loyalty in all those we chatted to. Yet we're sad to report that, in some cases, fervour to appear loyal and chipper bordered on disregard for those who have now left the firm. *"The firm is going from strength to strength,"* said one. *"The redundancies are a minor blip. It was typical of this firm that they were fair about it." "It was quick, painless, open."* Just like public guillotinings in the French Revolution.

We asked trainees about the firm's aims for the future, and while we were assured that *"everyone is aware of what the plan is,"* few could explain it to us with any certainty. *"We're focusing on four key sector areas,"* said one, *"banking, energy, property finance and...oh, I can't remember."* That would be financial institutions, real estate, energy and infrastructure, and technology, media and telecommunications.

ready for take-off

The asset finance group is divided into two: the *"slightly glamorous aircraft delivery, complete with Monte Carlo champagne receptions and parties"* and the *"less sexy middle-ticket leasing stuff."* On hearing about being sent on aircraft deliveries, we chuckled at images of trainees carrying aeroplanes in pizza warmers. Okay, so the trainee is carried by the plane, not the other way around, but at least you get a guided tour and a free meal...not to mention a nice pair of polyester sockettes. Middle-ticket leasing involves smaller assets like combine harvesters and JCB tractors – less glamorous but the legal structures are quite interesting and often as complex as those for aircraft financings.

In insolvency litigation, trainees encounter research tasks, preparing court bundles, drafting petitions, taking witness statements and helping with discovery. Some of our sources even did their own small pieces of advocacy, while the otherwise dull task of delivering documents was made all the sweeter with occasional trips abroad. Employment is, as ever, a popular choice: *"It lives up to the hype."*

flying high ...

Secondments are available to clients such as RBS. Strap on that parachute because here you can expect *"extreme responsibility."* Okay, you won't be abseiling down the Grand Hotel in Brighton or climbing Mount Kilimanjaro, but you'll get an adrenalin hit from 40 of your own files. Your work will range from decisions on loans to directors to drafting facility agreements and novation agreements (replacing existing loans with new ones). The responsibility you'll get in the corporate seat is less than on a client secondment (*"it's a fact of life when you're acting on larger matters"*), but you can make up for it in real estate where trainees have charge of their own smaller matters and assist on larger files. *"I was really involved;"* said one, *"my input was valued."* And happily no two files are the same. *"Even though I did five leases for the same client, I never felt that I was just pushing them through."*

The firm's TMT department has suffered setbacks, with the departure of most of the music law team. However, it retains strength in broadcasting and film finance, so trainees with a secret passion for the movies can still sample the heady delights of the silver screen. Recently, the firm has been involved in high-profile film financings including *Harry Potter and the Chamber of Secrets, Die Another Day, Tomb Raider II – The Cradle of Life* and *Terminator 3: Rise of the Machines*. Not to mention that ode to the morose, *The Hours*.

Of course, overseas seats are the highlight for some trainees. On offer – stints in Dubai, Hong Kong, Tokyo and Paris .

but not that high

Trainees described themselves as *"extremely laid back."* But banish those images of smoke-filled rooms, this is not a case of incapacitation or apathy, but instead a refreshing lack of *"airs and graces."* Trainees reported that *"there's no elitism here, no kudos attached to Oxford over Hull."* There is a palpable sense of pride among the DWS bunch and they're certainly not about to be intimidated by meetings at magic circle firms: *"We can hold our own."* Trainees were delighted to find that the firm is in many respects, *"the antithesis of the 'swinging dicks' City firm." "There's none of that designer suits, fast car lifestyle here,"* and for many, the attraction was the genuine diversity of the firm. We heard from our colleagues on *Chambers UK* that the firm's Africa group, for example, is headed by a Scottish partner, and includes Egyptian, Nigerian, Ghanaian and English lawyers. Among the trainees, many have had previous careers. Said one: *"I wasn't a standard candidate, and they appreciated what I could bring to the firm."*

The social calendar is full, but not compulsory. Said one source: *"The beauty of it is that you can take it or leave it, and there is no penalty to pay."* A trainee social committee organises three major events during the year, although perhaps out of sensitivity to those who have been laid off, and certainly to assist with budgeting, the summer ball was cancelled this year. Corney & Barrow is still the pub of choice firm-wide and there are quiz nights and the requisite sporting groups including hockey, softball and five-a-side football. Trainees are encouraged to mix with clients, *"adding another angle to the social scene,"* and DWS continues to sponsor the City of London Road Run.

and finally...

This year, the floundering economy has caused difficulties for most commercial law firms. Denton Wilde Sapte is certainly not the only one to have announced redundancies and poor NQ retention figures. Yet, despite the bad-news stories, the trainees we spoke to were happy with their lot, insisting: *"It would be a shame not to apply here because of a bad patch."*

Dickinson Dees

the facts

Location: Newcastle-upon-Tyne, Stockton-on-Tees
UK ranking by size: 53
Total number of trainees: 28
Seats: 4x6 months
Alternative seats: Brussels, secondments

Dickinson Dees is a sensation. Ask any experienced legal pundit to name the five best-regarded independent law firms outside London and they'll certainly come up with our current subject.

snowballs

Dickinson Dees has top-dog status in the North East and a growing influence beyond. One explanation for its success is the calibre of lawyer that is attracted to the firm, be they home grown or exiles from London, and another is the firm's absolute commitment to the region in which it is based. For Dickinson Dees, the future looks bright. Roll a snowball across fresh snow and it grows effortlessly; impress other lawyers and you attract even more of them to the firm. Factor in a regional renaissance and it becomes even easier to understand why the feel-good factor is running sky high at the moment. As if to provide formal validation, the firm earned itself the honour of becoming the second highest placed law firm in *The Sunday Times'* '100 Best Companies to Work For' poll in 2003.

First things first, do you have to be a Geordie to secure a coveted training contract with Dickie Dees? No, but in practice most trainees have grown up in the North East of England, many in Newcastle itself. We asked how someone would fare as a newcomer to the city. *"There are a few people who have come up here from the South,"* one source told us, *"the locals are very friendly and people are always going to be made welcome."* The firm, we heard, was *"embracing with new people"* and the professional community was synthesising to a greater degree than ever before. *"We are a founding member of the Newcastle Young Professionals Forum, which is for 20 to 35-year-olds. It's going to mean more and more events at which we can interact with other professionals."* No chance of becoming a Billy No-mates then.

baaaah

You can come to Dickinson Dees without any idea of where you want to specialise after qualification. The client base stretches from wealthy individuals and large landed estates and trusts (the source of *"the sheep and tweed reputation which we've had. There's a certain element of that at Dickie Dees and there always will be"*) to plcs and multinational companies. No ungulates or itchy plus fours to be found on the commercial side of the client list, which has names like Go-Ahead Group, Teesside International Airport, Parkdean Holidays, the Environment Agency, Black & Decker, Northumbria Police, Northern Electric, and several venture capital companies and banks.

Training is delivered in four six-month helpings. Each trainee must complete compulsory seats in coco, property and litigation; the fourth will be either a private client seat or a return visit to one of the three main commercial departments. *"You're encouraged to go around and talk to people, and then if you say that you want to be with X then they will put you there if possible."* This hasn't translated into a political approach to seat allocation and we heard no complaints on the issue. We also heard that the firm was open to requests for first-seat placements from trainees.

men in tights

The firm is twice the size it was five years ago and now has 60 partners and around 700 staff. *"Sometimes you hear wistful comments about how the firm used to be, but they want to retain a sense of identity and they are keen for people to attend evening events and things...quiz nights, the annual dinner dance, departmental do's."*

The annual *Stars in their Eyes* competition is not to be missed. Where else could you see the former head of corporate (*"a civilised gent normally"*) dressed up in full Rocky Horror garb doing 'The Time Warp'? We heard the offering from the pensions team was *"pretty diabolical,"* but we're unsure if they entered as The Bee Gees or Bucks Fizz or some other caterwauling collective. Hopefully the judges didn't get so drunk at this year's newly renamed Firm Academy event held at the city's Live Theatre. Acts included the Cheeky Girls, Whitney Houston and a trainee as Will Young.

Having rejected the idea of opening up a second office in London, the firm plumped for Stockton-on-Tees, some 35 miles away. When we interviewed trainees, three seats were offered in the 'Tees Valley' office – private client, coco and litigation. *"The Tees Valley office is developing as a smaller mirror image of the Newcastle office,"* one source said. A mini-me Dickie Dees, we suggested. *"Quite!"*

location, location, location

Trainees share a room with their supervisor. *"A very senior partner might have a lot of things on so you'll get supervision from others in the department as well. If you're sitting with a less senior person, you'll get more direct attention."* It is rare to work longer than 6pm, although most of our sources started work earlier than the required 9am. Reports on the quality of work handed to trainees were generally excellent, and as one trainee put it: *"You feel like a valuable resource to the firm. It's a case of you genuinely being a help to them rather than being found spare tasks."* Another said that the firm *"tries to balance learning with the commercial reality."*

We asked trainees what they'd like to change about the place, but suggestions were thin on the ground. One thought that the appraisal system *"although it does work,"* is *"relaxed...maybe a little too relaxed."* Another wanted a bigger salary, although at £30,000 NQs are paid only £2,000 or £3,000 less than their counterparts in Leeds, Manchester and Birmingham, and they are doing rather better than most of their peers in provincial southern England, especially when you consider that it's possible to buy a decent first house for £90,000 in Newcastle.

keep it buzzing

Having used up all available space in St Ann's Wharf, Dickie Dees' enormous, glitzy HQ on the Quayside, the residential property department has moved to Eldon Court in the city centre. Most staff, however, are housed in the main premises, which boasts great views (particularly from partners' rooms!) over the Tyne to the Baltic Flour Mills. As well as the culture and cafés of The Baltic, trainees will soon be able to enjoy The Sage, *"which is going to be a music venue and a home for the Northern Symphonia. Both the Baltic and the Sage are good additions as traditionally the city has been a bit deprived culture-wise."* Our sources described The

Sage in intriguing terms: "*It's almost like three turtle shells rising up, with the roofs smashed in and replaced with glass...almost like a spaceship.*" If you say so!

Despite losing out to Liverpool in its bid to be the next European Capital of Culture, Newcastle is not defeated and continues along the path to greater civic pride. One source employed the city's slogan, saying: "*In Newcastle people are still keen to 'Get with the Buzz'.*"

steamy stories

Every winter, one trainee gets the chance to do a Brussels competition seat and share a five-storey house (with basement sauna) with trainees from Pinsents. Interested first-years are flown over to Brussels and put up for a weekend at the firm's expense. Others can take up client secondments and a number of our interviewees spoke of trips to London and other cities for meetings and completions. While one trainee confessed that the only downside to the firm was that Newcastle was "*not London,*" for most this is an undisguised blessing. The firm's crown as king of the retention stats slipped in September 2003, when one of the 14 qualifiers didn't stay on at the firm.

and finally...

Quite simply, for anyone thinking about the North East this is a brilliant firm.

DLA

the facts

Location: Birmingham, Leeds, Liverpool, London, Manchester, Sheffield, Glasgow, Edinburgh
UK ranking by size: 5
Total numbers of trainees: 171
Seats: 6x4 months
Alternative seats: Overseas seats, secondments
Extras: Pro bono – The Prince's Trust

DLA is a large national firm that makes a lot of noise...but it has much to shout about.

magic circle? rubbish!

It's not hard to see why this ambitious national firm has been nicknamed the Yorkshire Terriers. In 1996, Sheffield firm Dibb Lupton Broomhead merged with Leeds firm Alsop Wilkinson. Two years later, Dibb Lupton Alsop announced that within three years it would be a top-ten firm in London, and in 2001 it claimed it would be a top-five European firm by 2006. Recently it took full-page adverts in *The Times*, *FT* and *Telegraph* to boost its image. Now it's focusing on Asia and talking of opening up in the US. Potential trainees take note: DLA is a firm on a mission. Aggressive reputation aside, DLA boasts over a thousand fee earners, a network of European offices and a client list that wouldn't embarrass any City firm. No wonder DLA trainees are among the happiest in the country – the regional offices see an excellent quality of work, and the London office offers a more intimate experience of the City than is possible at the magic circle.

"*We're DLA, we don't want to be anyone else!*" announced one trainee. This was the major theme of DLA's recent ad campaign. The firm has made its name doing good-quality everyday work for FTSE 100 and 250 clients, leaving the highest value and most complex deals for the magic circle. According to one of its clients: "They're Ryanair to Slaughter's British Airways." Moving work out of London and into the regions ensures that, for trainees, "*the work you see in Leeds won't be any different from what you get in the City.*" The drawback to a constant stream of high-quality work is that hours can be long, although in the view of one trainee: "*If you're good you can do great work and still get home in time for Eastenders.*"

mini me

To understand the firm is to understand managing partner and beloved leader, Nigel Knowles – simply 'Nigel' to DLA acolytes. He'll be there on the first night of your trainee induction, he'll take you out to dinner when you qualify, and he'll e-mail you (and the rest of the firm) from time to time about charity work. And every so often, Nigel will have another *"vision"* about the firm's future. Trainees tell us that even if you don't get Nigel in the flesh *"he'll send the video of himself along."* But far from being commercial law's equivalent to David Icke, Nigel knows exactly what he's doing. He's presided over a firm that has doubled its turnover in the last five years and expanded from its Sheffield roots into Europe, Thailand, Singapore and China. Trainees find him a genuine (if slightly cultish) source of inspiration. *"He's grown up with the firm – that's tremendously motivating,"* said one. *"You can tell he's really passionate about DLA," "he's been a DLA man from day one." "Maybe we're all mini-Nigels,"* mused one source. This is not a firm for anyone without a stomach for corporatespeak. Trainees referred to *"The DLA Way," "our values"* and *"our ambition."* The culture of the firm is strong.

northern soul

In case you were worried they'd all been brainwashed, most of the trainees *"take the visions and the marketing with a pinch of salt."* Despite the marketing guff, they spoke of a *"no-nonsense"* feel about the firm: *"It's down to earth."* Furthermore, *"there's quite a northern feel about the offices."* Even trainees in London *"appreciate the northern heritage."* We felt they shared a stronger egalitarian sense than most. As one put it: *"Relations between everyone in the office are very close and level – as they should be – there's a real mutual respect."* By the same token, *"partners don't consider themselves too important to chat about the football in the lift."*

A significant number of trainees in the regional offices had local roots or had gone to university there. Because? *"They don't want people who see staying in the regions as a second choice."* That said, trainees were a diverse bunch and every office included a range of backgrounds and ages. Above all it seems that confidence, commercial sense and *"an ability to do a bit of marketing"* are what DLA is looking for.

one firm

All new recruits (including those from Scotland, Hong Kong and Brussels) start their careers together on a residential induction course. After this there's a series of departmental induction sessions around the country. *"It's good because you know the trainees who'll be starting in your department in the other offices – you can always give them a ring with your questions,"* plus *"you get to stay in really nice hotels and everyone can have a few drinks."* Trainees also get to go on the firm-wide departmental training weekends in Amsterdam and Brussels, which is a good opportunity to *"see everyone in the wild."* All this bonding means relations between offices are good. Of course, geographical proximity means that some offices are more familiar with each other – trainees in Manchester and Liverpool see each other a bit more, and Sheffield and Leeds apparently have *"a Yorkshire connection,"* whatever that means.

London is the biggest office and its trainees are deemed to be a little more cliquey than their northern counterparts. The atmosphere was described as *"more competitive than elsewhere,"* and trainees socialised amongst themselves rather than with partners or assistants. Friday nights are usually spent in The City Pipe, and on office nights out, *"partners always put a card behind the bar."* There was a certain feeling in other offices that being at the epicentre of DLA Group led the London trainees to *"think they are at the centre of the universe!"* No different to any other City trainee then!

behind bars

Leeds is said to be run *"more independently"* than other offices (although we could draw out few details on this point). Its projects and banking departments are widely admired and it boasts *"the best premises in the DLA network."* Having visited them last year, we'd add that the firm has the best digs in Leeds. Very flash. Friday nights at The Lowry are popular and, once again, when partners come out *"they put a card behind the bar."* Can anyone see a trend?

Being the office from which the great leader emerged, Sheffield is the spiritual home of DLA. It's strong in litigation and, according to trainees, other Sheffield firms remain *"jealous"* of its success. Last year we suggested that a city-wide public holiday and a statue of Nigel in the main square would be appropriate. Alas, neither has materialised. Birmingham has a popular employment seat and a strong pensions department. The open-plan office promotes an easy atmosphere. On firm nights out *"no one's scared to have a few drinks,"* but the biggest problem is that *"nights out always seem to be on a Thursday."* Ouch!

Manchester is on a split site and the buildings *"could be nicer,"* but the quality of work is consistently high in the corporate department. The presence of a Pitcher & Piano directly underneath one of the buildings was quickly pointed out by several trainees. Occupying an old school overlooking the docks, the Liverpool office is the smallest in the network. It is just about to be refurbished and is said to enjoy the best address and view in Liverpool. Its particular specialism is marine law. Socially, everyone piles into the same pub on Friday nights and other trainees rate the Liverpool recruits as having the best sense of humour in the firm.

bein's believin'!

Last year we reported on the hand-clapping, flag-waving character of DLA and its predilection for a certain 80s classic theme song. Think welder chick by day, go-go dancer by night. (Almost) unbelievably, DLA considers itself the legal profession's answer to *Flashdance*. *"It's not like they play it through the speakers every morning and we all stand up,"* but reports are that from time to time it gets played at the end of the night at a firm jolly. One trainee even admitted to buying his own copy. We suspect he's not the only one. In fact, we predict DLA is poised to lead a legwarmer revival.

Let's get serious for a moment. You'll probably want to know how coercive all of this pep talking and rallying actually is? Without wishing to detract from a fantastic achievement for which we congratulate the firm, let us examine the firm's recent and much publicised charity walk from Land's End to John O'Groats – the Well Child Walk. Some thought it a perfect example of how the firm can pull together and make big things happen; others felt *"definite pressure to participate."* The firm encourages pro bono and charitable work, but a few trainees felt their preferences and/or efforts had been overshadowed by the firm's *"narrower,"* well-publicised charitable endeavours. For some, independence has been lost in the drive for firm-wide achievement.

The main gripe we heard in our interviews related to the lack of opportunities to work abroad. Basically, it's one Brussels seat twice a year. Those hell-bent on international placements won't necessarily find what they are looking for here just yet, but this isn't deterring any of the current crop: in September 2003, an impressive 67 of the 71 qualifiers kept the faith.

on the road to damascus

The chances are you'll know whether or not DLA is the right firm for you. Our favourite conversion story was of the trainee who received an offer of a training contract on his mobile as he travelled on a train down to London for an interview with a magic circle firm. *"He accepted on the spot, got off the train at the next station and went straight back home."* Many lawyers in the City have sneered at the visionary statements that emanate from this firm. Certainly, as its recent ad campaign illustrates, DLA has its own way of manoeuvring around the Square Mile. It hasn't got the sleekness or panache of certain established City firms, but many applicants will be only too glad of that. As one trainee commented rather dryly: *"You might not want to be typecast as being not quite good enough for the magic circle…or northern."*

and finally…

If anyone tells you DLA is an aggressive firm, don't for one minute believe that this is a comment about the internal culture; after all, it earned itself the highest place of any law firm in the *Sunday Times'* '100 Best Companies to Work For' survey of 2003. DLA is not for the faint-hearted, nor anyone with a strong streak of cynicism; however, if you're right for the firm and you do get The Call, you can count yourself lucky. Exciting times lie ahead.

DMH

the facts

Location: Brighton, Crawley, London, Worthing
UK ranking by size: 152
Total number of trainees: 13
Seats: 4x6 months
Alternative seats: None

Training at DMH is a bit like having one of those double ice cream cones. You get to sample two different flavours of legal practice and the proximity of the beach will give you that holiday feeling every day.

donkeys on the beach

The largest office is in Brighton. Here you'll find the PI, family, trusts, tax and probate departments as well as a clutch of residential conveyancers and some commercial. The Crawley office is commercially focused and plays host to coco, commercial property, employment and innovation and media groups. Crawley is seen as the newer, *"more slick"* upstart to the well-established Brighton HQ, which has a distinguished pedigree as well as a *"hilarious"* and *"really quite old"* family department with *"a few fee earners and secretaries who've been around for donkey's years."* Cheeky...

Make no mistake, this firm is neither old fashioned nor quaintly regional: trainees tell us that potential applicants *"shouldn't think that because we're not a London firm we haven't got modern ideas."* In fact, they feel the firm is *"really branded"* and *"vibrant."* Its lime green website certainly gives this impression, so stay well clear if you have a hangover. Other consciously modern touches include 'supergroups', sadly nothing to do with either wearing your underwear over your clothes or nicking your dad's 70s prog rock albums, but, rather, multidisciplinary teams of lawyers that work together for clients in specific industry sectors.

pearly kings and pearly whites

The firm also fishes in the London legal pond. Having merged a couple of years ago with personal injury specialists Fairbairn Morris, the office in the capital works in PI, commercial property and now insolvency following the hire of a specialist in this field. There are now two seats in London and trainees are encouraged to visit. Most switch between Brighton and Crawley, but rarely go to Worthing.

We were assured there were no compulsory seats: *"They basically assess which departments need trainees and then ask us which areas we would like to have a seat in."* But that doesn't mean you'll have a completely free hand: *"You would struggle if you just want to do commercial work, and because there's so much contentious work, everyone does a lot of it."* Typically in your first or second seat you might be billeted to the residential property department, which although perceived to be a bit of a drudge seat, can actually be really beneficial. *"It's hectic and you're given files from a very early stage, but it's a good seat to start with as it gets you familiar with the firm and with case management."* PI is the other high-volume seat that first-years find themselves in; here you'll get your own caseload and work side by side with experienced paralegals, mainly on road traffic accidents and 'trip and slip' cases. The good news is that you'll also get a crack at more complicated stuff such as dental negligence.

On the commercial side, you might do a standard coco seat, assisting on commercial contracts or M&A transactions around the £10 million mark. If you're lucky, you might wangle a seat in the popular employment department. This *"excellent team"* is top banana in the South according to *Chambers UK*, and it'll work you hard and train you well. Training partner Rustom Tata is in charge of this group, and according to one former charge: *"He takes his responsibility quite seriously"* and *"wanted to educate me."* Expect plenty of earnest half-hour chats about the finer points of your work! Mainly acting for employers, the department handles a mix of contentious and non-contentious instructions and all the advocacy is done in-house. There are fewer opportunities for courtroom drama in the commercial litigation department, which tends to use counsel for its relatively high-value matters. You will have some of your own small files there, but as one trainee admitted: *"There's lots of scope for dogsbody work."* That's litigation for you... Trainees weren't grumbling about the shape of the working day. *"There are only a few people at their desks after 5.15pm,"* although another admitted: *"I have done some late nights, but working until after 6.30pm is always my own choice."*

brighton rocks

DMH is aware of the world beyond the law. In both the open-plan Brighton and Crawley offices, *"the entire reception is given over to artwork."* Modern pieces by local artists feature most prominently, although it has to be said: *"Some are better than others!"* Whether it's Prince Harry A-level standard or Picasso-esque, it's *"always a talking point and good for breaking the ice with clients."* The firm is also prepared to nurture the creative instincts of its own staff; at the AGM, motivational talks and presentations are interspersed with fun. This year's Pollock-style painting session was variously described as *"expressing yourself through paint marks as a team"* and *"200 people in white boiler suits throwing paint around."*

So how do you go about booking your deckchair at DMH? Trainees reckon the firm *"quite likes the idea that people have had other experiences in life apart from school, university and the LPC."* You'll certainly find mature trainees here, both migrants from other careers and those who've finally hung up their backpacks. DMH has established ties with Sussex University and tries to recruit people who have connections to the area because *"they'll be more likely to stay on qualification."* This year seems no exception; of the five September 2003 qualifiers, four stayed.

We love the idea of working in Brighton and, at DMH, there's even a little bit of the beach in the office. There's no sand under the desks, but most departments have a sea view and when the weather gets hot and the air con isn't working, there'll be free ice lollies in the freezer. Trainees think this trendy seaside town is *"a brilliant place to live – it's very young and there's so much going on."* However, they also told us that Brighton is so full of *"people with money who don't work and creatives"* that there's a danger that you'll *"feel like a plonker in your suit."* By contrast, *"totally charmless," "concrete and horrible"* new town Crawley isn't the place to spend a sunny day. This commercial town near Gatwick Airport is great for attracting clients, but isn't much good for keeping trainees entertained after work. Because most employees live elsewhere and drive to work, there's a *"Coke and go home"* culture.

Back in Brighton, the beach is *"a lovely break from work"* and when the sun goes down there are plenty of watering holes to choose from. Trainees tend to go out every Friday and were still potty about uniquely decorated old favourite, The Pond. Its popularity rests on its proximity and the fact that *"one of the partners is mates with the landlord."* If your group hits its financial targets, the firm stumps up the cash for a night out. It has also organised visits to the capital for flights on the London Eye and trips down the Thames. More regularly, there are golf days, five-a-side football, cricket and tennis – and every year there's a summer party. One trainee sniffed at the efforts of the DJ. What were you expecting, Fatboy Slim?

and finally...

Sun, sea and suing. If you like the sound of this firm, dig out that old set of poster paints and get working on a masterpiece of a CV.

DWF

the facts

Location: Liverpool, Manchester, Warrington
UK ranking by size: 59
Total number of trainees: 14
Seats: 2x6 + 3x4 months
Alternative seats: None

DWF sees itself as young, energetic and on the up. Once an insurance litigation firm, like many in their mid-20s, it has outgrown the single-mindedness of youth and now focuses on advising corporate clients.

ain't no stopping us now

Though many trainees were blissfully unaware of the firm's roots in insurance (Royal & SunAlliance, Zurich, etc), it is still the powerhouse of the firm, *"a vast machine"* that cranks out around a third of the profits, much of it deriving from lower value work such as personal injury and home insurance claims.

The commercial dispute resolution, property and particularly corporate departments are catching up with the insurance department, and the firm has grown significantly in these areas in recent years, winning clients such as PwC and Bank of Scotland. To match the change in the client base, some would say that DWF has changed beyond recognition: *"The firm has become much more businesslike. We've now got proper HR, marketing and IT departments and regular training."* It doesn't stop there. DWF is *"constantly looking to expand,"* even if this means poaching from the neighbours: *"We've had a period of being quite acquisitive and getting people in from elsewhere."* However, many of the partners have been with the firm since it was a high street practice and trainees feel that the philosophy is still to *"recruit and retain people who will grow with us."* Supporting this, DWF's retention statistics are pretty solid; of the eight September 2003 qualifiers, seven stayed with the firm.

local firm for local people

Despite the firm's ambition and its trumpeting of international connections such as membership of the EU-LUX network (can we do our laundry there?), DWF is still very much a North West firm acting for North West clients – Liverpool John Moores University, Manchester Airport, and food manufacturers Princes and Burton Foods, among others. Again and again trainees told us they applied to the firm because they were committed to and from the region. One said: *"It's all a bit League of Gentlemen!"* – thankfully they didn't elaborate. We certainly sensed they loved where they lived: *"You won't get left out or shunned in Liverpool or Manchester if you're not from round here, but it makes it easier if you're mad keen."* In the Mersey office, a passion for football will get you a long way and you'll have ample opportunity to win tickets to watch Liverpool play as the firm is forever holding raffles.

Apart from local connections, trainees were also keen to stress that they were for the most part state educated and confident. *"You can't be a wallflower here,"* one thought, because of the focus DWF places on marketing. For these trainees, *"in today's legal world, everyone knows you've got the qualifications to be a good lawyer; whether you get the business comes down to people skills."* How right they are.

maximising potential?

DWF's seat system is a little unusual: your first seat is a standard six months long but is followed by three shorter, four-month seats before you finish off with a final six-month seat. Last year, the firm sent the new intake to spend their first six months in the exciting sounding DWF Maxima, which turns out to be a *"process-driven legal services unit"* in a business park just outside Warrington. This office has a high turnover of low-value insurance work. We're told that this is not likely to be a permanent feature of the training scheme, although those who did the seat got a good grounding in the basics of lower value work before moving onto more complicated multi-track cases. They also liked the fact that the whole intake got to know each other before being split between the Manchester and Liverpool offices.

Once you're brought back to the relatively civilised environs of Manchester or Liverpool, you'll typically do three seats taken from insurance litigation, corporate, commercial property or commercial dispute resolution. When we asked trainees if there was much jostling for seats, they were keen to distance themselves from what they perceived to be the more cut-throat approach of their peers in London firms, saying: *"You wouldn't fit in if you're a jumped-up pin-striped type – it's no good if you fancy yourself."* But make no mistake, although trainees don't feel the firm is *"stab you in the back ambitious,"* when it comes to seat allocation, we got the impression that you still have to make sure that your views are heard. If you want to do a specialised seat, for example IP instead of corporate, you must make this known as soon as possible.

The employment seat is a particularly popular choice. As a trainee, you'll be doing a mixture of contentious and non-contentious work on issues such as wrongful dismissal and termination packages. Property also gets the trainees' seal of approval: *"There are some real characters in that department."* When they're not exchanging banter, trainees get stuck into a wide variety of work and report feeling very involved in everything from property finance to reviewing commercial leases to residential transactions. The insurance litigation departments in Liverpool and Manchester handle more complex, higher value claims. *"If you want to qualify into insurance, they will fast-track you and give you very good stuff,"* so pipe up as soon as you like. Your final six-month seat is generally a run-in seat in the area you want to qualify into, but if there's something you still want to try then it's possible that this can be arranged instead.

visiting rights

You won't be jetting off to Paris or Hong Kong if you train with DWF, but if you start off in Liverpool and you fancy a stint in Manchester or vice versa then this is perfectly possible. The profile of each office is similar and at trainee level (particularly among those who've been banged up together in Warrington) links are very good. One Liverpool trainee enthused that their Manchester peers *"might as well be down the corridor."* More generally, an in-house magazine and video-conferencing keeps everyone in touch, but as one source said: *"You're never going to get the same level of bonding if you don't all work in one office."*

Trainees like the central Manchester location, but we think the Liverpool lot would be more entertaining if they ever got on *Changing Rooms*. Some raved about the wood panelling in the main boardroom (*"It would be a crime to take it out"*), while others complained about getting hopelessly lost in the *"rabbit warren"* that has been added on to the building at the back of the main Liverpool office. When they do manage to find their way out, the Liverpool trainees love being a part of the city that's not only won the title European Capital of Culture 2008, but has also been dubbed the capital of cool by *Tatler*. Free drinks are laid on every Friday, so you know the weekend's begun when an enterprising trainee gets the key and *"raids the booze store."* Although these soirees have been known to last until after midnight, usually the action moves on to News Bar or The Living Room. Bumping into *Hollyoaks* stars is a highlight, but footballers are two a penny; one trainee complained: *"Every time I go out, I see John Barnes."*

In *"cosmopolitan"* Manchester the social scene is less frantic; trainees tell us it's *"laid back"* and everyone usually just ends up in the local All Bar One, although there have been rebel factions trying to break with tradition and colonise Persia across the road. Today Peter Street, tomorrow Persepolis.

and finally...

If you love the North West and want a broad commercial training, although still heavy on insurance lit, you could do a lot worse than DWF. If you're not afraid to work hard and to make your voice heard in this lively and mercantile young firm, you'll have a whale of a time. Meet you at the Gates of Xerxes, ours is a pint.

Edwards Geldard

the facts

Location: Cardiff, Derby, Nottingham
UK ranking by size: 78
Total number of trainees: 21
Seats: 6x4 months
Alternative seats: None

This is a firm of two halves. In Wales, it stomps over most of the opposition and wins hefty instructions from leading clients. In the East Midlands, it competes in a larger field, but packs a decent punch.

game of two halves

Before we detail the ins and outs of training, let's give you a rundown of the sort of client that instructs Edwards Geldard. On the Cardiff lawyers' Christmas card list we found the Welsh Development Agency, Powell Duffryn, Admiral Insurance, S4C, Western Power Distribution and Citibank, while over in the East Midlands the firm acts for the likes of Powergen, Chubb, John Deere, Derbyshire County Council, Pendragon and Balfour Beatty. Trainees go on a day trip to visit *"the other side"* in their first week, but after that *"there's not much contact – the offices don't have much to do with each other."* You'll train at one or other site, completing six four-month seats. This system has *"swings and roundabouts."* You get to see a wider range of practice areas, although, as one trainee put it: *"It's good for a boring seat because it never gets too tedious, but then for good seats you feel like it's all over too soon."*

In the East Midlands, trainees move between Derby and Nottingham and though some complained of feeling *"shuffled about,"* the moves were mostly welcomed: *"because we've worked in both offices, we're the ones introducing people to each other."* While Derby and Nottingham are only 16 miles apart and it's hardly a life-changing move, it does help to have your own car as public transport links *"aren't great."* Even though there are no compulsory seats, trainees tend to undertake at least one stint in each of the litigation, corporate and property departments. As preparation for qualification, the firm then *"gets you back to where you want to qualify."* There is room for flexibility, *"but you have to be the one to approach them,"* and be prepared to lobby if you feel strongly about doing a particular seat in a particular location. As one trainee advised us, *"everyone does things they don't want to,"* so it helps to take *"a philosophical attitude."*

Matters are simpler in Cardiff, where everything is under the one roof. In your first year, you *"get what you're given;"* after this EG cuts trainees some slack: *"In the second year we sort it out between ourselves."* In both halves of the firm, employment remains the favourite seat, though litigation is a popular choice in Cardiff, perhaps because there's loads of advocacy, often through agency work for other firms. Certain seats carry reputations and these no doubt influence trainees' choices. For example, *"some of the partners in commercial property in Derby have an aggressive reputation,"* yet *"commercial property in Nottingham is known for giving good training."* Additionally, *"the insolvency seat in Nottingham has a reputation of 'anything goes',"* whereas, in Cardiff, *"IP has the worst reputation – the people are fine, but the hours are bad because you have to be seen to be working hard."* Take all of this with a pinch of salt; all firms have these differences, it's just that these trainees were more open about such matters.

sprechen sie welsh?

In terms of the responsibility trainees are given, *"it's a nice amount, not too much."* In smaller departments you have your own files under close supervision. In bigger departments, *"they don't want to let you loose on clients, but as your training progresses you get to see more of them."* The experiences seem to be similar in both regions, although East Midlands trainees have enjoyed greater exposure to marketing – go-karting, golf days, five-a-side football, even a dinner with an *Emmerdale* actress. Perhaps envious, the Welsh trainees have asked for more involvement and our sources were hopeful that more corporate jollies would now be on the agenda.

In the East Midlands office there's a collection of German lawyers and the firm's website can now be read in either English or Deutsch. Actually, we were surprised it couldn't also be read in Welsh as this is the first language of several of those who work in the Cardiff office. Trainees felt that *"there's an ambitious feel about the firm, a sense that you're part of something that is going somewhere."* One of our sources suggested that a Bristol office might be on the cards, and although we can't confirm the veracity of his claim, we do know that the firm is keen to develop business links with the US. Trainees were well up on the business plan, but some felt EG could afford to be more aggressive – *"There's not really a sense of 'let's go out and get it' more 'let's go to lunch and see what happens'."*

bring it on

In most cases, the training environment was felt to be *"supportive"* and *"responsive,"* but we heard of one or two incidents where people felt they had been *"caught in the firing line."* The general consensus was that trainees had been prepared well for life after qualification. As one put it: *"There's not much I'd be intimidated by now."* Feedback from supervisors is good, if a little haphazard. Trainees are meant to have appraisals midway through and at the end of their seats. *"When it's done, it's taken seriously, but it's getting people to do it…"* This, dear reader, is something we hear quite often. Cardiff trainees felt the best looked after: *"In your mid-seat appraisal, you can say what you haven't done and they'll go out of their way to make sure you do it."*

In terms of selection, trainees thought that their firm regarded personality and a well-rounded CV to be as important as academic credentials. *"You're expected to get involved in all aspects of the firm's life,"* commented one source. *"It sounds cheesy, but someone who didn't want to muck in would find it pretty difficult here."* In sum, *"you need to be an all-rounder, not just 100% lawyer. It's not just get in, head down, billable hours."* In September 2003, seven of the 13 qualifying trainees stayed with the firm.

playtime

The East Midlands offices each have their own character. Nottingham occupies *"three houses knocked into one."*The trainee who described it as *"a gorgeous old building in a lovely part of town"* could have a career in estate agency if they ever tire of the law. Derby lawyers, meanwhile, enjoy purpose-built offices with *"a really nice break room with a big telly in the middle."* Lucky old them, we've just got a rogues gallery of our 'favourite' lawyers. The drawback is the location *"on an industrial estate outside Derby."* One source said: *"There's not much to do. A few people use the gyms and one guy used to drive to Toys R Us to play on the Playstations at lunchtime!"* Perhaps reflecting the appearance of each office, *"in Derby you're in at nine or you're in trouble, and lunch doesn't spill over or you're in trouble. Nottingham is more results driven and less procedure driven."* In Wales, the office was summed up as *"four storeys, big central spiral staircase, glass panelling, very modern."* Its city centre location is *"tough on the purse strings."*

The Cardiff office has a fuller social programme. Among the highlights of the last year there was a beach party featuring partners dressed up in grass skirts. *"We're famous in Cardiff for having more Christmas parties than any other firm. There's the trainees' party, a fancy dress party, departmental parties and then a whole firm party."* Think that's enough? Oh no, there's an annual trainee ski holiday, video nights, theatre trips, shopping in London, and barbecues at weekends. Yet, the Welsh trainees are creatures of habit – as we reported last year, and the year before, they spend most Friday nights in Ha!Ha!…along with half of Cardiff's legal community. The social life in Nottingham and Derby is less frenzied, but trainees maintained that they too had *"a really good laugh."*

and finally…

A number of our sources had been recruited through Edwards Geldard's vacation scheme; others had gone for an initial interview and then been offered a week-long placement. Either way, if you're interested in the firm, a vac scheme seems a good way forward.

Eversheds

the facts

Location: Birmingham, Cambridge, Cardiff, Ipswich, Leeds, London, Manchester, Norwich, Nottingham.
UK ranking by size: 1
Total number of trainees: 201
Seats: varies between offices
Alternative seats: Overseas seats, secondments.
Extras: Pro bono – Streetlaw

With over 4,000 staff, Eversheds is the UK's largest firm. From the late 1980s it grew by taking over good regional firms and then rebranding them as Eversheds offices.

merging markets

Now the 'franchise' phase is at an end, Eversheds is on a drive to attain national integration and uniform service standards. In the last year it has been 'merging' some offices. There's a triumvirate in the East of England; Leeds and Manchester operate as a double act; and Birmingham and Nottingham have been conceptually fused. A national intranet system is in place, cross-office departmental meetings are commonplace, and trainees from right across the UK complete much of the PSC as a group. This year, around 120 of them descended on Birmingham's Hilton Hotel for three days of advocacy and...well, quite a few assessments were done with fuzzy heads.

Almost without exception, and right across the UK, we found Eversheds trainees to be *"grounded, easy-going"* individuals. Even those who had previously worked in high street firms said: *"We are straightforward. We're not stuffy in our dealings."* The dress-down policy and open-plan set up in most offices each contribute to glorious normality.

london: b.y.o. whale song

As the largest Eversheds office, on 1 May 2003 London was (*"regrettably,"* according to Birmingham trainees) made the administrative hub of the firm. In terms of the City muscle league, Eversheds comes in at number 21 by size, but trainees told us that they'd shunned the biggest City firms in favour of one where *"it's not so big that you get swallowed up...it's not a sweat shop."*

Trainees are offered a broad array of seats and pro bono secondments. Interestingly, tax law emerged as the surprise hit of the year, with trainees praising the variety and intellectual challenge of the work. As in many other seats, you get the sense of being part of a national team, with lawyers across the UK videoconferencing once a month to discuss developments. The London office is a respected force in medium-sized corporate deals, although corporate is, as ever, a cyclical beast, and you have to be lucky to catch the best work. The flow of property work has been more reliable, and trainees appreciated the chance to manage their own files as well as assist on larger transactions. A seat in something more specialist, like construction litigation, can satisfy the contentious seat requirement, and the general commercial lit department allows some trainees to go on a three-month secondment to the Mary Ward Legal Centre.

The fêted employment lawyers win the prize for being the most sociable team, although we never did find out how well they did in the recent and bizarrely named Photopoly challenge. Our sources described a treasure hunt in which participants dress up in costume and take photos of themselves in various locations around London. If the excitement of Photopoly gets a bit much, you can always retire to the office's serene meeting rooms, decorated in blue tones with aquatic images adorning the walls. It seems appropriate, then, that The Seahorse (or the Purple Pony as it's affectionately known) remains the after-work watering hole of choice.

midlands: a choice of fillings

The Birmingham and Nottingham offices have recently 'merged' together, thus formalising a phase of cross-office working and staff movement. Real estate is a major strength, and the Midlands' team is the largest nationwide. Accordingly, the demand for trainees is high, and although it's not strictly compulsory, Birmingham recruits should expect a seat there. In Birmingham, plush new digs are laid out with open-plan work areas, which, according to trainees has brought *"a real buzz about the place."* We must confess that to us it sounded, at times, rather like a call centre. After work, trainees head round the corner to Digress or the new Summer Row complex.

Nottingham is possibly best known for its projects/PFI work. The firm's national head is based here, and the group is particularly well respected for its schools and rail work. It recently acted on the Potters Bar crash investigation on behalf of Jarvis. But it's not all domestic work: the team has handled infrastructure projects as far afield as Ghana. There's also a sizeable environmental and regulatory department, spread over the two Midlands offices. Be aware that some of the sexier seats, including contentious IP, are not available in Nottingham. However, strengthened ties with Birmingham mean that Nottingham trainees can do seats in Birmingham and vice versa. Since our last edition, it seems that The Rotunda near to the Nottingham office has suffered a tragic decline, having been usurped as the pub of choice by The Castle. We must also report that Nottingham is the poor relation in the sandwich stakes – there is no in-house café.

east of england: big ears

The Cambridge, Ipswich and Norwich offices have long operated as a single group, with trainees undertaking seats in at least two locations. For some, the resulting commute is an irritant, and we did hear pleas for seat allocations to be announced earlier. In its defence, the firm is clear from the outset about its policy: *"They tell you that you'll have to move, and they mean it."* Happily, they will pick up the tab for your relocation costs, if you choose to move home.

Many of the UK's largest biotech companies are to be found in East Anglia's Silicon Fen, and the Cambridge office (a *"big, efficient machine"*) houses a specialist biosciences group. There is fierce competition for places here as trainees get involved in IP work. In the hotly contested employment group, you might help to prepare witness statements, draft submissions for employment tribunals and prepare case assessments. The group handles work for schools, colleges and hospitals, and trainees can often expect to be first point of contact for clients. Corporate is another popular choice, and on the subject of popular things, we're told the Cambridge staff café serves fantastic food – roast pork, lamb shanks, tiramisu...whoops, just drooled on the keyboard!

Norwich is the most traditional of the three offices. Its corporate seat is made popular by the quality of trainee tasks and some outstanding supervisors. The building is located within the Cathedral Grounds, so in summer lunch hours you can stretch out on the lawns or eat ice cream in the shade of the Norman architecture. Any night of the week you can find trainees in one of *"five or six bars within spitting distance"* of the office. This old city is well geared-up for young people, and on Friday nights the Riverside complex is heaving.

In the summer of 2002 Ipswich was transformed from a full-service to a specialist office, offering construction, projects and litigation. In projects, you might find yourself involved in big-ticket PPP or PFI work for large national clients – this is City-standard work in a rural setting. It's a notoriously hard-working and successful *"flagship department,"* and as a trainee, you'll be travelling to London frequently for client meetings. If you're nervous about getting involved in big transactions, don't be. Partners are *"happy to explain everything in Noddy and Big Ears-speak."* The litigation group handles volume work for insurance and banking clients. Ipswich has a beautiful glass office and a young vibe. Proving they're just big kids, last summer staff headed off to Alton Towers.

the north: cross-dressing

Uniquely, in the Leeds and Manchester offices trainees encounter six four-month seats. On the positive side, you see a wider variety of departments, and it gives trainees the chance to do their final four months in their intended qualification department. The downside is that four months is quicker than the blink of an eye in a seat you love. Increasingly, lawyers are dividing their time between the two sides of the Pennines and trainees are moving back and forth for different seats.

Both Leeds and Manchester have excellent IP/IT departments. IP litigation is much sought after, with trainees getting involved in international cybersquatting disputes, amongst other things. Over in mainstream corporate, you'll assist on decent-sized deals and have the opportunity to meet clients. One of Manchester's drawcards is an outstanding planning and property group. Regular client contact and visits to construction sites are a bonus. (Hard hats and wellies compulsory.) In Manchester, the offices are brand new and pretty spectacular, being located around a central atrium and library. If you can ever drag yourself away, Rain Bar is just next door.

Local government work is a particular strength in Leeds, where lawyers act for around 400 local authorities across the UK. Trainees undertake a fair bit of research, much of it preparation for client newsletters. In real estate, you'll have some of your own files, but the pace is not too hectic and our sources appreciated *"those breaks in the day when you just chat with the supervisors, rather than ploughing on with work."* As you might expect, commercial litigation offers an experience more akin to that of an *"assistant than a proper fee earner on a file,"* although where there was grunt work to be done, *"they tried to involve you in the bigger picture."* Although the Leeds office lacks the glamour of Manchester, the firm is scouting around for new digs, and will move in 2005. In its favour, the Leeds office is only five minutes from the train station, and is smack-bang in the city centre. The nightlife is *"fantastic,"* with trainees getting out regularly. Some (including boys!) broke out the fishnets for a visit to the Rocky Horror Show. Usually, trainees start out at...nobody could remember the name of the bar but *"it does the job"*...before heading on to Life or Tiger Tiger. Grrrr!

the freezing north: put a coat on

In Newcastle, the litigation group is *"a baptism of fire,"* with heaps of responsibility and client contact. PFI transactions involving NHS trusts and the MoD are the order of the day in commercial projects, while over in clinical negligence you'll be doing snippets of work on large files. Unfortunately it's rare to see a matter through from beginning to end, but as one trainee told us, if you want to know how it all fits together, just ask. Banking offers consistently long hours, but a good team ethic. This is a successful group, acting for clients such as Bank of Scotland in biggish-ticket financings. Even in corporate, a department rarely known for quality trainee work, the firm lets you *"have a go."* Over in real estate, the pace is more relaxed. Although you'll be running up to 50 of your own files, *"you might send out a letter and two weeks later someone might get back to you."* Trainees assured us that they were almost guaranteed to get the seats they wanted.

Don't be deceived by the dicky photograph on the website: the Newcastle office is an architectural triumph. Overlooking the Tyne and its Quayside, it boasts spectacular views from the open-plan floors. Newcastle is a veritable nirvana of bars and clubs, heaving with scantily clad angels of the north. Trendy bars positively lay siege to the office, all with names like Revolution, Centurion and Destination. The more traditionally named Telegraph and Long Bar are also popular with trainees. When they're not dancing down the cobbles of Bigg Market, trainees partake of that other traditional Geordie pastime – dragon boat racing. The firm took part in the recent Corporate Games in Newcastle, and although they failed to secure any medals, we're assured that if men's gymnastics were made an event, Eversheds would have scooped the pool – one trainee competed in the last Commonwealth Games.

cardiff: b.y.o welsh song

There are three law firms in Wales that carry off the medals in all matters corporate and commercial. No prizes for guessing that Eversheds is one of them. If there's a big deal to be done on this side of the border then there's a very good chance Eversheds will be on the case. That said, the office handles plenty of non-Welsh work too. Corporate and employment are the most popular trainee seats, although there are remarkably few squabbles over the best spots. A year ago, Cardiff moved into impressive new premises, which you can see from your window as you approach Cardiff train station. The office is completely open plan, and boasts spectacular views over Cardiff Bay from its full-length windows. By all accounts, the restaurant has top nosh.

Don't get too excited. We feel duty-bound to inform you that despite all the attractive Eversheds gents busy seducing you with freebie gifts and impressing you with their yo-yoing dexterity at law fairs, when we rang the Cardiff office there were only two male trainees out of a total of 16. Understandably, the Cardiff office wants *"people with a connection, or at least, a strong desire to be in Wales,"* but this still doesn't explain where all the boys have gone.

what's in a name?

A word of caution: don't assume that all Eversheds offices are the same. If you desire a particular location and know what area of work you want to specialise in, check that Eversheds is your best bet over other local rivals. As often as not it will be, but Eversheds does not mean the same thing in all practice areas in all locations. Internationally, there are two seats available in Paris and Brussels, although the firm has pulled out of Monaco, now that it has effectively shelved private client work.

We interviewed shedloads of trainees, yet we heard no complaints about the standard of training. On the contrary, our sources were glowing in their praise for supportive supervisors, who *"take a real interest in you."* Despite its size, there's an inclusive feel to the firm, and few feel *"lost in a vast machine."* There are annual 'Have Your Say' sessions, in which feedback from individual offices is channelled through to central management. On qualification, trainees can put the theory behind a unified national firm to the test as they are permitted to apply for vacancies in any office in the network. 75 out of the 100 qualifiers stayed on in September 2003.

The firm's motto is: *"straightforward, enterprising and effective."* On training matters, that seems pretty accurate to us.

and finally...

"Best of both worlds" is how one trainee summed up the Eversheds experience. You have the backup and resources of a vast national firm, while working from a medium-sized office. The bottom line for most trainees: *"I can work for a national and international firm in a region that I love."* Sound good?

Farrer & Co

the facts

Location: London
UK ranking by size: 81
Total number of trainees: 13
Seats: 6x4 months
Alternative seats: Occasional secondments

Farrer & Co is famed for its royal connections and private client work. While this sets it apart from most, it also tends to overshadow the firm's achievements in commercial areas of practice. Just like its office – Georgian town house overlooking Lincoln's Inn Fields on one side and modern office block overlooking Kingsway on the other – there's more than one side to good old Farrers.

the seating plan

During your six seats, you'll do property (commercial, private and estates options), charities or private client, commercial (including banking and employment) and litigation (family, media or general commercial), followed by a 'wild card', which can be used anywhere. The final four months is a second helping of the department into which you hope to qualify. *"The idea of the last four months is to iron out those remaining niggles and worries...it's an incredibly steep learning curve, but it's all about getting to grips with the work before I'm charged out at £10,000 an hour or whatever it is!"*

Like any good dinner party host, Farrers puts a lot of thought into the invitations and the seating plan. It's clear that guests are selected such that their proclivities will make for an interesting evening and they won't fight over the last portion of dessert. So is it advisable to make your interest in a department known when you apply? Yes and no. If you're drawn generally to the private client side of the firm then our sources recommend you highlight this. If it's something more specific about Farrers that's attracted you, say sports law (governing bodies and sports association clients) or heritage work, guard against giving the impression that you'll be an impolite guest who'll pull a face at the other four courses. If the commercial teams are of greater appeal then take comfort in the knowledge that you can take a commercial route through your training, only stopping briefly on the private client side. That said, don't underestimate the volume of private and charitable/institutional clients that use the firm and be aware that many of the corporate deals are done for wealthy entrepreneurs and not FTSE-listed companies.

winning numbers

Trainees usually come to Farrers for a reason. For some it is the firm's impeccable reputation for family, heritage or private client matters. In these departments, lawyers mingle with the great, the good and the moneyed, fixing all manner of problems and generally fulfilling the role of a good old-fashioned 'man of affairs'. Such lawyers are not anachronisms; wealthy people want them now as much as ever before. There's so much private client work that they've had to split the lawyers into three separate teams: international, private capital and heritage. The latter concentrates on clients whose wealth is chattel-rich and offered one trainee a four-month secondment to auctioneer client, Christie's.

Continuing on a cultural bent, the charities department handles work for galleries and museums as well as a host of schools and other educational establishments. *"It's a wonderful department,"* enthused one former resident. *"It's got three partners who are totally on top of their game"* and you can wade around in constitutional issues and advice on lottery fund distribution. In the past, some trainees have been seconded to the Science Museum and the London Business School.

The family department offers contact with yet more wealthy clients. The issues that crop up are much the same as those dealt with by a high street firm, although with clients from country estates in Gloucestershire not sink estates in Peckham, the pot of money at stake is often vast and there tends to be less domestic violence. Without wishing to stereotype: *"Often the wife won't have a bloody clue what the husband has been doing with the money for the last 30 years. What they want is really good legal advice...and you don't need to move in their world to do that."* And a good job too, because Farrers is no longer just recruiting People Like Us or People Like The Clients.

eton rifled?

Our calls to Farrers' trainees put us in contact with the well-spoken privately educated and the undaunted from comprehensive schools. Class warriors aside, we get the impression that a person from any background could make their way here.

You probably don't know this, but in 1694 the Charter of the Bank of England was sealed in the firm's Peacock Room. This momentous occasion took place well before Farrers took up residence though. It didn't move in until 1790, following the demise of the Duke of Newcastle, who lived at 66 Lincoln's Inn Fields throughout much of his life. Farrers takes pride in its home and the family trees of the Duke of Newcastle and his in-laws the Marlboroughs are on display in the reception. These days the Peacock Room serves as the venue for client seminars and parties. At times you may find it bristling with school bursars. One source said: *"Pretty soon I got to know the names of all the boarding schools in the south of England, although at first all the terminology was a totally different language to me."* And on the subject of complex languages, you might also have to get to grips with the vernacular of *The Sun*. Which brings us to Farrers' media litigation department, which handles top-level defamation work for the aforementioned title, amongst others.

the tweedies

Each year after speaking to Farrers' trainees we always come to the same conclusion: the firm has bags and bags of character. At partner level there are a fair few eccentrics (don't shoot the messenger) who are *"treated with the respect they deserve"* (whatever that means). *"It is normalising a bit! People who have been here for a long time will have seen it change in size certainly and in ethos slightly. It's not a rebranding, but more a sideways movement...it's trying to shift from the public school, upper middle-class image that it has had, but it doesn't want to lose the originality which is its selling point."* Ah ha...

If any of this report makes the place appear as the exclusive preserve of paid-up tweedies then we've done Farrers an injustice. One trainee said: *"I've lost count of the number of people who've come up to me at law fairs with this irritating view of Farrers as a bastion of the old school."* So let's be clear: parts of the firm are old school and parts are developing their own momentum and culture. One thing is for sure, no matter how much the firm changes, no one seems to want to give up the old premises. *"There will come a time when we can't have the whole firm in here, but we will never move the whole firm out of the building. The day Farrers goes into a New York-style glass building is the day it will end."*

Hurrah! No end in sight for the youngsters. All eight of September 2003's qualifying trainees stayed with the firm. Offers were made early, pay deals sorted and contracts of employment all signed up before we'd even picked up the phone to the firm in May. A job well done, we feel.

just joshing

The collegial nature of the firm and the idiosyncrasies of the partnership become apparent at the Christmas party, when first-years undergo an initiation ritual called '*The Christmas Revue*'. Forget unkind tarring and feathering, this is much worse...or so it may feel at the time. First-years act out skits written by second-years and censored by defamation supremo and senior partner, Robert Clinton. By all accounts Mr C takes a bullish view on the script and the partners come in for some bone-close ribbing. We did try to elicit a few details, but our sources were a discreet bunch and those titbits we did get were far too racy for this publication.

Those more attuned to sport can play cricket against the Royal Household and Mr Murdoch's tabloids, and rugby against bankers Coutts. We should also report on an easy-going social scene, with work teams regularly decamping to the nearby branch of the Jamies chain or the more traditional White Horse. Sunny days see trainees picnicking together on Lincoln's Inn Fields. This is the sort of place where you will take a lunch break and you will almost always have the evening to do as you please.

and finally...

The personal touch required to be a good private client lawyer seems to have infused the firm as a whole. City friends will make more money, but in terms of practical legal experience, a Farrers' training will leave you a high net worth individual.

Field Fisher Waterhouse

the facts

Location: London
UK ranking by size: 36
Total number of trainees: 24
Seats: 2x6 and 3x4 months
Alternative seats: Secondments

Field Fisher Waterhouse offers its trainees a balanced diet of traditional corporate, property and finance work, spiced up with some great niches, including IP, IT and, rather unusually, claimant clinical negligence.

no news is good news

The firm's commercial lawyers act for household names including plcs and public sector bodies, sometimes on transactions with a cross-border dimension. While this appeals to those seeking *"better quality work in a smaller firm,"* the trainees we spoke to generally agreed that *"medical negligence is the most sought after work."* Other specialist teams are brought together under the brands, technology, media and telecommunications banner. Yet while niche practices are a real strength, trainees were quick to remind us that *"it is a City firm, and corporate work is its bread and butter."*

Teetering on the fence between ever so slightly traditional and ever so slightly trendy we wondered if this year there would be news of a decisive leap into one camp or the other? Apparently not. In fact, no news at all. Despite racking up a few meaty deals, FFW has managed to avoid the gossips of the legal press, and continues to conduct business as usual. The firm has spent the year cautiously picking its way through rough economic terrain, and we suspect that its softly-softly approach has been wisely calculated.

Our hopes were raised when trainees mentioned *"the merger,"* but were quickly dashed when we realised they were referring to the merger of Field Fisher & Martineau and Waterhouse & Co...in 1989. While most of us were, in those days, pairing off Barbie with our brother's Action Man, the joint venture of these two firms has proved to be a more fruitful partnership. Many of FFW's current partners have their roots in one or other of the original firms and trainees tell us that *"you can work out who came from where."* We're astonished. Trainees are *"aware of the firm's history, and it would be a shame to lose it entirely."* However, *"though a more traditional mentality may linger, it has been jazzed up over the last few years."* With an eye on the future, FFW has joined a European alliance of law firms in Germany, France, Ireland and Scotland, and although it has had no direct impact on the training experience as yet, our sources hoped that it would open up secondment opportunities.

vital statistics

The FFW training is divided into five seats. Described as *"an extra bite at the cherry,"* the fifth seat can be taken in a new department or used for the purpose of getting extra practice in before qualification. The only requirement is that one seat is spent in corporate or banking & finance; however, with a mix of six and four-month seats, *"if you know you will hate it, they make it quite easy for you – they are happy for you to wangle a four-month seat there."* On the subject of qualification, nine of the ten September 2003 NQs stayed on.

It is in contentious work that the niche departments come into their own. As an alternative to mainstream com lit, there is clin neg, travel & tourism, IP/IT, or the professional regulatory group, which acts for the General Medical Council, nursing bodies and the new General Social Care Council.

Expect abundant responsibility: trainees in property, for example, run their own files, but elsewhere they get to meet clients and are involved in even the most high-profile House of Lords appeals. Generally, *"the responsibilities crank up as you go along."* Formal training takes the form of internal and external speakers giving regular lunchtime and evening seminars, and each department also runs its own programme. As and when, there are secondments to clients including the BBC and the GMC.

perfectly proportioned

Our sources were all consistent in their choice of *"a City firm without the reputation of the harder grinders."* As one said: "*I didn't want to be on my own, nor one of a hundred – I wanted the support of others, but also to be able to make an impact.*" Another added: *"It is very easy to create an impression here."* Given the recruitment brochure features images of impossibly large, pin-headed people leaping over buildings, we were amused to hear that *"a sense of proportion"* is a valuable asset at FFW. There are *"no wallflowers"* here, nor *"obnoxious types."* These are *"not crazy people,"* but *"the firm wouldn't recruit on the basis of an outstanding CV alone."* We reckon the firm does a good job of recruiting in keeping with its not-too-traditional-not-too-wacky image. As one trenchant character pointed out: *"It's just law. We're just lawyers."* Indeed. Another source pondered: *"The firm likes the sexy image that it thinks it has in media circles, but whether the banking and corporate departments are seen in the same light I really don't know."*

The firm's dual personality isn't helped by a dress code that would put most people in a blind panic every morning. Basically, everyone is suited and booted except for the media and IT bods, who have dress-down Fridays all year round, and all week throughout June, July and August…we think. *"Corporate also makes allowances for the weather,"* but *"it is all a bit discretionary."* As if it helps, the odd well-phrased e-mail has been known to go round reminding people of the rules. You could just keep a suit in the office in case of client meetings or court; many trainees play it safe and wear a suit every day.

the joke's on you

Inevitably, the longest hours are found in the corporate department, but generally people work from about 9am to 6pm or 6.30pm. The firm *"prefers you to bust a gut during the day and get out at 6pm;"* there are no prizes for all-nighters. Anyone still kicking around at 7pm will have to have a good reason and *"if you are still there at midnight people think you are a bit sad."*

Trainees get appraised at the end of each seat and *"you can ask for a mid-seat appraisal too."* Inevitably, the volume and quality of feedback varies between supervisors, but generally it is forthcoming. We were told that *"nobody minds being asked a 'duh' question"* and if partners laugh at you then it's *"good natured."* The shoe is on the other foot come Christmas though. The annual pantomime is a production of epic proportions, and last year's performance of Law Wars saw fee earners and trainees all mucking in to take the mickey out of partners and whole departments. While no expense is spared on costumes, the sharing of one light sabre seems to have passed unnoticed in the face of songs about IP rights and a partner shoved into the back end of a pantomime horse costume.

If am dram isn't your thing, FFW fields cricket, rugby, softball and netball teams, and a couple of squash courts in the basement have spawned a league. In addition to firm-wide parties, trainees have their own budget, which is frittered away without much trouble on visits to Walthamstow Dog Track, boat trips and dinners. Regular haunts include The Fine Line, Bar 38 and The Emperor, and decent Indian and Thai restaurants are a stone's throw away.

Squash courts aside, one source described the office as *"not aesthetically pleasing but perfectly functional."* The basement is also home to The Bolthole, where you can lounge on comfy sofas in front of a plasma screen TV between one completion and the next. Last year we reported on a section of London Wall that runs through the basement; this year we were assured that *"the tourists can't get past security."*

and finally...

Respected IP and IT practices have bolstered the firm's image, but at heart this is a solid medium-sized City practice offering traditional commercial training. Although *"it's not a sugary-sweet, huggy firm"* it will provide a well-supported, well-balanced training for anyone whose head is not too big.

Foot Anstey Sargent

the facts

Location: Plymouth, Exeter
UK ranking by size: 121
Total number of trainees: 12
Seats: 4x6 months
Alternative Seats: None

Foot Anstey Sargent is respected for its work across a broad range of practice areas from corporate finance, insolvency, litigation and property to family, media, crime and shipping. This growing firm has a stated ambition to be the best in the West Country.

best foot forward

Having bedded down its merger (February 2000: Anstey Sargent & Probert of Exeter and Budleigh Salterton meets Foot & Bowden of Plymouth and Exeter), the firm is striding forward and aggressively pursuing commercial clients, both in the region and nationally. No surprise, then, that there is *"a real buzz about the place."* This is a firm with a *"strong desire to be seen as first rate, not as provincial or second rate."* Trainees see it as *"forward thinking"* and *"happy to grab hold of trends."*

Provided you fulfil the law society's requirements, you can more or less pick and choose your seats, and how long you spend in them. One trainee spent half her time in the family and childcare department, while another focused more on property. Foot Anstey clients range from the great and the good of the business world to the downright destitute and desperate of the local community. But it's the commercial side that's being pushed and most trainees will find themselves in commercial seats. Choices include company/commercial, commercial property, employment, insolvency, banking and property litigation. The client roster proudly boasts names like Bank of Scotland, University of Plymouth, Wrigley and Tamar Science Park. Of particular note is a nationally recognised media practice, with lawyers acting for Northcliffe Newspaper Group, which has hundreds of regional titles.

learning to walk

Don't expect to be running your own show from day one; this firm takes a *"baby steps"* approach to trainee work and responsibility. *"I was never forced to do anything that was beyond me,"* one trainee assured us. *"If you can't cope, you can always tell your supervisor,"* with whom you share an office. Expect to see your share of grunt work such as photocopying, compiling bundles of documents and gophering to court, but play your cards right and the responsibility will grow. Employment is a particularly popular seat: *"It's one of those areas of law that is beautifully simple for trainees."* Here you'll draft letters and get stuck into the occasional compromise agreement. Meanwhile, over in insolvency you might even find yourself doing a bit of detective work, including digging the dirt on dodgy directors. Trainees positively raved about the advocacy training they received – a six-week course run by a former barrister, now a partner at the firm. Performances are videotaped, so you can gasp in horror at your double chins and nervous shuffling.

There are monthly meetings with the training principal, during which trainees can vent their spleen, share experiences and get a better idea of the different departments. *"You hear what sort of work people are doing, and even who's a nightmare to work for!"* Always have your best permasmile handy though. Trainees are expected to be active client entertainers at evening seminars, starting with handing out drinks and progressing to idle chit-chat.

kick up your heels?

While the region's nightlife may not be exactly rug cutting, you can console yourself with the undeniable charms of living and working in the West Country. Many trainees in these parts seem to prefer either a quiet life or a healthy life. Employees are encouraged to pursue their interests outside the office and their hours are an accommodating 9am-5.15pm, with the (very) occasional late night when the work demands. *"There's no jacket on the back of the chair mentality here."* At the prospect of working weekends, one trainee exclaimed in horror: *"Never! Good Lord no!"* And you get *"positively shoo-ed out of the office at lunchtime,"* which is probably why trainees make the effort to go for a group lunch each week.

The Plymouth lads boast a rather successful football team, although certain other attempts at sporting glory have been ill fated – both cricket matches were rained out last year. Would-be Paula Radcliffes take note: the firm has begun a competition to locate the fittest person in the firm. But leave your sweets at home. The mere mention of dress-down Friday had trainees guffawing in disapproval. *"It's pretty sad isn't it? So middle-aged. It's like 'Let's wear jeans and jumpers and act fun for the day!'"*

The Exeter office is in a charming, if freezing cold, terrace, which is *"a bit of a rabbit warren."* How appropriate – you'll be hopping up and down the stairs since there are no lifts. Promised new digs have not yet materialised so, for the moment, the Exeter colony will be huddling together for warmth. Plymouth, meanwhile, is a former television studio, complete with soundproofed rooms where nobody will hear you stutter like a novice into your Dictaphone. For lunch you can take your sangers to the waterfront and *"listen to the seagulls and watch the boats"* – it beats queuing up with 200 others at Starbucks in Moorgate. On weekends, Dartmoor is on your doorstep for walking or visiting friends in prison.

getting a foothold

Some of us on the *Student Guide* have a sideline in psychological profiling, so we asked ourselves: 'Who is the archetypal Foot Anstey trainee?' While diverse in age, background and education, most have a strong connection to the region or, even better, to the firm itself. Some were paralegals before applying for training contracts; one had done unpaid work experience, while another won a Foot Anstey-sponsored university prize. The preference for locals is entirely understandable given the risk of NQ *"brain drain."* You can imagine the firm's frustration when trainees skip off to Lovells immediately on qualification. It seems that *"people who come from other areas generally only experience the South West as a holiday destination, tend to qualify and leave fairly quickly."* The message is: if you think only sailors visit the Plymouth Hoe, best stick to London. This firm wants people *"who understand the area and who realise that Plymouth and Exeter aren't London, and they're not Bristol either!"* One of the two qualifiers stayed with the firm in September 2003.

the sweet smell of success

Mature applicants, breathe a sigh of relief. Your skills, experience and past lives are positively welcomed here. The oldest trainee is a 48-year-old defector from the police force; another is a former marketing manager with IBM and a mother of two; and yet another is a drama graduate who managed a chiropractor's office. *"They are imaginative enough to realise that a mature trainee might have something to offer,"* commented one source. The favour is returned with gratitude from trainees who feel a *"great sense of loyalty to the firm."* There is also the usual school-university-gap year-training contract bunch.

The selection process is famously rigorous, and that's how the masochists in grad recruitment like it. *"We like to put them under pressure and make them sweat a bit."* Crack out that roll-on, because you'll be subjected to an assessment day with the works: an interview and written test, conducted alongside 20 other perspiring hopefuls. The five or so who make the cut are invited back to give a short presentation on a person of their choosing. Your deepest darkest psychoses will then be exposed in a psychometric test. Yikes!

The firm pays well compared to others in the region, *"but they expect you to deliver."* Of the firm's 27 partners, a very healthy eight of them are women, including the managing partner.

and finally...

Foot Anstey Sargent is a firm with a clear vision of its future as a regional leader, so if you share its ambition and commitment to the West Country, get your skates on. It's as simple as that.

Ford & Warren

the facts

Location: Leeds
UK ranking by size: 150
Total number of trainees: 11
Seats: 4x6 months
Alternative seats: None

Ford & Warren is a no-nonsense northern firm. Based in the centre of Leeds, it has an excellent reputation in transport law, employment and commercial litigation and is managing to expand at a time when many other firms are suffering.

mucking in

"You're not going to get glossy work here," said one trainee, presumably referring to an absence of *FT* headline deals. What you will get is the chance to sample a wide variety of seats from corporate to family. The firm is particularly strong on transport law and

acts for clients including First Great Western, Travel West Midlands and the Road Haulage Association. Employment is another highly rated group; it represents, among others, Leeds City Council and various NHS trusts. Seats in employment are very popular, (*"good reputation, good people"*) as are stints in commercial litigation (*"it's interesting, there's lots of variety and you don't get treated like a battery hen"*). You're quite likely to spend time in private client, a positively Tardis-like group where you could be doing anything from investment work to acting in clinical negligence cases for clients suffering from cerebral palsy.

Property comes a lot lower down in the pecking order. Most of those we spoke to belonged to the property-allergic school, calling it *"tiresome and tedious,"* and *"a sausage machine operation where I was counting down from day one."* The main problems seem to be long hours and repetitive work; the trainees moaned about acres of proofreading and having to make endless phone calls to environmental health officers. Poor old property, does it get good press anywhere?

crop rotation

In terms of seat allocation, most of our sources were satisfied, although we did hear of one or two problems like having to extend or truncate seats when you least wanted to. Some felt there could be a bit more consultation and flexibility when it came to dividing up the spade work: *"I get the impression that there is a plan and you can't really say no when they've decided where to put you."* When it came to the appraisal system, trainees spoke very positively, with most having chats with their supervisors every few days and more formal feedback every month. Trainees also liked sitting together in trainee banks in the open-plan office, saying: *"It's really good to have the support system when you have a question you'd feel stupid asking your supervisor."* The firm's offices also get a big thumbs-up; trainees wax lyrical about the location right in the centre of Leeds. F&W has recently expanded into the whole of its building, which we choose to visualise as a seven-storey castle, since it was described that way last year.

reap what you sow

In a relatively small firm like this *"there's nowhere to hide,"* so forget playing sardines with your supervisor at lunchtime. Of course, this is a serious point – nearly every trainee told us that at F&W *"you get out what you put in."* Hard work will be acknowledged and appreciated; on the flipside: *"It's no good if you're rubbish. If you don't seem that bothered, it will come across. People aren't daft here."* You gotta love those no-nonsense Yorkshire folk! We heard of partners being reluctant to dish out good work if they felt the effort wasn't being put in, and trainees also told us they felt the need to work late in the run-up to qualification. Trainees feel confident of not being thrown out into the snow on qualification. Even if it's not able to offer a permanent job, the firm still looks after its NQs; in the past some have been found stopgap jobs until a place comes up in the department they want, or until they can find something at another firm. In September 2003, two of the four qualifiers stayed with the firm.

trained to perfection

The working day runs from around 9am till 6pm, but as the firm's website tells us: "There's no such thing as a free lunch." Trainees confirm this: *"The place has a 100% work ethic. Everyone's very conscientious and I'm being trained to reach perfection.'* For some, F&W could do with more *"social exchange;"* others couldn't have disagreed more. Thankfully for our researcher, they all agreed that the firm is about *"good lawyering"* not *"getting headlines,"* something that is reflected in the firm's policy not to market its services aggressively, but to rely on word of mouth. The firm shies away from flashiness on its back-to-basics website...and in its dress code: you won't find anyone trying to be trendy by slipping on a pair of chinos on Friday. Moreover, on occasion e-mails have even been circulated when the powers that be have noticed the trainee flock looking undergroomed.

F&W certainly has a personality all of its own – and it's the managing partner. Everyone had something to say about the man, especially the girls. In the past we've heard whispers that he's a bit of a practical joker; this year we got the sense that stand-up comic would be nearer the mark. *"He's one of the best public speakers I've ever seen,"* said one source. Another declared: *"He has a cheeky face"* and *"just amuses me."* If he ever wants to give up the law to goof around on the *Student Guide,* our editor will give him a try out.

The firm organises cricket and football teams and there's a well-attended Christmas party. More informal socialising tends to centre around departmental groupings; the trainees don't really do that much together. Perhaps they don't need to huddle together for fun – they all seem to have local connections, so going out with workmates isn't always a priority. We sensed a split between those involved in social activities (*"a hard-core group…who go out every Friday"*) and those who aren't, but as we always say, there's nothing wrong with Channel 4 sitcoms or a good book at the end of a hard week.

and finally…

With its no mess, no fuss approach, Ford & Warren will give you a solid training, but you'll have to earn your keep. If anyone tries to talk you into a training contract with the firm, we reckon you can believe what you hear.

Fosters

the facts

Location: Norwich, Bungay, Wymondham
UK ranking by size: 324
Total number of trainees: 13
Seats: 3x12 months
Alternative seats: None
Extras: Pro-bono – CABx, free legal surgery

Fosters is essentially an elite East Anglian high street firm with the broad spread of family, personal injury, litigation, property and probate work that you'd expect. Look more closely and you'll also spot a distinctive training contract.

family planning

Fosters is growing; one trainee even said: *"It has doubled in size since I've been here."* Although the roll-call isn't quite Paris, New York, Hong Kong etc, Fosters lays claim to seven offices across East Anglia. All but the three main ones referred to in the fact box are *"outposts"* used only for client meetings. Norwich is the HQ and this is where most trainees spend the entirety of their training contracts. Bungay offers mainly mediation services and Wymondham concentrates on property and PI cases. But things are about to change; a new building in Wymondham is *"ten times the size"* of the current office and *"the aim is to get someone from every department there."*

While Fosters' traditional strengths lie in family law, an ongoing campaign to beef up the commercial department means it has swelled from two to five fee earners and now *"rivals other firms targeting small and medium-sized businesses."* Trainees tell us *"the firm is on the move"* and that *"vast numbers of trainees are being taken on."* We also heard that Fosters has sometimes felt like it's at *"saturation point – they didn't know where to put us all,"* but it also means the firm has a youthful atmosphere. For those among you planning world domination (or at least a legal career in Norfolk), it's not unheard of to make the leap from humble NQ to feet-on-the-desk partner in just three years.

three for all

Fosters has an unusual training scheme that our sources described as a *"rare and valuable"* opportunity. No one we spoke to could remember anyone not being offered a job on qualification and, for this reason, Fosters insists on doing things *"the Fosters way"* – a three-year training. This means that, in the eyes of the Law Society, your first year at Fosters is technically a paralegal year. However, as far as the firm is concerned, it's very much best foot forward from day one. In family, property and litigation, you can expect to be running your own files within a month or so. Each training seat lasts for a full year and, as a result, our sources said they felt like – and were treated as – NQs by the end of the seat. Actually, why mess around with that whole rotation business if you don't want to? As long as you fulfil Law Society requirements, trainees can spend as long as they want in a particular seat. Many of them come to Fosters because they have a strong interest in family or crime, but the system still caters for those who aren't sure what will ultimately suit them. Despite the fact that you'll emerge with a lot of experience, the extra year of training can make the whole process feel like a bit of a slog, especially as the extra year means trainee pay.

In many smaller general practice or 'high street' firms, the trade-off for buckets of responsibility is that you won't get as much formal training as your peers in commercial practice. However, Fosters' managing partner Andrew Saul is *"very hot"* on training and runs a two-day client skills course for everyone in the firm. In addition, at regular trainee meetings, speakers from various departments present sessions on topics of interest. Nevertheless, the bottom line is that *"if you like learning on the job then Fosters will suit you."*

Because trainees are recruited on a rolling basis to start straight away or even a year or two in advance, seat rotation isn't always a perfectly synchronised ballet. Indeed, *"people might not know they're moving until a few days before."* Physical seating problems generally get resolved quickly, but trainees felt that more advance warning was needed so they could wind up their caseload before moving on. The word on the street is that seat allocation is indeed going to become more formalised.

godfathers of norwich

Family is the biggest department and *"the good majority of trainees end up doing a seat there."* As well as giving divorce, cohabitation and custody advice, you could also be seeking injunctions against the perpetrators of domestic violence and liaising with housing associations and women's refuges. It's all *"good stuff"* and you'll even get to go to court to do your own directions hearings. The client base includes people who are paying privately and those receiving legal aid.

When we were told that there's a lot of overlap at Fosters between family and crime, our first thought was of the Mafia. But no, these trainees had no time for our silliness and put us straight right away: *"The obvious example of shared clients comes in something like domestic violence cases or when a client is sent to prison and there's an issue of access to children."* But for those with a taste for serious crime, the firm takes on all kinds of juicy cases including murders, drugs conspiracy and serious fraud. Even as a trainee you can assist in these cases, but as a newly qualified the matters you'll deal with solo would be less serious, eg drunk and disorderly charges and traffic offences on which *"you get to do the talking in court."* Seats are available in the commercial, PI and property departments, and there are small mental health and private client groups.

night owls and pointy hats

Officially the hours are a straight up nine to five and in some departments everyone sticks to this religiously. But we found trainees who really care about their work and some chose to do late nights that were worthy of the City's magic circle firms. One trainee told us: *"My record is five in the morning!"* In crime, if you're on the police station duty you may be called out at any time of the day or night, but you'll get paid for it.

The firm has a fiercely contested bowling trophy that is fought over twice a year, and there are men's and women's soccer teams (*"if you like football, you'll be OK here!"*). Friday night drinks, usually at local hot spots Delaney's and Orgasmic, are generally well attended, and staff birthdays always turn into a big night out. The firm is closely involved with the local community, runs free legal advice sessions and sends all trainees down to the local CAB. The Lord Mayor's Parade in Norwich is also something that Fosters enthusiastically supports, this year dressing all staff in Harry Potter-style robes and pointy hats.

and finally...

Fosters may not be Hogwarts, but it offers three years of intense training.

Freethcartwright LLP

the facts

Location: Nottingham, Leicester, Derby
UK ranking by size: 70
Total number of trainees: 14
Seats: 4x6 months
Alternative seats: None

With offices in Nottingham, Leicester and Derby, Freethcartwright is one of the largest law firms in the East Midlands. It handles commercial property, corporate and commercial services, private client and personal litigation (clinical negligence, product liability and personal injury). If you like the idea of *"a big firm without the big city,"* read on…

flexible friends

Trainees are based in Nottingham, where the firm is split between four sites, though most also spend some time in Leicester or Derby. With no compulsories, they are given a free(ish) rein over seat selection, although one of our sources felt that having so much choice caused anxiety. In the past, the firm's top-notch reputation for clinical negligence and PI have seen trainees rushing to be first in line and, last year, commercial property was also deemed to be one of the coolest places to hang out. This year there seems to have been less of a scramble for particular seats. Also on offer in Nottingham are commercial services and employment law. Trainees venture to Leicester for private client, and more clin neg and PI, while a new slot in Derby offers commercial property and construction.

Our sources appreciated that the firm *"does its level best"* for them when it came to their training, and this flexible approach seemed to extend beyond the allocation of seats. While a one-week vacation placement is a relatively common route into a training contract, an increasing number start out as paralegals. We also understand that, though the exception rather than the rule, the firm's flexibility has extended to giving a part-time training contract to one young mum. Most trainees have some experience of Nottingham before joining the firm, be this at one of the two universities or because they grew up in the area.

i'm sticking like glue…

When Freethcartwright rebranded a few years ago and lost the gap in its name, we asked ourselves whether the firm was as closely bonded in reality as the consonants in its name. This year a troop of devotees described a wholly unified firm, which has won their long-term loyalty. To fill you in on the back-story, a little while ago Freeths rearranged itself from a many-sided object into a simpler, sleeker, more commercial entity. In so doing, it also *"constructed a better image."* Trainees are acutely aware of the firm's commercial push; one source went so far as to tell us: *"There is nothing of the old firm left."* Trainees think one more thing would cement the new look: *"A brand spanking new building, bringing the commercial division under one roof."* How convenient: that is precisely what is on the agenda for November 2003.

Most of Freeths' commercial clients are Midlands-based private companies and owner-managed businesses, but there are also some plcs. Names like HMV Media and Waterstones are among the most recognisable. A £15 million deal would be seen as a healthy instruction; however, the firm has received one as big as £65 million. The property department has grown enormously across the three locations and, with clients including the likes of Nottinghamshire County Council and John Mowlem, it is fast becoming a flagship practice area. It recently hired a chartered town planner to add weight to the planning and environmental side of things.

The construction team was boosted by the arrival of new lawyers from Wragge & Co and Farrer & Co, and saw client wins to add to a list filled with a number of public bodies and universities. It recently developed an association with leading niche London construction firm, Fenwick Elliott in order to promote new business. Litigation and other forms of dispute resolution are staples, and the firm is recognised for its expertise in this area. And if sport is your thing, how about a team handling international motorsport, cricket, football and rugby matters.

With a new chairman holding the reins and recently acquired LLP (limited liability partnership) status, trainees describe a firm that is profit-driven and ambitious. So does this mean it's all MBOs, MBIs and 80-page commercial leases? Certainly not. Top-flight negligence actions, such as the Leicester cervical smear fiasco and the case of Wayne Jowett, who died after being given a drug by injection that should have been given orally, keep Freethcartwright's profile high. The clin neg team also leads the Trilucent breast implant settlement scheme and is working on the MMR multiparty claim. All of this suggests that the new image is certainly not one-dimensional.

have a nice trip

Talking to trainees, it was hard to ignore the not so subliminal *"work hard, play hard"* message we heard replayed, again and again...and again. The most popular answer to a variety of questions, we wondered if this phrase was some new management slogan, or even the mantra of the Gospel according to Saint Freeth. However, there does seem to be an element of truth in the message. Though *"there are no guns held to heads"* (we should hope not), and *"no photocopying"* (ditto) none of the trainees we spoke to felt they had soft-pedalled through their time at the firm. Everyone just *"gets on with their stuff and keeps their head down."* An abundance of client contact comes with comensurate supervision, and *"while the firm will let you trip, it will never let you fall."* In addition to a comprehensive appraisal system, open-plan offices also make it easier for trainees to learn the ropes more quickly. While the office layout helps seniors *"keep a close eye"* according to one source, others felt it helped them *"to be kept in the loop, ask questions and chat."* About work, we trust...

kiss and tell

If you're wondering where all the hard play fits in, the answer is in The Slug & Lettuce next door to the Low Pavement office in Nottingham. Our trainees told us that *"bizarrely, after spending a week in the office with you, there will always be freeths people there who are pleased to see you."* Other trainee, departmental and firm-wide jollies seem to be rather overshadowed by the Christmas Party where the annual trainees' sketch this year saw Abba taking on the Spice Girls (and taking off the partners) in Popstars The Rivals fashion. Such raucous behaviour was put down to an unpoliced drinks voucher system, and beds for the night at the hotel venue. The Summer BBQ, we are assured, is a more sedate affair.

Despite an old reputation for being *"pretty big drinkers,"* the Derby representative amongst our interviewees quashed the rumour, saying that while a few people might go for a quick drink occasionally, there were *"no secret drinking clubs."* The same cannot be said of the 'up for it' Leicester contingent; reliable sources tell us that, not satisfied with one festive frenzy, each Christmas they surreptitiously sneak off to a large marquee on an airfield to join a throbbing mass of 1,000 other professional revellers. Play hard? We think so.

When it comes to playing hard to get, however, it is an altogether different story. With a male to female ratio of 1:3, the city of Nottingham was always destined to be a hotbed of passion; we quickly cottoned on to the romance in the air at Freethcartwright. *"It is a little bit incestuous,"* one source revealed, *"but nobody minds, as long as you're not nipping off to the stationery cupboard all the time!"* While we would never recommend picking a firm based on your chances of finding true love, Freeths has got to be a hot bet. In September 2003, six of the eight qualifying trainees stayed with the firm.

and finally...

For top-flight clinical negligence and personal injury work, Freethcartwight is a winner. Those looking to be trained in commercial practice, with a view to settling into a career in the East Midlands, will also find an excellent training.

Freshfields Bruckhaus Deringer

the facts

Location: London
UK ranking by size: 6
Total number of trainees: 181
Seats: 3 or 6 months long
Alternative seats: Overseas seats, secondments
Extras: Pro bono – RCJ CAB, Tower Hamlets Law Centre, FRU, death row appeals, language training

Sitting in the magic circle, Freshfields Bruckhaus Deringer radiates quality on a global scale. For an utterly respectable training in an utterly respectable corporate deal-driven firm, get ready to impress.

mix and match

For multibillion-pound corporate deals, follow the sign that says 'Freshfields'. Its clients include the biggest names – ICI, Kingfisher Group, Reuters, Powergen, Tesco and Reed Elsevier. Its recent deals include the $2.5bn acquisition of Enex Resources and Duiker Mining by Xstrata, the £712m sale of Travel Lodge and Little Chef by Compass Group, and the $2.3bn cash sale of ABB's structured finance business to GE Capital. The firm is also a high flyer in a host of supporting areas such as environment, pensions, competition, tax and public international law. If it's an international training you are after, the firm has feathered nests as far afield as Moscow and Madrid, Bangkok and Bratislava, Hanoi and Ho Chi Minh. Even if you stay put in Ol' Blighty, you can expect to be working on cross-border matters for much of your two years, especially in the corporate department.

The seat system mixes seats of six months with seats of three. Your first assignment is chosen for you and thereafter, *"they do ask you for your preferences"* though time in litigation, corporate and finance are all compulsory. Do not expect to get by on less than nine months of corporate and finance work in your two years. This year employment and litigation proved most popular; *"lots of people went for litigation on qualification – over 20 people applied for very few places."* More generally, the message is that *"the niche departments are small and sometimes they simply don't recruit. Full stop."* Never forget what the firm's main business actually is. If you are dead set on being, say a litigator or an employment lawyer, ask yourself why you aren't considering firms that specialise in these areas.

long haul

On the subject of the litigation experience, one trainee told us: *"Apart from the advocacy course, you would be very lucky to even see it, let alone do it."* However, wherever you are in the firm, you will be seeing and doing plenty of other training through a rigorous programme that includes a three-week induction, departmental sessions and optional courses on public speaking and presentation and grooming skills.

As for the flexible seat system, for every source telling us *"six months means you can raise your profile with partners and prove yourself a bit more,"* there was someone else saying *"with three-month seats you get to see more of the firm."* You decide. Most people who want to work abroad do so in their final seat. New York offers largely finance work; Hong Kong and Singapore offer corporate seats; Moscow offers more of a mix. There's no way we could detail it all here, so let's just say the choice of postings is wide. Freshfields also offers client secondments to IBM, Morgan Stanley and Reuters among others. While they may not be as glamorous as six months in an exotic location, for the right person they provide valuable insights into the clients' perspective. *"If you ask to go abroad or on secondment, they will expect a bit more sway in where they put you before that...this is where bargaining power comes in."*

bluebirds

Just like Freshfields' trainees, we've grown weary of talking about the stereotypes in the City, but we thought one trainee was too modest for their own good when they said: *"Freshfields was once the firm of blues and blondes. I don't have a blue. I am a brunette. And I am also quite ugly."* True, the firm has a high percentage of trainees, assistants and partners who attended Oxbridge colleges – as do the other top City firms – but these particular alma maters are not a prerequisite. The current trainee population is drawn from 45 universities across the UK and beyond.

Never a victim of *"management marketing gimmicky stuff,"* the firm has long maintained the Freshfield family crest as its logo. It's a slightly outdated symbol of a blue angel that brings to mind private healthcare or perhaps missionary activities overseas. Neither notion is far off the mark: Freshfields offers excellent service for those prepared to pay for it, and has most certainly been spreading the word across the globe. Our *"scrupulously honest"* sources made no bones about telling us that *"someone who wanted to save the world would be coming to the wrong place."* Here, *"you aren't using the law to protect the little people, you are just serving your clients."*

Time and again we were told about Freshfields' emphasis on teamwork. This is a firm where partners were sent on training days to learn how to change tyres on racing cars and to mimic the honking noises made by geese as a sign of encouragement during flight. Apparently *"the whole focus is on the team"* and there is a *"very collegiate feel."* And a jolly good thing too. No matter how honourable, decent and gentlemanly a firm may be, at 4am when you haven't been home for three days and you're up to your neck in it you'll be glad of all the camaraderie.

the hitch

Let's be clear, in any top-flight City firm, you will have to work hard. Very hard. Freshfields has carried a reputation for having *"the worst hours in the City,"* but we find no evidence to say they are worse than anywhere else in the magic circle. One wise sage advised students to be *"aware of the work ethic, so you aren't shocked – some coming through are a little blind."* Indeed. Have your eyes open when you go in, and a box of matchsticks at the ready. A quick straw poll suggests that *"50 hours per week is par for the course and that can go up to 80 just as a trainee."* There is no obvious guilt culture, though one source hit the nail on the head, by saying: *"You do feel weird walking out at 5.30pm. It happens so rarely that you feel like a part-timer if you do."* Everyone has a horror story to tell, but Freshfields' trainees are a philosophical bunch. While *"you will have to learn how to cancel social functions"* and *"you are expected to work the hours without complaining,"* the firm does give time off in lieu after particularly gruesome spells. *"They recognise that they do make extreme demands, and therefore treat you as a valuable asset."* And the infamous M&S shirt vouchers after a sweaty night of proofreading? One person suggested that *"there is a shirt buying system if needed;"* another refuted the claim: *"I have long counted the times when I have had to soldier on in the same shirt."* Whatever. What we do know is that trainees here get *"corporate discounts at TM Lewins and Hatton Garden jewellers, which are useful if you are planning on getting engaged."* Oh, that it were so easy...

The firm offers *"superb support."* Freshfields has fewer trainees than at close rival Linklaters and more paralegals than you could shake a stick at. When we asked, the firm conducted a headcount and came up with a grand total of 126. *"If your computer breaks down at 3am there is someone there to fix it."* On the topic of doing/avoiding grunt work, one source told us: *"You won't be running a multimillion pound transaction on your own, but you should be doing things that add value. If it were otherwise, we would be the most expensive photocopiers in the City."* While one source said: *"It is sometimes hard to sniff out the really good work, if you are lucky you will get it,"* another described the firm's small-team approach to deals as a *"baptism of fire."* When we were told: *"You won't get client interaction in a meaningful sense of the words,"* we couldn't help but wonder if that is because Freshfields' trainees do actually know the meaningful sense of the words. Troops of paralegals and support staff will not pave your way to the front line of a huge international transaction, but they will keep you from falling behind in a mire of Tipp-Ex and toner.

Trainees have developed an expectation of proper grown-up work and to be referred to as *"my colleague"* rather than *"my trainee."* With this comes proper, grown-up feedback: there is *"constructive criticism and constructive praise"* and *"it is rare for work to go by without being commented on."* You will share an office with either a partner or an associate and *"supervisors are more like mentors."* Respectful, receptive…and a whole lot of honking.

timeless classics

While the firm is *"traditional in the sense of values and the way we work"* it is *"not antiquated."* This is not high fashion, and probably never will be, but who cares? If you believe the best outfits are the ones that you can keep for years, bring out for every first date/job interview/dinner with parents and know that every time you wear it someone will say "Wow, you look fantastic!" then you may well be Freshfields material. Its application form is infamous for *"that blank sheet of paper."* Applicants are given the opportunity to write about themselves in their own style, without the restrictions of formulaic questions, tiny boxes and uncompromising word-counts. Surprised? Don't be. We were told: *"They do want the best people, but they don't mind where those people come from. You sink or swim by your own efforts, not by your background. The firm is successful, but not elitist."*

Trainees believe that *"everyone has their feet on the ground"* and *"everyone has worked hard to get here."* These were the kids at school who not only pulled top grades, but also ran sports teams, the debating society and the drama club. *"There is no arrogance or complacency"* and *"people don't pull rank."* Of course, *"there is a hierarchy and the partners pretty much rule the roost,"* but while *"you are always aware of where you stand in the pecking order, the barriers are fairly fluid."* We asked our sources why they chose Freshfields over other magic circle firms. At first many disputed that there was much between the firms, but after a while we sensed that Freshfields' well-mannered approach had played a part. That and the fact that *"when you have one of the best law firms in the world offering you a place and good money, you generally don't turn your nose up at it."* Nothing trendy, nothing brash, nothing controversial, no crowd-pleasing moves. Freshfields will not spin plates and jump through hoops to get your attention.

Like most corporate firms, this has not been the sweetest year for Freshfields, with a lower number of qualifiers than usual staying on (89 out of 98 in 2003) and press headlines about the loss of two large clients, we were unsurprised to hear of *"a slightly demoralised feeling."* More generally, this is a firm where people say: *"Okay, that's bad news. Let's just keep going."*

the good life

The firm has enough sports teams to field an Olympic squad, plus a fair number of theatre and museum trips, departmental Christmas and summer parties to keep the team spirit alive. More usually, it's just ad hoc drinks at The Witness Box or The Cheshire Cheese on Fleet Street. On the work hard, play hard cliché, we were warned: *"It is more the former than the latter."* A day in the office could incorporate yoga, aerobics or spinning (cycling variety, rather than the Tom and Barbara variety). The snug gym has recently been refurbished – it's no bigger we're afraid, but it is nevertheless now more pleasant.

The premises were built at two different times and our sources sheepishly admitted that they prefer the older of the two that fronts onto Fleet Street. Why? *"The new one is all very white and sterile – it looks like a lunatic asylum or a spaceship."* Attention to detail is everything: there's a doctor, a dentist and a masseur on site, you have cabs to take you home at the end of a long night, and the kitchens contain *"nine or ten different types of tea, and coffee, biscuits of course, oh, and fruit."* All this in addition to a *"wonderful canteen"* and an onsite Costa Coffee. Spoilt rotten!

and finally...

Freshfields wants high flyers. Applicants to the firm want world-class work. Both parties know they have to deliver the goods.

Galbraith Branley

the facts

Location: London
UK ranking by size: >500
Total number of trainees: 10
Seats: number varies
Alternative seats: None

This small north London outfit specialises in crime, family, personal injury, mental health work, prison law and police actions. If you don't mind late nights, hectic days and mixing it up with those living on the margins, Galbraith Branley can offer training of unparalleled personal challenges.

thick as thieves

Crime remains the firm's biggest drawcard. The trainees we spoke to were *"not really office people,"* and all got a thrill out of interacting with clients from the troubled elements of society. The work is challenging and often stressful, but exciting and varied: *"No two days are the same and you never know how your day will end up."* One trainee had charge of nine Crown Court and 25 magistrates' court files – no mean feat for a beginner. If the hard-boiled glamour and grit of crime appeals to you, just be aware that *"the gloss wears off at 5am in Kilburn police station."*

Mental health law is a fast-growing area, so much so that the firm recently opened a second office to house its flourishing mental health and PI groups. Lawyers celebrated a high-profile victory last year regarding human rights violations of patients sectioned under the Mental Health Act; meanwhile trainees cut their advocacy teeth by representing clients at managers meetings, where patients can appeal against being sectioned. Even where their case seems hopeless, you may still have the chance to improve the quality of your client's life. The PI seat is a more conventional experience, but still offers opportunities to turn around the fortunes of individuals who have suffered because of an accident. The family department handles the usual range of matrimonial and children's law matters, giving trainees the chance to assist clients through a miserable time of life. Wherever trainees sit, research and file management work is balanced with getting out of the office and visiting prisons, police stations, hospitals and courts.

At Galbraith Branley, you learn by doing. No photocopying or grunt work here, just plunging head first into the deep end. In your first week you'll make a start on gaining your police station accreditation by learning how to interview clients in custody. Although trainees are allocated a supervisor, supervision is a task shared among all the lawyers in the office. The firm is young (its youngest partner is 31 and its oldest is in his early 40s) and buzzing with energy, and trainees soon learn that they can approach anyone for assistance. Newly qualifieds, in particular, are an invaluable source of advice and support.

the mean streets

Trainees have *"personal contact with the sort of people 99% of society don't see,"* which requires resilience and excellent communications skills. Clients range from the dangerous (*"one guy threatened to throw a punch at me"*) to the benign (*"some are quite decent people you wouldn't mind having a pint with."*) Clients aside, we heard of the frustrations of dealing with the CPS and of sometimes thorny interactions with the police. No matter how tricky or infuriating it may sometimes feel when dealing with the criminal justice machinery, trainees must learn to avoid personal animosity.

the big sleep?

You wish! Forget *"slow immersion;" "the first six weeks are like being electrocuted."* Crime in particular is very fast moving and pressurised. One trainee, who told his mentor that he was too exhausted to go out after work was informed: *"You'll be knackered for the rest of your life. Get used to it."* Although you'll often wake up tired, you'll never dread work. Mind you, *"you can't go to the police station with your brain like putty, you would be compromising someone's future."* This is *"tougher than your average job,"* but the Galbraith Branley set thrive on it and there is plenty of laughter in the office *"to deflect the stress."* If you check out the firm's website, you'll see it features remarkably attractive and well-rested lawyers posing in glamorous surrounds. We were suspicious. Sure enough, we discovered they were models. *"But our staff are very good looking!"* the practice manager assured us.

crime doesn't pay

While an economic downturn usually spells excess capacity in commercial practices, it's a boon for the criminal lawyer. Through a series of breathless, harried interviews, we began to understand just how busy our trainee sources were. Unlike their peers languishing in corporate opulence, the crime trainee is in the office at 8am, and often doesn't leave until 7.30pm. Many then take work home with them. As a criminal lawyer, you'll be on call 24 hours a day, three times a month, and much to their chagrin, trainees do not get paid overtime. Even though the salary doesn't even begin to match City money, none of those we spoke to had any complaints. There are annual bonuses, as well as extras like mobile phones and paid expenses, but the value of job satisfaction, excitement and sense of real achievement is hard to quantify. All three 2003 qualifiers stayed with the firm.

mens rea

Socially, the firm doesn't mess around. Everyone goes to the pub after work to relax, unwind and debrief. They also chew the fat on the biggest bone of contention within the firm – the football team. We're told that after *"bringing down the standard of competition,"* women were ejected from the team and now have to content themselves with cheering (or is that jeering?) from the sidelines. The firm is bloke-heavy, it has to be said, but that's surely no excuse for depriving the women of a chance to shine on the pitch.

Applicants for training contracts should have a minimum 2:1 degree and a commendation or a distinction in the LPC, but we understand that the main factor in recruitment is performance at interview. Stamina, energy and a commitment to the firm's areas of practice are absolutely essential and the firm looks favourably on applicants who worked throughout university and those who have experience of juggling multiple roles. Trainees must also own a car.

We encountered public school and state-educated trainees; several Londoners and a number from different parts of the UK. All our sources were refreshingly free of pretension: *"We're not here to change the law, we know we're operating within the system. We just try to do the best by our clients."* All were non-judgmental: *"Some people might have a problem defending a particular client. I don't care what they've done. I'm not there to judge them."* A few trainees have had family or friends caught up on the wrong side of the mental health or criminal justice systems, while others simply thrive on the challenge and rewards of the job, especially when *"you come across clients who you genuinely like, or who clearly don't deserve their lot."*

and finally...

Galbraith Branley is a firm for those who'd thrive in a casual but highly pressured work environment made bearable by lots of irreverent jokes and football talk.

Gateley Wareing

the facts

Location: Birmingham, Leicester, Nottingham
UK ranking by size: 121
Total number of trainees: 13
Seats: 4x6 months
Alternative seats: None

This commercial firm is not seeking to steal the thunder of the Birmingham bigwigs, but it is working hard to sew up the market for Midlands' business. Gateley Wareing has already garnered a lot of respect for its entrepreneurial approach in acting for smaller companies, venture capital providers and clearing banks.

otorhinolaryngology

This is a firm on a mission. In August 2003, Gateley Wareing's Birmingham HQ moved to larger, more prominent digs after investing some £12 million trimming the nasal hair from the city's former Ear, Nose and Throat Hospital. Trainees saw this move as indicative of a new sense of ambition and direction, saying: *"It is symptomatic of the firm's forward push towards bigger and better. It shows that the firm is moving up rather than standing still."* The sense of optimism was further enhanced by the news that all five of September 2003's qualifying trainees would be staying with the firm and that additional newly qualifieds were being recruited from outside the firm.

The client base, which already included some great names (Lloyds TSB Development Capital, Barclays Bank, Bank of Scotland), is expanding too. The firm has recently entered the plc market, following the recruitment of new partners, including four from national giant Hammonds.

the drapes of paradise

When it comes to new recruits, Gateley Wareing really pushes the boat out. Like the proverbial prodigal son, you'll be welcomed into the fold with open arms, food and parties. Even before you start your contract, you'll be invited to a summer party and a pizza night with your soon-to-be work buddies. When September finally comes, you'll need to pack your new briefcase and prepare to be an office celebrity. At the trainee welcome night, before the entire firm, the second year trainees will give a presentation on their supervisors, so you'll know what you're in for. The atmosphere is light-hearted and cheeky. One source recalled: *"Everyone was drinking and heckling the supervisors. There was no pressure on us – the heat was really on the partners!"* After hearing that, we weren't surprised to learn that the firm is proud of a non-hierarchical atmosphere and few among its ranks stand on ceremony.

While lawyers at some firms aspire to being *"that mystical figure behind the curtains pulling the strings,"* GW encourages its trainees, clients, you, anyone to venture behind the curtain to witness the firm's inner workings for themselves. Cue 'Backstage'— an informal part of the website containing film and gig reviews alongside interviews with partners. Depending on your viewpoint it is either a confusing and terrifying alternative universe in which lawyers are actually cool or a law firm version of being backstage at a Cliff Richard concert. Property associate Iain Davies is snapped awkwardly cradling an electric guitar, looking about as comfortable as a man in a lingerie shop; meanwhile Ishaq Kayani, looking like an extra from *Reservoir Dogs*, holds a clapperboard and offers cinematographic insights. The partner profiles feature Testino-esque black and white photos of beaming lawyers, complete with autographs. Collect all 25! But as one trainee told us: *"At least the firm is trying!"* We would agree, but it's our contractual duty to poke fun at the firm.

please sir...

On offer are the usual four seats of six months, with corporate an almost essential element. The firm also *"prefers"* trainees to do a seat in either property or construction. Property is perennially popular, largely because trainees find themselves running their own files and handling client queries. *"You feel like you're really doing your clients a service,"* said one. Insolvency is a heady cocktail of contentious and non-contentious work that most trainees also find irresistible.

While you get just a dash of client contact in insolvency, the construction seat is client-heavy. Here trainees find themselves doing plenty of drafting and being fully involved in dispute resolution. *"It was nice when we won an adjudication and I realised that a lot of it was my own work."* The recently botoxed corporate department is an exciting place, but it is not for everyone: *"You have to be the sort of person who gets excited by deals and loves working through the night."* One trainee joked that corporate don't even start meetings until 7pm, *"just to show how hard they are!"*

If it's more work you want, you need only ask for it. One trainee concluded: *"If you're seen to be asking for work, people will think of you when they have work, and they are often the nicer jobs."* Trainee chores are almost always of a good quality and fit for a person who's completed a legal education. (Hurrah!) One trainee told us proudly: *"I haven't done any menial tasks. Actually I've paginated only one lever arch file."* Indeed: *"I've seen fee earners do their own pagination!"* It seems that *"the automatic instinct is not to give the bad work to trainees."* And don't expect to be *"tapping gently on the partners' doors, waiting scared, for them to look up,"* here you can kick down the door and march right in! Apparently.

Most of our sources had a connection with the Midlands and a real sense of regional loyalty. The archetypal trainee is also seriously hardworking and seriously sociable – *"We're never looking for an excuse to get out of social events."* You must be prepared to slot into a lively, firm-wide culture, so *"if you're shy, you might not like it."*

centre stage

Trainees were attracted by the firm's compact size and the quality of its work. One, who had worked at a Birmingham giant, described it as *"so big you kind of got lost, but you never feel lost in the system here."* And all this gave trainees a sense of *"greater opportunity." "We are really pushed to the forefront, not in the background doing nasty work."* Our sources all wanted to avoid the tireless slog of the capital, yet the hours at Gateley Wareing are not to be underestimated. Trainees are in the office by 8.30am and although they are out by 6pm most days, late nights are on the cards in corporate. We suspect that hard work is the norm. Indeed, if their availability in May 2003 is any indication, trainees work flat out most of the time.

Our sources indicated that the firm's lawyers were once notorious for their *"work hard, play hard, drink hard"* mentality, and although Gateley Wareing is still a famously sociable firm, the *"out every night"* reputation is fading. Trainees sit on the firm's social committee helping to organise events. There's a local bash once a month, and every third month the offices get together for a firm-wide knees-up. Transport is provided for the Leicester and Nottingham crews, so there's no excuse for non-attendance. Events vary from drinks and buffets to quizzes, casino nights and fancy dress parties. The quizzes get very competitive.

Last year, we reported a stark gender imbalance in the partner ranks. We can report that the firm has been redressing (so to speak) the balance. In 2002 five female trainees were taken on, and with recent lateral hires the number of female partners has increased to three, with several rising female associates.

and finally...

Gateley Wareing is a buzzing hive and the noises emanating from it are getting louder. If it's diverse training in a successful and fast-growing Midlands commercial firm you're after, you might want to make a beeline for this one.

Gosschalks

the facts

Location: Hull
UK ranking by size: 205
Total number of trainees: 8
Seats: 4x6 months
Alternative Seats: None

Vying for top billing with a couple of other commercial firms in Hull, Gosschalks defines itself by the ties it enjoys with local business, but it also acts for national companies and has a stellar licensing practice.

the hull story

Despite having been important as a port, an industrial centre and a strategic royalist stronghold in the civil war, Kingston-upon-Hull tends to be an afterthought in the national consciousness, not least because of its geographical isolation. At the end of the M62, the end of the railway line, in the middle of one of the flattest bits of the country, Hull seems destined to be deeply unfashionable in comparison to the more glamorous cities of Leeds and York. If you think this means it has little to offer budding lawyers, you'd be very wrong.

Some people are born in Hull and stay, others come to Hull and stay. The folk at Gosschalks are no exception to this principle and have shown devotion to the city since Maurice Victor Gosschalk founded the firm back in the late 19th century. As well as recruiting natives, it is happy to take on trainees from further afield who have succumbed to the Hull effect. Our sources emphasised the importance of Gosschalks' position as *"a main player in Hull"* and the need to *"be able to relate to people from all walks of life."* Then another trainee told us: *"We pride ourselves on our client interaction"* and our northern-cliché-o-meter flicked immediately to 'straight-talking northern values' alert. A klaxon sounded in the office (we quickly muffled it with a coat) but we already knew what we'd be in for over the next two days – stories of a firm with a no-nonsense approach and its feet on the ground.

Unlike a certain Hull rival, Gosschalks does not have historical connections with shipping; instead it has developed relationships with emerging local businesses and grown with them. Dixon Motors is a good example – it started as a small Hull-based company, but attained national status and was bought by outside concerns. It continues to consult the firm on various matters, wherever they arise in the UK.

pub talk

One source described being encouraged to experience *"a broad range of training,"* and it soon became clear that the scope of the firm's work made that a realistic proposition. The firm operates a four-seat system with no compulsories and the usual end-of-seat appraisals. Commercial property is by far the largest department, although unfortunately it's the least favoured by trainees because it involves *"little client contact, a lot of research, a lot of drafting, a lot of title investigations."* That'd be property law for you. There are two seats in the department, succinctly defined by one trainee as: *"One for the pub side, one for the non-pub side."* That'd be straight talking for you. If you consider that most pub chains have scores of properties, then you can easily imagine the attendant workload when your firm acts for several. As for the non-pub seat, we hear it covers *"construction and new developments."* But, knowing just how prominent Gosschalks' licensing department was, we wanted to talk more about pubs... Wizard Inns and Spirit (formerly Punch Taverns), for example, use the firm for their licensing requirements, as do bookies William Hill. Due to the nature of the department's work it is not usual for seats to be offered, but we believe that handwringing and begging might just swing things for you. The pub companies bring in a lot of work for the commercial and employment departments as well as the property department, and so trainees do get plenty of exposure to them. Seats in the closely allied commercial and employment departments are very popular, despite the fact that in the former you tend to be *"a small cog."* However, one source told us: *"The involvement was enough for my abilities."* Trainees assist with *"small internal company transactions, share purchases, statutory books and board minutes"* on deals in the several thousand to several million pound bracket.

The *"ton of client contact"* makes the litigation department an especially attractive prospect, offering trainees the chance to take on small files *"from opening to completion"* and to tackle a little advocacy. We learned that autonomy was most likely on PI matters, but that commercial litigation also *"gives you the chance to get your hands dirty."* After feedback from previous generations of trainees, the family law seat has been restructured so as to give *"a lot more responsibility more quickly."* One trainee's account said it all: *"At first I shadowed a partner for every court hearing and interview, then I started taking first interviews on my own, then took whole files myself."* The department also has what may be a national first, a fledgling nursery law team, which aims initially to target local childcare companies in the wake of new legislation. Who knows, maybe it'll go national like the licensing team, but at this stage it illustrates something that Gosschalks is generally very good at – cross-selling. *"Nursery law will hopefully get us a lot of local business and will also sell the firm as a package,"* one source confirmed.

larkin' around

Not known for pretension, the city's slogan was for many years 'It's never dull in Hull'. We were also reminded of one of the city's most famous lifelong residents, Philip Larkin, who was scarcely noted for joy and ebullience either in word or deed. Hull has not experienced the sort of renaissance that has transformed some cities' centres and psyches in recent years, but there is certainly life and fun to be had here. Friday night generally sees a motley crew of trainees, lawyers, partners and other staff making for Lloyds or the Jazz Bar. The firm is typified by a relaxed hierarchy at work and at leisure; each year the youngest trainee is forced to give a speech at the Christmas party, which usually involves public humiliation on the part of the partners. Last year the senior partner was in the mood for a speech too, only he decided to impart his words of wisdom while dressed in drag.

Situated slap bang in the middle of the city centre, standing atop a reclaimed dock, Gosschalks' purpose-built offices have recently been refurbished and an extra floor was created to ease the pressures of growth. With average working hours of 8.30am to 5.30pm, there's plenty of time for late-night shopping at The Only Shopping Centre on Stilts in the Universe™, Princess Quay. If you do need to ask for directions, make sure you speak Hull...you'll be looking for Prinny Keh. Unfortunately, in September 2003, the firm was only able to retain one of its three September qualifiers. The figure is usually higher.

and finally...

Gosschalks offers an excellent breadth of training and a sophistication of work that might not be expected in the region. If you've read this far, you'll probably already know Hull and you might even know about the firm. Even if neither are familiar, don't write them off – you won't be excluded.

Halliwell Landau

the facts

Location: Manchester, London, Sheffield
UK ranking by size: 34
Total number of trainees: 27
Seats: 5x21 weeks
Alternative seats: Secondments
Extras: Pro bono – Manchester Uni Advice Centre

Was this the year when the Halliwell Landau bubble finally burst? Did its super soar-away success come a cropper with attendant disarray, like a teenager discovering last month's growth spurt means his prized twisted Levis just don't fit any more? Absolutely not. In a depressed market you just can't argue with the achievement of becoming The UK's Most Profitable Regional Firm™. This Manchester firm's success story has a few chapters in it yet.

resistance is futile

So, the Halliwells blitzkrieg has continued unchecked: we've seen lateral expansion in the newer London site combined with vigorous growth in Manchester, where, for example, the addition of a specialist environment team is proof of the firm's zest for the new. It's clear there's precious little laurel-sitting going on here, and trainees had plenty to say about Halliwells' expansion: seeing the firm as *"vibrant, going places, progressive and ambitious;"* they even suggested competitors are *"scared of the firm,* [it's] *well known for driving things forward."*

Manchester is no longer big enough to contain this firm, and once we'd figured it out, we rather liked one trainee's (complex) analysis of the plans for future growth. *"It is now as important, if not more important, that Halliwells' significance as a national firm becomes entrenched, than the expansion of the Manchester operation continues."* The firm recruits into both its Manchester and London offices, and it's worth mentioning that it is now several years into a successful scheme whereby promising paralegals can take up training contracts.

can i have a p please, bob

Now, whilst Halliwells' publicity material might have you believe that its offices are a futuristic hive of automated, voice-activated gadgets and web-linked client management systems, all piloted by a stellar crew of half-human machines bent on national domination, by contrast its website reminds us of the classic TV quiz, *Blockbusters*. And from the accounts of the teething troubles experienced with the new five seat system implemented this year, it would be too easy to assume it was modelled on just such an example of cosy British inefficiency. According to our sources, trainees often had only *"one or two weeks' notice of seats. People have had no idea where they are going."* But let's not be too quick to judge; on further investigation we learned that efforts to slot fifth-seaters into the most appropriate pre-qualification seat was the reason for the delay. Getting it right takes time.

The IP and employment departments remain the most popular; however, they are small and they offer fewer seats. Of the larger departments, property was universally praised as *"a glamorous department,"* and litigation is *"especially popular in the London office."* Corporate was mentioned as the least popular department, but given the great variety of chemical, sports, manufacturing and insurance companies from whom the firm receives some rather good instructions, we really hope this is an aberration. Most importantly, trainees describe the firm as *"prepared to accommodate people"* in their choices and confirm there are no strictly compulsory seats.

With the expansion of the London office, it is becoming increasingly common for Manchester trainees to spend a seat in the capital or vice versa, and seats are available in the Sheffield insurance litigation office should anyone want one. Furthermore, if your tastes run towards a secondment in an industry position, then your chances are pretty good: AstraZeneca regularly takes trainees and we were told about one lucky so and so who spent six months at Umbro working on the England Football Team contract, acquiring a quantity of signed merchandise into the bargain.

a mellow moment

Halliwells is described by many outsiders as an aggressive firm. It hates the description, fearing that it may be attributed to its office culture as well as its pursuit of business. So we decided to ask trainees just how exactly things slid down to the junior end of the corporate grease pole. As one put it: *"Cases are approached aggressively with a determination to win. Internally this is reflected in an awful lot of responsibility for trainees from day one. But we don't feel it's bill, bill, bill in the partners' minds."* Trainees paint a self-portrait of *"ambitious people" "who know where they're going"* and *"have something to say about themselves;"* people who are up to the challenge of *"a steep learning curve."* Here's an illustrative comment, barked sharply down the phone by one trainee: *"Autonomy, what do you call autonomy? I like to make sure everything is checked before it goes anywhere. But within that I get lots of autonomy. I deal directly and liaise with clients myself."* Once we had stopped shaking and emerged tremulously from under the desk, it occurred to us that this rigorous, can-do, go get 'em, self-starting attitude is typical of Halliwells' trainees. We stopped for a coffee break and toasted their verve.

It's definitely more supportive than sink or swim, but if you do keep your head above water, expect to be rewarded with a few extra lengths of the pool. *"The workload can be overwhelming; I do get stressed,"* admitted one hardy soul, whilst several spoke of *"late nights and the pressure to get things done."* However, with an average working day of 9am to 7ish, and the majority of late nights around deal completions, the overall feeling was that the training is *"really getting me ready for the real world."*

to equilibrium and beyond

If we've given the impression that trainees are left to fend for themselves, then think again. It's one of the inherent contradictions of this firm that its management style is a cross between Sir Alec Ferguson and our old friend, kindly host of *Blockbusters*, Bob Holness – ie a boot in the eye and a friendly hint about the starter question. There is a comprehensive programme of training sessions covering everything from phone technique to networking, and more seminars than you can shake a stick at. Trainees are expected to attend as much as possible, but the system is far from fascistic and it is generally up to the individual to decide what is relevant to them.

Day-to-day feedback coupled with a healthy *"leave you to get on with it"* attitude, allows most trainees to feel comfortable in *"progressing to your equilibrium and beyond."* As evidence of this, trainees are let loose to dazzle clients at corporate events and spoke of *"being given a voice from day one; you feel more than just a trainee."* The three-stage system of pre-seat objective setting, mid-seat review and end-of-seat-appraisal is laudable in theory, but we did hear one or two complaints that, in practice, it was not always achieved. As one individual pointed out: *"It's fine if nothing's going wrong, but it can be frustrating if you only get feedback after the event."* In sharp contrast, there was high praise for the firm's responsiveness to any individual's problems. We heard tell of one trainee who was painlessly and sensitively moved to a new seat.

In September 2003, six out of the ten qualifiers stayed on. Nevertheless, the overall impression is of a firm training people it sees as integral to its future ambitions.

halliwell mambo

The Monday to Thursday *"smart or suit"* dress code is contrasted by dress-down Friday, concerning which, the occasional e-mail shrills: *"No jeans, no logos, no trainers!"* And whilst the central Manchester offices (*"not opulence, not grimy"*) are somewhat cramped, a move remains Halliwells' chimera. Thinking about it, it could have been their close proximity in the office that led to the *"sense of bonding"* among trainees. One thing's for sure, it absolutely wasn't a tear that trickled down our researcher's cheek as one interviewee said: *"I've definitely made friendships that will endure for life."*

The social side of Halliwells is excellent, offering an outlet in which office hierarchy matters very little. There are sports teams, trainee outings, departmental parties and firm-wide events. Last year's Christmas party saw several partners stripped down to their underwear, salsa dancing for the delectation of the assembled company. Don't say we didn't warn you! On a more relaxed note, Chez Gerard remains the firm's local; patronised by partners and employees alike, it's a good place to do a little light networking.

and finally...

If you're ready to take on the challenge of a firm where *"the ambitious can make their mark quickly,"* then Halliwell Landau is almost certainly for you. If you're hoping to coast along, look elsewhere. Talking to these trainees, we couldn't help but like the place.

Hammonds

the facts

Location: London, Leeds, Manchester, Birmingham
UK ranking by size: 11
Total numbers of trainees: 87
Seats: 6x4 months
Alternative seats: Overseas seats, secondments
Extras: Pro bono – Paddington Law Centre

This big national firm offers a unique multi-site training that is designed to promote a seamless culture across the firm. Respected in each of its four locations, it has plenty to offer an open-minded applicant.

taking it up a gear

In 2000, staunchly northern firm Hammond Suddards got busy. In the last three years it has swallowed up Birmingham/London firm Edge Ellison, niche sports practice Townleys and specialist insolvency lawyers Wilde & Partners. All this while resisting renaming itself Ham & Egg or Wilde Edge. UK mergers done and dusted, the firm embarked on a programme of overseas expansion, (think several European capitals and Hong Kong) and is generally thought to have kicked up a gear in terms of its clients and work. Some partner losses aside (particularly from Birmingham and due to the departure of the insurance litigation practice), trainees are happy with the change: *"It's become a better, stronger firm,"* said one. The joins are no longer visible: *"At first it was 'Are you Edge or are you Hammonds?' but now it's not such an issue."* But there remain *"small differences"* in the character of the Edge and Hammond Suddards alumni: the bold, chatty former HS recruits contrasted quite sharply with the more cerebral and laid-back Edge recruits we spoke to. We suspect Hammonds' recruiters are attracted to the HS-type – straight-talking, outgoing, and up for it.

magical mystery tour

From a trainee's perspective, the most controversial aspect of the merger was the adoption of a distinctive 'location rotation' training scheme that saw trainees doing six seats in a minimum of three offices around England. This came as a shock to the Edge recruits who'd signed up for four seats in Birmingham and HS recruits who'd planned on a northern training. Not surprisingly *"there was a lot of moaning"* when they were told to go and live somewhere else for four months... and then somewhere else for another four. The tour of Britain appealed more to younger applicants who were quite happy to live out of a suitcase in company flats shared with fellow trainees. The scheme is still in place, but perhaps having acknowledged that some talent was being lost at the application stage, the fixed-location training is back on the agenda and you now have a choice as to which scheme to embark upon. Each regional office will offer five fixed-location contracts.

Rotating trainees state a preference for the seats they want to do and the office they want to do them in. Corporate finance, litigation and property are compulsory, but beyond that there's a lot on offer. Bottlenecks tend to occur around the London corporate seat and the usual suspect – employment – is a hot favourite everywhere. Competition and sports law are also oversubscribed. Like guilty parents sending their children to boarding school, the firm goes out of its way to try to make sure trainees get their first choice of either location or department and most felt they'd been *"lucky"* with the way their contracts had panned out. Inevitably there's potential to be sent somewhere you don't want to go, but a surprising number of the trainees we spoke to had been happy to let the firm decide on the location of their first seat and *"get a surprise"* after the induction course.

back to the future

Given that some readers will elect to go on tour we'll report on the pros and cons. A common pattern was for trainees to move around more in their first year and then, as qualification loomed, to return to the department into which they hoped to qualify. On the plus side, with six seats your horizons are widened; however, most trainees found four-month seats *"just long enough to settle down,"* saying: *"It's just as you start to get more responsibility that you finish"* and *"you rarely see things through."* The system favours those who *"take to new jobs quickly,"* and *"can fit into teams easily."* It also sounds like hard work.

The firm has been strict about trainees undertaking the three compulsory seats and visiting a minimum of three locations, but there is room for manoeuvre. Trainees told us that client secondments count as locations, but actually grad recruitment confirmed that they only did if they were actually in a different location. Seats abroad definitely count as different locations. We spoke to people who'd used the system as an opportunity to sample life in London and to see if the rat race was for them. Inveterate nomads can really exercise (or even exorcise) itchy feet: with seats in Brussels, Paris, Berlin and Turin as well as in the four UK offices, it's possible to go somewhere totally new every four months, though we heard of only one trainee who'd managed to do this. Bear in mind that the Paris and Berlin offices work in the local language and trainees must be fluent to degree level before they can go.

just good friends

To minimise the trauma of moving, Hammonds sorts out accommodation. In London trainee apartments are in Docklands. In Manchester they live in Salford Quays, and the Leeds digs are in Horsforth. In Birmingham trainees had flats in a luxury block with a gym, sauna and roof terraces. All in all, the firm treats you to the type of pad you won't be able to afford again for a good few years. If you're going away for your first seat you'll live on your own or be thrown in with someone chosen at random, but from there on in you can nominate who you'd like to share with. Living and socialising with workmates might be overkill for some, yet many of the ever-resilient Hammonds trainees we spoke to welcomed the opportunity to make *"good friends not just colleagues."* Some said the system had created tight groups that *"tended to move together." "It's a bit like an extension of being a student;"* commented one, *"the accommodation is like posh halls of residence. Everyone just gets on with it and has a laugh."*

Moving about can be unsettling. *"You're in a new city, sometimes living with people you don't know, and you're starting a new department. Basically only the letterhead stays the same."* The second seat is the hardest: *"By that time you've made some friends and things are just settling down, and then you think 'I've got to do it all again'." "It gets easier over the two years,"* but trainees who were in long-term relationships or had mortgages suffered the most. One trainee said: *"It's frightening the number of relationships that have broken down."* We found evidence to show it's perfectly possible to get through a Hammonds training and stay in a relationship, but be prepared to spend a lot of time commuting and make sure your partner understands the wisdom of the tour of duty. The firm makes allowances: *"If you're in an office away from home, it's fine to go at 5.30pm on a Friday to catch a train, but it can wear you down."*

home from home

The four UK offices were described as being *"pretty much identical,"* although Birmingham was deemed to be the most relaxed – perhaps a legacy from the Edge Ellison days. Manchester used to be considered the least popular, but its small size is now a big selling point. *"It's like one big department,"* commented one trainee, *"and the partners there are the ones who started it so it's like their baby."* Leeds is *"busy"* and boasts the most active social committee. Of all the offices, London differed the most, mainly because trainees seemed to socialise less with each other and more with other friends. Trainees also found the office reflected *"the more cut-throat life of the City."* Like other national firms, the work in the regional offices was felt to be *"standard for the regions;"* London, however, brought the mixed blessing of *"bigger deals," "bigger clients"* and *"longer hours." "Everyone wants to go to London at some point,"* commented one. As a consequence the competition for seats and qualification jobs there is stiff. It's possible that this is another reason behind the reintroduction of fixed location training contracts in the regions – *"They're a bit wary of losing everyone to London. It can be seen as a back door route into the City."*

Depending on where you are, you may share a room with a partner, assistant solicitor or even another trainee, and some departments work open plan. But whatever the set-up, you're likely to feel well supervised and find it easy to work with your seniors. Perhaps because supervisors have been trained for their role, our sources reported that they'd received a good level of work. In litigation in London, for example: *"I was always going off to court for masters' appointments – time extensions, striking outs, charging orders."* And in corporate, another had taken responsibility for closure letters and gone to client meetings. Beyond fee earning, *"trainees usually go on all external marketing events. From sit down dinners to drinks, the firm does try and bring you in early on the marketing side."*

who ate all the pies?

As you may have guessed, this training contract suits sociable and confident people. Typically we heard comments like: *"I'm quite an extrovert"* and *"I tend to say what I think."* Factor in shared accommodation and plenty of socialising and it's no surprise it all leads to lawyerly high jinks. "*We had a party at the firm's flats – the assistants came and the other trainees travelled up from other offices,*" one source remembered. Another told us: "*We had a 13-flat flat crawl. It was film themed; you went from Harry Potter to Gosford Park to Jaws to Fight Club and Austin Powers.*" Not content with all this, some trainees had even enjoyed a Black Country booze tour – bussing around pubs and finishing off in a pie factory.

In september 2003, 34 of the 48 qualifying trainees stayed with the firm.

and finally...

The trainees who enjoyed the Hammonds merry-go-round were those who were "*determined to make the best of things*" or had started with no fixed ideas. Now the firm is also offering fixed-location training, we believe it will suit a greater variety of applicants.

Harbottle & Lewis LLP

the facts

Location: London
UK ranking by size: 132
Total number of trainees: 8
Seats: 4x6 months
Alternative seats: Secondments

You're Will Young and you're looking for a lawyer to represent your interests. Or you're Chris Evans and you want someone to handle your multimillion pound action against the purchasers of your radio station. Then again, you might be Richard Branson and you need a firm that can look after…well…everything including your airline. They all picked Harbottle & Lewis. Should you?

no business like show business

The firm was founded in the 1950s by City man Brian Lewis and Laurence Harbottle, who was keen to combine his legal career with his film and theatre interests. This combination can still be detected in the shape of the firm today, strong on media work but also with a good reputation for its corporate practice.

It's important to remember the breadth of the firm's work when you're sending off that CV; you're applying to a law firm not *Pop Idol* and you won't be hobnobbing with the stars all the time. As one trainee reminded us: "*Lots of the clients are celebrities, but much of what you're doing is the same kind of work as you'd get elsewhere.*" In the corporate department you might assist on the sale of a film company, but it's still M&A. In litigation you'll have more luck with your autograph book: "*This is the department where you might get to work with the people you read about in the papers.*" Trainees were keen to stress the firm's strengths in IT and IP work: it has done much to protect Robbie Williams' personality and image rights, including obtaining court orders against cybersquatters.

best seats in the house

In this training scheme, "the menu is varied enough to make it innovative without being outlandish." OK, so we copied that from partner Robert Porter's review of client Jamie Oliver's new restaurant Fifteen, but we felt it was apt. You'll almost certainly get the trainee's staple diet of litigation, property and corporate seats, yet these will be spicier than average as the work may come from the music, broadcasting, leisure, aviation and advertising industries. There will also be some tasty morsels on the side. For the fourth six-month serving, IP and IT is "*a really excellent seat;*" alternatively you could work in entertainment or sports law.

A popular secondment to Virgin offers anything from commercial contracts to deciding whether a drunken incident a mile high (no, not that sort!) constitutes a criminal offence. The journey out to Gatwick every day is a hassle, but past secondees were full of praise for the experience. "*It has a steep learning curve; people don't really know you're a trainee – the title is just legal adviser.*" The seat most lacking in critical acclaim was property: *"I wasn't a big fan. Personally, property doesn't really excite me and I know of a couple of other people who didn't have the best time there."* Trainees disliked the large amounts of residential conveyancing and being left to fend for themselves: *"It wasn't the case that the support wasn't there, it was just less apparent and you had to do more asking."*

The showbiz seats are in high demand, particularly music. *"It's partly the glamour, but also lots of people have a strong interest in music and want to be music lawyers."* We even heard of some fee earners hitting the decks at the Christmas party – Judge Jules watch out! You'll find lots of lawyers with extra-curricular interests matching their work: we hear that the sports department is populated entirely by Arsenal fans.

show times

"When you first join you are given a timetable with the seats you're going to be doing. There's some consultation beforehand, but after that it's up to you to say if you're happy or unhappy." There's only so much the good folk in HR can do to give everyone what they want, when they want. *"If you change your mind, the firm would be flexible, as long as you weren't causing problems for another trainee. Whether you get to do a different seat also depends on how busy the department you want to move to is."*

A careful appraisal system amounts to monthly chats with the training partner to examine feedback from your supervisor, and an end-of-seat review based on the comments of all those you've worked for. We're told the firm's size is *"a double-edged sword."* Although sometimes you'll be able to get far more involved with the work than you would at a bigger firm, equally you might end up doing more of the grunt work because there are fewer paralegals and resources. The litigation department was the major culprit here, with one trainee telling us they'd had their fill of photocopying and another speaking of paginating into the wee hours. Normally, weariness is not an issue though and the official working day follows the 10am till 6pm pattern that's tradition in the theatre. Don't count on slipping away in time for curtain up every night: *"If there's work around then you have to get it done,"* and in litigation in particular a 9pm exit isn't unusual. The show must go on!

changing the scenery

No such thing as a free lunch? Harbottles begs to differ. All fee earners are invited to eat together every day at one (though not at Fifteen…). In the dining room, *"we're encouraged not to have departmental tables and it's a good chance to get to know everyone."* The Duke of York is a favourite haunt and there's also a monthly drinks party and some departmental socialising. We hear the corporate department is *"pretty chummy – I guess they're all burning candles at the same time!"* There was a characteristic element of showbiz fun at the firm's Christmas party last year when a table magician was brought into entertain the guests. However, the mood of the firm was *"a bit downbeat"* in March when the firm had to make redundancies, we're told for the first time in its history. *"There was some shock initially, but things have been picking up again in recent months."* Both trainees qualifying in September 2003 stayed at the firm.

With some prime picnic spots close by and John Lewis opposite, the firm's period building is in an *"unbeatable"* West End location in Hanover Square. A *"cosy"* building with a *"scary cellar,"* it's certainly got character: *"Part of the reason why it's so fun is because it's so ramshackle; there are always things that should be done to it."* And as you roam the corridors, you may well bump into Mr Harbottle himself (*"very friendly, extremely funny"*), who still works as a consultant and likes to pop in every week or so.

and finale…

Harbottle & Lewis will give you an excellent all-round training, jazzed up with some work that (confidentiality allowing) you'll be able to brag about to your friends without boring them. It will work you hard, but if you perform well, you can expect a long and successful run.

Herbert Smith

the facts

Location: London
UK ranking by size: 7
Total number of trainees: 180
Seats: 4x6 months
Alternative seats: Overseas seats, secondments
Extras: Pro bono – Privy Council death row appeals, Whitechapel Legal Advice Centre, language training

Big, bold and profitable, Herbert Smith is commonly mistaken for a magic circle firm. But looks, smells and work can be deceiving. Another misconception is that Herbies is mainly a litigation firm. While litigation has long been its flagship department and currently accounts for around 40% of turnover, the firm's corporate and banking practices are charging ahead.

opposing views

Although it has diversified in recent years, this *"enormous litigation beast"* (to borrow the words of one client) continues to be regarded as the best in the City for contentious matters. If mammoth disputes float your boat, this firm is going to be on your shortlist. Recent instructions include acting for Equitable Life in its £2 billion action against former auditors and directors, and for Virgin Radio in its fracas with Chris Evans. But Herbert Smith should never be viewed as just a litigation outfit. Its corporate and banking practices have come on in leaps and bounds following a major campaign to compete as a transactional firm: recent deals include the $3.5 billion sale of PwC Consulting. It has also made inroads into the investment banking sector and now acts for CSFB, Merrill Lynch and Morgan Stanley.

Many of the new recruits start trainee life in the real estate department. News of a seat in real estate is often met with groans of despair, but our sources spoke warmly of this *"friendly, down-to-earth"* group where they found themselves managing their own small files and working with a team on larger matters. Some even attended planning enquiries and liaised with counsel. The hours are kind, and since there are around 20 trainees in the department at any one time, it's a terrifically social group. When we phoned, one trainee was about to nip off for drinks with their team.

Six months in the corporate department is compulsory for all. This year, experiences in the department varied wildly. Some sources spoke of *"terrific responsibility"* and almost no grunt work; others had spent days on particularly banal tasks. Some enjoyed client contact; others had not met a single client. Sadly, for many, this is the reality of corporate work across the City, but there is hope. We gathered that the tough, the persistent, and those who simply asked for superior work, received a better deal. Trainees told us that mergers and acquisitions is the *"sexiest"* of the corporate groups, where some lucky trainees revelled in *"great responsibility,"* even *"doing the first drafts on agreements."*

bones of contention

This year, the firm's new head of litigation, David Gold, overhauled the department's structure, and now it is divided into four groups. Litigation A and B handle a broad spread of commercial disputes; C is the insurance law group; and D deals with energy law and arbitrations. Litigation is renowned for being more traditional than other departments: referring to the hierarchy, one trainee said: *"It's almost like a barristers chambers."* We laughed at tales of beleaguered trainees paying the taxi fare and lugging boxes and files into court as partners and counsel *"stride ahead,"* and then realised our sources weren't joking. Insurance litigation in particular came in for criticism. Some sources lamented the group's hierarchical atmosphere, in which *"partners speak to partners, assistants speak to assistants and trainees..."* well, trainees just shut up. The group, however, is famously industrious, and *"everyone sits working solidly all day."* It's also felt to have a particularly individualistic working environment, yet some sources found the trade-off worthwhile: *"I got great responsibility and better work than in many other departments. It was worth it."* Again, the experiences of trainees varied from the blissful to the banal. Some *"paginated only 30 pages"* in their entire six months; others were not so lucky. An almost unique public international law practice, headed by the charismatic Robert Volterra, is especially popular.

Rumours have long abounded about tensions between the corporate and litigation departments. And it's not surprising, given that the litigation department, historically the firm's power base, was criticised in the past for acting against prospective corporate or banking clients. According to one trainee: *"It's more a light-hearted rivalry anyway."* To ease this light-hearted rivalry, this year the firm reviewed its strategy and litigation is now pitching for work alongside corporate and banking.

beyond the norm

Beyond the mainstays of corporate, finance, litigation and real estate, smaller niche departments welcome trainees. Employment, for example, was described as *"a lovely, lovely group. Not actually female dominated, but about half and half. Very, very friendly."* Trainees see both contentious work (preparing for and attending tribunal hearings) and non-contentious (compromise agreements and corporate support jobs). Instead of having trainees working for a single supervisor, the three partners delegate work to assistants who then get the trainees involved. The net result? *"You feel more a part of a group as a whole."*

Any trainee wanting to spend time overseas has an excellent chance of doing so. There are 16 foreign seats at any one time, indicative of the importance Herbert smith places on its international business. Hong Kong and Singapore are particularly prized, but European seats, like those in Paris and Brussels, are also popular. The firm's approach to lawyering overseas has resulted in the establishment of foreign offices of its own and 'best friend' alliances with excellent firms in other countries, notably Germany and Belgium. With its alliance firms, Stibbe and Gleiss Lutz, Herbies is now sharing offices in cities across Europe including Moscow, Prague, Shanghai and Warsaw. Client secondments are also available, including BSkyB, Coca-Cola, Cable & Wireless and IBM, as well as two placements for judicial assistants at the Court of Appeal.

Formal training? It's all good. *"You could drown under training if you wanted to, or you can dip your toe in now and again."* Appraisals? Our sources also praised the three-monthly system. One trainee who was disillusioned by not having met clients in corporate was comforted by the knowledge that their comments were taken on board following appraisal. Of course, one of the best things about working for a firm of Herbert Smith's size is *"the support."* Said one trainee: *"You don't have to reinvent the wheel every time you are asked to draft a document. You just have a look on the database and there will be one there already."* The firm's extensive library also came in for praise, although one trainee wished that staff would return books more promptly.

come along, watkins

Herbert Smith has had a reputation for being aggressive in its style of working. We asked our sources for their thoughts on whether this was fair, and if they thought that this translated into a tough working environment. We've got to hand it to these trainees, every year they speak candidly about life at the firm. We were left in no doubt that to thrive in this environment, you'll need to be a fairly *"robust"* person. It's all a bit 'pull yourself together, Watkins', 'stiff upper lip' and all that. There are few *"softies who burst into tears at the slightest provocation,"* since *"you wouldn't get much sympathy for that."* And if you need constant encouragement, love and thanks, you will not get it in all quarters. On the positive side, the result is an energetic, no-nonsense office populated by real characters, both good and evil. One trainee who adored the firm told us: *"I'm someone who just gets on with it. Possibly the firm looks for people like that."* Our sources spoke of a hierarchical atmosphere, and while some accepted *"the trainee place in the scheme of things,"* others lamented the difficulty of asking questions of some partners.

In September 2003, 51 of the 61 qualifiers took jobs at the firm. We heard that *"if you want to do corporate, you're supported and almost guaranteed a job."*

bagels and bugs

The offices are in the classic Gordon Gekko corporate style – plenty of wood and black leather. No wall-to-wall plasma screens in reception, no murals painted by eight-year-olds, no shell collections. Despite the comic Love Bug connotations of the name Herbies, this is less the souped up Volkswagon and more the Mercedes Benz of law firms. At lunch time, many trainees eschew the firm's restaurant in favour of a sandwich in Exchange Square or Spitalfields market, or bagels on Brick Lane. Indeed a number of trainees have descended upon Brick Lane where they live like cuckoos amidst the *"tax dodgers"* (Herbies-speak for creative types). We're sure the 'tax dodgers' and the Bengali community are thrilled to have them.

According to our sources, the social life consists largely of visits to the firm's local, Davids (formerly Futures). Alas, few eulogised about the place, affectionately describing it as *"just awful. Not that I'd wish to libel their establishment."* Of course not. Said one trainee: *"I'm trying to think of something we do that doesn't involve going on the lash. It's all on the lash, basically."* Those preferring healthier pursuits have plenty of options ranging from hockey to rugby sevens and cricket on Hampstead Heath. To get new intakes of trainees bonding, there's a traditional treasure hunt that sees them racing around the City.

and finally...

Herbert Smith is a terrifically successful firm. It is stealing a march on rivals in a number of practice areas and the days of Herbert Smith being *"just a litigation firm"* are long gone. That said, if you want to train at one of the biggest firms in the City, but are worried about the positively anorexic litigation experiences on offer at some, it is still a top pick. If you're a *"robust"* character who doesn't mind *"mucking in,"* this tough, ambitious firm has plenty to offer.

Hill Dickinson

the facts

Location: Liverpool, Manchester, Chester, London
UK ranking by size: 52
Total number of trainees: 19
Seats: 4x6 months
Alternative seats: Secondments

Hill Dickinson has had a presence in Liverpool since 1810 when international trade meant the port city's activities eclipsed those of London. One thing's for sure, it's not all cotton traders and sailing ships these days...

the long voyage

Naturally Hill Dickinson has changed immeasurably in 200 years. It's gained three more offices and moved into diverse areas of law; yet, even today, in the Liverpool office its roots poke through quite clearly. And it's not just the *"ship in a box"* in reception. *"You do feel a sense of the firm's history in the Liverpool office, but actually, only in its older departments – insurance and marine."* Apparently the marine department handled work relating to the great, but ill-fated, transatlantic cruise liners, the Titanic and the Lusitania.

These days the firm boasts a large and popular healthcare department, which acts for both the public and private sectors. Most notably it is one of only 15 firms on the panel of the NHS Litigation Authority, thus enabling it to conduct clinical negligence defence work. For some trainees, particularly if they have a healthcare background, this is the main reason for choosing the firm. Others have flocked for its overall emphasis on litigation work, be this insurance-related or general commercial cases. *"The defendant insurance work is very much the heart of the firm,"* one source confirmed. All manner of litigation is on offer, ranging from asbestosis and mesothelioma claims to bankruptcy and insolvency disputes. In insurance litigation your supervisor's caseload may contain two or three hundred claims and you'll possibly even have your own share of them to manage. "*It's all good experience*" and you can even expect to go to court to do your own small hearings.

our friends in the north

Movement between the firm's three northern offices is common. One source told us that the firm likes all trainees to spend at least one seat away from the Liverpool base. Moving around is no big deal as Manchester is just 30 or so miles from Liverpool and Chester is even closer. How different things are after qualification, when there doesn't seem to be much interaction between offices at all...other than an annual away weekend (business plus fun on Saturday, recovery on Sunday). However, at trainee level there are monthly meetings with the five-partner training committee. Anything goes at these meetings: niggling issues are raised, speakers are invited to impart their wisdom, and trainees themselves take turns to give short presentations. The whole thing is video linked to the London trainees.

A high proportion of the trainees have roots or an education in the North West, many of them are from the Wirral (which us ignorant southerners have learned is the posh bit south of the River Mersey). One source felt that the southerners who moved up to train were less likely to stay: "*I imagine that the firm wants to know they'll be able to keep hold of you on qualification and that you're not just treading water until then.*"

liverpool: mersey beat

There's no doubt that the Liverpool office is Hill Dicks' beating heart. It's the one with most on offer and up to 80% of the trainees work there at any one time. It's described as a lively place with plenty of e-mail banter and end-of-week socialising in the local bar, Trials. "*We always start there before progressing down Victoria Street.*" Our sources all stressed that the working ethos was relaxed with most people away from their desks by six in the evening.

On the partners: "*Some are quite young, but obviously some have been here for years.*" Rather like the office furniture then. Actually we did ask trainees about the firm's location and its decor. They had little positive to say on the internal appearance of the place, but we suspect they weren't the sort to get precious on the subject. Close to the Mersey and the Liver Building, and opposite the courts, Hill Dicks is right in the thick of things.

manchester: on the up

Busy? Since merging with Gorna & Co in 2002, the Manchester office has bounced in and out of the legal press with news items announcing the arrival of this or that new partner. "*It's the fastest growing office and definitely the one they are marketing,*" confirmed one clued-up trainee. Gorna & Co had a strong property law base and the merger quashed any notions of the Manchester branch of Hill Dickinson remaining a PI outpost. Of late there has been a push on family work and media clients (no doubt targeted at the super rich of Cheshire as well as the run-of-the-mill chattering classes of Didsbury and Chorlton). But don't get carried away – it's commercial work that the firm is really after.

As in Liverpool, Hill Dicks in Manchester is a sociable place. "*We tend to go out for a drink every Friday night, usually to one of three or four bars in Deansgate Lock.*" It also shares a full-time formal dress code; however, in decor terms, the Manchester office looks newer and fresher than its Mersey counterpart.

chester: runners and riders

The firm acquired this office through the takeover of a local firm in the 1990s. Depending on who we spoke to, they determined that its prime function was to cater for the residential conveyancing and private client needs of the local populace, or to make life easier for commercial clients who didn't want to drive into Liverpool or Manchester. Most trainees who go to Chester undertake a commercial litigation seat, but here's a little-publicised fact: if you are desperate to try your hand at one or two criminal matters, this is the office to go to. Let's make it perfectly clear that we are not referring to pilfering from the stationery cupboard. Excellent news: *"The head of private client has a horse!"* As you can imagine, an enthusiastic Hill Dicks crowd attends race days at the Chester and Aintree courses to cheer Streamstown on to the finish line. Alas, we cannot confirm reports that the horse runs in Hill Dicks' corporate colours.

london: blackbird pie

The London office sings from its own song sheet and has always recruited its tiny trainee intake separately. It has clear appeal for someone with an interest in one of its few core areas: marine (goods in transit or yachting) or personal injury. There is also a tiny one-partner corporate and commercial team offering non-contentious experience. *"There's not much seat choice,"* one source confirmed. *"It's more a case of choosing the order that you do them in."* There's a certain sort of trainee that thrives in an environment where they get a lot of attention and everyone knows who they are...you'll need to be one of them. *"You have to be gregarious and willing to help,"* because by all accounts your supervisor will get you involved very quickly.

Like other marine and insurance practices, Hill Dicks is located close to Lloyds of London on Cornhill, *"and near the Royal Exchange for expensive shopping!"* After work, you won't have to go far to catch up with colleagues for a drink. *"The Counting House across the road is where we watched much of the World Cup last year and it's where we go when anyone has a birthday."* This sounds like a sociable office that knows that one of its greatest strengths is cohesion, but trainees should expect relatively little interaction with friends in the North. In September 2003, firm-wide, six of the eight qualifiers were retained.

and finally...

Hill Dickinson no longer sees its future as just an insurance firm. That side of the work will continue to have prominence, but the firm is carefully tending its burgeoning healthcare work plus new shoots in both the commercial and the private client sectors.

Hodge Jones & Allen

the facts

Location: London
UK ranking by size: 167
Total number of trainees: 8
Seats: 4x6 months
Alternative seats: None

One of north London's most successful firms, Hodge Jones & Allen serves up high street legal advice and, increasingly, it is catering for some commercial clients.

london's other zoo

Canals, railways and gin all helped to grow Camden Town. And just as these things are all associated with the word 'decline', by the end of the 1960s, Camden Town had reached the decrepit state portrayed so well in *Withnail and I*. Then in the empty wharves and warehouses at Camden Lock, idealistic seventies artisans sowed the seeds of a new future. Camden's music venues started to break big-name bands and the media came to town. First TV AM, then MTV and others. For every rock-bottom street drunk and drug addict, there's a professional or celebrity resident. For every crack house, an overpriced canalside apartment.

So where is Hodge Jones & Allen in all of this? A Camden brand since 1977, it was started up by three lawyers – Henry Hodge is now Chief Immigration Adjudicator and married to Government minister, Margaret Hodge; Mr Jones we know little about; and Patrick Allen is still at the firm today. A trainee explained: *"The firm was founded on principles of social justice and access to the law for people who can't afford to pay for it. Those principles are still very clearly here today."*

sharp objectives

Trainees secure positions at HJA through one of two routes: they either apply for the job a year in advance or they make the grade as a paralegal. A four-seat system usually means six-month stints chosen from crime, family, PI, employment, commercial or residential property and housing law. The firm has always stressed that successful applicants will need to display commitment to its principal areas of work, and in the past many have had experience as volunteer advisors in law, community advice and housing centres. In an increasingly wintry climate for publicly funded legal advice, HJA is no longer putting all its eggs in the community law basket. These days you'll find it chasing more profitable commercial property and employment law business. And there's been another cultural change: *"We've just started doing enforcement work for Camden Council – parking fines, etc. – for the first time we are prosecuting people."* Apparently some at the firm have a purist view of what HJA should and shouldn't do but those in management have taken a pragmatic approach. As one source said: *"At its heart it is a legal aid firm, but its head has to be commercial as well."*

21 seconds, 17 years

The biggest department is crime and, apparently, *"crime rocks!"* Most trainees spend a seat here, working on everything from road traffic charges to serious assaults, rape and murder. And, believe us, there's plenty of murder and mutilation going on in this neck of the woods. The firm hooks some high-profile clients and cases: in the last couple of years it's acted for So Solid's Asher D and the defendants on the BBC/IRA bomb. It also acted for cousins Michael and Vincent Hickey in their claim for compensation having spent 17 years wrongfully imprisoned after the Carl Bridgewater case. Usually trainees sign up to the rota for 24-hour police station coverage and the Police Station Accreditation Scheme, which enables them to advise suspects in custody (and earn extra cash). When not behind bars, they'll meet clients in the office and attend magistrates' and Crown Court hearings with qualified lawyers. The crime department was described by one source as *"the belly"* of the firm. It's a lively place that brings you into contact with all manner of people, particularly if the crime happens at the bus stop in front of the office. *"We noticed a kerfuffle and then half an hour later Kentish Town police phoned us up to get someone to the station!"*

Traditionally oriented towards tenants, the housing department must now negotiate the complex landscape of Registered Social Landlords (housing associations – for which it also acts) and new local authority schemes. Housing law is no longer just about protecting tenants from unscrupulous landlords and defending rent arrears claims. Personal injury is normally handled on a no win, no fee basis. Leading charities such as Headway and the Spinal Injuries Association refer clients, so it's by no means all low-value RTA and slip-and-trip litigation. The client base in the family department is now half privately paying and half legally aided. Several of the lawyers have their own specialism – child abductions, injunctions against violent husbands, financial settlements etc. If you fancy trying out some of their work, your supervisor will allow you, and there's ample opportunity to attend court to clerk care cases or attend mediation hearings.

take your partner by the hand

Some departments have a very pronounced work ethic, which means that long hours are on the cards. Thankfully, this is balanced out by a good quality of work and tedious photocopying jobs are rare: *"We have clerks who do most of this, but occasionally you do it for your own cases. Generally you don't get lumbered with dull jobs."* But don't assume that you can get away without spending time on administrative matters. Legally aided cases now come with an awful lot of red tape.

Most trainees sit with a partner and also receive advice and encouragement from other fee earners and a mentor. Monthly appraisals are supplemented by regular file reviews with *"your training principal checking the majority of your work and discussing things in general."* We heard how the office has *"an efficient feel"* (with public funding franchise standards to maintain, how could it be otherwise?) and is *"quite workmanlike."* Of seat changes, one source said: *"We all do-si-do every six months."* Apparently, everyone will do crime;

most people want family; and new trainees must accept that they will do a non-legally aided seat – at present, employment or commercial property.

a walk in the park?

After a long, hard week you don't need to go far for liquid refreshment. Opposite the office is the luridly painted Mac Bar; easier on the eye (and our personal favourite) is The Camden Brewing Company with its Belgian beer and pub table philosophy; and for the traditionalists there's The Old Eagle. We were upset to hear that the annual charabang to the seaside has fallen by the wayside – a half-day picnic in Regent's Park had to suffice in 2003. The social committee is a busy one, organising mixed football, wine tasting, and for the girls, regular beauty treatment evenings. *"A group of people go kickboxing up the road,"* we heard, *"and there are always raffles for charity. Sometimes the prize is a day off."* We approve! On the NQ job front: in September 2003, three of the four qualifiers stayed on.

and finally...

The area in which Hodge Jones & Allen works is certainly gritty and full of surprises. HJA will suit energetic and open-minded applicants who don't mind a bit of commercial property with their crime.

Holman Fenwick & Willan

the facts

Location: London
UK ranking by size: 74
Total number of trainees: 18
Seats: 4x6 months
Alternative seats: Overseas seats, secondments

Holman Fenwick & Willan was set up in 1883 by a family of merchant adventurers who were ready to switch tide tables for case reports. Alas, much as we'd like there to be, we can find no evidence pointing to a piratical past.

coffee houses and carriage by sea

The late Victorian era was a time of stability and prosperity. Britannia ruled the waves, and shipping and international trade were big business. Wealthy individuals had long been underwriting marine risk in the coffee houses around the City, but in 1871 the Society of Lloyd's was formally incorporated and set up business in the Royal Exchange. It's easy to see how the original partners built a practice on advice to those involved in the transportation of goods and the sharing of the inescapable risks of sailing the high seas. And HF&W has continued to do exactly this for the last 120 years. *"There's a sense of heritage,"* one trainee mused, *"and a sense of tradition, but without it being an old, dry, fusty, out-of-date piece of machinery."*

When a firm is especially successful in an area of work, it's easy for its other activities to be overshadowed. The trainees we interviewed stressed that the firm is developing and promoting its non-shipping, non-insurance, non-contentious work. They talked of new groups like the energy, transport and infrastructure department, and of the new lawyers that have been laterally hired into corporate. But don't allow yourself to be swept away on the tide of enthusiasm for new, non-core business – around 80% of the firm's revenue still comes from litigation cases for shipping, insurance and international trade clients.

cutlasses at dawn

Every year we hear of trainees who come to the law from a maritime background or after a spell in the insurance industry. For them, choosing HF&W makes perfect sense, and quite often they will tailor their training contracts towards the appropriate departments. Don't worry if you forgot to become an underwriter or earn your master mariner's certificate: the firm also awards training contracts to fresh graduates. Apparently, it's all part of the plan. *"The various trainees suit different parts of the firm and go to make the whole picture."* Trainees talk quite openly with each other, so *"you sort of know what other people are aiming for"* and this cuts down on squabbling for seats.

In past years trainees always undertook three contentious seats and a non-contentious one in the company finance department. "*Company is a mix of all our non-contentious areas. Last time round, it had six or seven trainees including one who sat with the new energy partner and two trainees doing EU work.*" As an umbrella for all manner of transactional lawyers, this department even includes the tiny property team. These days it is more likely that a trainee could ask for, and get, two non-contentious seats.

shiver me timbers

There are those who come to HF&W with little more than vague curiosity for an area of law they assume will be "*romantic*" (even if they have no idea what a bill of lading is and there turns out to be no free cocktails at a charter party). One trainee described the appeal of 'wet' shipping work: "*It's the urgency, the immediacy of the whole thing.*" Exciting? You bet!

We got the impression that, rather like the firm's founding fathers, many HF&W lawyers were adventurous types. It seems to be true of the Admiralty department, with its thrills-and-spills-on-the-high-seas cases and in-house mariner-consultants (actual ship's captains, and not necessarily lawyers). But other parts of the firm don't fit the stereotype so easily, and not everyone considers that being helicoptered off to a sinking ship or handling an act of piracy beats drafting loan agreements.The dry shipping litigation department is somewhat calmer than Admiralty and concentrates on exercising intellectual muscles. "*It's law-heavy, but practical and very lucrative.*" We chuckled when certain partners were described as "*intellectually ostentatious,*" but then we reminded ourselves how many of the heavyweight cases in English law are shipping-related. Yet it's over in the reinsurance department that you find the real planet-sized brains, working on cases that go on for years, such as high-profile arbitrations between Lloyd's syndicates re 9/11 liabilities, business interruption claims arising out of the Hatfield rail incident, and cases concerning losses arising out of the Iraqi invasion of Kuwait.

voyage of discovery

On big litigation there's inevitably a requirement for trainees to handle administrative tasks. Despite all the discovery, bundling and photocopying etc, one of them told us how he felt "*close to the law and not a document monkey.*" Most of our sources accepted more menial tasks with good grace; others hinted that the firm could consider hiring more paralegal support in the busier times. Importantly, and administrative chores aside, there are good levels of responsibility to be had in all departments, and trainees had no shortage of examples of work they were proud of completing. The descriptions of their high points were usually something along the lines of: "*Being asked for input and being able to deliver it and feel that I was working as part of the team.*" Client contact is frequent, both on day-to-day case conduct and at the weekly seminars.

The international nature of the practice is a big draw for trainees. HF&W has offices in Paris, Piraeus, Hong Kong, Singapore and Shanghai. There's a good chance a trainee will go to one of the first three and qualified assistants can work abroad both long and short-term. The firm is especially delighted to receive applications from students with foreign language skills. Speak something unusual and you might find you are asked to help out with small pieces of translation work. As for the baffling lexicon of shipping and insurance – your ignorance will be quickly swept aside by a wave of training sessions.

the munch bunch

You know the case about the crew who ate the cabin boy…well don't worry: you'll not be eaten alive by the partners. "*Everybody is very, very accommodating and I am especially pleased by that,*" said one relieved trainee. Moreover, he went on to add: "*It feels slightly like a second family, people are pretty tolerant.*" However, we advise against getting so comfortable that you accidentally call your supervisor 'Dad'. Don't think it never happens! In certain ways the firm smacks of tradition. The dress code is formal and the girls have few senior female role models (*"Clearly 30 years ago few women were being attracted to the law by 350,000-tonne oil tankers"*). But can you expect anything different from a firm with a long pedigree in this type of business? *"Historically the firm has been a little public school, rah! and crusty,"* said one trainee. *"But this is changing and, especially among the younger partners, there are some pretty cool and down-to-earth characters."*

You'll get to know partners quickly, be it through work or social events. Every fortnight they host a buffet lunch for staff from all levels of the firm, and they can also be found out and about in the nearby pubs after work. *"The Admiralty lot are out of the office by 6.30pm and in the pub by 6.35pm. In reinsurance it's more like out of the office by 8pm and in the pub by 8.05pm."*

in dry dock?

Occupying two offices in Lloyd's Avenue, the firm couldn't be better placed. Its main premises is a terrace of three buildings with *"a traditional facade, but all done up inside."* The interior of the office has been overhauled from *"top to bottom,"* and it is now described as *"smart and subtle."* Interesting…seeing as the partnership is also undergoing a bit of a refit: some shifting around of practice groups, deliberate attempts to diverge from the old stalwarts of insurance and shipping, new blood at assistant level, new managing and senior partners. Someone's plotting a different course.

When they're not sailing in Docklands after work, the Pitcher & Piano, All Bar One and any number of chain bars are popular. More recently a newer bar, Thai Square, has become popular with the trainees, but a few of them also talked of a place called Milo's that once operated underneath the office. After a short spell as a lap-dancing club, it was closed down and the space has now been incorporated into HF&W's office and is used as meeting rooms. Why do we keep imagining clients stuffing tenners down their lawyer's trousers?

Six of the ten qualifying trainees stayed with the firm in September 2003.

and finally…

Holman Fenwick & Willan is a firm with a heavy litigation bias that is anchored to the international shipping and insurance industries. Its desire to win more non-contentious work will undoubtedly mean a more varied experience for trainees, but, just like one of those big oil tankers, this is a firm that will change course very slowly.

Hugh James

the facts

Location: Cardiff, Merthyr Tydfil, Blackwood, Treharris
UK ranking by size: 84
Total number of trainees: 17
Seats: 4x6 months
Alternative Seats: None

Having shrugged off the after effects of its recent demerger from West Country insurance practice Ford Simey, Welsh firm Hugh James has pushed forward with a process of modernisation. It has made some important commercial client gains while maintaining an excellent reputation in specialist industrial disease work and serious injury claims.

same-same but different

There's no easy answer to the question 'What does Hugh James do?' Forty-plus years of practice have seen it constantly evolving, diversifying and specialising. As several sources indicated: *"It is constantly updating. It is always looking for the latest technology and the newest business opportunities."* This urge for self-improvement spans the entire range of its practice, encompassing coco, commercial property, lender services, IP and IT, employment, commercial litigation, e-commerce, PI, insurance services…we could go on and on. One trainee summed it up perfectly: *"There's an atmosphere of wanting to keep Hugh James at the forefront of all its fields."*

The firm's organic growth has led to a structure that seems a little complex to the outside eye. Trainees say the offices feel similar in atmosphere, but distinct in method. From one: *"I expected day-to-day procedures and practices to be the same, but they were very different."* At the next level down, they said: *"Departments are all distinct"* and in extension *"each little pocket is specialised."* As an illustration, in PI you might work with 100 claimants who've suffered a miscellany of accidents, or you might work with the catastrophic head injuries team who have had the same clients for years. There are four overarching divisions: claimant; publicly funded; business litigation and business services. Each holds regular divisional conferences and social events with the net effect that all the constituent bits *"feel like parts of a larger entity."*

little guys and big buys

Having entered this monkey puzzle, how will you spend your four six-month seats? Unsurprisingly, the answer is that the type of experience and degree of responsibility you'll get depends on the department, location and field of practice. In commercial property in Cardiff, you could deal with multimillion-pound site acquisitions for clients like Nationwide Building Society or Barratts, while in Merthyr Tydfil you might be helping someone purchase their council house under the 'right-to-buy' scheme.

The trainees' favourite, employment, covers all contentious and non-contentious bases, so you might find yourself drafting contracts and termination agreements or running your own files *"up to and including tribunal hearings."* Opt for family law in Merthyr and you'll have *"a ton of client contact"* and cases covering everything from residency applications to divorces. Wherever you do claimant litigation, expect *"an excellent experience, but a load of photocopying and bundling too."* Finally, if you draw the short straw and get the dreaded lender services seat, repossession hearings and property title checking may be your lot. We should add that although this seat has been talked down by trainees for the last few years, it can offer the chance to work as assistant to the head of department, in which case *"you do get to assist on secured lending arrangements and on conveyancing matters."* Generally, wherever they worked, trainees viewed the firm as having *"an accommodating and supportive atmosphere, but it gives you lots of autonomy."* There is no single typical trainee experience at Hugh James; instead there are opportunities to grasp responsibility and specialise as you develop.

pleidiol wyf i'm gwlad

Having recently closed its offices in Bargoed and Talbot Green, the firm is gathering its numbers in the more important centres of Cardiff and Merthyr. The Blackwood branch remains important, taking trainees in family, licensing or criminal law; nevertheless when trainees told us *"it's unusual to see out your contract without a seat at a branch,"* it was quickly apparent that they no longer meant a sojourn in a small 'valleys' office. Now working outside Cardiff usually means time in Merthyr. As a homage to the lost valleys' experience, the whole *Student Guide* team gathered together and, after some coaching from the editor's dad, belted out *Land of My Fathers* from the roof of our EC1 office. It has to be said: the Treorchy male voice choir has nothing to worry about.

In the summer of 2003, the Cardiff office moved to *"glamorous and corporate-looking"* offices with acres of plate glass, glass elevators and beautiful views of Cardiff Castle and the Millennium Stadium. A few ingrates moaned about the open-plan seating now on offer, but more perceptive trainees suggested this is part of *"a drive to modernise and to move towards a more corporate practice."* Cardiff is where the majority of the firm's corporate lawyers are based, in addition to niche practices like the highly esteemed sports law team, that represents the Welsh Rugby Union authorities, the catastrophic head injuries team, and the IP/IT team, whose expertise put Hugh James on the panel for Future Firecrest – one of the FCO's most important IT projects. However, there are disadvantages to working on more important projects and deals: expect less autonomy as *"you are a small element of a larger process,"* and be prepared to work longer hours.

evans the solicitor

One trainee (who'd obviously eaten a dictionary for lunch) described the Merthyr office as *"more relaxed, but certainly not phlegmatic about law."* Based in purpose-built offices it may have *"a more local and high street-based feel,"* but it's certainly not stuck in its ways. It attracts a lot of PI and family law clients who walk in off the street and is also prominent in class actions involving miners' compensation claims for Vibration White Finger and other industrial diseases. It was described by one source as *"eager to be at the forefront of research"* on such matters. However, the local community remains important and the office building is named Martin Evans House after the old Merthyr firm Hugh James took over.

makin' whoopi

Our sources were generally happy with the support the firm offered them during their two years of training, although there were a few suggestions that appraisals *"should be every three months not six; it makes more sense to have the chance to put feedback into practice."* That aside, the warmth of the firm and its family-oriented atmosphere were roundly praised. The trainees are a tight-knit group: *"Of course there is healthy competition, but never nastiness; we're all really close."* Six of the seven trainees who qualified in September 2003 remain at the firm.

Ha!Ha! (*"the trendiest bar in Cardiff"*) is a regular haunt post-work and trainees also go clubbing together at the weekend. But it's at the Christmas parties, that the whole firm pulls together to deliver spectacular entertainment. Last year, the Cardiff bash involved everyone from partners to secretaries in a Grease-themed extravaganza. Meanwhile, up the road in Merthyr, a legendary group of extroverted partners pulled off a routine that, depending on whose account you believe, was either a take on Michael Jackson's Thriller or a Madness medley. We won't for a minute suggest that the quality of performance left it open to interpretation. And then, in our view best of all, an entire valleys office came to the Cardiff party as the choir from Sister Act.

and finally...

For breadth of practice in Wales, we don't think you could do much better.

Ince & Co

the facts

Location: London
UK ranking by size: 90
Total number of trainees: 24
Seats: 4x6 months
Alternative seats: Piraeus

Founded in 1870, Ince & Co has grown to become one of the world's best shipping firms. But it's not all plain sailing as the firm profits from disaster. Oil spills, shipwrecks, plane crashes, piracy and war are all grist for the mill. When disaster strikes, clients need only press the big red "Emergency Response" button on the firm's website for an Ince & Co lawyer to peel away the Saville Row pinstripe suit, leap into the batmobile and commence the rescue mission.

action stations!

Ince & Co has acted for the shipping and insurance industries for more than 130 years, and work for these sectors will dominate your training. The first thing to note is that there are no seats per se. Every six months you'll move into the office of a different partner. At the beginning of each new residency you get a list of partners whom you should approach for work, and it is entirely up to you to cultivate relationships with them. From the outset you'll be expected to network furiously and win the trust of your seniors. As one source told us: *"When there's a big disaster, or when a good case comes in, there can be a race for the relevant partner's office."* This is a hunter/gatherer style training in which fortune favours the brave and you become responsible for the development of your own practice. Trainees are told to think of themselves as individual businesses, not unlike barristers, and to think of partners as clients. *"You have a complete spread of work,"* for example, you might work for shipping, insurance and pollution partners all at the same time. And you could even find yourself doing bits and pieces of private client work for, say, shipowners, *"selling the odd house, doing some wills and probate."*

It's a fact of life in litigation that sometimes a total dud of a matter will land in your lap. In other firms you can hand these lemons over to the next trainee. Not so at Ince. There'll be no under-desk middle-finger farewells to that frustrating case; instead you'll carry it with you and keep it for as long as it takes. If this sounds like an ordeal, look away now. If the idea excites you, then you're clearly one of life's completers so read on.

batspeak

Amazingly, many of the firm's trainees arrived with little knowledge of shipping. *"I didn't know one end of a boat from another,"* said one. Fear not though; following the PSC, you'll be given a two-week intensive introduction to shipping law and lore. The idea is that by the end of it you'll know your pier from your ear and your quoin from your ... oh, forget it. If you like the sound of a particular introductory session, it's the perfect opportunity to collar the partner and introduce yourself. But surely some young players can fall through the cracks, finding themselves washed up and as idle as a painted ship upon a painted ocean? To combat this threat, each month a committee assesses who is busy and who has capacity. But, *"if by the end of two years, you're still not busy, it's a pretty good indication that you're not working out."*

Ince & Co lawyers are renowned for being *"plain speaking"* and well connected. The shipping world is one in which reputation matters and clients are notoriously demanding. Perhaps it's because partners are totally preoccupied with winning work and then delivering the goods that Ince's offices are unassuming and, well, *"rather shabby." "Ally McBeal it ain't!"* said one source. But we sense that clients prefer the premises to look like *"a real lawyers' office and not a trendy advertising firm's."* If the art collection is any indication, clients will love it – the walls are adorned with pictures of ships, oilrigs and planes. As for kit, trainees now get all the usual PCs, and Dictaphones etc, but there is a notable absence of voicemail. Consequently, we found it nigh impossible to get through to many of them, but those we did manage to speak to were all *"a bit pressed, actually,"* or *"very very busy on disclosure."* Being busy in the current climate can only be considered a good sign. Indeed, in 2003 the firm recently made up six new partners. At NQ level, seven of the ten trainees stayed on after qualification.

le havre and beyond

The firm has a truly international practice, with offices in Hamburg, Hong Kong, Le Havre, London, Paris, Piraeus, Shanghai and Singapore. Trainees can do a stint in Piraeus, taking shipping courses, visiting oilrigs and meeting clients. It *"puts your work into perspective,"* one trainee told us. *"It makes you realise you're working for real people with real problems."*

Ince & Co is an indisputably traditional firm from its mature wooden desks and filing cabinets, and its steadfast refusal to adopt an organised seating system, to its limited number of female partners (three out of 50 in London). Despite trainees' praise for The Ince Way, this is most certainly not the firm for everyone. One trainee told us: *"It's like being back at school."* But you won't be told to tuck in your shirt, and you won't find too many people pulling rank with trainees. *"You're never made to feel more junior than anyone else."* To its credit, this old-school approach is changing, albeit gradually, and despite its reputation for conservatism, this is not an oppressively hierarchical firm. You'll work directly with partners, sometimes very senior ones, and you can expect to be a central part of the cases you work on. In this sense, it is perhaps more enlightened than most.

On the second Thursday of the month, the partners host drinks at local bar Foxtrot Oscar. Everyone from print room staff to senior partners show up; some move on to a club afterwards and *"there are often a few sore heads on Friday."* Sailing and football go some way to bringing about a healthy booze/sports balance. Our final comment on the status of trainees concerns admin support. The trainee group shares three secretaries, and boy do they earn their money! One of our interviewees explained the relationship: *"I normally ring her and get her to come and get the work. Or I'll e-mail her and get her to print something off and bring it to me. They do a lot of walking around."* Given that the alternative is to share a partner's secretary (thus being relegated to the position of remora fish in the secretarial food chain), we suspect that trainees spend hours figuring out the best way to win 'most favoured trainee status' with their three secretaries. And if trainees begin to put on fat from lack of exercise, well they can always get onto one of those sports teams!

and finally...

To succeed at Ince & Co, you need to be *"tenacious, confident, practical and streetwise."* Not to mention self-reliant and rather enterprising because you will effectively have *"your own little law practice."* Shy or overly self-effacing applicants need not apply.

Irwin Mitchell

the facts

Location: Sheffield, Leeds, Birmingham, London, Newcastle-Upon-Tyne
UK ranking by size: 50
Total number of trainees: 30
Seats: 4x6 months
Alternative seats: None
Extras: Pro bono – Free Law, Docklands Legal Advice Service

Irwin Mitchell has turned into a giant among law firms. Since its early days in pre-WW1 Sheffield, it has grown to the point where it employs around 1,600 staff. From the ordinary man on the street to huge corporations, IM's client base is such that the training on offer is as varied as can be found anywhere. And just in case you were interested, in 2003 IM posted the third highest partner profits figure for a national or regional firm.

hundreds and thousands

Many of the firm's 1,000 fee earners are part or non-qualified case handlers processing high-volume, low-value PI and conveyancing cases. Aside from telling you that nearly 100 of them are training for ILEX qualifications, for the purposes of this feature we'll ignore that side of the business as it doesn't impact on the trainee experience. Instead, we'll concentrate on more complex, higher value claimant PI and clinical negligence work, other types of private client services and IM's business law functions. The main Sheffield HQ and the Leeds and London offices each offer a full range of services, while the Birmingham branch limits itself to PI and clin neg. A Newcastle office opened in 2003 with a mission to clean up on PI and clin neg in the North East.

disasters r us

Every year we trot out the same list of high-profile cases because they illustrate perfectly the type and calibre of matters on which IM's reputation has been built. Lockerbie, The Marchioness sinking, the Piper Alpha oilrig explosion, the King's Cross Fire, vCJD and miners' disease claims have made the firm what it is today. These and much more are detailed in IM's training brochure (a piece of literature that stands out from most because of its unspun factual approach). Less publicised, but equally important are the cases handled by the catastrophic injuries department, particularly those relating to brain trauma and spinal injuries. Among the trainees we interviewed were several who had targeted this work. *"I take the view that we are there to help these people. If you're getting them compensation or interim payments that will fund therapy and a move into more suitable accommodation then you are helping.*" The job can be heart wrenching at times, but you must stay as detached as possible. "*Paediatrics is the hardest; you just think 'God, that poor kid.*" Many fee earners become involved with related charities.

Not all of IM's private clients have suffered injury. The Leeds and Sheffield offices have family law teams; increasingly, each is being tilted towards privately paying rather than publicly funded clients. Employment lawyers act for individuals referred by their trade unions and work on larger, more wide-reaching issues for the organisations themselves. "*Lots of the union clients stemmed from Michael Napier* [senior partner], *and that spirit of community mindedness is carried through in the firm.*"

getting down to business

While it's rare for trainees with a purely commercial focus to join the firm, many accept a training contract at IM because they have yet to decide between different types of practice. As one source put it: "*I wanted to see both sides of the coin.*" On offer on the commercial side: insolvency, IP, commercial and technology, property, commercial litigation, and two quasi-commercial seats – business crime and public sector. Some seats involve a combination of more than one of the above, so earning names like 'Transactions Yorkshire'. The corporate team acts mainly for SMEs and owner-managed businesses, while the banking lawyers list several retail banks among their clients. Additionally, the firm acts for local authorities and charities.

Trainees in commercial litigation seats encounter everything from noisy neighbours, licensing and defamation to large commercial contract claims. It is normal practice for trainees to attend court to conduct hearings, for example mortgage repossessions, and there's a good supply of smaller cases for them to conduct by themselves under supervision. In only a few seats is there any likelihood of spending lengthy periods of time on routine tasks. Business is getting bigger at IM. "*It's fair to say there's more money to be made on the commercial side of things and that's definitely expanding the most rapidly...but that's not to say we can't capitalise more on the PI side too.*"

say what you mean

Most trainees are in their late twenties; the oldest this year was 38 and many were paralegals before starting their contracts. One experienced commentator told us: "*I have been impressed by the breadth of people I have encountered since I have been here.*" Another summed up the trainee group as "*liberal in their thinking, compared to those at a lot of big firms.*" Trainees are not looking for an easy life, it's just that earning the highest salaries or working in the most fashionable city isn't so important to them. Apparently, the IM way "*is a Yorkshire thing – honest, straightforward, direct – saying what you think, knowing where you stand.*" One trainee mused on whether the PI side is "*keeping the commercial side of the practice grounded.*" It's a nice idea.

an offer you can't refuse

Many of the trainees populating the two Yorkshire offices had pre-existing links with the region, and we found the same was the case in the Birmingham office, but there is no policy of local recruiting. Indeed, ideally you will be one of life's rolling stones because you are quite likely to move between offices. All this will be discussed with you at interview, and trainees advise applicants to think carefully on the matter before simply agreeing to do absolutely anything to get the job. Some trainees spend all their time in one office; some have spent time in three. There are no hard and fast rules as to who moves where or when, but the watchword is flexibility.

Head of training, Sue Lenkowski, has a tough job on her hands keeping up to 30 trainees happy with seat allocation. As in any firm you'll find winners and losers, but overall most get to do what they want most of the time, indeed, some trainees do two seats in the department that they eventually qualify into. However, one recurring criticism was that the amount of notice given prior to seat changes was too short, particularly if you need to quit your current accommodation and find new digs.

In September 2003 the firm awarded jobs to all but one of the 13 qualifiers.

out and about

The Sheffield office is the daddy – in all respects. Now with over 800 staff, it has outgrown its main premises in the town centre and is now split over two sites. After work you might head to Bar Sola with departmental colleagues; this is not a firm where the trainees herd together to the exclusion of others.

Open since 1989, the Birmingham branch has reversed out of commercial work and now specialises in PI and clin neg. Reflecting this new sate of affairs, there were just five trainees in the city when we rang and, again, their social life is departmental-based. Nearby is the Brum lawyer's favourite, The Old Joint Stock. And be careful with that credit card at lunchtime, the locale is *"dangerous for shopping."*

The London office was set up in 1995 and recently moved to larger premises in Chancery Lane. It's a retrograde step in terms of bars and restaurants, so the office-wide Friday Night Pub Club wanders back to its old Farringdon stomping ground. More seat options are now available – business crime, C&T, commercial litigation, employment and catastrophic injury, and the office recently welcomed new lawyers from niche travel litigation firm Lorenzo Zurbrugg.

Five years ago IM moved into Leeds, having acknowledged the city's position as the commercial centre of Yorkshire. The purpose-built premises are not quite as central as the Sheffield office, but they are smarter and less crowded. The social scene is a bit buzzier too, and younger lawyers can often be found hanging out in Babylon on a Friday night.

wannabes

Wherever they are in the IM network, staff have been able to compete in their very own version of *Pop Idol.* From secretaries to partners, from the accomplished to the downright awful, regional heats were open to all comers. At the grand finale, celebrity judge Matthew Marsden (*Corrie*, *Blackhawk Down*) helped pick the winner. Rumours that all male lawyers have now adopted the famous Cowell high-waisted trouser look are unconfirmed.

and finally...

Irwin Mitchell is a very good choice of firm for any applicant with a desire to experience *"the vanguard of the firm"* – high-calibre PI and/or clinical negligence work, while retaining the option of becoming a commercial lawyer. It will also appeal to anyone who wants to take on commercial-style work for 'non-corporate' organisations.

Jones Day Gouldens

the facts

Location: London
UK ranking by size: 55
Total number of trainees: 40
Seats: Non-rotational system
Alternative seats: None
Extras: Pro bono – Waterloo Advice Centre

In February 2002, fiercely independent and widely respected London commercial firm Gouldens voted to merge with the largest litigation firm in the United States, Cleveland-based giant Jones Day.

the beef

The trainees we spoke to unanimously acknowledged the merger to be *"a de facto takeover"* of the lean 40-partner Londoner by the 400-partner US heavyweight. Almost immediately there followed a wave of redundancies and we have watched as the word 'Gouldens' has buckled beneath a dominant 'Jones Day' on the website and letterhead. However, the departing assistants and associates were predominantly from the Jones Day side and we got the sense that the spirit of Gouldens was not for breaking. It's way too early to pass judgement on how the merger will bed down, but what we can say is that an international network, combined with the unique Gouldens' training regime, should prove a heady mix for bold, ambitious trainees.

Gouldens has been one of the golden circle of City firms, positioned below the big City players, but (forgive our use of the hackneyed phrase) felt to be punching above its weight. Its name is often mentioned alongside those of Travers Smith Braithwaite and Macfarlanes. Although well known for its lean, mean and successful corporate practice, Gouldens also built its reputation by paying its people – from trainees right up to partners – stacks of cash. Sure, it's been accused of being mercenary, but there's no disputing the chutzpah and hard work of its lawyers.

sharp suits

Clients have praised the firm's *"focused"* approach and its advisors, who *"get on with it."* Now our colleagues on *Chambers UK* report that the merger has endowed Gouldens with the transatlantic capabilities necessary for cross-pond deals. So now, in addition to Jones Day's London lawyers, Gouldens has access to a vast worldwide network, including 12 offices in the US, seven in Europe and eight in Asia. This trans-Atlantic capability can already be seen at work: London partners are working alongside DC partners for Russia's third largest oil company, TNK, in its US$6.75 billion joint venture with BP. And the firm recently advised US energy companies Aquila and FirstEnergy on the intended disposal of their interests in electricity distributor Midlands Energy.

JDG's London IP practice is doing well, in particular on trademark work where it acts for Glaxo and Boehringer Ingelheim in ongoing trademark litigation against parallel importers. For those who fantasise about the inimitable Ms Croft, the IP group acts for software publishers Eidos, best known for *Tomb Raider*. And JDG is also acting for some "trendy" (their words, their quotation marks, their everything) clothing manufacturers including Acupuncture, Ted Baker and Nike in licensing deals. Other practice areas are on the up, including litigation, which is widely seen by clients to have received a shot in the arm from the merger. Real estate and environment are among other bubbling departments.

and the lotus

So far so good, yes? Except changes are afoot in the newly merged outfit including the introduction of the Jones Day IT systems (Lotus Notes instead of Outlook), and billing matters now being run from Cleveland. The US billing culture is a notoriously onerous one when compared to the UK's, and there have been a few sharp intakes of breath at the prospect of meeting the new, hiked target of 2,000 chargeable hours a year. How appropriate that the world's first mechanical cash register was invented in Ohio.

What effect will the merger have on Gouldens' unique non-rotational training regime? While we heard that *"Jones Day partners and senior associates have a different view of trainee work,"* sources assured us that Gouldens' partners *"are fighting the corner"* to protect the old regime. To this end, they have delivered *"a series of talks on delegation."* In short, while there may be some dilution of the distinctive Gouldens' culture, the training scheme remains intact for now. Hurrah!

flying solo

What, then, has made the Gouldens' training so unique? On day one you are allocated your own office and total (well, almost) freedom. No shifting departments every six months, no sharing your space with a supervisor, no waiting hopefully for the work to come your way. It's almost as if you're treated like a sole practitioner in the sense that you've to hunt and gather your own work. Over the course of the two years, you must fulfil certain experience requirements, but there's no need to spend six months in any one practice area. Instead, trainees build up relationships with the partners and associates who do work that interests them. In practice, although *"everyone knows that there's a new batch of trainees, ensuring that you get approached with work,"* you will nevertheless be *"encouraged to bang on doors and introduce yourself to people."* The result is that *"you need to be responsible for yourself."* To ensure that trainees don't slip through the cracks, there are twice-weekly training seminars in the first year, which become weekly in the second.

"There's no doubt that you will get more work from the department [in which your office is located]." However, if you feel that you're receiving too much in an area that doesn't turn you on, take heart: *"It's not uncommon for people, after a year, to think 'I'm worried that I'm getting too much corporate'"* and to move to a room in another department. For bold, self-assured trainees, this can be a wonderfully challenging and liberating training experience. They have the pleasure of managing their own workloads, and are less likely to be at the beck and call of partners. According to one: *"A lot of my friends in larger firms turn up to work and do nothing until 3pm, then find that they have to stay until 10pm. Here, some people turn up at 7am, hit the road with their work and leave at 5pm."* For those who work out, this training creates confident and capable NQs. But it can also *"lead to a certain arrogance."* One source told us: *"Some people compare themselves and the work they're doing to that of their friends and say 'I must be great'."*

To survive this training regime you must be tough, confident and organised. If our interviews were any indication, the JDGouldens lot have these qualities in spades. Insightful, funny and unafraid to speak their minds, they were a pleasure to interview. Even when one castigated our fearless researcher with the words *"That statement is just preposterous!"* He had clearly forgotten our appointment as devil's advocate.

aristocrats?

There is an expression that likens managing lawyers to herding cats. At Gouldens it must be especially difficult. The idea of kowtowing to the Americans hasn't left everyone purring; said one trainee: *"I'm not fifth in line to be an earl or anything, but I'm English and the US set up doesn't appeal to me."* This was a firm that prided itself on its lack of restrictive administration, and according to one source: *"Before, we had a large degree of autonomy on files and general admin. Now it's a lot more constrained, and everything has to go through Cleveland."* Said another: *"There are tight controls on things like staplers now, whereas at Gouldens you just rocked up and took four."*

And yet, amidst all the changes, some things stay the same: the firm still gathers on the roof of its Old Bailey office building for drinks in summer, and in winter *"it will be back to the local pub,"* the Smokey Irish – Seamus O'Donnell's to use its real name. It's not just on pay day that the high-earning partners flash the cash for staff; in the pub, too, they are famous for being generous and gregarious.

In 2003, the firm kept on 11 of its 17 qualifying trainees.

and finally...

If the idea of running your own show appeals, Jones Day Gouldens will put you in the spotlight. If you have a strident, go get 'em attitude, this is a firm to consider. But don't take our word for it. When we asked trainees what advice they'd give to prospective applicants, they told us: *"Do a summer placement here, and another at a large City firm. See which suits you best."*

Kendall Freeman

the facts

Location: London
UK ranking by size: 177
Total number of trainees: 15
Seats: 4x6 months
Alternative seats: Secondments

On 1 May 2003 Kendall Freeman was born out of the popular firm DJ Freeman. It seems that having celebrated its 50th birthday, the DJ Freeman project had gone as far as it was ever going to and it was time to retire from the decks.

them's the breaks

Last year we felt a touch guilty about describing the old DJ Freeman as the legal equivalent of a Ford Mondeo. We suggested that the firm's management might consider lowering the suspension and souping up the engine. We'll confess to being as surprised as anyone when five months later, after some serious soul searching on the part of the executive committee, the decision was made to break up the firm. The reason it gave was "an insufficient strategic fit with the ongoing business." Many of the firm's property and technology & media lawyers moved over to Olswang. The remaining lawyers (about 40% of the partnership) now operate under the Kendall Freeman banner and are free to concentrate on litigation and commercial services aimed at the insurance industry.

We used to tie ourselves up in knots trying to explain (and even understand) the old DJ freeman business model, so we'd like to extend our thanks to the big men at KF for making our lives easier this year. Readers will obviously want to know what the new firm's business amounts to. A lot of litigation and arbitration for a start. Obviously, a good deal of it for its extensive list of insurance and reinsurance clients – AXA, Munich Re, Direct Line, HSBC Insurance Brokers, Equitable Life of the United States, Chubb, St Paul and Global Aerospace to name a few. Then there's general commercial litigation for clients like Shell, TotalFinaElf, Invensys and Corus, and the extra special work of the public international law team. The PIL lawyers represented the Nigerian Government in the International Court of Justice in its land and maritime boundary dispute with Cameroon. They are also advising Somaliland in its bid for independence. If you get offered a seat with the team, you should appreciate what a fantastic opportunity it represents – many people would sell their grannies for this work.

So far it sounds like a very litigation-heavy firm. It is, but there are transactional and commercial lawyers too, because as with any other type of business, insurance companies get involved in M&A and funding issues, plus they need regulatory, tax, insolvency and employment advice. The firm has stated its aim to develop its corporate and finance teams, so there's no need to write off the firm just because you don't intend to be a litigator. We couldn't help but think about what's going on at other insurance-focused firms (like Reynolds Porter Chamberlain and Barlow Lyde & Gilbert for example) – it's much the same diversification story. Of late, the insurance sector has been quite active in the AIM market and the firm's corporate lawyers had enjoyed some very decent work, including, in 2002, the PRI Group £130 million fundraising (the largest ever AIM flotation).

losing weight

Well, this is all well and good for the architects of the new firm, but what does it mean for trainees? *"The focus of the firm has been narrowed and so this obviously means the range of seats has narrowed."* We checked with the grad recruitment team and the following seats are currently on offer: insurance litigation, construction, company/commercial, general commercial litigation, PIL, insolvency and employment. Not a bad selection. So long as you don't want property, of course. There were one or two regrets that property was off the menu: *"Some are disappointed as they were expecting to do a seat there."*

"There's not too much fighting for seats," and our sources were certainly happy with the quality of work, supervision and feedback they were getting. Often trainees sit with senior assistants and work for more than one person, so ensuring their field of vision isn't too narrow. One reported: *"I've had day-to-day contact with clients and consultants; it's one of the things I've most enjoyed about the work."* Naturally, when you are working on a big litigation matter, there's a danger of becoming overwhelmed by bundling and pagination. Thankfully, *"there's a very good paralegal support team – a dedicated unit – they've always been a lifesaver in these situations, but trainees do their share."* Of course! On a £10 million claim, you're not going to get given the whole file, but you will be given *"discrete aspects of it, for example correspondence regarding disclosure. You always get the*

supervision you want, but you'll have a first go at something and it will then get cleaned up." In all respects, *"you must be willing to take on responsibility. At a smaller firm, you are no bit part."*

battling on

Our sources took a pragmatic view of their employer's reincarnation. *"To exist for 50 years and then to suddenly change – everybody was quite shocked really, it was initially an unsettling period. I was then quite surprised at how smoothly the transition went and how everything fell into place."* And as any wise 'new' firm knows, the first thing you do is make as big a splash as possible. *"We had a client event right at the beginning and the different departments have all been doing their own client events."* The feeling is that KF can now be more successful because it has *"no distractions. Clients see more resources focused on what they want to do."*

Now *"tighter and smaller,"* the firm fits neatly into the largest and best equipped of DJF's three former offices. 43 Fetter Lane was always the base for the insurance lawyers, so in effect it was business as usual on 1 May. Same desks, same next door neighbours, same cases and clients, just fewer people on the internal phone list and some new notepaper. The new branding is *"more classy, sleeker"* than the various DJF offerings of recent years. The firm has its own special blue – *"D52-6 or something. It's like going to Dulux!"* We clicked onto the KF website to see. "It's navy blue basically, isn't it?" we said. Our source agreed. We wondered if new, navy blue Kendall Freeman (which is, after all, a firm that wants to be more profitable than before) is going to lose the cuddly image people ascribed to DJF. *"That image is still fair,"* we heard. *"In a smaller firm, you do get to know people more easily. There are no partners who wouldn't know who I was…I could be sitting in the canteen with a couple of partners opposite."*

Not forgetting to keep spirits high amongst staff, the firm has also been throwing parties for its own benefit. As well as a spate of softball matches over the summer months, there was a party on the HMS Belfast. After hours, The Cartoonist vies for KF business with old-man pub The Mucky Duck and a couple of places on Farringdon Road. As one trainee put it: *"There's quite a bit of social action up and down the ranks."* And on the subjects of rank, we hear the men's five-a-side football team has a bit of a reputation in the London Legal league. *"We manage to finish second every time…actually, we've broken that now – we're fourth!"*

One trainee described the new firm as *"a leap in the dark,"* adding: *"Four months down the line, everyone is much happier."* From another: *"Job security has gone through the roof compared to what it was!"* And that can't be bad. In September 2003, six of the eight qualifying trainees stayed with the firm.

and finally...

Kendall Freeman makes sense where DJ Freeman had stopped making sense. Twelve months from now, we'll have figured out what model of car it is!

KLegal

the facts

Location: London
UK ranking by size: 29
Total number of trainees: 28
Seats: 4x6 months
Alternative seats: Brussels, Scotland, NI

KLegal was set up in 1999 as the legal arm of international accounting giant KPMG. Its brief history has seen super-rapid growth and a merger with leading Scots firm McGrigor Donald, but the last four years have also brought drama.

brave new world?

The Holy Grail of MDP (multidisciplinary practice) was KLegal's original raison d'être. The principles behind MDP centre on bringing accountants, lawyers, tax advisers and financial experts together to work in unison for clients. In the late 1990s, the MDP was seen by some as the brave new world of legal practice, and a number of lawyers, both young and experienced, jumped ship from traditional firms to come on board. But then came Enron. Once the seventh largest company in the US, it filed for bankruptcy and its auditor, KPMG's rival, Arthur Andersen, was implicated in the mess that followed. The downfall of both Andersen and its legal arm provided a salutary lesson for other accountancy practices and their tied law firms. In response to Enron, the US Government passed a piece of legislation called the Sarbanes-Oxley Act, which has had wide-reaching effects. We'll leave you to do some more research on the topic but, in short, it restricts the ability of accountancy firms to perform other expert services, including legal services, for their clients contemporaneously with audits.

Redundancies, partner defections and training contract deferrals (which have occurred at a number of leading firms) have prompted front-page headlines, but our sources were confident that *"the worst is behind us."* Dramas or no, our interviews left us concluding that KLegal offers an excellent training – this year many of the trainees we spoke to were among the most informed and commercially astute we encountered in our research. Perhaps it was a case of *"controversy pulling people together,"* but our sources were proud of their firm, and keen to speak up for its training.

donald, where's your troosers?

Finding that the professional landscape was changing around it, in 2002 KLegal merged with leading Scottish firm McGrigor Donald. The liaison brought a new client base, independent of KPMG, including a strong banking clientele with names such as Royal Bank of Scotland and HSBC. The merger also injected a more traditional law firm feel and internal systems, which some of our sources thought were *"more user friendly for lawyers."* So, although ties to KPMG remain strong, *"KLegal has come closer to being like any other law firm in London."* As one trainee concluded: *"KLegal needed a merger and McGrigors were up for it."*

A conventional partnership, McGrigor Donald is highly successful north of the border and was already in possession of an established London branch. But it also saw the tie-up with KLegal as a way of gaining access to extensive international links and resources. McGrigors has never been used to taking orders and it seems that, since merger, it has not taken them from its younger spouse. Examining the composition of the management of KLegal, it seems to us that McGrigors is wearing the trousers. Said one of our sources: *"You hear snipey remarks like 'This wouldn't have happened when it was just McGrigor Donald'."* But, to be fair to our other sources, we also heard that *"it took a while for two cultures to come together and become one happy family; everything is going smoothly and people are working together as a team."*

It's difficult to write a feature like this, knowing that the firm is unlikely to be in the same state and condition when readers will be ready to start their training contracts in 2006. The likely outcomes? A) KLegal will emerge older and wiser from the current market uncertainty as to the future of accountancy-tied legal practice. B) The influence of McGrigor Donald's Scottish decision-makers will continue to grow, while the bond with KPMG loosens. Just a week after we spoke with trainees, we heard that the third of the six founding KLegal partners had left the firm, making him the ninth KLegal partner to leave since the McGrigor Donald merger. We're prepared to be wrong, but our money would be on outcome B. And if our punt is right, readers may wish to spend a little time conducting some research on the Scots firm's client base and activities. As usual, we can refer them to *Chambers UK*.

rub-a-dub-dub

But let's put the crystal ball away and concentrate on the here and now – KLegal has some high-profile engagements. The firm acted for Tesco in its grey goods (parallel imports) dispute with Levi Strauss, and other notable clients include Tottenham Hotspur FC, Royal & SunAlliance, mobile service provider O2, Volvo and chemical company Akzo Nobel. Despite changes (brought by McGrigors and in the wake of Sarbanes-Oxley), KLegal still bears the hallmarks of MDP working. It's still the case that, rub-a-dub-dub-style, lawyers, accountants and financial advisers are rowing the same craft, albeit that the professional lines are clearer. KLegal and KPMG's offices are separate, but all within walking distance, and staff still get together on a weekly basis to discuss transactions. Trainees here are in regular contact with other professionals over the phone and by e-mail, and it's *"not unusual"* to find accountants, lawyers and tax consultants together in client meetings. But the stereotypes endure: *"You can spot an accountant a mile off,"* one trainee told us. *"They're the ones leaving at 5pm."*

in the slips

Trainees are permitted to select each of their four seats including, unusually, the first. Tax, tax litigation and IP are all popular, and each offers close integration with KPMG. When in the tax seat, most of your clients will be drawn from KPMG's tax consultancy, and the tax litigation seat brings you into contact with its *"rather technical"* tax experts. On offer is a mixture of High Court litigation and tax investigations work, which means plenty of *"hands-on"* experience, drafting, and issuing and serving claims. The work can be tricky, so it's perhaps best to save it for your second or a subsequent posting. The IP seat is in a transactional group with strong ties to KPMG's specialist intellectual property services team. Expect to be *"looking at the value of IP rights and how they fit in, in terms of tax and corporate wind-ups."* Again, the work can be complex, but trainees appreciated the responsibility they were given. You'll deal with accountants and patent attorneys on a daily basis and will also get some good, basic client contact.

The clients of the London corporate group are drawn from both McGrigor Donald's and KPMG's rosters. Trainees feel very included on deals, and although they see their fair share of document review tasks, there are perks – we heard a story about one trainee who went to Moscow for a completion, after which the clients took the whole team to the Bolshoi Ballet. In the banking seat, you'll be working for major banks on, amongst other things, property finance and PFI transactions. Here, trainees have good contact with clients and the opposing team's lawyers and attend their fair share of completion meetings.

In the pensions law seat, trainees see an awful lot of the KPMG folk, since the firm works on tax-based employee remuneration schemes. In the projects group, as in pensions, far from supporting the accountants and tax experts, lawyers *"go head to head with them to come up with solutions."* Full marks for the trainee supervisors in litigation, where the youngsters are let loose on client correspondence and appear in the High Court on small applications in front of masters. Although employment, or 'People Services' to use Kparlance, was no longer the top-choice department for trainees this year, the group continues to do high-profile work, including matters for Swiss International Air Lines and BP. Secondments are available to McGrigor Donald in Scotland and Northern Ireland or to Brussels. In September 2003, ten of the 15 qualifiers were retained.

what's my name?

McGrigor Donald kept its name after the merger, but we suspect that these feisty Scots weren't going to relinquish their respected 200-year-old moniker for anyone. Indeed, it seems that if anyone's going to be changing its name, it will be KLegal. We heard from some that we should expect a name change by the end of 2003. What will it be, we wondered. *"I don't mind,"* one trainee quipped, *"so long as it's not McLegal."*

Many people head to the pub together on Friday nights, and there are official firm-wide drinks once a month. Our sources also told us of a visit they were planning to the dog track. The *Student Guide* team would like to pass on a couple of tips. First, Sean Me Boy is a little beauty (we won over £80 on him at Walthamstow Stadium), and second, any dog that performs its ablutions just before the race is set for glory.

and finally...

The future of accountancy-tied law firms depends very much on the response of clients, and whether they continue to choose to instruct law firms that are linked with their auditors. It strikes us that KLegal has two dogs on which to place its bet – the accountancy firm that brought it into being and the Scottish law firm that is increasingly calling the shots.

Lawrence Graham

the facts

Location: London
UK ranking by size: 48
Total number of trainees: 35
Seats: 4x6 months
Alternative seats: Monaco

If you're interested in Lawrence Graham you now have two choices: read on or, if you'd rather, read our 2002 or 2001 reports. Not much has changed at this happy, mid-sized, property-plentiful firm.

white water and chips

"The firm will be a very different place in five years' time." Hmmm...convince us. *"It's becoming more City and more slick. It's very noticeable that we're trying to smarten up and give a better service. Everything is becoming more organised."* The reception has just been redecorated and last October the firm's logo and letterhead came back from the dry cleaners looking entirely different: *"Every scrap of paper in the office was whipped away at midnight and changed."* However, *"the changes are not just cosmetic – there've been changes in the firm's culture as well."* Trainees feel the firm has some great new ideas such as taking clients white-water rafting and holding casino nights – *"not just a bog-standard drinks party."*

In truth, LG hasn't always been great at publicising itself; some trainees told us the firm should be better known in the legal world. The property department is hot, and the tax and private capital department is very highly regarded, earning a top ranking in *Chambers UK* for its contentious work. This department has recently boosted its international presence (drum roll please) since scooping a Monaco office from Eversheds. Trainees can now spend three months there wooing new clients and taking lady luck out for nights at the tables. Martinis all round!

Back in London, property is the largest department; it drives the firm and brings in a significant proportion of the corporate work. You'll definitely do a property seat, and indeed some trainees do two and not always through choice. Trainees who wanted to qualify there raved about the great people and the interesting work – mostly projects for large property management companies. Those who were less keen still appreciated running their own, smaller files, the client contact and the strictly nine-to-six days.

stranded

You'll find people doing similar hours across LG, but the corporate department is a possible exception to the 'lawyer by day, well-rounded individual by night' culture. Here, you can expect *"to work until 10pm or later quite regularly,"* and we heard tales of working till 2am plus weekends. But guess what, trainees loved it, particularly the excitement of *"running on adrenalin."* Unsurprisingly, you'll see lots of property finance in this seat, and you'll work for companies aiming to get listed on AIM.

Litigation seats were also popular, bringing a spread of cases from contract claims to unjust enrichment and defamation. Clients include the Football League, brewers Scottish & Newcastle, and the liquidators of BCCI. There's a chance you'll be billeted at the firm's small outpost in St Mary's Axe near the Lloyds building, whch handles insurance, reinsurance and shipping work. Trainees are usually apprehensive about being exiled from the Strand mothership, but generally enjoy the seat. Back on the Strand, there are also more niche seats, such as employment and construction, and on occasion niche seats have even been created for people.

a word in your ear

Appraisals are pretty thorough; at your end-of-seat review, you'll be numerically graded on a whole host of professional and personal attributes. Just like the best reality TV, there's always high drama, laughter and tears – but training partner Hugh Maule isn't exactly Davina and no one gets voted off. If things do get bumpy, you can always turn to your mentor partner for advice or support. The only real gripe from the LG gang was that the seat allocation system is a tad erratic. Because second-years get priority, you'll get no consultation at all about your first seat and after that, *"the ball is very much in the trainees' court."* It'll be up to you to approach the training partner and drop a few hints before declaring your official preference in your mid-seat review. The system can work, but *"you have to be slightly pushy to get what you want. Stick to your guns. If you give an alternative and someone else wants your first choice, you won't get it."* The root of the problem seems to be too few litigation and corporate seats.

Qualification jobs are allocated in the same informal way. Most other firms have more transparent processes, but as always at LG, if it ain't broke... It certainly worked in 2003, as 15 out of the 16 qualifying trainees were made offers by the firm and 14 accepted.

whistle while you work

One trainee told us the air conditioning was so cold in her office that, on the baking August day when we spoke to her, she'd put her heating on as well. It could be said that this reflects the way in which LG trainees want the best of both worlds. Possibly this leaves them feeling a bit lukewarm: they dithered over the character of the firm. Basically, they didn't want us (or you) to think they're not hard working and ambitious, but they're big fans of *"this work/life balance malarky"* too. Trainees tell us: *"People take an interest in stuff you do outside work – you're almost expected to have something to talk about apart from the job."* Apparently some sections of the firm are *"quite sporty"* with lots of keen marathon runners, whereas in private client in particular, you're likely to find *"theatrical characters"* – one supervising partner even trained as an opera singer. Any chance of a song? Apparently not.

Expect *"an element of fun"* in the office and *"a bit of banter."* What kind exactly? *"Just generally not taking things too seriously...*[among the trainees] *it's never 'Oh my God, I've got to do this', but more 'I know I've got to do this, don't know quite how, but never mind!'"*

decorating with dinosaurs

Regarding the office, the word that fell most readily from trainees' lips was *"concrete."* How we chuckled when we heard about the lovely 'seventies' decor –*"green and white patterned wallpaper"* and *"carpet tiles."* However, trainees quite like the modern art in the spanking new reception area and the great views *"over the dreaming spires of the High Court."* The rumour mill indicates LG may move in the next year or so, quite possibly away from the West End and closer to Liverpool Street or Bishopsgate.

You can't talk to anyone for very long about the firm's social life before Daley's come up. This wine bar has been an unofficial extension to the office since time began: *"Every year the trainees resolve they're going to start going somewhere else...it never happens!"* And every year, there are departmental Christmas parties, client events and a summer soirée on the office roof. The highlight is the annual summer ball, this year held at the Natural History Museum – *"we ate our dinner underneath a dinosaur."* Unlike the prehistoric relics, romance is alive and well at LG and among the 16 second-years we found three couples. The annual trainee party is notorious: *"At both of the last two, someone got pissed before dinner and had to be carried home. It's kind of disappointing it didn't happen this year!"*

and finally...

Lawrence Graham may not be the most distinctive or cutting-edge firm, but it has interesting clients and some great work. If you don't want your enthusiasm for work and your personal life to be extinct by the time you hit your mid-twenties, you'll love it here.

Laytons

the facts

Location: Bristol, Guildford, London, Manchester
UK ranking by size: 109
Total number of trainees: 11
Seats: 4x6 months
Alternative seats: None

Laytons has evolved from a firm founded in the City of London 125 years ago into a four-site national commercial firm. Each office has its own distinctive flavour and something to shout about.

the matrix

Since the word 'matrix' aptly describes Laytons' network of independent yet interlinked offices, we couldn't resist the comparison with the blockbuster film. Unlike the sequel, however, each of Layton's incarnations has earned critical acclaim. Each attracts staff and clients from its own region, while pursuing a policy of cultivating relationships across the network.

We spoke to trainees in each location and noted a keen awareness of the activities of their colleagues in different parts of the country, not least because of the wonders of modern teleconferencing. For those with a desire to experience an area of practice not offered in their home office, there is the opportunity to enter the matrix and be teleported away for six months.

guildford: neo

Trainees normally spend six months in four departments chosen from coco, property, litigation, employment, and technology and media. Since merging with Lochners, the most prominent IP firm in the region, Laytons hasn't looked back and now boasts an unparalleled reputation in the South East for IP and IT. This year it reaffirmed its position by pulling off a deal for long-standing client Samsung, advising it on a movie/mobile partnership with Orange that will allow handset owners to download images, games and ringtones related to *The Matrix: Reloaded*. Whether in TMT or any other department (coco and property are also "*particularly busy*"), trainees like the fact that "*you are kept on your toes because you get good exposure to work and clients and can be expected to run your own files.*"

Apparently, "*it's not that you have to be an intellectual here, but you need to be very switched on.*" And speaking of intellectuals, we must mention the Guildford partners who, like Matrix hero Neo, have adopted powerful motorcycles as their preferred mode of transport. It's an absolute certainty that they pack more brains in their helmets than dear, sweet Keanu. Top clients include Harley-Davidson, Remmington and Nokia.

Socially, Old Orleans and The Star Inn remain popular for meals, Yates for a quick drink. The town centre location makes lunchtime chores easy, and a large Sainsbury's just two minutes walk away is also useful "*for ducking out to when you've forgotten the milk.*"

london: morpheus

In London every trainee will do the same four seats – property, coco, private client and litigation, the only difference being the order in which they are completed. Like Laurence Fishburne's character in *The Matrix*, Laytons' London wisdom comes from its considerable experience in the capital's legal hub. It is not officially the head office, but performs head office-type functions, such as the management of the trainee recruitment process. Coco is the largest department and boasts some plcs on its books, which in turn brings in some international work. The property group can also be proud of its client base, but as one source stressed: "*I wouldn't say any department really dominates the rest. There's definitely parity across the groups and so there are no superiority complexes...at least as far as I can see.*"

Plenty of extremely wealthy private clients liaise with Laytons London, and this seat is popular for its hands-on nature. One of our sources spoke of her most satisfying professional experience to date: "*I worked on a major contentious probate matter in court in place of a partner and got my first exhilarating experience of advocacy in front of a master. That's happened a few times since."* However, we did hear one gripe concerning the supervision and appraisal system: *"I think it's all a little unstructured. You actually have to ask a supervising partner for an appraisal and though you're likely to get one, it's not very reassuring. I felt that I was drifting somewhat, not knowing what the quality of my work was sometimes."*

Located on the upper floors of the superb Carmelite building on Victoria Embankment, the offices, particularly the client meeting areas and boardroom, have *"an unbeatable view of the best stretch of the Thames."* The locale ain't half bad from a social point of view either, with The Harrow, The Evangelist and The Witness Box close by.

manchester: trinity

Typically, trainees spend six months in the coco, litigation, property and family departments. Of course in *The Matrix: Reloaded*, Carrie-Anne Moss' Trinity character really wants to get it on and then settle down with Neo, perhaps even to have a couple of little wooden Keanu kids. If it all goes wrong, one or other party might consider instructing Laytons' Manchester family law team as it's top ranked for its work with wealthy individuals in the North West by *Chambers UK*. Family seat trainees really learn the meaning of client care, a skill they can take into commercial seats. Corporate remains the largest department and offers trainees a good client mix of listed and private companies. *"Over and above the usual basics, there's a fairly engaging amount of client contact and responsibility when it comes to drafting documents."* Our sources indicated that this is also true of the smaller litigation and property divisions. With a city centre that's easy to negotiate, the social scene in Manchester can scarcely be addressed in a paragraph. Bar 38 and Walkabout do a brisk trade with Laytons lawyers, as does lunchtime favourite, tapas bar El Rincon, situated just behind the office.

bristol: tank

Bristol trainees spend six months in coco, property/construction and litigation, and then a fourth six-month period is either spent back in coco or with the employment team. Just like Tank in *The Matrix*, the Bristol office really understands the design and build concept – its strength in construction law is evident and the department acts for a range of leading housebuilders, contractors and construction companies. Perhaps even more than the other offices, we sensed that Laytons Bristol gives trainees a *"very high level of exposure to clients"* and encourages a supportive environment in which they can manage their own files and act as the client's first port of call. On supervision and appraisal, one source said: *"It's definitely one of the selling points of the business. The supervision is brilliant and you are really made to feel important. There are monthly and mid-term appraisals, everyone has a training supervisor as well as the partner you sit with, and you can arrange additional conversations yourself if necessary."* Of all the seats, litigation appears to be the current favourite as trainees particularly enjoyed attending court with fee earners.

Lawyers here aren't spoilt with an over-abundance of flash facilities in the office: *"It isn't particularly swanky, but there's plenty of modern art on the walls, new furniture, greenery and a kitchen on both floors. Oh, and a tuck shop."* Bristol is certainly a lively city and we were told that you're *"highly likely"* to find Laytons' staff in The Three Sugar Loaves on Friday nights. An active social committee is always organising drinks, barbecues or the office party, which in 2003 was an energetic barn dance: *"It didn't matter if you could line dance or not. Everyone went the whole hog, partners included."*

Across the firm, six of the eight September 2003 qualifiers stayed with the firm.

and finally...

The best way of assessing whether Laytons is right for you would be to compare whichever of the offices you are interested in with the local competition. What they all have in common is good clients and a positive attitude to the role of the trainee. As in the movies, acting talent is not essential.

LeBoeuf, Lamb, Greene & MacRae LLP

the facts

Location: London
UK ranking by size: 218
Total number of trainees: 8
Seats: 4x6 months
Alternative seats: None

Now eight years old, the London office of US firm LeBoeuf, Lamb, Greene & MacRae has around 60 English and American lawyers. It is tiny compared to the New York office, which has been doing business since 1929, but it's an important stepping-stone to Europe for this global player.

the names of the game

The key to understanding what makes LeBoeuf (pronounced Lebuff) tick is knowing that its main focus is on two industry sectors. As one source explained: *"They want all the offices around the world to be the same, to concentrate on insurance and energy."* However, another source provided an equally important insight: *"The actual work you do doesn't really depend on the client; it's still, say, an acquisition, it's just that many of the clients happen to be in energy and insurance."* Obviously there is specialised work going on in the office, *"North Sea stuff,"* for example, but as a trainee you're not going to be floating on a sea of insurance claims or mentally clambering aboard oil rigs every day for two years.

The office is organised into two main departments – litigation and corporate. All trainees do a seat in each and then try out one of the more specialised groups – currently project finance, property, tax, and competition. The fourth seat will normally be in their qualification department. The client list is chock-a-block with insurance companies; having attracted good partners from a number of other firms, LeBoeuf can boast panel positions with CGNU, Lloyd's, Zurich Re, Royal & SunAlliance and...well the list just goes on and on. It specialises in technically complex cases, reinsurance and insolvency. At present it is deeply involved in issues arising out of the World Trade Center disaster.

banana splits

Proving that it's not all insurance-related claims, the litigation team was proud to have been instructed on a juicy matter that made legal headlines in 2002. The Noboa saga involved a family dispute over the inheritance of a US$1 billion Ecuadorian fruit company. Having ditched both sets of legal advisors, the parties turned to LeBoeuf and Herbert Smith to save the day. By all accounts the High Court trial was rather eventful.

Having been boosted by a team from Weil Gotshal, the project finance group continues to advise clients in Africa, the Middle East and Eastern Europe. The Maputo Port project in Mozambique has finally closed, with LeBoeuf acting for the various lenders who stumped up £45 million. The corporate team also expanded, with the arrival of a partner from Denton Wilde Sapte. One source was keen to point out that her arrival now meant that the office was no longer populated entirely by male partners. The recently arrived energy team has also settled into its stride. Many of the firm's current energy projects relate to Africa, such as the Ghanaian Volta River project and the restructuring of the electricity industry in Uganda.

small is beautiful

All our sources chose the firm because of their distaste for the factory farming of trainees in the City behemoths . *"With so few trainees here you can't hide, but in the same way, if you do well you are noticed. You are accountable for what you do; I suppose this firm is suitable for someone who doesn't mind people relying on them."* The scale and international nature of much of the firm's work does mean that trainees commonly take a supporting role, but occasionally smaller matters do come their way. Last year we reported on trainees' calls for paralegal help with the inevitable grunt elements in litigation. The firm has taken one on, but there is still plenty of bundling, copying and pagination to get through. However, there are three trainees in litigation at any one time, and qualified lawyers will roll their sleeves up and get stuck in too.

mid-atlantic accents

Trainees have six-monthly appraisals with the managing partner and one other. Training sessions occur monthly, many of them emanating from the New York office and patched through by video conference facilities. Trainees rated London sessions, but were less convinced of the usefulness of the American imports. One said: *"I wouldn't come here if you are expecting a large, structured training programme."* Each September a new batch of trainees is flown to New York for an orientation week, but while it's not necessarily the only overseas trip they'll make, there are no secondments to any of the 23 other offices.

One source pronounced the London office to be mid-Atlantic, confirming that pay was higher than standard for London (so true!), but lower than NY rates. The hours and billing targets are comparable with conventional City firms; and for trainees this means an average 9.30am to 7.30pm day. *"When jobs need to be done late at night or over a weekend, you don't just get an e-mail from an unknown person; people will come in and speak to you."* When we asked what influences had crossed the Atlantic, one source said: *"There aren't really any Americanisms, especially in the litigation department, which is very English. Saying that, we do have Americans over here in the corporate department and working for Lloyd's."* Another source felt that the firm did have one distinctive US trait in its London outpost – *"greater business aptitude."*

puppy dog tales

Described last year as a *"Gothicy building,"* there are a couple of things you need to know about LeBoeuf's premises. First, you must pay attention when using the lift because LeBoeuf occupies the sixth, ninth and twelfth floors. One trainee chuckled: *"There have been times I have come out of the lift and realised 'That's not right, I'm in someone else's office!'"* Second, LeBoeuf shares office space with a particularly evil lady. *"Our building is the one featured in 101 Dalmatians; it's Cruella De Ville's office."* There's a full-time business casual dress code, but a two-tone coiff is not recommended.

Staff usually go out once a week for drinks in local bars down Mark Lane. Attendance by partners is relatively rare, not because they are stand-offish – they probably just want to spend time with their families. *"Even at office parties they tend to just stay for a couple of drinks and then leave us to it."* A summer party is held on a Thames riverboat and at Christmas there's a black-tie bash. Three of the four September 2003 qualifiers have stayed to be around for the next one.

and finally...

LeBoeuf offers a highly paid training that definitely ticks the 'international' box. It will suit antone who hates being part of the crowd and/or wants to avoid highly specialised banking products. Just remember the insurance and energy focus.

Lester Aldridge

the facts

Location: Bournemouth, Southampton
UK ranking by size: 111
Total number of trainees: 11
Seats: 4x6 months
Alternative seats: Occasional secondments

The forecast for Lester Aldridge is clear skies and calm seas as it continues to take the south coast by storm.

flotsam and jetsam

Lester Aldridge was described by one trainee as *"a potential stepping stone to both the high street and the City."* Clients range from private individuals and small, local businesses to large banks and corporations. Combine this range with a *"drive towards being progressive"* and you are looking less at a mixed offering of flotsam and jetsam and more at *"a great base for a legal career."* Oh, and there's a beach.

The employment, corporate, property development and asset finance and banking practices are split between Southampton and Bournemouth, while fast track litigation (low value debt recovery) and residential conveyancing are handled in an office at Bournemouth International Airport. The trusts, tax and wills department is expanding from its Bournemouth base with fee earners also settling in Southampton too. Though Bournemouth is the main base, most trainees get a taste of this second office.

Rapid expansion in the last two years has seen LA develop a corporate outlook that sits better in the slick commercial hub of Southampton rather than grockle central by Bournemouth beach. And while this approach and an influx of new lawyers have not rocked the boat, this particular vessel has certainly changed tack. LA now cites names like Biffa and UGC cinemas as well as locals like Poole Pottery as clients.

like rabbits

Our sources felt the four-seat system worked well, saying: *"If you want to do something, you will get the chance to,"* though *"you might have to kick up a fuss to get family or marine law."* Described as *"a baptism of fire followed by working like a dog,"* the fast-track seat wasn't undertaken this year (Phew!), which left our interviewees without much to say on the subject of unpopular seats. A clear idea of what you want, and an even clearer voice seems to avoid disappointment. All six qualifying trainees were offered jobs at the firm and accepted them (although one is having a baby first).

We struggled to find anyone who was in much before 9am or left after 6pm. The corporate team has been known to keep people until 9pm occasionally, but *"the firm plays on the location to attract people, and there's no point in being in that location if you can't make the most of it."* Approximately half of the trainees share with another trainee, while the rest have their own rooms. Generally, interviewees preferred sharing as it made for a less lonely existence, and one source suggested fewer people would sit alone in the future, as *"they are multiplying like rabbits."* We moved swiftly on.

more beans, less counting

None of our sources was particularly concerned about billing targets. One told us she never looked at her time sheet and panicked – *"You are told not to worry about it at that stage."* And while grunt work does exist (one trainee mentioned a week spent manning the photocopier), generally *"you are encouraged to delegate"* to PAs and admin assistants. With billable hours comes a degree of autonomy and file management, and we got the impression there was a healthy balance of responsibility and supervision.An enthusiastic training director is held responsible for the bombardment of e-mails regarding extra training. Formal programmes vary between departments, but the added incentive of food at the sessions seemed standard and the odd glass of wine at the trainees' quarterly meetings with the managing partner was also seen as a way of *"getting trainees to spill the beans."*

shocking or normal?

LA once ran a marketing campaign under the banner 'Shockingly Normal' and we can only conclude that it was recruiting in keeping with this philosophy. One trainee declared: *"The firm has always been keen to promote normal people first, and lawyers second."* An unpretentious bunch, our sources struggled to spot any common traits amongst them, but it was obvious to us that the sea air and south coast lifestyle was a major draw in all cases. Around half the trainees are from the area and many attended Southampton Uni.

When we asked if there is anything they would want to change about the good ship LA, one trainee summed up the thoughts of the whole group: *"I would move my desk to the top floor where you get a great sea view."* (Actually one guy said he'd move his desk to the beach.) And what would they spy from the crow's nest? No longer a pleasure cruiser but an ocean liner, scattering its eccentricities in its wake. Photos of partners ironing or boogie boarding while fully suited and booted are now absent in promotional literature. The infamous PJ of Big Brother 3 fame (did he or didn't he?) was a no show for his training contract in September 2002, and what of Sparkle the pet pooch who has become the focal point of our interviews each year? Still around in the office, we hear, but no longer entertaining staff with her sandwich-eating tricks. We wonder if the 'shocking' has been lost from the equation as the firm turns its attention to bigger business.

One eccentricity trainees would happily throw overboard, is the *"cringeworthy"* AGM sketch. Unsurprisingly, as the firm grows, their desire to dress up and perform in front of the entire staff is waning. Our sources talked of mutiny and promised to keep us posted. This reluctance doesn't stretch to all fancily dressed occasions: the Christmas party had a star-studded 'stage and screen' theme last year and dress-down Fridays *"really are dress-down; there's no Friday chinos and loafers uniform here."*

all that snazz

As well as cricket and football, trips to Alton Towers, a summer ball, sailing and coastal walks are among the many events on offer. Friday nights see people in Downes in Bournemouth, and then perhaps in Toko's (apparently a *"vast improvement"* on former haunt Jumping Jacks). Socials see trainees mixing with partners, especially *"when the partners are buying the drinks."* The story is slightly different in Southampton; without the same number of people and the same established watering hole, the social life is less predictable. Yet Southampton definitely has its plus side. In a modern building on a Georgian crescent, the *"snazzy, clean and new"* appearance of the Southampton office *"reflects the way the firm is going."* Sadly, the sea views from the top floor must remain the greatest asset of Russell House in Bournemouth.

and finally...

"London ideals and a better lifestyle," is how trainees sum up Lester Aldridge. If you want a broad training (and sunbathing on the beach), drop anchor.

Lewis Silkin

the facts

Location: London
UK ranking by size: 98
Total number of trainees: 13
Seats: 4x6 months
Alternative seats: None

Each year we delve into Lewis Silkin hoping to unravel the mystery of Silkiness – the enigmatic quality that this firm looks for in its recruits. While that particular yarn remains a knotty issue, the firm is spinning a golden thread in several areas of practice.

from peckham to pukka

Lewis Silkin's cultural roots are in Westminster and a left wing of Peckham, but since 2000 the firm has been plying its trade from offices on the edge of the City. It was founded by the post-war Labour government minister Lewis Silkin, who lent his name and was succeeded by his sons. This history now seems dim and distant, particularly to trainees, yet it goes some way to explaining the firm's current guise: *"A real mix of social and not."* The firm of the noughties covers property, corporate finance, litigation, IP and construction in addition to three supersonic niche practices.

A first-class advertising and marketing practice goes part way to explaining why the firm is so media savvy. Assist on copy clearance advice and you'll never again regard commercial breaks as an opportunity to put the kettle on. Recently the firm represented ad agency Mother in its custody battle with the administrator of ITV Digital for Monkey's IP rights. Unfortunately, when we checked Monkey's current value on ebay, he was going for a paltry 38 quid. The team also advised Abbott Mead Vickers BBDO in relation to Jamie Oliver's work with Sainsbury's.

fair play

Niche number two might be just the thing to satisfy the social welfare campaigner in you. The housing group acts for countless housing associations and trusts on things like inner-city regeneration schemes, transfers of local authority housing and care homes, large-scale property funding and PFI projects.

Niche three can hardly be called a niche at all. The highly rated employment practice has grown to such an extent that it now makes up almost a third of the firm. Instructed by Harrods, Pizza Express, Pret a Manger, *FT*, Fiat, Sony Music and several leading law firms, the team has set its sights on worldwide business, having joined Jus Laboris, an international alliance of employment law firms. To date this new alliance has culminated in little more than a trip to South America for the firm's footie players (and subsequent humiliation at the hands of an Argentine team), but in the long run it is expected to reap benefits.

ooh ahh (just a little bit)

Given the firm's achievements in these three areas, we were surprised that our sources had picked Lewis Silkin for somewhat vaguer reasons…that elusive Silkiness perhaps. So, what is it? "*Ermm…I don't know.*" Anyone else? "*It's about being an individual and being able to be who you are, but working collectively.*" Apparently, it's about "*being a bit more alternative, a bit more off the wall, a bit more different and standing out a bit.*" Sounds terribly bitty. Could be time for some brand identity training for the kids.

Although the firm unpinned its red rosette some time ago, we are told it is "*straightforward, straight talking and quite political. They like people who will express opinions on politics and are interested in current affairs.*" That said, none of our sources came across as rollicking rabble-rousers. The bunch we spoke to subscribed to middle ground views on…everything.

You don't have to worry about being outspoken when it comes to the seat system. Some indicated that there were three compulsory seats…sort of…with a fourth taken anywhere you choose: "*Corporate, property and litigation are vaguely what you have to do, it is very much up to you.*" The demand for employment is met easily as there are three seats and IP is also popular; however, construction ("*fights about windows and buildings*") is not top of everyone's wish list, nor this year is property, though, "*those who have done social housing have loved it.*" Apparently, "*everyone is keen on litigation.*"

suits you, sir

While in property you will be running your own files, in corporate you'll get a smaller supporting role. Our sources stressed: "*You aren't just there to be a dogsbody,*" but "*you are expected to roll your sleeves up and hit the photocopier from time to time.*" Trainees' experiences vary a great deal; one said they'd been on site visits alone and attended client meetings, others felt they fulfilled a less vital role. Striking a happy medium (as ever in this firm) we heard: "*If you're willing to take on responsibility, and have the ability to do so, they will give you a lot.*"

Departments organise their own training and always invite trainees along. Mid and end-of-seat appraisals are padded out with encouragement and support: "*You are never left to wonder and they are very quick with thanks.*" There is also a monthly meeting between trainees, HR and a training partner, which starts in the office, and usually ends up in the pub. The hours are "*not unduly onerous*" and "*by 7pm it is pretty much deserted.*" The feeling is that "*the firm holds itself out as appreciating people;*" it is "*not intimidating.*"

The firm has a liberal approach to dress. While the litigation lawyers opt for suits, in employment and IP things are "*a bit more casual.*" The idea is that "*each department has its own culture and dresses accordingly.*" Bearing in mind that these interviews took place in the hottest week of the year, we weren't surprised that partners were walking around the office in shorts.

and the winner is…

Most trainees have followed the school-degree-LPC superhighway to a training contract. It has to be said, our sources were a very nice, straightforward bunch, but we wondered what had happened to all those opinions and "*that little something extra*" they claimed the firm looked for. If this sounds harsh, let us reflect.

This is a firm that is *"quite quirky."* It prides itself on its award-winning Christmas cards – each year, without fail, *The Times* bestows praise on the firm for its ingenuity. This is also a firm that offers massages in the lunch hours and *"tries to introduce things that people want."* A firm that has special taps in the kitchens dispensing sparkling water (*"for sparkling people"*). And a firm with top banana niche work that's expanding faster than its offices can bear. In September 2003, four of the six qualifiers remained at the firm to continue their quest for Silkiness.

The Friday night social life revolves around the nearby bars like Hodgsons in Chancery Lane and The Cheshire Cheese, and a social committee organises film nights, football, cricket and theatre visits. The annual summer bash this year had a 007 theme, prompting the arrival of several catsuited laydeez and a partner dressed up as Blofeld, complete with furry feline accessory. The office in cobbled Gough Square, near to Dr Johnson's House is deemed to be *"standard"* but *"nice and modern;"* its ground floor meeting rooms and canteen double up as a venue for tequila nights and cocktail parties. Gough Square itself seems to be another party venue and general gathering place during sunny lunchtimes.

For all its niches and quirks, it's important to remind yourself that there are plain old regular law firm experiences to be had here. You'll record your time, draft letters, research, bundle and proofread just like your peers all over the City. The fact is, the runaway success of the niche groups has overshadowed good corporate finance, commercial property and general commercial litigation, which actually make up the bulk of the work. If you just want to be a regular lawyer doing regular deals, there's room for you too.

and finally...

A-1 advertising, employment and social housing work; quality mainstream practice; and a healthy philosophy on the relative importance of work. Just add sparkling water.

Linklaters

the facts

Location: London
UK ranking by size: 4
Total number of trainees: 250
Seats: 4x6 months
Alternative seats: Overseas seats, secondments
Extras: Pro bono – Disability Law Service, death row appeals, RCJ CAB, Mary Ward, Toynbee Hall, Hackney and Southwark Law Centres, Liberty, lang. training

This City king is, according to its brochure, "recruiting for talent." For big deals, rigorous training, hard work and high standards, Linklaters says "good enough isn't good enough." Simon Cowell eat your heart out.

school dazed

When you sign up with Linklaters, you also sign up for top-notch formal training. Recruits receive a week-long pre-LPC business foundation course run by Manchester Business School. Your vacation may be cut short by a week, but the course will be a useful primer for the City LPC, when you'll also receive constant attention from the firm. The grad recruitment team go on a LPC 'liaison tour' and meet with each future trainee twice during the LPC. If you're not doing well, you 're going to have to explain why.

The pre-contract training sets the standard for the next two years. The PSC course is swiftly executed in a two-week block up front and is then followed by an induction to the inner workings of the firm. Teams of trainees are put through their paces on a task called the 'All Night Scenario', which has the newbies shut in offices with crashing computers, broken printers, an onslaught of irate client calls and a deal to close. In the middle of the nightmare a bright young student calls to ask about applying to Linklaters. Come on in (if you're hard enough). Thereafter trainees are treated to a liberal scattering of lunchtime lectures, departmental training sessions and group case studies that fit in around departmental work.

Linklaters recently underwent a makeover and adopted a new shade of pink for its logo. Don't be fooled: Barbie has not taken over as managing partner. In the legal world, this place is known as Castle Greyskull and the pink image belies a top-flight corporate powerhouse that, along with its magic circle peers, subscribes to the hard-graft school of thought.

magic moments

Linklaters continues to command respect for handling some of the highest profile work around. It won a Queen's Award for International Enterprise, and conducts business on a global scale for clients such as Shell, Vodafone, Hewlett-Packard, BA, Merrill Lynch and BT. The focus is primarily corporate and its name is tied to big-ticket work like the £21 billion acquisition by Network Rail of Railtrack, the €8.5 billion merger of Innogy with RWE and the £15.1 billion merger between Lattice and National Grid. We're talking FTSE 100. We're talking Blue Chip. We're talking Big Deal.

And Linklaters is a very big deal. It has a very large trainee population (although we did note that it is smaller by 44 people this year, which may be a result of deferrals in 2003). When quizzed about the firm's tendency in recent years to recruit more trainees than its direct competitors, some sources implied:*"It is a bit of a cloaked attempt to get all the good people in."* Or as one source put it: *"It's like picking all the apples on the tree without knowing what you are going to do with them. Inevitably, some of them end up rotting."* Most of our sources echoed the words of one trainee who said: *"You are not competitive with the other trainees."* But then we heard of a new breed of trainee coming in; the sort who seems *"extremely competitive and serious – much more career driven."* Is this the net result of all the intense and City-focused pre-contract schooling?

help yourself

The training follows a standard four by six-month seat rotation. A spell in a contentious department is no longer required for those who would prefer to attend a five-week litigation training programme at the College of Law in Store Street. Corporate is the only compulsory seat, although there are options here. For example, work in the investment management group offers alternative investment funds, private equity, real estate funds and reconstruction work, and in quieter times a client secondment may take the place of six months in the corporate dept. That said, mainstream corporate finance seats are popular as *"that is where the big work is and that is what Links does."* Your first seat is allocated and then in a meeting with HR you'll plan out the remainder of your contract. However, *"they are flexible, and your seating plan doesn't have to stay the same at all."* Our sources recognised the benefit of a helping hand: *"You can have a lot of say in your plan as long as you are wise in the way you play it, and if you get a partner on your side then it helps."*

The firm offers plenty of overseas seats and client secondments. We checked the stats: at any one time 30-35 trainees are abroad and the same number will be on client secondments. In the past, international postings have been the preserve of third-seaters; now trainees are encouraged to head off in their final seat, thus giving them more time back at base to work out where they want to qualify. Think smart if you want to jet off to one of the more popular destinations: Singapore, Hong Kong or Paris. We were told, quite categorically, that *"you don't get away with just fancying a seat in Hong Kong – it needs to fit in with your longer term aims."* Of course, *"people do have a laugh living as an expat in any of these countries"* and the experience is a refreshing change. Though *"you can feel less supported, it is less stressful"* and *"while it can feel like an outpost, you get plenty of good work and are well looked after."*

If this suggests that behind the gnashing jaws of Castle Greyskull it's just one long battle with the photocopier, fear not. In the past we have commented on a dearth of paralegals, and our sources told us that cutbacks have made them an even rarer breed; however, for every source describing night-long proofreading sessions as *"the trainee's lot"* someone else told us: *"Some good work is given over to you to manage on your own."* Sure, *"you will get crap trainee jobs, but it is up to you to build up trust and show you are keen and able."* If you sign up for a magic circle training, you also sign up to stints as the highest paid, most overqualified Document Facsimile Production Technician in the City. Then again, *"after a big deal, when you open the* [newspaper] *and see it, it makes it all worthwhile."* We were once again reminded of the story of the Cape Canaveral cleaner who, when asked by the US President what he did for NASA, replied "I'm helping to put a man on the moon."

After qualification, you can take a six-month sabbatical to *"learn something, or help a community, or save turtles and stuff."* Links pays 20% of your NQ qualified salary for the duration, but stipulates that a week of good deeds followed by a holiday is not an option. Although eight people had taken up the offer in 2003, most of our sources were somewhat cynical about the scheme, feeling that six months was too long to be out of the frame. *"People would prefer to just have a couple of months holiday instead."* Turtle haters.

masters of the universe

We jest. It is always tempting to despise the He-Mans and She-Rahs of the corporate world, but Links trainees really are some of the most articulate, strong-willed, philosophical and witty recruits the City has to offer. Confident, enthusiastic and competitive, these are the boys and girls who *"excelled at school by putting pressure on themselves."* Top-flight universities are the main suppliers, with *"Oxbridge popping up more than others."* Life's achievers come to Linklaters to *"push and stretch themselves"* in this *"very merit-based firm."* They are people who *"self-impose"* and understand the benefits of having *"a great training, great support, great clients and a great name on your CV."*

We were told of *"a certain corporate personality that likes the pressure"* and this is certainly what the firm's own recruitment material suggests it wants. One lucid source noted that *"the firm expects a lot, and sometimes people scare themselves by moving out of their comfort zone."* Another wasn't talking about cheap office furniture when they said: *"It is not so much scary, as uncomfortable sometimes."* Challenging, *"driven and high-pressured;"* trainees warn: *"You need to be realistic about the environment you're coming into."* We concur.

All that said, *"there is a social element, and there is always a lot of good banter."* In addition to an appraisal system that follows the standard mid and end-of-seat format, trainees praised levels of feedback and the approachability of senior staff. Post-deal evaluations give everyone a chance to chip in, and trainees say 'upward feedback' is appreciated. On top of that, fee earners do genuinely seem to appreciate trainees' efforts. Each shares an office with their supervisor and *"you can ask stupid questions."* There does not seem to be an overt guilt culture associated with hours, but everyone had a horror story to tell – two working weekends in two years was about average for our sources. You will have to cancel some evenings out, and you will have to go without sleep on occasion, but perhaps this is where a plentiful supply of trainee bodies to share the load works to your advantage.

high rollers

If feng shui roof terraces, basement swimming pools and Turner Prize winning art are your thing, Links' office decor won't do it for you. Described as *"big, grey and austere"* the premises offer *"nothing wacky."* But the shop floor is light and spacious, totally appropriate for a self-proclaimed corporate powerhouse with no pretentions to be a theme park. The in-house restaurant, Silks, produces very decent food, the gym has been extended, and there are all the necessary services to sustain a busy City lifestyle: doctor, dentist, manicurist…there's even a cash machine. In fact *"you don't ever have to leave – everything you would ever need is here."*

The social scene takes a secondary role to business, but departmental drinks on a Friday (and a clink-clinking trolley that does the rounds after deal closures) keep people topped up. For the sporty there are tennis, football and softball teams among other things. However, those with a masochistic desire for Cowell-style abuse may find the judges in the annual talent comp, LinkIdol, a little too kind. For trainees there is also an annual ball, which puts drinks in the The King's Head or Corney & Barrow deep in the shade. Post-deal client dinners were also mentioned, and trainees appreciated being invited to these.

While 54 of the 65 qualifiers were retained in September 2003, as in all magic circle firms, there is a general trend for solicitors to reassess their position after another two or three years. *"Trainees probably don't see themselves as partners here."* Why not? *"Because it is damned hard to go the whole hog here."* Is Linklaters a victim of its own success? Here is a top-notch firm, recruiting the cream of the trainee crop, yet down the line this can be problematic. *"Many of the people they recruit would be interested in working for a firm that has places to go, rather than one that is sitting at the top fighting off the competition. These trainees aren't boring academic types, they don't want a stale experience. It's not that it is better anywhere else, it's just that you want a change of scene; you want to cash your chips in to see what you'll get."* Trust us – you'll get a lot.

and finally...

If you want to be trained to within an inch of your life as one of a legion of high achievers, you should consider Linklaters.

Lovells

the facts

Location: London
UK ranking by size: 10
Total number of trainees: 119
Seats: 4x6 months
Alternative seats: Overseas seats, secondments
Extras: Pro bono – The Prince's Trust, Community Links, Caribbean death row appeals, FCO pro bono, language training

Top-notch corporate and commercial firm Lovells has long been a popular choice for training contract applicants. It slipstreams the biggest firms in the City, and in the summer of 2002 it took a physical and psychological leap forward when it moved into new offices on Holborn viaduct.

lex and the city

The atrium in Lovells' new home contains Europe's tallest water sculpture. And it swings. We asked if Angela Conner's seven-storey high creation said anything about the firm and were told that *"there's a whole kinetic energy idea going on, but there is nothing deep and insightful about it."* Trainees told us the *"comedy pendulum"* made them *"slightly seasick,"* and had a *"hypnotic effect."* Assuming this was not the original intention, we wondered if it is more a comment on *"the sense that Lovells is going places"* and *"the momentum in the firm."* Then again, we know we think too much.

Previously we've described Lovells as the perpetual corporate bridesmaid, implying that she'd never succeeded in marrying herself into the magic circle. All this talk of energy and momentum led us to wonder if Lovells wasn't now hoping to dash up the aisle. Some trainees described a *"management revolution,"* a *"sharpened image"* and *"an undertone of ambition and drive that has come more to the forefront."* However, others were adamant that *"Lovells isn't your hardball player,"* and seemed more comfortable with the Lovely White & Clean label it acquired when it was known as Lovell White & King. Perhaps the new office says more about Lovells' willingness to feather its singleton nest. Perhaps it's more interested in independent ventures and enjoying life as the successful and single Samantha Jones of the legal world.

the bottom line

Lovells is at base a corporate and commercial law firm. You need go no further than the sleeping pods in the basement (*"more for partners than trainees with a migraine"*) to know that it is as serious about the bottom line as any other City firm. It acts on enormous deals including the £2.6 billion merger of Granada and Carlton, the £750 million acquisition of Littlewoods by LW Investments and the London Underground PPP. It is not afraid to try something new: Lovells has pioneered the 'Mexican Wave' whereby it accepts all the work for property client PruPIM, and farms out lower value stuff to smaller firms.

However, it's not all corporate grind and power naps. Below stairs there's also a staff gym and restaurant and upstairs in the engine room, the firm offers a broad array of alternatives to the hard slog in the corporate department. Niche departments abound at Lovells and, in the past, we've always heard plenty about the IP group. While it continues to do the business for big names like Mars, Estée Lauder and Nintendo, trainees told us: *"IP is off the boil."* Apparently, *"it was perceived to be a trendy, cool area of law, but actually, it isn't all champagne receptions, and you can be doing cutting-edge stuff in other departments instead."*

We heard that *"litigation is more popular."* Perhaps swayed by the firm's involvement in the ING Barings case and its continued defence of British American Tobacco on health-related claims, trainee heads had clearly been turned by this part of the practice. Despite less chance of client contact and a greater threat of a peripheral role, the area has trainees fighting for the opportunity to be in on the high-profile cases.

The staff restaurant received mixed reviews. While it is widely regarded as a great place to catch up with friends, we were warned to *"avoid the world food counter: it is expensive and odd."* Thankfully, trainees feel no xenophobia when it comes to Lovells' international practice. In the last few years it's picked up offices across the globe through a series of mergers and start-ups. The most recent addition is an office in Shanghai, which brings the tally to 24 foreign offices..

swivel seats

Six floors of offices at Lovells sit around the atrium, so trainees either get the goldfish experience looking in towards the centre of the building, or a view out towards Smithfield or Holborn. The individual offices are a pretty standard affair – every trainee shares with their supervisor. Likewise, the seat system adopts a no-frills, functional approach: trainees do compulsory seats in litigation and corporate or finance, and then indicate preferences for the other two. There are few unhappy customers: *"There is a reasonable amount of flexibility, you just have to push a bit for what you want."*

Secondments to clients like Esso, Barclays, John Lewis and Egg are both common and *"super."* Although some trainees are *"reluctant to take them for fear of being out of the office,"* others welcomed the *"depth of experience and responsibility that you struggle to get elsewhere."* International seats provide a *"less London centric"* view of both legal practice and Lovells. Hong Kong and New York remain favoured destinations, as are Brussels and Paris, but Frankfurt and Milan are also offered.

Lovells' formal training has long been regarded as excellent. One source said: *"If I had £50 for every training course I had been on I would take the money and run."* In addition to a thorough induction and in-house PSC, throughout the two years additional sessions come in *"a glut at the start of each seat"* and monthly thereafter. Alongside the training, recruits get thorough appraisals. Monthly training records are discussed with supervisors, who also conduct end-of-seat appraisals and mid-seat reviews (if they have time). Generally, regular feedback is forthcoming, and while we got the feeling that trainees might not be receiving gushing praise or outright insults, they are always kept on the straight and narrow. They repeatedly told us that they felt supported. The sheer size of the firm and its work means that Lovells is not the place to come for an overdose of responsibility or scores of your own files. Except in property where you are likely to have *"a whole host of them."* Even in the corporate and litigation seats it's not all grunt work; intriguingly, we were told that *"if you are doing the photocopying, it is almost certainly your own fault."*

However, we got the impression that the firm gives as much as it takes, and while we did hear of poor souls passing up New Year revelries and Valentines dinners for an evening in the office, *"in terms of hours, they tend to ask rather than demand."* Inevitably there will be late nights and weekends, but it is rare for trainees to be left alone into the wee hours.

smartie pants

On each fee-earning floor there are 'Smartie Rooms'. Designed for internal meetings, the rooms are furnished with brightly coloured chairs around big glass tables, and some even proffer bowls of Smarties. If this all sounds a bit like playschool, rest assured, you will not be expected to dress the part or raise your hand when you need the loo. The firm subscribes to the suited and booted school of thought, but you are allowed to dress up on occasion – namely the annual ball. A no expense-spared fancy dress fandangle, this year's Oscars-theme saw partners dressing up as Pavarotti and Trinity from the Matrix, and *"there were a whole heap of Dolly Partons."* Others translated the Oscar theme more literally. With prizes of plane tickets to Paris and dinners at the Ritz, *"it is definitely worth taking your clothes off and spraying yourself gold."*

An enviable trainee budget gets people involved in dragon boat racing, trips to the dogs or the theatre, archery or horse riding. For drinks after work, most people head to the Bottlescrue, but more enticing bars in Smithfield are close at hand. Trainees mainly socialise within their intake, but also with their departments, some of which down tools for tea and cakes on a Friday afternoon.

hawks and doves

The top floors of Atlantic House have been kitted out as a swanky client area with *"loos like something out of Ideal Home."* But for whom is this home ideal? Despite a propensity for Oxbridge candidates on vacation schemes, the recruitment process ensures a *"liberal sprinkling"* of successful candidates from other universities. Our sources came up with various different reasons for having chosen Lovells. Many were strategic – the firm offered the range of practice areas that they were after, and a City/international experience without (they assumed) the hard graft psyche or bad-boy reputation of the magic circle. It would be wrong to cast Lovells as a soft, girly firm, but there is no escaping the appeal of the label that says 'a friendly face in the City'. We put the 'Lovely' stereotype to our sources and they were quite clear that, while *"friendliness pervades, they don't stand any nonsense,"* and *"there are no group hugs."* One source went further, saying: *"The stereotype gives a rose-tinted, comic perception."* So is the firm trying to shake off its girl-next-door reputation? *"No, we're very professional, but there is still a human touch."* Not smiles all round in September 2003 though: only 25 of the 35 qualifiers stayed on with the firm.

At the very top of Atlantic House is an oriental roof garden complete with a pigeon scaring hawk called Hermione. If you go for an interview at Lovells, you might want to step outside to separate your ying from your yang before facing partners.

and finally...

Lovells' pendulum swings between its long-established, yet slightly misleading 'nice' reputation and the reality of a driven firm approaching 21st century international practice head-on. This is a firm for people who appreciate a warm welcome to hard work.

Macfarlanes

the facts

Location: London
UK ranking by size: 57
Total number of trainees: 45
Seats: 4x6 months
Alternative seats: Secondments
Extras: Pro-bono – Cambridge House & Talbot Advice Centre, Caribbean death row appeals, language training

Its reputation, clients and profitability are the envy of many in the City. *"Small but perfectly formed,"* it's easy to see why Macfarlanes is the choice of the more discerning trainee.

renaissance training

Macfarlanes has adopted the Mutant Ninja Turtles approach to staffing: "Leonardo leads, Donatello does machines. Raphael is cool but rude, Michaelangelo is a party dude!" Check out the student pages of the firm's website and you'll see what we mean – well-rounded trainees, and we don't mean in the Rubensesque sense. The Macfarlanes stable boasts a stack of outstanding scholars, athletes, linguists and more – sometimes packaged up in one individual. Together they are a potent force, and if our interviews are anything to go by, individually they seem jolly good sorts. As in the rest of the firm, there are some *"corporate ball breakers,"* a few *"charmers"* and the essential *"academic boffins."* What Macfarlanes trainees all share is commercial nous and a willingness to work hard. It's a *"no-nonsense firm. People do their job and don't shout about it loudly."* Well, not too loudly.

city life

Trainees will typically rotate through the litigation, property and corporate departments, with the fourth seat in private client or another, more specialised, area of corporate law. The City is quiet these days and there's not a great deal happening on the M&A front, so fortunately or unfortunately, depending on your view, the traditionally intense and stressful corporate seat has been a fairly civilised experience of late. But in times of plenty, you'd better have stamina. In addition to M&A, private equity is a pillar of its practice and, employing smaller teams, it frequently competes with magic circle firms on important deals. Led by the energetic and pragmatic Charles Martin and featuring cigar-chomping City man, Robert Sutton, the corporate practice blazes the Macfarlanes trail. If you want to go far, then this is your department.

Recent headlines have included the creation of a €2 billion fund by HSBC Private Equity, the £374 million disposal of Go for 3i, and a clutch of private equity deals for Advent, Alchemy, Candover, and other funds. Any of you with a Nectar loyalty card may wish to think of the firm next time you're buying petrol or baked beans – it advised on the scheme.

Naturally, some trainees will find they are better suited to other departments. In property, you'll handle your own files and deal with clients from day one. As a first seat, property can be *"a baptism of fire. From the moment you walk in to the office, at least ten clients phone you up thinking you're in charge."* Employment, meanwhile, has a gentler introduction. In the current market, it's seen a lot of senior executive redundancies, which *"provides interesting human drama."* Perhaps symbolically, the private client team is housed separately from the firm's main building. Not all trainees acquire a taste for this work – tax, wills and trusts with a sideline in immigration – but those who do get to work with a top-ranked team.

i think i can. i think i can

Almost every trainee ever born will tell you that partners at their firm are "accessible" and "approachable," and the Macfarlanes set are no different. Certainly among their peers and clients, Macfarlanes' lawyers are renowned for being "good to deal with," and for showing a "can-do" (thank you *Chambers UK*) attitude. Bring that attitude along with you on your first day and the firm will take things from there. There is an intensive programme of educational seminars, but if you prefer to learn by doing, then this is an ideal training ground. *"Trainees have quite a high profile in the office,"* and if our sources are right in their perceptions, they get more responsibility than many of their City peers. We have it on good authority that a Macfarlanes deal is never knowingly overlawyered, and this means plenty of juicy tasks for even the lowliest of trainees. *"At the end of the two years, you should come out really feeling like a lawyer."*

Don't come here expecting international seats. The firm concentrates on doing well at home and cultivating 'best friend' relationships with firms overseas. And that's how the trainees like it: *"The lure of international seats goes through your mind, but the most important thing is to get the best training. There are lots of firms offering seats abroad, but it's basically a holiday."*

Nonetheless, language skills are valued, and if you're a frühaufsteher or you simply want to brush up on your vocab, the firm offers French and German classes at 8.15am on Tuesdays. And if you're desperate for time away from the office, you can spend three months of your litigation seat working as an assistant to a judge in the Court of Appeal or try for a client secondment to 3i. Most trainees can expect to be offered a job at the end of their two years. In 2003, all 16 of the qualifiers stayed on.

country life

Macfarlanes is renowned as a rather old school and conservative (with a small 'c') place. Look at the grown-up, client-oriented part of its website, where images of stone lions and earnest lawyers accompany words such as "strength" and "trust" and you'll get the picture. Its offices resemble a *"plush, unstyled, old-fashioned hotel with Country Life magazine."* All this instils and perpetuates a reputation that the firm seems otherwise desperate to dispel, at least among students. Several years ago the firm enlisted the help of Beanie Man (imagine Where's Wally? meets a baked bean) to market itself to prospective trainees. The little fella is doing a fine job, so far as we can tell.

One trainee described the firm as *"traditional in the best sense."* Indeed, it has a very English *"no-nonsense"* attitude. But don't be fooled, Macfarlanes is far from stuffy. The trainees we spoke to all described the *"relaxed, non-hierarchical"* culture, and one praised the firm's knowledgeable support staff. Even if the premises were decorated by someone's gran, the firm does have virtu and it houses one of the best corporate art collections in the City.

legal gentlemen

No partner has ever left in order to join another firm and there is no written partnership agreement. Why would you need one when a gentleman's agreement will suffice? Like Leonardo da Vinci's unsinkable double-hulled ship, Macfarlanes is sturdy, established and indestructible. Trainees loved the fact that *"it's the same firm I applied to five years ago, only better."* There's no chance of turning up to work on a Monday morning to find that you've merged with a US giant.

But far from resting on its laurels, this firm is seriously ambitious. There is a *"total rejection of complacency"* within the firm and among its trainees. It's not called Macfastlanes for nothing. Working hours are a standard 9am to 6pm or 7pm, with some late nights. Sadly, we must report that the trainees are a pretty lazy bunch when it comes to post-work revelry: *"We usually end up at The Castle."* In summer, there's a five-a-side football tournament and a sailing weekend. If you hate the idea of forced fun and chain bar crawls with your intake of 100+, you'll feel right at home. And if the City gets too much for you, then how about a hike in the country? This year, a group of 15 staff trudged 46 miles up and down mountains in the Lake District for the firm's favourite charity. One read the map, one took control of the compass, one carried the thermos…

and finally…

One gets the overwhelming impression that, in spite of the important role played by Beanie Man, Macfarlanes isn't going to change. But when you've found a winning formula, why would you?

Manches

the facts

Location: London, Oxford
UK ranking by size: 80
Total number of trainees: 20
Seats: 4x6 months
Alternative seats: None

One day they'll make a TV mini-series based on Manches, the London and Oxford law firm that's topped the family law league tables for years and held its own among mid-sized commercial practices.

the dynasty

Visualise a drama set in the cinematic surrounds of the Aldwych in London's West End. Providing the backdrop are the BBC, the London School of Economics, the Royal Courts of Justice and Covent Garden. Grand hotels and theatres add glamour to thronging streets in which lawyers rub shoulders with students, shoppers and tourists. This is the tale of one family's law firm, from its pre-WWII beginnings, when it was founded by Sydney Manches to its present day success under the helmswomanship of his daughter.

Much as we'd love to spend time on episodes one and two, you must allow us to jump straight to the present day, when family law partner Jane Simpson has just taken over as chairman from her former husband Alasdair Simpson, who had enjoyed the role for some 20 years. Mrs Simpson's brother, Louis Manches heads the large property department.

family matters

The grandeur of the setting and the clientele of the superior family law practice have translated into a reputation for being exclusive and elitist, however, we found the trainee recruitment policy to be anything but. The clearest common denominator among the trainee group is their desire to be a part of a firm that can offer them a middle way between the intense corporate focus of the City and the sometimes bitterly exposed experience of high street practice. *"I wanted general and commercial practice all rolled into one. People like me get to tour around the departments."*

The family department is so successful that it tends to dominate others' perceptions of the firm, yet the reality is that most business takes place in commercial areas of practice, and this is where trainees spend most of their four six-month seats. Some trainees elect to spend all four in commercial practice areas, while those that seek six months in family are assured of getting it (and some even do 12 months). The client base of the family practice includes the rich, the famous and the super rich and super famous. This can sometimes mean that partners are protective of their clients, however, overall trainees reported favourably on the experience. *"You don't get your own files, but you can really get involved in your supervisor's work. Most of it is ancillary relief and there's a lot of drafting of consent orders etc. I also went to court quite a lot."* This is the long-hours department, and with so many exceptional lawyers there, a trainee's performance needs to be up to scratch. An ideal place to learn all manner of lawyerly qualities, *"the regime is rigorous in its requirements."*

retail therapy

In law, as in life, few things are guaranteed. Except, that is, a stint in property. The department has a strong retail property bent; the average high street is chock-a-block with its clients. It has had an eventful 18 months, worthy of a secondary plot line in our legal drama. After some musical differences with the management, seven partners quit and, in a move to fill the gap they left behind, the firm has been considering mergers with smaller property-heavy firms. In the meantime, trainees have plenty to get on with, assisting on assignments, licences and funding issues. Up to four or five trainees sit in the department at any one time and the first thing they do in the morning is to open, sort and distribute the department's post. It's a task that irritates some, but pleases those who find sticky-beaking the mail an excellent way in which to learn more about the department's work.

Trainees reported that their time in the corporate department had been affected by the general downturn in the market, nevertheless they displayed no lack of enthusiasm for it. In busier times, we suspect that a corporate seat would be likely for most, with the experience offering component tasks on larger transactions and general company secretarial jobs such as buying and converting shelf companies and drafting board minutes. *"I did experience a 2am deal completion, but then at other times I was able to go from room to room to have coffee and chat to people and to read up on things."*

Employment pleased our critics no end. The team, and one senior assistant in particular, was praised for its dedicated and inclusive approach to training. *"The supervisor really takes an interest in you and gives plenty of feedback, guiding you and challenging you."* Employment work is *"very law heavy,"* and as it is constantly changing this means *"a tremendous amount of research."*

The quality of work in the litigation department can be more of a lottery, depending on what matters are on the lawyers' desks and what stage of the process they are at. One trainee gushed: *"I was so busy, I did a lot of drafting, attended conferences with barristers, and proofed witnesses. There was a good spread of smaller and medium-sized matters and the trainees in litigation get to do masters' appointments, which is good for you."* Indeed it is. More masters' appointments and possession hearings in property litigation resulted in a thumbs-up from another source, but sometimes a litigation seat can involve mountains of documentation to photocopy and bundle.

oxford blues?

There are four recruits in the smaller Oxford office, which might almost be described as a separate firm so far as the training goes. Our sources saw little of their peers in London beyond the first week induction and the occasional PSC session. Work-wise there isn't much crossover either, and Oxford is rather like a mini-Manches London, just without a tax department and with a private client team. Oxford trainees seemed delighted to have found London quality work amongst the dreaming spires. Litigation, property and corporate are all more than likely with a fourth seat spent in either private client, family or IP. An element of elasticity in the seat system suits the firm's business needs and (mostly) suits the trainees.

In addition to having a good publishing base, the Oxford office is targeting the biomedical and biotech firms that are spinning out of the university and occupying the city's hinterland. In this sense, it has the edge on its parent in London, but its premises definitely fall short. Located in five separate buildings, the office feels rather fragmented. *"We've talked about trying to move into one building, but there's not a lot available in the city right now."* Litigation was described as having a family atmosphere, while corporate was *"quiet and serious."*

Out of hours, a relaxed social scene means cricket and football, and the occasional bowling night or riverboat cruise. And Manches is, of course, famous for its sponsorship of a sailing regatta at Cowes each summer. No *"nasty kagoul"* jibes from trainees this year, in both Oxford and London they thought the event was a lot of fun.

dramatis personae

We sensed that the Oxford office rather enjoyed its independence from London, which sounded to us like a slightly political place. Such notions are easier to explain once you appreciate just how many big characters have collected in the firm, and it doesn't stop at the Manches family; *"it's loaded with big characters."* Yet those of our sources who felt this way were also happy to describe a friendly firm where fee earners and partners were easy to approach. *"There's very little hierarchy, except at the top."*

After interviewing a third of the firm's trainees we've concluded that the firm takes to strong characters who have plenty to say. Our sources ranged from the acerbic to the dutiful, but to a (wo)man they were talkative and decisive in their views. They told us the firm was recruiting people who were *"self-motivated"* and possessed of *"a bit of nous; someone who picks up ideas and doesn't need hand holding."* Manches might be misconstrued because it doesn't follow fads and fashions such as casual dress (*"Oh God! No!"*), nor has it adopted the macho work-till-you-drop attitudes of the City. So look beyond those things. You should also note that there have been multiple partner departures in the last 18 months, but it was good news on the NQ front in 2003: six of the seven qualifiers stayed.

and finally...

One of our most astute sources said: *"Manches is a hard one to pitch – it's still thought of as a family firm and quite posh and slightly old fashioned, yet it's more of a corporate firm than people think."*

Martineau Johnson

the facts

Location: Birmingham, London
UK ranking by size: 90
Total number of trainees: 22
Seats: 6x4 months
Alternative seats: None

If we gave this Birmingham-based firm a school report it would probably read "turning in solid work in corporate, property and litigation, and performing superbly in charities, education and private client."

the curriculum

We're as aware as anyone that there are problems right across the legal profession at the moment, but at this firm trainees do seem to be feeling the pinch. Three of those due to be starting in September 2003 were deferred, as well as seven of the 2004 starters. Things haven't been that hot for newly-qualifieds either – six out of eleven left the firm in September 2003. However, despite this, even the trainees we spoke to who were leaving the firm were loyal and had good things to say about their training. Martineaus runs a six-seat system: *"It's good because it gives you a bit more variety,"* and *"if you don't like a seat you won't get stuck – six seats is the way forward!"* Where the system works best is when it gives trainees a taste of several areas and then allows them to go back and spend their fifth and sixth seats where they want to qualify. Four months zips by, so just like in a good game of netball, you have to *"keep on your toes"* and some trainees cautioned that jumping around so much might mean that you can't get stuck into a seat.

There are four compulsory seats: corporate or banking; litigation (including employment); property and private client (or education). Corporate, litigation and employment are all popular and usually the province of second-years, but *"overall most people get what they want in the end."* Almost all the training takes place in Birmingham; the small London office concentrates on banking and litigation and a little property work, and *"if you want to do a seat there you can."*

religious education

Education law is quite academic; rather than handling your own files, you'll do *"loads of research."* The firm only acts for universities and colleges, not students, and you could end up doing anything from looking at constitutions and royal charters to advising an institution on its powers to combat on-site drug dealing. You might also be involved in responding to accusations of racial bias or being firm with students *"trying to shift the blame"* when they haven't got the exam results they wanted. You'll have to be on your best behaviour in the private client department, as you'll be involved in wills and probate work for the Midlands' wealthiest folk. Dig out that hymnbook from assembly as you may also get a spot of ecclesiastical law.

In a straight commercial seat, you may do pure corporate, pure banking or a mixture of both. The technical nature of banking work tends to mean that the juicy stuff is left to the prefects – sorry, the partners – but trainees felt a bit more involved in corporate transactions. Typical tasks include the transfer of shelf companies or drafting board minutes. Trainees generally enjoyed time in the commercial property department and praised most of the supervisors: *"Mine spent an hour a day talking me through things."*

teaching standards

We see that one issue has not yet been resolved to the satisfaction of trainees. Basically, some partners are not as good as others at supervising them and are *"difficult to work with and demanding."* To be fair, these moans could be attributed to the firm's insistence on high standards; one told us *"you have to be prepared to feel you have a long way to go."* Again, striving for fairness, we must report that the firm is taking steps to improve things and a 'Rough Guide' to being a supervisor' has been produced. Trainees describe it as *"spot on,"* but one of them also added: *"It isn't part of the culture of the firm to make partners do anything."*

The appraisal system works well. A few weeks after the end of each seat, supervisors fill in a report and targets for the next seat are agreed with the trainee. The firm has also instigated an upward appraisal system, a chance to give the partner you've been working with their marks out of ten. Trainees can also raise issues at six-monthly meetings with the managing partner and the good folk from HR. People start filing into the office at 8.30am and for most 5.30pm is going home time, although as elsewhere, you might do longer hours in corporate or banking. Late nights and weekends are a rarity.

business studies

The firm is all set to move to *"swanky new offices "* in 2004. The open-plan building will come complete with *"snazzy new furniture"* including *"flat computer screens"* and *"state of the art chairs."* Trainees tell us the new offices *"smell fresh,"* which is always reassuring. When we asked them if the shift to free-range working would affect the culture of the firm, some thought it could only be a good thing. From one straight talking source: *"The stuffy, traditional approach will fly out of the window…It's what the firm needs."* Other trainees thought that communication within the firm would improve. The minority view was the firm would lose something in becoming more modern: *"There'll be fewer characters and we'll become a bit more bland,"* and (the final twist of the knife) *"a bit more Eversheds."*

We heard about the *"loud"* and *"happy"* secretaries who are *"the driving force behind the humour"* and *"the hub of the firm."* We also heard about some eccentric partners. Trainees feel the firm is *"not amazingly fast-moving or dynamic;"* or as one saw it, *"a bit fuddy-duddy, but basically a good firm that cares about its trainees and wants to make changes."* The considered opinion of another was that *"we can match national firms on quality of work and undercut them on rates, but we're not clued-up on client marketing."* But the wheels of change are in motion and some departments, particularly employment and education, have organised more client breakfast meetings and *"hand-shaking"* events like go-karting and trips to the races. The key, one source said, is to *"sell the firm whilst not appearing to do so."* Sneaky!

be a good sport

Friday nights might mean The Old Joint Stock where partners and fee earners enjoy a pint with trainees. More energetic souls are *"constantly"* in Digress for the dance floor. A social committee organises karaoke nights and quizzes. Trainees wouldn't be drawn on any juicy details, but did confirm that *"corporate partners are very bad singers."* An active Birmingham TSG is *"the final mop-up,"* and Martineaus' trainees are heavily involved on the committee. If all this fun isn't enough for you, there's always hotly-contested sporting events between various firms. One trainee grumbled: *"Wragges are storming away and we hate losing."* Those who prefer amateurism to on-field aggression should save themselves for the BTSG summer sports day, which always includes wheelbarrow and sack races and an egg and spoon dash.

and finally…

This year has not been Martineau Johnson's finest, but we highlight it to anyone who wants a really interesting training. It represents an alternative to the national firms that patrol the Birmingham legal scene.

Masons

the facts

Location: London, Bristol, Leeds, Manchester Glasgow, Edinburgh
UK ranking by size: 26
Total number of trainees: 43
Seats: 4x6 months
Alternative seats: Secondments

In terms of its work for the construction and engineering industries, Masons is a juggernaut of a law firm. Its information and technology practice is also very successful and it has additional specialisms in projects and energy law. Masons has offices in Asia, Scotland and Ireland, but we report here on its English offices.

constructing a career

Following an internal shake up, Masons is now structured into four departments: UK construction and engineering; international and energy; capital projects; and technology and business services. This latter division is popular with trainees and incorporates areas such as dispute resolution, property, coco, information and technology, employment, tax, health and safety, insolvency and pensions. The seat system for trainees now runs on a six-month basis and everyone should expect a seat in UK construction and engineering. While a few have any experience of construction before joining the firm, any student in possession of either a relevant degree or related career experience would be well advised to hot foot it to Masons' door. Every year we hear the same story from trainees: *"I chose the firm because I really liked the people I met on the assessment day."* When we ask if they were aware of the firm's industry focus, the answer is normally *"sort of"* or words to that effect. Our advice is to do your research so that you understand the nature of Masons' business and its client base.

The construction department occupies the whole of the third floor of Mason's stunning, modern office building in London's trendy Clerkenwell. *"It's buzzing there,"* one source told us, *"all the guys are working together and doing well."* It has an almost infinite list of top clients, including AMEC, Jarvis, John Mowlem, Siemens, Southern Water, Wates and Wembley National Stadium. You name it, it does it.

projects, schemes and plans

The projects department suffered a blow in September 2002 when two of its most senior partners left to go to Norton Rose. From one source who had noticed the effects: *"The department was going through a change and it wasn't my best seat. There was a lot of research and the nature of the work affects the type of client contact you can have."* In a tougher PFI market, all eyes are on Masons and other firms with a commitment to PFI to see which ones end up as winners. We think our money is safe on Masons. Proving its commitment to projects work, in 2003, it hooked up with Californian firm Thelen Reid & Priest to form Masons Thelen Reid, an LLP joint venture to focus on international projects in emerging markets like China and South America.

The public law team (property, planning and environment) is praised for its warmth and the quality of supervision that young partners give to trainees. Non-core areas like employment, tax, and corporate are also favoured by trainees and client secondments come up on an ad hoc basis.

Commercial litigation got a round of applause too. *"I had a couple of small cases I worked on and shadowed partners on massive pieces of litigation. When I did do bundling and pagination, I was always made aware of what they were for."* Energy is less popular. Why? *"There's been a downturn across the market and there wasn't that much work on,"* said one source. *"I did help out by taking notes of meetings and telecons and writing articles."* As in the projects seat, matters come in large-scale, long-term format and as an inexperienced trainee it can sometimes be hard to relate to them. This is perhaps where the new six-month seats will assist by allowing trainees just that little bit more time to get their heads around deals. One source told us: *"Energy has merged with the international department and now the firm has got its ducks all in a row on that."*

attack of the clones

Trainees share an office with their supervisor – either a partner or a senior associate. Mid and end-of-seat appraisals are scheduled with the trainee's supervisor, in addition to six-monthly appraisals with the training manager or training principal. For the most part, relations between partners, solicitors, trainees and support staff are good and each Christmas the partners offer themselves up for public lampooning at the trainee revue. The preparations for the show are a good way for first-years to get to know second-years and to catch up on all the highlights of the previous year. *"Nothing is ever censored because we always give the script to generally liberal junior partners."* Last year's show had a comedic James Bond theme and culminated in a stage full of John Bishops. Mr B had just announced he was moving to head up the Hong Kong office after 12 years at the helm in London.

Our sources were very clear about the sort of applicant who'd be right for Masons. *"There's definitely an idea that to be successful, you have to show real enthusiasm and be competent...you have to give the perception that you will work as hard as you can."* One trainee explained: *"People realised it wasn't going to be a boat ride being a trainee and that you had to take control and grab the experience in the time you had and as positively as you could."*

wave physics

The offices in Leeds and Manchester are together known as Masons Northern. The Leeds office is small in terms of staff numbers and seat choices. *"You do a seat in contentious construction, one in capital projects and non-contentious construction, and a seat in energy."* After this you must *"show a degree of flexibility and be prepared to travel." "Unfortunately, I&T disappeared and relocated to different offices,"* one trainee said rather regretfully, but you can request a secondment to North Yorkshire County Council or another Masons office. There's plenty of space to run around in, an *"impressive, if impractical"* spiral staircase between floors and a funky staff room. *"There's an overlap of departments, so it's all hands on deck. You definitely need to be a team player."* Apparently most staff in the Leeds office are settled or married: *"We had a wave of engagements, a wave of marriages and then a wave of pregnancies!"*

The Manchester office is bigger and has more to offer by way of seat choices. That said, our sources *"didn't appreciate how much construction work there would be"* and we heard that a seat in energy feels much the same as one in construction. To compensate, we understand the firm relaxed its four-seat rule for some trainees, allowing them to sample a greater number of practice areas, including information law, pensions, property, capital projects and public law (environment, health and safety etc). Trainees appreciated the high standard of work that the office was winning and knew that they were being given good quality tasks. *"When you first start you can do a lot of paginating and bundling, but they are apologetic about it and you also get to draft witness statements and attend interviews."* The comment that the Manchester office was *"all on one level"* applied not only to the *"swanky"* premises in Barbirolli Square, but also to the interaction between partners and staff. As in London, the two northern offices get together for a Christmas party and the trainees perform a *"cheeky"* revue at the partners' expense. Someone muttered something about David Brent and Ali G. We got the picture.

with bells on

In Bristol, trainees do a construction seat plus commercial property, projects and finance, and property litigation (*"an area in which the Bristol office excels"*). A move to another office is possible – when we rang, one trainee had just flown off to Dublin for six months. The Georgian premises are not too far from Broadmead. On the last Friday of each month, staff are allowed to leave the suit and tie at home and there are office-wide drinks in a local bar. The Bristol managing partner seems to influence office culture, although whereas last year he was described as laid back, this year he's now *"competitive and sporty."* As in all other Masons offices, staff and partners are the sort *"you can speak to on a level,"* and with just 40-50 people in this office, *"everybody knows everybody"* and *"there's no formal rigmarole"* when you need to sort something out. There's just a slight sense that London doesn't remember Bristol often enough (*"No one told us the Christmas party in London had a Hogwarts theme – we all went as morris dancers"*), but such communication breakdowns in no way detract from the pride in being part of a world-beating specialist firm.

Again this year, there was a mixed bag of results for qualifying trainees. Bristol kept none of its three qualifiers; Leeds and Manchester each kept two from three, and in London 11 out of 16 stayed. *"It was sad to see people go,"* one London source said, adding: *"We are all hoping the market will turn."* In the immediate term, Masons is doing what a number of competitors are – deferring the start of some training contracts.

and finally...

If Masons areas of practice interest you, then get yourself on a vac scheme asap

Mayer, Brown, Rowe & Maw LLP

the facts

Location: London
UK ranking by size: 24
Total number of trainees: 50
Seats: 4x6 months
Alternative seats: Brussels, secondments
Extras: Pro Bono – RCJ CAB, Bar Pro Bono Unit, Liberty, Islington, Tooting and Toynbee Hall Law Centres, language training

Eyebrows were raised across the City when, in January 2002, the very British Rowe & Maw pulled off a merger with US firm Mayer Brown & Platt. The American groom now has English breeding, refinement and a foothold in the important London market. The bride, meanwhile, has broadened her international horizons and now boasts a sterling name worldwide. And she's retained her independence.

the paper anniversary

With its first anniversary celebrations already a memory, the newly wedded MBRM is striding ahead. Is this a match made in heaven? The initial signs are positive. Rowe & Maw retained her name on both sides of the Atlantic, won places for three partners on the worldwide management board, and in London has preserved her British flavour. The US arm has, at least for the moment, adopted a laissez-faire approach to London, leaving the office to determine key operational issues such as billing targets and hourly rates. London senior partner Paul Maher is widely credited with the coup. His hard work and charisma are renowned across the City, as is his ego, apparently; there were jokes circulating that the new firm would be named Maher, Brown, Rowe & Maw.

The small Mayer Brown litigation team left for the London office of a rival US firm as they'd originally joined MB because they wanted to work in a small US-style practice, not a conventional City practice. There is a message here: if you dream of working in a small intimate London office of a US law firm, look at the others. Aside from this, there was no major fallout post-merger and it's been pretty much business as usual in R&M's offices, with the MB lawyers having, to a large extent, to adapt to R&M's ways. According to one trainee: *"It doesn't feel like it's different except now we're part of this giant that's tenth largest in the world."* Others told us: *"Now you get e-mails from all over the world. There is a sense of being part of a global network."* That global network is 16 offices strong: eight in the Americas; six in Europe and two in China. Alas, the only overseas seat for trainees is Brussels – not so glamorous but at least the beer is good.

the dowry

Closer to home, *"we have more clout in the city. My friend at Linklaters said they were getting more documents with Mayer, Brown, Rowe & Maw on them."* From the BCCI litigation to multibillion-euro claims concerning antitrust activities in the vitamins market, from the merger of Cambridge Antibody Technology Group with Oxford Glycosciences to the €1 billion outsourcing of BT's global communications infrastructure to Unilever, the firm is winning great work. The client list is impressive: Nestlé, Rothschild, easynet, Cable & Wireless, Bank of America, Volkswagen, Dow Chemical, HMV, Virgin, Nationwide Building Society and endless others. Trainees are able to go on secondment to Unilever, AstraZeneca, Marsh & McLennan and Reuters. These visits offer good work and a sense of real importance. *"They treated me like an expert!"*

cinderella

The seating system is the usual four by six-month affair, with a compulsory stint in corporate, and of course, a contentious seat. Again this year, the corporate department came in for criticism and trainees bemoaned their *"untapped potential."* The experience of many can be summed up as follows: *"The hours were quite long, and I had a very very poor level of work. I didn't know what I'd be doing from day to day. I did a lot of proofing, indexing documents, putting together data rooms, and managing data rooms. As far as I'm aware there are no paralegals in corporate. I know the Mayer Brown side had maybe one or two, but they were not at the disposal of the group as a whole."* The problem in a nutshell is this: *"My supervisor operates a pyramid system. He gives work to his team and then the team gives me work, so often I end up with dregs."* Why operate this way? *"That system works. Part of me thinks 'This is crap', but everyone has to start somewhere."* Grad recruitment wants to resolve matters.

The legacy R&M partners could learn from their MB colleagues in terms of supervision, guidance and levels of responsibility accorded to trainees. The message from our sources: try to sit with a legacy MB partner. It's not all bad – corporate has a *"nice culture,"* and it's easy to get on with people, indeed it's renowned for being the most sociable part of the firm. Formal training sessions are also to be commended and those who'd completed a finance seat before heading into coco felt their experience was all the better for that reason. *"I became a sort of bridge between finance and corporate on one particular deal,"* said one. Someone who'd had an excellent time in corporate told us: *"I can see that others would have been disappointed. You get assigned to a project, so if you're not on one that's all guns blazing, you may be left to yourself."* The ingredients are there for a good experience; they just need to be weighed better.

elevating experiences

The American influence is strongest in the finance practice. *"The Mayer Brown side has a certain reputation for being on more sexy deals – Uzbekistan refinancings as opposed to building societies in Holborn."* Sexy deals or not, finance seats bring a decent cross section of work for finance houses alongside corporate support and property finance. Trainee tasks are *"sufficient and commensurate"* with trainees expectations. The insurance litigation seat in a satellite office in the Lloyd's building (*"Those glass lifts wake you up in the morning!"*) offers good responsibility and interesting cases in a relaxed and informal atmosphere. Ditto construction. Here, you might find yourself interviewing witnesses and preparing their statements, liaising with other professionals or drafting simple contracts.

And so to the general litigation and dispute resolution group. Handling megabucks instructions is all well and good, unless you're a trainee who ends up stuck in the middle of a mammoth disclosure exercise. As one trainee said: *"We're working on what will be the biggest ever case before English courts – the liquidation of BCCI – it's a huge matter worth hundreds of millions of pounds. There are boring jobs that have to be done and we're the ones that have to do it. I've been to interviews with key witnesses and I've been to High Court hearings, which were interesting, but I was working on just the one case."*

IP is favoured for its *"refreshingly stimulating"* work. In this department supervisors earned top marks for giving challenging assignments and plenty of guidance. Real estate is another popular seat because trainees run their own files and are often the first point of contact for clients. It may not seem like much, but *"you could see a task through to the end."*

all american smiles

Mid and end-of-seat appraisals involve a form that is *"not unnecessarily lengthy, but certainly probing."* Trainees' performances are graded, from 4 (unsatisfactory) up to 1 (outstanding), with 3 being standard. One source likened the system to a *"smiley face tick box. Smiley face, indifferent face, unhappy face. Indifferent face covers everything from not utterly shocking to not utterly magnificent. You can stick any trainee into that category."*

If a law firm is a family, then a merger is a Brady Bunch-style second marriage involving step kids, a couple of houses and potential for squabbles. Aside from the fact that the MB lawyers lost a sartorial battle and must now wear suits to work except on Fridays, there's little evidence of the latter. We learned that the trainees hired by R&M are generally seen as *"more compliant and accepting,"* while the MB recruits are more like grown-up kids who are *"used to being included."* The fusion of the two has been an eye-opener: the R&M trainees have learned to crave more individual responsibility, while their MB peers have had to adjust to being one of the crowd. In September 2003, 11 of the 17 qualifiers took jobs at the firm.

After work, The Evangelist is still the den of choice. If your budget won't stretch to £5 for a glass of wine, you might go downmarket to The Rising Sun, but be warned: it's been the ruin of many a poor boy.

and finally...

The firm has swanky new offices and a new-found confidence. As to the future, we'll leave you with a stream of consciousness from one of our sources: *"If the intention is to really challenge magic circle firms...and there's an underlying assumption that that is what we're going for...should we make that a stated aim? At least then people will know where they stand. The long-term plan is to get up there with the big boys in terms of revenues. As much as they don't like to say so, we're an American firm. Is that where we are headed? Or are we transatlantic, which I sense they want us to be."* Whatever. It's all looking good.

McCormicks

the facts

Location: Leeds
UK ranking by size: 311
Total number of trainees: 8
Seats: 4x6 months
Alternative seats: None

Currently celebrating its 20th anniversary, McCormicks is a youthful Yorkshire outfit that's far from jejune; while maintaining a commitment to private client work, it regularly outpaces larger rivals in the commercial field and possesses an enviable reputation for its media and sports practice.

it's a hard knock life

Napoleon, Danny DeVito, Frankie Dettori, Sneezy, the entire cast of *The Time Bandits*, those cheery Day-Glo Umpah Lumpahs working to within an inch of their tiny lives in Willy Wonka's capitalist chocolate sweatshop... Being small can be a hindrance, but history and fiction offer ample proof that low stature or status is often the catalyst that transforms the itsy-bitsy into world-beaters. One glance at the McCormicks website is evidence enough that the firm would like to write itself into this trend. Festooned with pictures of boxers and swordsmen, it proudly styles itself as "a fearless law firm with a fearsome reputation." *"The larger Leeds firms fear our fighting character, we're small and young, but we get the big clients,"* enthused one trainee. Others told us about Peter McCormick's hardcore first-day motivational sessions: everyone is made to do 1,000 press-ups *"and he kept telling us 'We punch above our weight'."* OK, we made up the bit about press-ups, but the slogan and the sentiment it embodies, really is stressed from day one.

sparks fly

Our sources were refreshingly direct, honest and bright. One of them admitted: *"This firm has personality in abundance, for better or worse!"* You can guess our thoughts on that one. We are all too used to hearing trainees tell us their firm is inclusive, friendly and supportive, blah blah blah... McCormicks trainees were no different, but at least they had a million examples to prove their point. We particularly liked the sound of the 9am daily meetings for the entire firm, at which a senior partner will regale staff with a humorous tale or ask people to list *"five things I wish I hadn't done at the weekend."* Compliance seems fraught with danger to us, however, one trainee reflected as follows: *"Like any place, sometimes you come into work and you're pissed off and you can't be bothered, but it really gets you into the mood for work."* And in the mood for winning new business from the sound of things. Trainees are expected to involve themselves in marketing from early on.

a sporting chance

McCormicks offers a good range of practice areas including property, coco, corporate crime, private client, employment, IP, family and commercial litigation, though we were warned that *"if you're really interested in banking or the largest commercial work you might want to look elsewhere."* However, the same cautious head also noted that *"at trainee level, the practical experience would be just as good here."* Much of McCormicks' cachet lies in the clients it represents. It boasts a top-notch media/broadcasting and sports law practice that acts for showbiz and football folk, as well as larger media and sports organisations. It has advised Brilliant Independent Media Specialists and Leeds United FC, and handles a significant amount of broadcasting, sponsorship, image rights and commercial contract work for the Premier League and its member clubs. If the idea of sports law lures you to McCormicks, then rejoice! *"All the trainees can get involved in sports matters because they tend to be large."*

Proving that not everything it does is glamorous, the corporate client base includes *"lots of smaller businesses,"* and this means trainees will spend time *"drafting partnership agreements and minutes etc."* By contrast, seats in corporate recovery are anything but workaday. Here you'll probably get a shot at advocacy as the firm advises national insolvency practitioners on individual and company bankruptcies.

Office hours are a reasonable 9am-ish to 6pm-ish. However, you can expect a few late nights in the corporate crime and risk team and the commercial litigation department. *"They work you bloody hard and, when deadlines come up, you have to put the hours in."* Both give a good degree of autonomy and variety; the trainees we interviewed had obtained witness statements, prepared Crown Court briefs and attended magistrates' courts on trading standards prosecutions. The firm's commitment to private client practice was described as *"unique amongst the larger firms in Leeds,"* (we'll add the word 'almost' to that statement) exposing trainees to the usual range of trusts and probate matters and Family Court hearings. The team receives client referrals through its links with Age Concern, one of the firm's many charitable clients.

ourfirm

Several trainees told us about the firm's stated aim to double in size. Apparently it is averse to the term 'expansion' and prefers to see itself as 'stretching'. Accordingly, we'll describe the recent purchase of new office space as 'loosening up'. The firm is currently divided between premises at Britannia Chambers and Oxford House. The former is *"homely, but definitely an office,"* and just like an older home it has *"dodgy plumbing."* Oxford House is a modern abode that is *"more what you'd expect for this firm."*

McCormicks' trainees have recently started up a group called MyLaw, which provides them with an internal support group and aims to help them forge business links in the region. They've had the full support of the firm, and you can even find details of the group on the firm's website. Fluffy name maybe, but this is no tame group. Following a MyLaw request for greater transparency, the partners now circulate reports detailing the reasons behind partnership decisions. Power to the people! In September 2003, two of the three qualifying trainees took jobs with the firm.

"At the end of the day it's suits away." Old favourite, The Vic, has been forsaken following an influx of *"city types."* New favourite, The Courtyard, holds the promise of cheap wine (in the best sense of the words) and outdoor tables. An active social committee organises events including comedy nights and trips to the dogs, and anyone wanting to show off their sporting prowess can choose between tennis, squash and football teams. In the summer, *"the boys try and play cricket."* We're told the 2003 Yuletide party will have a plain old 80s karaoke theme. Why? Here's why: *"The party is partly to help new trainees meet the rest of the firm,*

and it's hard to know who the partners are when they're in full Donald Duck costume."

and finally...

Do we really need to sum up this firm in two sentences? Could we?

Mills & Reeve

the facts

Location: Cambridge, Norwich, Birmingham, London
UK ranking by size: 41
Total number of trainees: 39
Seats: 6x4 months
Alternative seats: Occasional secondments

No longer just the largest firm in East Anglia, Mills & Reeve is now in Birmingham, and has a newly opened office in London. Quality work and dogged ambition characterise this well-respected firm.

do you want fries with that?

The firm has long been recognised as the leading name in the east of England, and in this part of its territories it offers considerable breadth of practice. From wills and trusts to AIM listings, M&R has put itself in pole position for the receipt of quality instructions from decent clients. Trainees can request seats in any one of the four locations, and *"the firm tries to make it as easy as possible to move around"* by assisting with accommodation and travel expenses.

Despite its expansion out of East Anglia, the firm has no plan to *"do an Eversheds or a McDonald's"* and open outlets across the UK. Birmingham started life in 1998 as a *"niche"* office catering to healthcare clients. The firm *"saw an opportunity and went to Birmingham to chase it."* The gamble has paid off, although the office was dealt a severe blow when it lost its lucrative work for the NHS Litigation Authority. Having recovered and diversified, its turnover increased by almost 65% in 2003. (Firm-wide profits were up 22%.) As well as litigation work there is now a decent coco capacity following the recruitment of new partners, including the head of commercial contracts from Eversheds Birmingham. Meanwhile, the fledgling London office is *"clear in its objective"* of serving insurance clients.

Rivalry between the Norwich and Cambridge offices is as old as the cities themselves, and the atmosphere of each is reflective of its client base. For history buffs: the firm's Norwich arm was founded in 1880 to serve the agricultural sector in the region. Just over a hundred years later, following either a fantastic feat of crystal ball gazing or a wonderful piece of good luck, the Cambridge office was founded in what would become 'Silicon Fen'. This pumped-up glamour girl has taken over as the administrative hub of the firm; powered along by its university and technology clientele, it is buzzing and intense. It's all *"jackets on the backs"* here. Chair backs, that is. The vibe from partners is, in the words of one trainee, *"fee, fee, fee!"* The hours, the clients and the work ensure that Cambridge is *"more driven, more City-like in its culture."* Well ... by Cambridge standards at least. If, on the other hand, it's the quiet life you're after, the Norwich office is the place for you. For some, *"a sleepy backwater"*, while for Alan Partridge *"an island in a bog," "Norwich is not just a way of life, it's an attitude."* Grab your wellies, because a client base consisting of regional businesses, farmers and landed estate owners ensures that a *"traditional"* character prevails.

smorgasbord

The training contract is divided into six four-month chunks, and while they won't get a choice for the first couple of seats, thereafter trainees are able to stipulate preferences. The degree to which choices are accommodated depends on the office. In Cambridge, competition for IP is sizzling hot, so second-years are given priority. Employment is popular everywhere (isn't it just), as is the firm's new regulatory and defence department, which acts for professional and public bodies in the health and education sectors. If it's diversity you're after, M&R has a veritable buffet table groaning with juicy dishes. You can complete seats in areas like family, agriculture, insurance and healthcare as well as the meaty departments —corporate, property and commercial litigation.

proper cooked dinner

So what of those main meal seats? One trainee had a message for all prospective trainees: *"You miss out on a rounded legal training without a property seat. It's a cornerstone of legal practice."* Trainees can expect to run their own files involving everything from residential sales and leasing of commercial properties to rights of way, boundary disputes and researching the title of properties stretching back 400 years.

If doing a property seat is like eating your greens, then corporate is the meat and litigation the spuds. In Norwich, a litigation seat can mean a *"nerve-wracking start,"* with trainees handling advocacy on procedural hearings. Surviving a bout in front of a district judge is a real badge of honour (or so it feels at the time), and one you'll wear proudly in front of your peers. In Cambridge, high-tech companies feature strongly in the client stable, which is perfect for trainees who want their contentious training to feature patent litigation. If you have a pagination phobia, rest assured, M&R *"doesn't believe in giving trainees grunt work." "They don't look at a trainee and see a photocopier."*

Being spread over four offices means regular inter-office socialising is a rarity. Trainees, however, see each other at training sessions. Still, *"there are always faces you don't recognise."* Each office has its own social committee. Birmingham trainees kick their heels up at monthly quizzes and evenings of revelry at local bar, Horts. In Cambridge, the *"cosy"* Flying Pig remains the pub of choice despite the ever present threat from invading hordes of Eversheds lawyers. And over in Norwich, you can spend your Friday nights at the startlingly named Orgasmic bar. The Norwich social scene is, however, orgasmic in name only; *"there's not a lot of scandal, unfortunately."* The preponderance of female trainees *"cuts down on the romance potential, for better or for worse."* Rather like marriage then.

the writing's on the wall

Each office has its own distinctive feel, yet there remains an overarching Mills & Reeve culture. The sartorial code is professional with no dress-down day, a sore point with some trainees. *"There aren't many egos here,"* we heard. *"Even in London, where it's all guns blazing,"* the firm is still not as stratified as some others. Still, ambition oozes from every pore, and the firm's entrepreneurial spirit is embodied in its business plan entitled M&R 2004. In case you need to refer to it for inspiration, it'll be pinned up next to your desk.

As in most firms north of Watford, lawyers arrive earlier and leave earlier than in London. Most are in by 8.45am and work until 6pm, although in corporate, the hours fluctuate with the deals. In Birmingham, trainees have the benefit of flexitime with core hours from 10am to 4pm. Since the early days of the *Student Guide*, we've watched Mills & Reeve change from a straightforward East Anglian success story into a firm brimming with opportunities in four locations. What hasn't changed a jot is the satisfaction of trainees and the recognition accorded to the firm by other lawyers. In September 2003, 13 of the 17 qualifiers stayed on at the firm.

and finally ...

Mills & Reeve is a stellar firm. Just be aware that the offices can feel like different countries and, at times, getting the seat you want may feel like a fight on pension day at the Hobson Street bingo hall.

Mishcon de Reya

the facts

Location: London
UK ranking by size: 97
Total number of trainees: 16
Seats: 4x6 months
Alternative seats: None
Extras: Pro bono – death row appeals, language training

A smaller commercial practice in Bloomsbury, Mishcon de Reya's size belies a punchy family practice and rip-roaring, headline-grabbing litigation. For *"individuality, ambition and exciting clients,"* step this way.

larceny

Mishcon de Reya refuses to submit to the *"predictable corporate environment."* This is clear from its work: a steady diet of property, family, corporate/commercial and litigation is spiced up with specialist work in fields such as sport, art, immigration, media and entertainment, business ethics and most recently IP fraud. The firm acted in the libel case brought against clients Deborah Lipstadt and Penguin by right-wing historian David Irving; it was also involved in Neil Hamilton v Mohammed Al Fayed. More recently, it's been instructed on the repatriation of works of art stolen during the holocaust, and has been carrying out anti-counterfeiting work for Microsoft. All this gives the firm plenty to shout about, as does a client list that includes Craig David, Zöe Ball and Holly Vallance.

This eclectic portfolio, along with *"some very strong personalities"* caused us, two years ago, to wonder if Mishcons wasn't the legal equivalent of a Far Side cartoon: slightly off the wall, but nevertheless tickling ribs you never knew you even had. This year there was a backlash against our theory: *"There are some fairly flamboyant characters, but they take their lawyering really seriously."* We never doubted it. One trainee, keen to impress that the firm wasn't afraid of controversy, told us: *"We aren't publicity whores, but we love the challenge and do it because we can think outside the box."* That told us.

art for art's sake

Mishcons follows the standard four six-month seat system and trainees enjoy relatively free rein over where they go. *"Litigation is very popular...and a number of people also proactively seek to be in the art law group."* This unique practice deals with art and cultural property issues including export regulations, the recovery of stolen cultural objects, provenance and copyright. However, and it's a big however, there is only one seat available there. Media litigation and defamation also appeal because of the glamour factor. But be warned: *"Doing it, I didn't feel like a film star. And considering the hours I was putting in, I didn't look like one either!"* No seats that are avoided like the plague, though *"most people have a prejudice against property, and family elicits the same kind of response, probably even more so."*

The family department mainly acts for wealthy individuals and celebrities, commonly handling international divorces and child abductions. The coco department may not bask in quite the same media coverage as some of its counterpart departments, however, *"the firm is going through an identity change – we have tried to become more corporate friendly."* Its lawyers act for household names including Trinity Group, Portman Building Society, Blacks Leisure Group and Storm Model Management.

swimming lessons

Trainees share an office with a supervisor, but may receive work from several sources. We were told that *"you get thrown in at the deep end – it is incredibly intense."* Running your own small files and meeting clients, there is no chance of you *"getting lost behind the photocopier,"* though one reflected (tongue firmly in cheek) that the lack of photocopier duties was *"unfortunate."* These are not people who shy away from hard work, and though it is *"very, very challenging and scary, it is exciting."* That said, we didn't come across any trainees who'd tried their hand at advocacy. Though some sources vaguely suggested you might get a go in family, others were adamant that *"it's a big disappointment – the firm is not nearly advanced enough here. If you push and are lucky you might do the really basic stuff."* Formal training earns applause though. All trainees attend a plethora of firm-wide and departmental seminars as well as trainee sessions, which means *"most weeks there is something going on."* In the main, supervisors do a proper job of giving guidance and feedback, although reading between the lines we sensed some were more complex to deal with than others.

A particularly relaxed approach to dress-down Fridays means "*there is no list of banned clothes.*" Likewise, trainees typically work from around 9am till 6.30pm, and while everyone had experienced long hours on occasions, "*it is not because it is macho or expected.*" The firm does not advertise other perks in the training package, although we did hear of some trainees who had been on client secondment. "*If you had a suitable offer and found yourself something, the firm wouldn't immediately dismiss it.*" This seems to have backfired this year. Two of its eight qualifying trainees ended up taking jobs with clients (the others stayed).

young bohemians

In 2002 Mishcons moved to Red Lion Square. Its art deco building has been immaculately restored – marble floors and all – and receives rave reviews. What Mishcons lacks in size, it more than makes up for on style with "*loud artwork, bright furniture and attention-grabbing flowers.*" As for the trainees, few appear to have trod the school-law degree-LPC path; one source volunteered that only a quarter of trainees had read law at university, adding: "*There is a big thing on the application form about legal philistines...they like broad arts backgrounds.*" As one source put it: "*They look for people with other prongs to their fork.*" We also hear that Mishcons' folk are "*culture vultures,*" but while "*the generic corporate types*" might not fit in, we suspect there's room for more than art buffs and opera boffins.

If this all sounds a bit highbrow, rest assured, people do still pop out for a simple pint. On Friday nights, a group usually makes its way to The Overdraft, and the social committee also organises 'mingles' for the whole firm. The annual summer party fell by the wayside in 2003, but the firm did push the boat out last Christmas with a black-tie dinner dance. And last year a talent competition saw staff dressing up as Moulin Rouge characters and partners exercising their vocal chords. "*People were so shocked by the embarrassment levels that there were no volunteers this year!*" In the past, Mishcons has seemed very willing to embrace its slightly off-the-wall image; however, the firm's celebrated dog, Lottie the Lurcher, is no longer a regular visitor ("*there are a fair few children, but no dogs*") and the fact that this year people are less willing to cancan for their Christmas dinner may be telling.

and finally...

While the training may not see you stepping into the Far Side it is definitely not a stroll through the standard corporate landscape.

Morgan Cole

the facts

Location: Cardiff, Swansea, Oxford, Reading, London
UK ranking by size: 28
Total number of trainees: 31
Seats: 4x6 months
Alternative seats: Secondments

Morgan Cole excels in Wales and sweeps up through the Thames Valley into London.

ups and downs

Back in November 1998, with much optimism and fanfare, Welsh firm Morgan Bruce merged its Cardiff, Swansea and London offices with Oxford and Reading partnership Cole & Cole. It quickly absorbed niche London insurance firm Fishburn Boxer. The aim was to create the pre-eminent firm in the M4 corridor, with particular emphasis on insurance litigation, energy and technology. In 2000, a Croydon office was added to handle lower value insurance claims work.

As it stands today, Fishburn Boxer has reclaimed its independence and over 50 partners have left the firm since the merger. In 2003, there has been a change in management and recent press reports indicated that average profits per partner had plummeted. Yet, in spite of all of this, our enquiries at the firm were met with openness and honesty; trainees were quite capable of communicating their views on a partnership struggling to act in unison, while reporting favourably on the quality of their training. Readers should consider the firm's best points in tandem with the bad news.

assembled in wales

There are three top commercial firms in Wales and Morgan Cole is one of them. For corporate finance, it remains pre-eminent, and earlier this year the firm celebrated a major coup when it snatched the role of law firm to the Welsh National Assembly from its previous advisers, Eversheds. It also earns top rankings in several other commercial areas of practice. There is a fair amount of interchange between the Cardiff and Swansea offices, and many trainees spend time in both. One trainee summarised Morgan Cole's office in the Welsh capital as *"a great place to train with good work, good office atmosphere and a great location."* Adding: *"That goes for people who are not Welsh too!"*

The flagship corporate department keeps trainees on their toes assisting teams on M&A transactions such as the acquisition of Teacrate by PHS Group. As one trainee said: *"My CV now looks really good."* The commercial department handles a *"broad church"* of work and trainees can sample work from the projects, IP and competition groups. Since the supervisors here are *"particularly approachable," "if you wanted to do a bit more IP or competition or projects, you can just speak to the relevant partner and they will give it to you."*

The litigation department now goes under the banner 'dispute management' and is filled with famously feisty and humorous characters. It's a tight-knit department in which many of the fee earners and partners trained together, and while it's not exactly cliquey, *"you do have to be good at your one-liners to fit in."* Trainees attend client meetings with their supervisors and draft instructions to counsel, witness statements, application notices and claim forms. The firm takes on agency work for firms outside Cardiff, thus enabling trainees to get advocacy experience in smaller hearings including mortgage repossessions. The contentious element of the training contract can also be satisfied by a construction litigation seat with what is regarded by some as *"the friendliest team in Cardiff."* Although the work *"is a bit specialised for a trainee,"* our sources enjoyed shadowing supervisors to meetings or court. We thought the following comment about a client meeting was quite telling of the general attitude towards trainees: *"I didn't have the confidence to say much, but if I wanted to, I don't think they'd have minded. They'd probably encourage me to speak, so I didn't look like a spare brick."*

The employment group is, as ever, a very popular choice. It's a young, vibrant team in which lawyers are *"happy to work for an extra hour at the end of the day, if it means you can have a chat and a laugh during office hours."* One trainee confessed: *"I enjoyed going to work, which is a novelty for me."* Our sources described a *"partner-heavy"* property group that, in contrast to the jokers in employment or litigation, *"has a reputation for being quite sombre."* Perhaps in an attempt to liven up the group and *"make it more fun,"* the firm has organised social events and provided whoopee cushions to all.

rooms with a view

Overlooking the marina, the Swansea branch occupies a shimmering new purpose-built office that boasts *"balconies and a lot of glass."* The move has had a tremendous impact on the mood of staff, which is described as optimistic and upbeat. We also heard that it is *"more Welsh"* in flavour than the Cardiff office. The work in Swansea ranges wildly from matters involving major corporate clients to local people with mortgage disputes. The property seat prompted mixed reviews; some trainees thought it *"a great introduction"* to property law, but would have liked more support and background info on the work. The group shares an impressive client base with the Cardiff property team including major corporates (Canary Wharf, BP) to the man on the street who simply needs a right of way over someone else's back garden.

Things haven't changed much in Wales since our last report. Cardiff trainees can still be found in Ha!Ha! or Bar Med before they head over to Bar Cuba on a Friday night, and in Swansea you can stroll on the beach after work. Trainees enjoy a good quality of life – as one said: *"If you look at the partners' car park in Cardiff at 7pm, there are never more than a few cars there."*

the thames valley

For trainees' purposes, the Oxford and Reading offices are regarded as almost interchangeable. Oxford, we're told, has *"a more traditional"* vibe than Reading. It is *"a bit out on a limb"* near to the ring road on the Botley Road side of the city and, as a consequence, the social life suffers somewhat. By contrast, the Reading office is right next to the train station in Apex Plaza. Its central location, and the fact that all staff work together on a single open-plan floor, makes for a *"relaxed, informal atmosphere."*

Most of the Oxford corporate team has left the firm, and what remains is now located in Reading, although *"the corporate lawyers go to Oxford on an almost daily basis."* The work consists of standard corporate fare – share acquisitions, management buyouts and shareholder agreements for a diverse clientele. Trainees can also undertake an IP or employment seat in Reading. An opportunity to go on secondment to ICI Paints in Slough gets trainees involved in commercial, corporate and employment matters.

The Thames Valley property team has consolidated in Oxford and offers a mixture of residential and commercial work. There is also an IP unit where trainees focus on trademarks work. Unusually for a firm of its size, the Oxford branch offers a family seat. A legacy of the old Cole & Cole, the department is now an important *"bolt-on"* to the commercial practice. The clients are largely wealthy individuals, and our sources appreciated the intellectual stimulation of the work. Said one: *"I like things I can physically touch or associate with. Property and family are areas that everyone has had personal experience of."* Employment and dispute management seats are also offered.

the fishburn that got away

"It was that big!" And yes, it was. A top insurance and reinsurance practice with 12 partners, Fishburn Boxer was a cracking firm with a cracking client base. Only three years after Morgan Cole hooked it, Fishburns broke free and now swims alone. Unfortunately, the mood in the London office is, in the words of one source, *"awful."* From the trainees' point of view, the range of seat options is now disappointingly limited. The property group has absconded, rendering an analysis of the training in that department largely unnecessary. Landlord and tenant litigation continues and trainees can also undertake a seat in dispute management, working on commercial claims. At the time of writing, secondments to Fishburns were available, offering trainees top-grade insurance litigation. Employment is a tiny department, but has been instructed to advise a group of some 130 former ITV Digital employees. A BP secondment offers general commercial work.

The firm states that it is concentrating its efforts on building a corporate finance practice in London. How successful it will be, only time will tell. No London trainees were retained on qualification in September 2003, although two NQs took jobs with Fishburn Boxer. Just before we went to press, we learned that the London office was quitting its Fleet Street address for smaller premises in Clerkenwell.

a curious cocktail

Morgan Cole is at the top of its game in Cardiff and Swansea. In the Thames Valley, despite a partner exodus, it retains many *"bright, dynamic"* lawyers, and having become accustomed to drama and departures, trainees in these two offices are hardy souls. One of them said: *"We feel a bit let down by the prospects at the firm."* In London, it's impossible to ignore the shrinking training opportunities. In September 2003, 12 out of the 19 trainees took jobs on qualification: nine of these were in Wales; two were offered in Oxford and two transferred to Fishburns.

and finally...

We were tempted to write three separate features to cover the three distinct regions in which Morgan Cole works. As one source told us: "*There is little interplay between the offices, apart from in the Thames Valley. I could walk into Cardiff and people wouldn't know me from Adam. The cultures are very different.*" If the case, it goes some way to explaining why the last five years have not run as smoothly as hoped by the architects of the merger.

Nabarro Nathanson

the facts

Location: London, Reading, Sheffield
UK ranking by size: 19
Total number of trainees: 62
Seats: 6x4 months
Alternative seats: Brussels, secondments
Extras: Language training

"A large and well-established firm offering a broad range of services to major national and international corporate, governmental, public sector and institutional clients." Thus speaketh the recruitment brochure. Spot-on too, but can't any large firm boast this? We decided to dig around to find out what's so special about Nabarro Nathanson.

bubbly

NN has long been known for its property expertise, something that's still very much in evidence – the likes of British Land, Hammerson and Slough Estates number amongst its clients. But, in keeping with its move to Holborn offices in 2000, the firm has been making a conscious effort to be seen as much more than just a property outfit. The corporate department is a recognised advisor to leading medium-sized and AIM-listed companies, venture capitalists and mid-market finance houses. This sector was badly buffeted by the economic downturn, but is now showing promising signs of rejuvenation. Other respected divisions are TMT (acting for Oracle, Siemens and Sun Microsystems) and employment, which boasts HSBC, BAA and McArthurGlen amongst its clients.

Right from the outset, from a vacation scheme that puts students into a single department for three weeks to advice on choosing which law school to attend, Nabarros sets out to welcome new recruits into the fold. Even before starting work, future trainees are invited by their assigned 'buddy trainee' to attend social events, thus ensuring that thoughts of NN are never far away. And after joining, a 'partner mentor' is there to provide general help and career advice. "*My mentor was actually very helpful and, moreover, was very well briefed about me,*" one source told us. A graduate recruitment contact, with whom every trainee can expect regular chats, means that, current seat supervisor included, there are four people on hand with a vested interest in an individual's progress.

A six-seat system has now been adopted, and although the system has its detractors, you won't find many of these at NN. It must all be working beautifully, because everybody we spoke to seemed so happy. In fact, we quickly became suspicious that the firm's offices had been cunningly sited so as to receive its water supply from underground Volvic springs.

meat, potatoes, veg

Of the six seats, commercial property, corporate and litigation are compulsory; beyond that, trainees get a say in where they go. As one source remarked: "*There are definitely plenty of other growing, yet already respected, departments to choose from, especially IP & IT, tax, employment and pensions.*" Steady on, let's talk turkey before we talk cranberry sauce and stuffing.

At every seat rotation, there's a good helping of training for the first couple of weeks, after which the firm lets trainees take on client-facing duties, particularly in property. One veteran said: "*You get loads of client contact in property, more than I thought you would. Even though there are plenty of more senior lawyers around, I've been to a couple of client meetings on my own.*" Another enthused: "*So far, I've run with a number of live files and have been very busy with leases, licenses, due diligence and with meetings and conversations with other solicitors, contractors and surveyors.*" Hectic!

Feedback about life in the corporate department was varied. One trainee felt that, in contrast to the property department, *"in my corporate seat I was definitely more like a single cog in a very big wheel."* Another noted: *"Though I've been extremely lucky only to have worked one weekend in two years, I know that others have found it tough going."* Litigation seemed a more popular destination: *"I did my fair share of grunt work here – bundling and photocopying – but you get that everywhere and in other respects, this seat was a great learning curve."*

it's all gravy

No one showed undue worries about seat allocation and the variety available mitigates the fact that the overseas seats are limited. For now it's just Brussels, but the firm might be considering an arrangement with a friendly firm in Germany. Client secondments are available to Siemens and Oxford University.

In past years we'd heard that trainees were sharing rooms with solicitors with relatively few years post-qualification experience under their belts. This is now a matter only for historical debate since the system has been modified such that supervisors are now between four and six years qualified. Trainees are happy with this, said one: *"I think this just goes not so much towards breaking the trainee/supervisor barriers down as discarding them altogether. You just never feel stupid asking what might be a relatively straightforward question and the supervisors happily take time to go beyond the call of duty with their help."* Factor in thorough mid and end-of-seat appraisals and you've got a pretty sweet deal.

enterprise and perseverance

Two words which aptly describe the weekly lives of the NN trainee, and that's also where you'll find most of them of a Friday evening. These two local hostelries are very popular with the firm's lawyers, partners, secretaries, post room staff, accounts clerks, Uncle Tom Cobbleigh and all. Hang on; do we smell a bouquet of rosy comments about down-to-earth, approachable partners and open-door policies? Indeed we do! *"Everyone is so down to earth and approachable, and I've worked in industry and commerce before, so am not looking through rose-tinted glasses. There's an open-door policy with partners, they are easy-going and feel that outside activities are important."* Bingo! A full set of clichés.

Busy bursts aside, decent hours are a selling point. Some trainees were very lucky indeed: *"In two years I've never felt that I have to stay if I've finished my work. Even the secretaries say that; though they could arguably earn more elsewhere, they wouldn't leave for anything."* Another trainee commented: *"So far, I've seen a partner working hard in the office, chatting to everyone at a summer party, and then in a language class looking suitably sheepish, like every other lawyer in there who'd for whatever reason failed to do their homework!"*

Within the pleasant, airy offices, light relief can be found in the informal Breakout area, which with its bright and breezy interior and leather couches was described as ***** (insert name of preferred coffee chain). And we'd never forgive ourselves for omitting a heaped spoonful of praise for 'Contact NN' – a forum for networking with peers in different professions through social gatherings and functions. Many valuable links have been forged over the years after rounds of human-sized Jenga and Scalextrics, wine tastings and useful talks and seminars.

heading for reading

If anyone has a burning desire to work in Reading (or Sheffield for that matter), then this preference can be indicated on the training contract application form. If two years is too long, it's also possible for London trainees to do a single seat in Reading, and for anybody with a keen interest in IP and IT, this may be worth pursuing since the locale is a hotbed of hi-tech talent. This regional office is *"perfectly self-governing"* and services a client base consisting of both local businesses and referrals from London. Also, the range of seats available for Reading trainees is good; corporate, litigation and property remain compulsory, with charities, employment, IT and IP making up the balance. The levels of supervision in Reading mirror those in

London, and the levels of client contact and frontline involvement are also similar, if not higher. *"I've been in meetings on my own and have handled due diligence and disclosure agreements from beginning to end. It's not that the help's not been available. I've just felt encouraged to make strides myself."*

The modern offices are small, but large enough to house around 30 lawyers. The benefit of this, in the words of one trainee, is that *"you definitely feel more a part of the business."* After hours, the Oracle is a popular destination for relaxation, socialising and shopping, being only two minutes' walk away. If there's one potential downside to Reading life, it would be that *"it's not as convenient to socialise after hours as in London, since people here tend to disperse more quickly, living that bit further away."*

feng shui in sheffield

Another proud office, Sheffield 'as everything that t'London office 'as, ta very much. And possibly more in fact, with an especially steely construction practice and a popular PI seat (a throwback to when many of the lawyers worked as an in-house unit for British Coal). PI gives trainees perhaps the greatest chance of some hands-on advocacy work. Otherwise, the seat regime is the same as London and Reading. The wonders of video conferencing mean that trips to London can be avoided and training sessions can be taken to a new interactive level. The ethos is, unsurprisingly, cordial and laid back. One trainee could name their entire London, Reading and Sheffield peer intake and recall the salient facts about each trainee. *"I don't really think that's impressive! We're all in contact, at least by e-mail and telephone, all of the time."*

The offices are *"light and airy"* and well situated opposite the canal and near to the Bluewater and Hilton Hotel bars. It scarcely merits comment here that Sheffield is a lively city, and the good news is that a version of Contact NN flourishes. A hugely successful summer ball was this year held in conjunction with an investment management firm, and the institution continues to promote a healthy mix of seminars and socials. Recently the trainees and their chums have been attending feng shui sessions designed to promote greater harmony in working conditions. By 'eck! In our day, you got a wooden crate to sit on and a beat-up old typewriter. And you were 'appy!

In September 2003, 19 of the 21 trainees were very 'appy to stay at the firm post-qualification.

and finally...

You won't find it on the front cover of the *FT* advising on record-breaking, transglobal deals, but the associated demands of such things are not everybody's cup of tea. If, instead, you are looking for a blend of hard work and variety, and you're happy with the property element, Nabarros is well worth considering.

Nelson and Co

the facts

Location: Leeds
UK ranking by size: 351
Total number of trainees: 9
Seats: 6x4 months
Alternative seats: None

With strong roots in insurance litigation, Nelson & Co is a mid-rank Leeds outfit that values its connections to the city and its people. It is actively working to expand its commercial presence.

dusting off the cobwebs

The trainees we spoke to gave us the impression that the firm has effected a good old-fashioned spring clean in the last few years, putting its house in order and (if you'll forgive our slide into a gardening metaphor) preparing the ground for the growth that is just beginning to take hold. The old training partner and his slightly 'unpredictable' methods has been tidied away and replaced by a shiny new, wipe-clean version that functions with greater efficiency. Trainees have welcomed a new six-seat system, which offers *"a great chance to experience a variety of work,"* and a new feedback and appraisal system that has encouraged reciprocity and responsiveness. Clarity extends to seat allocation too; the first three seats are chosen for trainees prior to their arrival, but decisions about how they will spend their second year are made *"organically"* after consultation between firm and individual. Said one source: *"They really listen to you and try to adapt to your needs."* Most trainees take their final seat in the area in which they hope to qualify.

roll with it

Insurance litigation has been the bedrock of the firm's practice, but the overhaul has signalled a change of focus, flagged up by one source as *"a move to coco, new image, new stationery, marketing hard."* This doesn't mean the firm has suddenly mutated into a hard-nosed and overly aggressive place; it still values *"local links and being part of the community."* In fact, we thought the summary by this trainee a balanced one: *"It's got more corporate and commercial-based, but keeps the medium-sized touches."* Or as we'd put it, not so much a revolution as a gentle roll. Insurance litigation is still important, however, and trainees undertaking a seat in the field can expect varied work in a department that makes an effort with them. Our sources talked of days spent work-shadowing partners in meetings, as well as drafting documents, taking witness statements and even running small files under supervision. The department handles PI claims for local people, as well as industrial disease cases. Alas, claimant litigation is regarded as old news and not many trainees angle for a seat here.

The newly refocused corporate, commercial and employment departments, and the nascent tax structuring department are the buzz areas of the firm at the moment. While a seat in coco involves a lot of work of the *"small cog in a big machine"* variety, the attraction lies in working directly for partners on big cases. Nelson & Co recently advised a leading supermarket chain on its acquisition of a property company and also lists clients like Omega and Ebuyer UK on its roster. The tax department supports the corporate department in transaction negotiations, whilst also handling a lot of tax planning for wealthy individuals. Its small size allows trainees more responsibility and client contact: *"The partners are often out securing new work, so you offer continuity for the client in the office."* The employment team offers busy days, the prospect of taking on some simple advocacy and *"really interesting cases that you can empathise with."*

Even though it is not at the top of every trainee's wish list, the property department (incorporating residential and commercial matters) is an important earner for the firm. Here a *"highly pressured"* environment dictates that the average hours of 8.30am to 6pm are likely to be stretched.

Trainees delighted us by stating the obvious. Concerning the trend for less litigation and more corporate work, they told us Nelson & Co is probably now looking for *"less litigation-type people and more corporate-type people."* If the truth be told, we applaud this simple approach to explaining the firm – at least they managed to avoid the cheesy clichés we're usually expected to swallow. We filled in a few blanks and decided they also meant that, to suit its new-found commercial ambitions, the firm may be looking for go-getting types with an interest in the commercial and transactional aspects of law. Both of the September 2003 qualifiers stayed on.

rhubarb and custard

Having closed down two smaller branch offices, in April 2003, the firm moved into a purpose-built canalside office in the LS1 postcode. Our sources told us it is *"an area where there's a lot of development. It'll be trendy in a few years' time, but it's a bit dead now."* They may be glad to hear that this was exactly the kind of move made by the top firms in both Bristol and Newcastle. Staff at Nelson & Co do have the advantage of an hour-and-a-half lunch break in which to make the five-minute trek to the bustling city centre, and the new office has all the usual mod cons including abstract art in the corporate department. Just as our researcher was gearing up for a discourse on the significance of said pieces, trainees told him: *"We don't actually know what it's meant to be."* Hands up anyone who understands the hidden meaning in the vivid shades of yellow and purple in the kitchen.

We're told the nearest decent pub is some distance away, but trainees do enjoy drinks on a Friday at The Wellington. Rest assured, when they do rouse themselves and make a night of it, the bars and clubs in Leeds are plentiful. A social club takes up a lot of the slack, co-ordinating events such as go-karting, paintballing and a booze cruise. The latter sounded good for juicy gossip, but although we were disappointed on that score, one trainee's clever deflection (*"I can't quite recall exactly what happened"*) suggested that, this year at least, the night was far from dull.

and finally...

Nelson & Co is gathering momentum. Students hoping for a broad-based Leeds training in a smaller firm might want to consider hopping on board.

Nicholson, Graham & Jones

the facts

Location: London
UK ranking by size: 87
Total number of trainees: 19
Seats: 4x6 months
Alternative seats: Occasional secondments
Extras: Pro bono – Battersea Legal Advice Centre

We've said something similar before, but if you put all those friendly, down-to-earth, work hard, play hard, medium-sized City firms in a blender and whizzed them together, the result would probably taste something like this firm. That's not a criticism – the firm encapsulates much of what's good in this sector – but it's sometimes hard to say what makes NGJ stand out. This doesn't bother its trainees, who claim they they've discovered the perfect cocktail.

balanced diet

Said one trainee of NGJ's broad practice: *"The firm has no real area of specialisation."* Accordingly, you'll get a meat and two veg training contract; the menu may not be that original, but it covers all the major food groups and it'll keep you satisfied. The three main departments are coco, litigation and property, and chances are you'll spend your first three seats here.

Corporate seats (including tax and banking) go down well. The firm mainly acts for AIM-listed clients and the odd FTSE 250 company and trainees get their teeth into some drafting and research on share purchase deals or partnership work. The only gripe was that there simply wasn't enough work to go round. NGJ was forced to lose three lawyers in the corporate department this spring as well as a handful of fee-earners and support staff in other departments. All we'll say is that the economic downturn has meant corporate departments everywhere are going hungry.

The property department acts for some big clients, including HSBC and London Underground. Property trainees are able to run their own files for landlords, helping to administer small licences and assignments, while also assisting partners on more complex matters. Many of our sources deemed the seat to be *"good fun"* and *"very useful – I was given lots of responsibility in dealing with clients, completing sales and purchases on my own, and it was also useful in terms of negotiation and time-management skills. It taught me what it was to be busy!"* The firm is particularly well known for property finance and recently advised the Bank of Scotland on the English property aspects of a £335 million loan to a fund comprising 11 shopping centres.

Much of NGJs litigation is focused on financial disputes; we heard of one trainee who was able to work on a juicy cross-border money laundering case. But don't get too excited; as with litigation departments everywhere, trainees must endure their fair share of the potato peeling, especially if it's a first or second seat. *"There was a lot of photocopying and bundling,"* one trainee confessed. Towards the end of your time in the department, you can expect to get a few files – perhaps debt collection – and you'll be able to make small applications in court. As an alternative to litigation, you could take a seat in employment or in the firm's first-class travel department, which acts for regulators such as ABTA and recently met with success in its defence of the first substantial PI action brought against a snowboarding holiday company.

If sport's your thing, you might also be tempted to NGJ by its highly regarded sports law team, which deals with commercial contracts, sponsorship and advice to players and clubs on image rights. Clients include Puma and Ryder Cup Limited, and the firm recently acted as sponsor and legal advisor to the British 10K Road Race. We suspect you'll also be tempted by the freebies – tickets to Arsenal games, cricket with clients at Lords and *"an excellent golf day."*

from the top

A cool and calm working day doesn't put too much strain on anyone: *"9am until 6pm is typical across the firm,"* although, as in any City firm, you might find yourself doing a few late nights when the work piles up. The only things that soured trainee life at NGJ were a couple of awkward supervisors and a few problems concerning who gets what seats. Trainees are generally happy with the level of responsibility they receive, saying: *"you're definitely valued as a member of the team."* They also commented on the fact that *"everyone knows each other,"* making it easy to chat to people as you walk around the firm and *"handy for cross-selling and interdepartmental issues."* Trainees might also be beaming at the moment because eight out of the nine qualifiers were retained in September 2003. Having said that, three had only been given six-month contracts on a wait-and-see basis.

One trainee was keen to point out that the firm was *"not ultra-modern and happy-clappy like Eversheds."* An interesting view of the national giant, but we think we understood what they were saying. Basically, NGJ is more like a nice cup of tea than, say, a skinny mochaccino. The office is traditionally laid out, with none of that open-plan nonsense and you'll sit with a partner, which means proper table manners at all times. One trainee admitted that *"it might be nice to sit with an assistant sometimes; they're more easy going and a bit of a laugh,"* but recognised that *"in terms of my career it's better this way. You get involved more and hear stuff from the top, not the middle."* If trainees do need to escape, there's always the canteen. Just like in your sixth-form common room, you'll find vending machines and a TV, and it's ideal for *"a bit of a gossip or a bicker."*

gene simmons r.i.p.

This is the point at which we were looking forward to writing about the annual country house weekend. Unfortunately, budgetary constraints have meant that, this summer, the extravagnza (which includes an elaborate costume party) was cancelled. So, no cross-dressing Spice Girl partners and no KISS look-alikes. The substituted event was a drinks party in the boardroom. Determined to find evidence of the firm's tendency to put its hair up before letting it down, we used our toughest interrogation techniques. Alas, we must rely on historical accounts, as karaoke seems to be the entertainment of choice this year. Nevertheless, partners are still able to make trainees cringe: *"Seeing a partner, who is normally very businesslike, getting up and singing 'I'm Too Sexy', unbuttoning his shirt and doing a bit of a strut is quite amusing."* If you say so.

When they're not doing their little turn on the catwalk, you might find the NGJ crowd in The Fine Line or The Red Lion near their Cannon Street offices. Trainees prefer going out en masse to mingling with the rest of the firm: *"On Fridays, we tend to go off on our own because we all get on. We'll see the others down the pub, but we just go out as a big group with boyfriends and girlfriends coming along."* Some are closer than others, we hear. Apparently, *"there are always a couple of trainees in each intake who end up going out with each other."*

and finally...

NGJ is the archetypal friendly, mid-sized, broad church, London commercial firm and trainees are very happy with that profile.

Norton Rose

the facts

Location: London
UK ranking by size: 14
Total number of trainees: 147
Seats: 6x4 months
Alternative seats: Overseas seats, secondments
Extras: Pro bono – Tower Hamlets Law Centre, CAB, FRU, Capital Case Panel, language training

Norton Rose is a top-ten City firm with loads of international offices. We suspect this is all some students want to know, but if you're thinking of applying, we'd recommend you read on...

it's getting hot in here...

Every year we're saved from detailing the complexities of the seat plan by writing this report on a sweltering Friday afternoon when lethargy is the perfect excuse to refer readers to the firm's own literature. This year fate dictates otherwise: a storm has cut through the heat and it's only Tuesday. Here goes...

During your first 16 months you'll complete three compulsory seats – corporate, banking and litigation – and an optional seat in something more specialised. You must then decide how to spend your remaining eight months, choosing between two new areas or one single four-month voyage into uncharted waters plus a return visit to the practice area that best floats your boat. From seat three onwards you can apply for an overseas posting.

...and teamy

Fresh out of the rebranding clinic, NR now sports a perky new look on its notepaper and website, having abandoned its traditional compass logo. Oh dear...how will trainees now navigate their way through the seat options? Cue the handy 'Rough Guide', written by and based on feedback from those who've already done each seat. The trainee grapevine also goes into overdrive prior to each rotation.

Departments are split into teams, and because these are central to the way NR functions, it is as important to find a team you fit into as it is to find a practice area you enjoy. *"You could get one team that is very male-dominated and doesn't like women wearing trousers to meetings."* But then, in another team, *"it really doesn't matter what kind of person you are – partners have a balanced attitude as to what's important in life and really get you involved."* It's horses for courses, clearly. A number of our sources spoke of the training contract as a quest to find the right team for qualification. Find that team early and you can build the rest of your training contract around it by choosing seats to enhance your knowledge base.

Everyone who wants to go abroad gets the chance, and while there's no ideal time to go (unless you're working around the climate or sporting fixtures), you should really complete a relevant corporate or banking seat in London beforehand. As expected, our sources confirmed that the international aspect of the firm is a big part of its appeal. You don't have to flee the country for international work though; this is a staple in the London HQ. Client secondments to Exxon Mobil are available for those who can't bear to leave loved ones or don't trust them to tape the *EastEnders* omnibus every Sunday for four months.

cash cow pie

We found a handy pie chart indicating the breakdown of fee income between the different departments. This showed that at the end of 2002 banking and corporate finance accounted for 55% of business, with litigation adding another 22%. Property came in at 9% and the remainder of the filling comprised other supporting departments like IP, employment and pensions, competition, and tax. You should realise that your training experience will be reflective of the firm's core business; it's unlikely you'll flit from one niche area to another to another. If you burn for a particular non-core area of work, however, you have a very good chance of getting a seat there and, overall, seat allocation is seen to be fair.

Your quality of life in the big powerhouse departments will depend on the team you end up in, as well as the type and volume of work it is handling. A massive transaction can be pretty exciting if you hit it at its climax, but four months of foreplay can mean heaps of document management. That said, none of our sources felt they'd done more than their fair share of bundling, proofing, copying or guarding the data room and all gave us examples of tasks that were worthy of their years of legal study. The asset finance team was particularly praised for rewarding work: *"I ran lots of small deals myself. The minute they see you are capable, you get a good amount of responsibility."*

One pragmatist, who had taken his share of *"mundane trainee jobs...on the chin,"* also had plenty to say about the *"scary buzz"* of drafting and the *"excellent responsibility"* of running certain discrete aspects of an international deal. Training in a City firm necessarily involves both types of task; as to the balance between the two, one source said: *"I'm a firm believer that it's down to the individual trainee. Sometimes you are automatically given good quality work and sometimes you need to push for it."* Another agreed: *"Supervisors aren't psychic."*

mind the gap

NR worked on the PPP of London Underground, so next time you're stuck on the Misery Line, spare a thought for the trainees. *"I think every trainee worked on that deal at some point,"* one of our interviewees chuckled. He then told us that the six-seat system meant trainees could sometimes *"meet the same deals from different angles."* Working on the same matter in different departments must surely help you decide what kind of lawyer you want to be. It also has the added bonus of putting you alongside old teammates. The LU PPP involved trainees in corporate, project finance, construction, property, and environment and planning, among others. We wanted to start a rumour that they were all given smart blue uniforms, but we know most readers are now wise to our puerile pranks.

And so to one of NR's best selling points: trainees and partners breathe the same air – literally. *"We usually share a room with a partner and that means you can develop some serious banter with them. They are not just some high-level person in an office around the corner."* Additionally, when they start, each trainee is assigned to a mentor-partner, who is there to monitor their progress and give advice on how to get through a tricky seat. The value of post-appraisal check-ups and regular lunches are not to be underestimated, and *"if it ever does come to fighting your corner, they do."* When it works – and it usually does – *"it's a great system...I was able to be totally open with my mentor."* But a few poor souls suffer from neglect and one trainee felt their mentor had been *"more of a hindrance than a help."* Note to training partner: retire some mentors, award merit badges to others. On the subject of performance, the end-of-seat trainee appraisals come with formal grades attached. *"It used to be from 'outstanding' to 'unsatisfactory' but now it's 1-6."* Like a school report? *"It is a bit, but one with more bearing on your future!"* 26 of the 32 qualifiers were kept on in September 2003.

Keen to discover if the new pink arrow branding was more appropriate than olde worlde nautical compass, we canvassed views. *"The firm is still quite traditional, but with a big will to change from some people."* Also: *"There's no dress down except on charity days,"* and the concession for summer is that *"girls wear tops and not blouses."* Don't get us wrong, this is not a stuffy firm, but in some respects it is conventional. A few people told us how NR had been in a state of flux, leading to internal changes and restructuring; others were more reticent on the subject of the firm's aims and direction. We thought it a fair topic, given that many of our sources joined the firm on the back of its 1999 mission statement to be 'Top Five by 2005'. This bold aspiration isn't one we hear about now, but we do see the firm focusing on its European network and carefully targeting its corporate and finance practices. *"We all went to an internal presentation and I now understand why we're pursuing certain companies, certain countries and certain structures,"* said a helpful source. Doubtless the much vaunted and valuable new instructions from Nestlé are exactly the sort of result the firm wants.

the stone roses

The firm's Kempson House HQ is close to Bishops House and opposite Stone House, but the litigation department is over in Margate…er, sorry, Moorgate…a ten-minute walk away. This fragmentation is the one thing trainees would change about the firm. Word has it that the lease on Kempson House is up in a year and this may prompt an office move.

Below Stone House is the bar formerly known as The Old Monk: trainees imply it had all the appeal of an aged friar's undergarments, yet they couldn't kick the habit. Now called The Stonehouse, there's a new menu, but otherwise it's the same as before. Alternatively there's The Light in Shoreditch or chain bars closer to hand. Every Monday evening the firm provides free drinks: *"It's meant to be for trainees, but assistants won't get thrown out."* There are sports teams for almost everything, and each year the firm organises a European office footie tournament based in the previous winner's city. *"Last time it was in Amsterdam; London won that tournament, but next time we're really hoping it'll be Milan!"* Um…isn't that what Posh said?

and finally...

Norton Rose represents a good alternative to the magic circle for those looking for international practice, quality training and a decent name for their CV.

Olswang

the facts

Location: London, Reading
UK ranking by size: 36
Total number of trainees: 46
Seats: 4x6 months
Alternative seats: Brussels, secondments
Extras: Pro bono – Toynbee Hall and Tower Hamlets Law Centres

One of the fastest-growing firms in the last ten years, Olswang has a first-rate reputation for TMT work and wins applause in more traditional areas. It's also cultivated a cool media-savvy reputation.

winning hearts, training minds

The training at Olswang follows the standard four by six-month seat system. There are no compulsories, but you will divide your time between coco, entertainment, litigation and property. Typically, most trainees get to sample the practice areas they are interested in, and we heard of few disappointments. Trainees admitted that media and entertainment work for the biggest names in film and TV was an attractive prospect, but confessed: *"It is not the main reason for being here, nor the lifeblood of the firm anymore."*

The property department has been through an explosive period of growth, benefiting greatly from the arrival of a sizeable chunk of the DJ Freeman team after that firm disbanded. Work for clients like Green Property, Woolworths, Land Securities Trillium, and companies in the media industry has won the hearts of many trainees, particularly as it is where you are most likely to get to run your own files. The bunch we spoke to were clearly not enamoured with corporate work, but we would suggest that has more to do with the type of person that Olswang had previously recruited than with what is going on in that department. That said, trainees who are interested in corporate law, are likely to find themselves with decent roles on deals, rather than 24/7 document management, although one source did point out that *"greater involvement and bigger responsibility does come at the expense of multi-billion pound deals."*

study leave

Last year we reported on the new 'Know-How' programme – a three-month period of research/admin during which trainees write legal updates, look for breaking law or assist in the amendment of precedents. The programme continues to receive mixed reviews. While some trainees said they *"dread it – you get the really rotten research work,"* others were more receptive, saying: *"It gives you a real in-depth knowledge."* Though some argue that Know-How takes you away from the clients, others found themselves explaining new legal developments to clients.

While not a dead cert, secondments to clients may crop up, giving trainees the chance to see what happens behind the scenes at the British Phonographic Institute, *The Mirror* or the BBC. A seat in Brussels is also up for grabs, offering largely corporate and EU work; however, if this is a priority for you, make sure you've brushed up your French first. The firm's newer Reading office currently has four trainees, one or two of whom are usually on secondment to the London office.

staying up past bedtime

Typically, levels of responsibility accorded to trainees vary depending on the nature of the department and the work it handles but, generally, our sources were fairly content with their lot. Though *"you very rarely get to run your own file because the work is too big, you get given elements of it,"* and while *"sometimes you have to do trainee gimp work, that is offset by the high points of the training contract."* The same philosophy applies to working hours. In the past Olswang has had a reputation for subscribing to the hard-graft school of thought, and our sources proudly told us that they *"work damned hard."* We don't doubt it – they spoke of 1am, 3am, even 5am finishes. But don't be alarmed: nobody was working through the night on a regular basis, and one source even sounded quite enthusiastic about the late nights, saying: *"After hours, people play music and take time out and stuff."*

could do better

In a firm where the chief executive is 30-something, and the senior partners have discovered the secret of eternal youth, it is perhaps unsurprising that trainees don't feel intimidated by them. While one pointed out: *"There definitely is a hierarchy,"* another said: *"You don't crawl past partners on your knees hoping they won't strike you down with a thunderbolt."* All trainees sit with an assistant solicitor or partner, and most find this an invaluable part of the learning process. In addition to three-monthly appraisals, *"as long as people aren't busy you will get more frequent feedback – people are very honest."* So what happens when people are busy? Well, often you need to push for information, and there's a feeling that, at times, appraisals weren't taken as seriously as they should be. Nevertheless, everyone gave the firm an 'A' for effort for its handling of the qualification process in 2003. Even those who weren't lucky enough to be kept on agreed that *"the firm now has a great system of giving information early."* We also give the firm good marks for its much-improved retention rate. After two years of poor stats, in September 2003, 17 out of the 23 qualifiers stayed.

too cool for school?

We wondered if Olswang was looking for grade-A swots with a Snoopy thermos and black plimsolls, or cool kids with a telly in their bedroom and a full set of pokémon cards? If its 'yoof' training brochure has been anything to go by, unless you are in possession of your own decks and an extensive selection of white labels, you should get in line for a bogwash. A shame really, because the trainees we spoke to weren't the kind of kids who would have intimidated the likes of us on the *Student Guide* team out of our dinner money.

Such a youthful, energetic firm inevitably *"wants your enthusiasm and excitement,"* but otherwise, its criteria seem quite oblique. You don't need to wear any particular trainers at Olswang (in fact, the dress code sidelines them to the gym) and you don't need to tread any particular path to get there. Trainees come from a variety of universities, are at varying stages in life, and have a wealth of different backgrounds. When we asked for an archetype, our sources described someone *"easy-going and business-minded, conversational and passionate."* Although not in a behind-the-bike-sheds kind of way.

So if kiss-chase isn't their thing, what do Olswang trainees get up to at playtime? The departmental skiing holidays of the dot.com boom have fallen by the wayside, replaced by the more typical offerings of summer parties and, of course, the Christmas party. Christmas is when *"Olswang does get trendy"* – last year fake tattoos were on offer. It sure beats paper hats and party poppers. There are netball, football and softball teams, and the inevitable Friday night out is a firm fixture. Since moving to new offices on High Holborn, the drinking contingent has yet to establish a regular pub, but Torts is *"a good place to start."*

bye bye bossa nova?

After a couple of tough years brought on by the tech slump, Olswang has welcomed a year of change and growth, and the move to the new, state-of-the-art office on High Holborn has marked this watershed. It offers flat screen computers, *"aerodynamic chairs,"* (presumably for high-flyers), glass walls, cappuccino bars and the O-Zone (a restaurant where trainees' waistlines are put to the test). The new building brings all the staff under one roof.

One of our sources hit the nail on the head: *"We've moved into a big new building and we've grown up..."* Instead of *"purple fittings and shiny stuff,"* it's now *"cream walls and a bit of wood panelling."* Last year, whenever we phoned we always got Bossa Nova hold music; this year we often ended up with Rigoletto and the New World Symphony. Has Olswang just emerged from self-conscious, cool-conscious adolescence?

If this is not what you were hoping to hear, don't worry – we are reliably informed that in one meeting room, the conference table has been replaced by table-football, and in the corporate department, Folf (a football/golf hybrid) is still played in the corridor. Olswang has not thrown its techie toys out of the pram, but this bright young prospect has serious work to do in other, more traditional, areas of law. The arrival of the DJ Freeman lawyers seems to have secured the firm a bigger foothold in the serious world of property, and the management has plans elsewhere too. Trainees spoke of *"stability and sustainable expansion."* Or, as we like to put it, growth without adolescent acne and heartache.

barley sugar, anyone?

In the past we have advised that you look beyond the image and, now more than ever, the firm's own recruits seem to agree. At law fairs, you may have seen cool Olswang trainees handing out funky brochures in cool CD-sized tins. Look again and you will see a normal young person handing out the kind of tin your gramps keeps his travel sweets in.

and finally...

While Olswang still has the *"wow factor,"* now it is based more on the deals it does for clients than urban myths about playing pinball with your supervisor. Consider it if you're after a firm that has sensible plans for the future and a tidal wave of really good lawyers.

Osborne Clarke

the facts

Location: Bristol, London, Reading
UK ranking by size: 23
Total number of trainees: 40
Seats: 4x6 months
Alternative seats: Overseas seats, secondments
Extras: Language training

Osborne Clarke is well known for its work for technology clients and has undergone a period of European expansion. Yet, in the current economic climate, we've seen it concentrating on more traditional practice and renewing its interest in its old Bristol hunting ground.

the great leap forward

Osborne Clarke developed a super name in the 1990s as it charged ahead with the likes of Taylor Wessing,

Olswang and Bird & Bird into the brave new world of the tech sector. Like each of these firms, the strategy was to provide a 360-degree service for TMT companies, while also acting for other clients. It was through the tech boom that the growth of its London and Reading offices was most noticeable, and this burgeoning market sector also fuelled the development of a European network and an office in California's Silicon Valley.

OC's overseas network now comprises its own offices in Barcelona, Madrid, Copenhagen, Cologne and California and associated firms in Brussels, Paris, the Netherlands, Russia and the Baltic region. Our sources were well aware of the European dimension, and not only because some of them go on three or six-month placements to Cologne or California. In the California seat you'll get an insight into *"many of the things you usually can't learn during a training contract. It's primarily a marketing role, so you do presentations…make referrals of new work to the European offices and…read the newspapers to see which start-up companies are going for, or have just won, new investment."*

clawing back

It's not the only firm to have suffered as a result of the tech slump in the last two years, but it is fair to say that OC has been noticeably hit. Having failed to spot the change in the market early enough, it carried on recruiting partners and assistants after it should have stopped. Faced with no alternative but to let people go, the firm then pushed through a round of redundancies and 'managed out' 14 partners. Another 11 partners quit the firm voluntarily, some of them big billers. All in all, it's been a tough old time at OC, especially in the London office. It was notable that of the 16 jobs available for the 25 second-years coming up to qualification in September 2003, only one was in London. The vast majority were in Bristol and three were in Reading.

real estate bonanza

Aside from the Law Soc's contentious requirement, no seat is compulsory, *"but everyone seems to do company"* and some people suggested a seat in commercial property was becoming inevitable. This department is going great guns at the moment, having won panel positions with some big property companies – Warner Estate, Lafarge Redland and Gazeley (the property arm of Asda-Walmart). Trainees had plenty to say on the benefits of six months in the department. *"I had huge responsibility in that seat,"* one told us. Another said it had presented him with *"the steepest learning curve. At the start I was on a large securitisation, which was a bit mind-numbing…lots of deeds scheduling. That completed and suddenly I got into some really good work: licences to assign and things like that…there was plenty of drafting and client handling."*

Litigation wins the hearts of many: *"I had a number of diverse cases in commercial litigation, and I got to see things at a variety of stages. I even went to court by myself."* Additionally, in Bristol, trainees are encouraged to spend an afternoon with a District Judge in the County Court. It's an experience that allows them to learn, pain-free, from others' mistakes. The accepted view is that you should undertake a selection of seats that will give you a broad experience. A few second-years split seats, although this is often linked with an overseas placement or an oversubscribed seat. Most trainees stay put in one office, but are encouraged to try a seat elsewhere. *"Obviously they need a certain number of trainees in each place, and if there's not enough in the right places, then they will ask people to go."*

no place like home?

Is Bristol where it's at these days? *"Yes, definitely."* Almost all the Bristol trainees we interviewed had been to a uni in the South West or grown up in the region. Every one of them had a real passion for the city. One source simply said: *"I love Bristol and I want to stay here."* Which brings us rather nicely to the new mood of Bristol-centricity at OC, a strong theme running through our interviews. One trainee explained: *"Since Simon Beswick has taken over as managing partner, there has been a conscious push to focus on the home market. The partner in my team often talks about it."*

In the last year, the firm has moved all its Bristol staff under the one roof of a brand new open-plan HQ next to Temple Meads train station. From the main conference room on the top floor *"you can see terrific views out over Bristol." "Someone once described it as a prison – there are all these balconies around the outside and when people are on them..."* Can we have a more palatable description? *"It's all light and airy inside with splashes of corporate orange and purple...but tastefully done."* Glad to hear it. The staff restaurant (*"No, no – they like to call it a cafe"*) serves the usual sandwiches, salads and hot food from breakfast time until 4pm. Apparently, decisions as to furniture and food for the eatery were made by a committee drawn from across the payroll – a nice touch and one that is indicative of the inclusive ethos of the firm.

Each month, the Bristol office used to have 'First Friday' nights, when all staff were issued with two drinks tokens (named 'Perrins' after the former managing partner). Alas, a new, more prudent approach to household budgeting meant that when we rang First Fridays were on hold. Additionally, in 2002 there was no firm-wide Christmas party, but we're happy to report that the OC fancy dress tradition was indulged wholeheartedly at a summer ball. Anticipating the event, one trainee mused: *"It's a Caribbean theme, which is difficult unless you want to go with a pineapple on your head!"* Thrill seekers take note: *"Osborne Clarke does know how to throw a good party."*

the valley five

The Thames Valley office (or TVO as they like to call it) is the smallest of the three and offers seats to around five trainees, although these are not limited to its core practice areas of IT and e-commerce. Since the litigation partner departed the firm, *"there's no lit seat,"* but slots are available in corporate, commercial, banking and employment. Reading is a close-knit office where people who like to know who's who and what's what will thrive. As one source said: *"There are about 50 of us here, so it's a pretty relaxed environment. Everyone has a laugh and a joke and we always have pizzas and Coke at our monthly meetings with management."* At these meetings, staff catch up on *"firm-wide and office-wide messages. We even spent an hour on the subject of how to spend our social budget."* More pizza and Coke maybe?

trimming cat fat

While we encountered great disappointment among trainees whose time at OC was about to come to an end, all our sources were very happy to recommend their employer to students, although we soon sensed that our remit was to flag-wave for the Bristol and Reading offices and to leave the jury in the deliberation room on the subject of the London office. And so that's where we are. On a lighter note, one of our interviewees was kind enough to pass on a delightful snippet about the big orange cat that graces the firm's notepaper. We're still unsure whether it's a puma or a panther, or some other breed (trainees don't seem to know either), but apparently the famous feline had *"a millimetre sliced off his tummy a few years ago. The firm didn't want people saying it was a fat cat."*

It's very clear to us what kind of trainee OC wants to recruit. *"The firm is looking for open, lively characters,"* one trainee explained, and we wholeheartedly endorse this self-portrait. We found our interviewees to be bright, enthusiastic, analytical and communicative. In tricky times, trainees often clam up in *True Picture* interviews, but we sensed that the firm's stated values of transparency and straightforwardness must have rubbed off on those we spoke to...or maybe that's how it recruits them in the first place.

and finally...

Trainees choose Osborne Clarke in part because of its famously pleasant atmosphere, and it's a credit to the firm that this atmosphere has survived, largely intact, despite a difficult 18 months. If, like our interviewees, you feel that Bristol's where it's at right now, then put your best paw forward.

Pannone & Partners

the facts

Location: Manchester
UK ranking by size: 62
Total number of trainees: 19
Seats: 4x6 months
Alternative seats: None

Pannone & Partners seems to have it all: 150 years of history, a profile that's higher than ever, a thriving commercial practice and a superb reputation in claimant PI and clinical negligence.

the hare and the tortoise

Pannone's clients are split evenly between companies and individuals and the two practices run like parallel streams. The personal legal services side is like a bubbling brook in perpetual motion. Alongside the flagship claimant PI and clinical negligence practices are trusts and probate, family, liquor licensing and residential property. Although PI is a major department, trainees assured us that they were neither forced nor expected to do a seat there. But if they do, they find themselves running around 30 of their own files and assisting partners on larger matters.

One thing that struck us about this firm is the sense of genuine care for clients. Many of those it acts for in the trusts and probate department are elderly or mentally ill; it is for this latter type of client that a partner acts as a panel receiver under the Mental Health Act. In this seat you'll have endless client contact and will even visit your clients in their homes. "*You have to be patient and gentle,*" said one trainee. And you should also be partial to the odd cup of tea and a natter with Gladys or Mabel. Budding Dr Seusses might also find their calling: one long standing client has a tortoise, which lives under her living room rug; so do be careful where you tread.

the fisherman and the little fish

By contrast, work in the commercial stream is fast flowing and can sweep a fresh-faced trainee off their feet and away. If acronyms like MBO and MBI make you shiver with pleasure rather than shudder with dread, you've certainly found the right place. Lawyers primarily act for a non-listed company client base but, big or small, clients are valued. You will get the chance to splash around with big-name clients, and many of them very big – Manchester Airport, English Tourist Board, Greater Manchester Passenger Transport Executive, Newell Rubbermaid, Texaco, York City FC and Sharp (UK), to name a few. Recently it received instructions to act for the five British men released from a Saudi prison, having been previously convicted of a series of bombings.

Litigation offers a massive spread of work – everything from commercial contract disputes to consumer claims. Trainees undertake research assignments, drafting, the inevitable bundling and document management and, we're pleased to report, they also get to attend court to take notes and make small applications.

the lion and the mouse

The firm operates a four by six-month seat system and listens to trainees' requests as to the departments they want to sit in. Second-years' preferences prevail over those of first-years and most trainees manage to engineer things such that their final six months are spent in the area into which they want to qualify. Nothing is compulsory, but if you want a shot at the prized clin neg department it is helpful to do a PI seat beforehand. If that side of the business is not why you joined the firm, fear not: you can follow a purely commercial path through your training. Sharpen your elbows if you're interested in employment though; it is the most coveted of all the seats.

Our sources waxed lyrical about the benefits of Pannone's high partner-to-trainee ratio, saying: "*They have time to train you.*" They also praised the firm's open culture, and all felt comfortable raising issues with the training partner. This is a firm that doesn't stand on ceremony. It also seems to be aware of the old adage 'Little friends may prove great friends.' As one pointed out: *"There's no point acting like you're better than the secretaries – they know more than you."*

Particularly in the personal legal services departments, the work is more than merely problem solving for distant, unknown clients. One trainee told us: *"People here genuinely care about the outcome for their client." "The partners inspire me. They're very passionate about their work,"* said another. And this attitude, we're told, pervades the entire firm. Applicants looking to find a firm with an abundance of female role models will be pleased to note that around one third of the partners, including the firm's managing partner, are women. She, the *"absolutely fantastic"* Joy Kingsley, works hard to keep the firm's name out there and to ensure that *"everybody feels a part of the machinery."* To its credit, Pannone seems to be encouraging staff to contribute in whatever way they can; through partner-free lunch meetings it asks staff what improvements could be made to the running of the firm. Perhaps Ms K inspires more than she realises because our sources expressed a desire to get more involved in the firm's marketing themselves, since *"we're the future of the firm after all."* In September 2003, five of the seven qualifiers stayed with the firm.

the bundle of sticks

Through the Pannone Law Group, the firm has links with firms around the world, including Brazil and several European jurisdictions. Whoah! Before you rush out to buy a thong and some factor 40, you should be aware that the chances of an overseas seat is even slimmer than the chances of Dale Winton and Nell McAndrew hearing the patter of little feet. The good news is that you won't always be chained to Manchester. Shortly after we interviewed trainees at Pannone, its football team, unlike Becks, was due to visit Milan for a few games. Major respect to the firm: out of the 70 people who were going, only 20 were on the squad. Just like true footballers' wives, *"the professional shoppers are hanging on."*

the hare with many friends

Sport and shopping, it seems, both feature heavily in Pannone's social calendar. For those who can't be bothered to slip into the changing rooms for team sports there are nights at the Bellevue Dog Races. For those who like nothing better than hanging around in changing rooms, last year there was a weekend of Christmas shopping in Edinburgh. Monthly drinks evenings and a Christmas and Summer Ball are supplemented by informal nights out in Manchester, a city that trainees confirmed is *"coming on in leaps and bounds."* Of course Manchester has many claims to fame and these days it's rare to hear it referred to as one of those grim places up north. With good reason, its cultural heritage and current offerings seem to overshadow its reputation as the gun capital of Britain. Among the many things the city has to offer, its unique contribution to popular music, its traditional position as the home of the free press and its recent successes at hosting the Commonwealth Games all build into a palpable sense of pride. Pannone has a strong Mancunian identity and the vast majority of trainees are born, raised or educated in the North West. If you know the area, you'll not be surprised to learn that places like Didsbury and Chorlton are the natural habitat of the Pannone set.

Lots of people have found love at the firm and there are even a few marriages. Amongst the trainees, however, we noted a distinct lack of action. Undeterred, one trainee vowed to *"keep plugging away. That's my ethos."* Slow and steady wins the girl, eh? Actually, the secret to general career success at Pannone is not hard: *"Be passionate about the work, be ambitious, and give the impression you're enjoying it!"*

and finally...

If you're wedded to Manchester, whatever your tastes, you'll find something to suit at Pannone & Partners, be this commercial practice or top-notch clinical negligence and PI. All this and the occasional spot of football or shopping, what more could you wish for?

Penningtons

the facts

Location: London, Basingstoke, Godalming, Newbury
UK ranking by size: 67
Total number of trainees: 22
Seats: 4x6 months
Alternative Seats: None

Penningtons offers a training that values breadth of experience over early specialisation. Trainees can dabble in anything from commercial transactions to claimant PI, family or private client. The firm has cohesion across its offices and gives equal focus to the capital and the Home Counties.

clout without the lout

Trainees reflected on the lustre projected by the Penningtons name when they'd been applying for contracts. Rather than simply assuming voodoo expertise on the part of the firm's recruiters, we pressed for specifics. The message came loud and clear: having experienced magic circle firms either at interview, on placement, or through reports from friends, trainees chose Penningtons for *"the name and status of a city firm, very good-quality work and a more relaxed work-life culture."* The firm certainly doesn't see itself as a poor cousin of larger City operations, and, especially in London, you can reasonably expect to be locking horns with them. Any hint that it deserves underdog status is a challenge the firm and trainees relish, as this anecdote illustrates: *"The other side in a recent litigation case was a top-five firm. They thought they had us easily licked. And they didn't. There are very good brains at this office and we shouldn't be underestimated."*

In London, Penningtons offers gentlemanly working without the hours and brash corporate fascism that can be a downer in the megafirms. The regional offices *"benefit from a slightly more relaxed culture,"* each having their own specialisms and characters whilst also taking work from the London office. The quality of trainee life in the provinces defers only to the specific vagaries of the location; the trainees are a fairly homogenous group. Do you recognise the following traits in yourself? *"A sound academic grounding, a certain enthusiasm, no feeling of a God-given right to be a trainee, a willingness to work."*

petits fours

Over the course of your four six-month seats, Penningtons pushes you towards time in litigation and a spell in property, which is viewed unfavourably by many trainees. Nevertheless, property is the biggest department, dealing with landlord and tenant matters as well as advising national house builders, commercial developers and property investment companies. In the second year, the firm tries to accommodate your developing interests, with emphasis placed on the third seat as a time to test your instincts about qualification. Although the emphasis is on a broad training, if you get the bit between your teeth for something specific, you can move in that direction. *"I wanted two litigation seats in my second year and got them,"* one source told us. The firm covers too many areas for us to go into detail on each, but suffice it to say that private client is particularly important and good-quality corporate work, IP and the ubiquitously popular employment are all on offer. The firm also has an immigration team and a nice line in corporate baking...sorry banking – nothing to do with cooking the books.

Mundane trainee tasks are balanced out by more interesting matters. PI in Basingstoke may involve a fair share of RTAs, but there's also a partner specialising in cerebral palsy negligence claims. By the same token, processing visa applications for finance houses may not make immigration exciting, but a high-profile deportation case will certainly spice things up.

hurry on sundown

In the late 1980s Penningtons was tipped for greatness, but it's probably fair to say that it has not changed greatly in the last two decades and a generation of partners who shaped the firm at that time still dominate today. *"There are few junior partners and a lot of control rests with half-a-dozen older partners. It's very partner-led and is not so good at marketing,"* was one appraisal, whilst another went further, saying: *"I'm not sure the firm knows where it's headed."* By way of contrast, we did learn that the firm has seen a 14% rise in turnover to £21.2 million this last year, so we'll leave you to balance out these different viewpoints.

Near to Bank and described as *"the ugliest building in London,"* the head office prompted one trainee to remark gnomicially: *"It is what it is, and it does what it does!"* We concluded this meant function over form. In recent hot weather there was a dress-down policy for a few months, *"and I mean dress-down, really relaxed,"* which might be considered surprisingly liberal for an office described by several years' worth of interviewees as *"conservative."* Apparently, one partner came to work during this period in *"knee-high socks and shorts."* Fabulous!

For all the building's functionality, there are enough offices to go around (trainees usually sit with a partner) and you can't sniff at the location in the heart of the City. A social committee arranges trips to the theatre and the like, although we heard a few murmurs about the need to *"get a greater cross-section of the firm out."* One trainee joked that *"trainees aren't treated like pariahs, no one throws stones at us!"* adding that *"NQs up to three years qualified come out, but drinking with partners is rare."* A regular office-based event known as Sundowners is a chance to schmooze with the older generation. At trainee level, the office also plays host to the monthly 'First Monday' training lectures for all trainees, which inevitably concludes in a local hostelry. The favourite for an after-work snifter is Balls Brothers just below the office.

the counties set

In each of the three county offices, seats are available in litigation, coco, property and private client. Neatly positioned equidistant from London and the south coast, Godalming is the most luxurious residence in Penningtons' portfolio, and with a select trainee population of four, training here will challenge. Almost inevitably, there are more opportunities *"to be noticed and take responsibility,"* especially in PI and clin neg. Agricultural issues are also a niche strength, with a team advising farms, estates and agribusiness managers for clients like Clydesdale Bank. Admittedly, the social scene is less than frantic, but there are organised trips and wine-tasting evenings. Here, as across the firm, isolation is not an option: monthly meetings with your supervisor, regular meetings with your 'buddy' and end-of-seat appraisals all mean that people are keeping tabs on your mental, physical, work and social well-being. It's probably safe to say your supervisor won't ring you at home to check you're eating properly, but you never know.

Along the M3 in Hampshire, Basingstoke takes on the same number of trainees. Its private client team handles some international instructions – two dual-qualified UK/French lawyers work closely with the small Paris office on trusts, personal tax and some property work The office has a quantity of new, younger partners and our sources suggest it epitomises a more dynamic side of the firm. Clearly, there are partners who want to *"lose some of the traditional orientation and drag the firm into the 21st century."* In the past we've suggested that a local connection is important to train here, but we were told one of the current trainees lives in the town during the week and returns to London for weekends. If you are new to the area, you could play catch-up through involvement with local young professionals' organisations. The firm encourages all trainees to get involved *"to help build connections for the firm in the future."* The Basingstoke branch has new, central offices within easy reach of Festival Place. An even more attractive prospect is the foamy hand-drawn ale at Barton's Mill, one of Old Basing's *"nice little country pubs."*

Newbury is firmly planted in Berkshire, and the nearby racecourse seems to have an influence on office life – some partners wear tweeds, we're told; one has interpreted dress-down Friday as *"a day to wear a cravat instead of a tie."* There is an *"excellent"* and not-too-formal office culture. According to our informants, you're just as likely to be displaying revolutionary zeal in Bar Cuba on a Friday night with a partner as with a fellow trainee, and bimonthly drinks parties help the work atmosphere shimmy along effortlessly. The standard quartet of litigation, property, private client and coco seats holds sway.

If you are considering the firm, it would probably be best to fix on one office and make a sustained assault, rather than go for the scattershot approach. Nine out of the 11 trainees who qualified in September 2003 stayed.

and finally...

Penningtons gives excellent training. Whether you want the comfort of the counties or to test yourself in London, you'll be able to explore what the profession has to offer before you specialise.

Pinsents

the facts

Location: Birmingham, Leeds, London, Manchester
UK ranking by size: 13
Total number of trainees: 64
Seats: 4x6 months
Alternative seats: Brussels, secondments
Extras: Language training

In the year since we last checked in on Pinsents, it's undergone some changes: not so much a full makeover as a general spruce-up and the purchase of a few new accessories. And rather like the UK populace, it's getting its head around this new-fangled idea that we're a part of Europe.

the game plan

The story starts with the 1995 merger of respected Birmingham firm Pinsent & Co with big Leeds player Simpson Curtis. The union spawned a small London office, which in turn joined forces with City boutique Biddle in 2001, giving the firm a decent presence in the capital. A year later, more action when Pinsent Curtis Biddle came to the rescue of a rapidly imploding Garretts, scooping its entire Midlands contingent into the tight embrace of the PCB Birmingham office. Eager to grow yet further, the firm then opened up a small office in Manchester.

Legal pundits watched all this with interest, nodding at appropriate moments, noting the firm's growth. Like an experienced chess pro making strategic moves, Pinsents (unlike most chess champs, it has now obligingly simplified its name) has kept our interest, but never caused us to break out into a nervous sweat wondering 'What next?'. The most we've asked is 'When will it push its pawns into Europe?' Pinsents is a classy player, not usually prone to impulsive moves, overbearing tactics or flamboyant outbursts, and through subtlety and shrewdness it's held its own and hung onto its vital pieces. There have been some partner departures, but we assume that the firm is in control of the moves. At the junior end in September 2003, the London qualifiers fared worse than their peers in Leeds and Birmingham, but overall 23 out of 33 stayed.

All the while, Pinsents has been edging away from its long-held reputation for technical, academic lawyering; in its place we see a greater emphasis on strategy and marketing – hence the decision to focus on and organise itself around 'chosen markets'. These chosen markets are financial institutions & insurance, government, manufacturing, real estate, services and technology. *"We are the chosen market generation,"* one trainee quipped. It's also worth noting that the firm has now shown an interest in European business, creating alliances with firms in France, Germany and Sweden (although most of our sources struggled to name more than one of the firms).

fighting dragons

Training contracts are offered in all offices, with most trainees staying put in one. Anyone can request a transfer; indeed we noted at least one migrant in each office and several in London. The official line is that no seat is compulsory, although trainees tell us: *"You are herded through some kind of corporate seat, but that's OK because to work here you do need a good grounding in corporate structures."* Beyond this, a contentious seat is a must and then it's mostly up to you. Most sources were satisfied with seat allocation: some notching up extra time in favoured departments; others taking advantage of client secondments or a trip to Brussels firm, Renouf & Co; others still doing split seats.

Commonly, trainees told us they had undertaken work for a number of fee earners in each department. Then again, we all know that possession is nine-tenths of the law and this is especially true if you have a possessive supervisor. Sometimes, when trainees claim to be a team resource, what they actually mean is that they are farmed out to anyone with a job too menial to do themselves. Not so here. Indulging our request for the intricate details of their daily lives, trainees reported good work and direct relationships with partners. A London source said: *"No partner is God and there's no culture of fear…no one can be that much of a dragon as the other partners would round on them."*

our friends in the north (and south)

Consciously or not, large-scale donkey jobs are shared between trainees, so ensuring plenty of time for more researching, drafting board minutes and simple documents, tagging along to meetings, and helping to administer deal completions. One trainee assured us that she was *"doing the work of a newly qualified in the magic circle."* However, nothing is ever perfect and we did hear that a large number of trainees (mostly first-years) had been drawn into a project that ran between October 2002 and April 2003. This involved them in the review of an important client's asset base, a mammoth task that diverted some from the work they had hoped to be handling. Not everyone was best pleased, but we understand it was a one-off exercise.

Monthly appraisals earned the trainees' thumbs-up. In addition to cross-office departmental training sessions, twice a year there are events called National Trainee Days when the whole group gathers for professional education and edification before a big night out. Then *"we all stay at each others' houses."* Having become acquainted during an initial two-week induction, these away days are perfect for maintaining friendships and collecting party invitations.

london: biddle goodbye

When we rang, the big news in London was the departure of (ex-Biddle partner) David Hooper and his defamation team. This came at much the same time as all trace of the Biddle name was removed from Pinsents' branding. Sources who had been hired by Biddle before the merger felt that it was part and parcel of the Pinsentisation of their office. One trainee concluded: *"When we joined it was managed by London partners, but increasingly it feels like a national firm and dictats come down from Birmingham."* Another agreed: *"We have to keep reminding people that London is the capital because Birmingham is definitely the head office."* Yet logic dictates that the London office must surely grow in stature and influence in the coming years. Since we first carried out interviews there four years ago, the number of trainee seats has multiplied. The choice now includes pensions, insurance, employment, corporate finance, private equity, banking, tech & media, litigation, property and major projects.

Pinsents' primary London home in a large and excessively brown office block near Liverpool Street boasts great views from reception. When we visited, the thing that struck us most was a neat row of umbrellas hanging from the wall behind the reception desk. Biddle's City gent influence or symbolic of Pinsents' innate caution? Either way, telling. Actually you don't need a brolly to make it home and dry to the local pub. Those who don't do *"dingy and smokey"* might prefer one of several chain bars nearby. The dress code is *"quite smart"* with Fridays *"not particularly dressed down."*

birmingham: olives

Just as Birmingham is undergoing structural alterations, so is Pinsents' office, although when we called the decision as to whether or not to go open plan had not been made. A full spread of seats was keeping the Brum trainees purring. We must offer an apology to the 2001-2003 trainee cohort for implying they had no truck with the Birmingham TSG. The truth of the matter is that, in contrast to their predecessors, this particular year group has fully involved itself with the organisation, some individuals even taking up committee posts. Olive anyone? Even after attending all TSG jollies there's still time for more intimate evenings out with colleagues in bars like Digress and the newcomer Aprés.

leeds: softball's for softies

The Leeds office operates open plan. Our sources spoke favourably of the set-up, saying that even senior figures were close to hand. *"I have not been concerned or inhibited about going to talk to anyone. I've never been blanked or sent away; even when people are busy they are at least courteous towards you."* The full complement of seats reflects the fact that the Leeds office covers all bases; however, PFI and projects work is particularly strong, as is property litigation. One-time official Pinsents haunt, the Slug & Lettuce, has lost much of its custom to new kid on the block, Firefly. Friday e-mails act as a rallying call for end-of-the-week revellers, and sometimes it's the partners who lead the charge. Just as in other offices, there are teams for football, hockey and softball (although one source suggested the latter was *"for jessies"*).

manchester: new order

Speaking of Pinsents' new venture in Manchester, one trainee told us: *"The office is fantastically go-getting – you really notice the conviviality. Trainees and partners are cracking jokes between themselves."* The office was built around several lateral hires, most notably private equity lawyers. Expect the office to continue to grow at a pace.

and finally...

Once seen as a firm of eggheads and rather technical in its approach, the firm is shedding that image. Now the archetype is simply *"someone who is affable and wants to get the job done properly."* 'Pinsent Courteous' we used to call it; the new name may have left us short of a pun but the sentiment is still there.

Prettys

the facts

Location: Ipswich
UK ranking by size: 234
Total number of trainees: 9
Seats: 4x6 months
Alternative seats: None

Prettys may be in Ipswich, but geographically and culturally it's just a short hop to London and beyond. If you fancy living somewhere where you can be a big fish in a small pond, then read on…

intergalactic

"If you come here" said one trainee, *"you won't be moving to a straw town to do Joan Smith's probate."* Prettys means business: *"The firm's quite commercially oriented anyway and has become more corporate even in the time I've been here."* The firm has well-established commercial, insurance, employment and private client departments. One trainee felt that the breadth of the firm's work meant greater job security: *"If one area is down, then another will be up."* A well-established local client base doesn't mean its horizons only stretch as far as Bury St Edmunds: in litigation you might find yourself involved in matters going before the county court, but you might also be dealing with clients referred from a European Chamber of Commerce. More proof of foreign interests comes in the form of niche French property and shipping departments. Furthermore, Prettys helped to set up Galexy, an international association of lawyers, and the office is positively polyglot.

sitting pretty

The firm will allocate the first of your four seats, and after that it's a case of dropping hints and asking nicely. Second-years get priority so *"if you want to do a particular seat, you'll probably get it eventually,"* but *"be prepared to go anywhere"* because in a smaller firm there's sometimes not much room for manoeuvre. However, you'll also get some of the benefits of being at a compact and bijou organisation – for instance, most trainees were managing their own caseload, sometimes even in their first seat. *"There's not really an average pattern of seats"* but you'll do corporate, insurance and probably property. Two or even three of your seats are likely to be heavy on litigation as this is a core strength. Commercial litigation is seen as particularly tasty and is *"always sought after"* for both the work (*"good varied exposure, good clients"*) and the people (*"the supervising partner is excellent"*). You might be involved in property matters or bankruptcy cases and will be able to go to court at least once a month. The seat can be hard work as *"you can't do anything about court deadlines,"* though bear in mind that a late night usually means staying in the office past 6pm. Is that hollow laughter we hear from the Square Mile?

Employment is seen as *"a sexy area,"* and a new IP/IT seat is sprouting out of the corporate department, which means trainees can now see copyright and trademark issues as well as e-commerce and data protection. In the corporate seat, you'll get your teeth into decent transactions and competition issues. Trainees say there's no difference between the type of work done here and in the City, saying: *"About half our work is London work – our overheads are lower so we charge less for the same stuff and the clients are loving it."* While we don't doubt their enthusiasm, we are wary of allowing readers to regard the Prettys experience in the same light as the Linklaters experience.

sutton who?

Ipswich. You'll know if you don't want to live here; you'll know if you do. But what if you just don't know anything at all about the place? Suffolk is most certainly an underrated part of the country. Think pretty villages, acres of countryside and easy access to the coast. But Ipswich isn't a buzzing metropolis: *"There's a nice marina with some swanky new flats"* and you'll find *"plenty to keep you amused until 11pm,"* although *"if you're heavily into clubbing I wouldn't recommend it."* Most of the trainees we spoke to felt the need to pop down to London fairly often, but by rail the journey's only about an hour so chances are you can make it to a City pub before your friends working at London firms can escape from their desks. Three of the four trainees who qualified in September 2003 stayed with the firm.

Traditionally, Prettys trainees have been heavily involved in the local Trainee Solicitors Group, which organises careers talks, charity events and an annual ball with *"vast alcohol consumption."* Recently Prettys' own events have included dragon boat racing, a quiz night and a walking weekend. Proper walking boots walking that is. On Fridays, *"there's always a big trail of people"* heading down to local bar Manning's.

Although officially your hours will be a very nice 9am to 6ish, trainees tended to find themselves getting embroiled in the firm's many marketing events – *"You have to want to get involved with the firm and the local community."* Not that anyone was complaining. Prettys lays on champagne receptions, trips to Newmarket races and an annual client party, this year held at local Anglo-Saxon burial site, Sutton Hoo. Bearing no similarity to the digging up of old relics, these events are *"a mixture of work and play. You have to be on your best behaviour, but you can still enjoy it. It's nice to have a non-work-related chat with the clients and it means when you next speak to them on the phone it's easier."*

i feel pretty...

Traditionally, the old boys' network has reigned supreme on the marketing front at Prettys, with golf and football matches galore. Now, as one female trainee put it: *"We're getting power!"* You'll find the girls playing netball matches against local businesses and, quite frankly, the men just can't compete. *"We invite them to play with us and a couple came once but they weren't much use – they just waved their arms about a bit."*

and finally...

If you want big city life then forget it, but if you fancy an interesting mix of work in a go-getting commercial firm with a bit of local colour, then dig out that netball kit or those golf clubs.

RadcliffesLeBrasseur

the facts

Location: London, Leeds
UK ranking by size: 89
Total number of trainees: 13
Seats: 4x6 months (2x12 in Leeds)
Alternative seats: None
Extras: Pro bono – Battersea Legal Advice Centre

If RadcliffesLeBrasseur was a car, it would be the front of a Bentley welded to the back of a new Beetle.

straight to video

In 2001, the old-school, wood-panelled Westminster firm Radcliffes merged with more *"happening"* Covent Garden firm Le Brasseur J. Tickle. The previous year Radcliffes had swallowed up a small specialist property firm, Jay Benning & Peltz. Now it has a toehold in the north of England in the shape of a Leeds office and a big practice in London that covers healthcare, corporate, charities, property, tax, private client and family work. Trainees can still see the joins from the merger – *"it's easy to tell which partner came from which firm"* – and the match was *"hardly natural,"* but the work is good and the training opportunities are varied. Current trainees reckon it's the firm's biggest selling point, saying *"you'd be hard pushed to get such different work under the same roof anywhere else."*

To save everyone from the agony of points failures/leaves on the line, contact between the two offices is regularly made via video-link. This has caused some confusion amongst trainees, one of whom said: *"At a firm drinks party I thought one of the partners was a real celebrity. Then I remembered I'd only seen him on the internal TV."* In general, relations are warm and the trainees all keep in touch.

be prepared

RadcliffesLeBrasseur's London trainees complete four six-month seats. Although *"the rumour is you have to do property – it's the firm's bread and butter work,"* there are no compulsories. There is *"no choice at all for the first seat,"* but the closer you get to qualification, the greater your chances of getting what you want. A fair degree of flexibility is evident and some trainees loved certain seats so much that they chose to do them twice, which just goes to show that variety isn't always the spice of life. The smaller Leeds office operates a system whereby trainees sit in just two departments – property and healthcare law. Unless you've known since birth that's what you wanted to do, you should think carefully about applying.

Following the national trend, employment remains popular: *"The team's got a friendly reputation and there's a lot of human interest there."* Healthcare is popular too. But be warned, *"you have to have a strong stomach as some of the work can be pretty grim, especially medical negligence photos."* The property department has earned a reputation for being a slog; apparently *"they've got work coming out of their ears."* The upside is you get to run your own files (one trainee boasted of 25), but the downside is the hours can be longer than the standard 8.30am – 6.30pm; hence *"if you get given property, it's a case of 'OK then' rather than 'Woo-hoo!'"*

While our sources had spent time in seats across the firm, they all had one experience in common – responsibility. Bags of it. Radcliffes isn't the sort of firm to choose if your heart races at the thought of seeing a client. It's the sort of place you go to if you think walking into a room full of new clients unaccompanied is *"fun."* Client meetings, phone calls, even client schmoozing are not beyond the courageous Radcliffes trainees. And for those that want it, the firm offers opportunities for advocacy. Our sources recounted tales of going before masters in the High Court for consent orders, time extensions and small claims, and of sitting with counsel on more crucial hearings. *"It can be daunting; I found myself up against a barrister of seven years' call in the RCJ. But it's great experience,"* remembers one first-year.

as plucky as ever

Trainees know the firm is *"distinguished and accomplished – they pay attention to detail,"* but *"they don't expect you to know everything straight from law school."* To aid the learning process, trainees sit with their supervisors. *"The responsibility is big, and you know the work you're doing is important, but you know your work will be checked so you can feel confident about doing it."* There are appraisals every three months, at which you can hold your hands up to needing more support. *"I said that I did and they took it on board. I still had the same work, but they were more responsive."* Reportedly, the partners are even willing to advise their trainees on anything from their personal lives to car maintenance. *"It's a place where partners will stop to have a chat with you. You're really able to feel at home,"* gushed one source.

We've said before, and we'll say it again, the recruits at Radcliffes are a plucky bunch. While there is no room for arrogance, those who thrive at the firm have the assured confidence that comes with knowing who you are and what you are about. Radcliffes' trainees describe themselves as *"organised, willing to have a go and confident;"* they're the type of people who *"tend to take on responsibility voluntarily"* and *"expect a lot of themselves."* We'd bet they're the ones who always end up organising theatre tickets and restaurant reservations for their friends.

on the pull

This is a sociable firm both north and south of the Watford Gap. Things are less hectic in Leeds, due to its smaller size, yet *"if anyone wants to go for a drink, be it secretaries, fee earners or office juniors, everyone goes out."* In London, things are livelier, though trainees claim they're *"not a particularly crazy bunch."* They are *"quite happy to leave work behind on a Friday night."* End-of-week wind-downs at the nearby Marquis of Grandby are well attended, as are trainee lunches. For those seeking fame, Radcliffes is handily located close to Parliament Square, *"right where they do the TV interviews with politicians."* It also offers views of the annual Commons vs. Lords tug-of-war contest (almost unbelievable isn't it?) and the ever-present possibility of bumping into the likes of Michael Portillo in your lunch hour.

Most trainees see the firm as a good bet for the long term. *"There's a sense that partnership is really possible,"* said one, *"and the best thing is the partners aren't all burnt out and divorced. They have outside interests and families."* In September 2003, five out of the six qualifiers stayed on.

and finally...

If you feel that being thrown in at the deep end only makes you a stronger swimmer, and you've always quite fancied a cut-and-shunt Bentley/Beetle, you might just have found your match.

Reed Smith

the facts

Location: London, Coventry.
UK ranking by size: 131
Total number of trainees: 12
Seats: 4x6 months
Alternative seats: None

This Pittsburgh-based firm has pursued an aggressive expansion policy over the past few years, merging with other US practices in California, Virginia and New York, and in 2001 with UK firm Warner Cranston. Two years after her union with the US firm, little Warner Cranston has given up her name.

lovelly

Founded by three young Lovells partners back in the 1970s, the legacy Warner Cranston was considered a rather progressive firm. By all accounts, not much has changed since the merger, apart from the introduction of a more aggressive US-style billing culture. But far from feeling ripped off by the firm's merger, trainees who applied to the legacy Warner Cranston have really hit the big time. Billing targets aside, the merger has *"added an extra dimension,"* with the opportunity to travel to the States to meet up with the American cousins. One junior associate has also spent nine months in the States on secondment and the firm expects opportunities like this to grow as it is intending to open up offices in France and Germany.

where streets are paved with gold

London trainees spend a year in the business and finance department and six months in litigation before choosing between real estate or employment. The business and finance department is large, and allows for specialisation in insurance, tax, corporate securities, intellectual property, company secretarial or a more general commercial seat. This year in IP, trainees assisted in the research and writing of legal handbooks, but on the billable side, worked mostly on trademark applications. Brush up on that GCSE French, because many of the firm's clients are just that. Reed Smith has been advising Eurostar on its brand relaunch (alas, no reported sightings of a beret-wearing Kylie) and phone manufacturer Sagem. Elsewhere, the business and finance group acted for Sara Lee in manufacturing joint ventures in Sri Lanka, and McDonald's on its sale of the Aroma coffee chain. Other clients include giant chemical manufacturer Akso Nobel, jewellery retailer Tiffany (Oooooh!) and a pop star (who we cannot name). You should be getting the picture by now that this is quality work for major clients. Happily, *"trainees are encouraged to build up relationships with clients and counsel,"* and many found themselves flying around the country for meetings. Although the business and finance department is at the heart of the training scheme, the rules of rotation are not set in stone. *"If you show enthusiasm for a certain area, they try to embrace that."*

The American influence is perhaps most strongly felt in litigation, where the firm is encouraging fee earners to gain higher rights of audience. One young Australian associate, Helen Mulcahy, was advocate in the High Court in the star-studded CZJ/Douglas spat with *Hello!* magazine. (The firm acted for the photographic agency, and the Marquesa de Varela, the now infamous snapper of the cake-eating photo.) Further down the food chain, trainees attend court and meet clients and counsel. And this, let's face it, is the best thing about working for a US firm – the responsibility and the quality of work. *"You can take on as much as you like,"* we heard, but trainees were relieved to find they were *"not left totally on their own."*

full english

The office near London Bridge is open plan and has acres of glass from floor to ceiling. On one side, it overlooks St Paul's and the Thames, on the other Tower Bridge and away to Canary Wharf. The office is right next door to Borough Market for lunchtime strolls and celebrity chef-spotting. Tragically, the nearby greasy spoon, Maria's, has closed down, but not before the lawyers threw a big party and presented Maria with a photo of all the regulars, many of whom had eaten there since the early days of Warner Cranston. But while *"there's nothing to rival Maria's iconic fry-up,"* we were relieved to hear that the London office is not *"totally without grease,"* and continues its traditional Friday Fry-Up ritual in another cafe.

Fry-ups aside, the London trainees are a healthy bunch, and you're as likely to find them on the softball pitch as in the pub. Once a week in the summer, players and spectators bowl up to Primrose Hill with a case of beer and some wine. Despite claims of *"not taking softball very seriously,"* when we called them the team was unbeaten. Of course, in football and cricket matches against clients, the best result can be a gracious defeat.

nest-building materials

Warner Cranston originally set up shop in Coventry to service the property and debt collection needs of Sara Lee. Today, the office is on a drive to become full service, and trainees rotate through four different seats – business and finance, real estate, litigation and employment. The older, established departments (real estate and lit) have thus far been better training grounds. In real estate, you'll be working autonomously on your own files and helping out on larger matters. Responsibility builds gradually, as *"you slowly take over a file."* The group is soon to move across the road to new premises, since the current digs are *"bursting at the seams."* Litigation offers occasional minor court appearances, some research, and a smattering of bundling or other grunt work. One partner in particular, Jonathan Hofstetter, won resounding praise for his excellent supervision and the quality of his international practice. Note to management: make JH a permanent training fixture.

It would be remiss of us not to tell you that the other two departments are fledglings hatched at the worst possible time – during a serious cold spell in the market. Employment is a one-woman show, and trainees found it a fairly quiet seat. In the business and finance practice, things have been pretty quiet on the deal side, so trainees were mostly involved in contract review and drafting terms and conditions.

sister act

The atmosphere in Coventry differs wildly from that of London. The relaxed nine-to-five vibe contrasts with the energy of the capital, where *"there are more loud characters"* and the hours are longer. In Coventry things are quieter; most people drive home, thus hampering Friday drinks. But the firm is making an effort to ensure more contact between the two offices and has an annual mystery celebration. In 2002, staff from both offices were taken on a Thames boat cruise, before returning to the office for music and dancing. This year, rumour has it that a Coventry-based event has been planned. The smart money is on Warwick Castle. The contrast between the offices is clear when the London juggernaut rolls into Coventry, but make no mistake, Coventry can offer things London never can. One trainee described a heavenly ten-minute commute to work, *"through beautiful green fields,"* before finding a parking space right outside the office.

We couldn't help but think that little 'ol Coventry doesn't quite fit the firm's glamorous international image. The Lynne Slater to London's Kat, Coventry sometimes loses the limelight to her louder sister, and to some extent, trainees were just a little envious of their sibling. Yet the Coventry office offers *"a sense of belonging to something big, but with the friendliness and support of a small firm."* In the three years since it started its training scheme, no qualifiers have been retained, however, we sense that this will change now Coventry is recruiting trainees with local ties. In London this year, three out of the four NQs stayed on.

and finally...

Like *EastEnders'* Slater sisters, the London and Coventry offices share the same name while being very different in character. If Coventry is in your neck of the woods, this smaller office comes recommended. The buzzing London office should appeal to those who want lots of attention. All up, definitely a firm to watch.

Reynolds Porter Chamberlain

the facts

Location: London, Tiverton
UK ranking by size: 53
Total number of trainees: 20
Seats: 4x6 months
Alternative seats: Occasional secondments

"When times are good people will litigate and when times are bad people will litigate." So went the good news story at Reynolds Porter Chamberlain. It may be one of the UK's most respected insurance and reinsurance firms, but that's not all it is.

california dreaming

"We have a really good reputation," said one trainee, *"but we're not one of the law factories."* Nicely put. The contentious side of the practice dominates and most trainees will spend three quarters of their training contract in such seats. This went down well with our sources, one of whom said his inspiration had come from *LA Law*. Not such a far-fetched comparison – trainees spend a lot of time in court. While in contentious departments, each of them is placed on a court duty rota, which involves both small appearances on RPC cases and agency work for other firms.

Back in the office, litigation seats expose trainees to *"both ends of the scale"* in terms of responsibility. *"On the big cases you do document management, bundles etc...all trainees have to do it. Then in professional liability I had five or six of my own files, mostly worth about £200K."* A large chunk of RPC's income comes from professional negligence, be this solicitors', accountants' or cases deriving from the slip-ups of other advisors. While no specific seat is compulsory, you can safely bet on a stint in this area. Clinical negligence is an interesting option, and one that's available in only a limited number of firms since the NHS Litigation Authority slashed its defence panel. Construction claims (again acting for insurers) are another speciality of the house, and those looking for more complex work will jump at reinsurance.

the white stripes

Underscoring the importance of the insurance industry, RPC has a second 'City Office' in Leadenhall near Lloyd's of London. The number of seats in this office has doubled to four and consequently, there is no longer a sense that trainees are 'exiled' there. *"It's hard work there and longer hours, but people are happier to go there than they were before."* The atmosphere is more pinstriped and less relaxed. *"It's how people expect the stereotype of the City law office to be. The people who have gone over there to work are more old-school Oxbridge types and it's quite intense. Here in our main office in Chichester House there's more of a blend of characters."* Holborn's greater diversity stems, it seems, from a broader client base and a wider range of activities.

If you're puzzling over the reference to Tiverton in the factbox, RPC absorbed a niche insurance firm, SJ Cornish in 2003. The move doesn't affect trainees.

it's a wonderful life

On the non-contentious side RPC has some decent clients – AstraZeneca, *The Daily Mail*, Northcliffe Newspapers (local titles) and some venture capital companies, and over in property Cancer Research UK, Three Valleys Water, Vivendi, The Arts Council of England and others. As they offer the only non-contentious seats, these two departments will host all trainees. Usually, coco is the preferred choice. *"The corporate lawyers are busy and making their targets, and they're actually recruiting, which is fairly odd at the moment!"* one source said proudly. Admittedly, if you're looking for something very corporate or very international, this is not the firm for you, but *"it doesn't market itself as that."*

A seat in the family department offers the right trainee an excellent six months. *"James Stewart* [the partner] *has major clients and has achieved some ground-breaking decisions. The work even involves international child abduction cases."* Trainees can focus on either the financial side or the children's law side, or they can sample both. And there's more. Taking up a seat in the media department will put you alongside a super defamation group (even more so since the arrival of David Hooper and team from Pinsents). But don't confuse a training contract with anything approaching celebrity – the work is interesting, but when there's paper to be pushed, you won't feel even D list!

In most departments, you'll receive work from several people but will report to the department's training partner to discuss your diary: *"It's taken very seriously...although there are variations between departments as to how seriously."* One of the strongest relationships you'll form during your training will be with your minder – a partner from the training committee who will oversee your gradual transformation into a qualified solicitor. A trainee forum meets with the HR team a few times a year to discuss issues of wider importance to the group, and there's been a recent development following the arrival of a dedicated training bod (previously at Norton Rose) to pep up departmental training and initiate a trainee-specific programme.

left around the table

"RPC isn't a firm that's going to merge with someone else and become characterless," one source pronounced. In the past it's had an old boys' club reputation, albeit a very pleasant one. There's still a partner's dining room, and it wasn't so long ago that port was still being served after meals. *"I do think that reputation is fading quite quickly now,"* one trainee told us.*"It's becoming a much more driven and ambitious firm."* Another trainee described the typical RPC lawyer as *"quite sociable. Our approach tends to be a lot less argumentative than some firms. We don't do things to deliberately aggravate the other side."* We delved deeper: *"The firm is really keen on coming across as ultraprofessional and will happily spend more time than they should on doing things better than they need to."*

Following a spot of navel-gazing, departments are meeting with each other more regularly, a newsletter, 'In Future', is used to spread information between groups and interdepartmental drinks take place in one of the boardrooms or nearby pub, The Bunghole. *"In terms of communication, it's not bad. The assistants asked for and the partners gave them the medium term business plan. The partnership is open to a degree...and anyway, the firm is small so things do get around."* Eight out of the ten qualifying trainees accepted the firm's offer of a job in September 2003.

no views is good news

Last year the main Holborn office was described as a 1960s block with little to recommend it other than swish client areas. This year we learned of new unisex superloos in reception (*"They were a talking point at first, but now we're not so sure clients want to go in them!"*) and acres of cream-coloured carpets. Surely they get dirty quickly? *"Yes, they're always having them cleaned."* In between shaking 'n' vacing, someone's also spruced up the rest of the building in RPC's blue orange and white colours. Alas, you won't get a great view from Chichester House. *"All the windows are mirrored...actually it's quite useful for doing your hair."*

The working day is very manageable. This is the beauty of being a litigation lawyer; generally you can plan your day or your week, so avoiding ambush just as you're thinking about what to have for dinner. *" If you were working till 9pm every night for a week, that would be defined as getting absolutely beasted."*

never mind the bollards

Many staff have a healthy interest in sports or socialising. Of course, often the two can be combined, as they are each summer at the Manches Cup sailing regatta in Cowes. About 35 people went down for the weekend at the firm's expense this year, and we hear that only one trainee had to be dragged back on board after an unscheduled dip in the drink. Back in London, despite Covent Garden having more variety (and style) to offer the post-work drinker, people head for Pendrells Oak. *"It's not great, but it's close, the beer's cheap and there are massive tables downstairs."* Proximity, economy and functionality...we wondered if these were guiding principles of the RPC social scene, but then we heard about the 2002 Jubilee-themed summer party. *"Five or six partners turned up as punks. One of them is a titled aristocrat and he had a pink mohican."*

and finally...

We rather liked one trainee's modest comments on Reynolds Porter Chamberlain's relative buoyancy in the current economic climate: *"There's a certainty factor here, the firm is not having a shocker...we are plodding on and doing well."* Anyone who ever dreamed of being Grace Van Owen or Michael Kuzak should apply.

Richards Butler

the facts

Location: London
UK ranking by size: 46
Total number of trainees: 44
Seats: 4x6 months
Alternative Seats: Overseas seats, secondments

On the London legal scene for over 80 years, Richards Butler is a City firm with an indisputable international presence. Its varied interests have much to offer trainees hankering after cosmopolitan warmth.

a lean and nimble vessel

Richards Butler's strategy is to target mid-tier businesses, both at home and abroad, and to keep itself at the top of the game in shipping-related and media-related law. In the last year the dispute resolution practice boosted the firm's overall financial health with a 20% rise in profits, whilst the corporate and finance practices managed to more than hold their own in unhelpful market conditions. We like to envisage the firm as one of the more nimble vessels in a City sea dominated by cumbersome frigates.

Our colleagues on *Chambers UK* consistently award the firm a top ranking for commodities work, an area in which international arbitrations govern disputes over trade finance, credit risks, and the confiscation and misappropriation of goods in transit. If the futures markets and derivatives trading appeal, then step on up; this is another area in which the firm shines, acting for two European exchanges and several commodities brokers. In more general litigation matters the firm is reaping the benefits of independence from the investment banking sector, thus enabling it to act on behalf of those in dispute with financial institutions.

water, water everywhere...

Contrary to popular belief, the firm is not awash with ancient mariners, nor are you likely to see film stars in the lobby every day. So here are a few facts...Yes, the media division is well respected and offers much sought-after secondments to the BBC, MTV and Rank. No, the media division is not the firm's biggest source of revenue (not by some way, as it happens), nor is the Beeb the firm's biggest client. (Try Boeing) Yes, there are a limited number of seats in media. Two in fact, one each in contentious and non-contentious groups and a third with a potential media flavour in the commercial dispute group, which occasionally deals with media litigation issues.

No, shipping is not the firm's greatest source of income either, though the firm is even better known for this than for media work. Yes, it offers trainees seats in the maritime nerve centres of Athens and Piraeus for six months. No, the master mariners to be found at the firm aren't all pinstriped Captain Birdseyes with white beards and pipes, but they are indeed great sources of shipping-specific knowledge, and the firm is very proud of them.

Maritime law is not a subject typically covered either at uni or on the LPC, so trainees were thankful for the firm's intensive induction course covering the essentials of shipping. One said: *"I had an especially intensive blitz in shipping in the first week and benefited from the monthly know-how and lunchtime sessions too."* The result? *"I felt pretty comfortable at the end of it and there was a nice international feel to the seat."* It's not all sweetness and light though: *"The brown carpet in the shipping department is vile!"*

meze

There are no specific compulsory seats, though everyone is expected to do at least one in property, shipping or litigation. Perhaps RB's most attractive feature is its wealth of niches, and by niche we mean anything other than general corporate, commercial litigation and commercial property. These mainstream departments are certainly there for all, but there's also a whole heap of beyond-the-norm work for eager young recruits – employment, insolvency and planning to name three. Having switched to a four-seat system, there's now the option to split a seat into two. One source recalled: *"I was very lucky with my split seats, both of them being enormously popular. The partners in both were really helpful, and in my media seat I was the only trainee so it felt like a fully-fledged role. I was in frequent contact with producers and film financiers and was copied in on most correspondence, which pleasantly surprised me. They even had me working as a helpline for producers."*

There are ample opportunities to work abroad. If the prospect of a Greek shipping seat doesn't get you smashing plates and dancing down to the passport office, there are also commercial slots in Paris for French speakers, Sao Paulo for Portuguese speakers and Abu Dhabi and Hong Kong for everyone else. This firm didn't earn a Queen's Award for Enterprise in International Trade in 2002 for nothing.

it's good to talk

As is the case with most firms, the corporate department usually demands the longest hours. In the words of one trainee: *"There have been peaks and troughs, which makes it difficult to predict when you are likely to be in late,"* so to compensate, *"the supervisors won't expect you to stay late during a quiet patch."* Another source did qualify thoughts about the 'glamorous' media seat by adding: *"It's hard work. I've been kept very busy, typically finishing at about 8pm. There've been no weekends at work yet, but there has been one all-nighter and a couple of midnight finishes."*

RB offers a proper system of supervision, feedback and appraisal. One trainee recalled a common problem: *"Something that presented itself early on for me was how best to prioritise two pieces of work from different partners, when it wasn't always clear which was the more pressing. I mentioned this and was talked through the protocols."* Our sources welcomed the firm's open invitation to suggest ways in which supervisors could improve, and were pleased that action is more often than not taken on suggestions. *"Some of us felt that we needed more information about how seats are assigned and what the options are upon qualification. The result was that RB wasted no time in making the situation more transparent for us."*

poets' corner

RB's current pride and joy is a new super hi-tech 'knowledge centre', which was conceived as a way of bringing information services together, both legal and IT. The 'Dome' was converted from a suite of meeting and function rooms into a state-of-the-art library with wings leading to IT training facilities and breakout rooms. Just like the ill-fated Dome in Greenwich, there was a cracking party thrown to celebrate the opening.

RB's office boasts a pretty roof garden that's *"very popular for summer barbecues"* and a staff restaurant called Writs (who says lawyers don't have a sense of humour?) For those who enjoy drinks with colleagues, the monthly 5:31 Club is still going strong, so at least in theory tools are downed and glasses raised 60 seconds after knocking off time. The social scene is supplemented by departmental drinks – one trainee confided: *"In shipping, I could set my clock by the clinking of the drinks tray at 5pm every other Wednesday."* Rum rations all round, we trust.

In previous guides we've mentioned the popularity of three local pubs, commonly referred to as the Purple and the Orange Poets (the Green having been consumed by an equally popular Slug & Lettuce a couple of years ago). We can report that the picture remains accurate today, although the nearby Old Tea Warehouse bar and Brick Lane compete for trainee salaries.

who works in a place like this?

"This is not the place for the super-competitive, aggressive trainee," we heard; instead, you are likely to find charming and quietly determined individuals of different ages and backgrounds, from different parts of the country, not to say the world. Remember the bright, sporty, easy-going boy at school whom the students voted to be Head of School, but the headmaster overlooked in favour of the rich lad whose father was managing director of ICI? He's here. And this year, like most years, he's staying. In September 2003, 11 of the 13 qualifiers took jobs with the firm.

and finally...

If you don't fancy stepping on board one of the legal warships for two years of scrubbing the corporate decks, and you're wary of the creaky unnamed vessels that chug back and forth across the nearest inland waterway, you might be ripe for Richards Butler. It won't be plain sailing every day and you must be prepared to climb the rigging in all weathers, but we suspect the view is great from the top.

Russell-Cooke

the facts

Location: London
UK ranking by size: 132
Total number of trainees: 10
Seats: 4x6months
Alternative seats: None

Putney-based Russell-Cooke combines the best bits of the high street with commercial practice...and a walk on the heath or a stroll by the river after work.

spoilt for choice

The firm offers a plethora of training seats including PI, crime, family, commercial and contentious property, professional regulatory matters, coco and employment. If all that isn't enough to whet your appetite, the client base is split evenly between private individuals and commercial organisations. Household names rub shoulders with national charities, and start-up ventures with public bodies. The firm's respected crime department has an excellent reputation and handled Colin Stagg's defence. Alongside murders, firearm offences, drug importation and conspiracy trials, the team is also developing a niche with football hooligans. The charity practice, which serves Barnardos and UNICEF, was recently bolstered by a merger with Sinclair Taylor & Martin. While these are small departments, they are certainly a big draw for trainees.

With such variety and lawyers spread over five sites in Putney, Holborn and Kingston, you could be forgiven for wondering if the firm isn't a little disparate. One source assured us: *"It all gels."* It is the variety that attracts most trainees, although one did tell us: *"I was convinced I wanted to do crime when I started, and didn't expect to enjoy other things – now I'm unsure what I want to qualify into."* You can't win can you?

life is like a box of chocolates

Within the four six-month seats *"it is pretty much accepted that you will do conveyancing or commercial property."* While *"ultimately it is determined by where the firm needs people,"* we didn't hear too many grumbles about seat allocation. Trainees' advice: *"You have to plug away – people who push for things generally get them."* The group we spoke to couldn't agree on which seats were especially popular, or conversely, which was the strawberry cream in the selection. However, we heard rumour that the firm is eyeing up the hard nuts and chewy toffees – its gaze is fixed on corporate and commercial matters so don't go thinking this is just a box of soft centres.

Depending on the department, trainees share their office with a partner or assistant, with fellow trainees, or sometimes no one at all. Supervisors are forthcoming with feedback so, by the time you got to your three-monthly appraisal (which usually takes the form of a pub lunch), *"you should already know how you are getting on."* The hours are nothing short of blissful: one source, who said he worked a 9am–6pm day, got the impression he stayed later than he should. Though business attire is the norm, *"it is quite relaxed and unenforced – you just strike a happy medium."*

A new training co-ordinator is keeping everyone on their toes with a lunchtime programme and evening seminars once a week. Our sources also enthused about the amount of responsibility they got. In addition to being given their own files from day one, *"trainees aren't locked away – they aren't afraid of letting you out."* Your most abiding memory of the two years will not be of pressing the green button on the photocopier.

pick 'n' mix

Historically the realm of duels and highwaymen, and better known as the start for the annual boat race between Oxford and Cambridge, Putney is the administrative centre of the firm and the venue for most trainee seats. The Putney lawyers are spread over three sites, but the firm recently commandeered an extra floor in the largest and *"plushest,"* so while it may be a *"rabbit warren,"* it is certainly not a chicken coop.

The Holborn branch is situated on tree-lined Bedford Row and mainly serves corporate clients, but also offers seats in commercial property and crime. Recently, its old-fashioned desks were replaced with modern furnishings. Out in Kingston, modern offices are situated by the river and house much of the firm's family practice as well as crime and residential conveyancing teams.

Trainees spend at least a year in Putney, going elsewhere according to which seats they undertake, so don't expect to wangle two years in Holborn…not that you'd want to once you've taken a few deep breaths of fresh air in Putney. We asked if any of the offices suffered from poor relation syndrome. We received a resounding 'no' in response. Trainees described a certain *"independence"* of the outlying offices in Kingston and Holborn, but were clear that *"though you kind of forget about them sometimes, when you walk into each office, you get the same feel for the firm."*

fun size

SW15 is the worst postcode for prompt mail delivery, served by the least punctual train service in London, plagued by traffic jams and inhabited by rowing types. Things weren't looking good. Then a Putneyite chirped up and painted an entirely different picture of a lively but pleasant neighbourhood sandwiched between the Thames and the open countryside. If you get an interview with Russell-Cooke, why not make a day of it and check things out for yourself.

Our sources were also quick to endorse a healthy social life centring on the pubs and bars of the High St. The Fox is the closest and most regular haunt, while The Coat & Badge is a safe bet for long summer evenings with *"a group of the willing."* Firm-wide summer and Christmas parties provide everyone with the opportunity to *"let their hair down,"* and an annual training weekend (last year Cambridge, this year Paris) combines teambuilding and brainstorming with plenty of partying. Bedford Row is widely regarded to be the most sociable of the offices, with people going out more than once a week and *"twice on Fridays."* A fairly athletic bunch, the firm is riddled with sailing enthusiasts and a netball team looks set for a revival.

tuck in

The Russell-Cooke brand of trainee is *"determined not to fit that hard City lawyer stereotype,"* so *"if your career is your life, you should go elsewhere."* We also heard that *"there is no one who is stand-offish"* and *"you have to be outgoing."* This is a pretty standard response, but in this instance we would agree. This isn't a firm where your dream training contract is going to be handed to you on a plate: *"If you want to just do your job and tick off your time sheet, it probably isn't for you."* Two of the three September 2003 qualifiers stayed with the firm.

The firm fits a low-key, straightforward bill, but looks to be changing. While trainees griped about prehistoric technology, Russell-Cooke is not *"bogged down by its history,"* and while it currently seems to be perched on the fence between its commercial face and its niche strengths, our sources perceived a more commercial future for the firm. This year, trainees did not view any future refocusing as a bad thing; in fact, one went so far as to say: *"The growth of the firm makes it even more attractive now than when I applied."* However, generally they hoped that growth would not be *"at the expense of public service work and the niche departments."*

and finally...

If you want London life but are inclined to steer clear of the City, hop on the No.337. Chances are, you won't look back.

Shadbolt & Co

the facts

Location: London, Reigate
UK ranking by size: 167
Total number of trainees: 8
Seats: 4x6 months
Alternative seats: Paris, secondments

Shadbolt & Co's reputation as a Reigate-based construction practice, belies a broadening commercial offering that extends to London, Paris, Athens and Tanzania.

bricks and mortar

There is no escaping this firm's stellar reputation for construction work –" *it sells the firm more than anything else*" and is very much "*the lifeblood of the firm.*" Here, household names including the BBC, Shelter, Amey/Mouchel, GallifordTry, Taylor Woodrow and WS Atkins are represented in both contentious and non-contentious matters. However, though the construction department forms a pretty solid foundation, "*the firm is trying to build up the other departments – they were originally servicing construction clients, but now they are getting their own clients and branching out on their own.*" Non-contentious teams handle PFI, corporate and commercial, IT, IP and e-commerce, employment and aviation matters.

The nature of the construction and engineering industries mean that much of the work in this field is international and Shadbolts' Paris office is pretty hot on international arbitration. The London office deals mainly with construction, but also handles some corporate work; Reigate is home to everything else. Though the firm has associated offices elsewhere, trainees do not get long stints on Greek beaches or African safaris. Instead secondments to clients are the most likely reason for time away from the UK offices. "*Working in-house is encouraged; they find that when trainees are given more responsibility they use their initiative more and confidence grows.*"

division of labour

Training follows the standard four six-month seat format, and "*the firm really goes out of its way to accommodate trainees' choices.*" Our sources told us there was no formal application process, and "*you negotiate through chatting to people... and a bit of lobbying.*" No seats are obviously compulsory, though "*contentious construction is done by everyone.*" Basically, "*you go to the firm knowing that it is their stronghold and you expect to get it.*" The people who didn't choose Shadbolts for its construction work "*tend to be linguists who like the Paris opportunities.*" By virtue of its small size, the French office has a slightly different atmosphere, but "*you still feel closely connected to the firm.*" Reigate is the most relaxed of the offices, whereas, with only one or two trainees in London at any one time, "*it is a bit isolated and can be hard going.*"

Apparently, training at the firm is "*very much hands-on and you work stuff out as you go along. There are talks in every department, but the reality is that you learn by doing.*" Shadbolts is not a place to come to if you want to be cosseted – you may well find yourself advocating at hearings, meeting clients, running your own files...and we even heard of clients contacting trainees directly for repeat work. The firm "*gives you as much responsibility as you can cope with,*" which is "*brilliant!*" Inevitably, "*there is a certain amount of bundling to be done, but you accept that as part of the job.*" And why wouldn't you, if it meant having a break from all that grown-up client handling and document drafting malarkey? Our sources appreciated the fact that "*there is no patronising attitude*" at the firm: three-monthly appraisals provide a high level of feedback, and "*you always know how you are getting on.*" Throw some very decent working hours into the equation (a late night Shadbolts-style is 9pm) and the firm seems to be offering its young brickies an apprenticeship made in heaven.

men at work

You could be forgiven for thinking all Shadbolt's recruits are called Bob, but in fact "*there is a 50-50 split between those who went there for construction and those who went there with an open mind."* Contrary to the suburban myth that the trainees all wear hard hats and fluorescent jackets and that *"steel toecaps are standard issue,"* the dress code dictates smart attire.

The firm's senior figures are largely *"really strong personalities who have walked out of big City firms of various shades."* The strong personalities do filter down to trainee level and Shadbolts does not nurture *"single-minded cardboard cut-out lawyer figures."* All our sources denied any laddish, builder-culture, but freely admitted that *"you won't fit in if you aren't the type of person who could get on with a brickie."* In truth, while all our sources were happy to play along with our childish (yet screamingly funny) builder stereotypes, the real common denominators are an interest in construction and international work...and a robust, self-deprecating sense of humour. All three September 2003 qualifiers stayed on with the firm.

a breath of fresh air

The Reigate base is a 1930s listed building, boasting *"photocopiers, water coolers and kitchens with kettles."* It's a far cry from the towering edifices of big City firms with their in-house restaurants, dentists and gyms, but none of our sources gave a stuff about such trappings. Instead their office is within easy reach of the town centre and a stone's throw from a park boasting *"wide open spaces, a lake, squirrels and lots of oxygen."* Many staff, including trainees, commute from London. Reigate itself (*"very twee, very Surrey"*) offers *"just about enough to keep young people interested"* – a surplus of Italian restaurants, quick access to the M25 and a reasonable social life. On Fridays trainees head over the road to The Venture Inn and occasionally go out for lunch together. Sport seems to be quite a big thing, though all our sources agreed:*"The football team is diabolical and the cricket scores are appalling."* For those with poor hand-eye co-ordination, the summer barbecue and Christmas parties have greater appeal and Christmas also throws up the annual trainee revue. Our sources were suspiciously vague on the details, but it would seem that their *"pastiche of partners' foibles"* has prompted acts of retribution (thankfully also of the thespian variety). Sounds ugly.

Such high jinks could probably be attributed to the firm's stock of *"eccentric"* characters. No one was willing to proffer details, but we got the feeling that while Reigate is *"not like the bright lights of London,"* this lot like to let their hair down at times. However, while *"sometimes the partners are the life and soul of the party, they do want you to work hard too – sometimes it is difficult to know where you stand."* We think this mix of brain-aching responsibility and side-splitting humour is quite appealing, if a touch confusing for new recruits.

and finally...

For top-flight construction work plus serious international arbitration in sufficiently broad commercial setting – and a healthy dose of dry wit – catch the 08:12 from London Waterloo.

Shoosmiths

the facts

Location: Northampton, Nottingham, Reading, Solent, Milton Keynes, Basingstoke, Birmingham
UK ranking by size: 41
Total number of trainees: 23
Seats: 4x6 months
Alternative seats: Secondments

A national firm with offices stretching from the south coast right up to the Midlands, Shoosmiths has taken the unusual step of shunning the capital. Perhaps it feels that the testosterone and traffic fumes of the City would mess with its mojo...

girls on top

Shoosmiths has two main divisions – commercial services and personal injury. Of the two, trainees usually spend most of their time in the latter, the PI business being largely a volume operation where lower value matters are handled by non-solicitors. The nerve centre of the firm is in Northampton, where the widest selection of seats is available. By contrast the new Birmingham office had just one trainee in the summer of 2003. Trainees can either spend all four seats in the one office or move to another for work that isn't handled in their home location.

When preparing for the mammoth exercise of interviewing trainees the length and breadth of Shooland, we noticed that the firm had recruited 20 girls and just three boys. The new starters in September 2003 had pushed the number of boys up to six, but still fewer than at most firms. The girls on top phenomenon is one that we see in a number of firms, but only once this year to quite the same degree (Eversheds' Cardiff office). Trainees told us that it's because good male applicants all want to go to London; we're not so sure this is quite the whole story. It's a chicken and egg conundrum, of course, but we sensed that the vibe Shoosmiths has put out in the past may have been too soft boiled for some applicants. Last season's grad recruitment brochure looked more like pages from *Elle* or *Vogue*. Its pictures of clear-skinned models in white dresses left us looking for the free perfume sample. Perhaps this year's CD ROM will be more hard hitting.

Speaking to trainees, we were left with the impression that they fall very much into two camps. Some of them implied they'd chosen the firm for shorter hours and feel-good factor alone; their ambitions seemed – how can we put this delicately – low-flying. Others clearly had a good deal more to say for themselves, and we are delighted to report that they see Shoosmiths as a firm that is *"ambitious and allows initiative."* While we are genuinely pleased for the former group, we do sometimes wonder if there isn't more to being a trainee than wanting to have a nice place to go from Monday to Friday. So hurrah for the trainees with tales of daring do and reports of fired-up partners. A number of them pointed to the likes of Oliver Brookshaw the superstar corporate partner in Nottingham. *"The firm is prepared to invest in people who are ambitious; they have made the firm attractive to people who have spent time in the City. Oliver came from Linklaters and he doesn't even get going until midnight!"*

the gathering of the clan

The trainee population is fragmented between six offices, but every two months they all get together for the national training day, usually held in Northampton, sometimes Nottingham or elsewhere. There are talks from partners and assistants in the morning and after lunch, more practical, interactive skills sessions. Once a year, trainees also gather for a night out in London, although nobody could remember exactly where they ate or stayed last time round. And each year lawyers and trainees in the commercial services division all gather for a national training weekend in a hotel in Northamptonshire. Regional variations aside, we got the impression that the same experiences are there for the taking in all parts of the firm. Occasionally, client secondments crop up with the likes of Abbey National, DaimlerChrysler and Hogg Robinson, and the firm's client list also includes Barclays Bank, BP and Nike.

northampton, milton keynes, brum

This year, we noticed there were fewer trainees working in the firm's Northampton HQ at The Lakes. One of our sources quickly explained that this was because Northampton-based trainees were now highly likely to take seats in the Milton Keynes office *"just 20 minutes away"* and the new Birmingham office, which currently offers one property seat but is likely to expand. *"Milton Keynes and Northampton seats are interchangeable,"* they told us,*"a lot of fee earners are some days here and some days there."* Between them, the three offices offer plenty of choice – claimant PI and clin neg, banking litigation and debt recovery, construction, commercial litigation, commercial property and landlord and tenant litigation, IP and regulatory law, planning and corporate. With such a full menu and no compulsories, we weren't surprised when one trainee told us: *"I wanted a firm that would encourage me to find my own feet."*

What 'finding your own feet' actually means depends on who you talk to. For some it means taking tiny steps, for others it means striding forwards to qualification and beyond. For example, some trainees indicated that standing up and making an application in front of a county court district judge was a terrifying ordeal to be avoided at all costs; others volunteered as often as they could. One Northampton trainee put many others to shame with their enthusiasm for sniffing out challenging work – had we spotted a partner of the future? Maybe, but before anyone gets too carried away, let's just make one thing clear: even the most go-ahead trainees have to knuckle down to the chore of trial bundling. *"I had quite a few of those to do, but at least there were apologies beforehand,"* said one source. Show enthusiasm and more rewarding tasks are offered – drafting, telephone negotiations and sitting with counsel in court.

Every Friday evening, the firm hosts a drinks party at the Lakes. To an extent it makes up for the fact that the office is in a business park just off the M1 and a few miles from Northampton and *"we don't have many bar options open to us."* Where The Lakes scores well is in its proximity to country pubs for *"relaxed lunches"* and a tennis court and Astroturf footie pitch next to the office car park. *"We have a few sports teams; our women's five-a-side football team beat Clifford Chance in the Legal Fives tournament. And an ex-partner has a cricket pitch in the grounds of his house – clients love it!"* We bet they do.

nottingham

Located centrally in a modern building next to the canal in Nottingham, we sensed more energy in this office than in past years. Trainees undertake seats in commercial litigation, coco, employment and commercial property, with their only choice being the order in which they do them. The tectonic plates have been shifting at Shoosmiths and the Nottingham office is now the home of the national corporate finance team as well as a large commercial property team. If you are the type who thrives on adrenalin, we suggest this might be your office. Yet some trainees found corporate was too much like hard work: one pronounced it to be *"a lot of late nights for not a lot of reason, as far as I can tell."* The commercial property seat will bring you into contact with important clients such as Boots and WH Smith. Trainee tasks in property may not always be that exciting (land registry searches and the like), but if you allow yourself, you can get caught up in the buzz of bigger projects.

reading and southampton

In Reading, seats are available in coco, property, litigation, construction and employment, and it's a short hop to Shoosmiths' special injuries unit in Basingstoke. Just five or six minutes' walk from the Oracle shopping and leisure complex, the Reading office has a distinctive IT flavour, reflecting the business focus of the Thames Valley hinterland. The trainee population has grown to six, in part because of the loss last year of the Banbury office.

Located in another business park, the Southampton office is close to Fareham on the side of the M27. Seats can be taken in litigation, property, coco and landlord and tenant. Tesco and TGI Friday are nearby, and if you get your binoculars out you might even spot the trainees at Blake Lapthorn Linnell over on the other side of the motorway. Turn your binoculars around 180 degrees and you can make your supervisor seem much further away than they really are.

and finally...

If you just don't click with the London firms you visit, or if you would prefer to stay close to your home territory, Shoosmiths is to be considered. In September 2003, only four out of ten qualifying trainees stayed with the firm, but you should appreciate that this is not typical.

Sidley Austin Brown & Wood

the facts

Location: London
UK ranking by size: 106
Total number of trainees: 15
Seats: 4x6 months
Alternative seats: None

In 2001, Chicago's Sidley Austin merged with New York-based Brown & Wood. It's now an international firm with six US, five Asian and two European offices, of which the London office is the primary one.

a date with the desktidy

Finance and corporate deals power the London office, and your training will have a strong finance flavour. All trainees undertake a seat in the international finance group, where capital markets work is a core part of the business. *"The firm likes you to do at least six months and often nine in IFG."* Again this year, our sources told us that your first challenge is getting to grips with its alien terminology, but it has a strong team ethos: *"It's where I got the most interaction with people and I thrive on that,"* said one source. Reporting on the securitisation seat, one trainee told us: *"Initially I worked on transaction management stuff – document management a lot of the time, liaising with parties, getting documents together, proofing, organising closings and signings and so on. And then preparing bibles of transaction documents and getting everything signed properly. Very varied. Very commercial. Very client oriented,"* such that *"if a client wants a document produced by the following day, you will be required to stay."* But while the work schedule and the hours can be demanding, trainees appreciated that their presence in the office wasn't taken for granted. *"The associates would ask 'Are you free tonight?' rather than just expecting you to be free."*

Just a week before we rang trainees in July 2003, the firm had lost a team of four partners and 21 structured finance associates and support staff to the new London office of Gide Loyrette Nouel. The departures still left Sidleys with 17 finance partners, so although it will have been a blow, the group wasn't exactly wiped out. *"There's been a big reshuffle internally,"* one discreet source acknowledged.

Beyond IFG, three seats are taken in the remaining departments – corporate and commercial, corporate securities, property and tax. The coco group is smaller and very popular with trainees, although it relies heavily on the IFG lawyers for its work and clients. One trainee had spent time looking at shareholder and acquisition agreements, drafting board minutes, filing documents with Companies House and general research. Trainees with *"an appetite for tax work"* reported being able to feast on mouth-watering and *"intellectually demanding"* research in that department. With so much of the office's work being multi-jurisdictional, nothing is straightforward and you'll need to put your clever head on in the mornings.

acacia avenue

The property group receives funding instructions from US and UK investment and retail banks including Merrill Lynch and Bank of New York. Much of the team's time is spent supporting the IFG and corporate group and trainees get involved largely with document amendment and proofreading, and *"talking directly to clients twice or three times a day."* The firm gets trainees to do residential conveyancing as a favour to corporate clients; they usually find these smaller matters a refreshing change.

Clever readers will have noticed that we've not referred to a litgation seat. There isn't one. To satisfy the Law Society's demands for contentious training, trainees can hope that a piece of litigation hits one of the lawyer's desks at just the right time. If not, the firm simply sends trainees off on a litigation course run over four weekends at Nottingham Law School's London branch. If you're unsure as to whether transactional or contentious work will turn out to be your cup of tea, you should think carefully before applying to Sidleys.

just blew in from the windy city

For some trainees, 'US firms' are the Holy Grail of legal practice. Said one: *"I like the ethos of American firms. They look after their people. I know they work you hard, but they give a lot back as well."* And so, we come to the crux of the debate on whether or not to train at an American firm: at its barest, the argument goes as follows – US firms inflict long hours on their staff and compensate them with stratospheric pay packets. Our interviewees insisted that there were no aggressive Wall Street types at Sidley in London. As for the hours, it's no cakewalk, but you shouldn't expect that in any firm handling high-calibre international work. An average day runs from 9am to 7pm – on a par with other City firms – but when a transaction kicks off, you'll not be home for the late news. On many US-led or US-fed deals, things kick off when the Americans arrive in the office, and the injustice of this was not lost on one trainee, who whined: *"I mean, why can't they just arrive at work five hours earlier instead of expecting us to stay back for them?"* V funny!

The reality is that 'US firms' in London are a breed on their own. For most trainees, the firm doesn't really feel like an American outfit. Although *"there are American accents floating around,"* few of our sources could point to any particularly American cultural influences. And while the smart-casual dress code will delight the chino-men among them, many trainees choose to wear a suit every day. Because? *"Just because I like it."* In a sort of legal version of *Wife Swap*, the London office has exchanges with its American cousins, whereby qualified lawyers in IFG can spend six months in Chicago, and Windy City associates who are so inclined can spend six months in our fine capital. While Chicago has Frank Lloyd Wright, Buckingham Fountain (the world's largest) and the Dan Ryan Expressway, London offers Christopher Wren, Buckingham Palace and the M25. We're not sure who gets the better deal.

Trainees rhapsodised about the firm's informal atmosphere where pretty soon everyone knows your name. Having spoken to a number of trainees, we can honestly say we can't spot a particular Sidley type. Some were straight out of university, others had switched careers; some had graduated with a First, others had a 2:2. Said one: *"They cared about my previous experience and about me, not just my results."* The most we can do to define the type is to say that they are *"positive, affable and willing to help."* In September 2003, three of the four qualifiers took jobs with the firm.

why don't we paint the town?

The firm's main Threadneedle offices are decked out in the sort of traditional dark wood that Americans imagine grows on trees in the UK. Said one budding Laurence Llewelyn-Bowen: *"It's all about subdued, muted colours for that understated atmosphere."* You won't find plasma screens or stainless steel in this office: *"The televisions are hidden behind wooden doors."* We're loving that look! A second office on Princes Street (a hangover from the pre-merger days) is just three minutes away. By early 2004, the two tribes should be united in the one office.

Currently, there's no canteen on-site, but both the offices are just by Royal Exchange, which has plenty of cafes offering standard sandwich fare. The social life isn't riotous, but it sure is pleasant enough. Most Friday nights, the Sidley posse can be found in the Jamaica Wine House or at Jamies on Gresham Street. And in fine weather staff and partners might slip upstairs to the roof terrace for a couple of drinks and to watch the sun setting over the City. A recent Thames boat cruise went off without drama, and we are pleased to report that unlike their counterparts at [CENSORED], no keys or recently consumed dinners were lost over the side of the boat.

and finally...

This isn't a broad training contract, but for the right applicant it should more than satisfy. Expect a handsomely paid and difficult job that will give you a head start in international finance law and *"a firm with real people who might do mad hours!"*

Simmons & Simmons

the facts

Location: London
UK ranking by size: 20
Total number of trainees: 111
Seats: 4x6 months
Alternative seats: Overseas seats, secondments
Extras: Pro bono – Battersea Legal Advice Centre, RCJ CAB, language training

Attracting plenty of interest from students, Simmons & Simmons is a corporate and finance-led firm with some excellent niche practices.

taste test

Trainees select their seats from three categories. Two seats must come from the group containing corporate and financial markets work, one must be contentious in nature, and the remaining seat will come from a list comprising departments such as tax, property, environment and private client. There's a preference for taking your favoured seat at either the second or third rotation, before the point at which you will want to apply for an NQ position. This arrangement has been in place for over two years and we sensed no dissatisfaction amongst trainees.

Seats in the stellar employment and IP practices are undoubtedly attractive to trainees, however, each one falls into the contentious seat category, so you can't do both. Furthermore, it is important to remember that neither department is the linchpin of the firm, and essentially, Simmons' training is a corporate and finance-oriented experience. In keeping with the firm's desire to bolster these elements, increasingly new trainees are perceived to be corporate-minded in their tastes. While some of our sources did not sound especially enamoured of corporate work, most acknowledged that the firm had moved on since they originally applied; the business strategy has shifted, and future hires are less likely to be as intent on a career in niche areas.

pie and chips

The firm has long been known for its association with Railtrack and acts for a wide range of blue-chip clients, including FTSE 100 companies and financial institutions. A tough economic climate may not have enabled it to show its true colours but big names like Vivendi, MoD and Interbrew keep the firm's proverbial finger in some pretty large pies. For example, it advised KPMG on the acquisition of Andersen Worldwide's business consulting units, and Brake Bros on its strategic review and subsequent sale of shares to CDRP Acquisition.

The firm is acknowledged for its extensive international network. From Europe to Asia, Simmons' overseas offices enhance the firm's ability to handle cross-border transactions as well as generating work locally. Trainees are able to apply for six-month placements in most overseas offices, although inevitably some are more sought after than others; Hong Kong and Tokyo are the most popular. Overseas seats usually go to third or fourth-seaters and for European offices, you need to be able to speak the relevant language. Secondments to clients also occur with regularity and are valued by trainees with no previous commercial experience. Last year UBS Warburg and the Commonwealth Development Corporation and others received visits from trainees.

all for free

Pro bono work raised a glimmer of enthusiasm from even the most lacklustre of those we interviewed. The opportunity to work in advice centres for members of the public who would otherwise not be able to afford legal services was widely perceived as an opportunity to touch up client skills and take on more responsibility. But ultimately, this is a City training, with all the associated perks and pitfalls. One source noted, rather dramatically, that in the capital markets department, *"clients are abroad and the hours get complicated. If you are dealing with people on the East Coast* [that's New York not Newcastle] *and in the Far East, you might die."* Surely not. Joking aside, the work ethic at Simmons is no different to most of the other City firms – certain departments inevitably keep you later, but when there is work to be done, everyone chips in. Referring to a trainee ruse that has taken on the status of urban myth, one source advised us that, at Simmons, *"you would never leave your jacket on the back of your chair so people think you are there when you are not."* For late nighters, there is a free dinner at 8pm, and free taxis after 9pm.

one-liners

It's not all free meals and free rides though, and particularly since the firm has shed much of its paralegal contingent, trainees do their fair share of grunt work. Described by one as *"the trainee's lot,"* there are no hard feelings about the odd day of page-turning, which is seen to be at a level in keeping with peers at other large City firms. *"The bottom line of cost-cutting,"* grunt work is the trade off for being in on the big deals. Inevitably levels of responsibility vary between departments, and according to supervisors. While one person may rewrite everything down to the last one-line e-mail, others will see you running your own small files with the odd glance and nod of approval. Although one trainee warned that someone hoping for masses of responsibility might fare better in a smaller firm, another suggested: *"If you show willing and have the capability, you will be given more work to do."*

The programme of formal training sessions won applause from our interviewees. No one could fault departmental training, which involves weekly sessions followed by a presentation to colleagues. Appraisals and feedback are also *"pitched pretty well."* A three-monthly appraisal system is rigorously enforced and informal feedback is forthcoming in the majority of cases, though as in any firm there's always room for a personality clash.

lambs to the slaughter

Generally trainees apply to the firm for City salaries, overseas opportunities and big deals. Commonly, our sources spoke of their desire to become a part of the City legal scene while sidestepping what they viewed as the corporate cutting edge of the magic circle. Indeed, when asked to describe themselves as a group, they were clearer on what they weren't like than what they were like. Our sources were reluctant to be pigeonholed, and were tripping over qualifiers (*"might be...sort of...quite..."*) to avoid being branded with the heavy-hitting, blood-spattered corporate iron. Their view was that boisterous, bragging rugger-bugger types or anyone *"too individualistic or too keen on advancing themselves"* need not apply.

As students, many of our sources had appreciated the firm's 'CV only' application policy. This has since been replaced by a short application form, the format of which seems to support the idea that the firm is looking for *"extremely academic people."* A *"rigorous"* assessment day that includes a tough scenario-based document exercise also confirms that this is not a firm for the academically faint-hearted. We certainly would not herd them into that pen. Our gut feeling: these are content, undemanding, decent people from decent universities, and many of them chose Simmons for what it is not, rather than what it is.

cut up cows

Current trainees perceive that *"increased recruitment into the corporate department will fairly quickly change the face and culture of the firm,"* but for now, this remains a collegiate, cerebral place to be. According to one trainee, *"people are more interested in being good lawyers with good clients than subscribing to the 'eat what you kill' mentality."* Sitting on the fence at Simmons, *"everything is based on traditional ideologies – it is forward thinking, but within boundaries – there are no gimmicky initiatives."* In short, Simmons offers *"a nice ride."*

What it lacks in gimmicky initiatives it more than makes up for with its art collection. While one trainee claimed: *"There is nothing zany or way-out going on here,"* with a collection of Damien Hirsts in the restaurant, we beg to differ. However, our sources were quick to assure us that *"none of it is incredibly radical –*

it is all the more neutral stuff." Furthermore, before you go and swot up your Hanson and Hiroshi, your Emin and Ofili, none of our sources were self-proclaiming art buffs. Something had changed since we had interviewed trainees 18 months earlier because now we heard: *"No one madly sings its praises"* and *"It brightens up a room and is good for clients."*

Simmons' CityPoint office never fails to inspire. A glass structure in the heart of the City, trainees describe it as *"very shiny and steely, and all mod cons inside."* It boasts a popular restaurant that, despite commanding greater praise for its atmosphere than its food, has a loyal following amongst its trainees. Smoking rooms on every floor and excellent showers suggest that the building caters for everyone.

hot dogs

A social committee organises events, and the majority of social activities take place on a departmental level. The firm-wide Christmas party is a very big deal with *"no expense spared"* – last year's event at the Royal Artillery grounds included a funfair. Departmental events include trips to the Walthamstow Dog Track, barbecues and dinners at The Ivy (filled with fishcake-eating slebs, nigh impossible to get a booking). More generally, the Corney & Barrow below the office and other nearby bars serve the day-to-day needs of trainees, who tend to stick together when it comes to socialising. Various sports teams, including cricket, rugby and running, see people mixing up a bit more, as do departmental Friday afternoon rituals. The employment department has its own sofa, which comes into its own on Fridays when drinks and nibbles are served, while IP goes for tea and cakes. An ice cream trolley roams the corridors on hot afternoons, and the restaurant staff need no excuse to produce themed meals: Independence Day, Chinese New Year, Thai Day…

Last year we reported on the positive effects of the firm's move to CityPoint, with trainees sounding buoyant and enthusiastic about the new-look firm. This year, the mood was calmer with a lot less hype, a lot less gush. Trainees were satisfied with their lot and, in contrast to our last round of interviews, perhaps felt no need to bombard us with enthusiasm. In September 2003, 23 of the 31 qualifiers stayed with the firm.

and finally…

For good work and good clients across the board and truly exceptional opportunities in employment and IP work, Simmons & Simmons offers trainees a well-managed training without the blood, sweat and tears they feared would be rampant elsewhere in the City.

SJ Berwin

the facts

Location: London
UK ranking by size: 22
Total number of trainees: 78
Seats: 4x6 months
Alternative seats: Overseas seats, secondments

Established by seven ex-Berwin Leighton lawyers, SJ Berwin is today a substantial and ebullient corporate player. In between high-powered closings, and with a furtive skull from the champagne bottle, it has now celebrated its 21st birthday. Through boundless energy, entrepreneurial spirit and sheer nerve, it has elbowed its way into the London top 20 and has set up a cluster of European offices. The question now is 'Where to from here?'

rocky! rocky! rocky!

It's a truism that SJ Berwin cares less about who you are than what you can achieve. Whether from Cambridge or Hull universities, this is a firm that will *"make you feel wanted."* SJ Berwin is the Rocky Balboa of law firms; a robust underdog punching above its weight, and if you're very hardworking, very ambitious and very determined, it might just put you into the ring.

If *"the client is King"* at SJ Berwin, the trainee can sometimes feel like the serf. Or, after a week of all-nighters, like a pack mule on a high-altitude trek. But there's no doubting it, SJ Berwin is a clients' dream. One trainee put it perfectly: *"We lack the size of the top ten firms, but we have clients to make them jealous. We feel that we have to give the same service as the magic circle to hold onto our clients, and when you're not as big, that can mean tough working hours."* While a lot is expected of trainees, most enjoyed the feeling of *"having something invested in the business."* Serfs maybe, but not reduced to nibbling on the crumbs that fall off a matter – *"You get your own slice."* To borrow a line from Rocky: "You're going to eat lightning and crap thunder." And if you're anything like the SJ Berwin set, you're going to love it.

the bitter pill?

The seat pattern is the usual four by six-month affair, with enormous variations between seats. *"It was like working in four different firms,"* said one trainee. You should know that you'll be required to spend two seats in the firm's mainstay corporate department (which can include tax, banking and financial services), a fact that many trainees found hard to swallow. But if corporate is not your cup of tea, you should probably take your business elsewhere. It's been a roller coaster time for trainees in the City, so we weren't surprised when one told us: *"I know some people who've had hell on earth being here."* Why? The private equity group ('Corporate 3' and hugely important to the firm) can deliver killer hours, some *"abrasive"* personalities, and the bulk of your two-year allocation of grunt work. But it can also deliver thrilling experiences. You might find yourself working on drafts of refinancing documents or taking part in strategic discussions. *"You get thrown in the deep end,"* commented one satisfied customer, *"and if you swim, they give you as much responsibility as you can handle."*

The Public M&A group (or 'Corporate 1' as it's known) is a cyclical beast. When it's busy, *"it's very very busy."* When it's not, *"you just sit around all day."* As with corporate departments across the City, there are routine chores – bibling, data room duty, compiling board minutes – and it's the lot of the trainee to do them, but you'll also get to see the sexy cut and thrust of big-ticket deals. You may not be Bruce Willis saving the world from juggernaut asteroids, but you might find yourself (and colleagues and opponents), getting *"rather hysterical"* at 4am on your fifth all-nighter on a deal.

Despite it having taken up residence in a satellite up the road from SJB's 222 HQ, the property department has been central to the firm's growth and success. If you want to work for clients like Quintain (which is redeveloping Wembley Stadium), Marks & Spencer, NHS Estates, London & Regional Properties and British Land, or if you want to witness the cross-fertilisation of real estate and corporate skills on deals worth well over £100 million, then you need to get on over there.

sexy and appealing

Litigation was another surprise favourite with this year's trainees, who spoke of matters ranging from boundary disputes for favoured corporate execs to vast international matters. From wrestling pandas (World Wrestling Federation taking on the World Wide Fund for Nature in the Court of Appeal) to battling Russian aircraft (a Dutch/Russian case concerning ownership of the world's largest cargo plane), many of the team's biggest cases are multi-jurisdictional. Competition for the non-corporate seats can be fierce, and you may struggle to get exactly the ones you want. One trainee told us: *"I know people who've not been able to get close to what they wanted to do."* Others felt that they weren't always consulted with seating arrangements. Don't expect the powers that be to read your mind; you have to be smart – let them know exactly what you want and be willing to bargain for it. One savvy trainee told us: *"I threw my hands up at the start of the training contract and told them that I would do anything to get the seat I wanted."* Thankfully it involved nothing undignified.

The seats with greatest sex appeal are employment, media and EU/competition, where there's a chance of a three-month stint in Brussels. Media, meanwhile, is one of the consistently busy areas, bringing regular 12-hour days on film financings, production house work and music and TV contracts. If you come to SJ Berwin with the dream of qualifying into a popular niche department then your training contract may be even more exhausting than most. You'll have to perform in your corporate seats (aside from having no option to do otherwise, you'll want to get good results in appraisals), and you'll have to bust a gut in your favourite seat to impress the relevant partners. Bear in mind, also, that others will be following exactly the same strategy.

omnibus philosophy

It's best to remember that working in a large commercial firm can be like catching a bus. Some days you get to the stop and, glory of glories, the number 19 arrives immediately. Other days you wait in the rain with a broken heel and dripping mascara, only to clamber on board and realise you've left your travel card at home. With law, as with buses, you need good organisation and a small streak of luck to catch the best work. Timing is crucial. However, in this enterprising firm, wise trainees rely on more than luck. If you ask, negotiate, even badger, for more responsibility and show some *"get up and go,"* it will come. And that goes for overseas seats too.

the antigone...

It's tough for any firm looking to limit its NQ intake, and we weren't surprised to find some slightly downbeat sources when we rang in May 2003, shortly before the qualification jobs were announced. 'When will you know if you've been given a reprieve?' we asked. One trainee answered, in reference to tragic heroine Antigone: *"Probably too late, after we've all hanged ourselves."* That said, no one could fault the firm's commitment to fairness in selecting the lucky winners. It interviewed for all NQ positions and trainees were comforted by the knowledge that *"there's not much 'nod and wink' going on."* To its credit, the firm has a trainee solicitors group through which people can vent their spleen, but sadly the partner in charge of training is *"a bit distant."* Don't get us wrong, the retention stats for SJ Berwin in September 2003 were about average for the current market – 23 of the 38 qualifiers stayed.

...and the ecstasy!

The firm's partners are renowned for being *"real characters"* and come in a variety of styles and packages. The same could be said of trainees too. One told us: *"The mix of people is refreshing."* If there's a unifying characteristic, it's *"ambition,"* although there aren't too many Macbeths knifing their best mates in the back. Despite a competitive environment, the trainees are still a cohesive bunch. Close friendships form at this firm, and trainees spend time together outside work and on weekends. *"Because you all work very hard, there is a sense of shared experience, of teamwork,"* one said. Another, clearly a king of sardonic comments, suggested that in the days before qualification it could also be as simple as *"crisis bringing people closer."* Readers may be interested to hear that each year we consider researching the SJ Berwin *True Picture* feature as a reward to be enjoyed after a few weeks of hard work. It's rare that we encounter a funnier, more insightful and enthusiastic bunch.

There isn't an excessive amount in the way of organised social life, although the firm continues its fine tradition of rollicking good Christmas and summer parties, and trainees still meet up at Centro opposite the office, where buying a round will require you to mortgage your folks' house. As we've mentioned the office, lets try and figure out why it's in the less than glamorous surrounds of Gray's Inn Road. Um...nope, we can't. Basically, it's a ten-minute walk from anything – King's Cross and Chancery Lane tubes, the Royal Courts of Justice, decent shops – and a cab ride to the Square Mile. Nevertheless, a brisk walk from the tube station in the morning will get you pumped up for the day ahead. Chances are by the time you get to the firm, it'll have moved *"somewhere further Cityish but not exactly in the City."*

and finally...

You don't need us to tell you that there is a hard-working ethos at SJ Berwin – a firm doesn't grow the way it has in just 21 years by sitting around filing its nails. Some trainees sensed that the firm is at a cross-roads. According to one: *"If it wants to continue this pace of growth, it's going to have to do a bit of M&A itself."* Whatever the future holds, if you're looking for a challenge, grab your gloves.

Slaughter and May

the facts

Location: London
UK ranking by size: 15
Total number of trainees: 162
Seats: 4x6 months
Alternative seats: Overseas seats
Extras: Pro bono – Islington Law Centre, lang. training

Slaughter and May: a slightly ominous name, a slightly ominous image, a slightly ominous hush one would normally associate with the British Library or a gentlemen's outfitters. We ventured in to break the silence, measure the ambient air temperature...and snatch a handful of jelly babies.

toto, we're not in kansas anymore

Let's get one thing straight, Slaughter and May does things its own way. This firm has staunchly refused to submit to jazzy corporate branding, soundbites, buzzwords and freebies in its search for talent. While other firms bombard students with glossy publications, corporate entertainment and lots of feel-good fun, at Slaughters you get a *"very classy and understated"* brochure, in which the graphics are limited to maps and there are 26 pages of straightforward narrative. Elsewhere you may be required to complete an application form explaining why you would most like to be Dorothy in *The Wizard of Oz*, or detailing the many acts of heroism you've managed to fit into your young life. For Slaughters, a simple CV and a form listing your grades will suffice. Other firms will subject you to *"long psychological recruitment programmes;"* here *"you turn up for a 45-minute chat and try not to spill the biscuits down your front."*

Let's get something else straight, Slaughters' way is the best way – certainly that's what our sources say. *"There is a widespread and commonly held assumption that we are the best...hmmm...that's quite arrogant isn't it?"* If you say so. In short, *"we don't care how others do things, but we are going to do it right."* So is Slaughters' haughtiness in fact a front for well-meaning, honourable intentions? *"Yes. I can understand why people think we are arrogant and obstinate, but there have been no major cock-ups so far, so we must be doing something right."* Fair point well made. We stand corrected.

hitting the big time

And what exactly is this firm doing right? You need look no further than our parent publication *Chambers UK* to see the Slaughters standard imprinted on the biggest deals for top clients. Some of the biggest gigs in town – the Carlton/ITV Digital case and the Safeways sale – tripped effortlessly off the tongues of our sources. If you aspire to the highest standards in corporate law, you need to sit down and ask yourself if you want to train at Slaughter and May...with all that this entails.

Never forget the corporate orientation of this firm. One trainee posed the rhetorical question: *"If you don't want to do corporate work, why would you come here?"* Why indeed? The standard four-seat system breaks down into a minimum of two corporate seats (though some of our sources did three), and the remaining time is spent doing contentious work and a niche area such as property, pensions and employment, IP or tax. These peripheral departments exist to support the corporate groups, and many of our sources only spent three months in them. Splitting a six-month seat into two is common with, say tax or litigation, but *"you can't split corporate seats."* Trainees appear to be generally happy with what they get. *"People nag personnel if they are particularly interested in something, and they usually get it."*

According to our sources, Slaughters has *"a spirit of excellence."* The firm adopts a generalist approach to law that sets it apart from its magic circle counterparts. As a corporate lawyer you will be initiated into this tradition and not packaged as a specialist the moment you've phoned your mum to tell her you've qualified. Almost uniquely, the firm eschews billing targets. In its customary, honourable, gentlemanly and discreet way, the firm *"gets on with its legal tasks"* and leaves the hype and aggro of targets to its rivals. The absence of targets has certainly killed off the competitive edge between trainees, as have traditionally high retention rates on qualification.

While the firm has *"quite a fearsome reputation in terms of hours,"* in the summer of 2003 we struggled to find anybody who had really suffered. It goes without saying that signing up to the magic circle means signing a portion of your life away, but here *"there isn't any idea of face time."* Of course, we write this at a time of economic malaise; in a more buoyant market we may well have heard a different story. There's a thorough programme of training in the first 18 months, as well as plenty of departmental sessions for trainees, all of which take place during normal business hours. In addition, there are pro bono opportunities and language classes, though *"these aren't rammed down your throat."*

global stage

Slaughters' international strategy is a classic example of how the firm likes to do things in its own way. Rather than battling for global domination with the likes of Clifford Chance, the firm has developed an international network of 'best friends'. It has five of its own overseas offices in the main commercial centres, and combines these with rock-solid relationships with top foreign firms. Our sources proudly told us that *"in terms of our international strategy, we are out on our own."* The idea is that all the firms concentrate on what they do best: Slaughters does English law, Uría y Menéndez does Spanish law and Hengeler Mueller German law etc. It's much like shopping for clothes at Selfridges, where you get all the best concessions under one roof, rather than Marks & Spencer, where you only get one brand and it just isn't the same.

While the international strategy is working well for the firm, it isn't really doing it for trainees. We heard various grumbles from people who had applied unsuccessfully for a six-month secondment either to a Slaughters office overseas or to a best friend firm. From some, we heard that *"the possibilities of going abroad aren't that wide,"* so we counted – 12 trainees on our list were in overseas seats. Even less common are client secondments, and when they do occur they tend to be in corporate seats.

All this said, generally, trainees had few grumbles about their experiences. Inevitably, *"it is swings and roundabouts."* As one person explained: *"On some transactions you are a minute, insignificant speck on the radar, but in other deals you get more of a kick."* It's the same story anywhere in the magic circle – if you are after a front-row seat to watch the world's best performers work on the world's biggest transactions, you are going to have to accept that Buttons will not be calling you up on stage to take a bow, even if it is your birthday.

carrots and sticks

The magic circle may sound like the sequel to *The Magic Roundabout*, but take it from us there is no tinkly theme tune or tripped-out happy hugs here. At Slaughters there is an end-of-seat appraisal, which one source made sound like a fairly gruelling battle of wills, and that's all you're guaranteed. While some trainees confirmed they had received regular and positive feedback from supervisors, others said you had to ask for it, and *"they make no bones about telling you when you are wrong."* This 'backwards in coming forwards' approach to dishing out pats on the back doesn't surprise us in a firm that trainees admit is *"traditional and hierarchical."* We were told time and again that *"people don't stand on ceremony, but you know where you are."* One source commented: *"I have never tugged my forelock for Nigel Boardman,"* but went on to say: *"While he talks very softly, and walks very softly, he carries a very big stick."* Thankfully, this separation cuts both ways, and while trainees may have to cope with *"a pecking order,"* they also described how at social functions *"partners often disappear before the end of the evening, so you can make a fool of yourself in peace and quiet."* Phew!

Until recently, Slaughters was the only firm where the average equity partner took home a million notes each year. In true Slaughters' fashion, none of our interviewees begrudged their seniors this recompense, in fact it was barely mentioned at all. One noted: *"Some assistants work incredibly hard for the outside chance that they will be made a partner and earn their cool million, but you have to have real burning ambition to stay and do that."* For those who already know they won't be staying at the firm long term, there's an appreciation that a Slaughters training *"makes you very saleable."* In the short term, Slaughters has a near perfect report card for NQ retention. Even in a lousy market, in September 2003 it offered jobs to 44 of its 47 qualifiers and only one chose to decline.

politeness costs nothing

"We all have haircuts our mothers would be proud of!" one source chuckled. Well mannered, slightly bookish and often softly spoken, these are the people who were on first-name terms with the school librarian and never clocked up fines. Slaughters kids were the sort who held doors open for teachers, not because they were keen, but because it was polite. Slaughters kids' homework was never, ever eaten by the dog. This firm's lawyers are understated, precise, witty, articulate and independent of thought – if you like *"team-building exercises and open-plan offices"* look elsewhere.

We heard a funny story from a vac scheme student. Our source was sitting with an assistant when an older partner walked into the room. He offered his hand and introduced himself as "[Xyz] *College, Oxford." "Nice to meet you,"* our source replied. The assistant cringed. The Oxbridge stereotype fits many, although these days *"there are many trainees who haven't been to Oxbridge."* The make-up of the trainee population is less a reflection of a leaning towards the dreaming spires and more the result of a bent for academic excellence. In keeping with the firm's *"pernickety"* demands, trainees need to be *"quite rigorous"* and *"good at black letter law."* Trainees also told us: *"They aren't keen on people who are too loud or too overconfident,"* so *"you shouldn't bring your ego with you."*

When trainees are *"treated like adults,"* they inevitably adopt a more mature outlook compared to their peers. Slaughters' trainees typically *"don't like enforced fun."* Don't expect alcopop-fuelled karaoke or any other aberration in the name of team building; these are people who enjoy *"simple stuff,"* maybe a drink after work with select friends at St Paul's Tavern or the nearest Corney & Barrow, or perhaps a game of rugby. The annual Christmas dinner dance at The Grosvenor is a black-tie affair where you may hear the odd self-conscious S&M joke, but *"people rarely make them because they aren't that funny."*

shedding light on the issue

Since moving to stylish new offices in Bunhill Row in 2002, trainees have enjoyed *"an unobtrusive environment"* of varying shades of grey. The most precise description of the decor was *"pale bluey-greyish-kinda-simple."* There's no gym, no manicurist and no masseur, but you get to work in a room with natural light and your very own supervisor. In the lobby, a now infamous floor-level water feature fools the odd victim running for the lift, and spare black socks are kept behind reception for clients who stray. As is a remote-controlled hovercraft for a certain partner's amusement. The staff entrance offers a sculpture that is scathingly referred to as *"the most expensive piece of driftwood in the world,"* and in the restaurant there is a jukebox, described by one dry wit as *"a token of fun in our dreary lives."* We hear there are so many rules about when it can be used that no one has ever tried.

It's not all silence and steely looks; Slaughters definitely has a lighter side. Our vac scheme spy chose the firm because they sensed a frisson and originality absent in lawyers at the other magic circle firm they'd investigated. So why doesn't it rail against the frosty image? According to one source: *"Stereotypes only take hold because there is an element of truth in them."* And here, perhaps, we get somewhere near the heart of the matter. Slaughters is sufficiently self-assured that it doesn't need to appear fluffy or recreate itself with the veneer of a new corporate colour, logo or typeface. Many firms seem to forget that today's 21-year-olds have been bombarded with advertising and marketing guff all their lives and the most perceptive among them are sick of it. Yet, in a self-aware gesture that delights us enormously, there are jelly babies *"scattered around the client area."* Who'd have thought humble confectionery could be satirical?

and finally...

Quite simply, Slaughter and May offers *"a really good, thorough grounding with no corners cut."* Focus on getting the best exam results you can and be sure you want a full-on corporate training. It's that simple.

Speechly Bircham

the facts

Location: London
UK ranking by size: 81
Total number of trainees: 10
Seats: 4x6 months
Alternative seats: None

"Hello, Slinky Pictures!"
"Um…is that Speechly Bircham?"
"No, Slinky Pictures!"

We're not sure what sort of cinema Slinky Pictures peddles, but we can be sure that the good folk at Speechly Bircham have never starred. This is an *"honest, unpretentious"* firm that eschews the glamour of the spotlight. A mid-sized firm well known for its private client work, it also has solid real estate, employment, litigation and corporate practices. Just be careful you dial its phone number correctly…

nothing artificial

Trainees were attracted to the firm's *"plain, homespun"* approach to recruitment. One source could have been reading our minds when he said: *"All the firms claimed to be collegiate with an open-door policy. Once you've heard this three or four times, you know it doesn't ring true."* Speechlys, by comparison, *"didn't make any outstanding claims. No masses of Forbes' clients, no New York seats. You're pleasantly surprised that they're not trying to over-egg the pudding. It's quite refreshing, really!"* Indeed. The firm is proud of its no-frills approach, and clients in particular appreciate the straightforward 'can do' attitude of its lawyers. There are no pretensions at Speechlys: *"You know what they're about and you get on with it."*

The firm takes only five trainees a year, so there's little chance of getting lost in the machinery; all our interviewees felt *"included"* at the firm. If client entertainment is your thing, Speechlys is *"more than happy"* for you to get involved. *"It's all part of trying to groom us into being fee earners."*

musical chairs

The training contract is divided into four six-month seats and most people will end up in the firm's well-known private capital (private client) group at some point. Lawyers advise the great, the good, and the plain old rolling in it on tax efficient wills and trust schemes and count among their high-profile clientele Howard de Walden Estates, Lord Lloyd-Webber, Alexander Thyssen and the chairmen of major UK plcs. Clients have the option of using prêt-a-porter tax-based wills packages, and trainees are involved in updating these services from day one. There was universal praise for the group's lawyers, who *"have a real passion for trusts and tax,"* and *"are happy to explain it."* And we're assured that while *"it sounds nerdy, it's really quite fun."* As well as the research, trainees enjoy a good dose of client contact. *"You chat to clients and really get to know them."* But the work is not for everyone, and the *"gentle"* pace may leave some trainees crying out for *"an adrenalin injection."*

If the idea of free tickets to *Cats* doesn't appeal, you can always get your claws into the firm's highly rated financial services group, which is renowned for its work with investment funds and, for its sins, recently acted for the Ecclesiastical Insurance Group on the reconstruction of the £155 million St Andrew Investment Trust. This is an area in which the firm excels and it is seen to be the equal of firms like Allen & Overy, Mayer Brown, Rowe & Maw and Travers Smith Braithwaite.

Dispute resolution offers *"a baptism of fire"* that's absolutely relished by most. Here, you'll be responsible for the day-to-day running of about a dozen of your own files and chances are you'll get to appear in a county court before a district judge or in the High Court before a master. In addition to conducting bite-sized matters under the supervision of more senior lawyers, trainees also take more of a back-seat role in larger disputes. Our sources raved about the supervision, and the junior lawyers in particular, who are *"always on hand to answer questions."*

first footing

In real estate litigation, a smaller department with only two partners, trainees can cut their teeth on smaller debt recovery files for large real estate portfolio owners. Collecting rent arrears is par for the course, but fear not, you won't need to feel bad about it as for the most part these are *"wealthy people living overseas who've simply forgotten to pay the rent on their London pied-à-terre."* Half their luck. Again, trainees attend county court hearings regularly. As many of the clients' property portfolios contain London properties, you'll often go and inspect them for yourself. The cases on which you'll work are by no means all tiddlers – one trainee was lucky enough to be involved in a successful appeal to the House of Lords.

On the non-contentious side, a seat in commercial property guarantees you personal conduct of 20 or so files, and you'll become a first point of contact for institutional landlord clients. It can be intimidating at first, and as one trainee said: *"You're dealing with clients with 20 years' experience so you have to sound like you have more than six months in law!"* Trainees delighted in the responsibility they were given; we heard that one had ended up making a New Year's Eve cannonball run to Paris to do an exchange of documents. He just made it back on the last train in time for Auld Lang Syne.

home sweet home

Speechly Bircham occupies six floors of a seven-floor office building overlooking St Andrew's Church in Holborn. Each floor is colour-coded, so you know where you are. (*"Although the numbers usually tell you that anyway."*) While there are the obligatory floor-to-ceiling glass windows and modern decor, in true Speechlys' style, *"it's not trying to be trendy."* And this leads us to an important point. While trainees told us of the firm's *"relaxed"* atmosphere, they were adamant that *"it doesn't trade on that."* It hasn't jumped on the 'work-life balance' bandwagon to attract new lawyers, and it doesn't employ the latest marketing jargon to attract good work. It just is what it is.

The firm-wide sports and social committee does just what the name says. The three rugby playing trainees are holding out for the day when a three-a-side legal league is formed. Until then, the thick-necked ones must content themselves with cricket in the summer and football in winter. Every two months, there's a drinks evening in one of the firm's meeting rooms, catered with prawn cutlets and other nibbley delights by the excellent firm chef. And there is such a thing as a free lunch at this firm – it's available once a month for all assistant solicitors and trainees. On a less formal basis, many people pop over to The Bottlescrue for an outdoor drink on Thursdays or Fridays. The recently opened Last Bar has proved popular, although when we spoke to them, trainees were feeling *"a bit over it,"* having been there every Friday for the past two months.

In September 2003, only one of the five qualifying trainees stayed with Speechlys, yet not one trainee we spoke to had a bad word to say about the place. Said one: *"Despite the fact that I'm leaving, I think it's a great firm. When I joined, one of the things they boasted about was their good retention rate, but there's no accounting for the market."* Indeed not.

and finally...

If you want quality training in an intimate and unpretentious environment, this is a top choice. Speechly Bircham is an honest-to-goodness law firm that does just what it says on the tin.

steeles

the facts

Location: Norwich, London, Diss
UK ranking by size: 266
Total number of trainees: 11
Seats: 4x6 months
Alternative seats: None
Extras: Pro bono – Citizens Advice Bureaux, FRU

Having undergone the proverbial corporate makeover, Steele & Co sports a new, trimmer look as steeles. The svelte appearance stops with the name though, as the firm is still spread over offices in Norwich, Diss and London.

comedy nose, big shoes

The Norwich office has a *"dominating presence"* and is the HQ. From here it handles everything from agriculture to e-commerce and has designs on higher value work for larger clients. With names like Campbell Foods, Start-Rite Shoes, BirdsEye Walls and a score of local authorities on its books, the firm seems to be well on its way and has even had the pleasure of handling Ronald McDonald's copyright concerns. The London office is home to commercial litigation for local authorities, employment law, commercial property and a new music and media department.

There are no compulsory seats within the four-seat system, so allowing for a bespoke training contract: you can conjure up a commercially oriented experience or, conversely, select a family and private client ensemble. In the past, a successful employment department has been a big draw, and that trend looks set to continue, as does trainees' current interest in coco. Unsurprisingly, *"there is a bit of a queue forming"* at the door of the music and media department and this seems to be one reason why *"the trend for trainees wanting to stay in Norwich has stopped – now everyone wants to go to London."*

The trend cannot be entirely attributed to a thumping bass line – the London office's move from Vauxhall to Holborn coincides with an expansion programme that makes it less an outpost and more of a focus for the firm. As such, trainees can expect to work in both locations and, if interested (and if the firm's needs allow), they may also get a spell in Diss handling civil litigation for private individuals, or even a crime seat in the firm's former Thetford office, which has hived off and now operates as ACT LLP. There is no hard and fast rule on where trainees spend their time, although one said: *"If you start training in London, you are deemed to be a Londoner with the option of going to Norwich if you want to, and vice versa."* Moving is optional; *"you are not forced to go anywhere, but for certain seats you have to move."*

town mouse, country mouse

While London is certainly proving itself to be a *"force to be reckoned with,"* Norwich remains the administrative centre and professional face of steeles and also has *"the main equity partners who rule the roost."* This makes for a slightly more hierarchical atmosphere, but bear in mind that trainees stressed the youthfulness of the firm and said they were *"definitely made to feel like an integral part of the place."* By contrast, *"there's a bit more of a buzz, a more relaxed and social atmosphere in London."* We wondered if the two separate identities should be a cause for concern, but were reassured that *"there is no rift, it is just that the different cultures of the two locations impose on the two offices."* Certainly, trainees could see the benefits of both: the faster pace and flexible work ethos of London is a good foil for the open countryside and calmer pace of Norfolk. In short, steeles offers trainees the chance to sample regional and City training in one contract.

day one, deals to be done

Applicants shopping around for a hands-on training need look no further. All our sources described enviable levels of experience, with one source telling us: *"I did an exchange of contracts on a property on the first day of my first seat."* Another described running 75 files single-handedly, while a third said: *"In my first seat I was in court nearly every day."* It is a case of *"sink or swim"* but *"they only give you complete responsibility if you've proved you can cope."* Trainees sit with or near their supervisor depending on whether or not they are working in an open-plan department, and mid- and end-of-seat appraisals are bolstered by ongoing feedback. *"It is a very encouraging place to work; if you do something wrong you get told, but you also get told how to put it right – it's very constructive."* We heard that the training programme has been slightly ad hoc in the past, but now there appears to be a more regular diet of internal lectures and presentations.

Steeles has *"an efficient culture rather than a guilt culture;"* a typical day, across the firm, is 9am-5.30pm and apparently *"it is rare to see people still at work after 6pm."* You won't get away from late nights scot-free though – the latest we heard of anyone staying was *"nearly midnight."* On that occasion, the people involved were given time off in lieu. Not bad. So what's the catch? Well, our candid sources told us *"salary is the only issue."* Steeles' trainees are by no means earning the least in legal circles, but a lack of financial support through law school and a modest wage may be inhibiting factors for some. One source said: *"People who have to do the CPE will go elsewhere because they can't afford to come here."* We did notice a propensity of law graduates.

i was just passing

Norfolk wins the hearts of many UEA students and steeles reaps the benefit, though an East Anglian background or education is far from obligatory. All the trainees we spoke to were cheerful, open and articulate – an interviewer's dream, in fact. We heard that *"strong characters won't go down well if they aren't prepared to muck in,"* yet confidence is a valuable trait as you'll be dealing with clients from day one. Trainees are allowed to contribute to the daily business of the firm in many ways, even to the extent that they sit in on interviews for future trainees.

The Norwich office's out-of-town location makes popping out for a pint after work a little tricky; however, *"there are views over open fields"* and Norwich as a City is quite lively when they do manage to get out. On the plus side: weekends by the sea, country walks, good shopping and the inevitable youth buzz of a university town. The downside: *"You are out on a limb in Norfolk. People don't really drop by."*

The London office has made The Duke of York its second home. A *"retro-traditional"* watering hole, trainees and fee earners gather there fairly regularly after work and for *"the odd cheeky lunch."* The Holborn offices offer pretty standard facilities, but are *"brand spanking new, trendy and open plan."*

In the past, the three offices have shared annual summer and Christmas parties, but this year due to the firm's growth in size, there were two summer boat parties – one on the Norfolk Broads and one on the Thames. Trainees could understand the logic of this decision, but did say *"it was a shame as some people never get to meet the crowd at the other offices."* That said, the firm is encouraging more trainee events. In 2003, three of the four September qualifiers stayed with the firm.

and finally...

If you're yearning for a relationship with the photocopier, steeles is not for you. This is a firm where you can stretch yourself in any number of directions.

Stephenson Harwood

the facts

Location: London
UK ranking by size: 51
Total number of trainees: 30
Seats: 4x6 months
Alternative seats: Overseas seats
Extras: Pro bono – Hoxton and Camden Law Centres, language training

Stephenson Harwood has had an interesting and high-profile history. Everyone knows the name, but defining the firm sometimes feels like an exercise rather akin to painting the Forth Bridge.

plans galore

Having made the transition to commercial practice in the 1970s, Stephenson Harwood was once among the largest of City practices. Like most City firms, it has grown significantly in the last couple of decades, though it has not expanded to the giant proportions of some of its peers. A good job too, according to its trainees, who had invariably chosen the firm for its mid-size appeal and relative intimacy. Since taking up a commercial outlook, SH has developed a broad-church profile, becoming particularly respected in asset finance, shipping and commercial litigation. And offering trainees a niche experience in private client work (called private capital), there's more than a whiff of the past still wafting along the corridors.

In 1999, SH announced it was to follow a three-year plan that would see it focus on transactional business, particularly mainstream corporate and work deriving from the international financial markets. There followed a curious wave of change: not a tsunami as such, but certainly one that altered the landscape of the firm. A lot of partners left, some because their practice area was no longer in keeping with the new look SH, others because they were regarded as dead wood and yet more who believed they could earn more elsewhere, having seen profits drop. Speaking of the three-year plan, one trainee confirmed: "*Corporate was going to be the daddy and that didn't happen.*" So the plan was modified and, after announcing its 'Positive Action Plan' in late 2003 the firm has set about concentrating on four target sectors: the financial industry, maritime services, the tech world and the property market.

BAFfled

SH operates a four by six-month seat system with no compulsories other than to satisfy Law Society requirements for both contentious and non-contentious work. In January 2002, the banking department fused with the ship finance department to form BAF (banking and asset finance). SH's merger with shipping practice Sinclair Roche & Temperley the following May further enhanced the capabilities of the department, whose clients include banks (often in syndicates) lending money for the acquisition of ships (and now aeroplanes too), as well as shipowners leasing their vessels to others. Clients come from places like Russia, Germany, Scandinavia, Greece and Korea...as do the trainees these days, especially since the merger with SRT. Judging from the numbers of BAF seats on offer at any one time you should view a seat in the department as more likely than not. One source shared his enthusiasm for the seat: "*It was a brilliant experience. I chose it because it was the busiest department. I had my own small files and on the bigger matters the loan agreements and major drafting was done by senior associates but the drafting of the security documents and conditions precedent were left to me.*"

The litigation team has long been well regarded in the market and is ranked in the top band of the medium-sized firms table by *Chambers UK*. It has recently restructured itself into four groups: offshore, financial, P&I (shipping) and insurance. Last year a team of litigators met with success in Standard Bank London v Canara Bank, a complex action involving a banking syndicate that provided useful judgment on the law of restitution among other things. It is interesting to note that the advocacy was handled in-house by resident QC John Higham. Obviously, it's impossible for trainees to take a lead role on such matters, and their function is a supporting role in the management of the large volume of documents, but our sources were happy to report that wherever possible they had been allocated smaller files, allowing them to see more of the litigation process.

passports at the ready

Some trainees reported that winning your favourite seat could be a political game requiring you to win the approval of the relevant partners, yet when we put this idea to other trainees, particularly first-years, they disagreed. It seems that if your desires are mainstream, you'll easily fulfil them, but you may need to push in the right places for something popular (say employment or biztech) or if you want to get a seat out in one of the firm's three Asian offices.

Around half of the trainee group (which is smaller than in recent years following some deferrals and the easing of a post-merger bulge) go abroad to one of SH's offices in Piraeus (ship finance), Hong Kong (mainly corporate) or Singapore (ship finance and shipping litigation). The Shanghai office could potentially offer a seat to the right trainee, but Madrid is now off the menu permanently since that office was taken over by DLA. As such, a rousing rendition of *Viva Espania* is not recommended at interview. Overall there's not an excessive amount of competition for overseas placements, so assume that you will get to go if you want to, although language skills may give you the edge over others for the Asian seats.

clocking off

Former SRT recruits aside, most trainees had joined the firm because they'd done a vac scheme and it had seemed like such a nice place. *"It was friendlier than the other firms and I chose it on that basis alone."* In this sense, SH is a place that is most commonly chosen not for its practice orientation but for its high score on the comfort scale. Trainees generally report an ease of interaction with their seniors on social occasions as well as in the office. The hours themselves are considered to be pretty good although there were mixed reactions to an e-mail from HR reminding trainees that the job was not a 9.30am to 5.30pm commitment. Official hours are 9.30am to 5.30pm; however, our sources said the average day runs to about 7pm. *"You don't feel right clocking off before about half six,"* one confirmed.

The retention rate for qualifiers was rather grim in September 2003 – seven out of 16 were given jobs. In truth, this is the second poor year for SH.

up on the roof

Opposite the front entrance to St Paul's Cathedral, the SH office is in one of the best locations in the City, in fact *"it's the only place in the City that gives a perfect view over St Paul's – any TV crew needing to film it will do so from our roof."* In the months after the SRT merger, some lawyers were trapped *"in the awful bunkers of Royex House"* but now everyone is together in One St Paul's Churchyard. At lunchtime in the summer, you can go up on the roof to catch some rays or you might take your sarnies into the crypt of St Paul's if you prefer your egg and cress with extra enlightenment.

Trainees spoke of after work trips to Shaws The Booksellers (a pub not a purveyor of literature) and at end-of-month drinks, staff make the most of that view from the roof. Three cheers for the football team: *"SH FC does pretty well in the London legal league"* despite the fact that the captain has fewer player options than his counterparts at the league-beating firms – Slaughter and May and KPMG. What about the giant Clifford Chance? *"No, they're not up to scratch."* The kit on the pitch may be prescribed, but in the office there's a permanent business-casual dress code. Gentlemen are advised to keep a suit in the office for client meetings or court.

thanks, but no thanks

While some people refused our request for an interview because they felt their contributions would be unhelpful, the characters we did speak to ranged from the somewhat stiff and chalky to the hilariously cheesy. Good academics have always been a must, and remain so, yet it seems that SH is now seeking something more. "*They are keen for trainees to push the marketing side more than they were before.*" If you have potentially useful contacts, don't be afraid to flash them at interview for fear of looking showy. Of course, to market the firm one must be fully up to speed on the course that's been set by management and the progress made. In this respect, some of our sources felt they needed to know more and that it would be easier to speak up for the firm if they understood more about the events affecting it. Yet, just to muddy the waters, one trainee told us: "*Every month we get an e-mail of the managing partner's thoughts, called 'Business Talk' – I usually delete it.*" Which just goes to show that you can't please all of the people all of the time.

We'd like to award our 'wit of the week' medallion to the trainee who had us in stitches as he mulled over the abandoned merger talks with New York firm Holland & Knight. "*...what were they called? Holland & Barratt?*" Multivits and wheatgerm with every lease. Sir, you know who you are and we hope we'll be in touch again next year. Interestingly, another source came to the conclusion that a US merger would be ideal for the firm, although there was nothing to suggest that this is being pursued.

and finally...

Stephenson Harwood has had a rough ride in the legal press and on certain message boards recently, nevertheless, most of our sources took a robust view on this, pointing to the firm's successes in asset finance, shipping and litigation. None of them had joined the firm for a hard-boiled corporate law training and, if your interests lie in SH's core practice areas, they suggest that you find out more about the firm.

Taylor Vinters

the facts

Location: Cambridge
UK ranking by size: 141
Total number of trainees: 10
Seats: 4x6 months
Alternative seats: Brussels

"*A grey bunker*" with an impressive female managing partner and the odd official secret to boot. You could be forgiven for mistaking Taylor Vinters for a clandestine MI5 operation, but step inside and you'll find an open-plan office where the only real enigma is the location of the secret beer fridge.

on the case

Taylor Vinters' vast array of practice areas is seen by trainees as a key strength of the firm, as well as invaluable to their own experience. Commercial work (especially for start-up technology enterprises) rubs alongside rural business (including bloodstock and equestrian services), matrimonial, private client, personal injury, employment, IP and property. The firm doesn't shy away from specialist fields, and also includes a food group in its repertoire.

First-years start with a seat in either PI or property. PI had won the hearts of all the trainees we spoke to. Described by one as "*a confidence-building seat,*" even those trainees who hadn't initially expressed interest in PI appreciated that it was "*trainee-friendly,*" and the nature of the work fostered core skills. In this seat "*you can be let loose a bit, and get stuck in at an early stage.*" Property does not receive quite such unanimous acclaim, but the high volume of work means that most trainees are encouraged into the department. A property seat could be in rural or commercial property, planning, or construction and development. An open mind will serve you well; while one trainee admitted property work was "*like sawdust,*" another was "*eating his hat*" having found that he really enjoyed it. While PI may kick-start you into handling low-value caseloads, you are unlikely to have quite the same role on a corporate transaction. However, across the board, trainees are encouraged to get out and meet clients, and in the departments where it is possible, to handle their own matters.

our man in...

From the second six months onwards, individuals' preferences are taken into account in seat allocation. Usually, there's competition for corporate, IP and employment, but this year's trainees were more diverse in their interests, making for fewer disappointments. A new technology seat is expected to become a permanent fixture. Our sources appreciated the firm's choice of young training principals and the fact that *"all the departments put in as much effort for trainees."* No seats to avoid like the plague then...

As if all this choice wasn't enough, there's also a three-month secondment to Brussels firm Renouf & Co, which has long-established relationships with a number of UK firms. A posting to Brussels involves an eclectic mix of issues, ranging from environment to employment, and a healthy dose of EU issues. The extensive UK trainee network in the city and a flat shared with another trainee means *"you are plugged into the social network immediately."*

inside q's gadget lab

TV's distinctive client base makes for a unique workload. Cambridge isn't the place to go for billion-pound deals, nonetheless, set in the heart of Silicon Fen, the firm has its finger on the hi-tech/biotech pulse. In addition to clients like Dr Reddy's Laboratories and Bayer CropScience, the firm also takes instructions from Cambridge University, many of its colleges and other institutional clients.

We became so used to the 'game on' attitude of our interviewees that we weren't in the least surprised to hear hardened techno fans and corporate aspirants extolling the virtues of private client practice. When we asked how private client work fitted in with the firm's culture, we were told it was *"a perfect match."* Though the department does act for the more traditional private client, it also picks up a fair bit of business from senior execs of its corporate paymasters. Expect to be mixing your green-wellied landowners with greenback-fingered scientists.

the debriefing

We spoke to some very satisfied customers on the subject of supervision and feedback. Thorough appraisals take place every three months, but perhaps more importantly, trainees felt comfortable with lawyers *"across the board, from juniors right up to the managing partner." "Nobody pulls rank"* and we sensed a strong mentoring culture. This is not intended to sound happy-clappy – if there is one thing this firm is not, it is fluffy around the edges – but TV's decisive, well-structured approach is backed up by a healthy dose of transparency that seems to flow down from the very top of the management structure. If there is something amiss, trainees know what procedures to instigate: whatever the problem, *"if you go through the right channels, it can be sorted. They will never brush things under the carpet."*

the hidden bunker

We asked for an artists' impression of Taylor Vinters' HQ. The outside? Responses varied from *"a bit grey"* to *"very grey"* to *"so grey that on a grey day you can't find it."* And the inside? *"Less grey."* Set on the outskirts of Cambridge and overlooking the Science Park, the whole firm is under one roof and benefits from a car park, which appealed greatly to the one interviewee who said he didn't like to make a habit of walking places. However, it lacks a canteen. Despite Phil's sandwich van parking up over the road every day (it even boasts a cappuccino machine) and a lady who brings sandwiches round, trainees did say: *"We end up craving a Starbucks. It's pathetic really."* You said it.

Nobody denies that the post-work social life suffers a bit from being out of reach of the city nightlife, however, groups of younger staff and trainees do make an effort to meet up in Cambridge from time to time. Mixed hockey, five-a-side football and cricket all provide opportunities for mixing with clients. A recent cricket tour to Cornwall gave the guys *"a chance to get legless with their colleagues and see a new side to them."* What about the girls? *"The girls are too lazy to organise themselves."* If you don't know your box from your bails, you'll be relieved to hear that the social life does not revolve exclusively around the cricket pitch. Trips to London and Calais, the dog track, karaoke and bingo nights, and the Christmas party and panto are all fixtures on the calendar. Oh no they aren't. Oh yes they are. But the highlight remains race day, where a coach load of lawyers and staff pursues a vanload of booze up the A14 to Newmarket. There's a permanent dress-down policy, but you are expected to be suitably attired for meeting clients. Keep a tie in your desk drawer, boys.

top secret secrets

For those of you who have only persevered with this report for news on the secret beer fridge, we can only confirm that for an open-plan office, this is a very closely guarded secret. When asked about the fridge (uncovered during last year's research), the reaction of one was: *"Oh my God! Oh my God! Oh my God!"* while another simply said: *"I am sworn to secrecy."* Try as we might, no one was going to enlighten us further as to its whereabouts, though one trainee warned us that *"the person who spilled the beans has no future at the firm."* Blimey! Best we ask no more.

On the face of it, the trainee group lacks any defining features. They describe themselves as *"a pretty sardonic bunch,"* which we wouldn't argue with, but we would also say they are unruffled, honest, well informed and a positive delight to chat with. Four of the five September 2003 qualifiers remain with the firm to chat another day.

and finally...

Taylor Vinters is quietly confident about its place in both the local and broader marketplaces and has much to recommend it.

Taylor Walton

the facts

Location: Luton, St Albans, Hemmel Hempstead, Harpenden
UK ranking by size: 167
Total number of trainees: 10
Seats: 4x6 months
Alternative seats: None

Over time, Taylor Walton has grown more interesting and, after a hat trick of small mergers, it's now the dominant commercial/general practice law firm in the northern Home Counties.

four of hearts

Four offices, fours seats. Usually trainees spend 12 or 18 months in Luton and the remainder of their time in one or two of the other offices. *"I consider the firm as one entity as I know lots of people in all offices,"* one source said. *"But those who work in one office all the time may look at it in a more partisan way."* It's easy to blow this concept of separation out of proportion: Luton, St Albans and Harpenden are all in a straight line, none is more than six or seven miles from another, and Hemmel is only eight or so miles away. You could do the route on your bike, if you wanted.

"The Luton office is the commercial hub" and the largest in the firm by far. Ah, Luton! In truth, the town has *"an awful reputation, but it is not as bad as all that...although it's as if everyone stopped caring 15 years ago."* Unsurprisingly, the airport has a significant impact on the local economy, and we noted the firm has bags of clients in both the aviation sector and related ancillary services. Away from Luton, St Albans is a leafy commuter town packed with private clients, some of them quite wealthy. The same can be said of Harpenden. As for Hemmel Hempstead, well there's not that much to be said about Hemmel...

The trainees aren't all local to Herts; several are from London and others come from as far afield as deepest darkest west Wales. A few of them had legal work experience before starting their training and one was an accountant before turning to the law. As for the ideal applicant, one source told us: *"It's somebody who's a bit eclectic. If you are hell bent on thing x or thing y, then it's maybe not the best place for you. It would also help to be a little bit outgoing."* A broad and flexible interest in legal practice is required as *"there are few areas Taylor Walton doesn't do. Well, there's crime, but short of that it can cater for everything."* OK, maybe not specialised capital markets transactions or shipping law, but you know what they're saying.

different suits

Training seminars are organised by department and we heard no complaints on that score. Nor were there any real grumbles about the quality of work allocated to our sources, although in commercial litigation we sensed that trainees had the least amount of self-determination. *"I was working for various fee earners doing small tasks under tight supervision."* A couple of small applications in court go part of the way towards compensating for the inevitable spells of document administration; however, there's less likelihood of getting your own files than in other seats.

Corporate brings a bit more responsibility. *"It feels more inclusive – I'd get the bare bones of a deal explained to me and learn what documents were needed. I found myself working very closely with fee earners, researching, drafting and putting together a suite of documents for a deal. It's fairly complicated, but I did get to go to client meetings."* With five partners, commercial property is the largest department and offers the usual mixture of post completion formalities and deeds management plus a decent amount of drafting.

PI work in the Hemmel office is a different kettle of fish altogether. Private clients and referrals from claims companies see trainees *"learning how to process volume work."* With all those RTAs, slips and trips and accidents at work comes oodles of client contact over the phone, much of it explaining the ins and outs of conditional fee agreements. Some found the seat a little monotonous, but *"the people were great to work with."* In the family department (Harpenden and St Albans), there are plenty of publicly funded and child law cases. Here, you'll assist fee earners with their caseloads: *"I was preparing briefs and sitting behind the barrister in court…even doing small hearings."*

cutting the pack

The head office in Luton is *"very modern, stylish and recently redecorated."* The branch offices are more traditional on the whole, although trainees do note change. All four sites benefit from the firm's keen interest in IT and communications. *"We've seen a rolling programme of improvements,"* said one trainee. *"This is not the sort of firm to buy a software package and not use it to its full capacity. They like to constantly improve the systems, including the database, and they are always asking staff for their ideas."* Full marks.

The managing partner, David Fry, is fairly young and started as a trainee at the firm. A private client practitioner, his position in this key role is perhaps indicative of the value that Taylor Walton places on private clients. Yes, it is pushing for growth in its commercial practice (hence the last merger), but *"they are encouraging all departments to expand and there's a big emphasis on cross-selling between them."* Very often with firms of this size, especially in the Home Counties, we find there are two types of partners – the forward planners (younger, often refugees from City firms) who want change, and the traditionalists (older, at the firm man and boy) who become increasingly sidelined. *"Here, the majority of partners do want to go forward."* And what of the others? *"They will be left behind or retire."* At the junior end, three of the five qualifying trainees stayed with the firm in 2003.

house rules

There's a football team and a cricket team, which (depending on who we spoke to) is either *"quite good"* or *"pretends that it's good."* Matches are played against local professionals…accountants and other lawyers, not Watford FC. Sporting fixtures and quiz nights (get on the team with the partner who has a photographic memory) act like glue, bonding together people from different offices and different levels of the firm. Most trainees work little beyond their contractual hours of 9am–5.15pm, although on rare occasions (mostly in Luton) client matters dictate otherwise. All agreed a few 10pm finishes are a far cry from selling your soul. After work, groups of fee earners from the smaller branch offices slip into local bars and brasseries, although certainly not every night of the week. In Luton, *"the conveyancers have their pub across the road from the office."* Called The Office, this pub is not to the tastes of all, so it's a good job there's a large Weatherspoons at the end of the street.

Dress-down? *"Ooh no, they wouldn't entertain that."* OK. Ways to improve Taylor Walton? *"The solicitors who supervise trainees should all have training themselves and be advised of how important their role is."* Anything else? *"A bit more ongoing feedback."* Anything else? *"The salary."* Oh, yes? *"It requires you to be...philosophical...although it's more than enough to survive on."*

and finally...

Taylor Walton is making more noise and showing steady growth across all sectors. We don't expect any sudden change in direction, which is rather comforting in a legal market that's throwing up more surprises than a night out with Derren Brown.

Taylor Wessing

the facts

Location: London, Cambridge
UK ranking by size: 32
Total number of trainees: 48
Seats: 4x6 months
Alternative seats: Brussels, secondments
Extras: Language training

Taylor Wessing has a stonking good reputation in IP and very solid achievements in general commercial spheres.

going deutsch

In July 2002, the firm transformed itself into an Anglo-German operation following the merger of Taylor Joynson Garrett with Wessing, which had offices in Berlin, Düsseldorf, Frankfurt, Hamburg and Munich. As for the firm's focus, well this seems to depend on the advice of PR people at the time you ask. Until recently it has declared an IP and technology focus with the capacity to offer an all-round service to the technology and life sciences clients, be they European or one of many that instruct the firm from the US. These days it sells itself as a commercial firm that happens to have a stack of techy and IP clients. While it's a difference of degree only, it has led to some confusion. As most students probably won't care either way, we're going to follow their lead.

When we asked our sources what impact the merger was having on their lives, in the main they said it was making little or no difference. The most analytical of our sources said: *"There's a change in the approach to marketing the firm – they are pushing the European thing – and there's a feeling that when you qualify you may get to go over. But because Wessing are over in Germany and it wasn't two London rivals muscling in on each other, it's mostly a conceptual change."* Another agreed: *"It's too early to say what the merger will evolve into. The German angle is not that obvious to me on a day-to-day basis, although there are assistants and partners toing and froing."* Basically, bratwurst isn't on the menu in the canteen, German classes are optional and the pronunciation of the German name Wessing (with a 'v' sound) has been changed to a 'w' sound to suit Anglo-Saxon tongues. There were no overseas seats in Germany at the time of writing but these are coming. For now, trainees can go to Brussels.

The Wessing merger came on the back of the opportunist acquisition of the old Andersen Legal Cambridge office and the absorption of a number of partners and assistants from that firm's London office. The Cambridge tech focus (lots of university spin-out companies and hi- and biotech clients in Silicon Fenn) certainly seemed to fit the bill, but mixed fortunes in the TMT sector have meant that Cambridge hasn't transformed the firm to any noticeable degree. Business as usual then? Alas no. Like other technology-facing firms such as Olswang and Bird & Bird, profits have suffered in the last two years, there have been redundancies and four TMT partners have quit. But on the positive side, just before we went to press, we learned that the firm had swiped Osborne Clarke's Frankfurt lawyers.

a bowl of cherries

Before we move onto the training scheme, there's one other item of news. The firm has a new grad recruitment manager whose last job was at Linklaters. Her arrival came not a minute too soon as, frankly, we'd got the impression that the lunatics had taken over the asylum, both before and during a period of caretaker managers. The task at hand is to impose a system on partners who've effectively had carte blanche to cherry pick the trainees they wanted, even to the extent that some were asking for trainees of a particular gender. Trainees, meanwhile, assumed it was their God-given right to select their next supervisor. At times, these two opposing patterns of behaviour caused upset and confusion, and led to an air of competition.

What's now being put in place is a fairer system where nobody throws their weight around or has to play politics. New trainees meet with HR at the outset to discuss a plan for their four seats (it can be revisited later, if necessary). Nominating a department will be OK, nominating a supervisor will not. As for partners picking trainees, there are likely to be only limited circumstances in which this is justifiable – IP partners specialising in patent litigation will be able to call for trainees with a scientific background. Our sources felt that a cultural change was also needed. "*Certain partners view trainees as dogsbodies, hardly speaking to them and not passing much work on. Some are genuinely nice but don't involve the trainee enough.*" Younger partners and senior associates are generally seen to be better, and to be fair there are many supervisors who "*want to be seen to be good and training focused.*"

oversized bath towels

A corporate seat is compulsory and the department has an interesting range of work on offer from smaller venture capital investments in new technology and biotech companies to inward investment work from the US. There's also the usual M&A and restructuring work. Undertaking a finance and projects seat will count as a stint in corporate, if you want it to. One source described this department as "*an amalgam of banking and corporate projects work…a lot of PFI in transport and energy.*" Another said of banking work: "*I didn't think I would like it, but I surprised myself. I attended many meetings and was always introduced to clients. Yes there was dirty work – copying and proofing and setting up bibles – I got a decent amount of that sort of work, but I was always brought along to completions.*" We noted that the firm handles quite a bit of real estate finance too, often acting for European banks. If you're ever lucky enough to stay at Hotel George V in Paris, you can thank the TW team that acted on its most recent refinancing.

A contentious seat is also compulsory and can be taken in one of the five groups in the department: general commercial (contractual, fraud and professional indemnity), construction litigation, personal injury, property litigation and insolvency. An employment or IP seat also ticks the contentious box. One trainee thought litigation was "*pretty good in terms of the work you are given. Obviously there are the trainee jobs of bundling and discovery, and we only have one paralegal at the moment, but plans are afoot to have a senior paralegal running a team of junior ones.*" Depending on which seat you get, other trainee tasks include drafting witness statements and small particulars of claim, sitting behind counsel or a senior lawyer in court, and if you're lucky, even making your own small applications in front of a master.

café mocha frappé

Described as a well-kept secret last year, this year we heard rave reviews about the family seat ("*old money families and new money clients*") and private client (trusts, tax, wills and probate and bags of high-value residential conveyancing). Commercial property also goes down well with those who actively choose it. Depending on which partner you are allocated to, your work might be purely transactional or it might include a large chunk of planning and environmental advice with compulsory purchase cases thrown in for good measure. Expect *"great client contact and a chance to run some of your own files."*

As usual, employment is very popular, partly because of excellent supervisors with a real knack for involving trainees. IP is also popular and seats are plentiful. Soft IP seats cover trademarks, copyright and data protection issues. Hard patent litigation seats are a different kettle of fish and it's easy to see why a scientific background is needed. It may wish to be seen as a general commercial firm these days, but there's no denying the excellence and the importance of TW's IP department. It is currently acting for Amgen and Ortho Biotech in their high-profile litigation regarding the patent for the DNA sequence for genetically engineered erythropoietin. On the soft side, the firm acts for Haagen Dazs.

london eyeful

You know when you watch a movie that's set in London, particularly one that's made by a Hollywood studio, they have a tendency to make all the best landmarks look impossibly close to each other. Well, it's much the same when you look at the river view from TW's reception area: Tower Bridge, Tate Modern, Blackfriars Bridge, the Oxo Tower, the National Theatre, the London Eye. Watching the riverboats and the red double-deckers stream past, you'll know you're in the heart of London alright. The glass and steel office itself is just as impressive; we sensed you'd want to wear your smartest suits to feel like you fit in. Perhaps this is why there's no dress-down except on Fridays.

The hours are as expected in a City practice, and no one complained. Formal training sessions also earned favourable comment, and departments put on a thorough induction programme for all new trainees. In truth, there's a lot to shout about here. Yet it's unfortunate that, for the second year in a row, the retention of newly qualifieds is nothing special (this year 15 out of 23 stayed). Some of our sources had a sense that to be a winner at TW, trainees must be motivated and enthusiastic: *"This will stand you in good stead."* While the firm is always keen to recruit trainees with science backgrounds, don't worry if you were one of the kids at school who never saw the white lab coat as a good look. Come with a PhD or even a BSc, however, and you'll feel you're made of gold dust.

The continued popularity of The Witness Box is evidence of a healthy social scene. Every year there's a formal black-tie dinner dance and the trainees still have a social budget, even in these times of belt tightening. Recently there was a school disco at Brodies.

and finally...

Taylor Wessing is a successful and very professional firm with plenty of plans for the future. Like many, it's been bitten on the behind by the economic downturn and the slump in the TMT sector, but these things are temporary.

Teacher Stern Selby

the facts

Location: London
UK ranking by size: 260
Total number of trainees: 9
Seats: usually 4x6 months
Alternative seats: None
Extras: Pro bono – Toynbee Hall Legal Advice Centre

While it is Teacher Stern Selby's ground-breaking education litigation that makes most headlines, a broad range of property work has always been, and remains, the beating heart of this composed West End practice.

not so hard times

Walking down Bedford Row to the period buildings occupied by the firm for the entirety of its 30-year history, you could be forgiven for thinking that you had slipped through an errant wormhole into a Dickensian dimension of London existence. But don't be misled by serene surroundings, for although there is an old-world quality to the TSS ethos, this is a thriving practice, expanding and developing at a self-dictated pace. What's more, the only cheeky urchins you are likely to see will be trainees heading to their homes, which we're willing to bet heavily will be neither workhouses nor cotton mills.

Property is without question the mainstay of the practice and where the big-hitting, seven-zero deals are made. Trainees undertake a six-month seat in this department as well as two other seats in company and commercial and litigation, before usually returning to the department into which they hope to qualify. Trainees stressed: "*Our clients come to us for property then use us for their other needs, so the litigation and commercial work often tends to be property-related.*" Described as a "*nice, gentle*" department, property actually offers a lot of responsibility to trainees. Expect to be "*given your own files, because the nature of the work is often such that trainees can comfortably take on transactions.*" Our sources were kept busy with property management tasks and undertook small sales and purchases, some of them auction transactions. Having pushed aside visions of David 'Day-Glo' Dickinson, we heard there is also plenty of large-scale work to get your teeth into (albeit in a lesser capacity), including multimillion-pound acquisitions of hotels and retail property portfolios.

you should coco

The company and commercial department has had its fair share of big transactions and deals recently, notably advising the AIM-listed owners of Watford FC on a new share offer. You are more likely to work on specific elements of such transactions rather than having your own caseload, but if the trade-off is autonomy, the payback is variety. "*The first couple of months was very transactional; I worked on asset purchases, share purchases and a corporate start-up, but now I'm advising private clients and drafting articles of association and maternity leave policies.*" This is definitely the place to be, if you place importance on "*a lot of face-to-face meetings.*" As one fan enthused: "*It's the most taxing department, you really engage your brain.*"

contentious, moi?

In recent years TSS, and more particularly the "Godfather of education" (*Chambers UK*) Jack Rabinowicz, has taken the field of education litigation by storm, having grown the practice out of the firm's existing medical negligence caseload. Several trainees have taken a seat with JR in the last few years, experiencing negligence claims relating to exclusion, tuition fees and bullying cases, some of which have gone all the way to the House of Lords, including the much-publicised Leah Bradford-Smart case in 2001. If you've already started trembling with excitement, we can confirm that this seat is regularly available.

Landlord and tenant matters make up a large proportion of the litigation department's work, and trainees' experiences reflect this. On top of this, there are also employment matters, the majority of which involve negotiating severance deals for high-flying executives. And now for the killer punch – we've left it until last, largely because the firm plays its cards close on the matter – the department runs a nice line in defamation law, having advised some notable celebrities and footballers. These are cases you would remember, but sadly we're obliged to keep schtum. You might think this explains the popularity of the department, but don't get knock-kneed with anticipation just yet, because the trainees we interviewed admitted they had "*almost no contact with that side of the litigation.*" Indeed, as a timely glass of water in the face, consider this statement: "*I spent my first ten days of litigation doing bundling...I did get quite good with the paginator!*"

we are family

Although one source told us: *"It has grown tremendously in terms of fee earners and work in the last four years,"* our impression was that the *"family-based atmosphere"* is a structural principle. Comments like *"there's a strong work ethic,"* sat easily alongside *"they don't want you working silly hours,"* and together they made even more sense when we learned it's not a case of *"seven hours to be billed a day before you can leave."* Quite simply, *"people have families and lives outside work."*

The four floors of the relatively small office building have just been refurbished to everyone's satisfaction, and despite it being an intimate workspace, trainees don't feel they are sat in their supervisor's pockets. *"You get feedback when you want it,"* and *"it's very easy to gauge and manage your own workload."* This year was our first major encounter with TSS, but we quickly sensed a culture that is permissive and supportive. As one source said: *"They expect you to ask questions as they don't expect you to know all the answers."* Average working hours of 9am-6.30pm promote a healthy work life/home life balance. Weekly office-wide drinks in the boardroom on Friday evenings are a good chance to unwind and catch up with partners, associates and fellow trainees, especially in summer. In winter, we're told, a number of staff and partners head home to observe the Sabbath. There were events for trainees on their arrival, and the firm's Christmas and summer parties were uniformly praised, but beyond that it is *"pretty much left to us as to whether we want to socialise after work. Lots of people have families."* Nevertheless, nights out in Covent Garden and the West End, or even illicit office tea parties, do all add to the training experience. Contraband cupcake, anyone?

The September 2003 retention figure of one from six did provoke some consternation and surprise among trainees, and one of them confirmed that *"most people would have liked to have stayed on at the firm."* Those who do stay are aware that *"you can make partner very early on, maybe only three or four years after qualification, if you're good enough."*

and finally...

It would be too easy to tag Teacher Stern Selby as a typical West End firm and to leave it at that. We found a well-organised outfit with solid connections to a diverse client base, both at home and overseas, especially in Canada, Israel and Eastern Europe. Definitely not just kids' stuff!

Thomas Eggar

the facts

Location: Chichester, Horsham, Worthing, London, Reigate
UK ranking by size: 87
Total number of trainees: 12
Seats: 4x6 months
Alternative seats: None

What on earth have West Sussex and Surrey got to offer a budding lawyer? Thomas Eggar that's what. Acting for commercial concerns and private individuals, the law firm and its sister company, Thesis Asset Management plc, have made very good names for themselves.

the history lesson

It took one trainee ages to talk us through all the various mergers that Thomas Eggar had been through. The nutshell version is that the Eggar bit started in Brighton in 1881 and merged with two other firms in the 1980s. Meanwhile, in a galaxy far, far away called Worthing, there was a merger between two other small firms. By 1989 they'd all got together. Still with us? Great, we're only half way there... In 1986, a London firm dating back to 1746 merged with an even older Reigate practice. Eventually, in 1998 the first merged group collided with the second, resulting in the current happy union. Of course, in firms like this there's a danger of ending up with a really unwieldy name, but thankfully some genius in marketing came up with the simple moniker that we see today.

Private client work accounts for around 50% of TE's business – high compared to other firms of stature in the region. "*They are very keen to maintain the private client side…the firm is half and half private client and commercial.*" The South East is already heavily populated and, if Government plans come to fruition, the region can expect a million new homes – that's a lot of potential new clients. In 2003, TE bucked the national trend by increasing turnover by 18%. Is its strategy beginning to make sense to you?

military campaigns

The training system is run pretty military style by an ex-army chap. One source informed us: "*A couple of months before you start your training contract you get given your whole seat plan.*" Some thought the advantages outweighed the "*lack of flexibility*" and were pleased to avoid the twice-yearly stress of not knowing where they'd be in the coming months. "*It gives you confidence when you start,*" we heard. Trainees are allocated to either the 'southern circuit' of Chichester, Horsham and Worthing or to the 'northern circuit' of London and Reigate. We'd call the latter a straight line, but who are we to quibble over semantics?

Trainees are supposed to undertake the same four seats: private client, litigation, company/commercial and commercial property. As to what's on offer, "*there are comparables on the different circuits,*" although, for our money, Chichester offers most. Trainees are billeted according to where they live…sort of. London residents take the northern circuit and south coasters the southern. Problems arise if you live somewhere in between and you don't get the one that suits you best. Time for a concerted campaign of begging and alliance forging. We also heard that "*being forthright*" has earned some people time in departments that hadn't normally taken trainees.

Although it's hard to get anyone to say outright that there is a head office, the signs points to Chichester. However, training contract applications are handled in London; most of the partners' meetings are held in Horsham and accounting and admin functions are spread across the offices. We'll confess that we had to sit down with a pen and paper and work out who was where and doing what to whom.

the death zone

"*The market is desperate for good private client lawyers,*" one wised-up youngster reported. After discussing the myopia of the City firms that had axed their private client teams, he said: "*Fantastic clients have come to us from across the City.*" And perhaps this explains why the firm has kept so many smaller offices instead of consolidating into one or two larger ones. Clients come from across the region and prefer their lawyers to be close to home. Somewhere like Horsham, for example, is rich in well-paid commuters and out of town there are plenty of wealthy landowners. On the subject of private client work, trainees fall into two and a half camps: those who are fairly neutral; those who embrace it; and those who try to wriggle out of it. Each of the five offices has its own team of specialists and, it seems, several have acquired a cruel nickname: in Worthing we heard them referred to as "*coffin dodgers*" and in Reigate as "*the death zone.*" Harsh!

alive and kicking

Litigation in Worthing is a Liquorice Allsorts experience involving claimant PI, probate disputes, fraud and insolvency, and good old boundary disputes. In most seats you'll do most of your work for just one person, but here trainees are a shared resource. The department is full of "*young go-getters*" and quite female-dominated due to the presence of around 20 litigation assistants working on PI claims. Trainees spoke of plenty of responsibility, including the management of small files and even court appearances.

Company and commercial work for smaller and medium-sized regional businesses is ideal for trainees. We're sure there's many a magic circle trainee who'd give their eye teeth to get the kind of client exposure on offer here. One source said: "*I picked up a chap off the street who wanted to sell his small business and I was able to handle a lot of it, even client meetings*." This is not to say that trainees flounder around on their own, just that under the guidance of their supervisor they can take a key role on some deals. Apparently there are *"a few superstars in corporate."* Neil Hart was one of those awarded 'most favoured supervisor' status by several sources. We're sure he and his partners don't spend too much of their time on chaps who walk in off the street; after all, someone's got to handle the AIM listings and the banks, insurance companies and pharmaceuticals and technology clients. And it's not all domestic deals – through the Bridge Group in the US and AvrioAdvocati in Europe, alliances with foreign firms ensure a modest flow of cross-border work.

Commercial property is an important source of revenue and the department boasts big name clients. Land Registry forms aren't the most entertaining thing on a long Friday afternoon, yet some trainees just click with property, discovering personal achievement and independence in amongst the office leases and assignments. In Horsham, we heard that *"supervision is excellent…a really hands-off approach."*

sticky situations

Most trainees have friends living in the area and so it's not surprising that trainee nights out are infrequent. Lunch is much easier to organise, particularly as the firm sticks them all together in one room once a quarter for trainee meetings. No prizes for guessing that the talk is of salaries, seats and travel expenses. Trainees tell us that the firm listens to them. Indeed, it was hard to contain them when on the subject of the new managing partner, Tony Edwards. What is it with this man? He inspires adulation on a scale not seen since the days of David Cassidy's first UK tour. (Ask your mum). *"He is the future of the firm!"* one trainee declared joyously. A more analytical commentator said: *"He takes notice and he is assertive."*

And so we come to the oddly named 'glue and branding' sessions. Following the Tony Hart method, the Thomas Eggar strategists gave all staff and partners crayons and asked them to draw their ideal view of the firm. The pictures were to be pinned up for all to see *"on the Grand Day Out, when they will tell us their vision for the future."* Sounds intriguing. We love all these *"state-of-the-nation"* presentations, and it's always nice to see trainees involved in them. All four 2003 qualifiers continue at the firm.

and finally…

If you'll be happy living and working in the South East in a firm that has a London office but is not London driven, this is definitely one to consider.

Thring Townsend

the facts

Location: Bath, Swindon, Newbury
UK ranking by size: 139
Total number of trainees: 12
Seats: 4x6 months
Alternative seats: None

Three years on from a merger between Swindon and Newbury firm Thrings & Long and Townsends of Bath and Frome, Thring Townsend is establishing itself as a commercial player in the south of England.

is it somethring i said?

David Brentism No.30: Set out to leave the first vapour trail in the blue-sky scenario.

Trainees complete four six-month seats and no department is compulsory. We found people who'd concentrated only on commercial work and those who'd focused almost exclusively on private client departments. The list of trainees that the firm sent to us also contained a handy breakdown of the departments on offer, and this in turn gave us confirmation of the firm's orientation. Four seats were available in commercial litigation; two in company/commercial; two in commercial property; and one each in employment, wealth strategy (private client for rich folk), conveyancing, family and PI. Our sources stressed that the system was *"not super-organised but flexible"* – exactly what trainees expect, and want, from firms of this size. Based either in Swindon or Bath, most do at least one seat at the other office and may also be asked to work in Newbury. Nearly all trainees live in or near to Swindon, so the firm pays the train fare for the half-hour journey to Bath or a petrol allowance.

Perhaps honouring S Club, one trainee gave us a 'reach for the stars' analysis of Thrings' activities of late. Last year we reported that all its engines had been switched on. This year you'll need to have fastened your seatbelt because the firm is taxiing down the runway of change. *"After a long period of biding their time and seeing how things integrated, now they want to cut back on certain areas."* To clarify: *"It is styling itself as a commercial practice and some of the less commercial departments are shrinking. Probate and parts of family and residential conveyancing have shrunk."*

For some, this has meant turbulence, particularly in Swindon, which is at the forefront of the shift into more commercial work. When a law firm implements a new strategy, it often loses staff. For example, *"residential conveyancing in Swindon used to have about 20 people and now there are two of them. They've moved that work over to Bath."* This can have a dampening impact on morale, and we did sense exactly this. But – and it's a big but – these changes make perfect sense for a firm intent on the big time. In September 2003. two of the four qualifiers stayed on.

thrings that make you go hmmm

David Brentism No.13: Accept that some days you are the pigeon, and some days you are the statue.

"Bath and Swindon are supposed to mirror each other in terms of departments, but some are bigger, like PI in Swindon and property in Bath." PI in Swindon has a reputation for serious head and spinal injuries, and we saw reports of a successful case concerning the asbestos-related death of a former British Rail employee. Property is big in Bath and Newbury. *"Commercial property is one of the, if not the, largest department in the firm. It earns the highest fees,"* thought one source. Commercial litigation and coco have joined forces to create a super team to service the growing client base of regional businesses and nationals/multinationals with offices nearby. *"A huge telecoms company"* was frequently mentioned, alongside more run-of-the-mill corporates. *"Our corporate deals might be anything from a few hundred thousand pounds to several million,"* one trainee revealed. And on the other side of matters? *"Most of the other solicitors are regional practices – the Osborne Clarkes and Bevan Ashfords – smaller firms and occasionally some of the big boys, including the magic circle."*

The Swindon office (and some of the Bath office) is open plan, with trainees sitting next to or within range of their supervisors. It's totally dependent on the department as to whether you work for one supervisor or are more of a team resource and, similarly, whether your working day is a standard 9am to 5.30pm or unfolds into the evening. However, one thing all our sources agreed on was the high level of responsibility available to trainees. Small claims matters (less than £5,000) enable you to have almost exclusive conduct of cases, or you'll be assigned tasks on higher-value claims or transactions. There will be some donkey work as preparing bundles for trial and photocopying has to be done by someone. *"In Swindon there's a good photocopying service but they don't have that in Bath. It is a down point* [in some seats] *and secretaries are quite busy."* But this sort of thing can be raised at appraisals with the head of HR and the training partner, and also at monthly group meetings. Those keen on getting involved with clients and new business will be pleased to hear that *"as a trainee you are encouraged to do your own marketing."* Such as? *"Going off to Business Link...seminars and free initial advice to small businesses."*

wild thrings

David Brentism No.33: Is your work done? Are all pigs fed, watered and ready to fly?

Bath and Swindon have cultural differences. *"The Bath lot are a lot more sociable. The conveyancing depart-*

ment in Bath are all very young and obviously they want to go out and have a laugh. In Swindon, staff are older and many of them have young families." To illustrate this phenomenon: *"The social committee in Swindon was organising a trip to Alton Towers next weekend, but it has been cancelled due to lack of interest."* While over in Bath: *"There's a yearly 'Pride of Bath' boat trip* [it's the name of a boat, not a city-wide gay carnival], *which is popular and everybody goes out on a Friday. The vouchers for drinks at the Green Park Brasserie are definitely an incentive to get people over there."*

The social behaviour of staff in each office is in keeping with the feel of each town. Bath is a gorgeous Georgian affair, designed and built for pleasure seekers. It's just as smart as it ever was and the price of property reflects that. Swindon is an entirely different collection of roundabouts and business parks. The butt of many a cruel joke, one's arrival in the land of Brunel and his railways is likely to be stamped in the memory along with the words: *"God, there's nothing here!"* Yet, in time, it's easy to see what the place has to offer – cheaper accommodation, easy access to motorways for weekend getaways and a town centre that's being massively redeveloped. Thrings has made a conscious decision to create a particular image for its Swindon office. After years in cramped premises in the Old Town, it selected a location away from the centre, leased a state-of-the-art building, complete with intelligent brickwork that obviates the need for AC and a tall palm tree-type centrepiece growing up through the main atrium. An in-house restaurant means staff don't have to trudge down the dual carriageway for a sandwich, although on Thursdays they can take a free bus into town to do their shopping or go to the pub during an extended 75-minute lunch break.

Before summing up, we'd just like to give a nod of respect to a coco team that's managed to resist the usual self-importance of corporate lawyers. Inspired by their surnames, all the lawyers go by the first names of female celebrities. You jokers…next you'll be setting staplers in jelly.

and finally...

In summing up the firm and its direction, one trainee put it like this: *"Generally we'll do anything, but we don't encourage the lower-value end of the market."* Such succinct matter-of-factness is refreshing, and you'll see plenty more of it on the firm's website, so you know what to do next…

TLT Solicitors

the facts

Location: Bristol
UK ranking by size: 107
Total number of trainees: 15
Seats: 4x6 months
Alternative seats: None

It's been three years since the merger of Trumps and Lawrence Tucketts in Bristol. The resultant firm, TLT Solicitors, worked hard to establish itself as *"Bristol's third firm."* But do we sense that it's no longer satisfied with the bronze gong? Will it now try to muscle in on Bristol's big boys' territory?

massive attack

Trainees talked to us about how the firm is *"closing the gap."* But what evidence is there? Well, it is expanding its banking, construction, retail, leisure and employment practices and, to this end, it recently appointed five new partners in its commercial services group, taking the total partner count to 37. We at the *Student Guide* were intrigued, so we decided to pester the firm's *"young, energetic"* managing partner, David…er…Pester. And what a lovely chap he is! *"Sixty per cent of our clients are from outside the region,"* he told us. *"When we merged, we had two FTSE 100 clients and now we have 11."* We also learned that the firm's winning strategy rests, in part, on competitive pricing.

It's important to set TLT's goals in their proper context. The two firms it is trying to make ground on (Burges Salmon and Osborne Clarke) are heavyweights that have, to an extent, turned their back on regional businesses in the quest to work for City, national and international clients. This has allowed room for another strong commercial outfit in Bristol, one that is happy to try and clean up on all the best commercial work in the region. The questions now are to what extent has this been achieved by TLT and to what extent does it want more? Actually, if you get an interview with the firm, these would be jolly good questions to ask.

Perhaps it's because TLT is still quite new that trainees feel instrumental in its future. Each team has an 'away day', attended by everyone from support staff to partners. In the morning, partners discuss figures and business plans and then give the others the opportunity to share their ideas. "*Everyone's point of view is valued.*" Trainees value this "*consultative*" management style and they have a "*fair idea of why decisions are made and of the firm's aims for the future.*"

the banking quarter

The firm has traditionally been "*reasonably flexible*" about trainee seats, but recently there has been some rather undignified musical chairs-style "*clambering*" for the popular ones. Employment remains the most sought-after place to plonk your derrière. Luckily, the team is expanding, and is said by rivals to be strengthening its position in the market. Trainees can take the lead from in-house advocates who represent regional and national employers on discrimination claims and trade union disputes. Prove your worth and you'll be running your own files, conducting research, liaising with clients and attending tribunals.

Although not fought over by trainees, banking and lender services is an expanding department, recently winning an appointment to Barclays' corporate recovery panel. Banking clients are a core part of TLT's business, accounting for some 25% of its revenue. The "*slower pace*" and largely private client base in the tax and probate department doesn't appeal to everyone, either. This is probably the last year that we will interview trainees who had applied to either of the legacy firms. We suspect that in the future TLT recruits will be even more commercially oriented in their preferences. That said, the firm has one of the best family law practices in the South West and it should always retain appeal for those trainees seeking high-value matrimonial experience.

Seats are also available in commercial property and planning, where you'll be carrying out searches, preparing pre-contract inquiries and piecing together chains of title stretching back through the centuries. If that sounds a bit too much like titchy residential conveyancing work then you should note that TLT acts for some very big property clients. For example, First Choice holidays and the Punch pub chain instruct the firm for real estate management work.

Over in corporate, the team advised the Ethical Property Company on its £4.2 million public share issue. Other clients include Blackwell's the academic booksellers, Wahl Clipper Corporation (bet they got a buzz out of that), Bristol Rovers and The World Professional Billiards and Snooker Association (no balls jokes, please).

trump towers

Until recently, TLT remained split between its Bush House and Redcliff Street offices, but this post-merger transition period in housing is coming to an end. Everyone has now been united under one roof in the refurbished and "*rather palatial*" waterfront offices on Redcliff Street. Ditching the 'two houses' approach was perhaps the final act of unification. One trainee told us: "*I wouldn't be able to tell you which firm someone came from, we're all TLT now.*" The building boasts the best views in Bristol, and the modern glass reception area features sexy new plasma screens. "*I have no idea what they're for,*" one perplexed trainee told us, "*but apparently they show Sky.*" There is also an enormous staff area, complete with sofas and kitchen. If TLT trainees once felt "*less grand*" than their peers at bigger Bristol rival firms, they now feel "*quite fancy*" when they walk into work in the mornings. The offices are open plan so you won't be far from support if you need it. And the best part is that, as a trainee, there'll be no tapping timidly on doors waiting for partners to deign to speak to you. You can bowl right over and ambush them at their workstations.

Monthly get-togethers in one of the conference rooms see trainees nibbling on *"posh sandwiches"* and asking questions of the training partner and the HR mob. After this, the partner departs, giving trainees *"a chance to moan about the firm…if we want to."* Moan? Surely not when there's Sky TV and partners who are described as *"young, progressive and optimistic."*

the bristol sound

The TLT trainees are a varied bunch, ranging from fresh-faced law graduates to a former Sainsbury's manager. This year we noted recruits came in all ages from their early twenties right up to a 40-year-old with children. What they share is a desire for a commercial legal training and good levels of support. We noted a general disdain for the stress and grime of London, but more importantly we noted a passion for Bristol and a commitment to the South West. While we could find no overt policy of recruiting those with a local connection, as with any Bristol firm, we recommend that you understand fully the reasons why you want to start (and continue) your career in this city. In 2003, two of the three qualifying trainees stayed with the firm.

The firm has a social committee to arrange monthly do's, which are usually spectacular affairs. Past events have included trips to Alton Towers and Paris, although not on the same weekend, of course. A recent karaoke night was a hit, with everyone from partners down involved. *"There were some fairly sheepish people on the Monday,"* we heard. Oh and don't we know that feeling…our editor loves a good warble, but soul diva she ain't. Our tip: it's best to stick with something where the original artist sounded rubbish to begin with…Vanilla Ice or Gina G, for example. Those who don't wish to humiliate themselves in front of colleagues can look forward to evenings in one of the city's many trendy bars – the partners will even run a tab from time to time. Alas, the move to a single office spelled tragedy for two public houses. The Shakespeare and The Shakespear (if you're confused, just dig out a couple of older editions of this book) have suffered *"something of a fall from grace"* as trainees and lawyers have been seduced by fashionable new offerings on the waterfront. As to which of these will become the main watering hole is still a hot topic at TLT. We, however, shall mourn the sad decline in appreciation for the bard.

and finally…

TLT is an optimistic and forward-moving firm. Increased profitability and the appointment of five new partners at a time of general market uncertainty and heavy outlay on swanky new premises are positive signs indeed. As one trainee told us: *"It feels good to know you're at a firm that's going places."* As a trainee, you won't be driving this fast-moving vehicle; however, you're almost certain to be helping out with directions.

TMK Solicitors

the facts

Location: Southend, Basildon, Chelmsford
UK ranking by size: 484
Total number of trainees: 9
Seats: 1x12 and 3x4 months
Alternative seats: None

Just a stone's throw from Southend's waterfront you'll find people's champion TMK. Already the largest crime firm in Essex, it has also successfully grown its civil and family work.

more than fancy lights

Southend is commonly defined by its Golden Mile, but the seafront with its bright lights and amusements is not the only thing that glistens – if medals were awarded to law firms then TMK would be the local Steve Redgrave. As we noted last year, in this part of the world, the letters T, M and K are synonymous with the word solicitor. *"We pride ourselves on good relationships with the court and having high levels of professionalism."* This reputation has been built on a strong foundation in criminal law, and now extends to matrimonial and children's law services, personal injury, civil litigation, employment, housing, mental health and immigration.

top marks

A particular sort of trainee is attracted to this firm. Somewhat surprisingly, local ties are not essential; however, *"there is a lot of similarity between us in terms of single-mindedness."* We repeatedly heard the words *"hard-working," "motivated"* and *"enthusiastic"* during our research interviews, and our sources had a clear idea from the outset what kind of firm appealed to them... *"On the interview day they are pretty honest about how you are expected to perform, and I left saying 'That's the firm I want'."* As well as being *"businesslike,"* these trainees can cope with whatever is thrown at them. Which includes demanding, and sometimes unpredictable, clients: *"It's about being able to make contact with people who have very strong emotions; emotions which sometimes get in the way of being objective."*

Trainees typically spend the first year in one department and the remainder in the other parts of the firm that pique their interest. They also spend an awful lot of time at court, particularly when in the criminal department. *"There's loads of advocacy...It's not the sort of firm where you can spend your training contract photocopying and keeping your head down – they expect you in court."* Unless you're up for it, this can be a strain; as one source said: *"You are down the court as much as a qualified solicitor, so if you have a lacklustre attitude, or your appearances aren't professional, it is noticed. It's a small town and you can very soon get a reputation for not being keen or professional."*

Don't panic – you'll have plenty of coaching. One of the partners, John Twitchen, knows a thing or two about courtroom conduct. Not only did he put the T in TMK, but he also sits as a district judge. *"He's very good at schooling you on how to prepare, and that comes to the fore, not only in court, but also on the PSC when you realise you are streets ahead of trainees at the large firms in London."* Another source confirmed (with more than a hint of a smirk): *"When we go to the College of Law for the PSC, our advocacy marks are usually among the highest."* Trainees who want to specialise in crime are advised to complete the Police Accreditation Scheme, and will quickly become familiar with trips to the station to interview clients. Real clients and lots of them: *"On an average Thursday at the magistrates' court you will probably speak to a dozen clients and take their instructions. It's the only way to learn."*

This level of client exposure is echoed in the other main departments. Working with the childcare team, trainees see *"a lot of care proceedings...going along with the principal to court or to meetings to discuss how the children are doing in placements. It's very interesting."* On the civil side the sentiment was repeated. *"You get to start a lot of cases; I've had quite a lot of experience on that. I've seen a few hearings, trials and an inquest."*

full diary

The TMK training extends far beyond advocacy. One of our informants explained: *"We have training diaries to fill out every week, and it's not like writing out 'I went to the toilet, scratched my back' that sort of thing – we bullet-point names of files we have worked on and the type of work we have done."* Reporting and monitoring is regular. Every two weeks in the first year, trainees meet with their supervisor and hand in a written assignment or bring along a current file for discussion. This becomes a monthly occurrence in the second year. But it doesn't stop there. In readiness for weekly departmental meetings, you'll sometimes have presentations to prepare.

And TMK has its own version of the SATs. After each seat there are tests in spelling (yes, you did just read that), mental arithmetic and current affairs. The spelling and maths are clearly useful because, often without secretarial support, trainees type their own letters to clients. *"In fairness they are doing an adminis-*

trative overhaul, introducing lots more pro formas and standard letters to give a certain uniformity and to guarantee clients the same style, whichever fee earner is dealing with it." Does all this training ever get too much? *"Yes, you sometimes think 'Oh bloody hell, I have so much on, I could do without this…'"*

shifting with the tide

Presently, a large slice of TMK's work is publicly funded, but *"they are looking to move the family department more towards privately funded work."* The free advice line that ran last year has stopped, as have free 30-minute consultations. An interviewee said: *"They are being a lot more selective and realistic as to what we can actually deal with."* Wait a minute, isn't the firm known for its legal aid work? According to one source: *"The firm is always looking for new ways to move on and stay with the times, without wishing to leave behind any of the clients we have."*

This mood shift is not entirely new. Offices at Basildon (*"in a business suite and quite plain"*) and Chelmsford (*"small and really quaint inside"*) already provide scope for expansion, and the Southend HQ was fully refurbished in 2002. From something that resembled a large family home, *"it looks lovely now with wood flooring and a pinkish 'candyfloss' wash on the walls."* Moreover, we heard that the three main departments, which previously seemed to operate in their own spheres, are slowly finding the same focus. *"They are coming into line a lot more in regard to how they deal with cases,"* said a source, *"and there is a more corporate attitude in how the firm portrays itself."*

TMK made up five new partners this year, but growth at the senior end was not reflected at the junior end in 2003, where only two of the five qualifiers stayed on. Nevertheless, those who spoke to us before they left seemed confident about their prospects. As one told us: *"Given the experience I have, recruitment agencies are happy to consider me for one-year-PQE jobs."*

The office closes its doors at 5.15pm and trainees reported finishing by sixish. On a Friday you need look no further than the Inane Café, where it's not uncommon for partners to get their credit cards out. *"The firm recognises that some people are from outside the area and is quite keen on firm events and organising nights out."* Last summer there was a fun run, rounders games, a quiz and a trip to France with *"lots of beer and wine on the way back."* Bien sur.

and finally…

If you're searching for an established, energetic 'people's firm' with a training scheme that brings new meaning to the word thorough, TMK is just the job.

Travers Smith Braithwaite

the facts

Location: London
UK ranking by size: 57
Total number of trainees: 42
Seats: 4x6 months
Alternative seats: Paris
Extras: Pro bono – ICSL Advice Centre, Caribbean death row appeals, Paddington Law Centre, language training

Travers Smith Braithwaite is a corporate-driven firm with a subtlety and understatement rarely encountered in the City. It is regularly engaged in high-profile transactions, frequently winning work that larger rivals would be proud to handle.

birds of a feather

Boasting one of the highest staff retention rates in the City, Travers is *"like being in a small class in a very good school."* Like a Hermès knit, it is very tight and exclusive. It has no plans to expand through merger or go on a hiring spree; instead its strategy is *"to grow organically by hand-picking the people we want."* Travers' website proclaims: "Peacocks need not apply." Certainly, it's a quiet and self-assured firm, so we felt it unusually immodest of one trainee when they announced: *"We don't have to make a lot of noise to prove we're really good. Everyone is of an exceptionally high level."*

The firm runs a four-seat training scheme with compulsory stints in corporate, property and something contentious. Interestingly, trainees always sit with a partner and change offices every three months. The idea is to give you access to a broader range of work and to ensure you see plenty of different working styles. Property is a *"good place to start trainee life;"* our sources were pleased to report that, even in the first week, they had a good deal of client contact. *"You feel valued from the first moment,"* said one, as you'll be managing your own files, speaking to clients and drafting documents. *"Within three months, you feel like a lawyer."* In this firm as in every other, employment is the sexy department offering loads of client contact and the chance to undertake a mixture of contentious and non-contentious work for employer clients. Six months in this seat can satisfy the Law Society's contentious requirement, saving trainees from having to visit the litigation department, if they really don't want to. It's a smaller group in which trainees *"feel like part of a family."* That old adage 'the family that plays together stays together' holds true for this department: social outings are a regular feature.

In commercial litigation, you'll be researching, attending conferences with counsel and clients, drafting the occasional letter, filing documents in court, and *"of course, there's always bundling to be done."* Few trainees come to Travers for its litigation prowess, but those who were keen to make a stop there had enjoyed the buzz of working on important matters that sometimes made it into the press. Travers is a bit hush hush about many of its cases but we were able to gather that it does a lot of work for KPMG, and has handled claims made by a number of local authorities against pension fund managers for failing to manage the funds with proper care and skill. It has also been acting for a bank on Enron-related issues and has continued representing the Mirror Group Pension Trustees in Maxwell-related litigation

private party

At the moment, in the firm's mainstay corporate department, private equity work is at the centre of the practice. Our sources confirmed that in addition to the lengthy chores involved in due diligence and the dreaded stints of managing data rooms, they were also allowed to assist in the negotiation of key documents and were kept in the loop on the business side of transactions. Despite a deflated market, the corporate department had a reasonably busy year in 2002, being involved in some 85 completed transactions with an aggregate value of £15.2 billion. It was also fully engaged with the task of refinancing NTL for £12.7 billion.

We've said it before, and we'll say it again, tax is the new black. As one trainee explained: *"If you're keen on academic, black letter law, it's a good area to get your head around."* Trainees enjoy a good combination of *"getting stuck in on deals and restructurings on the one hand, and really getting to know the law on the other."* And happily *"it has all the sexy and fun advantages of a corporate department with the lifestyle benefits of something nerdy."* Pensions is another academic group, in which trainees relish *"having to think things through."* The stimulating nature of the work lends itself to a *"quieter culture in the department"* – a perfect antidote to more energetic departments such as corporate.

You should be aware that while it's great at home, Travers only offers one overseas seat in Paris. Whether it's the chicken or the egg that comes first, we're not sure, but this firm tends to attract the quintessentially English trainee who is comfortable in the City and has no head for world domination.

breeders

One look at the firm's graduate recruitment website, and you'll think you've entered not a law firm but a horse stud. Travers Smith Braithwaite is, in its own words, "a breeding ground for some of the best lawyers in the City." And they mean it. The firm is renowned for being rather…how shall we put it…insular when it comes to mating. *"We're naturally drawn to each other,"* one trainee told us, so don't be surprised if you find yourself drafting commercial property leases to the peal of wedding bells. The firm is keen to preserve the integrity of both the Travers culture and its gene pool, and strives to avoid *"a dilution of both our culture and the quality of our service."*

Travers trainees are by and large a young group. Mostly straight out of university, some boasting the occasional gap year, there aren't too many mature trainees here. Our sources acknowledged that the firm recruits from a limited number of universities – Oxbridge and top redbricks or London colleges. One told us: *"I wouldn't look further than Oxbridge or redbricks for the brightest people. Bright people tend to go to good universities."* Thankfully, this firm has stuck with the traditional letter and CV application system, and its selection process – a straightforward interview – was also well received by trainees.

Whether it's their youth or a healthy respect for tradition, the Travers set are an enthusiastic and uncomplaining lot. Said one trainee: *"People here tend to get on with it. There aren't too many grumbles about management or the work."* With a steady stream of seminars and lectures to keep you on point and regular appraisals from supervisors, their training needs are certainly well catered for. Unfortunately, this year the firm was not able to boast its usual high retention rate: 12 out of the 18 qualifiers stayed in September 2003.

healthy living

The firm's appetites are well catered for by the staff restaurant, and its wholesome image is reflected in a commitment to sporting prowess. It plays all the usual team games like rugby sevens, hockey and cricket, and there's even a ladies' football team. On top of that there are a few golfers, the usual gaggle of softball players (although we all know that softball games are a poor excuse for lounging around in a park with a beer or two after work) and every year a group head off to Paris to run a half marathon. Not surprisingly, the Travers sporting kit is *"fairly conservative,"* and the best thing is it gets washed every week. As they have since the dawn of time, Travers' trainees can be found at the nearby Bishop's Finger on a Friday night. And if they're feeling particularly daring, they venture to the bars of Clerkenwell afterwards.

and finally...

Travers Smith Braithwaite wants to be seen as a premium brand and an alternative to the law factories. Thus far, it's succeeding. With less than 25 trainees recruited annually, it's not fibbing when it says "We don't want many, we just want the best." If you're of the Travers mould, this firm can offer a collegiate and very fulfilling work environment.

Trowers & Hamlins

the facts

Location: London, Manchester, Exeter
UK ranking by size: 61
Total number of trainees: 28
Seats: 4x6 months
Alternative seats: Overseas seats
Extras: Pro bono – Toynbee Hall Legal Advice Centre

Trowers & Hamlins is a mid-sized London firm that excels at social housing and public sector work. It is also the dominant international law firm in the Middle East, having been there since the 1970s. Yet, amazingly, the vast majority of trainees are attracted not by the firm's indubitable success in these areas, but purely and simply by its size and location.

projecting into the future

Your four six-month seats will *"inevitably"* include a property seat. *"You have to do litigation because of the Law Society and, Trowers being Trowers, you will do property."* If it's corporate-corporate-corporate and *FT* headlines you are after, then go instead to one of the megafirms in the heart of the City. There are few guarantees with any training contract, but one thing we can promise is that you'll never be set adrift without access to partners, core involvement in their work and even a small spot in the limelight. That's the beauty of a firm where the trainee intake is the size of a rugby team (although not in the neck department, of course). This place is a refuge for those wanting to avoid the magic circle and firms of that ilk. As one trainee said: *"I wasn't interested in the large firms. I chose Trowers because it was medium sized but not stagnating."*

In the last couple of years there's been a push from the firm's corporate and construction and projects departments. New partners have been hired and there's a definite buzz about the place. One name mentioned over and over again by trainees was that of construction head David Mosey, and he's probably a good person to illustrate how Trowers goes about its business. Not so long ago our man Mosey pioneered a new 'partnering contract' that is now widely used in housing and other projects by Government, both central and local. The firm has handled well over £5 billion worth of this kind of business. One deal involved the transfer of 23,000 homes from a local authority to an Arm's Length Management Organisation (ALMO) at a cost of £520 million. Then, to follow on from the initial refurbishment of these properties, there's a ten-year maintenance contract worth another £100 million. If you thought social housing was small-beer landlord and tenant disputes then think again. This firm tosses around the millions like it's monopoly money.

under the flag

However, all of this flag-waving work poses a problem for the firm. The shadow cast by the housing-related work is huge. Some of the trainees we spoke to spent much of the interview reinforcing the idea that the housing side of the practice was just that – only one side. With regard to graduate recruitment material, one said: *"The marketing is based around the public sector and social housing, but the corporate side of it is a very good training as well."* That trainee also told us that, given the chance to be managing partner: *"I would address the external misconception of this firm as a cuddly housing firm."* Another acknowledged the importance of the social housing work, but said: *"There's a tendency to imagine those clients as cardigan-wearing liberals, yet these are commercial people. They have limited funds and they are doing the best they can with those funds."* In reality, acting for this type of client is no different to acting for a large company except there are additional regulatory, charitable and constitutional angles to take into account.

What kind of things might a trainee do for an RSL (Registered Social Landlord)? Our sources helped us out: *"In housing I was involved in charging* [mortgaging] *exercises…moving great swathes of properties from one funder to another."* As well as preparing reports on title for properties, this sometimes involves *"deeds scheduling and getting dusty."* But it's not all gargantuan funding projects and development schemes. Trainees also talked about having near full control of files, input into client meetings and court appearances, perhaps on things like repossession cases.

So where does the truth lie? How much of the firm's work is for the housing and public sectors and how much is for the private sector? Perhaps the best we can do is to set out a list of the trainee seats available as at March-September 2003. So here it is. Corporate and commercial seats: 3. Employment: 1. Gulf and international seats: 6. Litigation, including property litigation: 4. Housing projects: 4. Projects and construction (for both private and public sector plus housing clients): 2. Public sector team: 2. Commercial property: 3. Private client: 1.

gulf veterans

The most unique thing about Trowers & Hamlins is its dominant presence in the Middle East. Abu Dhabi is a small, skyscrapered island oozing oil wealth and tolerant to Western culture. Dubai, on the UAE's coast is less developed yet is growing noticeably. Its commercial activities are broader and it is home to a more mixed population of Arabs, westerners and migrant workers from Asia. Further north in the Persian Gulf, Bahrain is a larger island floating on oil and banking revenues. And then bordering UAE is Oman, whose capital, Muscat, offers a calmer and culturally richer experience. Each of these cities welcomes trainees on six-month placements and up to half of each intake take up the offer. Our sources who'd been out to the Gulf all spoke enthusiastically about the responsibility they'd shouldered and the lifestyle they'd enjoyed during their six months abroad. When asked if the posting had benefited them professionally, one trainee said: *"Yes, a huge amount! I'd barely stuck my toes in the water in London and I was off on a plane. I really noticed the benefits when I came back."* It was exactly as a colleague had predicted when they'd said: *"Good Lord, you are going to come back as a real lawyer!"*

If you are an Arabophile then this is undoubtedly your firm. Each year, at least one newly qualified lawyer chooses to spend a few years in one of the overseas offices, and the firm seems delighted to send them there. Trowers also has an office in Cairo and recently embarked on a new joint venture with a local firm in Qatar. Neither office takes trainees. Closer to home, Trowers has branches in Exeter and Manchester. A London trainee could take a property or a litigation seat up north.

dramatically different?

Trowers is not your usual City experience. Instead it prefers to hover on the fringe and do it's own thing. Its pink triangular building at Sceptre Court overlooks the Tower of London from two sides and an unfortunate, grey concrete building and a car park from the third. The decor is described as *"rhubarb-coloured on the first and second floors,"* with *"artwork that looks like a school kid has done it."* (Harsh!) And then, in a total turnaround, the sixth floor *"looks like a Clinique counter; all frosted glass and Clinique green."* Once every quarter it is the venue for *"billing drinks,"* which, if you were wondering, is when the firm pops a few corks to celebrate the latest wave of invoices that have left the building.

Last year trainees all mentioned Bar 38 as the favoured watering hole, however, this year it was simply described as *"nasty."* The Assembly got most votes from this year's fickle mob, although there are also a couple of other bars on The Minories that get a look in. Perhaps confused as to where they were, one trainee told us: *"Tower Hill has been a bit of a desert until recently,"* and yet another remarked: *"It's not out on a limb exactly, but I wouldn't like to go any further east."*

red menace

There's always a catch isn't there? No matter how positive our sources were about the firm and their training, we are saddened to have to report a serious mistake on the part of management. The staff cafeteria, 'Treats', plays Heart FM to jolly people along. But as one despairing trainee explained: *"The last thing you need is Mick Hucknall when you are trying to eat your sandwiches."* A treat? We think not.

"There's no one-up-manship between trainees," said one source, who then went on to judge the ideal applicant as *"someone who is balanced and reasonable."* For what it's worth, the *Student Guide* team concurs. We encountered bright, well-adjusted, adaptable characters for whom the motivations and shortcomings of their magic circle peers – money, kudos, and a touch of arrogance – don't blip their radar. Call it a reluctance to head for the big time, the big hours and the big money or call it a smart move…whatever you call it, all our trainees were eager to stay at the firm post-qualification and 11 of the 14 qualifiers did manage just that in September 2003.

and finally...

It's simple really: if Trowers' areas of excellence interest you then you absolutely must make this your number one target, and if you're in the market for a mid-sized commercial employer in the City add it to your shortlist.

Veale Wasbrough

the facts

Location: Bristol
UK ranking by size: 90
Total number of trainees: 13
Seats: 4x6 months
Alternative seats: None
Extras: Pro bono – Bristol Law Centre, Young Enterprise

Chances are when you see the letters VW you'll think of something practical, reliable, well engineered, fun and crossing classes in an 'everyman' kind of way. Even if you were thinking of the cars, these adjectives are equally applicable to Bristol-based Veale Wasbrough. From its core commercial practice through to the niche education practice, the firm services a wide range of clients from mid-sized businesses to large not-for-profit and public sector organisations.

vw - new model unveiled

The trainees at VW were eager to tell us how much their firm has changed of late. It's now a sleeker machine – lawyers have shuffled themselves around, forming more logical groups with closer ties, and VW is making a concerted effort to raise its profile. Trainees also told us the firm has been more aggressive with its tenders for work recently, although *"is not an aggressive firm and we don't portray ourselves that way."*

A slim majority of VW's activities are in the non-contentious commercial field, with the rest an even split between contentious commercial work and personal legal services. Company/commercial, property, education, construction, employment, commercial litigation, technology, PI and estates & tax planning could all feature in the course of your training contract. Among the commercial and institutional clients you could encounter on your two-year journey are Esso, British Nuclear Fuels and several others in the power generation and supply sector, a million and one local authorities, the Treasury Solicitor, MoD, Police Federation, PwC and Allied Irish Bank.

comfortable seating

None of the four seats which trainees complete are strictly compulsory, but *"they like you to do property as it is our biggest department."* One trainee said: *"They encourage a property seat and a coco seat, and they are keen on you doing a PI seat as it is contentious."* However, another's experience was *"exactly as I would have wanted it."* Their advice is: *"If you make your preference known early enough you will probably get it."*

At the moment, *"everybody wants to do employment, and the coco seats are quite popular because that's where the money is."* Not only that, but *"the coco team is quite into the European stuff"* and *"there is an international team trying to move things on."* We discovered that in the last two years the team has increased its turnover by nearly 75% and hired the former heads of corporate from Bristol rival Clarke Willmott & Clark and Swindon/Bath firm Thring Townsend.

driving school

Last year we reported that *"nobody wants to do PI,"* but there's been something of a turnaround in the seat's appeal. As one source put it: *"In any commercial firm it is a little looked down on, but I think it is perhaps the best training you can get."* In PI, a large volume of work comes from a union client, the TGWU. Here, *"you run your own files from start to finish and get to know them really well,"* enthused one trainee. If it's client contact and court appearances you want, this is definitely the seat to go for.

One satisfied customer said of commercial litigation: *"It's the best seat, with fantastic supervision...I got to meet lots of clients, did lots of debt enforcement work from the very beginning; initial applications right through to default judgments."* Another area that is in demand is education. Although it doesn't provide a regular seat, *"it's a really good department. Robert Boyd, the partner who heads it, is at the top of his field. It's a real niche market and we are very good at it."* Indeed you are – *Chambers UK* ranks VW top in the South and South West. The team boasts schools like Rugby and Millfield among the 700 institutions on its books.

soft suspension

Let's get back to the TGWU for a moment. The firm provides a free legal advice line to the union's members, and this in turn provides excellent opportunities for trainees to cut their teeth on some pretty diverse work. *"A lot of trainees get involved in the scheme; you could be asked to advise on anything, absolutely anything. You get to meet the client, interview them, and then it's a good opportunity to go and meet the partners around the firm as you'll go to them for advice."*

VW trainees were also keen to talk to us about a number of local pro bono and charitable activities with which they were involved, and we reckon this soft-hearted side to the firm perfectly reflects the type of people it attracts. A big fat salary is not top of the list for folk at VW – the work on offer and the life they can lead in Bristol is more important to them. Ah, Bristol! You've got to love the place. Throughout our interviews we heard horns, mad people shouting and diesel engines at our end of the line, but wheeling seagulls at theirs. While we get blackened sinuses and shirt cuffs, the good lawyers of Bristol have a very good reason not to wear black.

good handling, nice feedback

While you might expect all this talk of responsibility to cause some trainees to apply the brakes, our sources were happy to go full throttle, safe in the knowledge that they're well protected by close supervision. *"It is a supportive environment and you don't feel that you've been left on your own to get on with things,"* said one. But no vehicle is maintenance free, and at VW we did hear the odd knocking sound from under the bonnet. *"Supervisors sometimes don't ask 'Have you got enough to do?' and it can be difficult to go around the department scrounging."* Judging by previous performance, we're confident the VW 'mechanics' will soon fix the problem – a year back they found a dodgy supervisor and quickly fitted a new one...

Our interviewees had nothing but praise for the way in which they had been steered through the four-seat training pattern. Because of its size, VW is in a position whereby it can be responsive to trainees' needs and demands. As well as end-of-seat reviews, the firm has introduced *"mid-seat reviews attended by your supervisor and the graduate recruitment manager."* Department-specific checklists (*"updated by trainees leaving the seat"*) were introduced and these enable trainees *"to give feedback on supervisors and comment on the work we have and haven't done. It's all very organised."*

local journeys

It seems that quality of work and free time are high on the average trainee wish list. Like many mid-sized regional practices, the firm attracts applicants from the local area: *"It is fantastic to work in a firm where many of the partners are Bristolian too...I talk to people and realise they went to Bristol Uni; you can share stories about common lecturers and stuff."* Another Bristolian concurred: *"We have a lot in common, and it is a lot more tight knit than I imagine it is in the City."* They could have a point. In September 2003, the firm retained three of its five qualifying trainees.

Local bars Evolution and the Pitcher & Piano still attract a fair crowd, as does new fave haunt BRB. Worryingly, however, we heard that romance is getting in the way: *"There is less going on in the week this year – more of the current intake are coupled up."* Thank goodness for the *"three or four partners who are the main instigators of Friday nights and curries."* The firm boasts a range of sports teams including men's and ladies' football and a crew for dragon boat racing. *"We wanted a netball team and they stumped up the cash."* Top that with membership in the Bristol TSG (one of VW's trainees recently organised the annual ball) and you have a pretty impressive social itinerary.

and finally...

If you are looking for a souped-up experience in the City, don't apply to Veale Wasbrough as a fallback option. It is designed and built for those with a real passion for Bristol. And for them it has more than enough under the bonnet. Once again, we award the firm a *Student Guide* MOT certificate.

Walker Morris

the facts

Location: Leeds
UK ranking by size: 71
Total number of trainees: 31
Seats: 6x4 months
Alternative Seats: Occasional secondments

Independent. Stalwart. Walker Morris is one of Leeds' 'big six' commercial firms. Yorkshire pride, directness and realism are all found here, alongside clarity, consistency, good lawyering and decent deals.

leeds untied

Most top-rung commercial law offices in Leeds are tied to national firms and managed from elsewhere in the country. Walker Morris, however, famously adheres to a single-site strategy. Independence has served it well, and for some years it has been among the most profitable firms outside London, although this is partly to do with the limited number of equity partners. Even in 2003's tough market it posted an 11% increase in profits. On the 'all together' topic, trainees have plenty to say, and they understand the benefits. One told us: *"Being in a single office makes it quite united. You can communicate with the whole firm just by walking up the stairs,"* while another said: *"It has a unified identity. I have seen or spoken to the majority of people who work here. You don't have to video conference."*

Unlike Terry Venables last season, this Leeds operator manages to hang on to its star players: a high proportion of the partners and assistants have been with the firm, man and boy…and girl. Qualifying trainees have enjoyed good retention rates, even in the last two, tougher years. In September 2003, 11 of the 13 accepted jobs. This tendency to stick with the firm probably comes from the fact that most lawyers have made a lifestyle decision to build their career in Leeds and, once through the door, they see no reason to trade firms.

six-shooter

We're assured they exist, yet we've never actually spoken to a Walker Morris trainee who didn't have a pre-existing link with Yorkshire. *"The quality of London life is not for me,"* one of our sources neatly summarised the drudgery of the capital. *"And I didn't fancy being just a number; I am one of only 17 trainees in my year."* It isn't hard to get your face known, whether or not you want that, and pretty quickly you'll end up rubbing shoulders with even the most senior of partners. This is made possible partly by the six-seat rotation that sends trainees to at least five different practice groups and most of the six different floors in the firm's modern city-centre HQ.

"The plan is that one seat in each of the compulsory departments [property, corporate and dispute resolution] *is done in your first year,"* and then in your second you get to try out a couple more seats, finally finishing off with a return visit to the department where you hope to qualify. Expect zero input into your first three destinations, but total involvement in seat allocation for your second three, when you'll get together with your peers to divvy up the available seats. In past years we've heard of Mexican standoffs, but this year the process went as smooth as, and no one even had to raise a voice, let alone a paginator, in anger.

Ranging from the lower-profile private client to the high-profile, hard-core commercial, the variety of seats is to be commended. First-years commonly get thrown into slots like retail property (*"Lots of small-time matters that are good and challenging, although you're not going to change the world!"*) or banking and insolvency, which is described as *"a very commercial seat where you can see the practical side of things."* Second-years opt for niche seats like IP and employment, plus perennially popular mainstream corporate and commercial litigation. Those hankering after time out of the office can request a client secondment for one month or even a whole seat. Recently, trainees have spent time with BUPA and financial services company Cattles.

eager beavers

"It definitely pays to be enthusiastic here, as everyone else is." One trainee said quite simply that to get on at the firm you must really want to be successful. Others were less strident in their comments: *"What you get out of the firm is down to you as an individual. If you want to be Walker Morris, Walker Morris, Walker Morris all the time and go out and market the firm then that's fine, but it's not forced. There are also the people who stay in the background and just work."* One source said: *"'Driven' is a DLA sort of word. I don't think this firm is overpowered by the urgency to make money – they are keener that you just get into the work."* Whatever your style, it's clear that you must be making an effort and *"not swinging the lead."* This doesn't necessarily translate into *"massive massives"* – 8.30am until 6–6.30pm seemed common for those we interviewed, and no one had pulled more than one all-nighter.

Business suits (*"Everyone knows where they stand."*) suit this business. Ah ha! This is the Walker Morris we recognise: straight talking, straightforward, quite robust, and somewhat fiery at times, but *"a firm that's not up its own arse."* Apparently, *"a few pleases and thank yous wouldn't go amiss,"* but most of the time our sources spoke of an environment in which *"there's a flexible and individual approach to trainees."* Steady: the lunchtime 'trolley ladies' are not yet delivering group hug therapy with the sandwiches...

get off my land

Expect a partner to supervise you in almost all your seats. *"You can listen to them on the phone, and you can pick your moments to put questions to them. When you sit with them its easier to get to know them as a person and build up a relationship."* Appraisals at the end of each seat are supplemented by mid-seat chats with supervisors, perhaps over lunch or a drink. *"Some partners are very good at communicating with trainees, and others aren't."* The partnership is *"a real mix – there's room for all sorts and as a trainee you have to learn to adapt to all types. You've got to know where you are in the chain of things, although it's not Dickensian in any way!"*

All our sources had seen bags of good work. A number of them talked of taking small meetings and interviewing clients on their own, and some had experience of advocacy, including proceedings to evict squatters, various pre-trial hearings and directions hearings in employment tribunals. *"Partners like to test you to see how you can cope,"* one source said. Another revealed that *"You get quite a lot of responsibility quite early and you get kept busy...you are expected to use your common sense and think things through."*

hanging out

Those with a taste for client schmoozing can get involved in things like local business groups, dinners, client seminars and sporting events. Walker Morris' internal social scene also sounds lively. On the last Thursday of every month local bar, Babylon, plays host to firm-wide *"sponsored drinks."* Within stumbling distance of the office, Wharf Street is WM's very own cradle of civilisation. On most nights you can stick your head around the door and find someone you know. The trainees have a large social budget, which, *"like a council, you have to rush to spend before end of year."* Trips to the dogs, bowling, comedy nights, Laser Quest and tickets to the Leeds TSG Ball all take care of the money. Trainees find all this helpful in 'partner bonding', which by all accounts is less sticky than it sounds. At the end of August there's a welcome dinner for the new intake of trainees plus the existing trainees and a few of the most relevant grown-ups. The message from trainees is clear: *"It's important to interact and socialise and become involved."*

poster paints and pixels

When we first looked on the firm's website we were puzzled by the word 'art' hovering randomly on the home page. Walker Morris, it seems, is a patron of the arts, from highbrow to Hollywood – it has sponsored a student show at London's Royal Academy and the Art of Star Wars exhibition. Local artists get a leg-up too: Leeds primary schoolchildren enter their paintings into a competition run by the firm, and the winners' efforts are reproduced in a calendar. *"Their pictures are also blown up and hung around the office in meeting rooms. Paintings by nine-year-olds – clients love it!"*

If splodges of primary colours move you less than a careful layout in Verdana, then you'll be pleased to hear that Walker Morris has a passion for the internet. It has an award-winning interactive client information service and clients can monitor the progress of cases handled by the conveyancing, PI and debt collection divisions of the firm.

and finally...

Walker Morris is undoubtedly a very successful firm and we don't expect that to change. *"You're not going to come in and have and easy ride of it,"* one trainee told us of the dedicated, work-hard attitude of the firm. But if you have a strong desire to get stuck into your career, and you want a Leeds-based commercial training, you'll get on just fine.

Ward Hadaway

the facts

Location: Newcastle-upon-Tyne, South Shields
UK ranking by size: 83
Total number of trainees: 15
Seats: 4x6 months
Alternative seats: None

Ward Hadaway is a lively Newcastle firm that's grown significantly in size and standing. It has a top-of-the-tree reputation in contentious matters.

bulging in all the right places

This firm has grown by over 1000% since 1990 and shows no sign of slowing down. Last year we reported on the arrival of partners from various leading firms in the north of England, and this year we see that two more have arrived from Pinsents. *"Ward Hadaway is so up-and-coming,"* one source said, *"you never know what's going to happen next. It's getting bigger and bigger and that will carry on."* Blimey!

Our parent publication *Chambers UK* has it newly ranked in construction law, holding on to its top ranking in commercial litigation and performing rather well across the board in non-contentious practice areas, private client, clinical negligence and family law. Out in the real world it has won a position on the Government's newly created panel of solicitors for IT, telecoms and e-commerce advice, and of course it remains just one of 15 firms to which the NHS Litigation Authority send its defence work. Private sector clients include Pride Valley Foods, Barratt Homes, Bellway Homes and Persimmon Homes plus smaller investors, technology start-ups, privately managed businesses and retail and leisure companies.

tomorrow's world

Perhaps we should explain something about the pecking order in legal Newcastle. Ward Hadaway's close neighbour on the Quayside is rival firm Dickinson Dees. It's seen as the big daddy in the city, however, we sensed no envy from our sources: *"We are very different to Dickinson Dees. They are a traditional firm and have been around for many years, so they have a wealth of experience and roots in Newcastle. By comparison, we are relatively young."* This relative youth was seen as an advantage: *"We've not got a long history to get in the way of progress."* For Ward Hadaway, it would seem that the future is everything.

The four-seat training system allows for a degree of flexibility; no bad thing seeing as new starters are asked to give an idea of where they want to qualify, and the training is then built around their answers. As any newly qualified lawyer will tell you, very often your ideas of what you'll enjoy and what you won't are challenged during your training contract. While we're on the subject, six out of the eight September 2003 qualifiers took jobs with the firm.

Trainees are expected to do seats in the property, litigation and commercial departments. *"Some avoid corporate finance as it has a reputation for longer hours;"* although those who choose it are *"involved all the way through a transaction, although at the due diligence and disclosure stages there's more legwork for trainees."* WH has taken the unusual step of employing three accountants (formerly at Ernst & Young and Deloittes) *"to help broker deals and enable a one-stop-shop approach."*

a little bit of what you fancy

A seat in business services will provide a varied diet of shareholder disputes and company start-ups etc, while a stint in property (seen as an excellent first seat) offers both residential and commercial deals and your very own files to manage. The banking seat brings you into contact with large national financial institutions like Barclays and Bank of Scotland, while over in insolvency you'll be acting for the regional offices of large insolvency practitioners. Trainees in this seat attended meetings in London, Leeds and Manchester on a fairly frequent basis. While banking might not permit masses of responsibility, the opposite was found to be the case in insolvency.

IP and IT are popular, as is the 'now seat' in planning law —maybe it's because you have to get your wellies on and make site visits that makes this *"the sexy side of property."* Actually there's a considerable amount of property development going on in and around the city – while it may have failed in its bid to become the European Capital of Culture (boo hiss to Liverpool!), nothing's going to stop Newcastle from evolving into a city fit for the 21st century. We almost wished we hadn't asked one of our sources to tell us what's so great about the place...six pages of notes later we had to stop her!

Matrimonial and clinical negligence provide a good alternative for those leaning more towards human interest cases. *"I think you really want to have to do it,"* said one source of clin neg work. *"It's not that the work is too...graphic...but it's not something that I would want to do again."* With two seats available and plenty of trainees preferring commercial areas of practice, anyone who wants a clin neg seat should be able to get one easily. And for the full-on private client experience, you could try a stint in the firm's smaller 'neighbourhood' office in South Shields.

may the fees be with you

The firm quickly outgrew its waterfront premises at Sandgate House, spilling over into another building directly behind called Keel Row. *"I've never been to the Dark Side,"* one source assured us. Er, excuse us? *"That's what we call Keel Row."* Far from being dingy, it is a new open-plan office (the Sandgate set-up has lawyers in separate rooms) that houses the corporate finance and business services departments. Keel Row has acquired its Lucas-esque nickname *"because of its reputation for long hours and being quite tough."* And because the head of corporate is known as Darth Vader... that is, when he's not being referred to as God.

Sandgate, or perhaps we should name it The Rebel Alliance, has brilliant views of the Tyne and Millennium Bridges, and is directly opposite the recently refurbished pleasure dome that is the old Baltic Flour Mills. Actually it's not at all dome-like, but next door to it is something that is, sort of... The Armadillo (The Sage if you want its proper name) is a new Sydney Opera House-style music venue that will eventually be a home to the Northern Symphonia. *"The firm took a risk when it first moved to the Quayside but it's really paid off,"* one trainee told us. *"I love working where we work rather than being stuck in the middle of town. You feel like you're in the posh part...there's a fresh feeling here."*

Back inside, *"the canteen doesn't serve fresh food, I mean it has vending-machine food as opposed to yesterday's food."* If a bag of Quavers just won't do it, there are bars and restaurants aplenty on the Quayside. If you're prepared to spend more than a couple of quid on a sandwich, Est Est Est offers pasta and pizza or you could pop over to the *"okay"* tapas place for some chorizo and montado.

name-calling

We interviewed trainees on a Friday and as we got closer to lunchtime we sensed a quickening of speech. *"Last year you described the regular Friday trainee lunch as a religious experience,"* one told us. *"And it is!"* We made sure that we released our noon interviewee in plenty of time to join the congregation for their devotions at the Pitcher & Piano. After work the bars on the Quayside are buzzing, and trainees mix with colleagues and friends at other firms like Dickinson Dees. *"We call them Ridiculous Fees and they call us Hadaway & Shite."* Apparently it's a Newcastle joke; whatever it means exactly, we think it's probably a bit rude!

After hours, trainees can also get involved with the local TSG, which organises several events each year, and for sporty types the firm pitches one department against another in mixed football. We also hear that most trainees tend to live reasonably close to each other: *"The main suburbs that young professionals live in are Sandford, Gosforth and Jesmond; Heaton too, but that's a bit more studenty."* This clustering means it's really easy to pop round to a colleague's house for dinner on a school night. The majority of WH trainees have a pre-existing relationship with Newcastle, having grown up nearby or through attendance at one of the two universities; however, there are trainees with no prior history in the city and our sources stressed that being a Geordie is most definitely not a requirement for successful applicants.

and finally...

This is a firm with places to go, people to hire and deals to do. We sense that it wants to recruit trainees who are not only passionate about the North East but who are also prepared to invest themselves in the firm's future. If the Angel of the North visits you in a dream one night, listen closely – she may just be whispering Ward Hadaway's name.

Watson, Farley & Williams

the facts

Location: London
UK ranking by size: 99
Total number of trainees: 20
Seats: 6x4 months
Alternative seats: Overseas seats

This year, amidst cake, candles and keys, Watson, Farley & Williams celebrated its 21st birthday. While still buoyed by matters nautical and deeply rooted in the shipping industry, having reached its majority, it now offers expertise in a broader range of areas. From asset finance to energy and natural resources, the firm is expanding its core practice areas.

frustration?

Originally a ship finance practice, the firm counts banks, shipowners and related industry organisations among its clients. Accordingly, much of your work as a trainee is *"linked to shipping."* And shipping, let's not forget, is inextricably bound up with world trade and international affairs. Right now, WFW is engaged in disputes stemming from the refusal of some chartered ships to deliver goods in the Persian Gulf prior to the outbreak of hostilities in Iraq.

Trainees undertake six seats of four months each. These include three compulsories – finance, litigation and corporate – plus three optional placements. Far from being a frenzied game of musical chairs, the system allows them to *"try a little bit of everything"* and breathe the air in different departments. And the air, we're told, can be thick with responsibility. Of course, the great benefit of working in a smaller firm is that there are fewer trainees to battle for popular seats. Chances are you won't suffer the frustration of waiting in vain for that coveted seat to be vacated, and if there is a particular partner you want to be near (or far!) from, just ask. Proving that there's more to the firm than asset finance and shipping work, the seat menu also offers banking, tax, employment, projects, EU, corporate, property and IP. A lion's share of WFW's work is international, so whether it's ship financings or litigation, you'll encounter plenty of foreign clients, be they Greek shipping magnates or Bulgarian bankers. Happily, WFW does not keep its trainees below decks, so you can expect to be attending client meetings and closings, sometimes in exotic locations.

back to school

There is an intensive trainee lecture circuit, and you'll be expected to attend all seminars that take place on the premises. *"The fact that they're compulsory makes you resentful of going sometimes,"* one source confided. *"It's like being at school,"* said another, although *"sometimes they can be useful."* A good job as, at times, they can occupy two lunchtimes per week. To soften the blow, they are accompanied by wine and food.

Curiously, trainees told us that at WFW, *"people tend to hide their commitment and ambition quite well. They don't put it in your face."* Try as they might to downplay their efforts, we suspected that, like elegant swans, our sources were paddling away furiously beneath the surface. One trainee summarised the firm's ethos as *"relaxed, but quietly determined"* married with *"straightforward and commercially minded."*

We started rolling our eyes when we heard that *"Watson, Farley & Williams is a firm that listens,"* however, there is supporting evidence for the claim. When trainees called out for the introduction of a mentoring system, that's exactly what they got. A handful of junior partners (*"ones who have a direct line to the powers that be, but who can remember what it's like to be an assistant or even a trainee and not know a whole lot"*) stepped forward for the job. Trainees also approved of department meetings at which staff from all levels can express their ideas and hear about developments in the practice. As if all that weren't enough, there's a trainee forum for their own specific issues. And this year there was little of the teeth gnashing that went on in many firms, ten of the 13 qualifiers stayed with the firm in September 2003, spreading themselves across several departments.

vive la difference!

Given the firm's focus, it's no surprise that most trainees have an international outlook. It's not necessary to be fluent in Esperanto or to have won a round-the-world yacht race, but a second language certainly won't hurt and most trainees have travelled or lived abroad. *"We're a pretty mixed bunch. Geographically, educationally and ethnically, we are very diverse."* This and good academics aside, confidence is what really unites the WFW set. *"Confidence and the ability to handle yourself!"* Some of those we spoke to freely admitted to being *"confrontational,"* and loved the *"challenge of an argument."* Just as well too since shipping clients are renowned for *"not pulling any punches."* One source told us that you *"need to be a fairly tough soul"* to get by; another agreed: *"I love the fact that I'm not mollycoddled."* At the same time, in a firm that prides itself on its commerciality, you'll also need to be pretty down to earth and practical. And flexible. Here's a test for you. Would you be thrilled or terrified by the idea of jetting off to Bangkok for a four-month seat at only three days notice? OK, that's a one-off example – most overseas postings come with more notice – but you can expect some business-related foreign trips to pop up out of the blue.

For most, the prospect of spending four months in an exotic location was a major attraction. *"I appreciated the fact that I was virtually guaranteed a foreign seat,"* one said. Since losing the bulk of its seven-partner Paris office to Orrick, Herrington & Sutcliffe, the firm has been busily rebuilding its French outpost, and recently poached partners from Weil, Gotshal & Manges. Trainees hankering after Grenache and Gauloises can breathe easy as a chaise in the city of romance is secure. Alternatively they can sample life in Bangkok, Singapore or Piraeus, often in their first year. Foreign offices are smaller and you'll find yourself getting *"a lot more exposure than you'd get as a trainee in London."* SARS Update: the firm's Singapore office remained open for business and staff had their temperatures taken twice daily. Under the tongue or up the…never mind.

set sail

So if the firm wants practical, down-to-earth and confident applicants, what draws trainees to the firm? Our sources had eschewed the vast machinery of the magic circle in favour of this more intimate experience. One told us: *"I didn't want to be a tiny cog lost in the mechanisms, but nor did I want to be in a firm so small that there was no time to learn."*

In a radical, morale-boosting exercise that would only be feasible in a smaller firm, founding partner Martin Watson has taken to poking his head around doors and grinning dryly: *"Good morning! I hear that smiling keeps the assistants happy!"* It seems to be working. Trainees spoke of a *"congenial"* atmosphere, and WFW was rated happiest firm in the 2002 *Legal Business* assistants' survey. Jolly good. As you were.

Far from scraping by on dry biscuits and battling scurvy, we hear that the in-house restaurant, has *"improved vastly,"* though until we're invited round for lunch (hint hint), we'll have to rely on hearsay. The laideez especially appreciated it when Le Chef *"goes all French on us"* with rich desserts. Luckily, you can work off that fourth crème brûlée on the sporting field with the firm's football or cricket teams. Those of a more cerebral persuasion can join in the regular quiz nights. In terms of bars, the firm is relatively chained in, and trainees usually end up at All Bar One. But we're assured that *"it's not an Ally McBeal situation."* No dancing babies; no impromptu karaoke; no shared toilet facilities. Alas, no snogging Jon Bon Jovi either. To compensate, über trendy Hoxton and Great Eastern Street are close by, so when the excitement of All Bar One gets too much, you can always pop round to Cantaloupe.

and finally...

Fancy a magic circle salary and international training without the hours? Trainees at Watson, Farley & Williams claim to have just that. On the downside, if being associated with one of the biggest brand names is important to you, you may struggle with those outside the shipping, asset finance and energy sectors.

Wedlake Bell

the facts

Location: London
UK ranking by size: 126
Total number of trainees: 10
Seats: 4x6 months
Alternative seats: None

Wedlake Bell is your classic West End firm; a bit of old money, some solid property and corporate work for up-and-coming businesses, a generous dash of clients you might actually read about outside the *FT* and all done in time for a couple of pints in nearby Covent Garden.

a nice bit of gorgonzola

The firm divides itself between the services it provides to its business clients (banking and corporate finance, property, employment, litigation) and its private clients (*"titles and aristocrats, not Richard Branson"*) for whom the firm sorts out tax and wealth protection issues. The firm also has an outpost in Guernsey for offshore matters.

Of your four seats, you'll do one in litigation, one in property and, usually, corporate finance. As with litigation everywhere, there's a whole lot of paginating to be done. *"In litigation, easily 50% of what I was doing was grunt work. At first that's great as you get to know how everything works, but you get cheesed off towards the end."* Usually though, trainee tasks are a little more interesting.

Talking of cheese, the IP lawyers recently negotiated on behalf of Aardman Animations in connection with the use of Wallace and Gromit in computer games. Property also sounds like fun; it's a *"very nice team"* offering *"a very good training"* – you should end up running your own files. The department's big-name clients include Surrey County Cricket Club and Dairy Crest. You'll be reined in a bit more in corporate finance where, because of the size of the transactions, *"you can't be let loose on so much stuff."*

You'll get some company secretarial work to do by yourself and those who think that sounds like typing should go and thumb through an LPC manual right now. The corporate team's clients tend to be private companies, including *"AIM and those aiming for AIM."*

lychee martinis

Apart from the mainstream seats, there's plenty else for you to have a stab at. How about going to Mipcom? No, not a trendy cocktail bar or cybercafe, but rather the firm's up-and-coming media, IP and commercial group. In a way, though, this team is the lychee martini to the round of pints that is property and finance; recent clients include Select Model Management on behalf of Helena Christianson. We understand the group works on other matters for further *"household names"* but, alas, trainees had been sworn to secrecy. Head of department Jonathan Cornthwaite (*"a very nice chap"*) has been nicknamed 'The Brain' – *"all the departments have smart people, but he's in a different league and has high expectations."*

A seat in the firm's well-regarded private client department is *"very hands-on"* and you can expect to run your own files in due course, as well as participating in work on bigger trusts. If you're interested then speak up as soon as possible – not all trainees get a seat here.

plum job

After asking for your seat preferences, HR will map out your training in the first few weeks. That said, nothing is set in stone and the system seems to be more hit than miss. Among current second-years, *"everyone's got the one thing they really wanted to do"* and we heard of lots of swapping and trading among the first-years. Once installed in a new seat, *"responsibility is initially low, but you do get your own files when you're ready."* Support is forthcoming and partners *"don't treat you like muck;"* even if they're doing something important, *"if you're in a pickle"* they will drop it and help you out. There's ample formal feedback. Every month, you'll sit down with your supervisor for a chat and to check that you're covering all the areas of law that you should, and at the end of your seat you'll meet with the training panel. Trainees like the good partner to fee-earner ratio, which means that partners can be accessed at work very easily and *"you feel you can socialise with them on an equal level."*

As we've found in previous years, to fit in at Wedlake Bell, *"a personable nature is essential."* Why is it so important here? *"Because of the amount of client contact. You are meeting clients from day one and everyone gets on very well with them."* Another trainee told us: *"The younger partners have been through Wedlake Bell themselves and want to be able to take you to a meeting and have you fit in, not sit there like a plum."* There's plenty of socialising between trainees and partners; one trainee seemed surprised that *"friends at other firms don't go out with their boss at all!"* We certainly got the sense that the firm likes to recruit the kind of chaps they'll get on with down the pub.

grape expectations

The place to meet at 5.30pm on a Friday for a beer is (*"unfortunately"*) still The Lamb and Flag in Covent Garden. Trainees tell us: *"It's a bit of a bloke's pub"* and *"an acquired taste – I think the toilets put people off."* If they move on from there, it's usually to The Spot, which is also *"pretty awful,"* but has the advantage of a late licence. Trainees perked up when we asked them about sport: *"The partners play golf, obviously,"* but there are football and cricket friendlies against other firms and clients, and fiercely contested softball in the summer. At the Christmas party – last year in the Hilton – you can expect *"a meal, lots of booze and a raffle."* All four of the trainees who qualified in September 2003 are staying with the firm to try for the big prize in the next draw.

Wedlake Bell is all set to make a small geographical but huge cultural move from Covent Garden to High Holborn in summer 2004. While trainees believe *"it will be a shame to leave Covent*

Garden," they were nevertheless looking forward to *"sussing out some new pubs"* and seemed excited about the move. Staff were asked for some input into how the new office should look. Top on the wish list were showers, bike stores and chill-out rooms, so if they end up working in a youth hostel they only have themselves to blame. As we interviewed, *"chair trials"* were taking place, so we look forward to reporting on the results next year. The new office will be in the highly distinctive *"modern classic"* style, beloved of first-class hotels everywhere. The explanation is simple: *"We have a large, traditional private client base and don't want to alienate anyone."* The best-loved features of the old office will remain, including the private dining room. Although the firm doesn't have a canteen for everyday use, *"we have a kitchen and a chef who comes in when needed. The food and wine is fantastic."*

and finally...

If you believe the personal touch of a firm like Wedlake Bell would suit you better than the law factories of the City and you have the requisite people skills, then don't hesitate to apply.

Weil, Gotshal & Manges

the facts

Location: London
UK ranking by size: 79
Total number of trainees: 20
Seats: 4x6 months
Alternative Seats: Overseas seats, secondments
Extras: Pro bono – RJC CAB, FRU, Bar Council and Solicitors pro bono units

Weil, Gotshal & Manges has come a long way from its roots in 1930s New York. It has 15 offices worldwide, and the London outpost that opened in 1996 now has a pivotal role in the development of the firm's European business.

killer weil?

When US firms arrived in London and started recruiting trainees, all manner of rumours circulated amongst students. Generally they went something like this: [sharp intake of breath/shake of head as if plumber/mechanic on first inspection of your pipes/big end] "You'll have a huge salary but no life...US firms can't train you properly...You'll become unmarketable...US firms will all leave town when the going gets tough." Well listen...at WGM the hours are no worse than at the magic circle, it offers a broad-based and well-supervised training contract, and the saloon doors aren't swinging on an empty room, even after a downturn in the market.

chapter 11 and beyond

We get e-mails from students who love the US so much that they will only consider applying to American firms, but most candidates base their decision on other considerations. So let's look at WGM's work. In the US it is **the** firm for insolvency and reconstruction matters. Take Enron, WorldCom and Global Crossing for example. Each company landed themselves in a big ol' multibillion-dollar mess and WGM has taken a prominent role in sorting out liabilities and salvaging something worthwhile from each. However, this is not the prime business of the firm's London office. Over here, corporate finance and private equity work are key. The value of certain client relationships must not be underestimated, especially leveraged buyout house Hicks, Muse, Tate & Furst, GE Capital and Tommy. It was Hicks Muse that instructed the office on the £2.1 billion buyout of Yell.com from BT.

Trainees all do corporate, litigation and finance seats. Beyond these they choose another from property (in a team of five), EU (new in 2003), tax (complex, but some love it), technology, environmental and employment, restructuring (now taking two trainees and growing) and securitisation and international corporate finance.

weil you were out

The firm celebrates 4th July and puts on a good spread at Thanksgiving, but no one's going to make you dress up as a pumpkin on Halloween. Trainees are quite certain that *"it feels like an English firm."* Almost all the London lawyers practice UK law, and only around 10% are American. We were delighted to see that one of them had pinned the Stars and Stripes to his door…as if we'd have not noticed him otherwise!

Any which way you look at it, this is an international law firm handling international work. Without wishing to downplay the London office's stand-alone business, it should also be viewed as the US practice's gateway to European business. Trainees talked of plenty of contact with the French and Frankfurt offices, and it will be interesting to see how business with the EU accession nations develops. Doubtless WGM has positioned itself in Warsaw, Prague and Budapest with exactly this in mind. If working overseas is important to you then how about a seat in New York (corporate plus a taste of life in the Midtown mother ship) or Silicon Valley (patent litigation plus your own car to cruise down to Big Sur and along Monterey's 17-Mile Drive). The firm doesn't rule out secondments elsewhere – Paris is on the cards and, if you have the relevant foreign language skills, so are other European offices. In past years there has also been a secondment to GE Capital.

where's the middle man?

Situated right above the Marks & Spencer store between Finsbury Square and Moorgate, there's a danger that you'll become spoiled and unable to lower yourself to shop in a normal supermarket ever again. We're unsure where the lawyers actually buy clothes, however, WGM's dress code allows for everything from chinos to pinstripes. This is indicative of the lack of stuffiness in the London office, which is unsurprising when you consider that it's only been around for seven years and lawyers moved there from other City firms because they wanted a change of environment…something fresher and, for many, more lucrative.

Most of the partners started their careers at Clifford Chance or other magic circle firms, but according to our sources you'll have greater access to partners than will your peers in the magic circle. *"The gap between you and the high end – the structuring of the deals – is not so great. There are not two tiers of separation between you and the partners…you'll know, and will have a relationship with, partners directly."* The firm is still attracting good names to the partnership, but it must be said that it has also lost a few. Early days…

Sessions on hard law come around at least weekly, and then there's also soft skills training: stress management, marketing, getting the best from appraisals and that kind of thing.

be prepared

It may be the influence of the NY office, but WGM is making strides in London on issues of diversity, staff welfare and commitment to pro bono. There's the usual blurb on pro bono in the grad recruitment brochure, which you might want to read. Occasionally we drop our cynicism about the publicity given by firms to their eleemosynary behaviour. Sshhh…that might be the sound of it hitting the floor right now.

"In terms of ambience it is quite informal. They want you to be relaxed, at ease and affable." You'll pick up on this, if you are fortunate enough to do a vac scheme or visit the firm. At the same time, it's the way of the firm to be *"prepared for every eventuality. It's not a place that's slow to react to things, like what's happening in the market and the world."* As an example (which you must promise to not get spooked by), all staff are issued with a fluorescent orange 'disaster pack' containing various items, such as a whistle, a torch and water. It's not paranoia; it's more a case of trying to do the best by people.

Stop! Are you trying to wear us down with corporate niceness? You've got to be pulling the profits out of the bag, right? Too right. Staff are expected to perform and there's absolutely no room for slackers. *"Getting a deal done can be quite a strain on you, but you do get an adrenalin rush from finishing it. It's probably more physical than mental…but that's the nature of working in the City. Bankers are very demanding people!"* But the good news for trainees is that smaller teams mean that you're less out of the loop on the way the deal is going and your intended role: *"Usually you can see it coming when you're going to be busy – you prepare for it."*

having a weil of a time

Four times a year the top man, Mike Francies, invites all staff to his quarterly review. Anyone who wants to know how the firm is doing, what it is doing and where it is going is recommended to attend. Of course, the review at the Christmas party gets more laughs, usually at the expense of partners who look a little bit like celebrities. We think we've spotted one they haven't…cheap as chips? We don't think he is.

Every other year, all the lawyers head off somewhere sunny for the annual retreat. Last year they had flamenco lessons in Barcelona and next year they are off to Cannes. Closer to home, trainees and junior associates gather for Friday night drinks in the bars around CityPoint, among them Corney & Barrow, Barola and new *"in place"* Digress. *"It's dark, underground and almost like being in a nightclub."* Or a coal mine perhaps? Every couple of months there are office drinks. *"We usually go out to a bar. We used to have them in the atrium in the office, but it tends to be reserved for client events and graduate recruitment events now."* We have it on good authority that it's kept for special occasions, as people were apt to stagger carelessly into the floor-level water feature. *"Perhaps that's why it was always being drained,"* mused one source.

and finally…

Drained is one thing that September 2003 qualifiers didn't feel. All eight of them were offered and accepted jobs in their first-choice departments. The trainee who talked about how the firm was *"embedded"* in London was spot on. If you want a full-on City training, but worry that you might rage against a big machine, Weil, Gotshal & Manges is a serious option. Oh and in case you were wondering, Manges rhymes with the river Ganges.

White & Case

the facts

Location: London
UK ranking by size: 69
Total number of trainees: 38
Seats: 4x6 months
Alternative seats: Overseas seats
Extras: Language training

With 39 offices in 26 countries, White & Case has long outgrown its US heritage. Having put down roots in London in 1972, the firm is a popular and established force in our capital and across most parts of the globe. Be prepared to work very hard and play even harder…

wherever I lay my hat

Founded in 1901 in New York, White & Case started life as a banking and finance outfit, based on the friendship of one of the era's most influential men JP Morgan financier, Henry P 'Harry' Davison. During WWI, the British and French Governments hired White & Case's main client, JP Morgan, to purchase arms on their behalf from the United States. The firm acted on most of the armament contracts for the war and in 1926, on the strength of the relationships it had built in Paris, opened its first international office there. When the Berlin wall fell in 1989, White & Case was quick to open offices in Eastern Europe, including Prague, Budapest, Warsaw and Moscow. Work for the Indonesian Republic during its debt crisis helped establish the firm's famous 'sovereign practice', which acts for heads of states and governments. White & Case has advised more countries in sovereign-related projects than any other law firm, particularly in (ex) communist and poorer countries.

This is a bold firm that's unafraid of new horizons, and yet it's true to say that wherever it goes, White & Case wins friends. Our colleagues at *Chambers Global* speak of a firm that is well integrated in local markets. According to our colleagues, it is widely respected for "maintaining Western standards" while "nurturing local talent into the partnership." Unlike some other firms, White & Case does not seek to stamp its culture on the map. According to one trainee, this is unnecessary since *"we're already a blend, a hybrid."*

touching

The London training scheme uses the four-seat model, and although technically no area of law is compulsory, everyone does at least one variety of finance seat. Usually this will be described simply and generally as banking and finance, though a more specialised asset finance seat may suffice in some cases. The other areas that you're very likely to come across are corporate and capital markets. Those trainees who go overseas (and that's going to be everyone – it would be an odd thing to choose this firm, if you didn't want to spend time abroad), often get involved in large-scale projects work. This year, Singapore and Eastern European offices seemed to be the most commonly visited, but there are also seats in Paris, Milan, Brussels and Hong Kong. Trainees get a spectacular deal in Singapore, where the accommodation provided has tennis and squash courts, a swimming pool, gym and even a put-put golfing green. Expect to spend every penny on weekend travel, and perhaps even to hire a private island for a weekend with your peers in other firms.

In asset finance, trainees get involved in big-ticket aircraft leasing, although few knew exactly what this was when they started. When they're not getting involved in some complex and meaty drafting (*"it wasn't just a case of cutting and pasting from precedents"*), trainees find themselves completing aircraft deliveries over the phone. *"It's pretty funny,"* giggled one source, *"the client is standing on the tarmac in, say Charles de Gaulle, their plane comes in and you tell them to put their hand on it. That's delivery!"* In banking, trainees told us they play an *"integral part"* in major international financings. Mostly, you can expect to be involved in proofing and preparing closing certificates, although you'll also get a chance to work on the first draft of an agreement. It is, said one trainee, *"a phenomenal experience."*

Tax, according to one besotted source, is *"fab, just fab."* The work involves large, complex cross-border transactions, *"not piddling about with sending letters to Inland Revenue."* The work is so cerebral, *"it's mind-boggling sometimes,"* but for the right trainee, it can offer unrivalled challenges. Speaking of things intellectual, how about a seat in the IP department? The work here is both contentious and non-contentious, and includes trademark applications, patent disputes and technology arbitrations, ensuring that trainees can see a decent spread of work. The litigation lawyers are seen as a *"really good, cohesive group."* One trainee, who had previously been dead set against contentious work eulogised about a department that *"is just so much fun."* The work is very international and there is a pronounced slant towards banking and finance disputes. For example, White & Case in London acted for US-based client International Finance Corporation against Utexafrica in a claim based on an alleged moratorium arising from the political and economic situation in the Congo.

monkey business

There are legal assistants to take the brunt of the grunt work in corporate. None of our sources had engaged in any serious photocopying or *"monkey work."* According to one trainee: *"They're quite particular about that here."* Indeed they are. Trainees must complete weekly reports detailing the work they have done and these are submitted to the training partner for scrutiny. Far from being a way of keeping watch over the hapless crew, he uses the reports to ensure that trainees aren't stuck at the photocopier or suffering pagination-related cramp. This is a firm in which *"we're very much treated as trainees, not used as legal assistants or secretaries."* After all, *"that's how you learn to be a lawyer."*

It all sounds too good to be true, doesn't it? Where's the downside? Well, lets talk about how hard you're going to have to work. The average time to leave the office is 7.30pm. *"Because of the international nature of the work, you are expected to be present in the office at unusual times."* We did hear of the odd 80-hour week, and the hours can be especially difficult if you are working with the US or, say, Brazil. To summarise, be prepared to work long and hard, but also to be well compensated for your efforts. In September 2003, eight of the nine qualifiers stayed with the firm.

The trainees we spoke to were adamant that White & Case is *"absolutely not a US firm." "It's a truly global firm,"* said one. And while the IT help desk switches over to New York after 6pm London time (*"a fun touch"*), there are few other American touches in the London office. Only seven of the partners speak with that funny accent and, indeed, today around half the firm's worldwide partners hail from outside the United States.

let your hair down

In spring 2004, the firm's four London offices will be united under one *"snazzy"* roof in Lion Plaza near Bank. The firm took the staff consultation process pretty seriously and we heard about eight-page questionnaires and discussion sessions to gauge people's views on whether there should be an open-plan layout or individual offices. They were also bombarded with questions on points relating to the canteen and the gym. Said one: *"They showed us pictures of chesterfield sofas and asked if we like them. Then they showed us chrome."* Did they then do the Rorschach inkblot test we wondered? Apparently not, yet the project has helped the London office to establish a self-identity. And the offices? We are assured that *"they won't look like a bar."*

Did someone mention a bar? On Thursday nights, our subject lawyers can be found by the briefcaseful at the local Corney & Barrow. Like that iconic 80s hairdo the mullet – or 'hockey hair' as our North American friends would call it – White & Case is all business up front, all party at the back. (For more in-depth socio-political insights on the mullet, we refer readers to www.mulletsgalore.com.) The firm is renowned for its hectic social calendar: there's the annual skiing trip for those who want to get on the piste with partners, an annual boat party and Christmas party in addition to a non-stop schedule of departmental do's and marketing events. And of course, there are the usual sporting teams, sailing weekends, macramé classes and Esperanto workshops. Or there might be, if you ask nicely.

and finally...

Those who train at White & Case will usually have flirted with the magic circle. The decision to eschew one of the established London giants can feel risky, but it's a decision that some students need to make. A summer placement at White & Case and one at a City giant should help you decide which style of firm suits you best.

Withers LLP

the facts

Location: London
UK ranking by size: 76
Total number of trainees: 23
Seats: 4x6 months
Alternative seats: Possibly Milan
Extras: Language training

Top-ranked in London for private client and agriculture work, Withers was always the place to come if you wanted to sell your grouse moor or put a few million in a trust fund for your heirs. But far from sitting back and feeling smug, the firm has been thinking ahead and expanding internationally. It's keen to do what it takes to stay top dog.

charmed life

Around 40% of the firm's work is handled by the private client department, with the rest divided fairly evenly between the family, litigation, corporate and property departments. There is a green-welly element to the client base (*"we basically act for rich people"*), but trainees confirm that the firm is *"moving forward,"* and targeting entrepreneurs and established businessmen. Withers' long-standing Italian links have always meant that its English persona is as much holiday home in Lombardy as rainy estate in Wiltshire, and since merging with a New York/New Haven firm in January 2002, we can also factor in a swish Park Avenue apartment and a New England beach house.

Partly as a result of the American connection, the firm is bang up to date with technological wizardry. Rather like pulling the right brick to get into Diagon Alley, if you say the magic word when you approach the old-school listed façade of Withers' office, you'll be whisked into a new world where video conferencing rules and dictations are emailed from office to office to be typed while you sleep (generally by secretaries rather than house elves). The buzz around the merger has added to a feeling of optimism at Withers: *"We haven't suffered that much in the market downturn,"* said one source, *"we're on the up when everyone else is treading water."* Positive thinking certainly worked for the September 2003 qualifiers (unless they bewitched the training partner, that is); all ten accepted jobs at the firm.

Although it is possible to avoid a stint, in practice most trainees spend time in the private client department and implied it would be odd to apply to Withers if you had no interest in it at all. Muggles beware: *"Private client is a peculiar and strange area of law. You find yourself dealing with many weird and wonderful things."* But before you get too carried away with that magic wand, remember that much of the work revolves around tax planning, which means, *"you have to sit down and read the bloody statutes!"* Trainees see the department as *"intellectual"* rather than *"conservative,"* though one trainee cautioned that *"if you like urgency and excitement, then private client may not be for you."* In this seat, you might also encounter charities law as the firm has a number of important ones, such as Macmillan Cancer Relief and Great Ormond Street Hospital, on its books.

Trainees tell us that to a certain extent corporate is a support department for private client; the work of the two departments overlap and it's worth bearing in mind that, *"if you get impressed by big macho deals, then Withers isn't the place for you."* You won't be doing big-ticket M&A here: *"It's not like a typical corporate department"* – you're more likely to get stuck into tax structures and investment funds. If this aspect of corporate work interests you, there's no reason why you shouldn't pick this firm hoping to become a corporate lawyer.

mixing the right potion

Most of the departments in the firm provide different legal services to a core group of private clients (and their corporate entities), but the family department's client base is slightly separate. *"People only tend to get divorced once,"* explained one trainee, *"although actually we do get some clients who have got divorced twice or more – sometimes from the same people."* It certainly seems to be the place for a good gossip (all in strict confidence, of course), and in contrast to the *"much quieter and more academic"* atmosphere of private client, trainees felt that the family department was the most *"buzzy and dynamic"* part of the firm. This can be daunting; trainees told us that starting a seat here was very much jumping *"in at the deep end,"* but fear not, someone always comes to the rescue. *"If you don't know what the bloody hell you're doing, you can just say 'Help!' I found people were falling over themselves to answer my questions!"* Steady on!

You'll find some *"huge personalities"* in the family department: *"They're incredible, charismatic people,"* and that makes for a high-decibel working environment. Partners and fee earners were described as *"exuberant," "expressive"* and *"people you could trust to make a noise in a bar."* Withers seems to recognise the importance of personality to successful family work: *"All the partners are quite different, so when Withers takes on a new client, they pick a personality to suit; for instance, if we get a film or West End actress there's a very kissy partner with a luvvy boyfriend who gets the job. If you're a wealthy husband or if you're aristocratic, there are also specific partners who you might get allocated to."* The department mainly does top-notch divorce and custody work, usually with several million pounds to play for, and often with a complicated international dimension. Withers also has expertise in complex cases at the cutting edge of family law, including international surrogacy and rights for same-sex cohabitees. Partners and assistants are often involved in writing textbooks, so don't be surprised if your supervisor asks you to give them a hand. Just don't expect a share of the royalties…

wearing the trousers

It was clear to us that trainees loved their work. But they were also honest about the downsides: *"The work can be hard and stressful because you're doing a huge variety of things. You get work from the whole department and so you're quite often doing things that you haven't done before."* Although one supervisor will be responsible for you, you are a trainee for the whole department. This actually enables you to gravitate towards the work you're interested in, something that is encouraged by the firm. Whatever you end up doing, standards are high. Quite simply, *"everyone is keen to be perfect – we want to stay at number one."* Be warned: although people will not usually stay past 7pm, there may be raised eyebrows in some departments if you try to sneak out at 5.30pm on a regular basis.

"Dynamic" chairman, Diana Parker, keeps an eye on the finer details, for instance resisting the dress-down movement so fashionable elsewhere. However, far from being conservative, trainees feel she has played a big part in pushing the firm forwards and tell us her attitude is indicative of the firm's culture as a whole. *"Even the old farts support her!"* Like Professor McGonagall, this lady can be fierce at times (*"even my supervisor is scared of her"*), but has universal respect (*"she's wicked, really cool"*). Apparently, to get on her good side just ask about her allotment.

Withers' office is evidence that innovation and good old-fashioned standards can co-exist. Behind the traditional exterior, you'll find *"a slick, modern building"* complete with a *"glass atrium"* and *"lots of windows"*…shaped like a pair of trousers. (Yes, you did read that right.) For once, the *Student Guide* stakes no claim on this particular piece of silliness – the comparison is universally used by everyone in the firm. As one trainee sniggered: *"You'll say 'My office is on the second floor, right hand-pocket' or 'Take this to so-and-so in the left leg'."* Trainees also speak fondly of the subsidised canteen – the girls like the 20p salads; fish and chips on Friday get the boys' vote. High-fibre diet? Low fat? Low carb? Home-made biscuits for your client meetings? The kitchen's got it sorted and even provides a 'zest for life' dish, the Withers version of the philosopher's stone.

favourite things

As a group, the Withers trainees may not be the biggest party animals, in fact we suspect they prefer to keep their social lives separate from work, although there may be lunches or drinks together (and all of one intake recently attended the wedding of one of their number). They seem to be a mature and sussed bunch, describing themselves as *"sorted," "independent"* and *"happy to let each other be."* Yet the firm as a whole is a bit of a Weasley-style happy family. Among the partners, we hear there are four married couples, and the various branches of the Withers clan keep in touch through a firm-wide newsletter that always includes a recipe from the Italian office and translations of more obscure English legal terminology for the Americans.

The most fun seems to be had at the annual departmental parties: *"They're generally something quite crazy, never just dinner."* We thought the property department's walking tour round the witch-burning sites of Smithfield sounded like a giggle, but for sheer entertainment value you can't beat the family department's outing to *Sing-A-long-A Sound of Music*. *"Everybody dressed up – the head of department went as a nun and one supervisor was a brown paper parcel tied up with string."* As if all this wasn't enough, there are also summer parties, Christmas parties and every-now-and-again parties.

and finally...

Withers may require trainees to work at the pointy end of private client and family work, but as a firm with no sharp edges, we suspect that it's a very comfortable place to be.

Wragge & Co

the facts

Location: Birmingham, London
UK ranking by size: 18
Total number of trainees: 48
Seats: 4x6 months
Alternative seats: Brussels, secondments
Extras: Pro bono – College of Law, BERAL, LaWWorksWeb, language training

Pride of the Midlands, Wragge & Co is a real success story. Since the mid-nineties it has grown from its humble, mid-sized, local beginnings into a big, bold regional firm that competes with leading London players. Having originally declared itself a one-city firm, it has now begun an assault on the capital itself.

potato days...

Our interviewees admitted that it was Wragges' kick-arse reputation, combined with its warm bedside manner that attracted them. Few firms can lay claim to this sort of growth and still inspire intense loyalty and enthusiasm in staff, but Wragges has done just that. Under the leadership of Quentin Poole and John Crabtree, it earned a reputation for a caring attitude to staff. Crabtree has now retired as senior partner, Poole has climbed into his chair and partner Richard Haywood has taken up the managing partner reigns, but the policy remains the same. This is a firm that takes staff development and consultation seriously, and there is a focus group for almost everything. When the firm was considering new computer software, it took sample testers from right across the firm. And by popular demand, Wragges is soon to have a staff canteen. *"They consulted us about the food...we've settled on baked potatoes and posh coffee."* Trainees are delighted to be part of an institution where they feel *"consulted and enfranchised."* Said one: *"They involve you in discussing strategy and business plans. They explain the partnership to you. It's refreshing to know where you're going."* Others applauded the *"honesty and transparency"* of a firm where *"everything is explained – the reasons for mergers, transfers, appointments, everything."* It may not seem like such a big deal, but believe us, there are plenty of firms where the attitude to staff is one of 'not in front of the children.'

The firm basks in an impressive reputation across almost all areas of practice. Our colleagues at *Chambers UK* rank it in 37 practice areas. And its client list is equally impressive, including such major names as 3i, Cadbury Schweppes, British Airways, Lloyds TSB and Alliance & Leicester.

...and pepperoni nights

The training scheme is the usual four-seat affair: trainees spend compulsory time in the commercial, property and litigation departments and a fourth seat can be taken anywhere. If it's long hours you're after, corporate can sure provide, but happily, few trainees found themselves doing grunt work. *"I didn't do photocopying or ordering pizza,"* said one. Instead, *"I had a serious contribution to make."* Even on late nights, *"when everyone else went home and it was just the core team, it was fun. I enjoyed the camaraderie and team spirit."*

The property department gets the thumbs-up from trainees. It offers autonomy on around 20 of their own files and a good dose of responsibility. In projects, trainees get involved in PFI and PPP work. Here the firm advises on matters such as rail privatisations in Africa and, closer to home, the London Underground. And while you probably won't be jetting off to Mozambique, in true Wragges' style, trainees are given a good dose of client contact. To satisfy the contentious training requirement, there are seats in property, construction or commercial litigation. Property litigation involves possession proceedings and even the odd public inquiry for a compulsory purchase order, while over in commercial litigation, trainees loved the "*human slant*" to director disqualification work.

boys in glasses

We've always had a sneaking suspicion that tax law is the new employment law…sexy! (OK, so the chicks on the *Student Guide* love studious boys in glasses.) We don't know if the tax group at Wragges would leave us breathless, but we're told it is "*well aware that tax is complicated and daunting,*" and to compensate there are "*loads of one-to-one training sessions.*" Sure, in some departments, the work is so embarrassingly easy that a chimpanzee with monthly training sessions and a set of Thomas Pink cufflinks can get by just fine (yes, we are joking!), but corporate tax is heavy going, and you'll need those twice-weekly sessions for trainees. By the end of it, our sources were thrilled to discover they knew more than they realised.

In September 2003, the firm retained all its newly qualifieds. True, some of them are now working in second-choice departments, but we hear that this is a firm where switching specialisms one, two, three or more years post-qualification is supported by the firm. There's evidence of flexibility pre-qualification too – we heard of a trainee working three days a week in one department and two in the other. In a volatile market, Wragges has refused to lay off staff, instead taking a longer-term view of profits.

After years of stratospheric growth, the pace of change has slowed somewhat. When we put this to our sources, it was easy to see that they were well informed on the subject and happy to speak candidly. As one admitted: "*When I first arrived, there was a real buzz about the place, but with the corporate slowdown, people aren't as happy not having enough work.*" But far from going backwards, trainees insisted the firm is now in a period of "*consolidation.*" The limelight is shifting to the newer London office. Legal pundits found it bemusing when the firm first announced its merger with a small niche IP practice in the capital; we'd been told Wragges was a single-site operation. Then some corporate lawyers joined them. The firm proclaimed that it would never go full service in London…just before it added real estate and employment groups. Our tough *Student Guide* interrogation techniques extracted the following gem from one trainee: "*Of course, they're saying they won't go full service in the City, but I think they will. They just don't want to do it all in one go – it doesn't make business sense.*" A confession at last! Let's hope they send some tax lawyers our way.

swagger and spin

Wragges has perfected the art of putting a sparkling optimistic gloss on even the dourest of news. For example, earlier this year, the firm responded to a bleak legal market by sending staff on client secondments and putting others into non-fee earning positions. The management admitted that while the secondments were used to manage the downturn, they also fitted with the firm's training culture. And last year, we reported on how it cleverly turned its office space shortage into a team-building, open-plan system.

In 2003, Wragges was once again ranked in *The Sunday Times'* '100 Best Companies to Work For' survey, one of only seven law firms. It's easy to dismiss such things as pretentious self-promotion, but the firm's perpetual optimism and commitment to its staff has had a noticeable impact on clients. The approach has enabled it to recruit and retain high-calibre lawyers who have a certain confidence that clients simply love. "It gives them an edge in negotiations," said one. "They're sharper, stronger and better for it," they told our colleagues at *Chambers UK*. The firm's *"non-hierarchical"* environment also ensures that staff feel comfortable taking responsibility upon themselves. One trainee reported: *"What makes my job easy is that there seem to be a lot of self-starters here, people just seem to do things off their own bat."*

hothouse flowers

Many regional firms have a policy of recruiting heavily from their local community. This helps to insure the firm against the cuckoo's nest syndrome in which trainees use a hapless regional firm for training and then cruelly ditch it two years later to move to Clapham and experience the daily delights of the Northern Line en route to Lovells. Not so at Wragges. This is a firm that many lawyers move to Birmingham for. Certainly, Brum is *"by no means a Sydney or a Rio,"* but it's come a long way in the last decade. The trainee group is an eclectic bunch: there are the straight-out-of-university types, those who have taken time to travel to exotic and far-flung locations like the real Sydney and the real Rio, and yet more who have already had a previous career. Happily, at Wragges, having a past is far from being considered a curse: among the current crop of trainees there's a former local authority surveyor and even a ballerina. In September 2003, all 17 qualifying trainees embarked on NQ careers at the firm. We just thought we ought to mention that once again!

Socially it's an exciting firm and there's *"a lot of meeting up in town after work."* Some practice groups are more sociable than others: this year litigation and the real estate group won special praise for their commitment to partying. Trainees get together casually *"once or twice a week,"* there are quarterly trainee meals organised by the trainee social committee (Yes, another committee), and last year the sports and social club arranged trips to Ascot and Wimbledon. The past few Birmingham TSG balls have been held in the Birmingham Botanical Gardens. *"It's a lovely venue,"* said one trainee. *"You can walk through hothouses."* Hot but not too steamy – we understand that while there was a bit of snogging in dark corners, there were few conga lines and even fewer incidents of table dancing. Honestly, trainees these days, no get up and go…

If you're a sportsman, there are a few things you should know about hockey in legal Brum. Firstly, hitting the ball has been outlawed since *"the boys would just smash the ball and ruin the game for everyone."* Secondly, there is one law firm team (whose name might begin with an E) that (allegedly) routinely hits the ball out of play and refuses to collect it. Refusing to take the bait, we're told the Wragges players simply laugh it off since *"it makes for a good bit of gossip in the office."*

and finally…

When we asked the trainees for some final sage words, one said: *"I was primarily looking at London firms before I considered Wragge & Co. Pause and think very carefully about whether City life is actually what you want."* Brum forever then? *"Yes!"* Well, unless you end up moving to the firm's London office…

Solicitors A-Z

Addleshaw Goddard

150 Aldersgate Street, London, EC1A 4EJ
25 Cannon Street, London, EC4M 5TB
Sovereign House, PO Box 8, Sovereign Street, Leeds LS1 1HQ
100 Barbirolli Square, Manchester, M2 3AB
Tel: (0161) 934 6000 / (020) 7606 8855
Fax: (0161) 934 6060 / (020) 7606 4390

firm profile

Addleshaw Goddard is a leading national law firm with the capability to provide excellent service to global clients. The result of a merger between two independently successful firms, Addleshaw Booth & Co and Theodore Goddard in May 2003, the cultural heart of Addleshaw Goddard will be driven by their passion for delivering the highest quality advice and service. The firm's aim is to set standards of client commitment which are valued by clients and admired by competitors.

main areas of work

The firm has five main business divisions, finance, commercial, corporate, litigation and employment and property. Within these divisions as well as the main practice areas it also has specialist areas such as sport, media and entertainment and private client services such as family and trust and tax.

trainee profile

Graduates who are capable of achieving a 2:1 and can demonstrate commercial awareness, motivation and enthusiasm. Applications from law and non-law graduates are welcomed, as are applications from mature students who may be considering a change of direction.

training environment

During each six month seat, there will be regular two-way performance reviews with the supervising partner or solicitor. Trainees have the opportunity to spend a seat in one of the firm's other offices and there are a number of secondments to clients available. Seated with a qualified solicitor or partner and working as part of a team, enables trainees to develop the professional skills necessary to deal with the demanding and challenging work the firm carries out for its clients. Practical training is complemented by high quality training courses provided by the in-house team and the College of Law.

sponsorship & benefits

CPE and LPC fees are paid, plus a maintenance grant of £4,500. Benefits include corporate gym membership, season ticket loan, subsidised restaurant, pension.

vacation placements

Places for 2004/5 - 75; Duration - 2 weeks; location - all offices; Apply by 13 February 2004.

Partners 170
Associates 500+
Trainees 99

contact

Mrs Simran Foote
Graduate Manager

selection procedure

Interview, assessment centre

closing date for 2006

31 July 2004

application

Training contracts p.a. **50**
Applications p.a. **3,000**
% interviewed **10%**
Required degree grade **2:1**

training

Salary
1st year (2002)
Manchester/Leeds £20,000
London £28,000
2nd year (2002)
Manchester/Leeds £22,000
London £30,000
Holiday entitlement **25 days**
% of trainees with a non-law degree p.a. **45%**

post-qualification

Salary (2002)
Manchester/Leeds £33,000
London £48,000
% of trainees offered job on qualification (2003) **81%**

other offices

Leeds, London, Manchester and Brussels

Allen & Overy

One New Change, London EC4M 9QQ
Tel: (020) 7330 3000 Fax: (020) 7330 9999
Email: graduate.recruitment@allenovery.com
Website: www.allenovery.com/careeruk

firm profile

Allen & Overy is one of the world's premier international law firms, with major strengths in banking, corporate and international capital markets. All departments work closely together to meet the needs of clients which include governments, financial institutions, businesses and private individuals.

main areas of work

Corporate; banking; international capital markets; litigation; real estate; private client; tax; employment and related areas.

trainee profile

Intellectual ability is a prerequisite but as Allen & Overy is a commercial firm it also looks for people with a good level of business understanding. The firm looks for creative, problem solving people who can quickly identify salient points without losing sight of detail. You will need to be highly motivated, demonstrate initiative and the ability to alternate between leading and being part of a team.

training environment

Within a highly pressurised environment, trainees obtain a balance of practical and formal tuition. You will experience at least four different areas of work, but will spend a significant amount of time in at least two of the following departments: banking, corporate and international capital markets. Your preferences will be balanced with the firm's needs. Seminars provide practical advice and an introduction to each area of law. Overseas placements are available. A positive, open and co-operative culture is encouraged both professionally and socially. A range of sporting activities are available.

benefits

Private healthcare scheme, private medical insurance, season ticket loans, subsidised restaurant, gym membership, six weeks unpaid leave on qualification.

vacation placements

Places for 2004: 90; Duration: 3 weeks; Remuneration: £250 p.w.; Closing Date: 31 January2004. Places available in London.

sponsorship & awards

CPE and LPC fees and £5,000 maintenance p.a. (£4,500 outside London, Oxford and Guildford).

Partners 439*
Associates 1409*
Trainees 429*
Denotes world-wide number

contact
Graduate Recruitment

method of application
Application form & online

selection procedure
Interview

closing date for 2006
CPE candidates
End Jan 2004
Law students **End Aug 04**

application
Training contracts p.a. **120**
Applications p.a. **4,000**
% interviewed p.a. **10%**
Required degree grade **2:1**

training
Salary
1st year (2003) £28,500
2nd year (2003) £32,000
Holiday entitlement **25 days**
% of trainees with a non-law degree p.a. **50%**
No. of seats available in international offices
32 seats twice a year and 5 client secondments

post-qualification
Salary (2003) **£50,000**
% of trainees offered job on qualification (as at 31/3/03) **90%**
% of partners (as at 31/1/03) who joined as trainees **49%**

international offices
Amsterdam, Antwerp, Bangkok, Beijing, Brussels, Bratislava, Budapest, Dubai, Frankfurt, Hamburg, Hong Kong, Luxembourg, Madrid, Milan, Moscow, New York, Paris, Prague, Rome, Shanghai, Singapore, Tirana, Tokyo, Turin, Warsaw

Arnold & Porter

Tower 42, 25 Old Broad Street, London EC2N 1HQ
Tel: (020) 7786 6100 Fax: (020) 7786 6299
Email: graduates@aporter.com
Website: www.arnoldporter.com

firm profile

With eight offices and almost 700 lawyers worldwide practising in over 25 practice and industry areas Arnold & Porter is able to bring clients a sophisticated understanding of changing environments at the intersection of business, law and public policy. The firm was established in Washington DC in 1946 and the London office was initially opened in 1997, but has grown rapidly over the past two years. As of mid-2003 there are almost 40 lawyers in the London office.

main areas of work

Arnold & Porter is a full-service law firm providing legal services worldwide. In the London office the practice areas include litigation, telecommunications, information technology, intellectual property, competition, corporate, life sciences, product liability and healthcare. The firm's clients include multinationals, UK and European concerns ranging from start-ups to Fortune 500 companies. Chambers and Partners presented the firm with their 'USA Antitrust Firm of the Year' Award in 2003, for the second time in the last three years.

trainee profile

The firm's commitment to excellence means that it expects its trainees to be well-rounded individuals with an outstanding academic background.

training environment

The London office reflects the environment of the firm generally. It has a collegial and informal atmosphere which is enhanced by twice-weekly informal social gatherings and other events, a casual dress policy and team-based assignment policies. Trainees will be expected to work on several matters at once and to assume responsibility quickly. The office emphasises teamwork and trainees will be quickly exposed to working for a variety of partners and fee-earners throughout the office and the firm. In the US, the firm is rated as the number one choice for new associates. The London office offered training contracts for the first time in 2002, and the firm's first trainees start in September 2004.

sponsorship & benefits

Sponsorship is provided for CPE/LPC. Private health insurance, a season ticket loan and life assurance are amongst the benefits offered by the firm.

vacation placements

Summer vacation schemes are on offer. Please apply on the firm's application form by 6 February 2004.

Partners	12
Assistant Solicitors	23
Total Trainees	0

contact
Graduate Recruitment

method of application
Application on firm's application form

selection procedure
Interview

closing date for 2006
6 August 2004

application
Training contracts p.a. 3-5
Required degree grade 2:1

training
Salary minimum £30,000
Holiday entitlement 25 days

post-qualification
Salary £59,000

overseas/regional offices
Washington DC, New York, Denver, Los Angeles, Century City, Northern Virginia, Brussels

ARNOLD & PORTER

asb *law*

Innovis House, 108 High Street, Crawley, West Sussex RH10 1AS
Tel: (01293) 603603 Fax: (01293) 603666
Email: human.resources@asb-law.com
Website: www.asb-law.com

firm profile

The firm asb *law* is a full-service law firm providing a range of specialist legal services to private clients, businesses, financial institutions, governments and public sector bodies. It has now established itself as one of the leading firms in the South of England. It is one of the largest and strongest commercial law firms in the region with unrivalled service coverage throughout Kent, Surrey and Sussex.

main areas of work

Principal areas of work are banking, corporate finance, commercial contracts, travel and aviation, commercial litigation, commercial property and planning, debt recovery, employment, environmental, family, information technology, insolvency and corporate recovery, intellectual property, licensing, personal injury, including clinical negligence, claimant and defendant actions, personal tax, wills, trusts and probate and residential property.

trainee profile

The firm is looking for bright, ambitious individuals who are client focused, commercial minded, polished and articulate. asb *law* are keen to recruit and retain individuals who have team values, a sense of fun and integrity.

training environment

The firm provides high quality training where individuals are positively encouraged to learn, take responsibility and have an active involvement with clients from an early stage. Training is divided into four seats (six months per seat). The firm's aim is to keep students with them as newly qualified solicitors so that through continual learning and development, students will have a challenging and rewarding long term career with the firm.

sponsorship & benefits

Life assurance, private medical insurance, 25 days holiday. An interest free loan is available for the LPC which is repayable over the period of the training contract.

Partners	49
Assistant Solicitors	54
Total Trainees	10

contact
Ms Gill Whensley
Tel: (01293) 601441

method of application
CV/covering letter; may be required to complete an application form with effect from 1st September 2003

selection procedure
2 interviews, psychometric test and written exercise

closing date for 2005
28 February 2004

closing date for 2006
28 February 2005

application
Training contracts p.a. **10**
Applications p.a **500 %**
interviewed **12%**
Required degree grade **2:1**

training
Year 1 **£16,750**
Year 2 **£18,750**

post-qualification
Salary **£27,500**

Ashurst Morris Crisp

Broadwalk House, 5 Appold St, London EC2A 2HA
Tel: (020) 7638 1111 Fax: (020) 7859 1800
Email: gradrec@ashursts.com
Website: www.ashursts.com

firm profile

An international City practice, smaller than its principal competitors, yet consistently ranked amongst the top few firms in terms of the work in which it is involved and clients for whom it acts.

main areas of work

Company/commercial, real estate, litigation, international finance, tax and energy, transport and infrastructure, with specialist groups in competition; construction; employment, incentives and pensions; environment; insolvency; insurance and reinsurance; intellectual property; life sciences; planning; product liability; property litigation; sport; technology; and telecommunications.

trainee profile

Candidates should want to be involved in the highest quality work that a City firm can offer. The firm is looking for high achievers academically as the work is intellectually challenging. Candidates should show common sense, good judgement, a willingness to take on responsibility, a sense of humour and an outgoing nature.

training environment

The training contract consists of four six month seats, one of which is a general corporate seat. Two seats are then spent in any two of the remaining main areas of practice. This will typically leave trainees with six months to choose one other department or specialist area of law in which they would like to gain experience. Trainees also have the opportunity to spend one of their seats abroad or in-house with a major client.

benefits

Benefits include private health insurance, pension, life assurance, interest-free season ticket loan, gym membership and 25 days holiday per year during training.

vacation placements

Places for 2004: 2 week Easter placement scheme primarily aimed at final year non-law undergraduates and all graduates. Two 3 week summer placement schemes primarily aimed at penultimate year law undergraduates. Remuneration £250 p.w. Closing date 31 January 2004.

sponsorship & awards

CPE and LPC funding, plus £5,000 maintenance allowance p.a. (£4,500 outside London and Guildford). LPC Distinction award of £500. Language tuition bursaries.

Partners	150
Assistant Solicitors	466
Total Trainees	100

contact
Stephen Trowbridge
Graduate Recruitment

method of application
Online

selection procedure
Interview with 1 assistant followed by interview with 2 partners

closing date for 2006
31 July 2004

application
Training contracts p.a. **50**
Applications p.a. **2,500**
% interviewed p.a. **20%**
Required degree grade **2:1**

training
(2003)
First six months
£28,000
Second six months
£29,000
Third six months
£31,000
Fourth six months
£32,000
Holiday entitlement **25 days**
% of trainees with a non-law degree p.a. **45-50%**
Number of seats abroad available p.a. **10**

post-qualification
Salary (2003) **£48,000**
% of trainees offered job on qualification (2003) **94%**

overseas offices
Brussels, Frankfurt, Madrid, Milan, Munich, New Delhi, New York, Paris, Singapore, Tokyo

Baker & McKenzie

100 New Bridge Street, London EC4V 6JA
Tel: (020) 7919 1000 Fax: (020) 7919 1999
Email: london.graduate.recruit@bakernet.com
Website: www.ukgraduates.bakernet.com

firm profile

Baker & McKenzie is a leading global law firm with more than 65 offices in 36 countries. In London, Baker & McKenzie is an established City firm of solicitors with a strong domestic and foreign client base providing legal services to multinational and domestic corporations, financial institutions, governments and entrepreneurs.

main areas of work

Corporate; commercial; dispute resolution; banking and finance; EC, competition and trade; employment; intellectual property and information technology; pensions; tax; projects; property. In addition the firm has cross-departmental practice groups, such as e-commerce and communications, insurance and reinsurance, business recovery and environmental law.

trainee profile

The firm is looking for trainee solicitors who are stimulated by intellectual challenge and want to be 'the best' at what they do. Effective communication together with the ability to be creative and practical problem solvers, team players and to have a sense of humour are qualities which will help them stand out from the crowd.

training environment

Four six month seats which include corporate and a contentious seat, usually within the firm's highly regarded dispute resolution department, together with the possibility of a secondment abroad or with a client. During each seat you will have formal and informal reviews to discuss your progress as well as subsequent seat preferences. Your training contract commences with a highly interactive and practical induction programme which focuses on key skills including practical problem solving, interviewing, presenting and the application of information technology. The firm's training programmes include important components on management and other business skills, as well as seminars and workshops on key legal topics for each practice area. There is a Trainee Solicitor Liaison Committee which acts as a forum for any new ideas or problems which may occur during the training contract. Trainees are actively encouraged to participate in a variety of pro bono issues and outside office hours there is a varied sporting and social life.

benefits

Permanent health insurance, life insurance, private medical insurance, group personal pension, subsidised gym membership, season ticket loan, subsidised staff restaurant.

Partners	70
Assistant Solicitors	196
Total Trainees	60

contact
Natalie McGourty

method of application
Letter & application form. Online applications also welcome

selection procedure
Candidates to give a short oral presentation based on the facts of a typical client problem, interview with 2 partners, meeting with a trainee

closing date for 2006
Non-law **18 Feb 2004**
Law **31 July 2004**

application
Training contracts p.a. **30**
Applications p.a. **2,000**
% interviewed p.a. **10%**
Required degree grade **2:1**

training
Salary
1st year (2003) £28,000 + £3,000 'golden hello'
2nd year (2003) £32,000
Holiday entitlement **25 days**
% of trainees with a non-law degree p.a. **Approx 50%**
No. of seats available abroad p.a. **Variable**

post-qualification
Salary (2003)
£50,000–£52,000
% of trainees offered job on qualification (2003) **72%**
% of partners (as at 1/9/03) who joined as trainees **40%**

Baker & McKenzie continued

vacation placements

London Summer Placement - Places for 2004: 30; Duration: 3 weeks; Remuneration: £250 p.w.; Closing date: 31 January 2004.

International Summer Placement - Places for 2004: 3-5; Duration: 6-12 weeks divided between London and an overseas office; Remuneration: £250 p.w.; Closing date: 31 January 2004.

sponsorship & awards

CPE funding: fees paid plus £5,000 maintenance.

LPC funding: fees paid plus £5,000 maintenance and choice to receive either an additional £2,000 or a laptop computer.

additional information

As mentioned, trainees have the opportunity to spend three months working in one of the firm's overseas offices. Trainees have already been seconded to its offices in Sydney, Hong Kong, Frankfurt, Chicago, Washington, Brussels and Moscow. In addition, the firm also operates an Associate Training Programme which enables lawyers with 18-24 months pqe to spend between 6-24 months working in an overseas office.

trainee comments

"Baker & McKenzie's global presence was apparent from my very first day here and has given me the opportunity to work closely with lawyers from many different jurisdictions. The quality of training here is second to none - trainees are given a lot of responsibility but never so much as to feel out of their depth. In addition to this, the professional yet friendly approach of everyone here has created an excellent working environment where you truly feel a valued member of the team. On a lighter note, the many and varied social events as well as the opportunities for joining in many different activities, from sporting teams to fund-raising committees, ensure that that there is always plenty to do outside the office". Nicole Kearley [2nd Seat Trainee]

"My training so far has involved working on a broad range of complex issues and I have had plenty of opportunity to take on challenging responsibilities. There has been friendly support available from all areas of the firm and this has been a great encouragement to me during my first months. The range of international work I undertake on a day to day basis remains exciting and makes the occasional request to down tools and catch a flight all the more enjoyable." Ben Crook [1st Seat Trainee]

"Throughout my training contract, I have been struck by the quality of training. As well as the formal training we receive at a firm-wide and departmental level, we are given continual guidance and feedback from associates and partners-the firm's "open-door" policy means that there is always someone to ask for advice. We are also encouraged to be pro-active in seeking out the kinds of work we are particularly interested in, and we have regular (formal and informal) meetings with our supervisors and departmental training partners to ensure that we are gaining the experience that we want. It is an extremely supportive and friendly atmosphere in which to work." Jo McGarvey [2nd Seat Trainee]

overseas offices

Almaty, Amsterdam, Bahrain, Baku, Bangkok, Barcelona, Beijing, Berlin, Bogotá, Bologna, Brasilia, Brussels, Budapest, Buenos Aires, Cairo, Calgary, Caracas, Chicago, Dallas, Düsseldorf, Frankfurt, Geneva, Guadalarjara, Hanoi, Ho Chi Minh City, Hong Kong, Houston, Hsinchu, Juarez, Kyiv, Madrid, Manila, Melbourne, Mexico City, Miami, Milan, Monterrey, Moscow, Munich, New York, Palo Alto, Paris, Porto Alegre, Prague, Rio de Janeiro, Riyadh, Rome, St Petersburg, San Diego, San Francisco, Santiago, São Paulo, Shanghai Singapore, Stockholm, Sydney, Taipei, Tijuana, Tokyo, Toronto, Valencia, Vienna, Warsaw, Washington DC, Zürich

Barlow Lyde & Gilbert

Beaufort House, 15 St Botolph Street, London EC3A 7NJ
Tel: (020) 7247 2277 Fax: (020) 7643 8500
Email: grad.recruit@blg.co.uk
Website: www.blg.co.uk

firm profile

Barlow Lyde & Gilbert is a leading international business law firm with more than 300 lawyers and 80 partners. The firm's principal office in the UK is in Aldgate in the City of London. BLG is particularly well known for its expertise in insurance law having first started to practise in this area in the 19th century. The firm has long been recognised as pre-eminent in all aspects of this field and it has formed the bedrock from which the firm has expanded into virtually all areas of business law. Today BLG is widely-based with strong practices in corporate, financial and commercial law, as well as in all kinds of commercial litigation. The firm also has highly rated aerospace, shipping and international trade, information technology and employment teams.

trainee profile

BLG recruits 16-18 trainees each year and looks for intelligent and motivated graduates with good academic qualifications and with the social skills that will enable them to communicate effectively and get along with their colleagues and clients.

training environment

During your training contract you will have six month seats in four different areas of the firm. The firm will always try to accommodate a trainee's preference for a particular type of work and there may be opportunities to spend time in its other offices, on secondment with clients or on exchange programmes with overseas law firms. A capable trainee will be given responsibility from an early stage in his or her training, subject of course to supervision, and will have to deal regularly with clients. Social activities play an important role for BLG and successful candidates can look forward to a variety of sporting and social events which ensure that people in different parts of the firm have a chance to meet and stay in contact with each other. Trainees are also encouraged to participate in the firm's various pro bono activities.

vacation placements

An increasing number of BLG's trainees come to the firm through its vacation schemes. Whether you are a law or non-law student the firm will introduce you to a City practice. You will be given the opportunity to become really involved and you can even choose which department you want to spend time in. The closing date for applications is 27 February. The firm also runs open days and drop in days throughout the year. Application is by way of a covering letter and application form.

sponsorship & awards

Full payment of fees and a maintenance grant are provided.

Partners	80
Assistant Solicitors	185
Total Trainees	35

contact
Caroline Walsh
Graduate Recruitment & Development Manager

method of application
Application form & covering letter

selection procedure
Interview day

closing date for 2006
30 July 2004

application
Training contracts p.a. **16-18**
Applications p.a. **2,000**
% interviewed p.a. **10%**

training
Salary
1st year £28,000
2nd year £30,000
Holiday entitlement
5 weeks

post-qualification
Salary **£47,000**
% of trainees offered job on qualification (2003) **72%**

other offices
Hong Kong, Shanghai

BLG
Barlow Lyde & Gilbert

Beachcroft Wansbroughs

100 Fetter Lane, London EC4A 1BN
Tel: (020) 7242 1011 Fax: (020) 2831 6630
Email: bwtrainee@bwlaw.co.uk
Website: www.bwlawfutures.com

firm profile

Beachcroft Wansbroughs is a progressive law firm with an ethos of team working and a reputation for being approachable. The firm prides itself on getting to know and understand its clients business as well as its clients do. In this way the firm anticipates clients' needs and delivers commercially tailored solutions to their problems and challenges.

main areas of work

The firm is managed in three divisions: Litigation, Commercial and Mutual Law. In addition it runs two consultancy services for Financial Services and Risk Management. The firm aims to provide an integrated and seamless service nationally, offering its clients a complete service in both contentious and non-contentious matters.

The firm has created a partnership with a strong sense of purpose and shared value; client service is its guiding principle. It has cultivated a reputation for leading rather than following and this is evident in its IT applications and approach to training.

trainee profile

The firm looks for outgoing, commercially minded people preferably with 2:1 honours degree in any subject. Students will need to be excellent team players, possess a mind capable of analysing, interpreting and applying complex points of law.

training environment

Training takes place over a two year period in London, Bristol, Manchester or Leeds, during which time students pursue a demanding study programme, whilst occupying 4 x 6 months seats in some of the key areas of commercial law. Responsibility will come early and the firm provides the supervision and support to enable students to develop and grow. The firm also runs an in-house training schedule open to trainees to attend which provides additional skills training to the PSC.

benefits

The firm operates a flexible benefits scheme, allowing students to buy and sell certain aspects of their benefits package, including holiday, pension and private health care. This gives students individual choice, depending on their current needs and circumstances.

sponsorship & awards

Beachcroft Wansbroughs provides payment for LPC, PgDL and £3,500 bursary.

Partners	130
Assistant Solicitors	375
Total Trainees	52

contact
Naomi Birch
Graduate Recruitment and Development Officer
Admin Centre
PO Box 2048
One Redcliff Street
Bristol BS99 7UR
Email: bwtrainee@bwlaw.co.uk

method of application
Apply online at www.bwlawfutures.com for an application form

selection procedure
Assessment centre and panel interview

closing date
1 August each year

application
Training contracts per annum
26
Required degree
2:1 preferred

training
Salary
1st year, regions-£19,500 pa
2nd year, regions-£22,000 pa
1st year, London-£27,000 pa
2nd year, London-£29,500 pa

offices
Birmingham, Bristol, Brussels, Leeds, London, Manchester, Winchester

Berwin Leighton Paisner

Adelaide House, London Bridge, London EC4R 9HA
Tel: (020) 7760 1000 Fax: (020) 7760 1111
Email: traineerecruit@blplaw.com
Website: www.blplaw.com

firm profile

Berwin Leighton Paisner is a top 15 City practice. It is a commercial law firm with expertise in many major industry and service sectors. The firm is a modern growing practice that puts a premium on commercial, as well as technical advice, client relations and transactional care. The firm is entrepreneurial and innovative.

main areas of work

Corporate finance; tech media; commercial; employment; commercial property; planning; environment; regulatory; construction and engineering; banking and capital markets; property finance; PFI/projects; and litigation and dispute resolution.

trainee profile

The firm is looking for intelligent, energetic, positive and hard working team players who have an interest in business and gain a sense of achievement from finding solutions.

training environment

Training starts with an induction covering all the practical aspects of working in a law firm from billing to client care. Comprehensive technical education programmes have been developed for each department and trainees attend weekly seminars supplemented by trainee lunches and skills sessions. You will undertake a tailor-made Professional Skills Course which is run in-house. Trainees spend six months in four seats and your progress will be reviewed every three months. The office environment is relaxed and friendly and trainees can enjoy early responsibility secure in the knowledge that they are fully supervised.

benefits

Flexible benefits package including permanent health insurance, private medical insurance, subsidised conveyancing, subsidised gym membership, 25 days holiday a year.

vacation placements

Places for 2004: Interviews held during March and April at either university campus or the firm's London office, application by online application form before 28 February 2004. The interviews could lead to a two week placement in the summer vacation. There are 50 places available on the summer placement scheme.

sponsorship & awards

CPE/PgDL and LPC fees paid and £4,500 maintenance p.a.

Partners	122
Assistant Solicitors	172
Total Trainees	66

contact
Debbie Campion

method of application
Firm application form online

selection procedure
Assessment day & partner interview

closing date for 2006
31 July 2004

application
Training contracts p.a. **35**
Applications p.a. **2,000**
% interviewed p.a. **5%**
Required degree grade **2:1**

training
Salary
1st year (2003) £28,000
2nd year (2003) £32,000
Holiday entitlement **25 days**
% of trainees with a non-law degree p.a. **27%**
No. of seats available abroad p.a. **0**

post-qualification
Salary (2003) **£48,000**
% of trainees offered job on qualification (2003) **80%**
% of assistants who joined as trainees (2003) **43%**
% of partners who joined as trainees (2003) **30%**

european offices
Brussels, associated office in Paris

SJ Berwin

222 Gray's Inn Road, London WC1X 8XF
Tel: (020) 7533 2268 Fax: (020) 7533 2000
Email: graduate.recruitment@sjberwin.com
Website: www.sjberwin.com/gradrecruit

firm profile

Since its formation in 1982, SJ Berwin has established a strong reputation in corporate finance. It also has a number of niche specialisms in areas such as private equity and film finance. Much work is international and clients range from major multinational business corporations and financial institutions to high net worth individuals.

main areas of work

Corporate 45%; property 20%; litigation 17%; EU and competition 8%; commercial media and IP 7%; tax 3%.

trainee profile

The firm wants ambitious, commercially-minded individuals who seek a high level of involvement from day one. Candidates must be bright and determined to succeed. They should be likely to achieve a 2:1 or first.

training environment

Four seats of six months each will be completed, and the seats are set, ideally, to the needs of the trainee. Two seats will be in the corporate finance arena, which includes Frankfurt, Paris and Madrid. The firm has a dedicated training department and weekly training schedules coupled with training designed specifically for trainees allow a good grounding in legal and non-legal skills and knowledge. Overseas seats are available in Paris, Madrid, Brussels, Munich and Frankfurt.

benefits

Corporate sports membership, free lunch, health insurance.

vacation placements

Places for 2004: 60; Duration: 2 weeks; Remuneration: £225 p.w.; Closing Date: 31 January 2004.

sponsorship & awards

PgDL and LPC fees paid and £4,500 maintenance p.a.(£5,000 in London).

Partners	119
Assistant Solicitors	270
Total Trainees	80

contact
Graduate Recruitment Team

method of application
online application form

selection procedure
2 interviews (early September)

closing date for 2006
31 July 2004

application
Training contracts p.a. **35**
Applications p.a. **2,500**
% interviewed p.a. **10%**
Required degree grade **2:1**

training
Salary
1st year £28,000
2nd year £32,000
Holiday entitlement
50 days over 2 years
% of trainees with a non-law degree p.a. **40%**
No. of seats available abroad p.a. **8**

post-qualification
Salary **£48,000**
% of trainees offered job on qualification (2003) **60%**
% of assistants who joined as trainees **26%**
% of partners who joined as trainees **12%**

overseas offices
Brussels, Frankfurt, Madrid, Berlin, Paris, Munich

Bevan Ashford

35 Colston Avenue, Bristol BS1 4TT
Tel: (0117) 918 3050 Fax: (0117) 918 8954
Email: hr.training@bevanashford.co.uk
Website: www.bevanashford.co.uk; www.bevan-ashford.com

firm profile

Bevan Ashford is one of the highest regarded national practices in the UK with a network of seven offices in Bristol, Birmingham, Exeter, London, Plymouth, Taunton and Tiverton. With 92 experienced partners, each of whom is a specialist in their field, and a total staff of over 750, the firm is able to provide clients with an efficient, professional and cost-effective service. Its national reputation means that the firm's client base ranges from multinational corporations and institutions through to smaller businesses, partnerships and individuals. Its success in attracting and keeping quality clients is achieved by the firm's complete commitment to total client care. By recruiting, training and keeping top quality personnel the firm believes it can continue its culture of client care and offer its clients the individual standards of service they require.

main areas of work

Healthcare 27%; commercial property 20%; commercial litigation 15%; company and commercial 16%; private client 17%; other work 5%.

trainee profile

Bevan Ashford is only as strong as its people. The firm's success is achieved by attracting and keeping enthusiastic, bright people with sound common sense, plenty of energy and the ability to work and communicate well with others plus a sense of humour! Language and IT skills are also desirable.

training environment

The core of your training will be practical work experience in conjunction with an extensive education programme consisting of talks, lectures and a residential weekend seminar to back-up the practical work. The training is aimed at developing attitudes, skills and legal and commercial knowledge essential for your career success. Your practical work experience will be reviewed on a regular basis by your supervising partner and you will be encouraged to take on as much work, and responsibility, as you wish. The firm is friendly with an open door policy with a wide range of social, sporting and cultural activities plus an active social club.

vacation placements

Places for 2004: 80. Closing Date: 31 March 2004.

sponsorship & awards

Available for LPC and in some cases PgDL (CPE).

Partners 92
Total Trainees 45

contact
HR and Training
(0117) 918 3050

method of application
Application form (available from the firm's website)

closing date for 2006
31 July 2004

application
Training contracts p.a. **25**
Required degree grade **2:1**

post-qualification
% of trainees offered job on qualification (2002) **95%**

other offices
Birmingham, Bristol, Exeter, London, Plymouth, Taunton, Tiverton

Bircham Dyson Bell

50 Broadway, Westminster, London SW1H 0BL
Tel: (020) 7227 7000 Fax: (020) 7222 3480
Email: trainee@bdb-law.co.uk
Website: www.bdb-law.co.uk

firm profile

Founded in 1834, the firm has particular strength in private client, charity and property work, together with thriving litigation and company commercial practices. It includes the leading parliamentary agency and public law and planning specialists (which previously practised under the name of Dyson Bell Martin). The firm is a member of the Lexwork International Group and has associate offices in 20 European countries.

main areas of work

Private client, charities, property, company commercial, litigation, parliamentary, public law and planning.

trainee profile

The firm is looking for mature, well-rounded candidates with high professional standards, a commercial approach and confidence. Bircham Dyson Bell recruit people whom they hope will have a successful future with the firm after qualifying.

training environment

Trainees will spend six months in four of the firm's five main departments: private client, parliamentary public law and planning, property, company commercial and litigation. They will be allotted their first seat, but the firm encourages trainees to express a preference for their remaining seats. Trainees share a room with a partner or senior solicitor, so that they can be involved in their supervisor's work and hear how matters are handled on a day-to-day basis. The firm provides training which offers trainees the opportunity to take responsibility, run their own files and meet clients, secure in the knowledge that their work is carefully supervised. There is always someone to answer questions and provide guidance and help.

benefits

Pension scheme; life assurance; private healthcare scheme.

Partners	**42**
Solicitors	**45**
Total Trainees	**10**

contact
Neil Emerson
Training Principal

method of application
CV & covering letter

selection procedure
2 interviews with partners from different departments and Head of Personnel

closing date for 2005
31 March 2004

application
Training contracts p.a. 6
Required degree grade 2:1

training
Salary
1st year (2003) £26,000
2nd year (2003) £27,000
Holiday entitlement 22 days

post-qualification
% of trainees offered job on qualification
Aims for 100%

Bircham Dyson Bell

Bird & Bird

90 Fetter Lane, London EC4A 1JP
Tel: (020) 7415 6000 Fax: (020) 7415 6111
Website: www.twobirds.com

firm profile

Bird & Bird is a 108 partner international law firm, employing approximately 600 staff including 30 trainees with offices in Brussels, Dussseldorf, Hong Kong, London, Milan, Paris, Stockholm and The Hague. The firm's size ensures a friendly but stimulating environment where legal, business and inter-personal skills can be developed and recognised. The firm has a clear business focus to provide a full range of legal services to specific industry sectors: communications, IT, life sciences, media, sports, e-commerce, banking and financial services, and aviation. This focus, combined with the firm's international ability, will enable you to work across borders and within fast movng industry sectors.

main areas of work

Company 56%; intellectual property 23%; litigation 12%; property 8%; private client 1%.

trainee profile

The firm looks for high calibre recruits – confident individuals capable of developing expert legal skills and commercial sense.

training environment

Following an introduction course, you will undertake four seats of six months. The choice of final seat is yours. You will share an office with a partner or senior assistant who will guide and advise you. You will hone drafting and legal research skills and gain familiarity with legal procedures. The firm encourages you to make an early contribution to case work and to meet clients immediately. Internal seminars and external lectures are arranged to cover the PSC. Trainees are welcome to join the number of sports teams at the firm and to attend various social events and outings.

benefits

BUPA, season ticket loan, subsidised sports club membership, life cover, PHI, pension.

vacation placements

Places for 2004: 18; Duration: 3 weeks; Remuneration: £220 p.w.; Closing Date: 30 January 2004.

sponsorship & awards

LPC and CPE fees paid and a yearly maintenance grant of £3,500.

Partners	108*
Assistant Solicitors	268*
Total Trainees	30*

** denotes worldwide figures*

contact
Lynne Walters
lynne.walters@twobirds.com

method of application
Online application form

selection procedure
Assessment mornings

closing date for 2006
30 July 2004

application
Training contracts p.a. **14**
Applications p.a. **1,500**
% interviewed p.a. **10%**
Required degree grade **2:1**

training
Salary
1st year (2003) £26,000
2nd year (2003) £28,000
Holiday entitlement
25 days
% of trainees with
a non-law degree p.a.
Varies

post-qualification
Salary (2003) **£43,000**
% of trainees offered job on qualification (2003) **75%**
% of assistants (as at 1/9/03) who joined as trainees **20%**
% of partners (as at 1/9/03) who joined as trainees **17%**

overseas offices
Brussels, Dusseldorf, Milan, Hong Kong, Paris, Sweden, Stockholm, The Hague

Blake Lapthorn Linnell

New Court, 1 Barnes Wallis Road, Segensworth, Fareham, PO15 5UA
Tel: (01489) 579990 Fax: (01489) 579126
Website: www.bllaw.co.uk

firm profile

Blake Lapthorn Linnell is a leading regional law firm with five offices in key locations in the South of England. Many solicitors who joined the firm as trainees are now partners. In addition a good proportion of the legal personnel have joined from major city law firms. With an enviable client base that includes many national companies, local authorities, government agencies, financial and non-profit organisations, the firm prides itself on its high value service, working closely with its clients to understand their needs and provide practical solutions. The breadth of the firm's business offers trainees all the challenges and opportunities of a big City firm, yet with all the advantages of a regional firm.

main areas of work

Company/commercial; commercial property; litigation; private client.

trainee profile

In addition to excellent academic achievements, the firm values previous experience, which has developed maturity and a wider perspective. Commercial awareness, teamworking and well-developed communication skills are also an advantage as well as familiarity with the use of IT.

training environment

Five to seven trainees are recruited each year and have a minimum of four placements lasting three or six months. Trainees' preferences are taken into account as far as possible, but the firm believes in providing well-rounded training supplemented with in-house education and regular appraisals and reviews with the Training Principal. Trainees are also allocated a 'mentor' for the duration of the contract.

Partners	79
Assistant Solicitors	175
Total Trainees	20

contact
Lynn Ford
graduateinfo@bllaw.co.uk

method of application
Firm's application form

selection procedure
Assessment Centre with interview then possible second interview

closing date for 2006
31 July 2004

application
Training contracts p.a. **5-7**
Applications p.a. **500**
% interviewed p.a. **10%**
Required degree grade **2:1**

training
Salary
1st year (2003) £16,500
2nd year (2003) £18,000
Holiday entitlement **25 days**

post-qualification
Salary (2003) **£29,000**
% of trainees offered job on qualification (2003) **75%**

Boyes Turner

Abbots House, Abbey Street, Reading RG1 3BD
Tel: (0118) 959 7711 Fax: (0118) 957 3257
Email: graduates@boyesturner.com
Website: www.boyesturner.com

firm profile

Boyes Turner is a leading Thames Valley practice, renowned for its insolvency and medical negligence work and well respected for corporate and commercial, commercial property, intellectual property, employment, personal injury, family law, planning, wills, private. While the focus for growth has been commercial work, the firm retains a commitment to its private clients.

main areas of work

Company/commercial (including employment) 20%; commercial property 20%; medical negligence/personal injury 20%; litigation 15%; insolvency 10%; family 5%; private client 10%.

trainee profile

Boyes Turner regards its trainees of today as its assistant solicitors and beyond of tomorrow and expects a high level of commitment, hard work and resourcefulness. Trainees must be responsive to the firm's mission to provide an excellent quality of service to both commercial and individual clients and also contribute to the team-working philosophy.

training environment

Training seats are currently organised into four six month seats; trainees gain experience in both commercial and private client practice areas. Work covers both individual and commercial clients, with as much client contact as possible, supervised by a partner or a senior solicitor. Andrew Chalkley, the Training Principal and Helen Barnett, the HR Manager oversee all aspects of the programme, while each trainee is assigned a tutor (one of the partners) who reviews their progress monthly. This is on two levels – first in assessing how the trainee is developing as a lawyer and secondly how the trainee is developing as an individual, including communication and negotiating skills.

benefits

Firm pension scheme, life assurance, 25 days holiday.

sponsorship & awards

LPC loan of £3,000 and only one loan per applicant. Interest free and repaid over training contract.

Partners	23
Assistant Solicitors	26
Total Trainees	8

contact
Graduate Recruitment Team

method of application
Letter & CV, online facility via website

selection procedure
2 interviews & 1 week work placement

closing date for 2006
31 May 2004

application
Training contracts p.a. **4**
% interviewed p.a. **1%+**
Required degree grade **2:1**

training
Salary
1st year (2003) £17,500
2nd year (2003) £18,500
Holiday entitlement **25 days**
% of trainees with a non-law degree p.a. **Varies**

post-qualification
% of trainees offered job on qualification (2002) **100%**
% of assistants (as at 1/9/03) who joined as trainees **42%**
% of partners (as at 1/9/03) who joined as trainees **17%**

B P Collins

Collins House, 32-38 Station Road, Gerrards Cross SL9 8EL
Tel: (01753) 889995 Fax: (01753) 889851
Email: jacqui.symons@bpcollins.co.uk
Website: www.bpcollins.co.uk

firm profile

B P Collins was established in 1965, and has expanded significantly to become one of the largest and best known legal practices at the London end of the M4/M40 corridors. At its main office in Gerrards Cross, the emphasis is on commercial work, with particular strengths being company/commercial work of all types, commercial conveyancing and general commercial litigation. Alongside this there is a highly respected private client department specialising in tax planning, trusts, charities, wills and probates, and an equally successful family law team.

main areas of work

Company/commercial, employment, IT/IP, civil and commercial litigation, commercial conveyancing, property development, private client and family law.

trainee profile

Most of the partners and other fee-earners have worked in London at one time or another but, tired of commuting, have opted to work in more congenial surroundings and enjoy a higher quality lifestyle. Gerrards Cross is not only a very pleasant town with a large number of high net worth private clients but it is also a convenient location for serving the extremely active business community at the eastern end of the Thames Valley including West London, Heathrow, Uxbridge, Slough and Windsor. The firm therefore looks for trainees who are likely to respond to this challenging environment.

training environment

The firm aims to have six trainee solicitors at different stages of their training contracts at all times. Trainees serve five months in four separate departments of their choice. The final four months is spent in the department handling the sort of work in which the trainee intends specialising. The firm has a training partner with overall responsibility for all trainees and each department has its own training principal who is responsible for day to day supervision. There are regular meetings between the training principal and the trainee to monitor progress and a review meeting with the training partner midway and at the end of each departmental seat. The firm also involves its trainees in social and marketing events including golf and cricket matches, go-karting and racing and other sporting and non-sporting activities and has its own six-a-side football team.

sponsorship & awards

50% LPC costs refunded once trainee starts contract.

Partners	18
Assistant Solicitors	22
Total Trainees	6

contact
Jacqui Symons

method of application
Handwritten covering letter & CV

selection procedure
Screening interview & selection day

training
Salary
1st year £17,000
2nd year £18,000

Brabners Chaffe Street

1 Dale St, Liverpool L2 2ET
Tel: (0151) 600 3000 Fax: (0151) 227 3185
Brook House, 77 Fountain Street, Manchester M2 2EE
Tel: (0161) 236 5800 Fax: (0161) 228 6862
7-8 Chapel Street, Preston PR1 8AN
Tel: (01772) 823921 Fax: (01772) 201918
Email: trainees@brabnerscs.com
Website: www.brabnerschaffestreet.com

firm profile

One of the top North West commercial firms, Brabners Chaffe Street, in Liverpool, Manchester and Preston, has the experience, talent and prestige of a firm that has a 200-plus-year history. Brabners Chaffe Street is a dynamic, client-led specialist in the provision of excellent legal services to clients ranging from large plcs to private individuals.

main areas of work

The firm carries out a wide range of specialist legal services and Brabners Chaffe Street's client base includes plcs, public sector bodies, banks and other commercial, corporate and professional businesses. Brabners Chaffe Street is organised into five client-focused departments: corporate (including commercial law); employment; litigation (including media); property (including housing association and construction); private client.

trainee profile

Graduates and those undertaking CPE or LPC, who can demonstrate intelligence, intuition, humour, approachability and commitment.

training environment

The firm is one of the few law firms that holds Investor in People status and has a comprehensive training and development programme. Trainees are given a high degree of responsibility and are an integral part of the culture of the firm. Seats are available in the firm's five departments and each trainee will have partner level supervision. Personal development appraisals are conducted at six monthly intervals to ensure that trainee progress is valuable and informed. The training programme is overseen by the firm's Director of Training and Development, Dr Tony Harvey, and each centre has a designated Trainee Partner. It is not all hard work and the firm has an excellent social programme.

Partners	42
Assistant Solicitors	46
Total Trainees	16

contact
Liverpool office:
Dr Tony Harvey
Director of Training and Development

method of application
Application form (please request by email, fax or post only)

selection procedure
Interview & assessment day

closing date for 2006
Apply by 31 July 2004 for training contracts commencing in September 2006

application
Training contracts p.a. 7
Required degree grade
2:1 or post-graduate degree

training
Salary:
1st year (2003) £17,000
Holiday entitlement 25 days

offices
Liverpool, Manchester, Preston

Brachers

Somerfield House, 59 London Road, Maidstone ME16 8JH
Tel: (01622) 690691 Fax: (01622) 681430
Email: info@brachers.co.uk
Website: www.brachers.co.uk

firm profile

Brachers is a leading firm in the South East with an established City office. The firm is principally involved in corporate and commercial work although it has a niche private client practice. The firm has a leading healthcare team, one of 14 on the NHSLA panel.

main areas of work

Company/commercial, general litigation, medical negligence, commercial property, employment, private client and family.

trainee profile

Candidates need to have a strong academic background, common sense and be team players. Both graduates in law and non-law subjects are considered as well as more mature candidates.

training environment

Trainees have four six-month seats out of company/commercial, property, general civil litigation, defendant insurance, medical negligence, family, employment, and private client. Trainees have two appraisals in each seat. The firm has an open door policy and is committed to developing a long term career structure. Social events are organised.

sponsorship & awards

LPC/CPE £6,000 discretionary award.

Partners 21
Assistant Solicitors 26
Total Trainees 8

contact
Mary Raymont

method of application
Handwritten letter & CV

selection procedure
Interview day with partners

closing date for 2006
31July 2004

application
Training contracts p.a. 6
Applications p.a. 400
% interviewed p.a. 7.5%
Required degree grade 2:1

training
Salary:
1st year (2003) £16,650
2nd year (2003) £18,200
Holiday entitlement 23 days

post-qualification
Salary (2003)
£27,500-£30,000
% of trainees offered job on qualification 90%

regional offices
Maidstone & London only

Bristows

3 Lincoln's Inn Fields, London WC2A 3AA
Tel: (020) 7400 8000 Fax: (020) 7400 8050
Email: info@bristows.com
Website: www.bristows.com

firm profile

Bristows specialises in providing legal services to businesses with interests in technology or intellectual property. The firm acts for some of the largest companies in the world and helps protect some of the most famous brands. Its work reaches beyond intellectual property law to corporate and commercial law, property, tax, employment law and litigation.

main areas of work

Intellectual property 54%; company/corporate finance/commercial 15%; IT 16%; commercial litigation (including employment) 10%; commercial property (including environmental) 5%.

trainee profile

Bristows is looking for applicants with outstanding intellects, with strong analytical skills and engaging personalities. It is also looking for people who will contribute to the ethos of the firm. Bristows is a very friendly firm and believes that you get the best from people if they are in a happy and supportive working environment.

training environment

The firm's training programme gives you the knowledge and skills to build on the extensive hands-on experience you will gain in each of its main departments. You will be working closely with partners, which will accelerate your training. Part of this training may also involve a secondment to one of a number of leading clients. With the international spread of its clients, the probability of overseas travel is high, especially upon qualification.

benefits

Excellent career prospects, a competitive package, firm pension scheme, life assurance and health insurance.

vacation placements

Schemes are run for one week during Christmas and Easter breaks, two weeks during the Summer break. Remuneration: £200 p.w.; Closing Date: Christmas –29 November; Easter/Summer – 28 February.

sponsorship & awards

CPE/LPC fees plus £5,000 maintenance grant for each.

Partners	26
Assistant Solicitors	59
Total Trainees	17

contact
Graduate Recruitment Officer

method of application
Application form

selection procedure
2 individual interviews

closing date for 2006
31 January 2004 for February interviews,
31 August 2004 for September interviews

application
Training contracts p.a. **Up to 10**
Applications p.a. **3,500**
% interviewed p.a. **6%**
Required degree grade **2:1 (preferred)**

training
Salary
1st year (2003) £26,000
2nd year (2003) £28,000
Holiday entitlement **4 weeks**
% of trainees with a non-law degree p.a. **71%**

post-qualification
Salary (2003) **£43,000**
% of trainees offered job on qualification (2002) **71%**
% of assistants (as at 1/9/01) who joined as trainees **41%**
% of partners (as at 1/9/01) who joined as trainees **53%**

Browne Jacobson

44 Castle Gate, Nottingham NG1 7BJ
Tel: (0115) 976 6000 Fax: (0115) 947 5246
Aldwych House, 81 Aldwych, London WC2B 4HN
Tel: (020) 7404 1546 Fax: (020) 7836 3882
102 Colmore Row, Birmingham B3 3AG
Tel: (0121) 237 3900 Fax: (0121) 236 1291
Email: info@brownejacobson.com
Website: www.brownejacobson.com

firm profile

Browne Jacobson is a substantial business and insurance services law firm, which has a practical approach providing a first class client service. Acknowledged as a leading regional practice offering a comprehensive range of services, the firm has continued to develop a nationwide reputation for quality and has a growing international presence. It operates from Nottingham, London and Birmingham. International development is driven primarily through London and Paris where the firm has an associated office and through key relationships with selected US law firms.

main areas of work

Insurance Services: Personal injury litigation; professional indemnity; public authority and defendant medical negligence.

Business Services: Corporate and commercial; tax and financial planning; commercial property; commercial litigation and employment.

trainee profile

The firm's trainees are bright, have high academic ability and bring enthusiasm and commitment to its practice. Personable and practical, they are able to work as part of a team whilst accepting individual responsibility.

training environment

Training at Browne Jacobson is practical and structured. You will spend four periods of six months working in all practice areas of the firm to obtain an overview and experience many new challenges. You will have a programme of skills training during which you will be strongly supported by Browne Jacobson's training team.

sponsorship & awards

PgDL, LPC.

Partners	48
Assistant Solicitors	91

contact
Carol King
Training Manager

method of application
CV & covering letter to Carol King, or via website

selection procedure
Assessment Centre

closing date for 2006
31 July 2004

application
Training contracts p.a. 8
Applications p.a. 1,500
% interviewed p.a. 5%
Required degree grade 2:1

training
Salary £18,500
Holiday entitlement 20 days
% of trainees with a non-law degree p.a. 5%

post-qualification
Salary Regional variations
Holiday entitlement 5 weeks

A-Z SOLICITORS

Burges Salmon

Narrow Quay House, Narrow Quay, Bristol BS1 4AH
Tel: (0117) 902 2766 (brochure) (0117) 902 7733 (enquiries) Fax: (0117) 902 4400
Email: alex.van-hattum@burges-salmon.com
Website: www.burges-salmon.com

firm profile

"...the Firm has managed to win work that other national rivals would kill for, and all with out sacrificing quality on the altar of ambition. With client wins such as EMI Group, Reuters, and Coca Cola HBC, Burges Salmon has quietly built the elite firm outside London." - A Leading Awards Body (2003).

Based in Bristol, with a facility in London, Burges Salmon is one of the UK's leading law firms offering an exceptional quality of life combined with a concentration of legal talent unsurpassed by any other firm in the country. More than 75% of its top 100 clients are based outside the South West, and the firm is consistently ranked amongst the UK's most profitable. Burges Salmon's success is based on a simple strategy: a focus on quality people, a breadth of practice areas and a single site approach. This ensures a cohesive culture combining skill, professionalism, enthusiasm and a supportive environment which attracts and retains staff and clients alike.

main areas of work

Burges Salmon provides national and international clients with a full commercial service through five main departments: company commercial, property, tax and trusts, commercial litigation, and agriculture, property litigation and environment (APLE). Specialist areas include: banking, competition, corporate finance, employment, IP and IT, and transport. The firm is ranked top tier by Chambers and Partners for 16 of its practice areas.

trainee profile

Successful candidates are motivated and hardworking, with a high degree of commercial acumen alongside a genuine enthusiasm for the law. They must show evidence of a strong academic background as well as significant achievements in non academic pursuits which demonstrate an ability to build relationships with clients as well as colleagues.

training environment

The Law Society recently accredited the firm's training programme with six points of good practice where the previous maximum in assessments of other firms had been two. This underlines Burges Salmon's reputation for having one of the best training programmes in the country. Training is personalised to suit each individual, and the firm's six seat structure means that you are given the opportunity to experience a wider range of practice areas before making a decision on qualification. This dedication to trainees is highlighted by a high retention rate, which is well above the industry average.

Partners	55
Assistant Solicitors	150
Total Trainees	40

contact
Alexandra Van-Hattum
Graduate Recruitment Manager

method of application
Employer's application form available on website

selection procedure
Penultimate year law students, final year non-law students, recent graduates or mature candidates are considered for open days, vacation placements and/or training contracts

closing date for 2006
31 July 2004

application
Training contracts p.a. **20-25**
Applications p.a. **1,500**
% interviewed p.a. **10%**
Required degree grade **2:1**

training
Salary
1st year (2003) £20,000
2nd year (2003) £21,000
Holiday entitlement **24 days**
% of trainees with a non-law degree p.a. **40%**

post-qualification
Salary (2003) **£34,000**
% of trainees offered job on qualification (2003) **90%**
% of assistants who joined as trainees (2003) **60%**
% of partners who joined as trainees (2003) **30%**

Burges Salmon continued

Trainees are given early responsibility balanced with an open door policy for advice and guidance. Supervisors are partners or senior lawyers who are highly trained to ensure trainees get as much as possible out of every seat and will tailor the workload to fit with each individual's interests and abilities. There are many opportunities for trainees to take an active role in cases involving high profile clients including Orange, Ministry of Defence, and Honda, as well as running their own files on smaller cases. Secondments to many of these clients are also encouraged to offer new perspectives on the profession as well as enabling trainees to build relationships with clients.

benefits

Annually reviewed competitive salary, 24 days paid annual leave, bonus scheme, Christmas gift, pension scheme, private heath care membership, mobile phone, laptop, corporate gym membership, sports and social club.

vacation placements

Places for 2004: 40, Duration: 2 weeks, Remuneration £175/wk, Closing Date: 30 January 2004. Selection for Vacation Placements is via Open Days which take place on 13 and 20 February 2004.

sponsorship and awards

The firm pays PgDL and LPC fees at the institution of your choice. Maintenance grants of £4,500 are paid to LPC students, and £7,000 to students studying for both the PgDL and LPC (£3,500 p.a.).

comments

"Burges Salmon has one of the most proactive practices I have come across. Their style, culture and professionalism are very hard to beat, and these qualities are very important to Honda." Christopher Morgan, Head of Legal, Honda UK.

"The firm employs a relatively small number of trainees which means that you feel very highly valued. The emphasis on trainng and development ensures you will not be left doing menial tasks which are a waste of your time, and a waste of the firm's investment in you. Trainees are able to enjoy a high level of responsibility due to the time supervisors and other lawyers are willing to invest in providing you with the support you need for each case." Luke Bowery, 2nd Year Trainee.

Cadwalader, Wickersham & Taft LLP

265 Strand, London WC2R 1BH
Tel: (020) 7170 8700 Fax: (020) 7170 8600
Email: hrdept@cwt-uk.com
Website: www.cadwalader.com

firm profile

Cadwalader, Wickersham & Taft LLP is a major New York based law firm, recognised for its innovative approach to legal and commercial matters. The London office, established in September 1997, is renowned for its expertise in capital markets, financial restructuring, corporate, banking and finance, project finance, litigation and real estate. The office services clients interested in capitalising on the European and worldwide markets, as well as those seeking US-style investment banking services and access to American capital markets.

main areas of work

Capital markets, financial restructuring, project finance, corporate, litigation, real estate and banking and finance.

trainee profile

Candidates need to demonstrate that they are intellectually bright and ambitious, have good communications skills and a commitment to the law. The firm looks for well-rounded individuals with a desire to succeed and a robust and resilient personality.

training environment

Training consists of four six month seats taking into account trainees' preferences. Responsibility and exposure to client meetings will take place at an early stage. Trainees share an office with a partner or associate, who supervise, review performance and provide feedback on a regular basis. Formal reviews will be carried out every six months. Elements of the PSC will occur at the start of the training contract; the remainder will take place over the following two years. The firm is friendly and supportive with an open door policy, operating a business casual dress down code all year round. There is also a varied sporting and social calendar.

benefits

Permanent health insurance, season ticket loan, BUPA (dental and health) and life assurance.

sponsorship & awards

CPE Funding: Fees paid plus £4,500 maintenance.
LPC Funding: Fees paid plus £4,500 maintenance.

Partners	11
Assistant Solicitors	45
Total Trainees	8

contact
HR Department

method of application
CV & covering letter

selection procedure
2 interviews

closing date for 2006
31 August 2004

application
Training contracts p.a. **6-8**
Applications p.a. **400**
% interviewed p.a. **6%**
Required degree grade **2:1**

training
Salary
1st year (2003) £30,000
2nd year (2003) £33,600
Holiday entitlement **24 days**

post-qualification
Salary **(2003) £65,000**
% of trainees offered job
on qualification (2002) **100%**

overseas offices
New York, Washington, Charlotte

Capsticks

77-83 Upper Richmond Road, London SW15 2TT
Tel: (020) 8780 2211 Fax: (020) 8780 4811
Email: career@capsticks.co.uk
Website: www.capsticks.com

firm profile

Rated as the country's leading healthcare law firm by the Chambers Guide and other leading directories, CAPSTICKS handles litigation, administrative law, employment, commercial and property work for a wide range of healthcare bodies, including over 150 NHS Trusts, PCTs and Strategic Health Authorities, and many private sector providers, healthcare-related charities and regulatory bodies.

main areas of work

Clinical law 54%; commercial 6%; commercial property 15%; dispute resolution 7%; employment law 18%.

trainee profile

Successful candidates possess intellectual agility, good interpersonal skills and are capable of taking initiative.

training environment

Six four-month seats, which may include clinical negligence/personal injury; commercial property; contract and commercial; employment law and commercial/property litigation. Trainees take responsibility for their own caseload and are involved in client meetings from an early stage. There are also opportunities to contribute to the firm's marketing and management processes. There are numerous in-house lectures for all fee earners. There is an open door policy, and trainees receive informal feedback and supervision as well as regular appraisals. Despite the firm's rapid expansion, it has retained a friendly atmosphere and a relaxed working environment. There are numerous informal social and sporting activities.

benefits

Bonus scheme, pension, PHI, death in service cover, interest-free Season Ticket Loan.

vacation placements

Places for 2004: Yes; Duration: 2 weeks; Closing Date: 28 February 2004.

sponsorship & awards

Scholarship contributions to CPE and LPC courses.

Partners	29
Assistant Solicitors	42
Total Trainees	12
Other Fee-earners	5

contact
Sue Laundy

method of application
Application form

selection procedure
Candidates are encouraged to participate in the firm's summer placement scheme. Final selection is by interview with the Training Principal & other partners

closing date for 2006
31 July 2004

application
Training contracts p.a. **4-5**
Applications p.a. **c.200**
% interviewed p.a. **c.18%**
Required degree grade
2:1 or above

training
Salary
1st year TBA
2nd year TBA
Holiday entitlement
22 days p.a. (increased by 1 day p.a. to max 25 days)
% of trainees with a non-law degree p.a. **60%**

post-qualification
Salary (2003)
£40,500 + benefits
% of trainees offered job on qualification (2003) **58%**
% of assistants (as at 1/9/03) who joined as trainees **45%**
% of partners (as at 1/9/03) who joined as trainees **7%**

Charles Russell

8–10 New Fetter Lane, London EC4A 1RS
Tel: (020) 7203 5000 Fax: (020) 7203 5307
Website: www.cr-law.co.uk

firm profile

Charles Russell is one of the UK's top 50 firms, providing a full range of services to UK and international companies and organisations, while its renowned private client and family practices continue to thrive. It has regional offices in Guildford and Cheltenham. The firm is known for its client care, high quality, expertise and friendly approach. The strategy is simple – to help clients achieve their goals through excellent service. Many of the lawyers are ranked as leaders in their field. Experienced in carrying out cross-border corporate and commercial work, the firm also provides clients with access to 150 recommended law firms across the world as part of the two major legal networks, ALFA International and the Association of European Lawyers. The firm's lawyers and staff are highly motivated and talented people. The firm's commitment to training and development and strong team spirit is a key ingredient to being known as a friendly firm to work with and work at. This is reflected in a recent survey of assistant lawyers which ranked the firm in the top six best law firms to work for in the UK.

main areas of work

75% of the firm's work is commercial. The principle areas of work include media and communications, employment and pensions, charities, private client/family, corporate, intellectual property, litigation/commercial dispute resolution, commercial property and insurance/reinsurance.

trainee profile

Trainees should be balanced, rounded achievers with an excellent academic background and outside interests.

training environment

For a firm of its size, a small number of Trainees are recruited each year. This allows Trainees to undergo the best possible training. Trainees spend six months in four of the following training seats – litigation, company/commercial, property, private client, family, employment and intellectual property. Wherever possible the firm will accommodate individual preference. Trainees will be seated with a partner/senior solicitor. Regular appraisals are held to discuss progress and direction. Trainees are encouraged to attend extensive in-house training courses. The PSC is taught both internally and externally. Trainees are encouraged to take on as much responsibility as possible. A social committee organises a range of activities from quiz nights through to sporting events.

benefits

BUPA; PHI and life assurance; pension plan; season ticket loans; dress down on certain days; eye tests; dry cleaning collection service; 25 days holiday and additional day for house moves; croissants and muffins available 8am to 9am each Friday.

sponsorship & awards

CPE/PgDL/LPC fees paid. Annual maintenance of £4,500 (under review) to London Trainees. One off grants in LPC year paid to Cheltenham and Guildford Trainees.

Partners	83
Associates	23
Assistant Solicitors	126
Total Trainees	26

contact
Jo-Anne Ratcliffe
Graduate Recruitment
Line: (020) 7203 5353

method of application
Covering letter & application form or online application

selection procedure
Assessment days to include an interview & other exercises designed to assess identified performance criteria

closing date for 2006
30 July 2004

application
Training contracts p.a. **8-10**
Applications p.a.
Approx 2,000
% interviewed p.a. **3%**
Required degree grade **2:1**

training
Salary
1st year (2003) £27,000
2nd year (2003) £29,500
Holiday entitlement
25 days + additional day for house moves

post-qualification
Salary (2003) **£44,000**

regional offices
Also offers training contracts in its Cheltenham & Guildford offices. Applications are dealt with by the London office

Clarks

One Forbury Square, The Forbury, Reading RG1 3EB
Tel: (0118) 958 5321 Fax: (0118) 960 4611
Email: contact@clarkslegal.com
Website: www.clarkslegal.com

firm profile

Founded in 1913, Clarks is a commercial law firm with a proven track record across the UK and overseas (with 17 partners and 13 associates). Clients range from small to medium sized enterprises to multinational companies. Clarks is particularly recognised for the number of international FTSE 250 clients who have chosen to use its services. Based in Reading, Clarks has taken full advantage of the rapid commercial and professional expansion of this thriving 'capital' of the Thames Valley.

main areas of work

Commercial property; corporate and technology; litigation; employment; planning; insolvency; private client; environmental and energy.

trainee profile

Candidates must have a consistently good academic record and should have effective interpersonal skills. Language skills are an advantage.

training environment

On joining Clarks, trainees will receive a full induction programme. Trainees immediately become part of a team and are encouraged to have direct involvement with clients and to play a part in building long-term relationships with them. Training usually consists of seats of six months in four of the following teams: property, corporate and technology, litigation, and employment. Within each seat you will have a mentor (a partner or an associate) who will have responsibility for guiding and encouraging you through that seat. In addition to training within a workgroup you are also encouraged to attend the firm's in-house weekly seminars. Clarks also supports you in your professional skills courses. Clarks is a classic yet innovative firm with an open, friendly culture. It retains a high number of trainees upon qualification and a significant number have progressed through the firm to become associates or partners.

sponsorship & benefits

LPC fees are paid, plus a maintenance grant. Benefits include pension, free conveyancing.

Partners	17
Solicitors	38
Total Trainees	7

contact
Denise Taylor
HR Officer

method of application
Application form (on website) or by letter and CV

selection procedure
Open day/interview and second interview (with limited written tests)

closing date for 2006
No closing date

application
Training contracts p.a. **3-4**
Applications p.a. **1,000**
% interviewed p.a. **10%**
Required degree grade
Usually 2:1 or above (but will consider lower grade if extenuating circumstances)

training
Salary
1st year (2003) £17,750
2nd year (2003) £19,000
Holiday entitlement **20 days**

post-qualification
% of trainees offered job on qualification (2003) **75%**
% of assistants who joined as trainees (2003) **40%**
% of partners who joined as trainees (2003) **40%**

overseas offices
Affiliated to TagLaw worldwide - ability to second to foreign office possible, subject to appropriate language skills

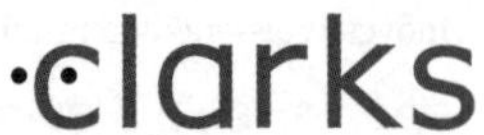

Clifford Chance

10 Upper Bank Street, London, E14 5JJ
Tel: (020) 7006 1000 Fax: (020) 7006 5555
Email: graduate.recruitment@cliffordchance.com
Website: www.cliffordchance.com/grads

firm profile

Clifford Chance is the world's first fully integrated law firm with 32 offices throughout Europe, Asia and America. It delivers legal services to powerful and influential businesses and financial institutions around the globe, working across international borders to shape the deals that make the news. This means trainees will gain breadth and depth in their experiences.

main areas of work

Banking and finance; capital markets; corporate; litigation and dispute resolution; real estate; tax, pensions and employment.

trainee profile

Consistently strong academic profile (minimum 2:1 degree), a broad range of interpersonal skills and extra curricular activities and interests, commitment to the career.

training environment

The Clifford Chance training contract has been devised to provide students with the technical skills and experience needed to contribute to the firm's success on a daily basis, to achieve professional qualification and to progress to a rewarding career. The two year training contract consists of four six month seats. Most trainees will spend a seat on a secondment at an international office or with a client. In each seat trainees will be working alongside senior lawyers. Trainees are encouraged to use initiative to make the most of expertise and resources available to the firm. Three-monthly appraisals and monitoring in each seat ensure trainees gain a range of work and experience.

benefits

Prize for first class degrees and distinction in LPC, interest-free loan, private health insurance, subsidised restaurant, fitness centre, life assurance, occupational health service, and permanent health assurance.

vacation placements

Places for 2003-2004: Christmas, Easter and summer break. There is a strong social element to the programme; Duration: 2-4 weeks; Remuneration: £270 pw; Closing Date: 14 November 2003 for Christmas scheme; 31 January 2004 for other schemes. A number of international placements will also be available during the summer. Selected candidates will have the opportunity to spend two weeks in London, followed by two weeks in one of the firm's European offices.

sponsorship & awards

CPE and LPC fees paid and currently £5,000 maintenance p.a. for London, Guildford and Oxford, £4,500 p.a. elsewhere.

London office

Partners	245
Lawyers	810
Trainees	235

contact
Louise McMunn
Graduate Recruitment

method of application
Online application

selection procedure
Assessment day comprising an interview with a partner & senior solicitor, a group exercise & a verbal reasoning test

application
Training contracts p.a. **125**
Applications p.a. **2,000**
% interviewed p.a. **25%**
Required degree grade **2:1**

training
Salary
1st year £28,500
(Aug 2003)
2nd year £32,000
Holiday entitlement **25 days**
% of trainees with a non-law degree p.a. **35%**
No. of seats available abroad p.a. **86**

post-qualification
Salary (Aug 2003) **£48,000**
% of trainees offered job on qualification (2003) **90%**

overseas offices
Amsterdam, Bangkok, Barcelona, Beijing, Berlin, Brussels, Budapest, Dubai, Düsseldorf, Frankfurt, Hong Kong, Los Angeles, Luxembourg, Madrid, Milan, Moscow, Munich, New York, Padua, Palo Alto, Paris, Prague, Rome, San Diego, San Francisco, São Paulo, Shanghai, Singapore, Tokyo, Warsaw, Washington DC

Clyde & Co

51 Eastcheap, London EC3M 1JP
Tel: (020) 7623 1244 Fax: (020) 7623 5427
Email: careers@clyde.co.uk
Website: www.clydeco.com

firm profile

A major international commercial firm with over 900 personnel worldwide and a client base spanning more than 100 countries. It is a leading practice in international trade, insurance, reinsurance, shipping and energy, and has experienced a high level of growth in corporate and finance. UK offices are in London, Guildford and Cardiff, with trainee solicitors recruited for London and Guildford.

main areas of work

Insurance/reinsurance; banking, corporate commercial and tax; marine and transport; general commercial litigation; property; employment.

trainee profile

The firm has no stereotypical trainee. Non-law graduates are welcome, especially those with modern languages or science degrees. The firm places as much importance on finding candidates with an outgoing, interesting personality as it does on academic credentials.

training environment

Trainees are immediately given as much responsibility as they can handle. They are also encouraged to take on as much client contact as possible, and are involved in developing business relationships. The PSC is run in-house and there is a full programme of lectures, seminars, courses, workshops and educational visits.

benefits

Subsidised sports club, interest free ticket loan, staff restaurant and weekly free bar.

legal work experience

The firm runs a Summer Vacation Placement scheme for 3 weeks in July. Closing Date: 27 February 2004.

sponsorship & awards

CPE and LPC fees paid and maintenance grant. Sponsorship provided where no LEA funding available.

Partners	120
Fee-earners	424
Total Trainees	41

contact
Claire Kohler
Graduate Recruitment Manager

method of application
Application form & covering letter

selection procedure
Assessment session with Graduate Recruitment followed by interview with 2 partners

closing date for 2006
13 August 2004

application
Training contracts p.a. **20**
Applications p.a. **1,300 +**
% interviewed p.a. **12%**
Required degree grade **2:1**

training
Salary
1st year (2003) **£27,000**
2nd year (2003) **£30,000**
Holiday entitlement **25 days**
% of trainees with a non-law degree p.a. **50%**
No. of seats available abroad p.a. (2003) **5**

post-qualification
Salary (2003) **£46,000**

overseas offices
Belgrade, Caracas, Dubai, Hong Kong, Nantes, Paris, Piraeus, Singapore, St Petersburg*
** Associated office*

CMS Cameron McKenna

Mitre House, 160 Aldersgate Street, London EC1A 4DD
Tel: (0845) 300 0491 Fax: (020) 7367 2000
Email: gradrec@cmck.com
Website: www.law-now.com

firm profile

CMS Cameron McKenna is a major full-service UK and international commercial law firm advising businesses and governments on transactions and projects particularly in the UK, continental Europe, the Asia Pacific region, North America and Southern Africa. It has particular strengths in a number of industry sectors such as banking and international finance, corporate, construction, projects, energy, healthcare, bioscience, insurance and real estate. The firm is modern, entrepreneurial and innovative and is strong on achievement.

main areas of work

Banking; corporate; insurance; energy, projects and construction; real estate and commercial.

trainee profile

The firm looks for high-achieving team players with good communication, analytical and organisational skills. You will need to show initiative and be able to accept personal responsibility, not only for your own work, but also for your career development. You will need to be resilient and focused on achieving results.

training environment

The firm is friendly and supportive and puts no limits on a trainee's progress. It offers four six month seats, three of which will be in the firm's main area of practice. In addition you may gain experience of a specialist area or opt for a secondment to a national or international client. In each seat you will be allocated high quality work on substantial transactions for a range of government and blue-chip clients. Regular appraisals will be held with your seat supervisor to assess your progress, skills and development needs. The three compulsory modules of the PSC will be completed before joining, allowing trainees to become effective and participate on a practical level as soon as possible. The Professional Skills Course is complemented by a comprehensive in-house training programme that continues up to qualification and beyond.

vacation placements

Places for 2003/2004: 55; Duration: 2 weeks; Remuneration: £225 p.w.

sponsorship & awards

PgDL and LPC Funding: Fees paid and a maintenance grant of £5,000 (London, Guildford and Oxford), £4,500 (elsewhere).

Partners	180
Assistant Solicitors	460
Total Trainees	112

contact
Graduate Recruitment Team (0845) 300 0491

method of application
Online application form www.law-now.com

selection procedure
2 stage selection procedure. Initial interview and verbal reasoning test followed by assessment centre

closing date
Continuous recruitment

application
Training contracts p.a. **80**
Applications p.a. **1,500**
% interviewed p.a. **27%**
Required degree grade **2:1**

training
Salary
1st year (2003) £28,000
2nd year (2003) £32,000
Holiday entitlement
25 days + option of flexible holiday
% of trainees with a non-law degree p.a. **40%**
No. of seats available abroad p.a. **Currently 15**

post-qualification
Salary (2003) **£48,000**
% of trainees offered job on qualification (2003) **90%**

CMS Cameron McKenna continued

additional information

Every trainee has a PC on their desk with email connection and access to legal and business databases. The firm financially supports trainees who wish to learn or improve a foreign language. There will be the opportunity to become involved in a number of sporting and social events.

trainee comments

"The firm has an incredibly wide base of areas to choose from, varying from healthcare and biotechnology to energy, projects and construction to the more traditional areas of banking, corporate and litigation. You'll find yourself in a pleasant and down to earth working environment where you'll be offered a variety of different opportunities, both in and out of work." (Trainee solicitor, Real Estate).

"Compared to other firms where I have friends it's very friendly and unstuffy here. It has retained the smaller firm environment even though we're now a top ten firm. Some firms pay lip service to the 'open door' idea but it really happens here. My best moment so far was helping the team who pitched against four of the top ten City firms for one of two places to do work for the Post Office - and we were appointed." (Trainee solicitor, Commercial).

"The most rewarding thing about the international opportunities here, whether it's before or after qualification, is the sheer scope the firm can offer you. There is no doubt that an international perspective is a massive selling point for law firms. Clients don't want to be dealing with one firm in London and any number of others overseas. And that's great news when you're a trainee because you have more chance to travel during your training contract, and then after qualification. My overseas experience was an invaluable part of my contract. I completed a seat in Hong Kong in our Corporate Recovery Group and worked in Orissa, India on the restructuring of the electricity industry. I doubt I'd get those kind of opportunities elsewhere." (Solicitor, Corporate).

branch offices

Visit www.law-now for further information

C/M/S/ Cameron McKenna

Cobbetts

Ship Canal House, King Street, Manchester M2 4WB
Tel: (0161) 833 3333 Fax: (0161) 833 3030
Trafalgar House, 29 Park Place, Leeds LS1 2SP
Tel: (0113) 246 8123 Fax: (0113) 244 2863
Email: lawyers@cobbetts.co.uk
Website: www.cobbetts.co.uk

firm profile

The firm continues to place high quality and long term relationship building with clients at the forefront of its strategy for success – a strategy which resulted in controlled sustained growth of around 20% p.a. This has been achieved through good management, and an emphasis on the needs of the clients, intermediaries and the firm's own personnel. In the 2002 Legal Business Assistants Satisfaction survey, Cobbetts was ranked highest outside London and fourth overall. In terms of skills training, Cobbetts was ranked second overall. Cobbetts believes in relationships, quality of environment and job satisfaction for all. Job satisfaction for trainees is shown by its trainee policy 'Recruit -Train - Retain'. Those three words say it all.

main areas of work

Commercial property 35%; company/commercial 29%; litigation 26%; private client 10%.

trainee profile

Law and non-law graduates.

training environment

Four six month seats are available. Typically these include one property, one litigation and one commercial/corporate seat. There is an opportunity for one trainee each year to spend three months in Brussels.

benefits

Social club and LA Fitness pool and gym.

vacation placements

Places for 2004: six placements are available during April, 24 during July and August.

sponsorship & awards

PgdL and LPC grant available.

trainee comments

"I would highly recommend Cobbetts as a firm to train with if you are looking for a challenging but enjoyable work environment together with a fun social life."
"Large enough and commercial enough to be one of the big players in the business, but yet relaxed enough and personal enough to make that difference to your training contract."
"I loved the firm on interview and was desperate to get in."

Partners	81
Fee-earners	112
Total Trainees	24

contact
Richard Webb
Trainee Recruitment Partner

method of application
Application form (available on request/via Internet)

selection procedure
Half day assessments

closing date for 2006
31 July 2004

application
Training contracts p.a. **15**
Applications p.a. **1,000**
% interviewed p.a. **10%**
Required degree grade **2:1**

training
Salary
1st year
Competitive rate
2nd year
Reviewed each year
Holiday entitlement **23 days**
% of trainees with a non-law degree p.a. **30%**
No. of seats available abroad p.a. **1**

post-qualification
% of trainees offered job on qualification (2002) **90%**
% of assistants (as at 1/9/00) who joined as trainees **75%**
% of partners (as at 1/9/01) who joined as trainees **60%**

overseas offices
Brussels

Coffin Mew & Clover

Fareham Point, Wickham Road, Fareham PO16 7AU
Tel: (01329) 825617 Fax: (01329) 825619
Email: saralloyd@coffinmew.co.uk
Website: www.coffinmew.co.uk

firm profile

Founded more than a century ago, the firm has grown to become one of the larger legal practices in the South East with major offices located in the cities of Portsmouth and Southampton and just off the M27 Motorway at Fareham. The firm is in the enviable position of operating a balanced practice offering private client and business services in approximately equal volume and is particularly noted for a number of niche practices with national reputations.

main areas of work

The firm is structured through eight core departments: corporate/commercial; employment; commercial litigation; personal injury; commercial property; family/crime; residential property; trust/probate. Niche practices include intellectual property; finance and business regulation; social housing; medical negligence and mental health.

trainee profile

The firm encourages applications from candidates with very good academic ability who seek a broad-based training contract in a highly progressive and demanding but friendly and pleasant environment.

training environment

The training contract is divided into six seats of four months each which will include a property department, a litigation department and a commercial department. The remainder of the training contract will be allocated after discussion with the trainee concerned. The firm aims to ensure that the trainee spends the final four months of his or her training contract in the department in which he or she hopes to work after qualification.

benefits

CPE and LPC funding available by discussion with candidates.

vacation placements

Open week in July each year; application as per training contract.

Partners 20
Assistant Solicitors 28
Total Trainees 9

contact
Sara Lloyd
Director of HR & Administration

method of application
CV & covering letter

selection procedure
Interview

closing date for 2006
31 July 2004

application
Training contracts p.a. **4-5**
Applications p.a. **400+**
% interviewed p.a. **5%**
Required degree grade
2:1 (save in exceptional circumstances)

training
Salary
1st year
Competitive market rate
2nd year
Competitive market rate
Holiday entitlement **20 days**
% of trainees with a non-law degree p.a. **25%**

post-qualification
Salary (2003) **£26,000+**
% of trainees offered job on qualification (2003) **100%**
% of assistants who joined as trainees **25%**
% of partners who joined as trainees **50%**

Coudert Brothers

60 Cannon Street, London EC4N 6JP
Tel: (020) 7248 3000 Fax: (020) 7248 3001
Email: recruitlondon@coudert.com
Website: www.coudert.com

firm profile

150 Years of Excellence, Innovation and Global Service. Founded in 1853, Coudert Brothers is a global partnership with 30 offices in 18 countries worldwide. In London the firm was one of the first English multinational partnerships of English solicitors and registered foreign lawyers. The firm advises on all aspects of national and international business law.

trainee profile

The quality and complexity of legal work undertaken by the firm demands that it recruits only individuals of the highest calibre. It is essential that trainees are enthusiastic, confident and outward going individuals, able to perform in a fast-moving and challenging environment. Early responsibility is routine and broad-based experience guaranteed. Coudert Brothers accepts law and non-law graduates. Applicants should have at least three A-level passes at grades A and B and a 2:1 degree. In view of the international nature of the firm's work and clients, language skills are an advantage, but not essential.

training environment

The training at Coudert Brothers comprises four six month placements. Three of these will be with the firm's core practices: corporate and commercial, banking and finance, litigation and property. The fourth will be drawn from one of the firm's other disciplines: energy and utilities, telecommunications, tax and funds and competition law. There is an opportunity for a secondment to one of the firm's overseas offices, usually Brussels. Partners and senior assistants ensure that trainees gain practical experience in research, drafting, procedural and client-related skills by working closely with them during each placement. There are regular appraisals during the two year training contract. Legal and professional training is provided through an in-house training programme and external conferences.

benefits

Pension, health insurance, subsidised gym membership, season ticket loan, private medical and dental care.

sponsorship & awards

CPE Funding: Fees paid plus £4,000 p.a. maintenance (discretionary).
LPC Funding: Fees paid plus £4,000 p.a. maintenance (discretionary).

Partners	10
Assistant Solicitors	20
Total Trainees	7

contact
Simon Cockshutt

method of application
Letter & CV

selection procedure
2 interviews with partners

closing date for 2006
31 July 2004

application
Training contracts p.a. 4
Required degree grade 2:1

training
Salary (Subject to review)
1st year (2003) £28,000
2nd year (2003) £32,000
Holiday entitlement 20 days

post-qualification
Prospects are good as the firm only takes a small number of trainees each year

overseas offices
Almaty, Antwerp, Bangkok, Beijing, Berlin, Brussels, Frankfurt, Ghent, Hong Kong, Los Angeles, Milan, Moscow, Munich, New York, Palo Alto, Paris, Rome, San Francisco, Shanghai, Singapore, Stockholm, St Petersburg, Sydney, Tokyo, Washington DC

associated offices
Budapest, Prague, Mexico City, Jakarta

Covington & Burling

265 Strand, London WC2R 1BH
Tel: (020) 7067 2000 Fax: (020) 7067 2222
Email: graduate@cov.com
Website: www.cov.com

firm profile

Covington & Burling is a leading international law firm, founded in Washington in 1919, with over 500 lawyers and offices in London, Washington, New York, San Francisco and Brussels. The firm's London office was established in 1988 and is growing at a steady rate. It is known for its expertise in cutting-edge fields, including information technology and e commerce, software, telecommunications, healthcare and life sciences and, in such work, the firm represents many household names.

main areas of work

The major practice areas include corporate and commercial work such as mergers and acquisitions, venture capital and private equity transactions, securities and finance, licensing and strategic alliances, intellectual property, information technology, competition, food and drug regulatory law, employment, litigation and arbitration, insurance and tax. There is no formal demarcation between practice areas and, at a firm level, practice areas spread across offices.

trainee profile

The firm is looking for outstanding students who are committed to providing quality legal advice in an imaginative way. In this way the firm will be able to maintain its ability to respond to the evolving needs and expectations of its clients. The firm obviously looks for team players, but above all else it also looks for intellectual distinction, imagination and integrity. In return the firm believes that the future will bring even more challenging and dynamic opportunities for Covington lawyers.

training environment

Trainees will spend six months in each of corporate, IT/IP and litigation practice areas. The fourth seat will be spent within the food and drug or the tax practice areas. The firm encourages junior members to take responsibility at an early stage of their career.

benefits

Pension, permanent health insurance, private health cover, life assurance and season ticket loan.

vacation placements

16 places during summer vacation. Closing date for applications 28 February 2004.

sponsorship & awards

CPE, PgDL and LPC fees paid. Maintenance grant of £5,000 per annum.

Partners: 163*
Associate Lawyers & Other Fee-earners: 345*
Total Trainees: 4 (2004)

** denotes worldwide figures*

contact
Graduate Recruitment Manager
(020) 7067 2091
graduate@cov.com

method of application
Application form & covering letter

selection procedure
1st & 2nd interview

closing date for 2006
31 July 2004

application
Training contracts p.a. 4
Required degree grade 2:1

training
Salary:
1st year £28,000
2nd year £32,000
(subject to review)

overseas offices
Brussels, New York, San Francisco, Washington

COVINGTON & BURLING

Cripps Harries Hall

Wallside House, 12 Mount Ephraim Road, Tunbridge Wells TN1 1EG
Tel: (01892) 506006 Fax: (01892) 506360
Email: aol@crippslaw.com
Website: www.crippslaw.com

firm profile

A leading regional law firm and one of the largest in the South East, the firm is recognised as being amongst the most progressive and innovative regional practices. Although long-established, this is a young firm where the atmosphere is professional and forward-thinking while friendly and informal. The firm is regarded by many businesses, institutions and wealthy individuals as the natural first choice among regional law firms. The firm achieved the Lexcel quality mark in January 1999, the first 'Top 100' firm to do so.

main areas of work

Commercial 44%, dispute resolution 31%, private client 25%. Its associated company, Cripps Portfolio, provides financial services.

trainee profile

Individuals who are confident and capable, with lively but well organised minds and a genuine interest in delivering client solutions through effective and pragmatic use of the law; keen to make a meaningful contribution both during their contract and long term career with the firm; and ambitious to build a career combining 'quality work' with 'quality life'.

training environment

The firm offers a comprehensive induction course, a well structured training programme, frequent one to one reviews, regular in-house courses and seminars, good levels of support and real responsibility. The training programme is broader than most other firms and typically includes six seats in both commercial and private client areas. Trainees will usually share a room with a partner and gain varied and challenging first hand experience.

sponsorship awards

Discretionary LPC funding: Fees – 50% interest free loan, 50% bursary.

Partners	38
Assistant Solicitors	51
Total Trainees	14

contact
Annabelle Lawrence
Head of Human Resources

method of application
application form available on website

selection procedure
1 interview with Managing Partner and Head of Human Resources

closing date for 2006
31 July 2004

application
Training contracts p.a. **8**
Applications p.a. **Up to 750**
% interviewed p.a. **6%**
Required degree grade **2:1**

training
Salary
1st year (2003) £17,000
2nd year (2003) £19,000
Holiday entitlement **25 days**
% of trainees with a non-law degree p.a. **7%**

post-qualification
Salary (2003) **£30,000**
% of trainees offered job on qualification (2003) **75%**
% of assistants/associates (as at 1/5/03) who joined as trainees **30%**
% of partners (as at 1/5/03) who joined as trainees **16%**

associated firms
A network of independent law firms in 18 European countries. Cripps Portfolio

CRIPPS HARRIES HALL

Cumberland Ellis Peirs

Columbia House, 69 Aldwych, London WC2B 4RW
Tel: (020) 7242 0422 Fax: (020) 7831 9081
Email: nicolawaldman@cep-law.co.uk
Website: www.cep-law.co.uk

firm profile

A central London firm of solicitors with a varied practice. The firm has a broad base of commercial and institutional clients including those involved in the media and information technology, quasi government councils, sporting associations, charities, City Livery companies, housing associations and landed estates, as well as having an established reputation for its private client services.

main areas of work

Company/commercial; commercial property; litigation, employment, family and private client.

trainee profile

Law and non-law graduates who have a consistently strong academic record. Individuals who can work with and relate well to others; who are commercially aware, with an ability to think creatively and to make a contribution to the firm. The firm is looking for candidates who have presence and enthusiasm, who are outgoing and articulate and who have a broad range of outside interests. IT skills are important.

training environment

Trainees spend time in each of the firm's departments under the supervision of a partner or senior assistant. Trainees are fully involved in all aspects of the work of the departments. Client contact and early responsibility for handling your own caseload are encouraged, subject to necessary guidance and supervision. There are a number of social, sporting and marketing activities going on during the course of the year and life outside the office is encouraged. An open door policy applies and the firm has a friendly and informal environment. Where possible the firm aims to recruit its trainees at the end of the training contract. The PSC is taught externally at the College of Law.

benefits

Season ticket loan, luncheon vouchers.

sponsorship & awards

It is not the firm's policy to offer vacation placements or sponsorship.

Partners	11
Assistant Solicitor	13
Total Trainees	4

contact
Nicola Waldman

method of application
Letter & covering CV (adding reference to 'Chambers')

selection procedure
2 interviews with partners

closing date for 2006
30 September 2004

application
Training contracts p.a. 2
Applications p.a. 500
% interviewed p.a. 3%
Required degree grade 2:1

training
Holiday entitlement
20 days

Davenport Lyons

1 Old Burlington Street, London W1S 3NL
Tel: (020) 7468 2600 Fax: (020) 7437 8216
Email: dl@davenportlyons.com
Website: www.davenportlyons.com

firm profile

Davenport Lyons is a leading entertainment and media law practice and combines this work with strong company/commercial (including IP/IT), litigation, property and private client departments. The firm adopts a keen commercial and practical partner-led approach and builds on long-term partnership with its clients.

main areas of work

Media/entertainment, music; litigation (defamation/IP/IT/contentious/property/general commercial/dispute resolution/insolvency/entertainment licensing); company and commercial (IP/IT); commercial/residential property; tax and trust; matrimonial; employment.

trainee profile

2:1 or above; interesting background; business acumen; practical with breadth of interests; sociable; knowledge of foreign languages an advantage.

training environment

Four seats of six months each. Three-monthly assessments. Supervision from within departments. Ongoing programme of in-house lectures and professional skills training. Davenport Lyons offers interesting hands-on training. Trainees are treated as junior fee-earners and are encouraged to develop their own client relationships and to handle their own matters under appropriate supervision.

benefits

Season ticket loan; client introduction bonus; contribution to gym membership; discretionary bonus; 23 days holiday.

vacation placements

Places for 2004: 10; Duration: 2 weeks; Remuneration: £175 p.w.; Closing Date: January 2004.

sponsorship & awards

The firm does not normally offer financial assistance.

Partners	30
Assistant Solicitors	46
Total Trainees	11

contact
Ann Goldie
HR/Training Manager
Michael Hatchwell
Training Partner

method of application
CV & covering letter

selection procedure
Interviews

closing dates
Closing date for 2005
December 2003
Closing date for 2006
July 2004

application
Training contracts p.a. **5**
Applications p.a. **1,500**
% interviewed p.a. **2%**
Required degree grade **2:1**

training
Salary
Currently under review
Holiday entitlement **23 days**
% of trainees with a non-law degree p.a. **40%**

post-qualification
% of trainees offered job on qualification (2002) **75%**
% of assistants (as at 2003) who joined as trainees **15%**
% of partners (as at 2003) who joined as trainees **3%**

DAVENPORT LYONS 

Davies Arnold Cooper

6–8 Bouverie Street, London EC4Y 8DD
Tel: (020) 7936 2222 Fax: (020) 7936 2020
Email: daclon@dac.co.uk
Website: www.dac.co.uk

Partners	49
Total Fee-earners	126
Total Trainees	9
Total Staff	335

firm profile

Davies Arnold Cooper specialises in a broad range of contentious and non-contentious legal services - always with the focus on pragmatism and the realties of business. The firm interprets the law with particular business context in mind; it doesn't just provide 'text book' answers. It is extremely proud of its reputation for providing high quality legal advice that delivers practical, commercial solutions. The firm acts for some of the leading public and private companies, both in the UK and abroad. The client list includes many large UK and international companies across a broad range of industry sectors from insurance and financial institutions (including Lloyds's), to property, retail, shipping, pharmaceuticals, energy, mining and construction.

main areas of work

The firm advises in relation to insurance and reinsurance (including fraud, professional indemnity, directors and officers liabilities and property and construction insurance); property; property finance; planning; product liability; construction and energy; health, safety and environmental law; international trade and competition law; insolvency and business recovery services; shipping; corporate and commercial; sports law and travel.

training environment

At Davies Arnold Cooper the firm likes to foster a culture that appeals to those who enjoy life. There is an atmosphere which lacks the formality and stuffiness of some more 'traditional' practices. However, at the same time the firm also ensures that it embraces the ethos of 'work hard, play hard'.

trainee programme

The firm's induction and training schemes are widely admired and trainees receive a comprehensive grounding in core legal skills. As a medium-sized firm it offers a flexible training programme with the opportunity for early responsibility within a supportive environment.

Dechert

2 Serjeants' Inn, London EC4Y 1LT
Tel: (020) 7775 7625 Fax: (020) 7775 7322
Email: application@dechert.com
Website: www.dechert.com

firm profile

Dechert is a leading international law firm with a full-service practice in the City of London. It specialises in a wide range of legal areas, including business, commercial property and litigation. With a total staff of over 1,500, based in 15 offices throughout Europe and the United States it competes successfully in the national and international arenas. Increasingly Dechert's London Practice represents clients from the United States and Continental Europe, alongside its UK client base. It has particular strengths in banking and securitisation, construction, corporate, defamation, employment, financial services, intellectual property, insurance, property finance, real estate and tax. The firm has offices in Boston, Brussels, Frankfurt, Harrisburg, Hartford, London, Luxembourg, Newport Beach, New York, Palo Alto, Paris, Philadelphia, Princeton, San Francisco and Washington. The largest offices are in Philadelphia, London, New York and Washington.

main areas of work – London

Business law (including areas such as corporate, financial services, banking, securitisation and IP) 43%, litigation 33% and property 24%.

trainee profile

Candidates should be able to empathise with a wide range of people, as their clients come from all walks of life. Dechert looks for enthusiasm, intelligence, an ability to find a practical solution to a problem and for powers of expression and persuasion. Also wanted are those with a desire and ability to promote the firm's business at every opportunity. Dechert wants people who will remain on qualifying and make their careers with the firm.

training environment

Unusually training is divided into six four-monthly periods, giving trainees the chance to sample a wide range of work. Your supervisor will participate with you and a Trainee Panel Partner (who will be responsible for your well-being throughout your training contract) in a formal oral and written assessment of your work towards the end of each seat. Trainees have the opportunity to spend four months in the firm's office in Brussels and some trainees now spend a period in their second year in one of the US offices. The greater number of seats makes it easier to fit in with any special requests to work in specific areas of the firm. The firm has a dedicated training programme managed by its Director of Training (the former Director of the College of Law, London). The PSC is provided in a tailored format by the firm, with some modules taking place in-house. That apart there is an extensive training programme in which trainees are encouraged to participate (numerous aspects being particularly aimed at trainees).

Partners (London) 40
Assistant Solicitors (London) 74
Total Trainees (London) 27

contact
Lynn Muncey

method of application
Application form via website

selection procedure
Communication exercises & interviews with partners & assistant solicitors

closing date for 2006
30 July 2004

application
Training contracts p.a. **18**
Applications p.a. **Over 1,500**
% interviewed p.a. **Approx 9%**
Required degree grade
2:1 (or capability of attaining a 2:1)

training
Salary
1st year (2003) £28,000
2nd year (2003) £32,000
(to be reviewed September 2004)
Holiday entitlement **20 days**
% of trainees with a non-law degree p.a. **Varies**
No. of seats available abroad p.a. **3 (plus shorter secondments to US offices)**

post-qualification
Salary (2003) **c.£48,000**
(to be reviewed July 2004)
% of trainees offered job on qualification (2002) **93%**
% of partners (as at 1/7/03) who joined as trainees **30%**

Dechert continued

benefits

Free permanent health and life assurance, subsidised membership of local gym and interest-free season ticket loans.

vacation placements - 2 programmes

Date: 12-23 July 2004 and 26 July to 6 August 2004; Places for 2004: 12 (6 on each programme); Remuneration: no less than £225 p.w.; Closing Date: 27 February 2004.
Assessment days: Dates: 30 March 2004 and 6 July 2004; Number of places: 20-30 on each.

sponsorship & awards

LPC fees paid and £4,500 maintenance (where local authority grants unavailable).

trainee comments

"The four month seat system at Dechert provides experience in a diverse mix of legal areas before deciding on a specific area for qualification. Seat rotations can be geared towards your career plans, Bernard George is always on hand to guide those uncertain of their path. Levels of supervision are sensible enough to make you feel you have a support network to fall back on, however you do get a sufficient level of responsibility depending on department (especially in litigation and property). This style of supervision develops confidence, particularly as a result of the high level of daily contact with both clients and other solicitors. Training and support throughout the training contract are of a very high standard and the six seat system allows the flexibility I sought for my contrac." (Ian Benjamin, Newly Qualified, read Classics at Nottingham).

"As one of a relatively small number of trainees at Dechert, training contracts are almost tailor-made. Trainees do six seats and are always able to do one or two seats in the area of law that interests them most. All supervisors are not only good at their jobs but also have a desire to teach you all they know. Trainees are encouraged to learn by experience, they can have a high level of contact with clients and other solicitors and are entrusted with relatively high levels of responsibility. However, supervisors and other members of each department are always willing to provide support and assistance when required. In addition, trainees receive training throughout the training contract on general points of law as well as training specific to their seats." (Claudia Nannini, Newly Qualified, read Law at Kings College London).

"Dechert's training programme is structured over six seats so trainees experience more areas of the law before deciding in which area to qualify. This was an important consideration for me in choosing Dechert over other firms since it was a priority for me to develop my capability as quickly and as fully as possible. Dechert's commitment to quality supervision is also significant, the firm places a high value on trainee development. Responsibility is delegated as you demonstrate an ability and willingness to assume it. Investment in trainees is a significant undertaking for the firm - its own future, as much as that of the trainees, is dependant on the success of its training programme. " (Nick Watson, Newly Qualified, read Spanish and German at Birmingham).

overseas offices
Boston, Brussels, Frankfurt, Harrisburg, Hartford, London, Luxembourg, Newport Beach, New York, Palo Alto, Paris, Philadelphia, Princeton, San Francisco, Washington

Denton Wilde Sapte

Five Chancery Lane, Clifford's Inn, London EC4A 1BU
Tel: (020) 7242 1212 Fax: (020) 7320 6555
Email: trainingcontracts@dentonwildesapte.com
Website: www.dentonwildesapte.com

firm profile

Denton Wilde Sapte is a large international law firm with particular strengths in banking and finance, corporate, energy and infrastructure, technology, media and telecommunications, real estate and dispute resolution: the firm's practice areas are as strong and diverse as its client list. The firm has offices in Europe, the Middle East, Asia and the CIS.

main areas of work

Denton Wilde Sapte provides the full range of legal services to the Real Estate, Technology, Media and Telecommunications, Energy and Financial Institution sectors.

trainee profile

The firm looks for candidates from any degree discipline with a strong academic and extra curricular record of achievement who are good team players. They should also have excellent interpersonal skills and the flexibility to grow with the firm. Languages are an advantage, but not essential.

training environment

Four six month seats, one of which may be spent in one of the firm's international offices. Two week induction at the beginning of contract including PSC core modules completed by October. Remaining electives should be completed by the end of the first year. The firm works to maintain a collegiate and open working environment where ideas are shared and people work together to achieve goals.

benefits

Flexible benefit scheme (choices include private health cover, sports membership, permanent health insurance, life assurance, dental insurance); meal away from home allowance; season ticket loan; holiday entitlement 24 days.

vacation placements

Approximately 25 places available on Open Days during December 2003 and 45 places available on Information Weeks during June and July 2004. Closing date for applications for Open Days is 5 December 2003 and for Information Weeks 27 February 2004. Closing date for 2006 training is 31 July 2004.

sponsorship & awards

CPE and LPC tuition fees covered plus £4,500 maintenance grant for each year of study, £5,000 if studying in London.

Partners	196
Fee-earners	666
Total Trainees	100

contact
Jo Wilson

method of application
Application form

selection procedure
First interview; selection test; second interview

closing date for 2006
31 July 2004

application
Training contracts p.a. **35**
Applications p.a. **2,000**
% interviewed p.a. **10-15%**
Required degree grade **2:1**

training
Salary
1st year £27,000-£28,000
2nd year £30,000-£31,000
Holiday entitlement **24 days**
% of trainees with a non-law degree p.a. **40%**
No. of seats available abroad p.a. **Currently 10**

post-qualification
Salary (2002) **£48,000**
% of trainees offered job on qualification (2002) **80%** (2003) **65%**

overseas offices
Abu Dhabi, Almaty, Beijing, Cairo, Dubai, Gibraltar, Hong Kong, Istanbul, Moscow, Muscat, Paris, Singapore, Tashkent, Tokyo

Devonshires

Salisbury House London Wall London EC2M 5QY
Tel: (020) 7628 7576 Fax: (020) 7256 7318
Email: training@devonshires.co.uk
Website: www.devonshires.com

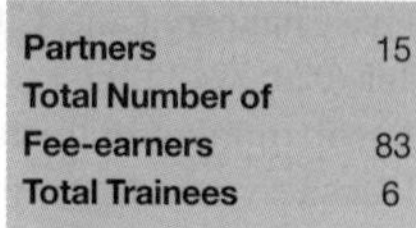

Partners	15
Total Number of Fee-earners	83
Total Trainees	6

contact
Angela Hall
Human Resources Manager
(020) 7628 7576

method of application
Online application form at www.devonshires.com

application
Training contracts p.a. **6**
Applications p.a. **400**
% interviewed p.a. **5%**
Required degree grade
2:1 and higher

training
salary for each year of training **£ market rate**
holiday entitlement **22 days**

post-qualification
Salary **negotiable**
% of trainees offered job on qualification (2003) **80%**

firm profile

Devonshires has been in the City of London for more than 150 years. The firm prides itself on its reputation for providing all its clients - who are based throughout England, Wales and the Channel Islands - with expert, cost-effective advice. The firm is a recognised leader in the social housing market and currently advises over 220 registered social landlords. The firm also advises financial institutions and stock exchange listed debt issuers; charities; corporations; government - domestic and international; insolvency practitioners; NHS trusts; private clients; professional service providers; property developers and investors - including financial institutions.

main areas of work

Property 30%; litigation 25%; banking and corporate 20%; PPP/PFI 10%; construction 5%; employment 5%; religious charities 5%.

trainee profile

The firm recruits high calibre trainees who are all-rounders. You don't have to be a law graduate - the firm welcomes applications from all disciplines and all universities. What you must have are keen commercial and technical qualities and proven academic abilities. You will also be able to show a demonstrable interest in a legal career and have a wide range of interests outside the office.

training environment

Training usually involves four seats of six months each, working with partners and senior staff in departments such as banking (company and commercial), church/charity, construction, employment, family/matrimonial, housing management litigation, litigation/dispute resolution, PFI and property. You will be required to cover a minimum of three practice areas and have a minimum of three months contentious experience.

benefits

Interest-free season ticket loans, healthcare scheme membership, subsidised health-club membership, dress down Fridays.

sponsorship & awards

Consideration for LPC funding.

Dickinson Dees

St. Ann's Wharf, 112 Quayside, Newcastle upon Tyne NE99 1SB
Tel: (0191) 279 9000 Fax: (0191) 279 9100
Email: law@dickinson-dees.com
Website: www.dickinson-dees.com

firm profile

One of the largest firms in the North East, Dickinson Dees has developed a national reputation for both commercial and private client services. The firm has premises on Newcastle's Quayside, in the City Centre and in the Tees Valley. The firm has an associated office in Brussels with opportunities for trainees to spend time on secondment there.

main areas of work

Corporate 30%; property 30%; private client 20%; litigation 20%.

trainee profile

Good academic and analytical ability. Good commercial and business sense. Confident, personable and adaptable with good communication skills with the ability to fit into a team.

training environment

Trainees are relatively few for the size of the practice. You are fully integrated into the firm and involved in all aspects of firm business. The training contract consists of four seats - one in each of the commercial property, company/commercial and litigation departments. You are able to specialise for the fourth seat. Trainees sit with their supervisors and appraisals are carried out every three months. The firm has its own Training Manager as well as a Graduate Recruitment Officer and a Graduate Programme Officer. There are induction courses on each move of department with opportunities for trainees to get involved in the firm's training programme. The firm offers a tailored in-house Professional Skills Course which is run in conjunction with the College of Law. The working environment is supportive and friendly with the benefits of working on the vibrant, bustling Quayside yet within 15 minutes from unspoilt countryside.

vacation placements

Places for 2004: 36; Duration: 1 week; Remuneration: £125 p.w.; Closing Date: 29 February 2004. Apply online or contact the Graduate Recruitment Team for an application form.

open days

Open days will be held in the Christmas vacation 2003, and the Easter and Summer vacations 2004. Closing date: 14 November 2003 for Christmas Open Day, 29 February 2004 for Easter Open Day and 30 April 2004 for Summer Open Days. Apply online or contact the Graduate Recruitment Team for an application form.

Partners	60
Total Staff	660
Total Trainees	30

contact
Graduate Recruitment Team

method of application
Apply online or contact Graduate Recruitment Team

selection procedure
Interview, in-tray exercise, negotiation exercise, personality questionnaire

closing date for 2006
31 July 2004

application
Training contracts p.a. **15**
Applications p.a. **700**
% interviewed p.a. **10%**
Required degree grade **2:1** in either law or non-law

training
Salary
1st year (2003) £18,000
2nd year (2003) £19,500
Holiday entitlement **23 days**
% of trainees with a non-law degree p.a. **50%**
No. of seats available abroad p.a. **1**
(3 month secondment)

post-qualification
Salary (2003) **£30,000**
% of trainees offered job on qualification (2003) **94%**
% of partners (as at 1/9/03) who joined as trainees **34%**

other offices
Tees Valley, Brussels

Dickinson Dees continued

sponsorship & awards

CPE/LPC fees paid and £4,000 interest free loan.

trainee comments

"Right from my very first visit I knew I had found the firm where I wanted to complete my training; Dickinson Dees has the strength and depth in its commercial practice areas to match most backgrounds and aspirations plus a genuine commitment to your training, great clients and informal, friendly colleagues -what else do you need?!" (Nicholas Payne, second year trainee in 2002-03, read Zoology at Oxford University)

"I was impressed at how everyone treated me as an important member of the team from the start, rather than just an extra pair of hands". (Mihoko Hirano, second year trainee in 2002-03, read Japanese Law at Chuo University, Tokyo).

"As soon as I had completed my work experience placement, I knew where I wanted to train. Dickinson Dees has the breadth of practice of a leading City firm, while offering a friendly and dynamic working environment and excellent training. As a linguist, I have also been able to use my language skills on several occasions". (Hilary Thorpe, first year trainee in 2002-03, read Law Exempting Degree with French Law at Northumbria University).

"Dickinson Dees promised me City quality work, real responsibility within a supportive and friendly environment and a life outside the office as well! What surprised me when joining was that the 'façade' did not fade – if anything they undersold themselves. This is a magnificent place to work where every member of the firm is made to feel an integral part of the team. I have received quality hands-on experience and client contact whilst maintaining a life of my own. What more could any trainee ask for?" (Rob Butler, first year trainee in 2002-03, read Law at Newcastle University).

"From my very first day at Dickinson Dees I felt a valued part of the team - I have undertaken work of the highest quality and have been given high levels of responsibility yet at the same time have received support through excellent supervision. Add to this the friendly and relaxed environment within the office and a social life which involves all members of the firm, from trainee to senior partner, and you soon realise why I chose Dickinson Dees. A fantastic firm within a fantastic city!" (Kevin Bell, first year trainee in 2002/03, read law at Durham University).

DLA

Victoria Square House, Victoria Square, Birmingham B2 4DL
Tel: (020) 7796 6677 Fax: (0121) 262 5793
Email: recruitment.graduate@dla.com
Website: www.dla.com/recruitment

firm profile

DLA is one of the UK's largest commercial law firms with offices in Birmingham, Edinburgh, Glasgow, Leeds, Liverpool, London, Manchester and Sheffield. With modern values and a clear strategy for the future DLA is a firm that is going places. Last year's fee income totalled £234 million. DLA was ranked 16th in the 'Sunday Times 100 Best Companies to Work for 2003' survey and has been awarded the prestigious 'Investors in People' standard.

main areas of work

DLA has the following practice groups: banking; business support and restructuring; commercial and projects; corporate; human resources; insurance; litigation; marine, aviation and reinsurance; real estate; regulatory; technology, media and communications.

trainee profile

The firm wants exceptional people as good academic ability alone is no longer sufficient. DLA values individuality and wants to recruit people from different backgrounds with a wide range of skills. Successful candidates will believe in themselves, relate well to other people, have an appetite for life and a desire to succeed in business.

training environment

The firm deliberately takes on a relatively small number of trainees. This enables it to offer a broad range of experience, a high level of responsibility and excellent prospects on qualification. During their training contract, trainees complete four six month seats in different commercial areas, learning through observation and practice. Through-the-job training is complemented by an ongoing commercial skills training programme and by the Professional Skills Course, which is run in-house.

benefits

Contributory pension scheme, health insurance, life assurance, 25 days holiday, good sports and social facilities and car scheme.

vacation placements

Places for 2004: 200; Duration: 1 week; Remuneration (2003 figures): £210 per week (London), £160 per week (Regions and Scotland); Closing Date: 28 February 2004.

sponsorship & awards

Payment of full fees during the PgDL and LPC years, plus a maintenance grant in both years.

Partners	322
Associates	241
Assistant Solicitors	426
Total Trainees	156

contact
Sally Carthy
National Graduate Recruitment Manager

method of application
Application form

selection procedure
First interview, second interview assessment afternoon

closing date for 2006
31 July 2004

application
Training contracts p.a. **85+**
Applications p.a. **2,000**
% interviewed p.a. **15-20%**
Required degree grade **2:1**

training
Salary (2003)
1st year £28,000 (London)
£20,000 (Regions)
£16,000 (Scotland)
2nd year £31,000 (London)
£22,000 (Regions)
£18,000 (Scotland)
% of trainees with a non-law degree p.a. **40%**

post-qualification
Salary (2003)
£48,000 (London)
£33,000 (Birmingham)
£32,500 (Other regional offices)
£30,000 (Scotland)
% of trainees offered job on qualification 2003 **94%**

overseas offices
Antwerp, Bangkok, Brussels, Madrid, Singapore, Shanghai plus associated offices across Europe & Asia

DMH

100 Queens Road, Brighton BN1 3YB
Tel: (01273) 744270 Fax: (01273) 744404
Email: personnel@dmh.co.uk
Website: www.dmh.co.uk

firm profile

DMH is an approachable and innovative firm with an open culture which encourages personal development and provides its personnel with a high level of support in order to achieve this. The firm offers expertise and service comparable to City firms to a range of commercial organisations, non-profit institutions and individual clients. By focusing on the client's needs DMH provides practical and creative solutions. DMH operates from offices in Brighton, Crawley and London.

main areas of work

Corporate/commercial; commercial property, planning and environmental; employment, intellectual property/IT; litigation; residential conveyancing; personal injury; private client.

trainee profile

The firm welcomes applications from motivated graduates from all backgrounds and age groups. Enthusiasm, a mature outlook and commercial awareness are as prized as academic ability, and good communication skills are a must. Ideal applicants are those with the potential to become effective managers or strong marketeers.

training environment

Usually four six month seats taken from the following areas: employment, intellectual property/IT, corporate/commercial, planning and environmental, commercial property, commercial litigation, property litigation, personal injury, civil litigation, residential conveyancing and private client. Trainees are closely supervised by the partner to whom they are attached but have every opportunity to work as part of a team and deal directly with clients.

vacation placements

Places for Summer 2004: Priority given to trainee interviewees with a limited number of unpaid places; Duration: 1 week; Closing Date: 31 January 2004.

Partners 32
Assistant Solicitors 26
Total Trainees 9

contact
Jessica Leigh-Davis

method of application
Application form
Selection Procedure: First interview and assessment day (March/April), work experience, then second interview (August).

closing date for 2005
31 December 2003

application
Training contracts p.a. **6-7**
Applications p.a. **400**
% interviewed p.a. **4%**
Required degree grade **2:1**

training
Salary
1st year (2003) £17,000
2nd year (2003) £19,500
Holiday entitlement **23.5 days**
% of trainees with a non-law degree p.a. **66%**

post-qualification
Salary (2003) **£29,000**
% of trainees offered job on qualification (2003) **100%**
% of assistants (as at 1/7/03) who joined as trainees **46%**
% of partners (as at 1/7/03) who joined as trainees **47%**

DWF

5 Castle Street, Liverpool L2 4XE
Tel: (0151) 907 3000 Fax: (0151) 236 3088
Email: trainees@dwf-law.com
Website: www.dwf.co.uk

firm profile

DWF delivers a complete menu of legal services for businesses, specialist technical know-how and industry sector expertise. It has a reputation for efficient and business-friendly service and for delivering outstanding value for money. DWF is a top tier law firm of choice for businesses based or operating in England and Wales – with a credible and effective national and international capability. Through its work with successful and growing businesses, DWF has become one of the fastest growing law firms in the UK.

main areas of work

Services for business clients, delivered by specialist teams – including leading experts in their field – supported by state-of-the-art technology. DWF's clients span the entire range of industry types but there are clusters of clients in certain sectors. To maximize the support for these clients, DWF had launched a number of industry sector groups, drawing together the firm's know-how and experience in the sector to deliver best practice and commercial advantage to the businesses concerned. Established industry sector groups are the DWF Finance Group, the DWF Food Group, the DWF Insurance Group, the DWF Property Group and the DWF Science Group. DWF is known for service innovation, as its BusinessBoost, DWF HRhorizons, DWF Maxima and Advantage services demonstrate. Information about the industry sector groups and innovative services can be found at www.dwf.co.uk.

trainee profile

DWF wants trainees to play a part in building on its success. The firm is looking for trainees who enjoy working as part of a busy team, who respond positively to a challenge and think they have what it takes to deliver results for clients. The firm is looking for its partners of the future.

training environment

All trainees commence life at DWF with a welcome programme designed to provide a clear picture of the firm and its services before moving to their first seat. The firm provides a flexible seat rotation including corporate, property, commercial litigation and insurance with agreed options which focus on post-qualification aspirations. This is supplemented by general training as well as specific training relevant to the particular seat which may be run in-house or using external courses. Appraisals are carried out during each seat to review progress and development. Trainees will have the opportunity to join in the busy social life within the office and with local trainee solicitors' groups.

Partners	55
Assistant Solicitors	119
Total Trainees	18

contact
Sarah Fielding
HR Officer
(Manchester address)

method of application
DWF application form

selection procedure
2 stage interview/selection process

closing date for 2005/2006
2 August 2004

application
Training contracts p.a. **6**
Applications p.a. **c.1000**
% interviewed p.a. **5%**
Required degree grade **2:1 in any subject preferred**

training
Salary
1st year (2003) £16,750
Holiday entitlement
23 days p.a. minimum

post-qualification
% of trainees offered job on qualification (2003) **100%**

benefits
Life Assurance, pension scheme

vacation placements
Open day events at each office

sponsorship & awards
LPC funding for tuition fees

Edwards Geldard

Dumfries House, Dumfries Place, Cardiff CF10 3ZF
Tel: (029) 2023 8239 Fax: (029) 2023 7268
Email: info@geldards.com
Website: www.geldards.com

firm profile

Edwards Geldard is one of the leading regional law firms. In the United Kingdom the firm's offices are located in Cardiff, Derby and Nottingham. Whilst continuing to expand the traditional areas of work in the company and commercial, commercial property, dispute resolution and private client departments, the firm has acquired particular expertise in a variety of 'niche' areas of legal work. These include mergers and acquisitions, corporate finance and banking, intellectual property, public law, planning and environmental law, energy law, rail and transport law, construction contracts and building arbitration, employment law, insolvency, trusts and tax, secured lending, property litigation and clinical negligence. The firm's growth in recent years has been characterised by an expansion of its work for major Stock Exchange listed clients and for City of London based organisations and by the growing reputation of its work for public sector bodies.

main areas of work

Company/commercial 40%; property 25%; litigation 20%; other 15%.

trainee profile

Candidates should be motivated and hardworking with a strong academic background. A sense of humour is essential, as is involvement in extra curricular activities and interests which show evidence of a balanced and well-rounded individual.

training environment

Training is divided into six four month seats in the firm's main practice areas. Trainees are allocated to a particular team and are supervised by the lead partner or senior solicitors working within the team. An 'open door' policy applies and trainees are regarded very much as an integral part of the team to which they have been allocated. A dedicated partner within each office has responsibility for the trainees in that office. A senior partner monitors consistency, progress and development across the three offices. Training is reviewed every three months. Your formal training will be a combination of external courses and internal seminars. Early contact with clients is encouraged in both work and social environments, as is the acceptance of responsibility. The atmosphere is friendly and the firm encourages its own social and sporting functions outside the office.

benefits

Life assurance at three times salary, 25 days holiday entitlement per annum.

sponsorship & awards

Full-funded LPC and up to £3,000 towards the CPE.

Partners	43
Assistant Solicitors	63
Total Trainees	23

contact
Owen M. Golding
Head of HR and Training

method of application
Application form

selection procedure
Interview & Summer Placement

closing date for 2006
For summer placements March 1 2004, otherwise end of July 2004

application
Training contracts p.a. **8**
Applications p.a. **400**
% interviewed p.a. **20%**
Required degree grade
2:1 desirable

training
Salary
1st year (2003) £16,000
2nd year (2003) £17,000
Holiday entitlement **25 days**
% of trainees with a non-law degree p.a. **Varies**

post-qualification
Salary (2003)
Not less than £29,000
% of trainees retained (2003) **60%**

Eversheds

Senator House, 85 Queen Victoria Street, London EC4V 4JL
Tel: (020) 7919 4761 Fax: (020) 7919 4919
Application Form Online at www.eversheds.com
Email: gradrec@eversheds.com
Website: www.eversheds.com

firm profile

Eversheds LLP has over 2000 legal and business advisers providing services to the private and public sector business and finance community. Access to all these services is provided through the firm's network of offices. Eversheds combines local market knowledge and access with the specialisms, resources and international capability of one of the world's largest law firms.

main areas of work

Corporate, commercial, litigation and dispute management, real estate, human resources (employment and pensions) and legal systems group. In addition to these core areas each office provides expertise in a further 30 business and industry sectors.

trainee profile

Eversheds' people are valued for being straightforward, enterprising and effective. The firm listens to its clients. It likes to simplify rather than complicate. It expects trainees to be business-like, unstuffy and down-to-earth. You will need to display commercial acumen, imagination and drive and, above all, you will need to be results-driven. As a trainee you will get as much responsibility as you can handle and will benefit from the 'hands on, learning by doing' philosophy. The firm takes your training very seriously but expects it to be fun too.

training environment

You will be encouraged to play a major part in the direction your training and development takes, with advice and supervision always available. In each department you will sit with a partner or a senior assistant and participate from an early stage in varied, complex and high-value work. Eversheds aims to retain as many trainees as possible on qualifying and many of the partners were trainees with the firm. A steep learning curve begins with a week of basic training followed by departmental seats – three of which will cover the firm's main practice areas. During your training you will also complete an Eversheds designed Professional Skills Course and, on qualification, follow a progressive career structure.

benefits

Regional variations.

vacation placements

Places for 2004: 150; Duration: 2 weeks; Remuneration: regional variations; Closing Date: 31 January 2004.

sponsorship & awards

CPE/LPC fees and maintenance grants.

Partners	400+
Assistant Solicitors	2,000+
Total Trainees	200+

contact
Jacqueline Speight
Graduate Recruitment Team

method of application
Apply online at
www.eversheds.com

selection procedure
Selection days include group and individual exercises, presentations and interview

closing date for 2006
31 July 2004

application
Training contracts p.a. **92**
Applications p.a. **4,000**
% interviewed p.a. **15%**
Required degree grade **2:1**

training
Salary
1st year London (2002)
£28,000
2nd year London (2002)
£31,000
Holiday entitlement **23 days**
% of trainees with a non-law degree p.a. **45%**
No. of seats available abroad p.a. **Up to 12**

post-qualification
Salary London (2003)
£46,000
% of trainees offered job on qualification (2002) **86%**

offices
Birmingham, Brussels, Cambridge, Cardiff, Copenhagen*, Hong Kong*, Ipswich, Kuala Lumpur*, Leeds, London, Manchester, Milan*, Newcastle, Norwich, Nottingham, Paris, Rome*, Singapore*, Sofia*

** Associated office*

Farrer & Co

66 Lincoln's Inn Fields, London WC2A 3LH
Tel: (020) 7242 2022 Fax: (020) 7242 9899
Email: trainees@farrer.co.uk
Website: www.farrer.co.uk

firm profile

Farrer & Co is one of the UK's leading law practices. It provides a range of specialist advice to private, institutional and corporate clients.

main areas of work

The firm's breadth of expertise is reflected by the fact that it has an outstanding reputation in fields as diverse as matrimonial law, offshore tax planning, employment, heritage work, charity law and defamation.

trainee profile

Trainees are expected to be highly motivated individuals with keen intellects and interesting and engaging personalities. Those applicants who appear to break the mould – as shown by their initiative for organisation, leadership, exploration, or enterprise – are far more likely to get an interview than the erudite, but otherwise unimpressive, student.

training environment

The training programme involves each trainee in the widest range of cases, clients and issues possible in a single law firm taking full advantage of the wide range of practice areas at Farrer & Co by offering six seats, rather than the more usual four. This provides a broad foundation of knowledge and experience and the opportunity to make an informed choice about the area of law in which to specialise. A high degree of involvement is encouraged under the direct supervision of solicitors and partners. Trainees attend an induction programme and regular internal lectures. The training principal reviews trainees' progress at the end of each seat and extensive feedback is given. The firm has a very friendly atmosphere and regular sporting and social events.

benefits

Health and life insurance, subsidised gym membership, season ticket loan.

vacation placements

Places for 2004: 32; Duration: 2 weeks at Easter, three schemes for 2 weeks in summer; Remuneration: £220 p.w.; Closing Date: 31 January 2004.

sponsorship & awards

CPE Funding: Fees paid plus £4,500 maintenance. LPC Funding: Fees paid plus £4,500 maintenance.

Partners	55
Assistant Solicitors	58
Total Trainees	14

contact
Graduate Recruitment Manager

method of application
Firm's application form and covering letter

selection procedure
Interviews with Graduate Recruitment Partner and partners

closing date for 2006
31 July 2004

application
Training contracts p.a. **8**
Applications p.a. **1,500**
% interviewed p.a. **2.5%**
Required degree grade **2:1**

training
Salary
1st year (2003) £26,000
2nd year (2003) £28,000
Holiday entitlement **25 days**
% of trainees with non-law degrees p.a. **42%**

post-qualification
Salary (2003) **£40,000**
trainees offered job on qualification (2003) **90%**
% of assistants (as at 1/9/01) who joined as trainees **72%**
% of partners (as at 1/9/01) who joined as trainees **70%**

Field Fisher Waterhouse

35 Vine Street, London EC3N 2AA
Tel: (020) 7861 4000 Fax: (020) 7488 0084
Email: kmd@ffwlaw.com
Website: www.ffwlaw.com

firm profile

Field Fisher Waterhouse is a city law firm with a reputation for providing a quality service to an impressive list of UK and international clients. In April 2002 it formed The European Legal Alliance with four other European law firms in Scotland, Ireland, Germany and France, giving it a full-service presence in 12 European cities. The firm prides itself on its collegiate atmosphere, its creative and commercial approach to law and its constructive approach to career development.

main areas of work

The firm has particular strengths in its key commercial areas of finance, corporate, commercial property, and brands, technology, media and telecommunications. It is also highly regarded for its expertise in commercial litigation, medical negligence and personal injury, aviation, travel and tourism, employment, pensions, private client, tax, competition law, energy, investment funds and products and professional regulation.

trainee profile

The firm is looking to recruit ambitious individuals with ability, enthusiasm and determination, who will be able to respond creatively and commercially to its clients' needs. It values strong personal qualities as well as academic achievement and welcomes applications from both law and non-law students.

training environment

Training will be split into five seats to enable you to gain the widest possible exposure to the firm's broad range of practice areas. In each seat you will work with several partners and assistants to gain a wide experience of the department. Feedback is ongoing and you will participate in a formal assessment at the end of each seat. The firm aims to develop your grasp of legal principles and to foster your commercial awareness. Your training will combine practical hands on experience and a comprehensive training programme of in-house lectures and external seminars. Staff enjoy the benefits of a busy sports and social committee, a 'Bolt Hole' lounge and dining area and squash courts.

sponsorship & benefits

Tuition fees and maintenance grant paid for CPE/PgDL and LPC. 25 days annual holiday, interest free season ticket loan, private medical insurance and life assurance.

vacation placements

Places for 2004: A summer vacation scheme will be run during July 2004. Application by CV and covering letter, between 1 January 2004 and 28 February 2004.

Partners	81
Assistant Solicitors	113
Total Trainees	24

contact
Karen Danker

method of application
Firm's own application form & covering letter

selection procedure
Interview

closing date for 2006
31 August 2004

application
Training contracts p.a. **10-12**
Applications p.a. **2,000**
Required degree grade **2:1**

training
Salary
1st year (2003) **£26,000**
2nd year (2003) **£29,120**
Holiday entitlement **25 days**
% of trainees with a non-law degree p.a. **50%**

post-qualification
Salary (2003) **£43,000**
% of trainees offered job on qualification (2003) **90%**
% of assistants (2003) who joined as trainees **40%**
% of partners (2003) who joined as trainees **40%**

Finers Stephens Innocent

179 Great Portland St, London W1N 6LS
Tel: (020) 7323 4000 Fax: (020) 7580 7069
Email: gradrecruitment@fsilaw.co.uk
Website: www.fsilaw.co.uk

firm profile

Finers Stephens Innocent is an expanding practice based in Central London providing a range of high quality legal services to corporate and commercial clients. The firm offers a range of services focused to meet the requirements of its primarily commercial client base. The firm's philosophy includes close partner involvement and a commercial approach in all client matters. Dedicated teams create services that are supplied in a cost effective manner with a working style which is personable, client supportive and informal. The firm is a member of the Network of Leading Law Firms and of Meritas.

main areas of work

Commercial property; litigation; media; employment; family; defamation; company/ commercial; private client. See the firm's website for further details.

trainee profile

The firm looks for academic excellence in applicants. It also looks for maturity, an interesting personality, strong communication skills, ability to think like a lawyer and an indefinable 'it' which shows that you have the potential to become a long-term member of the firm's team. Mature applicants are especially encouraged.

training environment

After your induction programme, you will complete four six month seats, sharing a room with either a Partner or Senior Assistant. The firm has two Training Partners who keep a close eye on the welfare and progress of trainees. There are regular group meetings of trainees and an appraisal process which enables you to know how you are progressing as well as giving you a chance to provide feedback on your view of your training.

benefits

20 days holiday, pension, private medical insurance, life insurance, long-term disability insurance, season ticket loan.

sponsorship & awards

LPC and CPE course fees.

Partners	33
Assistant Solicitors	34
Total Trainees	8

contact
Personnel Department

method of application
CV & covering letter

selection procedure
2 interviews with the Training Partners

closing date for 2006
30 June 2004

application
Training contracts p.a. 4
Applications p.a. 1,200
% interviewed p.a. 3%
Required degree grade 2:1

training
Salary
1st year
Highly competitive
2nd year
Highly competitive
Holiday entitlement 20 days
% of trainees with a non-law degree p.a. 0-50%

post-qualification
Salary
Highly competitive
% of trainees offered job on qualification (2003) 33%

Fladgate Fielder

25 North Row, London W1K 6DJ
Graduate Recruitment Line: (020) 7462 2299 Fax: (020) 7629 4414
Email: gradrec@fladgate.com
Website: www.fladgate.com

firm profile

Fladgate Fielder is an innovative, progressive and thriving law firm based in the heart of London's West End. The firm's business covers the whole spectrum of commercial activities. It provides a full range of legal services to a client base drawn from all sectors of commerce and industry in the UK and overseas, including multinationals, major institutions and listed companies, clearing banks, lenders and entrepreneurs.

main areas of work

The firm's four main departments comprise property, corporate, litigation and tax. These are complemented by cross-departmental units focusing on sports, media and technology, employment and benefits, intellectual property and insolvency.

trainee profile

In addition to a strong academic record, your extra-curricular activities and personal qualities are important to us; the firm's trainees will have commercial acumen, enthusiasm, leadership potential, excellent interpersonal skills and a genuine interest in the law. Fladgate Fielder is keen to attract candidates with developed language skills, particularly French, German and Italian.

training environment

You will normally be given the opportunity to complete six months in each of the firm's main departments: corporate, litigation, property and tax. In each seat you will sit with and be supervised by a partner or senior solicitor. In addition to on-the-job training and the PSC (undertaken externally), your career development will be encouraged through a number of activities. Each department runs a programme of talks and seminars covering legal and skills training; cross-departmental sessions are held on a regular basis. There is also the opportunity to attend sessions covering such topics as networking and time management.

benefits

Pension, permanent health insurance, life assurance, season ticket loan, sports club loan, bonus scheme.

Partners	32
Assistant Solicitors	36
Total Trainees	6

contact
Sharon Xenophontos

training
The firm operates a biennial recruitment programme and will be recruiting for its intakes of 2006 and 2007 in Summer 2005

Foot Anstey Sargent

21 Derry's Cross, Plymouth PL1 2SW
Tel: (01752) 675000 Fax: (01752) 675500
4-6 Barnfield Crescent, Exeter EX1 1RF
Tel: (01392) 411221 Fax: (01392) 218554
Email: training@foot-ansteys.co.uk
Website: www.foot-ansteys.co.uk

firm profile

Foot Anstey Sargent is one of the leading full-service law firms in the South West and has a strong reputation and prominence in the region. With a growing national and international client base the firm is recognised for its expertise in many sectors.

main areas of work

Commercial property, property litigation, commercial litigation, company and commercial, criminal advocates, family and childcare and private client. Niche areas include banking, employment, insolvency, media and marine.

trainee profile

The firm welcomes applicants from all law and non-law graduates who have a strong academic background, established communication skills and who are committed to achieving excellent standards of customer service. A strong team ethos is paramount to the firm. Trainees can expect to be welcomed into a friendly and supportive environment where they will find the quality and variety of work both challenging and rewarding.

training environment

The wide range of legal services provided offers trainees opportunities in many areas of law, sitting in either the Exeter or Plymouth offices. Trainees undertake four seats of six months and excepting the first, trainees are normally able to select their seat. All trainees attend an induction course. Individual monthly meetings are held with supervisors and a group meeting with the training principal. Appraisals are conducted quarterly. A non-partner acts as a confidential and objective counsellor. Regular communication between the trainees and supervisors ensures an open and friendly atmosphere. The PSC is taught externally. The firm holds an Investors in People accreditation and has an excellent training and development programme.

benefits

Contributory pension, 25 days holiday.

vacation placements

The deadline for the summer placement scheme is 31 March 2004.

sponsorship & awards

£8,000 grant towards LPC and living expenses.

Partners 26
Assistant Solicitors 47
Total Trainees 16

contact
Richard Sutton
(01752) 675151

method of application
CV and covering letter to Richard Sutton at the Plymouth office address. Alternatively email it to: training@foot-ansteys.co.uk or apply online at www.foot-ansteys.co.uk

selection procedure
Assessment day

application
Training contracts p.a. 8
Required degree grade 2:1 (preferred)

closing date for 2006
24 August 2004

training
Salary
1st year (2002) £15,600
2nd year (2002) £17,680
Holiday entitlement 25 days

post-qualification
Salary (2002) £27,825
% of trainees offered job on qualification (2002) 100%
% of assistant solicitors who joined as trainees (as at 30/04/03) 20%
% of partners who joined as trainees (as at 30/04/03) 30%

Forbes

Marsden House, 28-32 Wellington Street (St. Johns), Blackburn BB1 8DA
Tel: (01254) 662831 Fax: (01254) 681104
Email: Siobhan.hardy@forbessolicitors.co.uk

firm profile

Forbes is one of the largest and most respected practices in the north with 23 partners and over 300 members of staff based in nine offices across the north of England. The firm has a broad based practice dealing with both commercial and private client work and can therefore provide a varied and exciting training contract. The firm is however especially noted for excellence in its company/commercial; civil litigation; defendant insurer; crime; family and employment departments. It has a number of Higher Court Advocates and the firm holds many Legal Service Commission Franchises. Underlying the practice is a strong commitment to quality, training and career development – a commitment underlined by the fact that Forbes was one of the first firms to be recognised as an Investor in People and its ISO 9001 accreditation. For applicants looking for a 'city' practice without the associated hassles of working in a city then Forbes could be it. The firm can offer the best of both worlds. - a large firm with extensive resources and support combined with a commitment to quality, people and the personal touch.

main areas of work

Company/commercial, civil litigation, defendant insurer, crime, family and employment services.

trainee profile

Forbes looks for high-calibre recruits with strong local connections, good academic records, who are also keen team players.

training environment

A tailored training programme involves six months in four of the following: crime, civil litigation, defendant insurer, matrimonial, and non-contentious/company commercial.

Partners	23
Assistant Solicitors	65
Total Trainees	13

contact
Siobhan Hardy

method of application
Handwritten letter and CV

selection procedure
Interview with partners

closing date for 2006
31 July 2004

application
Training contracts p.a. **4**
Applications p.a. **350 plus**
% interviewed p.a. **Varies**
Required degree grade **2:1**

training
Salary
1st year At least Law Society minimum
2nd year (2003) £16,600
Holiday entitlement
20 days pa

post-qualification
Salary
Highly competitive
% of trainees offered job on qualification (2003) **100%**

Ford & Warren

Westgate Point, Westgate, Leeds, LS1 2AX
Tel: (0113) 243 6601 Fax: (0113) 242 0905
Email: clientmail@forwarn.com
Website: www.forwarn.com

firm profile

Ford & Warren is an independent, single office commercial law firm based in Leeds. Over the last 10 years the firm has sustained a rapid and generic growth without mergers or acquisitions so that it now occupies the whole of the prestigious Westgate Point office block in the heart of the commercial centre of Leeds. The firm has 24 partners, 88 solicitors and para-legals and a total staff of over 200. Ford & Warren has the following departments: Employment; Road and Rail; Transportation; Corporate; Commercial Litigation; Commercial Property; Insurance and PI; Tax and Inheritance; Matrimonial. The firm has a significant presence in the public sector particularly in health and education. The firm has areas of high specialisation where its lawyers have a national reputation and its client base includes the largest limited companies and PLCs. These areas include transportation and the licensed and leisure industries.

main areas of work

Employment and industrial relations; road and rail transportation; corporate; insurance and personal injury; commercial property/real estate; public sector; tax and inheritance; matrimonial. The Dispute Resolution/Commercial Litigation Department has five sections: commercial dispute resolution, property litigation, finance litigation, insolvency and debt recovery.

trainee profile

The firm is looking for hard working, self-reliant and enthusiastic individuals who will make a contribution to the firm from the outset. Applicants must have a strong academic background, a genuine enthusiasm for the law and the social abilities required to work effectively with colleagues and clients. The majority of lawyers practising at the firm joined as trainees.

training environment

The firm offers seats in employment, commercial litigtion, corporate, insurance and personal injury, commercial property and private client. Usually, trainees will undertake four seats of six months, although split seats may sometimes be available. The final six months takes place in the department into which the trainee wishes to qualify. The firm has a comprehensive in-house trainig programme for all lawyers and the PSC is also provided internally.

selection procedure

First interviews and exercise held with Practice Manager and a Partner in September and early October. Successful candidates are invited to a second interview with the Managing Partner, including a further exercise and presentation.

Partners	24
Assistant Solicitors	88
Total Trainees	12

contact
Caroline Verriez

method of application
Handwritten letter and CV

selection procedure
Interviews and exercise

closing date for 2006
31 August 2004

application
Training contracts p.a. **6**
Applications p.a. **700**
Required degree grade **2:1**

Forsters

67 Grosvenor Street, London W1K 3JN
Tel: (020) 7863 8333 Fax: (020) 7863 8444
Email: ajfairchild@forsters.co.uk
Website: www.forsters.co.uk

firm profile

Forsters opened for business in 1998 with 11 of the 22 founding partners previously being partners of Frere Chomley Bischoff. It is a progressive law firm with a strong reputation for its property and private client work as well as thriving commercial and litigation practices. The working atmosphere of the firm is friendly and informal, yet highly professional. A social committee organises a range of activities from quiz nights to sporting events as Forsters actively encourages all its staff to have a life outside of work!

main areas of work

The firm has a strong reputation for all aspects of commercial and residential property work. The groups handle investment funding; development; planning; construction; landlord and tenant; property taxation and residential investment and development. Forsters is also recognised as one of the leading proponents of private client work in London with a client base comprising a broad range of individuals and trusts in the UK and elsewhere. The firm's commercial practice specialises in acquisitions and financing for technology, communication and media companies whilst its litigation group conducts commercial litigation and arbitration and advises on a broad spectrum of matters.

trainee profile

Successful candidates will have a strong academic background and either have attained or be expected to achieve a good second class degree. The firm considers that factors alongside academic achievements are also important. The firm is looking for individuals who give a real indication of being interested in a career in law and who the firm feels would readily accept and work well in its team environment.

training environment

The first year of training is split into three seats of four months in three of the following departments: commercial property, private client, company commercial or litigation. In the second year the four month pattern still applies, but the firm discusses with you whether you have developed an area of particular interest and tries to accommodate this. The training is very 'hands on' as you share an office with a partner or assistant who will give you real responsibility alongside supervision. At the end of each seat your progress and performance will be reviewed by way of an appraisal with a partner from the relevant department.

sponsorship & benefits

22 days holiday p.a., season ticket loan, permanent health insurance, life insurance, subsidised gym membership. No sponsorship for CPE or LPC courses is currently provided.

Partners 22
Assistant Solicitors 40
Total Trainees 6

contact
Alison Fairchild

method of application
Application form

selection procedure
First interview with HR Manager & Graduate Recruitment Partner; second interview with 2 partners

training
Salary
1st year (2003) £24,500
2nd year (2003) £26,500
Holiday entitlement **22 days**

post-qualification
Salary (2003) **£41,000**
% of trainees offered job on qualification (2002) **100%** (2003) **75%**

Freethcartwright LLP

Willoughby House, 20 Low Pavement, Nottingham NG1 7EA
Tel: (0115) 936 9369 Fax: (0115) 859 9603
Email: carole.wigley@freethcartwright.co.uk
Website: www.freethcartwright.co.uk

firm profile

Tracing its origins back to 1805, Freethcartwright LLP became Nottingham's largest firm in 1994 with successful offices now established in Derby and Leicester. Whilst Freethcartwright LLP is a heavyweight commercial firm, serving a wide variety of corporate and institutional clients, there is also a commitment to a range of legal services, which includes a substantial private client element. This enables it to give a breadth of experience in training which is not always available in firms of a similar size.

main areas of work

Property and construction, commercial services, private client and personal litigation.

trainee profile

Freethcartwright LLP looks for people to bring their own perspective and individuality to the firm. The firm needs people who can cope with the intellectual demands of life as a lawyer and who possess the wider personal skills which are needed in its diverse practice.

training environment

Freethcartwright LLP is committed to providing comprehensive training for all its staff. The firm's training programme is based on in-house training covering technical matters and personal skills, supplemented with external courses where appropriate. The firm endeavours to give the best possible experience during the training period, as it believes that informal training on-the-job is the most effective means of encouraging the skills required in a qualified solicitor. One of the firm's senior partners takes responsibility for all its trainees and their personal development, overseeing their progress through the firm and discussing performance based on feedback. Normally, the training contract will consist of four six month seats in different departments, most of which are available in the firm's Nottingham offices, although it is possible for trainees to spend at least one seat in another location.

Members	54
Assistant Solicitors	67
Total Trainees	14

contact
Carole Wigley

method of application
Application form

selection procedure
Interview & selection day

closing date for 2006
31 July 2004

training
Starting salary (2003)
£16,000

branch offices
Nottingham, Leicester, Derby

Freethcartwright LLP

Freshfields Bruckhaus Deringer

65 Fleet Street, London EC4Y 1HS
Tel: (020) 7936 4000 Fax: (020) 7832 7001
Email: graduaterecruitment@freshfields.com
Website: www.freshfields.com/graduaterecruitment

firm profile

Freshfields Bruckhaus Deringer is a leading international firm with a network of 28 offices in 18 countries. The firm provides first-rate legal services to corporations, financial institutions and governments around the world.

main areas of work

Corporate; mergers and acquisitions; banking; dispute resolution; joint ventures; employment, pensions and benefits; asset finance; real estate; tax; capital markets; intellectual property and information technology; project finance; private finance initiative; US securities; antitrust, competition and trade; communications and media; construction and engineering; energy; environment; financial services; restructuring and insolvency; insurance; international tax; investment funds.

trainee profile

Good academic qualifications, good record of achievement in other areas, common sense and creative thinking. Language and computer skills are also an advantage.

training environment

The firm's trainees receive a thorough professional training in a very broad range of practice areas, an excellent personal development programme and the chance to work in one of the firm's international offices or on secondment with a client in the UK or abroad. It provides the professional, technical and pastoral support necessary to ensure that you enjoy and make the most of the opportunities on offer – during your training contract and beyond.

benefits

Life assurance; permanent health insurance; group personal pension; interest-free loan; interest-free loan for a season travel ticket; free membership of the firm's private medical insurance scheme; subsidised staff restaurant; gym.

vacation placements

Places for 2004: 100; Duration: 2 weeks; Remuneration: £500; Closing Date: 14 February 2004 but apply as quickly as possible after 1 December 2003 as there may not be places left by the deadline.

sponsorship & awards

CPE and LPC fees paid and £5,000 maintenance p.a. for those studying in London and Oxford and £4,500 p.a. for those studying elsewhere.

Partners 518
Asst Solicitors 1,702
Total Trainees 180
(London-based)

contact
Maia Riley

method of application
Application form

selection procedure
1 interview with 2 partners & written test

closing date for 2006
24 July 04
(non-law graduates)
24 August 04
(law graduates)

application
Training contracts p.a. **100**
Applications p.a. **c.2,500**
% interviewed p.a. **c.10%**
Required degree grade **2:1**

training
Salary
1st year (2002) £28,000
2nd year (2002) £32,000
Holiday entitlement **25 days**
% of trainees with a non-law degree p.a. **c.40%**
No. of seats available abroad p.a. **c.48**

post-qualification
Salary (2002) **£50,000**
% of trainees offered job on qualification (02/03) **98%**

overseas offices
Amsterdam, Bangkok, Barcelona, Beijing, Berlin, Bratislava, Brussels, Budapest, Cologne, Düsseldorf, Frankfurt, Hamburg, Hanoi, Ho Chi Minh City, Hong Kong, Madrid, Milan, Moscow, Munich, New York, Paris, Rome, Shanghai, Singapore, Tokyo, Vienna, Washington DC

Gateley Wareing

One Eleven Edmund Street, Birmingham, B3 2HJ
Tel: (0121) 234 0121 Fax: (0121) 234 0079
Email: www.gateleywareing.com
Website: wwarburton@gateleywareing.com

firm profile

A 25-partner, Midlands-based practice with an excellent reputation for general commercial work and particular expertise in corporate, plc, commercial, employment, property, tax, commercial dispute resolution, construction, insolvency and banking. The firm is expanding (175 staff) and offers a highly practical, commercial and fast-paced environment. The firm prides itself on its entrepreneurial style and its work hard/play hard reputation. The firm focuses on owner-led businesses, but also counts some household names and internationals amongst its clients.

trainee profile

Applications are invited from second year law students and final year non-law students. Applicants should have (or be heading for) a minimum 2.1 degree, and should have at least three Bs (or equivalent) at A-level. Individuals should be hardworking team players capable of using initiative and demonstrating commercial awareness.

training environment

Four seats of six months each with ongoing supervision and appraisals every three months. PSC taken internally. In-house courses on skills such as time management, negotiation, IT, drafting, business skills, marketing, presentation and writing in plain English.

benefits

Bonus scheme (up to 10% of salary), a current trainee offered as a 'buddy' - a point of contact within the firm, library available, invitation to summer party prior to joining.

vacation placements

12 two week placements over the summer. Deadline for vacation placement scheme is 13 February 2004 and for training contracts is 31 July 2004. Apply immediately by requesting an application form or online at www.gateleywareing.com.

sponsorship & awards

LPC with maintenance grant of £4,000: CPE.

Partners	25
Vacancies	6
Total Trainees	12
Total Staff	175

contact
Mrs Wendy Warburton
HR Manager

closing date for 2006
Vacation placements:
13 February 2004
Training contracts:
31 July 2004

training
Salary
1st year £18,500
2nd year £20,500

post-qualification
Salary **£32,000**

offices
Birmingham, Leicester, Nottingham

Goodman Derrick

90 Fetter Lane, London EC4A 1PT
Tel: (020) 7404 0606 Fax: (020) 7831 6407
Email: mail@gdlaw.co.uk
Website: www.gdlaw.co.uk

firm profile

Founded in 1954 by Lord Goodman, the firm now has a broad commercial practice and is well known for its media and defamation work, particularly relating to television.

main areas of work

Media 12%; commercial and general litigation 22%; corporate 32%; property 21%; charities/private client 5%; employment 8%.

trainee profile

Candidates must show that they will quickly be able to handle responsibility and deal directly with clients. They must be suited to the firm's work environment, present themselves confidently and be quick thinking and practically-minded.

training environment

Training at the firm is based on direct and active involvement with the work of the practice. The PSC is partly carried out at the start of the training contract, with some courses taking place over the following two years, coupled with the firm's general training programme. Trainees are in addition expected to initiate personal research if specialist knowledge needs to be gained for a particular piece of work. Periods of six months are spent in four of the following departments: company/commercial, media, property, litigation and employment. Work groups within these main departments allow trainees to experience further specialist fields. Trainees' own preferences and aptitude will be monitored by the supervising partner and discussed at monthly meetings and at three-monthly appraisals. The firm has a very friendly and informal environment.

benefits

Medical health insurance, season ticket loan, pension scheme.

sponsorship & awards

LPC fees plus maintenance grant.

Partners	18
Assistant Solicitors	8
Total Trainees	7

contact
Nicholas Armstrong

method of application
CV & covering letter

selection procedure
2 interviews

closing date for 2006
End of July 2004

application
Training contracts p.a. **2/3**
Applications p.a. **900**
% interviewed p.a. **3%**
Required degree grade
Min. 2:1

training
Salary
1st year (2002) £24,500
2nd year (2002) £25,750
Holiday entitlement **25 days**
% of trainees with a
non-law degree p.a. **50%**

post-qualification
% of trainees offered job
on qualification (2003) **75%**
% of assistants (as at 2003)
who joined as trainees **70%**
% of partners (as at 2003)
who joined as trainees **33%**

Halliwell Landau

St. James's Court, Brown St, Manchester M2 2JF
Tel: (0161) 836 5613 Fax: (0161) 828 5613
Email: ctaylor@halliwells.co.uk

firm profile

Halliwell Landau is the largest independent commercial law firm in the North West. Over the last few years the firm has increased substantially in both size and turnover and now has in excess of 200 fee-earners and 67 partners. This development leads to a continuing requirement for solicitors and has given rise to more internal promotions to partnerships.

main areas of work

Corporate/banking 24%; commercial property 18%; commercial litigation 22%; insurance litigation 16%; intellectual property 4.8%; trust and estates 4.5%; employment 3.7%; financial institutions 6.9%.

trainee profile

Candidates need to show a good academic ability but do not necessarily need to have studied law at university. They should demonstrate an ability to fit into a hardworking team. In particular, Halliwell Landau is looking for candidates who will continue to develop with the firm after their initial training.

training environment

Each trainee will have five seats in at least three separate departments. These will usually include commercial litigation, corporate and commercial property. Individual requests from trainees for experience in a particular department will be accomodated where possible. The trainee will work within one of the department's teams and be encouraged to assist other team members to help broaden their experience. Specific training appropriate to each department will be given and trainees are strongly encouraged to attend the firm's regular in-house seminars on legal and related topics. A supervisor will be assigned to each trainee to support their development throughout the seat. Each trainee will be assessed both mid-seat and end of seat.

benefits

A generous pension scheme plus a subsidised gym membership is available.

vacation placements

40 places are available for Summer 2004. There are four schemes each lasting for two weeks. Schemes commence first week in July. Renumeration £126 per week. Closing date for applications is 31 March 2004.

sponsorship & awards

The firm pays PgDL fees and LPC fees plus a £2,000 maintenance grant.

Partners	67
Assistant Solicitors	104
Total Trainees	27

contact
Carrie Taylor
(Graduate Recruitment Assistant)
ctaylor@halliwells.co.uk

method of application
Application form only

selection procedure
Written paper, presentation and interview

closing date for 2006
31 July 2004

application
Training contracts p.a. **10**
Applications p.a. **1,000**
% interviewed p.a. **5%**
Required degree grade **2:1**

training
Salary
1st year (2003) £21,000
2nd year (2003) £22,000

post-qualification
Salary (2003) **£32,000**
% of trainees offered job on qualification (2003) **99%**

Hammonds

Rutland House, 148 Edmund Street, Birmingham B3 2JR
7 Devonshire Square, Cutlers Gardens, London EC2M 4YH
2 Park Lane, Leeds LS3 1ES
Trinity Court, 16 Dalton Street, Manchester M6O 8HS
Tel: (0870) 839 0000 Fax: (0870) 839 3666
Website: www.hammonds.com

firm profile

Hammonds is one of the UK's largest commercial law firms, with offices in London, Birmingham, Leeds, Manchester, Brussels, Paris, Berlin, Munich, Rome, Milan, Madrid, Turin and Hong Kong. The firm has nearly 2,000 staff, including 208 partners, 600 solicitors and 86 trainees, and is regarded as innovative, opportunistic and highly successful in the markets in which it operates.

main areas of work

Corporate; commercial dispute resolution; construction; engineering and projects; employment; EU and competition; finance law (including banking); intellectual property and commercial; media/IT; pensions; property; sports law; tax.

trainee profile

Hammonds seeks applications from all disciplines for both vacation work and training contracts. It looks for three characteristics: strong academic performance, work experience in the legal sector and significant achievement in non-academic pursuits.

training environment

Around 40 trainee solicitors are recruited each year who each carry out six four month seats during their training contract. There are both fixed location and rotational training contracts available. Trainees on a rotational contract are eligible for subsidised accomodation and experience three UK locations during the contract. Trainees can choose their seats as they progress through the training contract.

benefits

Subsidised accommodation for rotational trainees. Flexible benefits scheme which allows trainees to choose their own benefits from a range of options.

vacation placements

Places for 2004: 64; Duration: 3 weeks; Remuneration: £230 p.w. (London), £180 p.w. (Leeds, Manchester, Birmingham); Closing Date: 29 February 2004.

sponsorship & awards

PgDL and LPC fees paid and maintenance grant of £4,500 p.a.

Partners	208
Assistant Solicitors	600
Total Trainees	86

contact
The Graduate Recruitment Team

method of application
Online application form

selection procedure
2 interviews

closing date for 2006
31 July 2004

application
Training contracts p.a. **40**
Applications p.a. **1,800**
% interviewed p.a. **6%**
Required degree grade **2:1**

training
Salary
1st year (2003) £20,500+ subsidised accommodation for rotational contract
2nd year (2003) £23,000+ subsidised accommodation for rotational contract
Holiday entitlement **23 days**
% of trainees with a non-law degree p.a. **25%**
No. of seats available abroad p.a. **12**

post-qualification
Salary (2003)
London £46,500
Other £33,000-£34,000
% of trainees accepting job on qualification (2003) **80%**

overseas offices
Brussels, Paris, Berlin, Munich, Rome, Milan, Turin, Hong Kong, Madrid

Harbottle & Lewis LLP

Hanover House, 14 Hanover Square, London W1S 1HP
Tel: (020) 7667 5000 Fax: (020) 7667 5100
Email: kathy.beilby@harbottle.com
Website: www.harbottle.com

firm profile

Harbottle & Lewis LLP is recognised for the unique breadth of its practice in the entertainment, media, travel (including aviation) and leisure industries. It undertakes significant corporate commercial and contentious work for clients within these industries including newer industries such as digital mixed media.

main areas of work

Music, film and television production, theatre, broadcasting, computer games and publishing, sport, sponsorship and advertising, aviation, property investment and leisure.

trainee profile

Trainees will have demonstrated the high academic abilities, commercial awareness, and initiative necessary to become part of a team advising clients in dynamic and demanding industries.

training environment

The two year training contract is divided into four six month seats where trainees will be given experience in a variety of legal skills including company commercial, litigation, intellectual property and real property, working within teams focused on the firm's core industries. The firm has a policy of accepting a small number of trainees to ensure they are given relevant and challenging work and are exposed to and have responsibility for a full range of legal tasks. The firm has its own lecture and seminars programme in both legal topics and industry know-how. An open door policy and a pragmatic entrepreneurial approach to legal practice provides a stimulating working environment.

benefits

Lunch provided; season ticket loans.

sponsorship & awards

LPC fees paid and interest-free loans towards maintenance.

Partners	19
Assistant Solicitors	49
Total Trainees	7

contact
Kathy Beilby

method of application
CV & letter

selection procedure
Interview

closing date for 2006
31 July 2004

application
Training contracts p.a. **4**
Applications p.a. **800**
% interviewed p.a. **5%**
Required degree grade **2:1**

training
Salary
1st year £24,250 (2003)
2nd year £25,250 (2003)
Holiday entitlement
in the first year **23 days**
in the second year **26 days**
% of trainees with
a non-law degree p.a. **40%**

post-qualification
Salary (2003) **£41,000**
% of trainees offered job
on qualification (2003) **100%**

Henmans

116 St. Aldates, Oxford OX1 1HA
Tel: (01865) 722181 Fax: (01865) 792376
Email: welcome@henmans.co.uk
Website: www.henmans.co.uk

firm profile

Henmans is a well-established Oxfordshire based practice with a strong national reputation, serving both corporate and private clients. Henmans' philosophy is to be extremely client focused to deliver exceptional levels of service. The firm achieves this through an emphasis on teamwork to ensure clients always have access to a specific partner with specialist support, and through an ongoing programme of recruitment and training to guarantee clients optimum advice and guidance. Henmans has invested heavily in IT and has implemented a case management system to enhance services and client care. Henmans' policy of bespoke services and controlled costs ensure that both corporate and private clients benefit from City level litigation standards at competitive regional prices. The firm is now accredited as an Investor in People

main areas of work

The firm's core service of litigation is nationally recognised. The personal injury and clinical negligence litigation is strong, as is professional negligence work. Professional negligence and commercial litigation: 29%; personal injury: 26%; property: 17%; private client (including family)/charities/trusts: 16%; corporate/employment: 12%.

trainee profile

Commercial awareness, sound academic accomplishment, intellectual capability, IT literate, able to work as part of a team, good communication skills.

training environment

Trainees are introduced to the firm with a detailed induction and overview of the client base. Experience is likely to be within the PI. Property, family, professional negligence/ commercial litigation and private client departments. The firm values commitment and enthusiasm both professionally and socially as an integral part of its culture. The firm provides an ongoing programme of in-house education and regular appraisals within its supportive friendly environment.

Partners	**22**
Assistant Solicitors	**35**
Total Trainees	**6**

contact
Viv J Matthews (Mrs)
MA FCIPD
Human Resources Manager

method of application
Application form on website

selection procedure
Interview with HR Manager & partners

closing date for 2006
31 July 2004

application
Training contracts p.a. **3**
Applications p.a. **450**

training
Salary
1st year (2003) £16,275
2nd year (2003) £17,850
Holiday entitlement **20 days**
% of trainees with a non-law degree p.a. **30%**

post-qualification
Salary (2003) **£27,000**
% of assistants who joined as trainees **28%**
% of partners who joined as trainees **15%**

Herbert Smith

Exchange House, Primrose Street, London EC2A 2HS
Tel: (020) 7374 8000 Fax: (020) 7374 0888
Email: graduate.recruitment@herbertsmith.com
Website: www.herbertsmith.com

firm profile

Herbert Smith is an international law firm with over 1,000 lawyers and a network of offices in Europe and Asia. It has a distinctive reputation for providing the highest quality corporate, finance and dispute resolution advice. Clients include major corporations, financial institutions and governments. The working environment is strongly team-orientated, friendly and informal. Herbert Smith has a formal alliance with the German firm, Gleiss Lutz, and the Dutch and Belgian firm, Stibbe.

main areas of work

Corporate (including international mergers and acquisitions); finance and banking (including capital markets); international litigation and arbitration; energy; projects and project finance; EU and competition; real estate; tax; employment and trusts; construction and engineering; insurance; investment funds; IP and IT; US securities.

trainee profile

Trainees need strong academic records, common sense, self-confidence and intelligence to make their own way in a large firm. They are typically high-achieving and creative thinking – language skills are an advantage.

training environment

Structured training and supervision are designed to allow experience of a unique range of contentious and non-contentious work. You will be encouraged to take on responsibilities as soon as you join the firm. You will work within partner-led teams and have your own role. Individual strengths will be monitored, developed and utilised. On-the-job training will be divided into four six-month seats; one seat will be in the corporate division, one in the litigation division and you will have a choice of specialists seats such as IP/IT or EU and competition, as well as an opportunity to go on secondment to a client or an overseas office. Great emphasis is placed on professional and personal development and the firm runs its own legal development programme.

sponsorship & benefits

CPE and LPC fees are paid plus a £5,000 maintenance grant p.a. Benefits include profit share, permanent health insurance, private medical insurance, season ticket loan, life assurance, subsidised gym membership, group personal accident insurance and matched contributory pension scheme.

vacation placements

Places for 2003/04: 115. Christmas 2003 (non-law students only), Easter and Summer 2004 (law and non-law students). Closing Dates: 14 November 2003 for Christmas scheme; 30 January 2004 for Easter and Summer schemes. Opportunities in some of the firm's European offices.

Partners	202
Fee-earners	575
Total Trainees	202

contact
Kerry Jarred

method of application
Application form, available online or hard copy on request

selection procedure
Case study and interview

closing date for Sept, 2006/March 2007
31 July 2004

application
Training contracts p.a. up to 100
Applications p.a. **1,139**
% interviewed p.a. **31%**
Required degree grade **2:1**

training
Salary
1st year £28,500
2nd year £32,000
Holiday entitlement
25 days, rising to 27 on qualification
ratio of law to non-law graduates is broadly equal

post-qualification
Salary (2003) **£50,000**
% of trainees offered job on qualification (Mar & Sept 2003) **84% (based on no. of jobs offered)**

overseas offices
Bangkok, Beijing, Brussels, Hong Kong, Moscow, Paris, Shanghai, Singapore, Tokyo

associated offices
Amsterdam, Berlin, Frankfurt, Jakarta, Munich, New York, Prague, Stuttgart, Warsaw

Hewitsons

42 Newmarket Road, Cambridge CB5 8EP
Tel: (01604) 233233 Fax: (01223) 316511
Email: mail@hewitsons.com (for all offices)
Website: www.hbslaw.co.uk (for all offices)

firm profile

Established in 1865, the firm handles mostly company and commercial work, but has a growing body of public sector clients. The firm has three offices: Cambridge, Northampton and Saffron Walden.

main areas of work

Three sections: corporate technology, property and private client.

trainee profile

The firm is interested in applications from candidates who have achieved a high degree of success in academic studies and who are bright, personable and able to take the initiative.

training environment

The firm offers four six month seats.

benefits

The PSC is provided during the first year of the training contract. This is coupled with an extensive programme of Trainee Solicitor Seminars provided by specialist in-house lawyers.

vacation placements

Places for 2004: A few placements are available, application is by way of letter and CV to Caroline Lewis; Duration: 1 week.

sponsorship & awards

Funding for the CPE and/or LPC is not provided.

Partners	51
Assistant Solicitors	43
Total Trainees	14

contact
Caroline Lewis
7 Spencer Parade
Northampton NN1 5AB

method of application
Firm's application form

selection procedure
Interview

closing date for 2006
End of August 2004

application
Training contracts p.a. **8**
Applications p.a. **1,400**
% interviewed p.a. **10%**
Required degree grade
2:1 min

training
Salary
1st year (2003) £17,500
2nd year (2003) £18,500
Holiday entitlement **22 days**
% of trainees with a non-law degree p.a. **50%**

post-qualification
Salary (2003) **£31,500**
% of trainees offered job on qualification (2003) **70%**
% of assistants (as at 1/9/03) who joined as trainees **54%**
% of partners (as at 1/9/03) who joined as trainees **32%**

Hill Dickinson

Pearl Assurance House, 2 Derby Square, Liverpool L2 9XL
Tel: (0151) 236 5400 Fax: (0151) 236 2175
Email: law@hilldickinson.com
Website: www.hilldickinson.com

firm profile

Hill Dickinson is one of the leading commercial law firms in the UK, providing legal advice to both the domestic and international markets from each of its four offices in London, Liverpool, Manchester and Chester. Delivering a highly professional and added value service the firm is alert to the ever changing and increasing demands being placed upon different markets and is well positioned to support its clients in all aspects of their legal requirements.

main areas of work

With a wealth of specialists, the firm advises a range of clients including corporates, the private sector, individuals and the public sector and is structured into four specialist groups: commercial, insurance and litigation, health, and marine and transit. Specialisms include sport and media, corporate law, European law, employment, pensions, PFI, intellectual property and technology, private client, professional indemnity, fraud and policy and regulation, clinical negligence, mental health, shipping, goods in transit and yachting, to name a few.

trainee profile

Commercial awareness and academic ability are the key factors, together with a desire to succeed. Trainees are viewed as the partners of the future and the firm is looking for personable individuals with whom it wants to work.

training environment

Trainees spend six months in each of the four departments (commercial, insurance and litigation, health and marine and transit) and will be given the chance to specialise in specific areas. You will be given the opportunity to learn and develop communication and presentation skills, legal research, drafting, interviewing and advising, negotiations and advocacy. Trainees are encouraged to accept responsibility and are expected to act with initiative. The practice has an active social committee and a larger than usual selection of competitive sporting teams.

vacation placements

One week structured scheme with places available for 2004. Apply by CV and covering letter to Philip Bradbury (Partner) by 30 April 2004.

sponsorship & awards

LPC funding provided. Further funding and maintenance awards are under review.

Partners	90
Assistant Solicitors	93
Total Trainees	19

contact
Peter Barlow
Partner
law@hilldickinson.com

method of application
CV with supporting letter by email

selection procedure
Assessment day

closing date for 2006
15 July 2004

training
Salary
1st year (2002) £17,500
2nd year (2002) £19,000
Salaries are currently under review
Holiday entitlement
4 weeks

post-qualification
% of trainees offered job on qualification (2002) **80%**

offices
Chester, Liverpool, London, Manchester

Holman Fenwick & Willan

Marlow House, Lloyds Avenue, London EC3N 3AL
Tel: (020) 7488 2300 Fax: (020) 7481 0316
Email: grad.recruitment@hfw.co.uk

firm profile

Holman Fenwick & Willan is an international law firm and one of the world's leading specialists in maritime transportation, insurance, reinsurance, energy and trade. The firm is a leader in the field of commercial litigation and arbitration and also offers comprehensive commercial advice. Founded in 1883, the firm is one of the largest operating in its chosen fields with a team of over 200 lawyers worldwide, and a reputation for excellence and innovation.

main areas of work

The firm's range of services include marine, admiralty and crisis management, insurance and reinsurance, commercial litigation and arbitration, international trade and commodities, energy, corporate and financial.

trainee profile

Applications are invited from commercially minded undergraduates and graduates of all disciplines with good A levels and who have, or expect to receive, a 2:1 degree. Good foreign languages or a scientific or maritime background are an advantage.

training environment

During your training period the firm will ensure that you gain valuable experience in a wide range of areas. It also organises formal training supplemented by a programme of in-house seminars and ship visits in addition to the PSC. Your training development as an effective lawyer will be managed by the Recruitment and Training Partner, Ottilie Sefton, who will ensure that your training is both successful and enjoyable.

benefits

Private medical insurance, permanent health and accident insurance, subsidised gym membership, season ticket loan.

vacation placements

Places for 2004: 16; Duration: 2 weeks. Dates: 28 June - 9 July / 19 July - 30 July; Remuneration (2003): £250 p.w.; Closing Date: Applications accepted 1 Jan - 14 Feb 2004.

sponsorship & awards

PgDL Funding: Fees paid plus £5,000 maintenance; LPC Funding: Fees paid plus £5,000 maintenance.

Partners 80+
Other Solicitors & Fee-earners 120+
Total Trainees 16

contact
Graduate Recruitment Officer

method of application
Application form

selection procedure
2 interviews with partners & written exercise

closing date for 2006
31 July 2004

application
Training contracts p.a. **8**
Applications p.a. **1,000**
% interviewed p.a. **5%**
Required degree grade **2:1**

training
Salary (Sept 2003)
1st year £28,000
2nd year £30,000
Holiday entitlement **22 days**
% of trainees with a non-law degree p.a. **50%**

post-qualification
Salary TBA
% of trainees offered job on qualification (Sept 2002) **75%**

overseas offices
Hong Kong, Nantes, Paris, Piraeus, Rouen, Shanghai, Singapore

Howes Percival

Oxford House, Cliftonville, Northampton NN1 5PN
Tel: (01604) 230400 Fax: (01604) 620956
Email: katy.pattle@howespercival.com
Website: www.howespercival.com

firm profile

Howes Percival is a 34 partner commercial law firm with offices in Leicester, Milton Keynes, Northampton and Norwich. The firm's working environment is young, progressive and highly professional and its corporate structure means that fee-earners are rewarded on merit and can progress to associate or partner status quickly. The type and high value of the work that the firm does places it in a position whereby it is recognised as being a regional firm by location only. The firm has the expertise, resources, and partner reputation that match a city firm.

main areas of work

The practice is departmentalised and the breakdown of its work is as follows: corporate 30%; commercial property 25%; commercial litigation 20%; insolvency 10%; employment 10%; private client 5%.

trainee profile

The firm is looking for six well-educated, focused, enthusiastic, commercially aware graduates with a minimum 2:1 degree in any discipline. Howes Percival welcomes confident communicators with strong interpersonal skills who share the firm's desire to be the best.

training environment

Trainees complete four six month seats, each one in a different department. Trainees joining the Norwich office will remain at Norwich for the duration of their training contract. Within the East Midlands region, there is the opportunity to gain experience in each of the three East Midlands offices. Trainees report direct to a partner and after three months and again towards the end of each seat they will be formally assessed by the partner training them. Trainees will be given every assistance by the fee-earners in their department to develop quickly and will be given responsibility as soon as they are ready.

benefits

Contributory pension scheme. Private health insurance. LPC/CPE funding.

vacation placements

Vacation placements are available in July and August. Please apply to Miss Katy Pattle at the above address for further details.

Partners	34
Assistant Solicitors	25
Total Trainees	10

contact
Miss Katy Pattle
HR Assistant

method of application
Letter, CV and firm's application form

selection procedure
Assessment centres including second interview with training principal and partner

closing date for 2006
31 July 2004

application
Training contracts p.a. **7**
Applications p.a. **300**
% interviewed p.a. **10%**
Required degree grade **2:1**

training
Salary
1st year (as at June 2003) £18,750
2nd year (as at June 2003) £20,000
Holiday entitlement
23 days p.a.

post-qualification
% of trainees offered job on qualification (2003) **50%**
% of assistants (as at 1/9/02) who joined as trainees **42%**
% of partners (as at 1/9/01) who joined as trainees **7.5%**

Hugh James

Hodge House, 114-116 St. Mary Street, Cardiff CF10 1DY
Tel: (029) 2022 4871 Fax: (029) 2038 8222
Email: training@hughjames.com
Website: www.hughjames.com

firm profile

Hugh James is one of the UK's leading regional law firms and has experienced phenomenal growth and success since it was formed in 1960. It has for many years been one of only a handful of firms to dominate the legal scene in Wales. Hugh James is placed high in the table of the top 100 law firms in the UK. The firm offers its clients a comprehensive service covering the whole of South Wales through its five offices.

main areas of work

The practice is divided up into four divisions: business litigation (26%); business services (32%); claimant litigation (28%); public funded (14%). Specialist teams have been established to service niche areas of the law and the firm has a multidisciplinary approach to the provision of legal services.

trainee profile

Hugh James welcomes applications from law and non-law undergraduates with a good class degree. Candidates must exhibit first class legal and practice skills and good interpersonal and IT skills are essential. The majority of trainees are retained upon qualification and are seen as an integral part of the future of the firm. Hugh James is proud of the fact that most of its present partners were trained at the firm.

training environment

Trainees generally undertake four seats of not less than six months which may be in any of the firm's offices. Broadly, experience will be gained in all four main work categories. The breadth of work dealt with by the firm enables it to ensure that over-specialisation is avoided.

benefits

Company contribution to stakeholder pension scheme.

vacation placements

Places for 2004 available.

Partners	47
Assistant Solicitors	53
Total Trainees	16

contact
John McManus
HR Director

method of application
Application form available from HR Manager

selection procedure
Assessment day

closing date for 2006
31 March 2004

application
Training contracts p.a. 7
Applications p.a. 350
% interviewed p.a. 30%
Required degree grade 2:2

training
Salary
Competitive & reviewed annually

other offices
Merthyr Tydfil, Bargoed, Blackwood, Talbot Green, Treharris

Ince & Co

Knollys House, 11 Byward Street, London EC3R 5EN
Tel: (020) 7623 2011 Fax: (020) 7623 3225
Email: claire.kendall@ince.co.uk

firm profile

Since its foundation in 1870, Ince & Co has specialised in international commercial law and is best known for its shipping and insurance work.

main areas of work

Shipping, aviation and international trade, 44%; insurance/reinsurance/professional indemnity, 27%; energy and construction, 19%; business and finance group including corporate/private client/property, 10%.

trainee profile

Hard working competitive individuals with initiative who relish challenge and responsibility within a team environment. Academic achievements, positions of responsibility, sport and travel are all taken into account.

training environment

Trainees sit with four different partners for six months at a time throughout their training. Under close supervision, they are encouraged from an early stage to meet and visit clients, interview witnesses, liaise with counsel, deal with technical experts and handle opposing lawyers. They will quickly build up a portfolio of cases from a number of partners involved in a cross-section of the firm's practice and will see their cases through from start to finish. They will also attend in-house and external lectures, conferences and seminars on practical and legal topics.

benefits

STL, corporate health cover, PHI, contributory pension scheme.

vacation placements

Places for 2004: 18; Duration: 2 weeks; Remuneration: £250 p.w.; Closing Date: 13 February 2004.

sponsorship & awards

LPC fees, £4,750 grant for study in London, £4,000 grant for study elsewhere. Discretionary sponsorship for CPE.

Partners	62*
Assistant Solicitors	85*
Total Trainees	24*

** denotes worldwide figures*

contact
Claire Kendall

method of application
Typed/handwritten letter & CV with contact details of 2 academic referees

selection procedure
Interview with HR professional & interview with 2 partners from Recruitment Committee & a written test

closing date for 2006
31 July 2004

application
Training contracts p.a. 8
Applications p.a. 1,500
% interviewed p.a. 5%
Required degree grade 2:1

training
Salary
1st year (2001) £27,000
2nd year (2001) £30,000
Holiday entitlement 22 days
% of trainees with a non-law degree p.a. 55%

post-qualification
Salary (2003) £47,000
% of trainees offered job on qualification (2003) 70%. All accepted!
% of partners (as at 2002) who joined as trainees Approx 73%

overseas offices
Hamburg, Hong Kong, Le Havre, Paris, Piraeus, Shanghai, Singapore

Irwin Mitchell

St. Peter's House, Hartshead, Sheffield S1 2EL
Recruitment Line: (0114) 274 4580
Email: enquiries@irwinmitchell.co.uk
Website: imonline.co.uk

firm profile

Irwin Mitchell is a rapidly expanding national practice with 82 partners and over 1,650 employees with offices in Birmingham, Leeds, London, Newcastle and Sheffield. It is particularly well known for commercial law, commercial litigation, insurance law, business crime and claimant personal injury litigation. The firm's strong reputation for dealing with novel and complex areas of law and handling developmental cases such as vibration white finger, CJD and the Matrix-Churchill 'arms to Iraq' affair means that it can offer a broad range of experience within each of its specialist departments, giving trainees a high standard of training.

main areas of work

Corporate services 27%; claimant personal injury 27%; insurance litigation 35%; private client 11%.

trainee profile

The firm is looking for ambitious, well motivated individuals with a real commitment to the law and who can demonstrate a positive approach to a work life balance. It recruits law and non-law graduates. Foreign languages and IT skills are an asset. Irwin Mitchell believes trainees to be an investment for the future and endeavour to retain trainees upon qualification.

training environment

The two year training contract consists of four seats. The firm's trainees also benefit from a structured induction programme, monthly training events and the Professional Skills Course which is run in-house and financed by the firm. Each trainee has a quarterly review with their supervising partner to focus on performance and development ensuring progress is on track.

vacation placements

Places for 2004: 50; Duration: 1 week; Remuneration: £75 p.w.; Closing Date: 31 January.

sponsorship & awards

Payment of PgDL and LPC fees plus a £3,000 maintenance grant.

Partners	82
Assistant Solicitors	175
Total Trainees	27

contact
Sue Lenkowski

method of application
Firm's application form & covering letter, go online or call the recruitment line between 1 April & 31 July to request a recruitment pack

selection procedure
Assessment centre & interview during September. Successful candidates invited to attend second interview

closing date for 2006
31 July 2004

application
Training contracts p.a. **15**
Applications p.a. **1,000**
% interviewed p.a. **7%**

training
Salary
1st year £17,500
2nd year £19,500
(outside London)
reviewed annually
Holiday entitlement
24.5 days
% of trainees with a non-law degree p.a. **25%**

post-qualification
% of trainees offered job on qualification **91%**
% of assistants who joined as trainees **41%**
% of partners (2003) who joined as trainees **22%**

Jones Day Gouldens

10 Old Bailey, London, EC4M 7NG
Tel: (020) 7583 7777 Fax: (020) 7583 6777
Brochure Request Hotline: 0800 0856 750
Email: recruit.london@jonesday.com
Website: www.gouldens.com/recruit

firm profile

Jones Day Gouldens is a key part of the international partnership, Jones Day, a global law firm with 29 offices worldwide. The firm has around 200 lawyers in London, which means that the office retains the intimacy and atmosphere of a medium sized City firm. The firm offers a full range of legal services to major clients from the UK and overseas.

main areas of work

Jones Day Gouldens has four core departments: corporate, real estate, litigation and tax. There are specialist groups for banking and finance, competition, construction, environment, planning, insolvency, insurance, intellectual property, employment, employee benefits and pensions.

trainee profile

Candidates should have obtained or be predicted a 2.1 degree in any discipline. They should be willing to accept the challenge of responsibility in an atmosphere where not only technical expertise but flair, originality and enthusiasm are rewarded.

training environment

The firm operates a unique, non-rotational system of training and trainees receive work simultaneously from all departments in the firm. The training is designed to provide freedom, flexibility and responsibility from the start. Trainees are encouraged to assume their own workload, which allows early responsibility, a faster development of potential and the opportunity to compare and contrast the different disciplines alongside one another. Work will vary from small cases which the trainee may handle alone (under the supervision of a senior lawyer as a mentor) to larger matters where they will assist a partner or an associate solicitor. The firm runs a structured training programme with weekly seminars to support the thorough practical training and regular feedback that trainees receive from the associates and partners they work with.

vacation placements

Places for 2003/04: Christmas 2003 (non-law): 16; 2 weeks; £275; closing date 31 October.
Easter 2004 (non-law): 16; 2 weeks; £275; closing date 14 February.
Summer 2004 (law): 40; 2 weeks; £275; closing date 14 February.

benefits

Private healthcare, season ticket loan, subsidised sports club membership, group life cover.

sponsorship & awards

CPE/PgDL and LPC fees paid and £5,000 maintenance p.a.

Partners	54
Assistant Solicitors	90
Total Trainees	40

contact
Lisa Holmes
Recruitment Manager

method of application
CV and letter online at www.gouldens.com/recruit

selection procedure
2 interviews with partners

closing date for 2006
31 August 2004 - please apply by end of July to ensure an early interview slot

application
Training contracts p.a. **20**
Applications p.a. **1,700**
% interviewed p.a. **12%**
Required degree grade **2.1**

training
Salary
1st year (2003) £33,000
2nd year (2003) £37,000
Holiday entitlement
5 weeks

post-qualification
Salary (2003) **£55,000**
% of trainees offered job on qualification (2003) **65%**

overseas offices
Continental Europe, Asia, North America

Kendall Freeman

43 Fetter Lane, London, EC4A 1JU
Tel: (020) 7583 4055 Fax: (020) 7353 7377
Email: graduaterecruitment@kendallfreeman.com
Website: www.kendallfreeman.com

firm profile

Kendall Freeman launched on 1 May 2003. It was formerly D J Freeman. The firm handles high value and complex matters for clients in the insurance and reinsurance industry, banks, corporates and the public sectors.

main areas of work

Arbitration, ADR, banking, charities, commercial litigation, company and commercial, construction, corporate finance, corporate tax, employment, insolvency, restructuring, insurance/reinsurance, mergers and acquisitions and international law.

trainee profile

The firm is small by City standards, with 21 partners, but successfully competes and acts alongside the largest international and UK firms of solicitors in its work. It can therefore offer excellent training with high quality work in a more personal environment than the larger firms. The firm seeks commercial and energetic individuals with initiative who do not want to be one of a crowd. Trainees will have early client interaction so require excellent people skills with a very strong academic bacground to enable you to provide effective commercial advice to the firm's clients.

training environment

Trainees spend six months of their training contract in four of the firm's major practice areas and once a month are able to discuss their progress with a partner. Believing supervised, practical experience to be the best training, the firm soon gives trainees the chance to meet clients, be responsible for their own work and join in marketing and client development activities. Regular workshops in each seat help develop basic skills in the different practice areas. There is a trainee solicitors' committee which meets regularly and which is attended by two trainee representatives where any suggestions or concerns can be voiced. Each trainee is also allocated a partner as a mentor.

vacation placements

From 2004 the firm will offer summer placements to university students both in law and other disciplines. Applications are particularly encouraged from law students who are about to start their last year at university and students in other disciplines who are about to commence the law conversion course. Placements are for two weeks and students will receive a weekly sum to cover expenses. There are 12 places for 2004. Closing date: end of February 2004.

sponsorship & awards

CPE/GDL and LPC funding and a maintenance grant.

Partners	21
Assistant Solicitors	31
Total Trainees	15

contact
Graduate Recruitment
(020) 7583 4055

method of application
Firm's online application form

selection procedure
One interview with two partners

closing date for 2006
31 July 2004

application
Training contracts p.a. **6-7**
Minimum required degree grade **2:1**

training
Salary
1st year £26,000
to increase by £1,000 at six month intervals until qualification

post-qualification
Salary (2003) **£48,000**
% of trainees offered job on qualification (2003) **60%**

KENDALL FREEMAN

Keoghs

2 The Parklands, Bolton BL6 4SE
Tel: (01204) 677000 Fax: (01204) 677111
Email: info@keoghs.co.uk

firm profile

Keoghs is one of the UK's leading insurance litigation firms offering national coverage to clients and acts for most of the UK's major insurance companies. The company and commercial team specialise in commercial business advice serving a client base ranging from the private individual to small growing businesses and national blue chip organisations. The high standard of service given to new and existing clients has enabled the firm to achieve ISO 9001 accreditation. Keoghs ranked 49th in the 2003 Sunday Times 100 best companies to work for.

main areas of work

The main practice areas are personal injury litigation, commercial litigation and company commercial (which includes corporate, employment, intellectual property commercial property and private client).

trainee profile

The firm is looking to recruit the partners of the future and indeed many current partners and assistant solicitors joined the firm as trainees. Applicants should be able to demonstrate a high academic standard (at least a 2:1 degree but not necessarily in law), an ability to work in a team, and good communication and decision making skills. The firm welcomes commercially aware, enthusiastic and self motivated candidates with good IT skills and a sense of humour.

training environment

Trainees undertake a flexible programme of six month periods in each of the firm's three main practice areas of defendant personal injury litigation, commercial litigation and company commercial work. A final six months can then be spent in the department of the trainee's choice. The trainee will work as part of a specialist team, receiving specific training from their departmental supervisor. The supervisor will also assess the trainee during and at the end of their placement to review progress and development of their drafting, research, communication, advocacy and negotiation skills. The firm's Training and Development department runs a comprehensive programme of in-house training designed to complement the compulsory Professional Skills Course.

Partners	29
Trainees	8
Total Staff	364

contact
Mrs Frances Cross
Director of HR

method of application
Apply by sending a CV & covering letter

selection procedure
By 2 stage interview

closing date for 2006
August 2004

application
Training contracts p.a. **3 in Bolton, 1 in Coventry**
Applications p.a. **800**
% interviewed p.a. **3.5%**
Required degree grade **2:1**

training
Salary for each year of training
Currently under review (in excess of Law Society minimum)
Holiday entitlement
25 days + 8 statutory days

post-qualification
Salary (2003) **£27,500**
% of trainees offered job on qualification **The firm aims for 100%**

regional offices
Bolton, Coventry

KLegal

1-2 Dorset Rise, London EC4Y 8AE
Tel: (020) 7694 2500 Fax: (020) 7694 2501
Website: www.klegaltrainees.co.uk

firm profile

Founded in July 1999, KLegal is the law firm associated with KPMG in England. Through organic growth and the tie-up with McGrigor Donald, KLegal has grown to be one of the top 30 law firms in the UK.

main areas of work

One of the firm's main areas of focus is on developing its legal expertise in practice areas that complement the service offered by KPMG. These include banking and finance, corporate, dispute resolution, employment, intellectual property, IT and telecommunications, private equity, projects/PPP, real estate and tax litigation. The firm's membership of KLegal International means much of its work has an international dimension.

trainee profile

KLegal is looking for outstanding candidates with ambition who share the firm's vision and who are capable of helping the firm achieve this. The firm is a constantly changing environment and is looking to those who see the opportunities this provides both for themselves as individuals and for their colleagues in general.

training environment

KLegal's training is based upon a standard rotation of seats of six months in four main practice areas. The firm's trainees are encouraged to spend a seat in Edinburgh or Glasgow rather than spend a full two years in London. The firm provides opportunities for trainees to learn their legal skills as part of multi-disciplinary teams helping them to become among the best commercially-minded lawyers in the City. The firm has a well established training and development programme specifically for trainees in addition to a broad programme for qualified staff. KLegal's commitment is to provide an enjoyable experience, allowing individuals to maximise both their own personal and professional development.

benefits

KLegal offers life assurance, pension, a daily lunch allowance and 25 days holiday. Flextra, the firm's flexible benefit scheme, allows staff the opportunity to shape their own reward package by indicating their preferences.

vacation placements

Places for 2004: 10; duration: 4 weeks; remuneration: £250 p.w; closing date: 21st February 2004.

sponsorship & awards

CPE Funding: Fees paid plus maintenance of £4,500. LPC Funding: Fees paid plus maintenance of £4,500.

Partners	64
Trainees	63
Total headcount	520

contact
Georgina Bond
HR Department

method of application
Apply via website at www.klegaltrainees.co.uk

selection procedure
2 interviews & assessment centre

closing date for 2006
31 July 2004

application
Vacancies **10-12**
Required degree grade **2:1**

training
Salary (Reviewed annually)
1st year £28,000
2nd year £32,000

offices
Two McGrigor Donald offices in Scotland and one in Belfast. A member of KLegal International with offices in over 50 jurisdictions

Lawrence Graham

190 Strand, London WC2R 1JN
Tel: (020) 7759 6694 Fax: (020) 7379 6854
Email: graduate@lawgram.com
Website: www.lawgram.com

firm profile

Lawrence Graham is a leading London based firm with an outstanding reputation in commercial property transactions and mid-market corporate transactions. The firm's main departments are commercial property and company and commercial. The firm also has a top rated tax and private capital department and a highly regarded litigation department. Through Lawrence Graham International, the firm works with a number of independent law firms in Europe. Lawrence Graham also works with a number of US firms.

main areas of work

Property 35%; company and commercial 29%; litigation 21%; tax and private client 14%.

trainee profile

The firm is looking for individuals who can demonstrate a commitment to a career in the commercial application of law and an understanding of the rigours of professional practice. A strong academic track record with a minimum 2.1 degree is a basic requirement. In addition, the firm expects a good record of achievement in other areas, indicative of the ability to succeed in a demanding career. Evidence of team working skills and the ability to handle responsibility are also essential.

training environment

Under partner supervision students will be given early responsibility. Training is structured to facilitate the ability to manage one's own files and interact with clients. In addition to the Professional Skills Course, there are departmental training and induction sessions. Training consists of four six-month seats. A property, corporate and contentious seat are compulsory. The final seat can be either in tax and private capital or back to either commercial property or company and commercial as they are the largest departments.

benefits

Season ticket loan, on-site gym.

vacation placements

Places for 2004: 40; Duration: 2 weeks during Easter break and 4 x 2 weeks between June and August; Remuneration: £220 p.w.; Closing Date: 31 January 2004.

sponsorship & awards

GDL Funding: Course fees and £4,000 maintenance grant.
LPC Funding: Course fees and £4,000 maintenance grant.

Partners 86
Assistant Solicitors 103
Total Trainees 36

contact
Graduate Recruitment Officer

method of application
Firm's application form.
For law **After 2nd year results**
For non-law **After final results**

selection procedure
Interview

closing date for 2006
31 July 2004

application
Training contracts **18**
Applications p.a. **1,000**
Required degree grade **2:1**

training
Salary
1st year (2003) £28,000
2nd year (2003) £32,000
% of trainees with a non-law degree p.a. **40%**

post-qualification
Salary (2003) **£46,000**
% of trainees offered job on qualification (2003) **98%**
% of assistants (as at 1/9/01) who joined as trainees **42%**
% of partners (as at 1/9/01) who joined as trainees **32%**

Laytons

Carmelite, 50 Victoria Embankment, Blackfriars, London EC4Y 0LS
Tel: (020) 7842 8000 Fax: (020) 7842 8080
Email: london@laytons.com
Website: www.laytons.com

firm profile

Laytons is a growing commercial law firm operating as a single national team through its offices in Bristol, Guildford, London and Manchester, each of which draws on the strengths of the national firm with the benefit of excellent IT and communications. The firm's distinctive culture and approach is the product of a tradition of hardworking, straightforward lawyering, crafted from a firm founded in the City of London over 125 years ago. The firm's approach to legal issues is practical, creative and energetic. Laytons builds strong relationships with its clients and provides them with high quality advice, drawing on a range of complementary specialist skills relevant to the firm's primary focus - dynamic business. The firm's long term support for clients is matched by its internal culture of support and encouragement, long term career development and its 'single team' approach.

main areas of work

Corporate and commercial, commercial property (including land development and construction), dispute resolution, debt recovery, insolvency, employment, technology, media and intellectual property, private client and trusts.

trainee profile

Successful candidates will be balanced, rounded individuals who are commercially aware, have a sound academic background and will be enthusiastic and committed members of the team.

training environment

Trainees are generally placed in four six month seats in appropriate practice groups. All trainees have contact with clients from an early stage, working on a wide variety of matters in a close working relationship with partners and qualified staff. Trainees will soon be responsible for their own files, although they are always supported and have regular appraisals throughout the training contract. Trainees are also encouraged to participate in business development and marketing activities. The firm recruits trainees with a view to retaining them at the end of the training contract. The nature of the training is that the work is sufficiently defined in scope to be of high quality and give reasonable depth of experience, yet sufficiently general within that scope to give breadth of experience. The working environment of the firm is supportive and interactive and trainees - as does everyone - greatly benefit from this.

vacation placements

Places for Summer 2004: 6. Duration: 1 week. Closing Date: 31 March 2004.

sponsorship & awards

LPC and CPE funding: consideration given.

Partners	43
Assistant Solicitors	48
Total Trainees	12

contact
Anita Coaster (Bristol)
David Knight (Guildford)
Stephen Cates &
Lisa McLean (London)
Christine Barker (Manchester)

method of application
Application form

selection procedure
Usually 2 interviews

closing date for 2006
31 August 2004 (although posts are filled as soon as suitable candidates are identified)

application
Training contracts p.a. **8**
Applications p.a. **2,000**
% interviewed p.a. **5%**
Required degree grade
1 or 2:1

training
Salary
1st year (2003) Market rate
2nd year (2003) Market rate
Holiday entitlement
22 days on entry

post-qualification
Salary (2003) **Market rate**
% of trainees offered job on qualification (2003) **86%**
% of assistants (as at 1/9/03) who joined as trainees **42%**
% of partners (as at 1/9/03) who joined as trainees **33%**

regional offices
Training contracts are offered in each of Laytons' offices. Apply directly to desired office. See website for further details: www.laytons.com

LeBoeuf, Lamb, Greene & MacRae

1 Minster Court, Mincing Lane, London EC3R 7YL
Tel: (020) 7459 5000 Fax: (020) 7459 5099
Email: traineelondon@llgm.com
Website: www.llgm.com

firm profile

LeBoeuf, Lamb, Greene & MacRae is an international law firm with some 650 lawyers worldwide in offices across Europe, the US, Africa, Middle East and Asia. The London office, established as a multinational partnership in 1995 employs almost 60 lawyers and is the hub office for the firm's European and international practice. The London office handles varied, interesting work and will suit people who want early responsibility in a relaxed but hard working environment.

main areas of work

General corporate, litigation, energy, corporate finance, project finance, capital markets, private equity, insurance, insolvency, property, tax, intellectual property, employment, trusts and estates.

trainee profile

LeBoeuf, Lamb, Greene & MacRae is looking for outstanding people in the broadest possible sense. The firm welcomes applications from varied, non-traditional backgrounds. Inter-personal skills are very important: the firm likes bright, engaging people. Linguistic skills are useful (but not crucial). The firm wants proactive people who will contribute from day one.

training environment

Trainees spend six months in four seats. The firm's training programme is comprehensive and covers an induction programme, participation in internal seminars and training sessions and attendance at external courses, including the Professional Skills Course. You will be encouraged to act on your own initiative from an early stage. Trainees sit with a senior lawyer, often a partner, who can give ongoing feed back and guidance and progress is reviewed every six months.

benefits

Private medical insurance, season ticket loan, subsidised restaurant.

sponsorship & awards

Full payment of CPE/LPC fees and maintenance grant of £4,500 provided.

Partners	13
Counsel	6
Assistant Solicitors	24
Total Trainees	8

contact
Andrew Terry

method of application
CV & covering letter

selection procedure
2 interviews

closing date for 2006
31 August 2004

application
Training contracts p.a. 4
Applications p.a. 1,000
% interviewed p.a. 3%
Required degree grade 2:1

training
Salary
1st year (2003) £33,000
2nd year (2004) £37,000
Holiday entitlement 20 days
% of trainees with a non-law degree p.a. 50%

post-qualification
Salary (2003) £65,000

overseas offices
Albany, Almaty, Beijing, Bishkek, Boston, Brussels, Denver, Harrisburg, Hartford, Houston, Jacksonville, Johannesburg, Los Angeles, Moscow, New York, Newark, Paris, Pittsburgh, Riyadh, Salt Lake City, San Francisco, Washington

Lee Bolton & Lee

1 The Sanctuary, Westminster, London SW1P 3JT
Tel: (020) 7222 5381 Fax: (020) 7222 7502
Email: enquiries@1thesanctuary.com
Website: www.leeboltonlee.com

firm profile

Founded in 1855, Lee Bolton & Lee is a successful medium-sized firm based in Westminster. It is closely associated with parliamentary agents and solicitors, Rees and Freres, who provide a specialist service in parliamentary, public and administrative law.

main areas of work

Commercial; property; private client; litigation; charity; education work.

trainee profile

The firm seeks to recruit trainees with a good degree (2:1 or above), first class communication skills, motivation, professionalism, initiative, enthusiasm, and a sense of humour.

training environment

Trainees spend six months in each of four seats: private client, property/commercial property, litigation and public law, with either a senior solicitor or a partner. Training is comprehensive and covers a full induction programme, participation in internal seminars and training sessions and attendance at external courses, including the Professional Skills Course. Trainees are given responsibility for their own files from the beginning, and whilst this might at first seem daunting, the firm operates an open door policy and help is never far away. Progress is reviewed monthly by your elected Supervisor and every three months by the Training Principal. There are various sporting and social events.

benefits

Season ticket loan, non-guaranteed bonus.

sponsorship & awards

A contribution towards LPC funding but dependent upon being offered a training contract.

Partners	12
Assistant Solicitors	14
Total Trainees	5

contact
Susie Hust

method of application
Letter & CV

selection procedure
Panel interview

closing date for 2006
End July 2004

application
Training contracts p.a. **3**
Applications p.a. **800**
% interviewed p.a. **3%**
Required degree grade **2:1**

training
Salary (2003)
1st year £21,000
2nd year £22,000
Holiday entitlement **22 days**
% of trainees with a non-law degree p.a. **50%**

post-qualification
Salary (2003) **£39,000**
% of trainees offered job on qualification (2003) **50%**
% of assistants (as at 1/9/03) who joined as trainees **40%**
% of partners (as at 1/9/03) who joined as trainees **15%**

Lester Aldridge

Russell House, Oxford Road, Bournemouth BH8 8EX
Tel: (01202) 786161 Fax: (01202) 786110
Email: juliet.milne@LA-law.com
Website: www.lesteraldridge.com

firm profile

Based on the South Coast, Lester Aldridge is a dynamic business providing both commercial and private client services across central southern England. The firm also operates in a number of niche markets nationally including asset finance, corporate finance, licensing and marine. The effective corporate management structure ensures LA is focused on delivering pragmatic solutions to their clients. LA places great emphasis on a positive working environment, and the work/life balance, understanding that this will ultimately be of benefit to clients.

main areas of work

Corporate, banking and finance 32%; litigation 30%; private client 21%; commercial prorerty 12%; investments 5%.

trainee profile

Candidates should have strong intellectual capabilities, be commercially aware, resourceful and able to relate easily to other people. IT skills and a team approach are also required.

training environment

Training consists of four six-month seats across the firm. About half-way through each seat trainees discuss their preferences for the next seat and every attempt is made to match aspirations to the needs of the firm. Trainees have a training principal for the duration of the contract who will discuss progress every month. They receive a formal comprehensive appraisal from their team leader towards the end of each seat, and the managing partner meets all trainees as a group every three months.

benefits

Life assurance and pension schemes.

vacation placements

Places for 2004: 8; Duration: 2 weeks; Remuneration: £75 p.w.; Closing Date: 31 March 2004.

sponsorship & awards

LPC (discretionary loan).

Partners	35
Total Trainees	11
Total Staff	320

contact
Juliet Milne

method of application
Letter, CV & completed application form

selection procedure
Interview by a panel of partners

closing date for 2006
13 August 2004

application
Training contracts p.a. **5**
Applications p.a. **300**
% interviewed p.a. **5%**
Required degree grade **2:1**

training
Salary
Starting: **£16,500 at present, increasing by £500 after each seat**
Holiday entitlement **22 days**
% of trainees with a non-law degree p.a. **20%**

post-qualification
Salary (2003) **£29,000**
% of trainees offered job on qualification (2003) **100%**
% of assistants (as at 1/9/01) who joined as trainees **30%**
% of partners (as at 1/9/03) who joined as trainees **25%**

offices
Bournemouth (2), Southampton

Lewis Silkin

12 Gough Square, London EC4A 3DW
Tel: (020) 7074 8000 Fax: (020) 7832 1200
Email: train@lewissilkin.com

firm profile
Lewis Silkin places the highest priority on its relationship with clients, excellent technical ability and the commercial thinking of its lawyers. As a result, it is a profitable and distinctive firm, with a friendly and lively style.

main areas of work
The firm has a wide range of corporate clients and provides services through four main departments: corporate, employment and incentives, litigation and property. The major work areas are: construction; corporate services, which includes company, commercial and corporate finance; commercial litigation and dispute resolution; employment; housing and project finance; marketing services, embracing advertising and marketing law; property; technology and communications, which includes IT, media and telecommunications.

trainee profile
The firm looks for trainees with keen minds and personality, who will fit into a professional but informal team. Law and non-law degrees considered.

training environment
Lewis Silkin provides a comprehensive induction and training programme, with practical 'hands-on' experience in four six month seats. At least three of these seats will be in one of the main departments. The fourth seat can be in one of the specialist areas. Trainees usually sit with a partner who can give ongoing feedback and guidance and progress is formally reviewed every three months. Trainees have the opportunity to get involved in the firm's social and marketing events and also to represent the firm at local trainee solicitors' groups and Law Centres.

benefits
Life assurance, critical illness cover, health insurance, season ticket loan, group pension plan, subsidised gym membership.

vacation placements
Places for 2004: None.

sponsorship & awards
Full fees paid for LPC.

Partners	39
Assistant Solicitors	53
Total Trainees	13

contact
Lucie Rees
HR Officer

method of application
Application form

selection procedure
Assessment day, including an interview with 2 partners & an analytical exercise

closing date for 2006
30 July 2004

application
Training contracts p.a. 6
Applications p.a. 1,000
Required degree grade 2:1

training
Salary
1st year £27,000
2nd year £29,000
Holiday entitlement 25 days

post-qualification
Salary (2003) £43,000

Linklaters

One Silk Street, London EC2Y 8HQ
Tel: (020) 7456 2000 Fax: (020) 7456 2222
Email: graduate.recruitment@linklaters.com
Website: www.linklaters.com/careers/uk

firm profile

Linklaters is a global law firm that advises the world's leading companies, financial institutions and governments. With offices in major business centres in Europe, Asia and the Americas, the firm specialises in innovative solutions for its clients' most challenging deals and transactions.

main areas of work

Linklaters' business covers three core areas - corporate, finance and projects, and commercial - within which there are over 20 different practice areas where trainees can gain experience. These include corporate/M&A, capital markets, banking, projects, asset finance, real estate and construction (including environment and planning), litigation and arbitration, intellectual property, IT and communications, EU/competition, employment, pensions and incentives, financial markets, investment management and tax.

trainee profile

Linklaters' lawyers work as part of a globally integrated team of problem solvers. Trainees will learn from colleagues at the peak of their profession, from different countries and cultures. They benefit from being part of a firm with solid coaching and a supportive ethos. The firm's open-door policy ensures that trainees will always have access to a mentor, because Linklaters prides itself on strong teamwork, both within the firm and with its clients.

training environment

Training is a top priority. Before starting the LPC, students will complete a unique week-long Business Foundation Course, which focuses on improving commercial awareness. Linklaters also keeps in touch with its trainees at Law School through its LPC Liaison Programme. Linklaters will then agree a seat plan of four, six-month seats. Almost all Linklaters trainees spend time in one of the firm's international offices or on client secondment.

sponsorship & benefits

PgDL and LPC fees are paid in full, plus a maintenance grant of £4,500-£5,000. Profit- and performance-related bonus schemes; 25 days' holiday; health and worldwide travel insurance; life assurance; pension scheme; interest-free season ticket loan; subsidised gym membership.

vacation placements

Christmas scheme for 30 final year non-law students and two summer schemes for 60 penultimate year law students. £250 pw. Summer schemes offer opportunity to spend two weeks in another European office.

Partners	500
Associates	1,500
Trainees	250*
*(London)	

contact
Dominique Eisinger

method of application
Application form (available online)

selection procedure
2 interviews plus commercial case study (same day)

application
Training contracts p.a. **125**
Applications p.a. **2,500**
% interviewed p.a. **20%**
Required degree grade **2:1**

training
Salary
1st year (2003) £28,500
2nd year (2003) £32,000
Holiday entitlement **25 days**
% of trainees with a non-law degree p.a. **33%**
No. of seats available abroad p.a. **75**

post-qualification
Salary **£50,000 + performance related bonus**
% of trainees retained on qualification (2003) **82%**

offices
Alicante, Amsterdam, Antwerp, Bangkok, Beijing, Berlin, Bratislava, Brussels, Bucharest, Budapest, Cologne, Frankfurt, Hong Kong, Lisbon, London, Luxembourg, Madrid, Malmö, Milan, Moscow, Munich, New York, Paris, Prague, Rome, São Paulo, Shanghai, Singapore, Stockholm, Tokyo, Warsaw

Lovells

Atlantic House, Holborn Viaduct, London EC1A 2FG
Tel: (020) 7296 2000 Fax: (020) 7296 2001
Email: recruit@lovells.com
Website: www.lovells.com

firm profile

Lovells is one of the world's leading international law firms based in the City of London, with offices in Asia, Europe and North America. The firm's strength across a wide range of practice areas sets it apart from most of its competitors.

main areas of work

The firm's core areas of practice are corporate, litigation, commercial property and specialist groups (including EU/competition, intellectual property, media and telecommunications, employment, tax).

trainee profile

High calibre candidates who can demonstrate high academic ability, ambition, energy and good communication skills.

training environment

Trainees spend six months in four different areas of the practice to gain as much experience as possible. They have the option of spending their third seat in an international office or on secondment to the in-house legal department of a major client. A comprehensive programme of skills training is run for trainees both in-house and externally, placing a particular emphasis on advocacy and communication. Trainees are offered as much responsibility as they can handle as well as regular reviews, six monthly appraisals and support when they need it.

benefits

PPP medical insurance, life assurance, PHI, season ticket loan, in-house gym, staff restaurant, in-house dentist, doctor and physiotherapist, discounts at local retailers.

vacation placements

Places for 2003: 90. Placements available at Christmas 2003 (closing date 14 November), Easter and Summer 2004 (closing date 13 February).

sponsorship & awards

CPE and LPC course fees are paid, and a maintenance grant is also provided of £5,000 for London and Oxford and £4,500 elsewhere. In addition, £500 bonus on joining the firm; £1,000 advance in salary on joining; £500 prize for a First Class degree result.

Partners	350
Assistant Solicitors	1500
Total Trainees	172

contact
Clare Harris
Recruitment Manager

method of application
Online application form

selection procedure
Assessment day: critical thinking test, group exercise, interview

closing date for 2006
31 August 2004

application
Training contracts p.a. **75**
Applications p.a. **1,500**
% interviewed p.a. **18%**
Required degree grade **2:1**

training
Salary
1st year (2002) £28,000
2nd year (2002) £32,000
Holiday entitlement **25 days**
% of trainees with a non-law degree p.a. **40%**
No. of seats available abroad p.a. **18**

post-qualification
Salary (2003) **£50,000**

international offices
Alicante, Amsterdam, Beijing, Berlin, Brussels, Budapest, Chicago, Düsseldorf, Frankfurt, Hamburg, Ho Chi Minh City, Hong Kong, London, Milan, Moscow, Munich, New York, Paris, Prague, Rome, Singapore, Shanghai, Tokyo, Vienna, Warsaw, Zagreb

Lupton Fawcett

Yorkshire House, Greek Street, Leeds LS1 5SX
Tel: (0113) 280 2000 Fax: (0113) 245 6782
Email: elizabeth.brown@luptonfawcett.com
Website: www.luptonfawcett.co.uk

firm profile

Lupton Fawcett is a well-established yet dynamic and integrated practice. The firm offers a full range of legal services to both commercial and private clients alike on a quality-driven and client-led basis with the emphasis on providing first-class cost-effective and practical solutions which exceed the clients expectations. The firm was one of the first in Leeds to hold both Investors in People and the Law Society's Lexcel quality standard.

main areas of work

The commercial division offers the chance to gain experience in corporate, commercial property, employment, intellectual property, insolvency and commercial and chancery litigation. On the private client side, opportunities are available in financial services, trusts and probate, family and residential conveyancing. Further specialist areas of the firm include employment, licensing and advocacy, IT and e-commerce, sports law, debt recovery, insurance litigation and specialist personal injury.

trainee profile

Although strong academic achievements are required, the firm places a high value on previous experience and interests which have developed commercial awareness, maturity and character. Trainees will also be able to demonstrate enthusiasm, confidence, good interpersonal and team skills, humour, initiative, commitment and common sense.

training environment

Training at Lupton Fawcett is normally split into four six month seats. Trainees office share with the partner or associate with whom they are working and are an integral part of the team, assuming a high degree of responsibility. Appraisals following each seat take place to ensure that progress is monitored effectively. A full in-house training programme enables continual development as well as from training gained from excellent hands-on experience. Trainees will have the chance to meet clients and be responsible for their own work, as well as being involved in and actively encouraged to join in marketing and practice development initiatives. There is a full social programme in which the trainees are encouraged to participate as well as sporting events organised by the office and an excellent informal social culture.

benefits

Health insurance, season ticket loans, interest free loans towards LPC funding available by discussion with candidates.

Partners	27
Assistant Solicitors	26
Total Trainees	5

contact
Paul Forster
(0113) 280 2134 or
Liz Brown
(0113) 280 2251

method of application
Employer's application form & handwritten letter

selection procedure
Interviews & assessment days

closing date for 2006
31 July 2004

application
Training contracts p.a. **2-3**
Applications p.a. **300**
% interviewed p.a. **10**
Required degree grade **2:1** preferred

training
Salary
Competitive with similar size/type firms
Holiday entitlement **20 days**

post-qualification
Salary
Competitive with similar size/type firms
% of trainees offered job on qualification (2002-03) **85%**

Mace & Jones

19 Water Street, Liverpool L2 0RP
Tel: (0151) 236 8989 Fax: (0151) 227 5010
Email: donal.bannon@maceandjones.co.uk
14 Oxford Court, Bishopsgate, Manchester M2 3WQ
Tel: (0161) 236 2244 Fax: (0161) 228 7285
Website: www.maceandjones.co.uk

firm profile

Mace & Jones is a leading regional practice in the North West and remains a full service firm while enjoying a national reputation for its commercial expertise, especially in employment, litigation/insolvency, corporate and property. The firm's clients range from national and multinational companies and public sector bodies to owner managed businesses and private individuals, reflecting the broad nature of the work undertaken. Sound practical advice is given always on a value for money basis.

main areas of work

Commercial litigation/insolvency 15%; commercial property 15%; company/commercial 15%; employment 35%; personal injury/private client/family 20%.

trainee profile

The firm seeks to recruit highly motivated trainees with above average ability and the determination to succeed. The right calibre of trainee will assume responsibility early in their career. The firm provides a comprehensive internal and external training programme.

training environment

Trainees complete an induction course to familiarise themselves with the work carried out by the firm's main departments, administration and professional conduct. Training consists of four six month seats in the following departments: company/commercial, employment, commercial litigation/personal injury litigation, property law, family law. Strenuous efforts are made to ensure that trainees are able to select the training seat of their choice. A trainee will normally be required to share an office with a partner who will supervise their work and review the trainee's progress at the end of the seat. The PSC is taught externally. The firm operates an open door policy and has various social events.

Partners 34
Assistant Solicitors 50
Total Trainees 14

contact
Donal Bannon
Liverpool Office

method of application
Covering letter & typed CV which should indicate individual degree subject results

selection procedure
Interview with partners

closing date for 2005
31 March 2004

application
Training contracts p.a. **varies**
Applications p.a. **1,500**
% interviewed p.a. **2%**
Required degree grade **2:1**

training
Salary
1st year (2003) £15,000
2nd year (2003) £15,500
Holiday entitlement **20 days**
% of trainees with a non-law degree p.a. **40%**

post-qualification
Salary (2003) **Negotiable**
% of trainees offered job on qualification (2003) **75%**
% of assistants (as at 1/7/03) who joined as trainees **30%**
% of partners (as at 1/9/03) who joined as trainees **30%**

Macfarlanes

10 Norwich Street, London EC4A 1BD
Tel: (020) 7831 9222 Fax: (020) 7831 9607
Email: gradrec@macfarlanes.com
Website: www.macfarlanes.com

firm profile

A leading City firm serving national and international commercial, industrial, financial and private clients.

main areas of work

Corporate 51%; property 22%; litigation 14%; private client 13%.

trainee profile

Any degree discipline. Actual or predicted 2:1 or better.

training environment

Macfarlanes divides the training contract into four six month periods. You will usually spend time in each of the firm's four main departments (corporate; litigation; property; private client). There is an extensive in-house training programme. Trainees have responsibility for real work and make a contribution that is acknowledged and appreciated.

benefits

21 working days holiday in each calendar year (rising to 26 days upon qualification); interest free season ticket loan; pension; free permanent health insurance*; free private medical insurance*; subsidised conveyancing; subsidised health club/gym membership; subsidised firm restaurant; subscription paid to the City of London Law Society or the London Trainee Solicitors' Group.

*After 12 months service.

vacation placements

Places for 2004: 40; Duration: 2 weeks; Remuneration: £250 p.w.; Closing Date: 27 February 2004 but applications considered and places offered from the end of January 2004.

sponsorship & awards

CPE and LPC fees paid in full and a £5,000 maintenance allowance for courses studied in London, Guildford and Oxford and £4,500 for courses studied elsewhere. Prizes for those gaining distinction or commendation for the LPC.

Partners	61
Assistant Solicitors	125
Total Trainees	45

contact
Graham Stoddart

method of application
Online via website

selection procedure
Assessment day

closing date for 2006
30 July 2004

application
Training contracts p.a. **25**
Applications p.a. **1,500**
% interviewed p.a. **15%**
Required degree grade **2:1**

training
Salary
1st year (2003) £28,000
2nd year (2003) £32,000
Holiday entitlement **21 days**
% of trainees with a non-law degree p.a. **45%**

post-qualification
Salary (2003) **£50,000**
% of trainees offered job on qualification (2003) **100%**
% of assistants (as at 1/9/02) who joined as trainees **60%**
% of partners (as at 1/9/02) who joined as trainees **65%**

Manches

Aldwych House, 81 Aldwych, London WC2B 4RP
Tel: (020) 7404 4433 Fax: (020) 7430 1133
Email: sheona.boldero@manches.co.uk
Website: www.manches.com

firm profile

Manches is a London and Oxford-based commercial firm with strengths across a range of services and industry sectors. The firm's strategy has seen a greater concentration and focus on the firm's core commercial industry sectors of technology and media, property, construction and retail, while continuing to be market leaders in family law. The firm offers 10 trainee places each September.

main areas of work

Industry Sectors: Technology and media, property and construction.

Legal Groups: Corporate finance (emphasis in technology); commercial property; commercial litigation; construction; family; trusts and estates (Oxford office only); employment; intellectual property; information technology; biotechnology (Oxford office only).

trainee profile

Manches looks for candidates with a consistently good academic record who are enthusiastic, committed and with an outgoing engaging personality. They should display a strong sense of commercial awareness, the ability to think for themselves and excellent interpersonal/social skills.

training environment

The firm provides high quality, individual training. Trainees generally sit in four different seats for six months at a time (one of which is usually in a niche practice area). The firm's comprehensive in-house training programme enables them to take responsibility from an early stage, ensuring that they become confident and competent solicitors. Trainees have the opportunity to actively participate in departmental meetings and briefings and receive regular appraisals on their progress.

benefits

Season ticket loan, BUPA after six months, permanent health insurance, life insurance, pension after three months.

vacation placements

Places for 2004: 24 approx.; Duration: 1 week; Remuneration: Under review.; Closing Date: 31 January 2004.

sponsorship & awards

CPE/PgDL and LPC fees are paid in full together with an annual maintenance allowance (currently £4,000 p.a. - under review).

Partners	48
Assistant Solicitors	62
Total Trainees	20

contact
Sheona Boldero
Tel. (020) 7872 8690
(Graduate Recruitment line)

method of application
Application form

selection procedure
Interview with 2 partners. Possible second interview & assessments

closing date for 2006
31 July 2004

application
Training contracts p.a. **10**
Applications p.a. **1,000**
% interviewed p.a. **5%**
Required degree grade **2:1**

training
Salary (Under review)
1st year (2003)
London £26,500
2nd year (2003)
London £30,000
Holiday entitlement **22 days**

post-qualification
Salary (Under review)
London £40,250 (2003)
% of trainees offered job on qualification (2003) **86%**

Martineau Johnson

St. Philips House, St. Philips Place, Birmingham B3 2PP
Tel: (0121) 678 1417 Fax: (0121) 633 7433
Email: anna.swift@martjohn.co.uk
Website: www.martineau-johnson.co.uk and www.graduates4law.co.uk

firm profile

Martineau Johnson combines a dynamic and commercial approach with a traditional and caring attitude. It is set to move to the most prestigious offices in Birmingham city centre, where there will be room for the expansion planned by the firm and where staff will benefit from the latest working methods. And it also has growth plans for its London office too. Its vision is built on matching legal know-how to clients' needs through building partnerships with them and based on detailed understanding and knowledge of their businesses.

main areas of work

Commercial 25%; corporate services 23%; commercial disputes management 18%; property 15%; private client 19%.

trainee profile

Trainees are vital to Martineau Johnson's future and no effort is spared to give the best possible experience and support to them, whilst treating them as individuals. There is a very high retention rate at the end of training contracts, when trainees are generally offered roles in their preferred departments and specialisms.

training environment

Martineau Johnson's aim is to work in partnership with trainees, providing them with mentoring, supervision, support and an exposure to the key areas of the firm's practice. Trainees are actively encouraged to be an integral part of the team delivering legal solutions to its clients whilst benefiting from quality work, flexible seat rotation in a small and friendly team environment. Generally, the firm's trainees are given experience in its chosen sectors: commercial, corporate services, commercial disputes management, property and private client - they are then given the opportunity to carry out further work in areas of their choice and specialism. There are opportunities for Birmingham-based trainees to be exposed to the London scene. Trainees benefit from a structured career training programme tailored to their personal development needs – and it covers not only legal technical matters, but also a business and commercial approach which have never been more central to successful professional careers. In giving training and offering experience that matches the best city firms, Martineau Johnson offers a rare opportunity for trainees to lay great foundations for their legal career in a fast moving, ever changing but caring environment.

sponsorship & awards

LPC fees paid, CPE interest free loan and a maintenance grant of £3,500.

Partners	42
Assistant Solicitors	85
Total Trainees	22

contact
Anna Swift

method of application
Online application form
www.graduates4law.co.uk

selection procedure
Assessment centre - half day

closing date for 2006
31 July 2004

application
Training contracts p.a. **10-12**
Applications p.a. **650**
% interviewed p.a. **15%**
Required degree grade **2:1**

training
Salary
1st year (2003) £18,000
2nd year (2003) £19,500
Holiday entitlement **23 days**
% of trainees with a non-law degree (2003) **40%**

post-qualification
Salary (2003) **£33,000**
% of trainees offered job on qualification (2003) **65%**
% of assistants (as at 1/9/03) who joined as trainees **66%**
% of partners (as at 1/9/03) who joined as trainees **42%**

Masons

30 Aylesbury Street, London EC1R 0ER
Tel: (020) 7490 4000 Fax: (020) 7490 2545
Email: graduate.recruitment@masons.com
Website: www.masons.com and www.out-law.com

firm profile

Masons is one of the most highly regarded specialist law firms in Europe and the Asia Pacific region. The firm's aim is to be recognised as pre-eminent advisers providing a complete range of legal services to businesses operating in the construction and engineering, projects, energy and infrastructure industries and to users and suppliers of information and technology.

main areas of work

Masons provides a complete legal service to clients operating in the construction and engineering, projects, energy and infrastructure industries and to users and suppliers of information and technology. Masons' lawyers provide a comprehensive service in these sectors, as well as to other clients, in the areas of: capital projects; commercial property and development, construction and engineering; corporate and commercial, e-commerce/new media; employment, data protection, dispute resolution (property and commercial), environment, facilities management, freedom of information; health and safety; information technology, insolvency, pensions, planning, project finance and taxation.

trainee profile

Applications are welcome from both law and non-law students with a minimum 2:1 degree and 24 UCAS points. Please apply online at www.masons.com/graduaterecruitment.

training environment

After induction, your two year training contract will be divided into a number of 'seats'. Each seat will involve sharing an office with a partner or solicitor selected from one of the practice areas outlined above. Your rotation throughout the firm will ensure that you are exposed to a range of areas of law and to a variety of approaches. Wherever possible the firm tries to tailor the arrangement to meet individual needs.

benefits

Life assurance, private health care (all offices), subsidised restaurant and season ticket loan (London).

vacation placements

Places for 2004: Approx 18 in London, approx 5 in Manchester; Duration: 2 weeks between mid-June and the end of August; Closing Date: 20 February 2004.

sponsorship & awards

Fees are paid for CPE and LPC courses and maintenance grants.

Partners	102
Total Staff	653
Total Trainees	48

contact
Graduate Recruitment Team, London Office

method of application
Apply online EAF

selection procedure
Assessment day & an interview

closing date for 2006
31 July 2004

application
Training contracts p.a. **15-17 across UK**
Applications p.a. **1,600**
% interviewed p.a. **5%**
Required degree grade **2:1**

training
Salary
£25k-£27k in London. Please note that salaries & benefits vary throughout UK offices
Holiday entitlement
23 days (1st year)
24 days (2nd year)

post-qualification
Salary **£43,000 in London**

overseas offices
Brussels, Dublin, Hong Kong, Shanghai

UK offices
Bristol, Edinburgh (LSS), Glasgow (LSS), Leeds, London, Manchester

Mayer, Brown, Rowe & Maw LLP

11 Pilgrim Street, London EC4V 6RW
Tel: (020) 7248 4282 Fax: (020) 7782 8790
Email: graduaterecruitment@mayerbrownrowe.com
Website: www.mayerbrownrowe.com/london/careers/gradrecruit

firm profile

Mayer, Brown, Rowe & Maw LLP is one of the ten largest law practices in the world. The practice serves its international client base from its 13 offices worldwide, including representation in the world's major financial centres: London, Paris, Frankfurt and New York. The practice has a reputation for delivering pragmatic commercial advice, and is praised for its professionalism.

main areas of work

The practice's client base is diverse and includes blue-chip corporates, multinationals, private companies, partnerships, financial institutions and intermediaries. The practice has an excellent reputation in a diverse range of practice areas, receiving recognition in numerous prestigious legal awards. Major practice areas include: construction; competition and trade; corporate and securities; employment; environment; finance and banking; insurance and reinsurance; intellectual property; litigation and arbitration; oil and gas; pensions; real estate; regulated industries, securitisation and tax.

trainee profile

The practice is interested in motivated students with a good academic record and a strong commitment to law. Commercial awareness gained through legal or business work experience is an advantage.

training environment

Students looking for a leading international law practice that offers exposure to a multitude of blue chip companies and a wide range of international work, combined with the confidence of knowing they have a place in its future, should contact Mayer, Brown, Rowe and Maw LLP. Trainees will participate in a lively, energetic and positive business culture, spending time in four six-month seats including the corporate and litigation departments. The practice's culture of getting immersed in a client's business means that there are excellent secondment opportunities. In addition to the Professional Skills Course, the practice offers an individual professional development and training programme. Three monthly appraisals assist trainees in reaching their true potential.

benefits

Benefits include 25 days holiday per annum, interest free season ticket loan, subsidised sports club membership and private health scheme.

vacation placements

Places for 2004: 25; Duration: 2 weeks during Easter and summer vacations. Experience in two of the principal work groups plus a programme of seminars, visits and social events.

sponsorship & awards

GDL and LPC fees, plus a maintenance grant of £4,500 (£5,000 for London and Guildford).

Partners	100
Assistant Solicitors	170
Total Trainees	48

contact
Sophie Wood

method of application
Online application form

selection procedure
Selection workshops including an interview, a business analysis exercise & a group exercise

closing date for 2006
31 July 2004

application
Training contracts p.a. **Approx 25-30**
Applications p.a. **720**
% interviewed p.a. **9%**
Required degree grade **2:1**

training
Starting salary (2003) **£28,000**
Holiday entitlement **25 days**
% of trainees with a non-law degree p.a. **45%**
No. of seats available abroad p.a. **1**

post-qualification
Salary (2003) **£50,000**
% of trainees offered job on qualification (2003) **79%**
% of partners who joined as trainees **35%**

overseas offices
Brussels, Charlotte, Chicago, Cologne, Frankfurt, Houston, London, Los Angeles, Manchester, New York, Palo Alto, Paris, Washington DC

McCormicks

Britannia Chambers, 4 Oxford Place, Leeds LS1 3AX
Tel: (0113) 246 0622 Fax: (0113) 246 7488
Wharfedale House, 37 East Parade, Harrogate HG1 5LQ
Tel: (01423) 530630 Fax: (01423) 530709
Email: l.Jackson@mccormicks-solicitors.com
Website: www.mccormicks-solicitors.com

firm profile

McCormicks is a unique legal practice at the heart of a vibrant commercial region. With core traditional values of integrity, technical excellence and hard work, the firm is committed to deliver an unrivalled quality of service and innovation to its clients and quality of life to its people. McCormicks combines the full range and depth of skills across its entire practice with the firm's renowned fearlessness and ability to punch above its weight in order to deliver the best possible result.

main areas of work

With a diverse range of clients from private individuals to high profile international organisations its work is never dull. Trainees are exposed to all its practice areas including sports law, media and entertainment law, corporate and commercial, commercial property, commercial litigation, charity work, family, corporate crime, insolvency and intellectual property.

trainee profile

Intellectual achievement, ambition, a sense of humour and commitment to hard work are crucial qualities of a McCormicks trainee. The firm will challenge you but support you at every step of the way.

training environment

Trainees are assigned to one of five departments and supervised throughout by a mentor. The firm's training work will develop skills, knowledge and ambition within a friendly, progressive and supportive environment. Your development will be reviewed regularly by the mentor, team supervisor and the training partner. There is an open door policy and a great team spirit.

vacation placements

Places for 2004: Available in summer vacation. Closing Date: Application forms by 27 February 2004.

Partners	12
Assistant Solicitors	17
Total Trainees	7

contact
Linda Jackson

method of application
Application form

selection procedure
Interview with two partners

closing date for 2006
30 July 2004

application
Training contracts p.a. 4
Applications p.a. 300
% interviewed p.a. 8%
Required degree grade 2:1

training
Salary
1st year (2003)
Highly competitive

post-qualification
Salary (2003)
Highly competitive
trainees offered job on qualification (2003) 2 of 3
% of partners (as at 1/1/2003) who joined as trainees 50%

McDermott, Will & Emery

7 Bishopsgate, London EC2N 3AR
Tel: (020) 7577 6900 Fax: (020) 7577 6950
Website: www.mwe.com/london
Email: graduate.recruitment@europe.mwe.com

firm profile

McDermott, Will & Emery is a leading international law firm with offices in Boston, Chicago, Düsseldorf, London, Los Angeles, Miami, Munich, New York, Orange County, San Diego, Silicon Valley and Washington, DC. The firm's client base includes some of the world's leading financial institutions, largest corporations, mid-cap businesses, and individuals. The firm represents more than 75 of the companies in the Fortune 100 in addition to clients in the FTSE 100 and FTSE 250. Rated as one of the leading firms in The American Lawyer's Top 100, by a number of indicators, including gross revenues and profits per Partner.

London Office: The London office was founded less than five years ago. It is already recognised as being in the top 10 of the 100 US law firms operating in London by the legal media. The firm has about 60 lawyers at present in London, almost all of whom are English-qualified. The firm provides business oriented legal advice to multinational and national corporates, financial institutions, investment banks and private clients. Most of the firm's partners were head of practice at their former firms and are recognised as leaders in their respective fields by the most respected professional directories and market commentators.

main areas of work

Banking and finance; corporate, including international corporate finance and M&A; EU/competition; employment, IP, IT and e-business; litigation and arbitration; pensions and employee benefits; taxation; telecoms and US securities. London is the hub for the firm's European expansions. The firm opened its continental European offices in January 2002 in Munich, Düsseldorf in September 2002 and more will follow.

trainee profile

The firm is looking for the brightest, best and most entrepreneurial trainees. You will need to convince the firm that you have made a deliberate choice.

training environment

The primary focus is to provide a practical foundation for your career with the firm. You will experience between four and six seats over the two year period and the deliberately small number of trainees means that the firm is able to provide a degree of flexibility in tailoring seats to the individual. Trainees get regular support and regular feedback.

benefits

Private medical and dental insurance, life assurance, permanent health insurance, season ticket loan, subisidised gym membership, employee assistance programme, 25 days holiday.

sponsorship & awards

CPE and LPC funding and mainenance grant.

Partners	550*
	18 (London)
Associate Lawyers & Other Fee-earners	397*
	39 (London)
Total Trainees	3 in 2002
	2 in 2003

** denotes worldwide figures*

method of application
CV & covering letter

closing date for 2006
31 July 2004

training
Salary
1st year (2003) £30,000

McDermott, Will & Emery

Mills & Reeve

112 Hills Road, Cambridge CB2 1PH
Tel: (01223) 222336 Fax: (01223) 335848
Email: graduate.recruitment@mills-reeve.com
Website: www.mills-reeve.com

firm profile

Mills & Reeve is one of the largest UK commercial law firms and works for a range of household names. It operates throughout England and Wales from offices in Birmingham, Cambridge, London and Norwich.

main areas of work

The firm offers a full range of corporate, commercial, property, litigation and private client services to a mix of regional and national businesses. The firm is a regional leader in corporate and commercial work and a national specialist in the insurance, higher education, health, agriculture, hi-tech and bio-tech industries.

trainee profile

The firm seeks trainees with a strong academic background, maturity, energy and initiative. Candidates will be willing to accept responsibility and drive the business forward.

training environment

Trainees are based in the Birmingham, Cambridge or Norwich office. The firm seeks to give its trainees experience in a broad range of practice areas, in as many different parts of the business as possible. Subject to the overriding needs of the business, the firm seeks to ensure that its trainees undertake seats in the work areas in which they are most interested. The firm is happy for those trainees with a desire to undertake a seat not practised in their base office to temporarily move to another office, including London, and supports the move with an accommodation allowance. During each seat, trainees sit with a partner or experienced solicitor and their performance is reviewed via a mix of formal and informal appraisals. Staff at all levels are friendly and approachable and excellent support services allow trainees to concentrate on high quality work. A full induction integrates trainees quickly into the firm and ongoing in-house lectures and training by Professional Support Lawyers support the PSC.

benefits

Life assurance at two times pensionable salary, a contributory pension scheme, 25 days holiday, bonus scheme, discounted gym and discounted rate for BUPA.

vacation placements

Applications for two week placements during the summer must be received by 1 March.

sponsorship & awards

The firm pays the full costs of the CPE/DGL and LPC fees and offers a maintenance grant for the LPC year.

Partners	66
Assistant Solicitors	176
Total Trainees	39

contact
Graduate Recruitment

method of application
Firm's application form

selection procedure
Normally one day assessment centre

closing date for 2006
31 July 2004 for training contracts
1st March 2004 for work placements

application
Training contracts p.a. **15-20**
Applications p.a. **Approx 500**
% interviewed p.a. **13%**
Required degree grade **2:1**

training
Salary
1st year (2003) £20,000
2nd year (2003) £21,000
Holiday entitlement
25 days p.a.
% of trainees with a non-law degree **40%**

post-qualification
Salary **£31,500-£32,500**
% of trainees offered job on qualification (2003) **93%**
% of assistants (as at 1/9/03) who joined as trainees **20%**
% of partners (as at 1/9/03) who joined as trainees **24%**

Mishcon de Reya

Summit House, 12 Red Lion Square, London WC1R 4QD
Tel: (020) 7440 7198 Fax: (020) 7430 0691
Email: graduate.recruitment@mishcon.co.uk
Website: www.mishcon.co.uk

firm profile

Mishcon de Reya is a commercial law firm, run by lawyers who understand business. It is an energetic, open and innovative practice committed to providing intelligent and creative legal advice.

main areas of work

Mishcon de Reya provides legal services to a wide range of corporate, entrepreneurial and individual clients. The firm's work falls into four main departments: Corporate and Commercial, Litigation, Property and Family. The firm has also developed specialist groups to meet the demands and opportunities of a constantly evolving business environment, including art, banking and finance, brands and rights, defamation, employment, fraud, immigration, media, music, reputation management, sport and wealth management.

trainee profile

Those who read nothing but law books are probably not the right trainees for this firm. The firm wants people who can meet the highest intellectual and business standards, while maintaining outside interests. Candidates should be cheerful, enterprising and ambitious – they should see themselves as future partners.

training environment

Trainees have the opportunity to experience four different 'seats' of six months each. All trainees get exposure to at least three of the four core departments and are also able to gain experience in specialist groups during their time with the firm. Trainees share a room with a partner or assistant solicitor and the firm's style is friendly and informal. Because of the relatively few training contracts offered, trainees can expect to be exposed to high quality work with early responsibility. In order to support this, the firm has a wide-ranging training programme and provides extensive internal training in addition to the Professional Skills Course. Three-monthly appraisals and monitoring in each seat ensures trainees gain a range of work and experience.

benefits

Medical cover, subsidised gym membership, season ticket loan, permanent health insurance, life assurance and pension.

vacation placements

Places for 2004: 12; Duration: 2 weeks; Expenses: £200 p.w.; Closing Date: 14 March 2004.

sponsorship & awards

CPE and LPC funding with bursary.

Partners	43
Assistant Solicitors	53
Total Trainees	17

contact
Human Resources Department

method of application
Application form

closing date for 2006
31 July 2004

application
Training contracts p.a. 6
Applications p.a. 800+
% interviewed p.a. 5%
Required degree grade 2:1

training
Salary
1st year £25,000
2nd year £27,000
Holiday entitlement
25 days p.a.
Occasional secondments available

post-qualification
% of trainees retained (2003) 75%
% of assistants who joined as trainees 42%
% of partners who joined as trainees 15%

Morgan Cole

Apex Plaza, Forbury Road, Reading RG1 1AX
Tel: (0870) 3664610 Fax: (0870) 3662653
Email: recruitment@morgan-cole.com
Website: www.morgan-cole.com

firm profile

Morgan Cole is one of the leading commercial law practices in the country, providing a comprehensive service to both individual and corporate clients in both the public and private sectors. The firm has a reputation for excellence and therefore attracts the highest quality of staff from all fields. The firm enjoys strong connections throughout the UK and the USA and is a founder member of the Association of European Lawyers, one of five leading UK law firms responsible for establishing a network of English speaking lawyers throughout Europe. The firm's areas of work are covered by ten practice areas: commercial; corporate and banking; employment; insurance; private client; construction; health; landlord and tenant; commercial property; and dispute management. As a modern practice, the firm strives to meet the legal needs of clients in all sectors of industry, but places a specific emphasis on four main sectors: insurance; energy; health; and technology. Within these practice areas the firm's work includes: acquisitions and disposals; technology and intellectual property work; corporate finance; employment; energy; information technology; insolvency; joint ventures; management buy-outs and buy-ins; partnerships; PFI; sports law; public law; commercial property; construction; environmental/planning/health and safety; heath and social care (including medical negligence); commercial litigation; licensing; family and alternative dispute resolution.

trainee profile

Successful candidates should be commercially aware, self motivated individuals with drive and initiative who are able to apply a logical and common-sense approach to solving client problems. The firm is seeking applications from graduates/undergraduates in both law and non-law subjects, preferably with at least a 2:1 degree.

training environment

Trainees spend six months in four different practice areas, and since each practice area handles a wide variety of work within its constituent teams, there is no danger of over-specialisation. Trainees also have the opportunity to be seconded to some of the firm's major clients for one of their seats.

open days

Six in total: two in London, two in Oxford and two in Cardiff. Applications to be made online before 31 March 2004.

sponsorship & awards

The firm offers full funding of fees for attendance on the CPE/PgDL and LPC as well as making a contribution towards maintenance.

Partners	67
Lawyers	346
Total Trainees	28

contact
Guy Constant
Training Principal

method of application
Apply online at www.morgan-cole.com/careers

selection procedure
Assessment Centre & interview

closing date for 2006
31 July 2004

application
Required degree grade
Preferably 2:1

training
Salary
1st & 2nd year (2003)
Competitive for the London, Thames Valley and South Wales regions which are reviewed annually in line with market trends

other offices
Cardiff, Croydon, London, Oxford, Swansea

Nabarro Nathanson

Lacon House, Theobald's Road, London WC1X 8RW
Tel: (0800) 056 4021 Fax: (020) 7524 6524
Email: graduateinfo@nabarro.com
Website: www.nabarro.com

Partners	**107**
Assistant Solicitors	**219**
Total Trainees	**63**

contact
Sally Bridges

method of application
Application form

selection procedure
Interview & assessment day

closing date for 2006
31 July 2004

application
Training contracts p.a. **30**
Applications p.a. **1,500**
Required degree grade **2:1**

training
Salary
1st year (2003)
London & Reading £28,000
Sheffield £20,000
2nd year (2003)
London & Reading £32,000
Sheffield £22,000
Holiday entitlement **25 days**

post-qualification
Salary (2003)
London £46,000
Sheffield £31,000
(reviewed annually)

overseas offices
Brussels

firm profile

One of the UK's leading commercial law firms with offices in London, Reading and Sheffield. The firm is known for having an open but highly professional culture and expects its lawyers to have a life outside work.

main areas of work

Company and commercial law; commercial property; planning; pensions and employment; corporate finance; IP/IT; commercial litigation; construction; PFI; environmental law.

trainee profile

Nabarro Nathanson welcomes applications from law and non law undergraduates. Candidates will usually be expecting a minimum 2:1 degree. As well as strong intellectual ability graduates need exceptional qualities. These include: enthusiasm, drive and initiative, common sense, strong interpersonal skills and teamworking skills.

training environment

Trainees undertake six four-month seats which ensures maximum exposure to the firm's core practice areas (company commercial, commercial property and litigation). The firm aims to retain all trainees on qualification. In addition to the core seats, trainees have the opportunity to gain further experience by spending time in specialist areas (eg pensions, IP/IT, tax, employment), possibly in Germany or Brussels, or completing a further seat in a core area. In most cases trainees will return to the seat they wish to qualify into for the remaining four months of their contract. This ensures a smooth transition from trainee to qualified solicitor.

benefits

Trainees are given private medical insurance, pension, 25 days holiday entitlement per annum, a season ticket loan, access to a subsidised restaurant and subsidised corporate gym membership. Trainee salaries are reviewed annually.

vacation placements

Places for 2004: 60; Duration: 3 weeks between mid-June and end of August; Closing Date: 28 February 2004.

sponsorship & awards

Full fees paid for CPE and LPC and a maintenance grant (London and Guildford: £5,000; elsewhere: £4,500).

Nicholson Graham & Jones

110 Cannon Street, London EC4N 6AR
Tel: (020) 7648 9000 Fax: (020) 7648 9001
Email: traineerecruitment@ngj.co.uk
Website: www.ngj.co.uk

firm profile

A successful mid-sized City law firm which has a strong commercial practice but also acts for private individuals.

main areas of work

The firm is divided into industry sector groups: finance; real estate and construction; projects; technology, media and sport; travel and leisure; manufacturing, distribution and retail.

trainee profile

Highly motivated intelligent graduates of any discipline.

training environment

Trainees spend six months in four of the following training seats: company; litigation; intellectual property; construction; private client and property. The firm aims to allow choice of seats where possible. Each trainee sits with a supervisor and is allocated an additional mentor to ensure all round supervision and training. The firm has a wide induction scheme and recently won an award for its career development programme. Trainees are encouraged to participate fully in all the activities of the firm. High importance is placed on the acquisition of practical skills with considerable emphasis on client contact and early responsibility. The training programme consists of weekly legal education seminars, workshops and a full programme of skills electives. Language training is also available. The annual training weekend is a popular event when the firm gets together for broader skills based training and socialising.

benefits

Life assurance, season ticket loan, subsidised gym membership and BUPA.

vacation placements

The firm runs Open Days in the Easter and Summer Vacations. Online application.

sponsorship & awards

CPE and LPC fees paid plus annual maintenance grant £4,000 (2003).

Partners	52
Assistant Solicitors	52
Total Trainees	18

contact
Tina Two

method of application
Online only

selection procedure
Interview & assessment

closing date for 2006
31 July 2004

application
Training contracts p.a. **10**
Applications p.a. **1,500**
% interviewed p.a. **5%**
Required degree grade **2:1**

training
Salary
1st year (2003) £28,000
2nd year (2004) £31,000
Holiday entitlement **25 days**
% of trainees with a non-law degree p.a. **Varies**

post-qualification
Salary (2003) **£44,000**
% of trainees offered job on qualification (2003) **90%**

overseas offices
Brussels

Norton Rose

Kempson House, Camomile Street, London EC3A 7AN
Tel: (020) 7283 6000 Fax: (020) 7283 6500
Email: grad.recruitment@nortonrose.com
Website: www.nortonrose.com

firm profile

Norton Rose is a leading city and international law firm. They provide an integrated business law service from a network of offices located across Europe, Asia and the Middle East. The firm works primarily for international corporates and financial institutions on large, complex, cross-border transactions, offering them the full range of business legal services.

main areas of work

Corporate finance; banking; dispute resolution; property, planning and environmental; taxation; competition; employment, pensions and incentives; intellectual property and technology.

trainee profile

Successful candidates will be commercially aware, focused, ambitious and team-orientated. High intellect and international awareness are a priority, and language skills are appreciated.

training environment

Norton Rose operates an innovative six-seat system. The first four seats (16 months) include one seat in each of the firm's core departments - corporate finance, banking and dispute resolution - plus an optional seat in one of the firm's other, non-core, departments - employment, pensions and incentives, tax, competition and EC, intellectual property and technology, or property, planning and environmental. The remaining eight months can be spent in the department in which you wish to qualify, or you can visit a different practice area for four months to help you to decide, and spend the last four months in your qualification seat. Alternatively, from your third seat onwards, you can elect to spend four months in one of the firm's international offices or apply for a client secondment. The firm's flexible seat system makes the transition from trainee to qualified solicitor as smooth as possible. The system has won the firm's trainees' approval, and from their point of view, develops associates with the adaptability and expertise the firm need for its future.

benefits

Life assurance (21+), private health insurance (optional), season ticket loan, subsidised gym membership.

vacation placements

Places for 2004: 45 Summer, 15 Christmas; Duration: Summer: Three weeks, Christmas: Two weeks; Remuneration: £250 p.w.; Closing Date: 31 January 2004 for Summer, 1 November 2003 for Christmas. Five or six open days per year are also held.

sponsorship & awards

£1,000 travel scholarship, £800 loan on arrival, four weeks unpaid leave on qualification. LPC/CPE fees paid plus a £5,000 maintenance grant.

Partners 213*
Assistant Solicitors 600*
Total Trainees 147
** denotes worldwide figures*

contact
Shaun Savory

method of application
Employer's application form (available on-line)

selection procedure
Interview and group exercise

closing date for 2006
1 August 2004

application
Training contracts p.a. 70
Applications p.a. 3,500+
% interviewed p.a. 7%
Required degree grade 2:1

training
Salary
1st year (2003) £28,500
2nd year (2003) £32,000
Holiday entitlement 25 days
% of trainees with a non-law degree p.a. 40%
No. of seats available abroad p.a. 22 (per seat move)

overseas offices
Amsterdam, Athens, Bahrain, Bangkok, Beijing,* Brussels, Cologne, Dubai, Frankfurt, Greece, Hong Kong, Jakarta,* London, Milan, Moscow, Munich, Paris, Piraeus, Prague,* Singapore, Warsaw
** Associated office*

Olswang

90 High Holborn, London WC1V 6XX
Tel: (020) 7067 3000 Fax: (020) 7067 3999
Email: graduate@olswang.com
Website: www.olswang.com

firm profile

Forward thinking and progressive, Olswang's ethos has always focused on realising the potential of its clients, of all of its people and the potential within every situation. The firm's aim is simple: to be the preferred law firm of leading companies in the technology, media, telecommunications and property sectors. Olswang knows the players, knows the business and above all, understands the issues. This has brought rapid growth. Olswang is a 500+ strong team committed to providing innovative business solutions through legal excellence.

main areas of work

Advertising; banking; bio-sciences; commercial litigation; corporate and commercial; media litigation; e-commerce; employment; EU and competition; film finance and production; information technology; intellectual property; music; private equity; property; sponsorship; sport; tax; telecommunications; TV/broadcasting.

trainee profile

Being a trainee at Olswang is both demanding and rewarding. The firm is interested in hearing from individuals with a 2:1 degree and above, exceptional drive and relevant commercial experience. In addition, it is absolutely critical that trainees fit well into the Olswang environment which is challenging, busy, energetic, individualistic, meritocratic and fun.

training environment

Olswang wants to help trainees match their expectations and needs with those of the firm. Training consists of four six month seats in the company, media and communications, litigation or property groups. You will be assigned a mentor, usually a partner, to assist and advise you throughout your training contract. In-house lectures supplement general training and six monthly appraisals assess development. Regular social events with the other trainees not only encourage strong relationship building but adds to the fun of work.

benefits

After six months: pension contributions, medical cover, life cover, dental scheme, season ticket loan, subsidised gym membership. After 12 months: PHI.

vacation placements

Places for 2004: June, July, August; Duration: 2 weeks; Remuneration: £250 p.w.; 15 students per scheme; Closing Date: 1 March 2004.

sponsorship & awards

LPC and CPE fees paid in full. Maintenance grant of £4,500 (inside London), £4,000 (outside).

Partners	70
Assistant Solicitors	136
Total Trainees	53

contact
Victoria Edwards
Graduate Recruitment Manager

method of application
Online

selection procedure
Business case scenario, interview, psychometric test and written exercises

closing date for 2006
2 August 2004

application
Training contracts p.a. **Up to 20**
Applications p.a. **2,500**
% interviewed p.a. **4%**
Required degree grade **2:1**

training
Salary
1st year (2003) £26,500
2nd year (2003) £30,000
Holiday entitlement **24 days**
% of trainees with a non-law degree p.a. **33%**

post-qualification
Salary (2003) **£46,000**

overseas offices
Brussels

Orchard

6 Snow Hill, London EC1A 2AY
Tel: (020) 7246 6100 Fax: (020) 7246 6101

firm profile

Established in 1995, Orchard has quickly made its name as one of the newest, most vibrant firms in London. Built on the expertise of a highly experienced team, Orchard has already won the business of many household name clients. The firm is committed to growth through focussed recruitment.

main areas of work

Commercial litigation, corporate finance, mergers and acquisitions, banking, financial services, corporate insolvency, commercial, commercial property, employment, IT / telecommunications and media.

trainee profile

Successful candidates will immediately form part of the professional team and gain early client contract alongside partners and qualified solicitors. Orchard's trainees are valued, fee-earning, members of the team, responsible for managing their own caseloads as well as assisting others. In a firm of Orchard's size, trainees have the opportunity to make a significant contribution to the running of the firm and its development. High standards of academic achievement are important but so too are commercial awareness and enthusiasm. Essential qualities are flexibility of approach and a sense of humour.

training environment

Trainees will spend six months in four of the firm's main practice areas sitting with a partner. Trainees benefit from a system which allows them to work both independently and as part of a team. Each trainee is assigned a personal mentor to assist them throughout their contract period and regular appraisals are conducted on both an informal and formal basis. Continuing education is encouraged and is supplemented by in-house seminars. Trainees are invited to join in the busy social life within the office and take part in client entertaining.

benefits

Under review.

vacation placements

Individual arrangements may be made in writing with Lisa Mills at:
lisa.mills@orchardlaw.com.

Partners	17
Assistants	20
Total Trainees	6

contact
Lisa Mills

method of application
Application form

selection procedure
Two interviews

closing date for 2006
March/September 2004

application
Training contracts p.a.4-6
Applications p.a. 350
% interviewed p.a. 8%
Required degree grade 2:1

training
Salary
1st year: market rate
2nd year: market rate
Holiday entitlement 20 days
% of trainees with a non-law degree p.a. 50%

post-qualification
% of trainees offered permanent employment
100%

Osborne Clarke

2 Temple Back East, Temple Quay, Bristol BS1 6EG
Hillgate House, 26 Old Bailey, London EC4M 7HW
Apex Plaza, Forbury Road, Reading RG1 1AX
Tel: (0117) 917 4322
Email: graduate.recruitment@osborneclarke.com
Website: www.osborneclarke.com

firm profile

Osborne Clarke will challenge your preconceptions about law firms. Described by its clients as dynamic, informal, straightforward and professional, the culture of the firm sets it apart from others as a great place to work. Osborne Clarke looks after its people, encourages individual thinkers and has just two surprisingly simple objectives: to exceed its clients' expectations and, second only to that, to provide interesting and rewarding careers for all its people. As an accredited Investor in People, that objective is taken seriously.

main areas of work

Principal areas of work include corporate, banking, commercial, property, employment, pensions and incentives, dispute resolution and tax. Osborne Clarke acts on sector 'insider' knowledge, bringing educated market solutions to the legal advice given. Sectors include construction, financial services, leisure, media, natural resources, retail, technology and telecoms and transport.

trainee profile

Take it as read that you should have intelligence, commercial focus and the ability to communicate with clients and colleagues alike. To succeed at Osborne Clarke you should also be down to earth, enthusiastic, committed and able to think independently. Trainees come from a wide background, with some joining after a first, or even second career.

training environment

Trainees can expect early responsibility. The firm takes an individual approach to ensure training is relevant to each trainee and offers a well-structured programme. Trainees are encouraged to spend time in at least two of the UK offices, in addition to which international opportunities to Europe and the US are available.

benefits

25 days holiday entitlement, employer's pension contributions, private healthcare cover, season ticket loan, permanent health insurance, group life assurance cover.

vacation placements

20–25 one week placements in April or July 2004, during which you will meet trainees, solicitors and partners, get involved with some real work and experience first-hand life at Osborne Clarke. Remuneration: £175 - £200 per week, depending on location. Closing date: 31 January 2004.

sponsorship & awards

CPE/PgDL and LPC course fees paid and £3,000 maintenance grant for each, some conditions apply.

Partners	**101**
Solicitors	**219**
Trainee Solicitors	**40**
Total Staff	**727**

contact
Graduate Recruitment Team

method of application
Online application form

selection procedure
Assessment day: group exercises, one-to-one interview and selection testing. Final stage: one-to-one partner interview and presentation

closing date for 2006
31 July 2004

application
Training contracts p.a. **20-25**
Applications p.a. **1,000-1,500**
% interviewed p.a. **8%**
Required degree grade
2:1 preferred

training
Salary (2003)
1st year £25,000
London & Thames Valley,
£19,000
Bristol
Holiday entitlement **25 days**
% of trainees with a non-law degree p.a. **Approx 40%**

post-qualification
Salary (2003)
£34,000 Bristol
£47,000 London
£43,000 Thames Valley

overseas offices
Germany: Cologne;
USA: Silicon Valley;
International (Alliance Member) Locations:
France (Paris), Belgium (Brussels), Spain (Barcelona, Madrid), The Netherlands (Rotterdam), Nordic Region (Copenhagen, Helsinki, Tallinn) and Russia (St Petersburg)

Pannone & Partners

123 Deansgate, Manchester M3 2BU
Tel: (0161) 909 3000 Fax: (0161) 909 4444
Email: julia.jessop@pannone.co.uk
Website: www.pannone.com

firm profile

A high profile Manchester firm continuing to undergo rapid growth. The firm prides itself on offering a full range of legal services to a diverse client base which is split almost equally between personal and commercial clients. The firm was the first to be awarded the quality standard ISO 9001 and is a founder member of Pannone Law Group – Europe's first integrated international law group.

main areas of work

Commercial litigation 19%; personal injury 30%; corporate 12%; commercial property 7%; family 9%; clinical negligence 8%; private client 11%; employment 4%.

trainee profile

Selection criteria include a high level of academic achievement, teamwork, organisation and communication skills, a wide range of interests and a connection with the North West.

training environment

An induction course helps trainees adjust to working life, and covers the firm's quality procedures and good practice. Regular trainee seminars cover the work of other departments within the firm, legal developments and practice. Additional departmental training sessions focus in more detail on legal and procedural matters in that department. Four seats of six months are spent in various departments and trainees' progress is monitored regularly. Trainees have easy access to support and guidance on any matters of concern. Work is tackled with gusto here, but so are the many social gatherings that take place.

vacation placements

Places for 2003: 50; Duration: 1 week; Remuneration: None; Closing Date: Easter 30 January 2004, Summer 27 February 2004.

sponsorship & awards

Full grant for LPC fees.

Partners	67
Assistant Solicitors	59
Total Trainees	19

contact
Julia Jessop

method of application
Application form & CV

selection procedure
Individual interview, second interview comprises a tour of the firm & informal lunch

closing date for 2006
2 August 2004

application
Training contracts p.a. **10**
Applications p.a. **700**
% interviewed p.a. **9%**
Required degree grade **2:1**

training
Salary
1st year (2003) £19,000
2nd year (2003) £21,000
Holiday entitlement **23 days**
% of trainees with a non-law degree p.a. **20%**

post-qualification
Salary (2003) **£32,000**
% of trainees offered job on qualification (2003) **85%**
% of assistants who joined as trainees **35%**
% of partners who joined as trainees **33%**

Payne Hicks Beach

10 New Square, Lincoln's Inn, London WC2A 3QG
Tel: (020) 7465 4300 Fax: (020) 7465 4400
Email: apalmer@paynehicksbeach.co.uk
Website: www.paynehicksbeach.co.uk

firm profile

Payne Hicks Beach is a medium-sized firm based in Lincoln's Inn. It provides specialist tax, trusts and probate advice and also specialises in matrimonial, commercial litigation, property and corporate and commercial work.

main areas of work

Private client 41%; matrimonial 22%; property 17%; commercial litigation 13%; corporate and commercial 7%.

trainee profile

The firm looks for law and non-law graduates with a good academic record, an ability to solve practical problems, enthusiasm and an ability to work hard and deal appropriately with their colleagues and the firm's clients.

training environment

Following an initial induction course, trainees usually spend six months in four of the firm's departments. Working with a partner, they are involved in the day to day activities of the department, including attending conferences with clients, counsel and other professional advisers. Assessment is continuous and trainees will be given responsibility as they demonstrate ability and aptitude. To complement the PSC, the firm runs a formal training system for trainees and requires them to attend lectures and seminars on various topics.

benefits

Season travel ticket loan, life assurance 4 x salary, permanent health insurance, contribution to personal pension plan.

sponsorship & awards

Fees for the CPE and LPC are paid.

Partners	28
Assistant Solicitors	21
Total Trainees	5

contact
Mrs Alice Palmer

method of application
Letter & CV

selection procedure
Interview

closing date for 2006
1 August 2004

application
Training contracts p.a. **3**
Applications p.a. **1,000**
% interviewed p.a. **3%**
Required degree grade **2:1**

training
Salary
1st year (2002) £25,000
2nd year (2002) £27,500
Holiday entitlement
4 weeks
% of trainees with a non-law degree p.a. **50%**

Penningtons

Bucklersbury House, 83 Cannon Street, London EC4N 8PE
Tel: (020) 7457 3000 Fax: (020) 7457 3240
Website: www.penningtons.co.uk

firm profile

A London and South East law firm, with offices in the City, Basingstoke, Godalming, Newbury and Paris. There are four main departments. Specialist units cover industry sectors and key overseas jurisdictions, including North America, South Africa, Italy, France and India.

main areas of work

Property 37%; litigation 28%; corporate/commercial 21%; private client 14%.

trainee profile

Penningtons is looking for bright, enthusiastic, highly motivated and well rounded individuals with a keen interest in the practice of law.

training environment

Six month seats are provided in three or four of the following departments: corporate/commercial, property, litigation, and private client. Individual preference is usually accommodated in the second year. Trainees are given a thorough grounding in the law. International opportunities do arise. There are in-house lectures and reviews and appraisals occur regularly. The firm aims to utilise trainees' talents to their full, but is careful not to overburden them. All staff are supportive and the atmosphere is both professional and informal.

benefits

Subsidised sports and social club, life assurance, private medical, season ticket loan.

vacation placements

Places for 2004: 60 on London open days at Easter; Remuneration: Expenses; Closing Date: 15 February 2004. Some summer vacation placements out of London, closing date 15 April 2004.

sponsorship & awards

Full fees and maintenance for the LPC. Awards are given for commendation or distinction in LPC.

Partners 59*
Assistant Solicitors 100*
Total Trainees 22
** denotes worldwide figures*

contact
Lesley Lintott

method of application
Covering letter, CV & application form

selection procedure
1 interview with a partner & director of studies

closing date for 2006
31 July 2004

application
Training contracts p.a. **11**
Applications p.a. **1,000**
% interviewed p.a. **5%**
Required degree grade **2:1**

training
Salary
1st year (2003)
£25,500 (London)
2nd year (2003)
£27,500 (London)
Holiday entitlement **23 days**
% of trainees with a non-law degree p.a. **50%**

post-qualification
Salary (2003)
£38,000 (London)
% of trainees offered job on qualification (2003) **90%**
% of assistants (as at 1/9/01) who joined as trainees **45%**
% of partners (as at 1/9/01) who joined as trainees **40%**

overseas offices
Paris

Pinsents

Dashwood House, 69 Old Broad Street, London EC2M 1NR
3 Colmore Circus, Birmingham B4 6BH
1 Park Row, Leeds LS1 5AB
The Chancery, 58 Spring Gardens, Manchester M216 1EW
Email: gradrecruiting@pinsents.com
Website: www.pinsents.com/graduate

firm profile

Pinsents is a leading corporate law firm that is committed to sector growth through its industry-recognised business model: the Chosen Market Strategy. This strategy aligns the firm to specific business sectors to achieve market-leading positions. As a result the firm has developed a successful and innovative approach to building strong, broad and deep corporate relationships. Client service is the cornerstone of the Pinsents business.

main areas of work

Corporate; dispute resolution and litigation; employment; insurance and reinsurance; pensions; projects and commercial; property; tax; technology and media.

trainee profile

The firm welcomes applications from both law and non-law graduates with a good honours degree. In addition to a strong academic background the firm is looking for problem solvers with a sharp commercial acumen, who as committed team players can use their initiative and common sense to get to the heart of the clients' business and legal needs.

training environment

Trainees sit in four seats of six months across the practice groups and are supervised by partners or associates. There are also opportunities for trainees to be seconded to clients. There is a supportive team structure where hands-on experience is an essential part of the learning process, with early responsibility and contact with clients encouraged. In addition to the PSC the firm has a structured development programme designed to broaden trainee business and legal knowledge. This is the first stage of the firm's focused legal management development programme that supports individuals through to partnership. The firm has an open-door policy and informal atmosphere with a positive focus on work life balance.

summer vacation placements

Places for 2004: 90; Duration: 2 weeks; Closing Date: 20 February 2004.

sponsorship & awards

CPE/ LPC fees are paid. In addition to this, maintenance grants of £3,000 for CPE and £5,000 for LPC are offered.

Partners 175
Assistant Solicitors 294
Total Trainees 70

contact
Ms Maxine Jayes
Recruitment Hotline:
(0845) 300 3232

method of application
Online application form

selection procedure
Assessment centre
including interview

closing date for 2006
31 July 2004

application
Training contracts p.a. **35**
Applications p.a. **2,000**
Required degree grade **2:1**

training
Salary
1st year (2003) £28,000
2nd year (2003) £32,000
Holiday entitlement **25 days**

post-qualification
Salary (2003)
Approx £48,000
% of trainees offered job
on qualification (2003) **70%**

Prettys

Elm House, 25 Elm Street, Ipswich IP1 2AD
Tel: (01473) 232121 Fax: (01473) 230002
Email: agage@prettys.co.uk
Website: www.prettys.co.uk

firm profile

Prettys is one of the largest and most successful legal practices in East Anglia. The firm is located in the centre of the East Anglian business community, with the expanding hi-tech corridor between Ipswich and Cambridge to the west, Felixstowe to the east and the City of London 60 minutes away to the south. The firm's lawyers are approachable and pragmatic. It provides expert advice to national and regional businesses.

main areas of work

Prettys' broad-based practice allows it to offer a full-service to all its clients. Business law services: company, commercial, shipping, transport, construction, intellectual property, information technology, property, employment, commercial litigation, insurance, professional indemnity, health and safety and executive immigration. Personal law services: French property, personal injury, clinical negligence, financial services, estates, agriculture, conveyancing and family.

trainee profile

Prettys' trainees are the future of the firm. Applicants should be able to demonstrate a desire to pursue a career in East Anglia. Trainees are given considerable responsibility early on and the firm is therefore looking for candidates who are well motivated, enthusiastic and have a good common sense approach. Good IT skills are essential.

training environment

A two week induction programme will introduce you to the firm. You will receive continuous supervision and three monthly reviews. Training is in four six-month seats with some choice in your second year and the possibility of remaining in the same department for two seats. Trainees work closely with a partner, meeting clients and becoming involved in all aspects of the department's work. Frequent training seminars are provided in-house. The PSC is taken externally.

additional information

One day placements are available (apply to Angela Gage). Apply by the end of July 2004 to begin 2006.

sponsorship & awards

Discretionary.

Partners	15
Total Trainees	8-10

contact
Angela Gage

method of application
Application letter & CV

closing date for 2006
Apply by the end of July 2004 to begin 2006

application
Training contracts p.a. 4-5
Required degree grade 2:1 preferred in law or other relevant subject. Good A Levels

training
Salary
Above Law Society guidelines

Pritchard Englefield

14 New St, London EC2M 4HE
Tel: (020) 7972 9720 Fax: (020) 7972 9722
Email: po@pritchardenglefield.eu.com
Website: www.pritchardenglefield.eu.com

firm profile

A medium-sized City firm practising a mix of general commercial and non-commercial law with many German and French clients. Despite its strong commercial departments, the firm still undertakes family and private client work and is known for its strong international flavour.

main areas of work

All main areas of commercial practice including litigation, company/commercial (UK, German and French), property and employment, also estate and trusts, personal injury and family.

trainee profile

High academic achievers with fluent German and/or French.

training environment

An induction course acquaints trainees with the computer network, library and administrative procedures and there is a formal in-house training programme. Four six month seats make up most of your training. You can usually choose some departments, and you could spend two six month periods in the same seat. Over two years, you learn advocacy, negotiating, drafting and interviewing, attend court, use your language skills and meet clients. Occasional talks and seminars explain the work of the firm, and you can air concerns over bi-monthly lunches with the partners comprising the Trainee Panel. PSC is taken externally over two years. Quarterly drinks parties number amongst popular social events.

benefits

Some subsidised training, luncheon vouchers.

sponsorship & awards

Full funding for LPC fees.

Partners	22
Assistant Solicitors	11
Total Trainees	6

contact
Graduate Recruitment

method of application
Standard application form available from Graduate Recruitment or online

selection procedure
1 interview only in September

closing date for 2006
31 July 2004

application
Training contracts p.a. 3
Applications p.a. **300–400**
% interviewed p.a. **10%**
Required degree grade
Generally 2:1

training
Salary
1st year (2003) £20,750
2nd year (2003) £21,250
Holiday entitlement **25 days**
% of trainees with a non-law degree p.a. **Approx 50%**

post-qualification
Salary (2003)
Approx £34,000
% of trainees offered job on qualification (2002) **75%**
% of assistants (as at 1/9/03) who joined as trainees **50%**
% of partners (as at 1/9/03) who joined as trainees **40%**

overseas offices
Hong Kong

RadcliffesLeBrasseur

5 Great College Street, Westminster, London SW1P 3SJ
Tel: (020) 7222 7040 Fax: (020) 7222 6208
Email: gradrec@rlb-law.com
Website: www.rlb-law.com

firm profile

RadcliffesLeBrasseur combines traditional values of integrity and prompt response with a client focused approach to everything that it does. It has a wide and varied client base which includes healthcare services providers, public and private companies, property companies, charities, banks, institutions, public authorities and private individuals. Along with its offices in Westminster, the firm also has offices in Leeds and Cardiff.

main areas of work

The firm is organised into departments and experts within them integrate their knowledge in the firm's specialist market facing groups, health, corporate (including litigation), property, charities, tax and private client.

trainee profile

Its aim is to recruit trainee solicitors who have a real prospect of becoming future partners. The firm seeks not just academic but also extra curricular activities, self-confidence, determination and a sense of humour.

training environment

Trainees are introduced to the firm with a full induction week.

benefits

Health insurance, season ticket loan, life assurance, PHI and pension scheme.

vacation placements

Places for 2004: 20 (London only); Duration: 2 weeks; Remuneration: travel expenses; Closing Date: 31 March 2004.

sponsorship & awards

LPC fees paid.

trainee comments

"From day one, after the induction week, you have your own files and actually do the work."
"It's a thoroughly commercial firm, so it's no good being academically brilliant but financially naive."
"I liked the way people worked together to get jobs done, rather than working all hours on their own to make some kind of individual point."

Partners	55
Assistant Solicitors	47
Total Trainees	13

contact
Graduate Recruitment

method of application
CV & covering letter

selection procedure
2 Interviews with partners

closing date for 2006
31 July 2004

application
Training contracts p.a. 4 (London 3; Leeds 1)
Applications p.a. 1,000
% interviewed p.a. 9%
Preferred degree grade 2:1

training
Salary
1st year (2002)
£23,500 (London)
£15,000 (Leeds)
2nd year (2002)
£26,000 (London)
£16,500 (Leeds)

post-qualification
Salary (2003) £38,000 (London)
% of trainees offered job on qualification (2003) 80%
% of assistants (as at 1/9/03) who joined as trainees 45%

Reed Smith

Minerva House, 5 Montague Close SE1 9BB
Tel: (020) 7403 2900 Fax: (020) 7403 4221
Email: tclaxton@reedsmith.co.uk
Website: www.reedsmith.co.uk

firm profile

Reed Smith is a leading international law firm with 16 US offices and two UK offices located in London and the Midlands. The UK is known for its international work and handles all types of commercial transactions for well-known clients.

main areas of work

The firm is divided into four core departments: business and finance; international litigation; real estate; employment.

trainee profile

Enthusiastic, proactive, bright, commercially-minded graduates who want to work in a friendly atmosphere where personality, a sense of humour and a hands-on approach are encouraged.

training environment

To help trainees build a strong career, the firm invests heavily in training (approximately one training session per week) covering a range of skills including advocacy, drafting and marketing. The firm provides an informal but fast-paced working environment where trainees are immediately given access to clients and fulfilling work, often with an international bias. Trainees who are fluent French speakers will be given opportunities to develop these skills. The firm has four seats available in business and finance, international litigation, real estate and employment. Progress is reviewed regularly by a senior partner.

benefits

BUPA, IFSTL, life assurance, permanent health insurance, pension contributions (after qualifying period).

vacation placements

Places for Summer 2004: 12; Duration: 4 weeks (London), 2 weeks (Midlands); Remuneration: £800 (London), £300 (Midlands); Closing Date: 31 January 2004.

sponsorship & awards

CPE/LPC fees and maintenance grant plus interest-free loan.

Partners	31
Assistant Solicitors	34
Total Trainees	12

contact
Tassy Claxton
Recruitment Co-ordinator

method of application
Application form & covering letter

selection procedure
Assessment day:
2 interviews, aptitude test & presentation

closing date for 2006
31 July 2004

application
Training contracts p.a.
6 (London 4, Coventry 2)
Applications p.a. **1,000**
% interviewed p.a. **3%**
Required degree grade **2:1**

training
Salary
1st year (2002) £27,000
2nd year (2002) £31,000
Holiday entitlement **25 days**
% of trainees with a non-law degree **25%**

post-qualification
Salary (2003) **£48,000**

Reynolds Porter Chamberlain

Chichester House, 278-282 High Holborn, London WC1V 7HA
Tel: (020) 7242 2877 Fax: (020) 7242 1431
Email: training@rpc.co.uk
Website: www.rpc.co.uk/training

firm profile

Reynolds Porter Chamberlain is a leading commercial law firm with approximately 250 lawyers. In addition to its main offices in Holborn, the firm has an expanding office at Leadenhall Street in the City which serves its insurance clients. Best known as a major litigation practice, particularly in the field of professional negligence and insurance/reinsurance, RPC also has thriving corporate, commercial property, private client and construction departments. Another rapidly expanding part of the firm is its media and technology practice. This handles major defamation actions and has dealt with some of the biggest internet deals to date.

main areas of work

Litigation 60%; corporate 10%; commercial property 10%; construction 10%; media and technology 5%; family/private client 5%.

trainee profile

The firm appoints ten trainees each year from law and non-law backgrounds. Although proven academic ability is important (the firm requires a 2:1 or above), RPC also values flair, energy, business sense, commitment and the ability to communicate and relate well to others.

training environment

As a trainee you will receive first rate training in a supportive working environment. You will work closely with a partner and be given real responsibility as soon as you are ready to handle it. At least six months will be spent in each of the three main areas of the practice and the firm encourages trainees to express a preference for their seats. This provides a thorough grounding and the chance to develop confidence as you see matters through to their conclusion. In addition to the internally provided Professional Skills Course the firm provides a complimentary programme of in-house training.

benefits

Four weeks holiday, bonus schemes, private medical insurance, income protection benefits, season ticket loan, subsidised gym membership, active social calendar.

vacation placements

Places for July 2004: 12; Duration: 2 weeks; Remuneration: £250 p.w.; Closing Date: 27 February 2004.

sponsorship & awards

CPE/PgDL Funding: Fees paid plus £4,000 maintenance; LPC Funding: Fees paid plus £4,000 maintenance.

Partners	62
Assistant Solicitors	183
Total Trainees	20

contact
Kate Gregg
Graduate Recruitment Officer

method of application
Online application system

selection procedure
Assessment days held in September

closing date for 2006
14 August 2004

application
Training contracts p.a. **10**
Applications p.a. **1,000**
% interviewed p.a. **4.5%**
Required degree grade **2:1**

training
Salary
1st year (2003) £27,000
2nd year (2003) £29,000
Holiday entitlement **20 days**
% of trainees with a non-law degree p.a. **Approx 25%**

post-qualification
Salary (2003) **£45,000**
% of trainees offered job on qualification (2003) **100%**
% of assistants (as at 1/9/03) who joined as trainees **30%**
% of partners (as at 1/9/03) who joined as trainees **35%**

Richards Butler

Beaufort House, 15 St. Botolph Street, London EC3A 7EE
Tel: (020) 7247 6555 Fax: (020) 7247 5091
Email: gradrecruit@richardsbutler.com

firm profile

Established in 1920, Richards Butler is noted for the exceptional variety of its work. It has acknowledged strengths in commercial disputes, commodities, competition, corporate finance, energy law, insurance, media/entertainment, property and shipping, in each of which it has international prominence. Over two thirds of the firm's work involves cross border deals and the firm's contribution to international trade was recognised when it was awarded the Queen's Award for Enterprise in 2002.

main areas of work

Banking/commercial/corporate/finance 27%; insurance/international trade and commodities/shipping 29%; commercial disputes 30%; commercial property 14%.

trainee profile

Candidates should be players rather than onlookers, work well under pressure and be happy to operate as a team member or team leader as circumstances dictate. Candidates from diverse backgrounds are welcome, including mature students with commercial experience and management skills.

training environment

Four or five seat rotations enable Richards Butler to provide practical experience across as wide a spectrum of the law as possible. Trainees can also apply for secondment to one of the firm's overseas offices, Hong Kong, Paris, Abu Dhabi, São Paulo, Piraeus or to one of their client in-house legal teams.

benefits

Performance related bonus, life insurance, BUPA, interest-free season ticket loan, subsidised staff restaurant, staff conveyancing allowance.

vacation placements

Places for 2004: 30; Duration: 2 weeks; Remuneration: £200 p.w.; Closing Date: 13 February 2004. In addition, the firm offers overseas scholarships to Paris, Hong Kong, Abu Dhabi and Athens. The scholarship consists of a return airfare, accomodation, living expenses and two weeks of work experience. Please see website for further information.

sponsorship & awards

CPE Funding: Fees paid plus £5,000 maintenance.
LPC Funding: Fees paid plus £5,000 maintenance.

Partners	112*
Fee-earners	436*
Total Trainees	68*

** denotes worldwide figures*

contact
Mark Matthews

method of application
Online application form

selection procedure
Selection exercise & interview

closing date for 2006/07
31 July 2004

application
Training contracts p.a. **20**
Applications p.a. **2,000**
% interviewed p.a. **5%**
Required degree grade **2:1**

training
Salary
1st year (2003) £28,000
2nd year (2003) £31,000
Holiday entitlement **25 days**
% of trainees with a non-law degree p.a. **33%**
No. of seats available abroad p.a. **10**

post-qualification
Salary (2003)
£48,000 plus bonus
% of assistants who joined as trainees **59%**
% of partners who joined as trainees **54%**

overseas offices
Abu Dhabi, Athens, Beijing, Brussels, Doha*, Hong Kong, Muscat*, Paris, Piraeus, São Paulo
** Associated office*

Salans

Clements House, 14-18 Gresham Street, London EC2V 7NN
Tel: (020) 7509 6000 Fax: (020) 7726 6191
Email: london.recruitment@salans.com

firm profile

Salans is a multinational law firm with full-service offices in the City of London, Paris and New York, together with further offices in Moscow, St Petersburg, Warsaw, Kyiv, Almaty and Baku. The firm currently has over 500 fee-earners, including over 120 partners.

main areas of work

London Office: Banking and finance; corporate; litigation; employment; real estate; insolvency and corporate recovery; information technology and communications; betting and gaming; media and film finance.

trainee profile

Candidates need to have high academic qualifications, including good A-Level (or equivalent) results, along with the ability to approach complex problems in a practical and commercial way. The firm looks to recruit those who demonstrate an ability and a willingness to assume responsibility at an early stage, possess common sense and good judgement. Relevant work experience demonstrating a desire to pursue a career in law will be viewed positively, and language and computer skills are also valued.

benefits

Private healthcare, pension, season ticket loan.

sponsorship & awards

LPC tuition fees paid.

Partners 120
Assistant Solicitors
(Worldwide) 250+
Total Trainees
(London) 7

contact
Vicky Williams
HR Manager

method of application
Handwritten letter & CV

selection procedure
interview programme and selection workshop

closing date for 2006
31 July 2004

application
Training contracts p.a. **3-4**
Applications p.a. **500+**
% interviewed p.a. **5%**
Required degree grade **2:1**

training
Salary
1st year (2003) £26,500
2nd year (2003) £28,500
Holiday entitlement **25 days**
% of trainees with a non-law degree p.a. **Variable**
No. of seats available abroad p.a. **None at present**

post-qualification
Salary (2002) **Variable**
% of trainees offered job on qualification (2002) **100%**

overseas offices
Almaty, Baku, Kyiv, Moscow, New York, Paris, St Petersburg, Warsaw

Shadbolt & Co

Chatham Court, Lesbourne Road, Reigate RH2 7LD
Tel: (01737) 226277 Fax: (01737) 226165
Email: mail@shadboltlaw.com
Website: www.shadboltlaw.com

firm profile

Established in 1991, Shadbolt & Co is an award winning dynamic, progressive firm committed to high quality work and excellence both in the UK and internationally. The atmosphere at the firm is friendly, relaxed and informal and there are various social and sporting activities for staff. The firm's qualified staff have a high level of experience and industry knowledge and some are widely regarded as leading practitioners in their field.

main areas of work

The firm is well known for its strengths in major projects, construction and engineering and dispute resolution and litigation with expansion into corporate and commercial, employment, commercial property and IT and e-commerce. The firm's client list includes some of the world's best known names in the construction and engineering industries.

trainee profile

Applicants must demonstrate that they are mature self-starters with a strong academic background and outside interests. Leadership, ambition, initiative, enthusiasm and good interpersonal skills are essential as is the ability to play an active role in the future of the firm. Linguists are particularly welcome as are those with supporting professional qualifications. The firm welcomes non-law graduates.

training

Four six month seats from construction and commercial litigation, arbitration and dispute resolution, major projects and construction, employment, corporate and commercial and commercial property. Where possible individual preference is noted. Work has an international bias. There are opportunities for secondment to major clients and work in the overseas offices. Trainees are treated as valued members of the firm, expected to take early responsibility and encouraged to participate in all the firm's activities, including practice development.

sponsorship & benefits

Optional private healthcare, permanent health insurance, group life assurance, paid study leave, season ticket loan, discretionary annual bonus, paid professional memberships and subscriptions, 50% refund of LPC upon commencement of training contract, PSC fees paid.

vacation placements

Places for 2004: 6; Duration: 2 weeks; Remuneration (2003): £170 p.w.; Closing Date: 16 March 2004; Interviews: April 2004.

Partners	21
Assistant Solicitors	25
Total Trainees	8
Total Staff	105

contact
Andrea Pickett

method of application
Application form

selection procedure
Interview & written assessment

closing date for 2006
31 August 2004 (interviews September 2004)

application
Training contracts p.a. **4**
Applications p.a. **100**
% interviewed p.a. **15%**
Required degree grade **2:1 (occasional exceptions)**

training
Salary
1st year (2002) £22,000
2nd year (2002) £26,000
Holiday entitlement
20 days rising to 25 on qualification
% of trainees with a non-law degree p.a. **50%**
No. of seats available abroad p.a. **1**

post-qualification
Salary (2003) **£35,000**
% of trainees offered job on qualification (2003) **100%**
% of assistants (2003) who joined as trainees **64%**
% of partners (2003) who joined as trainees **0%**

other offices
Reigate, City of London, Paris, Dar es Salaam, Athens

Shearman & Sterling LLP

Broadgate West, 9 Appold Street, London EC2A 2AP
Tel: (020) 7655 5000 Fax: (020) 7655 5500

firm profile

Shearman & Sterling LLP is one of New York's oldest legal partnerships, which has transformed from a New York-based firm focused on banking into a diversified global institution. Recognised throughout the world, the firm's reputation, skills and expertise are second to none in its field. The London office, established in 1972, has become a leading practice covering all aspects of English and European corporate and finance law. The firm employs over 130 English and US trained legal staff in London and has more than 1,000 lawyers in 18 offices worldwide.

main areas of work

Banking, leveraged finance and securitisation (primary and secondary structured debt, bridging facilities, debt trading and financial restructuring). Project finance (all aspects, in the power, oil, gas, telecommunications, mining and transport infrastructure sectors). M&A (public and private cross-border transactions on a pan-European scale). Global capital markets (structuring and execution of high-yield debt and equity-linked financing). International arbitration and litigation (international commercial law on a global scale). Tax (all direct and indirect tax aspects of structured finance and securitisations, domestic and international banking, capital markets issues, M&A and reorganisations). EU and competition (cross-border and UK M&A transactions, restrictive practices and abuse of dominance, competition litigation, state aid, public procurement and utility regulation).

trainee profile

The firm's successful future development calls for people who will relish the hard work and intellectual challenge of today's commercial world. You will be a self-starter, keen to assume professional responsibility early in your career and determined to become a first-class lawyer in a first-class firm. The firm's two year training programme will equip you with all the skills needed to become a successful commercial lawyer. You will spend six months in each of four practice areas, with an opportunity to spend six months in Hong Kong or Singapore. You will be an integral part of the London team from the outset, with your own laptop and mobile phone. The firm will expect you to contribute creatively to all the transactions you are involved in. The firm has an informal yet professional atmosphere. Your enthusiasm, intellect and energy will be more important than what you wear to work. The firm will provide you with a mentor, arrange personal and professional development courses and give you early responsibility. The firm wants to recruit people who will stay with it; people who want to become partners in its continuing success story.

sponsorship & awards

Sponsorship for the CPE and LPC courses, together with a maintenance grant of £4,500.

Partners	23
Assistant Solicitors	100
Total Trainees	5

contact
Kirsten Davies
Tel: (020) 7655 5082

method of application
Application form

selection procedure
Interviews

closing date for 2006
31 July 2004

application
Training contracts p.a. 6
Required degree grade 2:1

training
Salary
1st year (2003) £30,000
2nd year (2003) £34,000
Holiday entitlement
24 days p.a.
% of trainees with non-law degree p.a. **50%**
No of seats available abroad **2**

post-qualification
Salary (2003) **£55,000**
% of trainees offered job on qualification (2003) **100%**

overseas offices
Abu Dhabi, Bejing, Brussels, Düsseldorf, Frankfurt, Hong Kong, Mannheim, Menlo Park, Munich, New York, Paris, Rome, San Francisco, Singapore, Tokyo, Toronto, Washington DC

Shoosmiths

The Lakes, Bedford Road, Northampton NN4 7SH
Tel: (0870) 086 3223 Fax: (0870) 086 3001
Email: join.us@shoosmiths.co.uk
Website: www.shoosmiths.co.uk

firm profile

Growing steadily, with eight offices across the country, 62 partners and 1,200 staff, Shoosmiths is one of the big players outside of London. By joining the firm you can expect to experience a full range of interesting and challenging commercial work. In a demanding legal market, Shoosmiths has developed exciting, even radical, services helping it to exceed the highest expectations of its clients. The firm supports and encourages its people to develop exhilarating, balanced careers. Shoosmiths' workplace culture offers a stimulating environment, time for family and the opportunity to put something back into the community.

main areas of work

Corporate/commercial; dispute resolution; employment; planning; commercial property; banking; financial institutions; private client; personal injury.

trainee profile

You will be confident, motivated and articulate with natural intelligence and the drive to succeed, thereby making a real contribution to the firm's commercial success. You will want to be a part of a winning team and will care about the kind of service you give to your clients, both internal and external.

training environment

You will be involved in 'real' work from day one of your training contract. Sitting with a partner who will oversee your training and career development, you will have direct contact with clients and will draft your own letters and documents. Your experience will build through your daily, practical, workload complemented by the training you would expect from a leading national law firm. In addition to the compulsory Professional Skills Course, the firm offers a comprehensive internal training programme that includes managerial, legal and IT training as standard. Over the course of two years, you will complete four seats of six month duration, to help you decide which area you would like to qualify into.

benefits

Flexible holidays, pension (after 3 months service), life assurance, various staff discounts, Christmas bonus.

vacation placements

Places for 2004: 30; Duration: 2 weeks; Remuneration: £160 p.w.; Closing Date: 28 Feb 2004.

sponsorship & awards

LPC funding: £12,500 – split between fees and maintenance.

Partners	62
Assistant Solicitors	106
Total Trainees	23

contact
Sarah Woods

method of application
Application form via website

selection procedure
Selection centre - full day

closing date for 2006
31 July 2004

application
Training contracts p.a. **10**
Applications p.a. **1,000**
% interviewed p.a. **10%**
Required degree grade **2:1**

training
Salary
Competitive
Holiday entitlement
23 days + option to flex

post-qualification
Salary **Market rate**

offices
Northampton, Nottingham, Reading, Fareham, Milton Keynes, Basingstoke, Birmingham

Sidley Austin Brown & Wood

1 Threadneedle Street, London EC2R 8AW
Princes Court, 7 Princes Street, London EC2R 8AQ
Tel: (020) 7360 3600 Fax: (020) 7626 7937
Email: idrummond@sidley.com
Website: www.sidley.com

firm profile

Sidley Austin Brown & Wood is one of the world's largest full-service law firms combining the strengths of two exceptional law firms. With more than 1,300 lawyers practising in 13 offices on three continents (North America, Europe and Asia), the firm provides a broad range of integrated services to meet the needs of its clients across a multitude of industries. The firm has over 100 lawyers in London and is expanding fast.

main areas of work

Corporate securities; corporate finance; investment funds; tax; banking regulation; securitisation and structured finance; corporate reconstruction; property and property finance.

trainee profile

Sidley Austin Brown & Wood is looking for focused, intelligent and enthusiastic individuals with personality and humour who have a real interest in practising law in the commercial world. Trainees should have a 2:1 degree (not necessarily in law) and three A levels at A and B grades. Trainees would normally be expected to pass the CPE (if required) and the LPC at the first attempt.

training environment

Sidley Austin Brown & Wood is looking to recruit six to eight trainee solicitors to start in September 2006/March 2007. The firm is not a typical City firm and it is not a 'legal factory' so there is no risk of being just a number. The team in London is young, dynamic and collegiate. Everyone is encouraged to be proactive and to create their own niche when they are ready to do so. Trainees spend a period of time in the firm's specialist groups: international finance, corporate securities, corporate commercial, tax and property. Sidley Austin Brown & Wood in London does not have a separate litigation department, although some litigation work is undertaken. The firm does, however, organise external litigation training for all trainees. In each group trainees will sit with a partner or senior associate to ensure that students receive individual training that is both effective and based on a real caseload. In addition, there is a structured timetable of training on a cross-section of subjects and an annual training weekend.

benefits

Healthcare, disability cover, life assurance, contribution to gym membership, interest-free season ticket loan.

sponsorship & awards

CPE and LPC fees paid and maintenance p.a.

Partners	26
Assistant Solicitors	74
Total Trainees	16

contact
Isabel Drummond, Legal and Graduate Recruitment Manager

method of application
Covering letter & employee application form

selection procedure
Interview(s)

closing date for 2006
30 July 2004

application
Training contracts p.a. 6-8
Applications p.a. 500
% interviewed p.a. 15
Required degree grade 2:1

training
Salary
1st year (2003) £28,500
2nd year (2003) £32,000
Holiday entitlement 25 days
% of trainees with a non-law degree p.a. 50%

overseas offices
Beijing, Chicago, Dallas, Geneva, Hong Kong, London, Los Angeles, New York, San Francisco, Shanghai, Singapore, Tokyo, Washington DC

Simmons & Simmons

CityPoint, One Ropemaker Street, London EC2Y 9SS
Tel: (020) 7628 2020 Fax: (020) 7628 2070
Email: recruitment@simmons-simmons.com
Website: www.simmons-simmons.com

firm profile

Simmons & Simmons is a worldclass law firm providing advice to financial institutions, corporates, public and international bodies and private individuals through its international network of offices. It provides a comprehensive range of legal services with strength and depth. The ability to provide technically excellent, commercial and high quality advice is expected of leading law firms. Simmons & Simmons aims to provide an additional dimension by focusing on the way it works with its clients and by shaping its services to fit the clients' needs.

main areas of work

The firm provides a range of legal services including: commercial, corporate, dispute resolution, EU and competition, employment and benefit, finance, intellectual property, projects, real estate and environment and tax. The firm works with particular focus in eight key industries: aerospace and defence, consumer goods, energy and utilities, financial markets, pharmaceutical and biotechnology, real estate and construction, TMT and transport.

trainee profile

While a good academic record and sound commercial judgement is important, strength of character and outside interests are also taken into consideration.

training environment

The firm will make sure students have the right skills to join the firm's team of worldclass legal professionals. The firm really wants students to succeed so trainees will find a warm welcome as well as genuine levels of support from new colleagues. Simmons & Simmons have put together a friendly, supportive and approachable team of people who will accompany trainees throughout their training. There will be a supervisor to help with everyday work and also a dedicated personnel officer who looks after each trainee from the minute they join.

benefits

Season ticket loan, fitness loan, group travel insurance, group accident insurance, death in service, medical cover, staff restaurant.

vacation placements

Places for 2004: 30–40; Duration: 4 weeks; Remuneration: £250 p.w.; Closing date: 20 February 2004.

sponsorship & awards

In the absence of local authority funding LPC fees and PgDL/CPE fees are paid, plus a maintenance grant of £5,000 for London, Oxford or Guildford and £4,500 elsewhere.

Partners	212
Assistant Solicitors	490
Total Trainees	191

contact
Vickie Chamberlain

method of application
Online application

selection procedure
Assessment days: Document exercise, interview & written exercise

closing date for 2006
13 August 2004

application
Training contracts p.a. **50-60**
Applications p.a. **2,700**
% interviewed p.a. **15%**
Required degree grade **2:1**

training
Salary
1st year (2003) £28,000
2nd year (2003) £32,000
Holiday entitlement **25 days**
% of trainees with a non-law degree p.a. **50%**
No. of seats available abroad p.a. **26**

post-qualification
Salary (2003) **£48,000**
% of trainees offered job on qualification (2003) **80%**

overseas offices
London, Rotterdam, Paris, Lisbon, Milan, Rome, Dusseldorf, Frankfurt, Brussels, Madrid, Padua, Oportu, Madeira, Abu Dhabi, Hong Kong, Shanghai, Tokyo, New York. The firm is also opening an office in Qatar in September.

Slaughter and May

One Bunhill Row, London EC1Y 8YY
Tel: (020) 7600 1200 Fax: (020) 7090 5000
Website: www.slaughterandmay.com

firm profile

One of the leading law firms in the world, Slaughter and May enjoys a reputation for quality and expertise. The corporate and financial practice is particularly strong and lawyers are known for their business acumen and technical excellence. Much of the firm's work spans the globe with transactions involving not only the firm's overseas offices but also leading independent law firms in other jurisdictions with whom the firm has long standing established relationships. No London partner has ever left the firm to join a competing practice.

main areas of work

Corporate and financial; tax; competition; financial regulation; litigation and arbitration; technology; media and telecommunications; intellectual property; commercial real estate; environment; pensions and employment.

trainee profile

The work is demanding and the firm looks for intellectual agility and the ability to work with people from different countries and walks of life. Common sense, a mature outlook and the willingness to accept responsibility are all essential. The firm expects to provide training in everything except the fundamental principles of law, so does not expect applicants to know much of commercial life. Trainees are expected to remain with the firm on qualification.

training environment

Four or five seats of three or six months duration. Two seats will be in the corporate and financial department with an option to choose a posting overseas (either to one of the firm's offices or to a "best friend" firm), competition or financial regulation, a commercial real estate seat is optional, and one seat in either litigation, intellectual property, tax or pensions and employment. In each seat a partner is responsible for monitoring your progress and reviewing your work. There is an extensive training programme which includes the PSC. There are also discussion groups covering general and specialised legal topics.

benefits

BUPA, STL, pension scheme, subsidised membership of health club, 24 hour accident cover.

vacation placements - summer 2004

Places: 60; Duration: 2 weeks; Remuneration: £250 p.w.; Closing Date: 6 February 2004 for penultimate year (of first degree) students only.

sponsorship & awards

CPE and LPC fees and maintenance grants are paid.

Partners	127
Associates	417
Total Trainees	165

contact
Charlotte Houghton

method of application
Either online (via website) or by posting to the firm a CV and covering letter

selection procedure
Interview

application
Training contracts p.a. **Approx 85**
Applications p.a. **2,500+**
% interviewed p.a. **20%**
Required standard **Good 2:1 ability**

training
Salary (May 2003)
1st year £29,000
2nd year £32,500
Holiday entitlement **25 days p.a.**
% of trainees with a non-law degree **Approx 50%**
No. of seats available abroad p.a. **Approx 35-40**

post-qualification
Salary (May 2003) **£50,000**
% of trainees offered job on qualification (2003) **95%+**

overseas offices
Paris, Brussels, Singapore, Hong Kong, New York

Speechly Bircham

6 St Andrew Street, London EC4A 3LX
Tel: (020) 7427 6400 Fax: (020) 7353 4368
Email: trainingcontracts@speechlys.com
Website: www.speechlys.com

firm profile

Speechly Bircham is a mid-sized City law firm with an excellent client base. Its strong commercial focus is complemented by a highly regarded private client practice. The firm handles major transactions as well as commercial disputes and has a good reputation for several specialist advisory areas, notably private client and corporate tax. Speechly Bircham's strengths lie in the synergy of the relationships between its four main departments, private client, corporate and tax, litigation and property.

main areas of work

Corporate and tax 25%; property 25%; litigation 25%; private client 25%.

trainee profile

Both law and non-law graduates who are capable of achieving a 2:1. The firm seeks intellectually dynamic individuals who enjoy a collaborative working environment where they can make an impact.

training environment

Speechly Bircham divides the training contract into four six month seats. Emphasis is given to early responsibility and supervised client contact providing trainees with a practical learning environment.

benefits

Season ticket loan, private medical insurance, life assurance.

vacation placements

Places for 2004: 12. The firm's summer placement scheme for students gives them the chance to experience a City legal practice. In a three-practice placement, students will be asked to research and present on a legal issue at the end of their placement; Duration: 3 weeks; Remuneration: £250 p.w.; Closing Date: 14 February 2004.

sponsorship & awards

CPE and LPC fees and a maintenance grant.

Partners	45
Assistant Solicitors	65
Total Trainees	10

contact
Nicola Swann
Human Resources Director

method of application
Application form (available by request or online)

selection procedure
Interview

closing date for 2006
31 July 2004

application
Training contracts p.a. **5**
Applications p.a. **1,000**
% interviewed p.a. **5%**
Required degree grade **2:1**

training
Salary
1st year (2003)
£26,000-£27,000
2nd year (2003)
£28,000-£29,000
Holiday entitlement **20 days**
% of trainees with a non-law degree p.a. **50%**

post-qualification
Salary (2003) **£45,000**

steeles

2 Norwich Business Park, Whiting Rd, Norwich NR4 6DJ
Tel: (01603) 274700 Fax: (01603) 274728
Email: personnel@steele.co.uk
Website: www.steeleslaw.co.uk

firm profile

steeles is an innovative and progressive commercial firm with a growing national client base. It is recognised in particular for the strength of its employment and commercial practitioners and for the range and quality of its services to local authorities and business.

main areas of work

The firm offers a full range of corporate, property, litigation and public sector services. The firm is dedicated to delivering high quality value for money services to its clients regardless of location.

trainee profile

Candidates will be highly motivated, commercially astute, with a strong academic record and previous relevant experience.

training environment

The aim is to ensure that every trainee will wish to continue their career with the firm. The training programme consists of four six month seats in the following departments: company commercial, commercial property, civil litigation, commercial disputes, employment, family and public sector. You will have some choice in the order of your seats. Trainees are encouraged to take on as much responsibility as possible with considerable client contact early on in their training contract. Bi-monthly meetings provide a forum for discussion of topical issues. The offices are open-plan, providing a supportive and learning environment which reflects the firm's accreditation to both ISO 9001 and Investor in People. Trainee solicitors are appraised at the end of each seat and are included in the firm's mentor scheme. There is an active sports and social life.

benefits

Pension, accident insurance, legal services, interest-free season ticket loan, gym membership loan.

vacation placements

Places for 2004: Places offered throughout the Summer vacation.

Partners	13
Assistant Solicitors	31
Total Trainees	10

contact
Ann Chancellor
Human Resources Manager

method of application
Online or CV & covering letter

selection procedure
Interview/assessment day

application
Training contracts p.a. **6**
Applications p.a. **300-400**
Required degree grade **2:1**

post-qualification
% of trainees offered job on qualification (2003) **100%**

Stephenson Harwood

One St Paul's Churchyard, London EC4M 8SH
Tel: (020) 7329 4422 Fax: (020) 7606 0822
Email: graduate.recruitment@shlegal.com

firm profile

Established in the City of London in 1828, Stephenson Harwood has developed into a large international practice, with a commercial focus and a wide client base.

main areas of work

Corporate (including corporate finance, funds, corporate tax, business technology); employment, pensions and benefits; banking and asset finance; dry and wet shipping litigation; commercial litigation; property; and private capital.

trainee profile

The firm looks for high calibre graduates with excellent academic records and an outgoing personality.

training environment

As the graduate intake is relatively small, the firm gives trainees individual attention, coaching and monitoring. Your structured and challenging programme involves four six month seats in areas of the firm covering contentious and non-contentious areas, across any department within the firm's practice groups. It may also involve a secondment to one of the overseas offices or to a client in London. These seats include 'on the job' training, sharing an office and working with a partner or senior solicitor. In-house lectures complement your training and there is continuous review of your career development. You will have the opportunity to spend six months abroad and have free language tuition where appropriate. You will be given your own caseload and as much responsibility as you can shoulder. The firm plays a range of team sports, has its own gym, subsidised membership of a City health club (or a health club of your choice) and has privileged seats for concerts at the Royal Albert Hall and the London Coliseum and access to private views at the Tate Gallery.

benefits

Subsidised membership of health clubs, private health insurance, BUPA membership, season ticket loan and 25 days paid holiday per year.

vacation placements

Places for 2004: 16; Duration: 2 weeks; Remuneration: £250 p.w.; Closing Date: 20 February 2004.

sponsorship & awards

Fees paid for CPE and LPC and maintenance awards.

Partners 100*
Assistant Solicitors 358*
Total Trainees 46
** denotes world-wide figures*

contact
Graduate Recruitment

method of application
Application form only

selection procedure
assessment centre

closing date for Sept 2006/ March 2007
31 July 2004

application
Training contracts p.a. **16-18**
% interviewed p.a. **10%**
Required degree grade **2:1**

training
Salary
1st year (2003) £26,000
2nd year (2003) £29,000
Holiday entitlement **25 days**
% of trainees with a non-law degree p.a. **46%**
No. of seats available abroad p.a. **10-12**

post-qualification
Salary (2003) £46,000
% of trainees offered job on qualification (2002) **75%**
% of assistants (as at 1/9/01) who joined as trainees **37%**
% of partners (as at 1/9/01) who joined as trainees **46%**

overseas offices
Bucharest, Paris, Piraeus, Singapore and in the People's Republic of China - Guangzhou and Hong Kong, with an associated office in Shanghai.

Stevens & Bolton

The Billings, Guildford, Surrey GU4 1YD
Tel: (01483) 302264 Fax: (01483) 302254
Email: gradrec@stevens-bolton.co.uk
Website: www.stevens-bolton.co.uk

firm profile

Stevens & Bolton is a leading South East law firm based in Guildford with over 120 staff in total. For prospective trainees, it can be difficult to know how regional law firms differ from each other apart from size. Steven & Bolton firmly believes that one thing that distinguishes it from other firms is its working environment. For example the firm encourages open, two-way communication enabling everyone to have an involvement in the firm's direction and planning. Over the past five years the firm has grown rapidly and is one of the major practices in the region. 80% of the firm's work is commercial, the other 20% is advising medium and high net worth individuals on private client matters. The firm has a reputation for providing a high quality commercial service, comparable with that of national and City firms.

main areas of work

Corporate and commercial, property, litigation and dispute resolution, employment, private client and family.

trainee profile

The firm requires a good academic record and individuals who have other interests such as music, sport, travel and work experience and who have a genuine enthusiasm to work in the law.

training environment

You will be supervised by and will sit with a partner. There is a comprehensive cross-departmental training programme and regular reviews of performance. The experience you gain will be rewarding, as you will get real responsibility early on.

benefits

Private medical insurance, life assurance, pension, rail or car park season ticket loan, permanent health insurance.

vacation placements

The firm does not run a vacation scheme.

sponsorship & awards

£5,000 towards CPE/GDL and LPC fees, (if no grant is available) and a £4,000 maintenance grant per annum.

Partners 22
Assistant Solicitors 36
Total Trainees 6

contact
Julie Bounden
(01483) 302264

method of application
Graduate application form and covering letter, available from the website or by request

selection procedure
Two interviews

closing date for 2006
31 August 2004

application
Training contracts p.a. **3**
Applications p.a. **600**
% interviewed **6%**
Required degree grade **2:1 & one grade A at 'A' Level**

training
Salary
1st year (2003) £20,000
2nd year (2003) £22,000
Holiday entitlement **25 days**

post-qualification
Salary (2003) **£38,000**
% of trainees offered job on qualification (2003) **70%**

overseas/regional offices
Guildford only

Tarlo Lyons

Watchmaker Court, 33 St John's Lane, London EC1M 4DB
Tel: (020) 7405 2000 Fax: (020) 7814 9421
Email: trainee.recruitment@tarlolyons.com
Website: www.tarlolyons.com

firm profile

Tarlo Lyons is a modern London firm focused on delivering creative commercial solutions for technology driven business. The firm believes in leveraging the expertise and talent it has assembled to provide benefits for clients across a range of sectors. The firm has five main sectors that it focuses on - the banking, insurance and financial services sector, the hotel, leisure and gaming sector, the outsourcing companies sector, the IT Services sector and the development and healthcare sector. It is proud to be one of the few City law firms with Investors in People accreditation.

main areas of work

Commercial technology; intellectual property; commercial property; dispute resolution (including technology litigation); employment and resourcing; corporate; gaming and licensing and business crime.

trainee profile

Applicants should have a sound academic record and a natural inquisitiveness and intellectual curiosity. An interest or background in information technology or commercial ventures is an advantage, as is a gap year or work undertaken outside of law. Applicants should also have common sense, resourcefulness and a good sense of humour.

training environment

Trainees will gain work experience in all the main areas of the practice. The PSC is taught externally and trainees also attend internal seminars. Trainees meet regularly with both a supervisor and the training partner and formal reviews are conducted every two months. The firm has a friendly, open-door policy and trainees are encouraged to take part in a wide range of marketing, sporting and social events.

benefits

Tarlo Lyons offers competitive compensation and salary may be enhanced by an annual discretionary bonus. The firm offers membership of a private health scheme, participation in a pension plan and subsidised membership of a nearby health club.

sponsorship & awards

LPC fees paid.

Partners	24
Assistant Solicitors	19
Total Trainees	7

contact
Trainee Recruitment Co-ordinator

method of application
Application form available from website

selection procedure
2 interviews with partners & skills assessment

closing date for 2006
7 August 2004

application
Training contracts p.a. 3
Applications p.a. 300
% interviewed p.a. 10%
Required degree grade 2:1

training
Salary
1st year (2003) £25,000 on average
2nd year (2003) £28,000 on average
Holiday entitlement 25 days
% of trainees with a non-law degree p.a. 50%

post-qualification
Salary (2002) £42,000
(Salary levels may increase subject to market conditions)

Taylor Walton

28-44 Alma Street, Luton LU1 2PL
Tel: (01582) 731161 Fax: (01582) 457900
Email: luton@taylorwalton.co.uk
Website: www.taylorwalton.co.uk

Partners	25
Assistant Solicitors	44
Total Trainees	10

contact
Jim Wrigglesworth

method of application
CV with covering letter

selection procedure
First & second interview with opportunity to meet other partners

closing date for 2006
30 September 2004

application
Required degree grade
2:1 or above

firm profile

Strategically located in Luton, Harpenden, St Albans and Hemel Hempstead, Taylor Walton is a major regional law practice advising both businesses and private clients. Its strengths are in commercial property, corporate work and commercial litigation, whilst maintaining a strong private client side to the practice. It has a progressive outlook both in its partners and staff and in its systems, training and IT.

main areas of work

Company/commercial 15%; commercial property 20%; commercial litigation 15%; employment 5%; personal injury 5%; family 5%; private client 10%; residential property 20%; direct conveyancing 5%.

trainee profile

Candidates need to show excellent intellectual capabilities, coupled with an engaging personality so as to show that they can engage and interact with the firm's clients as the practice of law involves the practice of the art of communication. Taylor Walton sees its partners and staff as business advisers involved in clients' businesses, not merely stand-alone legal advisers.

training environment

The training consists of four six month seats. The training partner oversees the structural training alongside a supervisor who will be a partner or senior solicitor in each department. The firm does try to take trainees' own wishes in relation to seats into account. In a regional law practice like Taylor Walton you will find client contact and responsibility coupled with supervision, management and training. There is an in-house training programme for all fee-earning members of staff. At the end of each seat there is a post seat appraisal conducted by the training partner, the trainee and the supervisor. The PSC is taught externally. The firm is friendly with an open door policy and there are various sporting and social events.

vacation placements

Places for 2004: 8; Duration: Up to 4 weeks; Remuneration: Agreed with trainee; Closing Date: 30 April 2004.

Taylor Wessing

Carmelite, 50 Victoria Embankment, Blackfriars
London EC4Y 0DX
Tel: (020) 7300 7000 Fax: (020) 7300 7100
Website: www.taylorwessing.com

firm profile

Taylor Wessing enjoys an enviable reputation for corporate, finance, intellectual property/technology, real estate and projects advice, providing the full range of legal services to major corporations, financial institutions, growing enterprises and wealthy families.

main areas of work

Corporate, dispute resolution, employment and pensions, finance and projects, intellectual property, private client and real estate.

trainee profile

High intellectual ability is paramount and the firm seeks a minimum of ABB grades at A Level and a 2.1 degree in any discipline. The firm looks for team players who have excellent communication skills, energy, ambition, an open mind and a willingness to learn. Applicants will also need to demonstrate a comittment to a career in law and genuine interest in business and awareness of the commercial implications of decisions.

training environment

Trainees will have six month seats in four different departments, with the possibility of a placement to another office or a client. Trainees will work closely with a number of partners and associates in the departments and will be provided with plenty of opportunity for early responsibility. Trainees will receive regular feedback and be appraised in the middle and at the end of each seat, and have meetings to discuss which practice areas they would like to experience. All trainees attend the Professional Skills Course, which is run in-house, and other training courses as necessary during the two years.

benefits

Private medical care, permanent health insurance, season ticket loan, subsidised staff restaurant, non-contributory pension scheme.

vacation placements

Places for 2004: 24; Duration: 2 weeks; Remuneration: £225 p.w.; Closing date: 20 February 2004.

sponsorship & awards

PgDL and LPC fees paid in full. Maintenance grant £4,500 per annum.

Partners	103
Fee-earners	307
Trainees	48 (UK)

contact
Graduate Recruitment Department

method of application
Firm's application form

selection procedure
two interviews, one with a partner

closing date for 2006
6 August 2004

application
Training contracts p.a. **24**
Applications p.a. **1,600**
% interviewed p.a. **10%**
Required degree grade **2:1**

training
Salary
1st year (2002) £26,000
2nd year (2002) £29,000
Holiday entitlement **25 days**
% of trainees with a non-law degree p.a. **30%**

post-qualification
Salary (2003) **£48,000**
% of trainees offered job on qualification (2002-03) **65-70%**

overseas offices
Berlin, Brussels, Cologne Dusseldorf, Frankfurt, Hamburg, Munich, and representative offices in Alicante and Shanghai

Teacher Stern Selby

37-41 Bedford Row, London WC1R 4JH
Tel: (020) 7242 3191 Fax: (020) 7242 1156
Email: r.raphael@tsslaw.com
Website: www.tsslaw.com

firm profile

A central London-based general commercial firm, with clientele and caseload normally attributable to larger firms. It has a wide range of contacts overseas.

main areas of work

Commercial litigation 25%; commercial property 38%; company and commercial 16%; secured lending 12%; private client 4%; clinical negligence/education/judicial review 5%.

trainee profile

Emphasis falls equally on academic excellence and personality. The firm looks for flexible and motivated individuals, who have outside interests and who have demonstrated responsibility in the past.

training environment

Trainees spend six months in three departments (company commercial, litigation and property) with, where possible, an option to return to a preferred department in the final six months. Most trainees are assigned to actively assist a partner who monitors and supports them. Trainees are fully involved in departmental work and encouraged to take early responsibility. Trainees are expected to attend in-house seminars and lectures for continuing education. The atmosphere is relaxed and informal.

vacation placements

Places for 2004: Approximately 10 places to those that have accepted or applied for training contracts.

sponsorship & awards

Possible but unlikely.

Partners	21
Assistant Solicitors	17
Total Trainees	12

contact
Russell Raphael

method of application
Letter & application form

selection procedure
2 interviews

closing date for 2006
31 October 2004

application
Training contracts p.a. **3-6**
Applications p.a. **1,000**
% interviewed p.a. **5%**
Required degree grade
2:1 (not absolute)

training
Salary
1st year (2006) **£24,000**
Holiday entitlement
4 weeks
% of trainees with a non-law degree p.a. **50%**

post-qualification
Salary (2003) **£35,000**
% of trainees offered job on qualification (2003) **16%**
% of assistants (as at 1/5/03) who joined as trainees **35%**
% of partners (as at 1/5/03) who joined as trainees **38%**

Thomson Snell & Passmore

3 Lonsdale Gardens, Tunbridge Wells, Kent TN1 1NX
Tel: (01892) 510000 Fax: (01892) 549884
Email: solicitors@ts-p.co.uk
Website: www.ts-p.co.uk

firm profile

Established in 1570, Thomson Snell & Passmore continues to be regarded as one of the premier law firms in the South East. The firm has a reputation for quality and a commitment to deliver precise and clear advice which is recognised and respected both by its clients and professional contacts. It has held the Lexcel quality mark since January 1999. The firm is vibrant and progressive and enjoys an extremely friendly atmosphere. Its offices are located in the centre of Tunbridge Wells and attract clients locally, nationally and internationally.

main areas of work

Commercial litigation 25%; corporate and commercial property 17%; private client 21%; personal injury/clinical negligence 15%; residential property 14%; family 8%.

trainee profile

Thomson Snell & Passmore regards its trainees from the outset as future assistants, associates and partners. The firm is looking for people not only with strong intellectual ability, but enthusiasm, drive, initiative, strong interpersonal and team-working skills, together with good IT skills.

training environment

The firm's induction course will help you to adjust to working life. As a founder member of Law South your training is provided in-house with trainees from other Law South member firms. Your two year training contract is divided into four periods of six months each. You will receive a thorough grounding and responsibility with early client exposure. You will be monitored regularly, receive advice and assistance throughout and appraisals every three months. The Training Partner will co-ordinate your continuing education in the law, procedure, commerce, marketing, IT and presentation skills. Trainees enjoy an active social life which is encouraged and supported.

sponsorship & awards

Grant and interest free loan available for LPC.

Partners	20
Assistant Solicitors	55
Total Trainees	8

contact
Pauline Tobin
Personnel Manager
Tel: (01892) 510000

method of application
Handwritten letter & firm's application form available from website

selection procedure
1 interview with Training Partner & 1 other partner

closing date for 2006
31 July 2004

application
Training contracts p.a. 4
Applications p.a.
Approximately 500
% interviewed p.a. 5%
Required degree grade
2:1 (any discipline)

training
Salary for each year of training
1st year (Sept 2003)
£16,500
2nd year (Sept 2003)
£18,000
Holiday entitlement **25 days**

post-qualification
Salary **£27,500 (Sept 2003)**
% of trainees offered job on qualification (2003) 75%

overseas/regional offices
Network of independent law firms throughout Europe and founding member of Law South

TLT Solicitors

One Redcliff St, Bristol BS99 7JZ
Tel: (0117) 917 7777 Fax: (0117) 917 7778
Email: lbevan@TLTsolicitors.com
Website: www.TLTsolicitors.com

firm profile

Over the past three years TLT has grown rapidly to become one of the largest law firms in Bristol and amongst the top 100 in the country.

main areas of work

Corporate, including corporate finance, acquisitions, disposals, JVs, stock exchange and a substantial amount of AIM and OFEX work; banking, including corporate lending, all types of banking litigation, mortgage documentation, insolvency, in addition to volume recoveries and conveyancing; employment, including strategic employment work, HR consultancy services, specialist pensions expertise and management training; property, including secured lending, development, planning, landlord and tenant, dispute resolution, management of property portfolios and estates; dispute resolution, including handling a wide range of heavyweight domestic and international litigation, as well as a substantial amount of ADR work, particularly mediation and arbitration. TLT's client list also includes high net worth individuals whom it advises on family matters, tax and trusts. The firm's family team is widely regarded as the best in the region.

trainee profile

A strong academic background is preferred and a resourceful personality is also a consideration.

training environment

Training is administered by the training principal and the trainee supervisor. It is divided into four six month periods. Wherever possible, the seats are settled in consultation with the trainee, preference being given to second year trainees. All trainees sit with another lawyer but in every case the work will be drawn from all parts of the team giving the widest experience. Monitoring meetings are held bi-monthly.

benefits

Pension, subsidised health insurance, subsidised sports and health club facility, life assurance.

vacation placements

Eight paid summer placements available, each lasting one week.

sponsorship & awards

LPC fees paid plus maintenance grant.

Partners	37
Assistant Solicitors	30
Total Trainees	16

contact
Liz Bevan
Human Resources

method of application
Firm's application form

selection procedure
Assessment day

closing date for 2006
15 August 2004

application
Training contracts p.a. 8
Applications p.a. 750
% interviewed p.a. 5%
Required degree grade
2:1 prefered
Holiday entitlement 25 days
% of trainees with a
non-law degree p.a. 50%

post-qualification
Market rate

Travers Smith Braithwaite

10 Snow Hill, London EC1A 2AL
Tel: (020) 7295 3000 Fax: (020) 7295 3500
Email: graduate.recruitment@traverssmith.com
Website: www.traverssmith.com

firm profile

A City firm with a major corporate/commercial practice. A high proportion of the firm's work has an international dimension - this is dealt with through the firm's Paris and Berlin offices. The firm attracts high quality work, but offers a professional yet relaxed working environment.

main areas of work

Corporate law (including takeovers and mergers, financial services and regulatory laws), commercial law (which includes competition and intellectual property), dispute resolution, corporate recovery/insolvency, tax, employment, pensions, banking and property.
The firm also offer a range of pro bono opportunities within individual departments and on a firm wide basis. The firm is an active member of the Caribbean Capital Cases Committee and has a long history of acting for prisoners on death-row.

trainee profile

Travers Smith look for people who combine academic excellence with plain common sense; who are articulate, who think on their feet, are determined and self motivated and who take their work but not themselves seriously. Applications are welcome from law and non-law graduates.

training environment

The firm has a comprehensive training programme which ensures that trainees experience a broad range of work. All trainee solicitors sit in rooms with partners and assistants, receive individual and extensive training from experienced lawyers and enjoy client contact and the responsibility that goes with it from the beginning of their training contract. The firm operate an exchange programme for assistant solicitors with US and European law firms.

benefits

Private health insurance, permanent sickness cover, life assurance cover, season ticket loans, refreshment credit, subsidised sports club membership.

vacation placements

45 places for summer 2004; Duration: two weeks; Remuneration: £250; Closing Date: 31 January 2004. The firm also offers Christmas and Easter vacation placements.

sponsorship & awards

LPC and CPE fees paid and maintenance of £5,000 p.a. (£4,500 outside London).

Partners	53
Assistant Solicitors	110
Total Trainees	42

contact
Germaine VanGeyzel

method of application
CV and covering letter

selection procedure
Interviews (2 stage process)

closing date for 2006
31 July 2004

application
Training contracts p.a. **Up to 25**
Applications p.a. **2,500**
% interviewed p.a. **12%**
Required degree grade **2:1**

training
Salary
1st year (2003) £28,000
2nd year (2003) £32,000
Holiday entitlement **20 days**
% of trainees with a non-law degree p.a. **Approx 50%**

post-qualification
Salary (2003) **£48,000**
% of trainees offered job on qualification (2003) **70%**
% of assistants (as at 1/9/03) who joined as trainees **64%**
% of partners (as at 1/9/03) who joined as trainees **61%**

Trowers & Hamlins

Sceptre Court, 40 Tower Hill, London EC3N 4DX
Tel: (020) 7423 8000 Fax: (020) 7423 8001
Email: gradrecruitment@trowers.com
Website: www.trowers.com

firm profile

Trowers & Hamlins is a substantial international firm. A leader in housing and public sector law, the firm also has a strong commercial side. The firm has regional offices in the UK, offices in the Middle East and links with Jordan, Yemen, Singapore, USA and Europe.

main areas of work

Property (housing, public sector, commercial) 40%; company and commercial/construction 29%; litigation 24%; private client 7%.

trainee profile

Personable, enthusiastic candidates with a good academic record and wide-ranging outside interests. The ability to work under pressure and with others, combined with versatility, are essential characteristics.

training environment

Trainees will gain experience in four seats from: company/commercial, construction, property, international, litigation, employment and private client. Trainees are encouraged to learn from direct contact with clients and to assume responsibility. The training programme is flexible and, with reviews held every three months, individual preferences will be considered. A training officer assists partners with the training programme and in-house lectures and seminars are held regularly. There are opportunities to work in Manchester and the Middle East. The firm encourages a relaxed atmosphere and blends traditional qualities with contemporary attitudes. Activities are organised outside working hours.

benefits

Season ticket loan, private healthcare after six months service, Employee Assistance Programme and discretionary bonus, Death in Service.

vacation placements

Places for 2004: 25-30; Duration: 2 weeks; Remuneration: £225 p.w.; Closing Date: 1 March (Summer). Open Day: June/July.

sponsorship & awards

CPE and LPC fees paid and £4,250-£4,500 maintenance p.a.

Partners	69
Assistant Solicitors	112
Total Trainees	30

contact
Graduate Recruitment Office

method of application
Letter, application form & CV

selection procedure
Interview(s), essay & practical test

closing date for 2006
1 August 2004

application
Training contracts p.a. **12–15**
Applications p.a. **1,600**
% interviewed p.a. **4%**
Required degree grade **2:1+**

training
Salary
1st year £26,000
2nd year £27,500
Holiday entitlement **25 days**
% of trainees with a non-law degree p.a. **40%**
No. of seats available abroad p.a. **Between 4-6**

post-qualification
Salary (2003) **£43,500**
% of trainees offered job on qualification (2003) **80%**
% of assistants (as at 1/9/02) who joined as trainees **45%**
% of partners (as at 1/9/02) who joined as trainees **45%**

overseas offices
Abu Dhabi, Dubai, Oman, Bahrain, Cairo

Walker Morris

Kings Court, 12 King Street, Leeds LS1 2HL
Tel: (0113) 283 2500 Fax: (0113) 245 9412
Email: traineerecruit@walkermorris.co.uk
Website: www.walkermorris.co.uk

firm profile

Based in Leeds, Walker Morris is one of the largest commercial law firms in the North, providing a full range of legal services to commercial and private clients. It is increasingly gaining an international reputation.

main areas of work

Commercial litigation 30%; commercial property 25%; company and commercial 25%; building societies 16%; private clients 2%; tax 2%.

trainee profile

Bright, articulate, highly motivated individuals who will thrive on early responsibility in a demanding yet friendly environment.

training environment

Trainees commence with an induction programme, before spending four months in each main department (commercial property, corporate and commercial litigation). Trainees can choose in which departments they wish to spend their second year. Formal training will include interactive role plays, interactive video, lectures, workshops and seminars. The PSC covers personal work management, advocacy and professional conduct plus a variety of specially tailored skills programmes. Individual IT training is provided. Opportunities can also arise for secondments to some of the firm's major clients. Emphasis is placed on teamwork, inside and outside the office. The firm's social and sporting activities are an important part of its culture and are organised by a committee drawn from all levels of the firm. A trainee solicitors' committee also organises events and liaises with the Leeds Trainee Solicitors Group.

vacation placements

Places for 2004: 45 over 3 weeks; Duration: 1 week; Remuneration: £150 p.w.; Closing Date: 28 February 2004.

sponsorship & awards

LPC fees plus maintenance of £4,500 and PgDL fees plus maintenance of £3,500.

Partners	40
Assistant Solicitors	88
Total Trainees	30

contact
Nick Bates

method of application
Application form

selection procedure
Telephone & face-to-face interviews

closing date for 2006
31 July 2004

application
Training contracts p.a. **15**
Applications p.a.
Approx. 800
% interviewed p.a.
Telephone **16%**
Face to face **8%**
Required degree grade **2:1**

training
Salary
1st year (2003) £20,000
2nd year (2003) £22,000
Holiday entitlement **24 days**
% of trainees with a non-law degree p.a.
30% on average

post-qualification
Salary (2003) **£32,000**
% of trainees offered job on qualification (2003) **85%**
% of assistants (as at 1/9/03) who joined as trainees **55%**
% of partners (as at 1/9/03) who joined as trainees **53%**

Ward Hadaway

Sandgate House, 102 Quayside, Newcastle upon Tyne NE1 3DX
Tel: (0191) 204 4000 Fax: (0191) 204 4098
Email: recruitment@wardhadaway.com
Website: www.wardhadaway.com

firm profile

Ward Hadaway is one of the most progressive commercial law firms in the North of England. The firm is firmly established as one of the North East region's legal heavyweights.

main areas of work

Litigation; property; company/commercial; private client.

trainee profile

The usual academic and professional qualifications are sought. Sound commercial and business awareness are essential as is the need to demonstrate strong communication skills, enthusiasm and flexibility. Candidates will be able to demonstrate excellent interpersonal and analytical skills.

training environment

The training contract is structured around four seats (property, company/commercial, litigation and private client) each of six months duration. At regular intervals, and each time you are due to change seat, you will have the opportunity to discuss the experience you would like to gain during your training contract. The firm will always try to give high priority to your preferences. You will share a room with a partner or associate which will enable you to learn how to deal with different situations. Your practical experience will also be complemented by an extensive programme of seminars and lectures. All trainees are allocated a 'buddy', usually a second year trainee or newly qualified solicitor, who can provide as much practical advice and guidance as possible during your training. The firm has an active Social Committee and offers a full range of sporting and social events.

benefits

23 days holiday (26 after five years service), death in service insurance, pension.

vacation placements

Applications for summer vacation placements should be received by 30 April 2004. Duration 1 week.

sponsorship & awards

LPC fees paid and £2,000 interest-free loan.

Partners 45
Total Trainees 16

contact
Carol Butts
Human Resources Manager

method of application
Application form & handwritten letter

selection procedure
Interview

closing date for 2006
31 July 2004

application
Training contracts p.a. **8**
Applications p.a. **400+**
% interviewed p.a. **10%**
Required degree grade **2:1**

training
Salary
1st year (2002) **£17,000**
2nd year (2003) **£18,000**
Holiday entitlement **23 days**
% of trainees with a non-law degree p.a. **Varies**

post-qualification
Salary (2002)
£30,000 minimum

wardhadaway

Watson, Farley & Williams

15 Appold Street, London EC2A 2HB
Tel: (020) 7814 8000 Fax: (020) 7814 8017
Email: graduates@wfw.com
Website: www.wfw.com

firm profile

Established in 1982, Watson, Farley & Williams has its strengths in corporate, banking and asset finance, particularly ship and aircraft finance. The firm aims to provide a superior service in specialist areas and to build long-lasting relationships with its clients.

main areas of work

Shipping; ship finance; aviation; banking; asset finance; corporate; litigation; e-commerce; intellectual property; EC and competition; taxation; property; insolvency; telecoms; project finance.

trainee profile

Outgoing graduates who exhibit energy, ambition, self-assurance, initiative and intellectual flair.

training environment

Trainees are introduced to the firm with a comprehensive induction course covering legal topics and practical instruction. Seats are available in at least four of the firm's main areas, aiming to provide trainees with a solid commercial grounding. There is also the opportunity to spend time abroad, working on cross-border transactions. Operating in an informal, friendly and energetic atmosphere, trainees will receive support whenever necessary. You will be encouraged to take on early responsibility and play an active role alongside a partner at each stage of your training. The practice encourages continuous learning for all employees and works closely with a number of law lecturers, producing a widely-read 'digest' of legal developments, to which trainees are encouraged to contribute. All modules of the PSC are held in-house. The firm has its own sports teams and organises a variety of social functions.

benefits

Life assurance, PHI, BUPA, STL, pension, subsidised gym membership.

vacation placements

Places for 2004: 30; Duration: 2 weeks; Remuneration: £200 p.w.; Closing Date: 27th February 2004.

sponsorship & awards

CPE and LPC fees paid and £4,500 maintenance p.a. (£4,000 outside London).

Partners	56
Assistant Solicitors	150
Total Trainees	23

contact
Graduate Recruitment Manager

method of application
Online application

selection procedure
Assessment centre & Interview

closing date for 2006
27 July 2004

application
Training contracts p.a. **12**
Applications p.a. **1,000**
% interviewed p.a. **10%**
Required degree grade
Minimum 2:1 & 24 UCAS points or above

training
Salary
1st year (2003) £28,500
2nd year (2003) £32,500
Holiday entitlement **22 days**
% of trainees with a non-law degree p.a. **50%**
No. of seats available abroad p.a. **12**

post-qualification
Salary (2003)
Not less than £50,000 at the time of writing
% of trainees offered job on qualification (2003) **80%**
% of assistants (as at 1/9/03) who joined as trainees **60%**
% of partners (as at 1/9/03) who joined as trainees **4%**

overseas offices
New York, Paris, Piraeus, Singapore, Bangkok, Rome

Wedlake Bell

16 Bedford Street, Covent Garden, London WC2E 9HF
Tel: (020) 7395 3000 Fax: (020) 7836 9966
Email: recruitment@wedlakebell.com
Website: www.wedlakebell.com

firm profile

Wedlake Bell is a medium-sized law firm providing legal advice to businesses and high net worth individuals from around the world. The firm's services are based on a high degree of partner involvement, extensive business and commercial experience and strong technical expertise. The firm has over 80 lawyers in central London and Guernsey, and affiliations with law firms throughout Europe and in the United States.

main areas of work

For the firm's business clients: Banking and asset finance; corporate finance; commercial property; media, IP and commercial; internet and e-business; employment services; pensions and share schemes; construction; litigation and dispute resolution.
For private individuals: Tax, trusts and wealth protection; offshore services.

trainee profile

In addition to academic excellence, Wedlake Bell looks for commercial aptitude, flexibility, enthusiasm, a personable nature, confidence, mental agility and computer literacy in its candidates. Languages are not crucial.

training environment

Trainees have four seats of six months across the following areas: corporate finance, banking, construction, media and IP/IT, employment, litigation, property and private client. As a trainee the firm encourages you to have direct contact and involvement with clients from an early stage. Trainees will work within highly specialised teams and have a high degree of responsibility. Tainees will be closely supervised by a partner or senior solicitor and become involved in high quality and varied work. The firm is committed to the training and career development of its lawyers and many of its trainees continue their careers with the firm often through to partnership. Wedlake Bell has an informal, creative and co-operative culture with a balanced approach to life.

sponsorship & benefits

LPC and CPE fees paid and £2,500 maintenance grant where local authority grant not available. During training contract: pension, travel loans, subsidised gym membership. On qualification: 25 days holiday, life assurance, medical insurance and PHI.

vacation placements

Places for 2004: 6; Duration: 3 weeks in July; Remuneration: £150 p.w.; Closing Date: End of February.

Partners	35
Assistant Solicitors	37
Total Trainees	10

contact
Natalie King

method of application
CV & covering letter

selection procedure
Interviews in September

closing date for 2006
End August 2004

application
Training contracts p.a. **4-6**
Required degree grade **2:1**

training
Holiday entitlement
1st year **20 days,**
2nd year **21 days**
% of trainees with a non-law degree p.a. **50%**

post-qualification
% of trainees offered job on qualification (2003) **100%**
% of assistants (as at 1/9/03) who joined as trainees **25%**

overseas offices
Guernsey

Weightman Vizards

India Buildings, Water Street, Liverpool L2 0GA
Tel: (0870) 241 3512 Fax: (0151) 227 3223
Email: HR@weightmanvizards.com
Website: www.weightmanvizards.com

firm profile

Weightman Vizards is a top 100 UK law firm with 78 partners and nearly 600 staff. With offices in Birmingham, Leicester, Liverpool, London and Manchester, the firm offers a comprehensive range of legal services to both public sector organisations and private sector companies. In addition to being one of the largest litigation practices in the UK, the firm has a thriving commercial practice. The firm develops successful relationships with its clients, based on a spirit of partnership and trust. The firm encourages innovation and strives to achieve excellence in all its activities. Above all, it listens, keeps its promises, and dedicates itself to providing a complete value for money service for every client, large or small.

main areas of work

The firm's areas of commercial expertise include company commercial, commercial litigation, property, employment, licensing, construction, intellectual property and IT. Litigation expertise includes workplace, transport and large loss claims. Specialist teams within the firm service the healthcare, professional indemnity, public sector and police markets.

trainee profile

Weightman Vizards is a friendly firm, with a strong commitment to a team environment and a culture that encourages early, decisive and effective action from all its staff. The firm is looking for enterprising commercially-minded people, who share its commitment to client service and will contribute to the spirit of the firm by demonstrating their support for its values. Applications from a wide variety of academic backgrounds are considered. Those with a track record that demonstrates an ability to study with discipline and common sense to achieve results will have a distinct advantage. The firm believes in rewarding all of its people well. It pays a highly competitive salary that is reviewed annually. The firm offers a benefits package, which includes a pension, health cover and life assurance. If you are offered a Training Contract, the firm will pay all course/study fees for LPC and CPE study.

training environment

Weightman Vizards' expects its trainees to make a positive contribution from the outset. Four 6-month seats, with focused training and regular review meetings, provides a progressive learning environment for its young lawyers.

Partners	78
Assistant Solicitors	112
Trainees p.a.	12

method of application
online with
www.weightmanvizards.com

closing date for 2006
31 July 2004

other offices
Birmingham, Leicester, London, Manchester

Weil, Gotshal & Manges

One South Place, London EC2M 2WG
Tel: (020) 7903 1074 Fax: (020) 7903 0990
Email: graduate.recruitment@weil.com
Website: www.weil.com

firm profile

Weil Gotshal & Manges is a premier international law firm, with over 1,100 lawyers worldwide and a reputation for providing first-class US and European legal advice that meets the commercial needs of its international corporate and finance clients. Worldwide, the firm has over 220 partners and 555 associates. The London office has 25 partners, 82 associates and 21 trainees.

main areas of work

The firm's practice in London bridges the traditional divides between US and UK corporate and finance law, encompassing acquisition finance, asset finance and leasing, banking business finance and restructuring, capital markets, commercial litigation and arbitration, competition, consumer finance, corporate, environmental, financial services, healthcare, mergers and acquisitions, pensions, private equity, real estate, securitisation, structured finance, taxation and technology.

trainee profile

The firm is looking for trainees with the commercial acumen and energy to become legal experts providing high quality client service and advice to complex international transactions. It needs people who have a genuine contribution to make to the continued success in the development of the London office. It aims to recruit down-to-earth people with the intelligence, personality and drive to be happy and successful in an entrepreneurial environment.

training environment

Trainees who join the firm in 2006 will usually complete four six month seats, one of which may be in an overseas office. In order to ensure its trainees receive adequate support and on-the-job training, they each work closely with a senior associate or partner. The practical experience gained through exposure to client work is enhanced by regular internal seminars. Legal staff are also assisted by an excellent team of support staff. The firm aims to keep all trainees on qualification.

benefits

Performance-related bonus, well woman/man health screens, pension, permanent health insurance, private health care, life assurance, subsidised gym membership, season ticket loan. The firm will pay tuition fees and a maintenance allowance for CPE and LPC.

vacation placements

Places for 2004: 12 in summer vacation. Closing date for applications by EAF: 14 February 2004.

Partners	25
Assistant Solicitors	82
Total Trainees	21

contact
Jillian Singh

method of application
online application form

closing date for 2006
31 July 2004

application
Training contracts p.a. **12**
Required degree grade **2:1**

training
Salary
1st year (2003) £35,000
Holiday entitlement **23 days**

overseas offices
Austin, Boston, Brussels, Budapest, Dallas, Frankfurt, Houston, Silicon Valley, Miami, New York, Paris, Prague, Singapore, Warsaw, Washington DC

White & Case

7-11 Moorgate, London EC2R 6HH
Tel: (020) 7600 7300 Fax: (020) 7600 7030
Email: trainee@whitecase.com
Website: www.whitecase.com

firm profile

White & Case is a law firm with over 1,600 lawyers in 38 offices worldwide. The London office has been open for over 30 years and boasts over 100 UK and US qualified lawyers who work with financial institutions, multinational corporations and governments on major international corporate and financial transactions and complex disputes.

main areas of work

In the London office: acquisition finance, arbitration, asset and aircraft finance, banking, capital markets, corporate finance, construction, employment, intellectual property, litigation, M&A, project finance, structured finance and securitisation, tax, and telecoms media and technology.

trainee profile

Trainees should be enthusiastic, be able to show initiative and work closely with others in a team environment. You should also have an understanding of international commercial issues and have a desire to be involved in innovative and high profile legal matters.

training environment

The firm's trainees are important and valued members of the London office and frequently work on multijurisdictional matters requiring close co-operation with lawyers throughout the firm's established global network. You will spend six months in each seat and cover the majority of work dealt with in the London office during the course of your training contract. You will sit with an associate or partner and hands-on experience will be supplemented by formal internal training sessions. You are encouraged to spend six months in one of the firm's overseas offices to gain a fuller understanding of the global network.

benefits

BUPA, gym membership contribution, life insurance, pension scheme, permanent health scheme, season ticket loan, discretionary bonus scheme, sign on bonus.

vacation placements

Places for 2004: 40-50; Duration: 2 weeks; Remuneration: £250; Closing Date: End of January 2004.

sponsorship & awards

CPE and LPC fees paid and £5,500 maintenance p.a. Prizes for commendation and distinction for LPC.

Partners	38
Assistant Solicitors	92
Total Trainees	38

contact
Ms Emma Falder

method of application
Online application via firm website

selection procedure
Interview

closing date for 2006
31 July 2004

application
Training contracts p.a.20-25
Applications p.a. 1,500
Required degree grade 2:1

training
Salary
1st year (2003) £33,000, rising by £1,500 every 6 months
Holiday entitlement 25 days

All trainees are encouraged to spend a seat abroad

post-qualification
Salary (2003) £60,000

overseas offices
Almaty, Ankara, Bangkok, Berlin, Bombay, Bratislava, Brussels, Budapest, Dresden, Düsseldorf, Frankfurt, Hamburg, Helsinki, Ho Chi Minh City, Hong Kong, Istanbul, Jakarta, Jeddah, Johannesburg, London, Los Angeles, Mexico City, Miami, Milan, Moscow, New York, Palo Alto, Paris, Prague, Riyadh, Rome, São Paulo, Singapore, Shanghai, Stockholm, Tokyo, Warsaw, Washington DC

Wiggin and Co

95 The Promenade, Cheltenham GL50 1WG
Tel: (01242) 224114 Fax: (01242) 224223
Email: law@wiggin.co.uk

firm profile

Based in Cheltenham, with offices in London and Los Angeles, Wiggin and Co is a 'city-type' niche practice. It specialises in private client (particularly in international tax planning for the super-rich individual), non-contentious and contentious media law (with particular emphasis on broadcast media and entertainment) and the company/commercial fields.

main areas of work

Private client 27%; media and entertainment 37%; corporate 18%; litigation 11%; property 7%.

trainee profile

Candidates will have a strong academic background, be personable and show a willingness to work hard individually or as part of a team.

training environment

The training is divided into four 'seats'. Trainees will spend time in four departments drawn from the company/commercial, private client, media (two 'seats'), litigation and property departments. Trainees are encouraged to take an active role in transactions, assume responsibility and deal directly with clients. In-house lectures and seminars are held regularly and training reviews are held every four months. The firm offers the attraction of Cheltenham combined with technical ability and experience akin to a large City firm. Its relatively small size encourages a personal approach towards staff and client relations.

benefits

Life assurance, private health cover, pension scheme, permanent health insurance.

sponsorship & awards

CPE and LPC fees and £3,000 maintenance p.a. Brochure available on request.

Partners	14
Assistant Solicitors	11
Total Trainees	6

contact
Simon Baggs

method of application
CV

selection procedure
2 interviews

closing date for 2006
21 August 2004

application
Training contracts p.a. **3**
Applications p.a. **300**
% interviewed p.a. **8%**
Required degree grade **2:1**

training
Salary
1st year (2003) £21,900
2nd year (2003) £29,700
Holiday entitlement **20 days**
% of trainees with a non-law degree p.a. **50%**

post-qualification
Salary (2003) **£41,600**
% of trainees offered job on qualification (2003) **33%**
% of assistants (as at 2003) who joined as trainees **36%**
% of partners (as at 2003) who joined as trainees **21%**

overseas office
Los Angeles

Withers LLP

16 Old Bailey, London EC4M 7EG
Tel: (020) 7597 6000 Fax: (020) 7597 6543
Email: emma.heycock@withersworldwide.com
Website: www.withersworldwide.com

firm profile

Withers' transatlantic merger with US firm Bergman, Horowitz & Reynolds in January 2002 has created the first international law firm dedicated to the business, personal and philanthropic interests of successful people, their families and advisers. The firm provides integrated answers to the US, UK and international legal and tax needs of its clients whether this means restructuring their own assets, buying or selling businesses and properties, coping with divorce, termination of their employment or setting up charitable foundations. The exciting mix of work creates a diverse and interesting training for the small number of trainees employed. Withers LLP has the largest team of specialist private client lawyers in Europe and more Italian speakers than any other City law firm. Last year the firm extended its presence in Milan, opening a new office there.

main areas of work

Private client and charities 40%; family 13%; litigation 21%; corporate, company and commercial 13%; property 13%.

training environment

Trainees spend six months in four of the firm's five departments (family, property, private client, corporate and litigation). On the job training is supplemented by the firm's departmental and trainee-specific training. Buddy and mentor systems ensure that trainees are fully supported from the outset.

benefits

Interest-free season ticket loan, private medical insurance, life assurance, Christmas bonus, social events, subsidised café facilities.

vacation placements

Easter and Summer vacation placements are available in the firm's London and Milan offices in 2004. Students spend two weeks in two different departments. The closing date for applications is 30 January 2004. The firm has 24 places available during summer and 6 at Easter.

sponsorship & awards

CPE/PgDL and LPC fees and £4,500 maintenance p.a. are paid. A cash prize is awarded for a distinction or commendation in the CPE/PgDL and/or LPC.

Partners	75
Legal Staff	229
Total Trainees	24

contact
Emma Heycock
Senior Recruitment Officer

method of application
Application form (available online)

selection procedure
2 interviews

closing date for 2006
training scheme:
30 July 2004
Closing date for 2004 vacation scheme:
30 January 2004

application
Training contracts p.a. **12**
Applications p.a. **1,200**
% interviewed p.a. **10%**
Required degree grade **2:1**

training
Salary
1st year (2003) £27,000
2nd year (2003) £29,000
Holiday entitlement **23 days**
% of trainees with a non-law degree p.a. **50%**

post-qualification
Salary (2003) **£45,000**

overseas offices
Milan, New York, New Haven

withers LLP

Wollastons

Brierly Place, New London Road, Chelmsford, Essex CM2 0AP
Tel: (01245) 211211 Fax: (01245) 354764
Email: recruitment@wollastons.co.uk
Website: www.wollastons.com

firm profile

Wollastons is a dynamic, regional law firm, widely recognised as the leading, commercial practice in Essex. Wollastons has a strong reputation as a forward thinking and energetic organisation, offering high levels of service to both businesses and private clients. The firm's first class resources, including sophisticated IT, and the lively atmosphere attracts high calibre lawyers, keen to work in a modern, professional environment. The Investors in People accreditation demonstrates a strong commitment to staff development and training at all levels.

main areas of work

Main practice areas include corporate and commercial; commercial property; commercial disputes; employment; planning and property disputes; private client and family.

trainee profile

Applications are welcomed from able and ambitious graduates with 24 UCAS points and a 2:1 degree. Candidates should have a commercial outlook, be confident, outgoing and able to demonstrate a wide range of interests. A link with the Essex area would be useful.

training environment

Trainees have four six month seats. These will normally include: company and commercial; commercial disputes; commercial property and employment. Trainees sit with a partner or a senior solicitor and form an integral part of the team. Trainees are fully involved in a wide range of interesting work and, although your work will be closely checked, you will be encouraged to take responsibility from an early stage. The firm is very friendly and informal and trainees receive a great deal of individual attention and support. Your progress will be kept under constant review with mid-seat and end of seat appraisals.

Partners	15
Fee-earners	21
Total Trainees	4 (2 p.a.)

contact
Jo Salt - HR Manager
(01245) 211253

method of application
CV and application form, see website for details

selection procedure
2 stage interview process

closing date for 2006
No fixed dates, currently recruiting for 2004 and 2005

application
Training contracts p.a. 2
Applications p.a. **Approx 500**
Interviewed p.a. **Approx 50**
Required degree grade
2:1 & 24 UCAS points

WOLLASTONS

INVESTOR IN PEOPLE

Wragge & Co LLP

55 Colmore Row, Birmingham B3 2AS
Tel: Freephone (0800) 096 9610
Email: gradmail@wragge.com
Website: www.wragge.com/graduate

firm profile

Wragge & Co is a top 20 UK law firm providing a full-service to some of the world's largest and most successful organisations. Only by providing the highest quality of work and excellent client service can the firm list 33 of the FTSE 100 as its clients. With its main base in Birmingham and offices in London and Brussels over 70% of the firm's work is generated outside the Midlands and over 25% is international. Much has been said and written about the firm's culture. People who work at Wragge & Co will tell you it has a strong culture based on: (a) Integrity and honesty - in the firm's relationships by working to a set of values and commitments. (b) Working as a team - by ensuring everyone at Wragge & Co feels valued, can play a part in the firm going forward and act as a single team. (c) Making a commitment to its people - by communicating openly so they understand the business they are contributing to and can buy into the firm's overall aims. Wragge & Co encourage a balanced and flexible approach to work which results in lower stress levels and greater retention rates. Wragge & Co is a 'relationship' firm. The firm was 34th in The Sunday Times "100 best companies to work for 2003" and 13th best workplace in the UK in a recent Financial Times survey. Wragge & Co was voted "The Law Firm With the Best Training Environment" at a leading lawyer awards ceremony in 2003 and was "Best in the Land" according to a leading legal publication in 2001.

main areas of work

The firm has a national reputation in many areas, including dispute resolution, employment, tax, media, project finance and transport and utilities. It also has the UK's third largest real estate group and leading practices in corporate, construction, banking and intellectual property. Other "top five" areas include EU/competition, public law and regulation and pensions. The quality of its work is reflected in the firm's client list, which includes AT&T, British Airways, Cadbury Schweppes, Cap Gemini Ernst & Young, Carlton UK Television, H J Heinz, HSBC, Marks & Spencer, McDonald's, Powergen, and Royal Bank of Scotland. The firm has over 1,000 employees, including 114 partners. While its main base remains in Birmingham the firm also has two other offices. Its Brussels office supports the EU/competition team, and the London office deals with intellectual property, private equity and real estate. You'll be given the opportunity to spend six months in one of these offices. More than a quarter of the firm's work is international and it is formally associated with German independent Graf von Westphalen Bappert & Modest. Many of its solicitors have broadened their experience and their language skills by undertaking international secondments in law firms across the world.

Partners	114
Assistant Solicitors	300
Total Trainees	46

contact
Julie Caudle
Graduate Recruitment & Training Manager

method of application
Applications are made online at www.wragge.com/graduate (paper application form available on request)

selection procedure
Telephone discussion & assessment day

closing date
Sept 2006/March 2007: 31 July 2004. If you are a non-law student, please return your form as soon as possible, as the firm will be running assessment days over the forthcoming year

application
Training contracts p.a. **25**
Applications p.a. **1,300**
% interviewed p.a. **15%**
Required degree grade **2:1**

training
Salary (Sept 2003)
1st year £21,000
2nd year £24,000
Holiday entitlement **25 days**
% of trainees with a non-law degree p.a. **Varies**

post-qualification
Salary (2003) **£33,000**
% of trainees offered job on qualification (2003) **100%**
% of assistants (as at 1/7/03) who joined as trainees **50%**
% of partners (as at 1/7/03) who joined as trainees **47%**

Wragge & Co LLP continued

trainee profile

The firm is looking for graduates of 2:1 standard at degree level, with some legal or commercial work experience gained either via a holiday job or a previous career. You should be practical, with a common sense and problem solving approach to work, and be able to show adaptability, enthusiasm and ambition.

training environment

The firm aims to transform its trainees into high quality, commercially minded lawyers. You will spend six months in four different practice areas, usually including real estate, corporate and litigation, with a chance to specialise in a seat of your choice. From day one, you will work on live files with direct contact with clients and other solicitors, and be responsible for the management of the transaction and its ultimate billing. The more aptitude you show, the greater the responsibility you will be given. You will be supported by the graduate recruitment team, with a partner who acts as a mentor to you throughout your training contract and a supervisor who will co-ordinate your work and give you weekly feedback. Introductory courses are provided at the start of each seat in addition to the professional skills course training requirements. This formal training complements "on the job" learning and it is more than likely that the firm's commitment to your development will extend well past the number of days recommended by the Law Society. Some of the courses will be residential, allowing you to reflect on your work practices, forge relationships and compare notes without the disturbances of your daily work. The firm's excellent trainee retention rates are the greatest testament to its training programme.

benefits

Wragge & Co's benefits include prizes for 1st class degree and LPC distinction, £1,000 interest free loan, pension scheme, life insurance, permanent health insurance, 25 days holiday a year, travel schemes, private medical insurance, sports and social club, independent financial advice, corporate gym membership rates and a Christmas gift.

sponsorship

The firm will provide your tuition fees for LPC and GDL (where relevant) and a maintenance grant of £4,500 for each year of study for LPC and GDL.

vacation placements

Easter and summer vacation placements are run at Wragge & Co. As part of its scheme, you will get the opportunity to experience different areas of the firm, attend client meetings and get involved in real files. There are also organised social events with the firm's current trainees. Again, you can apply on-line at www.wragge.com/graduate (paper application form available on request). The closing date for applications is 31 January 2004.

Wragge & co LLP is a Limited Liability Partnership

The Bar

BARRISTERS TIMETABLE

<table>
<tr><th></th><th>LAW STUDENTS • Penultimate Undergraduate Year</th><th>NON-LAW STUDENTS • Final Year</th></tr>
<tr><td>Throughout the year</td><td colspan="2">Think – do you want to be a barrister or a solicitor?
Research chambers & mini pupillages. Attend law fairs</td></tr>
<tr><td>By the end of January</td><td></td><td>Apply for the CPE</td></tr>
<tr><td>By the end of April</td><td colspan="2">Apply for a pupillage under the year early scheme on Olpas</td></tr>
<tr><td>May</td><td></td><td>Apply for a CPE scholarship from an Inn of Court.
If successful, join that Inn</td></tr>
<tr><td>June to September</td><td></td><td>Do pre-CPE mini-pupillages</td></tr>
<tr><td>September/October 2004</td><td>Start final year of degree</td><td>Start CPE</td></tr>
<tr><td>November</td><td colspan="2">By November apply through BVC Online for the BVC. Apply to an Inn of Court for a BVC scholarship</td></tr>
<tr><td>During final year/CPE</td><td colspan="2">Apply for pupillage to non-OLPAS sets.
Do mini pupillages</td></tr>
<tr><td>April</td><td colspan="2">Before 30th April apply for pupillage through OLPAS</td></tr>
<tr><td>June</td><td colspan="2">Apply for Inn membership</td></tr>
<tr><td>September 2005</td><td colspan="2">Start the BVC. Apply through the September tranche of
OLPAS; make further pupillage applications to non-OLPAS sets</td></tr>
<tr><td>April</td><td colspan="2">If unsuccessful last year, apply for pupillage before 30th April</td></tr>
<tr><td>June</td><td colspan="2">Finish BVC</td></tr>
<tr><td>September</td><td colspan="2">Apply for pupillage through OLPAS if you have yet to be successful</td></tr>
<tr><td>October 2006</td><td colspan="2">Start pupillage</td></tr>
<tr><td>June</td><td colspan="2">Be offered tenancy at your pupillage chambers or apply for it elsewhere</td></tr>
<tr><td>October 2007</td><td colspan="2">Start tenancy</td></tr>
<tr><td>2037</td><td colspan="2">Be appointed to the High Court Bench</td></tr>
</table>

thinking of the bar?

barcode

Don't let the often-curious terms used at the Bar confuse or intimidate you!

bar council – the professional body that regulates barristers
barrister – a member of the Bar of England and Wales; an advocate
bench – the judiciary
bencher – a senior member of an Inn of Court. Usually silks and judges, known as masters of the bench
brief – a case; the documents setting out instructions to a barrister
bvc online – the BVC online application system run by the Bar Council and GTI. CACH was the old disk based application system for the BVC (the old term is likely to linger for some time)
call – the ceremony whereby you become a barrister
chambers – a group of barristers in independent practice who have joined together to share common costs of practice such as clerks' fees and building rents; the word refers both to the physical building and to the group of barristers
clerk – administrator/manager in chambers who organises work for barristers and organises diaries, payment of fees, etc.
counsel – a barrister
devilling – (paid) work done by a junior member of chambers for a more senior member
inns of court – four ancient institutions, which alone have the power to 'make' barristers
junior – a barrister not yet appointed silk. Note: older juniors are known as senior juniors
mini pupillage – a short period of work experience spent in chambers
olpas – the Online Pupillage Application System run by the Bar Council
pupil – essentially a 'trainee'; a barrister in pupillage
pupillage – the year of training undertaken after Bar school and before tenancy. It is divided into two consecutive six-month periods, hence 'first six' and 'second six'. These are commonly taken at the same set of chambers but may, especially in Chancery practice, be taken separately. The main distinction is that a pupil can start earning for himself during second six. Occasionally, and particularly in criminal practice (such is the difficulty of attaining tenancy), a pupil may have to take a third six.
pupilmaster – a senior barrister with whom a pupil sits and who teaches the pupil and gives him work. The Bar Council is encouraging the term pupil supervisor.
QC – Queen's Counsel; a silk
set – as in a 'set of chambers'
silk – one of Her Majesty's Counsel, appointed on the recommendation of the Lord Chancellor; so named after the silk robes they wear. This year the Lord Chancellor announced he was considering scrapping the appointment.
tenant/tenancy – a tenant is a barrister who is a member of chambers. Tenancy is essentially 'the job', that is, permission from chambers to join their set and work with them. This means you have to pay your fair share of the rent, hence the word. A 'squatter' is someone who is permitted to use chambers' premises, but is not actually a member of the set. A 'door tenant' is someone who is affiliated with the set, but who does not conduct business from chambers' premises.
treasury counsel – barristers appointed to work for the Government. They are graded on various panels and there are different lists for different areas of practice. The top fella on a list is the Treasury Devil.

myth, magic and mystery

At university you'll hear plenty of myths about the Bar; the state it's presently in and the state it will be in before long. People will tell you it's an archaic profession that is impenetrable to anyone other than public-schooled, white, male, Oxbridge graduates. As Keith Vaz MP famously pointed out to Lord Chancellor Derry Irvine in a select committee meeting in April 2003, some 78% of the judiciary achieve a 'full house' on the above demographic criteria. This is the age-old stereotype of barristers and it puts many students off. But Bar school tells us a different story. The male:female ratio is now 50:50. And, in pupillage, a healthy 18%+ of places go to candidates from ethnic minorities. While many older barristers fit the stereotype, there is increasing diversity at the junior end of the Bar. In another ten years, the Vazes and the Irvines of the day will doubtless discuss different statistics; perhaps not radically different ones, but it's true to say that the Bar is becoming more modern and accessible.

But will there still be a Bar? Speak to some solicitors and they'll plead with you to be sensible and pragmatic about your future. The special and revered position of barristers is being eroded, they'll tell you, while muttering about higher rights of audience for solicitors. What you won't hear is that solicitors have been relatively slow in asserting their new rights of audience, and that the Bar seems to have survived great changes to the justice system. Lord Woolf's transformation of civil justice and the measures proposed following Sir Robin Auld's review of the criminal justice system are waking the Bar up to the need to modernise and they are doing just that. And there's even good news: like the increasing number of individuals and organisations who are now allowed 'direct access' to the Bar without needing to instruct solicitors.

Just as we have seen consolidation over on the solicitors' side of the fence, there is a trend for fewer, larger sets at the Bar. However, this seems to be the Bar's response to the demand for specialist advocates, backed up by experienced teams and sophisticated chambers' infrastructure.

Even the OFT has expressed its opinion on the Bar, questioning why sets do not operate as partnerships. This debate and others, such as the Lord Chancellor's musings on the scrapping of wigs and the title of QC, will rumble on in the coming years. It may have to adapt further, but it is inconceivable that the Bar will wither away. The demand for barristers will continue, both for those who specialise in advocacy and those who can advocate in specialist areas of law.

Broadly speaking, numbers at the Bar are reasonably stable, although there are reports showing that since the mandatory funding of pupillages post-January 2003, the number of pupillages has dropped. If this is true it should be put in the context of other changes – a number of the most successful sets are sponsoring students, pupils and very junior barristers like never before. This feast or famine picture is perhaps indicative of the Bar as a whole: very healthy in the Premiership, much less so in the Vauxhall Conference.

independence every day

As a barrister in independent practice you will be self-employed. You will be responsible for how hard you work, when you work, paying your own taxes and arranging your own pension. There are no company perks, no free lunches, no hiding behind colleagues, and no annual appraisals on which your next pay rise or bonus depends. In theory, you can work as hard as you like and as often as you like. If you want to take a ten-week honeymoon, no one is going to stop you. And if you want to be a full-time parent to your offspring, it is you who decides how long your maternity leave will be.

In our travels around the Inns of Court, we were left in no doubt that barristers treasure their independence. In theory, even the youngest junior is the equal of the most senior QC in chambers (although it won't usually feel that way!). Of course, in the early years, you'll be a slave to your clerks – your lifeline to new work and an income. It is they who assess which member of chambers is best suited to handle a particular instruction, so if you appear unwilling to take work, clerks will stop offering it to you and your practice could nosedive. Building a healthy practice takes a lot of hard work, but at good sets the financial rewards are apparent almost immediately.

Each set of chambers has a different ethos and this will certainly affect how you work. An ultra-modern set might be happy for you to work from home or to turn up in jeans. A more traditional set might want you to be in chambers regardless of what work you have to do and to wear a suit at all times. We hope that the weeks we spent exploring the Inns and beyond will help you understand how sets operate and the cultural differences between them. *"It's a bit like anthropology, isn't it?"* one barrister said after we'd interviewed him. It most certainly was. Our Chambers Reports section covers 24 sets, but if you want us to investigate any others then do e-mail us. If we receive enough interest we'll certainly go on a mission for you.

on the couch

Any student thinking of a career at the Bar needs to take a good hard look at themselves. Academic strength is essential. You must have real intelligence and the ability to analyse things in great detail. Sadly, too many of our contacts said: *"We see far too many students who don't have a hope in hell of getting pupillage."* Academic strength is almost always judged by way of your academic record. As a general rule, without good A-levels, without a 2:1 degree class (or, ideally, a First) and without having been to an established or respected university, you will struggle to get pupillage. This is not to say that those with weak A-levels, or those who have been to one of the newer universities, or those with less than a 2:1 don't ever get pupillage. But rarely will those that meet with success be disadvantaged in all three measures, and they will always possess redeeming and desirable qualities (such as having previous relevant industry or voluntary experience), which make them stand out as remarkable candidates.

You won't get pupillage or make a good barrister just by being bright. A range of other skills (which to a certain degree may be taught) are also essential, not least the ability to advocate and to think on your feet, and interpersonal skills that allow you to relate to clients, solicitors, judges and juries. But on top of this, you will need determination. Having stamina, tenacity and perseverance is crucial because, without them, the temptation to turn the pressure off and to stop battling will see you submerge in the pool of unsuccessful candidates.

Contrary to what you might think, the Bar is desperate to attract high-quality candidates, and it is hard for them to counter intense competition from solicitors firms offering fistfuls of cash, college sponsorship, and branded umbrellas and shot glasses. Add this to the negative comments that circulate about life at the Bar and it's easy to see why some students abandon long-held dreams of a career there.

It's simple really: academically gifted students with 'presence' and a real desire for advocacy will fare very well at the Bar. But if you don't feel confident that you tick each of these boxes, then do think again.

NUMBER OF:	1998-1999	1999-2000	2000-2001	2001-2002	2002-2003
BVC applicants	2,696	2,370	2,252	2,119	2,067
BVC enrolments	1,459	1,490	1,407	1,386	n/a
Students passing the BVC	1,238	1,201	1,110	1,182	n/a
First six pupils	706	681	695	812	n/a
Second six pupils	694	704	700	724	n/a
Pupils awarded tenancy	541	511	527	490	n/a

Bar Council statistics

mini pupillages

Mini-pupillages are the perfect opportunity to sneak a look at life as a barrister. Ranging from two days to a week, most sets take an informal approach to minis, while for others they will be an integral part of the selection of pupils. During an assessed mini-pupillage your performance and interaction with others are monitored and you will probably be asked to hand in a piece of written work. A few sets will require you to have undertaken a mini pupillage with them before they will even consider your pupillage application. In most chambers, however, a stream of students will be given the opportunity to test the waters, and the smartest will use their time in different chambers to compare types of practice and styles of working.

There is no central source of information on mini pupillages but chambers' websites flag up the correct application method and contact details. Usually a CV accompanied by a letter won't go far wrong.

what's the point?

Everyone agrees that doing at least one mini pupillage is essential; an application showing none suggests that the student hasn't properly considered his chosen profession. But myths perpetuate as to how many you should do and some students have been known to do up to a dozen. While every pupillage application will be assisted by a modest number of mini pupillages, chambers are quite likely to be put off if they see a huge number as it indicates a lack of direction. When we interviewed pupils in the UK's leading sets, we learned that most of them had on average done two or three, and all had completed one in the type of set they eventually ended up in. However, we found no evidence that pupils were usually selected by sets where they had completed minis. It seems that unless stated to be integral to recruitment, a mini is of more use to the student than the set.

are two days long enough?

Apparently so. *"You may not understand the work and you may be taken aback by the reams and reams of paper but that doesn't matter."* The important thing is to watch how the barristers behave with each other and clients, noting how they operate. Can you see yourself as one of them? Try to understand what approach they take to their work and what is being demanded of them. You'll see a world of difference between a crime set and a Chancery set, and you'll be much better suited to one than the other. As for the smaller differences between two sets handling similar work, they are there and you may be lucky enough to pick up on them. But do be aware that the mini pupillage scheme at a particular set may be a poor reflection of the place. We heard unfavourable reports about mini-pupillages at one set that were totally out of keeping with what we subsequently learned about it, all because the scheme was less user-friendly than at certain other sets. Our tip is to make the effort to chat to current pupils and very junior barristers, if you possibly can. They can give you a good sense of life at that set and what it is looking for in its pupils.

hanging around

Your time may be spent hanging around in the county court or in the corner of someone's room with a mountain of files that seem meaningless, yet in either case there's plenty to take in. Whether it's huddling in on court door discussions or witnessing a barrister in conference with his instructing solicitor, just look, listen and learn.

the inns of court

There are four ancient Inns of Court located around the Royal Courts of Justice on the Strand in London – Lincoln's Inn, Inner Temple, Middle Temple and Gray's Inn – originally formed as societies to provide legal training for barristers. In addition, like the Oxford colleges to which they bear more than a passing similarity, their function included providing board and lodging for both barristers and students. These institutions alone have the power to 'make' a barrister in a ceremony known as Call. Successful BVC student barristers are called by their Inn's Treasurer to the 'Degree of the Utter Bar'.

the inns today

Their teaching function has largely been delegated to the eight BVC providers, but the Inns still provide some advocacy training in addition to fulfilling their ancient role as providers of hospitality for student barristers. You must join an Inn by 30 June in the year in which your BVC commences. As well as passing the BVC, before you can be called it is necessary to 'keep term' at your Inn. This means you have to attend 12 qualifying sessions, but not so long ago students had to undertake 36. Largely, this means 'dining', but education days, introductory weekends and advocacy training all count as qualifying sessions.

dining – more than just dinner

Dining receives mixed reviews from students. *"Some think it is archaic, but others love it."* The best advice is to make the most of it, because if you approach it negatively, it will be all the more arduous. *"There are always some who complain about it and don't get involved."* Others find it expensive, although at an average of £10 a dinner, this will hardly break the bank and there are scholarships to cover the cost. Dining is more than eating – the evening may include a concert, a debate or moot, or sometimes even a disco. At least once a term there is mixed dining (often at a 'Domus Dinner') when Bar, Bench and students sit together, and also popular Guest Nights. The point of dining is to reinforce the collegiate nature of the Inn and maintain social contact within the profession. Smart students use it as an opportunity to network.

Students usually have to wear gowns for dinner and will arrive in Hall first. Masters of the Bench arrive last and sit at High Table on the dais at one end of Hall. Before the food is served, grace will be said, sometimes in Latin. Students often sit in 'messes' of four, with the 'mess captain' having to serve the other three members. After dinner each member of the mess will toast the others.

mentoring

Each Inn runs a mentoring scheme for its students. Seen as useful contacts by some students, others do not find mentors particularly helpful, especially if they've already secured pupillage. If you attend one of the provincial providers, make sure the Inn doesn't give you a London sponsor unless you request it.

whose inn and who's not?

Broadly, the Inns are much of a muchness, but there are subtle differences, so spend some time considering which would suit you best. Go and look around the Inns, meet the education department and talk to people. Students join for many different reasons – architecture, friends/family connections, the reputation of the chef, etc. All the Inns are friendly and assist their students, and although they try not to compete, we have managed to discern one or two differences. These days students need not rely on the old rhyme about the four Inns: "Inner Temple rich, Middle Temple poor; Lincoln's Inn for gentlemen, and Gray's Inn for a whore." (Or something like that!)

lincoln's inn

Lincoln's Inn is the oldest and largest of the four. Its Old Hall (once the out of term seat of the High Court of Chancery) is the opening setting of Dickens' *Bleak House*. It is fitting that *"those interested in full-blooded Chancery still tend to come here for historical reasons."* Lincoln's has plenty of international students, ensuring a lively and *"enriching"* community. Students find it *"informal and friendly"* and it has *"a lot going on."* Others appreciate its *"amazing surroundings and atmosphere."* It maintains a visible profile in the provinces and keeps in touch with students, providing money for functions.

inner temple

Third in size for number of members, Inner Temple is known to students as the *"party Inn"* and is home to the famous Pegasus Bar to which they often retire after dinner. As a smaller Inn, it is known to take a *"keen interest in student welfare."* The *"wild"* Cumberland Lodge weekends are *"more fun than with the other Inns – Inner Temple really lets its hair down!"* with Benchers and barristers joining in the fun. It built a bright, light Hall after its mediaeval buildings were destroyed during WWII.

middle temple

The second largest Inn by size. Middle Temple's *"splendid"* sixteenth century Hall is famous as the location for the first performance of Shakespeare's *Twelfth Night*. This thespian tradition continues today with the annual Middle Temple Revels in December – a comic musical production performed by students and barristers. Similarly, the Inn may have anything from *"jazz to opera to steel bands"* after dinner. Like Inner Temple, it is known to be very lively and after dining *"everyone goes to the bar."*

gray's inn

The smallest Inn and *"more personal."* Despite plenty of music and drama, the emphasis is still *"very much on dining."* Only natural then that it should be known for *"good food and lots of port."* Perceptive students say the Inn *"must surely be in breach of some human rights' point"* by not allowing anyone to leave Hall during dinner – not even for the loo. Some think it is *"very traditional."* While dining, it is not unheard of for a student to *"get told to stand up and debate"* or perform a forfeit for a breach of etiquette. Some think this is *"a nightmare, so intimidating;"* others comment that it is *"fantastic – what a great way to improve your advocacy."* It seems to have a lower profile in the provinces. ICSL is within its precincts, so proximity to its libraries might influence some students to join.

THE HONOURABLE SOCIETIES

	LINCOLN'S INN	INNER TEMPLE	MIDDLE TEMPLE	GRAY'S INN
Contacts	Tel: 020 7405 1393 www.lincolnsinn.org.uk	Tel: 020 7797 8250 www.innertemple.org.uk	Tel: 020 7427 4800 www.middletemple.org.uk	Tel: 020 7458 7800 www.graysinn.org.uk
Architecture	Everything from the mediaeval Old Hall to the neo-Classical Stono Buildings to the Victorian gothic Great Hall	12th-century Temple Church stands opposite the modern Hall built after the original was destroyed in WWII; otherwise the Inn largely resembles a car park	Splendid Elizabethan Hall tucked down an intricate maze of alleys and narrow streets	Suffered serious war damage and is largely a 1950s red-brick creation, albeit with its ancient Hall and Chapel intact
Gardens	Small and shaded; always open	Stretching down to the Thames. Croquet may be played	Small but handy for the bar	Famous walks provide recreation for nearby ICSL students, but only open at lunchtimes
Style	Friendly, international and large	Sociable and hard-working	Musical and arty	Intimate, traditional and formal
Gastronomy	A new chef means good food; lunch served every day	Wine left over after dining; lunch served every day but suits must be worn	The construction of new kitchens augurs well; lunch served every day	The emphasis is on the port not the food; lunch served every day
Accommodation	For scholars, in the Inn	Not for students	For scholars, in the Inn and in Clapham	Not for students
Bar	Briefs – fairly dismal and quiet. Open for lunches and snacks during the day	The Pegasus Bar has subsidised lunch for students and cheesy discos	New bar conveniently located beneath the library and adjacent to the gardens	Recently renovated
Old Members	Mohammed Jinnah Lord Hailsham LC Lord Denning MR	Judge Jeffreys of the 'Bloody Assizes' M K Gandhi	Sir Walter Raleigh William Blackstone Charles Dickens	Sir Francis Bacon Lord Birkenhead LC
Current Members	Cherie Booth QC Tony Blair MP Lady Thatcher	Lord Irvine of Laing LC Dame Elizabeth Butler-Sloss P Jack Straw MP	Lord Phillips of Worth Maltravers MR Edward Garnier QC MP	Lord Lane Lord Bingham David Pannick QC
Points of Interest	Together with the Royal Navy, Lincoln's Inn takes the Loyal Toast seated	Temple Church	Shakespeare's *Twelfth Night* first performed here in 1602	Shakespeare's *Comedy of Errors* first performed here. Wooden screen in Hall made with timbers from the Armada
Scholarship Interview Process	Applicants are selected for 20-minute interview but there is only one round	CPE scholars normally expect automatic funding for BVC, but can apply for higher award. Scholarships awarded on merit and bursaries on merit and financial need	Every applicant will be interviewed	Must have an upper second class degree to be eligible for BVC scholarship

money, money, money...

Why do you want to become a barrister? Do you have a love of the law and a passion for advocacy? Perhaps you want to help the disadvantaged and oppressed? Or is it because you want to earn pots of money? While you rarely meet an experienced barrister who's poor, earnings do vary wildly. There is no guarantee that you will earn a fortune, or indeed anything like that, and even if you do find the cash rolls in, when will you have the time to spend it?

But the one thing that is certain is the sheer cost of getting there. On top of law school fees, you will have to provide living expenses – often in London and therefore especially expensive. Likewise, although your pupillage will be funded in accordance with the Bar Council's new rules, £10,000 does not go far in your first year once you take off the cost of travelling to magistrates' and county courts halfway across the country. And even if you make it to tenancy, those initial receipts will be reduced by the hefty repayments on that fat loan you took out to pay for Bar school. You could end up with a worse lifestyle after starting work than when you were a student.

awards and scholarships

Bar school fees, books, Inn membership, dining fees, call fees, BVC Online fee, a wig and gown, suits, collars, shirts, shoes...it all adds up. Then there's rent and basic living expenses. It could easily swallow £20,000 that you simply don't have. There are several sources of financial assistance, and we've set out the main ones in the **Funding** section on pages 34 and 35. In addition to the range of loans from the high street banks (which if used wisely need not be the most painful option), the Inns have over three million pounds' worth of scholarships for the best students, details of which are set out in the following table. The application procedure varies from Inn to Inn, but usually it's a simple application form and interview. Gray's Inn requires at least a 2:1 degree; the others consider applications from those with at least a 2:2. There's no hard and fast policy on means testing, but you will have to answer questions about your finances and make a declaration of income. Scholarships would seem to be provided on merit first with means as a secondary consideration. Make your application look as impressive as possible as being shortlisted for interview is half the battle. The selection panel looks for academic ability, the likelihood you'll make a good advocate and, importantly, a commitment to the Bar. The last thing they want is to give several thousand pounds to someone who will then drop out of the BVC and join the circus.

It is very unlikely that you will be tested on substantive legal matters, although you should definitely be ready to discuss topical legal issues or to talk through an area of law that interests you. In addition to this, expect to be quizzed on which area of law you want to go into and what skills you can bring to the Bar.

funding from chambers

Some students will be lucky enough to have gained a pupillage funded in excess of the Bar Council's recommended minimum of £10,000, and an increasing number of these high-paying sets allow their pupils to draw down funds during the BVC. Finally, the Bar Council Scholarship Trust offers £5,000 interest-free loans to pupils.

SCHOLARSHIPS FROM THE INNS

NAME OF INN	FUNDS AVAIL.	CPE/BVC AWARDS	PUPILLAGE AWARDS	CONTACT DETAILS
Lincoln's Inn	£903,000 + subsidised accommodation	**CPE**: Up to 32 scholarships of up to £8,000 **BVC**: Up to 70 scholarships of between £6,000 and £15,000 each Up to 40 bursaries of up to £5,000 each 2 x £10,000 studentships 15 rooms in self contained flats **BVC/CPE**: Entrance awards-up to 100 awards for admission, call and dining	Up to 40 scholarships between £250 and £3,000 £3,000 for a place at European Court £3,000 for a place at European Court of Human Rights £10,000 bursary fund for overseas placements £2,000 for sundry prizes	Judith Fox Tel: 020 7405 0138 judith.fox@lincolnsinn.org.uk
Middle Temple	c. £700,000 + subsidised accommodation	**CPE**: 20-30 of between £1,000 and £8,000 **BVC**: 80 –100 of between £1,000 - £15,000 Subsidised accommodation for students	Approx 25 awards of between £500 and £5,000	Students Department Tel: 020 7427 4800 student_enquiries@middletemple.org.uk
Gray's Inn	c. £650k+	**CPE**: 6 x £7,500 max; 1 x £5,000 max **BVC**: 9 x £15,000 max 12 x £12,500 max 42 x £7,000 max	3 x £3,500 1 x £4,000 13 x £3,000 max At least 1 EU Stage award of £5,000 max	Rachael Isaac, PA to Deputy Under Treasurer (Students) Tel: 020 7458 7900 rachael.Isaac@graysinn.org.uk
		Up to £20,000 available in other misc awards		
Inner Temple	£858,000	**CPE**: 1 x £12,500 5 x £10,000 £77,500 in means-tested Exhibitions **BVC**: 1 x £17,500 1 x £20,000 1 x £15,000 4 x £12,500 20 x £11,000 Around 35 exhibitions of up to £10,000	£24,000 available for internships or similar	Clare Drewett Tel: 020 7797 8210 cdrewett@innertemple.org.uk
		50 x £160 for admission / call fees Various smaller scholarships and prizes £15,000 in disability grants for BVC or pupillage year Up to 12 Pegasus Scholarships to live and work abroad for 3 months (only available to tenants under 5 years' Call)		

practice areas at the bar

chancery

Chancery work is so named because cases are mostly heard in the Chancery Division of the High Court, as opposed to the Queen's Bench Division. In Chancery there is a strong emphasis on the application of the law and its principles, and its practitioners are viewed as lawyers' lawyers. The tools of their trade are legal arguments and their skills lie in applying these tools to real situations. Typically, you'll build up a wide practice for the first few years, but then aim to develop a reputation for specific expertise, thus making you more attractive to clients. Leading Chancery barristers have a reputation for being expensive and maybe a cut above, but this is an area in which only the highest quality advice is viable.

type of work

Chancery is divided into 'traditional' (trusts, probate, real property, charities, mortgages, partnerships) and 'commercial' (company cases, shareholdings, banking, pensions, financial services, insolvency, media and IP, professional negligence). But the distinction between the two is blurring and most sets now do both types of work. There are some fine brains at the Chancery Bar and it produces highly respected QCs and judges, but don't labour under the illusion that it's all paperwork and lofty academia. You'll have plenty of opportunity to develop your advocacy style, although the volume of court work tends to be higher in other practice areas. After a few years you may develop an overseas practice: the offshore tax havens are notorious for providing plenty of high-value work.

At first, property and commercial cases will take you to county courts across the UK and you'll cut your teeth on mortgage-related actions, landlord and tenant work and winding up applications. As time goes on, and particularly in the bigger sets of chambers, you'll be brought in on some substantial cases as a first or second junior, eg. a High Court trial on a matter relating to pensions, commercial trusts or professional negligence. Chancery barristers are increasingly taking on work that traditionally wouldn't have been seen as their preserve. For example, there are aspects of financial services, particularly pensions, which involve large trust funds.

skills needed

You need to be pretty bright to succeed within the Chancery Bar. As Joanne Wicks from Wilberforce Chambers says: *"The challenging intellectual nature of the work we do can't be over emphasised."* It requires complex problem solving together with the application of hard legal principles and a rigorous examination of facts. More importantly, you must be an excellent communicator. Solicitors will sometimes come to you with extremely complex and puzzling cases. These must be pulled apart and analysed. You must adore research and get a buzz from getting to the crux of interesting and intellectual questions. You then need to be able to interpret and communicate these conceptual ideas to your client in a practical and business-like matter. And you need to be confident in your findings. Joanne explains: *"Clients don't really want to know the details of the 1882 Conveyancing Act, they want to know whether they're going to win or lose."*

One day you could be acting for a plc with an entire team from a big City firm behind it. The next day might bring you a high street solicitor and a little old lady who's been conned into signing her house over to the window cleaner. It is unlikely that either the solicitor or the little old lady will have any experience of High Court litigation, so you'll need to do a lot of hand holding.

prospects

Most areas of the Bar are extremely competitive, and Chancery is no different. Joanne says: *"We always get a lot of very good applicants for pupillage and I'm sure it's the same at other Chancery sets,"* but *"there's always space for good people, and it's an area where there is a demand for our services and money is being generated, so recruitment is happening."*

CHANCERY: COMMERCIAL • London
1 **Maitland Chambers** (Lyndon-Stanford/Aldous)
2 **Serle Court** (Lord Neill of Bladen)
3-4 South Square (Crystal/Alexander)
4 Stone Buildings (Heslop)
Wilberforce Chambers (Nugee)
3 **New Square Chambers** (Purle)
24 Old Buildings (Mann/Steinfeld)
9 Old Square (Driscoll)
3 Stone Buildings (Vos)
11 Stone Buildings (Rosen)

CHANCERY: TRADITIONAL • London
1 **Wilberforce Chambers** (Nugee)
2 **5 Stone Buildings** (Harrod)
3 **11 New Square** (Proudman)
10 Old Square (Price)
4 **Maitland Chambers** (Lyndon-Stanford/Aldous)
New Square Chambers (Purle)
11 Old Square (Crawford/Simpkiss)
Serle Court (Lord Neill of Bladen)

Source: Chambers UK 2003 - 2004

commercial

In its purest sense, commercial work is dealt with in the Commercial Court or one of the County Court Business Courts. However, much of it is heard by the High Court (both Queen's Bench and Chancery Divisions) or dealt with by way of arbitration. There is an overlap of work with the Chancery Bar, reflecting the fact that commercial work is an umbrella term and not a rigidly defined practice area. Alternative methods of dispute resolution are increasingly employed to conclude business disputes as they often enable commercial relationships to continue undamaged by full-blown litigation. The commercial Bar handles a broad range of business disputes for a variety of industry sectors. Some barristers see industry specialisation as the way forward, but others prefer to remain generalists.

type of work

Instructions are generally paper and fact-intensive, and may involve huge sums of money and multiple parties. There is a perception that commercial work involves written advice as opposed to court work. Top QC Jeffrey Gruder, from Essex Court Chambers, explains: *"Compared to criminal barristers who are in court every day, we do less court work. However, on some cases you may find yourself in court for months on end."* Around 90% of his work is contentious. Of course, the majority of disputes settle, which limits opportunities for trial work, but interlocutory applications and, increasingly, jurisdictional questions, take commercial barristers into court fairly regularly.

Jeffrey's work encompasses shipping, insurance, general commercial contracts of various kinds, banking, commodity dealing, and even arbitrations concerning patents. As he says: *"The fundamentals of what we do are contract and tort."* The area remains heavily based on common law, with domestic and European legislation also coming into play. The continuing trend towards globalisation means commercial barristers are advising more and more on cross-border issues, which encompass competition law, international public and trade law and conflicts of laws.

Juniors handle smaller specialist disputes, such as shipping or insurance claims, as well as general commercial claims, such as sale of goods matters. Jeffrey confirms that these cases *"wouldn't come into the Commercial Court in the narrow sense but are nevertheless commercial in the wider sense."* On larger commercial cases, young barristers assist QCs as second or third junior on one or other of the aspects of the case. Such disputes might be high in value, complexity and profile and enable the junior to observe quality silks in action, while making a valuable contribution in terms of case preparation and direction. They will also gain a working knowledge of the higher courts, although as second or third juniors it's unlikely there would be any opportunities for oral advocacy. The good news is that there's a steady flow of arbitrations and County Court hearings during the first few years and juniors can also gain valuable experience in interlocutory applications and through deployment in a range of tribunals.

skills needed

The ability to work fast under pressure and to meet deadlines is important – not just court deadlines, but those of clients too. As Andy George of Blackstone Chambers says: *"It can differ from Chancery work in that your clients come from a commercial environment and expect answers and ideas within a sometimes unreasonably short time."* You need interpersonal skills that can be applied to all types of individual. Andy told us: *"During the course of an average day, my clients range from the East End rag trade to the City-based banking industry."* Jeffrey thinks: *"You need an ability to learn how businesses work and an understanding of business problems."* You also need to be on the same wavelength as your clients, and understand their needs and desires. A previous career in business may pay dividends but unlike, say patents, where a science qualification is almost mandatory, it's not vital to have had one and most haven't.

Illustrating the breadth of his practice, Jeffrey has an advanced knowledge of the shipping and insurance markets, but he also knows *"how recording companies deal with artists: what problems can arise and what the terms of the contracts are like."* No doubt this gives him a better idea than most as to what Will and Gareth got themselves into!

prospects

Competition for pupillage at the commercial Bar is fought out by some of the very best candidates. Jeffrey feels that *"if you get a junior tenancy at one of the top seven or eight commercial chambers, then most solicitors will regard this as a pretty good recommendation and will give you a try. Unless something goes terribly wrong, you should then have a reasonable career. Whether it's going to be really good will depend on your ability and your commitment."*

	COMMERCIAL LITIGATION • London
1	**Brick Court Chambers** (Clarke)
	Essex Court Chambers (Pollock)
	One Essex Court (Grabiner)
	Fountain Court (Brindle/Lerego)
2	**Blackstone Chambers** (Baxendale/Flint)
	3 Verulam Buildings (Symons/Jarvis)
3	**20 Essex Street** (Milligan)
	7 King's Bench Walk (Flaux/Kealey)

Source: Chambers UK 2003 - 2004 - 2004

common law

Common law comes from the precedents set in judicial decisions, rather than from statute. Most cases turn on principles of tort and contract and are dealt with in the Queen's Bench Division (QBD) of the High Court and the County Courts. Work blurs at the edges into both Chancery and commercial law.

type of work

A junior could have a very mixed caseload as many such sets also handle crime, family, employment, civil actions against police and housing matters. Early on, the work will involve drafting pleadings and attending hearings relating to matters ranging from RTAs and consumer credit debts to criminal hearings. There is less advocacy than at a criminal set, but greater than with Chancery or commercial. Tara Vindis of 9 Gough Square, says: *"The work is fairly advocacy-based. Certainly junior tenants in my set are in court at least once and sometimes twice a day."* Typically, a junior might start early in chambers doing last minute preparation and then travel to court – perhaps a 15-minute stroll down the road or a long train ride to Bristol. It might be a two-day trial or a half-hour standard directions appointment.

It's challenging – you won't necessarily know what you'll be doing from one day to the next. It's likely to terrify those who like their days to be structured and planned to the nth degree. Barrister's clerks juggle the chambers' diary deciding who's best placed to handle matters and sometimes instructions arrive late in the day. It's not unusual to receive a brief at 5pm the night before going to court. But, as Tara says: *"It's rewarding in the sense that you've got a lot of opportunity to be in court and have client contact."*

The growth of ADR and mediation has reduced the number of cases available to the common law Bar. In addition, the Woolf reforms changed the adversarial nature of claims, such that many preliminary hearings simply no longer take place. The effect of legal aid cutbacks is that junior barristers are now being instructed in relation to more conditional fee agreements (CFA, or no win, no fee). In practice, cases with poor prospects lead to barristers doing work and spending time on matters where fees become unrecoverable. It's not all gloom and doom though. According to Tara, there's *"plenty of case management conference work to be had, for civil actions in general and PI matters in particular."* Solicitor advocates crop up reasonably frequently at directions hearings, but they are rarely seen on trials.

skills needed

You must be flexible and not mind rushing here, there and everywhere. You might have something come in at 2pm that needs to be done by 5pm. Or you might have spent all day preparing a case for court the next day and then be told at the last minute that it's all off. Could you handle these situations with good grace? You must be a quick learner with a good short-term memory for facts and a long-term one for the law. This is particularly true during the early years when your practice will leapfrog between many different types of case. Perseverance is essential if you are to get to the stage where routine matters become familiar and straightforward and you can then specialise in a chosen area. Good people skills and an ability to adapt to a range of clients are both key. Tara makes the point that *"common law clients tend to be less high-flying than the clients in commercial sets."* Most won't be savvy company directors; they'll be ordinary people who just happen to have been involved in a traffic accident, tripped over or been sacked.

prospects

If work really is scarce in the early years, then you'll have to be impressive to secure your next instruction. Part of that will boil down to personality and how well you interact with clients. Common law sets will look closely at communication and people skills when recruiting pupils.

criminal

Rumpole... Kavanagh QC... even Judge John Deed manages to be a superb advocate (despite the fact that he's actually on the Bench!). But is the reality anywhere near as exciting as these fictional depictions? Maybe...

type of work

The first year or so will be a continual round of Magistrates' Court appearances on minor matters like motoring offences, committals to the Crown Court, sentencing, pleas in mitigation and directions hearings. Soon you'll progress to full trials, initially on smaller crimes such as common assault and the taking of motor vehicles, then graduating to ABH, robbery, indecent assault and possession of drugs with intent to supply. You may also get the opportunity to work with more senior barristers on matters such as white-collar crime, kidnapping, rape or murder. Bear in mind that juniors are asked to do unappealing work at times and you will often be required to travel a great deal with papers you have had little or no time to prepare. And how will you cope when you arrive promptly for trial, but your witnesses are nowhere to be seen?

Following pupillage, you may apply to be included on the CPS list, entitling you to receive instructions to prosecute as well as defend individuals. Some juniors also advise on Criminal Injuries Compensation and do voluntary work for legal advice centres or organisations such as Victim Support, the Free Representation Unit and Justice.

On the whole, the criminal Bar is not afflicted by a shortage of work. As Quentin Hunt, a junior at 2 Bedford Row, says: *"Crime is crime essentially. People will always commit crimes and people will always need criminal barristers. The work will always be there."* David Spens QC from 6 King's Bench Walk speaks for most when he says: *"It's massively competitive. There's obviously competition from other barristers and down at the bottom end (ie the Magistrates' Courts) there are also solicitor advocates, who are making quite an impact on the defence side."* On the prosecution side, there are solicitors from the Crown Prosecution Service who are doing "whole lists of cases," particularly in the Inner London Magistrates' Courts.

skills needed

As a criminal barrister, you really do need to know how to deal with people, particularly when conducting defence work. You will be dealing with defendants, the victims and witnesses of crimes, the juries that must reach verdicts, the solicitors instructing you, your opposing counsel and the professionals who administer justice. You'll encounter the whole spectrum of society: the real criminal underclass right through to aristocrats caught drink driving, so people skills are essential. Not everyone will be pleasant, not everyone will be sane. Not everyone will be an adult (in any sense of the word).

You need to be a good judge of character. You should also be comfortable with constantly being in the spotlight as an advocate. For Quentin: *"The best bit of the job is being in court every day doing lots of advocacy and lots of different cases."* If that's what you're looking for, then the criminal Bar is ideal. The flip side of this is the fact that there's a lot of waiting around. You might arrive at a busy court at 10am, but not actually have your matter come up till 3pm.

Hopefully, you'll be outgoing and personable as there's not much room for repressed academics at the criminal Bar, although you will have to keep on top of criminal evidence rules, which are ever changing. You also need to be able to express yourself clearly, particularly to lay people, and to be industrious in the sense of both managing detail and, at the same time, 'seeing the wood for the trees'.

CRIME • London	
1	**2 Bedford Row** (Clegg)
	Doughty Street Chambers (Robertson)
	Hollis Whiteman Chambers (QEB) (Bevan/Whiteman)
	6 King's Bench Walk (Amlot)
	3 Raymond Buildings (Nicholls)
2	**25 Bedford Row** (Tansey)
	2 Hare Court (Kramer)
	18 Red Lion Court (Rook)
3	**Atkinson Bevan Chambers** (Atkinson/Bevan)
	7 Bedford Row (Farrer)
	9-12 Bell Yard (Carlile)
	23 Essex Street (Miskin)
	Furnival Chambers (Mitchell)
	Two Garden Court (Davies/Griffiths)
	Matrix
	Tooks Court Chambers (Mansfield)
	2-4 Tudor Street (Ferguson)
4	**36 Bedford Row** (Pert)
	9 Bedford Row (Berry)
	10 King's Bench Walk (Nathan)
	187 Fleet Street (Trollope)
	5 Paper Buildings (Carey/Caplan)
	3 Temple Gardens (Goldberg)

Source: Chambers UK 2003 - 2004

prospects

The criminal Bar tends to award more pupillages than any other area. That said, Quentin told us that, of nine pupils at his chambers, only he and one other were given tenancy. Needless to say, competition remains fierce. Evidence of proven advocacy skill (if only from activities such as debating or mooting) would be advisable for anyone seeking a pupilage. David Spens describes criminal advocacy as being *"80% preparation, 10% luck and 10% performance on the day."* This emphasises two points well – you can't wing your cases and *"the charisma factor is the icing on the cake, and makes the difference between those who win and the also-rans."*

employment

Since 1997 the Labour Government has passed a raft of new employment legislation, and it's got even more planned for us – age discrimination and religious discrimination. Couple this with the public's growing awareness of employment rights and the net effect is more cases, particularly in relation to discrimination. Great news for the employment Bar! Legal representation is not required in employment tribunals, however, many people have household contents insurance with a significant legal expenses component and cases are often of such complexity that specialist legal advice is advisable. Tom Coghlin from Cloisters believes that *"in a case where there's more than several thousand pounds at stake, you'd be silly not to engage a barrister to represent you."*

type of work

It's usual for juniors to undertake a mixture of employment cases and other areas of work, mainly commercial and civil matters. While the 'cab rank rule' applies (ie barristers will do whatever work comes through the door), most junior employment barristers handle roughly even amounts of work for applicants (often individual employees) and respondents (often HR managers representing the employer company). This is the case even though the specialist sets tend to have links to either applicant or respondent oriented law firms. Bear in mind the fact that *"respondents generally pay better."*

With damages capped in all employment cases except those relating to discrimination, it rarely pays to get a senior barrister involved, so there's a good selection of work at the junior end. Straightforward tribunal work, such as unfair dismissals, discrimination cases and relatively low-value contract claims are interspersed with more difficult work, such as whistle blowing and cases concerning trade union activities. Sarah Moor from Old Square Chambers says that acting for an applicant sometimes means *"you'll be up against a party who can afford a senior barrister, which of course is a useful learning opportunity for you."*

There's plenty of advocacy, particularly at the junior end. This marks it out from an area like commercial, which tends to involve more documents and drafting. Generally, you'll appear in the informal setting of an employment tribunal or the Employment Appeals Tribunal, as opposed to the courts, and you may have three or four different tribunals a week. David Craig from Devereux Chambers explains: *"Because there are no costs consequences in tribunals, a lot of people will go to trial. Even if they lose, they've only got their own costs to bear, not the other side's. If people had more to lose, they might be keener to settle."*

Employment barristers have been in competition with solicitor advocates for some time. Tom says: *"I normally expect to be against a barrister in the employment tribunal, but often I'm against a solicitor or a litigant in person."* David stressed the expense factor again: *"Barristers' brief fees tend to be considerably lower than solicitors' fees for preparing, travelling, waiting and appearing in court, particularly if City solicitors have been instructed."* Solicitor advocates are rare in the higher courts, but they may draft the pleadings themselves.

skills needed

Decent advocacy skills and an engaging personality will take you a long way. You'll come across all types in your work and it's important to interact well with them, be they High Court judges, tribunal members, union officials, high-flying execs or dinner ladies. In tribunal hearings, you'll need a gentle touch if you're against a litigant in person, *"otherwise you can come across as a bully!"* and you need to be less legalistic in your language.

Perhaps more than most areas, you have to keep abreast of developments in the law. New directives, regulations and cases appear all the time and you'll be forever having your cases stayed while others with similar points are being heard on appeal. One disadvantage, according to Tom, is that *"very often briefs are delivered at half past four the afternoon before trial, usually because solicitors are holding out till the last minute for a deal and don't want to incur the cost of instructing counsel until they absolutely have to."* Consequently, you may have little time to prepare a case for trial. It's in these situations where you realise how important it is to know all the relevant law *"so you don't have to be researching it at midnight the night before."*

prospects

The area is incredibly competitive and there are few pupillages available. Tom says that experience in almost any environment other than the Bar is a good thing. *"At the Bar you're neither an employer nor an employee, yet as an employment barrister you're arguing what is reasonable behaviour by an employer. How can you do this if you've never seen or been a manager yourself?"*

The best advice we can give is to make sure you can demonstrate your interest and commitment. Sarah says: *"It's most disappointing to see a very bright candidate with an excellent degree who can't put together a rational explanation as to why they want to do employment work – even if it's more theoretical than practical at that stage."* David recommends that you *"think about doing some employment cases for the Free Representation Unit. You act for applicants and run a case from start to finish, which will clue you up on the law and give you terrific advocacy experience."*

EMPLOYMENT • London	
1	**11 King's Bench Walk** (Tabachnik/Goudie)
2	**Blackstone Chambers** (Baxendale/Flint)
	Cloisters (Cox)
	Devereux Chambers (Edelman)
	Littleton Chambers (Kallipetis)
	Old Square Chambers (Hendy)
3	**Essex Court Chambers** (Pollock)
	Matrix

Source: Chambers UK 2003 - 2004

family

Feuding couples and bitter child custody battles - can you handle these? Family law is a demanding practice area for a barrister, who will only be involved in the most complex or combative cases.

Daniel Bentham, a tenant at Queen Elizabeth Building, told us: *"It's a relatively small niche at the Bar, but it accounts for a whole division of the High Court."* A large amount of court time in England and Wales is allotted to divorce, separation, adoption, child residence and contact orders, financial provision and domestic violence. However, there has been an increase in mediation in an attempt to resolve disputes in a more efficient and less unsettling fashion. The family Bar had been concerned that this, and an increase in solicitor advocates, would lead to a downturn in work. With the exception of children's cases, in which solicitors have always been encouraged to do their own advocacy, work for the Bar appears to have continued largely unabated, although fees for publicly funded work have been reduced.

type of work

Barristers cut their teeth on simple County Court matters, progressing to complex matters in the Family Division of the High Court. In the early years, there will be a lot of private law children work (disputes between parents), which will consist of minor appointments, directions hearings and timetabling. More substantive work, including final hearings, will follow. Public law children's work (care proceedings between local authorities and parents) tends to be publicly funded where the barrister is acting for the parents and is less lucrative for the barrister.

Ancillary relief (financial arrangements) can be complex, so it helps to have a flair for things like pensions and shares and a good grounding in the basics of trusts and property. Specialising in matrimonial finance requires very different skills from children work. That said, some barristers build up excellent reputations in both areas.

Daniel does a lot of children's matters and directions hearings: *"If you want to be an advocate, it's a pretty good place to be... I'm in court about three times a week, generally for small cases or applications rather than big trials."* A significant component of the work of Nick Anderson, a tenant at One King's Bench Walk, involves seeking injunctions in domestic violence cases. These issues can upset and anger, so be sure that long-term exposure will not affect your own wellbeing.

The legislation affecting the area is comprehensive and well settled and there's also a large and flourishing body of case law (in the Family Law Reports). You must keep up with cases, but remind yourself that, while the basics remain the same in relation to the problems that couples and families experience, precedents are only useful to an extent. Unlike contracts, no two families are ever the same. The job is, therefore, more about negotiating general principles than strictly adhering to precedents.

skills needed

Whilst conflict is often deeply embedded in a case, the law requires an attempt at resolution through mediation. An adversarial approach is not appropriate and practitioners need to focus on client contact and genuine discussion. In children's cases, the paramount consideration is the child's best interests.

You can read the instructions or the brief, but often the case only comes alive when you meet the client. The ruling made or the settlement reached can have a massive impact on each of the lives touched by it and, consequently, it's vital that you find the appropriate course of action in each case and work with the solicitor in managing the case from an early stage. As Daniel says: *"A tactical, academic and practical approach to the matter needs to be combined with empathy for your client's situation you don't want to come across as a legal machine."* You need to stay objective, give clear-headed advice, but bear in mind that you are giving this advice to emotionally vulnerable clients.

Presentation and communication skills need to be tailored to different types of people. Nick told us: *"You will have clients ranging from a 17-year-old girl who's having her child taken into care, to a fairly well-off couple who are divorcing and dividing up their assets."* He added: *"It's very much a job for those who enjoy working with people. Hopefully we're achieving some good rather than just making money by pushing paper around for faceless corporations."*

prospects

It's a small area, so competition and standards are high. Even at specialist family sets, many pupils are not retained as tenants. Daniel says: *"Before you devote 25 years of your life to it, you should do some investigation and mini-pupillages will mark you out as being committed to the area."*

FAMILY/MATRIMONIAL • London	
1	**One King's Bench Walk** (Hacking)
	1 Hare Court (Blair)
	Queen Elizabeth Building (Baron)
2	**4 Paper Buildings** (Swift)
	29 Bedford Row Chambers (Francis)
	One Garden Court Family Law (Platt/Ball)
3	**14 Gray's Inn Square** (Turner)
	Renaissance Chambers (Jubb/Setright)

Source: Chambers UK 2003 - 2004

public law

Public bodies operate within statutory constraints and their decisions may be challenged on a number of grounds. Have they considered the relevant facts in reaching their decisions? Have the officers acted strictly in accordance with the correct procedure? Did the body or officer have the authority to make the decision in the first place? Will they reveal to you how and why they have made a decision? If these questions interest you and you are passionate about principles of justice and the advancement of the law, read on.

type of work

While the breadth of public law work is huge, by far the most common matters are the judicial review of immigration decisions, which account for approximately half of the Administrative Court's case list. Such work features prominently in a junior barrister's practice. Those building up a local authority clientele may find themselves acting for a number of different departments on a range of work, which will often lean heavily towards decisions concerning planning, housing or environmental matters and education, health and children. A recent growth area has been community care matters, concerning the provision of social services by local authorities. For example, a single mother with two disabled children who is seeking more assistance and a larger council flat might bring an action against the council.

At the other end of the spectrum sit some high-profile and contentious cases, such as that of 'Miss B', an irreversibly paralysed woman who successfully pursued a claim in the High Court for the right to have her life-support machine switched off.

Very few sets limit themselves to public law cases; most will combine the work with general common law, competition, criminal or employment as second strings to their public law bow. Additionally, many sets that do not hold themselves out as public law specialists carry out judicial review work. Andrew Blake, a tenant at 11 King's Bench Walk, makes the point that *"many sets link their public law work to their non-public law work."* For example, if a set does criminal work, its public law practice will often be in relation to prisons or breaches of procedure by police. Alternatively, if a set does commercial work, it might handle judicial reviews of DTI decisions.

Where an event is of great importance to society as a whole, or even just a segment of it, public inquiries are commissioned by the Government and then operate independently. The Bloody Sunday Inquiry, the recent inquiry into Heathrow Terminal 5 and the Hutton Inquiry into the death of David Kelly illustrate the different types of issue that come under scrutiny. All of these inquiries utilise the services of counsel, and sometimes multiple counsel. Bloody Sunday, for instance, has involved 18 barristers.

The Human Rights Act has undoubtedly affected public law. *"In theory the HRA can influence any public law case,"* says Andrew. *"It's had a stealth impact in some ways, in that it doesn't have to be expressly referred to in order to have an impact on a case. It's already laid down a few general principles that are now standard considerations for any case."*

Initially, pupillage at a public law set will see you drafting opinions and shadowing your pupilmaster. In the second six you'll get the chance to undertake some advocacy. The nature of this may depend on the work of your chambers, but may include criminal work or applications for urgent injunctions. It's not usual for the most junior barristers to handle judicial review cases, although juniors will be led by QCs when complex or important matters make it to court. After a few years you should have built a practice with a good balance of advice and advocacy. You'll see an interesting array of cases which, given their nature, are often reported in the newspapers. Andrew said: *"One day I could be doing an education case about exclusion from school, the next day I could be doing a case involving a prison, or an environmental or planning matter."* If you subscribe to the theory that variety is the spice of life, this could well be the area for you.

Public international law appeals to many students, but openings are very limited. Issues of note include border disputes (eg between Nigeria and Cameroon), the Lockerbie air crash, the UK and Spanish governments' Pinochet extradition dispute, and the Irish and UK governments' Sea Tribunal concerning the effects of Sellafield. Traditionally it's been the preserve of academics – the leading names are predominantly sitting or ex-professors at the top universities, but also include Foreign Office veterans and the occasional pure barrister. Governments want tried-and-tested counsel and will expect those they instruct to be recognised, published authors. This is not an area of work you'll fall into by accident, nor is it one you're likely to get into until you're much more experienced. If the academic route is not for you, seek a pupillage at a leading public law set.

skills needed

The job is all about understanding red tape and wanting to battle through it. You have to really care about the fundamental laws by which we live. In order to have a successful practice, you must develop a comprehensive knowledge of administrative and constitutional law, and you need to be au fait with the inner workings of central and local government generally. In addition, familiarity with EU and international law is becoming increasingly important. You should remember, though, that the work won't always involve close contact with your lay client. In many cases, the client doesn't attend the hearing in person at all.

The Administrative Court is one of the most inundated branches of the High Court, so you'll need to develop an efficient style of advocacy. Long and dramatic performances are rarely well received; you must learn how to cut to the chase and deliver the pertinent information, draw on the relevant case law or statutory regulations and present your arguments promptly. An inquiring and analytical mind is essential.

prospects

"It's definitely a growing area, particularly in relation to judicial review," says Andrew. *"This is partly due to the HRA, but it's also due to a growing awareness by the public of their ability to take legal action against Government decisions and that the government should be and can be held accountable for their actions."* It's always been competitive and the introduction of the HRA has made it more so. *"Human rights is a very trendy area of law, and lots of people are intrigued by the idea of placing limits on what the Government or the police or any public body can do."* Andrew suggests focusing your studies on constitutional law subjects as one way of demonstrating your enthusiasm for the area. In addition, doing plenty of pro bono work in the early stages of your tenancy is an ideal way to get involved in public law matters.

Rank	ADMINISTRATIVE & PUBLIC LAW • London
1	**Blackstone Chambers** (Baxendale/Flint)
2	**Brick Court Chambers** (Clarke)
	Doughty Street Chambers (Robertson)
	39 Essex Street (Davies/Wilmot-Smith)
	11 King's Bench Walk (Tabachnik/Goudie)
	Landmark Chambers (Clarkson)
	Matrix
3	**1 Crown Office Row** (Seabrook)
	Two Garden Court (Davies/Griffiths)

Rank	PUBLIC INTERNATIONAL LAW • London
1	**Blackstone Chambers** (Baxendale/Flint)
	Essex Court Chambers (Gordon Pollock QC)
	20 Essex Street (Iain Milligan QC)
2	**Matrix**

Rank	IMMIGRATION • London
1	**Two Garden Court** (Davies/Griffiths)
2	**Doughty Street Chambers** (Robertson)
	Matrix
3	**6 King's Bench Walk** (Kadri)
	Tooks Court Chambers (Mansfield)
4	**Blackstone Chambers** (Baxendale/Flint)
	39 Essex Street (Davies/Wilmot-Smith)
	Renaissance Chambers (Jubb/Setright)

Source: Chambers UK 2003 - 2004

olpas: the agony and the ecstasy of getting pupillage

OLPAS is the online application system for pupillage that was introduced by the Bar Council in 2001. Whether or not they participate in OLPAS, every set of chambers or employer is required to advertise each pupillage on **www.olpas.co.uk**. Students can then peruse the website for details of pupillages, chambers, levels of funding and so on. Details are also reproduced in the *Pupillage and Awards Handbook*, published in March each year to coincide with the opening of OLPAS and the National Pupillage Fair at Lincoln's Inn.

OLPAS operates in two rounds or 'seasons': summer and autumn. The summer season closing date is 30 April; three months are allowed for interviews, with chambers making offers from 31 July. The autumn season has a 30 September closing date and allows only one month for interviews with offers from 31 October. Students may apply for up to 12 pupillages in both rounds, but chambers can only offer pupillages in one round. Chambers and candidates communicate with each other by e-mail, which, unless you are careful, means that you end up checking for mail every 20 minutes.

The online application form requires details of your academic background, relevant work experience, motivation for being a barrister and referees. You complete the form just the once and it is sent automatically to all 12 sets. Some students feel that the form's 'box checking' format works against those who may have to explain poor results or a non-standard journey to the Bar. Others feel that the online form inhibits them from expressing their personality or style, but relax: there's ample opportunity to reveal the inner you in interview.

David Brent from *The Office* once said: "Avoid employing unlucky people – throw half of the pile of CVs in the bin without reading them." You'll be relieved to hear that we've been impressed by the time and effort put into pupillage selection by the many Bar recruiters we've spoken to. Applications are usually read by at least two members of chambers who each score them on a series of measures. Most sets expect a good 2:1 or even a First – they can afford to be picky – so if your degree result is unimpressive, your application will, in all likelihood, be seen that way too.

Commonly, leading sets receive at least 200 applications and possibly many more. Our research indicates that roughly one in every five applications will score an interview. Of course, some students get interviews from the majority of their preferred sets, while others get few or none at all. Max your chances by putting together a compelling reason for the set to select you. Peter Ratcliffe, a tenant at 3 Verulam Buildings, told us: *"It goes without saying that we expect candidates to know why they want to be a barrister, but we respond best to those who give the impression that they have thought about why they want to be a barrister at 3 Verulam Buildings in particular."* Amazingly, practically every chambers recruiter we spoke to confirmed that too many application forms end up in the bin purely because the student has failed to carry out any research into the set's activities. Peter also went on to say: *"Filling in the OLPAS application form is an exercise in diplomacy. It's not a good idea to trumpet your affection for any particular chambers in the main body of the form; you'll alienate the other sets you apply to. But when you get to the section headed 'Reasons for Applying to Chambers', take the opportunity to demonstrate that you have researched and thought about your application – tailor your response for each set you apply to."*

Remember to make applications through OLPAS in the year before pupillage is due to start. Thus, for pupillages starting in 2005, you must apply in April or September 2004. OLPAS permits chambers to recruit pupils a year earlier than normal (ie two years in advance of the start date) in the hope that this will afford students the security of knowing that they have a pupillage before committing to BVC fees. However, only some of the high-flying commercial sets have adopted this approach, owing to the fact that they are in direct competition with solicitors' firms for the very best candidates. Most sets want to know as much as possible about candidates and avoid making early offers before even the degree class is known for sure.

non-olpas sets

Many of the sets offering pupillage don't participate in OLPAS, preferring instead to invite applications on their own forms and at different times of year. You can make as many applications as you like to these non-OLPAS sets.

interviews

We've spoken to a string of pupillage committee members at a number of different sets, yet the drill is pretty much the same everywhere. Sets operating a two-round system will hold shorter and more informal first interviews, through which the pack will be cut down to a dozen or so candidates. A second interview will invariably involve an exercise, for which you'll have, say, 45 minutes to prepare. Other sets – especially those that put the emphasis on assessed mini-pupillages – may simply invite 20-25 people to attend a single interview. A set will happily explain the interview format to candidates who ask in order to prep for their big moment. You can probably also find out about the size of the panel and its make-up – eg seniority of the barristers and whether or not clerks sit on it.

A first interview is designed to establish whether or not you have presence and sufficient ability to communicate. In other words, how well you would come across to clients. To a degree, you either have it or you don't, but if you are worried that you haven't got enough of it then, assuming that you're reading this early enough, why not consider some sort of DIY training programme to polish up your presentation skills. Work on eradicating those unpleasant cuticle-picking habits, the tendency to *"Um..."* and *"Er..."* between sentences, and the nervous gabbling. Your friends will be brutally honest with you, if you ask them to be! And prepare your interview look well in advance – the right shirt and tie, shoes or accessories can improve your general appearance. These things alone won't win you a second interview, but they might stop you losing one. And remember, there's a good chance you'll have to discuss your CV so work out which experiences you want to stress and understand your motivation to be a barrister inside out. You may end up discussing current affairs, so keep on top of the news. Read the legal press and *The Times* on a Tuesday so that you can develop opinions on current or controversial topics in the area of law that you are looking to move into.

An interview that centres on a legal problem can benefit enormously from a bit of forward planning. We didn't quite believe what we were hearing when recruiters told us that law undergraduates often fare worse in these interviews than CPE students who may only have had a few short months of the course under their belts. Well, believe it! "Sorry, it's been ages since I did contract/tort" really messes up your prospects at a pupillage interview. Exercises are designed such that CPE students are not unfairly disadvantaged. CPE students spend their time mainlining the core principles of the law...so go back to the basics and master them. Invariably you'll have to give an oral answer, and you must expect the panel to come back at you. Don't panic if it presents an argument or a case you have not heard before or did not anticipate. In addition to your ability to spot the issues in a problem scenario, an important part of the interview is testing your ability to respond to the surprises. Anna Diamond, a tenant at Birmingham's No.5 Chambers, told us: *"Candidates are normally fine on the expected questions, but we need to see that they can think on their feet and be mentally agile…that they can change direction in mid-flow."* Remember that the panel is neither looking for, nor does it expect, ready-packaged barristers. What it wants to see is your potential.

Different chambers are looking for different things in their pupils. Some, like Doughty Street Chambers, for example, rarely take fresh-faced graduates, preferring those who have firmly demonstrated their commitment to human rights matters through some relevant post-degree activity. Blackstone Chambers stresses that it is looking for raw talent, whatever kind of package it comes in; many other sets freely admit they want someone who will be able to fit in with the existing members of chambers. Most sets tend to recruit in their own image…which, again, is why you need to do your research.

Chambers do not want robotic legal brains. Nor do they want cocky and arrogant students with no experience of life. And one final word of advice: don't embarrass yourself with a display of begging and hand wringing. Desperation never has been, and is unlikely ever to be, an attractive look.

the free representation unit (FRU)

Aspiring barristers listen up: if you're looking for ways to bolster your qualifications and get the pupillage you want, you simply must consider gaining advocacy experience through FRU. The organisation was established as a charity in 1972, and as the name suggests, it provides free legal representation to those who cannot afford to pay for it. FRU volunteers appear mainly before employment tribunals and social security tribunals, although the unit also undertakes Criminal Injuries Compensation Board and immigration work.

Besides providing a valuable service to members of the community, FRU also has an important training role for the legal profession, providing law students and young lawyers with first-hand case preparation and advocacy experience. Volunteers include CPE students, occasionally final-year law undergraduates, BVC students, trainee solicitors, pupils and qualified barristers. At all the sets we visited, barristers spoke glowingly of the unit's work, and many first-rate sets actively encourage their pupils and very junior tenants to take FRU cases. As a volunteer, you'll undertake a one-day induction during which you'll be introduced to social security and employment law. You'll then be asked to write an opinion on a typical FRU matter, and if it's up to scratch, you'll be accepted. If not, you can resit the test any time. Recruitment is ongoing and induction days are held three times a year in March, July and October.

The extent of your obligation to FRU is up to you – you take on cases only when you choose to. You can browse its current files and, if you like the look of something, you can ask to get involved. When we investigated, we found out that one FRU volunteer had done more than 60 cases, while others settled for fewer – around ten is not uncommon. FRU's Naomi Cunningham told us: *"You have the freedom to use FRU work to get the experience you want."* But apparently, *"the single most useful thing for the sake of your career is to get solid cross-examination experience."* In employment law matters, your experiences may range from the simplest advocacy work to challenging and demanding appellate advocacy before the Employment Appeals Tribunal. When handling Social Security Commission matters, there's even a possibility that a case may be reported and change the law.

And finally, a cautionary tale for pupils out there who think they don't need FRU. The FRU coordinator had a *"very meritorious case"* on her desk and called a reputable set to find someone to take the matter. The clerk offered the services of a first-year tenant, who phoned FRU back some days later to say she could not take the matter as she had never cross-examined before. An unusual decision we feel, after all, *"you don't want to walk into court with a client paying through the nose and you wearing great big L plates on your back!"*

pupillage and after...

So college is over, you've bagged the BVC and it's time to step out of the protective shadow of academia and into the harsh, testing light of pupillage. Will it be 12 months of stress-induced hair loss or will you be forged into a million-a-year advocate of the future?

Pupillage is a year of practical training under the supervision of a series of pupil supervisors (or as most sets still call them 'pupilmasters'). It is divided into two parts: the 'first six' is a non-practising period during which pupils shadow their pupil supervisor. This is followed by a practising 'second six' during which pupils can undertake work in their own right and appear in court on their own. That's the theory, but we've found that different chambers have different views on how the second six is best spent. Some push you onto your feet as early as possible while others restrain you until the end of pupillage. Incidentally, both sixes may be taken in the same set or at two different sets. In all sets there are compulsory professional training courses that must be undertaken.

Pupillage is demanding and competitive wherever you go and the learning curve is steep. Certain sets, like Brick Court and Blackstone, put pupils through their paces by setting regular, assessed exercises. Be it in a formal or informal way, and wherever you are, you will be assessed throughout. Additionally, in some chambers there's a strong emphasis on getting your face known and impressing all the right people. This can be an unwanted burden for pupils already stressed about producing good work for their supervisors. Our research has shown us that supervisors will happily give guidance on what is the best approach to getting tenancy. Whether it's: "Get to know the clerks as soon as possible" or "So and so is an important person to try and do good work for," take your lead from your supervisor and the 'baby juniors' who have won tenancy in the preceding year or two. Yes, you are in competition with your fellow pupils but we found that pupils who were able to create a support network for each other within their chambers were less stressed than those where internecine warfare was the order of the day. If you are made of the right stuff you will get tenancy, irrespective of the fate of your fellow pupils.

Crunch time comes when all members of chambers (or a committee) gather to decide who gets tenancy. Most sets decide nine or ten months into pupillage; a few let pupils know if they are successful as early as the end of the first six, so enabling those who are unsuccessful to continue pupillage at another set. In these circumstances we've found that chambers do assist pupils in finding a second six elsewhere. It is not unusual, especially in crime and family, for pupils to undertake a third six before tenancy becomes a realistic option. Some make the decision more than 12 months after pupillage started. For those pupils who are unsuccessful, this can be the darkest hour. We reproduced the Bar Council's statistics on students' prospects for the BVC, pupillage and tenancy on page 581, but don't get too gloomy: if you're good enough you'll succeed, however, you'll have to be proactive.

And if, ultimately, you decide the independent Bar is not for you, other options are open to you. You might consider working as a barrister employed by a firm of solicitors, or by a large corporation or bank. The Government also has positions for barristers in, for example, the CPS, the Government Legal Service, the Environment Agency and the Law Commission.

chambers reports

In spite of everything – less small-end work, the threat to the silk system, wigs on the endangered list – the *Student Guide* felt it was time to lift the lid on life at the Bar. Until now, students have had to rely on stereotypes and third-hand rumours in order to work out which sets they might want to apply to, be it for mini or full pupillage. No longer. We pestered around 30 sets in the hope they'd allow us to go in and ask all sorts of useful (and trivial) questions about life in chambers. We report on the 24 that were game and responded to us quickest. While the ones we've chosen are among the best, we aren't suggesting that they are the top two dozen. For example, how do you compare family set Queen Elizabeth Building with commercial set Fountain Court?

We took tours of chambers, sampled the coffee, interrogated pupillage committees, silks and pupilmasters, probed pupils, patted dogs and kissed baby juniors (okay, not really). The sets we visited were all successful businesses with plans for the future and a real desire to recruit bright and talented students. Whichever route they'd taken to the Bar, one thing all our sources had in common was a complete dedication to their careers. The pupils were often anxious as to how well they were performing and nervous of the looming tenancy decision, yet none of them regretted the decision to undertake pupillage. Finding the right set and type of practice for you is the key to career satisfaction and success. To some extent, chambers' recruiters will help you with this as they have a great deal of experience in spotting who is right for them. In the end, we've concluded that finding a pupillage is rather like embarking on a bizarre dating game – good luck!

NO.	SET	LOCATION	HEAD OF CHAMBERS	(QCS/JUNIORS)
1.	Blackstone Chambers	London	Baxendale/Flint	64 (28/36)
2.	Brick Court Chambers	London	Christopher Clarke	65 (29/36)
3.	Cloisters	London	Laura Cox	42 (4/38)
4.	Crown Office Chambers	London	Spencer/Purchas	78 (19/59)
5.	Devereux Chambers	London	Colin Edelman	46 (7/39)
6.	Doughty Street	London	Geoffrey Robertson	87 (21/66)
7.	Erskine Chambers	London	Robin Potts	24 (9/15)
8.	Essex Court Chambers	London	Gordon Pollock	64 (28/36)
9.	One Essex Court	London	Anthony Grabiner	53 (22/31)
10.	20 Essex Street	London	Iain Milligan	49 (20/29)
11.	Fountain Court	London	Brindle/Lerego	57 (20/37)
12.	Two Garden Court	London	Davies/Griffiths	80 (7/73)
13.	Hollis Whiteman Chambers	London	Bevan/Whiteman	52 (18/34)
14.	11 King's Bench Walk	London	Tabachnik/Goudie	42 (12/30)
15.	Maitland Chambers	London	Lyndon-Stanford/Aldous	43 (10/33)
16.	Matrix Chambers	London	n/a	44 (16/28)
17.	Queen Elizabeth Building	London	Florence Baron	26 (4/22)
18.	Serle Court	London	Lord Neill of Bladen	47 (14/33)
19.	4 Stone Buildings	London	Philip Heslop	26 (8/18)
20.	3/4 South Square	London	Crystal/Alexander	53 (18/35)
21.	3 Verulam Buildings	London	Symons/Jarvis	52 (21/31)
22.	Wilberforce Chambers	London	Edward Nugee	39 (16/23)
23.	No.5 Chambers	Birmingham	Gareth Evans	136 (12/124)
24.	St Philips Chambers	Birmingham	John Randall	141 (11/130)

Numbers of members taken from Chambers UK 2003-2004

Blackstone Chambers

the facts

OLPAS: summer season **Pupillages:** 5x12 months
Applications: 350 **mini pupillages:** 40
Interviews: 12
Award: £35,000, (£9,000 can be advanced for BVC)
Tenancies offered in 2003: 2
Chambers UK rankings: Administrative law, commercial litigation, employment, environment, financial services, civil fraud, human rights, immigration, media & entertainment, public international, sport

Blackstone Chambers has a dominant position in public law and leading commercial and employment practices. It has big-name QCs like Barbara Dohmann, Charles Flint and David Pannick, and you might be aware of co-head Presiley Baxendale's rebirth as a mediator. The set is instructed by all manner of firms from the magic circle to smaller provincial outfits. It also receives direct instructions from local authorities

Blackstone attracts all those who apply to the magic circle commercial sets and plenty more besides. For many students, it's the set's public law reputation but, whatever motivates you, be aware that pupillage and the first few years of tenancy will involve all aspects of the set's work. So, *"if you don't want commercial practice you'll get a nasty shock!"* The first step to admission is an assessed mini pupillage, from which 12 lucky candidates will step up for a pupillage interview. They should have plenty to talk about as there's a sincere attempt to integrate even mini-pupils into chambers life. Yet, despite lunches and drinks with members, the pupillage committee assures us that the process of selection is based solely on objective criteria. *"There's a temptation to want to work with people you like as, on the balance of probabilities, they will be here forever,"* but *"we're not trying to recreate the set's image for the next generation."* So what is it aiming for? According to one source: *"It's not a magic circle commercial set, but it desperately wants to be."* Don't assume you'll have to come from a 'standard' background. You need first-class ability but this doesn't always equate to a First in a law degree from Oxbridge. Among the juniors at Blackstone, there is an ex-banker, an ex-journalist and an ex-bouncer.

The process of selecting pupils is just the first in a long line of examples of this set's preoccupation with fairness...and systems to ensure fairness. Apparently, there's a rumour going round that the performance of pupils is displayed in a league table in the clerks' room. While a performance chart does exist (pupils are required to take two-day formal assessments every month), it is available only to the pupillage committee and is designed to ensure the tenancy decision is based on performance rather than favouritism and face time. Our sources spoke positively of this intense 'under the microscope' approach: *"It provides a framework and that's comforting in a way. It's so fair...sometimes it's too fair and you can perhaps feel that there's no room for personality to sway the decision."* Being constantly assessed may colour your pupillage year, but *"it cuts down the need for any internecine warfare between pupils...you're so much in the same boat."*

Four pupilmasters take pupils for three months each – last year, an employment guru, an insurance specialist and two barristers with mixed commercial/public law practices. Depending on which one you're with, you'll either be haring in and out of county courts and employment tribunals or you'll be more chambers-based, researching, writing advices and pleadings etc. Work for other members is banned, as is paid work. Expect to stay within the secure confines of a carefully structured scheme, free from the need to impress all and sundry. And there's no chambers tea to which you must dutifully troop in order to be seen but not heard.

Chambers is open and relaxed and, so long as you keep a *"scramble suit"* hanging behind your door, you can happily parade around in your 501s. *"The impression an outsider gets is of a very informal and lively bunch of people who have a great deal of affection and respect for each other. Wandering along the corridors you hear laughter and lively conversation."* This youth and vitality seems to have sprung into life in the 1990s when a constitution was established, along with a new mood for nurturing younger members and pupils. This latter phenomenon has been attributed to senior junior Pushpinder Saini, who started taking the kids out for lunch and drinks. It has now evolved into a full-blown social scene to which even senior members have attached themselves. Often, there are drinks in chambers on a Friday, and if it's a fine summer evening they'll retire to the roof to enjoy the view over the Thames. But spare a thought for the chambers' goldfish that only have a view of the clerks' room. We heard a fishy tale of clerks and barristers scrabbling around under desks following a piscine bid for freedom.

In 1998, when Blackstone moved to its current home, the set skipped a generation of older members and appointed the two (younger) current heads of chambers. It was *"a reflection of a desire to be modern and forward thinking. The set was very comfortable with having younger people as figureheads."* This is a set that no one (except maybe the fish) ever leaves. *"The last time someone went to the bench was in 1979...and then in the mid-80s someone became a Master of the Queen's Bench."* Why? *"Because we're argumentative and bloody-minded advocates!"* As for moving to other sets, that's not on either. *"Michael Beloff left. But then he came back."*

"We particularly pride ourselves on our advocates," one silk told us. *"That's where we outstrip the opposition."* Certainly the juniors are encouraged to experience advocacy as early as possible, and the volume of employment work assists in this aim. Of course, a toptastic academic record is absolutely essential for pupils, but unless you're the sort that enjoys questioning things and then standing up and arguing your point, you're not really Blackstone material. Some of the members run the Gray's Inn advocacy course for pupils as well as additional in-house advocacy training for Blackstone pupils.

The tenancy decision in the summer can be an emotional moment. One source told us: *"You worry that if you have to go somewhere else, you'll spend the first three months hating them for not being Blackstone."* So what do they fear they will miss? The support network of Julia Hornor, Doreen and her chocolate biscuits, fellow pupils and junior tenants, the opportunity to have *"blazing rows"* with your pupilmaster on work/non-work related topics (*"You're supposed to stand up for your views"*) and the notion that they belong to **the** set for public law matters.

Brick Court Chambers

the facts

OLPAS: summer season **Pupillages:** 4x12 months
Applications: 370 **Mini pupillages:** 110
First interview: 50 **Second interview:** 20-25
Award: £35,000 (funds can be advanced for BVC)
Tenancies offered in 2003: 2
Chambers UK rankings: Administrative, aviation, banking & finance, commercial litigation, competition/European law, energy & natural resources, environment, civil fraud, human rights, insurance, international arbitration, professional negligence

If you're aiming for top-level European, commercial or public law, then try Brick Court. It boasts some of the biggest names at the Bar, including Jonathan Sumption QC and five others in the million-a-year club. This magic circle set has a fearsome reputation for breadth of work and calibre of lawyers. Name a big commercial case from the last 15 years and there's a good chance Brick Court was involved.

EU law is in vogue with students and huge numbers of them apply for pupillage at this set. As one source told us: *"Applicants have to be outstanding in all areas; we can afford to be picky."* Wanted: *"Excellent brains and an ability to express oneself clearly in writing, while being articulate, attractive and persuasive orally."* Contrary to rumours, what is not required is a parent on the bench – this idea probably sprang from the fact that four senior members are the offspring of judges. Just like the Bar as a whole, this set is departing from the elitist, old-fashioned stereotype. That said, barristers don't dress in jeans and trainers, many still get the 'Mister' and 'Sir' treatment from clerks, and there's no attempt to convince the outside world of its being hip…or anything much else for that matter. Brick Court's work speaks for itself.

Some might say that the work is everything at Brick Court. People make friends, and two of the barristers have recently made a baby, but there's a take it or leave it approach to spending time with colleagues. *"There might be a chambers party or dinner once or twice a year, and there's a tradition that junior tenants arrange an evening out for pupils a couple of times a term."* There's no chambers tea (described by one pupil as an *"ordeal"* to be *"suffered"*) and no chambers lunch – togetherness is not force-fed. Sure, barristers are collaborative when it comes to discussing legal matters, but pulling together to raise the profile of chambers? No need. A common goal to take on other sets, to speed towards infinity and beyond? Already there. Take away the need to hype or heavily promote the set and you're left with the business of getting on with business. Unfortunately, this cool, calm and collected approach is sometimes misinterpreted by outsiders as coldness or austerity. There is a film of seriousness over the set; most of the pupils we spoke to were a shade more earnest (although possibly less anxious) than their peers elsewhere.

"Our USP is diversity of work," said a pupilmaster, cringing at her use of marketing jargon. And she's right: Brick Court has real variety in its commercial work, super-set status for EU matters and a thoroughly impressive record in public law. You can find sets of equal standing in each of these areas, but none that competes at the same level in all of them. Some of our sources stressed that while they felt they could get the calibre of public law experience elsewhere, they had no desire to mix it with employment work or even personal injury. They told us that for a commercial/public law pupillage Brick Court has to be the top choice. Those hell-bent on an EU/commercial caseload were even less tempted by other sets.

Each pupil sits with a pupilmaster for three months, also doing bits and pieces of work for other members. The pupillage committee has tight control of the demands on pupils and performance monitoring. *"There's enough stress on pupils already, so they shouldn't have to worry about being seen by the right people."* The system is designed to contain sufficient objective measures to nullify the 'face fits' phenomenon. As one pupil confirmed: *"The fitting-in thing is not a big requirement. People who make good barristers can be fun to be with or complete nerds who spend all their time in their rooms. It doesn't go against you to be friendly or nerdy."* Excellent news. Pupils rub along together quite well; indeed, three of them were nipping off for lunch together when we visited. *"People are human and so there is bound to be an element of comparison, but every effort is made so you don't feel like you are in direct competition."* Monthly, assessed advocacy exercises aren't divisive, even though pupil advocates against pupil. *"We're faced by a panel, who are all attempting to trip us up with awkward questions. We're all going through the same thing together."*

Advocacy exercises are all well and good, but you'll doubtless want the real thing. In your second six there's ample opportunity to represent clients on social security and possession proceedings through Law4All. Brick Court knows that much of its work is way beyond the reach of pupils and that 12 months spent researching discrete points of law on fragments of cases doesn't make for a rounded training. It might be *"inspiring"* to work with the big names and to *"see them in their thinking context"* but you'll need some smaller matters of your own. In July, the pupillage committee recommends who should be given tenancy, but three months beforehand, pupils will have had an indication of their long-term prospects. Whether or not it's good news, *"a pupillage here is recognised as a very good training,"* so even those who don't get the right signals usually stay a full year. While *"they can be quite hard-nosed about who they keep on,"* we understand the set is looking to grow at the junior end. And on the subject of youth, the two senior clerks are relatively young. One of their predecessors, a very famous clerk called Burley (*"Ah, yes, Burley"*) was a traditional and powerful figure, *"a mega-force in chambers."* And now? *"The power is definitely with the barristers."*

Brick Court inspires strong reactions. Intense praise from clients. Respect from competitors. Looks of abject horror from those who don't understand or would not be suited to the Brick Court style. That style is somewhat formal, efficient, clever and businesslike. It is not buffed and polished to catch the light and it is not seeking popularity for the sake of it. When a set becomes known for its profitability, its exceptional law-making cases and the variety of its activities, such distractions would seem ridiculous. If you're keen to build a serious career in one of Brick Court's core areas, apply for a mini pupillage (they are mandatory). A week here will give you all the insight you need.

Cloisters

the facts

OLPAS: autumn season **Pupillages:** 3x12 months
Applications: 450 **Mini pupillages:** 20
First interview: c.70 **Second interview:** 12-20
Award: £25,000 (£3,000 can be advanced for BVC)
Tenancies offered in 2003: 1
Chambers UK rankings: Clinical negligence, employment, product liability

Cloisters was founded 51 years ago with the goal of "fighting for the individual." Its well-known former head of chambers, Laura Cox, has recently been appointed as one of only seven female High Court judges out of a total of 107.

Located in the classical confines of Pump Court, Cloisters enjoys a tranquil existence next to Temple Church. Inside, the set has adopted a Sunday brunch approach to chambers decor: red-checked sofas and Utterly Butterly yellow wallpaper, *The Guardian* and *The Times* (each read many times over) strewn across the waiting room coffee table. It's bright, warm and welcoming, and very lived-in. It even doubles up as an art gallery, so who knows, you might walk away with legal advice and a new painting.

Cloisters delights in its reputation for *"creative"* legal argument and has long been associated with a commitment to difficult cases. Even before the introduction of the Human Rights Act, its members were active in civil liberties cases, *"extending the ambit of the law."* To this day, it retains a willingness to *"have a fight."* In particular, two members embody this ethos: disability and discrimination expert Robin Allen QC and the charming PI and employment guru Brian Langstaff QC. Members are currently acting for some 4,500 Chagossians who, in 1965, were expelled from the island of Diego Garcia by the British Government. True to its creative spirit, Cloisters' barristers are now attempting to bring about a brand new tort – that of unlawful exile.

Pupils sit with between two and four supervisors, but are encouraged to work for others in chambers, so exposing them to *"a spread of work and working styles."* There is an element of matching: if you're boisterous, you might find yourself sitting with an equally boisterous supervisor; *"if you are diffident, we'll sit you with someone who might bring you out."*

Your bread-and-utterly-butterly work will be immigration and employment matters, although pupils can play an instrumental role in major reported cases. When Brian Langstaff QC argued the leading case on capacity – Masterman-Lister v Jewell – a pupil assisted. Later, when it went before the Court of Appeal, she was again involved, this time as a tenant. Her name appears in the reported judgment. Although *"slow to start off,"* pupils can expect to be on their feet up to three times a week by the middle of their second six. A formal 'No Photocopying for Pupils' decree is policed vigorously.

Breathe easy, because during the first part of pupillage, you're free to make some mistakes. After this, pupils sit through formal assessments consisting of written and advocacy tests followed by an interview with the pupillage committee. Pupils are assessed against a universal standard, not each other, and any pupil who attains a final mark over 80% is automatically offered tenancy. It's a truism that this system avoids the culture of competition that can otherwise thrive like a noxious weed. Unsurprisingly, Cloisters is committed to transparent decision-making and pupils are free to examine the marking schedules.

In 2000, tired of paying for facilities they never used, Cloisters' criminal barristers left for another set. The absence of criminal work is one thing that now distinguishes Cloisters from its peers – 2 Garden Court and Tooks Court. But if criminal advocacy is important to you, you can participate in an exchange scheme with Tooks. Cloisters now regards its competitors as the big civil (and especially employment) sets and is marketing itself appropriately. In a bid to compete with them, it increased its pupillage award to £12,500 for the first six, with guaranteed earnings of £12,500 in the second. This caused some pique among existing pupils and juniors, while others felt that it might dilute the altruistic ethos of the set.

Cloisters receives bags of pupillage applications and can afford to be picky. Academic credentials are the single most important criteria for recruiters, but mooting, public speaking, legal or volunteer work are all considered favourably. In all, you must be bright, enthusiastic and curious. Cloisters says it's a diverse set, but look a little closer and an archetype emerges. Members here don't carry *"much truck for conventions or pomposity. We take things with a pinch of salt, we're nonconformist."* One pupil told us how she is not afraid to *"speak up at bail hearings or walk into the advocates' lounge and ask for advice."* This is a brave set, but one in which juniors feel comfortable asking questions and *"revealing the chink in their academic armour."*

Cloisters represents both claimants and defendants and it is perhaps because its feet are firmly planted in both camps that it is not *"on a political mission."* Whatever your politics, if you pass muster, you'll be accepted. The commitment to equal opportunities is notable and the set recently passed a resolution requiring each member to complete one week's worth of pro bono work per annum.

A dizzying social agenda has caused raised eyebrows among pupils' flatmates. One nicknamed Cloisters *"Bolly Chambers."* And not without good reason it seems. For its 50th anniversary year, chambers rent was increased by half a per cent to cover the anticipated increase in alcohol consumption. There are drinks to celebrate new artists being exhibited in chambers, welcoming parties for pupils and new tenants, and regular trips to local hostelries *"whenever someone's had a hell of a day."* Chez Gerard, Hodgsons, Gaucho Grill and The Cock are the usual suspects. On occasions, pupils even get together with the pupillage committee for breakfast.

The dress code is *"strictly informal."* Tenants *"never wear suits"* unless appearing in court or in conference. On the day we visited, juniors wore jeans and trainers. One of them told us about the time he forgot his court clothes and cobbled together a suit consisting of size nine shoes (waaaay too small), a jacket from here, trousers from there, and a tie from someone else. He won't make the same mistake again: *"It's hard to do the barrister's swagger when you're hobbling in shoes three sizes too small."* This sartorial informality is indicative of something deeper.

You'd never know that Cloisters is 51 years old. Like Isabella Rossellini, who was also born in 1952, it seems so much younger. The joking and jibing we witnessed between members was the perfect illustration of the collective spirit that binds this set. As we were leaving, we passed a little girl rolling over the red-checked sofas, and a suited man singing 'Baa Baa Black Sheep' to her. We're not sure quite why we're ending on this note, but somehow it seems appropriate.

Crown Office Chambers

the facts

OLPAS: No **Pupillages:** up to 4x12 months
Applications: 150 **Mini pupillages:** c.100
First interview: 30 **Second interview:** 15
Award: £30,000 (up to £5,000 advanced for BVC)
Tenancies offered in 2003: Not known
Chambers UK rankings: Clinical negligence, construction, personal injury, product liability, professional negligence

Crown Office Chambers came into existence in 2000, following the merger of One Paper Buildings with 2 Crown Office Row. It's a large set with an emphasis on personal injury, construction, professional and clinical negligence and product liability, topped off with general commercial and insurance/reinsurance cases. Among its silks are joint heads of chambers Michael Spencer and Christopher Purchas, Roger ter Haar and a number of other respected names. Members have been involved in most of the major product liability issues of recent years – tobacco, oral contraceptives, MMR, organophosphate sheep dip – as well as public enquiries into major rail crashes.

So why did the two sets merge? Basically, much of their work came from insurance companies and their solicitors, a sector that has seen a lot of consolidation and cost cutting. Each of the two legacy sets realised that they'd be better off working together instead of remaining as competitors. As plans go, it was a smart one.

The set has a long client list with half a dozen firms at its core: Berrymans Lace Mawer, Beachcroft Wansbroughs, CMS Cameron McKenna, Lovells, Morgan Cole and Vizards Wyeth. In addition to an army of PI lawyers, there are also specialists in construction and those handling general commercial cases. In the early years, and *"before people start fitting into one area,"* junior barristers remain generalists. Indeed, the bulk of pupillage applications come from students for whom this approach is the main attraction. Most practices at Crown Office Chambers sit neatly on the halfway point between the paper-intensive work of commercial sets and the rapid-response, court-every-day experience of crime sets.

Full marks to the pupilmasters, who are regarded by their charges as *"gateway guardians,"* only allowing other members to give pupils useful work. *"Their principal concern is that the requirements and demands on you are fair."* One pupil described the first weeks as *"like doing finals every day. You go to the Bar to be the master of your own destiny and, initially, you are absolutely not; you are totally apprenticed to your pupilmaster."* Another talked of *"excellent attention from pupilmasters. I've almost been embarrassed at how seriously I've been taken."* A PM told us: *"I make a point of talking to them about VAT and getting an accountant. They need exposure to all aspects of life as a barrister, including ethics."* In the event of there being something you don't particularly want to ask your PM, you can turn to one of the 'uncles and aunts' (junior tenant mentors) who will take you under their wing.

In the first six you'll have two PMs and your time will be split between observing them in court and settling pleadings on a variety of their matters – *"mostly PI, insurance and construction."* Additionally, each pupil undertakes standardised written assessments and four weeks of advocacy training, which all adds to the feeling of being under close supervision. This gives way to a *"radically different"* second six. Our pupil interviewees were just a few weeks into their second sixes, but had already met with the challenge of advocacy several times. They start off with RTA small claims trials (worth under £5,000, no wigs, no gowns) and quickly progress to fast-track hearings (worth up to £15,000 – eg an assessment of damages in a PI case). Pupils tell us that *"a lot is expected of you,"* but that getting stuck in is *"the only way you learn."*

Formal feedback at Easter gives pupils a hint as to their chances of securing tenancy. Determined by a committee rather than chambers as a whole, tenancy is certainly not guaranteed; however, the set is in expansion mode. Despite the absence of *"cultural presentism,"* pupils do experience long days and they clearly feel pressure to perform both well and consistently. We asked about the principles their guardians were instilling in them. *"Thoroughness," "taking pride in your work,"* and *"professional ethics"* won most mentions. Amusingly, we heard that it used to be said of 2 Crown Office Row that they took their work so seriously that *"every trial was a state trial."* One silk stressed: *"We try very hard to fulfil our ethical responsibilities. With pupils, we do draw particular attention to the fact that the primary duty is to the court."* Commendable.

Some barristers act only on the side of the angels – the disadvantaged and oppressed, those without culpability. Not here. Much of the time barristers defend insurance companies from claims brought by those seeking compensation for pain and suffering following an accident, medical malpractice or the use of a drug that is alleged to have been harmful. Their job is to minimise the amount their client must pay or to ensure that they are not held liable at all. *"You should make sure you are comfortable with that proposition,"* one source warned. When acting for the business interest in the business of misfortune, it's our guess that barristers need solid moral ground on which to stand. Is this why we found such a strong emphasis on professional ethics and conduct at Crown Office Chambers?

The set still occupies its two pre-merger addresses so, to assist integration, various members moved between the buildings. The southern end of the Temple is a beautiful location and, even though baby barristers get pokey rooms and QCs must often share the larger rooms with views of the Thames, overall there is a spacious feel to chambers. Good news for technophiles: the IT system is pretty hot, even down to a system which tells you who's got what from the library. We asked one junior if he ever visited the other building. *"Yes, to see my mates over there,"* he replied, so raising the topic of friendships within chambers. *"We're not in the pub every day"* trading *"gallows humour"* like criminal barristers, he said, but it sounds as if most members do rather like each other's company. Characters range from *"the profoundly intelligent to knockabout PI practitioners."* There's no forced bonding; instead it's more a case of easy interaction along the corridors, with people frequently swapping advice and insights. While we interviewed a number of barristers in their rooms, phones rang and heads poked around doors...a lot.

Although not a particularly traditional set, there are traditional elements to the place. Clerks call senior members 'Sir', but this practice has slipped at the junior end, and while it's proud of past members who've gone to the Bench, including Lord Justice Otton, who sat in the Court of Appeal, and High Court judges Popplewell and Tucker, there's no rogues gallery of portraits in reception. There's also no chambers tea and little to indicate that juniors are overly deferential towards their seniors. Hardcore traditionalism wouldn't wash with the set's major clients these days, we suspect. An executive committee of 11 barristers – some very junior – runs the place, with *"day-to-day matters 80% clerk-managed."* That's unsurprising given that both senior clerks have 25 years' experience and know the insurance market inside out. Rest assured that in your early years, they are more than capable of keeping you very busy in courts up and down the country. The pupillage selection process follows a standard two-interview pattern; however, don't be disarmed by a charming interview panel – you still need to show you're as sharp as a razor.

Devereux Chambers

the facts

OLPAS: summer season **Pupillages:** 2x12 months
Applications: c.300 **Mini pupillages:** through the year
First interview: 35-40 **Second interview:** 10-12
Award: £30,000 (£8,000 can be advanced for the BVC)
Tenancies offered in 2003: 2
Chambers UK rankings: Employment, insurance, personal injury

Employment, personal injury and general commercial cases are the building blocks of practice at Devereux and leading silk Colin Edelman QC and others also draw in major insurance matters. There is an even mix of claimant/applicant and defendant/respondent instructions, although much of the most profitable defendant work goes to senior tenants. Timothy Brennan QC has recently been acting for former Cantor Fitzgerald employee Steve Horkulak in his £1.5 million claim for constructive dismissal following abuse and bullying at work. Once, the set had key public law silk Richard Clayton among its number, but applicants looking for a public law set should be aware that there is now little work in this area. A solid institutional client base includes BT, Royal Mail, a number of trade unions and transport giant Stagecoach.

If you're visiting Devereux Chambers, take our advice and leave yourself an extra half-hour to find it. After you've wandered aimlessly around Middle Temple and the Queen Elizabeth Building, you'll need at least ten minutes to find your way up through Devereux Court, and then another ten to negotiate the hordes of tourists being led by a mockney-accented woman dressed in Victorian garb. But when you do locate chambers, down a cobbled alleyway opposite the Royal Courts of Justice, you'll be delighted. Behind the unassuming exterior, the reception room – coir matting, dark wood, sleek black leather – serves a set that is split over two premises. While most members and staff are in Devereux Court, a cluster of juniors occupies rooms in Queen Elizabeth Building on the Embankment.

On arriving at the room of one senior junior, he proudly proclaimed in a cry reminiscent of Axel Rose: *"Welcome to the dungeon!"* Actually, it was far from dungeon-like, with CDs scattered on the desk (The Streets, Tears For Fears, Jazz Greats) and a fan humming away in the corner. Instantly, you appreciate that Devereux prides itself on its *"friendly, unstuffy culture."* As the head of the pupillage committee told us: *"It's not our style to drone on with the 'hereinbefores' and the 'humbly craves'." "On the basis that advocacy is about communication, it works better if you're downbeat rather than highfalutin'."* This is a set that is *"not afraid of being funny in court,"* so long as it's not *"trivialising or disrespectful."* Indeed, a former member, now a judge, once said: *"One of the most effective things you can do as an advocate is make your tribunal like you."*

The set receives almost 300 pupillage applications each year. The usual academic and extra-curricular achievements are considered alongside *"a good turn of phrase."* Those who impress at first interview (CV-based discussion plus ethical conundrum) progress to a second, more rigorous, test of advocacy skills based on a problem handed out half an hour beforehand. This year's question was set in the fictional jurisdiction of Utopia, a place singularly unused to legal drama. Clarity of thought and expression are the main qualities recruiters seek. As one told us: *"You hear an awful lot of verbal ticks. That doesn't help. Obviously people are nervous, and this is why fluency and clarity are impressive."* More important than clarity of speech is clarity of analysis, since *"speaking can be learned more easily than thinking."*

Pupils rotate around the same three supervisors, one from each of the set's core areas of practice. The assessment regime has been *"smartened up"* in the past year and there are now formal tests throughout pupillage. There are two advocacy assessments in which pupils are given 24 hours to prepare a skeleton and present before a panel. One member of the panel is a judge, and pupils perform against a junior tenant who recently argued the same facts in court. It is, as one junior told us, *"terribly nerve-wracking,"* but great practice, and a way for pupils to hone their advocacy skills before embarking on real-life hearings. Despite the assessment regime, former pupils were adamant that pupillage did not feel like a miserable exercise in perpetual grovelling and self-abasement: *"You feel they want you to be* taken on. You feel they're on your side." To this end, feedback is *"honest and forthright"* and given with a view to improving the skills of pupils.

The tenancy decision is made in July, and pupils start working in their own name from the start of the second six. During this period, you can expect to be on your feet up to twice a week, feasting on a diet of small claims, RTAs and applications concerning expert evidence. Court appearances are mixed in with paper and advisory work for members of chambers. Second-six pupils also work closely with baby juniors to prepare them for tenancy. Employment and personal injury form the bread and butter for inexperienced juniors, who will also occasionally assist more senior members on larger commercial matters. There are no guaranteed minimum earnings for juniors, because there don't need to be. Happily, for the most part, they are busy from the outset and clients pay up relatively quickly.

Life at the Bar can be an isolated existence; indeed, many barristers tell us they are attracted by the idea of *"individual challenges."* As we sat in the stark office of one baby junior over in the QEB annexe, it was hard not to feel distanced from the action up in Devereux Court. That is until the dungeon keeper we'd met earlier cheerily poked his head through the open window: *"Just checking in on you!"* When barristers tell us that their set is *"like a family"* we're always a little wary; after all, families can bring out the worst in each other as well as the best. Yet, something rang true when we heard the claim at Devereux. It was a Friday afternoon when we visited and, as we said our goodbyes, members and staff were packing up and preparing to head to the pub. Aside from The Puzzle (run by one member's wife), The Edgar Wallace is a den of choice, as is 'The Dev', from which members can practically order beers from their office windows. We left the barristers standing around, drinks in hand, chatting in the mottled sunlight – just as they've probably done for hundreds of years.

Doughty Street Chambers

the facts

OLPAS: summer season **Pupillages:** 4x12 months
Applications: 200-300 **Mini pupillages:** 24
First interview: c.50 **Second interview:** 20
Award: £15,000
Tenancies offered in 2003: 1 to a pupil
Chambers UK rankings: Administrative & public law, clinical negligence, crime, human rights, immigration, personal injury, police law, product liability

"Defending freedom and citizens' rights" is this set's raison d'être. Founded in 1990, its reputation is inextricably linked with that of the inimitable Australian legal personality Geoffrey Robertson QC. Members are renowned as human rights' crusaders, advising in major prisoners' rights, sentencing, mental health, extradition and death row cases. Members were involved in the Hughes, Reyes and Fox cases that were influential in the abolition of mandatory life sentences in the Caribbean, while Geoffrey Robertson QC has been appointed as Appeal Judge for the new Special Court in Sierra Leone, set up to try cases of war crimes and crimes against humanity. Some members, including Geoffrey Robertson, feature in *Chambers UK*'s defamation rankings for their work with newspapers and journalists.

The self-proclaimed *"warm and cuddly"* end of the Bar, Doughty Street is, according to some, the ideal antidote to the stuffiness, conservatism and pomposity that characterises certain other sets. It prides itself on a commitment to equal opportunities so don't bother dry-cleaning the old school tie for your pupillage interview. It may be recognised for its egalitarian and rather self-consciously informal culture, but don't be deceived. Like the iron fist in the velvet glove, this is a seriously and ambitious set with a commitment to client service and quality, supported by an organised and efficient administration. As one pupil put it: *"The atmosphere is laid back, but work-wise, it's very intense."*

Seventy-four members are housed in a Georgian terraced property on the moral high ground of Doughty Street, not far from Russell Square. The area has as much in common with the arts and literature as the Bar: Charles Dickens published *The Pickwick Papers*, *Oliver Twist* and *Nicholas Nickleby* while living a few doors away. Could the ghosts of social crusaders past have swept through the set? The premises are basic, neutral and non-threatening; instead of grandiose oil paintings, there's just some fairly simple art adding a modicum of interest to the plain white walls. Think neat and tidy B&B or law centre.

Mini pupillages are structured as a week-long course, during which you'll follow a single case of your choosing. By day you'll conduct research, attend conferences and sit in court; each evening, there are seminars given by specialists in different areas of law. Academic credentials, while important, are by no means the be-all and end-all at this set. More importantly, applicants must demonstrate a commitment to welfare and human rights, either through voluntary or community work or overcoming personal challenges. Few pupils come fresh out of university, since the set *"tends towards people with more life experience."* The youngest pupil we spoke to was 26. Around a third of applicants make it to the first interview – a casual getting to know you. Those who reach stage two must give a presentation on a topical legal or ethical question. It is designed to test your knowledge of current affairs, analytical ability and presentation skills. Questions usually have a human rights or civil liberties bent, eg 'Do paedophiles have a right to privacy?' We doubt it's wise to respond 'No! They should all be outed on the evening news before being chemically sterilised.' And a word of advice: do not walk into this interview without having revised the Human Rights Act.

Your first six will be paper-intensive, and chances are you'll cut your teeth on smaller immigration matters. You will be given feedback on each piece of work you do, and while you're allocated a supervisor for the entire pupillage, pupils are also encouraged to do work for other members. Whereas some people believe pupils should be seen and not heard, those at Doughty Street are *"never made to feel small."* If you want to work with a particular tenant, just ask, and pupils are often included on the sexier international and human rights matters. Our sources spoke of a *"supportive"* atmosphere, with one junior tenant commenting: *"The preparation is incredible. As a junior, when I appear for someone else, the case is always amazingly well prepared...I never feel like I've been dropped in it."* And the support extends to a unique commitment to the personal and career development of members and staff. Apparently, most people feel comfortable telling clerks: *"I won't be in on Thursday this week, I'm doing voluntary work at a shelter."* This flexible approach enables members to work with international tribunals, on death row cases and in public interest matters. Tenants here are positively encouraged to have exciting, high-profile careers.

Pupils must go through the whole year before finding out about tenancy. The whole set makes the decision, basing it on a formal written assessment and an interview. Pupils are tested in a range of legal areas and papers are marked blind. You don't need us to tell you the process is hugely stressful, with only one in four pupils usually attaining tenancy. However, those we interviewed insisted that there is no tension between pupils. Friendships form around professional relationships, and where some sets boast formal afternoon tea, Doughty Street has Friday night drinks in the local pub, which often turn into late nights at one or other of the barristers' homes.

All pupils boast impressive resumés and all have had first-hand experience in human rights or welfare-related fields. When we visited, one was a trained mental health nurse and NHS consultant; one was a consultant on Russian development and two others taught in Africa. The junior tenant we spoke to worked for two years as a volunteer at the centre for Advice on Individual Rights in Europe (AIRE). He applied for pupillages prior to his work at AIRE and got nothing. Disheartened, he embarked on two years of penury as a volunteer and later found himself with a slew of offers from chambers. It's a lesson for anyone wanting to get into Doughty Street or similar sets.

Just remember that this is human rights at a distance: if it is direct client contact you want, you should consider going to a solicitors firm. But whether it's the set's inspirational and high-profile crusaders, its reputation for progressive attitudes or the *"electric"* energy of the place, for its pupils at least, Doughty Street remains the *"cool"* set.

Erskine Chambers

the facts

OLPAS: No **Pupillages:** 2x12 months
Applications: over 100 **Mini pupillages:** no limit
First interview: 10 **Second interview:** 4-5
Award: £35,000 (funds can be advanced for BVC)
Tenancies offered in 2003: 2
Chambers UK rankings: Banking & finance, company, financial services, insolvency

Erskine Chambers is a one-off. After a modest start in 24 Old Buildings, it moved in the 1980s to the premises in the north-east corner of Lincoln's Inn Fields, from which it took its name. We were greatly disappointed to learn this as we'd hoped the set's pedigree stretched back to the early 19th century Lord Chancellor Erskine who, rumour has it, trained his dog to wear a wig and sit with his paws on an open book.

To say that this is the leading company law set doesn't emphasise sufficiently its dominance of that field. So let's put it like this: no other set comes close to commanding the respect that Erskine does for advice and advocacy on company law matters. Its barristers are so in demand that some 70% of cases are fought against other members of the set. Nine members are QCs, including head of chambers Robin Potts. The previous head, Richard Sykes, was a real influence: *"In City circles he was an oracle and his advice would be treated with the respect it deserved."*

Erskine receives fewer applications than other leading commercial sets and it is seen by many students as too specialised, too company law-led and too advisory-based. We put this to the secretary of the pupillage committee. *"It's not true to say that all our stuff is out of the Companies Act,"* he told us. *"Traditionally we've had a leaning towards advisory work,"* but now *"most barristers here do a mix of advisory work and litigation."* If you have a general interest in business matters, this is a set to consider alongside the usual suspects of the commercial Bar.

Erskine barristers have adapted to the way in which their instructing solicitors do business. With the rise of IT systems and the general advance in the volume of corporate transactions over the last two decades, solicitors recycle the structures of deals wherever possible. This leaves the role of the company law barrister as that of underwriter. Where there is an issue on a point of principle or concerns about the effect or legality of changes made to a transaction, the call will go out to an Erskine barrister. *"It's not unusual to get that call at 5pm, and you've got to deal with it immediately because the client will want to complete the transaction that night."* Consequently to succeed here you've got to be *"responsive"* and *"commercially minded."*

On the contentious side, the work spills over into commercial disputes, especially where there is a company law angle. Indeed, an Erskine barrister may have the edge over their peers in that they might go looking for such an angle and find it before anyone else. Naturally twinned with company law, insolvency and corporate restructuring feature often, and in the early years you'll see more than your fair share of winding-up petitions, leading on to full-day court appointments and injunctions to prevent the advertisement of petitions. Directors' disqualifications and shareholder disputes will also come in thick and fast. *"We always have lots of little stocking fillers to keep them busy,"* a pupilmaster told us in typically understated style. Amazingly, we heard: *"We have no demand for dogsbodies to trawl through mountains of disclosure. If we do get it, we will get in a junior from another set."* Result!

And there's more: *"As a junior here, very quickly you'll find yourself against someone more senior."* But, *"we are good about not sending people into battle without the right armour."*

Erskine has a rather kindly approach to its pupils. It will keep them out of the spotlight during the initial three-month period with their first pupilmaster. In the second three months, another PM will gradually ease them into the mainstream and the pupil will also start to take on work for other members. Of PMs, one source said: *"Some have a more advisory leaning and others have more commercial litigation than pure company law cases."*

The set makes its tenancy decision after six months, allowing an unsuccessful pupil time to head off elsewhere for a second six. And how does the set know if it has picked a winner? *"It's a cocktail. You know when you see too much of one thing and too little of another."* Our interpretation of this cryptic comment is slightly bookish but with a businesslike mind, a steady, logical thinker, confident, calm and reassuring, happy to be alone much of the time, and very likeable. As for the work, ask yourself if you really enjoy the academic study of law. Think about how you'd enjoy *"some horribly knotty problem and spending a week or so tackling it to the exclusion of all else."*

In spite of – who knows, perhaps because of – the set's phenomenal success, it immediately strikes you as a calm and almost gentle place. No rushing around, no egos bumping off the corridor walls like pinball bearings. Our theory is that the frequency with which members act against each other has led to the erection of more Chinese walls than were ever built by the Ming Dynasty. They may take chambers tea at 5pm and chat about the weather and what judge so-and-so probably thought about such-and-such a case, but this is pretty much it for socialising and our younger sources found the job a fairly solitary experience. The doors to barristers' rooms were mostly closed when we visited, and we noted that the phone calls our sources received were almost always on their personal mobiles. This is definitely a set where you get your head down and work, and you learn to be self-reliant, yet there is a network of colleagues to call upon so you shouldn't feel like you've been set adrift.

Erskine's character is not heavily influenced by a handful of instructing firms; work comes from all quarters. It's a *"pretty egalitarian"* set that is member-driven and *"pretty close to one person, one vote."* At chambers tea, pupils tend to keep quiet in the early months, but if one did pipe up with something, *"it's not like everyone would turn around and stare as if the dog had just spoken!"* We must confess, we liked the place and we liked the people we met. In this quiet and measured chambers, carefulness and brainpower fuse into something utterly impressive.

Essex Court Chambers

the facts

OLPAS: summer season **Pupillages:** 4x12 months
Applications: not disclosed **Mini pupillages:** 30
Interviews: not disclosed
Award: £37,500 (funds can be advanced for BVC)
Tenancies offered in 2003: 2
Chambers UK rankings: Aviation, banking & finance, commercial litigation, employment, energy & natural resources, civil fraud, insurance, international arbitration, media & entertainment, public international law, shipping

Set up in 1961 by five *"bright but disparate self-made men"* who proceeded to have illustrious careers and took leading judicial positions, Essex Court Chambers is one of the magic circle of commercial sets. It boasts some of the big names at the Bar: QCs Gordon Pollock, VV Veeder and Andrew Hochhauser, and new silk Joe Smouha. Recent big cases include Lloyd's v Jaffray, Barings v Coopers & Lybrand and BCCI v Bank of England.

If you're wondering how Essex Court's practice differs from close rivals then note that, in addition to mainstream commercial work, there's a strong emphasis on insurance, reinsurance, shipping and international arbitration. Firms like Clyde & Co, Barlow Lyde & Gilbert, Ince & Co and Holman Fenwick & Willan instruct the set on behalf of clients that include foreign shipowners, P&I clubs and reinsurance companies. One of our more senior sources told us that his work was commonly *"off-beam – a bit more fun"* and required an *"imaginative"* approach.

In pupillage, the first six months is a period of observation when you'll work for your main pupilmaster for three months and then for a maximum of five others in your second three. All pupils work for the same group of barristers. Sometimes you'll be in court shadowing your PM, but it's more likely that you'll be in the library researching points of law or their room writing a skeleton argument or opinion. By the end of March you will be told whether or not you have a future at Essex Court. All our sources thought this to be an extremely practical arrangement. Unsuccessful pupils are not forced to leave, but are unlikely to stay as the advantage of moving to another set for the second six is clear. Clutching persuasive references, they commonly slip into other well-respected sets becoming *"cuckoos in the nest elsewhere."*

The pupils who stay can heave a sigh of relief and concentrate on another six months of learning...but not earning. *"We don't encourage paid work or advocacy in the second six,"* one pupilmaster told us. *"They cut their teeth on that once they are a tenant."* So while your peers at other sets will be on their feet in court, you'll still be at your master's side, observing and researching smaller points on their mega-sized, mega-value cases. Patience is required. Our sources assured us that the approach pays off. Occasionally, a second-sixer might be loaned out to a law firm or sent to visit Lloyd's of London for a spell. The average working day stretches from 8.30am-7pm, and although it's fair to say that some members choose to drive themselves rather hard, pupils don't appear to be bent out of shape by long hours.

The set's caseload is broad – some barristers specialise, but there is a prevailing generalist ethos, particularly at the junior end. It's not really possible to pigeonhole members either by background or personality: apparently, *"the poshest people around work alongside people with entirely working-class backgrounds."* Our sources used various words to describe the set: *"a meritocracy," "pink-tinged but with some Tories too,"* and *"a broad church/synagogue."* Whether you're *"left, right, snobbish or violently egalitarian,"* what counts is that you're talented. And confident. Brave even. We wondered if the idea of working with the big names at the commercial Bar was at all intimidating. *"No! That's what's great about it,"* a pupil explained. *"You've got to be in it to win it,"* another source said of his decision to apply to a set that's at the top of the commercial tree. *"The cost of trying is not that high, but the prize is huge."* Another benefit is an absence of competitive behaviour within chambers. *"People don't have things to prove to each other. At lesser sets, barristers are keen to let each other know how busy they are and how good they are."*

Having established that there are eccentrics, legendary advocates and highly academic boffins all co-existing within the set's five adjoining buildings on the north side of Lincoln's Inn Fields, we turned our attention to the eclectic premises. Visitors to the set (which people refer to as having broken away from the Temple) are first presented with the old: leather armchairs and marble columns in the waiting room, and then the new: stylish, modern conference rooms that feel more City than Inns of Court. As for the remainder of chambers, it's somewhat warren-like, and everyone's room is different – from ornamental trees, chandeliers and flowing curtains to shrines to minimalism and modern art.

There's no chambers tea; instead, on Fridays, 30-40 barristers will gather for lunch to chat about their cases...or maybe their weekend plans. Pupils are welcome and can end up in conversation with senior members quite easily. *"Gordon Pollock is always there telling stories,"* one pupil revealed. The social scene could never be described as big, but some of the juniors go out for drinks on Friday night.

Clerks generally call members by their surnames, particularly seniors, but with juniors this tradition is easing. Actually, no commentary on Essex Court would be complete without a reference to its impressive clerking. Senior clerk David Grief (who's been doing the business since 1980) is an important figure and highly respected in the profession. You'll meet him on the four to five-strong pupillage interview panel. Essex Court picks its pupils after a single interview, so you'll need to make the most of your one shot at getting into the set. It will be tough, but remember that the other applicants will be in the same boat. How you approach and tackle the problem question you'll be set is crucial. As is talent and a self-belief, so prepare as fully as you can and put your best foot forward.

One Essex Court

the facts

OLPAS: summer season **Pupillages:** 4 x12 months
Applications: 200-250 **Mini pupillages:** 20
Interview: 40
Award: £37,500 (2004); £40,000 (2005) (£12,500 can be advanced for BVC)
Tenancies offered in 2003: 3
Chambers UK rankings: Banking & finance, commercial litigation, energy & natural resources, civil fraud, intellectual property, international arbitration, tax

In the four decades since One Essex Court was established, it has transformed from a general common law set into one of the magic circle of commercial players. Its head of chambers is the inimitable Lord Grabiner QC; fellow silks, including Nicholas Strauss, Mark Barnes and Laurence Rabinowitz, also enjoy much of the limelight.

In the 1970s Sam Stamler QC and two of his former pupils, Grabiner and Strauss, took the lead in developing the set's commercial work, initially through a relationship with Slaughter and May. The way in which Stamler worked and taught his pupils is responsible for the set's approach today: *"One case at a time with plenty of preparation beforehand and gaps between cases…quality conscious and really rigorous."* The fees may be at the higher end of the scale, but *"you can absolutely rely on the barrister you have instructed being available to do the job properly."* 30 years on and important work still comes from Slaughters, as well as firms like Herbert Smith, Freshfields, Clifford Chance and Baker & McKenzie. Rather like Slaughters, OEC believes that the best lawyers can turn their hand to all manner of commercial matters. *"The generalist ethos is very strong."*

This set believes advocates are made not born, but as one pupilmaster stressed: *"We can turn someone into a fine advocate, but they have to get a buzz out of standing up and giving it some welly."* Don't underestimate the amount of written advocacy that will be required of you: *"Everything you do is advocacy; every opinion you write, every skeleton argument; they all require you to persuade."* The complexity of cases means that the most important thing a pupil can possess is a practical problem-solving ability. As one explained: *"The facts of cases can be so complicated; you might have up to 14 parties to a single case."*

Cerebral it may be but ivory-towered it isn't. *"We don't want a brain in a jar,"* said one barrister. *"It's not about giving dry legal advice; a client in conference wants a solution to their problem. How can we improve things? Where do we go from here?" "If you like things to be fast-paced and you are happy to work really hard,"* then *"you can be yourself."* We suspect it's important to be exactly that; a 40-year masquerade would certainly fray the nerves. Of his seniors, one pupil told us: *"Mostly they are smiling, chirpy people rather than great brooding intellects."* While we don't doubt that OEC is stuffed full of interesting and personable characters who show a healthy respect for each other, the very fact that pupils are experiencing life at the pointy end of the commercial Bar can induce a fair few knee wobbles. *"The biggest nightmare is doing something wrong for someone important."* Pupils have to work hard to adapt to the high standards of this set and to learn how to produce excellent work on complicated cases. All this and making sure you get your name known around chambers.

You'll have a minimum of three pupilmasters, each of whom will have a broad practice (although you might request an IP specialist if that were your bag). Your first six will be reasonably chambers-based – legal research, drafting opinions and skeleton arguments etc. *"It's not just disembodied parts of larger cases,"* we were told. In the second six you'll also tackle your own paid work. *"There's a huge emphasis on getting people on their feet in court – wherever or whatever – because hearing your own voice is crucial."* Many of the set's cases are huge, so juniors take a second or third counsel role, but the clerks also encourage smaller instructions, allowing juniors to run cases by themselves. Over 2,000 firms send instructions, although 35% of the fees come from half-a-dozen City firms. These clients expect their barristers to have plenty of confidence and to be decisive. Maybe this is why the pupillage interview was likened by one source to *"cruel torture."*

The decor at One Essex Court (and Nos.2, 3 and now 4) gives a nod to tradition, but we got the impression that this was simply the default setting for commercial sets in the Temple. OEC doesn't appear to be trying hard to create an image for itself. We'd also guess that precious little time is devoted to committees with a remit to expanding chambers' business. *"I don't think in terms of where I want chambers to be,"* one barrister told us. The fact is, OEC is already at the top of its game. Big-name barristers generate more than enough work for themselves, and an impressive clerking system obviates the need to put on a song and dance to attract clients. *"Solicitors love our clerks,"* one barrister boasted of the administrative team. *"Generous staffing levels"* reflect the set's unhurried approach. For 'unhurried' don't read 'slow', read 'calm'. Sources outside chambers say that the power of the senior clerks should never be underestimated at OEC; indeed, our sources inside the set readily admitted that they have a *"huge influence"* on all aspects of the business.

OEC doesn't parade a long list of old members who've gone to the bench: *"Most of us are people from pretty ordinary backgrounds who have done well academically...we like to think that we're not stuffy."* But as in most sets, there's the odd eccentric and the place is no doubt the richer for them. Pupillage literature indicates chambers tea is a once-weekly affair, but that might be overbilling the event. The wise pupil will attend Friday evening drinks in chambers. One-off events aside, this is where the social scene stops. However, *"you don't come in, clock on, do your timesheets and leave."* There is a reasonable amount of interaction between colleagues and *"plenty of e-mail exchanges!"* As for the dress code, the wise pupil errs on the side of the wardrobe where smart suits hang.

Some final advice: first, show a positive disposition at all times. In such a well-run set with such great opportunities, you really oughtn't to have anything to complain about. And second, good enough isn't actually good enough – chambers values complete attention to detail and rigour of analysis. Reflect these traits in your application.

20 Essex Street

the facts

OLPAS: summer season **Pupillages:** 3-5x12 months
Applications: 133 **Mini pupillages:** 17
First interview: 31
Award: £34,000 (£8,000 can be advanced for BVC)
Tenancies offered in 2003: 1
Chambers UK rankings: Banking & finance, commercial litigation, insurance, international arbitration, public international law, shipping

Established in 1926, 20 Essex Street is the UK's premier shipping and international law set. Huddled amidst the other commercial heavyweights in Essex Street, No.20 boasts some of the biggest names in their fields. Its list of members past and present reads like a Who's Who of international and shipping law. Former judges in the International Court of Justice Lord Arnold McNair and Sir Hersch Lauterpacht were door tenants, and international law gurus continue to pad the corridors today. Sir Elihu Lauterpacht maintains the family tradition, and Sir Arthur Watts QC has appeared in major international disputes, acting as counsel for New Zealand against France in the Nuclear Tests cases, and as counsel for Nigeria in its boundary dispute with Cameroon. But we must stop. While the set is undoubtedly outstanding in public international law, it is wary of *"over-promoting"* this area of practice to prospective pupils. *"You don't go into law and then decide to practice PIL. It's not like commercial law."* Most in this game have a diplomatic or academic career under their belts before embarking on practice.

While its reputation largely revolves around shipping and international law, this is more than just a shipping set. Yes, it is instructed by the biggest names in the shipping world – Holman Fenwick & Willan, Ince & Co, Richards Butler and Clyde & Co – but No.20 is now receiving more instructions from the likes of Linklaters, Allen & Overy and Herbert Smith. Its involvement in the £2.5 billion claim by Equitable Life against former auditors and directors is a perfect example of its general litigation.

Behind a Queen Anne façade, the interior of No.20 is refined, if not conservative. In reception, steel grey carpet meets walls of leather-bound law reports and, conforming to stereotype, the set has hung a gilt-framed oil depicting a lighthouse in a tempest. Sinking into a faded red damask sofa, visitors can leaf through *The Spectator*, *Country Life*, the *FT* or, the joker in the pack, *The Magnificent 92: Indiana Courthouses.* (And magnificent they are.) A potted palm sits motionless in the corner and the noise and flurry of Fleet Street seems a mile away from this silent room. Silent, but for the rhythmic tick-tock-tick of the clock and the shloop of pages turning slowly.

It should come as no surprise that in this law library atmosphere pupillage is a highly academic affair. If you're hankering after the cut and thrust of courtroom advocacy in your second six, go elsewhere. Read on if complex legal problems and opinion writing in an intellectual environment appeal.

No. 20 takes between three and five pupils annually, each of whom sit with a different pupilmaster each term. During your first 'finding your feet' term, your work will come almost exclusively from your PM and you'll be blessedly free of advocacy exercises. After the New Year, these begin and continue every month or two until the end of pupillage. Meanwhile, your PM's job becomes less about giving you work and more about supervising your diary. You will not work in your own name during your second six, and you certainly won't be on your feet. Shortly before the end of the first six, tenancy prospects are reviewed; those not making the grade are advised to set up a second six elsewhere. The tenancy decision is made in July and based on the views of anyone who has seen the work of pupils. As to whether or not there's a quota for tenancies: *"Good people will make a name for themselves. There's no point turning them away because there's not enough work at that particular time."* In the early years, you can expect to assist senior members, although clerks have built relationships with solicitors doing small, routine work for big commercial clients. You should also be aware that around half of the set's work is comprised of arbitrations.

On most days, pupils arrive at 8.30am and leave at around 6pm. Even if they wanted to work on weekends, they'd have some trouble, since no one gets a key to chambers until they are made a tenant.

The set receives only a modest number of pupillage applications, and this may in part be due to its fearsome reputation for intellectual vigour. *"It sounds terrible,"* one insider told us, *"but you need to be more than a solid 2:1 person to cope with our work."* No, not so terrible. What marks one excellent applicant out from the others is *"a well-rounded CV"* that shows you are *"more than just a library bookworm."* The interview consists of a problem question based on a real case that a member of chambers has worked on. It aims to identify an understanding of first principles, logical/analytical ability and interpretative skills. To introduce a spanner into the works, the panel will make regular interjections, not unlike those a judge would make in court. Time to produce the three 'C's – clarity, coherence and calm. Be sure to keep abreast of current issues: in 2003, the panel were unable to resist asking applicants for their views on the abolition of the Lord Chancellor's role and Blair's constitutional reshuffle. You'll need academic ability teamed with *"a personality that will be effective in court and effective in front of clients."*

One tenant remarked: *"We are a club, a collection of equals."* The social life is suitably warm and low-key. There is chambers tea at 4.30pm in the common room – a chance to have a cup of tea (*"and cake if we're lucky"*) in front of the cricket or the golf on Sky. Every now and then there are drinks parties and groups of juniors will occasionally head out for a beer together. Chambers football matches are a competitive affair; in the bitter rivalry between clerks and barristers, clerks seem to have the edge.

20 Essex Street is refined and academic without being arrogant. We found its members to be charming, polite and unassuming, but fiercely intelligent and legally gifted. Apparently, people used to say of this set: *"There are gentlemen and players, and you people are gentlemen."* And ladies, of course.

Fountain Court

the facts

OLPAS: summer season **Pupillages:** 4x12 months
Applications: 200 **Mini pupillages:** 30-40
First interview: 45 **Second interview:** 12
Award: £34,000 (funds can be advanced for BVC)
Tenancies offered in 2003: 3
Chambers UK rankings: Aviation, banking & finance, commercial litigation, energy & natural resources, civil fraud, insurance, international arbitration, professional negligence.

One of the Bar's magic circle of heavyweight commercial sets, Fountain Court straddles Essex Street and sits in the shadows of the RCJ. Originally a common law set, it moved into commercial work during the practising heyday of Lord Bingham (senior Law Lord, formerly Lord Chief Justice and Master of the Rolls), but still retains the generalist approach of its past. It boasts some big-name QCs, such as Anthony Boswood, new joint head of chambers Michael Brindle, new silk Bankim Thanki and the Attorney General, Lord Goldsmith.

Most members have a broad commercial practice, although a few specialise, most notably in insurance. Your pupillage experience will reflect this breadth, although you could sit with a specialist pupilmaster if their practice matched your career aspirations. In your first three months, you'll stick to your PM's side and can breathe easy as none of your gaffes will count against you in the following June's tenancy decision. In the second three, you'll see pupil-sized chunks of a new PM's work and you'll also do things for other members. After this, a third PM will be notionally responsible for you, and then for your final months (after the tenancy decision), you'll return to your first PM to show them just how far you've developed. Your diet of work will include banking, insurance, general commercial/contractual matters, aviation (eg the DVT case), professional negligence and, if you're lucky, perhaps some copyright or employment. Expect an average day of 9am-7pm.

Apply elsewhere if you want to be on your feet in court every other day, as *"mostly you'll be sitting at your desk doing paperwork."* Also, *"there's very little contact with* [lay] *clients; conferences are usually with the solicitor."* Very good relationships exist with magic circle firms like Freshfields, Slaughter and May and Linklaters, plus others like Barlow Lyde & Gilbert, CMS Cameron McKenna and Herbert Smith. Think big-money, high-profile instructions: BCCI and spin-offs including Three Rivers, Cape v Lubbe (first group action by foreign claimants and the largest), and the Britvic benzene contamination case. Your involvement as a pupil or very junior member of chambers will be low-level and paper-based. Patience is a virtue at Fountain Court.

A big, fierce and full-on set? Yes, no and sort of. Chambers is spread across three buildings – the main one behind the fountain in the appropriately named courtyard and just around the corner from Temple Church, the other two in annexes at 11 and 14 Essex Street. The premises appear neutral and business-like. The library in the basement is well organised, if a touch claustrophobic. The tearoom is modern and large enough to hold most members, but the 4pm tea ritual apparently declined after Lord Falconer (new Lord Chancellor and Secretary of State for Constitutional Affairs) left in 1997. Members are more likely to be in their rooms writing advices than gathering to discuss their day in court. The dress code? Most will be suited; others might opt for smart casual. The reaction of friends might be *"Oh God, you poor thing!"* when you tell them you've got pupillage here; they might see the set as *"a ruthless law machine where you'll be worked to death."* However, those we spoke to were categorical in their rebuttal. *"Pupillage is much better than I expected,"* said one. *"People are not stuffy and barristerial. Yes, they are keen and some are overachievers, but they are not arrogant."* As a seasoned member told us: *"People are quite decent to each other…considerate…pupils are well treated and respected. The job can be stressful so we make it as nice as it can be."*

Which sounds like a fair description of the first-round interview for pupillage. *"It was very informal with more junior people,"* said one pupil. *"I was quite surprised as it was more of a chat."* But be prepared for a more exacting experience if you are asked back. *"The second one is much more formal…and there will always be someone on the panel who will be devil's advocate."*

The ideal applicant will have a top-notch academic record. Those wondering if they are cut out for this set should ask themselves if they enjoy an academic challenge and can hold their own among those who are used to success. Do you relish the process of writing an essay – the research, structuring and argument and building up the end product? As with essays, the written work you'll handle in chambers requires that *"you enjoy the challenge for itself, irrespective of whether or not you are interested in the subject matter."* This is an intellectual set that prides itself on thorough preparation and impeccable conduct of the litigation process. *"People here are clever, but they wear it quite lightly."* Pushy, ruthless or over pompous types will soon encounter deflating comments, we heard, but we sensed a touch of self-satisfaction. Maybe that's fair – make it here and you've a lot to be satisfied with. Junior members are a mixed bag of old Etonians and the state educated and, to pass muster and make it as one of them, you must display *"consistency, thoroughness and a good written style."* Your 'solicitor appeal' is also crucial as litigators from the biggest City firms will instruct you on mammoth cases and you'll deal with them over extended periods of time. They must like and trust you, and you must be able to add something to their team…both intellectually and in terms of 'presence'.

While new pupils are welcomed with a drinks party, this is not a set that parties non-stop. The pupils we met hinted that they weren't joined at the hip and realised that, ultimately, they'd be in direct competition with each other for tenancy. However, generally, a collaborative ethos pervades chambers. Indeed, we were delighted to discover a Highgate Massive – quite a number of members live in this part of north London, some within a few streets of each other…even sharing the same cleaning lady. And while we're on the subject of cleaning, we are reliably informed that Tuesday is shoeshine day. Don't worry, pupils are not expected to run around with a tin of Kiwi – someone comes in to perform the task.

"This is not a clerk-driven set," we heard; members are definitely in control. In part, this means that clerks are less pushy in terms of foisting work on barristers or foisting particular barristers on instructing solicitors. Clerks do call members by their surnames, particularly seniors, although pupils were a bit unsure as to correct forms of address (or indeed if there were any). This is certainly not a stuffy old set, but we did sense pupils needed to ease themselves in to the place slowly and discreetly.

Two Garden Court

the facts

OLPAS: summer season **Pupillages:** 6x12 months
Applications: 700 **Mini pupillages:** 46
Interviews: 30-40
Award: £12,000 plus earnings
Tenancies offered in 2003: 1 (plus 4 lateral transfers)
Chambers UK rankings: Administrative & public law, crime, human rights, immigration, police law, social housing

Hatched in the liberal dreamscape of the mid-1970s, Two Garden Court has made good on its promise to undertake morally and socially progressive work. From its self-proclaimed *"revolutionary, if not subversive"* beginnings, the set has grown from six barristers pretty fresh out of pupillage to some 79 tenants. Its immigration practice is pre-eminent, boasting the man *Chambers UK* described as the *"guru and greatest brain in the field,"* Laurie Fransman QC. The courage and zeal of the set is reflected in its motto "Do right, fear no one."

Members and pupils pride themselves on working for *"vulnerable people,"* and although the set is unabashed about its values, it is not self-righteous or superior. Modesty is scarcely a barristerial trait, but we found a trace of it here. In age and ethnic background, the members are a diverse lot, and the fact that many joined the Bar later in life may explain the lack of *"Bar culture."*

The set's chief premises overlook the idyllic Garden Court and Middle Temple Hall. Yet we found that even the scent of roses and lavender wafting through the windows of the reception area did nothing to soften its alarming resemblance to the waiting room of an NHS dental surgery. The framed certificates on the walls (Quality Mark, Bar Mark, Certificate of Registration), and a pinboard boasting such fascinating reading as 'You and your barrister' and 'Having a job understanding employment law?' left us with a decided feeling of dental unease. Perhaps that's the way its clients like it – housing advice and root canal work all in one day.

Under its new regime, the set will offer six 12-month pupillages. There are no tenancies offered at the end of pupillage – if a place for a junior tenant arises, it is advertised to all-comers. The reasoning behind this system is to ensure equal opportunity for all and to guarantee that the set sees the best applicants. It means that this pupillage is regarded first and foremost as a training, rather than as the entry point for tenancy. Luckily, the set's pupils have a high success rate elsewhere and, if necessary, are welcome to stay for a third six while searching for permanent membership at another chambers.

Here, your expectations will be both fulfilled and confounded. The junior tenant we met was kitted out in a Gap T-shirt, rolled up jeans and sandals, but the senior member was suited. One of the pupils we met was a mature Oxbridge graduate, while the other was a 25-year-old from Aberdeen. And the work itself is diverse – from criminal to social housing, administrative and public law, family, human rights and immigration. Chambers tries to ensure that its pupils work in at least three areas of practice.

The set receives more applications than any other we've investigated, and to make it into the class of 30 or so that are interviewed, you must have a seriously impressive CV. A rare entity at the Bar, this appears to be a set that couldn't care less where you went to university. Furthermore, as one member of the pupillage committee told us: *"We don't care if someone had a poor degree when they were 21. We are looking for experience and commitment to the principles of the set."* And boy, have they found it. Those we spoke to own CVs that would make even Kofi Annan weep with envy. One enjoyed a successful career as a humanitarian monitor for the UN, Human Rights Watch and more non-government organisations than you can shake a stick at, while somehow managing to squeeze in a masters in international relations at Columbia University. Another worked for £12,000 a year at a legal charity, while studying part-time for an LL.M, before working as a volunteer on a capital punishment cases in New Orleans. There are several lessons to be learned from this. One is that, if at first you don't succeed (at getting pupillage), try, try again. Another is that age and experience are no impediment.

The pupillage interview consists of an advocacy exercise (eg a bail application) followed by a discussion of current legal issues. You should brush up on your knowledge of new and proposed criminal justice legislation and the HRA. As one member told us: *"Lack of knowledge and understanding of things in the wider world is a real turn-off for us."* And in keeping with its ethos of fairness and transparency, unsuccessful applicants can request feedback on their interview performance.

The set boasts a very organised and well-structured training scheme. Pupils are exposed to advocacy training and lectures on substantive areas of law, courtroom etiquette and legal developments. You'll change pupil supervisors after your first six, but are encouraged to maintain contact with your old mentor. In your second six, you'll have a two-week induction before appearing in court for the first time. After this, you'll be clerked for, on your feet, and *"on your own."* But not entirely. Pupils are encouraged to take the telephone numbers of members with them to court, and to use them. The set strives to ensure that second-sixers see a good dose of both criminal and civil (mostly immigration) work, to ensure remunerative equity. As you'd expect with criminal work, the hours are long as papers tend not to arrive until the end of the day.

With its elaborate bureaucracy and management structure (committees for the library, administration, personnel, professional administrators, the list goes on…), it is a quintessential child of the 70s. A largely member-driven and democratic set, even baby barristers can stroll into the lion's den of the clerk's room without fear. However, it's a large set and being spread over three sites puts it at a risk of fragmentation. As one member told us: *"If you are not careful, you risk seeing people only from your practice group."* Perhaps this is why there is a strong social dynamic, with organised dinners and weekends away. Chambers also organises women's nights out and annual summer and Christmas parties. The summer party – held in a nightclub – has achieved notoriety at the Bar.

Two Garden Court is replete with contradictions. While its motto may be "Do right, fear no one," it lacks the same reputation for all-out crusading of some of its competitors. The system of tenancy selection serves the set and outsiders well, but whether it is as ideal for its own pupils as it could be, we couldn't say. What we can say is that a pupillage here is extremely well regarded.

Hollis Whiteman Chambers

the facts

OLPAS: summer season **Pupillages:** 5x15 months
Applications: 250 **Mini pupillages:** available
First interview: 95 **Second interview:** 10
Award: £12,000 plus earnings
Tenancies offered in 2003: 2
Chambers UK rankings: Crime, criminal fraud

A leading crime set, Hollis Whiteman undertakes all areas of criminal law, both for the prosecution and defence. It has a particular emphasis on corporate and financial fraud, which has earned it top-dog status in *Chambers UK*. Recent high-profile matters include acting for the prosecution in the Sarah Payne murder trial, and in the trials of Meziane and Benmerzouga (Al Qaeda fundraising) and Paul Burrell. The set has recognised expertise in professional tribunals and public enquiries, appearing in the Victoria Climbié, Bloody Sunday and Stephen Lawrence enquiries.

The Hollis Whiteman story begins in 1947, when five barristers set up shop in Middle Temple Lane. By the 1950s, the set had grown to 12 and had to split to comply with Bar Council rules. The two sets later reunited to create a criminal megaset – the first with over 30 members – and moved into brand new premises at Queen Elizabeth Building next to the Thames and the greenery of Middle Temple Gardens. Chambers is decorated with the ubiquitous green upholstery and law reports lining the walls. Back issues of *Hello!* and *Better Homes & Gardens* are piled in the waiting room. It's traditional yet contemporary, conservative but not stifling.

Hollis Whiteman tenants are *"almost exclusively home grown,"* and while this has given it a reputation for *"self-containment and impenetrability,"* it has also lent it a *"harmonious family atmosphere."* Tenants are deeply loyal to the set and proud of its reputation for quality and commitment to *"the correct way of behaving."* Hollis Whiteman's identity is drawn from its ethos, rather than from a legacy of great names or eccentric characters. There are no prima donnas here: *"This set is bigger than the sum of its parts."* Members speak proudly of *"fairness in prosecution, honesty and diligence,"* and of a willingness to fight hard. *"Once work comes in, it will get done properly. There is a sense of pride in the name, and a collective responsibility for maintaining that."*

If it's advocacy training you're after, Hollis Whiteman is ideal. The pupillage lasts for 15 months and is organised into two parts. The first seven months of shadowing are paper-intensive, but you'll also receive weekly advocacy training and observe court hearings. Pupils share a room with their pupilmaster, but are encouraged to work for as many members as possible. After this, buy yourself some comfortable shoes, because you can expect to be on your feet every day for the next eight months. You're not alone, however, and remain under the guidance and support of your PM, who is there to allay any *"heebie-jeebies."*

We won't lie to you, the hours are long and the work can be stressful and challenging. Because Hollis Whiteman deliberately keeps pupil numbers low and refuses to accept squatters, pupils are on their feet and carry a lot of responsibility right from the outset. After a day in court or travelling, you should expect to return to chambers and perhaps end up staying until fairly late at night preparing for the next day in court. If the idea of *Law & Order*-style courtroom battles lured you to the Bar, you'll probably not find a better training ground, and by the end of pupillage, you will have appeared in at least 200 different hearings.

The tenancy decision is made in January, 15 months after the start of pupillage. This delay is to allow pupils the chance to work for the CPS, since to do this you must have completed 12 months of pupillage. There is no formal assessment procedure in determining who gets tenancy. Instead, pupils are observed on a daily basis throughout pupillage, are interviewed by the pupillage committee, and have a mock trial in the Old Bailey, during which aspiring Rumpoles *"get the chance to strut their stuff."* The opinions of tenants and clerks are canvassed, and uniquely, the committee also consults with solicitors, judges and Crown prosecutors.

The pupillage interview can take some applicants by surprise. You will be given a topical legal or ethical issue to address. Recent examples have included the separation of conjoined twins and the implications of holding suspected terrorists indefinitely without charge. One year, applicants were asked to pretend they were the public relations executive of Bristol Royal Infirmary and to explain why the hospital needed to take the organs of babies without their parents' consent.

It's probably OK for us to say that academic credentials are secondary to advocacy skills at Hollis Whiteman. The interview is designed to test applicants' clarity of thought and expression. It's also essential to know *"when to stop talking!"* Personality and a sense of humour are vital, since in criminal work barristers must be able to relate to *"drunks, jurors and judges"* alike. One member of the pupillage committee told us: *"You must make us laugh. The real test is: 'Do I want to spend the next 30 years in a room with this person?'"* Having said that, don't try and be Jim Carrey. The set wants pupils not court jesters.

Pupils are diverse in age, education and background, but share a confident, outgoing manner. These are advocates first and foremost, and they boast buckets of charm. Rather than antagonism and suspicion between pupils competing for tenancy, we sensed warmth amongst the Hollis Whiteman bunch. One pupil was given reams of urgent photocopying by her PM. She asked a fellow pupil to help and together the two of them stayed until 8pm. He was repaid when she introduced him to his current girlfriend that very night!

Pupils sometimes socialise with their PMs – one told us how she was taken to a gentleman's club. Push grotesque images of spearmint and rhinoceroses from your mind; this is the Reform Club, an ornate, Corinthian-columned monument to the passing of the 1832 Reform Act and its exponents. Keen sportsmen can participate in an annual chambers cricket match, while those more at home with a glass in their hand enjoy regular drinks with colleagues. There is little to indicate a rigid hierarchy here, and clerks address all barristers, whether juniors or silks, on a first-name basis. When asked to sum up the character of the set, one pupil described Hollis Whiteman as *"friendly and old-school."* Seems like a pretty accurate description to us.

11 King's Bench Walk

the facts

OLPAS: summer season **Pupillages:** 2-3x12 months
Applications: 177 **Mini pupillages:** 40
Interview: 10-12
Award: £27,000 (advance for BVC considered)
Tenancies offered in 2003: 1
Chambers UK rankings: Administrative & public law, education, employment, local government

Not to be confused with the common law set of the same name, 11 KBW, led by Eldred Tabachnik QC and James Goudie QC, is a highly regarded employment and public law set.

Despite its old-school appearance, 11 KBW is a relative baby among chambers. In 1981, former Lord Chancellor Derry Irvine founded the set with nine juniors, including Tony Blair. Today it has 41 tenants, ten of them silks. It is renowned for its strong cadre of juniors and for a helpful and professional clerking service. Situated in the Temple in a small terraced building, the premises are quaint, warm, low key, and very lived-in. Worn brown chairs line the walls of the waiting room and newspapers are scattered on a table, the French polish on which has seen better days. Members' rooms are dark and dusty, law reports clinging to every wall.

11 KBW's beginnings give the set a distinctive sense of pride and cohesion. The *"intellectually rigorous"* legacy of Derry Irvine remains to this day, and the set boasts a wealth of eminent practitioners who are respected for their academic excellence. In some senses, 11 KBW feels more like a law faculty than a barristers chambers. Legal debate is a part of the fabric of chambers; one pupil told us: *"Some tenants are quite donnish in their approach."*

An 11 KBW pupillage is intensely paper-driven. From your first day, you'll be in the library researching in order to go on to draft opinions, skeleton arguments and notes for cross-examination. The work is *"intellectually hardcore"* and, at times, of undeniable importance – one pupil prepared a skeleton argument for the House of Lords and was gutted when the matter settled. Pupils feast on a smorgasbord of work, consisting mainly of employment matters, but including a decent helping of public and commercial law. The idea is that you *"get the law right"* before embarking on advocacy; however, pupils are encouraged to get involved in FRU cases.

Pupils sit with a new pupilmaster every three months. Personality-wise, there is an element of matching PMs to pupils, although almost every pupil will sit with 'Treasury Devil' Philip Sales. He is the junior with possibly the most diverse and interesting practice in chambers, and a *"rigorous"* tutor. In the first three months, you'll belong entirely to your

PM, but thereafter, during each three-month period, you must aim to complete three pieces of work for your PM and six for other members. Written pieces for others are double marked, such that most tenants will have seen your work before the tenancy decision is made. This is a heavily assessed and highly academic pupillage: expect to spend most of your working hours in the library *"living out a permanent essay crisis!"* As one pupil put it: *"There is no learning by mistake here!"*

Despite being high achievers, all those we met were quietly spoken and unaffected. It's no secret that outstanding academic credentials are *"essential, non-negotiable"*– you'll probably need a First and you'll also need to demonstrate exceptional analytical skills and the ability to apply these in practice. Because of the nature of its work, the client base is varied. The set takes instructions from most of the leading City firms, and from central government, local government, NHS bodies and trade unions. Employment clients can range from low-wage, blue-collar workers to CEOs of large companies, so the ability to relate to a range of people is essential.

You'll be given an indication as to how you're getting on at the start of your second six. On the rare occasion that pupils are not performing, it will be suggested that they look for another set. The tenancy decision is made in July, and in addition to the assessed written work that pupils have produced, the committee considers their performance in an advocacy exercise – usually a mock EAT hearing. Pupils are assessed against *"a universal standard, not each other."* If accepted as a tenant, earnings will be good from the outset, and for the first year no chambers' fees are payable. Employment law is the bread and butter of juniors up to five years' call, with the possibility of some public law matters thrown in. Since 11 KBW has barristers on the Treasury Panels, juniors can also see some Treasury work.

Pupillage selection consists of a single, fairly rigorous interview lasting for about half an hour. Applicants, who will ideally already be known to the panel through a mini pupillage, are asked about a case or a law they would like to change, or a case they felt was wrongly decided. Far from being a test of knowledge, this is gauges your ability to reason with legal concepts and give your views persuasively. The ideal applicant will demonstrate *"strong academic ability, even if not expressed in legal terms,"* and the capacity to become a *"top-flight advocate."*

We found 11 KBW to be hospitable and gracious. This set is certainly not slick and modern like some, but it is modest and unaffected. If it's a kicking post-work social life you're after, look elsewhere: apart from a low-key Christmas dinner, the scene is far from riotous. Nevertheless, there is camaraderie between tenants, and silks will often join juniors and pupils for lunch in Hall. While a pupillage here will undoubtedly be challenging, for applicants of the highest academic calibre it will stimulate and reward.

Maitland Chambers

the facts

OLPAS: No **Pupillages:** up to 3x12 months
Applications: 200 **Mini pupillages:** 30
First interview: 30 **Second interview:** 10-16
Award: £40,000 (£10,000 can be advanced for BVC)
Tenancies offered in 2003: 2
Chambers UK rankings: Commercial Chancery, traditional Chancery, charities, company, insolvency, partnership, professional negligence, real estate

When 13 Old Square and 7 Stone Buildings merged in 2001, rebranding as Maitland Chambers, the Chancery Bar felt the effect. Immediately the new set secured an exclusive position in the top band in *Chambers UK* for commercial Chancery work and a very decent place in the traditional Chancery listings (although this work is scarcer here than at some other Chancery sets). If you're drawn to commercial Chancery work, you're going to be choosing between a small clutch of sets, and some at Maitland would say that this one offers the best environment in which to stand up and fight rather than sit down and draft opinions. At the time of the merger, it had former members sitting in each division of the High Court plus the Court of Appeal and the House of Lords.

The distinction between Chancery and straight commercial cases is blurring and Maitland's work spans both areas, with a large percentage of instructions coming from Herbert Smith, Lovells, A&O, and Slaughter and May. Of the £20 million fees billed in 2002, £1.4 million related to overseas cases, most notably in Hong Kong, the Isle of Man, the Cayman Islands and Singapore. Leading cases have included Lloyd's v Jaffray, BCCI v Bank of England and the Barings claim against Coopers & Lybrand & Ors.

So what can you expect as a new pupil? Your first six is predominantly chambers and paper-based. In your second six you might average a couple of days a week in court, but the rest will be spent sat at your desk. PMs are *"quite good at farming you out to others. One of the most important things is to impress as many people as you can."* We asked one PM what it took to succeed at Maitland. His answer: *"You need to really want to litigate, and you need to be fantastically determined and work hard."* After six months, all pupils undertake an advocacy test in front of the pupillage committee. It's part and parcel of the ongoing assessment, although it is *"handled to make it feel like training."* We've come to the conclusion that it's a mistake to consider pupillage at a Chancery set as a specialised training – *"The generalist tradition in this chambers is still going strong. Half the fun is that you never know what's coming through the door next!"* As a pupil, you'll cover company law, land law, trusts, insolvency (*"going to court to freeze assets"*), and *"possibly some landlord and tenant stuff depending on who you are sitting with."* The good news is that *"nearly everyone resists the temptation to take advantage of pupils."*

The set was named after the Victorian legal historian FW Maitland, in an attempt to come up with something independent of each of the two legacy sets. 13 Old Square and 7 Stone Buildings are a stone's throw from each other and both are beautiful architecturally. Parallel to Chancery Lane and just a moment from Lincoln's Inn Fields, the sweeping white terrace of Stone Buildings leads up to High Holborn, while the impressive redbrick houses in Old Square study each other across the cobbles. Just like the set's name, its premises give a nod to tradition, although the contemporary glass name board and up-to-the-minute IT network remind you that Maitland is a new venture...of sorts. Perhaps Chancery work begs tradition – the grand but not opulent country-house-drawing-room-style reception area; conference rooms with open fires; the rituals of afternoon tea and morning coffee in the library (*"as a pupil it is probably important to be seen there"* but to *"listen rather than talk"*) – these things fuel the notion that Maitland is a stuffy set. But is it really, or is the traditional image studied?

We perceived a hint of polite reserve in most of those we met in chambers but, then again, maybe it was nothing more than good manners. One source said there was *"no undue deference"* between seniors and juniors, but *"a degree of respect."* Almost everyone we met seemed to have arrived at the law via the classics, and a high proportion of members have earned a First. To say that people here are bright is a statement of the obvious: *"If your intellect is up to it, everyone in chambers will respect you. It's more important than where you come from. No one looks down their nose at anyone."* The recruitment process focuses on how well you present your views and arguments. Does your application communicate a good enough reason to get you an interview? The first interview tests how well you can express your views on current affairs (past examples include Jo Moore, Pinochet and Guantanamo Bay). Those who make it through to the second interview must tackle an unusual problem – one year, Wind in the Willows was subjected to the Badger Act. Applicants need to spot all the issues lurking within: *"It's not a test of law, but analytical ability."*

Clerks call senior members by their surnames, but increasingly juniors are insisting on first names. Pupils weren't entirely sure of the drill on nomenclature. In their first 12 months, tenants have a guaranteed minimum income of £70,000, yet pay nothing at all to chambers. The ethos was described by one established member as *"paternalistic."* We asked how decisions were made in chambers and learned that *"big decisions are made in general meetings: it's one man, one vote and everyone says exactly what they think in words of one syllable. You have to trust the people you work with."* That's not to diminish the role of a chief exec or any number of committees – Manco (management); Pupco (pupillage); Tenco (tenancy) and a relatively recent addition Pubco (Thursday night drinks).

To sum up Maitland you must overlay the benefits of the merger (economies of scale, increased market profile, a renewed focus on management practices) on the best of what the past held for each legacy set. You must also factor in the presence of more than 40 legal minds that can only be described as sharp, organised and elegant.

Matrix

the facts

OLPAS: summer season **Traineeships:** 2
Applications: 500 **Student placements:** 10
First interview: 50 **Second interview:** 15
Award: £25,000 (£5,000 can be advanced for BVC)
Tenancies offered in 2003: 2
Chambers UK rankings: Administrative and public law, crime, education, employment, environment, criminal fraud, human rights, immigration, police law, public international law

The first thing you are told upon entering Matrix is to get the phraseology right. *"We're trying to shake things up a bit. We don't want you to say clerk or pupillage. We have practice managers and traineeships."* Okey dokey! Established in May 2000, Matrix is a self-professed *"progressive"* set. It made a huge splash at its inception and has since grown to 43 members. *Chambers UK* puts it at the top of the human rights tree alongside its main rival, Doughty Street. High-profile engagements include acting for detainees at Camp X-Ray in Guantanamo Bay, and advising on the exclusion order on Nation of Islam minister Louis Farrakhan. One of its leading lights, Rabinder Singh, led the calls for a judicial inquiry into the legality of war on Iraq. The set also has a distinctly academic bent, and boasts many of the top academic minds in its areas of expertise. Among them, public international law gurus Professor James Crawford SC and Philippe Sands QC. Of course, another member, Cherie Booth QC is married to someone fairly high up in government.

"New century," "innovate," "value" and *"efficient business organisation"* are not words normally associated with the Bar, but these are the buzzwords at Matrix. This is a stylised, sleek organisation whose offices feel more advertising agency than barristers chambers. You'll find the set in a newly renovated former police station in Gray's Inn, now renamed the Griffin Building. Aside from some fairly impressive security measures, there is little else to remind the visitor that this was once a cop shop. The inside is a cross between a trendy Clapham bar and a fish tank – all iridescent blue, modern art and blond wood floors, followed by striking fuchsia walls in meeting rooms. Less charitable (and possibly envious) commentators have described it as *"like Apollo 13 – no atmosphere!"*

Although best known as a human rights set, Matrix lacks the righteousness of some competitors. Happy to act for both the Government and for applicants, it has come under criticism from some quarters for compromising its commitment to human rights. And so we arrive at an important issue. Matrix barristers, we learned, commonly take an academic, rather than a campaigning 'human' interest in human rights issues. We don't intend this to make the set sound overly clinical; it's more a case of fighting a cause on principles rather than naked passion or moral outrage. The set harnesses the brains and resources of academic lawyers, of which it boasts an impressive list as members. One junior told us: *"I can e-mail* [human rights lawyer] *Conor*

Gearty and he'll send me a list of articles on theory." This is a set that *"keeps engaged with academic thinking."*

Traineeships are divided into four three-month portions, each of which is spent with a different member of chambers, so allowing you to see different areas of specialism. Most trainees sit with specialists in employment, public law and human rights, although the traineeship committee will try and accommodate your preferences. While you are able to work for other members of chambers, it's rare for trainees to do too much for anyone other than their supervisor. Much of the time you'll be involved in legal research and drafting, writing opinions and observing court proceedings. There is nothing to stop you from getting on your feet from the first day of your second six, and trainees often get their first advocacy experience in small employment tribunal matters. The work is intellectually stimulating and conducted in a collegial atmosphere. The hours are a regular 9-6pm, and trainees who are seen in the office past 6.30pm are *"positively kicked out."*

The set receives a huge number of traineeship applications for its two places. From the outset, academic excellence is critical, yet Matrix strives to be inclusive and takes socio-economic background and other factors into consideration. A commitment to, and interest in, the work Matrix handles is vital, however, as one pupil told us: *"They're not worried if you haven't been to sub-Saharan Africa to save the world."* On the contrary, a member of the committee noted: *"Not everyone can afford to take a gap year."* In the first interview, conducted with three members, applicants may be asked to discuss a recent case that they find interesting. One year, applicants were asked what they would add to the new Criminal Justice Bill; in another they were asked about the challenges facing the Bar in the years ahead. The second interview involves a written test based on a legal problem, which is then followed by an interview with up to five members. It's a pretty intensive process, and one you can't prepare for, since the problem is deliberately based on an area of which few applicants will have any knowledge. One member of the traineeship committee told us: *"We're attracted to applicants with creative minds who think strategically...those with a lively intellect who are articulate."*

Trainees are formally assessed throughout the 12 months and, by the end of their first nine, will have completed two written and two oral assessments. There is no quota for membership, and the official policy is vague, but Matrix deliberately keeps its trainee numbers low. The set imposes a *"threshold of excellence"* and those who reach this threshold will be offered membership. For those lucky enough to become junior members, the hours are intensive; however, there is no *"culture of perpetual grind."* Barristers feel able to tell their practice manager when they're simply too busy to take instructions.

It could be because of this intense work ethic that the Matrix social scene is pleasant, without being full-on. There is a Christmas dinner and last year staff went ice-skating at Marble Arch. And although there are parties to celebrate the arrival or departure of staff, there are no regular Friday night drinks. The offices have a *"chill-out room"* complete with sofas, newspapers, and (soon!) a coffee machine and a float tank (Okay, not really).

Matrix prides itself on its innovation, progressive values, non-hierarchical structure, commitment to quality service and efficient management. It becomes palpably clear that this set runs itself as a business, and business ethics predominate. Those we spoke to were well aware of the set's almost Orwellian reputation (also described as *"snooty, sleek, businesslike and soulless"*), but they were adamant that *"this is absolutely not the case."* Certainly Matrix does seem to have a preoccupation with image and branding, but it feels it has something different to offer clients: a highly academic take on matters that is, at the same time, wrapped up in pragmatism and cool business efficiency. It is this melding of law as a business with law as a discipline that makes Matrix so distinctive. That and the fuchsia walls, of course.

Queen Elizabeth Building

the facts

OLPAS: summer season **Pupillages:** 3-4x12 months
Applications: 116 **Mini pupillages:** 40
Interview: 25
Award: £17,500 plus earnings
Tenancies offered in 2003: 3
Chambers UK rankings: Family

A long held reputation for excellence makes QEB a target for any crack Bar student looking for a family law pupillage. Unsurpassed on top-end financial cases, QEB barristers act for the wealthy, the famous and the influential.

QEB has just four QCs at present and this is in no small part due to the regularity with which senior members take up judicial appointments. The set has a long tradition in this regard, boasting names like Sir Harry Philimore (Nuremberg War Trials/Lord Justice of Appeal) and Sir Roger Ormerod (CA). The current head of chambers, Florence Baron QC, is universally admired and a popular figurehead for the set. White v White and Cowan v Cowan (if you don't know the cases by now, do your homework) were handled here, as were some of the highest profile divorces of the last few years: The Prince of Wales, Geldof v Yates, Jagger v Hall, Picasso and more. The work at the top end is distinctly big-money, frequently stylish and often has an international dimension. Matters pertaining to children figure less frequently. A few members handle PI and clinical or professional negligence, but don't head for QEB if this is what you are really after.

From the windows of QEB you'll survey the Thames and the full extent of Middle Temple Gardens. Once inside, it's hard to believe that chambers' home was built as recently as the 1950s. Its reception area is lined with enormous oil paintings of the venerable and ancient. Bewigged Lord Chancellors of centuries gone by glower down on well turned out and conservatively dressed members. *"There is a traditional side to QEB and they make an effort to maintain that – clients want that."*

QEB may appear traditional, but it is not oppressively so. Meeting junior members (who make up a very high proportion of the set) enables you to pull the buttoned-up public image apart from the set's internal workings. The hard edge to be found in commercial sets is softened by the type of person that is drawn to family work. Yet QEB barristers are no soft touch: our sources described characters ranging from *"the feisty to the gentle and calm; the pragmatic to the academic; and the ambitious to the not so."* One junior explained that while family work was commonly billed as *"children and care cases...happy-clappy social work,"* this was far from the reality at QEB. *"We're much more commercial in orientation and handle more moneyed clients. A lot of cases involve legal issues not immediately associated with family work: trusts, conflicts of law etc."* Indeed, when your clients are company directors with extensive assets (possibly overseas), you'll need to grapple with company law issues, pension rights and jurisdiction questions. Some juniors do handle divorces for ordinary folk, even those on legal aid, but this is how teeth are cut and not the end goal.

Top-ranked solicitors firms have instructed members of chambers since time immemorial and, provided you put the effort into maintaining these existing relationships, you'll receive quality instructions from them when you're ready. You can expect the best, but the best will be expected of you...after all, QEB has a reputation to protect. While this could feel like a burden, those we spoke to seemed unfazed and, importantly, lacked the arrogance that might come with such a prestigious position. *"That kind of attitude doesn't cut the mustard in Watford County Court,"* one junior remarked, reminding us that even the set's leading silks would have paid their dues in common or garden county court matters. Clerks may cling to the tradition of using surnames when addressing even the lowliest of pupils but, between themselves, barristers at all levels in this small set are supportive of each other. Perhaps the best example of the sense of camaraderie is the daily ritual of gathering for afternoon tea. *"It keeps everybody chatting"* and enables fresh-faced pupils to strike up conversation with senior members and even the odd High Court judge who's popped back for a cuppa.

In the last three or four years, the senior end of chambers has loosened its grip and committees have sprung up for everything – marketing, the library, pupillage selection etc. – yet the decision as to who gets tenancy is taken by the whole set. Officially, talent and hard work are the key to success. Unofficially, we heard: *"Working hard is not enough. There is an element of luck in what work you get, although chambers are fair. Try to build up contacts, but do so appropriately – don't be too forthright."* Aside from a couple of book groups, QEB isn't cliquey. It strives to make pupils feel a part of things, and in addition to their pupil supervisors (three for four months each), they will also have a very junior 'minder' who will frequently take them to court. Pupils are also able to work for any other member of chambers. Our sources reported days averaging 9am-6pm and, depending on the practice of their supervisor, anything from 2-4 days a week in court: *"Many clients are disappointed that we don't wear wigs!"*

We didn't leave QEB with the impression that you had to have the same background, tastes and attitudes as many of its very wealthy clients. Commitment to the family Bar, intellectual ability, a bit of charm and a knack for communication are what counts. The best advice we can give is to get relevant voluntary experience on your CV and a few mini pupillages. You could also read *Family Law* (monthly) so you know what cases are hot. At interview, remember the financial emphasis of work and show that you have the ability and confidence to interact with everyone from legally aided clients to Appeal Court judges. We'll leave the final word to the barrister who said: *"In your 25 or so years here, you and chambers will be involved in the best work the family Bar has to offer."*

Serle Court

the facts

OLPAS: No **Pupillages:** 2x12 months
Applications: 106 **Mini pupillages:** 30
First interview: 26 **Second interview:** 8
Award: £35,000 (£10,000 can be advanced for BVC)
Tenancies offered in 2003: 2
Chambers UK rankings: Banking & finance, commercial chancery, traditional chancery, company, civil fraud, insolvency, partnership, professional negligence

As we've mentioned before, the distinction between commercial and Chancery work is blurring. Serle Court epitomises that blur. In 2000, a Chancery set from 13 Old Square merged with a smaller commercial set, 1 Hare Court, taking Serle Court as its new home and its new name. The smaller set filled some gaps in the larger one and came dripping with quality silks, including Michael Briggs, the man who is ranked by *Chambers UK* in more practice areas than any other barrister.

Cases come from a wide range of instructing solicitors (Richards Butler, Bird & Bird and Clifford Chance are all good customers), and barristers deal with both commercial clients and individuals from all walks of life, including little old ladies with troublesome wills, and families and ex-lovers reduced to warring over the beneficial ownership of property. However, most of the bigger cases are for commercial clients and the set defines itself by its commercial work. Banking, financial services, company law, partnership law, professional negligence, insolvency and plain old contract disputes; it's all there. There's even a spot of public law and human rights work.

Standing outside in New Square, nothing suggests that Serle Court will offer anything other than the usual maze of barristers rooms and an old-fashioned waiting area. However, prior to moving in, the set asked award-winning architect Niall McLaughlin to leave his mark on its new home. The result is beautiful. Glass and pale wood are set off by large pieces of modern art painted by the wife of one of the barristers. Serle Court has also used this clean, calm and modern look in its branding. We sensed it was also reflective of the attitudes and approach of the barristers. *"High quality, modernity, and being receptive to customers' needs"* are, apparently, the guiding principles. You know that expression about tidy desk, tidy mind? That's the kind of feel Serle Court has.

One pupil explained his reason for choosing the set: *"I wanted interesting, high powered work in a comfortable environment."* Is it really that simple? Almost. The other important consideration is that, along with a few others, the set offers its pupillages *"far in advance of anyone else."* There it is again – simple, uncluttered logic. The recruitment process is the usual two-interview affair. Expect both outings to be fairly rigorous.

The set claims to offer *"one of the more progressive pupillages at the Bar,"* and we found supporting evidence. The interaction between members and pupils is particularly easy. Nowhere to be found are the awful school desk-sized folding tables at which some of their peers must sit, as if to reinforce a sense of lowliness. Pupils are invited to chambers parties and out for drinks even before they've finished Bar school, so *"the initial discomfort about starting pupillage is not there."* We were delighted to learn that groups of barristers regularly negotiate the vast open spaces of Chancery Lane to settle in the Gaucho Grill or slip into the nearby Seven Stars for a pint. *"It's a tradition that pupils are not allowed to spend a penny,"* we were told. To avoid any confusion we agreed to change the quote to *"...not allowed to spend any money."*

Another thing the Serle youngsters are not allowed to do is appear in court until they've completed a full 12 months of pupillage. It's seen as a time for learning not earning. This does lead to feelings of being *"left behind"* as *"friends are on their feet being barristers while I am still a pupil."* Instead, pupils undertake advocacy exercises within chambers in front of senior members who hold part-time judicial positions.

The two sixes do not differ greatly. In each, the pupil will have two PMs and will work for others in chambers. They tackle a mixture of real work and set pieces designed to test their progress. One told us: *"You are taught to be a quality product and to produce quality products...they are punctilious about written style."* And so we arrive at the crux of the matter: there's an awful lot of thinking and written work involved in this pupillage. A very junior tenant told us: *"You need self motivation and you mustn't mind sitting in libraries for hours, working on your own, buckling down."* But this is no ivory tower – good judgement and being *"rigorous in examining your client's case"* is key. Getting the right answer is only part of the job; it then needs to be turned into practical advice, which, after all, is why the client instructed you in the first place.

We looked for the quirks and scraps of humour that sometimes help define a set. Sadly our sources fell silent when asked for hilarious stories; they painted a rather earnest picture of daily life. That said, we must congratulate the prankster who tossed three yellow plastic ducks into the pigeon netting above the courtyard behind chambers. *"We're a serious business,"* one barrister told us. We thought about the ducks. We nodded.

Many sets sneer at the tradition of chambers tea, regarding it as anachronistic. This set loves it enough to also indulge in a morning coffee version, which it holds in the nearby St George's cafe. Apparently tea is a stand-up affair, but one sits down for coffee. *"It fosters a non-hierarchical atmosphere,"* a baby junior told us, *"...and yes, pupils can speak at tea!"* So, expect plenty of chattering – whether it's about work or football, it's all fair comment.

We were fortunate enough to collar one of the top bods on the management committee who, after discussing the leap that was made at the time of the merger, explained: *"Any change here is evolutionary; people are broadly happy with the set as it is, but we will continue recruiting talented people."* Broadly happy? We'd guess that the folk at Serle Court are utterly delighted with the way things are. Carry on.

3/4 South Square

the facts

OLPAS: No **Pupillages:** Up to 4x12 months
Applications: 300 **Mini pupillages:** Up to 10 funded
First interview: 40 **Second interview:** 20
Award: £35,000 (funds can be advanced for BVC)
Tenancies offered in 2003: 2
Chambers UK rankings: Banking & finance, Chancery, company law, insolvence

3/4 South Square is the UK's premier insolvency set and the first point of call for many clients. This is a good pick for anyone *"with an interest in the workings of business."* BCCI, Maxwell, Polly Peck, Olympia & York, Lloyd's of London, Barings, Enron, Railtrack, Marconi, NTL and Global Crossing – you name it, if it's a corporate disaster, 3/4 has been involved in some capacity.

The set is located in Gray's Inn, overlooking the blazing floral displays of South Square. When we visited, jarring late-80s decor was about to give way to a more contemporary look. But while the reception area was to be *"smartened up,"* we were assured that there would be no glitz, marble or *"Lovells-style great metal sculptures or towering atrium."* Said one senior member of chambers: *"We don't want our clients thinking we're prohibitively expensive."*

The set's core area of practice is insolvency, and most of its members specialise in one brand or other of insolvency law. Members relish work that requires you to *"go into a company for a time, understand its business, see the human drama and the whole range of problems of a business in distress."* And, invariably, some of these businesses will be at the centre of commercial drama and intrigue. Speaking of his work on the ITV Digital collapse, one member told us: *"That touched millions of people's lives...Not being able to watch the football makes life scarcely worth living!"*

If you're curious about life at the insolvency Bar, the set now has a system of funded mini pupillages, designed to give prospective pupils *"a feeling of what it's like to be here."* And it is, according to one QC, *"informal, friendly and approachable."* These clichés trip off the tongue very easily, but we saw no reason to doubt him. While the work is *"serious"* (*"there's no arsing about"*), this is a young set, defined by its relationships with clients. Said one member: *"The big thing is how you get along with them."* The work involves grappling with complex legal issues, nonetheless, *"it's not about finding an academic, theoretical solution."* *"We pride ourselves on offering practical business solutions. Our clients want to know what to do next."* Readers need only look at the set's website to get a taste of its practical approach. The 'Links' and 'London' pages in particular are packed with all the relevant information an out-of-town instructing solicitor or client would need: hotels, restaurants, travel info, weather etc. Someone's been thinking ahead...'What will a visitor from Hong Kong/Texas/Newcastle need to know?'

When we asked chambers' recruiters what qualities they sought in prospective pupils, the answer was *"a hybrid."* The editor of *Chambers UK* confirmed this hybrid theory, when she described insolvency barristers as both *"analytical and deal-driven."* *"There is a deal-doing mentality, but we're also there to help. After all, we're there to save the company in many cases."* And to do so, in court *"you have to be able to present a case clearly and attractively, and in the best possible light."* For fans of *The Simpsons* fantasising about Lionel Hutz-style court appearances, be warned: this is *"not stuff you can pick up five minutes beforehand."* The work is *"complicated, factually and legally,"* and your success will depend *"90% on preparation."*

Pupils are assigned to a different pupilmaster every 6-8 weeks, so enabling them to see a range of practices and working styles, and to ensure that as many members as possible see their work. During the second six, pupils spend more time interacting with the most junior tenants *"to give them a better picture of life at the junior end,"* but it'll be no holiday as you'll also do pieces of work for silks on major matters. If the cut and thrust of regular advocacy is what really appeals to you, this is perhaps not the best pupillage. Few pupils can expect to be on their feet at all during the second six, since *"the work is sufficiently demanding to require a full 12 months of training."* At the six-month mark, pupils are informed as to their chances of gaining tenancy, and some are advised to seek a second six elsewhere. There are no formal assessments: all your work will be taken into account, as will feedback from the pupilmasters and anyone else who has had dealings with you.

The set's main clients are City law firms, although for juniors there's an endless list of instructing firms from outside the capital. In their early years, juniors spend a lot of time *"traipsing around the county courts and district registries,"* and can expect a good cross-section of smaller corporate and personal insolvency matters — winding-up petitions, setting aside statutory demands, injunctions and the like. They can also expect to work as part of a team on much larger cases and, indeed, 3/4 South Square prides itself on its team ethos and team approach to staffing large matters. As one source stressed, while there are *"lots of good, competent people around,"* personality and the ability to work in a team will take you over the line.

Some chambers are highly individualistic in their style and culture; others are cohesive to the point of conformism. We sensed that 3/4 South Square is a mixture of both. The social life is full and fabulous for those who want it, but there is no element of compulsion. Except, that is, when it comes to an annual tradition whereby junior tenants take the wide-eyed, bushy-tailed pupils out and *"get them very drunk."* It's a way of demonstrating that the set is *"not just a place where you turn up and work."* There is also a chambers function once a term, at which everyone gets together.

Pupillage applicants with *"past lives"* are embraced. Among the members, we weren't surprised to hear of a former Bank of England employee and an actuary. The BBC producer and the hairdresser were an unexpected delight. As with most things at 3/4, there is generally an *"easy"* relationship with clerks. Overall, we sensed a warm, informal atmosphere in a set that is neither contrived nor unnervingly slick. Definitely one for those with a fascination for business.

4 Stone Buildings

the facts

OLPAS: No **Pupillages:** 3x6 months (pupillages may be extended to 12 months)
Applications: c. 90 **Mini pupillages:** 20
Interview: 20
Award: £30,000 (funds can be advanced for BVC)
Tenancies offered in 2003: 1
Chambers UK rankings: Commercial Chancery, company, energy & natural resources, financial services, civil fraud, insolvency/corporate recovery

4 Stone Buildings is a small but rock-solid company and commercial law set with a host of stars within its ranks. Brightest among them is head of chambers, Philip Heslop QC, who acted in such mammoth cases as Polly Peck and Guinness, and is now leading the charge for Bank of America in BCCI litigation. Years ago, another senior member, Peter Curry QC, left the Bar to set up the litigation department at Freshfields before jumping the fence again and joining 4 Stone Buildings.

Occupying elegant Georgian premises overlooking the green expanse of Lincoln's Inn Fields, the set's vibe is serene and traditional. Inside, Barristers 'R Us strike again on the decoration front. It's all law reports, spectacular marble fireplaces and French polish. 4 Stone Buildings started life as a Chancery set, but like other Chancery outfits, it recognised that to remain successful and profitable it needed to diversify. Over the last two decades, it has shifted its focus to company and commercial law, with a strong emphasis on corporate insolvency. The plan has paid off and today its members act in some of the highest profile and valuable international insolvencies. The set takes instructions from several leading City firms, and maintains strong contacts with regional firms.

Company law instructions cover takeover disputes, building society mergers, share transfers, directors duties, freezing injunctions and issues of management control (such as that of Tottenham Hotspur FC). Many of the cases are very large, requiring second or third juniors to assist a silk. The work necessitates close contact with instructing solicitors, bringing about a real team ethos. But this is not a case of barristers trying to replicate solicitors' offices. A pupil told us: *"I steered clear of solicitors' firms because of that group culture. I wanted a bit of that, but not to the extent of it being obligatory."* In a similar vein, a junior told us: *"I like the intellectual stimulation of the Bar, being out on your own and challenged individually."* A rolling stone gathers no moss, and neither, it seems do the members of this set. With strong international connections, barristers are active in such glamorous and exotic locations as Hong Kong, Bermuda, the Cayman Islands, Trinidad and Singapore. One lucky junior spent eight weeks in Bermuda on the BCCI insolvency, juxtaposing his time at work with relaxation on the beach.

Chambers' recruiters were adamant that they *"don't care what university you went to."* Additionally, *"we don't distinguish between a First and a 2:1,"* since *"often students with Firsts have no common sense."* And the job, we were informed, is as much about common sense as pure brains. Many sets make claims to fairness in recruitment, but 4 Stone Buildings is surely unique in that it phones the referees of every single applicant for pupillage, as *"references are really telling."* From here, the set interviews around 20 lucky applicants. The interview panel is large and includes the set's influential senior clerk, David Goddard. We won't lie to you, the interview process is rigorous and the questions fairly tough. This is a set that prides itself on its common sense and commerciality – *Chambers UK* doesn't describe it as *"user friendly"* for nothing – so you should argue with your client's needs in mind. We sneaked a peek at the 4 Stone Buildings recruitment guidelines – chief among the characteristics it seeks are *"quality, agility, fluency and potential."* As one junior tenant told us: *"Potential is the hardest thing to judge. We're trying to spot the next Lord Hoffman."* Following this, you'll have a general discussion with the panel, and you'll get your chance to avenge the recruiters with hard-hitting enquiries of your own. You might want to tone down the pomposity – *"Very occasionally we get someone who is full of themselves,"* and that doesn't appeal.

Although a mini pupillage is advisable, it's not a prerequisite (it seems that few things are!). *"It's a chance for students to decide whether they like us."* In keeping with this approach, minis are not assessed, although someone will write a brief appraisal of your work. Those pupillage interviewees who perform well, but have not undertaken a mini, will be invited to spend a couple of days in chambers to see how they rub along.

Chambers only offers six-month pupillages. At the end of the first six, the pupillage committee reviews your progress, and depending on your chances of tenancy, might offer you a second. While most comparable sets effectively offer 12-month pupillages with a break clause at six months, at 4 Stone Buildings, you're encouraged to have an alternative second six arranged beforehand. Until Christmas, you'll sit with your first pupilmaster, switching to a second in January. All work from other members of chambers passes through your PM, who will ensure it is appropriate. The assessment regime is light, since *"the emphasis is on training and work rather than marking."* You're unlikely to work in you own name during a second six; some pupils get on their feet during this time but, in this is a paperwork-heavy pupillage, it's far from the norm. As a junior you can expect to work on mammoth cases with senior members and to run your own smaller matters. Clerks maintain relationships with regional solicitors to ensure a good flow of baby junior-sized instructions. At this stage of your career, it is likely that insolvency work will feature heavily.

4 Stone Buildings prides itself on its warmth. There is chambers tea every afternoon, although we're told it bears no resemblance to the funereal affairs that have become the stuff of legend at the Bar. A pupil told us that 'Treasury Devil' Jonathan Crow *"tells the most amusing anecdotes at tea."* We're reliably informed that

the *"treacle-like"* liquid prepared by the clerks is unfit for human consumption. Apparently the recipe consists of 23 teabags for each member plus four for the pot. Outside work, there are occasional parties, ice-skating expeditions to Somerset House in winter, and every August the whole set goes out to lunch...in Paris. Apparently one member has earned his pilot's licence and is threatening to take everyone hot air ballooning.

Shortage of space in No.4 dictates that some members must reside in No.6 Stone Buildings. In spite of this separation, we found a set with a degree of intimacy and congeniality that is to be applauded. Courteous and traditional certainly, but far from stuffy, 4 Stone buildings is one of Lincoln's Inn's finest offerings.

3 Verulam Buildings

the facts

OLPAS: summer season **Pupillages:** 4x12 months (and 2x6 months unfunded for overseas practice)
Applications: 200 **Mini pupillages:** c.40
First interviews: 50 **Second interviews:** 20
Award: At least £33,000 (£11,000 can be advanced for BVC)
Tenancies offered in 2003: 4
Chambers UK rankings: Banking & finance, commercial litigation, financial services, civil fraud, insurance, international arbitration, media & entertainment, professional negligence

3 Verulam Buildings is best known for first-class banking and finance litigation; however, success stacks up in an impressive range of other commercial areas. Headed by John Jarvis QC and the immensely popular Christopher Symons QC, its notables include former FSA general counsel Michael Blair QC, William Blair QC (brother of Tony, no relation to Michael, and current chairman of the Commercial Bar Association), and a veritable brat pack of junior silks and senior juniors.

3VB's pre-WW1 roots lie in the Temple and we're sure it won't mind us saying that nothing much distinguished it until the late 1970s. At this time, the set underwent aggressive expansion under the leadership of Andrew Leggatt QC, who moved it away from common law in the Temple to commercial practice, more particularly financial cases, in Gray's Inn. Also worth mentioning is former head of chambers Mr Justice Cresswell who, with Bill Blair, recruited many of the current 'names' and continued the banking focus with a view to using it as a base from which to develop other commercial areas. Members have acted on Maxwell, BCCI, Prince Jefri, Polly Peck, and the undue influence cases of Barclays Bank v O'Brien and Royal Bank of Scotland v Etridge. Then there was the spat between Italian scooter manufacturer Aprilia and the Spice Girls, the Dubai Aluminium professional negligence action and the Britvic benzine product liability litigation.

The Bar is facing change on a number of fronts and 3VB strikes us as a set that understands the importance of adapting to these changes. Some sets boast a Hotel California ethos, which is to say that no one ever leaves. Not 3VB. While it has sucked in tenants from other good sets, when Matrix Chambers was formed, four members joined it to pursue public law practice amongst other like-minded souls. In a similar vein, it is interesting to note that the set has more than one ex-solicitor among its ranks and, intriguingly, in the past a couple of juniors have jumped the fence. The comings and goings at 3VB are not what defines it – it's hardly a revolving door scenario – but there's evidence to show that the set has a restless gene in its DNA.

When trying to identify a particular chambers' house style, it helps to know which firms of solicitors have aligned themselves with the set. Here, the Lovells link is strong, as is that with Herbert Smith and A&O. In large commercial cases, solicitors need the barristers they instruct to assist them by *"collaborating on the management of litigation,"* as if they were a part of the team. Perhaps this is why new tenants are commonly sent on secondment to City firms (Slaughter and May for one) to see things from the instructing solicitor's perspective. If there is a 3VB Way then it should perhaps be defined by the word 'efficiency'. Our sources all emphasised the importance of being well organised and prepared, and as a pupil that's just what you'll learn to be. After all, *"nobody wants to be taken be surprise."* Expect an emphasis on *"anticipating the needs of case timetables and work schedules."* It all sounds so precise, so Swiss. Just without the cuckoo clocks.

The clerking system operates around groups of barristers organised by practice area. Team clerking came in with the arrival of practice manager Nick Hill in 1999, and both he and Chris Symons are seen to be very much on top of the management game. Each practice group holds three-monthly review meetings and implements a programme of continuing education and marketing through seminars. It all smacks of a set that's continually assessing its own performance and following a plan. But, if all this is true, who's in the driving seat? In a fair approximation of democracy, committees are the order of the day. There's the management committee, the pupillage committee, the tenancy committee and so on, however, our favourite has to be the practice development committee (aka the family planning committee), which handles lateral hires and the set's direction and goals.

Boasting possibly the tiniest waiting room at the Bar, and occupying three and a half of five early 19th century townhouses just off Gray's Inn Road and backing onto Gray's Inn Walks, the premises can at best be described as modest. Rather like the set. *"It's not selling itself as a corporate hothouse: all glass and blond wood and Swedish chairs."* Equally, it is *"not Gordon Gekko-macho-bravado"* and *"not hard-nosed or uptight-establishment."* Fine. Some hints on how the set does see itself? *"Relaxed in its relations with people,"* but with *"a pretty serious ambition to make chambers a leading set in as many fields as possible."* One tenant communicated *"a strong sense of identity with chambers as a whole and what you do mattering for chambers. It matters to me if senior juniors and silks are doing well."*

As well as minding each other's business, these barristers are, it seems, lunching and visiting the local pub together. Some even go on the piste together.

We met two of the pupils, each of whom had studied masters' degrees at top overseas universities. Among the juniors there are those who've turned to the law after other careers, including a former philosophy lecturer and a film producer. Whether or not you possess a novel CV, only academic excellence will see you through to an interview, and then you're going to have to show that you have self-confidence and all the usual powers of analysis and reasoning that are essential at the commercial Bar. The first of the two interviews will be a relaxed stroll through your CV, and if the panel like what they see, you'll be invited back to tackle a problem-based interview. *"We're not overbearing,"* the pupillage committee secretary reassured us: *"It's not my experience as a barrister that you're bounced around the room."*

All four pupils rotate around the same group of pupilmasters, sampling banking, general commercial, telecoms, insurance and reinsurance, civil fraud and insolvency work as they go. After the first three months, pupils may take on matters from around chambers, and in the second six may also get started on bits and pieces of paying work – masters' appointments, small claims, etc. While *"a premium is placed on your drafting skills,"* it's not the case that you'll be chambers-bound with your nose to paper every day. Pupillage is *"not sedentary at all;"* what with your PM's conferences and sitting in on trials, you'll be *"out of chambers once or twice a week at least."* More often, we sensed, than their peers in magic circle sets. This is perhaps due to the involvement of shadow pupilmasters, a breed of mini-me PM, whose cases are smaller and more easily understood by pupils.

Inspite of its steadfast refusal to dress public areas in contemporary fashions, you leave this set with a strong sense that it is looking only at its future. None of the *"flash"* of some commercial sets, but instead *"a quiet confidence"* from people *"quietly focused and going about it."* As the magic circle of solicitors' firms has its aspirants, so too does the so-called magic circle of commercial sets. 3VB is clearly pursuing membership.

Wilberforce Chambers

the facts

OLPAS: No **Pupillages:** 2x12 months
Applications: 85 **Mini pupillages:** 21
First interview: 27 **Second interview:** 9
Award: £37,500 (up to £12,500 can be advanced for BVC)
Tenancies offered in 2003: 1
Chambers UK rankings: Commercial Chancery, traditional Chancery, intellectual property, pensions, professional negligence, real estate litigation

Although certain members will have additional specialisms, the main business is Chancery work. Even as a new pupil you'll be familiar with the names of the senior members: *"You meet the people you've been reading about in the law reports"* – QCs like Edward Nugee, Jules Sher, Michael Bloch, Terence Mowschenson. Notable cases of recent years include Grupo Torras, Barings, BCCI and Bermuda Fire & Marine. Members of chambers regularly work abroad in the Bahamas and the Cayman Islands.

In New Square's south-west corner, and just yards from Lincoln's Inn's Old Hall, No.8 is home to most of the set. As you descend from the newest tenants' tiny garret-like rooms on the fourth floor, down the broad wooden staircase you pass ever larger and grander accommodation until you reach the wood-panelled rooms of top QC's. The set has also taken over part of Nos.7 and 9 and a modern building on the other side of the square at No.16. Built on the site of 'The Boghouse' – communal toilets that dated back to 1693 – No.16 houses many of the juniors. It also plays host to afternoon tea, which is a very informal affair when anything up to a dozen people congregating outside the kitchen to chat about what they're up to. Chambers lunch (every fortnight for members) is when most people catch up. Social get-togethers tend to coincide with chambers' marketing events rather than having a strong life force of their own.

As we walked around chambers, we observed that some members were very smartly dressed while others had climbed out of the casual side of the bed. Michael Bloch sometimes brings his dog – Gladstone – into chambers, and Terence Mowschenson will occasionally be joined by his two King Charles Spaniels, Ruby and Carlo (who were lazing by an open fire when we dropped into their room). Our afternoon at Wilberforce left us with the feeling that we'd been to visit some rather welcoming long lost relatives, so we were intrigued when one pupilmaster said: *"We don't pretend we're a family; we're working colleagues. Being a family can make administration very difficult."* A sizeable proportion of the members have moved here from other sets, yet while no one has ever left except to go to the bench, *"we don't see ourselves as a tight knot who have been together forever and will be till death us do part..."* As for its self-image: *"We've ditched a lot of the old traditions that make you feel uncomfortable."* Instead, a modern management structure and a *"heads down"* ethos have been adopted. How different from the Dickens' portrayal of the Chancery Bar in *Bleak House*.

First six pupils move between pupilmasters every two months and work on papers that have recently come to their PM. Days are spent drafting opinions, skeleton arguments and particulars of claim or defence, or *"sometimes a QC will ask you to do a bit of research for them."* If their work is good enough, it may end up being used. *"Most pieces of pupil-friendly work are small self-standing matters."* No Jarndyce v Jarndyce stuff. Should you stay for a second six, you might receive noting briefs (to attend court to take notes) or smaller county court hearings. The firms that instruct chambers range from small high street practices to the giants of the magic circle and, consequently, the subject matter of the cases is extremely varied. Pensions, gas exportation, public law, overseas trusts, probate, property, landlord and tenant, housing associations... *"The work is cerebral – you're dealing with the more difficult areas of the law like land and trusts, but then you get into things like pensions and you soon realise that you'll not find much in a trusts book on pensions."* You do encounter the occasional little old lady with a will, but a lot of the time you'll be instructed by large commercial landlords. A junior whose practice contains traditional Chancery work will handle plenty of smaller cases, *"where you are in charge and not being led."* Commonly the cases relate to somebody's home or something very personal to them, but the cut and thrust of mainstream commercial work must not be underemphasised.

Anyone thinking of applying here has to be aware that success comes in *"a more complex package than a starred First."* Yes, pupils usually have near-perfect academic credentials, but they also have a fascination for the law. One source hinted that winning scholarships or essay prizes and mooting or debating competitions would look good on your application. Another explained the heightened degree of sophistication required by Chancery advocates as opposed to, say, their criminal colleagues. *"This is not the place for bluff and bluster. A jury advocate needs to grasp the layman's attention and not let it go for several days; in Chancery you need to get across difficult concepts to a judge – this requires poise."* Remember, open and shut cases are few and far between. Excellent paper advocacy is even more important, and a tip from one successful ex-pupil is that *"you need to be consistently good rather than occasionally amazing."* No need to clock up hours and hours of face-time: *"They're not looking for bumptious Lord Flashheart types."* Like many other leading sets, Wilberforce takes its tenancy decision after just six months so that those who are unsuccessful have the chance to move elsewhere for a second six. *"It's better than drinking in the last chance saloon, if you have to go for a third six!"* A word of recommendation: go all out for one of the mini pupillages.

In February 2003, esteemed former Law Lord Wilberforce (great-great-grandson of the social reformer William Wilberforce) died aged 95. His obituary in *The Guardian* portrayed him as *"One of the most civilised and balanced judges of the 20th century."* While no one we spoke to in chambers mentioned Lord Wilberforce, we concluded that civilised and balanced were words that described the set very well. Maybe it's the dogs. Maybe it's the people. Whatever it is, there's something pretty good going on at Wilberforce. If Dickens had met modern day Chancery barristers, *Bleak House* would have been a different book altogether...

No.5 Chambers, Birmingham

the facts

OLPAS: No **Pupillages:** 2x12 months
Applications: 200 **Mini pupillages:** c.50
First interview: 30 **Second interview:** 10-16
Award: £15,000 + earnings (advance considered for BVC)
Tenancies offered in 2003: 1 to a No.5 pupil
Chambers UK rankings: Employment, environment, personal injury, planning

Depending on what day of the week it is, this set may or may not be the largest in the UK. Birmingham's No.5 Chambers is an impressive and audacious set. A big, bold set like this needs big, noticeable words to describe it, and just over a decade ago one word that was used was 'Frankenstein'. The profession was shocked that barristers should choose to incorporate. Of course, they are now no longer alone...

A corporate structure is by no means the only thing that gets No.5 noticed. An ambitious growth strategy has seen the set climb from under 30 members in the early 1980s to nearly 140 today. No mergers here, it's a case of drawing in 'names' to continue feeding the six practice groups: commercial & Chancery (24 members); crime & licensing (35+); employment (18); Family (18); PI & clin neg (45 specialists); and planning and environment (12). Each of these teams has its own head, deputy, recruitment plan, marketing plan, budget and clerking team. Clerks get legal training too.

A whopping £18 million turnover puts it into the top ten sets in the UK, as measured by income. This income is supplemented by earnings from conferences and training as well as case handling; indeed the planning group managed an away weekend in Barcelona on the proceeds of one conference.

There was only one pupil at the time we investigated No. 5. His solitude was, at least, saving him from the Lord of the Flies-style moral disintegration that some London pupils get drawn into. (We did bump into a second pupil at a party in London some months after our visit to Birmingham. He'd only stayed a week, having discovered he'd left his soul in London.) Back in Brum, the pupil offered up his views on the set. His thoughts on the quality of management (*"the dark art of clerking"*) and the attention he'd received from pupilmasters confirmed our suspicions that this is the kind of place where no stone is left unturned in the quest to create good barristers. *"You have to be outgoing and independent in action and thought"* to survive here, but you will be welcomed by the set, particularly by junior members. Many of the barristers sit and eat lunch together in the common room; it's a good spot for picking up on the feel of the set. And that is? *"Well, even though there are people of exceptional talent who are highly focused on their jobs, chambers doesn't lose a certain lightness of being...especially on social occasions."*

At times you must expect to get lost in the labyrinthine premises. Perhaps a bag of breadcrumbs might assist in negotiating the endless corridors and stairs, most of which are parquet-floored and likely to inspire flashbacks to your old junior school assembly hall. Thankfully, in your first three months you'll stick closely to your pupilmaster. You'll do bits and pieces for other members when they are desperate for another pair of hands, but *"you are farmed out on only a very occasional basis."* Your PM is likely to take a *"Do it for yourself"* attitude. Working on their briefs, you'll be invited to go away and have a stab at producing something. *"The first six is good preparation for the second. By then you'll have experience of getting a brief, reading through it and handling things quickly."* After the first three months, you'll have two month-long spells with other PMs who can offer an insight into entirely different areas of practice. And then, as you creep towards your second, practising six, you'll have a month-long float with junior tenants from around chambers. *"So far, I've done commercial and Chancery, employment, crime and PI...in fact, everything apart from planning and family."*

The second six is going to be a whirl of briefs and court appearances, and it won't let up. You'll occupy the common areas of chambers, particularly the 'Bedouin Area'. The tenancy decision is made after ten months, and then you have *"two months grace to see out your triumph or to seek alternative employment."* And once tenancy is settled? *"Relative to other sets it's probably true that we specialise quite early. Juniors settle into their way and it happens quite naturally."* Never one to let things drift, practice director Tony McDaid (who should probably be called Tony McDude given his influence) has cosy *"tea and biscuits chats"* with members...regularly. As your career develops Mr McDude will ask you about where you want to go and what kind of work/life balance you're looking for. We heard that our man McDude sits with a copy of the Bar Guide putting crosses next to the barristers he'd like to draw to the set. Apparently he's got a good hit rate.

"No.5's outlook is a progressive one, couched within a more traditional appearance." A fair statement, we'd say. To illustrate: it has set up a London annexe; it has designs on a national network; it is diverse in all respects; and it embraces developments in practice management earlier than most sets. Barmark, Investors in People, an equal ops officer...No.5 gives a damn about these things, but it doesn't wear them as badges of correctness. And yet this is a set where clerks refer to barristers as 'Sir' and 'Miss', except on the football pitch or the golf course. There's a whiff of formality and traditionalism, which underscores the respect that the administrative corp accords to the lawyering corp, and it's easy

to misread such signals and assume austerity and backwardness. Avoid this trap.

Whichever one of the six core practice groups appeals to you, so long as you are prepared to commit to Birmingham, this set would be a canny choice. Early applications are encouraged and you should try for a mini pupillage. One pupilmaster described the set as *"courageous, principled and forward thinking."* We concur.

St Philips Chambers, Birmingham

the facts

OLPAS: No **Pupillages:** Up to 4x12 months
Applications: 250 **Mini pupillages:** Unlimited
First interview: 21 **Second interview:** 8
Award: £12,500 plus earnings
Tenancies offered in 2003: not known (6 in 2002)
Chambers UK rankings: Employment, environment, personal injury, planning

One of Birmingham's two super sets, St Philips has grown through a series of mergers. In 1998, No.s 7 and 2 Fountain Court merged and adopted chambers' current moniker. In 2002, it fused with criminal specialists No.1 Fountain Court and, in so doing, pumped its numbers up to match those of rival set No.5 Chambers. Currently it is home to 140 barristers and, at the time of writing, was the largest in the UK. In such a large set, structured practice groups become a necessity and this is exactly how St Philips has chosen to organise itself. The largest group is crime, boasting some 67 members of chambers. Following in its wake are the family, employment, commercial, immigration, public law and PI groups. The set's website gives an indication of the size of each.

The first thing that strikes you about St Philips (other than stuff of legend, Dave the doorman) is that it looks like a swanky solicitors firm with its spacious, hi-tech reception. Artwork is eschewed in favour of the blank walls and clean lines that appeared on the architect's drawing board. *"We're a business and we need to be different,"* is the explanation. *"We consciously took a modern, bold approach."* St Philips was an early participant in the trend for chambers to employ a chief executive and he, along with the five practice area heads, comprise the management committee. Taking administrative functions away from the barristers – the set has full-time staff to handle accountancy, IT, HR, marketing and library services – enables the barristers to get on with lawyering and adds a certain slickness to the operation. Nothing much, it seems, is the product of the past and the word 'tradition' is rarely spoken. As one pupil supervisor told us: *"There's a definite feeling that we're all in this big project together."* Abandoning the Birmingham Bar's traditional home in Fountain Court and moving to the present location was a wrench for some, but what has emerged is an organisation with more clout, more drive and more plans. *"Things don't evolve here, they are designed, and there's a system for everything. If a problem arises and there is no system to deal with it then a system is created."*

St Philips is incorporated: the barristers are the shareholders of the company and the company owns its own premises outright. Depending on how much they want to pay in 'rent', they choose between a room (most of which are shared by two barristers), dedicated desk space in an open-plan area, or fashionable vagrancy (ie hot-desking). It's a system that suits variable earnings within the set and there's a further graduated discount on fees for barristers of up to five years' call. We visited on a Friday afternoon when St Philips was having a mellow moment, but we understand that it can get cramped and rather busy. Over the road, extra space has been found in Windsor House, aka Bleak House as it scores much lower on the swish-o-meter.

Communal areas and a chambers-wide drinks party one Friday each month lend weight to the claim that *"people here go out of their way to be very friendly."* *"There's ample opportunity to chat, but chambers is too big to know everyone's business inside out,"* one pupil told us. Certain bars benefit from St Philips' brief fees:

Hotel du Vin (when your clerk has got a decent price for you), Utopia (if you're feeling sufficiently chic) and the Old Joint Stock (which packs enough lawyers to qualify as Dante's seventh circle of hell).

They didn't differ much from the London pupils we interviewed, but one thing struck us about St Philips' pupils: they were completely at ease with each other. It's relatively rare for a pupil to not get tenancy; consequently, they don't see pupillage as a lottery or 12 months of stiff competition with peers. Friendships grow easily between them, assisted by the fact that most live in one or other of the lawyerburbs of Harborne and Moseley. If chambers is not looking for winners and losers, it can concentrate on bringing all pupils on: *"Trying to get you to do your best."*

In your first three or four months, you'll work with your main pupil supervisor, accompanying them to court and getting a feel for paperwork – perhaps preparing a chronology for a multi-day employment case or drafting a statement of claim or defence on a PI matter. You'll then move in with two other supervisors for a month each to experience different areas of work. In the final couple of weeks of your first six, you'll hook up with more junior tenants to see first hand exactly what you'll be doing in your second, practising six. The second half of pupillage is when you'll be set loose, but previous supervisors will maintain a watching brief to ensure that you stay on the right track. In crime there's a fair bit of West Midlands Probation Service work in the Magistrates' Courts and mentions in the Crown Court. Some pupils have even undertaken three-month secondments to the CPS. On the civil side, small claims will see you in the County Courts and family work will centre around local authority care proceedings, contact orders and directions hearings. *"Everyone intends to specialise,"* we learned, *"but in your first three years you'll do a bit of everything; after all, you can't know what you want to do until you've tried things."* Tell that to pupils embarking on a specialist training in London...A more senior source told us: *"We've been debating offering specialist pupillages, but the view seems to be that general ones are better."*

Of course, you'll need to consider what practice in Birmingham has to offer you long term. Crime is the biggest practice group at St Philips, but commercial work is more profitable and the set is determined to edge itself in that direction. Maybe this is why the decision to deal crime specialists at 1 Fountain Court into the game was so hotly debated at the time. The real task ahead is to win more Midlands-based commercial instructions (around 65% of them still go to London sets), and there are signs that St Philips is making headway. Recent commercial highlights have included some hefty Mercantile Court cases, such as a £35 million Dunkin Donuts franchising dispute and a case between Landrover and one of its suppliers. About 80% of instructions come from firms within a 50-mile radius of the city and there will also be work from London solicitors with business in Birmingham courts. You'll not be restricted in where you work either; it's a case of 'have brief will travel' – Manchester, Leeds, Lincolnshire...the universe!

They may have been on the bliss pills before we met them, but our junior and pupil sources seemed very satisfied and quite at home, speaking of how their seniors and administrative staff made a positive effort to help them grow into chambers. *"There's a genuine mix of personalities within each group,"* one told us, *"so you're not taken on because you'll fit into one or other group."* If there's a St Philips Way then it was best put by the pupil who said: *"It's not about traditional values, it's about surviving at the modern Bar."* Whatever changes the Bar faces in the future – handling cases from cradle to grave, block-contract crime work from the Legal Services Commission – we'd bet St Philips will be there before most.

Bar A-Z

Blackstone Chambers (P Baxendale QC and C Flint QC)

Blackstone House, Temple, London EC4Y 9BW DX: 281
Tel: (020) 7583 1770 Fax: (020) 7822 7350
Email: clerks@blackstonechambers.com
Website: www.blackstonechambers.com

chambers profile

Blackstone Chambers occupies modern, fully networked premises in the Temple.

type of work undertaken

Chambers' formidable strengths lie in three principal areas of practice: commercial, employment and public law. Commercial law includes financial/business law, international trade, conflicts, sport, media and entertainment, intellectual property and professional negligence. All aspects of employment law, including discrimination, are covered by chambers' extensive employment law practice. Public law incorporates judicial review, acting both for and against central and local government agencies and other regulatory authorities, human rights and other aspects of administrative law. Chambers recognises the increasingly important role which mediation has to play in dispute resolution. Two members are CEDR accredited mediators.

pupil profile

Chambers looks for articulate and intelligent applicants who are able to work well under pressure and demonstrate high intellectual ability. Successful candidates usually have at least a 2:1 honours degree, although not necessarily in law.

pupillage

Chambers offers four (or exceptionally five) 12 month pupillages to those wishing to practise full-time at the Bar, normally commencing in October each year. Pupillage is divided into three or four sections and every effort is made to ensure that pupils receive a broad training. The environment is a friendly one; pupils attend an induction week introducing them to the chambers working environment. Chambers prefers to recruit new tenants from pupils wherever possible. Chambers subscribes to OLPAS; applications should be made for the summer season.

mini pupillages

Assessed mini pupillages are available and are an important part of the application procedure. Applications for mini pupillages must be made by 30 April; earlier applications are strongly advised and are preferred in the year before pupillage commences.

funding

Awards of £35,000 per annum are available. The pupillage committee has a discretion to consider applications for up to £9,000 of the pupillage award to be advanced during the BVC year.

No of Silks	28
No of Juniors	38
No of Pupils	5 (current)

contact

Ms Julia Hornor
Practice Manager

method of application

OLPAS

pupillages (p.a.)

12 months **4**
Required degree grade
Minimum 2:1
(law or non-law)

income

Award **£35,000**
Earnings not included

tenancies

Junior tenancies offered in last 3 years **100%**
No of tenants of 5 years call or under **11**

Erskine Chambers

33 Chancery Lane, London WC2A 1EN
Tel: (020) 7242 5532 Fax: (020) 7831 0125
Email: clerks@erskine-chambers.co.uk
Website: www.erskine-chambers.co.uk

chambers profile

Erskine Chambers is widely recognised as the leading specialist company law set and undertakes litigation and advisory work in all areas in which company law arises.

type of work undertaken

Company and related commercial law, including, in particular, shareholder disputes, corporate insolvencies, directors' duties, takeovers, corporate reconstructions, loan capital and banking securities, financial services, accounting and auditing, professional negligence and corporate fraud.

pupil profile

Chambers seek ambitious, intellectually able students, ordinarily with a first or upper second class degree and preferably some knowledge or experience of company law.

pupillage

Each pupil will spend three months with one pupil supervisor before moving to another pupil supervisor. Increasingly, they will begin to work for other members of Chambers. There are opportunities throughout for pupils to become involved in particularly interesting or high-profile work being done by members of Chambers.

mini pupillages

Available throughout the year on both an assessed and a non-assessed basis.

sponsorship & awards

Two awards of up to £35,000 are made each year in respect of the 12-month pupillage period. Applications should be made on Chambers' standard application form available from the above address. Applications for 2005/2006 should be made by 31 May 2004.

No of Silks	8
No of Juniors	16
No of Pupils	2

contact

Nigel Dougherty
(020) 7242 5532

method of application

Chambers' standard application form

pupillages (p.a.)

Up to 2, up to 12 months

tenancies

Up to 2

4 Essex Court (Nigel Teare QC)

4 Essex Court, Temple, London EC4Y 9AJ
DX: 292 London (Chancery Lane)
Tel: (020) 7653 5653 Fax: (020) 7653 5654
Email: pupillage@4sx.co.uk
Website: www.4sx.co.uk

chambers profile

4 Essex Court is one of the leading commercial chambers. Chambers offers a wide range of services to its clients within the commercial sphere specialising particularly in maritime and aviation law. 4 Essex Court is placed in the first rank in both specialisms by *Chambers Guide to the Legal Profession 2001-2002*. In shipping law seven silks and nine juniors were selected by *Chambers* as leaders in their field; in aviation *Chambers* concluded that "these highly commercial barristers are at the forefront of the aviation field". In both these areas the set had more 'leaders in their field' selected than any other set of chambers. Chambers advises on domestic and international commercial litigation and acts as advocates in Court, abitration and inquiries in England and abroad. Please note, in early 2004, Chambers will be moving to a new building. Details will be published on Chambers' website.

type of work undertaken

The challenging and rewarding work of Chambers encompasses the broad range of commercial disputes embracing arbitration, aviation, banking, shipping, international trade, insurance and reinsurance, professional negligence, entertainment and media, environmental and construction law. Over 70% of Chambers' work involves international clients.

pupil profile

4 Essex Court seeks high calibre pupils with good academic qualifications (at least a 2:1 degree) who exhibit good written and oral skills.

pupillage

Chambers offers a maximum of four funded pupillages of 12 months duration (reviewable at six months). Pupils are moved amongst several members of Chambers and will experience a wide range of high quality commercial work. Outstanding pupils are likely to be offered a tenancy at the end of their pupillage. Further information can be found on the website.

mini pupillages

Mini pupillages are encouraged in order that potential pupils may experience the work of Chambers before committing themselves to an application for full pupillage.

funding

Awards of £30,000 p.a. are available for each funded pupillage - part of which may be forwarded during the BVC, at the Pupillage Committee's discretion.

No of Silks 8
No of Juniors 31

contact
Secretary to Pupillage Committee

method of application
Chambers' application form

pupillages (p.a.)
1st 6 months **4**
2nd 6 months **4**
12 months
(Reviewed at 6 months)
Required degree
Good 2:1+

income
1st 6 months
£15,000
2nd 6 months
£15,000
Earnings not included

tenancies
Current tenants who served pupillage in Chambers **21**
Junior tenancies offered in last 3 years **6**
No of tenants of 5 years call or under **7**
Income (1st year)
c. £40,000

Furnival Chambers

32 Furnival Street, London EC4A 1JQ
Tel: (020) 7405 3232 Fax: (020) 7405 3322
Website: www.furnivallaw.co.uk

chambers profile

Furnival Chambers (previously 171 Fleet Street) is a young (established 1985), energetic and progressive leading criminal set and the leading set in the field of asset forfeiture and confiscation.

type of work undertaken

Members of Chambers regularly appear in high-profile cases (defending and prosecuting). Prosecution work includes work undertaken by Treasury Counsel at the Central Criminal Court. Many members undertake high-profile work on behalf of HM Customs and Excise, the Department of Trade and Industry, the Serious Fraud Office, the Department of Work & Pensions, Inland Revenue and the Crown Prosecution Service. The asset forfeiture team comprises approximately 10 members specialising in money laundering prosecutions, mutual assistance and confiscation proceedings in the criminal courts, and injunctive and receivership work in the civil courts. Members of the team include the authors of the leading practitioners' textbook and regularly conduct cases in Commonwealth and Caribbean jurisdictions.

pupil profile

Applicants are expected to have excellent academic qualifications and an ability to absorb complex documentary material.

pupillage

Pupillage follows a well-defined process so that the same opportunities are afforded to all at every level. Chambers have simple and robust procedures in place that ensure that decisions affecting pupils are fair, and reinforce these with a clear complaints procedure. Further information regarding Chambers' pupillage policy is available on the Chambers website. Chambers operate a compulsory in-house advocacy course which pupils must pass before being permitted to practise in their second six months. Pupils can, therefore, expect to be well prepared for an exceptionally busy second six.

mini pupillages

Assessed mini-pupillages are available. Mini-pupils must expect to travel to courts in London. Applications should be made in writing to Clara Milligan (Chambers Administrator) with accompanying CV. Student visits are not possible. Sponsored students are not accepted.

funding

Chambers offer three funded (12 month) pupillages at £15,000 (£7,500 payable at the beginning of each six).

contact
Clara Milligan (Chambers Administrator) cmilligan@furnivallaw.co.uk

method of application
OLPAS summer season 2004 for 2005

pupillages (p.a.)
3 Funded

income
1st 6 months
£7,500
2nd 6 months
£7,500

tenancies
6

2 Hare Court

2 Hare Court, Temple, London EC4Y 7BH
Tel: (020) 7353 5324 Fax: (020) 7353 0667
Email: clerks@2harecourt.com
Website: www.2harecourt.com

No of Silks	**11**
No of Juniors	**36**
No of Pupils	**3**

contact
Jeremy Benson QC

method of application
OLPAS (summer)

pupillages (p.a.)
Three 12 month pupillages
Minimum degree 2:1

tenancies
According to ability

annexes
None

chambers profile

2 Hare Court is well established as one of the leading sets specialising in criminal law. Members of Chambers defend and prosecute at all levels in London, throughout England and Wales and overseas, and are experienced in advising parties from the commencement of the investigation, including issues arising from international judicial assistance. Chambers has a strong tradition of representation both on the Bar Council and Criminal Bar Association.

type of work undertaken

Chambers has considerable experience in high profile cases involving murder, corporate manslaughter, terrorism, police corruption, drug trafficking, sexual offences and internet pornography as well as those involving child witnesses and has increasingly specialised in commercial fraud and international money laundering. Individual tenants also provide specialist expertise in associated fields including immigration, licensing and health and safety.

pupil profile

Chambers select as pupils articulate and well motivated individuals of high intellectual ability who can demonstrate sound judgement and a practical approach to problem solving. Candidates should have at least a 2.1 honours degree.

pupillage

Chambers normally offers three 12 month pupillages starting in September. The year is divided into two six month periods although pupils are assigned to a different pupil master for each of the four months to ensure experience in different areas of crime. Chambers pays for the "Advice to Counsel" course and runs their own in-house advocacy training.

mini pupillages

The programme runs throughout the year with one mini pupil taken each week and two each week in the summer. Applicants must be at least 18 years old and either be studying for Higher Education qualification or on or about to start CPE or BVC course.

funding

12 month pupils will be sponsored through a combination of an award scheme, guaranteed earnings and additional earnings. No clerks' fees or deductions are taken from earnings.

2 HARE COURT

2 MCB (Chambers of Guy Roots QC)

2 Mitre Court Buildings, Temple, London EC4Y 7BX
Tel: (020) 7583 1380 Fax: (020) 7353 7772
Email: clerks@2mcb.co.uk
Website: www.2mcb.co.uk

chambers profile

Chambers specialises in planning and local government law, employment law. All members appear at public inquiries, the Lands Tribunal and the courts. Comprises 19 tenants.

type of work undertaken

The main specialist areas practised by all members comprises planning and local government law which includes town and country planning, environmental law, compulsory purchase and compensation, rating and the council tax, utilities and infrastructure, local government, education, public and administrative law, parliamentary bills and transport and works act orders.

pupil profile

Those with sound academic ability, 2:1 degree or higher, professional aptitude and an interest in Chambers' specialisation.

pupillage

Two x 12 month pupillages, with change of pupil master every three months.

mini pupillages

On application direct to Chambers - throughout year.

sponsorship & awards

£25,000 for 12 month pupillage.

funding

Only £25,000 remuneration above.

No of Silks	**5**
No of Juniors	**14**
No of Pupils	**2**

contact
Michael Druce
(020) 7583 1380

method of application
OLPAS (Summer Season)

pupillages (p.a.)
Two x 12 months

tenancies
One per year

annexes
None

2MCB

Serle Court

Serle Court, 6 New Square, Lincoln's Inn, London WC2A 3QS
Tel: (020) 7242 6105 Fax: (020) 7405 4004
Email: pupillage@serlecourt.co.uk
Website: www.serlecourt.co.uk

No of Silks	**15**
No of Juniors	**34**
No of Pupils	**2**

contact
Hugh Norbury
Tel (020) 7242 6105

method of application
Chambers application form, available from website or Chambers.
Not a member of OLPAS

pupillages (p.a.)
Two 12 month pupillages

tenancies
Up to 2 per annum

chambers profile

'Excellent for all aspects of general business law…' Chambers & Partners Guide 2002-3
Serle Court is the largest commercial chancery set with 49 barristers including 15 silks. Widely recognised as a leading set, Chambers is recommended in 17 different areas of practice by legal directories. Chambers has a stimulating and inclusive work environment and a forward looking approach.

type of work undertaken

Litigation, arbitration, mediation and advisory services across the full range of chancery and commercial practice areas including: administrative and public law, banking, civil fraud, commercial litigation, company, financial services, human rights, insolvency, mediation, partnership, professional negligence, property, regulatory and disciplinary, trusts and probate.

pupil profile

Candidates are well-rounded people, from any background. Chambers looks for highly motivated individuals with first class intellectual ability, combined with a practical approach, sound judgment and the potential to become excellent advocates. Serle Court has a reputation for 'consistent high quality' and for being 'responsive and able team members' and seeks the same qualities in pupils.

pupillage

Pupils sit with different pupil supervisors in order to experience a broad a range of work. Two pupils are recruited each year and Chambers offers: An excellent preparation for successful practice; A genuinely friendly and supportive environment; The opportunity to learn from some of the leading barristers in their field; A real prospect of tenancy.

mini-pupillages

About 30 available each year. Apply with CV to pupillage@serlecourt.co.uk

funding

£35,000, of which £10,000 is available during the BVC year.

serle court

3/4 South Square

3/4 South Square, Gray's Inn, London WC1R 5HP
Tel: (020) 7696 9900 Fax: (020) 7696 9911
Email: pupillage@southsquare.com
Website: www.southsquare.com

No of Silks	**16**
No of Juniors	**28**
No of Pupils	**2**

contact
Pupillage Secretary
Tel (020) 7696 9900

method of application
CV with covering letter

pupillages (p.a.)
Up to four, 12 month pupillages offered each year

chambers profile

Chambers is an established successful commercial set, involved in high-profile international and domestic commercial litigation and advice. Members of Chambers have been involved in some of the most important commercial cases of the last decade including Barings, BCCI, Lloyds, Maxwell and Polly Peck.

type of work undertaken

3/4 South Square has a pre-eminent reputation in insolvency and reconstruction law and specialist expertise in banking, financial services, company law, professional negligence, domestic and international arbitration, mediation, European Union Law, insurance/reinsurance law and general commercial litigation.

pupil profile

Chambers seek to recruit the highest calibre of candidates who must be prepared to commit themselves to establishing a successful practice and maintaining Chambers' position at the forefront of the modern Commercial Bar. The minimum academic qualification is a 2:1 degree.

pupillage

Pupils are welcomed into all areas of Chambers' life and are provided with an organised programme designed to train and equip them for practice in a dynamic and challenging environment. Pupils sit with a number of pupil masters for periods of six-eight weeks and we look to recruit at least one tenant every year from our pupils.

mini pupillages

Chambers also offers funded and unfunded mini-pupillages – please see the set's website for further details.

sponsorship & awards

Currently £35,000 per annum (reviewable annually).

4 Stone Buildings

4 Stone Buildings, Lincoln's Inn, London WC2A 3XT
Tel: (020) 7242 5524 Fax: (020) 7831 7907
Email: d.goddard@4stonebuildings.com

No of Silks	**6**
No of Juniors	**21**
No of Pupils	**2**

contact
David Goddard
(020) 7242 5524

method of application
On Chambers own application form

pupillages (p.a.)
2 x six months

tenancies
At least 1 per year

annexes
None

chambers profile

An established friendly company/commercial set involved in high profile company/commercial litigation and advice.

type of work undertaken

4, Stone Buildings specialise in the fields of company law, commercial law, financial services and regulation and corporate insolvency.

pupil profile

Candidates are expected to have first class, or good second class degrees. But mere intellectual ability is only part of it: a successful candidate must have the confidence and ambition to succeed, the common sense to recognise the practical advice a client really needs, and an ability to get on well with clients, solicitors and other members of Chambers - and the clerks.

pupillage

The set aim to give all pupils the knowledge, skills and practical experience they need for a successful career at the Bar. They believe that it is important for all pupils to see as much as possible of the different kinds of work in Chambers. This enables pupils to judge whether their work suits them, and enables different members of Chambers to assess the pupils. Each pupil therefore normally spends time with two or more pupil-masters within any six month period. If other members of Chambers have particularly interesting cases in Court, pupils will be encouraged to work and attend Court with them. All pupils work in their pupil masters' rooms, read their papers, attend their conferences, draft pleadings and documents, write draft opinions and accompany their pupil masters to Court. Pupils are treated as part of Chambers, and are fully involved in the activities of Chambers while they are with 4 Stone Chambers.

mini pupillages

Up to 20 mini-pupillages offered per year of up to a weeks duration. Application by letter and cv.

sponsorship & awards

£15,000 per six months.

funding

As above.

3 Verulam Buildings (Christopher Symons QC/John Jarvis QC)

3 Verulam Buildings, Gray's Inn, London WC1R 5NT DX: LDE 331
Tel: (020) 7831 8441 Fax: (020) 7831 8479
Email: chambers@3vb.com
Website: www.3vb.com

chambers profile

3 Verulam Buildings is a large commercial set with a history of expansion by recruitment of tenants from amongst pupils. Over the past 10 years, on average, two of its pupils have become tenants every year. Chambers occupies recently refurbished, spacious offices overlooking Gray's Inn Walks with all modern IT and library facilities. Chambers prides itself on a pleasant, friendly and relaxed atmosphere.

type of work undertaken

A wide range of commercial work, in particular banking and financial services, insurance and reinsurance, commercial fraud, professional negligence, company law, entertainment, arbitration/ADR, as well as other general commercial work. Members of Chambers regularly appear in high profile cases and a substantial amount of Chambers' work is international.

pupil profile

Chambers looks for intelligent and ambitious candidates with strong powers of analysis and reasoning, who are self confident and get on well with others. Candidates should normally have at least a 2:1 grade in an honours subject which need not be law.

pupillage

Chambers seeks to recruit four funded 12 months pupils every year through OLPAS. Each pupil spends three months with four different members of Chambers to gain experience of different types of work. Chambers also offers unfunded pupillages to pupils who do not intend to practise at the Bar of England and Wales.

mini pupillages

Mini pupillages are available for university, CPE or Bar students who are interested in finding out more about Chambers' work. Chambers considers mini pupillage to be an important part of its recruitment process. Candidates should have, or expect to obtain, the minimum requirements for a funded 12 month pupillage. Applications are accepted throughout the year and should be addressed to Matthew Parker.

funding

In the year 2004-05 the annual award will be at least £33,000, up to £11,000 of which may be drawn during the BVC year.

No of Silks	8
No of Juniors	35
No of Pupils	4

contact
Mr Peter Ratcliffe (Pupillage)
Mr Matthew Parker (Mini Pupillage)

method of application
OLPAS, or for unfunded pupillage & mini pupillage CV & covering letter stating dates of availability

pupillages (p.a.)
12 months **4**
Required degree grade **2:1**

income
At least £33,000 per annum
Earnings not included

tenancies
Current tenants who served pupillage in Chambers **Approx 40**
Junior tenancies offered in last 3 years **7**
No of tenants of 5 years call or under **9**

Wilberforce Chambers

8 New Square, Lincoln's Inn, London WC2A 3QP
Tel: (020) 7306 0102 Fax: (020) 7306 0096
Email: lbillins@wilberforce.co.uk
Website: www.wilberforce.co.uk

No of Silks 16
No of Juniors 23
No of Pupils 3 (2003/04)

contact
Louise Billins
(020) 7304 2857

method of application
Online via website or in writing to Louise Billins, Pupillage Secretary

pupillages (p.a.)
Two x 12 months

tenancies
1 (2003)

chambers profile

As a leading commercial chancery Chambers, the set has 39 members (16 QC's) involved in some of the most commercially important and cutting edge advice and advocacy undertaken by the Bar today. Most of its members are recognised as leaders in their field by the key legal directories. Instructions come from top UK and international law firms with a complex and rewarding range of work for international companies, financial institutions, sports and media organisations, private individuals and well-known names. While clients demand high intellectual performance and client care standards the rewards are a successful career at the Bar. The atmosphere in Chambers is one of a united and friendly 'family' which it guards with great care.

type of work undertaken

Chambers commercial chancery practices include commercial litigation, company, financial services and banking, insolvency, pensions, trusts and tax, property litigation, planning, professional negligence, sports and media, intellectual property and charities work.

pupil profile

Trainees should possess high intellectual ability, strong motivation and excellent communication skills. They need to have maturity and confidence with the ability to work with others and analyse legal problems clearly, demonstrating commercial and practical good sense. Chambers looks for people who possess real potential to join Chambers as a tenant at the end of their pupillage. A 2.1 degree (in Law or another subject) is a minimum requirement. Chambers has a track record of taking CPE students.

pupillage

Chambers operates a structured pupillage programme with continual assessment aimed at giving you a broad experience of commercial chancery practice under several pupil masters with whom you are able to develop your skills. It offers 12-month terminable pupillages and aims to reach a decision about tenancy after six months of pupillage. Chambers website explains this programme in greater detail.

mini-pupillages

Chambers encourage interested students to visit for a week in order to learn how it operates, to meet members of Chambers and to see the sort of work it does. Chambers run three separate mini-pupillage weeks (two in December and one in July). See the website for more details.

funding

The award for 2004/2005 is £37,500 pa (£18,750 for a six-month pupillage). The award is paid monthly. A proportion of the pupillage award (up to £12,500) can be drawn down during the BVC year.

notes